INTRODUCTION TO
JAVA™
PROGRAMMING

COMPREHENSIVE VERSION
FIFTH EDITION

Y. Daniel Liang

School of Computing
Armstrong Atlantic State University

PEARSON

Prentice
Hall

Pearson Education International

Vice President and Editorial Director,
  ECS: *Marcia J. Horton*
Publisher: *Alan R. Apt*
Associate Editor: *Toni Dianne Holm*
Editorial Assistant: *Patrick Lindner*
Vice President and Director of Production
  and Manufacturing, ESM: *David W. Riccardi*
Executive Managing Editor: *Vince O'Brien*
Managing Editor: *Camille Trentacoste*
Production Editor: *John Keegan*
Director of Creative Services: *Paul Belfanti*
Art Director: *Jonathan Boylan*
Interior & Cover Designer: *Dina Curro*

Managing Editor, AV Management
  and Production: *Patricia Burns*
Art Editor: *Xiaohong Zhu*
Front Cover Photo: © *Rick Strange/AGE Fotostock Americ*
Director, Image Resource Center: *Melinda Reo*
Manager, Rights and Permissions: *Zina Arabia*
Manager, Visual Research: *Beth Brenzel*
Manager, Cover Visual Research
  and Permissions: *Karen Sanatar*
Manufacturing Manager: *Trudy Pisciotti*
Manufacturing Buyer: *Lisa McDowell*
Executive Marketing Manager: *Pamela Hersperger*
Marketing Assistant: *Barrie Reinhold*

© 2005, 2003, 2001, 1999, 1998 Pearson Education, Inc.
Pearson Prentice Hall
Pearson Education, Inc.
Upper Saddle River, NJ 07458

Printed in the United States of America

10   9   8   7   6   5   4   3   2   1

ISBN: 0-13-185721-5

Pearson Education Ltd., *London*
Pearson Education Australia Pty. Ltd., *Sydney*
Pearson Education Singapore, Pte. Ltd.
Pearson Education North Asia Ltd., *Hong Kong*
Pearson Education Canada, Inc., *Toronto*
Pearson Educación de Mexico, S.A. de C.V.
Pearson Education—Japan, *Tokyo*
Pearson Education Malaysia, Pte. Ltd.
Pearson Education, Inc., *Upper Saddle River, New Jersey*

To Samantha, Michael, and Michelle

PREFACE

In the past seven years, five editions of *Introduction to Java Programming* have been published. Each new edition substantially improved the previous edition in clarity, content, presentation, examples, and exercises, thanks to comments and suggestions by instructors and students. The Fifth Edition is a gigantic leap forward. I invite you to take a close look and be the judge. I am constantly improving the book. Please continue to send me your comments and suggestions to help further improve it.

Custom Versions

The book is published in a comprehensive version of twenty-nine chapters and can also be printed in custom versions with substantial savings for students. The first sixteen chapters form the custom core. You can customize the book by adding new chapters to the custom core. The following diagram summarizes the materials in the comprehensive version.

Introduction to Java Programming, 5E, Comprehensive Version

Part I Fundamentals of Programming
  Chapter 1 Introduction to Computers, Programs,
    and Java
  Chapter 2 Primitive Data Types and Operations
  Chapter 3 Control Statements
  Chapter 4 Methods
  Chapter 5 Arrays

Part II Object-Oriented Programming
  Chapter 6 Objects and Classes
  Chapter 7 Strings
  Chapter 8 Inheritance and Polymorphism
  Chapter 9 Abstract Classes and Interfaces
  Chapter 10 Object-Oriented Modeling

Part III GUI Programming
  Chapter 11 Getting Started with GUI
    Programming
  Chapter 12 Event-Driven Programming
  Chapter 13 Creating User Interfaces
  Chapter 14 Applets, Images, and Audio

Part IV Exception Handling and IO
  Chapter 15 Exceptions and Assertions
  Chapter 16 Simple Input and Output

Custom Core

Part V Data Structures and Collections Framework
  Chapter 17 Object-Oriented Data Structures
  Chapter 18 Java Collections Framework

Part VI Threads and Internationalization
  Chapter 19 Multithreading
  Chapter 20 Internationalization

Part VII Advanced GUI Programming
  Chapter 21 JavaBeans, Bean Events, and MVC
  Chapter 22 Containers, Layout Managers,
    and Borders
  Chapter 23 Menus, Toolbars, Dialogs, and
    Internal Frames
  Chapter 24 Advanced Swing Components

Part VIII Web Programming
  Chapter 25 Java Database Programming
  Chapter 26 Servlets
  Chapter 27 JavaServer Pages

Part IX Distributed Computing
  Chapter 28 Networking
  Chapter 29 Remote Method Invocation

Appendixes

Please contact your Prentice Hall sales representative or your Pearson Custom Editor to order custom versions.

Teaching Strategies

There are three popular strategies in teaching Java. The first, known as *GUI-first*, is to mix Java applets and GUI programming with object-oriented programming concepts. The second, known as *object-first*, is to introduce object-oriented programming (OOP) from the start. The third strategy, known as *fundamentals-first*, is a step-by-step approach, first laying a sound foundation on programming concepts, control statements, methods, and arrays, then introducing object-oriented programming, and then moving on to graphical user interface (GUI), applets, and finally to exception handling, simple I/O, and other advanced subjects.

GUI-first

The GUI-first strategy, starting with GUI and applets, seems attractive, but requires substantial knowledge of object-oriented programming and a good understanding of the Java event-handling model; thus, students may never fully understand what they are doing.

object-first

The object-first strategy is based on the notion that objects should be introduced first because Java is an object-oriented programming language. This notion, however, overlooks the importance of the fundamental techniques required for writing programs in any programming language. Furthermore, this approach inevitably mixes static and instance variables and methods before students can fully understand classes and objects and use them to develop useful programs. Students are overwhelmed by having to master object-oriented programming and basic rules of programming simultaneously in the early stage of learning Java. This is a common source of frustration for first-year students learning object-oriented programming.

fundamentals-first

From my own experience, confirmed by the experiences of many colleagues, I have found that learning basic logic and fundamental programming techniques like loops is a struggle for most first-year students. *Students who cannot write code in procedural programming are not able to learn object-oriented programming.* A good introduction on primitive data types, control statements, methods, and arrays prepares students to learn object-oriented programming. Therefore, this text adopts the fundamentals-first strategy, proceeding at a steady pace through all the necessary and important basic concepts, then moving to object-oriented programming, and then to the use of the object-oriented approach to build interesting GUI applications and applets with exception handling, simple I/O, and advanced features. The fundamentals-first approach can reinforce object-oriented programming by first presenting the procedural solutions and demonstrating how they can be improved using the object-oriented approach. Students can learn when and how to apply OOP effectively.

problem solving

This book is not simply about how to program, for it teaches, as well, how to solve problems using programs. Applying the concept of abstraction in the design and implementation of software projects is the key to developing software. The overriding objective of the book, therefore, is to teach students to use many levels of abstraction in solving problems and to see problems in small and in large. *The examples and exercises throughout the book foster the concept of developing reusable components and using them to create practical projects.*

Learning Strategies

practice

A programming course is quite different from other courses. In a programming course, you learn from examples, from practice, and from mistakes. You need to devote a lot of time to writing programs, testing them, and fixing errors.

programmatic solution

For first-time programmers, learning Java is like learning any high-level programming language. The fundamental point in learning programming is to develop the critical skills of formulating programmatic solutions for real problems and translating them into programs using selection statements, loops, and methods.

object-oriented programming

Once you acquire the basic skills of writing programs using loops, methods, and arrays, you can begin to learn object-oriented programming. You will learn how to develop object-oriented software using class encapsulation and class inheritance.

Java API

Once you understand the concept of object-oriented programming, learning Java becomes a matter of learning the Java API. The Java API establishes a framework for programmers to develop applications using Java. You have to use these classes and interfaces in the API and follow their conventions and rules to create applications. The best way to learn the Java API is to imitate examples and do exercises. The following diagram highlights the API covered in the book.

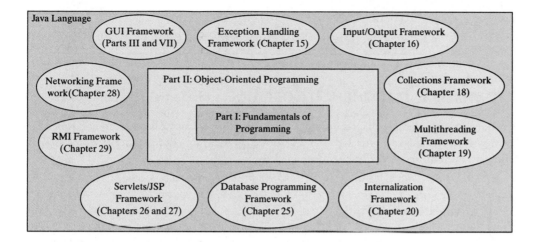

Pedagogical Features

The philosophy of the Liang Java Series is *teaching by example and learning by doing*. Basic features are explained by example so that you can learn by doing. The book uses the following elements to get the most from the material:

teaching by example
learning by doing

- ✦ **Objectives** list what students should have learned from the chapter. This will help them to determine whether they have met the objectives after completing the chapter.

- ✦ **Introduction** opens the discussion with a brief overview of what to expect from the chapter.

- ✦ **Examples**, carefully chosen and presented in an easy-to-follow style, teach programming concepts. Each example has a problem statement, solution steps, complete source code, sample run, and review.

- ✦ **Chapter Summary** reviews the important subjects that students should understand and remember. It helps them to reinforce the key concepts they have learned in the chapter.

- ✦ **Review Questions** are grouped by sections to help students track their progress and evaluate their learning.

- ✦ **Programming Exercises** are grouped by sections to provide students with opportunities to apply the skills on their own. The level of difficulty is rated easy (no asterisk), moderate (*), hard (**), or challenging (***). The trick of learning programming is practice, practice, and practice. To that end, the book provides a large number of exercises.

- ✦ **Interactive Self-Test** lets students test their knowledge interactively online. The Self-Test is accessible from the Companion Website. It provides more than nine hundred multiple-choice questions organized by sections in each chapter.

- ✦ **Notes, Tips,** and **Cautions** are inserted throughout the text to offer valuable advice and insight on important aspects of program development.

 NOTE
Provides additional information on the subject and reinforces important concepts.

 TIP
Teaches good programming style and practice.

🌺 **CAUTION**
Helps students steer away from the pitfalls of programming errors.

Flexible Chapter Orderings

The book provides flexible chapter orderings to enable GUI, IO, or Collections to be covered earlier. Many of the chapters after Chapter 14 can be covered immediately after Chapter 14. The following diagram shows the chapter dependencies.

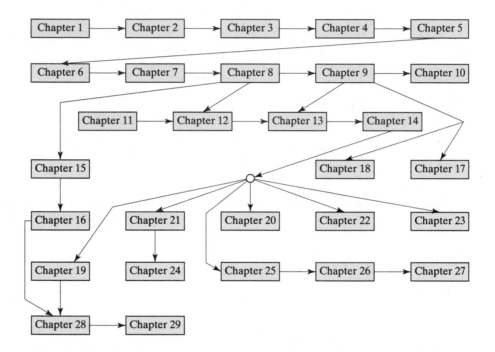

🌺 **NOTE**
Some of the optional examples and exercises in a later chapter may be dependent on earlier chapters. In such cases the examples and exercises can be omitted. For example, Chapter 25 has an example that uses JTable from Chapter 24. If you have not covered JTable, this type of examples and exercises can be skipped.

What's New in This Edition?

This edition improves upon *Introduction to Java Programming, Fourth Edition*. The major changes are as follows:

✦ The book is completely revised in every detail to improve clarity, content, presentation, examples, and exercises.

✦ The book provides many new illustrations and uses short examples to demonstrate concepts and techniques. Longer examples are presented in case studies with overall discussions and thorough line-by-line explanations.

✦ Part I, "Fundamentals of Programming," focuses on problem-solving and basic programming techniques with many new illustrations and practical examples. This part uses JOptionPane input dialog to receive input, but console input using the MyInput class and the JDK 1.5 Scanner class are also introduced to provide alternative ways for input.

✦ Part II, "Object-Oriented Programming," is expanded into five chapters to give a comprehensive introduction on OOP and how to use it to design programs. New organization improves the presentation of object-oriented programming and enables GUI programming to be covered earlier.

✦ Part III, "GUI Programming," is expanded into four chapters to introduce GUI programming, event-driven programming, creating user interfaces, and applets. Advanced GUI features are now covered in Part VII, "Advanced GUI Programming."

✦ Chapter 16, "Simple Input and Output," is completely overhauled. It first introduces the File class, then text I/O, binary I/O, object I/O, and random access files. Short examples are used to demonstrate concepts and techniques. Three cases studies on using various I/O classes are presented in this chapter.

✦ The comprehensive version covers the Java collections framework, threads, JavaBeans, advanced GUI components, JDBC, Servlets, JSP, networking, and RMI.

✦ Purely mathematical examples, such as computing deviations and matrix multiplications, have been replaced by practical examples, such as computing loan payments, taxes, and printing payroll statements.

✦ The number of exercises is almost doubled to cover a variety of problems with simple or complex solutions. The level of difficulty is rated easy (no asterisk), moderate (*), hard (**), or challenging (***).

✦ The book is updated to JDK 1.5.

How are the New Features in JDK 1.5 Treated?

There are already more features in Java than an introductory course can cover. This edition does not aim to cover all the new features in JDK 1.5. Nevertheless, some of the useful features of JDK 1.5 are appropriately introduced to beginners. Specifically,

✦ Formatted output (System.out.printf) is covered in Chapter 2.

✦ The enhanced for loop is covered in Chapters 5 and 18.

✦ The java.util.Scanner class is covered in Chapter 2 and Supplement T for console input, and in Chapter 7 to complement the StringTokenizer class.

✦ Boxing and unboxing of primitives is covered in Chapter 9.

✦ Static import is covered in Chapter 11.

✦ Generic types are covered in Chapter 18 and Supplement Q.

To facilitate the use of this book in courses based on JDK 1.4 and to enable instructors to choose JDK 1.5 topics freely, all the sections on JDK 1.5 are marked *JDK 1.5 Features* and can be skipped.

 NOTE

Sun MicroSystems recently renamed JDK 1.5 to JDK 5.0. Since most programmers are familiar with JDK 1.5, Sun uses JDK 5.0 and JDK 1.5 interchangeably. So does this book.

JDK 1.5 = JDK 5.0

Java Development Tools

You can use a text editor, such as the Windows Notepad or WordPad, to create Java programs, and compile and run the programs from the command window. You can also use a Java development tool, such as TextPad, JBuilder, NetBeans, or Eclipse. These tools support an integrated development environment (IDE) for rapidly developing Java programs. Editing, compiling, building, and executing programs are integrated in one graphical user interface. Using these tools effectively will greatly increase your programming productivity. TextPad is a primitive IDE tool. JBuilder, NetBeans, and Eclipse are more sophisticated. It may take a while to become familiar with a tool, but the time you invest will pay off in the long run. Tutorials on TextPad, JBuilder, NetBeans, and Eclipse are in the supplements on the Companion Website.

Companion Website

The Companion Website accessible from `www.prenhall.com/liang` contains the following resources:

◆ Interactive Self-Test

◆ Supplements

◆ Answers to review questions

◆ Solutions to even-numbered programming exercises

◆ Source code for the examples in the book

◆ Download links for JDK 1.5, JBuilder, NetBeans, Eclipse, TextPad, JCreator LE, JEdit, JGrasp, BlueJ, WinZip, MySQL, and Apache Tomcat.

Instructor Resource Website

The Instructor Resource Website accessible from `www.prenhall.com/liang` contains the following resources:

◆ Microsoft PowerPoint slides with interactive buttons to view full-color, syntax-highlighted source code and to run programs without leaving the slides.

◆ Sample exams. In general, each exam has four parts:

  1. Multiple-choice questions or short-answer questions (most of these are different from the ones in the Self-Test on the Companion Website)

  2. Correct programming errors

  3. Trace programs

  4. Write programs

◆ Solutions to all the exercises. Students will have access to the solutions of even-numbered exercises from the Companion Website.

◆ Quiz generator developed using Java.

Some readers have requested the materials in the Instructor Resource Website. Please understand that these are for instructors only. Such requests will not be answered.

Supplements

The text covers the core subjects. The supplements extend the text to introduce additional topics that might be of interest to readers. The following supplements are available from the Companion Website.

A. Installing and Configuring JDK 1.5
B. Compiling and Running Java from the Command Window
C. Compiling and Running Java from TextPad
D. Java Coding Style Guidelines
E. HTML Tutorial
F. Glossary
G. SQL statements for creating and initializing tables for Chapters 25, 26, 27, and 29
H. JBuilder Tutorial
I. NetBeans Tutorial
J. Eclipse Tutorial
K. Tutorial for MySQL
L. Tutorial for Oracle
M. Tutorial for Microsoft Access
N. Tutorial for Tomcat
O. Creating Shortcuts for Java Applications on Windows
P. Supplemental Case Study for Chapter 10: Design a `GenericMatrix` Class
Q. Creating Generic Types (JDK 1.5)
R. Enumerated Types (JDK 1.5)
S. Semaphores (JDK 1.5)
T. Obtaining Input from the Console Using the `Scanner` Class (JDK 1.5)

Acknowledgments

I would like to thank Ray Greenlaw, Chuck Shipley, and my colleagues at Armstrong Atlantic State University for enabling me to teach what I write and for supporting me in writing what I teach. Teaching is the source of inspiration for continuing to improve the book. I am grateful to the instructors and students who have offered comments, suggestions, bug reports, and praise. Their enthusiastic support has contributed to the success of my Java series.

This book was greatly improved thanks to outstanding reviews by James Chegwidden of Tarrant County College, Dan Lipsa of Armstrong Atlantic State University, Vladan Jovanovic of Georgia Southern University, Kenrick Mock of the University of Alaska—Anchorage, Ronald F. Taylor of Wright State University, and Lixin Tao of Pace University. Professors Mutsumi Nakamura and Lian Yu of Arizona State University are so kind to provide us with the errata and suggestions, which came just in time before the book is finished.

It is a great pleasure and privilege to work with the legendary computer science team at Prentice Hall. I would like to thank Alan Apt, Toni Holm, Patrick Lindner, Sarah Parker, Camille Trentacoste, John Keegan, Xiaohong Zhu, Pamela Hersperger, Barrie Reinhold, Toni Callum, Barbara Taylor-Laino, Meredith Maresca, and their colleagues for organizing, managing, and promoting this project, and to Robert Milch for copy editing.

During the production of this book, I was in Asia. I thank Pearson Education in Taiwan, Malaysia, and Singapore for their hospitality and valuable assistance.

As always, I am indebted to my wife, Samantha, for her love, support, and encouragement.

Y. DANIEL LIANG
liang@armstrong.edu
www.cs.armstrong.edu/liang/intro5e.html

BRIEF CONTENTS

CONTENTS

SUPPLEMENTS ARE POSTED ON THE COMPANION WEBSITE

PART I

FUNDAMENTALS OF PROGRAMMING

By now you have heard a lot about Java and are anxious to start writing Java programs. The first part of the book is a stepping stone that will prepare you to embark on the journey of learning Java. You will begin to know Java and will develop fundamental programming skills. Specifically, you will learn how to write simple Java programs with primitive data types, control statements, methods, and arrays.

Chapter 1
Introduction to Computers, Programs, and Java

Chapter 2
Primitive Data Types and Operations

Chapter 3
Control Statements

Chapter 4
Methods

Chapter 5
Arrays

Prerequisites for Part I

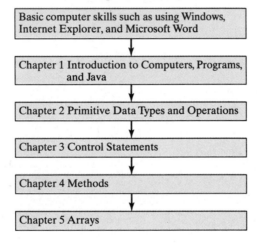

chapter

1

INTRODUCTION TO COMPUTERS, PROGRAMS, AND JAVA

Objectives

- ✦ To review computer basics, programs, and operating systems (§§1.2–1.4).

- ✦ To represent numbers in binary, decimal, and hexadecimal (§1.5 Optional).

- ✦ To understand the relationship between Java and the World Wide Web (§1.6).

- ✦ To know Java's advantages (§1.7).

- ✦ To distinguish the terms API, IDE, and JDK (§1.8).

- ✦ To write a simple Java program (§1.9).

- ✦ To create, compile, and run Java programs (§1.10).

- ✦ To know the basic syntax of a Java program (§1.11).

- ✦ To display output on the console and on the dialog box (§1.12).

1.1 Introduction

You use word-processors to write documents, Web browsers to explore the Internet, and e-mail programs to send e-mails over the Internet. Word-processors, browsers, and e-mail programs are all examples of software that runs on computers. Software is developed using programming languages. There are many programming languages. So why Java? The answer is that Java enables users to deploy applications on the Internet for servers, desktop computers, and small hand-held devices. The future of computing will be profoundly influenced by the Internet, and Java promises to remain a big part of that future. Java is *the* Internet programming language.

You are about to begin an exciting journey, learning a powerful programming language. Before the journey, it is helpful to review computer basics, programs, and operating systems, and to become familiar with number systems. You may skip the review in Sections 1.2, 1.3, and 1.4 if you are familiar with such terms as CPU, memory, disks, operating systems, and programming languages. You may also skip Section 1.5 and use it as reference when you have questions regarding binary and hexadecimal numbers.

1.2 What Is a Computer?

hardware
software

A computer is an electronic device that stores and processes data. A computer includes both *hardware* and *software*. In general, hardware is the physical aspect of the computer that can be seen, and software is the invisible instructions that control the hardware and make it work. Computer programming consists of writing instructions for computers to perform. You can learn a programming language without knowing computer hardware, but you will be better able to understand the effect of the instructions in the program if you do. This section gives a brief introduction to computer hardware components and their functionality.

A computer consists of the following major hardware components, as shown in Figure 1.1.

✦ Central Processing Unit (CPU)

✦ Memory (main memory)

✦ Storage Devices (disks, CDs, tapes)

✦ Input and Output Devices (monitors, keyboards, mouses, printers)

✦ Communication Devices (modems and network interface cards (NICs))

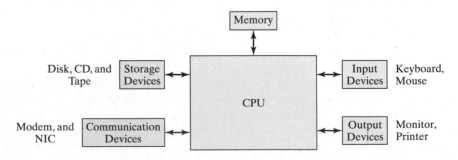

FIGURE 1.1 *A computer consists of a CPU, memory, hard disk, floppy disk, monitor, printer, and communication devices.*

1.2.1 Central Processing Unit

CPU

The *central processing unit* (CPU) is the brain of a computer. It retrieves instructions from memory and executes them. The CPU usually has two components: a *control unit* and an *arithmetic/logic unit.* The control unit controls and coordinates the actions of the other components. The arithmetic and logic unit performs numeric operations (addition, subtraction, multiplication, division) and logical operations (comparisons).

Today's CPU is built on a small silicon semiconductor chip with millions of transistors. The *speed* of the CPU is mainly determined by clock speed. Every computer has an internal clock. The clock emits electronic pulses at a constant rate, and these are used to control and synchronize the pace of operations. The faster the clock speed, the more instructions are executed in a given period of time. The clock speed is measured in *megahertz* (MHz), with 1 megahertz equaling 1 million pulses per second. The speed of the CPU has been improved continuously. If you buy a PC now, you can get an Intel Pentium 4 Processor at 3 *gigahertz* (1 gigahertz is 1000 megahertz).

megahertz

gigahertz

1.2.2 Memory

Computers use zeros and ones because digital devices have two stable states, referred to as *zero* and *one* by convention. Data of various kinds, such as numbers, characters, and strings, are encoded as a series of bits (*binary digits*: zeros and ones). *Memory* stores data and program instructions for the CPU to execute. A memory unit is an ordered sequence of *bytes*, each holding eight bits, as shown in Figure 1.2.

bit

byte

Memory address   Memory content

2000	01001010	Encoding for character 'J'
2001	01100001	Encoding for character 'a'
2002	01110110	Encoding for character 'v'
2003	01100001	Encoding for character 'a'
2004	00000011	Encoding for number 3

FIGURE 1.2 *Memory stores data and program instructions.*

The programmer need not be concerned about the encoding and decoding of data, which is performed automatically by the system based on the encoding scheme. The encoding scheme varies. For example, character 'J' is represented by 01001010 in one byte in the popular ASCII encoding. A small number such as 3 can be stored in a single byte. If a computer needs to store a large number that cannot fit into a single byte, it uses several adjacent bytes. No two data items can share or split the same byte. A byte is the minimum storage unit.

A program and its data must be brought to memory before they can be executed. A memory byte is never empty, but its initial content may be meaningless to your program. The current content of a memory byte is lost whenever new information is placed in it.

Every byte has a unique address. The address is used to locate the byte for storing and retrieving data. Since bytes can be accessed at any location, the memory is also referred to as *RAM* (random-access memory). Today's personal computers usually have at least 128 megabytes of RAM. A *megabyte* is about 1 million bytes. Like the CPU, memory is built on silicon semiconductor chips containing thousands of transistors embedded on their surface. Compared to the CPU chips, memory chips are less complicated, slower, and less expensive.

RAM

megabyte

1.2.3 Storage Devices

Memory is volatile, because information is lost when the power is off. Programs and data are permanently stored on storage devices and are moved to memory when the computer actually uses them. The reason for that is that memory is much faster than storage devices. There are three main types of storage devices:

- ✦ Disk drives (hard disks and floppy disks)
- ✦ CD drives (CD-R and CD-RW)
- ✦ Tape drives

drive

Drives are devices for operating a medium, such as disks, CDs, and tapes.

1.2.3.1   Disks

hard disk
floppy disk

There are two kinds of disks: *hard disks* and *floppy disks*. Personal computers usually have a 3.5-inch floppy disk drive and a hard drive. A floppy disk has a fixed capacity of about 1.44 MB. Hard disk capacities vary. The capacity of the hard disks of the latest PCs is in the range of 30 gigabytes to 120 gigabytes. Hard disks provide much faster performance and larger capacity than floppy disks. Both disk drives are often encased inside the computer. A floppy disk is removable. A hard disk is mounted inside the case of the computer. Removable hard disks are also available.

1.2.3.2   CDs

CD-R

CD-RW

CD stands for compact disc. There are two types of CD drives: CD-R and CD-RW. A *CD-R* is for read-only permanent storage, and the user cannot modify its contents once they are recorded. A *CD-RW* can be used like a floppy disk. A single CD can hold up to 650 MB. Most software is distributed through CD-Rs. Most new PCs are equipped with a CD-RW drive that can work with both CD-R and CD-W.

1.2.3.3   Tapes

Tapes are mainly used for backup of data and programs. Unlike disks and CDs, tapes store information sequentially. The computer must retrieve information in the order it was stored. Tapes are very slow. It would take one to two hours to back up a 1-gigabyte hard disk.

1.2.4   Input and Output Devices

The common input devices are *keyboards* and *mouses*. The output devices are *monitors* and *printers*. Input devices let the user talk to the computer. Output devices let the computer communicate to the user.

1.2.4.1   The Keyboard

A computer *keyboard* resembles a typewriter keyboard except that it has extra keys for certain special functions.

Function keys are located at the top of the keyboard with prefix F. Their use depends on the software.

Numeric keypad, located on the right-hand corner of the keyboard, is a separate set of number keys for quick input of numbers.

Arrow keys, located between the main keypad and the numeric keypad, are used to move the cursor up, down, left, and right.

Insert, delete, page up, page down keys, located above the arrow keys, are used in word processing for performing insert, delete, page up, and page down.

1.2.4.2   The Mouse

A mouse is a pointing device. It is used to move an electronic pointer called a cursor around the screen or to click on an object on the screen to trigger it to respond. In Java GUI programming, you can use the mouse to click on a button to trigger an event.

1.2.4.3 The Monitor

The monitor displays information (text and graphics). The resolution and dot pitch determine the quality of the display.

The *resolution* specifies the number of pixels per square inch. Pixels (short for "picture elements") are tiny dots that form an image on the screen. The resolution can be set manually. The higher the resolution, the sharper and clearer the image is.

The *dot pitch* is the amount of space between pixels. The smaller the dot pitch, the better the display.

resolution

dot pitch

1.2.5 Communication Devices

Computers can be networked through communication devices. The commonly used communication devices are the regular *modem*, *DSL*, cable modem, and *network interface card*. A regular modem uses a phone line and can transfer data at a speed up to 56,000 bps (bits per second). A DSL (digital subscriber line) also uses a phone line and can transfer data at a speed twenty times faster than a regular modem. A cable modem uses the TV cable line maintained by the cable company. A cable modem is as fast as a DSL. A network interface card (NIC) is a device that connects a computer to a *local area network* (LAN). The LAN is commonly used in business, universities, and government organizations. A typical NIC, called *10BaseT*, can transfer data at 10 mbps (million bits per second).

modem

DSL

NIC

LAN

mbps

1.3 Programs

Computer *programs*, known as *software*, are instructions to the computer. You tell a computer what to do through programs. Without programs, a computer is an empty machine. Computers do not understand human languages, so you need to use computer languages to communicate with them.

software

The language a computer speaks is the computer's native language or machine language. The *machine language* is a set of primitive instructions built into every computer. The instructions are in the form of binary code, so you have to enter binary codes for various instructions. Programming using a native machine language is a tedious process. Moreover, the programs are highly difficult to read and modify. For example, to add two numbers, you might have to write the instruction in binary like this:

machine language

```
1101101010011010
```

Assembly language is a low-level programming language in which a mnemonic is used to represent each of the machine language instructions. For example, to add two numbers, you might write an instruction in assembly code like this:

assembly language

```
ADDF3 R1, R2, R3
```

Assembly languages were developed to make programming easy. Since the computer cannot understand assembly language, however, a program called an *assembler* is used to convert assembly language programs into machine code, as shown in Figure 1.3.

assembler

Since assembly language is machine-dependent, an assembly program can only be executed on a particular machine. Assembly programs are written in terms of machine instructions with easy-to-remember mnemonic names. The high-level languages were developed in order to overcome the platform-specific problem and make programming easier.

The *high-level languages* are English-like and easy to learn and program. Here, for example, is a high-level language statement that computes the area of a circle with radius 5:

high-level language

```
area = 5 * 5 * 3.1415;
```

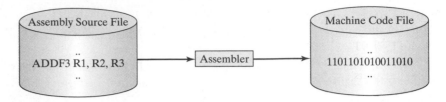

FIGURE 1.3 *Assembler translates assembly language instructions to machine code.*

There are over one hundred high-level languages. The popular languages used today are:

✦ Java

✦ COBOL (COmmon Business Oriented Language)

✦ FORTRAN (FORmula TRANslation)

✦ BASIC (Beginner All-purpose Symbolic Instructional Code)

✦ Pascal (named for Blaise Pascal)

✦ Ada (named for Ada Lovelace)

✦ C (whose developer designed B first)

✦ Visual Basic (Basic-like visual language developed by Microsoft)

✦ Delphi (Pascal-like visual language developed by Borland)

✦ C++ (an object-oriented language, based on C)

Each of these languages was designed for a specific purpose. COBOL was designed for business applications and now is used primarily for business data processing. FORTRAN was designed for mathematical computations and is used mainly for numeric computations. BASIC, as its name suggests, was designed to be learned and used easily. Ada was developed for the Department of Defense and is mainly used in defense projects. C combines the power of an assembly language with the ease of use and portability of a high-level language. Visual BASIC and Delphi are used in developing graphical user interfaces and in rapid application development. C++ is popular for system software projects like writing compilers and operating systems. The Microsoft Windows operating system was coded using C++.

source program
compiler

A program written in a high-level language is called a *source program*. Since a computer cannot understand a source program, a program called a *compiler* is used to translate the source program into a machine-language program called an *object program*. The object program is often then linked with other supporting library code to form an executable file. The executable file can be executed on the machine, as shown in Figure 1.4. On Windows, executable files have extension .exe.

You can port a source program to any machine with appropriate compilers. The source program must be recompiled, however, because the object program can only run on a specific

FIGURE 1.4 *A source program is compiled into an object file, and the object file is linked with the system library to form an executable file.*

machine. Nowadays computers are networked to work together. Java was designed to run object programs on any platform. With Java, you write the program once and compile the source program into a special type of object code known as *bytecode*. The bytecode can then run on any computer with a *Java Virtual Machine* (JVM), as shown in Figure 1.5. Java Virtual Machine is a software that interprets Java bytecode.

bytecode
JVM

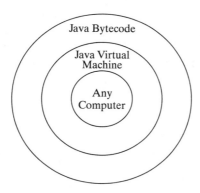

FIGURE 1.5   *Java bytecode can be executed on any computer with a Java Virtual Machine.*

1.4   Operating Systems

The *operating system* (OS) is the most important program that runs on a computer to manage and control its activities. You are probably using Windows 98, NT, 2000, XP, or ME. Windows is currently the most popular PC operating system. Application programs, such as an Internet browser or a word processor, cannot run without an operating system. The interrelationship of hardware, operating system, application software, and user is shown in Figure 1.6.

OS

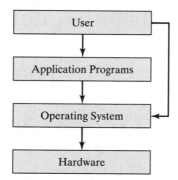

FIGURE 1.6   *The operating system is the software that controls and manages the system.*

The major tasks of the operating systems are:

✦ Controlling and monitoring system activities

✦ Allocating and assigning system resources

✦ Scheduling operations

1.4.1   Controlling and Monitoring System Activities

Operating systems are responsible for security, ensuring that unauthorized users do not access the system. Operating systems perform basic tasks, such as recognizing input from the keyboard, sending output to the monitor, keeping track of files and directories on the disk, and controlling peripheral devices, such as disk drives and printers. Operating systems also make sure that different programs and users running at the same time do not interfere with one other.

1.4.2   Allocating and Assigning System Resources

The OS is responsible for determining what computer resources (CPU, memory, disks, input and output devices) a program needs, and for allocating and assigning them to run the program.

1.4.3   Scheduling Operations

The OS is responsible for scheduling programs to use the system resources efficiently. Many of today's operating systems support such techniques as *multiprogramming, multithreading*, or *multiprocessing* to increase system performance.

multiprogramming

   Multiprogramming allows multiple programs to run simultaneously by sharing the CPU. The CPU is much faster than the other components. As a result, it is idle most of the time;—for example, while waiting for data to be transferred from the disk or from other sources. A multiprogramming OS takes advantage of this by allowing multiple programs to use the CPU when it would otherwise be idle. For example, you may use a word processor to edit a file while the Web browser is downloading a file at the same time.

multithreading

   Multithreading allows concurrency within a program, so that its subunits can run at the same time. For example, a word-processing program allows users to edit text and save it to a file at the same time. In this example, editing and saving are two tasks within the same application.

multiprocessing

   Multiprocessing, or parallel processing, uses two or more processors together to perform a task. It is like a surgical operation where several doctors work together on one patient.

1.5   Number Systems (Optional)

 NOTE
You can skip this section and use it as reference when you have questions regarding binary and hexadecimal numbers.

binary number

   Computers use *binary numbers* internally because storage devices like memory and disk are made to store 0s and 1s. A number or a text inside a computer is stored as a sequence of 0s and 1s. Each 0 or 1 is called a *bit*, short for *bi*nary *d*igit. The binary number system has two digits, 0 and 1.

decimal number

   Since we use *decimal numbers* in our daily life, binary numbers are not intuitive. When you write a number like 20 in a program, it is assumed to be a decimal number. The digits in the decimal number system are 0, 1, 2, 3, 4, 5, 6, 7, 8, and 9. Internally, computer software is used to convert decimal numbers into binary numbers, and vice versa.

   You write programs using decimal number systems. However, if you write programs to deal with a system like an operating system, you need to use binary numbers to reach down to the "machine-level." Binary numbers tend to be very long and cumbersome. *Hexadecimal numbers*

hexadecimal number

are often used to abbreviate binary numbers. The hexadecimal number system has sixteen digits: 0, 1, 2, 3, 4, 5, 6, 7, 8, 9, A, B, C, D, E, and F. The letters A, B, C, D, E, and F correspond to the decimal numbers 10, 11, 12, 13, 14, and 15.

1.5.1 Conversions Between Binary Numbers and Decimal Numbers

Given a binary number $b_n b_{n-1} b_{n-2} \ldots b_2 b_1 b_0$, the equivalent decimal value is

$$b_n \times 2^n + b_{n-1} \times 2^{n-1} + b_{n-2} \times 2^{n-2} + \cdots + b_2 \times 2^2 + b_1 \times 2^1 + b_0 \times 2^0$$

The following are examples of converting binary numbers to decimals:

Binary	Conversion formula	Decimal
10	$1 \times 2^1 + 0$	2
1000	$1 \times 2^3 + 0 \times 2^2 + 0 \times 2 + 0$	8
10101011	$1 \times 2^7 + 0 \times 2^6 + 1 \times 2^5 + 0 \times 2^4 + 1 \times 2^3 + 0 \times 2^2 + 1 \times 2 + 1$	171

To convert a decimal number d to a binary number is to find the bits b_n, b_{n-1}, $b_{n-2}, \ldots, b_2, b_1$, and b_0 such that

$$d = b_n \times 2^n + b_{n-1} \times 2^{n-1} + b_{n-2} \times 2^{n-2} + \cdots + b_2 \times 2^2$$
$$+ b_1 \times 2^1 + b_0 \times 2^0$$

These bits can be found by successively dividing d by 2 until the quotient is 0. The remainders are $b_0, b_1, b_2, \ldots, b_{n-2}, b_{n-1}$, and b_n.

For example, the decimal number 123 is 1111011 in binary. The conversion is done as follows:

Quotient →	61	30	15	7	3	1	0
	2 ⌐ 123	2 ⌐ 61	2 ⌐ 30	2 ⌐ 15	2 ⌐ 7	2 ⌐ 3	2 ⌐ 1
	122	60	30	14	6	2	0
Remainder →	1	1	0	1	1	1	1
	↓	↓	↓	↓	↓	↓	↓
	b_0	b_1	b_2	b_3	b_4	b_5	b_6

 TIP

The Windows Calculator, shown in Figure 1.7, is a useful tool for performing number conversions. To run it, choose *Programs, Accessories,* and *Calculator* from the Start button.

1.5.2 Conversions Between Hexadecimal Numbers and Decimal Numbers

Given a hexadecimal number $h_n h_{n-1} h_{n-2} \ldots h_2 h_1 h_0$, the equivalent decimal value is

$$h_n \times 16^n + h_{n-1} \times 16^{n-1} + h_{n-2} \times 16^{n-2} + \cdots$$
$$+ h_2 \times 16^2 + h_1 \times 16^1 + h_0 \times 16^0$$

Binary

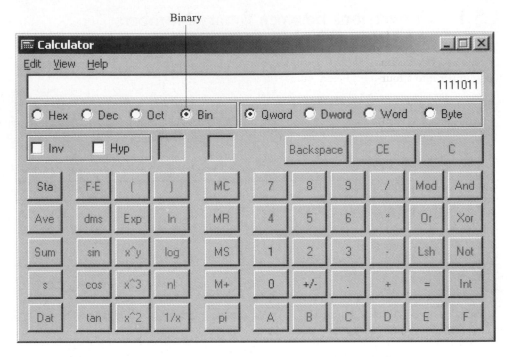

FIGURE 1.7 *You can perform number conversions using the Windows Calculator.*

The following are examples of converting hexadecimal numbers to decimals:

Hexadecimal	Conversion formula	Decimal
7F	$7 \times 16^1 + 15$	127
FFFF	$15 \times 16^3 + 15 \times 16^2 + 15 \times 16 + 15$	65535
431	$4 \times 16^2 + 3 \times 16 + 1$	1073

To convert a decimal number d to a hexadecimal number is to find the hexadecimal digits $h_n, h_{n-1}, h_{n-2}, \ldots, h_2, h_1,$ and h_0 such that

$$d = h_n \times 16^n + h_{n-1} \times 16^{n-1} + h_{n-2} \times 16^{n-2} + \cdots + h_2 \times 16^2$$
$$+ h_1 \times 16^1 + h_0 \times 16^0$$

These numbers can be found by successively dividing d by 16 until the quotient is 0. The remainders are $h_0, h_1, h_2, \ldots, h_{n-2}, h_{n-1},$ and h_n.

For example, the decimal number 123 is 7B in hexadecimal. The conversion is done as follows:

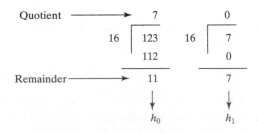

1.5.3   Conversions Between Binary Numbers and Hexadecimal Numbers

To convert a hexadecimal number to a binary number, simply convert each digit in the hexadecimal number into a four-digit binary number using Table 1.1.

TABLE **1.1**   Converting Hexadecimal to Binary

Hexadecimal	Binary	Decimal
0	0	0
1	1	1
2	10	2
3	11	3
4	100	4
5	101	5
6	110	6
7	111	7
8	1000	8
9	1001	9
A	1010	10
B	1011	11
C	1100	12
D	1101	13
E	1110	14
F	1111	15

For example, the hexadecimal number 7B is 1111011, where 7 is 111 in binary, and B is 1011 in binary.

To convert a binary number to a hexadecimal, convert every four binary digits from right to left in the binary number into a hexadecimal number.

For example, the binary number 1110001101 is 38D, since 1101 is D, 1000 is 8, and 11 is 3, as shown below:

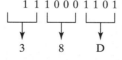

 NOTE
Octal numbers are also useful. The octal number system has eight digits, 0 to 7. A decimal number 8 is represented as 10 in the octal system.

1.6   Java, World Wide Web, and Beyond

This book introduces Java programming. Java was developed by a team led by James Gosling at Sun Microsystems. Originally called *Oak*, it was designed in 1991 for use in embedded consumer electronic appliances. In 1995, renamed *Java*, it was redesigned for developing Internet applications. For the history of Java, see `http://java.sun.com/features/1998/05/birthday.html`.

Java is a full-featured, general-purpose programming language that is capable of developing robust mission-critical applications. In recent years, Java has gained enormous popularity and has quickly become the most popular and successful programming language. Today, it is used not only for Web programming, but also for developing standalone applications across platforms on servers, desktops, and mobile devices. It was used to develop the code to communicate with and control the robotic rover that rolled on Mars. Many companies that once considered Java to be more hype than substance are now using it to create distributed applications accessed by customers and partners across the Internet. For every new project being developed today, companies are asking how they can use Java to make their work easier.

The World Wide Web is an electronic information repository that can be accessed on the Internet from anywhere in the world. You can use the Web to book a hotel room, buy an airline ticket, register for a college course, download the *New York Times*, chat with friends, or listen to live radio. There are countless activities you can do on the Internet. Many people spend a good part of their computer time surfing the Web for fun and profit.

The Internet is the infrastructure of the Web. The Internet has been around for more than thirty years, but has only recently become popular. The colorful World Wide Web and sophisticated Web browsers are the major reason for its popularity.

The primary authoring language for the Web is the Hypertext Markup Language (HTML). HTML is a markup language: a simple language for laying out documents, linking

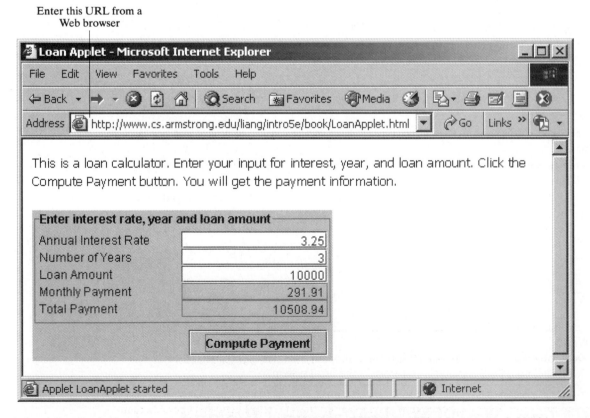

FIGURE 1.8   *A Java applet for computing loan payments is embedded in an HTML page. The user can use the applet to compute the loan payments.*

documents on the Internet, and bringing images, sound, and video alive on the Web. However, it cannot interact with the user except through simple forms. Web pages in HTML are essentially static and flat.

Java initially became attractive because Java programs can be run from a Web browser. Java programs that run from a Web browser are called *applets*. Applets use a modern graphical user interface with buttons, text fields, text areas, radio buttons, and so on, to interact with users on the Web and process their requests. Applets make the Web responsive, interactive, and fun to use. Figure 1.8 shows an applet running from a Web browser. To run applets from a Web browser, you need to use Netscape 7 or Internet Explorer 6, or higher.

applet

 TIP

For a demonstration of Java applets, visit `java.sun.com/applets`. This site provides a rich Java resource as well as links to other cool applet demo sites. `java.sun.com` is the official Sun Java Web site.

Java can also be used to develop applications on the server side. These applications, called *Java servlets* or *JavaServer Pages (JSP)*, can be run from a Web server to generate dynamic Web pages. The Self-Test Web site for this book, as shown in Figure 1.9, was developed using Java servlets. The Web pages for the questions and answers are dynamically generated by the servlets.

servlet
JSP

Enter this URL from a
Web browser

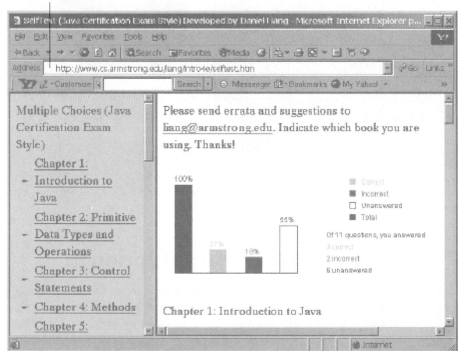

FIGURE 1.9 *Java was used to develop the self-test in the Companion Website for this book.*

Java is a versatile programming language. You can use it to develop applications on your desktop and on the server. You can also use it to develop applications for small hand-held devices, such as personal digital assistants and cell phones. Figure 1.10 shows a Java program that displays the calendar on a Palm PDA and on a cell phone.

FIGURE 1.10   *Java can be used to develop applications for hand-held and wireless devices, such as a Palm PDA (left) and a cell phone (right).*

1.7   Characteristics of Java (Optional)

Java has become enormously popular. Java's rapid rise and wide acceptance can be traced to its design and programming features, particularly its promise that you can write a program once and run it anywhere. As stated in the Java-language white paper by Sun, Java is *simple, object-oriented, distributed, interpreted, robust, secure, architecture-neutral, portable, high-performance, multithreaded,* and *dynamic.* Let's analyze these often-used buzzwords.

1.7.1   Java Is Simple

No language is simple, but Java is a bit easier than the popular object-oriented programming language C++, which was the dominant software-development language before Java. Java is partially modeled on C++, but greatly simplified and improved. For instance, pointers and multiple inheritance often make programming complicated. Java replaces the multiple inheritance in C++ with a simple language construct called an *interface*, and eliminates pointers.

Java uses automatic memory allocation and garbage collection, whereas C++ requires the programmer to allocate memory and collect garbage. Also, the number of language constructs is small for such a powerful language. The clean syntax makes Java programs easy to write and read. Some people refer to Java as "C++--" because it is like C++ but with more functionality and fewer negative aspects.

1.7.2   Java Is Object-Oriented

Java is inherently object-oriented. Although many object-oriented languages began strictly as procedural languages, Java was designed from the start to be object-oriented. Object-oriented programming (OOP) is a popular programming approach that is replacing traditional procedural programming techniques.

Software systems developed using procedural programming languages are based on the paradigm of procedures. Object-oriented programming models the real world in terms of objects. Everything in the world can be modeled as an object. A circle is an object, a person is an object, and a Windows icon is an object. Even a loan can be perceived as an object. A Java program is object-oriented because programming in Java is centered on creating objects, manipulating objects, and making objects work together.

Part I, "Fundamentals of Programming," introduces primitive data types and operations, control statements, methods, and arrays. These are the fundamentals for all programming languages. You will learn object-oriented programming in Part II, "Object-Oriented Programming."

One of the central issues in software development is how to reuse code. Object-oriented programming provides great flexibility, modularity, clarity, and reusability through encapsulation, inheritance, and polymorphism—all of which you will learn about in this book. For years, object-oriented technology was perceived as elitist, requiring a substantial investment in training and infrastructure. Java has helped object-oriented technology enter the mainstream of computing. Its simple, clean syntax makes programs easy to write and read. Java programs are quite *expressive* in terms of designing and developing applications.

1.7.3   Java Is Distributed

Distributed computing involves several computers working together on a network. Java is designed to make distributed computing easy. Since networking capability is inherently integrated into Java, writing network programs is like sending and receiving data to and from a file.

1.7.4   Java Is Interpreted

You need an interpreter to run Java programs. The programs are compiled into the Java Virtual Machine code called *bytecode*. The bytecode is machine-independent and can run on any machine that has a Java interpreter, which is part of the Java Virtual Machine (JVM).

bytecode

Most compilers, including C++ compilers, translate programs in a high-level language to machine code. The code can only run on the native machine. If you run the program on other machines, it has to be recompiled on the native machine. For instance, if you compile a C++ program in Windows, the executable code generated by the compiler can only run on the Windows platform. With Java, you compile the source code once, and the bytecode generated by a Java compiler can run on any platform with a Java interpreter. The Java interpreter translates the bytecode into the machine language of the target machine.

1.7.5   Java Is Robust

Robust means *reliable*. No programming language can ensure complete reliability. Java puts a lot of emphasis on early checking for possible errors, because Java compilers can detect many problems that would first show up at execution time in other languages. Java has eliminated certain types of error-prone programming constructs found in other languages. It does not support pointers, for example, thereby eliminating the possibility of overwriting memory and corrupting data.

Java has a runtime exception-handling feature to provide programming support for robustness. Java forces the programmer to write the code to deal with exceptions. Java can catch and respond to an exceptional situation so that the program can continue its normal execution and terminate gracefully when a runtime error occurs.

1.7.6   Java Is Secure

As an Internet programming language, Java is used in a networked and distributed environment. If you download a Java applet (a special kind of program) and run it on your computer, it will not damage your system because Java implements several security mechanisms to protect your system against harm caused by stray programs. The security is based on the premise that *nothing should be trusted*.

1.7.7   Java Is Architecture-Neutral

architecture-neutral
platform-independent

Java is interpreted. This feature enables Java to be *architecture-neutral*, or to use an alternative term, *platform-independent*. With a Java Virtual Machine (JVM), you can write one program that will run on any platform, as shown in Figure 1.5 on page 9.

Java's initial success stemmed from its Web-programming capability. You can run Java applets from a Web browser, but Java is for more than just writing Web applets. You can also run standalone Java applications directly from operating systems, using a Java interpreter. Today, software vendors usually develop multiple versions of the same product to run on different platforms (Windows, OS/2, Macintosh, and various UNIX, IBM AS/400, and IBM mainframes). Using Java, developers need to write only one version that can run on every platform.

1.7.8   Java Is Portable

Because Java is architecture-neutral, Java programs are portable. They can be run on any platform without being recompiled. Moreover, there are no platform-specific features in the Java language. In some languages, such as Ada, the largest integer varies on different platforms. But in Java, the range of the integer is the same on every platform, as is the behavior of arithmetic. The fixed range of the numbers makes the program portable.

The Java environment is portable to new hardware and operating systems. In fact, the Java compiler itself is written in Java.

1.7.9   Java's Performance

Java's performance is sometimes criticized. The execution of the bytecode is never as fast as it would be with a compiled language, such as C++. Because Java is interpreted, the bytecode is not directly executed by the system, but is run through the interpreter. However, its speed is more than adequate for most interactive applications, where the CPU is often idle, waiting for input or for data from other sources.

CPU speed has increased dramatically in the past few years, and this trend will continue. There are many ways to improve performance. Users of the earlier Sun Java Virtual Machine certainly noticed that Java was slow. However, the new JVM is significantly faster. The new JVM uses the technology known as *just-in-time compilation*. It compiles bytecode into native machine code, stores the native code, and reinvokes the native code when its bytecode is executed. Sun recently developed the Java HotSpot Performance Engine, which includes a compiler for optimizing the frequently used code. The HotSpot Performance Engine can be plugged into a JVM to dramatically boost its performance.

1.7.10 Java Is Multithreaded

Multithreading is a program's capability to perform several tasks simultaneously. For example, downloading a video file while playing the video would be considered multithreading. Multithread programming is smoothly integrated in Java, whereas in other languages you have to call procedures specific to the operating system to enable multithreading.

Multithreading is particularly useful in graphical user interface (GUI) and network programming. In GUI programming, there are many things going on at the same time. A user can listen to an audio recording while surfing a Web page. In network programming, a server can serve multiple clients at the same time. Multithreading is a necessity in multimedia and network programming.

1.7.11 Java Is Dynamic

Java was designed to adapt to an evolving environment. New class can be loaded on the fly without recompilation. There is no need for developers to create, and for users to install, major new software versions. New features can be incorporated transparently as needed.

1.8 The Java Language Specification, API, JDK, and IDE

Computer languages have strict rules of usage. If you do not follow the rules when writing a program, the computer will be unable to understand it. Sun Microsystems, the originator of Java, intends to retain control of this important new computer language—and for a very good reason: to prevent it from losing its unified standards. The Java language specification and Java API define the Java standard.

The Java language specification is a technical definition of the language that includes the syntax and semantics of the Java programming language. The complete reference of the Java language specification can be found at `java.sun.com/docs/books/jls`.

The *application program interface* (API) contains predefined classes and interfaces for developing Java programs. The Java language specification is stable, but the API is still expanding. At the Sun Java Web site (`java.sun.com`), you can view and download the latest version and updates to the Java API.

API

Java was introduced in 1995. Sun announced the Java 2 platform in December 1998. Java 2 is the overarching brand that applies to current Java technology. There are three editions of the Java API: *Java 2 Standard Edition (J2SE)*, *Java 2 Enterprise Edition (J2EE)*, and *Java 2 Micro Edition (J2ME)*. Java is a full-fledged and powerful language that can be used in many ways. J2SE can be used to develop client-side standalone applications or applets. J2EE can be used to develop server-side applications, such as Java servlets and JavaServer Pages. J2ME can be used to develop applications for mobile devices, such as cell phones. This book uses J2SE to introduce Java programming.

There are many versions of J2SE. The latest version is J2SE 5.0, which will be used in this book. Sun releases each version of J2SE with a *Java Development Toolkit* (JDK). For J2SE 5.0, the Java Development Toolkit is called JDK 5.0, formerly known as JDK 1.5. Since most Java programmers are familiar with the name JDK 1.5, this book uses the names JDK 5.0 and JDK 1.5 interchangeably.

J2SE 5.0

JDK 5.0
JDK 1.5

JDK consists of a set of separate programs for developing and testing Java programs, each of which is invoked from a command line. Besides JDK, there are more than a dozen Java development tools on the market today. The major development tools are:

✦ JBuilder by Borland (`www.borland.com`)

✦ NetBeans Open Source by Sun (`www.netbeans.org`)

> ✦ Sun ONE, a commercial version of NetBeans by Sun (`java.sun.com`)
>
> ✦ Eclipse Open Source by IBM (`www.eclipse.org`)

Java IDE

These tools provide an *integrated development environment* (IDE) for rapidly developing Java programs. Editing, compiling, building, debugging, and online help are integrated in one graphical user interface. Just enter source code in one window or open an existing file in a window, then click a button, menu item, or function key to compile the source code.

1.9   A Simple Java Program

application
applet

A Java program can be written in many ways. This book introduces Java applications and applets. *Applications* are standalone programs. This includes any program written with a high-level language. Applications can be executed from any computer with a Java interpreter. *Applets* are special kinds of Java programs that can run directly from a Java-compatible Web browser. Applets are suitable for deploying Web projects. Applets will be introduced in Chapter 14, "Applets, Images, and Audio."

Let us begin with a simple Java program that displays the message "Welcome to Java!"

EXAMPLE 1.1 A SIMPLE APPLICATION

Problem

Write a program that displays the message "Welcome to Java!" on the console.

Solution

Listing 1.1 gives the solution to the problem.

LISTING 1.1   Welcome.java (Displaying a Message)

```
// This application program prints Welcome to Java!

public class Welcome {    Class Name
    public static void main(String[] args) {

        System.out.println("Welcome to Java!");    String
    }
}
```

Comments →
Class heading →
Main method signature

Review

class name

Every Java program must have at least one class. Each class begins with a class declaration that defines data and methods for the class. In this example, the *class name* is `Welcome`.

main method

The class contains a method named `main`. The `main` method in this program contains the `System.out.println` statement. The `main` method is invoked by the interpreter.

console output

In this program, `println("Welcome to Java!")` is actually the statement that prints the message. So why use the other statements in the program? Because Java, like any other programming language, has its own syntax, and you need to write code that obeys the syntax rules. The Java compiler will report syntax errors if your program violates the syntax rules.

EXAMPLE 1.1 (CONTINUED)

 NOTE

You are probably wondering about such points as why the main method is declared this way and why System.out.println(...) is used to display a message to the console. Your questions cannot be fully answered yet. For the time being, you will just have to accept that this is how things are done. You will find the answers in the coming chapters.

1.10 Creating, Compiling, and Executing a Java Program

You have to create your program and compile it before it can be executed. This process is iterative, as shown in Figure 1.11. If your program has compilation errors, you have to fix them by modifying the program, then recompile it. If your program has runtime errors or does not produce the correct result, you have to modify the program, recompile it, and execute it again.

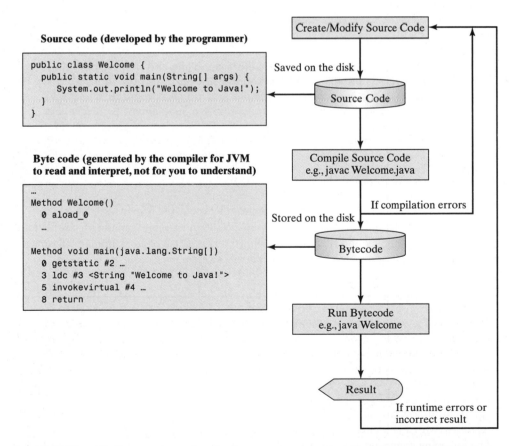

FIGURE 1.11 *The Java programming-development process consists of creating/modifying source code, compiling, and executing programs.*

editor

You can use any text *editor* to create and edit a Java source code file, or you can use an IDE like JBuilder and NetBeans. Figure 1.12 shows how to use the NotePad to create and edit the source code file.

```
Welcome - Notepad
File   Edit   Format   Help
public class welcome {
  public static void main(string[] args) {
    System.out.println("welcome to Java!");
  }
}
```

FIGURE 1.12 *You can create the Java source file using Windows NotePad.*

.java source file

This file must end with the extension .java and should have the exact same name as the public class name. For example, the file for the source code in Example 1.1 should be named Welcome.java, since the public class name is `Welcome`.

compile

To *compile* the program is to translate the Java source code into Java bytecode using the software called a *compiler*. The following command compiles Welcome.java:

```
javac Welcome.java
```

NOTE

You must first install and configure JDK before compiling and running programs. See Supplement A, "Installing and Configuring JDK 5.0," on how to install JDK and how to set up the environment to compile and run Java programs. If you have trouble compiling and running programs, please see Supplement B, "Compiling and Running Java from the Command Window." This supplement also contains information on how to use basic DOS commands and how to use Windows NotePad and WordPad to create and edit files. All the supplements are accessible from the Companion Website.

.class bytecode file

If there are no syntax errors, the *compiler* generates a bytecode file named `Welcome.class`. The bytecode is similar to machine instructions but is architecture-neutral and can run on any platform that has the Java interpreter and runtime environment. This is one of Java's primary advantages: *Java bytecode can run on a variety of hardware platforms and operating systems.*

CAUTION

Java source programs are case-sensitive. It would be wrong, for example, to replace main in the program with Main. Program filenames are case-sensitive on UNIX but generally not on PCs; JDK treats filenames as case-sensitive on any platform. If you try to compile the program using javac welcome.java, you will get a file-not-found error.

run

To execute a Java program is to run the program's bytecode. You can execute the bytecode on any platform with a Java interpreter.

The following command *runs* the bytecode:

```
java Welcome
```

Figure 1.13 shows the javac command for compiling Welcome.java. The compiler generated the Welcome.class file. This file is executed using the java command.

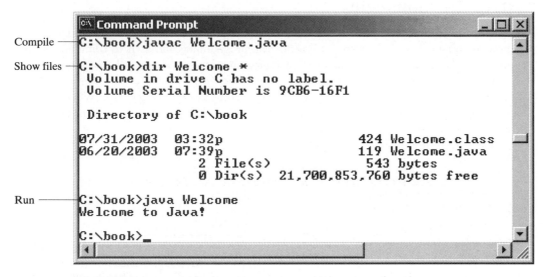

Compile —

Show files —

Run —

FIGURE **1.13** *The output of Example 1.1 displays the message Welcome to Java!*

 CAUTION

Do not use the extension .class in the command line when executing the program. The Java interpreter assumes that the first argument in the command is the filename and then fetches filename.class to execute. It would fetch filename.class.class if you used java filename.class in the command line.

 TIP

If you execute a class file that does not exist, a NoClassDefFoundError exception will occur. If you execute a class file that does not have a main method or you mistype the main method (e.g., by typing Main instead of main), a NoSuchMethodError will occur.

NoClassDefFoundError

NoSuchMethodError

1.11   Anatomy of the Java Program

The application program in Example 1.1 has the following components:

✦ Comments

✦ Reserved words

✦ Modifiers

✦ Statements

✦ Blocks

✦ Classes

✦ Methods

✦ The main method

To build a program, you need to understand these basic elements. They are explained in the sections that follow.

1.11.1   Comments

line comment

paragraph comment

The first line in welcome.java on page 20 is a *comment* that documents what the program is and how the program is constructed. Comments help programmers and users to communicate and understand the program. Comments are not programming statements and are ignored by the compiler. In Java, comments are preceded by two slashes (//) on a line, called a *line comment*, or enclosed between /* and */ on one or several lines, called a *paragraph comment*. When the compiler sees //, it ignores all text after // on the same line. When it sees /*, it scans for the next */ and ignores any text between /* and */.

Here are examples of the two types of comments:

```
// This application program prints Welcome to Java!
/* This application program prints Welcome to Java! */
/* This application program
   prints Welcome to Java! */
```

javadoc comment

 NOTE

In addition to the two comment styles, // and /*, Java supports comments of a special type, referred to as *javadoc comments*. javadoc comments begin with /** and end with */. They are used for documenting classes, data, and methods. They can be extracted into an HTML file using JDK's javadoc command. For more information, see java.sun.com/j2se/javadoc.

1.11.2   Reserved Words

reserved word

Reserved words, or *keywords*, are words that have a specific meaning to the compiler and cannot be used for other purposes in the program. For example, when the compiler sees the word class, it understands that the word after class is the name for the class. Other reserved words in Example 1.1 are public, static, and void. Their use will be introduced later in the book.

 TIP

case-sensitive

Because Java is *case-sensitive*, public is a reserved word, but Public is not. Nonetheless, for clarity and readability, it would be best to avoid using reserved words in other forms. (See Appendix A, "Java Keywords.")

1.11.3   Modifiers

modifier

Java uses certain reserved words called *modifiers* that specify the properties of the data, methods, and classes and how they can be used. Examples of modifiers are public and static. Other modifiers are private, final, abstract, and protected. A public datum, method, or class can be accessed by other classes. A private datum or method cannot be accessed by other classes.

1.11.4   Statements

statement

A *statement* represents an action or a sequence of actions. The statement System.out .println("Welcome to Java!") in the program in Example 1.1 is a statement to display the greeting "Welcome to Java!" Every statement in Java ends with a *semicolon* (;).

semicolon

1.11.5 Blocks

The braces in the program form a *block* that groups the components of the program. In Java, each block begins with an opening brace ({) and ends with a closing brace (}). Every class has a *class block* that groups the data and methods of the class. Every method has a *method block* that groups the statements in the method. Blocks can be *nested*, meaning that one block can be placed within another, as shown in the following code.

block

```
public class Test {
    public static void main(String[] args) {
        System.out.println("Welcome to Java!");  Method block
    }
}
```
Class block

1.11.6 Classes

The *class* is the essential Java construct. To program in Java, you must understand classes and be able to write and use them. The mystery of classes will be unveiled throughout the book. For now, though, it is enough to know that a program is defined by using one or more classes.

class

1.11.7 Methods

What is `System.out.println`? `System.out` is known as the *standard output object*. `println` is a *method* in the object, which consists of a collection of statements that perform a sequence of operations to display a message to the standard output device. If you run the program from the command window, the output from the `System.out.println` is displayed in the command window. The method can be used even without fully understanding the details of how it works. It is used by invoking a statement with a string argument. The string argument is enclosed in parentheses. In this case, the argument is `"Welcome to Java!"` You can call the same `println` method with a different argument to print a different message.

method

1.11.8 The `main` Method

Every Java application must have a user-declared `main` method that defines where the program begins. The `main` method provides the control of program flow. The Java interpreter executes the application by invoking the `main` method.

main method

The `main` method looks like this:

```
public static void main(String[] args) {
  // Statements;
}
```

1.12 Displaying Text in a Message Dialog Box

Example 1.1 displays the text on the console, as shown in Figure 1.13. You can rewrite the program to display the text in a message dialog box. To do so, you need to use the `showMessageDialog` method in the `JOptionPane` class. `JOptionPane` is one of the many predefined classes in the Java system that can be reused rather than "reinventing the wheel." You can use the `showMessageDialog` box to display any text in a message dialog box (or simply dialog), as shown in Figure 1.14.

JOptionPane

showMessageDialog

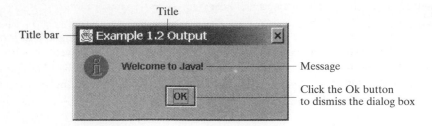

FIGURE 1.14 *The string Welcome to Java! is displayed in a message dialog box.*

EXAMPLE 1.2 USING MESSAGE DIALOG BOXES

Problem

Write a program that displays text in a message dialog box.

Solution

Listing 1.2 gives the solution to the problem. Figure 1.14 shows the text "Welcome to Java!" displayed in a message dialog box.

LISTING 1.2   WelcomeInMessageDialogBox.java (Displaying a Message in a Dialog)

paragraph comment

import

main method

display message

```
1   /** This application program displays Welcome to Java!
2    *  in a message dialog box.
3    */
4   import javax.swing.JOptionPane;
5
6   public class WelcomeInMessageDialogBox {
7     public static void main(String[] args) {
8       // Display Welcome to Java! in a message dialog box
9       JOptionPane.showMessageDialog(null, "Welcome to Java!",
10        "Example 1.2 Output", JOptionPane.INFORMATION_MESSAGE);
11    }
12  }
```

Review

The line numbers are not part of the program, but are displayed for reference purposes.

This program uses a Java class: JOptionPane (Line 9). Java's predefined classes are grouped into packages. JOptionPane is in the javax.swing package. It is imported to the program using the import statement in Line 4 so that the compiler can locate the class. Recall that you have used the System class in the statement System.out.println("Welcome to Java") in Example 1.1. The System class is not imported because it is in the java.lang package. All the classes in the java.lang package are implicitly imported in every Java program.

> **NOTE**
> If you replace JOptionPane on Line 9 with javax.swing.JOptionPane, you don't need to import it in Line 4. javax.swing.JOptionPane is the full name for the JOptionPane class.

EXAMPLE 1.2 (CONTINUED)

The showMessageDialog method is a *static* method. Such a method should be invoked by using the class name followed by a dot operator (.) and the method name with arguments. Static methods will be introduced in Chapter 4, "Methods." The showMessageDialog method can be invoked with four arguments, as in Lines 9–10.

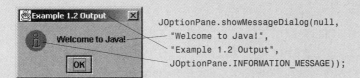

```
JOptionPane.showMessageDialog(null,
    "Welcome to Java!",
    "Example 1.2 Output",
    JOptionPane.INFORMATION_MESSAGE));
```

The first argument can always be null. null is a Java keyword that will be fully introduced in Part II, "Object-Oriented Programming." The second argument can be a string for text to be displayed. The third argument is the title of the message box. The fourth argument can be JOptionPane.INFORMATION_MESSAGE, which causes the icon () to be displayed in the message box.

 NOTE

There are several ways to use the showMessageDialog method. For the time being, all you need to know are two ways to invoke it. One is to use a statement, as shown in the example:

```
JOptionPane.showMessageDialog(null, x,
    y, JOptionPane.INFORMATION_MESSAGE));
```

where x is a string for the text to be displayed, and y is a string for the title of the message dialog box.

The other is to use a statement like this one:

```
JOptionPane.showMessageDialog(null, x);
```

where x is a string for the text to be displayed.

KEY TERMS

.java file   21
.class file   21
assembly language   7
binary numbers   10
block   25
byte   5
bytecode   9
cable modem   7
central processing unit (CPU)   4
comment   24
compiler   9
digital subscriber line (DSL)   7

dot pitch   7
hardware   4
hexadecimal numbers   10
high-level language   8
Integrated Development
   Environment (IDE)   20
interpreter   17
java command   23
javac command   22
Java Development Toolkit (JDK)   19
Java Virtual Machine (JVM)   9
just-in-time compiler   19

 NOTE

The above terms are defined in this chapter. Supplement G, "Glossary," lists all the key terms and descriptions in the book, organized by chapters.

Key Classes and Methods

✦ **java.lang.System** is a class that contains static methods for performing system functions, such as outputting a string to the console.

✦ **System.out.println (string)** outputs a string to the console.

✦ **javax.swing.JOptionPane** is a class that contains static methods for displaying dialog boxes.

✦ **JOptionPane.showMessageDialog(…)** displays a message dialog.

CHAPTER SUMMARY

✦ A computer is an electronic device that stores and processes data. A computer includes both *hardware* and *software*. In general, hardware is the physical aspect of the computer that can be seen, and software is the invisible instructions that control the hardware and make it work. The hardware of a computer consists of a CPU, memory, hard disk, floppy disk, monitor, printer, and communication devices.

✦ Computer *programs*, known as *software*, are instructions to the computer. You tell a computer what to do through programs. Computer programming consists of writing instructions for computers to perform. The language a computer speaks is the computer's native language or machine language.

✦ The *machine language* is a set of primitive instructions built into every computer. *Assembly language* is a low-level programming language in which a mnemonic is used to represent each of the machine-language instructions.

✦ *High-level languages* are English-like and easy to learn and program. There are over one hundred high-level languages. A program written in a high-level language is called a *source program*. Since a computer cannot understand a source program, a program called a *compiler* is used to translate the source program into a machine-language program called an *object program*. The object program is often then linked with other supporting library code before the object can be executed on the machine.

✦ The *operating system* (OS) is a program that manages and controls a computer's activities. Application programs, such as Internet browsers and word processors, cannot run without an operating system.

✦ Java was developed by a team led by James Gosling at Sun Microsystems. It is an Internet programming language. Since its inception in 1995, it has quickly become a premier language for building software.

✦ Java is platform-independent, meaning that you can write a program once and run it anywhere.

✦ Java is a simple, object-oriented programming language with built-in graphics programming, input and output, exception handling, networking, and multithreading support.

✦ Java programs can be embedded in HTML pages and downloaded by Web browsers to bring live animation and interaction to Web clients.

✦ Java source files end with the `.java` extension. Every class is compiled into a separate file called a bytecode that has the same name as the class and ends with the `.class` extension.

✦ To compile a Java source code file, use the `javac` command. To run a Java class, use the `java` command.

✦ Every Java program is a set of class definitions. The keyword `class` introduces a class definition. The contents of the class are included in a block. A block begins with an opening brace ({) and ends with a closing brace (}). Methods are contained in a class.

✦ A Java application must have a *main* method. The `main` method is the entry point where the application program starts when it is executed.

✦ You can display output to the console using the `System.out.println` method, or can display a message dialog box using the `JOptionPane.showMessageDialog` method.

REVIEW QUESTIONS

 NOTE
Answers to review questions are on the Companion Website.

Sections 1.2–1.4

1.1 Define hardware and software.

1.2 Define machine language, assembly language, and high-level programming language.

1.3 What is an operating system?

Section 1.5

1.4 Convert the following decimal numbers into hexadecimal and binary numbers.

100; 4340; 2000

1.5 Convert the following binary numbers into hexadecimal numbers and decimal numbers.

1000011001; 100000000; 100111

1.6 Convert the following hex numbers into binary and decimal numbers.

FEFA9; 93; 2000

Sections 1.6–1.8

1.7 Describe the history of Java. Can Java run on any machine? What is needed to run Java on a computer?

1.8 What are the input and output of a Java compiler?

1.9 List some Java development tools. Are tools like NetBeans and JBuilder different languages from Java, or are they dialects or extensions of Java?

1.10 What is the relationship between Java and HTML?

Sections 1.9–1.12

1.11 Explain the Java keywords. List some Java keywords you learned in this chapter.

1.12 Is Java case-sensitive? What is the case for Java keywords?

1.13 What is the Java source filename extension, and what is the Java bytecode filename extension?

1.14 What is a comment? What is the syntax for a comment in Java? Is the comment ignored by the compiler?

1.15 What is the statement to display a string on the console? What is the statement to display the message "Hello world" in a message dialog box?

1.16 Identify and fix the errors in the following code:

```
public class Welcome {
  public void Main(String[] args) {
    System.out.println('Welcome to Java!);
  }
}
```

1.17 What is the command to compile a Java program? What is the command to run a Java application?

1.18 If the exception NoClassFoundError is raised when you run a program from the DOS prompt, what is wrong?

1.19 If the exception "NoSuchMethodError: main" is raised when you run a program from the DOS prompt, what is wrong?

PROGRAMMING EXERCISES

1.1 (*Creating, compiling, and running a Java program*) Create a source file containing a Java program. Perform the following steps to compile the program and run it (see Section 1.10, "Creating, Compiling, and Executing a Java Program")

1. Create a file named Welcome.java for Example 1.1. You can use any editor that will save your file in text format.

2. Compile the source file.

3. Run the bytecode.

4. Replace "Welcome to Java" with "My first program" in the program; save, compile, and run the program. You will see the message "My first program" displayed.

5. Replace `main` with `Main`, and recompile the source code. The compiler returns an error message because the Java program is case-sensitive.

6. Change it back, and compile the program again.

7. Instead of the command `javac Welcome.java`, use `javac welcome.java`. What happens?

8. Instead of the command `java Welcome`, use `java Welcome.class`. What happens? (The interpreter searches for `Welcome.class.class`.)

chapter

2

PRIMITIVE DATA TYPES AND OPERATIONS

Objectives

✦ To write Java programs to perform simple calculations (§2.2).

✦ To use identifiers to name variables, constants, methods, and classes (§2.3).

✦ To use variables to store data (§§2.4–2.5).

✦ To program with assignment statements and assignment expressions (§2.5).

✦ To use constants to store permanent data (§2.6).

✦ To declare Java primitive data types: `byte`, `short`, `int`, `long`, `float`, `double`, `char`, and `boolean` (§§2.7–2.10).

✦ To use Java operators to write expressions (§§2.7–2.10).

✦ To know the rules governing operand evaluation order, operator precedence, and operator associativity (§§2.11–2.12).

✦ To represent a string using the `String` type (§2.13).

✦ To obtain input using the `JOptionPane` input dialog boxes (§2.14).

✦ To obtain input from the console (§2.16 Optional).

✦ To format output using JDK 1.5 `printf` (§2.17 Optional).

✦ To become familiar with Java documentation, programming style, and naming conventions (§2.18).

✦ To distinguish syntax errors, runtime errors, and logic errors (§2.19).

✦ To debug logic errors (§2.20).

2.1 Introduction

In the preceding chapter, you learned how to create, compile, and run a Java program. In this chapter, you will be introduced to Java primitive data types and related subjects, such as variables, constants, data types, operators, and expressions. You will learn how to write programs using primitive data types, input and output, and simple calculations.

2.2 Writing Simple Programs

To begin, let's look at a simple program that computes the area of a circle. The program reads in the radius of the circle and displays its area. The program will use variables to store the radius and the area, and will use an expression to compute the area.

Writing this program involves designing algorithms and data structures, as well as translating algorithms into programming codes. An *algorithm* describes how a problem is solved in terms of the actions to be executed, and it specifies the order in which the actions should be executed. Algorithms can help the programmer plan a program before writing it in a programming language. The algorithm for this program can be described as follows:

          algorithm

1. Read in the radius.

2. Compute the area using the following formula:

      area = radius $\times$ radius $\times$ π

3. Display the area.

Many of the problems you will meet when taking an introductory course in programming using this text can be described with simple, straightforward algorithms. As your education progresses, and you take courses on data structures or on algorithm design and analysis, you will encounter complex problems that require sophisticated solutions. You will need to design accurate, efficient algorithms with appropriate data structures in order to solve such problems.

Data structures involve data representation and manipulation. Java provides data types for representing integers, floating-point numbers (i.e., numbers with a decimal point), characters, and Boolean types. These types are known as *primitive data types*. Java also supports array and string types as objects. Some advanced data structures, such as stacks, sets, and lists, have built-in implementation in Java.

          primitive data types

To novice programmers, coding is a daunting task. When you *code*, you translate an algorithm into a programming language understood by the computer. You already know that every Java program begins with a class declaration in which the keyword `class` is followed by the class name. Assume that you have chosen `ComputeArea` as the class name. The outline of the program would look like this:

```
public class ComputeArea {
  // Data and methods to be given later
}
```

As you know, every application must have a `main` method that controls the execution of the program. So the program is expanded as follows:

```
public class ComputeArea {
  public static void main(String[] args) {
    // Step 1: Read in radius

    // Step 2: Compute area

    // Step 3: Display the area
  }
}
```

The program needs to read the radius entered by the user from the keyboard. This raises two important issues:

◆ Reading the radius.

◆ Storing the radius in the program.

variable

descriptive names

Let's address the second issue first. In order to store the radius, the program needs to declare a symbol called a *variable* that will represent the radius. Variables are used to store data and computational results in the program.

Rather than using x and y, choose *descriptive names*: in this case, radius for radius, and area for area. Specify their data types to let the compiler know what radius and area are, indicating whether they are integer, float, or something else. Declare radius and area as double-precision floating-point numbers. The program can be expanded as follows:

```
public class ComputeArea {
  public static void main(String[] args) {
    double radius;
    double area;

    // Step 1: Read in radius

    // Step 2: Compute area

    // Step 3: Display the area
  }
}
```

The program declares radius and area as variables. The reserved word double indicates that radius and area are double-precision floating-point values stored in the computer.

The first step is to read in radius. Reading a number is not a simple matter. For the time being, let us assign a fixed number to radius in the program. In Section 2.14, "Getting Input from Input Dialogs," you will learn how to obtain a numeric value from an input dialog.

The second step is to compute area by assigning the expression radius * radius * 3.14159 to area.

In the final step, print area on the console by using the System.out.println method.

The complete program is shown in Listing 2.1. A sample run of the program is shown in Figure 2.1.

LISTING 2.1 ComputeArea.java (Computing Area for a Circle)

```
1   public class ComputeArea {
2     /** Main method */
3     public static void main(String[] args) {
4       double radius;
5       double area;
6
7       // Assign a radius
8       radius = 20;
9
10      // Compute area
11      area = radius * radius * 3.14159;
12
13      // Display results
14      System.out.println("The area for the circle of radius " +
15        radius + " is " + area);
16    }
17  }
```

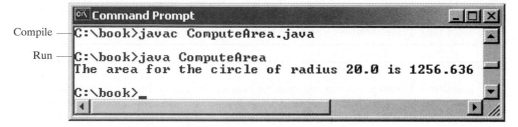

Compile
Run

FIGURE 2.1 *The program displays the area of the circle.*

The plus sign (+) is called a *string concatenation operator* if one of the operands is a string. The string concatenation operator connects two strings if two operands are strings. If one of the operands is a non-string (e.g., a number), the non-string value is converted into a string and concatenated with the other string. So the plus signs (+) in Lines 14–15 concatenate strings into a longer string, which is then displayed in the output. More on strings and string concatenation will be discussed in Section 2.13, "The String Type."

concatenating strings

concatenating strings with numbers

CAUTION

A string constant should not cross lines in the source code. Thus the following statement would result in a compilation error:

```java
System.out.println("Introduction to Java Programming,
  by Y. Daniel Liang");
```

To fix the error, break the string into substrings, and use the concatenation operator (+) to combine them:

breaking a long string

```java
System.out.println("Introduction to Java Programming, " +
  "by Y. Daniel Liang");
```

2.3 Identifiers

Just as every entity in the real world has a name, so you need to choose names for the things you will refer to in your programs. Programming languages use special symbols called *identifiers* to name such programming entities as variables, constants, methods, classes, and packages. Here are the rules for naming identifiers:

identifier

✦ An identifier is a sequence of characters that consists of letters, digits, underscores (_), and dollar signs ($).

✦ An identifier must start with a letter, an underscore (_), or a dollar sign ($). It cannot start with a digit.

✦ An identifier cannot be a reserved word. (See Appendix A, "Java Keywords," for a list of reserved words.)

✦ An identifier cannot be true, false, or null.

✦ An identifier can be of any length.

For example, $2, ComputeArea, area, radius, and showMessageDialog are legal identifiers, whereas 2A and d+4 are illegal identifiers because they do not follow the rules. The Java compiler detects illegal identifiers and reports syntax errors.

case-sensitive

 NOTE

Since Java is *case-sensitive*, X and x are different identifiers.

descriptive names

 TIP

Identifiers are used for naming variables, constants, methods, classes, and packages. Descriptive identifiers make programs easy to read. Besides choosing *descriptive names* for identifiers, there are naming conventions for different kinds of identifiers. Naming conventions are summarized in Section 2.18, "Programming Style and Documentation."

2.4 Variables

Variables are used to store data in a program. In the program in Listing 2.1, radius and area are variables of double-precision, floating-point type. You can assign any numerical value to radius and area, and the values of radius and area can be reassigned. For example, you can write the code shown below to compute the area for different radii:

```
// Compute the first area
radius = 1.0;
area = radius * radius * 3.14159;
System.out.println("The area is " + area + " for radius " + radius);

// Compute the second area
radius = 2.0;
area = radius * radius * 3.14159;
System.out.println("The area is " + area + " for radius " + radius);
```

2.4.1 Declaring Variables

Variables are for representing data of a certain type. To use a variable, you declare it by telling the compiler the name of the variable as well as what type of data it represents. This is called a *variable declaration*. Declaring a variable tells the compiler to allocate appropriate memory space for the variable based on its data type. Here is the syntax for declaring a variable:

declaring variable

```
datatype variableName;
```

Here are some examples of variable declarations:

```
int x;               // Declare x to be an integer variable;
double radius;       // Declare radius to be a double variable;
double interestRate; // Declare interestRate to be a double variable;
char a;              // Declare a to be a character variable;
```

The examples use the data types int, double, and char. Later in this chapter you will be introduced to additional data types, such as byte, short, long, float, char, and boolean. If variables are of the same type, they can be declared together, as follows:

```
datatype variable1, variable2, …, variablen;
```

The variables are separated by commas.

naming variables

 NOTE

By convention, variable names are in lowercase. If a name consists of several words, concatenate all of them and capitalize the first letter of each word except the first. Examples of variables are radius and interestRate.

2.5 Assignment Statements and Assignment Expressions

After a variable is declared, you can assign a value to it by using an *assignment statement*. In Java, the equal sign (=) is used as the *assignment operator*. The syntax for assignment statements is as follows:

assignment statement
assignment operator

```
variable = expression;
```

An *expression* represents a computation involving values, variables, and operators that evaluates to a value. For example, consider the following code:

expression

```
int x = 1;                      // Assign 1 to variable x;
double radius = 1.0;            // Assign 1.0 to variable radius;
a = 'A';                        // Assign 'A' to variable a;
x = 5 * (3 / 2) + 3 * 2;        // Assign the value of the expression to x;
x = y + 1;                      // Assign the addition of y and 1 to x;
area = radius * radius * 3.14159; // Compute area
```

The variable can also be used in the expression. For example,

```
x = x + 1;
```

In this assignment statement, the result of x + 1 is assigned to x. If x is 1 before the statement is executed, then it becomes 2 after the statement is executed.

To assign a value to a variable, the variable name must be on the left of the assignment operator. Thus, 1 = x would be wrong.

In Java, an assignment statement can also be treated as an expression that evaluates to the value being assigned to the variable on the left-hand side of the assignment operator. For this reason, an assignment statement is also known as an *assignment expression*. For example, the following statement is correct:

assignment expression

```
System.out.println(x = 1);
```

which is equivalent to

```
x = 1;
System.out.println(x);
```

The following statement is also correct:

```
i = j = k = 1;
```

which is equivalent to

```
k = 1;
j = k;
i = j;
```

 NOTE

In an assignment statement, the data type of the variable on the left must be compatible with the data type of the value on the right. For example, int x = 1.0 would be illegal because the data type of x is int. You cannot assign a double value (1.0) to an int variable without using type casting. Type casting is introduced in Section 2.8, "Numeric Type Conversions."

2.5.1 Declaring and Initializing Variables in One Step

Variables often have initial values. You can declare a variable and initialize it in one step. Consider, for instance, the following code:

```
int x = 1;
```

This is equivalent to the next two statements:

```
int x;
x = 1;
```

You can also use a shorthand form to declare and initialize variables of the same type together. For example,

```
int i = 1, j = 2;
```

 TIP

A variable must be declared before it can be assigned a value. A variable declared in a method must be assigned a value before it can be used.

Whenever possible, declare a variable and assign its initial value in one step. This will make the program easy to read and avoid programming errors.

2.6   Constants

constant

The value of a variable may change during the execution of the program, but a *constant* represents permanent data that never changes. In our `ComputeArea` program, π is a constant. If you use it frequently, you don't want to keep typing 3.14159; instead, you can define a constant for π. Here is the syntax for declaring a constant:

```
final datatype CONSTANTNAME = VALUE;
```

The word `final` is a Java keyword which means that the constant cannot be changed. For example, in the `ComputeArea` program, you could define π as a constant and rewrite the program as follows:

```
// ComputeArea.java: Compute the area of a circle
public class ComputeArea {
  /** Main method */
  public static void main(String[] args) {
    final double PI + 3.14159; // Declare a constant

    // Assign a radius
    double radius = 20;

    // Compute area
    double area = radius * radius * PI;

    // Display results
    System.out.println("The area for the circle of radius " +
      radius + " is " + area);
  }
}
```

naming constants

 CAUTION

A constant must be declared and initialized before it can be used. You cannot change a constant's value once it is declared. By convention, constants are named in uppercase: `PI`, not `pi` or `Pi`.

benefits of constants

 NOTE

There are three benefits of using constants: (1) you don't have to repeatedly type the same value; (2) the value can be changed in a single location, if necessary; (3) the program is easy to read.

2.7 Numeric Data Types and Operations

Every data type has a range of values. The compiler allocates memory space to store each variable or constant according to its data type. Java provides several primitive data types for numeric values, characters, and Boolean values. In this section, numeric data types are introduced.

Java has six numeric types: four for integers and two for floating-point numbers. Table 2.1 lists the six numeric data types, their ranges, and their storage sizes.

TABLE 2.1 Numeric Data Types

Name	Range	Storage Size
byte	-2^7 (-128) to $2^7 - 1$ (127)	8-bit signed
short	-2^{15} (-32768) to $2^{15} - 1$ (32767)	16-bit signed
int	-2^{31} (-2147483648) to $2^{31} - 1$ (2147483647)	32-bit signed
long	-2^{63} to $2^{63} - 1$ (i.e., -9223372036854775808 to 9223372036854775807)	64-bit signed
float	$-3.4E38$ to $3.4E38$ (6 to 7 significant digits of accuracy)	32-bit IEEE 754
double	$-1.7E308$ to $1.7E308$ (14 to 15 significant digits of accuracy)	64-bit IEEE 754

> **NOTE**
> IEEE 754 is a standard approved by the Institute of Electrical and Electronics Engineers for representing floating-point numbers on computers. The standard has been widely adopted. Java has adopted the 32-bit IEEE 754 for the `float` type and the 64-bit IEEE 754 for the `double` type. The IEEE 754 standard also defines special values and operations in Appendix F, "Special Floating-Point Values."

2.7.1 Numeric Operators

The operators for numeric data types include the standard arithmetic operators: addition (+), subtraction (−), multiplication (*), division (/), and remainder (%). For examples, see the following code:

operators +, −, *, /, %

```
int i1 = 34 + 1;        // i1 becomes 35
double d1 = 34.0 - 0.1; // d1 becomes 33.9
long i2 = 300 * 30;     // i2 becomes 9000
double d2 = 1.0 / 2.0;  // d2 becomes 0.5
int i3 = 1 / 2;         // i3 becomes 0; Note that the result is
                        // the integer part of the division
byte i4 = 20 % 3;       // i4 becomes 2; Note that the result is
                        // the remainder after the division
```

The result of integer division is an integer. The fractional part is truncated. For example, $5/2 = 2$, not 2.5, and $-5/2 = -2$, not -2.5.

The % operator yields the remainder after division. Therefore, 7 % 3 yields 1, and 20 % 13 yields 7. This operator is often used for integers but also can be used with floating-point values.

$\dfrac{2}{7}$
$\sqrt[3]{}$
$\dfrac{6}{1}$

Remainder is very useful in programming. For example, an even number % 2 is always 0 and an odd number % 2 is always 1. So you can use this property to determine whether a number is even or odd. Suppose you know that January 1, 2005 is a Saturday, you can find that the day for February 1, 2005 is Tuesday using the following expression:

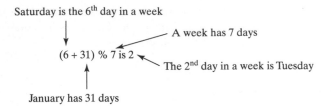

Saturday is the 6th day in a week

A week has 7 days

(6 + 31) % 7 is 2

The 2nd day in a week is Tuesday

January has 31 days

unary operator
binary operator

The + and − operators can be both unary and binary. A *unary operator* has only one operand; a *binary operator* has two operands. For example, the − operator in −5 can be considered a unary operator to negate number 5, whereas the − operator in 4 − 5 is a binary operator for subtracting 5 from 4.

approximation

> **NOTE**
> Calculations involving floating-point numbers are approximated because these numbers are not stored with complete accuracy. For example,
>
> ```
> System.out.println(1 - 0.1 - 0.1 - 0.1 - 0.1 - 0.1);
> ```
>
> displays 0.5000000000000001, not 0.5, and
>
> ```
> System.out.println(1.0 - 0.9);
> ```
>
> displays 0.09999999999999998, not 0.1. Integers are stored precisely. Therefore, calculations with integers yield a precise integer result.

2.7.2 Numeric Literals

literal

A *literal* is a constant value that appears directly in a program. For example, 34, 1,000,000, and 5.0 are literals in the following statements:

```
int i = 34;
long k = 1000000;
double d = 5.0;
```

2.7.2.1 Integer Literals

An integer literal can be assigned to an integer variable as long as it can fit into the variable. A compilation error would occur if the literal were too large for the variable to hold. The statement `byte b = 1000`, for example, would cause a compilation error, because 1000 cannot be stored in a variable of the `byte` type.

suffix L or l

An integer literal is assumed to be of the `int` type, whose value is between -2^{31} (-2147483648) and $2^{31} - 1$ (2147483647). To denote an integer literal of the `long` type, append the letter L or l to it (e.g., `2147483648L`). L is preferred because l (lowercase L) can easily be confused with 1 (the digit one). Since `2147483648` exceeds the range for the `int` value, it must be denoted as `2147483648L`.

octal and hex literals

> **NOTE**
> By default, an integer literal is a decimal number. To denote an octal integer literal, use a leading 0 (zero), and to denote a hexadecimal integer literal, use a

leading *0x* or *0X* (zero x). For example, the following code displays the decimal value 65535 for hexadecimal number FFFF:

```
System.out.println(0xFFFF);
```

Hexadecimal numbers, binary numbers, and octal numbers were introduced in Section 1.5, "Number systems."

2.7.2.2   Floating-Point Literals

Floating-point literals are written with a decimal point. By default, a floating-point literal is treated as a `double` type value. For example, 5.0 is considered a `double` value, not a `float` value. You can make a number a `float` by appending the letter `f` or `F`, and you can make a number a `double` by appending the letter `d` or `D`. For example, you can use `100.2f` or `100.2F` for a `float` number, and `100.2d` or `100.2D` for a `double` number.

suffix f or F
suffix d or D

 NOTE

The `double` type values are more accurate than the `float` type values. For example,

```
System.out.println("1.0 / 3.0 is " + 1.0 / 3.0);
```

displays 1.0 / 3.0 is 0.3333333333333333.

```
System.out.println("1.0F / 3.0F is " + 1.0F / 3.0F);
```

displays 1.0F / 3.0F is 0.33333334.

double vs. `float`

2.7.2.3   Scientific Notations

Floating point literals can also be specified in scientific notation; for example, 1.23456e + 2, the same as 1.23456e2, is equivalent to $1.23456 \times 10^2 = 123.456$, and 1.23456e − 2 is equivalent to $1.23456 \times 10^{-2} = 0.0123456$. E (or e) represents an exponent and can be either in lowercase or uppercase.

2.7.3   Arithmetic Expressions

Writing numeric expressions in Java involves a straightforward translation of an arithmetic expression using Java operators. For example, the arithmetic expression

$$\frac{3 + 4x}{5} - \frac{10(y - 5)(a + b + c)}{x} + 9\left(\frac{4}{x} + \frac{9 + x}{y}\right)$$

can be translated into a Java expression as:

```
(3 + 4 * x) / 5 - 10 * (y - 5) * (a + b + c) / x +
9 * (4 / x + (9 + x) / y)
```

The numeric operators in a Java expression are applied the same way as in an arithmetic expression. Operators contained within pairs of parentheses are evaluated first. Parentheses can be nested, in which case the expression in the inner parentheses is evaluated first. Multiplication, division, and remainder operators are applied next. If an expression contains several multiplication, division, and remainder operators, they are applied from left to right. Addition and subtraction operators are applied last. If an expression contains several addition and subtraction operators, they are applied from left to right.

integer vs. decimal division

 CAUTION

Be careful when applying division. Division of two integers yields an integer in Java. For example, the formula for converting a Fahrenheit degree is

$$\text{celsius} = \left(\frac{5}{9}\right)(\text{fahrenheit} - 32)$$

Because 5 / 9 yields 0 in Java, the preceding formula should be translated into a Java statement shown below:

```
celsius = (5.0 / 9) * (fahrenheit - 32)
```

2.7.4 Shortcut Operators

Very often the current value of a variable is used, modified, and then reassigned back to the same variable. For example, consider the following code:

```
i = i + 8;
```

This statement is equivalent to

```
i += 8;
```

shortcut operator

The += is called a *shortcut operator*. Other shortcut operators are shown in Table 2.2.

TABLE 2.2 Shortcut Operators

Operator	Name	Example	Equivalent
+=	Addition assignment	i += 8	i = i + 8
-=	Subtraction assignment	f -= 8.0	f = f - 8.0
*=	Multiplication assignment	i *= 8	i = i * 8
/=	Division assignment	i /= 8	i = i / 8
%=	Remainder assignment	i %= 8	i = i % 8

++ and --

There are two more shortcut operators for incrementing and decrementing a variable by 1. This is handy because that's often how much the value needs to be changed. These two operators are ++ and --. They can be used in prefix or suffix notation, as shown in Table 2.3.

TABLE 2.3 Increment and Decrement Operators

Operator	Name	Description
++var	preincrement	The expression (++var) increments var by 1 and evaluates to the *new* value in var *after* the increment.
var++	postincrement	The expression (var++) evaluates to the *original* value in var and increments var by 1.
--var	predecrement	The expression (--var) decrements var by 1 and evaluates to the *new* value in var *after* the decrement.
var--	postdecrement	The expression (var--) evaluates to the *original* value in var and decrements var by 1.

preincrement, predecrement

If the operator is *before* (prefixed to) the variable, the variable is incremented or decremented by 1, then the *new* value of the variable is returned. If the operator is *after* (suffixed to) the variable, the original *old* value of the variable is returned, then the variable is incremented or decremented by 1. Therefore, the prefixes ++x and --x are referred to, respectively, as the *preincrement operator* and the *predecrement operator*; and the suffixes x++ and x-- are referred to, respectively, as the *postincrement operator* and the *postdecrement operator*. The prefix form of ++ (or −−) and the suffix form of ++ (or --) are the same if they are used in isolation, but they have different effects when used in an expression. The following code illustrates this:

```
int i = 10;
int newNum = 10 * i++;
```
Same effect as →
```
int newNum = 10 * i;
i = i + 1;
```

In this case, i is incremented by 1, then the *old* value of i is returned and used in the multiplication. So newNum becomes 100. If i++ is replaced by ++i as follows,

```
int i = 10;
int newNum = 10 * (++i);
```
Same effect as →
```
i = i + 1;
int newNum = 10 * i;
```

i is incremented by 1, and the new value of i is returned and used in the multiplication. Thus newNum becomes 110.

Here is another example:

```
double x = 1.0;
double y = 5.0;
double z = x-- + (++y);
```

After all three lines are executed, y becomes 6.0, z becomes 7.0, and x becomes 0.0.

The increment operator ++ and the decrement operator −− can be applied to all integer and floating-point types. These operators are often used in loop statements. A *loop statement* is a structure that controls how many times an operation or a sequence of operations is performed in succession. This structure, and the subject of loop statements, is introduced in Chapter 3, "Control Statements."

 TIP

Using increment and decrement operators makes expressions short, but it also makes them complex and difficult to read. Avoid using these operators in expressions that modify multiple variables or the same variable multiple times, such as this one: int k = ++i + i.

 NOTE

Like the assignment operator (=), the operators (+=, -=, *=, /=, %=, ++, and --) can be used to form an assignment statement as well as an expression. Prior to Java 2, all expressions could be used as statements. Since Java 2, only the following types of expressions can be statements:

```
variable op= expression; // Where op is +, -, *, /, or %
++variable;
variable++;
--variable;
variable--;
```

The code shown below has a compilation error in Java 2:

```
public static void main(String[] args) {
  3 + 4; // Correct prior to Java 2, but wrong in Java 2
}
```

CAUTION

There are no spaces in the shortcut operators. For example, + = should be +=.

2.8   Numeric Type Conversions

Sometimes it is necessary to mix numeric values of different types in a computation. Consider the following statements:

```
byte i = 100;
long k = i * 3 + 4;
double d = i * 3.1 + k / 2;
```

converting operands

Are these statements correct? Java allows binary operations on values of different types. When performing a binary operation involving two operands of different types, Java automatically converts the operand based on the following rules:

1. If one of the operands is `double`, the other is converted into `double`.

2. Otherwise, if one of the operands is `float`, the other is converted into `float`.

3. Otherwise, if one of the operands is `long`, the other is converted into `long`.

4. Otherwise, both operands are converted into `int`.

For example, the result of 1/2 is 0, and the result of 1.0/2 is 0.5.

type casting

widening a type

narrowing a type

You can always assign a value to a numeric variable whose type supports a larger range of values; thus, for instance, you can assign a `long` value to a `float` variable. You cannot, however, assign a value to a variable of a type with smaller range unless you use *type casting*. Casting is an operation that converts a value of one data type into a value of another data type. Casting a variable of a type with a small range to a variable of a type with a larger range is known as *widening a type*. Casting a variable of a type with a large range to a variable of a type with a smaller range is known as *narrowing a type*. Widening a type can be performed automatically without explicit casting. Narrowing a type must be performed explicitly.

The syntax for casting gives the target type in parentheses, followed by the variable's name or the value to be cast. The code that follows is an example.

```
float f = (float)10.1;
int i = (int)f;
```

In the first line, the `double` value 10.1 is cast into `float`. In the second line, `i` has a value of 10; the fractional part in `f` is truncated.

CAUTION

possible loss of precision

Casting is necessary if you are assigning a value to a variable of a smaller type range, such as assigning a `double` value to an `int` variable. A compilation error will occur if casting is not used in situations of this kind. Be careful when using casting. Lost information might lead to inaccurate results, as will be shown in Example 2.3, "Monetary Units," in Section 2.15, "Case Studies."

NOTE

Casting does not change the variable being cast. For example, `d` is not changed after casting in the following code:

```
double d = 4.5;
int i = (int)d; // d is not changed
```

NOTE

To assign a variable of the `int` type to a variable of the `short` or `byte` type, explicit casting must be used. For example, the following statements have a syntax error:

```
int i = 1;
byte b = i; // Error because explicit casting is required
```

However, so long as the integer literal is within the permissible range of the target variable, explicit casting is not needed to assign an integer literal to a variable of the `short` or `byte` type. Please refer to Section 2.7.2.1, "Integer Literals."

2.9   Character Data Type and Operations

The character data type, `char`, is used to represent a single character. A character literal is enclosed in single quotation marks. Consider the following code:

```
char letter = 'A';
char numChar = '4';
```

char type

The first statement assigns character A to the `char` variable `letter`. The second statement assigns the digit character 4 to the `char` variable `numChar`.

 CAUTION

A string literal must be enclosed in quotation marks. A character literal is a single character enclosed in single quotation marks. So "A" is a string, and 'A' is a character.

char literal

2.9.1   Unicode and ASCII code

Computers use binary numbers internally. A character is stored as a sequence of 0s and 1s in a computer. To convert a character to its binary representation is called *encoding*. There are different ways to encode a character. How characters are encoded is defined by an encoding scheme.

character encoding

Java uses *Unicode*, a 16-bit encoding scheme established by the Unicode Consortium to support the interchange, processing, and display of written texts in the world's diverse languages. (See the Unicode Web site at www.unicode.org for more information.) Unicode takes two bytes, preceded by \u, expressed in four hexadecimal digits that run from '\u0000' to '\uFFFF'. For example, the word "coffee" is translated into Chinese using two characters. The Unicodes of these two characters are "\u5496\u5561". The following statement displays three Greek letters, as shown in Figure 2.2.

Unicode

```
JOptionPane.showMessageDialog(null, "\u03b1 \u03b2 \u03b3",
    "Display Greek Letters", JOptionPane.INFORMATION_MESSAGE);
```

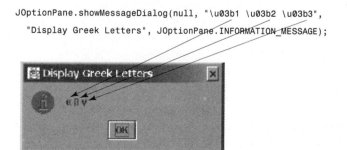

FIGURE 2.2   *You can use Unicode to represent international characters.*

Unicode can represent 65,536 characters, since FFFF in hexadecimal is 65535. Most computers use ASCII (American Standard Code for Information Interchange), a 7-bit encoding scheme for representing all uppercase and lowercase letters, digits, punctuation marks, and control characters. Unicode includes ASCII code, with '\u0000' to '\u007F' corresponding to the 128 ASCII characters. (See Appendix B, "The ASCII Character Set," for a list of ASCII characters and their decimal and hexadecimal codes.) You can use ASCII characters like 'X', '1', and '$' in a Java program as well as Unicodes. Thus, for example, the following statements are equivalent:

```
char letter = 'A';
char letter = '\u0041'; // Character A's Unicode is 0041
```

Both statements assign character A to char variable letter.

NOTE

The increment and decrement operators can also be used on char variables to get the next or preceding Unicode character. For example, the following statements display character b:

```
char ch = 'a';
System.out.println(++ch);
```

2.9.2 Escape Sequences for Special Characters

Java allows you to use escape sequences to represent special characters, as shown in Table 2.4. An escape sequence begins with the backslash character (\) followed by a character that has a special meaning to the compiler.

TABLE 2.4 **Java Escape Sequences**

Description	Character Escape Sequence	Unicode
Backspace	\b	\u0008
Tab	\t	\u0009
Linefeed	\n	\u000A
Formfeed	\f	\u000C
Carriage Return	\r	\u000D
Backslash	\\	\u005C
Single Quote	\'	\u0027
Double Quote	\"	\u0022

Suppose you want to print the quoted message shown below:

```
He said "Java is fun"
```

Here is how to write the statement:

```
System.out.println("He said \"Java is fun\"");
```

2.9.3 Casting between char and Numeric Types

A char can be cast into any numeric type, and vice versa. When an integer is cast into a char, only its lower sixteen bits of data are used; the other part is ignored. When a floating-point value is cast into a char, the floating-point value is first cast into an int, which is then cast into a char. When a char is cast into a numeric type, the character's Unicode is cast into the specified numeric type.

Implicit casting can be used if the result of a casting fits into the target variable. Otherwise, explicit casting must be used. For example, since the Unicode of '0' is 48, which is within the range of a byte, these implicit castings are fine:

```
byte b = '0';
int i = '0';
```

But the next casting is incorrect, because the Unicode \uFFF4 cannot fit into a byte:

```
byte b = '\uFFF4';
```

To force a casting, use explicit casting, as follows:

```
byte b = (byte)'\uFFF4';
```

Any positive integer between 0 and FFFF in hexadecimal can be cast into a character implicitly. Any number not in this range must be cast into a char explicitly.

 NOTE

All numeric operators can be applied to the char operands. The char operand is cast into a number if the other operand is a number or a character. If the other operand is a string, the character is concatenated with the string. For example, the following statements:

numeric operators on characters

```
int i = '1' + '2'; // (int)'1' is 49 and (int)'2' is 50
System.out.println("i is " + i);

int j = 1 + 'a'; // (int)'a' is 97
System.out.println("j is " + 98);
System.out.println(j + " is the Unicode for character " + (char)j);

System.out.println("Chapter " + '2');
```

display

```
i is 99
j is 98
98 is the Unicode for character b
Chapter 2
```

 NOTE

It is worthwhile to note that the Unicodes for lowercase letters are consecutive integers starting from the Unicode for 'a', then for 'b', 'c', ..., and 'z'. The same is true for the uppercase letters. Furthermore, the Unicode for 'a' is greater than the Unicode for 'A'. So 'a' - 'A' is the same as 'b' - 'B'. For a lowercase letter *ch*, its corresponding uppercase letter is (char)('A' + (ch - 'a')).

2.10 **boolean** Data Type and Operations

Often in a program you need to compare two values, such as whether i is greater than j. Java provides six *comparison operators* (also known as *relational operators*) in Table 2.5 that can be used to compare two values. The result of the comparison is a Boolean value: true or false. For example, the following statement displays true:

comparison operators

```
System.out.println(1 < 2);
```

TABLE 2.5 Comparison Operators

Operator	Name	Example	Answer
<	less than	1 < 2	true
<=	less than or equal to	1 <= 2	true
>	greater than	1 > 2	false
>=	greater than or equal to	1 >= 2	false
==	equal to	1 == 2	false
!=	not equal to	1 != 2	true

compare characters

 NOTE

You can also *compare characters*. Comparing characters is the same as comparing the Unicodes of the characters. For example, 'a' is larger than 'A' because the Unicode of 'a' is larger than the Unicode of 'A'.

(== vs. =)

 CAUTION

The equality comparison operator is two equal signs (==), not a single equal sign (=). The latter symbol is for assignment.

Boolean variable

A variable that holds a Boolean value is known as a *Boolean variable*. The boolean data type is used to declare Boolean variables. The domain of the boolean type consists of two literal values: true and false. For example, the following statement assigns true to the variable lightsOn:

```
boolean lightsOn = true;
```

Boolean operators

Boolean operators, also known as *logical operators*, operate on Boolean values to create a new Boolean value. Table 2.6 contains a list of *Boolean operators*. Table 2.7 defines the not (!) operator. The not (!) operator negates true to false and false to true. Table 2.8 defines the and (&&)

TABLE 2.6 Boolean Operators

Operator	Name	Description
!	not	logical negation
&&	and	logical conjunction
||	or	logical disjunction
^	exclusive or	logical exclusion

TABLE 2.7 Truth Table for Operator !

p	!p	Example
true	false	!(1 > 2) is true, because (1 > 2) is false.
false	true	!(1 > 0) is false, because (1 > 0) is true.

TABLE 2.8 Truth Table for Operator &&

p1	p2	p1 && p2	Example
false	false	false	(2 > 3) && (5 > 5) is false, because either (2 > 3) or (5 > 5) is false.
false	true	false	
true	false	false	(3 > 2) && (5 > 5) is false, because (5 > 5) is false.
true	true	true	(3 > 2) && (5 >= 5) is true, because (3 > 2) and (5 >= 5) are both true.

TABLE 2.9 Truth Table for Operator ¦¦

p1	p2	p1 ¦¦ p2	*Example*
false	false	false	(2 > 3) ¦¦ (5 > 5) is false, because (2 > 3) and (5 > 5) are both false.
false	true	true	
true	false	true	(3 > 2) ¦¦ (5 > 5) is true, because (3 > 2) is true.
true	true	true	

TABLE 2.10 Truth Table for Operator ^

p1	p2	p1 ^ p2	*Example*
false	false	false	
false	true	true	(2 > 3) ^ (5 > 1) is true, because (2 > 3) is false and (5 > 1) is true.
true	false	true	
true	true	false	(3 > 2) ^ (5 > 1) is false, because both (3 > 2) and (5 > 1) are true.

operator. The and (&&) of two Boolean operands is true if and only if both operands are true. Table 2.9 defines the or (¦¦) operator. The or (¦¦) of two Boolean operands is true if at least one of the operands is true. Table 2.10 defines the exclusive or (^) operator. The exclusive or (^) of two Boolean operands is true if and only if the two operands have different Boolean values.

The following statements check whether a number is divisible by 2 and 3, whether a number is divisible by 2 or 3 and whether a number is divisible by 2 or 3 but not both:

```
System.out.println("Is " + number + " divisible by 2 and 3? " +
  ((number % 2 == 0) && (number % 3 == 0)));

System.out.println("Is " + number + " divisible by 2 or 3? " +
  ((number % 2 == 0) ¦¦ (number % 3 == 0)));

System.out.println("Is " + number +
  " divisible by 2 or 3, but not both? " +
  ((number % 2 == 0) ^ (number % 3 == 0)));
```

2.10.1 Unconditional vs. Conditional Boolean Operators

If one of the operands of an && operator is false, the expression is false; if one of the operands of an ¦¦ operands is true, the expression is true. Java uses these properties to improve the performance of these operators.

When evaluating p1 && p2, Java first evaluates p1 and then evaluates p2 if p1 is true; if p1 is false, it does not evaluate p2. When evaluating p1 ¦¦ p2, Java first evaluates p1 and then evaluates p2 if p1 is false; if p1 is true, it does not evaluate p2. Therefore, && is referred to as the *conditional* or *short-circuit AND* operator, and ¦¦ is referred to as the *conditional* or *short-circuit OR* operator.

conditional operator
short-circuit operator

Java also provides the & and ¦ operators. The & operator works exactly the same as the && operator, and the ¦ operator works exactly the same as the ¦¦ operator with one exception: the & and ¦ operators always evaluate both operands. Therefore, & is referred to as the *unconditional AND* operator, and ¦ is referred to as the *unconditional OR* operator. In some rare situations, you can

unconditional operator

use the & and ¦ operators to guarantee that the right-hand operand is evaluated regardless of whether the left-hand operand is `true` or `false`. For example, the expression (`width < 2`) & (`height-- < 2`) guarantees that (`height-- < 2`) is evaluated. Thus, the variable `height` will be decremented regardless of whether `width` is less than 2 or not.

 TIP

Avoid using the & and ¦ operators. The benefits of the & and ¦ operators are marginal. Using them will make the program difficult to read and could cause errors. For example, the expression (x != 0) & (100 / x) results in a runtime error if x is 0. However, (x != 0) && (100 / x) is fine. If x is 0, (x != 0) is false. Since && is a short-circuit operator, Java does not evaluate (100 / x) and returns the result as false for the entire expression (x != 0) && (100 / x).

---

bitwise operations

 NOTE

The & and ¦ operators can also apply to *bitwise operations*. See Appendix G, "Bit Operations," for details.

 NOTE

As shown in the preceding section, a `char` value can be cast into an `int` value, and vice versa. A Boolean value, however, cannot be cast into a value of other types, nor can a value of other types be cast into a Boolean value.

Boolean literals

NOTE

`true` and `false` are literals, just like a number such as 10, so they are not keywords, but you cannot use them as identifiers, just as you cannot use 10 as an identifier.

2.11   Operator Precedence and Associativity

Operator precedence and associativity determine the order in which operators are evaluated. Suppose that you have this expression:

```
3 + 4 * 4 > 5 * (4 + 3) - 1
```

What is its value? How does the compiler know the execution order of the operators? The expression in the parentheses is evaluated first. (Parentheses can be nested, in which case the expression in the inner parentheses is executed first.) When evaluating an expression without parentheses, the operators are applied according to the precedence rule and the associativity rule. The *precedence* rule defines precedence for operators, as shown in Table 2.11, which contains the operators you have learned in this chapter. Operators are listed in decreasing order of precedence from top to bottom. Operators with the same precedence appear in the same group. (See Appendix C, "Operator Precedence Chart," for a complete list of Java operators and their precedence.)

precedence

associativity

If operators with the same precedence are next to each other, their *associativity* determines the order of evaluation. All binary operators except assignment operators are *left-associative*. For example, since + and − are of the same precedence and are left-associative, the expression

$$a - b + c - d \quad \underline{\text{equivalent}} \quad ((a - b) + c) - d$$

Assignment operators are *right-associative*. Therefore, the expression

$$a = b \mathrel{+}= c = 5 \quad \underline{\text{equivalent}} \quad a = (b \mathrel{+}= (c = 5))$$

TABLE 2.11   Operator Precedence Chart

Precedence	Operator
Highest Order	var++ and var-- (Postincrement and postdecrement)
	+, - (Unary plus and minus), ++var and --var (prefix)
	(type) (Casting)
	! (Not)
	*, /, % (Multiplication, division, and remainder)
	+, - (Binary addition and subtraction)
	<, <=, >, >= (Comparison)
	==, != (Equality)
	& (Unconditional AND)
	^ (Exclusive OR)
	¦ (Unconditional OR)
	&& (Conditional AND)
	¦¦ (Conditional OR)
Lowest Order	=, +=, -=, *=, /=, %= (Assignment operator)

Suppose a, b, and c are 1 before the assignment; after the whole expression is evaluated, a becomes 6, b becomes 6, and c becomes 5.

Applying the operator precedence and associativity rule, the expression 3 + 4 * 4 > 5 * (4 + 3) - 1 is evaluated as follows:

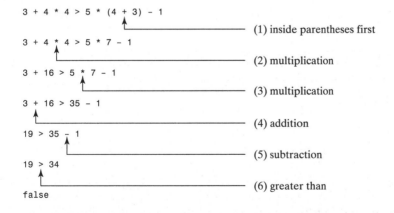

```
3 + 4 * 4 > 5 * (4 + 3) - 1
                                    (1) inside parentheses first
3 + 4 * 4 > 5 * 7 - 1
                                    (2) multiplication
3 + 16 > 5 * 7 - 1
                                    (3) multiplication
3 + 16 > 35 - 1
                                    (4) addition
19 > 35 - 1
                                    (5) subtraction
19 > 34
                                    (6) greater than
false
```

 TIP

You can use parentheses to force an evaluation order as well as to make a program easy to read. Use of redundant parentheses does not slow down the execution of the expression.

2.12   Operand Evaluation Order

The precedence and associativity rules specify the order of the operators but not the order in which the operands of a binary operator are evaluated. Operands are evaluated strictly from left to right in Java. *The left-hand operand of a binary operator is evaluated before any part of the right-hand*

from left to right

operand is evaluated. This rule takes precedence over any other rules that govern expressions. Consider this expression:

```
a + b * (c + 10 * d) / e
```

a, b, c, d, and e are evaluated in this order. *If no operands have side effects that change the value of a variable, the order of operand evaluation is irrelevant.* Interesting cases arise when operands do have a side effect. For example, x becomes 1 in the following code because a is evaluated to 0 before ++a is evaluated to 1:

```
int a = 0;
int x = a + (++a);
```

But x becomes 2 in the following code because ++a is evaluated to 1, then a is evaluated to 1:

```
int a = 0;
int x = ++a + a;
```

The order for evaluating operands takes precedence over the operator precedence rule. In the former case, (++a) has higher precedence than addition (+), but since a is a left-hand operand of the addition (+), it is evaluated before any part of its right-hand operand (e.g., ++a in this case).

evaluation rule

In summary, the rule of evaluating an expression is:

◆ Rule 1: Evaluate whatever subexpressions you can possibly evaluate from left to right.

◆ Rule 2: The operators are applied according to their precedence, as shown in Table 2.11.

◆ Rule 3: The associativity rule applies for two operators next to each other with the same precedence.

Applying the rule, the expression 3 + 4 * 4 > 5 * (4 + 3) - 1 is evaluated as follows:

```
3 + 4 * 4 > 5 * (4 + 3) - 1
```
(1) 4 * 4 is the first subexpression that can be evaluated from the left.

```
3 + 16 > 5 * (4 + 3) - 1
```
(2) 3 + 16 is evaluated now.

```
19 > 5 * (4 + 3) - 1
```
(3) 4 + 3 is now the leftmost subexpression that should be evaluated.

```
19 > 5 * 7 - 1
```
(4) 5 * 7 is evaluated now.

```
19 > 35 - 1
```
(5) 35 - 1 is evaluated now.

```
19 > 34
```
(6) 19 > 34 is evaluated now.

```
false
```

The result happens to be the same as applying Rule 2 and Rule 3 without applying Rule 1. In fact, Rule 1 is not necessary if no operands have side effects that change the value of a variable in an expression.

2.13   The **String** Type

The char type only represents one character. To represent a string of characters, use the data type called String. For example, the following code declares the message to be a string that has an initial value of "Welcome to Java":

```
String message = "Welcome to Java";
```

String is actually a predefined class in the Java library just like the System class and JOptionPane class. The String type is not a primitive type. It is known as a *reference type*. Any Java class can be used as a reference type for a variable. Reference data types will be thoroughly discussed in Chapter 6, "Classes and Objects." For the time being, you only need to know how to declare a String variable, how to assign a string to the variable, and how to concatenate strings.

As first shown in Listing 2.1, two strings can be concatenated. The plus sign (+) is the concatenation operator if one of the operands is a string. If one of the operands is a non-string (e.g., a number), the non-string value is converted into a string and concatenated with the other string. Here are some examples:

concatenating strings and numbers

```
// Three strings are concatenated
String message = "Welcome " + "to " + "Java";

// String Chapter is concatenated with number 2
String s = "Chapter" + 2; // s becomes Chapter2

// String Supplement is concatenated with character B
String s1 = "Supplement" + 'B'; // s becomes SupplementB
```

If none of the operands is a string, the plus sign (+) is the addition operator that adds two numbers.

The short hand += operator can also be used for string concatenation. For example, the following code appends the string " and Java is fun" with the string "Welcome to Java" in message:

```
message += " and Java is fun";
```

So the new message is "Welcome to Java and Java is fun".

The operator precedence order and associativity rule for the operators + and += apply to strings in the same way as to numbers. Suppose that i = 1 and j = 2, what is the output of the following statement?

```
System.out.println("i + j is " + i + j);
```

The output is "i + j is 12" because "i + j is " is concatenated with the value of i first. To force i + j to be executed first, enclose i + j in the parentheses, as follows:

```
System.out.println("i + j is " + (i + j));
```

2.14 Getting Input from Input Dialogs

In Listing 2.1, the radius is fixed in the source code. To use a different radius, you have to modify the source code and recompile it. Obviously, this is not convenient. You can use the showInputDialog method in the JOptionPane class to get input at runtime. When this method is executed, a dialog is displayed to enable you to enter an input, as shown in Figure 2.3.

showInputDialog

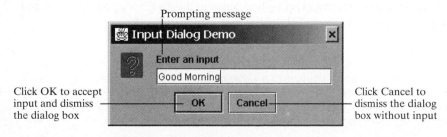

FIGURE 2.3 *The input dialog box enables the user to enter a string.*

After entering a string, click OK to accept the input and dismiss the dialog box. The input is returned from the method as a string. You can invoke the method with four arguments, as follows:

```
String input =
  JOptionPane.showInputDialog(null,
  "Enter an input",
  "Input Dialog Demo",
  JOptionPane.QUESTION_MESSAGE);
```

The first argument can always be `null`. The second argument is a string that prompts the user. The third argument is the title of the input box. The fourth argument can be `JOptionPane.QUESTION_MESSAGE`, which causes the icon () to be displayed in the input box.

---

showInputDialog method

> ### ✿ NOTE
>
> There are several ways to use the `showInputDialog` method. For the time being, you only need to know two ways to invoke it.
>
> One is to use a statement as shown in the example:
>
> ```
> String string = JOptionPane.showInputDialog(null, x,
>   y, JOptionPane.QUESTION_MESSAGE));
> ```
>
> where x is a string for the prompting message, and y is a string for the title of the input dialog box.
>
> The other is to use a statement like this one:
>
> ```
> JOptionPane.showMessageDialog(x);
> ```
>
> where x is a string for the prompting message.

2.14.1 Converting Strings to Numbers

The input returned from the input dialog box is a string. If you enter a numeric value such as 123, it returns "123". You have to convert a string into a number to obtain the input as a number.

Integer.parseInt method

To convert a string into an `int` value, use the `parseInt` method in the `Integer` class, as follows:

```
int intValue = Integer.parseInt(intString);
```

where `intString` is a numeric string such as "123".

Double.parseDouble method

To convert a string into a `double` value, use the `parseDouble` method in the `Double` class, as follows:

```
double doubleValue = Double.parseDouble(doubleString);
```

where `doubleString` is a numeric string such as "123.45".

The `Integer` and `Double` classes are both included in the `java.lang` package. These classes will be further discussed in Chapter 9, "Abstract Classes and Interfaces."

> ### ✿ NOTE
>
> You can also convert a string into a value of the `byte` type, `short` type, `long` type, `float` type, `char` type, or `boolean` type. You will learn the conversion methods later in the book.

EXAMPLE 2.1 ENTERING INPUT FROM DIALOG BOXES

Problem

This example shows you how to enter input from dialog boxes. As shown in Figure 2.4, the program prompts the user to enter a year as an int value and checks whether it is a leap year; then it prompts the user to enter a double value and checks whether it is positive.

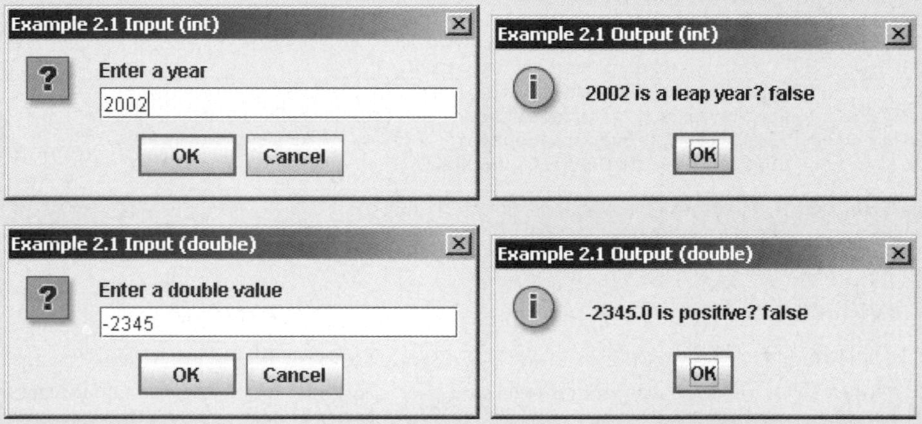

FIGURE 2.4 *The input dialog box enables the user to enter a string.*

Solution

A year is a *leap year* if it is divisible by 4 but not by 100 or if it is divisible by 400. So you can use the following Boolean expression to check whether a year is a leap year:

leap year

```
((year % 4 == 0) && (year % 100 != 0)) || (year % 400 == 0)
```

LISTING 2.2 InputDialogDemo.java (Entering Input from Dialogs)

```
1  import javax.swing.JOptionPane;
2
3  public class InputDialogDemo {
4    /** Main method */
5    public static void main(String args[]) {
6      // Prompt the user to enter a year
7      String yearString = JOptionPane.showInputDialog(null,
8        "Enter a year", "Example 2.1 Input (int)",
9        JOptionPane.QUESTION_MESSAGE);
10
11     // Convert the string into an int value
12     int year = Integer.parseInt(yearString);
13
14     // Check if the year is a leap year
15     boolean isLeapYear =
16       ((year % 4 == 0) && (year % 100 != 0)) || (year % 400 == 0);
17
```

show input dialog

convert to int

EXAMPLE 2.1 (CONTINUED)

show message dialog

```
18      // Display the result in a message dialog box
19      JOptionPane.showMessageDialog(null,
20        year + " is a leap year? " + isLeapYear,
21        "Example 2.1 Output (int)", JOptionPane.INFORMATION_MESSAGE);
22
23      // Prompt the user to enter a double value
24      String doubleString = JOptionPane.showInputDialog(null,
25        "Enter a double value", "Example 2.1 Input (double)",
26        JOptionPane.QUESTION_MESSAGE);
27
28      // Convert the string into a double value
29      double doubleValue = Double.parseDouble(doubleString);
30
31      // Check if the number is positive
32      JOptionPane.showMessageDialog(null,
33        doubleValue + " is positive? " + (doubleValue > 0),
34        "Example 2.1 Output (double)",
35        JOptionPane.INFORMATION_MESSAGE);
36    }
37  }
```

show input dialog

converting to double

show message dialog

Review

The `showInputDialog` method in Lines 7–9 displays an input dialog box titled "Example 2.1 Input (int)." Enter a year as an integer and click OK to accept the input. The integer is returned as a string that is assigned to the `String` variable `yearString`. The `Integer.parseInt(yearString)` (Line 12) is used to convert the string into an int value. If you entered an input other than an integer, a runtime error would occur. In Chapter 15, "Exceptions and Assertions," you will learn how to handle the exception so that the program can continue to run.

The `showMessageDialog` method in Lines 19–21 displays the output in a message dialog box titled "Example 2.1 Output (int)."

The `showInputDialog` method in Lines 24–26 displays an input dialog box titled "Example 2.1 Input (double)." Enter a floating-point value and click OK to accept the input. The floating-point value is returned as a string that is assigned to the `String` variable `doubleString`. The `Double.parseDouble(doubleString)` (Line 29) is used to convert the string into an int value. If you entered a non-numeric value, a runtime error would occur.

 NOTE
If you click *Cancel* in the input dialog box, no string is returned. A runtime error would occur.

2.15 Case Studies

In the preceding sections, you learned about variables, constants, primitive data types, operators, and expressions. You are now ready to use them to write interesting programs. This section presents three examples: computing loan payments, breaking a sum of money down into smaller units, and displaying the current time.

EXAMPLE 2.2 COMPUTING LOAN PAYMENTS

Problem

This example shows you how to write a program that computes loan payments. The loan can be a car loan, a student loan, or a home mortgage loan. The program lets the user enter the interest rate, number of years, and loan amount, and then computes the monthly payment and the total payment. It concludes by displaying the monthly and total payments.

Solution

The formula to compute the monthly payment is as follows:

$$\frac{loanAmount \times monthlyInterestRate}{1 - \dfrac{1}{(1 + monthlyInterestRate)^{numberOfYears \times 12}}}$$

You don't have to know how this formula is derived. Nonetheless, given the monthly interest rate, number of years, and loan amount, you can use it to compute the monthly payment.

Here are the steps in developing the program:

1. Prompt the user to enter the annual interest rate, number of years, and loan amount.

2. Obtain the monthly interest rate from the annual interest rate.

3. Compute the monthly payment using the preceding formula.

4. Compute the total payment, which is the monthly payment multiplied by 12 and multiplied by the number of years.

5. Display the monthly payment and total payment in a message dialog.
   The program follows, and the output is shown in Figure 2.5.

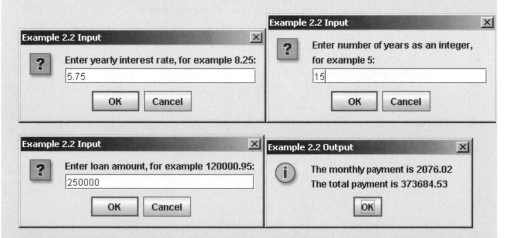

FIGURE 2.5 *The program accepts the annual interest rate, number of years, and loan amount, then displays the monthly payment and total payment.*

EXAMPLE 2.2 (CONTINUED)

LISTING 2.3 ComputeLoan.java (Computing Loan Payments)

```
1   import javax.swing.JOptionPane;
2
3   public class ComputeLoan {
4     /** Main method */
5     public static void main(String[] args) {
6       // Enter yearly interest rate
7       String annualInterestRateString = JOptionPane.showInputDialog(
8         null, "Enter yearly interest rate, for example 8.25:",
9         "Example 2.2 Input", JOptionPane.QUESTION_MESSAGE);
10
11      // Convert string to double
12      double annualInterestRate =
13        Double.parseDouble(annualInterestRateString);
14
15      // Obtain monthly interest rate
16      double monthlyInterestRate = annualInterestRate / 1200;
17
18      // Enter number of years
19      String numberOfYearsString = JOptionPane.showInputDialog(null,
20        "Enter number of years as an integer, \nfor example 5:",
21        "Example 2.2 Input", JOptionPane.QUESTION_MESSAGE);
22
23      // Convert string to int
24      int numberOfYears = Integer.parseInt(numberOfYearsString);
25
26      // Enter loan amount
27      String loanString = JOptionPane.showInputDialog(null,
28        "Enter loan amount, for example 120000.95:",
29        "Example 2.2 Input", JOptionPane.QUESTION_MESSAGE);
30
31      // Convert string to double
32      double loanAmount = Double.parseDouble(loanString);
33
34      // Calculate payment
35      double monthlyPayment = loanAmount * monthlyInterestRate / (1
36        - 1 / Math.pow(1 + monthlyInterestRate, numberOfYears * 12));
37      double totalPayment = monthlyPayment * numberOfYears * 12;
38
39      // Format to keep two digits after the decimal point
40      monthlyPayment = (int)(monthlyPayment * 100) / 100.0;
41      totalPayment = (int)(totalPayment * 100) / 100.0;
42
43      // Display results
44      String output = "The monthly payment is " + monthlyPayment +
45        "\nThe total payment is " + totalPayment;
46      JOptionPane.showMessageDialog(null, output,
47        "Example 2.2 Output", JOptionPane.INFORMATION_MESSAGE);
48    }
49  }
```

monthlyPayment (Line 35)

totalPayment (Line 37)

formatting numbers (Lines 40–41)

preparing output (Lines 44–47)

Review

Each new variable in a method must be declared once and only once. Choose the most appropriate data type for the variable. For example, numberOfYears is best declared as int (Line 24), although it could be declared as long, float, or double.

The method for computing b^p in the Math class is pow(b, p) (Lines 35–36). The Math class, which comes with the Java API, is available to all Java programs. The Math class is introduced in Chapter 4, "Methods."

pow method

EXAMPLE 2.2 (CONTINUED)

The statements in Lines 40–41 are for formatting the number to keep two digits after the decimal point. For example, if `monthlyPayment` is 2076.0252175, `(int)(monthlyPayment * 100)` is 207602. Therefore, `(int)(monthlyPayment * 100) / 100.0` yields 2076.02.

formatting numbers

The strings are concatenated into `output` in Lines 44–45. The linefeed escape character `'\n'` is in the string to display the text after `'\n'` in the next line.

EXAMPLE 2.3 MONETARY UNITS

Problem

Write a program that classifies a given amount of money into smaller monetary units. The program lets the user enter an amount as a `double` value representing a total in dollars and cents, and outputs a report listing the monetary equivalent in dollars, quarters, dimes, nickels, and pennies.

Your program should report the maximum number of dollars, then the maximum number of quarters, and so on, in this order.

Solution

Here are the steps in developing the program:

1. Prompt the user to enter the amount as a decimal number such as 11.56.

2. Convert the amount (e.g., 11.56) into cents (1156).

3. Divide the cents by 100 to find the number of dollars. Obtain the remaining cents using the cents remainder 100.

4. Divide the remaining cents by 25 to find the number of quarters. Obtain the remaining cents using the remaining cents remainder 25.

5. Divide the remaining cents by 10 to find the number of dimes. Obtain the remaining cents using the remaining cents remainder 10.

6. Divide the remaining cents by 5 to find the number of nickels. Obtain the remaining cents using the remaining cents remainder 5.

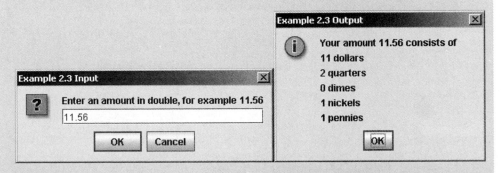

FIGURE 2.6 *The program receives an amount in decimals and breaks it into singles, quarters, dimes, nickels, and pennies.*

EXAMPLE 2.3 (CONTINUED)

7. The remaining cents are the pennies.

8. Display the result.

The program follows, and the output is shown in Figure 2.6.

LISTING 2.4   ComputeChange.java (Monetary Units)

```java
1 import javax.swing.JOptionPane;
2
3 public class ComputeChange {
4   /** Main method */
5   public static void main(String[] args) {
6     // Receive the amount entered from the keyboard
7     String amountString = JOptionPane.showInputDialog(null,
8       "Enter an amount in double, for example 11.56",
9       "Example 2.3 Input", JOptionPane.QUESTION_MESSAGE);
10
11    // Convert string to double
12    double amount = Double.parseDouble(amountString);
13
14    int remainingAmount = (int)(amount * 100);
15
16    // Find the number of one dollars
17    int numberOfOneDollars = remainingAmount / 100;
18    remainingAmount = remainingAmount % 100;
19
20    // Find the number of quarters in the remaining amount
21    int numberOfQuarters = remainingAmount / 25;
22    remainingAmount = remainingAmount % 25;
23
24    // Find the number of dimes in the remaining amount
25    int numberOfDimes = remainingAmount / 10;
26    remainingAmount = remainingAmount % 10;
27
28    // Find the number of nickels in the remaining amount
29    int numberOfNickels = remainingAmount / 5;
30    remainingAmount = remainingAmount % 5;
31
32    // Find the number of pennies in the remaining amount
33    int numberOfPennies = remainingAmount;
34
35    // Display results
36    String output = "Your amount " + amount + " consists of \n" +
37      numberOfOneDollars + " dollars\n" +
38      numberOfQuarters + " quarters\n" +
39      numberOfDimes + " dimes\n" +
40      numberOfNickels + " nickels\n" +
41      numberOfPennies + " pennies";
42    JOptionPane.showMessageDialog(null, output,
43      "Example 2.3 Output", JOptionPane.INFORMATION_MESSAGE);
44  }
45 }
```

dollars

quarters

dimes

nickels

pennies

Review

The variable amount stores the amount entered from the input dialog box (Lines 7–12). This variable is not changed because the amount has to be used at the end of the program to display the results. The program introduces the variable remainingAmount (Line 14) to store the changing remainingAmount.

EXAMPLE 2.3 (CONTINUED)

The variable `amount` is a `double` decimal representing dollars and cents. It is converted to an `int` variable `remainingAmount`, which represents all the cents. For instance, if `amount` is 11.56, then the initial `remainingAmount` is 1156. The division operator yields the integer part of the division. So 1156 / 100 is 11. The remainder operator obtains the remainder of the division. So 1156 % 100 is 56.

The program extracts the maximum number of singles from the total amount and obtains the remaining amount in the variable `remainingAmount` (Lines 17–18). It then extracts the maximum number of quarters from `remainingAmount` and obtains a new `remainingAmount` (Lines 21–22). Continuing the same process, the program finds the maximum number of dimes, nickels, and pennies in the remaining amount.

One serious problem with this example is the possible *loss of precision* when casting a `double` amount to an `int` `remainingAmount`. This could lead to an inaccurate result. If you try to enter the amount 10.03, 10.03 * 100 becomes 1002.9999999999999. You will find that the program displays 10 dollars and 2 pennies. There are two ways to fix the problem. One is to enter the amount as an `int` value representing cents (see Exercise 2.14); the other is to read the decimal number as a string and extract the dollars part and the cents part separately as `int` values. Processing strings will be introduced in Chapter 7, "Strings."

loss of precision

As shown in Figure 2.6, 0 dimes, 1 nickels, and 1 pennies are displayed in the result. It would be better not to display 0 dimes, and to display 1 nickel and 1 penny using the singular forms of the words. You will learn how to use selection statements to modify this program in the next chapter (see Exercise 3.1).

EXAMPLE 2.4 DISPLAYING THE CURRENT TIME

Problem

Write a program that displays the current time in GMT (Greenwich Meridian Time) in the format hour:minute:second, such as 1:45:19.

Solution

The `currentTimeMillis` method in the `System` class returns the current time in milliseconds since midnight, January 1, 1970 GMT (also known as the *Unix time* because 1970 was the year when the Unix operating system was formally introduced). You can use this method to obtain the current time, and then compute the current second, minute, and hour as follows.

currentTimeMillis
Unix time

1. Obtain the total milliseconds since midnight, Jan 1, 1970 in `totalSeconds` by invoking `System.currentTimeMillis()`.

2. Obtain the total seconds `totalSeconds` by dividing 1000 from `totalMilliseconds`.

3. Compute the current second in the minute in the hour from `totalSeconds % 60`.

4. Obtain the total minutes `totalMinutes` by dividing 60 from `totalSeconds`.

5. Compute the current minute in the hour from `totalMinutes % 60`.

EXAMPLE 2.4 (CONTINUED)

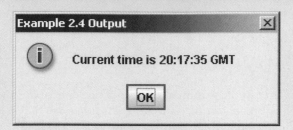

FIGURE 2.7   *The program displays the current time.*

6. Obtain the total hours `totalHours` by dividing 60 from `totalMinutes`.

7. Compute the current hour from `totalHours % 24`.

The program follows, and the output is shown in Figure 2.7.

LISTING 2.5   ShowCurrentTime.java (Displaying Current Time)

```
 1 import javax.swing.JOptionPane;
 2
 3 public class ShowCurrentTime {
 4   public static void main(String[] args) {
 5     // Obtain the total milliseconds since the midnight, Jan 1, 1970
 6     long totalMilliseconds = System.currentTimeMillis();
 7
 8     // Obtain the total seconds since the midnight, Jan 1, 1970
 9     long totalSeconds = totalMilliseconds / 1000;
10
11     // Compute the current second in the minute in the hour
12     int currentSecond = (int)(totalSeconds % 60);
13
14     // Obtain the total minutes
15     long totalMinutes = totalSeconds / 60;
16
17     // Compute the current minute in the hour
18     int currentMinute = (int)(totalMinutes % 60);
19
20     // Obtain the total hours
21     long totalHours = totalMinutes / 60;
22
23     // Compute the current hour
24     int currentHour = (int)(totalHours % 24);
25
26     // Display results
27     String output = "Current time is " + currentHour + ":"
28       + currentMinute + ":" + currentSecond + " GMT";
29
30     JOptionPane.showMessageDialog(null, output,
31       "Example 2.4 Output", JOptionPane.INFORMATION_MESSAGE);
32   }
33 }
```

totalSeconds

currentSecond

totalMinutes

currentMinute

totalHours

currentHour

preparing output

Review

When `System.currentTimeMillis()` (Line 6) is invoked, it returns the difference, measured in milliseconds, between the current time and midnight, January 1, 1970 GMT. This method returns the milliseconds as a `long` value.

This example finds the current time. To find the date (day, month, and year), see Exercise 4.18.

2.16   Getting Input from the Console (Optional)

The previous editions of this book used the MyInput class to let the user enter input from the command window. If you wish to use it, download MyInput.java from the Companion Website to the directory that contains your program. MyInput is like JOptionPane. JOptionPane is a class in the Java library, whereas I developed MyInput. You can use the methods in JOptionPane without knowing how the class is implemented. Likewise, you can use the methods in MyInput without having to be concerned about its implementation. The implementation of MyInput will be introduced in Chapter 7. You may also use the new JDK 1.5 Scanner class for console input. (See Supplement T, "Obtaining Input from the Console Using the Scanner Class."

MyInput

The MyInput class contains the methods readByte(), readShort(), readInt(), readLong(), readFloat(), readDouble(), readChar(), readBoolean(), and readString() to read numeric values, characters, boolean values, and strings from the console.

Listing 2.6 is an example that uses the methods in MyInput. A sample run of this program is shown in Figure 2.8.

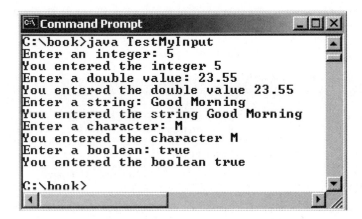

FIGURE 2.8   *You can enter input from a command window.*

LISTING 2.6   TestMyInput.java (Using Console Input)

```
1 public class TestMyInput {
2   public static void main(String args[]) {
3     // Prompt the user to enter an integer
4     System.out.print("Enter an integer: ");
5     int intValue = MyInput.readInt();
6     System.out.println("You entered the integer " + intValue);
7
8     // Prompt the user to enter a double value
9     System.out.print("Enter a double value: ");
10    double doubleValue = MyInput.readDouble();
11    System.out.println("You entered the double value "
12      + doubleValue);
13
14    // Prompt the user to enter a string
15    System.out.print("Enter a string: ");
16    String string = MyInput.readString();
17    System.out.println("You entered the string " + string);
18
19    // Prompt the user to enter a character
20    System.out.print("Enter a character: ");
21    char charValue = MyInput.readChar();
22    System.out.println("You entered the character " + charValue);
23
```

```
24      // Prompt the user to enter a boolean
25      System.out.print("Enter a boolean: ");
26      boolean booleanValue = MyInput.readBoolean();
27      System.out.println("You entered the boolean " + booleanValue);
28    }
29 }
```

 NOTE

The print method displays a string to the console. This method is identical to the println method except that println moves the cursor to the next line after displaying the string, but print does not advance the cursor to the next line when completed.

input from a file

TIP

One benefit of using the console input is that you can store the input values in a text file and pass the file from the command line using the following command:

```
java TestMyInput < input.txt
```

where input.txt is a text file that contains the data, as shown in Figure 2.9(a). The output of java TestMyInput < input.txt is shown in Figure 2.9(b).

(a)

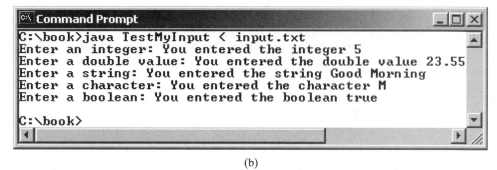

(b)

FIGURE 2.9 *(a) You can create a text file using NotePad. (b) The data in the text file are passed to the program.*

You can also save the output into a file using the following command:

output to a file

```
java TestMyInput < input.txt > out.txt
```

2.17 Formatting Output (JDK 1.5 Feature)

printf

You already know how to display console output using the print or println methods. JDK 1.5 introduced a new printf method that enables you to format output. The syntax to invoke this method is

```
System.out.printf(format, items)
```

specifier

where format is a string that may consist of substrings and format specifiers. A format *specifier* specifies how an item should be displayed. An item may be a numeric value, a character, a boolean value, or a string. Each specifier begins with a percent sign. Table 2.12 lists some frequently used specifiers:

TABLE 2.12 Frequently Used Specifiers

Specifier	Output	Example
%b	a boolean value	true or false
%c	a character	'a'
%d	a decimal integer	200
%f	a floating-point number	45.460000
%e	a number in standard scientific notation	4.556000e+01
%s	a string	"Java is cool"

Here is an example:

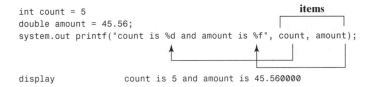

```
int count = 5
double amount = 45.56;
system.out printf("count is %d and amount is %f", count, amount);
```

```
display          count is 5 and amount is 45.560000
```

Items must match the specifiers in order, in number, and in exact type. For example, the specifier for count is %d, for (1 < 0) is %b, and for amount is %f. By default, a floating-point value is displayed with six digits after the decimal point. You can specify the width and precision in a specifier, as shown in the examples in Table 2.13.

TABLE 2.13 Examples of Specifying Width and Precision

Example	Output
%5c	Output the character and add four spaces before the character item.
%6b	Output the boolean value and add one space before the false value and two spaces before the true value.
%5d	Output the integer item with width at least 5. If the number of digits in the item is < 5, add spaces before the number.
%10.2f	Output the floating-point item with width at least 10 including a decimal point and two digits after the point. Thus there are 7 digits allocated before the decimal point. If the number of digits before the decimal in the item is < 7, add spaces before the number.
%10.2e	Output the floating-point item with width at least 10 including a decimal point, two digits after the point and the exponent part. If the displayed number in scientific notation has width less than 10, add spaces before the number.
%12s	Output the string with width at least 12 characters. If the string item has less than 12 characters, add spaces before the string.

 CAUTION

The items must match the specifiers in exact type. The item for the specifier %f or %e must be a floating-point type value such as 40.0, not 40. Thus, an int variable cannot match %f or %e.

TIP

The % sign denotes a specifier. To output a literal % in the format string, use %%.

2.18 Programming Style and Documentation

programming style

Programming style deals with what programs look like. A program can compile and run properly even if written on only one line, but writing it all on one line would be bad programming style because it would be hard to read. *Documentation* is the body of explanatory remarks and comments pertaining to a program. Programming style and documentation are as important as coding. Good programming style and appropriate documentation reduce the chance of errors and make programs easy to read. So far you have learned some good programming styles. This section summarizes them and gives several guidelines. More detailed guidelines on programming style and documentation can be found in Supplement D, "Java Coding Style Guidelines," on the Companion Website.

2.18.1 Appropriate Comments and Comment Styles

Include a summary at the beginning of the program to explain what the program does, its key features, its supporting data structures, and any unique techniques it uses. In a long program, you should also include comments that introduce each major step and explain anything that is difficult to read. It is important to make comments concise so that they do not crowd the program or make it difficult to read.

javadoc comments

Use javadoc comments (`/** ... */`) for commenting on an entire class or an entire method. These comments must precede the class or the method header, and can be extracted in a javadoc HTML file. For commenting on steps inside a method, use line comments (`//`).

2.18.2 Naming Conventions

Make sure that you choose descriptive names with straightforward meanings for the variables, constants, classes, and methods in your program. Names are case-sensitive. Listed below are the conventions for naming variables, methods, and classes.

name variables and methods

✦ Use lowercase for variables and methods. If a name consists of several words, concatenate them into one, making the first word lowercase and capitalizing the first letter of each subsequent word; for example, the variables `radius` and `area` and the method `showInputDialog`.

name classes

✦ Capitalize the first letter of each word in a class name; for example, the class names `ComputeArea`, `Math`, and `JOptionPane`.

name constants

✦ Capitalize every letter in a constant, and use underscores between words; for example, the constants `PI` and `MAX_VALUE`.

naming conventions

 TIP
It is important to become familiar with the *naming conventions*. Understanding them will help you to understand Java programs. If you stick with the naming conventions, other programmers will be more willing to accept your program.

naming classes

 CAUTION
Do not choose class names that are already used in the Java library. For example, since the `Math` class is defined in Java, you should not name your class `Math`.

TIP

Avoid using abbreviation for identifiers. Using complete words is more descriptive. For example, `numberOfStudents` is better than `numStuds`, `numOfStuds`, or `numOfStudents`.

using full descriptive names

2.18.3   Proper Indentation and Spacing

A consistent indentation style makes programs clear and easy to read. *Indentation* is used to illustrate the structural relationships between a program's components or statements. Java can read the program even if all of the statements are in a straight line, but it is easier to read and maintain code that is aligned properly. Indent each subcomponent or statement *two* spaces more than the structure within which it is nested.

indentation

A single space should be added on both sides of a binary operator, as shown in the following statement:

A single space line should be used to separate segments of the code to make the program easier to read.

2.18.4   Block Styles

A block is a group of statements surrounded by braces. There are two popular styles, *next-line* style and *end-of-line* style, as shown in Figure 2.10. The next-line style aligns braces vertically and makes programs easy to read, whereas the end-of-line style saves space and may help avoid some subtle programming errors. Both are acceptable block styles. The choice depends on personal or organizational preference. You should use a style consistently. Mixing styles is not recommended. This book uses the *end-of-line* style to be consistent with the Java API source code.

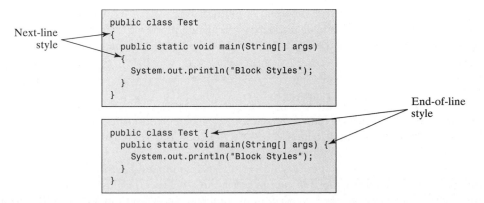

FIGURE 2.10   *The opening brace is placed at the beginning of a new line for next-line style and at the end of line for end-of-line style.*

2.19 Programming Errors

Programming errors are unavoidable, even for experienced programmers. Errors can be categorized into three types: syntax errors, runtime errors, and logic errors.

2.19.1 Syntax Errors

syntax errors

Errors that occur during compilation are called *syntax errors* or *compilation errors*. Syntax errors result from errors in code construction, such as mistyping a keyword, omitting some necessary punctuation, or using an opening brace without a corresponding closing brace. These errors are usually easy to detect, because the compiler tells you where they are and what caused them. For example, compiling the following program results in a syntax error, as shown in Figure 2.11.

syntax error

```java
// ShowSyntaxErrors.java: The program contains syntax errors
public class ShowSyntaxErrors {
  public static void main(String[] args) {
    i = 30;
    System.out.println(i + 4);
  }
}
```

```
C:\book>javac ShowSyntaxErrors.java
ShowSyntaxErrors.java:4: cannot resolve symbol
symbol  : variable i
location: class ShowSyntaxErrors
    i = 30;
    ^
ShowSyntaxErrors.java:5: cannot resolve symbol
symbol  : variable i
location: class ShowSyntaxErrors
    System.out.println(i + 4);
                       ^
2 errors

C:\book>
```

FIGURE 2.11 *The compiler reports syntax errors.*

Two errors are detected. Both are the result of not declaring variable i. Since a single error will often display many lines of compilation errors, it is a good practice to start debugging from the top line and work downward. Fixing errors that occur earlier in the program may also fix cascading errors that occur later.

2.19.2 Runtime Errors

runtime errors

Runtime errors are errors that cause a program to terminate abnormally. Runtime errors occur while an application is running if the environment detects an operation that is impossible to carry out. Input errors are typical runtime errors.

An *input error* occurs when the user enters an unexpected input value that the program cannot handle. For instance, if the program expects to read in a number, but instead the user enters a string, this causes data-type errors to occur in the program. To prevent input errors, the program should prompt the user to enter the correct type of values. It may display a message like "Please enter an integer" before reading an integer from the keyboard.

Another common source of runtime errors is division by zero. This happens when the divisor is zero for integer divisions. For instance, the following program would cause a runtime error, as shown in Figure 2.12.

```
// ShowRuntimeErrors.java: Program contains runtime errors
public class ShowRuntimeErrors {
  public static void main(String[] args) {
    int i = 1 / 0;                                              runtime error
  }
}
```

FIGURE 2.12 *The runtime error causes the program to terminate.*

2.19.3 Logic Errors

Logic errors occur when a program does not perform the way it was intended to. Errors of this kind occur for many different reasons. For example, suppose you wrote the following program to add number1 to number2:

```
// ShowLogicErrors.java: The program contains a logic error
public class ShowLogicErrors {
  public static void main(String[] args) {
    // Add number1 to number2
    int number1 = 3;
    int number2 = 3;
    number2 += number1 + number2;
    System.out.println(number2 is + number2);
  }
}
```

The program does not have syntax errors or runtime errors, but it does not print the correct result for number2. See if you can find the error.

2.20 Debugging

In general, syntax errors are easy to find and easy to correct, because the compiler gives indications as to where the errors came from and why they are there. Runtime errors are not difficult to find either, since the Java interpreter displays them on the console when the program aborts. Finding logic errors, on the other hand, can be very challenging.

Logic errors are called *bugs*. The process of finding and correcting errors is called *debugging*. A common approach to debugging is to use a combination of methods to narrow down to the part of the program where the bug is located. You can *hand-trace* the program (i.e., catch errors by reading the program), or you can insert print statements in order to show the values of the variables or the execution flow of the program. This approach might work for a short, simple program. But for a large, complex program, the most effective approach for debugging is to use a debugger utility.

bugs
debugging
hand-traces

JDK includes a command-line debugger (jdb), which is invoked with a class name. jdb is itself a Java program, running its own copy of the Java interpreter. All the Java IDE tools, such as JBuilder, NetBeans, and Eclipse, include integrated debuggers. The debugger utilities let you follow the execution of a program. They vary from one system to another, but they all support most of the following helpful features:

✦ **Executing a single statement at a time:** The debugger allows you to execute one statement at a time so that you can see the effect of each statement.

✦ **Tracing into or stepping over a method:** If a method is being executed, you can ask the debugger to enter the method and execute one statement at a time in the method, or you can ask it to step over the entire method. You should step over the entire method if you know that the method works. For example, always step over system-supplied methods, such as `System.out.println`.

✦ **Setting breakpoints:** You can also set a breakpoint at a specific statement. Your program pauses when it reaches a breakpoint and displays the line with the breakpoint. You can set as many breakpoints as you want. Breakpoints are particularly useful when you know where your programming error starts. You can set a breakpoint at that line and have the program execute until it reaches the breakpoint.

✦ **Displaying variables:** The debugger lets you select several variables and display their values. As you trace through a program, the content of a variable is continuously updated.

✦ **Displaying call stacks:** The debugger lets you trace all of the method calls and lists all pending methods. This feature is helpful when you need to see a large picture of the program-execution flow.

✦ **Modifying variables:** Some debuggers enable you to modify the value of a variable when debugging. This is convenient when you want to test a program with different samples but do not want to leave the debugger.

KEY TERMS

algorithm 33	increment operator (++) 43
assignment operator (=) 37	indentation 67
assignment statement 37	int type 39
backslash (\) 46	literal 40
Boolean value 47	logic error 69
boolean type 48	long type 39
byte type 39	narrowing (of types) 44
casting 44	operand evaluation order 51
char type 45	operator associativity 50
constant 38	operator precedence 50
debugging 69	primitive data type 33
decrement operator (--) 43	runtime error 68
double type 39	short type 39
encoding 45	short-circuit operator 49
final 38	syntax error 68
float type 39	Unicode 45
floating-point number 33	Unix time 61
expression 37	variable declaration 36
identifier 35	widening (of types) 44

Key Classes and Methods

✦ `java.lang.Math` is a class that contains static methods for mathematical operations.

✦ `Math.pow(a, b)` returns a raised to the power of b (a^b).

✦ `JOptionPane.showInputDialog(...)` displays an input dialog.

✦ `Integer.parseInt(string)` parses a string into an `int` value.

✦ `Integer.parseDouble(string)` parses a string into a `double` value.

✦ `System.currentTimeMills()` returns the current time in milliseconds since midnight, January 1, 1970 GMT (the Unix time).

CHAPTER SUMMARY

✦ Java provides four integer types (`byte`, `short`, `int`, `long`) that represent integers of four different sizes, and two floating-point types (`float`, `double`) that represent floating-point numbers of two different precisions. Character type (`char`) represents a single character, and `boolean` type represents a `true` or `false` value. These are called primitive data types. Java's primitive types are portable across all computer platforms. They have exactly the same values on all platforms. When they are declared, the variables of these types are created and assigned memory space.

✦ Java provides operators that perform numeric operations: + (addition) , - (subtraction) , * (multiplication) , / (division) , and % (remainder). Integer division (/) yields an integer result. The remainder operator (%) yields the remainder of the division.

✦ The increment operator (++) and the decrement operator (--) increment or decrement a variable by 1. If the operator is prefixed to the variable, the variable is first incremented or decremented by 1, then used in the expression. If the operator is a suffix to the variable, the variable is incremented or decremented by 1, but then the original old value is used in the expression.

✦ All the numeric operators can be applied to characters. When an operand is a character, the character's Unicode value is used in the operation.

✦ You can use casting to convert a value of one type into another type. Casting a variable of a type with a small range to a variable of a type with a larger range is known as *widening a type*. Casting a variable of a type with a large range to a variable of a type with a smaller range is known as *narrowing a type*. Widening a type can be performed automatically without explicit casting. Narrowing a type must be performed explicitly.

✦ The Boolean operators &&, &, ¦¦, ¦, !, and ^ operate with Boolean values and variables. The relational operators (<, <=, ==, !=, >, >=) work with numbers and characters, and yield a Boolean value.

✦ When evaluating p1 && p2, Java first evaluates p1 and then evaluates p2 if p1 is `true`; if p1 is `false`, it does not evaluate p2. When evaluating p1 ¦¦ p2, Java first evaluates p1 and then evaluates p2 if p1 is `false`; if p1 is `true`, it does not evaluate p2. Therefore, && is referred to as the *conditional* or *short-circuit AND* operator, and ¦¦ is referred to as the *conditional* or *short-circuit OR* operator.

✦ Java also provides the & and ¦ operators. The & operator works exactly the same as the && operator, and the ¦ operator works exactly the same as the ¦¦ operator with one exception: the & and ¦ operators always evaluate both operands. Therefore, & is referred to as the *unconditional AND* operator, and ¦ is referred to as the *unconditional OR* operator.

✦ The operands of a binary operator are evaluated from left to right. No part of the right-hand operand is evaluated until all the operands before the binary operator are evaluated.

✦ The operators in arithmetic expressions are evaluated in the order determined by the rules of parentheses, operator precedence, and associativity.

✦ Parentheses can be used to force the order of evaluation to occur in any sequence. Operators with higher precedence are evaluated earlier. The associativity of the operators determines the order of evaluation for operators of the same precedence.

✦ All binary operators except assignment operators are left-associative, and assignment operators are right-associative.

✦ You can receive input from an input dialog box using the method JOptionPane. showInputDialog. The input from an input dialog box is a string. To convert it to a double number, use the Double.parseDouble method; to convert it to an int value, use the Integer.parseInt method.

✦ You can use the Math.pow(a, b) method to compute a^b and use the System.current-TimeMillis() to return the current time in milliseconds since midnight, January 1, 1970 GMT (the Unix time).

✦ Programming errors can be categorized into three types: syntax errors, runtime errors, and logic errors. Errors that occur during compilation are called *syntax errors* or *compilation errors*. *Runtime errors* are errors that cause a program to terminate abnormally. *Logic errors* occur when a program does not perform the way it was intended to.

REVIEW QUESTIONS

Sections 2.2–2.6

2.1 Are the following identifiers valid?

applet, Applet, a++, --a, 4#R, $4, #44, apps

2.2 Which of the following are Java keywords?

class, public, int, x, y, radius

2.3 Declare an int variable count with initial value 100, and declare an int constant SIZE with value 20.

2.4 What are the benefits of using constants?

Section 2.7 Numeric Data Types and Operations

2.5 Assume that int a = 1 and double d = 1.0, and that each expression is independent. What are the results of the following expressions?

```
a = 46 / 9;
a = 46 % 9 + 4 * 4 - 2;
a = 45 + 43 % 5 * (23 * 3 % 2);
```

```
a %= 3 / a + 3;
d = 4 + d * d + 4;
d += 1.5 * 3 + (++a);
d -= 1.5 * 3 + a++;
```

2.6 Find the largest and smallest `byte`, `short`, `int`, `long`, `float`, and `double`. Which of these data types requires the least amount of memory?

2.7 What is the result of 25 / 4? How would you rewrite the expression if you wished the result to be a floating-point number?

2.8 Are the following statements correct? If so, show the output.

```
System.out.println("the output for 25 / 4 is " + 25 / 4);
System.out.println("the output for 25 / 4.0 is " + 25 / 4.0);
```

2.9 How would you write the following arithmetic expression in Java?

$$\frac{4}{3(r + 34)} - 9(a + bc) + \frac{3 + d(2 + a)}{a + bd}$$

2.10 Which of these statements are true?

a. Any expression can be used as a statement.
b. The expression x++ can be used as a statement.
c. The statement x = x + 5 is also an expression.
d. The statement x = y = x = 0 is illegal.
e. All the operators of the same precedence are evaluated from left to right.

2.11 Which of the following are correct literals for floating-point numbers?
12.3, 12.3e + 2, 23.4e − 2, −334.4, 20, 39F, 40D

2.12 Identify and fix the errors in the following code:

```
1  public class Test {
2    public void main(string[] args) {
3      int i;
4      int k = 100.0;
5      int j = i + 1;
6
7      System.out.println("j is " + j + " and
8        k is " + k);
9    }
10 }
```

Section 2.8 Numeric Type Conversions

2.13 Can different types of numeric values be used together in a computation?

2.14 What does an explicit conversion from a `double` to an `int` do with the fractional part of the *double* value? Does casting change the variable being cast?

2.15 Show the following output.

```
float f = 12.5F;
int i = (int)f;
System.out.println("f is " + f);
System.out.println("i is " + i);
```

Section 2.9 Character Data Type and Operations

2.16 Use print statements to find out the ASCII code for '1', 'A', 'B', 'a', 'b'. Use print statements to find out the character for the decimal code 40, 59, 79, 85, 90. Use print statements to find out the character for the hexadecimal code 40, 5A, 71, 72, 7A.

2.17 Which of the following are correct literals for characters?
'1' , '\u345dE', '\u3fFa', '\b', \t

2.18 How do you display characters \ and "?

2.19 Evaluate the following:

```
int i = '1';
int j = '1' + '2';
int k = 'a';
char c = 90;
```

Section 2.10 `boolean` Data Type and Operations

2.20 List six comparison operators.

2.21 Assume that x is 1, show the result of the following Boolean expressions:

```
(true) && (3 > 4)
!(x > 0) && (x > 0)
(x > 0) || (x < 0)
(x != 0) || (x == 0)
(x >= 0) || (x < 0)
(x != 1) == !(x == 1)
```

2.22 Write a Boolean expression that evaluates to true if the number is between 1 and 100.

2.23 Write a Boolean expression that evaluates to true if the number is between 1 and 100 or the number is negative.

2.24 Assume that x and y are int type. Which of the following expressions are correct?

```
x > y > 0
x = y && y
x /= y
x or y
x and y
(x != 0) || (x = 0)
```

2.25 List the precedence order of the Boolean operators. Evaluate the following expressions:

```
true | true && false
true || true && false
true | true & false
```

Sections 2.11–2.12

2.26 Show and explain the output of the following code:

a.

```
int i = 0;
System.out.println(--i + i + i++);
System.out.println(i + ++i);
```

b.

```
int i = 0;
i = i + (i = 1);
System.out.println(i);
```

c.

```
int i = 0;
i = (i = 1) + i;
System.out.println(i);
```

2.27 Assume that int a = 1 and double d = 1.0, and that each expression is independent. What are the results of the following expressions?

```
a = (a = 3) + a;
a = a + (a = 3);
a += a + (a = 3);
```

```
a = 5 + 5 * 2 % a--;
a = 4 + 1 + 4 * 5 % (++a + 1);
d += 1.5 * 3 + (++d);
d -= 1.5 * 3 + d++;
```

Section 2.13

2.28 Show the output of the following statements.

```
System.out.println("1" + 1);
System.out.println('1' + 1);
System.out.println("1" + 1 + 1);
System.out.println("1" + (1 + 1));
System.out.println('1' + 1 + 1);
```

Sections 2.14–2.16

2.29 How do you convert a decimal string into a `double` value? How do you convert an integer string into an `int` value?

2.30 How do you obtain the current minute using the `System.currentTimeMillis()` method?

Section 2.18

2.31 What are the specifiers for outputting a boolean value, a character, a decimal integer, a floating-point number, and a string?

2.32 What is wrong in the following statements?

a. `System.out.printf("%5d %d", 1, 2, 3);`

b. `System.out.printf("%5d %f", 1);`

c. `System.out.printf("%5d %f", 1, 2);`

2.33 Show the output of the following statements:

a. `System.out.printf("amount is %f %e\n", 32.32, 32.32);`

b. `System.out.printf("amount is %5.4f %5.4e\n", 32.32, 32.32);`

c. `System.out.printf("%6b\n", (1 > 2));`

d. `System.out.printf("%6s\n", "Java");`

Sections 2.19–2.20

2.34 How do you denote a comment line and a comment paragraph?

2.35 What are the naming conventions for class names, method names, constants, and variables? Which of the following items can be a constant, a method, a variable, or a class according to the Java naming conventions?

```
MAX_VALUE, Test, read, readInt
```

2.36 Reformat the following program according to the programming style and documentation guidelines. Use the next-line brace style.

```
public class Test
{
  // Main method
  public static void main(String[] args) {
  /** Print a line */
  System.out.println("2 % 3 = "+2%3);
  }
}
```

2.37 Describe syntax errors, runtime errors, and logic errors.

Comprehensive

2.38 Evaluate the following expression:

```
1 + "Welcome " + 1 + 1
1 + "Welcome " + (1 + 1)
1 + "Welcome " + ('\u0001' + 1)
1 + "Welcome " + 'a' + 1
```

2.39 Can the following conversions involving casting be allowed? If so, find the converted result.

```
char c = 'A';
i = (int)c;

boolean b = true;
i = (int)b;

float f = 1000.34f;
int i = (int)f;

double d = 1000.34;
int i = (int)d;

int i = 97;
char c = (char)i;

int i = 1000;
boolean b = (boolean)i;
```

2.40 Suppose that x is 1. What is x after the evaluation of the following expression?

```
(x > 1) & (x++ > 1)
```

2.41 Suppose that x is 1. What is x after the evaluation of the following expression?

```
(x > 1) && (x++ > 1)
```

2.42 Show the output of the following program:

```
public class Test {
  public static void main(String[] args) {
    char x = 'a';
    char y = 'c';

    System.out.println(++y);
    System.out.println(y++);
    System.out.println(x > y);
    System.out.println(x - y);
  }
}
```

PROGRAMMING EXERCISES

 NOTE

Solutions to even-numbered exercises are on the Companion Website. Solutions to all exercises are on the Instructor Resource Web site. The level of difficulty is rated easy (no star), moderate (*), hard (**), or challenging (***).

Sections 2.2–2.8

2.1 (*Converting Fahrenheit to Celsius*) Write a program that reads a Fahrenheit degree in double from an input dialog box, then converts it to Celsius and displays the result in a message dialog box. The formula for the conversion is as follows:

celsius = (5 / 9) * (fahrenheit − 32)

HINT

In Java, 5 / 9 is 0, so you need to write 5.0 / 9 in the program to obtain the correct result.

2.2 (*Computing the volume of a cylinder*) Write a program that reads in the radius and length of a cylinder and computes volume using the following formulas:

area = radius * radius * π
volume = area * length

2.3 (*Converting feet into meters*) Write a program that reads a number in feet, converts it to meters, and displays the result. One foot is 0.305 meters.

2.4 (*Converting pounds into kilograms*) Write a program that converts pounds into kilograms. The program prompts the user to enter a number in pounds, converts it to kilograms, and displays the result. One pound is 0.454 kilograms.

2.5* (*Calculating tips*) Write a program that reads the subtotal and the gratuity rate, and computes the gratuity and total. For example, if the user enters 10 for subtotal and 15 percent for gratuity rate, the program displays $1.5 as gratuity and $11.5 as total.

2.6** (*Summing the digits in an integer*) Write a program that reads an integer between 0 and 1000 and adds all the digits in the integer. For example, if an integer is 932, the sum of all its digits is 14.

 HINT

Use the % operator to extract digits, and use the / operator to remove the extracted digit. For instance, 932 % 10 = 2 and 932 / 10 = 93.

Section 2.9 Character Data Type and Operations

2.7* (*Converting an uppercase letter to lowercase*) Write a program that converts an uppercase letter to a lowercase letter. The character is typed in the source code. In Chapter 7, "Strings," you will learn how to enter a character from an input dialog box.

 HINT

In the ASCII table (see Appendix B), uppercase letters appear before lowercase letters. The offset between any uppercase letter and its corresponding lowercase letter is the same. So you can find a lowercase letter from its corresponding uppercase letter, as follows:

```
int offset = (int)'a' - (int)'A';
char lowercase = (char)((int)uppercase + offset);
```

2.8* (*Finding the character of an ASCII code*) Write a program that receives an ASCII code (an integer between 0 and 128) and displays its character. For example, if the user enters 97, the program displays character a.

Section 2.10 boolean Data Type and Operations

2.9* (*Validating triangles*) Write a program that reads three edges for a triangle and determines whether the input is valid. The input is valid if the sum of any two edges is greater than the third edge. For example, if your input for three edges is 1, 2, 1, the output should be:

```
Can edges 1, 2, and 1 form a triangle? false
```

if your input for three edges is 2, 2, 1, the output should be:

```
Can edges 2, 2, and 1 form a triangle? true
```

2.10 (*Checking whether a number is even*) Write a program that reads an integer and checks whether it is even. For example, if your input is 25, the output should be:

```
Is 25 an even number? false
```

If your input is 2000, the output should be:

```
Is 2000 an even number? true
```

2.11* (*Using the* &&, || *and* ^ *operators*) Write a program that prompts the user to enter an integer and determines whether it is divisible by 5 and 6, whether it is divisible by 5 or 6, and whether it is divisible by 5 or 6, but not both. For example, if your input is 10, the output should be

```
Is 10 divisible by 5 and 6? false
Is 10 divisible by 5 or 6? true
Is 10 divisible by 5 or 6, but not both? true
```

Section 2.15 Case Studies

2.12* (*Calculating the future investment value*) Write a program that reads in investment amount, annual interest rate, and number of years, and displays the future investment value using the following formula:

```
futureInvestmentValue =
    investmentAmount x (1 + monthlyInterestRate)^{numberOfYears*12}
```

For example, if you entered amount 1000, annual interest rate 3.25%, and number of years 1, the future investment value is 1032.98.

 HINT
Use the `Math.pow(a, b)` method to compute a raised to the power of b.

2.13* (*Payroll*) Write a program that reads the following information and prints a payroll statement, as shown in Figure 2.13.

Employee's full name (e.g., John Doe)

Number of hours worked in a week (e.g., 10)

Hourly pay rate (e.g., 6.75)

Federal tax withholding rate (e.g., 20%)

State tax withholding rate (e.g., 9%)

2.14* (*Monetary units*) Rewrite Example 2.3 to fix the possible loss of accuracy when converting a `double` value to an `int` value. Enter the input as an integer whose last two digits represent the cents. For example, the input 1156 represents 11 dollars and 56 cents.

Sections 2.16–2.17

2.15* (*Using the console input*) Rewrite Exercise 2.13 using the `MyInput` class.

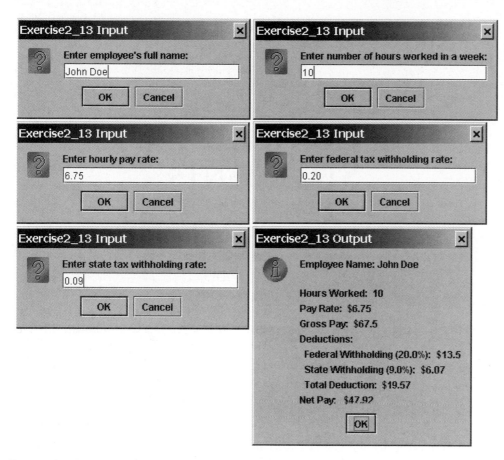

FIGURE 2.13   *The program prints a payroll statement.*

chapter

3

CONTROL STATEMENTS

Objectives

- ✦ To understand the flow of control in selection and loop statements (§§3.2–3.7).

- ✦ To use Boolean expressions to control selection statements and loop statements (§§3.2–3.7).

- ✦ To implement selection control using `if` and nested `if` statements (§§3.2.1-3.2.3).

- ✦ To implement selection control using `switch` statements (§3.2.4).

- ✦ To write expressions using the conditional operator (§3.2.5).

- ✦ To use `while`, `do-while`, and `for` loop statements to control the repetition of statements (§§3.4.1-3.4.3).

- ✦ To write nested loops (§3.4.4).

- ✦ To know the similarities and differences of three types of loops (§3.5).

- ✦ To implement program control with `break` and `continue` (§3.6).

3.1 Introduction

Program control specifies the order in which statements are executed in a program. The programs that you have written so far execute statements in sequence. Often, however, you are faced with situations in which you must provide alternative steps.

In Chapter 2, "Primitive Data Types and Operations," if you assigned a negative value for `radius` in Listing 2.1 ComputeArea.java, the program would print an invalid result. If the radius is negative, you don't want the program to compute the area. Like all high-level programming languages, Java provides selection statements that let you choose actions with two or more alternative courses. You can use selection statements in the following *pseudocode* (i.e., natural language mixed with Java code) to rewrite Listing 2.1:

pseudocode

```
if the radius is negative
  the program displays a message indicating a wrong input;
else
  the program computes the area and displays the result;
```

Like other high-level programming languages, Java provides iteration structures in order to control the repeated execution of statements. Suppose that you need to print the same message a hundred times. It would be tedious to have to write the same code a hundred times in order to print the message a hundred times. Java provides a powerful control structure called a *loop*, which controls how many times an operation or a sequence of operations is performed in succession. Using a loop statement, you simply tell the computer to print the message a hundred times without having to code the print statement a hundred times. Java has three types of loop statements: `while` loops, `do-while` loops, and `for` loops.

In this chapter, you will learn various selection and loop control statements.

3.2 Selection Statements

This section introduces selection statements. Java has several types of selection statements: simple `if` statements, `if ... else` statements, nested `if` statements, `switch` statements, and conditional expressions.

3.2.1 Simple `if` Statements

A simple `if` statement executes an action only if the condition is `true`. The syntax for a simple `if` statement is shown below:

```
if (booleanExpression) {
  statement(s);
}
```

if statement

The execution flow chart is shown in Figure 3.1(a).

If the `booleanExpression` evaluates as `true`, the statements in the block are executed. As an example, see the following code:

```
if (radius >= 0) {
  area = radius * radius * PI;
  System.out.println("The area for the circle of radius " +
    radius + " is " + area);
}
```

The flow chart of the preceding statement is shown in Figure 3.1(b). If the value of `radius` is greater than or equal to 0, then the `area` is computed and the result is displayed; otherwise, the two statements in the block will not be executed.

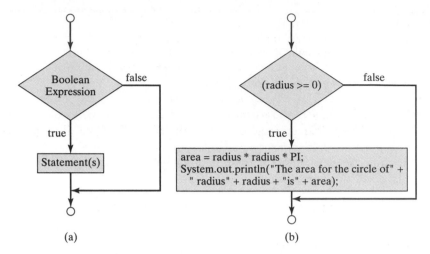

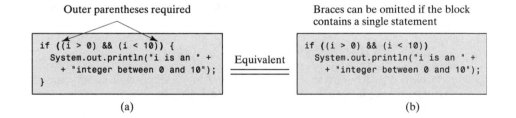

(a)   (b)

FIGURE 3.1 *An* `if` *statement executes statements if the* `booleanExpression` *evaluates as* `true`.

 NOTE

The `booleanExpression` is enclosed in parentheses for all forms of the `if` state-ment. Thus, for example, the outer parentheses in the following `if` statements are required.

Outer parentheses required

```
if ((i > 0) && (i < 10)) {
  System.out.println("i is an " +
    + "integer between 0 and 10");
}
```

Braces can be omitted if the block contains a single statement

```
if ((i > 0) && (i < 10))
  System.out.println("i is an " +
    + "integer between 0 and 10");
```

Equivalent

(a)   (b)

The braces can be omitted if they enclose a single statement.

 CAUTION

Forgetting the braces when they are needed for grouping multiple statements is a common programming error. If you modify the code by adding new statements in an `if` statement without braces, you will have to insert the braces if they are not already in place.

The following statement determines whether a number is even or odd:

```
// Prompt the user to enter an integer
String intString = JOptionPane.showInputDialog(
  "Enter an integer:");

// Convert string into int
int number = Integer.parseInt(intString);

if (number % 2 == 0)
  System.out.println(number + " is even.");

if (number % 2 != 0)
  System.out.println(number + " is odd.");
```

CAUTION

Adding a semicolon at the end of an `if` clause, as shown in (a) in the following code, is a common mistake.

Logic Error

```
if (radius >= 0);
{
  area = radius * radius * PI;
  System.out.println("The area "
    + " is " - area);
}
```
(a)

Equivalent

```
if (radius >= 0) { };
{
  area = radius * radius * PI;
  System.out.println("The area "
    + " is " + area);
}
```
(b)

This mistake is hard to find, because it is not a compilation error or a runtime error; it is a logic error. The code in (a) is equivalent to (b).

This error often occurs when you use the next-line block style. Using the end-of-line block style will prevent this error.

3.2.2 `if` ... `else` Statements

A simple `if` statement takes an action if the specified condition is `true`. If the condition is `false`, nothing is done. But what if you want to take alternative actions when the condition is `false`? You can use an `if` ... `else` statement. The actions that an `if` ... `else` statement specifies differ based on whether the condition is `true` or `false`.

Here is the syntax for this type of statement:

```
if (booleanExpression) {
  statement(s)-for-the-true-case;
}
else {
  statement(s)-for-the-false-case;
}
```

The flow chart of the statement is shown in Figure 3.2.

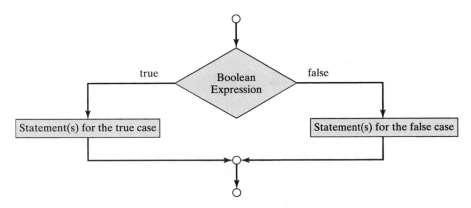

FIGURE 3.2 *An* `if` ... `else` *statement executes statements for the* `true` *case if the* `boolean` *expression evaluates as* `true`; *otherwise, statements for the* `false` *case are executed.*

If the booleanExpression evaluates as true, the statement(s) for the true case is executed; otherwise, the statement(s) for the false case is executed. For example, consider the following code:

```
if (radius >= 0) {
  area = radius * radius * PI;
  System.out.println("The area for the circle of radius " +
    radius + " is " + area);
}
else {
  System.out.println("Negative input");
}
```

If radius >= 0 is true, area is computed and displayed; if it is false, the message "Negative input" is printed.

As usual, the braces can be omitted if there is only one statement within them. The braces enclosing the System.out.println("Negative input") statement can therefore be omitted in the preceding example.

Using the if ... else statement, you can rewrite the code for determining whether a number is even or odd in the preceding section, as follows:

```
if (number % 2 == 0)
  System.out.println(number + " is even.");
else
  System.out.println(number + " is odd.");
```

This is more efficient because whether number % 2 is 0 is tested only once.

3.2.3 Nested if Statements

The statement in an if or if ... else statement can be any legal Java statement, including another if or if ... else statement. The inner if statement is said to be *nested* inside the outer if statement. The inner if statement can contain another if statement; in fact, there is no limit to the depth of the nesting. For example, the following is a nested if statement:

```
if (i > k) {
  if (j > k)
    System.out.println("i and j are greater than k");
}
else
  System.out.println("i is less than or equal to k");
```

The if (j > k) statement is nested inside the if (i > k) statement.

The nested if statement can be used to implement multiple alternatives. The statement given in Figure 3.3(a), for instance, assigns a letter grade to the variable grade according to the score, with multiple alternatives.

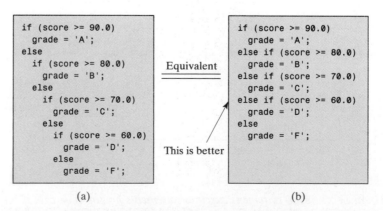

FIGURE 3.3 *A preferred format for multiple alternative if statements is shown in (b).*

The execution of this `if` statement proceeds as follows. The first condition (`score >= 90.0`) is tested. If it is `true`, the grade becomes `'A'`. If it is `false`, the second condition (`score >= 80.0`) is tested. If the second condition is `true`, the grade becomes `'B'`. If that condition is `false`, the third condition and the rest of the conditions (if necessary) continue to be tested until a condition is met or all of the conditions prove to be `false`. If all of the conditions are `false`, the grade becomes `'F'`. Note that a condition is tested only when all of the conditions that come before it are `false`.

The `if` statement in Figure 3.3(a) is equivalent to the `if` statement in Figure 3.3(b). In fact, Figure 3.3(b) is the preferred writing style for multiple alternative `if` statements. This style avoids deep indentation and makes the program easy to read.

NOTE

The `else` clause matches the most recent unmatched `if` clause in the same block. For example, the following statement in (a) is equivalent to the statement in (b):

matching `else` with `if`

```
int i = 1;
int j = 2;
int k = 3;

if (i > j)
    if (i > k)
        System.out.println("A");
else
        System.out.println("B");
```
(a)

Equivalent

This is better with correct indentation

```
int i = 1;
int j = 2;
int k = 3;

if (i > j)
    if (i > k)
        System.out.println("A");
    else
        System.out.println("B");
```
(b)

The compiler ignores indentation. Nothing is printed from the statement in (a) and (b). To force the `else` clause to match the first `if` clause, you must add a pair of braces:

```
int i = 1; int j = 2; int k = 3;

if (i > j) {
  if (i > k)
    System.out.println("A");
}
else
  System.out.println("B");
```

This statement prints B.

TIP

Often new programmers write the code that assigns a test condition to a `boolean` variable like the code in (a):

assign `boolean` variable

```
if (number % 2 == 0)
    even = true;
else
    even = false;
```
(a)

Equivalent

This is better

```
boolean even
    = number % 2 == 0;
```
(b)

The code can be simplified by assigning the test value directly to the variable, as shown in (b).

test boolean value

  CAUTION

To test whether a `boolean` variable is `true` or `false` in a test condition, it is redundant to use the equality comparison operator like the code in (a):

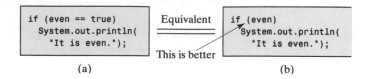

```
if (even == true)
    System.out.println(
        "It is even.");
```
(a)

Equivalent
━━━━━━━
This is better

```
if (even)
    System.out.println(
        "It is even.");
```
(b)

Instead, it is better to use the `boolean` variable directly, as shown in (b). Another good reason to use the `boolean` variable directly is to avoid errors that are difficult to detect. Using the = operator instead of the == operator to compare equality of two items in a test condition is a common error. It could lead to the following erroneous statement:

```
if (even = true)
    System.out.println("It is even.");
```

This statement does not have syntax errors. It assigns `true` to `even` so that `even` is always `true`.

EXAMPLE 3.1 COMPUTING TAXES

Problem

The United States federal personal income tax is calculated based on filing status and taxable income. There are four filing statuses: single filers, married filing jointly, married filing separately, and head of household. The tax rates for 2002 are shown in Table 3.1. If you are, say, single with a taxable income of $10,000, the first $6,000 is taxed at 10% and the other $4,000 is taxed at 15%. So your tax is $1,200.

TABLE 3.1   2002 U.S. Federal Personal Tax Rates

Tax rate	Single filers	Married filing jointly or qualifying widow/widower	Married filing separately	Head of household
10%	Up to $6,000	Up to $12,000	Up to $6,000	Up to $10,000
15%	$6,001–$27,950	$12,001–$46,700	$6,001–$23,350	$10,001–$37,450
27%	$27,951–$67,700	$46,701–$112,850	$23,351–$56,425	$37,451–$96,700
30%	$67,701–$141,250	$112,851–$171,950	$56,426–$85,975	$96,701–$156,600
35%	$141,251–$307,050	$171,951–$307,050	$85,976–$153,525	$156,601–$307,050
38.6%	$307,051 or more	$307,051 or more	$153,526 or more	$307–051 or more

Write a program that prompts the user to enter the filing status and taxable income and computes the tax for the year 2002. Enter 0 for single filers, 1 for married filing jointly, 2 for married filing separately, and 3 for head of household. A sample run of the program is shown in Figure 3.4.

EXAMPLE 3.1 (CONTINUED)

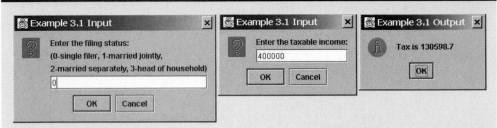

FIGURE **3.4** *The program computes the tax using* if *statements.*

Solution

Your program computes the tax for the taxable income based on the filing status. The filing status can be determined using if statements outlined as follows:

```
if (status == 0) {
  // Compute tax for single filers
}
else if (status == 1) {
  // Compute tax for married file jointly
}
else if (status == 2) {
  // Compute tax for married file separately
}
else if (status == 3) {
  // Compute tax for head of household
}
else {
  // Display wrong status
}
```

For each filing status, there are six tax rates. Each rate is applied to a certain amount of taxable income. For example, of a taxable income of \$400,000 for single filers, \$6,000 is taxed at 10%, $(27950 - 6000)$ at 15%, $(67700 - 27950)$ at 27%, $(141250 - 67700)$ at 35%, and $(400000 - 307050)$ at 38.6%.

Listing 3.1 gives the solution to compute taxes for single filers. The complete solution is left as an exercise.

LISTING **3.1 ComputeTaxWithSelectionStatement.java (Computing Tax)**

```
 1 import javax.swing.JOptionPane;                              import class
 2
 3 public class ComputeTaxWithSelectionStatement {
 4   public static void main(String[] args) {
 5     // Prompt the user to enter filing status
 6     String statusString = JOptionPane.showInputDialog(null,   input dialog
 7       "Enter the filing status:\n" +
 8       "(0-single filer, 1-married jointly,\n" +
 9       "2-married separately, 3-head of household)",
10       "Example 3.1 Input", JOptionPane.QUESTION_MESSAGE);
11     int status = Integer.parseInt(statusString);              convert string to int
12
13     // Prompt the user to enter taxable income
14     String incomeString = JOptionPane.showInputDialog(null,   input dialog
15       "Enter the taxable income:",
16       "Example 3.1 Input", JOptionPane.QUESTION_MESSAGE);
17     double income = Double.parseDouble(incomeString);         convert string to double
18
19     // Compute tax
20     double tax = 0;
21
```

EXAMPLE 3.1 (CONTINUED)

```
22      if (status == 0) { // Compute tax for single filers
23        if (income <= 6000)
24          tax = income * 0.10;
25        else if (income <= 27950)
26          tax = 6000 * 0.10 + (income - 6000) * 0.15;
27        else if (income <= 67700)
28          tax = 6000 * 0.10 + (27950 - 6000) * 0.15 +
29            (income - 27950) * 0.27;
30        else if (income <= 141250)
31          tax = 6000 * 0.10 + (27950 - 6000) * 0.15 +
32            (67700 - 27950) * 0.27 + (income - 67700) * 0.30;
33        else if (income <= 307050)
34          tax = 6000 * 0.10 + (27950 - 6000) * 0.15 +
35            (67700 - 27950) * 0.27 + (141250 - 67700) * 0.30 +
36            (income - 141250) * 0.35;
37        else
38          tax = 6000 * 0.10 + (27950 - 6000) * 0.15 +
39            (67700 - 27950) * 0.27 + (141250 - 67700) * 0.30 +
40            (307050 - 141250) * 0.35 + (income - 307050) * 0.386;
41      }
42      else if (status == 1) { // Compute tax for married file jointly
44        // Left as exercise
44      }
45      else if (status == 2) { // Compute tax for married separately
46        // Left as exercise
47      }
48      else if (status == 3) { // Compute tax for head of household
49        // Left as exercise
50      }
51      else {
52        System.out.println("Error: invalid status");
53        System.exit(0);
54      }
55
56      // Display the result
57      JOptionPane.showMessageDialog(null, "Tax is " +
58        (int)(tax * 100) / 100.0,
59        "Example 3.1 Output", JOptionPane.INFORMATION_MESSAGE);
60    }
61 }
```

compute tax

message dialog

Review

The `import` statement (Line 1) makes the class `javax.swing.JOptionPane` available for use in this example.

The program receives the filing status and taxable income. The multiple alternative `if` statements (Lines 22, 42, 45, 48, 51) check the filing status and compute the tax based on the filing status.

Like the `showMessageDialog` method, `System.exit(0)` (Line 53) is also a static method. This method is defined in the `System` class. Invoking this method terminates the program. The argument 0 indicates that the program is terminated normally.

Note that an initial value of 0 is assigned to `tax` (Line 20). A syntax error would occur if it had no initial value because all of the other statements that assign values to `tax` are within the `if` statement. The compiler thinks that these statements may not be executed and therefore reports a syntax error.

3.2.4   switch Statements

The `if` statement in Example 3.1 makes selections based on a single `true` or `false` condition. There are four cases for computing taxes, which depend on the value of `status`. To fully account for all the cases, nested `if` statements were used. Overuse of nested `if` statements makes a program difficult to read. Java provides a switch statement to handle multiple conditions efficiently. You could write the following switch statement to replace the nested if statement in Example 3.1:

```
switch (status) {
  case 0: compute taxes for single filers;
          break;
  case 1: compute taxes for married file jointly;
          break;
  case 2: compute taxes for married file separately;
          break;
  case 3: compute taxes for head of household;
          break;
  default: System.out.println("Errors: invalid status");
          System.exit(0);
}
```

The flow chart of the preceding switch statement is shown in Figure 3.5.

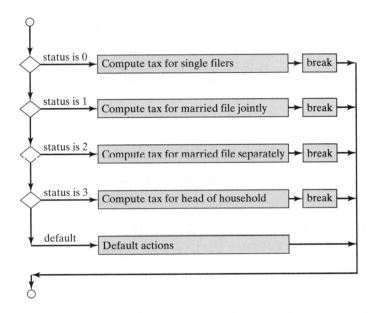

FIGURE 3.5 *The* switch *statement checks all cases and executes the statements in the matched case.*

This statement checks to see whether the status matches the value 0, 1, 2, or 3, in that order. If matched, the corresponding tax is computed; if not matched, a message is displayed. Here is the full syntax for the switch statement:

```
switch (switch-expression) {
  case value1: statement(s)1;
               break;
  case value2: statement(s)2;
               break;
  ...
  case valueN: statement(s)N;
               break;
  default:     statement(s)-for-default;
}
```

switch statement

The switch statement observes the following rules:

◆ The switch-expression must yield a value of char, byte, short, or int type and must always be enclosed in parentheses.

✦ The value1, ..., and valueN must have the same data type as the value of the switch-expression. Note that value1, ..., and valueN are constant expressions, meaning that they cannot contain variables in the expression, such as 1 + x.

✦ When the value in a case statement matches the value of the switch-expression, the statements starting from this case are executed until either a break statement or the end of the switch statement is reached.

✦ The keyword break is optional. The break statement immediately ends the switch statement.

✦ The default case, which is optional, can be used to perform actions when none of the specified cases matches the switch-expression.

✦ The case statements are checked in sequential order, but the order of the cases (including the default case) does not matter. However, it is good programming style to follow the logical sequence of the cases and place the default case at the end.

✿ **CAUTION**

without break

fall-through behavior

Do not forget to use a break statement when one is needed. Once a case is matched, the statements starting from the matched case are executed until a break statement or the end of the switch statement is reached. This phenomenon is referred to as the *fall-through behavior*. For example, the following code prints character a three times if ch is 'a':

```
switch (ch) {
  case 'a': System.out.println(ch);
  case 'b': System.out.println(ch);
  case 'c': System.out.println(ch);
}
```

✿ **TIP**

To avoid programming errors and improve code maintainability, it is a good idea to put a comment in a case clause if break is purposely omitted.

3.2.5   Conditional Expressions

You might want to assign a value to a variable that is restricted by certain conditions. For example, the following statement assigns 1 to y if x is greater than 0, and −1 to y if x is less than or equal to 0:

```
if (x > 0)
  y = 1
else
  y = -1;
```

Alternatively, as in this example, you can use a conditional expression to achieve the same result:

```
y = (x > 0) ? 1 : -1;
```

Conditional expressions are in a completely different style, with no explicit if in the statement. The syntax is shown below:

```
booleanExpression ? expression1 : expression2;
```

conditional expression

The result of this conditional expression is expression1 if booleanExpression is true; otherwise the result is expression2. Suppose you want to assign the larger number between variable num1 and num2 to max. You can simply write a statement using the conditional expression:

```
max = (num1 > num2) ? num1 : num2;
```

For another example, the following statement displays the message "num is even" if num is even, and otherwise displays "num is odd":

```
System.out.println((num % 2 == 0) ? "num is even" : "num is odd");
```

 NOTE

The symbols ? and : appear together in a conditional expression. They form a *conditional operator*. This operator is called a *ternary operator* because it uses three operands. It is the only ternary operator in Java.

3.3   Loop Statements

Loops are structures that control repeated executions of a block of statements. The part of the loop that contains the statements to be repeated is called the *loop body*. A one-time execution of a loop body is referred to as an *iteration of the loop*. Each loop contains a `loop-continuation-condition`, a Boolean expression that controls the execution of the body. After each iteration, the `loop-continuation-condition` is reevaluated. If the condition is `true`, the execution of the loop body is repeated. If the condition is `false`, the loop terminates.

loop body
iteration

The concept of looping is fundamental to programming. Java provides three types of loop statements: the `while` loop, the `do-while` loop, and the `for` loop.

3.3.1   The `while` Loop

The syntax for the `while` loop is as follows:

while loop

```
while (loop-continuation-condition) {
  // Loop body
  Statement(s);
}
```

The braces enclosing a `while` loop or any other loop can be omitted only if the loop body contains one or no statement. The `while` loop flow chart is shown in Figure 3.6(a).

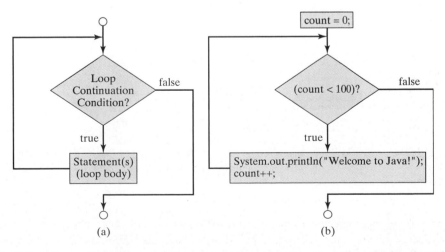

(a)   (b)

FIGURE 3.6 *The `while` loop repeatedly executes the statements in the loop body when the `loop-continuation-condition` evaluates as `true`.*

The `loop-continuation-condition`, a Boolean expression, must appear inside the parentheses. It is always evaluated before the loop body is executed. If its evaluation is `true`, the loop body is executed; if its evaluation is `false`, the entire loop terminates and the program control turns to the statement that follows the `while` loop. For example, the following `while` loop prints `Welcome to Java!` a hundred times.

```
int count = 0;
while (count < 100) {
  System.out.println("Welcome to Java!");
  count++;
}
```

The flow chart of the preceding statement is shown in Figure 3.6(b). The variable `count` is initially 0. The loop checks whether (`count < 100`) is true. If so, it executes the loop body to print the message `Welcome to Java!` and increments `count` by 1. It repeatedly executes the loop body until (`count < 100`) becomes false. When (`count < 100`) is false, the loop terminates and the next statement after the loop statement is executed.

 CAUTION

infinite loop

Make sure that the `loop-continuation-condition` eventually becomes `false` so that the program will terminate. A common programming error involves *infinite loops*. That is, the program cannot terminate because of a mistake on the `loop-continuation-condition`. For instance, if you forgot to increase `count` (count++) in the code, the program would not stop. To terminate the program, press CTRL+C.

EXAMPLE 3.2 USING `while` LOOPS

Problem

Write a program that reads and calculates the sum of an unspecified number of integers. The input 0 signifies the end of the input.

Solution

Listing 3.2 gives the solution to the problem. The program's sample run is shown in Figure 3.7.

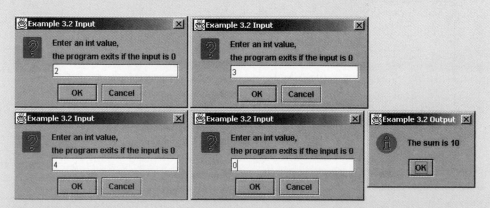

FIGURE 3.7 *Example 3.2 uses a `while` loop to add an unspecified number of integers.*

EXAMPLE 3.2 (CONTINUED)

LISTING 3.2 TestWhile.java (Using while Loop)

```java
1 import javax.swing.JOptionPane;
2
3 public class TestWhile {
4   /** Main method */
5   public static void main(String[] args) {
6     // Read an initial data
7     String dataString = JOptionPane.showInputDialog(null,
8       "Enter an int value, \nthe program exits if the input is 0",
9       "Example 3.2 Input", JOptionPane.QUESTION_MESSAGE);
10     int data = Integer.parseInt(dataString);
11
12     // Keep reading data until the input is 0
13     int sum = 0;
14     while (data != 0) {
15       sum += data;
16
17       // Read the next data
18       dataString = JOptionPane.showInputDialog(null,
19         "Enter an int value, \nthe program exits if the input is 0",
20         "Example 3.2 Input", JOptionPane.QUESTION_MESSAGE);
21       data = Integer.parseInt(dataString);
22     }
23
24     JOptionPane.showMessageDialog(null, "The sum is " + sum,
25       "Example 3.2 Output", JOptionPane.INFORMATION_MESSAGE);
26   }
27 }
```

input dialog

convert string to int

loop

message dialog

Review

If data is not 0, it is added to the sum (Line 15) and the next items of input data are read (Lines 18–21). If data is 0, the loop body is not executed and the while loop terminates.

Note that if the first input read is 0, the loop body never executes, and the resulting sum is 0.

 NOTE

The program uses the input value 0 as the end of the input. A special input value that signifies the end of the input, such as 0 in this example, is also known as a *sentinel value*.

sentinel value

 CAUTION

Don't use floating-point values for equality checking in a loop control. Since floating-point values are approximations, using them could result in imprecise counter values and inaccurate results. This example uses int value for data. If a floating-point type value is used for data, (data != 0) may be true even though data is 0.

numeric error

Here is a good example provided by a reviewer of this book:

```java
// data should be zero
double data = Math.pow(Math.sqrt(2), 2) - 2;

if (data == 0)
  System.out.println("data is zero");
else
  System.out.println("data is not zero");
```

> Like `pow`, `sqrt` is a method in the `Math` class for computing the square root of a number. The variable `data` in the above code should be zero, but it is not, because of rounding-off errors.

3.3.2 The `do-while` Loop

`do-while` loop

The `do-while` loop is a variation of the `while` loop. Its syntax is given below:

```
do {
  // Loop body;
  Statement(s);
} while (loop-continuation-condition);
```

Its execution flow chart is shown in Figure 3.8.

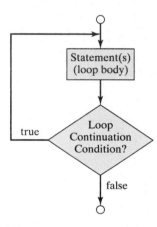

FIGURE 3.8 *The `do-while` loop executes the loop body first, and then checks the `loop-continuation-condition` to determine whether to continue or terminate the loop.*

The loop body is executed first. Then the `loop-continuation-condition` is evaluated. If the evaluation is `true`, the loop body is executed again; if it is `false`, the `do-while` loop terminates. The major difference between a `while` loop and a `do-while` loop is the order in which the `loop-continuation-condition` is evaluated and the loop body executed. The `while` loop and the `do-while` loop have equal expressive power. Sometimes one is a more convenient choice than the other. For example, you can rewrite Example 3.2 as shown in Listing 3.3.

LISTING 3.3 TestDo.java (Using do-while Loop)

loop

```
1 import javax.swing.JOptionPane;
2
3 public class TestDoWhile {
4   /** Main method */
5   public static void main(String[] args) {
6     int data;
7     int sum = 0;
8
9     // Keep reading data until the input is 0
10    do {
11      // Read the next data
```

```
12        String dataString = JOptionPane.showInputDialog(null,
13          "Enter an int value, \nthe program exits if the input is 0",
14          "TestDo", JOptionPane.QUESTION_MESSAGE);
15
16        data = Integer.parseInt(dataString);
17
18        sum += data;
19      } while (data != 0);
20
21        JOptionPane.showMessageDialog(null, "The sum is " + sum,
22          "TestDo", JOptionPane.INFORMATION_MESSAGE);
23    }
24 }
```

 TIP

Use the `do-while` loop if you have statements inside the loop that must be executed at least once, as in the case of the `do-while` loop in the preceding `TestDoWhile` program. These statements must appear before the loop as well as inside the loop if you use a `while` loop.

3.3.3   The `for` Loop

Often you write a loop in the following common form:

```
i = initialValue; // Initialize loop control variable
while (i < endValue) {
  // Loop body
  ...
  i++; // Adjust loop control variable
}
```

A `for` loop can be used to simplify the above loop:

```
for (i = initialValue; i < endValue; i++) {
  // Loop body
  ...
}
```

In general, the syntax of a `for` loop is as shown below:

```
for (initial-action; loop-continuation-condition;
     action-after-each-iteration) {
  // Loop body;
  Statement(s);
}
```

for loop

The flow chart of the `for` loop is shown in Figure 3.9(a).

The `for` loop statement starts with the keyword `for`, followed by a pair of parentheses enclosing `initial-action`, `loop-continuation-condition`, and `action-after-each-iteration`, and the loop body, enclosed inside braces. `initial-action`, `loop-continuation-condition`, and `action-after-each-iteration` are separated by semicolons.

A `for` loop generally uses a variable to control how many times the loop body is executed and when the loop terminates. This variable is referred to as a *control variable*. The `initial-action` often initializes a control variable, the `action-after-each-iteration` usually increments or decrements the control variable, and the `loop-continuation-condition` tests whether the control

control variable

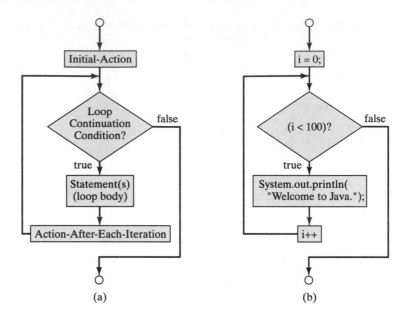

(a)   (b)

FIGURE 3.9 *A* `for` *loop performs an initial action once, then repeatedly executes the state-ments in the loop body, and performs an action after an iteration when the* `loop-continua-tion-condition` *evaluates as* `true`.

variable has reached a termination value. For example, the following `for` loop prints `Welcome to Java!` a hundred times:

```java
int i;
for (i = 0; i < 100; i++) {
  System.out.println("Welcome to Java!");
}
```

The flow chart of the statement is shown in Figure 3.9(b). The `for` loop initializes `i` to `0`, then repeatedly executes the `println` statement and evaluates `i++` if `i` is less than `100`.

The `initial-action`, `i = 0`, initializes the control variable, `i`.

The `loop-continuation-condition`, `i < 100`, is a Boolean expression. The expression is eval-uated at the beginning of each iteration. If this condition is `true`, execute the loop body. If it is `false`, the loop terminates and the program control turns to the line following the loop.

The `action-after-each-iteration`, `i++`, is a statement that adjusts the control variable. This statement is executed after each iteration. It increments the control variable. Eventually, the value of the control variable forces the `loop-continuation-condition` to become `false`.

The loop control variable can be declared and initialized in the `for` loop. Here is an example:

```java
for (int i = 0; i < 100; i++) {
  System.out.println("Welcome to Java!");
}
```

If there is only one statement in the loop body, as in this example, the braces can be omitted.

 TIP

The control variable must always be declared inside the control structure of the loop or before the loop. If the loop control variable is used only in the loop, and not elsewhere, it is good programming practice to declare it in the `initial-action` of the `for` loop. If the variable is declared inside the loop control structure, it cannot be referenced outside the loop. For example, you cannot reference `i` outside the `for` loop in the preceding code, because it is declared inside the `for` loop.

NOTE

The `initial-action` in a `for` loop can be a list of zero or more comma-separated variable declaration statements or assignment expressions. For example,

```
for (int i = 0, j = 0; (i + j < 10); i++, j++) {
  // Do something
}
```

The `action-after-each-iteration` in a `for` loop can be a list of zero or more comma-separated statements. For example,

```
for (int i = 1; i < 100; System.out.println(i), i++);
```

This example is correct, but it is not a good example, because it makes the code difficult to read. Normally, you declare and initialize a control variable as initial action, and increment or decrement the control variable as an action after each iteration.

NOTE

If the `loop-continuation-condition` in a `for` loop is omitted, it is implicitly true. Thus the statement given below in (a), which is an infinite loop, is correct. Nevertheless, I recommend that you use the equivalent loop in (b) to avoid confusion:

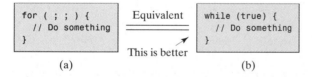

EXAMPLE 3.3 USING for LOOPS

Problem
Write a program that sums a series that starts with 0.01 and ends with 1.0. The numbers in the series will increment by 0.01, as follows: 0.01 + 0.02 + 0.03 and so on.

Solution
Listing 3.4 gives the solution to the problem. The output of the program appears in Figure 3.10.

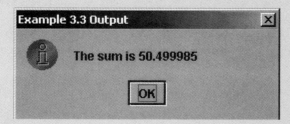

FIGURE 3.10 *Example 3.3 uses a* for *loop to sum a series from 0.01 to 1 in increments of 0.01.*

EXAMPLE 3.3 (CONTINUED)

LISTING 3.4   TestSum.java (Using for Loop)

```
1  import javax.swing.JOptionPane;
2
3  public class TestSum {
4    /** Main method */
5    public static void main(String[] args) {
6      // Initialize sum
7      float sum = 0;
8
9      // Add 0.01, 0.02, ..., 0.99, 1 to sum
10     for (float i = 0.01f; i <= 1.0f; i = i + 0.01f)
11       sum += i;
12
13     // Display result
14     JOptionPane.showMessageDialog(null, "The sum is " + sum,
15       "Example 3.3 Output", JOptionPane.INFORMATION_MESSAGE);
16   }
17 }
```

Review

loop

The for loop (Lines 10–11) repeatedly adds the control variable i to the sum. This variable, which begins with 0.01, is incremented by 0.01 after each iteration. The loop terminates when i exceeds 1.0.

The for loop initial action can be any statement, but it is often used to initialize a control variable. From this example, you can see that a control variable can be a float type. In fact, it can be any data type.

numeric error

The exact sum should be 50.50, but the answer is 50.499985. The result is not precise because computers use a fixed number of bits to represent floating-point numbers, and thus cannot represent some floating-point numbers exactly. If you change float in the program to double as follows, you should see a slight improvement in precision because a double variable takes sixty-four bits, whereas a float variable takes thirty-two bits:

```
// Initialize sum
double sum = 0;

// Add 0.01, 0.02, ..., 0.99, 1 to sum
for (double i = 0.01; i <= 1.0; i = i + 0.01)
  sum += i;
```

However, you will be stunned to see that the result is actually 49.50000000000003. What went wrong? If you print out i for each iteration in the loop, you will see that the last i is slightly larger than 1 (not exactly 1). This causes the last i not to be added in sum. The fundamental problem is that the floating-point numbers are represented by approximation. Errors commonly occur. To ensure that all items are added to sum, use an integer variable to count the items. Here is the new loop:

```
double item = 0.01;
for (int count = 0; count < 100; count++) {
  sum += item;
  item += 0.01;
}
```

After this loop, sum is 50.50000000000003.

3.3.4 Nested Loops

Nested loops consist of an outer loop and one or more inner loops. Each time the outer loop is repeated, the inner loops are reentered, and all the required iterations are performed.

EXAMPLE 3.4 DISPLAYING THE MULTIPLICATION TABLE

Problem

Write a program that uses nested `for` loops to print a multiplication table, as shown in Figure 3.11.

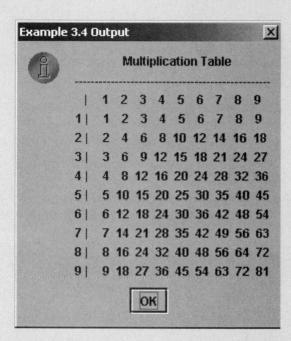

FIGURE 3.11 *Example 3.4 uses nested* for *loops to print a multiplication table.*

Solution

Listing 3.5 gives the solution to the problem.

LISTING **3.5** TestMultiplicationTable.java
(Using Nested for Loop)

```
 1 import javax.swing.JOptionPane;
 2
 3 public class TestMultiplicationTable {
 4   /** Main method */
 5   public static void main(String[] args) {
 6     // Display the table heading
 7     String output = " Multiplication Table\n";              table title
 8     output += "----------------------------------\n";
 9
10     // Display the number title
11     output += " | ";
12     for (int j = 1; j <= 9; j++)
13       output += "  " + j;
```

```
       EXAMPLE 3.4 (CONTINUED)

14
15      output += "\n";
16
17      // Print table body
18      for (int i = 1; i <= 9; i++) {
19        output += i + " | ";
20        for (int j = 1; j <= 9; j++) {
21          // Display the product and align properly
22          if (i * j < 10)
23            output += "  " + i * j;
24          else
25            output += " " + i * j;
26        }
27        output += "\n";
28      }
29
30      // Display result
31      JOptionPane.showMessageDialog(null, output,
32        "Example 3.4 Output", JOptionPane.INFORMATION_MESSAGE);
33    }
34 }
```

table body

nested loop

Review

The program displays a title (Line 7) on the first line and dashes (-) (Line 8) on the second line. The first for loop (Lines 12–13) displays the numbers 1 through 9 on the third line.

The next loop (Lines 18–28) is a nested for loop with the control variable i in the outer loop and j in the inner loop. For each i, the product i * j is displayed on a line in the inner loop, with j being 1, 2, 3, . . . , 9. The if statement in the inner loop (Lines 22–25) is used so that the product will be aligned properly. If the product is a single digit, it is displayed with an extra space before it.

3.5 Which Loop to Use?

The three forms of loop statements, while, do-while, and for, are expressively equivalent; that is, you can write a loop in any of these three forms. For example, a while loop in (a) in the following figure can always be converted into the for loop in (b):

```
while (loop-continuation-condition) {
  // Loop body
}
```
Equivalent
```
for ( ; loop-continuation-condition; ) {
  // Loop body
}
```

                (a)   (b)

A for loop in (a) in the next figure can generally be converted into the while loop in (b) except in certain special cases (see Review Question 3.20 for such a case):

```
for (initial-action;
     loop-continuation-condition;
     action-after-each-iteration) {
  // Loop body;
}
```
Equivalent
```
initial-action;
while (loop-continuation-condition) {
  // Loop body;
  action-after-each-iteration;
}
```

                (a)   (b)

I recommend that you use the loop statement that is most intuitive and comfortable for you. In general, a `for` loop may be used if the number of repetitions is known, as, for example, when you need to print a message a hundred times. A `while` loop may be used if the number of repetitions is not known, as in the case of reading the numbers until the input is 0. A `do-while` loop can be used to replace a `while` loop if the loop body has to be executed before the continuation condition is tested.

 CAUTION

Adding a semicolon at the end of the `for` clause before the loop body is a common mistake, as shown below in (a). Similarly, the loop in (b) is also wrong.

Logic Error   Logic Error

```
for (int i = 0; i < 10; i++);
{
  System.out.println("i is " + i);
}
```

(a)

```
int i = 0;
while (i < 10);
{
  System.out.println("i is " + i);
  i++;
}
```

(b)

In both cases, the semicolon signifies the end of the loop prematurely. These errors often occur when you use the next-line block style.

In the case of the `do-while` loop, the semicolon is needed to end the loop.

```
int i = 0;
do {
  System.out.println("i is " + i);
  i++;
} while (i < 10);  ◄─── Correct
```

3.6 Using the Keywords `break` and `continue`

Two statements, `break` and `continue`, can be used in loop statements to provide the loop with additional control.

✦ **break** immediately ends the innermost loop that contains it. It is generally used with an `if` statement. break statement

✦ **continue** only ends the current iteration. Program control goes to the end of the loop body. This keyword is generally used with an `if` statement. continue statement

You have already used the keyword `break` in a `switch` statement. You can also use `break` and `continue` in a loop.

EXAMPLE 3.5 DEMONSTRATING A `break` STATEMENT

Problem
Add the integers from 1 to 20 in this order to sum until sum is greater than or equal to 100.

Solution
Listing 3.6 gives the solution to the problem.

EXAMPLE 3.5 (CONTINUED)

LISTING 3.6   **TestBreak.java (Skipping Loop)**

```
 1 public class TestBreak {
 2   /** Main method */
 3   public static void main(String[] args) {
 4     int sum = 0;
 5     int number = 0;
 6
 7     while (number < 20) {
 8       number++;
 9       sum += number;
10       if (sum >= 100) break;
11     }
12
13     System.out.println("The number is " + number);
14     System.out.println("The sum is " + sum);
15   }
16 }
```

break

Review

Without the `if` statement (Line 10), this program calculates the sum of the numbers from 1 to 20. But with the `if` statement, the loop terminates when the sum becomes greater than or equal to 100. The output of the program is shown in Figure 3.12(a).

If you changed the `if` statement as shown below, the output would resemble that in Figure 3.12(b).

```
if (sum == 100) break;
```

In this case, the `if` condition will never be `true`. Therefore, the `break` statement will never be executed.

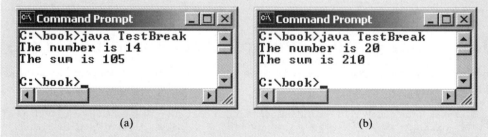

(a)   (b)

FIGURE 3.12 *(a) The* break *statement in the* TestBreak *program forces the* while *loop to exit when* sum *is greater than or equal to 100. (b) The* break *statement is not executed in the modified* TestBreak *program because* sum == 100 *cannot be* true.

EXAMPLE 3.6 DEMONSTRATING A continue STATEMENT

Problem

Add all the integers from 1 to 20 except 10 and 11 to sum.

Solution

Listing 3.7 gives the solution to the problem.

EXAMPLE 3.6 (CONTINUED)

LISTING 3.7   TestContinue.java (Skipping Iteration)

```
 1 public class TestContinue {
 2   /** Main method */
 3   public static void main(String[] args) {
 4     int sum = 0;
 5     int number = 0;
 6
 7     while (number < 20) {
 8       number++;
 9       if (number == 10 || number == 11) continue;
10       sum += number;
11     }
12
13     System.out.println("The sum is " + sum);
14   }
15 }
```

continue

Review

With the if statement in the program (Line 9), the continue statement is executed when number becomes 10 or 11. The continue statement ends the current iteration so that the rest of the statement in the loop body is not executed; therefore, number is not added to sum when it is 10 or 11. The output of the program is shown in Figure 3.13(a).

Without the if statement in the program, the output would look like Figure 3.13(b). In this case, all of the numbers are added to sum, including when number is 10 or 11. Therefore, the result is 210, which is 21 more than it was with the if statement.

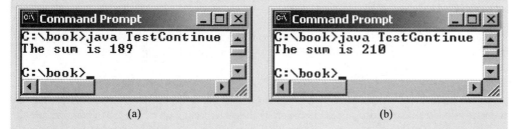

(a)   (b)

FIGURE 3.13   *(a) The* continue *statement in the* TestContinue *program forces the current iteration to end when* number *equals 10 or 11. (b) Since the modified* TestContinue *program has no* continue *statement, every number is added to* sum.

 NOTE

The continue statement is always inside a loop. In the while and do-while loops, the loop-continuation-condition is evaluated immediately after the continue statement. In the for loop, the action-after-each-iteration is performed, then the loop-continuation-condition is evaluated, immediately after the continue statement.

 TIP

You can always write a program without using break or continue in a loop. See Review Question 3.21. In general, it is appropriate to use break and continue if their use simplifies coding and makes programs easier to read.

3.6.1 Statement Labels and Breaking with Labels (Optional)

Every statement in Java can have an optional label as an identifier. Labels are often associated with loops. You can use a break statement with a label to break out of the labeled loop, and a continue statement with a label to break out of the current iteration of the labeled loop.

The break statement given below, for example, breaks out of the outer loop if (i * j > 50) and transfers control to the statement immediately following the outer loop:

```
outer:
  for (int i = 1; i < 10; i++) {
  inner:
    for (int j = 1; j < 10; j++) {
      if (i * j > 50)
        break outer;

      System.out.println(i * j);
    }
  }
```

If you replace break outer with break in the preceding statement, the break statement would break out of the inner loop and continue to stay inside the outer loop.

The following continue statement breaks out of the inner loop if (i * j > 50) and starts a new iteration of the outer loop if i < 10 is true after i is incremented by 1:

```
outer:
 for (int i = 1; i < 10; i++) {
 inner:
   for (int j = 1; j < 10; j++) {
     if (i * j > 50)
       continue outer;

     System.out.println(i * j);
   }
 }
```

If you replace continue outer with continue in the preceding statement, the continue statement would break out of the current iteration of the inner loop if (i * j > 50) and continue the next iteration of the inner loop if j < 10 is true after j is incremented by 1.

goto

> **NOTE**
>
> Some programming languages have a goto statement, but labeled break statements and labeled continue statements in Java are completely different from goto statements. The goto label statement would indiscriminately transfer the control to any labeled statement in the program and execute it. The break label statement breaks out of the labeled loop, and the continue label statement breaks out of the current iteration in the labeled loop.

3.7 Case Studies

Control statements are fundamental in programming. The ability to write control statements is essential in learning Java programming. *If you can write programs using loops, you know how to program!* For this reason, this section presents four additional examples of how to solve problems using loops.

EXAMPLE 3.7 FINDING THE GREATEST COMMON DIVISOR

Problem

Write a program that prompts the user to enter two positive integers and finds their greatest common divisor.

Solution

The greatest common divisor of the integers 4 and 2, is 2. The greatest common divisor of the integers 16 and 24, is 8. How do you find the greatest common divisor? Let the two input integers be n1 and n2. You know that number 1 is a common divisor, but it may not be the greatest common divisor. So you can check whether k (for k = 2, 3, 4, and so on) is a common divisor for n1 and n2, until k is greater than n1 or n2. Store the common divisor in a variable named gcd. Initially, gcd is 1. Whenever a new common divisor is found, it becomes the new gcd. When you have checked all the possible common divisors from 2 up to n1 or n2, the value in variable gcd is the greatest common divisor. The idea can be translated into the following loop:

GCD

```
int gcd = 1;
int k = 1;
while (k <= n1 && k <= n2) {
  if (n1 % k == 0 && n2 % k == 0)
    gcd = k;
  k++;
}
// After the loop, gcd is the greatest common divisor for n1 and n2
```

The complete program is given in Listing 3.8, and a sample run of the program is shown in Figure 3.14.

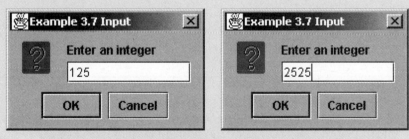

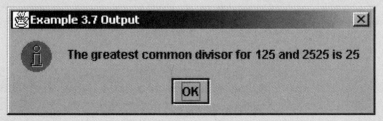

FIGURE 3.14 *The program finds the greatest common divisor for two integers.*

LISTING 3.8 GreatestCommonDivisor.java (Finding GCD)

```
1 import javax.swing.JOptionPane;
2
3 public class GreatestCommonDivisor {
4   /** Main method */
5   public static void main(String[] args) {
```

EXAMPLE 3.7 (CONTINUED)

input

input

gcd

```
 6      // Prompt the user to enter two integers
 7      String s1 = JOptionPane.showInputDialog(null, "Enter an integer",
 8        "Example 3.7 Input", JOptionPane.QUESTION_MESSAGE);
 9      int n1 = Integer.parseInt(s1);
10
11      String s2 = JOptionPane.showInputDialog(null, "Enter an integer",
12        "Example 3.7 Input", JOptionPane.QUESTION_MESSAGE);
13      int n2 = Integer.parseInt(s2);
14
15      int gcd = 1;
16      int k = 1;
17      while (k <= n1 && k <= n2) {
18        if (n1 % k == 0 && n2 % k == 0)
19          gcd = k;
20        k++;
21      }
22
23      String output = "The greatest common divisor for " + n1 + " and "
24        + n2 + " is " + gcd;
25      JOptionPane.showMessageDialog(null, output,
26        "Example 3.7 Output", JOptionPane.INFORMATION_MESSAGE);
27    }
28 }
```

output

Review

think before you type

How did you write this program? Did you immediately begin to write the code? No. It is important to *think before you type*. Thinking enables you to generate a logical solution for the problem without concern about how to write the code. Once you have a logical solution, type the code to translate the solution into a Java program. The translation is not unique. For example, you could use a `for` loop to rewrite the code as follows:

```
for (int k = 1; k <= n1 && k <= n2; k++) {
  if (n1 % k == 0 && n2 % k == 0)
    gcd = k;
}
```

multiple solutions

> **NOTE**
>
> A problem often has *multiple solutions*. The GCD problem can be solved in many ways. Exercise 3.20 suggests another solution. A more efficient solution is to use the classic Euclidean algorithm. See http://www.mapleapps.com/maplelinks/html/euclid.html for more information.

EXAMPLE 3.8 FINDING THE SALES AMOUNT

Problem

You have just started a sales job in a department store. Your pay consists of a base salary and a commission. The base salary is $5,000. The scheme shown below is used to determine the commission rate.

Sales Amount	Commission Rate
$0.01–$5,000	8 percent
$5,000.01–$10,000	10 percent
$10,000.01 and above	12 percent

EXAMPLE 3.8 (CONTINUED)

Your goal is to earn $30,000 a year. Write a program that finds out the minimum amount of sales you have to generate in order to make $30,000.

Solution

Since your base salary is $5,000, you have to make $25,000 in commissions to earn $30,000 a year. What is the sales amount for a $25,000 commission? If you know the sales amount, the commission can be computed as follows:

```
if (salesAmount >= 10000.01)
  commission =
    5000 * 0.08 + 5000 * 0.1 + (salesAmount - 10000) * 0.12;
else if (salesAmount >= 5000.01)
  commission = 5000 * 0.08 + (salesAmount - 5000) * 0.10;
else
  commission = salesAmount * 0.08;
```

This suggests that you can try to find the salesAmount to match a given commission through incremental approximation. For salesAmount of $0.01 (1 cent), find commission. If commission is less than $25,000, increment salesAmount by 0.01 and find commission again. If commission is still less than $25,000, repeat the process until the commission is greater than or equal to $25,000. This is a tedious job for humans, but it is exactly what a computer is good for. You can write a loop and let a computer execute it painlessly. The idea can be translated into the following loop:

```
Set COMMISSION_SOUGHT as a constant;
Set an initial salesAmount;

do {
  Increase salesAmount by 1 cent;
  Compute the commission from the current salesAmount;
} while (commission < COMMISSION_SOUGHT);
```

The complete program is given in Listing 3.9, and a sample run of the program is shown in Figure 3.15.

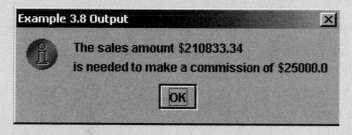

FIGURE 3.15 *The program finds the sales amount for the given commission.*

LISTING 3.9 FindSalesAmount.java (Finding Sales Amount)

```
1 import javax.swing.JOptionPane;
2
3 public class FindSalesAmount {
4   /** Main method */
5   public static void main(String[] args) {
6     // The commission sought
7     final double COMMISSION_SOUGHT = 25000;                    constants
8     final double INITIAL_SALES_AMOUNT = 0.01;
9     double commission = 0;
10    double salesAmount = INITIAL_SALES_AMOUNT;
```

EXAMPLE 3.8 (CONTINUED)

loop

```
11
12   do {
13     // Increase salesAmount by 1 cent
14     salesAmount += 0.01;
15
16     // Compute the commission from the current salesAmount;
17     if (salesAmount >= 10000.01)
18       commission =
19         5000 * 0.08 + 5000 * 0.1 + (salesAmount - 10000) * 0.12;
20     else if (salesAmount >= 5000.01)
21       commission = 5000 * 0.08 + (salesAmount - 5000) * 0.10;
22     else
23       commission = salesAmount * 0.08;
24   } while (commission < COMMISSION_SOUGHT);
25
```

prepare output

```
26   // Display the sales amount
27   String output =
28     "The sales amount $" + (int)(salesAmount * 100) / 100.0 +
29     "\nis needed to make a commission of $" + COMMISSION_SOUGHT;
```

output

```
30   JOptionPane.showMessageDialog(null, output,
31     "Example 3.8 Output", JOptionPane.INFORMATION_MESSAGE);
32   }
33 }
```

Review

The do-while loop (Lines 12–24) is used to repeatedly compute commission for an incremental salesAmount. The loop terminates when commission is greater than or equal to a constant COMMISSION_SOUGHT.

In Exercise 3.22, you will rewrite this program to let the user enter COMMISSION_SOUGHT dynamically from an input dialog.

You can improve the performance of this program by estimating a higher INITIAL_SALES_AMOUNT (e.g., 25000).

What is wrong if saleAmount is incremented after the commission is computed as follows?

```
do {
  // Compute the commission from the current salesAmount;
  if (salesAmount >= 10000.01)
    commission =
      5000 * 0.08 + 5000 * 0.1 + (salesAmount - 10000) * 0.12;
  else if (salesAmount >= 5000.01)
    commission = 5000 * 0.08 + (salesAmount - 5000) * 0.10;
  else
    commission = salesAmount * 0.08;

  // Increase salesAmount by 1 cent
  salesAmount += 0.01;
} while (commission < COMMISSION_SOUGHT);
```

off-by-one error

The change is erroneous because saleAmount is 1 cent more than is needed for the commission when the loop ends. This is a common error in loops, known as the *off-by-one* error.

constants

TIP

This example uses *constants* COMMISSION_SOUGHT and INITIAL_SALES_AMOUNT. Using constants makes programs easy to read and maintain.

EXAMPLE 3.9 DISPLAYING A PYRAMID OF NUMBERS

Problem

Write a program that prompts the user to enter an integer from 1 to 15 and displays a pyramid. If the input integer is 12, for example, the output is shown in Figure 3.16.

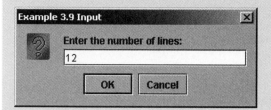

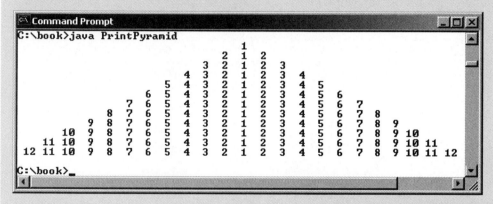

FIGURE 3.16 *The program uses nested loops to print numbers in a triangular pattern.*

Solution

Your program receives the input for an integer (`numberOfLines`) that represents the total number of lines. It displays all the lines one by one. Each line has three parts. The first part comprises the spaces before the numbers; the second part, the leading numbers, such as 3 2 1 on Line 3; and the last part, the ending numbers, such as 2 3 on Line 3.

Each number occupies three spaces. Display an empty space before a double-digit number, and display two empty spaces before a single-digit number.

You can use an outer loop to control the lines. At the nth row, there are (`numberOfLines` – n) * 3 leading spaces, the leading numbers are n, n–1, ..., 1, and the ending numbers are 2, ..., n. You can use three separate inner loops to print each part.

Here is the algorithm for the problem:

```
Input numberOfLines;

for (int row = 1; row <= numberOfLines; row++) {
  Print (numberOfLines - row) * 3 leading spaces;
  Print leading numbers row, row - 1, ..., 1;
  Print ending numbers 2, 3, ..., row - 1, row;
  Start a new line;
}
```

The complete program is given in Listing 3.10.

EXAMPLE 3.9 (CONTINUED)

LISTING 3.10 PrintPyramid.java (Printing Pyramid)

```
1 import javax.swing.JOptionPane;
2
3 public class PrintPyramid {
4   /** Main method */
5   public static void main(String[] args) {
6     // Prompt the user to enter the number of lines
7     String input = JOptionPane.showInputDialog(null,
8       "Enter the number of lines:", "Example 3.9 Input",
9       JOptionPane.QUESTION_MESSAGE);
10    int numberOfLines = Integer.parseInt(input);
11
12    if (numberOfLines < 1 || numberOfLines > 15) {
13      System.out.println("You must enter a number from 1 to 15");
14      System.exit(0);
15    }
16
17    // Print lines
18    for (int row = 1; row <= numberOfLines; row++) {
19      // Print NUMBER_OF_LINES - row) leading spaces
20      for (int column = 1; column <= numberOfLines - row; column++)
21        System.out.print("   ");
22
23      // Print leading numbers row, row - 1, ..., 1
24      for (int num = row; num >= 1; num--)
25        System.out.print((num >= 10) ? " " + num : "  " + num);
26
27      // Print ending numbers 2, 3, ..., row - 1, row
28      for (int num = 2; num <= row; num++)
29        System.out.print((num >= 10) ? " " + num : "  " + num);
30
31      // Start a new line
32      System.out.println();
33    }
34  }
35 }
```

print lines — (line 18)

print spaces — (line 20)

print leading numbers — (line 24)

print ending numbers — (line 28)

Review

The program uses the print method (Lines 21, 25, and 29) to display a string to the console. This method is identical to the println method except that println moves the cursor to the next line after displaying the string, but print does not advance the cursor to the next line when completed.

The conditional expression (num >= 10) ? " " + num : " " + num in Lines 25 and 29 returns a string with a single empty space before the number if the number is greater than or equal to 10, and otherwise returns a string with two empty spaces before the number.

Printing patterns like this one and the ones in Exercises 3.23 and 3.24 is my favorite exercise for practicing loop control statements. The key is to understand the pattern and to describe it using loop control variables.

The last line in the outer loop (Line 32), System.out.println(), does not have any argument in the method. This call moves the cursor to the next line.

EXAMPLE 3.10 DISPLAYING PRIME NUMBERS (OPTIONAL)

Problem

Write a program that displays the first fifty *prime numbers* in five lines, each of which contains ten numbers, as shown in Figure 3.17. An integer greater than 1 is *prime* if its only positive divisor is 1 or itself. For example, 2, 3, 5, and 7 are prime numbers, but 4, 6, 8, and 9 are not.

prime number

```
Command Prompt                                    _ □ ×

C:\book>java PrimeNumber
The first 50 prime numbers are

2 3 5 7 11 13 17 19 23 29
31 37 41 43 47 53 59 61 67 71
73 79 83 89 97 101 103 107 109 113
127 131 137 139 149 151 157 163 167 173
179 181 191 193 197 199 211 223 227 229

C:\book>_
```

FIGURE 3.17 *The program displays the first fifty prime numbers.*

Solution

The problem can be broken into the following tasks:

✦ Determine whether a given number is prime.

✦ For number = 2, 3, 4, 5, 6, ..., test whether the number is prime.

✦ Count the prime numbers.

✦ Print each prime number, and print ten numbers per line.

Obviously, you need to write a loop and repeatedly test whether a new number is prime. If the number is prime, increase the count by 1. The count is 0 initially. When it exceeds 50, the loop terminates.

Here is the algorithm for the problem:

```
Set the number of prime numbers to be printed as
  a constant NUMBER_OF_PRIMES;
Use count to track the number of prime numbers and
  set an initial count to 0;
Set an initial number to 2;

while (count < NUMBER_OF_PRIMES) {
  Test if number is prime;

  if number is prime {
    Print the prime number and increase the count;
  }

  Increment number by 1;
}
```

EXAMPLE 3.10 (CONTINUED)

To test whether a number is prime, check whether the number is divisible by 2, 3, 4, up to number/2. If a divisor is found, the number is not a prime. The algorithm can be described as follows:

```
Use a boolean variable isPrime to denote whether
  the number is prime; Set isPrime to true initially;

for (int divisor = 2; divisor <= number / 2; divisor++) {
  if (number % divisor == 0) {
      Set isPrime to false
      Exit the loop;
  }
}
```

The program is given as shown below.

LISTING 3.11 PrimeNumber.java (Printing Prime Numbers)

```
 1 public class PrimeNumber {
 2   /** Main method */
 3   public static void main(String[] args) {
 4     final int NUMBER_OF_PRIMES = 50; // Number of primes to display
 5     final int NUMBER_OF_PRIMES_PER_LINE = 10; // Display 10 per line
 6     int count = 0; // Count the number of prime numbers
 7     int number = 2; // A number to be tested for primeness
 8     boolean isPrime = true; // Is the current number prime?
 9
10     System.out.println("The first 50 prime numbers are \n");
11
12     // Repeatedly find prime numbers
13     while (count < NUMBER_OF_PRIMES) {
14       // Assume the number is prime
15       isPrime = true;
16
17       // Test if number is prime
18       for (int divisor = 2; divisor <= number / 2; divisor++) {
19         //If true, the number is not prime
20         if (number % divisor == 0) {
21           // Set isPrime to false, if the number is not prime
22           isPrime = false;
23           break; // Exit the for loop
24         }
25       }
26
27       // Print the prime number and increase the count
28       if (isPrime) {
29         count++; // Increase the count
30
31         if (count % NUMBER_OF_PRIMES_PER_LINE == 0) {
32           // Print the number and advance to the new line
33           System.out.println(number);
34         }
35         else
36           System.out.print(number + " ");
37       }
38
39       // Check if the next number is prime
40       number++;
41     }
42   }
43 }
```

count prime numbers

check primeness

exit loop

print if prime

EXAMPLE 3.10 (CONTINUED)

Review

This is a complex example for novice programmers. The key to developing a programmatic solution to this problem, and to many other problems, is to break it into *subproblems* and develop solutions for each of them in turn. Do not attempt to develop a complete solution in the first trial. Instead, begin by writing the code to determine whether a given number is prime, then expand the program to test whether other numbers are prime in a loop.

subproblem

To determine whether a number is prime, check whether it is divisible by a number between 2 and number/2 inclusive. If so, it is not a prime number; otherwise, it is a prime number. For a prime number, display it. If the count is divisible by 10, advance to a new line. The program ends when the count reaches 51.

 NOTE

The program uses the break statement in Line 23 to exit the for loop as soon as the number is found to be a nonprime. You can rewrite the loop (Lines 18–25) without using the break statement, as follows:

```
for (int divisor = 2; divisor <= number / 2 && isPrime;
    divisor++) {
  //If true, the number is not prime
  if (number % divisor == 0) {
    // Set isPrime to false, if the number is not prime
    isPrime = false;
  }
}
```

However, using the break statement makes the program simpler and easier to read in this case.

KEY TERMS

break statement   89, 101
conditional operator   91
continue statement   101
fall-through behavior   90
infinite loop   92
iteration   91
labeled break statement   104
labled continue statement   104

loop   91
loop-continuation-condition   91
loop body   91
nested loop   99
off-by-one error   108
selection statement   81
sentinel value   93

CHAPTER SUMMARY

✦ Program control specifies the order in which statements are executed in a program. There are three types of control statements: sequence, selection, and loop.

✦ Selection statements are used for building selection steps into programs. There are several types of selection statements: if statements, if ... else statements, nested if statements, switch statements, and conditional expressions.

✦ The various `if` statements all make control decisions based on a Boolean expression. Based on the `true` or `false` evaluation of that expression, these statements take one of two possible courses.

✦ The `switch` statement makes control decisions based on a switch expression of type `char`, `byte`, `short`, `int`, or `boolean`.

✦ The keyword `break` is optional in a switch statement, but it should be used at the end of each case in order to terminate the remainder of the `switch` statement. If the `break` statement is not present, the next `case` statement will be executed.

✦ There are three types of repetition statements: the `while` loop, the `do-while` loop, and the `for` loop. In designing loops, you need to consider both the loop control structure and the loop body.

✦ The `while` loop checks the `loop-continuation-condition` first. If the condition is `true`, the loop body is executed; if it is `false`, the loop terminates. The `do-while` loop is similar to the `while` loop, except that the `do-while` loop executes the loop body first and then checks the `loop-continuation-condition` to decide whether to continue or to terminate.

✦ Since the `while` loop and the `do-while` loop contain the `loop-continuation-condition`, which is dependent on the loop body, the number of repetitions is determined by the loop body. The `while` loop and the `do-while` loop are often used when the number of repetitions is unspecified.

✦ The `for` loop is generally used to execute a loop body a predictable number of times; this number is not determined by the loop body. The loop control has three parts. The first part is an initial action that often initializes a control variable. The second part, the `loop-continuation-condition`, determines whether the loop body is to be executed. The third part is executed after each iteration and is often used to adjust the control variable. Usually, the loop control variables are initialized and changed in the control structure.

✦ Two keywords, `break` and `continue`, can be used in a loop. The `break` keyword immediately ends the innermost loop, which contains the break. The `continue` keyword only ends the current iteration.

REVIEW QUESTIONS

Section 3.2 Selection Statements

3.1 Write a statement to determine whether an integer `i` is even or odd.

3.2 Suppose x = 3 and y = 2, show the output, if any, of the following code. What is the output if x = 3 and y = 4? What is the output if x = 2 and y = 2?

```
if (x > 2) {
  if (y > 2) {
    int z = x + y;
    System.out.println("z is " + z);
  }
}
else
  System.out.println("x is " + x);
```

3.3   Which of the following statements are equivalent? Which ones are correctly indented?

```
if (i > 0) if
(j > 0)
x = 0; else
if (k > 0) y = 0;
else z = 0;
```
(a)

```
if (i > 0) {
    if (j > 0)
        x = 0;
    else if (k > 0)
        y = 0;
}
else
    z = 0;
```
(b)

```
if (i > 0)
    if (j > 0)
        x = 0;
    else if (k > 0)
        y = 0;
    else
        z = 0;
```
(c)

```
if (i > 0)
    if (j > 0)
        x = 0;
    else if (k > 0)
        y = 0;
else
    z = 0;
```
(d)

3.4   Suppose x = 2 and y = 3, show the output, if any, of the following code. What is the output if x = 3 and y = 2? What is the output if x = 3 and y = 3? (Hint: indent the statement correctly first.)

```
if (x > 2)
  if (y > 2) {
    int z = x + y;
    System.out.println("z is " + z);
  }
else
  System.out.println("x is " + x);
```

3.5   Are the following two statements equivalent?

```
if (income <= 10000)
    tax = income * 0.1;
else if (income <= 20000)
    tax = 1000 +
        (income - 10000) * 0.15;
```

```
if (income <= 10000)
    tax = income * 0.1;
else if (income > 10000 &&
         income <= 20000)
    tax = 1000 +
        (income - 10000) * 0.15;
```

Section 3.2.4 `switch` Statements

3.6   What data types are required for a `switch` variable? If the keyword `break` is not used after a case is processed, what is the next statement to be executed? Can you convert a `switch` statement to an equivalent `if` statement, or vice versa? What are the advantages of using a `switch` statement?

3.7   What is y after the following `switch` statement is executed?

```
x = 3;
switch (x + 3) {
  case 6: y = 1;
  default: y += 1;
}
```

3.8   Use a `switch` statement to rewrite the following `if` statement:

```
if (a == 1)
  x += 5;
else if (a == 2)
  x += 10;
else if (a == 3)
  x += 16;
else if (a == 4)
  x += 34;
```

Section 3.2.5 Conditional Expressions

3.9 Rewrite the following `if` statement using the conditional operator:

```
if (count % 10 == 0)
  System.out.print(count + "\n");
else
  System.out.print(count + " ");
```

Section 3.3 Loop Statements

3.10 How many times is the following loop body repeated? What is the printout of the loop?

```
int i = 1;
while (i > 10)
  if ((i++) % 2 == 0)
    System.out.println(i);
```

```
int i = 1;
while (i < 10)
  if ((i++) % 2 == 0)
    System.out.println(i);
```

(a)   (b)

3.11 What are the differences between a `while` loop and a `do-while` loop?

3.12 Do the following two loops result in the same value in sum?

```
for (int i = 0; i < 10; ++i)
  sum += i;
}
```

```
for (int i = 0; i < 10; i++)
  sum += i;
}
```

(a)   (b)

3.13 What are the three parts of a `for` loop control? Write a `for` loop that prints the numbers from 1 to 100.

3.14 What does the following statement do?

```
for ( ; ; ) {
  do something;
}
```

3.15 If a variable is declared in the `for` loop control, can it be used after the loop exits?

3.16 Can you convert a `for` loop to a `while` loop? List the advantages of using `for` loops.

3.17 Convert the following `for` loop statement to a `while` loop and to a `do-while` loop:

```
long sum = 0;
for (int i = 0; i <= 1000; i++)
  sum = sum + i;
```

Section 3.6 Using the Keywords `break` and `continue`

3.18 What is the keyword `break` for? What is the keyword `continue` for? Will the following program terminate? If so, give the output.

```
int balance = 1000;
while (true) {
  if (balance < 9)
    break;
  balance = balance - 9;
}

System.out.println("Balance is "
  + balance);
```

```
int balance = 1000;
while (true) {
  if (balance < 9)
    continue;
  balance = balance - 9;
}

System.out.println("Balance is "
  + balance);
```

(a)   (b)

3.19 Can you always convert a while loop into a for loop? Convert the following while loop into a for loop:

```
int i = 1;
int sum = 0;
while (sum < 10000) {
  sum = sum + i;
  i++;
}
```

3.20 The for loop on the left is converted into the while loop on the right. What is wrong? Correct it.

```
for (int i = 0; i < 4; i++) {
    if (i % 3 == 0) continue;
    sum += i;
}
```

Converted

Wrong conversion

```
int i = 0;
while (i < 4) {
    if (i % 3 == 0) continue;
    sum += i;
    i++;
}
```

3.21 Rewrite the programs TestBreak and TestContinue without using break and continue (see Examples 3.5 and 3.6).

3.22 After the break outer statement is executed in the following loop, which statement is executed?

```
outer:
  for (int i = 1; i < 10; i++) {
  inner:
    for (int j = 1; j < 10; j++) {
      if (i * j > 50)
        break outer;

      System.out.println(i * j);
    }
  }
next:
```

3.23 After the continue outer statement is executed in the following loop, which statement is executed?

```
outer:
  for (int i = 1; i < 10; i++) {
  inner:
    for (int j = 1; j < 10; j++) {
      if (i * j > 50)
        continue outer;

      System.out.println(i * j);
    }
  }
next:
```

Comprehensive

3.24 Identify and fix the errors in the following code:

```
1 public class Test {
2   public void main(String[] args) {
3     for (int i = 0; i < 10; i++);
4       sum += i;
5
6     if (i < j);
7       System.out.println(i)
```

```
 7      else
 8         System.out.println(j);
 9
10      while (j < 10);
11      {
12         j++;
13      };
14
15      do {
16         j++;
17      } while (j < 10)
18   }
19 }
```

3.25. What is wrong with the following program?

```
1 public class ShowErrors {
2   public static void main(String[] args) {
3     int i;
4     int j = 5;
5
6     if (j > 3)
7        System.out.println(i + 4);
8   }
9 }
```

(a)

```
1 public class ShowErrors {
2   public static void main(String[] args) {
3     for (int i = 0; i < 10; i++);
4        System.out.println(i + 4);
5   }
6 }
```

(b)

3.26. Show the output of the following programs:

```
public class Test {
  /** Main method */
  public static void main(String[] args) {
    for (int i = 1; i < 5; i++) {
      int j = 0;
      while (j < i) {
        System.out.print(j + " ");
        j++;
      }
    }
  }
}
```

(a)

```
public class Test {
  /** Main method */
  public static void main(String[] args) {
    int i = 0;
    while (i < 5) {
      for (int j = i; j > 1; j--)
        System.out.print(j + " ");
      System.out.println("*****");
      i++;
    }
  }
}
```

(b)

```
public class Test {
  public static void main(String[] args) {
    int i = 5;
    while (i >= 1) {
      int num = 1;
      for (int j = 1; j <= i; j++) {
        System.out.print(num + "xxx");
        num *= 2;
      }

      System.out.println();
      i--;
    }
  }
}
```

(c)

```
public class Test {
  public static void main(String[] args) {
    int i = 1;
    do {
      int num = 1;
      for (int j = 1; j <= i; j++) {
        System.out.print(num + "G");
        num += 2;
      }

      System.out.println();
      i++;
    } while (i <= 5);
  }
}
```

(d)

3.27. Reformat the following programs according to the programming style and documentation guidelines proposed in Section 2.18. Use the next-line brace style.

```
public class Test {
  public static void main(String[] args) {
    int i = 0;
    if (i>0)
    i++;
    else
    i--;

    char grade;

    if (i >= 90)
      grade = 'A';
    else
      if (i >= 80)
        grade = 'B';
  }
}
```

(a)

```
public class Test {
  public static void main(String[] args) {
    for (int i = 0; i<10; i++)
      if (i>0)
        i++;
      else
        i--;
  }
}
```

(b)

PROGRAMMING EXERCISES

Section 3.2 Selection Statements

3.1 (*Monetary units*) Modify Example 2.4, "Monetary Units," to display the non-zero denominations only, using singular words for single units like 1 dollar and 1 penny, and plural words for more than one unit like 2 dollars and 3 pennies. (Use 23.67 to test your program.)

3.2* (*Sorting three integers*) Write a program that sorts three integers. The integers are entered from the input dialogs and stored in variables num1, num2, and num3, respectively. The program sorts the numbers so that num1 <= num2 <= num3.

3.3 (*Computing the perimeter of a triangle*) Write a program that reads three edges for a triangle and computes the perimeter if the input is valid. Otherwise, display that the input is invalid. The input is valid if the sum of any two edges is greater than the third edge (also see Exercise 2.9).

3.4 (*Computing taxes*) Example 3.1 gives the partial source code to compute taxes for single filers. Complete Example 3.1 to give the complete source code.

3.5* (*Finding the number of days in a month*) Write a program that prompts the user to enter the month and year, and displays the number of days in the month. For example, if the user entered month 2 and year 2000, the program should display that February 2000 has 29 days. If the user entered month 3 and year 2005, the program should display that March 2005 has 31 days.

3.6 (*Checking a number*) Write a program that prompts the user to enter an integer and checks whether the number is divisible by both 5 and 6, either or just one of them. Here are some sample output for input 10, 30, and 23.

```
10 is divisible by 5 or 6, but not both
30 is divisible by both 5 and 6
23 is not divisible by either 5 or 6
```

Section 3.3 Loop Statements

3.7* (*Counting positive and negative numbers and computing the average of numbers*) Write a program that reads an unspecified number of integers, determines how many positive and negative values have been read, and computes the total and average of the input values, not counting zeros. Your program ends with the input 0. Display the average as a floating-point number. (For example, if you entered 1, 2, and 0, the average should be 1.5.)

3.8 (*Conversion from kilograms to pounds*) Write a program that displays the following table (note that 1 kilogram is 2.2 pound):

Kilograms	Pounds
1	2.2
3	6.6
...	
197	433.4
199	437.8

3.9 (*Conversion from miles to kilometers*) Write a program that displays the following table (note that 1 mile is 1.609 kilometers):

Miles	Kilometers
1	1.609
2	3.218
...	
9	14.481
10	16.09

3.10 (*Conversion from kilograms to pounds*) Write a program that displays the following two tables side-by-side (note that 1 kilogram is 2.2 pounds):

Kilograms	Pounds	Pounds	Kilograms
1	2.2	20	9.09
3	6.6	25	11.36
....			
197	433.4	510	231.82
199	437.8	515	234.09

3.11 (*Conversion from miles to kilometers*) Write a program that displays the following two tables side-by-side (note that 1 mile is 1.609 kilometers):

Miles	Kilometers	Kilometers	Miles
1	1.609	20	12.430
2	3.218	25	15.538
...			
9	14.481	60	37.290
10	16.09	65	40.398

3.12** (*Computing future tuition*) Suppose that the tuition for a university is $10,000 this year and tuition increases 5% every year. Write a program that uses a loop to compute the tuition in ten years.

3.13 (*Finding the highest score*) Write a program that prompts the user to enter the number of students and each student's name and score, and finally displays the student with the highest score.

3.14* (*Finding the two highest scores*) Write a program that prompts the user to enter the number of students and each student's name and score, and finally displays the student with the highest score and the student with the second-highest score.

3.15 (*Finding numbers divisible by 5 and 6*) Write a program that displays all the numbers from 100 to 1000, ten per line, that are divisible by 5 and 6.

3.16 (*Finding numbers divisible by 5 or 6, but not both*) Write a program that displays all the numbers from 100 to 200, ten per line, that are divisible by 5 or 6, but not both.

3.17 (*Finding the smallest n such that* $n^2 > 12000$) Use a `while` loop to find the smallest integer n such that n^2 is greater than 12,000.

3.18 (*Finding the largest n such that* $n^3 < 12000$) Use a `while` loop to find the largest integer n such that n^3 is less than 12,000.

3.19* (*Displaying the ACSII character table*) Write a program that prints the 128 characters in the ASCII character table. Print ten characters per line.

Section 3.7 Case Studies

3.20* (*Computing the greatest common divisor*) Another solution for Example 3.7 to find the greatest common divisor of two integers n1 and n2 is as follows: First find d to be the minimum of n1 and n2, then check whether d, d-1, d-2, ..., 2, or 1 is a divisor for both n1 and n2 in this order. The first such common divisor is the greatest common divisor for n1 and n2.

3.21** (*Finding the factors of an integer*) Write a program that reads an integer and displays all its smallest factors. For example, if the input integer is 120, the output should be as follows: 2, 2, 2, 3, 5.

3.22* (*Finding the sales amount*) Rewrite Example 3.8, "Finding Sales Amount," as follows:

 ✦ Use a `for` loop instead of a `do-while` loop.
 ✦ Let the user enter `COMMISSION_SOUGHT` instead of fixing it as a constant.

3.23* (*Printing four patterns using loops*) Use nested loops that print the following patterns in separate programs:

```
Pattern I        Pattern II        Pattern III        Pattern IV
1                1 2 3 4 5 6                 1          1 2 3 4 5 6
1 2              1 2 3 4 5                 2 1            1 2 3 4 5
1 2 3            1 2 3 4                 3 2 1              1 2 3 4
1 2 3 4          1 2 3                 4 3 2 1                1 2 3
1 2 3 4 5        1 2                 5 4 3 2 1                  1 2
1 2 3 4 5 6      1                 6 5 4 3 2 1                    1
```

3.24** (*Printing numbers in a pyramid pattern*) Write a nested `for` loop that prints the following output:

```
                        1
                    1   2   1
                1   2   4   2   1
            1   2   4   8   4   2   1
        1   2   4   8  16   8   4   2   1
      1 2   4   8  16  32  16   8   4   2   1
    1 2   4   8  16  32  64  32  16   8   4   2   1
  1 2   4   8  16  32  64 128  64  32  16   8   4   2   1
```

🌸 HINT

Here is the pseudocode solution:

```
for the row from 0 to 7 {
    Pad leading blanks in a row using a loop like this:
    for the column from 1 to 7-row
        System.out.print("   ");

    Print left half of the row for numbers 1, 2, 4, up to
      2^row using a look like this:
    for the column from 0 to row
        System.out.print("   " + (int)Math.pow(2, column));

    Print the right half of the row for numbers
      2^row-1, 2^row-2, ..., 1 using a loop like this:
    for (int column = row - 1; column >= 0; col--)
        System.out.print("   " + (int)Math.pow(2, column));

    Start a new line
    System.out.println();
}
```

You need to figure out how many spaces to print before the number. This is dependent on the number. If a number is a single digit, print four spaces. If a number has two digits, print three spaces. If a number has three digits, print two spaces.

The Math.pow() method was introduced in Example 2.3. Can you write this program without using it?

3.25* (*Printing prime numbers between 2 and 1000*) Modify Example 3.10 to print all the prime numbers between 2 and 1000, inclusively. Display eight prime numbers per line.

Comprehensive

3.26** (*Comparing loans with various interest rates*) Write a program that lets the user enter the loan amount and loan period in number of years and displays the monthly and total payments for each interest rate from 5% to 8%, with an increment of 1/8. Suppose you enter the loan amount 10,000 for five years, display a table as follows:

```
Loan Amount: 10000
Number of Years: 5
    Interest Rate       Monthly Payment       Total Payment
    5%                  188.71                11322.74
    5.125%              189.28                11357.13
    5.25%               189.85                11391.59
    ...
    7.85%               202.16                12129.97
    8.0%                202.76                12165.83
```

3.27** (*Displaying the loan amortization schedule*) The monthly payment for a given loan pays the principal and the interest. The monthly interest is computed by multiplying the monthly interest rate and the balance (the remaining principal). The principal paid for the month is therefore the monthly payment minus the monthly interest. Write a program that lets the user enter the loan amount, number of years, and interest rate, and displays the amortization schedule for the loan. Suppose you enter the loan amount 10,000 for one year with an interest rate of 7%, display a table as follows:

```
Loan Amount: 10000
Number of Years: 1
Annual Interest Rate: 7%
```

```
Monthly Payment: 865.26
Total Payment: 10383.21

Payment#        Interest        Principal       Balance
1               58.33           806.93          9193.07
2               53.62           811.64          8381.43

11              10.0            855.26          860.27
12              5.01            860.25          0.01
```

 NOTE

The balance after the last payment may not be zero. If so, the last payment should be the normal monthly payment plus the final balance.

 HINT

Write a loop to print the table. Since monthly payment is the same for each month, it should be computed before the loop. The balance is initially the loan amount. For each iteration in the loop, compute the interest and principal, and update the balance. The loop may look like this:

```
for (i = 1; i <= numberOfYears * 12; i++) {
    interest = (int)(monthlyInterestRate * balance * 100) / 100.0;
    principal = (int)((monthlyPayment - interest) * 100) / 100.0;
    balance = (int)((balance - principal) * 100) / 100.0;
    System.out.println(i + "\t\t" + interest
    + "\t\t" + principal + "\t\t" + balance);
}
```

3.28* (*Demonstrating cancellation errors*) A cancellation error occurs when you are manipulating a very large number with a very small number. The large number may cancel out the smaller number. For example, the result of 100000000.0 + 0.000000001 is equal to 100000000.0. To avoid cancellation errors and obtain more accurate results, carefully select the order of computation. For example, in computing the following series, you will obtain more accurate results by computing from right to left:

$$1 + \frac{1}{2} + \frac{1}{3} + \cdots + \frac{1}{n}$$

Write a program that compares the results of the summation of the preceding series, computing from left to right and from right to left with $n = 50000$.

3.29* (*Summing a series*) Write a program to sum the following series:

$$\frac{1}{3} + \frac{3}{5} + \frac{5}{7} + \frac{7}{9} + \frac{9}{11} + \frac{11}{13} + \cdots + \frac{95}{97} + \frac{97}{99}$$

3.30** (*Computing π*) You can approximate π by using the following series:

$$\pi = 4\left(1 - \frac{1}{3} + \frac{1}{5} - \frac{1}{7} + \frac{1}{9} - \frac{1}{11} + \frac{1}{13} - \cdots - \frac{1}{2i - 1} + \frac{1}{2i + 1}\right)$$

Write a program that displays the π value for $i = 10000, 20000, \ldots,$ and 100000.

3.31** (*Computing e*) You can approximate e by using the following series:

$$e = 1 + \frac{1}{1!} + \frac{1}{2!} + \frac{1}{3!} + \frac{1}{4!} + \cdots + \frac{1}{i!}$$

Write a program that displays the e value for i   and 100000. (Hint: Since

$$i! = i \times (i - 1) \times \cdots \times 2 \times 1, \frac{1}{i!} \text{ is } \frac{1}{i(i - 1)!}.$$

Initialize e and item to be 1 and keep adding a new item to e. The new item is the previous item divided by i for $i = 2, 3, 4, \ldots$)

3.32** (*Displaying leap years*) Write a program that displays all the leap years, ten per line, in the twenty-first century (from 2000 to 2100). See page 55 regarding leap year.

3.33** (*Displaying first days of each month*) Write a program that prompts the user to enter the year and first day of the year, and displays the first day of each month in the year on the console. For example, if the user entered year 2005, and 6 for Saturday, January 1, 2005, your program should display the following output:

```
January 1, 2005 is Saturday
...
December 1, 2005 is Thursday
```

3.34** (*Displaying calendars*) Write a program that prompts the user to enter the year and first day of the year, and displays the calendar table for the year on the console. For example, if the user entered year 2005, and 6 for Saturday, January 1, 2005, your program should display the calendar for each month in the year, as follows:

```
            January 2005
        --------------------------
        Sun Mon Tue Wed Thu Fri Sat
                                  1
          2   3   4   5   6   7   8
          9  10  11  12  13  14  15
         16  17  18  19  20  21  22
         23  24  25  26  27  28  29
         30  31
        ...
            December 2005
        --------------------------
        Sun Mon Tue Wed Thu Fri Sat
                          1   2   3
          4   5   6   7   8   9  10
         11  12  13  14  15  16  17
         18  19  20  21  22  23  24
         25  26  27  28  29  30  31
```

chapter

4

METHODS

Objectives

✦ To create methods, invoke methods, and pass arguments to methods (§§4.2–4.4).

✦ To use method overloading and know ambiguous overloading (§4.5).

✦ To determine the scope of local variables (§4.6).

✦ To learn the concept of method abstraction (§4.7).

✦ To know how to use the methods in the Math class (§4.8).

✦ To design and implement methods using stepwise refinement (§4.10).

✦ To write recursive methods (§4.11 Optional).

✦ To group classes into packages (§4.12 Optional).

4.1 Introduction

In the preceding chapters, you learned about such methods as `System.out.println`, `JOptionPane.showMessageDialog`, `JOptionPane.showInputDialog`, `Integer.parseInt`, `Double.parseDouble`, `System.exit`, and `Math.pow`. A method is a collection of statements that are grouped together to perform an operation. When you call the `System.out.println` method, for example, the system actually executes several statements in order to display a message on the console.

This chapter introduces several topics that involve, or are related to, methods. You will learn how to create your own methods with or without return values, invoke a method with or without parameters, overload methods using the same names, write a recursive method that invokes itself, and apply method abstraction in the program design.

4.2 Creating a Method

In general, a method has the following syntax:

```
modifier returnValueType methodName(list of parameters) {
  // Method body;
}
```

Let's take a look at a method created to find which of two integers is bigger. This method, named `max`, has two `int` parameters, `num1` and `num2`, the larger of which is returned by the method. Figure 4.1 illustrates the components of this method.

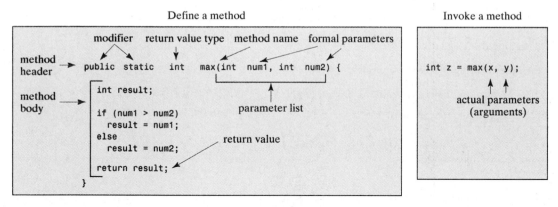

FIGURE 4.1 *A method declaration consists of a method header and a method body.*

The method header specifies the *modifiers*, *return value type*, *method name*, and *parameters* of the method. The modifier, which is optional, tells the compiler how to call the method. The static modifier is used for all the methods in this chapter. The reason for using it will be discussed in Chapter 6, "Objects and Classes."

A method may return a value. The `returnValueType` is the data type of the value the method returns. Some methods perform desired operations without returning a value. In this case, the `returnValueType` is the keyword `void`. For example, the `returnValueType` in the main method is `void`, as well as in `System.exit`, `Syste.out.println`, and `JOptionPane.showMessageDialog`.

The *parameter list* refers to the type, order, and number of the parameters of a method. The method name and the parameter list together constitute the *method signature*. Parameters are optional; that is, a method may contain no parameters. The variables defined in the method header are known as *formal parameters* or simply *parameters*. A parameter is like a placeholder. When a

void
parameter list

method signature

formal parameter

method is invoked, you pass a value to the parameter. This value is referred to as *actual parameter or argument*.

argument

The method body contains a collection of statements that define what the method does. The method body of the `max` method uses an `if` statement to determine which number is larger and return the value of that number. A return statement using the keyword `return` is *required* for a nonvoid method to return a result. The method terminates when a return statement is executed.

 NOTE

In certain other languages, methods are referred to as *procedures* and *functions*. A method with a nonvoid return value type is called a *function*; a method with a void return value type is called a *procedure*.

 NOTE

A `return` statement is not needed for a void method, but it can be used for terminating the method and returning to the method's caller. The syntax is simply

return

```
return;
```

This is rare, but sometimes useful for circumventing the normal flow of control in a void method. See Review Question 4.5.

 CAUTION

You need to declare a separate data type for each parameter. For instance, `int num1, num2` should be replaced by `int num1, int num2`.

4.3   Calling a Method

In creating a method, you give a definition of what the method is to do. To use a method, you have to *call* or *invoke* it. There are two ways to call a method; the choice is based on whether the method returns a value or not.

If the method returns a value, a call to the method is usually treated as a value. For example,

```
int larger = max(3, 4);
```

calls `max(3, 4)` and assigns the result of the method to the variable `larger`. Another example of a call that is treated as a value is

```
System.out.println(max(3, 4));
```

which prints the return value of the method call `max(3, 4)`.

If the method returns void, a call to the method must be a statement. For example, the method `println` returns void. The following call is a statement:

```
System.out.println("Welcome to Java!");
```

 NOTE

A method with a nonvoid return value type can also be invoked as a statement in Java. In this case, the caller simply ignores the return value. In the majority of cases, a call to a method with return value is treated as a value. In some cases, however, the caller is not interested in the return value. For example, many methods in database applications return a Boolean value to indicate whether the operation is successful. You can choose to ignore the return value if you know the operation will always succeed. I recommend, though, that you always treat a call to a method with return value as a value in order to avoid programming errors.

When a program calls a method, program control is transferred to the called method. A called method returns control to the caller when its return statement is executed or when its method-ending closing brace is reached.

The example shown below gives the complete program that is used to test the max method.

EXAMPLE 4.1 TESTING THE max METHOD

Problem

Write a program that demonstrates how to create and invoke the max method.

Solution

Listing 4.1 gives the solution to the problem. The output of the program is shown in Figure 4.2.

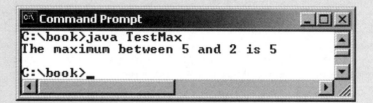

FIGURE 4.2   *The program invokes* max(i, j) *in order to get the maximum value between* i *and* j.

LISTING 4.1   TestMax.java (Declaring and Using a Method)

```
 1 public class TestMax {
 2   /** Main method */
 3   public static void main(String[] args) {
 4     int i = 5;
 5     int j = 2;
 6     int k = max(i, j);
 7     System.out.println("The maximum between " + i +
 8       " and " + j + " is " + k);
 9   }
10
11   /** Return the max between two numbers */
12   public static int max(int num1, int num2) {
13     int result;
14
15     if (num1 > num2)
16       result = num1;
17     else
18       result = num2;
19
20     return result;
21   }
22 }
```

main method

invoke max

declare method

Review

main method

This program contains the main method and the max method. The main method is just like any other method except that it is invoked by the Java interpreter.

EXAMPLE 4.1 (CONTINUED)

The `main` method's header is always the same, like the one in this example, with the modifiers `public` and `static`, return value type `void`, method name `main`, and a parameter of the `String[]` type. `String[]` indicates that the parameter is an array of `String`, a subject addressed in Chapter 5, "Arrays."

The statements in `main` may invoke other methods that are defined in the class that contains the `main` method or in other classes. In this example, the `main` method invokes `max(i, j)`, which is defined in the same class with the `main` method.

When the `max` method is invoked (Line 6), variable `i`'s value 5 is passed to `num1`, and variable `j`'s value 2 is passed to `num2` in the `max` method. The flow of control transfers to the `max` method. The `max` method is executed. When the `return` statement in the `max` method is executed, the `max` method returns the control to its caller (in this case the caller is the `main` method). This process is illustrated in Figure 4.3.

max method

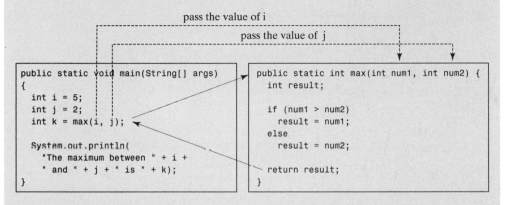

FIGURE 4.3 *When the* max *method is invoked, the flow of control transfers to the* max *method. Once the* max *method is finished, it returns the control back to the caller.*

 CAUTION

A `return` statement is required for a nonvoid method. The method shown below in (a) is logically correct, but it has a compilation error because the Java compiler thinks it possible that this method does not return any value.

```
public static int sign(int n) {
  if (n > 0) return 1;
  else if (n == 0) return 0;
  else if (n < 0) return -1;
}
```
(a)

Should be →

```
public static int sign(int n) {
  if (n > 0) return 1;
  else if (n == 0) return 0;
  else return -1;
}
```
(b)

To fix this problem, delete `if (n < 0)` in (a), so that the compiler will see a `return` statement to be reached regardless of how the `if` statement is evaluated.

NOTE

reusing method

One of the benefits of methods is for reuse. The `max` method can be invoked from any class besides `TestMax`. If you create a new class, `Test`, you can invoke the `max` method using `ClassName.methodName` (i.e., `TestMax.max`).

4.3.1   Call Stacks

stack

Each time a method is invoked, the system stores parameters and local variables in an area of memory, known as a *stack*, which stores elements in last-in first-out fashion. When a method calls another method, the caller's stack space is kept intact, and new space is created to handle the new method call. When a method finishes its work and returns to its caller, its associated space is released.

Understanding call stacks helps you to comprehend how methods are invoked. The variables defined in the main method are i, j, and k. The variables defined in the max method are num1, num2, and result. The variables num1 and num2 are defined in the method signature and are parameters of the method. Their values are passed through method invocation. Figure 4.4 illustrates the variables in the stack.

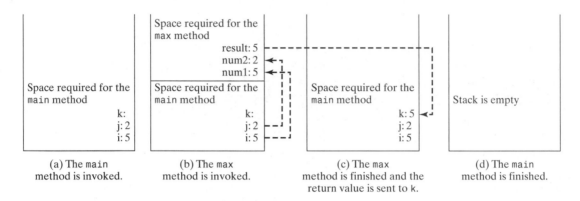

FIGURE 4.4   *When the* max *method is invoked, the flow of control transfers to the* max *method. Once the* max *method is finished, it returns the control back to the caller.*

4.4   Passing Parameters by Values

The power of a method is its ability to work with parameters. You can use println to print any string and max to find the maximum between any two int values. When calling a method, you need to provide arguments, which must be given in the same order as their respective parameters in the method specification. This is known as *parameter order association*. For example, the following method prints a message n times:

```
public static void nPrintln(String message, int n) {
  for (int i = 0; i < n; i++)
    System.out.println(message);
}
```

You can use nPrintln("Hello", 3) to print "Hello" three times. The nPrintln("Hello", 3) statement passes the actual string parameter, "Hello", to the parameter, message; passes 3 to n; and prints "Hello" three times. However, the statement nPrintln(3, "Hello") would be wrong. The data type of 3 does not match the data type for the first parameter, message, nor does the second parameter, "Hello", match the second parameter, n.

 CAUTION

The arguments must match the parameters in *order*, *number*, and *compatible type*, as defined in the method signature. Compatible type means that you can pass an argument to a parameter without explicit casting, such as passing an int value argument to a double value parameter.

When you invoke a method with a parameter, the value of the argument is passed to the parameter. This is referred to as *pass by value*. If the argument is a variable, the value of the variable is passed to the parameter. The variable is not affected, regardless of the changes made to the parameter inside the method. We will examine an interesting scenario in the following example, in which the parameters are changed in the method but the arguments are not affected.

pass by value

EXAMPLE 4.2 TESTING PASS BY VALUE

Problem

Write a program that demonstrates the effect of passing by value.

Solution

Listing 4.2 creates a method for swapping two variables. The swap method is invoked by passing two arguments. Interestingly, the values of the arguments are not changed after the method is invoked. The output of the program is shown in Figure 4.5.

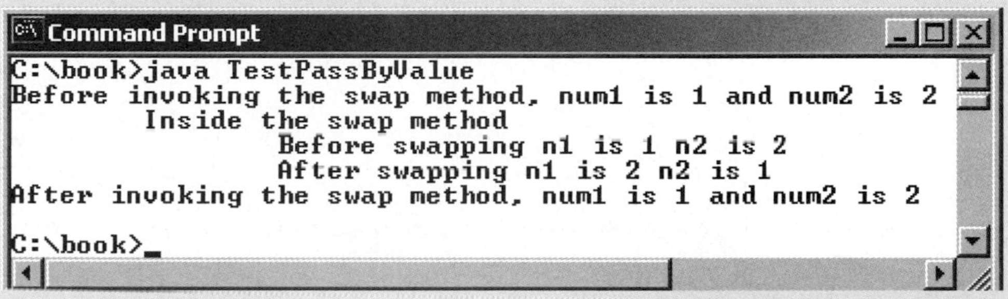

```
Command Prompt                                              _ □ X
C:\book>java TestPassByValue
Before invoking the swap method, num1 is 1 and num2 is 2
        Inside the swap method
                Before swapping n1 is 1 n2 is 2
                After swapping n1 is 2 n2 is 1
After invoking the swap method, num1 is 1 and num2 is 2

C:\book>_
```

FIGURE 4.5 *The contents of the arguments are not swapped after the* swap *method is invoked.*

LISTING **4.2** TestPassByValue.java (Passing by Value)

```java
 1 public class TestPassByValue {
 2   /** Main method */
 3   public static void main(String[] args) {
 4     // Declare and initialize variables
 5     int num1 = 1;
 6     int num2 = 2;
 7
 8     System.out.println("Before invoking the swap method, num1 is " +
 9       num1 + " and num2 is " + num2);
10
11     // Invoke the swap method to attempt to swap two variables
12     swap(num1, num2);
13
14     System.out.println("After invoking the swap method, num1 is " +
15       num1 + " and num2 is " + num2);
16   }
17
18   /** Swap two variables */
19   public static void swap(int n1, int n2) {
20     System.out.println("\tInside the swap method");
21     System.out.println("\t\tBefore swapping n1 is " + n1
22       + " n2 is " + n2);
```

false swap

EXAMPLE 4.2 (CONTINUED)

```
23
24      // Swap n1 with n2
25      int temp = n1;
26      n1 = n2;
27      n2 = temp;
28
29      System.out.println("\t\tAfter swapping n1 is " + n1
30        + " n2 is " + n2);
31   }
32 }
```

Review

Before the swap method is invoked (Line 12), num1 is 1 and num2 is 2. After the swap method is invoked, num1 is still 1 and num2 is still 2. Their values are not swapped when the swap method is invoked. As shown in Figure 4.6, the values of the arguments num1 and num2 are passed to n1 and n2, but n1 and n2 have their own memory locations independent of num1 and num2. Therefore, changes in n1 and n2 do not affect the contents of num1 and num2.

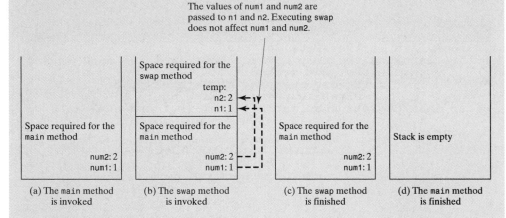

FIGURE 4.6   *The values of the variables are passed to the parameters of the method.*

Another twist is to change the parameter name n1 in swap to num1. What effect does this have? No change occurs, because it makes no difference whether the parameter and the argument have the same name. The parameter is a local variable in the method with its own memory space. The local variable is allocated when the method is invoked, and it disappears when the method is returned to its caller.

🌸 NOTE

For simplicity, Java programmers often say *passing an argument* x *to a parameter* y, which actually means *passing the value of* x *to* y.

4.5 Overloading Methods

The max method that was used earlier works only with the int data type. But what if you need to find which of two floating-point numbers has the maximum value? The solution is to create another method with the same name but different parameters, as shown in the following code:

```
public static double max(double num1, double num2) {
  if (num1 > num2)
    return num1;
  else
    return num2;
}
```

If you call max with int parameters, the max method that expects int parameters will be invoked; if you call max with double parameters, the max method that expects double parameters will be invoked. This is referred to as *method overloading*; that is, two methods have the same name but different parameter lists. The Java compiler determines which method is used based on the method signature.

method overloading

EXAMPLE 4.3 OVERLOADING THE max METHOD

Problem

Write a program that creates three methods. The first finds the maximum integer, the second finds the maximum double, and the third finds the maximum among three double values. All three methods are named max.

Solution

Listing 4.3 gives the solution to the problem. The output of the program is shown in Figure 4.7.

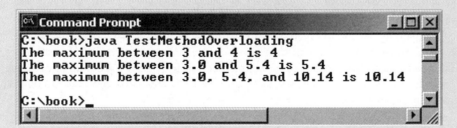

FIGURE 4.7 *The program invokes three different* max *methods that all have the same name:* max(3, 4), max(3.0, 5.4), *and* max(3.0, 5.4, 10.14).

LISTING 4.3 TestMethodOverloading.java (Overloading Methods)

```
1 public class TestMethodOverloading {
2   /** Main method */
3   public static void main(String[] args) {
4     // Invoke the max method with int parameters
5     System.out.println("The maximum between 3 and 4 is "
6       + max(3, 4));
7
```

EXAMPLE 4.3 (CONTINUED)

```
 8     // Invoke the max method with the double parameters
 9     System.out.println("The maximum between 3.0 and 5.4 is "
10       + max(3.0, 5.4));
11
12     // Invoke the max method with three double parameters
13     System.out.println("The maximum between 3.0, 5.4, and 10.14 is "
14       + max(3.0, 5.4, 10.14));
15   }
16
17   /** Return the max between two int values */
18   public static int max(int num1, int num2) {
19     if (num1 > num2)
20       return num1;
21     else
22       return num2;
23   }
24
25   /** Find the max between two double values */
26   public static double max(double num1, double num2) {
27     if (num1 > num2)
28       return num1;
29     else
30       return num2;
31   }
32
33   /** Return the max among three double values */
34   public static double max(double num1, double num2, double num3) {
35     return max(max(num1, num2), num3);
36   }
37 }
```

Review

When calling max(3, 4) (Line 6), the max method for finding the maximum of two integers is invoked. When calling max(3.0, 5.4) (Line 10), the max method for finding the maximum of two doubles is invoked. When calling max(3.0, 5.4, 10.14) (Line 14), the max method for finding the maximum of three double values is invoked.

Can you invoke the max method with an int value and a double value, such as max(2, 2.5)? If so, which of the max methods is invoked? The answer to the first question is yes. The answer to the second is that the max method for finding the maximum of two double values is invoked. The argument value 2 is automatically converted into a double value and passed to this method.

You may be wondering why the method max(double, double) is not invoked for the call max(3, 4). Both max(double, double) and max(int, int) are possible matches for max(3, 4). The Java compiler finds the most specific method for a method invocation. Since the method max(int, int) is more specific than max(double, double), max(int, int) is used to invoke max(3, 4).

 TIP

Overloading methods can make programs clearer and more readable. Methods that perform closely related tasks should be given the same name.

 NOTE

Overloaded methods must have different parameter lists. You cannot overload methods based on different modifiers or return types.

NOTE

Sometimes there are two or more possible matches for an invocation of a method, but the compiler cannot determine the most specific match. This is referred to as *ambiguous invocation*. Ambiguous invocation is a compilation error. Consider the following code:

ambiguous invocation

```java
public class AmbiguousOverloading {
  public static void main(String[] args) {
    System.out.println(max(1, 2));
  }

  public static double max(int num1, double num2) {
    if (num1 > num2)
      return num1;
    else
      return num2;
  }

  public static double max(double num1, int num2) {
    if (num1 > num2)
      return num1;
    else
      return num2;
  }
}
```

Both `max(int, double)` and `max(double, int)` are possible candidates to match `max(1, 2)`. Since neither of them is more specific than the other, the invocation is ambiguous.

EXAMPLE 4.4 COMPUTING TAXES WITH METHODS

Problem

Example 3.1, "Computing Taxes," uses `if` statements to check the filing status and computes the tax based on the filing status. Simplify Example 3.1 using methods.

Solution

Each filing status has six brackets. The code for computing taxes is nearly the same for each filing status except that each filing status has different bracket ranges. For example, the single filer status has six brackets [0, 6000], (6000, 27950], (27950, 67700], (67700, 141250], (141250, 307050], (307050, ∞), and the married file jointly status has six brackets [0, 12000], (12000, 46700], (46700, 112850], (112850, 171950], (171950, 307050], (307050, ∞). The first bracket of each filing status is taxed at 10%, the second at 15%, the third at 27%, the fourth at 30%, the fifth at 35%, and the sixth at 38.6%. So you can write a method with the brackets as arguments to compute the tax for the filing status. The header of the method is:

```
public static double computeTax(double income, ◄─────────── 400000
    int r1, int r2, int r3, int r4, int r5)
```

`[0, 6000]`, `[6000, 27950]`, `[27950, 67700]`, `[67700, 141250]`, `[141250, 307050]`, `(307050, ∞)`

For example, you can invoke `computeTax(400000, 6000, 27950, 67700, 141250, 307050)` to compute the tax for single filers with $400,000 of taxable income.

EXAMPLE 4.4 (CONTINUED)

Listing 4.4 gives the solution to the problem. The output of the program is similar to Figure 3.3.

LISTING **4.4** ComputeTaxWithMethod.java (Computing Tax)

```
1 import javax.swing.JOptionPane;
2
3 public class ComputeTaxWithMethod {
4   public static void main(String[] args) {
5     // Prompt the user to enter filing status
6     String statusString = JOptionPane.showInputDialog(
7       "Enter the filing status:");
8     int status = Integer.parseInt(statusString);
9
10    // Prompt the user to enter taxable income
11    String incomeString = JOptionPane.showInputDialog(
12      "Enter the taxable income:");
13    double income = Double.parseDouble(incomeString);
14
15    // Display the result
16    JOptionPane.showMessageDialog(null, "Tax is " +
17      (int)(computeTax(status, income) * 100) / 100.0);
18  }
19
20  public static double computeTax(double income,
21    int r1, int r2, int r3, int r4, int r5) {
22    double tax = 0;
23
24    if (income <= r1)
25      tax = income * 0.10;
26    else if (income <= r2)
27      tax = r1 * 0.10 + (income - r1) * 0.15;
28    else if (income <= r3)
29      tax = r1 * 0.10 + (r2 - r1) * 0.15 + (income - r2) * 0.27;
30    else if (income <= r4)
31      tax = r1 * 0.10 + (r2 - r1) * 0.15 +
32        (r3 - r2) * 0.27 + (income - r3) * 0.30;
33    else if (income <= r5)
34      tax = r1 * 0.10 + (r2 - r1) * 0.15 + (r3 - r2) * 0.27 +
35        (r4 - r3) * 0.30 + (income - r4) * 0.35;
36    else
37      tax = r1 * 0.10 + (r2 - r1) * 0.15 + (r3 - r2) * 0.27 +
38        (r4 - r3) * 0.30 + (r5 - r4) * 0.35 + (income - r5) * 0.386;
39
40    return tax;
41  }
42
43  public static double computeTax(int status, double income) {
44    switch (status) {
45      case 0: return
46        computeTax(income, 6000, 27950, 67700, 141250, 307050);
47      case 1: return
48        computeTax(income, 12000, 46700, 112850, 171950, 307050);
49      case 2: return
50        computeTax(income, 6000, 23350, 56425, 85975, 153525);
51      case 3: return
52        computeTax(income, 10000, 37450, 96700, 156600, 307050);
53      default: return 0;
54    }
55  }
56 }
```

input status

input income

compute tax

computeTax

overloaded computeTax

EXAMPLE 4.4 (CONTINUED)

Review

This program does the same thing as Example 3.1. Instead of writing the same code for computing taxes for different filing statuses, the new program uses a method for computing taxes. Using the method not only shortens the program, it also makes the program simpler, easy to read, and easy to maintain.

The program uses two overloaded `computeTax` methods (Lines 20, 43). The first `computeTax` method in Line 20 computes the tax for the specified brackets and taxable income. The second `computeTax` method in Line 43 computes the tax for the specified status and taxable income.

4.6   The Scope of Local Variables

The *scope of a variable* is the part of the program where the variable can be referenced. A variable defined inside a method is referred to as a *local variable*.

scope of variable

local variable

The scope of a local variable starts from its declaration and continues to the end of the block that contains the variable. A local variable must be declared before it can be used.

A *parameter* is actually a local variable. The scope of a method parameter covers the entire method.

parameter

A variable declared in the initial action part of a `for` loop header has its scope in the entire loop. But a variable declared inside a `for` loop body has its scope limited in the loop body from its declaration and to the end of the block that contains the variable, as shown in Figure 4.8.

`for` loop control variable

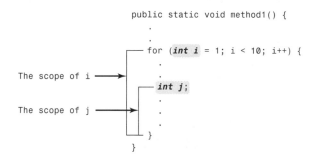

FIGURE 4.8   *A variable declared in the initial action part of a* `for` *loop header has its scope in the entire loop.*

You can declare a local variable with the same name multiple times in different non-nesting blocks in a method, but you cannot declare a local variable twice in nested blocks, as shown in Figure 4.9.

multiple declarations

 CAUTION

Do not declare a variable inside a block and then use it outside the block. Here is an example of a common mistake:

```
for (int i = 0; i < 10; i++) {
}

System.out.println(i);
```

The last statement would cause a syntax error because variable `i` is not defined outside of the `for` loop.

It is fine to declare *i* in two non-nesting blocks

It is wrong to declare *i* in two two nesting blocks

```
public static void method1() {
  int x = 1;
  int y = 1;

  for (int i = 1; i < 10; i++) {
    x += i;
  }

  for (int i = 1; i < 10; i++) {
    y += i;
  }
}
```

```
public static void method2() {

  int i = 1;
  int sum = 0;

  for (int i = 1; i < 10; i++)
    sum += i;
  }

}
```

FIGURE 4.9 *A variable can be declared multiple times in non-nested blocks, but can be declared only once in nesting blocks.*

4.7 Method Abstraction

method abstraction

information hiding

The key to developing software is to apply the concept of abstraction. You will learn many levels of abstraction from this book. *Method abstraction* is achieved by separating the use of a method from its implementation. The client can use a method without knowing how it is implemented. The details of the implementation are encapsulated in the method and hidden from the client who invokes the method. This is known as *information hiding* or *encapsulation*. If you decide to change the implementation, the client program will not be affected, provided that you do not change the method signature. The implementation of the method is hidden from the client in a "black box," as shown in Figure 4.10.

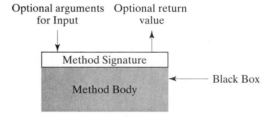

FIGURE 4.10 *The method body can be thought of as a black box that contains the detailed implementation for the method.*

You have already used the `System.out.print` method to display a string, the `JOptionPane.showInputDialog` method to read a string from a dialog box, and the `max` method to find the maximum number. You know how to write the code to invoke these methods in your program, but as a user of these methods, you are not required to know how they are implemented. The next section introduces the use of methods in the `Math` class.

4.8 The `Math` Class

The `Math` class contains the methods needed to perform basic mathematical functions. You have already used the `pow(a, b)` method to compute a^b in Example 2.3, "Computing Loan Payments." This section introduces other useful methods in the `Math` class. They can be categorized as *trigonometric methods*, *exponent methods*, and *service methods*. Besides methods, the `Math` class provides two useful `double` constants, `PI` and `E` (the base of natural logarithms). You can use these constants as `Math.PI` and `Math.E` in any program.

4.8.1 Trigonometric Methods

The Math class contains the following trigonometric methods:

```
public static double sin(double radians)
public static double cos(double radians)
public static double tan(double radians)
public static double asin(double radians)
public static double acos(double radians)
public static double atan(double radians)
public static double toRadians(double degree)
public static double toDegrees(double radians)
```

Each method has a single double parameter, and its return type is double. The parameter represents an angle in radians. One degree is equal to $\pi/180$ in radians. For example, Math.sin(Math.PI) returns the trigonometric sine of π. Since JDK 1.2, the Math class has also provided the method toRadians(double angdeg) for converting an angle in degrees to radians, and the method toDegrees(double angrad) for converting an angle in radians to degrees.

For example,

```
Math.sin(0) returns 0.0
Math.sin(Math.toRadians(270)) returns -1.0
Math.sin(Math.PI / 6) returns 0.5
Math.sin(Math.PI / 2) returns 1.0
Math.cos(0) returns 1.0
Math.cos(Math.PI / 6) returns 0.866
Math.cos(Math.PI / 2) returns 0
```

4.8.2 Exponent Methods

There are four methods related to exponents in the Math class:

```
/** Return e raised to the power of a (eᵃ) */
public static double exp(double a)

/** Return the natural logarithm of a (ln(a) = logₑ(a)) */
public static double log(double a)

/** Return a raised to the power of b (aᵇ) */
public static double pow(double a, double b)

/** Return the square root of a (√a) */
public static double sqrt(double a)
```

Note that the parameter in the sqrt method must not be negative.

For example,

```
Math.pow(2, 3) returns 8.0
Math.pow(3, 2) returns 9.0
Math.pow(3.5, 2.5) returns 22.91765
Math.sqrt(4) returns 2.0
Math.sqrt(10.5) returns 3.24
```

4.8.3 The Rounding Methods

The Math class contains five rounding methods:

```
/** x rounded up to its nearest integer. This integer is
  * returned as a double value. */
public static double ceil(double x)

/** x is rounded down to its nearest integer. This integer is
  * returned as a double value. */
public static double floor(double x)

/** x is rounded to its nearest integer. If x is equally close
  * to two integers, the even one is returned as a double. */
public static double rint(double x)
```

```
/** Return (int)Math.floor(x + 0.5). */
public static int round(float x)

/** Return (long)Math.floor(x + 0.5). */
public static long round(double x)
```

For example,

```
Math.ceil(2.1) returns 3.0
Math.ceil(2.0) returns 2.0
Math.ceil(-2.0) returns -2.0
Math.ceil(-2.1) returns -2.0
Math.floor(2.1) returns 2.0
Math.floor(2.0) returns 2.0
Math.floor(-2.0) returns -2.0
Math.floor(-2.1) returns -3.0
Math.rint(2.1) returns 2.0
Math.rint(2.0) returns 2.0
Math.rint(-2.0) returns -2.0
Math.rint(-2.1) returns -2.0
Math.rint(2.5) returns 2.0
Math.rint(-2.5) returns -2.0
Math.round(2.6f) returns 3 // Returns int
Math.round(2.0) returns 2 //  Returns long
Math.round(-2.0f) returns -2
Math.round(-2.6) returns -3
```

4.8.4   The min, max, and abs Methods

The min and max methods are overloaded to return the minimum and maximum numbers between two numbers (int, long, float, or double). For example, max(3.4, 5.0) returns 5.0, and min(3, 2) returns 2.

The abs method is overloaded to return the absolute value of the number (int, long, float, and double).

For example,

```
Math.max(2, 3) returns 3
Math.max(2.5, 3) returns 3.0
Math.min(2.5, 3.6) returns 2.5
Math.abs(-2) returns 2
Math.abs(-2.1) returns 2.1
```

4.8.5   The random Methods

The Math class also has a powerful method, random, which generates a random double value greater than or equal to 0.0 and less than 1.0 (0 <= Math.random() < 1.0). This method is very useful. You can use it to write a simple expression to generate random numbers in any range. For example,

```
(int) (Math.random() * 10)  ──────────▶  Returns a random integer
                                          between 0 and 9.

50 + (int) (Math.random() * 50)  ──────▶  Returns a random integer
                                          between 50 and 99.
```

In general,

```
a + Math.random() * b  ──────────▶  Returns a random number between
                                     a and a + b, excluding a + b.
```

🌼 **TIP**

view documentation online

You can view the complete documentation for the Math class online from http://java.sun.com/j2se/1.5.0/docs/api/index.html, as shown in Figure 4.11.

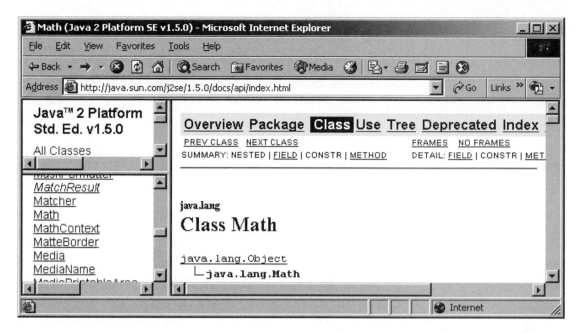

FIGURE 4.11   *You can view the documentation for Java API online at* `http://java.sun.com/j2se/1.5.0/docs/api/` `index.html`.

You can also download j2sdk-1_5_0-doc.zip from `http://java.sun.com/j2se/` `1.5.0/download.jsp#docs` and install it on your PC so that you can browse the documents locally.

 NOTE

Not all classes need a `main` method. The `Math` class and `JOptionPane` class do not have `main` methods. These classes contain methods for other classes to use.

4.9   Case Study: Generating Random Characters

Computer programs process numerical data and characters. You have seen many examples that involve numerical data. It is also important to understand characters and how to process them. This section presents an example for generating random characters.

As introduced in Section 2.9, every character has a unique Unicode between 0 and FFFF in hexadecimal (65535 in decimal). To generate a random character is to generate a random integer between 0 and 65535 using the following expression (note that since `0 <= Math.random() < 1.0`, you have to add 1 to 65535):

```
(int)(Math.random() * (65535 + 1))
```

Now let us consider how to generate a random lowercase letter. The Unicodes for lowercase letters are consecutive integers starting from the Unicode for `'a'`, then for `'b'`, `'c'`, . . . , and `'z'`. The Unicode for `'a'` is

```
(int)'a'
```

So a random integer between `(int)'a'` and `(int)'z'` is

```
(int)((int)'a' + Math.random() * ((int)'z' - (int)'a' + 1)
```

As discussed in Section 2.9.4, all numeric operators can be applied to the `char` operands. The `char` operand is cast into a number if the other operand is a number or a character. Thus the preceding expression can be simplified as follows:

```
'a' + Math.random() * ('z' - 'a' + 1)
```

and a random lowercase letter is

```
(char)('a' + Math.random() * ('z' - 'a' + 1))
```

To generalize the foregoing discussion, a random character between any two characters `ch1` and `ch2` with `ch1 < ch2` can be generated as follows:

```
(char)(ch1 + Math.random() * (ch2 - ch1 + 1))
```

This is a simple but useful discovery. Let us create a class named `RandomCharacter` in Listing 4.5 with five overloaded methods to get a certain type of character randomly. You can use these methods in your future projects.

LISTING 4.5   RandomCharacter.java (Generating Random Characters)

```
 1 public class RandomCharacter {
 2   /** Generate a random character between ch1 and ch2 */
 3   public static char getRandomCharacter(char ch1, char ch2) {
 4     return (char)(ch1 + Math.random() * (ch2 - ch1 + 1));
 5   }
 6
 7   /** Generate a random lowercase letter */
 8   public static char getRandomLowerCaseLetter() {
 9     return getRandomCharacter('a', 'z');
10   }
11
12   /** Generate a random uppercase letter */
13   public static char getRandomUpperCaseLetter() {
14     return getRandomCharacter('A', 'Z');
15   }
16
17   /** Generate a random digit character */
18   public static char getRandomDigitCharacter() {
19     return getRandomCharacter('0', '9');
20   }
21
22   /** Generate a random character */
23   public static char getRandomCharacter() {
24     return getRandomCharacter('\u0000', '\uFFFF');
25   }
26 }
```

Listing 4.6 gives a test program that displays one hundred lowercase letters.

LISTING 4.6   TestRandomCharacter.java (Using RandomCharacter)

```
 1 public class TestRandomCharacter {
 2   /** Main method */
 3   public static void main(String args[]) {
 4     final int NUMBER_OF_CHARS = 175;
 5     final int CHARS_PER_LINE = 25;
 6
```

constants

```
7      // Print random characters between '!' and '~', 25 chars per line
8      for (int i = 0; i < NUMBER_OF_CHARS; i++) {
9        char ch = RandomCharacter.getRandomLowerCaseLetter();
10       if ((i + 1) % CHARS_PER_LINE == 0)
11         System.out.println(ch);
12       else
13         System.out.print(ch);
14     }
15   }
16 }
```

lowercase letter

4.10 Stepwise Refinement (Optional)

The concept of method abstraction can be applied to the process of developing programs. When writing a large program, you can use the "divide and conquer" strategy, also known as *stepwise refinement*, to decompose it into subproblems. The subproblems can be further decomposed into smaller, more manageable problems.

divide and conquer

stepwise refinement

Suppose you write a program that displays the calendar for a given month of the year. The program prompts the user to enter the year and the month, and then displays the entire calendar for the month, as shown in Figure 4.12.

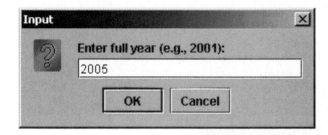
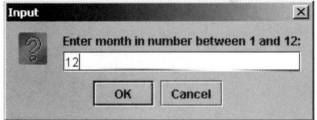

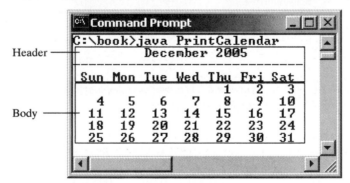

FIGURE 4.12 *After prompting the user to enter the year and the month, the program displays the calendar for that month.*

Let us use this example demonstrate the divide-and-conquer approach.

4.10.1 Top-Down Design

How would you get started on such a program? Would you immediately start coding? Beginning programmers often start by trying to work out the solution to every detail. Although details are important in the final program, concern for detail in the early stages may block the problem-solving process. To make problem-solving flow as smoothly as possible, this example begins by using method abstraction to isolate details from design and only later implements the details.

For this example, the problem is first broken into two subproblems: get input from the user, and print the calendar for the month. At this stage, the creator of the program should be concerned with what the subproblems will achieve, not with how to get input and print the calendar for the month. You can draw a structure chart to help visualize the decomposition of the problem (see Figure 4.13(a)).

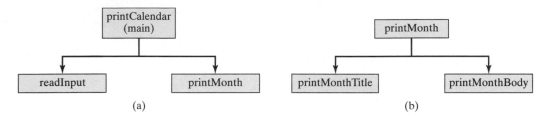

(a)   (b)

FIGURE 4.13 *The structure chart shows that the* printCalendar *problem is divided into two subproblems,* readInput *and* printMonth, *and that* printMonth *is divided into two smaller subproblems,* printMonthTitle *and* printMonthBody.

Use the JOptionPane.showInputDialog method to display input dialog boxes that prompt the user to enter the year and the month.

The problem of printing the calendar for a given month can be broken into two subproblems: print the month title, and print the month body, as shown in Figure 4.13(b). The month title consists of three lines: month and year, a dash line, and the names of the seven days of the week. You need to get the month name (e.g., January) from the numeric month (e.g., 1). This is accomplished in getMonthName (see Figure 4.14(a)).

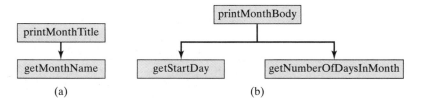

(a)   (b)

FIGURE 4.14 *(a) To* printMonthTitle, *you need* getMonthName. *(b) The* printMonthBody *problem is refined into several smaller problems.*

In order to print the month body, you need to know which day of the week is the first day of the month (getStartDay) and how many days the month has (getNumberOfDaysInMonth), as shown in Figure 4.14(b). For example, December 2005 has thirty-one days, and the first of the month is Thursday, as shown in Figure 4.12.

How would you get the start day for the first date in a month? There are several ways to find the start day. The simplest approach is to use the Calendar class in Section 9.3, "The Calendar and GregorianCalendar classes." For now, an alternative approach is used. Assume that you know that the start day (startDay1800 = 3) for January 1, 1800 was Wednesday. You could compute the total number of days (totalNumberOfDays) between January 1, 1800 and the first date of the calendar month. The start day for the calendar month is (totalNumberOfDays + startDay1800) % 7, since every week has seven days. So the getStartDay problem can be further refined as getTotalNumberOfDays, as shown in Figure 4.15(a).

To get the total number of days, you need to know whether a year is a leap year and the number of days in each month. So the getTotalNumberOfDays is further refined into two subproblems: isLeapYear and getNumberOfDaysInMonth, as shown in Figure 4.15(b). The complete structure chart is shown in Figure 4.16.

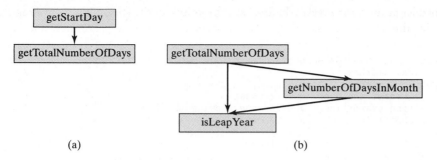

(a)   (b)

FIGURE 4.15 *(a) To* `getStartDay`, *you need* `getTotalNumberOfDays`. *(b) The* `getTotalNumberOfDays` *problem is refined into two smaller problems.*

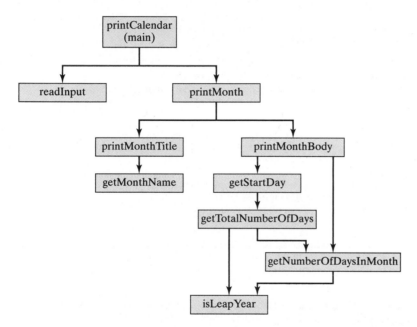

FIGURE 4.16 *The structure chart shows the hierarchical relationship of the subproblems in the program.*

4.10.2   Top-Down or Bottom-Up Implementation

Now we turn our attention to implementation. In general, a subproblem corresponds to a method in the implementation, although some are so simple that this is unnecessary. You would need to decide which modules to implement as methods and which to combine in other methods. Decisions of this kind should be based on whether the overall program will be easier to read as a result of your choice. In this example, the subproblem `readInput` can be simply implemented in the `main` method.

You can use either a "top-down" approach or a "bottom-up" approach. The *top-down approach* implements one method in the structure chart at a time from the top to the bottom. Stubs can be used for the methods waiting to be implemented. A *stub* is a simple but incomplete version of a method. The use of stubs enables you to test invoking the method from a caller. Implement the `main` method first, and then use a stub for the `printMonth` method. For

top-down approach

stub

example, let printMonth display the year and the month in the stub. Thus, your program may begin like this:

```java
public class PrintCalendar {
  /** Main method */
  public static void main(String[] args) {
    // Prompt the user to enter year
    String yearString = JOptionPane.showInputDialog(
      "Enter full year (e.g., 2001):");

    // Convert string into integer
    int year = Integer.parseInt(yearString);

    // Prompt the user to enter month
    String monthString = JOptionPane.showInputDialog(
      "Enter month in number between 1 and 12:");

    // Convert string into integer
    int month = Integer.parseInt(monthString);

    // Print calendar for the month of the year
    printMonth(year, month);
  }

  /** A stub for printMonth may look like this */
  public static void printMonth(int year, int month) {
    System.out.print(month + " " + year);
  }

  /** A stub for printMonthTitle may look like this */
  public static void printMonthTitle(int year, int month) {
  }

  /** A stub for getMonthName may look like this */
  public static String getMonthName(int month) {
    return "January"; // a dummy value
  }

  /** A stub for getMonthName may look like this */
  public static int getStartDay(int year, int month) {
    return 1; // a dummy value
  }

  /** A stub for getNumberOfDaysInMonth may look like this */
  public static int getNumberOfDaysInMonth(int year, int month) {
    return 31; // a dummy value
  }

  /** A stub for getTotalNumberOfDays may look like this */
  public static int getTotalNumberOfDays(int year, int month) {
    return 10000; // a dummy value
  }

  /** A stub for getTotalNumberOfDays may look like this */
  public static boolean isLeapYear(int year) {
    return true; // a dummy value
  }
}
```

Compile and test the program, and fix any errors. You can now implement the printMonth method. For methods invoked from the printMonth method, you can again use stubs.

bottom-up approach

The *bottom-up approach* implements one method in the structure chart at a time from the bottom to the top. For each method implemented, write a test program to test it. The top-down and bottom-up approaches are both fine. Both approaches implement methods incrementally, help to isolate programming errors, and make debugging easy. Sometimes they can be used together.

4.10.3   Implementation Details

The `isLeapYear(int year)` method can be implemented using the following code:

```
return (year % 400 == 0 || (year % 4 == 0 && year % 100 != 0));
```

Use the following fact to implement `getTotalNumberOfDaysInMonth(int year, int month)`:

✦ January, March, May, July, August, October, and December have thirty-one days.

✦ April, June, September, and November have thirty days.

✦ February has twenty-eight days during a regular year and twenty-nine days during a leap year. A regular year, therefore, has 365 days, whereas a leap year has 366 days.

To implement `getTotalNumberOfDays(int year, int month)`, you need to compute the total number of days (`totalNumberOfDays`) between Jan 1, 1800 and the first day of the calendar month. You could find the total number of days between the year 1800 and the calendar year and then figure out the total number of days prior to the calendar month in the calendar year. The sum of these two totals is `totalNumberOfDays`.

To print a body, first pad some space before the start day and then print the lines for every week, as shown for December 2005 (see Figure 4.12).

The complete program is given in Listing 4.7.

LISTING 4.7   PrintCalendar.java (Printing Calendar)

```
 1 import javax.swing.JOptionPane;
 2
 3 public class PrintCalendar {
 4   /** Main method */
 5   public static void main(String[] args) {
 6     // Prompt the user to enter year
 7     String yearString = JOptionPane.showInputDialog(
 8       "Enter full year (e.g., 2001):");
 9
10     // Convert string into integer
11     int year = Integer.parseInt(yearString);
12
13     // Prompt the user to enter month
14     String monthString = JOptionPane.showInputDialog(
15       "Enter month in number between 1 and 12:");
16
17     // Convert string into integer
18     int month = Integer.parseInt(monthString);
19
20     // Print calendar for the month of the year
21     printMonth(year, month);
22   }
23
24   /** Print the calendar for a month in a year */
25   static void printMonth(int year, int month) {
26     // Print the headings of the calendar
27     printMonthTitle(year, month);
28
29     // Print the body of the calendar
30     printMonthBody(year, month);
31   }
32
33   /** Print the month title, e.g., May, 1999 */
34   static void printMonthTitle(int year, int month) {
35     System.out.println("    " + getMonthName(month)
36       + " " + year);
37     System.out.println("---------------------------");
38     System.out.println(" Sun Mon Tue Wed Thu Fri Sat");
39   }
```

```
40
41    /** Get the English name for the month */
42    static String getMonthName(int month) {
43      String monthName = null;
44      switch (month) {
45        case 1: monthName = "January"; break;
46        case 2: monthName = "February"; break;
47        case 3: monthName = "March"; break;
48        case 4: monthName = "April"; break;
49        case 5: monthName = "May"; break;
50        case 6: monthName = "June"; break;
51        case 7: monthName = "July"; break;
52        case 8: monthName = "August"; break;
53        case 9: monthName = "September"; break;
54        case 10: monthName = "October"; break;
55        case 11: monthName = "November"; break;
56        case 12: monthName = "December";
57      }
58
59      return monthName;
60    }
61
62    /** Print month body */
63    static void printMonthBody(int year, int month) {
64      // Get start day of the week for the first date in the month
65      int startDay = getStartDay(year, month);
66
67      // Get number of days in the month
68      int numberOfDaysInMonth = getNumberOfDaysInMonth(year, month);
69
70      // Pad space before the first day of the month
71      int i = 0;
72      for (i = 0; i < startDay; i++)
73        System.out.print("   ");
74
75      for (i = 1; i <= numberOfDaysInMonth; i++) {
76        if (i < 10)
77          System.out.print("   " + i);
78        else
79          System.out.print("  " + i);
80
81        if ((i + startDay) % 7 == 0)
82          System.out.println();
83      }
84
85      System.out.println();
86    }
87
88    /** Get the start day of the first day in a month */
89    static int getStartDay(int year, int month) {
90      // Get total number of days since 1/1/1800
91      int startDay1800 = 3;
92      int totalNumberOfDays = getTotalNumberOfDays(year, month);
93
94      // Return the start day
95      return (totalNumberOfDays + startDay1800) % 7;
96    }
97
98    /** Get the total number of days since Jan 1, 1800 */
99    static int getTotalNumberOfDays(int year, int month) {
100     int total = 0;
101
102     // Get the total days from 1800 to year - 1
103     for (int i = 1800; i < year; i++)
104     if (isLeapYear(i))
105       total = total + 366;
106     else
107       total = total + 365;
108
```

```
109      // Add days from Jan to the month prior to the calendar month
110      for (int i = 1; i < month; i++)
111        total = total + getNumberOfDaysInMonth(year, i);
112
113      return total;
114    }
115
116    /** Get the number of days in a month */
117    static int getNumberOfDaysInMonth(int year, int month) {
118      if (month == 1 || month == 3 || month == 5 || month == 7 ||
119        month == 8 || month == 10 || month == 12)
120        return 31;
121
122      if (month == 4 || month == 6 || month == 9 || month == 11)
123        return 30;
124
125      if (month == 2) return isLeapYear(year) ? 29 : 28;
126
127      return 0; // If month is incorrect
128    }
129
130    /** Determine if it is a leap year */
131    static boolean isLeapYear(int year) {
132      return year % 400 == 0 || (year % 4 == 0 && year % 100 137 != 0);
133    }
134  }
```

The program does not validate user input. For instance, if the user enters a month not in the range between 1 and 12, or a year before 1800, the program would display an erroneous calendar. To avoid this error, add an if statement to check the input before printing the calendar.

This program prints calendars for a month but could easily be modified to print calendars for a whole year. Although it can only print months after January 1800, it could be modified to trace the day of a month before 1800.

NOTE

Method abstraction modularizes programs in a neat, hierarchical manner. Programs written as collections of concise methods are easier to write, debug, maintain, and modify than would otherwise be the case. This writing style also promotes method reusability.

TIP

When implementing a large program, use the top-down or bottom-up coding approach. Do not write the entire program at once. This approach seems to take more time for coding (because you are repeatedly compiling and running the program), but it actually saves time and makes debugging easier.

4.11   Recursion (Optional)

You have seen a method calling another method; that is, a statement contained in a method body calling another method. Can a method call itself? And what happens if it does? This section examines these questions and uses three classic examples to demonstrate recursive programming.

4.11.1   Computing Factorials

recursion

Recursion, a powerful mathematical concept, is the process of a function calling itself, directly or indirectly. Many mathematical functions are defined using recursion. The factorial of a number n can be recursively defined as follows:

```
0! = 1;
n! = n × (n - 1)!; n > 0
```

How do you find n! for a given n? It is easy to find 1! because you know 0! and 1! is 1 × 0!. Assuming that you know (n-1)!, n! can be obtained immediately using n × (n-1)!. Thus, the problem of computing n! is reduced to computing (n-1)!. When computing (n-1)!, you can apply the same idea recursively until n is reduced to 0.

stopping condition

Let factorial(n) be the method for computing n!. If you call the method with n=0, it immediately returns the result. The method knows how to solve the simplest case, which is referred to as the *base case* or the *stopping condition*. If you call the method with n>0, it reduces the problem into a subproblem for computing the factorial of n-1. The subproblem is essentially the same as the original problem, but is slightly simpler or smaller than the original. Because the subproblem has the same property as the original, you can call the method with a different argument, which is referred to as a *recursive call*.

recursive call

The recursive algorithm for computing factorial(n) can be simply described as follows:

```
if (n == 0)
  return 1;
else
  return n * factorial(n - 1);
```

A recursive call can result in many more recursive calls because the method is dividing a subproblem into new subproblems. For a recursive method to terminate, the problem must eventually be reduced to a stopping case. When it reaches a stopping case, the method returns a result to its caller. The caller then performs a computation and returns the result to its own caller. This process continues until the result is passed back to the original caller. The original problem can now be solved by multiplying n with the result of factorial(n - 1).

EXAMPLE 4.5 COMPUTING FACTORIALS

Problem

Write a recursive method for computing a factorial factorial(n), given n. The test program prompts the user to enter n.

Solution

Listing 4.8 gives the solution to the problem. A sample run of the program is shown in Figure 4.17.

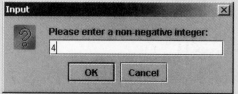
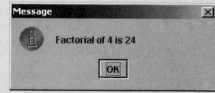

FIGURE 4.17   *The program prompts the user to enter a non-negative integer and then displays the factorial for the number.*

Example 4.5 (Continued)

Listing 4.8 ComputeFactorial.java (Computing Factorial)

```
1 import javax.swing.JOptionPane;
2
3 public class ComputeFactorial {
4   /** Main method */
5   public static void main(String[] args) {
6     // Prompt the user to enter an integer
7     String intString = JOptionPane.showInputDialog(
8       "Please enter a non-negative integer:");
9
10    // Convert string into integer
11    int n = Integer.parseInt(intString);
12
13    // Display factorial
14    JOptionPane.showMessageDialog(null,
15      "Factorial of " + n + " is " + factorial(n));
16  }
17
18  /** Return the factorial for a specified index */
19  static long factorial(int n) {
20    if (n == 0) // Stopping condition
21      return 1;
22    else
23      return n * factorial(n - 1); // Call factorial recursively
24  }
25 }
```

recursion

Review

The factorial method (Lines 19–24) is essentially a direct translation of the recursive mathematical definition for the factorial into Java code. The call to factorial is recursive because it calls itself. The parameter passed to factorial is decremented until it reaches the base case of 0.

Figure 4.18 illustrates the execution of the recursive calls, starting with n = 4. The use of stack space for recursive calls is shown in Figure 4.19.

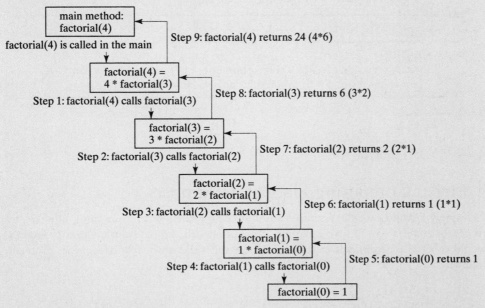

Figure 4.18 *Invoking* factorial(4) *spawns recursive calls to* factorial.

EXAMPLE 4.5 (CONTINUED)

1	Space Required for factorial(4)

2	Space Required for factorial(3)
	Space Required for factorial(4)

3	Space Required for factorial(2)
	Space Required for factorial(3)
	Space Required for factorial(4)

4	Space Required for factorial(1)
	Space Required for factorial(2)
	Space Required for factorial(3)
	Space Required for factorial(4)

5	Space Required for factorial(0)
	Space Required for factorial(1)
	Space Required for factorial(2)
	Space Required for factorial(3)
	Space Required for factorial(4)

6	Space Required for factorial(1)
	Space Required for factorial(2)
	Space Required for factorial(3)
	Space Required for factorial(4)

7	Space Required for factorial(2)
	Space Required for factorial(3)
	Space Required for factorial(4)

8	Space Required for factorial(3)
	Space Required for factorial(4)

9	Space Required for factorial(4)

FIGURE 4.19 *When* `factorial(4)` *is being executed, the* `factorial` *method is called recursively, causing memory space to dynamically change.*

 NOTE
All recursive methods have the following characteristics:

✦ One or more base cases (the simplest case) are used to stop recursion.

✦ Every recursive call reduces the original problem, bringing it increasingly closer to a base case until it becomes that case.

 CAUTION
Infinite recursion can occur if recursion does not reduce the problem in a manner that allows it to eventually converge into the base case.

4.11.2   Computing Fibonacci Numbers

Example 4.5 could easily be rewritten without using recursion. In some cases, however, using recursion enables you to give a natural, straightforward, simple solution to a program that would otherwise be difficult to solve. Consider the well-known Fibonacci series problem, as follows:

The series:	0	1	1	2	3	5	8	13	21	34	55	89	...
indices:	0	1	2	3	4	5	6	7	8	9	10	11	

The Fibonacci series begins with 0 and 1, and each subsequent number is the sum of the preceding two numbers in the series. The series can be recursively defined as follows:

```
fib(0) = 0;
fib(1) = 1;
fib(index) = fib(index - 2) + fib(index - 1); index >= 2
```

The Fibonacci series was named for Leonardo Fibonacci, a medieval mathematician, who originated it to model the growth of the rabbit population. It can be applied in numeric optimization and in various other areas.

How do you find `fib(index)` for a given `index`? It is easy to find `fib(2)` because you know `fib(0)` and `fib(1)`. Assuming that you know `fib(index - 2)` and `fib(index - 1)`, `fib(index)` can be obtained immediately. Thus, the problem of computing `fib(index)` is reduced to computing `fib(index - 2)` and `fib(index - 1)`. When computing `fib(index - 2)` and `fib(index - 1)`, you apply the idea recursively until `index` is reduced to 0 or 1.

The base case is `index = 0` or `index = 1`. If you call the method with `index = 0` or `index = 1`, it immediately returns the result. If you call the method with `index >= 2`, it divides the problem into two subproblems for computing `fib(index - 1)` and `fib(index - 2)` using recursive calls. The recursive algorithm for computing `fib(index)` can be simply described as follows:

```
if (index == 0)
  return 0;
else if (index == 1)
  return 1;
else
  return fib(index - 1) + fib(index - 2);
```

EXAMPLE 4.6 COMPUTING FIBONACCI NUMBERS

Problem

Write a recursive method for computing a Fibonacci number `fib(index)` for a given index. The test program prompts the user to enter index `index`, then calls the method and displays the result.

Solution

Listing 4.9 gives the solution to the problem. A sample run of the program is shown in Figure 4.20.

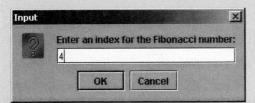
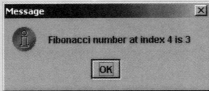

FIGURE 4.20 *The program prompts the user to enter an index for the Fibonacci number and then displays the number at the index.*

LISTING 4.9 ComputeFibonacci.java (Finding Fibonacci Number)

```
1 import javax.swing.JOptionPane;
2
3 public class ComputeFibonacci {
4   /** Main method */
5   public static void main(String args[]) {
```

recursion

EXAMPLE 4.6 (CONTINUED)

```
6       // Read the index
7       String intString = JOptionPane.showInputDialog(
8         "Enter an index for the Fibonacci number:");
9
10      // Convert string into integer
11      int index = Integer.parseInt(intString);
12
13      // Find and display the Fibonacci number
14      JOptionPane.showMessageDialog(null,
15        "Fibonacci number at index " + index + " is " + fib(index));
16    }
17
18    /** The method for finding the Fibonacci number */
19    public static long fib(long index) {
20      if (index == 0) // Stopping condition
21        return 0;
22      else if (index == 1) // Stopping condition
23        return 1;
24      else // Reduction and recursive calls
25        return fib(index - 1) + fib(index - 2);
26    }
27  }
```

Review

The implementation of the method is very simple and straightforward. The solution is slightly more difficult if you do not use recursion. For a hint on computing Fibonacci numbers using iterations, see Exercise 4.20.

The program does not show the considerable amount of work done behind the scenes by the computer. Figure 4.21, however, shows successive recursive calls for evaluating `fib(4)`. The original method, `fib(4)`, makes two recursive calls, `fib(3)` and `fib(2)`, and then returns `fib(3) + fib(2)`. But in what order are these methods called? In Java, operands are evaluated from left to right. The labels in Figure 4.21 show the order in which methods are called.

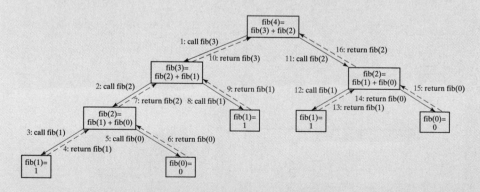

FIGURE 4.21   *Invoking `fib(4)` spawns recursive calls to `fib`.*

As shown in Figure 4.21, there are many duplicated recursive calls. For instance, `fib(2)` is called twice, `fib(1)` is called three times, and `fib(0)` is called twice. In general, computing `fib(index)` requires twice as many recursive calls as are needed for computing `fib(index - 1)`. As you try larger index values, the number of calls substantially increases.

Besides the large number of recursive calls, the computer requires more time and space to run recursive methods. For more discussion, see Section 4.11.4, "Recursion versus Iteration."

4.11.3 The Tower of Hanoi Problem

You have seen a recursive method with a return value. Here is an example of a recursive method with a return type of void.

The problem involves moving a specified number of disks of distinct sizes from one tower to another while observing the following rules:

✦ There are *n* disks labeled 1, 2, 3, ..., *n*, and three towers labeled A, B, and C.

✦ No disk can be on top of a smaller disk at any time.

✦ All the disks are initially placed on tower A.

✦ Only one disk can be moved at a time, and it must be the top disk on the tower.

The objective of the problem is to move all the disks from A to B with the assistance of C. For example, if you have three disks, as shown in Figure 4.22, the following steps will move all of the disks from A to B:

1. Move disk 1 from A to B.

2. Move disk 2 from A to C.

3. Move disk 1 from B to C.

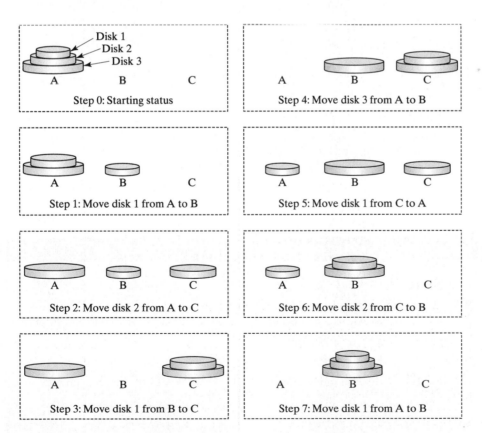

FIGURE 4.22 *The goal of the Towers of Hanoi problem is to move disks from tower A to tower B without breaking the rules.*

4. Move disk 3 from A to B.

5. Move disk 1 from C to A.

6. Move disk 2 from C to B.

7. Move disk 1 from A to B.

 NOTE

The Towers of Hanoi is a classic computer science problem. There are many Web sites devoted to this problem. The Web site `www.cut-the-knot.com/recurrence/hanoi.html` is worth seeing.

In the case of three disks, you can find the solution manually. However, the problem is quite complex for a larger number of disks—even for four. Fortunately, the problem has an inherently recursive nature, which leads to a straightforward recursive solution.

The base case for the problem is n == 1. If n == 1, you could simply move the disk from A to B. When n > 1, you could split the original problem into three subproblems and solve them sequentially.

1. Move the first n – 1 disks from A to C with the assistance of tower B.

2. Move disk n from A to B.

3. Move n – 1 disks from C to B with the assistance of tower A.

The following method moves *n* disks from the fromTower to the toTower with the assistance of the auxTower:

```
void moveDisks(int n, char fromTower, char toTower, char auxTower)
```

The algorithm for the method can be described as follows:

```
if (n == 1) // Stopping condition
  Move disk 1 from the fromTower to the toTower;
else {
  moveDisks(n - 1, fromTower, auxTower, toTower);
  Move disk n from the fromTower to the toTower;
  moveDisks(n - 1, auxTower, toTower, fromTower);
}
```

EXAMPLE 4.7 SOLVING THE TOWERS OF HANOI PROBLEM

Problem

Write a program that finds a solution for the Towers of Hanoi problem. The program prompts the user to enter the number of disks and invokes the recursive method moveDisks to display the solution for moving the disks.

Solution

Listing 4.10 gives the solution to the problem. A sample run of the program appears in Figure 4.23.

EXAMPLE 4.7 (CONTINUED)

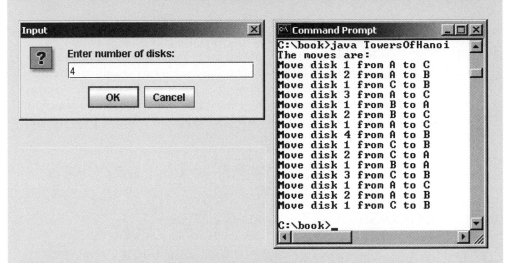

FIGURE 4.23 *The program prompts the user to enter the number of disks and then displays the steps that must be followed to solve the Towers of Hanoi problem.*

LISTING 4.10 TowersOfHanoi.java (Towers of Hanoi Problem)

```
1 import javax.swing.JOptionPane;
2
3 public class TowersOfHanoi {
4   /** Main method */
5   public static void main(String[] args) {
6     // Read number of disks, n
7     String intString = JOptionPane.showInputDialog(
8       "Enter number of disks:");
9
10    // Convert string into integer
11    int n = Integer.parseInt(intString);
12
13    // Find the solution recursively
14    System.out.println("The moves are:");
15    moveDisks(n, 'A', 'B', 'C');
16  }
17
18  /** The method for finding the solution to move n disks
19      from fromTower to toTower with auxTower */
20  public static void moveDisks(int n, char fromTower,
21      char toTower, char auxTower) {
22    if (n == 1) // Stopping condition
23      System.out.println("Move disk " + n + " from " +
24        fromTower + " to " + toTower);
25    else {
26      moveDisks(n - 1, fromTower, auxTower, toTower);          recursion
27      System.out.println("Move disk " + n + " from " +
28        fromTower + " to " + toTower);
29      moveDisks(n - 1, auxTower, toTower, fromTower);          recursion
30    }
31  }
32 }
```

EXAMPLE **4.7** (CONTINUED)

Review

This problem is inherently recursive. Using recursion makes it possible to find a natural, simple solution. It would be difficult to solve the problem without using recursion.

Consider tracing the program for n = 3. The successive recursive calls are shown in Figure 4.24. As you can see, writing the program is easier than tracing the recursive calls. The system uses stacks to trace the calls behind the scenes. To some extent, recursion provides a level of abstraction that hides iterations and other details from the user.

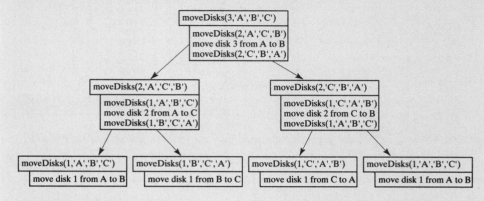

FIGURE **4.24** *Invoking* moveDisks(3, 'A', 'B', 'C') *spawns calls to* moveDisks *recursively.*

The fib method in the preceding example returns a value to its caller, but the moveDisks method in this example does not return a value to its caller.

4.11.4 Recursion versus Iteration

Recursion is an alternative form of program control. It is essentially repetition without a loop control. When you use loops, you specify a loop body. The repetition of the loop body is controlled by the loop-control structure. In recursion, the method itself is called repeatedly. A selection statement must be used to control whether to call the method recursively or not.

Recursion bears substantial overhead. Each time the program calls a method, the system must assign space for all of the method's local variables and parameters. This can consume considerable memory and requires extra time to manage the additional space.

Any problem that can be solved recursively can be solved nonrecursively with iterations. Recursion has many negative aspects: it uses up too much time and too much memory. Why, then, should you use it? In some cases, using recursion enables you to specify a clear, simple solution that would otherwise be difficult to obtain.

The decision whether to use recursion or iteration should be based on the nature of the problem you are trying to solve and your understanding of the problem. The rule of thumb is to use whichever of the two approaches can best develop an intuitive solution that naturally mirrors the problem. If an iterative solution is obvious, use it. It will generally be more efficient than the recursive option.

 NOTE

Your recursive program could run out of memory, causing a runtime error. In Chapter 15, "Exceptions and Assertions," you will learn how to handle errors so that the program terminates gracefully when there is a stack overflow.

> ### 🦋 Tɪᴘ
> If you are concerned about your program's performance, avoid using recursion, because it takes more time and consumes more memory than iteration. Commercial software generally do not use recursion.

4.12   Packages (Optional)

Packages are used to group classes. So far, all the classes in this book are grouped into a default package. You can explicitly specify a package for each class. There are four reasons for using packages.   *why packages?*

✦ **To locate classes.** Classes with similar functions can be placed in the same package so they can be easily located.

✦ **To avoid naming conflicts.** When you develop reusable classes to be shared by other programmers, naming conflicts often occur. To prevent this, put your classes into packages so that they can be referenced through package names.

✦ **To distribute software conveniently.** Packages group related classes so that they can be easily distributed.

✦ **To protect classes.** Packages provide protection so that the protected members of the classes are accessible to the classes in the same package, but not to the external classes.

4.12.1   Package-Naming Conventions

Packages are hierarchical, and you can have packages within packages. For example, `java.lang.Math` indicates that `Math` is a class in the package `lang` and that `lang` is a package in the package `java`. Levels of nesting can be used to ensure the uniqueness of package names.

Choosing a unique name is important because your package may be used on the Internet by other programs. Java designers recommend that you use your Internet domain name in reverse order as a package prefix. Since Internet domain names are unique, this prevents naming conflicts. Suppose you want to create a package named `mypackage` on a host machine with the Internet domain name `prenhall.com`. To follow the naming convention, you would name the entire package `com.prenhall.mypackage`. By convention, package names are all in lowercase.

4.12.2   Package Directories

Java expects one-to-one mapping of the package name and the file system directory structure. For the package named `com.prenhall.mypackage`, you must create a directory, as shown in Figure 4.25(a). In other words, a package is actually a directory that contains the bytecode of the classes.

(a)   (b)

Fɪɢᴜʀᴇ 4.25   *The package* `com.prenhall.mypackage` *is mapped to a directory structure in the file system.*

classpath
class directory

The com directory does not have to be the root directory. In order for Java to know where your package is in the file system, you must modify the environment variable classpath so that it points to the directory in which your package resides. Such a directory is known as the *class directory* for the class. Suppose the com directory is under c:\book, as shown in Figure 4.25(b). The following line adds c:\book into the classpath:

```
classpath=.;c:\book;
```

current directory

The period (.) indicating the *current directory* is always in classpath. The directory c:\book is in classpath so that you can use the package com.prenhall.mypackage in the program.

You can add as many directories as necessary in classpath. The order in which the directories are specified is the order in which the classes are searched. If you have two classes of the same name in different directories, Java uses the first one it finds.

The classpath variable is set differently in Windows and Unix, as outlined below.

✦ **Windows 98:** Edit autoexec.bat using a text editor, such as Microsoft Notepad.

✦ **Windows NT/2000/XP:** Go to the start button and choose control panel, select the system icon, then modify classpath in the Environment Variables.

✦ **UNIX:** Use the setenv command to set classpath, such as

```
setenv classpath .:/home/book
```

If you insert this line into the .cshrc file, the classpath variable will be set automatically when you log on.

 NOTE

On Windows 95 and Windows 98, you must restart the system in order for the classpath variable to take effect. On Windows NT and Windows 2000, however, the settings are effective immediately. They affect any new command-line windows, but not the existing command-line windows.

4.12.3   Putting Classes into Packages

Every class in Java belongs to a package. The class is added to a package when it is compiled. All the classes that you have used so far in this book were placed in the current directory (a default package) when the Java source programs were compiled. To put a class in a specific package, you need to add the following line as the first noncomment and nonblank statement in the program:

```
package packagename;
```

EXAMPLE 4.8 PUTTING CLASSES INTO PACKAGES

Problem

This example creates a class named Format and places it in the package com. prenhall.mypackage. The Format class contains the format(number, numberOfDecimal- Digits) method, which returns a new number with the specified number of digits after the decimal point. For example, format(10.3422345, 2) returns 10.34, and format (−0.343434, 3) returns −0.343.

EXAMPLE 4.8 (CONTINUED)

Solution

1. Create Format.java in Listing 4.11 and save it into c:\book\com\prenhall\mypackage.

LISTING 4.11   **Format.java (Formatting Numbers)**

```
1 package com.prenhall.mypackage;
2
3 public class Format {
4   public static double format(
5       double number, int numberOfDecimalDigits) {
6     return Math.round(number * Math.pow(10, numberOfDecimalDigits)) /
7       Math.pow(10, numberOfDecimalDigits);
8   }
9 }
```

specify a package

2. Compile Format.java. Make sure Format.class is in c:\book\com\prenhall\mypackage.

Review

A class must be defined as public in order to be accessed by other programs. If you want to put several classes into the package, you have to create separate source files for them because one file can have only one public class.

Format.java can be placed under anyDir\com\prenhall\mypackage and Format.class in anyOtherDir\com\prenhall\mypackage, and anyDir and anyOtherDir may be the same or different. To make the class available, add anyOtherDir in the classpath using the command:

```
set classpath=%classpath%;anyOtherDir
```

 NOTE

Class files can be archived into a single file for convenience. For instance, you may compress all the class files in the folder mypackage into a single zip file named mypackage.zip with subfolder information kept as shown in Figure 4.26. To make the classes in the zip file available for use, add the zip file to the classpath like this:

```
classpath=%classpath%;c:\mypackage.zip
```

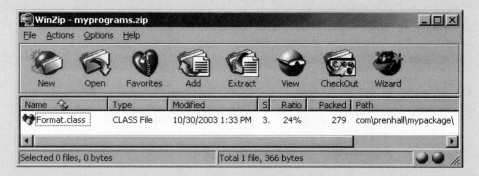

FIGURE 4.26   *Class files can be archived into a single compressed file.*

EXAMPLE 4.8 (CONTINUED)

 NOTE

An IDE such as JBuilder and NetBeans uses the *source directory path* to specify where the source files are stored and uses the *class directory path* to specify where the compiled class files are stored.

A source file must be stored in a package directory under the source directory path. For example, if the source directory is c:\mysource and the package statement in the source code is `package com.prenhall.mypackage`, then the source code file must be stored in c:\mysource\com\prenhall\mypackage.

A class file must be stored in a package directory under the class directory path. For example, if the class directory is `c:\myclass` and the package statement in the source code is `package com.prenhall.mypackage`, then the class file must be stored in c:\myclass\com\prenhall\mypackage.

4.12.4   Using Classes from Packages

There are two ways to use classes from a package. One way is to use the fully qualified name of the class. For example, the fully qualified name for `JOptionPane` is `javax.swing.JOptionPane`. For `Format` in the preceding example, it is `com.prenhall.mypackage.Format`. This is convenient if the class is used only a few times in the program. The other way is to use the `import` statement. For example, to import all the classes in the `javax.swing` package, you can use

```
import javax.swing.*;
```

An import that uses an * is called *an import on demand* declaration . You can also import a specific class. For example, this statement imports `javax.swing.JOptionPane`:

```
import javax.swing.JOptionPane;
```

The information for the classes in an imported package is not read in at compile time or runtime unless the class is used in the program. The import statement simply tells the compiler where to locate the classes. There is no performance difference between an import on demand declaration and a specific class import declaration.

EXAMPLE 4.9 USING PACKAGES

Problem

This example shows a program that uses the `Format` class in the `com.prenhall.mypackage.mypackage` package.

Solution

1. Create TestFormatClass.java in Listing 4.12 and save it into c:\book.

LISTING 4.12   **TestFormatClass.java (Using the Format Class)**

import class

```
1 import com.prenhall.mypackage.Format;
2
3 public class TestFormatClass {
4   /** Main method */
```

EXAMPLE 4.9 (CONTINUED)

```
5    public static void main(String[] args) {
6       System.out.println(Format.format(10.3422345, 2));
7       System.out.println(Format.format(-0.343434, 3));
8    }
9 }
```

2. Run TestFormatClass, as shown in Figure 4.27.

```
Command Prompt                                          _ ☐ ✕
C:\book\com\prenhall\mypackage>javac Format.java

C:\book\com\prenhall\mypackage>cd c:\book

C:\book>javac TestFormatClass.java

C:\book>java TestFormatClass
10.34
-0.343

C:\book>
```

FIGURE 4.27   *TestFormatClass uses* Format *defined in* com.prenhall.mypackage.

Review

TestFormatClass.java can be placed anywhere as long as c:\book is in the classpath so that the Format class can be found. Please note that Format is defined as public so that it can be used by classes in other packages.

The program uses an import statement to get the class Format. You cannot import entire packages, such as com.prenhall.*.*. Only one asterisk (*) can be used in an import statement.

🌸 NOTE

The format method can be invoked from any class. If you create a new class in the same package with Format, you can invoke the format method using ClassName.methodName (e.g., Format.format). If you create a new class in a different package, you can invoke the format method using packagename.ClassName.method (e.g., com.prenhall.mypackage. Format.format).

KEY TERMS

actual parameter   127
ambiguous invocation   135
divide and conquer   143
formal parameter (i.e., parameter)   126
information hiding   138
method abstraction   138
method overloading   133
method signature   126
modifier   126

package   159
pass by value   131
recursion   149
return type   126
return value   126
scope of variable   137
stub   145

KEY CLASSES AND METHODS

✦   **`java.lang.Math`** is a class that contains methods to perform trigonometric functions (`sin`, `cos`, `tan`, `acos`, `asin`, `atan`), exponent functions (`exp`, `log`, `pow`, `sqrt`), and some service functions (`min`, `max`, `abs`, `round`, `random`). All of these methods operate on `double` values; `min`, `max`, and `abs` can also operate on `int`, `long`, `float`, and `double`.

CHAPTER SUMMARY

✦   Making programs modular and reusable is one of the central goals in software engineering. Java provides many powerful constructs that help to achieve this goal. The methods are one such construct.

✦   The method header specifies the *modifiers*, *return value type*, *method name*, and *parameters* of the method. The modifier, which is optional, tells the compiler how to call the method. The static modifier is used for all the methods in this chapter.

✦   A method may return a value. The `returnValueType` is the data type of the value the method returns. If the method does not return a value, the `returnValueType` is the keyword `void`.

✦   The *parameter list* refers to the type, order, and number of the parameters of a method. The method name and the parameter list together constitute the *method signature*. Parameters are optional; that is, a method may contain no parameters.

✦   A return statement can also be used in a void method for terminating the method and returning to the method's caller. This is occasionally useful for circumventing the normal flow of control in a method.

✦   The arguments that are passed to a method should have the same number, type, and order as the parameters in the method definition.

✦   When a program calls a method, program control is transferred to the called method. A called method returns control to the caller when its return statement is executed or when its method-ending closing brace is reached.

✦   A method with a nonvoid return value type can also be invoked as a statement in Java. In this case, the caller simply ignores the return value. In the majority of cases, a call to a method with return value is treated as a value. In some cases, however, the caller is not interested in the return value.

✦   Each time a method is invoked, the system stores parameters, local variables, and system registers in a space known as a *stack*. When a method calls another method, the caller's stack space is kept intact, and new space is created to handle the new method call. When a method finishes its work and returns to its caller, its associated space is released.

✦   A method can be overloaded. This means that two methods can have the same name as long as their method parameter lists differ.

✦   The scope of a local variable is limited locally to a method. The scope of a local variable starts from its declaration and continues to the end of the block that contains the variable.

A local variable must be declared before it can be used, and it must be initialized before it is referenced.

✦ *Method abstraction* is achieved by separating the use of a method from its implementation. The client can use a method without knowing how it is implemented. The details of the implementation are encapsulated in the method and hidden from the client who invokes the method. This is known as *information hiding* or *encapsulation*.

✦ Method abstraction modularizes programs in a neat, hierarchical manner. Programs written as collections of concise methods are easier to write, debug, maintain, and modify than would otherwise be the case. This writing style also promotes method reusability.

✦ When implementing a large program, use the top-down or bottom-up coding approach. Do not write the entire program at once. This approach seems to take more time for coding (because you are repeatedly compiling and running the program), but it actually saves time and makes debugging easier.

✦ Recursion is an alternative form of program control. It is essentially repetition without a loop control. It can be used to specify simple, clear solutions for inherently recursive problems that would otherwise be difficult to solve.

✦ Recursion bears substantial overhead. Each time the program calls a method, the system must assign space for all of the method's local variables and parameters. This can consume considerable memory and requires extra time to manage the additional space.

REVIEW QUESTIONS

Sections 4.2–4.3

4.1 What are the benefits of using a method? How do you declare a method? How do you invoke a method?

4.2 What is the `return` type of a `main` method?

4.3 Can you simplify the `max` method in Example 4.1 using the conditional operator?

4.4 True or false? A call to a method with a `void` return type is always a statement, but a call to a method with a nonvoid return type is always a component of an expression.

4.5 What would be wrong with not writing a `return` statement in a nonvoid method? Can you have a `return` statement in a `void` method, such as the following?

```
public static void main(String[] args) {
  int i;
  while (true) {
    // Prompt the user to enter an integer
    String intString = JOptionPane.showInputDialog(
      "Enter an integer:");

    // Convert a string into int
    int i = Integer.parseInt(intString);
    if (i == 0)
      return;
    System.out.println("i = " + i);
  }
}
```

Does the `return` statement in the following method cause syntax errors?

```
public static void xMethod(double x, double y) {
  System.out.println(x + y);
  return x + y;
}
```

4.6 In some languages, you can define methods inside a method. Can you define a method inside a method in Java?

4.7 For each of the following, decide whether a `void` method or a nonvoid method is the most appropriate implementation:

✦ Computing a sales commission, given the sales amount and the commission rate.

✦ Printing the calendar for a month.

✦ Computing a square root.

✦ Testing whether a number is even, and returning `true` if it is.

✦ Printing a message a specified number of times.

✦ Computing the monthly payment, given the loan amount, number of years, and annual interest rate.

✦ Finding the corresponding uppercase letter, given a lowercase letter.

4.8 Identify and correct the errors in the following program:

```
 1 public class Test {
 2   public static method1(int n, m) {
 3     n += m;
 4     xMethod(3.4);
 5   }
 6
 7   public static int xMethod(int n) {
 8     if (n > 0) return 1;
 9     else if (n == 0) return 0;
10     else if (n < 0) return -1;
11   }
12 }
```

4.9 Reformat the following program according to the programming style and documentation guidelines proposed in Section 2.18, "Programming Style and Documentation." Use the next-line brace style.

```
public class Test {
  public static double xMethod(double i,double j)
  {
  while (i<j) {
    j--;
  }
  return j;
  }
}
```

Section 4.4 Passing Parameters

4.10 How is an argument passed to a method? Can the argument have the same name as its parameter?

4.11 What is pass by value? Show the result of the following programs:

```java
public class Test {
  public static void main(String[] args) {
    int max = 0;
    max(1, 2, max);
    System.out.println(max);
  }

  public static void max(
    int value1, int value2, int max) {
    if (value1 > value2)
      max = value1;
    else
      max = value2;
  }
}
```

(a)

```java
public class Test {
  public static void main(String[] args) {
    // Initialize times
    int times = 3;
    System.out.println("Before the call,"
      + " variable times is " + times);

    // Invoke nPrintln and display times
    nPrintln("Welcome to Java!", times);
    System.out.println("After the call,"
      + "variable times is " + times);
  }

  // Print the message n times
  public static void nPrintln(
    String message, int n) {
    while (n > 0) {
      System.out.println("n = " + n);
      System.out.println(message);
      n--;
    }
  }
}
```

(b)

```java
public class Test {
  public static void main(String[] args) {
    int i = 1;
    while (i <= 6) {
      xMethod(1, 2);
      i++;
    }
  }

  public static void xMethod(
    int i, int num) {
    for (int j = 1; j <= i; j++) {
      System.out.print(num + " ");
      num *= 2;
    }

    System.out.println();
  }
}
```

(c)

```java
public class Test {
  public static void main(String[] args) {
    int i = 0;
    while (i <= 4) {
      xMethod(i);
      i++;
    }

    System.out.println("i is " + i);
  }

  public static void xMethod(int i) {
    do {
      if (i % 3 != 0)
        System.out.print(i + " ");
      i--;
    }
    while (i >= 1);

    System.out.println();
  }
}
```

(d)

4.12 For (a) in the preceding question, show the contents of the stack just before the method max is invoked, just entering max, just before max is returned, and right after max is returned.

Section 4.5 Overloading Methods

4.13 What is method overloading? Is it possible to define two methods that have the same name but different parameter types? Is it possible to define two methods in a class that have identical method names and parameter lists with different return value types or different modifiers?

4.14 What is wrong in the following program?

```
public class Test {
  public static void method(int x) {
  }

  public static int method(int y) {
    return y;
  }
}
```

Section 4.6 The Scope of Local Variables

4.15 Identify and correct the errors in the following program:

```
1 public class Test {
2   public static void main(String[] args) {
3     nPrintln("Welcome to Java!", 5);
4   }
5
6   public static void nPrintln(String message, int n) {
7     int n = 1;
8     for (int i = 0; i < n; i++)
9       System.out.println(message);
10  }
11 }
```

Section 4.8 The Math Class

4.16 Which of the following is a possible output from invoking Math.random()?

323.4, 0.5, 34, 1.0, 0.0, 0.234

4.17 Write an expression that returns a random integer between 34 and 55. Write an expression that returns a random integer between 0 and 999. Write an expression that returns a random number between 5.5 and 55.5. Write an expression that returns a random lowercase letter.

4.18 Evaluate the following method calls:

A. Math.sqrt(4)
B. Math.sin(2 * Math.PI)
C. Math.cos(2 * Math.PI)
D. Math.pow(2, 2)
E. Math.log(Math.E)
F. Math.exp(1)
G. Math.max(2, Math.min(3, 4))
H. Math.rint(-2.5)
I. Math.ceil(-2.5)

J. Math.floor(-2.5)
K. Math.round(-2.5f)
L. Math.round(-2.5)
M. Math.rint(2.5)
N. Math.ceil(2.5)
O. Math.floor(2.5)
P. Math.round(2.5f)
Q. Math.round(2.5)
R. Math.round(Math.abs(-2.5))

Section 4.11 Recursion (Optional)

4.19 What is a recursive method? Describe the characteristics of recursive methods.

4.20 Show the output of the following program:

```
public class Test {
  public static void main(String[] args) {
    System.out.println("Sum is " + xMethod(5));
  }

  public static int xMethod(int n) {
    if (n == 1)
      return 1;
    else
      return n + xMethod(n - 1);
  }
}
```

4.21   Show the output of the following two programs:

```
public class Test {
  public static void main(String[] args) {
    xMethod(5);
  }

  public static void xMethod(int n) {
    if (n > 0) {
      System.out.print(n + " ");
      xMethod(n - 1);
    }
  }
}
```

```
public class Test {
  public static void main(String[] args) {
    xMethod(5);
  }

  public static void xMethod(int n) {
    if (n > 0) {
      xMethod(n - 1);
      System.out.print(n + " ");
    }
  }
}
```

Section 4.12 Packages (Optional)

4.22   What are the benefits of using packages?

4.23   If a class uses the package statement "package java.chapter4", where should the source code be stored, and where should the .class files be stored? How do you make the class available for use by other programs?

4.24   Why do you have to import JOptionPane not the Math class?

PROGRAMMING EXERCISES

Sections 4.2–4.3

4.1   (*Converting an uppercase letter to lowercase*) Write a method that converts an uppercase letter to a lowercase letter. Use the following method header:

```
public static char upperCaseToLowerCase(char ch)
```

For example, upperCaseToLowerCase('B') returns b.

4.2   (*Summing the digits in an integer*) Write a method that computes the sum of the digits in an integer. Use the following method header:

```
public static int sumDigits(long n)
```

For example, sumDigits(234) returns $2 + 3 + 4 = 9$.

 HINT

Use the % operator to extract digits, and use the / operator to remove the extracted digit. For instance, $234 \% 10 = 4$ and $234 / 10 = 23$. Use a loop to repeatedly extract and remove the digit until all the digits are extracted.

4.3   (*Computing the future investment value*) Write a method that computes future investment value at a given interest rate for a specified number of years. The future investment is determined using the formula in Exercise 2.11.

Use the following method header:

```
public static double futureInvestmentValue(
  double investmentAmount, double monthlyInterestRate, int years)
```

For example, futureInvestmentValue(10000, 0.05 / 12, 5) returns 12833.59.

Write a test program that prompts the user to enter the investment amount (e.g., 1000) and the interest rate (e.g., 9%), and print a table that displays future value for the years from 1 to 30, as shown below:

```
The amount invested: 1000
Annual interest rate: 9%
Years          Future Value
1              1093.8
2              1196.41
...

29             13467.25
30             14730.57
```

4.4 (*Conversions between Celsius and Fahrenheit*) Write a class that contains the following two methods:

```
/** Converts from Celsius to Fahrenheit */
public static double celsiusToFahrenheit(double celsius)

/** Converts from Fahrenheit to Celsius */
public static double fahrenheitToCelsius(double fahrenheit)
```

The formula for the conversion is:

```
fahrenheit = (9.0 / 5) * celsius + 32
```

Write a test program that invokes these methods to display the following tables:

Celsius	Fahrenheit		Fahrenheit	Celsius
40.0	104.0		120.0	48.89
39.0	102.2		110.0	43.33
...				
32.0	89.6		40.0	4.44
31.0	87.8		30.0	-1.11

4.5 (*Conversions between feet and meters*) Write a class that contains the following two methods:

```
/** Converts from feet to meters */
public static double footToMeter(double foot)

/** Converts from meters to feet */
public static double meterToFoot(double meter)
```

The formula for the conversion is:

```
meter = 0.305 * foot
```

Write a test program that invokes these methods to display the following tables:

Feet	Meters		Meters	Feet
1.0	0.305		20.0	65.574
2.0	0.61		25.0	81.967
...				
9.0	2.745		60.0	195.721
10.0	3.05		65.0	213.115

4.6 (*Computing GCD*) Write a method that returns the greatest common divisor between two positive integers using the following header:

```
public static int gcd(int m, int n)
```

Write a test program that computes gcd(24, 16) and gcd(255, 25).

4.7 (*Computing commissions*) Write a method that computes the commission using the scheme in Example 3.8. The header of the method is as follows:

```
public static double computeCommission(double salesAmount)
```

Write a test program that displays the following tables:

```
SalesAmount     Commission
10000           900.0
15000           1500.0
...
95000           11100.0
100000          11700.0
```

4.8   (*Displaying characters*) Write a method that prints characters using the following header:

```
public static void printChars(char ch1, char ch2, int numberPerLine)
```

This method prints the characters between ch1 and ch2 with the specified numbers per line. Write a test program that prints ten characters per line from '1' and 'Z'.

4.9*   (*Printing a tax table*) Use the computeTax methods in Example 4.4 to write a program that prints a 2002 tax table for taxable income from $50,000 to $60,000 with intervals of $50 for all four statuses, as follows:

Taxable Income	Single	Married Joint	Married Separate	Head of a House
50000	9846	7296	10398	8506
50050	9859	7309	10411	8519
...				
59950	12532	9982	13190	11192
60000	12546	9996	13205	11206

4.10*   (*Revising Example 3.9 "Displaying Prime Numbers"*) Write a program that meets the following requirements:

✦ Declare a method to determine whether an integer is a prime number. Use the following method header:

```
public static boolean isPrime(int num)
```

An integer greater than 1 is a *prime number* if its only divisor is 1 or itself. For example, isPrime(11) returns true, and isPrime(9) returns false.

✦ Use the isPrime method to find the first thousand prime numbers and display every ten prime numbers in a row, as follows:

```
2 3 5 7 11 13 17 19 23 29
31 37 41 43 47 53 59 61 67 71
73 79 83 89 97 ...
...
```

Section 4.8 The Math Class

4.11*   (*Displaying matrix of 0s and 1s*) Write a method that displays an *n* by *n* matrix using the following header:

```
public static void printMatrix(int n)
```

Each element is 0 or 1, which is generated randomly. Write a test program that prints a 3 by 3 matrix that may look like this:

```
0 1 0
0 0 0
1 1 1
```

4.12   (*Using the* Math.sqrt *method*) Write a program that prints the following table using the sqrt method in the Math class:

```
Number    SquareRoot

0            0.0000
2            1.4142
...
18           4.2426
20           4.4721
```

4.13*   (*The* MyTriangle *class*) Create a class named MyTriangle that contains the following two methods:

```
public static boolean isValid(
   double side1, double side2, double side3)
```

Returns true if the sum of any two sides is greater than the third side.

```
public static double area(
   double side1, double side2, double side3)
```

Returns the area of the triangle.

The formula for computing the area is

$$s = (side1 + side2 + side3)/2;$$
$$area = \sqrt{s(s - side1)(s - side2)(s - side3)}$$

Write a test program that reads three sides for a triangle and computes the area if the input is valid. Otherwise, display that the input is invalid.

4.14   (*Using trigonometric methods*) Print the following table to display the sin value and cos value of degrees from 0 to 360 with increments of 10 degrees. Round the value to keep four digits after the decimal point.

```
Degree    Sin        Cos
0         0.0        1.0
10        0.1736     0.9848
...
350       -0.1736    0.9848
360       0.0        1.0
```

4.15** (*Computing mean and standard deviation*) In business applications, you are often asked to compute the mean and standard deviation of data. The mean is simply the average of the numbers. The standard deviation is a statistic that tells you how tightly all the various data are clustered around the mean in a set of data. For example, what is the average age of the students in a class? How close are the ages? If all the students are the same age, the deviation is 0. Write a program that generates ten random numbers between 0 and 1000, and computes the mean and standard deviations of these numbers using the following formula:

$$mean = \frac{\sum_{i=1}^{n} x_i}{n} = \frac{x_1 + x_2 + \cdots + x_n}{n} \qquad deviation = \sqrt{\frac{\sum_{i=1}^{n} x_i^2 - \frac{\left(\sum_{i=1}^{n} x_i\right)^2}{n}}{n - 1}}$$

4.16** (*Approximating the square root*) implement the sqrt method. The square root of a number, num, can be approximated by repeatedly performing a calculation using the following formula:

```
nextGuess = (lastGuess + (num / lastGuess)) / 2
```

When `nextGuess` and `lastGuess` are almost identical, `nextGuess` is the approximated square root. The initial guess will be the starting value of `lastGuess`. If the difference between `nextGuess` and `lastGuess` is less than a very small number, such as 0.0001, you can claim that `nextGuess` is the approximated square root of `num`.

Sections 4.9–4.10

4.17* (*Generating random characters*) Use the methods in `RandomCharacter` in Listing 4.5 to print one hundred uppercase letters and then one hundred single digits, and print ten per line.

4.18* (*Displaying current date and time*) Example 2.5, "Displaying Current Time," displays the current time. Improve this example to display the current date and time. The calendar example in Section 4.10, "Stepwise Refinement," should give you some ideas on how to find year, month, and day.

Section 4.11 Recursion (Optional)

4.19 (*Computing factorials*) Rewrite Example 4.5, "Computing Factorials," using iterations.

4.20* (*Fibonacci numbers*) Revise Example 4.6, "Computing Fibonacci Numbers," using a nonrecursive method that computes Fibonacci numbers.

 HINT

To compute `fib(n)` without recursion, you need to obtain `fib(n - 2)` and `fib(n - 1)` first. Let `f0` and `f1` denote the two previous Fibonacci numbers. The current Fibonacci number would then be `f0 + f1`. The algorithm can be described as follows:

```
f0 = 0; // For fib(0)
f1 = 1; // For fib(1)
for (int i = 1; i <= n; i++) {
  currentFib = f0 + f1;
  f0 = f1;
  f1 = currentFib;
}
// After the loop, currentFib is fib(n)
```

4.21* (*Towers of Hanoi*) Modify Example 4.7, "Solving the Towers of Hanoi Problem," so that the program finds the number of moves needed to move *n* disks from tower A to tower B.

4.22* (*Computing greatest common divisor using recursion*) The `gcd(m, n)` can also be defined recursively as follows:

◆ If `m % n` is 0, `gcd (m, n)` is `n`.

◆ Otherwise, `gcd(m, n)` is `gcd(n, m % n)`.

Write a recursive method to find the GCD. Write a test program that computes `gcd(24, 16)` and `gcd(255, 25)`.

4.23* (*Printing message using recursion*) Write a method with the following header that displays a message *n* times using recursion.

```
public static void displayMessage(String message, int times)
```

4.24** (*Summing the digits in an integer using recursion*) Rewrite Exercise 4.2 using recursion.

4.25** (*Summing the series*) Write a recursive method and a nonrecursive method to compute the following function (for $i > 1$):

$$m(i) = \frac{1}{2} + \frac{2}{3} + \cdots + \frac{i}{i + 1}$$

Write a test program that displays the following table:

```
i       m(i)
2       0.5
3       1.1667
...
19      15.4523
20      16.4023
```

chapter

5

ARRAYS

Objectives

- ✦ To describe why an array is necessary in programming (§5.1).

- ✦ To learn the steps involved in using arrays: declaring array reference variables and creating arrays (§§5.2.1-5.2.2).

- ✦ To initialize the values in an array (§5.2.3).

- ✦ To access array elements using indexed variables (§5.2.4).

- ✦ To simplify programming using the JDK 1.5 enhanced for loop (§5.2.5).

- ✦ To declare, create, and initialize an array using an array initializer (§5.2.6).

- ✦ To copy contents from one array to another (§5.3).

- ✦ To develop and invoke methods with array arguments and return value (§§5.4–5.5).

- ✦ To sort an array using the selection sort algorithm (§5.6).

- ✦ To search elements using the linear or binary search algorithm (§5.7).

- ✦ To declare and create multidimensional arrays (§5.8.1).

- ✦ To obtain the lengths of multidimensional arrays (§5.8.2).

- ✦ To create ragged arrays (§5.8.3).

5.1   Introduction

why array?

Often you will have to store a large number of values during the execution of a program. Suppose, for instance, that you want to read one hundred numbers, compute their average, and find out how many numbers are above the average. Your program first reads the numbers and computes their average, and then compares each number with the average to determine whether it is above the average. The numbers must all be stored in variables in order to accomplish this task. You have to declare one hundred variables and repetitively write almost identical code one hundred times. From the standpoint of practicality, it is impossible to write a program this way. An efficient, organized approach is needed. Java and all other high-level languages provide a data structure, the *array*, which stores a fixed-size sequential collection of elements of identical types.

array

5.2   Array Basics

This section introduces how to declare array variables, create arrays, and process arrays.

5.2.1   Declaring Array Variables

To use an array in a program, you must declare a variable to reference the array and specify the type of array the variable can reference. Here is the syntax for declaring an array variable:

preferred syntax

```
dataType[] arrayRefVar;
```

or

```
dataType arrayRefVar[]; // This style is correct, but not preferred
```

The following code snippets are examples of this syntax:

```
double[] myList;
```

or

```
double myList[]; // This style is correct, but not preferred
```

 NOTE

The style `dataType[] arrayRefVar` is preferred. The style `dataType arrayRefVar[]` comes from the C language and was adopted in Java to accommodate C programmers.

5.2.2   Creating Arrays

Unlike declarations for primitive data type variables, the declaration of an array variable does not allocate any space in memory for the array. Only a storage location for the reference to an array is created. If a variable does not reference to an array, the value of the variable is `null`. You cannot assign elements to an array unless it has already been created. After an array variable is declared, you can create an array by using the `new` operator with the following syntax:

new operator

```
arrayRefVar = new dataType[arraySize];
```

This statement does two things: (1) it creates an array using `new dataType[arraySize]`; (2) it assigns the reference of the newly created array to the variable `arrayRefVar`.

Declaring an array variable, creating an array, and assigning the reference of the array to the variable can be combined in one statement, as shown below:

```
dataType[] arrayRefVar = new dataType[arraySize];
```

or

```
dataType arrayRefVar[] = new dataType[arraySize];
```

Here is an example of such a statement:

```
double[] myList = new double[10];
```

This statement declares an array variable, myList, creates an array of ten elements of double type, and assigns its reference to myList, as shown in Figure 5.1.

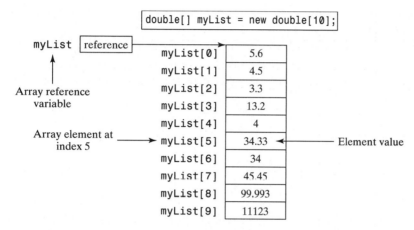

FIGURE 5.1 *The array* myList *has ten elements of* double *type and* int *indices from 0 to 9.*

  NOTE

An array variable that appears to hold an array actually contains a reference to that array. Strictly speaking, an array variable and an array are different, but most of the time the distinction between them can be ignored. Thus it is all right to say, for simplicity, that myList is an array, instead of stating, at greater length, that myList is a variable that contains a reference to an array of ten double elements. When the distinction makes a subtle difference, the longer phrase should be used.

array vs. array variable

5.2.3 Array Size and Default Values

When space for an array is allocated, the array size must be given, to specify the number of elements that can be stored in it. The size of an array cannot be changed after the array is created. Size can be obtained using arrayRefVar.length. For example, myList.length is 10.

array length

When an array is created, its elements are assigned the *default value* of 0 for the numeric primitive data types, '\u0000' for char types, and false for boolean types.

default values

5.2.4 Array Indexed Variables

The array elements are accessed through the index. Array indices are *0-based*; that is, they start from 0 to arrayRefVar.length-1. In the example in Figure 5.1, myList holds ten double values and the indices are from 0 to 9.

array index
0-based

index variables

Each element in the array is represented using the following syntax, known as an *indexed variable*:

```
arrayRefVar[index];
```

For example, myList[9] represents the last element in the array myList.

 NOTE

In Java, an array index must be an integer or an integer expression. In many other languages, such as Ada and Pascal, the index can be either an integer or another type of value.

 CAUTION

Some languages use parentheses to reference an array element, as in myList(9). But Java uses brackets, as in myList[9].

After an array is created, an indexed variable can be used in the same way as a regular variable. For example, the following code adds the value in myList[0] and myList[1] to myList[2]:

```
myList[2] = myList[0] + myList[1];
```

The following loop assigns 0 to myList[0], 1 to myList[1], ..., and 9 to myList[9]:

```
for (int i = 0; i < myList.length; i++)
  myList[i] = i;
```

5.2.5 Enhanced for Loop (JDK 1.5 Feature)

JDK 1.5 introduced a new for loop that enables you to traverse the complete array sequentially without using an index variable. For example, the following code displays all the elements in the array myList:

```
for (double value: myList)
  System.out.println(value);
```

In general, the syntax is

```
for (elementType value: arrayRefVar) {
  // Process the value
}
```

You still have to use an index variable if you wish to traverse the array in a different order or change the elements in the array.

5.2.6 Array Initializers

array initializer

Java has a shorthand notation, known as the *array initializer*, which combines declaring an array, creating an array, and initializing in one statement using the following syntax:

```
dataType[] arrayRefVar = {literal0, literal1, ..., literalk};
```

For example,

```
double[] myList = {1.9, 2.9, 3.4, 3.5};
```

This statement declares, creates, and initializes the array `myList` with four elements, which is equivalent to the statements shown below:

```
double[] myList = new double[4];
myList[0] = 1.9;
myList[1] = 2.9;
myList[2] = 3.4;
myList[3] = 3.5;
```

 CAUTION

The `new` operator is not used in the array initializer syntax. Using an array initializer, you have to declare, create, and initialize the array all in one statement. Splitting it would cause a syntax error. Thus the next statement is wrong:

```
double[] myList;
myList = {1.9, 2.9, 3.4, 3.5};
```

 NOTE

You can also create and initialize an array using the following syntax:

```
new dataType[]{literal0, literal1, ..., literalk};
```

For example, these statements are correct:

```
double[] myList = {1, 2, 3};
// Some time later you need assign a new array to myList
myList = new double[]{1.9, 2.9, 3.4, 3.5};
```

When processing array elements, you will often use a `for` loop. Here are the reasons why:

✦ All of the elements in an array are of the same type. They are evenly processed in the same fashion by repeatedly using a loop.

✦ Since the size of the array is known, it is natural to use a `for` loop.

EXAMPLE 5.1 TESTING ARRAYS

Problem

Write a program that reads six integers, finds the largest of them, and counts its occurrences. Suppose that you entered 3, 5, 2, 5, 5, 5, as shown in Figure 5.2; the program finds that the largest is 5 and the occurrence count for 5 is 4.

Solution

An intuitive solution is to first read the numbers and store them in an array, then find the largest number in the array, and finally count the occurrences of the largest number in the array.

EXAMPLE 5.1 (CONTINUED)

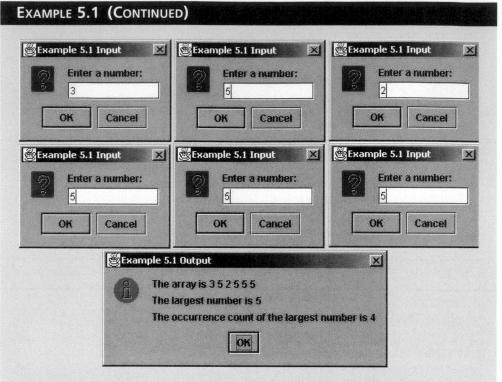

FIGURE 5.2 *The program finds the largest number and counts its occurrences.*

LISTING 5.1 TestArray.java (Using Arrays)

```
1 import javax.swing.JOptionPane;
2
3 public class TestArray {
4   /** Main method */
5   public static void main(String[] args) {
6     final int TOTAL_NUMBERS = 6;
7     int[] numbers = new int[TOTAL_NUMBERS];
8
9     // Read all numbers
10    for (int i = 0; i < numbers.length; i++) {
11      String numString = JOptionPane.showInputDialog(null,
12        "Enter a number:",
13        "Example 5.1 Input", JOptionPane.QUESTION_MESSAGE);
14
15      // Convert string into integer
16      numbers[i] = Integer.parseInt(numString);
17    }
18
19    // Find the largest
20    int max = numbers[0];
21    for (int i = 1; i < numbers.length; i++) {
22      if (max < numbers[i])
23        max = numbers[i];
24    }
25
26    // Find the occurrence of the largest number
27    int count = 0;
28    for (int i = 0; i < numbers.length; i++) {
29      if (numbers[i] == max) count++;
30    }
31
```

create array

store numbers

update max

count occurrence

EXAMPLE 5.1 (CONTINUED)

```
32     // Prepare the result
33     String output = "The array is ";
34     for (int i = 0; i < numbers.length; i++) {
35       output += numbers[i] + " ";
36     }
37
38     output += "\nThe largest number is " + max;
39     output += "\nThe occurrence count of the largest number "
40       + "is " + count;
41
42     // Display the result
43     JOptionPane.showMessageDialog(null, output,
44       "Example 5.1 Output", JOptionPane.INFORMATION_MESSAGE);
45   }
46 }
```

prepare output

output

Review

The program declares and creates an array of six integers (Line 7). It finds the largest number in the array (Lines 20–24), counts its occurrences (Lines 27–30), and displays the result (Lines 32–44). To display the array, you need to display each element in the array using a loop.

Without using the numbers array, you would have to declare a variable for each number entered, because all the numbers are compared to the largest number to count its occurrences after it is found.

🌿 CAUTION

Accessing an array out of bounds is a common programming error, which throws a runtime ArrayIndexOutOfBoundsException. To avoid it, make sure that you do not use an index beyond arrayRefVar.length - 1.

Programmers often mistakenly reference the first element in an array with index 1, so that the index of the tenth element becomes 10. This is called the *off-by-one error*.

ArrayIndexOutOfBounds Exception

off-by-one error

EXAMPLE 5.2 ASSIGNING GRADES

Problem

Write a program that reads student scores, gets the best score, and then assigns grades based on the following scheme:

Grade is A if score is $>=$ best -10;

Grade is B if score is $>=$ best -20;

Grade is C if score is $>=$ best -30;

Grade is D if score is $>=$ best -40;

Grade is F otherwise.

The program prompts the user to enter the total number of students, then prompts the user to enter all of the scores, and concludes by displaying the grades.

EXAMPLE 5.2 (CONTINUED)

Solution

The program reads the scores, then finds the best score, and finally assigns grades to the students based on the preceding scheme. Listing 5.2 gives the solution to the problem. The output of a sample run of the program is shown in Figure 5.3.

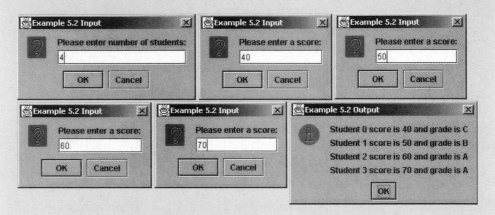

FIGURE **5.3** *The program receives the number of students and their scores, and then assigns grades.*

LISTING 5.2 **AssignGrade.java (Assigning Grades)**

```
1 import javax.swing.JOptionPane;
2
3 public class AssignGrade {
4   /** Main method */
5   public static void main(String[] args) {
6     int numberOfStudents = 0; // The number of students
7     int[] scores; // Array scores
8     int best = 0; // The best score
9     char grade; // The grade
10
11     // Get number of students
12     String numberOfStudentsString = JOptionPane.showInputDialog(
13       null, "Please enter number of students:",
14       "Example 5.2 Input", JOptionPane.QUESTION_MESSAGE);
15
16     // Convert string into integer
17     numberOfStudents = Integer.parseInt(numberOfStudentsString);
18
19     // Create array scores
20     scores = new int[numberOfStudents];
21
22     // Read scores and find the best score
23     for (int i = 0; i < scores.length; i++) {
24       String scoreString = JOptionPane.showInputDialog(null,
25         "Please enter a score:",
26         "Example 5.2 Input", JOptionPane.QUESTION_MESSAGE);
27
28       // Convert string into integer
29       scores[i] = Integer.parseInt(scoreString);
30       if (scores[i] > best)
31         best = scores[i];
32     }
33
```

declare array — line 7

create array — line 20

get a score — line 24

update best — line 30

EXAMPLE 5.2 (CONTINUED)

```
34     // Declare and initialize output string
35     String output = "";
36
37     // Assign and display grades
38     for (int i = 0; i < scores.length; i++) {
39       if (scores[i] >= best - 10)
40         grade = 'A';
41       else if (scores[i] >= best - 20)
42         grade = 'B';
43       else if (scores[i] >= best - 30)
44         grade = 'C';
45       else if (scores[i] >= best - 40)
46         grade = 'D';
47       else
48         grade = 'F';
49
50       output += "Student " + i + " score is " +
51         scores[i] + " and grade is " + grade + "\n";
52     }
53
54     // Display the result
55     JOptionPane.showMessageDialog(null, output,
56       "Example 5.2 Output", JOptionPane.INFORMATION_MESSAGE);
57   }
58 }
```

assign grade

Review

The program declares `scores` as an array of `int` type in order to store the students' scores (Line 7). After the user enters the number of students into `numberOfStudents` in Lines 12–17, an array with the size `numberOfStudents` is created in Line 20. The size of the array is set at runtime; it cannot be changed once the array is created.

The array is not needed to find the best score, but it is needed to keep all of the scores so that grades can be assigned later on, and it is needed when scores are printed along with the students' grades.

5.3   Copying Arrays

Often, in a program, you need to duplicate an array or a part of an array. In such cases you could attempt to use the assignment statement (=), as follows:

```
list2 = list1;
```

This statement does not copy the contents of the array referenced by `list1` to `list2`, but merely copies the reference value from `list1` to `list2`. After this statement, `list1` and `list2` reference to the same array, as shown in Figure 5.4. The array previously referenced by `list2` is no longer referenced; it becomes garbage, which will be automatically collected by the Java Virtual Machine.

copy reference

In Java, you can use assignment statements to copy primitive data type variables, but not arrays. Assigning one array variable to another array variable actually copies one reference to another and makes both variables point to the same memory location.

There are three ways to copy arrays:

✦ Use a loop to copy individual elements.

✦ Use the static `arraycopy` method in the `System` class.

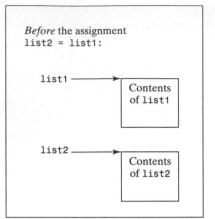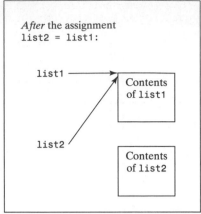

FIGURE 5.4 *Before the assignment statement,* list1 *and* list2 *point to separate memory locations. After the assignment, the reference of the* list1 *array is passed to* list2.

✦ Use the clone method to copy arrays; this will be introduced in Chapter 8, "Inheritance and Polymorphism."

You can write a loop to copy every element from the source array to the corresponding element in the target array. The following code, for instance, copies sourceArray to targetArray using a for loop:

```
int[] sourceArray = {2, 3, 1, 5, 10};
int[] targetArray = new int[sourceArray.length];
for (int i = 0; i < sourceArray.length; i++)
  targetArray[i] = sourceArray[i];
```

arraycopy method

Another approach is to use the arraycopy method in the java.lang.System class to copy arrays instead of using a loop. The syntax for arraycopy is as follows:

```
arraycopy(sourceArray, src_pos, targetArray, tar_pos, length);
```

The parameters src_pos and tar_pos indicate the starting positions in sourceArray and targetArray, respectively. The number of elements copied from sourceArray to target-Array is indicated by length. For example, you can rewrite the loop using the following statement:

```
System.arraycopy(sourceArray, 0, targetArray, 0, sourceArray.length);
```

The arraycopy method does not allocate memory space for the target array. The target array must have already been created with its memory space allocated. After the copying takes place, targetArray and sourceArray have the same content but independent memory locations.

 NOTE
The arraycopy method violates the Java naming convention. By convention, this method should be named arrayCopy.

5.4 Passing Arrays to Methods

Just as you can pass the primitive type values to methods, you can also pass the arrays to methods. For example, the following method displays the elements in an int array:

```java
public static void printArray(int[] array) {
  for (int i = 0; i < array.length; i++) {
    System.out.print(array[i] + " ");
  }
}
```

You can invoke it by passing an array. For example, the next statement invokes the `printArray` method to display 3, 1, 2, 6, 4, and 2:

```java
printArray(new int[]{3, 1, 2, 6, 4, 2});
```

 NOTE

The preceding statement creates an array using the following syntax: anonymous array

```java
new dataType[]{literal0, literal1, . . . , literalk};
```

There is no explicit reference variable for the array. Such array is called an anonymous array.

Java uses *pass by value* to pass arguments to a method. There are important differences between   pass by value
passing the values of variables of primitive data types and passing arrays.

◆ For an argument of a primitive type, the argument's value is passed.

◆ For an argument of an array type, the value of the argument contains a reference to an array; this reference is passed to the method.

Take the following code for example:

```java
public class Test {
  public static void main(String[] args) {
    int x = 1; // x represents an int value
    int[] y = new int[10]; // y represents an array of int values

    m(x, y); // Invoke m with arguments x and y

    System.out.println("x is " + x);
    System.out.println("y[0] is " + y[0]);
  }

  public static void m(int number, int[] numbers) {
    number = 1001; // Assign a new value to number
    numbers[0] = 5555; // Assign a new value to numbers[0]
  }
}
```

You will see that after m is invoked, x remains 1, but y[0] is 5555. This is because y and numbers reference to the same array, although y and numbers are independent variables, as illustrated in Figure 5.5. When invoking m(x, y), the values of x and y are passed to number and numbers. Since y contains the reference value to the array, numbers now contains the same reference value to the same array.

 NOTE

The JVM stores the array in an area of memory called *heap*, which is used for dy-   heap
namic memory allocation where blocks of memory are allocated and freed in an arbitrary order.

The following is another example that shows the difference between passing a primitive data type value and an array reference variable to a method.

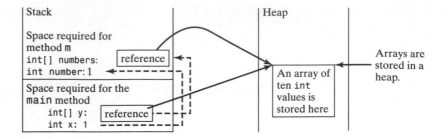

FIGURE 5.5 *The primitive type value in* x *is passed to* number, *and the reference value in* y *is passed to* numbers.

EXAMPLE 5.3 PASSING ARRAYS AS ARGUMENTS

Problem

Write two methods for swapping elements in an array. The first method, named swap, fails to swap two int arguments. The second method, named swapFirstTwoInArray, successfully swaps the first two elements in the array argument.

Solution

Listing 5.3 gives the program. Figure 5.6 shows a sample run of the program.

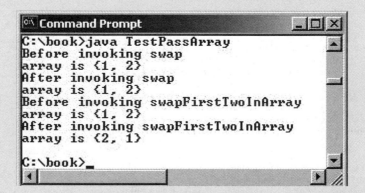

FIGURE 5.6 *The program attempts to swap two elements using the* swap *method and the* swapFirstTwoInArray *method.*

LISTING 5.3   TestPassArray.java (Passing Array Arguments)

```
 1 public class TestPassArray {
 2   /** Main method */
 3   public static void main(String[] args) {
 4     int[] a = {1, 2};
 5
 6     // Swap elements using the swap method
 7     System.out.println("Before invoking swap");
 8     System.out.println("array is {" + a[0] + ", " + a[1] + "}");
 9     swap(a[0], a[1]);
10     System.out.println("After invoking swap");
11     System.out.println("array is {" + a[0] + ", " + a[1] + "}");
12
```

false swap

EXAMPLE 5.3 (CONTINUED)

```
13      // Swap elements using the swapFirstTwoInArray method
14      System.out.println("Before invoking swapFirstTwoInArray");
15      System.out.println("array is {" + a[0] + ", " + a[1] + "}");
16      swapFirstTwoInArray(a);
17      System.out.println("After invoking swapFirstTwoInArray");
18      System.out.println("array is {" + a[0] + ", " + a[1] + "}");
19    }
20
21    /** Swap two variables */
22    public static void swap(int n1, int n2) {
23      int temp = n1;
24      n1 = n2;
25      n2 = temp;
26    }
27
28    /** Swap the first two elements in the array */
29    public static void swapFirstTwoInArray(int[] array) {
30      int temp = array[0];
31      array[0] = array[1];
32      array[1] = temp;
33    }
34  }
```

swap array elements

Review

As shown in Figure 5.6, the two elements are not swapped using the swap method. However, they are swapped using the swapFirstTwoInArray method. Since the parameters in the swap method are primitive type, the values of a[0] and a[1] are passed to n1 and n2 inside the method when invoking swap(a[0], a[1]). The memory locations for n1 and n2 are independent of the ones for a[0] and a[1]. The contents of the array are not affected by this call. This is pictured in Figure 5.7.

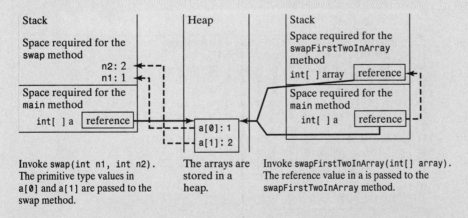

FIGURE 5.7 *When passing an array to a method, the reference of the array is passed to the method.*

The parameter in the swapFirstTwoInArray method is an array. As shown in Figure 5.7, the reference of the array is passed to the method. Thus the variables a (outside the method) and array (inside the method) both refer to the same array in the same memory location. Therefore, swapping array[0] with array[1] inside the method swapFirst TwoInArray is the same as swapping a[0] with a[1] outside of the method.

5.5   Returning an Array from a Method

You can pass arrays to invoke a method. A method may also return an array. For example, the method shown below returns an array that is the reversal of another array:

create array

```
 1 public static int[] reverse(int[] list) {
 2   int[] result = new int[list.length];
 3
 4   for (int i = 0, j = result.length - 1;
 5        i < list.length; i++, j--) {
 6     result[j] = list[i];
 7   }
 8
 9   return result;
10 }
```

return array

Line 2 creates a new array result. Lines 4–7 copies elements from array list to array result. Line 9 returns the array. For example, the following statement returns a new array list2 with elements 6, 5, 4, 3, 2, 1:

```
int[] list1 = {1, 2, 3, 4, 5, 6};
int[] list2 = reverse(list1);
```

EXAMPLE 5.4 COUNTING THE OCCURRENCES OF EACH LETTER

Problem

Write a program that does the following:

1. Generate one hundred lowercase letters randomly and assign them to an array of characters.

2. Count the occurrences of each letter in the array.

   Figure 5.8 shows a sample run of the program.

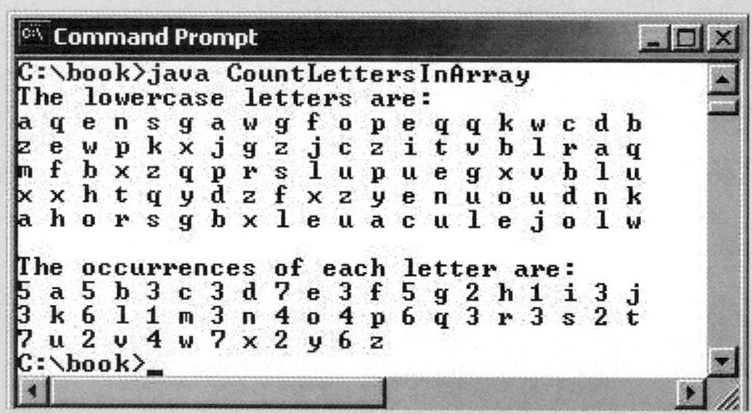

FIGURE 5.8   *The program generates one hundred lowercase letters randomly and counts the occurrences of each letter.*

Solution

1. You can obtain a random letter by using the getRandomLowerCaseLetter() method in the RandomCharacter class on page 142.

2. To count the occurrences of each letter in the array, create an array, say counts of twenty-six int values, each of which counts the occurrences of a letter. That is, counts[0] counts the number of a's, counts[1] counts the number of b's, and so on.

EXAMPLE 5.4 (CONTINUED)

LISTING 5.4   CountLettersInArray.java (Counting Letters)

```java
1  public class CountLettersInArray {
2    /** Main method */
3    public static void main(String args[]) {
4      // Declare and create an array
5      char[] chars = createArray();                              // create array
6
7      // Display the array
8      System.out.println("The lowercase letters are:");
9      displayArray(chars);                                       // pass array
10
11     // Count the occurrences of each letter
12     int[] counts = countLetters(chars);                        // return array
13
14     // Display counts
15     System.out.println();
16     System.out.println("The occurrences of each letter are:");
17     displayCounts(counts);                                     // pass array
18   }
19
20   /** Create an array of characters */
21   public static char[] createArray() {
22     // Declare an array of characters and create it
23     char[] chars = new char[100];
24
25     // Create lowercase letters randomly and assign
26     // them to the array
27     for (int i = 0; i < chars.length; i++)
28       chars[i] = RandomCharacter.getRandomLowerCaseLetter();
29
30     // Return the array
31     return chars;
32   }
33
34   /** Display the array of characters */
35   public static void displayArray(char[] chars) {
36     // Display the characters in the array 20 on each line
37     for (int i = 0; i < chars.length; i++) {
38       if ((i + 1) % 20 == 0)
39         System.out.println(chars[i] + " ");
40       else
41         System.out.print(chars[i] + " ");
42     }
43   }
44
45   /** Count the occurrences of each letter */
46   public static int[] countLetters(char[] chars) {
47     // Declare and create an array of 26 int
48     int[] counts = new int[26];
49
50     // For each lowercase letter in the array, count it
51     for (int i = 0; i < chars.length; i++)
52       counts[chars[i] - 'a']++;                                // count
53
54     return counts;
55   }
56
57   /** Display counts */
58   public static void displayCounts(int[] counts) {
59     for (int i = 0; i < counts.length; i++) {
60       if ((i + 1) % 10 == 0)
61         System.out.println(counts[i] + " " + (char)(i + 'a'));
62       else
63         System.out.print(counts[i] + " " + (char)(i + 'a') + " ");
64     }
65   }
66 }
```

EXAMPLE 5.4 (CONTINUED)

Review

The `createArray` method (Lines 21–32) generates an array of one hundred random lower-case letters. Line 5 invokes the method and assigns the array to `chars`. What would be wrong if you rewrote the code as follows?

```
char[] chars = new char[100];
chars = createArray();
```

You would be creating two arrays. The first line would create an array by using `new char[100]`. The second line would create an array by invoking `createArray()` and assign the reference of the array to `chars`. The array created in the first line would be garbage because it is no longer referenced. Java automatically collects garbage behind the scenes. Your program would compile and run correctly, but it would create an array unnecessarily.

Invoking `getRandomLowerCaseLetter()` (Line 28) returns a random lowercase letter. This method is defined in the `RandomCharacter` class on page 142.

The `countLetters` method (Lines 46–55) returns an array of twenty-six int values, each of which stores the number of occurrences of a letter. The method processes each letter in the array and increases its count by one. A brute-force approach to count the occurrences of each letter might be as follows:

```
for (int i = 0; i < chars.length; i++)
  if (counts[chars[i] == 'a') count[0]++;
  else if (counts[chars[i] == 'b') count[1]++;
  ...
```

But a better solution is given in Lines 51–52.

```
for (int i = 0; i < chars.length; i++)
  counts[chars[i] - 'a']++;
```

If the letter (`chars[i]`) is `'a'`, the corresponding count is `counts['a' - 'a']` (i.e., `counts[0]`). If the letter is `'b'`, the corresponding count is `counts['b' - 'a']` (i.e., `counts[1]`) since the Unicode of `'b'` is one more than that of `'a'`. If the letter is `'z'`, the corresponding count is `counts['z' - 'a']` (i.e., `counts[25]`) since the Unicode of `'z'` is 25 more than that of `'a'`.

Figure 5.9 shows the call stack and heap *during* and *after* executing `createArray`. See Review Question 5.14 to show the call stack and heap for other methods in the program.

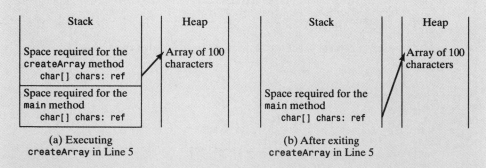

FIGURE 5.9 *(a) An array of one hundred characters is created when executing* `createArray`. *(b) This array is returned and assigned to the variable* `chars` *in the* main *method.*

5.6 Sorting Arrays

Sorting is a common task in computer programming. It would be used, for instance, if you wanted to display the grades from Example 5.2, "Assigning Grades," in alphabetical order. Many different algorithms have been developed for sorting. In this section, a simple, intuitive sorting algorithm, *selection sort*, is introduced.

selection sort

Suppose that you want to sort a list in ascending order. Selection sort finds the largest number in the list and places it last. It then finds the largest number remaining and places it next to last, and so on until the list contains only a single number. Figure 5.10 shows how to sort the list {2, 9, 5, 4, 8, 1, 6} using selection sort.

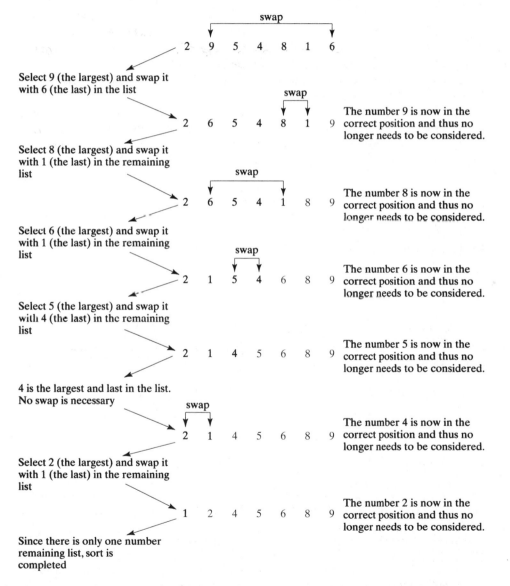

FIGURE 5.10 *Selection sort repeatedly selects the largest number and swaps it with the last number in the list.*

You know how the selection sort approach works. The task now is to implement it in Java. For beginners, it is difficult to develop a complete solution on the first attempt. I suggest that you write the code for the first iteration to find the largest element in the list and swap it with the last element, and then observe what would be different for the second iteration, the third, and so on. The insight this gives you will enable you to write a loop that generalizes all the iterations.

The solution can be described as follows:

```
for (int i = list.length - 1; i >= 1; i--) {
  select the largest element in list[0..i];
  swap the largest with list[i], if necessary;
  // list[i] is in place. The next iteration apply on list[0..i-1]
}
```

Listing 5.5 implements the solution.

LISTING 5.5 SelectionSort.java (Sorting Numbers)

```
1 public class SelectionSort {
2   /** The method for sorting the numbers */
3   public static void selectionSort(double[] list) {
4     for (int i = list.length - 1; i >= 1; i--) {
5       // Find the maximum in the list[0..i]
6       double currentMax = list[0];
7       int currentMaxIndex = 0;
8
9       for (int j = 1; j <= i; j++) {
10        if (currentMax < list[j]) {
11          currentMax = list[j];
12          currentMaxIndex = j;
13        }
14      }
15
16      // Swap list[i] with list[currentMaxIndex] if necessary;
17      if (currentMaxIndex != i) {
18        list[currentMaxIndex] = list[i];
19        list[i] = currentMax;
20      }
21    }
22  }
23 }
```

The selectionSort(double[] list) method sorts any array of double elements. The method is implemented with a nested for loop. The outer loop (with the loop control variable i) (Line 4) is iterated in order to find the largest element in the list, which ranges from list[0] to list[i], and exchange it with the current last element, list[i].

The variable i is initially list.length - 1. After each iteration of the outer loop, list[i] is in the right place. Eventually, all the elements are put in the right place; therefore, the whole list is sorted.

Please trace the method with the following statements:

```
selectionSort(new double[]{2, 1});
selectionSort(new double[]{2, 3, 1});
selectionSort(new double[]{1, 2, 1});
```

🌸 TIP

Since sorting is frequently used in programming, Java provides several overloaded sort methods for sorting an array of int, double, char, short, long, and float in the java.util.Arrays class. For example, the code shown below sorts an array of numbers and an array of characters:

```
double[] numbers = {5.0, 4.4, 1.9, 2.9, 3.4, 3.5};
java.util.Arrays.sort(numbers);

char[] chars = {'a', 'A', '4', 'F', 'D', 'P'};
java.util.Arrays.sort(chars);
```

5.7 Searching Arrays

Searching is the process of looking for a specific element in an array; for example, discovering whether a certain score is included in a list of scores. Searching, like sorting, is a common task in computer programming. There are many algorithms and data structures devoted to searching. In this section, two commonly used approaches are discussed, *linear search* and *binary search*.

5.7.1 The Linear Search Approach

The *linear search* approach compares the key element key with each element in the array. The method continues to do so until the key matches an element in the array or the array is exhausted without a match being found. If a match is made, the linear search returns the index of the element in the array that matches the key. If no match is found, the search returns - 1. The linearSearch method in Listing 5.6 gives the solution.

linear search

LISTING 5.6 **LinearSearch.java (Linear Search)**

```
1 public class LinearSearch {
2   /** The method for finding a key in the list */
3   public static int linearSearch(int[] list, int key) {
4     for (int i = 0; i < list.length; i++)
5       if (key == list[i])
6         return i;
7     return - 1;
8   }
9 }
```

Please trace the method using the following statements:

```
int[] list = {1, 4, 4, 2, 5, -3, 6, 2};
int i = linearSearch(list, 4); //  returns 1
int j = linearSearch(list, -4); // returns - 1
int k = linearSearch(list, -3); // returns 5
```

The linear search method compares the key with each element in the array. The elements in the array can be in any order. On average, the algorithm will have to compare half of the elements in an array. Since the execution time of a linear search increases linearly as the number of array elements increases, linear search is inefficient for a large array.

5.7.2 The Binary Search Approach

Binary search is the other common search approach. For binary search to work, the elements in the array must already be ordered. Without loss of generality, assume that the array is in ascending order. The binary search first compares the key with the element in the middle of the array. Consider the following three cases:

binary search

✦ If the key is less than the middle element, you only need to search the key in the first half of the array.

✦ If the key is equal to the middle element, the search ends with a match.

✦ If the key is greater than the middle element, you only need to search the key in the second half of the array.

Clearly, the binary search method eliminates half of the array after each comparison. Suppose that the array has *n* elements. For convenience, let n be a power of 2. After the first comparison, there are $n/2$ elements left for further search; after the second comparison, there are $(n/2)/2$ elements left for further search. After the kth comparison, there are $n/2^k$ elements left for further search. When k = log₂n, only one element is left in the array, and you only need one more comparison. Therefore, in the worst case, you need $\log_2 n + 1$ comparisons to find an element in the sorted array when using the binary search approach. For a list of 1024 (2^{10}) elements, binary search requires only eleven comparisons in the worst case, whereas a linear search would take 1024 comparisons in the worst case.

The portion of the array being searched shrinks by half after each comparison. Let low and high denote, respectively, the first index and last index of the array that is currently being searched. Initially, low is 0 and high is list.length - 1. Let mid denote the index of the middle element. So mid is (low + high)/2. Figure 5.11 shows how to find key 11 in the list {2, 4, 7, 10, 11, 45, 50, 59, 60, 66, 69, 70, 79} using binary search.

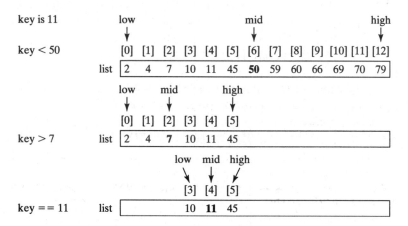

FIGURE 5.11   *Binary search eliminates half of the list from further consideration after each comparison.*

The binary search returns the index of the search key if it is contained in the list. Otherwise, it returns –insertion point −1. The insertion point is the point at which the key would be inserted into the list. For example, the insertion point for key 5 is 2, so the binary search returns −3; the insertion point for key 51 is 7, so the binary search returns −8.

You know how the binary approach works. The task now is to implement it in Java, as shown in Listing 5.7.

LISTING 5.7   BinarySearch.java (Binary Search)

```java
 1  public class BinarySearch {
 2    /** Use binary search to find the key in the list */
 3    public static int binarySearch(int[] list, int key) {
 4      int low = 0;
 5      int high = list.length - 1;
 6
 7      while (high >= low) {
 8        int mid = (low + high) / 2;
 9        if (key < list[mid])
10          high = mid - 1;
11        else if (key == list[mid])
12          return mid;
13        else
14          low = mid + 1;
15      }
16
17      return -low - 1;
18    }
19  }
```

You start to compare the key with the middle element in the list whose low index is 0 and high index is list.length - 1. If key < list[mid], set the high index to mid - 1; if key == list[mid], a match is found and return mid; if key > list[mid], set the low index to mid + 1.

Continue the search until low > high or a match is found. If low > high, return -1 - low, where low is the insertion point.

What happens if (high >= low) in Line 7 is replaced by (high > low)? The search would miss a possible matching element. Consider a list with just one element. The search would miss the element.

Does the method still work if there are duplicate elements in the list? Yes, as long as the elements are sorted in increasing order in the list. The method returns the index of one of the matching element if the element is in the list.

Please trace the program using the following statements:

```
int[] list = {2, 4, 7, 10, 11, 45, 50, 59, 60, 66, 69, 70, 79};
int i = binarySearch(list, 2); // returns 0
int j = binarySearch(list, 11); // returns 4
int k = binarySearch(list, 12); // returns - 6
```

NOTE

Linear search is useful for finding an element in a small array or an unsorted array, but it is inefficient for large arrays. Binary search is more efficient, but requires that the array be pre-sorted.

TIP

Since binary search is frequently used in programming, Java provides several overloaded binarySearch methods for searching a key in an array of int, double, char, short, long, and float in the java.util.Arrays class. For example, the following code searches the keys in an array of numbers and an array of characters:

```
int[] list = {2, 4, 7, 10, 11, 45, 50, 59, 60, 66, 69, 70, 79};
System.out.println("Index is " +
  java.util.Arrays.binarySearch(list, 11));

char[] chars = {'a', 'c', 'g', 'x', 'y', 'z'};
System.out.println("Index is " +
  java.util.Arrays.binarySearch(chars, 't'));
```

For the binarySearch method to work, the array must be pre-sorted in increasing order.

5.7.3 Recursive Implementation of Binary Search (Optional)

The preceding section implements binary search using iteration. You can also implement it using recursion in two overloaded methods, as follows:

```
/** Use binary search to find the key in the list */
public static int recursiveBinarySearch(int[] list, int key) {
  int low = 0;
  int high = list.length - 1;
  return recursiveBinarySearch(list, key, low, high);
}

/** Use binary search to find the key in the list between
    list[low] and list[high] */
public static int recursiveBinarySearch(int[] list, int key,
    int low, int high) {
  if (low > high) // The list has been exhausted without a match
    return -low - 1;
```

```
int mid = (low + high) / 2;
if (key < list[mid])
  return recursiveBinarySearch(list, key, low, mid - 1);
else if (key == list[mid])
  return mid;
else
  return recursiveBinarySearch(list, key, mid + 1, high);
}
```

The first method finds a key in the whole list. The second method finds a key in the list with index from `low` to `high`.

The first `binarySearch` method passes the initial array with `low = 0` and `high = list.length - 1` to the second `binarySearch` method. The second method is invoked recursively to find the key in an ever-shrinking subarray. It is a common design technique in recursive programming to choose a second method that can be called recursively.

There are two reasons why this is a good example of using recursion. First, using recursion enables you to specify a clear, simple solution for the binary search problem. Second, the number of recursive calls is less than the size of the list. So the solution is reasonably efficient.

5.8 Multidimensional Arrays

Thus far, you have used one-dimensional arrays to model linear collections of elements. You can use a two-dimensional array to represent a matrix or a table. Occasionally, you will need to represent n-dimensional data structures. In Java, you can create n-dimensional arrays for any integer n.

5.8.1 Declaring Variables of Multidimensional Arrays and Creating Multidimensional Arrays

Here is the syntax for declaring a two-dimensional array:

```
dataType[][] arrayRefVar;
```

or

```
dataType arrayRefVar[][]; // This style is correct, but not preferred
```

As an example, here is how you would declare a two-dimensional array variable `matrix` of `int` values:

```
int[][] matrix;
```

or

```
int matrix[][]; // This style is correct, but not preferred
```

You can create a two-dimensional array of 5 by 5 `int` values and assign it to `matrix` using this syntax:

```
matrix = new int[5][5];
```

Two subscripts are used in a two-dimensional array, one for the row, and the other for the column. As in a one-dimensional array, the index for each subscript is of the `int` type and starts from 0, as shown in Figure 5.12(a).

To assign the value 7 to a specific element at row 2 and column 1, as shown in Figure 5.12(b), you can use the following:

```
matrix[2][1] = 7;
```

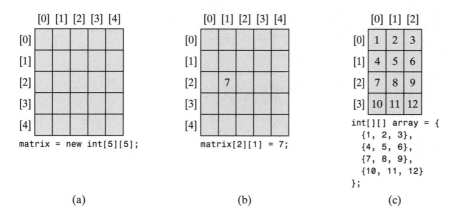

FIGURE 5.12   *The index of each subscript of a multidimensional array is an* int *value starting from 0.*

 CAUTION

It is a common mistake to use matrix[2, 1] to access the element at row 2 and column 1. In Java, each subscript must be enclosed in a pair of square brackets.

You can also use an array initializer to declare, create, and initialize a two-dimensional array. For example, the following code in (a) creates an array with the specified initial values, as shown in Figure 5.12(c). This is equivalent to the code in (a).

```
int[][] array = {
  {1, 2, 3},
  {4, 5, 6},
  {7, 8, 9},
  {10, 11, 12}
};
```

Equivalent

```
int[][] array = new int[4][3];
array[0][0] = 1; array[0][1] = 2; array[0][2] = 3;
array[1][0] = 4; array[1][1] = 5; array[1][2] = 6;
array[2][0] = 7; array[2][1] = 8; array[2][2] = 9;
array[3][0] = 10; array[3][1] = 11; array[3][2] = 12;
```

(a)   (b)

The way to declare two-dimensional array variables and create two-dimensional arrays can be generalized to declare *n*-dimensional array variables and create *n*-dimensional arrays for $n >= 3$. For example, the following syntax declares a three-dimensional array variable scores, creates an array, and assigns its reference to scores:

```
double[][][] scores = new double[10][5][2];
```

5.8.2   Obtaining the Lengths of Multidimensional Arrays

A multidimensional array is actually an array in which each element is another array. A two-dimensional array consists of an array of elements, each of which is a one-dimensional array. A three-dimensional array consists of an array of two-dimensional arrays, each of which is an array of one-dimensional arrays. The length of an array x is the number of elements in the array, which can be obtained using x.length. x[0], x[1], ..., and x[x.length - 1] are arrays. Their lengths can be obtained using x[0].length, x[1].length, ..., and x[x.length - 1].length.

For example, suppose x = new int[3][4], x[0], x[1], and x[2] are one-dimensional arrays and each contains four elements, as shown in Figure 5.13. x.length is 3, and x[0].length, x[1].length and x[2].length are 4.

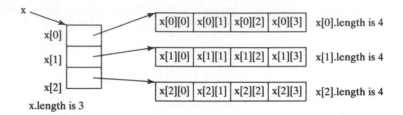

FIGURE 5.13 *A two-dimensional array is a one-dimensional array in which each element is another one-dimensional array.*

Suppose x = new int[2][2][5], x[0] and x[1] are two-dimensional arrays. X[0][0], x[0][1], x[1][0], and x[1][1] are one-dimensional arrays and each contains five elements. x.length is 2, x[0].length and x[1].length are 2, and X[0][0].length, x[0][1].length, x[1][0].length, and x[1][1].length are 5.

5.8.3 Ragged Arrays

ragged array

Each row in a two-dimensional array is itself an array. Thus the rows can have different lengths. An array of this kind is known as a *ragged array*. Here is an example of creating a ragged array:

```
int[][] triangleArray = {
  {1, 2, 3, 4, 5},
  {2, 3, 4, 5},
  {3, 4, 5},
  {4, 5},
  {5}
};
```

As can be seen triangleArray[0].length is 5, triangleArray[1].length is 4, triangle Array[2].length is 3, triangleArray[3].length is 2, and triangleArray[4].length is 1.

If you don't know the values in a ragged array in advance, but know the sizes, say the same as before, you can create a ragged array using the syntax that follows:

```
int[][] triangleArray = new int[5][];
triangleArray[0] = new int[5];
triangleArray[1] = new int[4];
triangleArray[2] = new int[3];
triangleArray[3] = new int[2];
triangleArray[4] = new int[1];
```

You can now assign random values to the array using the following loop:

```
for (int row = 0; row < triangleArray.length; row++)
  for (int column = 0; column < triangleArray[row].length; column++)
    triangleArray[row][column] = (int)(Math.random() * 1000);
```

 NOTE

The syntax new int[5][] for creating an array requires the first index to be specified. The syntax new int[][] would be wrong.

EXAMPLE 5.5 GRADING A MULTIPLE-CHOICE TEST

Problem

Write a program that grades multiple-choice tests. Suppose there are eight students and ten questions, and the answers are stored in a two-dimensional array. Each row records a student's answers to the questions. For example, the following array stores the test:

Students' Answers to the Questions:

```
            0 1 2 3 4 5 6 7 8 9
Student 0   A B A C C D E E A D
Student 1   D B A B C A E E A D
Student 2   E D D A C B E E A D
Student 3   C B A E D C E E A D
Student 4   A B D C C D E E A D
Student 5   B B E C C D E E A D
Student 6   B B A C C D E E A D
Student 7   E B E C C D E E A D
```

The key is stored in a one-dimensional array, as follows:

Key to the Questions:

```
      0 1 2 3 4 5 6 7 8 9
Key   D B D C C D A E A D
```

Your program grades the test and displays the result, as shown in Figure 5.14.

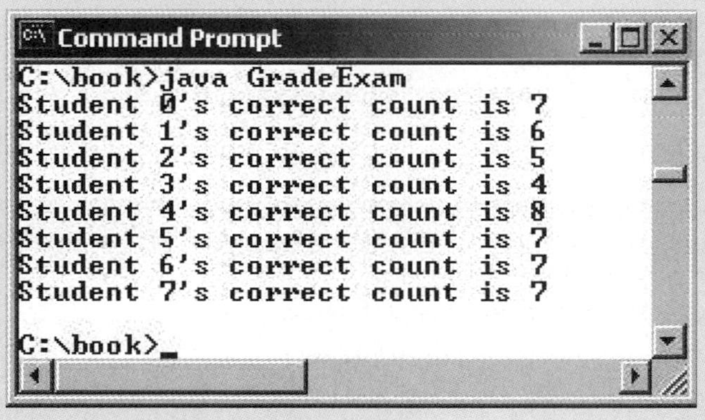

```
C:\book>java GradeExam
Student 0's correct count is 7
Student 1's correct count is 6
Student 2's correct count is 5
Student 3's correct count is 4
Student 4's correct count is 8
Student 5's correct count is 7
Student 6's correct count is 7
Student 7's correct count is 7

C:\book>
```

FIGURE 5.14 *The program grades students' answers to the multiple-choice questions.*

Solution

The program compares each student's answers with the key, counts the number of correct answers, and displays it. Listing 5.8 for the program is shown below.

LISTING 5.8 **GradeExam.java (Grading Exams)**

```java
1 public class GradeExam {
2   /** Main method */
3   public static void main(String args[]) {
4     // Students' answers to the questions
```

EXAMPLE 5.5 (CONTINUED)

```
 5   char[][] answers = {
 6     {'A', 'B', 'A', 'C', 'C', 'D', 'E', 'E', 'A', 'D'},
 7     {'D', 'B', 'A', 'B', 'C', 'A', 'E', 'E', 'A', 'D'},
 8     {'E', 'D', 'D', 'A', 'C', 'B', 'E', 'E', 'A', 'D'},
 9     {'C', 'B', 'A', 'E', 'D', 'C', 'E', 'E', 'A', 'D'},
10     {'A', 'B', 'D', 'C', 'C', 'D', 'E', 'E', 'A', 'D'},
11     {'B', 'B', 'E', 'C', 'C', 'D', 'E', 'E', 'A', 'D'},
12     {'B', 'B', 'A', 'C', 'C', 'D', 'E', 'E', 'A', 'D'},
13     {'E', 'B', 'E', 'C', 'C', 'D', 'E', 'E', 'A', 'D'}};
14
15   // Key to the questions
16   char[] keys = {'D', 'B', 'D', 'C', 'C', 'D', 'A', 'E', 'A', 'D'};
17
18   // Grade all answers
19   for (int i = 0; i < answers.length; i++) {
20     // Grade one student
21     int correctCount = 0;
22     for (int j = 0; j < answers[i].length; j++) {
23       if (answers[i][j] == keys[j])
24         correctCount++;
25     }
26
27     System.out.println("Student " + i + "'s correct count is " +
28       correctCount);
29   }
30 }
31 }
```

Review

The statement in Lines 5–13 declares, creates, and initializes a two-dimensional array of characters and assigns the reference to answers of the char[][] type.

The statement in Line 16 declares, creates, and initializes an array of char values and assigns the reference to keys of the char[][] type.

Each row in the array answers stores a student's answer, which is graded by comparing it with the key in the array keys. The result is displayed immediately after a student's answer is graded.

EXAMPLE 5.6 COMPUTING TAXES USING ARRAYS

Problem

Example 4.4, "Computing Taxes with Methods," simplified Example 3.1, "Computing Taxes." Example 4.4 can be further improved using arrays. Rewrite Example 3.1 using arrays to store tax rates and brackets.

Solution

For each filing status, there are six tax rates. Each rate is applied to a certain amount of taxable income. For example, from the taxable income of $400,000 for a single filer, $6,000 is taxed at 10%, (27950 − 6000) at 15%, (67700 − 27950) at 27%, (141250 − 67700) at 35%, and (400000 − 307050) at 38.6%. The six rates are the same for all filing statuses, which can be represented in the following array:

```
double[] rates = {0.10, 0.15, 0.27, 0.30, 0.35, 0.386};
```

EXAMPLE 5.6 (CONTINUED)

The brackets for each rate for all the filing statuses can be represented in a two-dimensional array as follows:

```
int[][] brackets = {
  {6000, 27950, 67700, 141250, 307050}, // Single filer
  {12000, 46700, 112850, 171950, 307050}, // married jointly
  {6000, 23350, 56425, 85975, 153525}, // married separately
  {10000, 37450, 96700, 156600, 307050} // head of household
};
```

Suppose the taxable income is $400,000 for single filers, the tax can be computed as follows:

```
brackets[0][0] * rates[0] +
(brackets[0][1] - brackets[0][0]) * rates[1] +
(brackets[0][2] - brackets[0][1]) * rates[2] +
(brackets[0][3] - brackets[0][2]) * rates[3] +
(brackets[0][4] - brackets[0][3]) * rates[4] +
(400000 - brackets[0][4]) * rates[5]
```

Listing 5.9 gives the solution to the program.

LISTING 5.9 ComputeTax.java (Computing Tax)

```
1 import javax.swing.JOptionPane;
2
3 public class ComputeTax {
4   public static void main(String[] args) {
5     // Prompt the user to enter filing status
6     String statusString = JOptionPane.showInputDialog(
7       "Enter the filing status:\n" +
8       "(0-single filer, 1-married jointly,\n" +
9       "2-married separately, 3-head of household)");
10    int status = Integer.parseInt(statusString);
11
12    // Prompt the user to enter taxable income
13    String incomeString = JOptionPane.showInputDialog(
14      "Enter the taxable income:");
15    double income = Double.parseDouble(incomeString);
16
17    // Compute and display the result
18    JOptionPane.showMessageDialog(null, "Tax is " +
19      (int)(computeTax(status, income) * 100) / 100.0);
20  }
21
22  public static double computeTax(int status, double income) {
23    double[] rates = {0.10, 0.15, 0.27, 0.30, 0.35, 0.386};
24
25    int[][] brackets = {
26      {6000, 27950, 67700, 141250, 307050}, // Single filer
27      {12000, 46700, 112850, 171950, 307050}, // Married jointly
28      {6000, 23350, 56425, 85975, 153525}, // Married separately
29      {10000, 37450, 96700, 156600, 307050} // Head of household
30    };
31
32    double tax = 0; // Tax to be computed
33
34    // Compute tax in the first bracket
35    if (income <= brackets[status][0])
36      return tax = income * rates[0]; // Done
37    else
38      tax = brackets[status][0] * rates[0];
```

EXAMPLE 5.6 (CONTINUED)

```
39
40     // Compute tax in the 2nd, 3rd, 4th, and 5th brackets, if needed
41     for (int i = 1; i < brackets[0].length; i++) {
42       if (income > brackets[status][i])
43         tax += (brackets[status][i] - brackets[status][i - 1]) *
44           rates[i];
45       else {
46         tax += (income - brackets[status][i - 1]) * rates[i];
47         return tax; // Done
48       }
49     }
50
51     // Compute tax in the last (i.e., 6th) bracket
52     return tax += (income - brackets[status][4]) * rates[5];
53   }
54 }
```

Review

The computeTax method computes the tax for the taxable income of a given filing status. The tax for the first bracket (0 to brackets[status][0]) is computed in Lines 35–38. The taxes for the second, third, fourth, and fifth brackets are computed in the loop in Lines 41–49. The tax for the last bracket is computed in Line 52.

EXAMPLE 5.7 CALCULATING TOTAL SCORES

Problem

Write a program that calculates the total score for the students in a class. Suppose the scores are stored in a three-dimensional array named scores. The first index in scores refers to a student, the second refers to an exam, and the third refers to a part of the exam. Suppose there are seven students, five exams, and each exam has two parts: a multiple-choice part and a programming part. scores[i][j][0] represents the score on the multiple-choice part for the i's student on the j's exam. scores[i][j][1] represents the score on the programming part for the i's student on the j's exam. Your program displays the total score for each student, as shown in Figure 5.15.

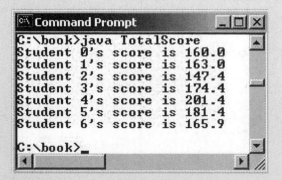

```
C:\book>java TotalScore
Student 0's score is 160.0
Student 1's score is 163.0
Student 2's score is 147.4
Student 3's score is 174.4
Student 4's score is 201.4
Student 5's score is 181.4
Student 6's score is 165.9

C:\book>_
```

FIGURE 5.15   *The program displays the total score for each student.*

EXAMPLE 5.7 (CONTINUED)

Solution

The program in Listing 5.10 processes the `scores` array for all the students. For each student, it adds the two scores from all exams to `totalScore` and displays `totalScore`.

LISTING 5.10   TotalScore.java (Computing Student Scores)

```
1 public class TotalScore {
2   /** Main method */
3   public static void main(String args[]) {    scores[0][3][1]  scores[0][4][1]
4     double[][][] scores = {
5       {{7.5, 20.5}, {9.0, 22.5}, {15, 33.5}, {13, 21.5}, {15, 2.5}},
6       {{4.5, 21.5}, {9.0, 22.5}, {15, 34.5}, {12, 20.5}, {14, 9.5}},
7       {{5.5, 30.5}, {9.4, 10.5}, {11, 33.5}, {11, 23.5}, {10, 2.5}},
8       {{6.5, 23.5}, {9.4, 32.5}, {13, 34.5}, {11, 20.5}, {16, 7.5}},
9       {{8.5, 25.5}, {9.4, 52.5}, {13, 36.5}, {13, 24.5}, {16, 2.5}},
10      {{9.5, 20.5}, {9.4, 42.5}, {13, 31.5}, {12, 20.5}, {16, 6.5}},
11      {{1.5, 29.5}, {6.4, 22.5}, {14, 30.5}, {10, 30.5}, {16, 5.0}}};
12
13    // Calculate and display total score for each student
14    for (int i = 0; i < scores.length; i++) {              scores[6][4][1]
15      double totalScore = 0;
16      for (int j = 0; j < scores[i].length; j++)
17        for (int k = 0; k < scores[i][j].length; k++)
18          totalScore += scores[i][j][k];
19
20      System.out.println("Student " + i + "'s score is " +
21        totalScore);
22    }
23  }
24 }
```

Review

To understand this example, it is essential to know how data in the three-dimensional array are interpreted. `scores[0]` is a two-dimensional array that stores all the exam scores for the first student. `scores[0][0]` is `{7.5, 20.5}`, a one-dimensional array, which stores two scores for two parts of the first student's first exam. `scores[0][0][0]` is 7.5, which is the score for the first part of the first student's first exam. `scores[5]` is a two-dimensional array that stores all the exam scores for the sixth student. `scores[5][4]` is `{16, 6.5}`, a one-dimensional array, which stores two scores for two parts of the sixth student's fifth exam. `scores[5][4][1]` is 6.5, which is the score for the second part of the sixth student's fifth exam.

The statement in Lines 4–11 declares, creates, and initializes a three-dimensional array of `double` values and assigns the reference to `scores` of the `double[][][]` type.

The scores for each student are added in Lines 16–18, and the result is displayed in Lines 20–21. The `for` loop in Line 14 process the scores for all the students.

KEY TERMS

KEY CLASSES AND METHODS

✦ `System.arraycopy(...)` copies the contents from a source array to a target array.

✦ `java.util.Arrays` is a class that contains static methods for manipulating arrays.

✦ `Arrays.sort(array)` sorts an array of `short`, `int`, `long`, `float`, `double`, and `char`.

✦ `Arrays.binarySearch(array, key)` uses the binary search method to search a key in the array of `short`, `int`, `long`, `float`, `double`, and `char`.

CHAPTER SUMMARY

✦ A variable is declared as an array type using the syntax `dataType[] arrayRefVar` or `dataType arrayRefVar[]`. The style `dataType[] arrayRefVar` is preferred, although `dataType arrayRefVar[] is legal`.

✦ Unlike declarations for primitive data type variables, the declaration of an array variable does not allocate any space in memory for the array. An array variable is not a primitive data type variable. An array variable contains a reference to an array.

✦ You cannot assign elements to an array unless it has already been created. You can create an array by using the `new` operator with the following syntax: `new dataType[arraySize]`.

✦ Each element in the array is represented using the syntax `arrayRefVar[index]`. An index must be an integer or an integer expression.

✦ After an array is created, its size becomes permanent and can be obtained using `arrayRefVar.length`. Since the index of an array always begins with 0, the last index is always `arrayRefVar.length - 1`. An out-of-bounds error will occur if you attempt to reference elements beyond the bounds of an array.

✦ Programmers often mistakenly reference the first element in an array with index 1, so that the index of the tenth element becomes 10. This is called the *index off-by-one error*.

✦ Java has a shorthand notation, known as the *array initializer*, which combines declaring an array, creating an array, and initializing in one statement using the syntax: `dataType[] arrayRefVar = {literal0, literal1, ..., literalk}`.

✦ When you pass an array argument to a method, you are actually passing the reference of the array; that is, the called method can modify the elements in the caller's original arrays.

✦ You can use arrays of arrays to form multidimensional arrays. For example, a two-dimensional array is declared as an array of arrays using the syntax `dataType[][] arrayRefVar` or `dataType arrayRefVar[][]`.

REVIEW QUESTIONS

Section 5.2 Array Basics

5.1   How do you declare and create an array?

5.2   How do you access elements of an array?

5.3   Is memory allocated when an array is declared? When is the memory allocated for an array? What is the printout of the following code?

```
int x = 30;
int[] numbers = new int[x];
x = 60;
System.out.println("x is " + x);
System.out.println("The size of numbers is " + numbers.length);
```

5.4   Indicate true or false for the following statements:

     ✦ Every element in an array has the same type.

     ✦ The array size is fixed after it is declared.

     ✦ The array size is fixed after it is created.

     ✦ The elements in an array must be of primitive data type.

5.5   Which of the following statements are valid array declarations?

```
int i = new int(30);
double d[] = new double[30];
char[] r = new char(1..30);
int i[] = (3, 4, 3, 2);
float f[] = {2.3, 4.5, 5.6};
char[] c = new char();
int[][] r = new int[2];
```

5.6   What is the array index type? What is the lowest index?

5.7   What is the representation of the third element in an array named a?

5.8   What happens when your program attempts to access an array element with an invalid index?

5.9   Identify and fix the errors in the following code:

```
1 public class Test {
2   public static void main(String[] args) {
3     double[100] r;
4
5     for (int i = 0; i < r.length(); i++);
6       r(i) = Math.random * 100;
7   }
8 }
```

Section 5.3 Copying Arrays

5.10   Use the `arraycopy()` method to copy the following array to a target array t:

```
int[] source = {3, 4, 5};
```

5.11   Once an array is created, its size cannot be changed. Does the following code resize the array?

```
int[] myList;
myList = new int[10];
// Some time later you want to assign a new array to myList
myList = new int[20];
```

Sections 5.4–5.5

5.12   When an array is passed to a method, a new array is created and passed to the method. Is this true?

5.13 Show the output of the following program:

```
1 public class Test {
2   public static void main(String[] args) {
3     int number = 0;
4     int[] numbers = new int[1];
5
6     m(number, numbers);
7     System.out.println("numbers is " + number +
8       " and numbers[0] is " + numbers[0]);
9   }
10
11  public static void m(int x, int[] y) {
12    x = 3;
13    y[0] = 3;
14  }
15 }
```

5.14 Where are the arrays stored during execution? Show the contents of the stack and heap during and after executing createArray, displayArray, countLetters, displayCounts in Example 5.4,

Section 5.6–5.7

5.15 Use Figure 5.10 as an example to show how to apply the selection sort approach to sort {3.4, 5, 3, 3.5, 2.2, 1.9, 2}.

5.16 What types of array can be sorted using the java.util.Arrays.sort method? Does this sort method create a new array?

5.17 Use Figure 5.11 as an example to show how to apply the binary search approach to search for key 10 and key 12 in list {2, 4, 7, 10, 11, 45, 50, 59, 60, 66, 69, 70, 79}.

5.18 To apply java.util.Arrays.binarySearch(array, key), should the array be sorted in increasing order, in decreasing order, or either?

Section 5.8 Multidimensional Arrays

5.19 Declare and create a 4×5 int matrix.

5.20 Can the rows in a two-dimensional array have different lengths?

5.21 What is the output of the following code?

```
int[][] array = new int[5][6];
int[] x = {1, 2};
array[0] = x;
System.out.println("array[0][1] is " + array[0][1]);
```

PROGRAMMING EXERCISES

Section 5.2 Array Basics

5.1 *(Analyzing input)* Write a program that reads ten numbers, computes their average, and finds out how many numbers are above the average.

5.2 *(Alternative solution to Example 5.1, "Testing Arrays")* The solution of Example 5.1 counts the occurrences of the largest number by comparing *each number* with the largest. So you have to use an array to store all the numbers. Another way to solve the problem is to maintain two variables, max and count. max stores the current max number, and count stores its occurrences. Initially, assign the first number to max and 1 to count. Compare each subsequent number with max. If the number is greater than max, assign it to max and reset count to 1. If the number is equal to max, increment count by 1. Use this approach to rewrite Example 5.1.

5.3   *(Reversing the numbers entered)* Write a program that reads ten integers and displays them in reverse order.

5.4   *(Analyzing scores)* Write a program that reads an unspecified number of scores and determines how many scores are above or equal to the average and how many scores are below the average. Enter a negative number to signify the end of the input. Assume that the maximum number of scores is 100.

5.5**   *(Printing unique numbers)* Write a program that reads in ten numbers and display unique numbers. *Hint:* Read a number and store it to an array if it is new. If the number is already in the array, discard it. After the input, the numbers in the array contains all the unique numbers.

5.6*   *(Revising Example 3.10 "Displaying Prime Numbers")* Example 3.10 determines whether a number n is prime by checking whether 2, 3, 4, 5, 6, ..., n/2 is a divisor. If a divisor is found, n is not prime. A more efficient approach to determine whether n is prime is to check whether any of the prime numbers less than or equal to $\sqrt{n}$ can divide n evenly. If not, n is prime. Rewrite Example 3.10 to display the first fifty prime numbers using this approach. You need to use an array to store the prime numbers and later use them to check whether they are possible divisors for n.

5.7*   *(Counting single digits)* Write a program that generates one hundred random integers between 0 and 9 and displays the count for each number. *Hint:* Use (int)(Math.random() * 10) to generate a random integer between 0 and 9. Use an array of ten integers, say counts, to store the counts for the number of 0's, 1's, ..., 9's.

Sections 5.4–5.5

5.8   *(Averaging an array)* Write two overloaded methods that return the average of an array with the following headers:

```
public static int average(int[] array);
public static double average(double[] array);
```

Use {1, 2, 3, 4, 5, 6} and {5.0, 4.4, 1.9, 2.9, 3.4, 3.5} to test the methods.

5.9   *(Finding the smallest element)* Write a method that finds the smallest element in an array of integers. Use {1, 2, 4, 5, 10, 100, 2, −22} to test the method.

5.10   *(Finding the index of the smallest element)* Write a method that returns the index of the smallest element in an array of integers. If there are more than one such elements, return the smallest index. Use {1, 2, 4, 5, 10, 100, 2, −22} to test the method.

5.11*   *(Computing deviation)* Exercise 4.15 computes the standard deviation of numbers. This exercise uses a different but equivalent formula to compute the standard deviation of n numbers.

$$mean = \frac{\sum\limits_{i=1}^{n} x_i}{n} = \frac{x_1 + x_2 + \cdots + x_n}{n} \qquad deviation = \sqrt{\frac{\sum\limits_{i=1}^{n}(x_i - mean)^2}{n-1}}$$

To compute deviation with this formula, you have to store the individual numbers using an array, so that they can be used after the mean is obtained. Use {1, 2, 3, 4, 5, 6, 7, 8, 9, 10} to test the method.

Sections 5.6–5.7

5.12**   *(Recursive selection sort)* Use recursion to rewrite the selection sort in Section 5.6.

5.13* *(Revising selection sort)* In Section 5.6, you used selection sort to sort an array. The selection sort method repeatedly finds the largest number in the current array and swaps it with the last number in the array. Rewrite this example by finding the smallest number and swapping it with the first number in the array.

5.14* *(Bubble sort)* Write a sort method that uses the bubble-sort algorithm. The bubble-sort algorithm makes several passes through the array. On each pass, successive neighboring pairs are compared. If a pair is in decreasing order, its values are swapped; otherwise, the values remain unchanged. The technique is called a *bubble sort* or *sinking sort* because the smaller values gradually "bubble" their way to the top and the larger values sink to the bottom.

The algorithm can be described as follows:

```
boolean changed = true;
do {
  changed = false;
  for (int j = 0; j < list.length - 1; j++)
    if (list[j] > list[j + 1]) {
      swap list[j] with list[j + 1];
      changed = true;
    }
}
while (changed);
```

Clearly, the list is in increasing order when the loop terminates. It is easy to show that the do loop executes at most list.length -1 times.

Use {5.0, 4.4, 1.9, 2.9, 3.4, 2.9, 3.5} to test the method.

5.15** *(Insertion sort)* Write a sort method that uses the insertion-sort algorithm. The insertion-sort algorithm sorts a list of values by repeatedly inserting an unsorted element into a sorted sublist until the whole list is sorted. The algorithm can be described as follows:

```
for (int i = 1; i < list.length; i++) {
  /** The elements in list[0..i - 1] are already sorted. To insert
    * the element list[i] into list[0..i - 1] is to move list[k] into
    * list[k + 1] for k <= i - 1 such that list[k] > list[i] */
  double currentElement = list[i];
  int k = i - 1;
  while (k >= 0 && list[k] > currentElement) {
    list[k + 1] = list[k];
    k--;
  }

  // Insert the current element into list[k + 1]
  list[k + 1] = currentElement;
}
```

Use {5.0, 4.4, 1.9, 2.9, 3.4, 2.9, 3.5} to test the method.

5.16** *(Sorting students)* Write a program that prompts the user to enter the number of students, and student names and their scores, and prints student names in decreasing order of their scores.

5.17** *(Finding the sales amount)* Rewrite Example 3.8, "Finding the Sales Amount," using the binary search approach. Since the sales amount is between 1 and COMMISSION_SOUGHT/0.08, you can use a binary search to improve Example 3.8.

Section 5.8 Multidimensional Arrays

5.18* *(Summing all the numbers in a matrix)* Write a method that sums all the integers in a matrix of integers. Use {{1, 2, 4, 5}, {6, 7, 8, 9}, {10, 11, 12, 13}, {14, 15, 16, 17}} to test the method.

5.19* *(Summing the major diagonal in a matrix)* Write a method that sums all the integers in the major diagonal in a matrix of integers. Use $\{\{1, 2, 4, 5\}, \{6, 7, 8, 9\}, \{10, 11, 12, 13\}, \{14, 15, 16, 17\}\}$ to test the method.

5.20* *(Sorting students on grades)* Rewrite Example 5.5, "Grading a Multiple-Choice Test," to display the students in increasing order of the number of correct answers.

5.21* *(Computing the weekly hours for each employee)* Suppose the weekly hours for all employees are stored in a two-dimensional array. Each row records an employee's seven-day work hours with seven columns. For example, the following array stores the work hours for eight employees. Write a program that displays employees and their total hours in decreasing order of the total hours.

	Su	M	T	W	H	F	Sa
Employee 0	2	4	3	4	5	8	8
Employee 1	7	3	4	3	3	4	4
Employee 2	3	3	4	3	3	2	2
Employee 3	9	3	4	7	3	4	1
Employee 4	3	5	4	3	6	3	8
Employee 5	3	4	4	6	3	4	4
Employee 6	3	7	4	8	3	8	4
Employee 7	6	3	5	9	2	7	9

5.22 *(Adding two matrices)* Write a method to add two matrices. The header of the method is as follows:

```
public static int[][] addMatrix(int[][] a, int[][] b)
```

In order to be added, two matrices must have the same dimensions and the same or compatible types of elements. As shown below, two matrices are added by adding the two elements of the arrays with the same index:

$$
\begin{pmatrix}
a_{11} & a_{12} & a_{13} & a_{14} & a_{15} \\
a_{21} & a_{22} & a_{23} & a_{24} & a_{25} \\
a_{31} & a_{32} & a_{33} & a_{34} & a_{35} \\
a_{41} & a_{42} & a_{43} & a_{44} & a_{45} \\
a_{51} & a_{52} & a_{53} & a_{54} & a_{55}
\end{pmatrix}
+
\begin{pmatrix}
b_{11} & b_{12} & b_{13} & b_{14} & b_{15} \\
b_{21} & b_{22} & b_{23} & b_{24} & b_{25} \\
b_{31} & b_{32} & b_{33} & b_{34} & b_{35} \\
b_{41} & b_{42} & b_{43} & b_{44} & b_{45} \\
b_{51} & b_{52} & b_{53} & b_{54} & b_{55}
\end{pmatrix}
$$

$$
=
\begin{pmatrix}
a_{11} + b_{11} & a_{12} + b_{12} & a_{13} + b_{13} & a_{14} + b_{14} & a_{15} + b_{15} \\
a_{21} + b_{21} & a_{22} + b_{22} & a_{23} + b_{23} & a_{24} + b_{24} & a_{25} + b_{25} \\
a_{31} + b_{31} & a_{32} + b_{32} & a_{33} + b_{33} & a_{34} + b_{34} & a_{35} + b_{35} \\
a_{41} + b_{41} & a_{42} + b_{42} & a_{43} + b_{43} & a_{44} + b_{44} & a_{45} + b_{45} \\
a_{51} + b_{51} & a_{52} + b_{52} & a_{53} + b_{53} & a_{54} + b_{54} & a_{55} + b_{55}
\end{pmatrix}
$$

5.23** *(Multiplying two matrices)* Write a method to multiply two matrices. The header of the method is as follows:

```
public static int[][] multiplyMatrix(int[][] a, int[][] b)
```

To multiply matrix a by matrix b, the number of columns in a must be the same as the number of rows in b, and the two matrices must have elements of the same or compatible types. Let c be the result of the multiplication, and a, b, and c are denoted as follows:

$$
\begin{pmatrix}
a_{11} & a_{12} & a_{13} & a_{14} & a_{15} \\
a_{21} & a_{22} & a_{23} & a_{24} & a_{25} \\
a_{31} & a_{32} & a_{33} & a_{34} & a_{35} \\
a_{41} & a_{42} & a_{43} & a_{44} & a_{45} \\
a_{51} & a_{52} & a_{53} & a_{54} & a_{55}
\end{pmatrix}
\times
\begin{pmatrix}
b_{11} & b_{12} & b_{13} & b_{14} & b_{15} \\
b_{21} & b_{22} & b_{23} & b_{24} & b_{25} \\
b_{31} & b_{32} & b_{33} & b_{34} & b_{35} \\
b_{41} & b_{42} & b_{43} & b_{44} & b_{45} \\
b_{51} & b_{52} & b_{53} & b_{54} & b_{55}
\end{pmatrix}
=
\begin{pmatrix}
c_{11} & c_{12} & c_{13} & c_{14} & c_{15} \\
c_{21} & c_{22} & c_{23} & c_{24} & c_{25} \\
c_{31} & c_{32} & c_{33} & c_{34} & c_{35} \\
c_{41} & c_{42} & c_{43} & c_{44} & c_{45} \\
c_{51} & c_{52} & c_{53} & c_{54} & c_{55}
\end{pmatrix}
$$

where

$$c_{ij} = a_{i1} \times b_{1j} + a_{i2} \times b_{2j} + a_{i3} \times b_{3j} + a_{i4} \times b_{4j} + a_{i5} \times b_{5j}$$

5.24*   *(TicTacToe board)* Write a program that randomly fills in 0s and 1s into a TicTacToc board, prints the board, and finds the rows, columns, or diagonals with all 0s or 1s. Use a two-dimensional array to represent a TicTacToe board. Here is a sample run of the program:

```
001
001
111
All 0's on row 0
All 1's on row 2
All 1's on column 2
```

5.25**   *(Checker board)* Write a program that randomly fills in 0s and 1s into an 8 × 8 checker board, prints the board, and finds the rows, columns, or diagonals with all 0s or 1s. Use a two-dimensional array to represent a checker board. Here is a sample run of the program:

```
10101000
10100001
11100011
10100001
11100111
10000001
10100111
00100001
All 0's on subdiagonal
```

5.26***   *(Playing a TicTacToe game)* In a game of TicTacToe, two players take turns marking an available cell in a 3 × 3 grid with their respective tokens (either X or O). When one player has placed three tokens in a horizontal, vertical, or diagonal row on the grid, the game is over and that player has won. A draw (no winner) occurs when all the cells on the grid have been filled with tokens and neither player has achieved a win. Create a program for playing TicTacToe, as follows:

✦ The program prompts the first player to enter an X token, and then prompts the second player to enter an O token. Whenever a token is entered, the program redisplayes the board and determines the status of the game (win, draw, or unfinished).

✦ To place a token, display two dialog boxes to prompt the user to enter the row and the column for the token.

PART II

OBJECT-ORIENTED PROGRAMMING

In Part I, "Fundamentals of Programming," you learned how to write simple Java applications using primitive data types, control statements, methods, and arrays, all of which are features commonly available in procedural programming languages. Java, however, is an object-oriented programming language that uses abstraction, encapsulation, inheritance, and polymorphism to provide great flexibility, modularity, and reusability for developing software. In this part of the book you will learn how to define, extend, and work with classes and their objects.

Chapter 6
Objects and Classes

Chapter 7
Strings

Chapter 8
Inheritance and Polymorphism

Chapter 9
Abstract Classes and Interfaces

Chapter 10
Object-Oriented Modeling

Prerequisites for Part II

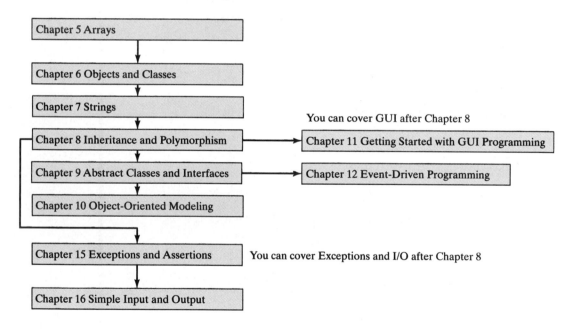

chapter
6

Objects and Classes

Objectives

- ◆ To understand objects and classes, and use classes to model objects (§6.2).

- ◆ To learn how to declare a class and how to create an object of a class (§6.3).

- ◆ To understand the roles of constructors and use constructors to create objects (§6.3).

- ◆ To use UML graphical notations to describe classes and objects (§6.3).

- ◆ To distinguish between object reference variables and primitive data type variables (§6.4).

- ◆ To use classes in the Java library (§6.5).

- ◆ To declare private data fields with appropriate get and set methods for data field encapsulation to make classes easy to maintain (§§6.6–6.7).

- ◆ To create immutable objects from immutable classes (§6.8).

- ◆ To develop methods with object arguments (§6.9).

- ◆ To understand the difference between instance and static variables and methods (§6.10).

- ◆ To determine the scope of variables in the context of a class (§6.11).

- ◆ To use the keyword this to refer to the calling object (§6.12).

- ◆ To store and process objects in arrays (§6.13).

- ◆ To apply class abstraction to develop software (§6.14).

- ◆ To declare inner classes (§6.17).

6.1 Introduction

Programming in procedural languages like C, Pascal, BASIC, Ada, and COBOL involves choosing data structures, designing algorithms, and translating algorithms into code. An object-oriented language like Java combines the power of procedural languages with an added dimension that provides more flexibility, modularity, clarity, and reusability through class encapsulation, class inheritance, and polymorphism.

In procedural programming, data and operations on the data are separate, and this methodology requires sending data to procedures and functions. Object-oriented programming places data and the operations that pertain to them within a single entity called an *object*; this approach solves many of the problems inherent in procedural programming. The object-oriented programming approach organizes programs in a way that mirrors the real world, in which all objects are associated with both attributes and activities. Using objects improves software reusability and makes programs easy to develop and easy to maintain. Programming in Java involves thinking in terms of objects; a Java program can be viewed as a collection of cooperating objects.

This chapter introduces the fundamentals of object-oriented programming: declaring classes, creating objects, manipulating objects, and making objects work together.

6.2 Defining Classes for Objects

object

data field
behavior
method

class

Object-oriented programming (OOP) involves programming using objects. An *object* represents an entity in the real world that can be distinctly identified. For example, a student, a desk, a circle, a button, and even a loan can all be viewed as objects. An object has a unique identity, state, and behaviors. The *state* of an object consists of a set of *data fields* (also known as *properties*) with their current values. The *behavior* of an object is defined by a set of *methods*. Figure 6.1(a) shows a diagram of a generic object with its data fields and methods. Invoking a method on an object is to ask the object to perform a task.

A `Circle` object, for example, has a data field, `radius`, which is the property that characterizes a circle. One behavior of a circle is that its area can be computed using the method `findArea()`. A `Circle` object is shown in Figure 6.1(b).

Classes are constructs that define objects of the same type. A Java class uses variables to define data fields and methods to define behaviors. Additionally, a class provides methods of a special

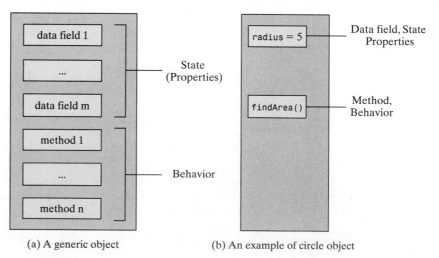

(a) A generic object   (b) An example of circle object

FIGURE 6.1 *An object has both a state and behavior. The state defines the object, and the behavior defines what the object does.*

type, known as *constructors*, which are invoked to construct objects from the class. A **constructor**, like a method, can perform any action, but constructors are designed to perform initializing actions, such as initializing the data fields of objects. Figure 6.2 shows an example of the class for `Circle` objects.

constructor

```
class Circle {
   /** The radius of this circle */
   double radius = 1.0;  ◄──────────── Data field

   /** Construct a circle object */ ─┐
   Circle() {                        │
   }                                 │
                                     ├──◄── Constructors
   /** Construct a circle object */  │
   Circle(double newRadius) {        │
      radius = newRadius;            │
   }                                ─┘

   /** Return the area of this circle */
   double findArea() {  ◄──────────── Method
      return radius * radius * 3.14159;
   }
}
```

FIGURE 6.2 *A class is a construct that defines objects of the same type.*

The `Circle` class is different from all of the other classes you have seen thus far. It does not have a main method and therefore cannot be run; it is merely a definition used to declare and create `Circle` objects. For convenience, the class that contains the main method will be referred to as the *main class* in this book.

main class

6.3 Constructing Objects Using Constructors

The constructor has exactly the same name as the defining class. Like methods, constructors can be overloaded, making it easier to construct objects with different initial data values.

overloading constructors

To construct an object from a class, invoke a constructor of the class using the new operator, as follows:

```
new ClassName(arguments);
```

For example, new `Circle()` creates an object of the `Circle` class using the first constructor defined in the `Circle` class, and new `Circle(5)` creates an object using the second constructor defined in the `Circle` class.

A class normally provides a constructor without arguments (e.g., `Circle()`). Such a constructor is called a *no-arg* or *no-argument constructor*.

no-arg constructor

A class may be declared without constructors. In this case, a no-arg constructor with an empty body is implicitly declared in the class. This constructor, called *a default constructor*, is provided automatically *only if no constructors are explicitly declared in the class*.

default constructor

NOTE

Constructors are a special kind of method, with three differences:

◆ Constructors must have the same name as the class itself.

constructor's name

no return type

new operator

✦ Constructors do not have a return type—not even void.

✦ Constructors are invoked using the new operator when an object is created. Constructors play the role of initializing objects.

 CAUTION

It is a common mistake to put the void keyword in front of a constructor. For example,

```
public void Circle() {
}
```

In this case, Circle() is method, not a constructor.

A class is a blueprint that defines what an object's data and methods will be. An object is an instance of a class. You can create many instances of a class (see Figure 6.3). Creating an instance is referred to as *instantiation*. The terms *object* and *instance* are often interchangeable. The relationship between classes and objects is analogous to the relationship between apple pie recipes and apple pies. You can make as many apple pies as you want from a single recipe.

instantiation

object

instance

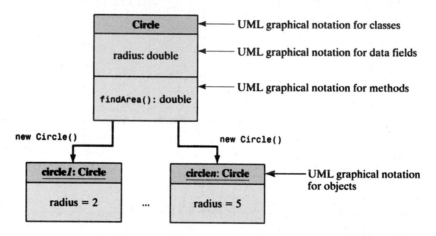

FIGURE 6.3 *A class can have many different objects.*

 NOTE

Figure 6.3 uses the graphical notations adopted in the Unified Modeling Language (UML) to illustrate classes and objects. UML has become the standard for object-oriented modeling. For more information on UML, see www.rational.com/uml/. For a summary of the graphical notations used in this book, see Appendix E, "UML Graphical Notations."

UML

6.4 Accessing Objects via Reference Variables

Newly created objects are allocated in the memory. How can they be accessed? The answer is given in this section.

6.4.1 Reference Variables and Reference Types

reference variable

Objects are accessed via object *reference variables*, which contain references to the objects. Such variables are declared using the following syntax:

```
ClassName objectRefVar;
```

A class defines a type, known as a *reference type*. Any variable of the class type can reference to an instance of the class. The following statement declares the variable `myCircle` to be of the `Circle` type:

```
Circle myCircle;
```

The variable `myCircle` can reference a `Circle` object. The next statement creates an object and assigns its reference to `myCircle`:

```
myCircle = new Circle();
```

Using the syntax shown below, you can write one statement that combines the declaration of an object reference variable, the creation of an object, and the assigning of an object reference to the variable:

```
ClassName objectRefVar = new ClassName();
```

Here is an example:

```
Circle myCircle = new Circle();
```

The variable `myCircle` holds a reference to a `Circle` object.

reference type

 NOTE

An object reference variable that appears to hold an object actually contains a reference to that object. Strictly speaking, an object reference variable and an object are different, but most of the time the distinction between them can be ignored. So it is fine, for simplicity, to say that `myCircle` is a `Circle` object rather than a more long-winded phrase stating that `myCircle` is a variable that contains a reference to a `Circle` object. When the distinction makes a subtle difference, the long phrase should be used.

object vs. object reference variable

 NOTE

Arrays are treated as objects in Java. Arrays are created using the new operator. An array variable is actually a variable that contains a reference to an array.

array object

6.4.2 Accessing an Object's Data and Methods

After an object is created, its data can be accessed and its methods invoked using the following dot notation:

✦ `objectRefVar.data` references an object's data.

✦ `objectRefVar.method(arguments)` invokes an object's method.

For example, `myCircle.radius` references the radius of `myCircle`, and `myCircle.findArea()` invokes the `findArea` method of `myCircle`. Methods are invoked as operations on objects.

The data field `radius` is referred to as an *instance variable* because it is dependent on a specific instance. For the same reason, the method `findArea` is referred to as an *instance method*, because you can only invoke it on a specific instance.

instance variable
instance method

 NOTE

Most of the time, you create an object and assign it to a variable. Later you can use the variable to reference the object. Occasionally, an object does not need to be referenced later. In this case, you can create an object without explicitly assigning it to a variable, as shown below:

```
new Circle();
```

or

```
System.out.println("Area is " + new Circle().findArea());
```

The former statement creates a `Circle` object. The latter statement creates a `Circle` object and invokes its `findArea` method to return its area. An object created in this way is known as an *anonymous object*.

anonymous object

EXAMPLE 6.1 DECLARING CLASSES AND CREATING OBJECTS

Problem

Write a program that constructs an object with radius 5 and an object with radius 1 and displays the radius and area of each of the two circles. Change the radius of the second object to 100 and display its new radius and area, as shown in Figure 6.4.

Solution

To avoid a naming conflict with several improved versions of the `Circle` class introduced later in this chapter, the `Circle` class in this example is named `SimpleCircle` and given in Listing 6.1.

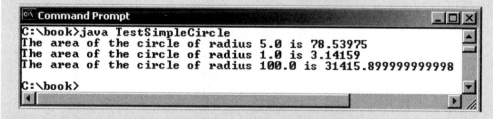

```
Command Prompt                                           _ □ ×
C:\book>java TestSimpleCircle
The area of the circle of radius 5.0 is 78.53975
The area of the circle of radius 1.0 is 3.14159
The area of the circle of radius 100.0 is 31415.899999999998

C:\book>
```

FIGURE 6.4 *The program constructs two circles with radii of 5 and 1, and displays their radii and areas.*

LISTING 6.1 TestSimpleCircle.java (A Simple Circle Class)

```
 1 public class TestSimpleCircle {
 2   /** Main method */
 3   public static void main(String[] args) {
 4     // Create a circle with radius 5.0
 5     SimpleCircle myCircle = new SimpleCircle(5.0);
 6     System.out.println("The area of the circle of radius "
 7       + myCircle.radius + " is " + myCircle.findArea());
 8
 9     // Create a circle with radius 1
10     SimpleCircle yourCircle = new SimpleCircle();
11     System.out.println("The area of the circle of radius "
12       + yourCircle.radius + " is " + yourCircle.findArea());
13
14     // Modify circle radius
15     yourCircle.radius = 100;
16     System.out.println("The area of the circle of radius "
17       + yourCircle.radius + " is " + yourCircle.findArea());
18   }
19 }
20
```

EXAMPLE 6.1   (CONTINUED)

```
21 // Define the circle class with two constructors
22 class SimpleCircle {
23   double radius;
24
25   /** Construct a circle with radius 1 */
26   SimpleCircle() {
27     radius = 1.0;
28   }
29
30   /** Construct a circle with a specified radius */
31   SimpleCircle(double newRadius) {
32     radius = newRadius;
33   }
34
35   /** Return the area of this circle */
36   double findArea() {
37     return radius * radius * 3.14159;
38   }
39 }
```

no-arg constructor

second constructor

Review

The program contains two classes. The first class, `TestSimpleCircle`, is the main class. Its sole purpose is to test the second class, `SimpleCircle`. Every time you run the program, the Java runtime system invokes the `main` method in the main class.

You can put the two classes into one file, but only one class in the file can be a public class. Furthermore, the public class must have the same name as the file name. Therefore, the file name is TestSimpleCircle.java if the `TestSimpleCircle` and `SimpleCircle` classes are both in the same file.

The main class contains the `main` method (Line 3) that creates two objects. The constructor `SimpleCircle(5.0)` was used to create `myCircle` with a radius of 5.0 (Line 5), and the constructor `SimpleCircle()` was used to create `yourCircle` with a radius of 1.0 (Line 10).

These two objects (referenced by `myCircle` and `yourCircle`) have different data but share the same methods. Therefore, you can compute their respective areas by using the `findArea()` method.

To write the `findArea` method in a procedural programming language like Pascal, you would pass radius as an argument to the method. But in object-oriented programming, radius and `findArea` are defined in the same class. The `radius` is a data member in the `SimpleCircle` class, which is accessible by the `findArea` method. In procedural programming languages, data and methods are separated, but in an object-oriented programming language, data and methods are defined together in a class.

The `findArea` method is an instance method that is always invoked by an instance in which the `radius` is specified.

There are many ways to write Java programs. For instance, you can combine the two classes in the example into one, as shown below:

```
public class SimpleCircle {
  /** Main method */
  public static void main(String[] args) {
    // Create a circle with radius 5.0
    SimpleCircle myCircle = new SimpleCircle(5.0);
    System.out.println("The area of the circle of radius "
      + myCircle.radius + " is " + myCircle.findArea());

    // Create a circle with radius 1
    SimpleCircle yourCircle = new SimpleCircle();
    System.out.println("The area of the circle of radius "
      + yourCircle.radius + " is " + yourCircle.findArea());
```

EXAMPLE **6.1**   (CONTINUED)

```
      // Modify circle radius
      yourCircle.radius = 100;
      System.out.println("The area of the circle of radius "
        + yourCircle.radius + " is " + yourCircle.findArea());
    }

    double radius;

    /** Construct a circle with radius 1 */
    SimpleCircle() {
      radius = 1.0;
    }

    /** Construct a circle with a specified radius */
    SimpleCircle(double newRadius) {
      radius = newRadius;
    }

    /** Return the area of this circle */
    double findArea() {
      return radius * radius * 3.14159;
    }

  }
```

Since the combined class has a `main` method, it can be executed by the Java interpreter. The `main` method creates `myCircle` as a `SimpleCircle` object and then displays radius and finds area in `myCircle`. This demonstrates that you can test a class by simply adding a `main` method in the same class.

> **CAUTION**
>
> invoking methods
>
> Recall that you use `Math.methodName(arguments)` (e.g., `Math.pow(3, 2.5)`) to invoke a method in the `Math` class. Can you invoke `findArea()` using `SimpleCircle.findArea()`? The answer is no. All the methods used before this chapter are static methods, which are defined using the `static` keyword. However, `findArea()` is non-static. It must be invoked from an object using `objectRefVar.methodName(arguments)` (e.g., `myCircle.findArea()`). More explanations will be given in Section 6.10, "Static Variables, Constants, and Methods."

6.4.3   The `null` Value

If a variable of a reference type does not reference any object, the variable holds a special Java value, `null`. `null` is a literal just like `true` and `false`. While `true` and `false` are literals for `boolean` type variables, `null` is for reference type variables.

default field values

The default value of a data field is `null` for a reference type, `0` for a numeric type, `false` for a `boolean` type, and `'\u0000'` for a `char` type. However, Java assigns no default value to a local variable inside a method. The following code displays the default values of data fields `name`, `age`, `isScienceMajor`, and `gender` for a `Student` object:

```
class Student {
  String name; // name has default value null
  int age; // age has default value 0
  boolean isScienceMajor; // isScienceMajor has default value false
  char gender; // c has default value '\u0000'

  public static void main(String[] args) {
    Student student = new Student();
    System.out.println("name? " + student.name);
```

```
        System.out.println("age? " + student.age);
        System.out.println("isScienceMajor? " + student.isScienceMajor);
        System.out.println("gender? " + student.gender);
    }
}
```

The following code has a compilation error because local variables x and y are not initialized:

```
class Test {
  public static void main(String[] args) {
    int x; // x has no default value
    String y; // y has no default value
    System.out.println("x is " + x);
    System.out.println("y is " + y);
  }
}
```

CAUTION

You must always create an object before referencing it through a reference variable. Referencing an object that has not been created would cause a runtime NullPointerException. Exception handling will be introduced in Chapter 15, "Exceptions and Assertions."

NullPointerException

6.4.4   Differences Between Variables of Primitive Types and Reference Types

Every variable represents a memory location that holds a value. When you declare a variable, you are telling the compiler what type of value the variable can hold. For a variable of a primitive type, the value is of the primitive type. For a variable of a reference type, the value is a reference to where an object is located. For example, as shown in Figure 6.5, the value of int variable i is int value 1, and the value of Circle object c holds a reference to where the contents of the Circle object are stored in the memory.

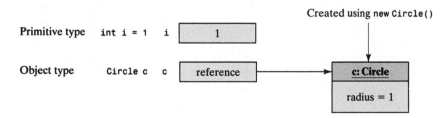

FIGURE 6.5   *A variable of a primitive type holds a value of the primitive type, and a variable of a reference type holds a reference to where an object is stored in the memory.*

When you assign one variable to another, the other variable is set to the same value. For a variable of a primitive type, the real value of one variable is assigned to the other variable. For a variable of a reference type, the reference of one variable is assigned to the other variable. As shown in Figure 6.6, the assignment statement i = j copies the contents of j into i for primitive variables, and the assignment statement c1 = c2 copies the reference of c2 into c1 for reference variables. After the assignment, variables c1 and c2 refer to the same object.

NOTE

As shown in Figure 6.6, after the assignment statement c1 = c2, c1 points to the same object referenced by c2. The object previously referenced by c1 is no longer useful and therefore is now known as *garbage*. Garbage occupies memory space.

garbage

garbage collection

The Java runtime system detects garbage and automatically reclaims the space it occupies. This process is called *garbage collection*.

 TIP

If you know that an object is no longer needed, you can explicitly assign `null` to a reference variable for the object. The Java Virtual Machine will automatically collect the space if the object is not referenced by any reference variable.

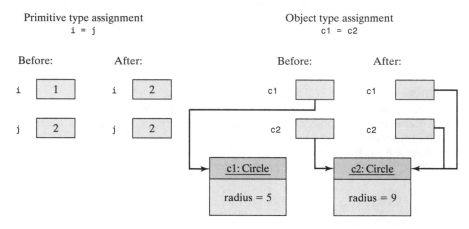

FIGURE 6.6 *Copying a reference variable to another variable does not make a copy of the object; it merely assigns the reference of the object to the other variable.*

6.5 Using Classes from the Java Library

Example 6.1 declared the `SimpleCircle` class and created objects from the class. You will frequently use the classes in the Java library to develop programs. In Example 2.5, "Displaying Current Time," you learned how to obtain the current time using `System.currentTimeMillis()`. You used the division and remainder operators to extract current second, minute, and hour. Java provides a system-independent encapsulation of date and time in the `java.util.Date` class. You can use the
`Date` class to create an instance for the current date and time and its `toString` method to return the date and time as a string. For example, the following code

Date class

```
java.util.Date date = new java.util.Date();
System.out.println(date.toString());
```

displays a string like `Sun Mar 09 13:50:19 EST 2003`.

When you develop programs to create graphical user interfaces, you will use Java classes to create frames, buttons, radio buttons, combo boxes, lists, and so on. Listing 6.2 is an example that creates two frames.

LISTING 6.2 TestFrame.java (Using Java API Classes)

creating an object
invoking a method

```
1 import javax.swing.JFrame;
2
3 public class TestFrame {
4   public static void main(String[] args) {
5     JFrame frame1 = new JFrame();
6     frame1.setTitle("Window 1");
7     frame1.setSize(200, 150);
8     frame1.setLocation(200, 100);
9     frame1.setVisible(true);
10
```

```
11    JFrame frame2 = new JFrame();
12    frame2.setTitle("Window 2");
13    frame2.setSize(200, 150);
14    frame2.setLocation(410, 100);
15    frame2.setVisible(true);
16  }
17 }
```

creating an object
invoking a method

The output of the program is shown in Figure 6.7.

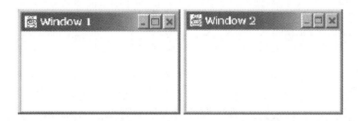

FIGURE 6.7 *The program creates two windows using the* JFrame *class.*

This program creates two objects of the JFrame class and then uses the methods setTitle, setSize, setLocation, and setVisible to set the properties of the objects. The setTitle method sets a title for the window (Lines 6, 2). The setSize method sets the window's width and height (Lines 7, 13). The setLocation method specifies the location of the window's upper-left corner (Line 9, 14). The setVisible method displays the window. You can add graphical user interface components, such as buttons, labels, text fields, combo boxes, lists, and menus, to the window. The components are defined using classes. GUI programming will be introduced in Part III, "GUI Programming."

A class usually provides many constructors with which users can initialize objects. For example, the JFrame class has a no-arg constructor, JFrame(), and another one, JFrame(String title), to initialize the title. You can use the following statement to create a frame entitled "Window 1":

```
JFrame frame1 = new JFrame("Window 1");
```

6.6 Visibility Modifiers, Accessors, and Mutators

Java provides several modifiers that control access to data, methods, and classes. This section introduces the public, private, and default modifiers.

✦ public makes classes, methods, and data fields accessible from any class.

public

✦ private makes methods and data fields accessible only from within its own class.

private

✦ If public or private is not used, then by default the classes, methods, and data are accessible by any class in the same package. This is known as *package-private* or *package-access*.

package-private

Figure 6.8 illustrates how public, default, and private data or methods in class C1 can be accessed from a class C2 in the same package, and from a class C3 in a different package.

If a class is not declared public, it can only be accessed within the same package, as shown in Figure 6.9.

```
package p1;

public class C1 {              public class C2 {
  public int x;                  C1 o = new C1();
  int y;                         can access o.x;
  private int z;                 can access o.y;
                                 cannot access o.z;
  public void m1() {
  }                              can invoke o.m1();
  void m2() {                    can invoke o.m2();
  }                              cannot invoke o.m3();
  private void m3() {          }
  }
}
```

```
package p2;

public class C3 {
  C1 o = new C1();
  can access o.x;
  cannot access o.y;
  cannot access o.z;

  can invoke o.m1();
  cannot invoke o.m2();
  cannot invoke o.m3();
}
```

FIGURE 6.8 *The private modifier restricts access to within a class, the default modifier restricts access to within a package, and the public modifier enables unrestricted access.*

```
package p1;

class C1 {            public class C2 {
  ...                   can access C1
}                     }
```

```
package p2;

public class C3 {
  cannot access C1;
}
```

FIGURE 6.9 *A non-public class has package-access.*

🌿 NOTE

An object cannot access its private members, as shown in Figure 6.10(b). It is OK, however, if the object is declared in its own class, as shown in Figure 6.10(a).

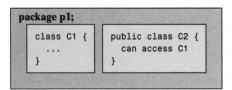

```
public class Foo {
  private boolean x;

  public static void main(String[] args) {
    Foo foo = new Foo();
    System.out.println(foo.x);
    System.out.println(foo.convert(foo.x));
  }

  private int convert(boolean b) {
    return x ? 1 : -1;
  }
}
```

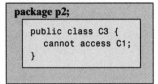

```
public class Test {
  public static void main(String[] args) {
    Foo foo = new Foo();
    System.out.println(foo.x);
    System.out.println(foo.convert(foo.x));
  }
}
```

(a) This is OK because object foo is used inside the Foo class

(b) This is wrong because x and convert are private in Foo.

FIGURE 6.10 *An object can access its private members if it is declared in its own class.*

🌿 NOTE

The modifier `private` applies solely to data or methods, not to classes (except inner classes). Inner classes will be introduced in Section 6.17, "Inner Classes." The various Java modifiers are summarized in the table in Appendix D, "Java Modifiers."

Visibility modifiers are used for the members of the class, not local variables inside the methods. Using a visibility modifier inside a method body would cause a compilation error.

 NOTE

In most cases, the constructor should be public. However, if you want to prohibit the user from creating an instance of a class, you can use a private constructor. For example, there is no reason to create an instance from the Math class because all of the data and methods are static. One solution is to define a dummy private constructor in the class. The Math class cannot be instantiated because it has a private constructor, as follows:

```
private Math() {
}
```

The Math class that comes with the Java system was introduced in Section 4.8, "The Math Class."

6.7 Data Field Encapsulation

Example 6.1 works fine, but it is not a good practice to allow the fields to be modified directly through the object reference (e.g., myCircle.radius = 5). Doing so makes the class difficult to maintain and vulnerable to bugs. Suppose you want to modify the Circle class to ensure that the radius is non-negative after other programs have already used the class. You have to change not only the Circle class, but also the programs that use the Circle class. Such programs are often referred to as *clients*. This is because the clients may have modified the radius directly (e.g., myCircle.radius = -5). To prevent direct modifications of properties through the object reference, you should declare the field private, using the private modifier. This is known as *data field encapsulation*.

client

data field encapsulation

A private data field cannot be accessed by an object through a direct reference outside the class that defines the private field. But often a client needs to retrieve and modify a data field. To make a private data field accessible, provide a *get* method to return the value of the data. To enable a private data field to be updated, provide a *set* method to set a new value.

 NOTE

Colloquially, a get method is referred to as a *getter* (or *accessor*), and a set method is referred to as a *setter* (or *mutator*).

accessor

mutator

A get method has the following signature:

`public returnType getPropertyName()`

If the returnType is boolean, the get method should be defined as follows by convention:

`public boolean isPropertyName()`

A set method has the following signature:

`public void setPropertyName(dataType propertyValue)`

Let us create a new Circle class with a private data field radius and its associated accessor and mutator methods, as follows:

LISTING 6.3 Circle.java (A Circle Class with Private Fields)

```
1 public class Circle {
2   /** The radius of the circle */
3   private double radius;
4
```

encapsulate radius

```
 5   /** Construct a circle with radius 1 */
 6   public Circle() {
 7     radius = 1.0;
 8   }
 9
10   /** Construct a circle with a specified radius */
11   public Circle(double newRadius) {
12     radius = newRadius;
13   }
14
15   /** Return radius */
16   public double getRadius() {
17     return radius;
18   }
19
20   /** Set a new radius */
21   public void setRadius(double newRadius) {
22     radius = (newRadius >= 0) ? newRadius : 0;
23   }
24
25   /** Return the area of this circle */
26   public double findArea() {
27     return radius * radius * 3.14159;
28   }
29 }
```

access method — Line 16: `public double getRadius() {`

mutator method — Line 21: `public void setRadius(double newRadius) {`

The getRadius() method (Lines 16–18) returns the radius, and the setRadius(newRadius) method (Line 21–23) sets a new radius into the object. If the new radius is negative, 0 is set to the radius in the object. Since these methods are the only ways to read and modify radius, you have total control over how the radius property is accessed. If you have to change the implementation of these methods, you need not change the client programs that use them. This makes the class easy to maintain. For this reason, most of the data fields in this book will be private.

Here is a client program that uses the Circle class to create a Circle object and modifies the radius using the setRadius method.

```
 1 // TestCircle.java : Demonstrate private modifier
 2 public class TestCircle {
 3   /** Main method */
 4   public static void main(String[] args) {
 5     // Create a Circle with radius 5.0
 6     Circle myCircle = new Circle(5.0);
 7     System.out.println("The area of the circle of radius "
 8       + myCircle.getRadius() + " is " + myCircle.findArea());
 9
10     // Increase myCircle's radius by 10%
11     myCircle.setRadius(myCircle.getRadius() * 1.1);
12     System.out.println("The area of the circle of radius "
13       + myCircle.getRadius() + " is " + myCircle.findArea());
14   }
15 }
```

The data field radius is declared private. Private data can only be accessed within their defining class. You cannot use myCircle.radius in the client program. A compilation error would occur if you attempted to access private data from a client.

Suppose you combined TestCircle and Circle into one class by moving the main method in TestCircle into Circle. Could you use myCircle.radius in the main method? See Review Question 6.12 for the answer.

 NOTE

When you compile TestCircle.java, the Java compiler automatically compiles Circle.java if it has not been compiled since the last change.

6.8   Immutable Objects and Classes

If the contents of an object cannot be changed once the object is created, the object is called an *immutable object* and its class is called an *immutable class*. If you delete the set method in the Circle class in the preceding example, the class would be immutable because radius is private and cannot be changed without a set method.

immutable class
immutable object

A class with all private data fields and no mutators is not necessarily immutable. For example, the following class Student has all private data fields and no mutators, but it is mutable:

```java
public class Student {
  private int id;
  private BirthDate birthDate;

  public Student(int ssn, int year, int month, int day) {
    id = ssn;
    birthDate = new BirthDate(year, month, day);
  }

  public int getId() {
    return id;
  }

  public BirthDate getBirthDate() {
    return birthDate;
  }
}

public class BirthDate {
  private int year;
  private int month;
  private int day;

  public BirthDate(int newYear, int newMonth, int newDay) {
    year = newYear;
    month = newMonth;
    day = newDay;
  }

  public void setYear(int newYear) {
    year = newYear;
  }
}
```

As shown in the following code, the data field birthDate is returned using the getBirthDate() method. This is a reference to a BirthDate object. Through this reference, the year of the birth date is changed, which effectively changes the contents of the Student object.

```java
public class Test {
  public static void main(String[] args) {
    Student student = new Student(111223333, 1970, 5, 3);
    BirthDate date = student.getBirthDate();
    date.setYear(2010); // Now the student birth year is changed!
  }
}
```

For a class to be immutable, it must mark all data fields private and provide no mutator methods and no accessor methods that would return a reference to a mutable data field object.

6.9 Passing Objects to Methods

So far, you have learned how to pass arguments of primitive types and array types to methods. You can also pass objects to methods. Like passing an array, passing an object is actually passing the reference of the object. The following code passes the myCircle object as an argument to the printCircle method:

```
public class TestPassObject {
  public static void main(String[] args) {
    Circle myCircle = new Circle(5.0);
    printCircle(myCircle);
  }

  public static void printCircle(Circle c) {
    System.out.println("The area of the circle of radius "
      + c.getRadius() + " is " + c.findArea());
  }
}
```

pass by value

Java uses exactly one mode of passing arguments: *pass by value*. In the preceding code, the value of myCircle is passed to the printCircle method. This value is a reference to a Circle object.

Let us demonstrate the difference between passing a primitive type value and passing a reference value with the program in Listing 6.4:

LISTING 6.4 TestPassObject.java (Object Arguments)

```
 1 public class TestPassObject {
 2   /** Main method */
 3   public static void main(String[] args) {
 4     // Create a Circle object with radius 1
 5     Circle myCircle = new Circle();
 6
 7     // Print areas for radius 1, 2, 3, 4, and 5.
 8     int n = 5;
 9     printAreas(myCircle, n);
10
11     // See myCircle.radius and times
12     System.out.println("\n" + "Radius is " + myCircle.getRadius());
13     System.out.println("n is " + n);
14   }
15
16   /** Print a table of areas for radius */
17   public static void printAreas(Circle c, int times) {
18     System.out.println("Radius \t\tArea");
19     while (times >= 1) {
20       System.out.println(c.getRadius() + "\t\t" + c.findArea());
21       c.setRadius(c.getRadius() + 1);
22       times--;
23     }
24   }
25 }
```

The program passes a Circle object myCircle and an integer value from n to invoke printAreas(myCircle, n) (Line 9), which prints a table of areas for radii 1, 2, 3, 4, and 5, as shown in Figure 6.11.

Figure 6.12 shows the call stack for executing the methods in the program. Note that the objects are stored in a heap.

When passing an argument of a primitive data type, the value of the argument is passed. In this case, the value of n (5) is passed to times. Inside the printAreas method, the content of times is changed; this does not affect the content of n. When passing an argument of a reference type, the reference of the object is passed. In this case, c contains a reference for the object that is also referenced via myCircle. Therefore, changing the properties of the object through c inside

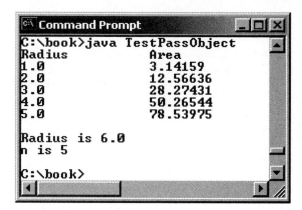

FIGURE 6.11   *The program passes a* Circle *object* myCircle *and an integer value* n *as arguments to the* printAreas *method, which displays a table of the areas for radii 1, 2, 3, 4, and 5.*

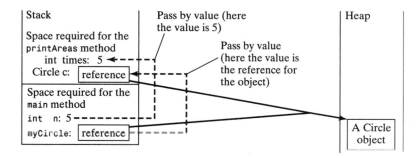

FIGURE 6.12   *The value of* n *is passed to* times, *and the reference of* myCircle *is passed to* c *in the* printAreas *method.*

the printAreas method has the same effect as doing so outside the method through the variable myCircle.

6.10   Static Variables, Constants, and Methods

The variable radius in the circle classes in the preceding examples is known as an *instance variable*. An instance variable is tied to a specific instance of the class; it is not shared among objects of the same class. For example, suppose that you create the following objects:

```
Circle circle1 = new Circle();
Circle circle2 = new Circle(5);
```

The radius in circle1 is independent of the radius in circle2, and is stored in a different memory location. Changes made to circle1's radius do not affect circle2's radius, and vice versa.

If you want all the instances of a class to share data, use *static variables*. Static variables store values for the variables in a common memory location. Because of this common location, all objects of the same class are affected if one object changes the value of a static variable. Java supports static methods as well as static variables. *Static methods* can be called without creating an instance of the class.

Let us modify the Circle class by adding a static variable numberOfObjects to track the number of circle objects created. The UML of the new circle class named CircleWithStatic

instance variable

static variable

static method

UML Notation:
    +: public variables or methods
    −: private variables or methods
    underline: static variables or methods

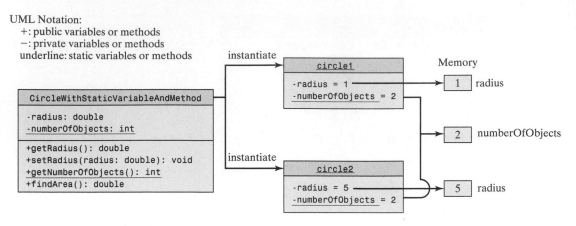

FIGURE 6.13   *The instance variables, which belong to the instances, have memory storage independent of one another. The static variables are shared by all the instances of the same class.*

VariableAndMethod is shown in Figure 6.13. The CircleWithStaticVariableAndMethod class defines the instance variable radius and the static variable numberOfObjects, the instance methods getRadius, setRadius, and findArea, and the static method getNumberOfObjects.

To declare a static variable or a static method, put the modifier static in the variable or method declaration. The static variable numberOfObjects and the static method getNumberOfObjects() can be declared as follows:

declare static variable

```
private static int numberOfObjects;
```

declare static method

```
public static int getNumberObjects() {
  return numberOfObjects;
}
```

When the first object of this class is created, numberOfObjects is 1. When the second object is created, numberOfObjects becomes 2, as shown in Figure 6.13.

To declare a class constant, add the final keyword in the static variable declaration. For example, the constant PI in the Math class is defined as:

declare constant

```
public final static double PI = 3.14159265358979323846;
```

The CircleWithStaticVariableAndMethod class can be declared as follows:

LISTING 6.5   CircleWithStaticVariableAndMethod.java (Static Fields and Methods)

```
 1 public class CircleWithStaticVariableAndMethod {
 2   /** The radius of the circle */
 3   private double radius;
 4
 5   /** The number of the objects created */
 6   private static int numberOfObjects = 0;
 7
 8   /** Construct a circle with radius 1 */
 9   public CircleWithStaticVariableAndMethod() {
10     radius = 1.0;
11     numberOfObjects++;
12   }
13
14   /** Construct a circle with a specified radius */
15   public CircleWithStaticVariableAndMethod(double newRadius) {
16     radius = newRadius;
17     numberOfObjects++;
18   }
19
```

```
20    /** Return radius */
21    public double getRadius() {
22      return radius;
23    }
24
25    /** Set a new radius */
26    public void setRadius(double newRadius) {
27      radius = newRadius;
28    }
29
30    /** Return numberOfObjects */
31    public static int getNumberOfObjects() {
32      return numberOfObjects;
33    }
34
35    /** Return the area of this circle */
36    public double findArea() {
37      return radius * radius * Math.PI;
38    }
39 }
```

Method getNumberOfObjects() in CircleWithStaticVariableAndMethod is a static method. Other examples of static methods are showMessageDialog and showInputDialog in the JOptionPane class, and all the methods in the Math class. In fact, so are all the methods used in Part I of this book, including the main method.

Instance methods (e.g., getRadius, setRadius, and findArea) belong to instances and can only be applied after the instances are created. They are called by the following:

```
objectRefVar.methodName();
```

Static methods (e.g., getNumberOfObjects()) are called by one of these syntaxes:

```
ClassRefVar.methodName(arguments); // Invoked from a class name
objectRefVar.methodName(arguments); // Invoked from a calling object
```

For example, method getNumberOfObjects can be invoked using CircleWithStatic VariableAndMethod.getNumberOfObjects() or circle1.getNumberOfObjects(), where circle1 is a variable declared as CircleWithStaticVariableAndMethod.

TIP

I recommend that you invoke a static method using ClassName.method-Name(arguments). This improves readability because the user can easily recognize the static method invoked with the class name.

The program in Listing 6.6 demonstrates how to use instance and static variables and methods, and illustrates the effects of using them. Its output is shown in Figure 6.14.

```
C:\book>java TestCircleWithStaticVariableAndMethod
Before creating circle2
circle1 is : radius (1.0) and number of Circle objects (1)

After creating circle2 and modifying circle1's radius to 9
circle1 is : radius (9.0) and number of Circle objects (2)
circle2 is : radius (5.0) and number of Circle objects (2)

C:\book>_
```

FIGURE 6.14 *The program uses the instance variable* radius *as well as the static variable* numberOfObjects. *All of the objects share the same* numberOfObjects.

LISTING 6.6   TestCircleWithStaticVariableAndMethod.java

```
1 public class TestCircleWithStaticVariableAndMethod {
2    /** Main method */
3    public static void main(String[] args) {
4      // Create circle1
5      CircleWithStaticVariableAndMethod circle1 =
6        new CircleWithStaticVariableAndMethod();
7
8      // Display circle1 BEFORE circle2 is created
9      System.out.println("Before creating circle2");
10     System.out.print("circle1 is : ");
11     printCircle(circle1);
12
13     // Create circle2
14     CircleWithStaticVariableAndMethod circle2 =
15       new CircleWithStaticVariableAndMethod(5);
16
17     // Change the radius in circle1
18     circle1.setRadius(9);
19
20     // Display circle1 and circle2 AFTER circle2 was created
21     System.out.println("\nAfter creating circle2 and modifying " +
22       "circle1's radius to 9");
23     System.out.print("circle1 is : ");
24     printCircle(circle1);
25     System.out.print("circle2 is : ");
26     printCircle(circle2);
27   }
28
29   /** Print circle information */
30   public static void printCircle(
31       CircleWithStaticVariableAndMethod c) {
32     System.out.println("radius (" + c.getRadius() +
33       ") and number of Circle objects (" +
34       c.getNumberOfObjects() + ")");
35   }
36 }
```

The main method creates two circles, circle1 and circle2 (Lines 5, 14). The instance variable radius in circle1 is modified to become 9 (Line 18). This change does not affect the instance variable radius in circle2, since these two instance variables are independent. The static variable numberOfObjects becomes 1 after circle1 is created (Lines 5–6), and it becomes 2 after circle2 is created (Lines 14–15). This change affects all the instances of the CircleWithStaticVariableAndMethod class, since the static variable numberOfObjects is shared by all the instances of the CircleWithStaticVariableAndMethod class.

Since numberOfObjects is private, it cannot be modified. This prevents tampering. For example, the user cannot set numberOfObjects to 100. The only way to make it 100 is to create one hundred objects of the CircleWithStaticVariableAndMethod class.

Note that Math.PI is used to access PI, and that c.numberOfObjects in the printCircle method (Line 34) is used to access numberOfObjects. Math is the class name, and c is an object of the Circle class. To access a constant like PI, you can use either the ClassName.CONSTANTNAME or the objectName.CONSTANTNAME. To access an instance variable like radius, you need to use objectRefVar.variableName.

I recommend that you invoke static variables and methods using ClassName.variable and ClassName.method. This improves readability because the user can easily recognize the static variables and methods. In this example you should replace c.getNumberOfObjects() in Line 34 by CircleWithStaticVariableAndMethod.getNumberOfObjects().

 CAUTION

Static variables and methods can be used from either instance or static methods in the class. However, instance variables and methods can only be used from instance methods, not from static methods, since static variables and methods belong to the class as a whole and not to particular objects. Thus the code given below would be wrong.

```
public class Foo {
  int i = 5;
  static int k = 2;

  public static void main(String[] args) {
    int j = i; // Wrong because i is an instance variable
    m1(); // Wrong because m1() is an instance method
  }

  public void m1() {
    // Correct since instance and static variables and methods
    // can be used in an instance method
    i = i + k + m2(i, k);
  }

  public static int m2(int i, int j) {
    return (int)(Math.pow(i, j));
  }
}
```

TIP

How do you decide whether a variable or method should be an instance one or a static one? A variable or method that is dependent on a specific instance of the class should be an instance variable or method. A variable or method that is not dependent on a specific instance of the class should be a static variable or method. For example, every circle has its own radius. Radius is dependent on a specific circle. Therefore, radius is an instance variable of the Circle class. Since the findArea method is dependent on a specific circle, it is an instance method. None of the methods in the Math class, such as random, pow, sin, and cos, is dependent on a specific instance. Therefore, these methods are static methods. The main method is static, and can be invoked directly from a class.

instance or static?

6.11 The Scope of Variables

Chapter 4, "Methods," discussed local variables and their scope rules. Local variables are declared and used inside a method locally. This section discusses the scope rules of all the variables in the context of a class.

Instance and static variables in a class are referred to as the *class's variables or data fields*. A variable defined inside a method is referred to as a local variable. The scope of a class's variables is the entire class, regardless of where the variables are declared. A class's variables and methods can be declared in any order in the class, as shown in Figure 6.15(a). The exception is when a data field

```
public class Circle {
  public double findArea() {
    return radius * radius * Math.PI;
  }

  private double radius = 1;
}
```

```
public class Foo {
  private int i;
  private int j = i + 1;
}
```

(a) variable radius and method findArea()   (b) i has to be declared before j because
    can be declared in any order   j's initial value is dependent on i.

FIGURE 6.15 *Members of a class can be declared in any order, with one exception.*

is initialized based on a reference to another data field. In such cases, the other data field must be declared first, as shown in Figure 6.15(b).

You can declare a class's variable only once, but you can declare the same variable in a method many times in different non-nesting blocks.

If a local variable has the same name as a class's variable, the local variable takes precedence and the class's variable with the same name is hidden. For example, in the following program, x is defined as an instance variable and as a local variable in the method:

```java
class Foo {
  int x = 0; // instance variable
  int y = 0;

  Foo() {
  }

  void p() {
    int x = 1; // local variable
    System.out.println("x = " + x);
    System.out.println("y = " + y);
  }
}
```

What is the printout for f.p(), where f is an instance of Foo? The printout for f.p() is 1 for x and 0 for y. Here is why:

✦ x is declared as a data field with the initial value of 0 in the class, but is also defined in the method p() with an initial value of 1. The latter x is referenced in the System. out.println statement.

✦ y is declared outside the method p(), but is accessible inside it.

TIP

As demonstrated in the example, it is easy to make mistakes. To avoid confusion, do not declare a variable twice in a class, except for method parameters and loop control variables in a for loop.

6.12   The this Keyword

hidden variable

Sometimes you need to reference a class's *hidden variable* in a method. For example, a property name is often used as the parameter name in a set method for the property. In this case, you need to reference the hidden property name in the method in order to set a new value to

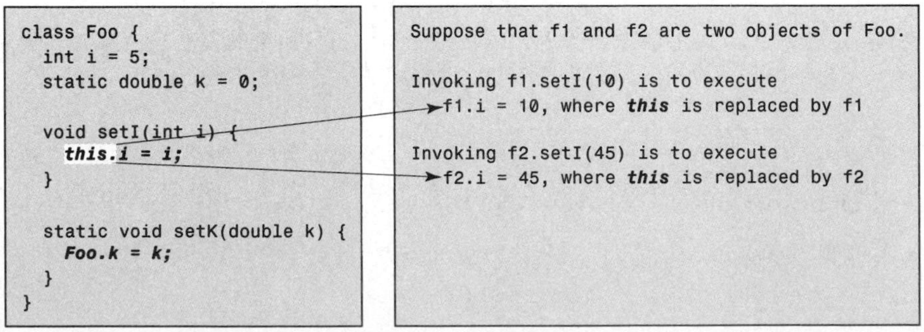

```java
class Foo {
  int i = 5;
  static double k = 0;

  void setI(int i) {
    this.i = i;
  }

  static void setK(double k) {
    Foo.k = k;
  }
}
```

(a)

```
Suppose that f1 and f2 are two objects of Foo.

Invoking f1.setI(10) is to execute
   f1.i = 10, where this is replaced by f1

Invoking f2.setI(45) is to execute
   f2.i = 45, where this is replaced by f2
```

(b)

FIGURE 6.16   *The this keyword serves as the proxy for the object that invokes the method.*

it. A hidden static variable can be accessed simply by using the `ClassName.StaticVariable` reference. A hidden instance variable can be accessed by using the keyword `this`, as shown in Figure 6.16(a).

The line `this.i = i` means "assign the value of parameter `i` to the data field `i` of the calling object." The keyword `this` serves as a proxy for the object that invokes the instance method `setI`, as shown in Figure 6.16(b). The line `Foo.k = k` means that the value in parameter `k` is assigned to the static data field `k` of the class, which is shared by all the objects of the class.

The keyword `this` can also be used inside a constructor to invoke another constructor of the same class. For example, you can redefine the `Circle` class as follows:

```
public class Circle {
  private double radius;

  public Circle(double radius) {
    this.radius = radius;
  }                             this must be explicitly used to reference the data
                                field radius of the object being constructed
  public Circle() {
    this(1.0);
  }                             this is used to invoke another constructor

  public double findArea() {
    return this.radius * this.radius * Math.PI;
  }                   Every instance variable belongs to an instance represented by this,
}                     which is normally omitted
```

The line `this(1.0)` invokes the constructor with a `double` value argument in the class.

 TIP

If a class has multiple constructors, I recommend that you implement them using `this(arg-list)` as much as possible. In general, a constructor with no or fewer arguments can invoke the constructor with more arguments using `this(arg-list)`. This often simplifies coding and makes the class easier to read and to maintain.

 NOTE

Java requires that the `this(arg-list)` statement appear first in the constructor before any other statements.

6.13 Array of Objects

In Chapter 5, "Arrays," arrays of primitive type elements were created. You can also create arrays of objects. For example, the following statement declares and creates an array of ten `Circle` objects:

```
Circle[] circleArray = new Circle[10];
```

To initialize the `circleArray`, you can use a `for` loop like this one:

```
for (int i = 0; i < circleArray.length; i++) {
  circleArray[i] = new Circle();
}
```

An array of objects is actually an *array of reference variables*. So invoking `circleArray[1].findArea()` involves two levels of referencing, as shown in Figure 6.17. `circleArray` references the entire array. `circleArray[1]` references a `Circle` object.

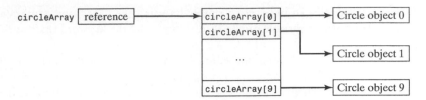

FIGURE 6.17 *In an array of objects, an element of the array contains a reference to an object.*

 NOTE

When an array of objects is created using the `new` operator, each element is a reference variable with a default value of `null`.

The example given below demonstrates how to use an array of objects.

EXAMPLE 6.2 SUMMARIZING THE AREAS OF THE CIRCLES

Problem

Write a program that summarizes the areas of an array of circles. The program creates `circleArray`, an array composed of ten `Circle` objects; it then initializes circle radii with random values, and displays the total area of the circles in the array.

Solution

Listing 6.7 gives the solution to the problem. The output of a sample run of the program is shown in Figure 6.18.

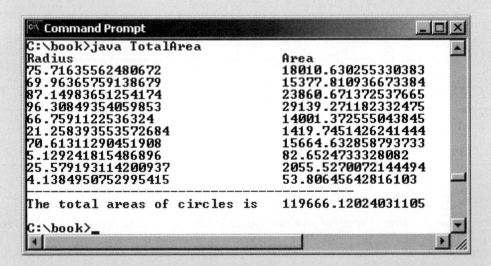

FIGURE 6.18 *The program creates an array of* `Circle` *objects, then displays their total area.*

LISTING 6.7 TotalArea.java (Array of Objects)

```
1 public class TotalArea {
2   /** Main method */
3   public static void main(String[] args) {
4     // Declare circleArray
5     Circle[] circleArray;
6
```

EXAMPLE 6.2   (CONTINUED)

```java
 7      // Create circleArray
 8      circleArray = createCircleArray();
 9
10      // Print circleArray and total areas of the circles
11      printCircleArray(circleArray);
12    }
13
14    /** Create an array of Circle objects */
15    public static Circle[] createCircleArray() {
16      Circle[] circleArray = new Circle[10];
17
18      for (int i = 0; i < circleArray.length; i++) {
19        circleArray[i] = new Circle(Math.random() * 100);
20      }
21
22      // Return Circle array
23      return circleArray;
24    }
25
26    /** Print an array of circles and their total area */
27    public static void printCircleArray
28        (Circle[] circleArray) {
29      System.out.println("Radius\t\t\t\t" + "Area");
30      for (int i = 0; i < circleArray.length; i++) {
31        System.out.print(circleArray[i].getRadius() + "\t\t" +
32          circleArray[i].findArea() + '\n');
33      }
34
35      System.out.println("----------------");
36
37      // Compute and display the result
38      System.out.println("The total areas of circles is \t" +
39        sum(circleArray));
40    }
41
42    /** Add circle areas */
43    public static double sum(Circle[] circleArray) {
44      // Initialize sum
45      double sum = 0;
46
47      // Add areas to sum
48      for (int i = 0; i < circleArray.length; i++)
49        sum += circleArray[i].findArea();
50
51      return sum;
52    }
53  }
```

Review

The program invokes `createCircleArray()` (Line 8) to create an array of ten `Circle` objects. Several `Circle` classes were introduced in this chapter. This example uses the `Circle` class introduced in Section 6.7, "Data Field Encapsulation."

The circle radii are randomly generated using the `Math.random()` method (Line 19). The `createCircleObject` method returns an array of `Circle` objects (Line 23). The array is passed to the `printCircleArray` method, which displays the radii of the total area of the circles.

The sum of the areas of the circle is computed using the `sum` method (Line 39), which takes the array of `Circle` objects as the argument and returns a `double` value for the total area.

6.14 Class Abstraction and Encapsulation

class abstraction

In Chapter 4, "Methods," you learned about method abstraction and used it in program development. Java provides many levels of abstraction. *Class abstraction* is the separation of class implementation from the use of a class. The creator of a class provides a description of the class and lets the user know how the class can be used. The collection of methods and fields that are accessible from outside the class, together with the description of how these members are expected to behave, serves as the *class's contract*. As shown in Figure 6.19, the user of the class does not need to know how the class is implemented. The details of implementation are encapsulated and hidden from the user. This is known as *class encapsulation*. For example, you can create a `Circle` object and find the area of the circle without knowing how the area is computed.

class encapsulation

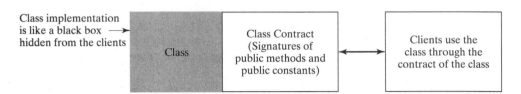

FIGURE 6.19 *Class abstraction separates class implementation from the use of the class.*

Class abstraction and encapsulation are two sides of the same coin. There are many real-life examples that illustrate the concept of class abstraction. Consider building a computer system, for instance. Your personal computer is made up of many components, such as a CPU, CD-ROM, floppy disk, motherboard, fan, and so on. Each component can be viewed as an object that has properties and methods. To get the components to work together, all you need to know is how each component is used and how it interacts with the others. You don't need to know how it works internally. The internal implementation is encapsulated and hidden from you. You can build a computer without knowing how a component is implemented.

The computer-system analogy precisely mirrors the object-oriented approach. Each component can be viewed as an object of the class for the component. For example, you might have a class that models all kinds of fans for use in a computer, with properties like fan size and speed, and methods like start, stop, and so on. A specific fan is an instance of this class with specific property values.

Consider getting a loan, for another example. A specific loan can be viewed as an object of a `Loan` class. Interest rate, loan amount, and loan period are its data properties, and computing monthly payment and total payment are its methods. When you buy a car, a loan object is created by instantiating the class with your loan interest rate, loan amount, and loan period. You can then use the methods to find the monthly payment and total payment of your loan. As a user of the `Loan` class, you don't need to know how these methods are implemented.

6.15 CASE STUDY: The Loan Class

Let us use the `Loan` class as an example to demonstrate the creation and use of classes. `Loan` has the data fields `annualInterestRate`, `numberOfYears`, `loanAmount`, and `loanDate`, and the methods `getAnnualInterestRate`, `getNumberOfYears`, `getLoanAmount`, `getLoanDate`, `setAnnualInterestRate`, `setNumberOfYears`, `setLoanAmount`, `monthlyPayment`, and `totalPayment`, as shown in Figure 6.20.

The UML diagram in Figure 6.20 serves as the contract for the `Loan` class. Throughout the book, you will play the role of both class user and class writer. The user can use the class without knowing how the class is implemented. Assume that the `Loan` class is available. Let us begin by writing a test program that uses the `Loan` class in Listing 6.8.

Loan
-annualInterestRate: double
-numberOfYears: int
-loanAmount: double
-loanDate: Date
+Loan()

+Loan(annualInterestRate: double,
   numberOfYears: int,
   loanAmount: double)

+getAnnualInterestRate(): double
+getNumberOfYears(): int
+getLoanAmount(): double
+getLoanDate(): Date
+setAnnualInterestRate(annualInterestRate: double): void
+setNumberOfYears(numberOfYears: int): void
+setLoanAmount(loanAmount: double): void
+monthlyPayment(): double
+totalPayment(): double

The annual interest rate of the loan (default: 2.5).
The number of years for the loan (default: 1).
The loan amount (default: 1000).
The date this loan was created.

Constructs a default loan object.
Constructs a loan with specified interest rate, years, and
   loan amount.

Returns the annual interest rate of this loan.
Returns the number of the years of this loan.
Returns the amount of this loan.
Returns the date of the creation of this loan.

Sets a new annual interest rate for this loan.

Sets a new number of years for this loan.

Sets a new amount for this loan.

Returns the monthly payment of this loan.
Returns the total payment of this loan.

FIGURE 6.20   *The Loan class models the properties and behaviors of loans.*

LISTING 6.8   TestLoanClass.java (Using the Loan Class)

```java
1 import javax.swing.JOptionPane;
2
3 public class TestLoanClass {
4   /** Main method */
5   public static void main(String[] args) {
6     // Enter yearly interest rate
7     String annualInterestRateString = JOptionPane.showInputDialog(
8       "Enter yearly interest rate, for example 8.25:");
9
10    // Convert string to double
11    double annualInterestRate =
12      Double.parseDouble(annualInterestRateString);
13
14    // Enter number of years
15    String numberOfYearsString = JOptionPane.showInputDialog(
16      "Enter number of years as an integer, \nfor example 5:");
17
18    // Convert string to int
19    int numberOfYears = Integer.parseInt(numberOfYearsString);
20
21    // Enter loan amount
22    String loanString = JOptionPane.showInputDialog(
23      "Enter loan amount, for example 120000.95:");
24
25    // Convert string to double
26    double loanAmount =  Double.parseDouble(loanString);
27
28    // Create Loan object
29    Loan loan =
30      new Loan(annualInterestRate, numberOfYears, loanAmount);
31
32    // Format to keep two digits after the decimal point
33    double monthlyPayment =
34      (int)(loan.monthlyPayment() * 100) / 100.0;
35    double totalPayment =
36      (int)(loan.totalPayment() * 100) / 100.0;
37
```

```
38      // Display results
39      String output = "The loan was created on " +
40        loan.getLoanDate().toString() + "\nThe monthly payment is " +
41        monthlyPayment + "\nThe total payment is " + totalPayment;
42      JOptionPane.showMessageDialog(null, output);
43   }
44 }
```

The `main` method reads interest rate, payment period (in years), and loan amount; creates a Loan object; and then obtains the monthly payment (Lines 33–34) and total payment (Lines 35-36) using the instance methods in the Loan class. Figure 6.21 shows the output of a sample run of the program.

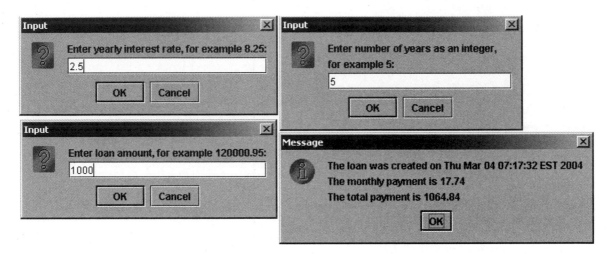

FIGURE 6.21 *The program creates a Loan instance with the annual interest rate, number of years, and loan amount, and displays the loan date, monthly payment, and total payment by invoking the methods of the instance.*

The Loan class is implemented in Listing 6.9.

LISTING 6.9 **Loan.java (The Loan Class)**

```
1 public class Loan {
2    private double annualInterestRate;
3    private int numberOfYears;
4    private double loanAmount;
5    private java.util.Date loanDate;
6
7    /** Construct a loan with interest rate 2.5, 1 year, and $1000 */
8    public Loan() {
9      this(2.5, 1, 1000);
10   }
11
12   /** Construct a loan with specified annual interest rate,
13       number of years and loan amount
14    */
15   public Loan(double annualInterestRate, int numberOfYears,
16       double loanAmount) {
17     this.annualInterestRate = annualInterestRate;
18     this.numberOfYears = numberOfYears;
19     this.loanAmount = loanAmount;
20     loanDate = new java.util.Date();
21   }
22
```

no-arg constructor

second constructor

```
23    /** Return annualInterestRate */
24    public double getAnnualInterestRate() {
25      return annualInterestRate;
26    }
27
28    /** Set a new annualInterestRate */
29    public void setAnnualInterestRate(double annualInterestRate) {
30      this.annualInterestRate = annualInterestRate;
31    }
32
33    /** Return numberOfYears */
34    public int getNumberOfYears() {
35      return numberOfYears;
36    }
37
38    /** Set a new numberOfYears */
39    public void setNumberOfYears(int numberOfYears) {
40      this.numberOfYears = numberOfYears;
41    }
42
43    /** Return loanAmount */
44    public double getLoanAmount() {
45      return loanAmount;
46    }
47
48    /** Set a newloanAmount */
49    public void setLoanAmount(double loanAmount) {
50      this.loanAmount = loanAmount;
51    }
52
53    /** Find monthly payment */
54    public double monthlyPayment() {
55      double monthlyInterestRate = annualInterestRate / 1200;
56      return loanAmount * monthlyInterestRate / (1 -
57        (Math.pow(1 / (1 + monthlyInterestRate), numberOfYears * 12)));
58    }
59
60    /** Find total payment */
61    public double totalPayment() {
62      return monthlyPayment() * numberOfYears * 12;
63    }
64
65    /** Return loan date */
66    public java.util.Date getLoanDate() {
67      return loanDate;
68    }
69 }
```

From a writer's perspective, a class is designed for use by many different customers. In order to be useful in a wide range of applications, a class should provide a variety of ways for customization through constructors, properties, and methods.

The Loan class contains two constructors, four get methods, three set methods, and the methods for finding monthly payment and total payment. You can construct a Loan object by using the no-arg constructor or the one with three parameters: annual interest rate, number of years, and loan amount. When a loan object is created, its date is stored in the loanDate field. The getLoanDate method returns the date. The three get methods, getAnnualInterest, getNumberOfYears, and getLoanAmount, return annual interest rate, payment years, and loan amount, respectively. All the data properties and methods in this class are tied to a specific instance of the Loan class. Therefore, they are instance variables or methods.

Recall that the java.util.Date can be used to create an instance to represent current date and time (see page 222). The Loan class contains the accessor method for loanDate, but no mutator method for it. Does this mean that the contents of loanDate cannot be changed? See Review Question 6.24.

IMPORTANT PEDAGOGICAL TIP

The UML diagram for the Loan class is shown in Figure 6.20. Students should begin by writing a test program that uses the Loan class even though they do not know how the Loan class is implemented. This has three benefits:

✦ It demonstrates that developing a class and using a class are two separate tasks.

✦ It makes it possible to skip the complex implementation of certain classes without interrupting the sequence of the book.

✦ It is easier to learn how to implement a class if you are familiar with the class through using it.

For all the examples from now on, I recommend that you first create an object from the class and try to use its methods and then turn your attention to its implementation.

✦ 6.16 CASE STUDY: The StackOfIntegers Class (Optional)

This section gives another example to demonstrate the creation and use of classes. Let us create a class for stacks.

stack

A *stack* is a data structure that holds objects in a last-in first-out fashion. It has many applications. For example, the compiler uses a stack to process method invocations. When a method is invoked, the parameters and local variables of the method are pushed into a stack. When a method calls another method, the new method's parameters and local variables are pushed into the stack. When a method finishes its work and returns to its caller, its associated space is released from the stack.

The UML diagram for the class is shown in Figure 6.22. Suppose that the class is available. Let us write a test program in Listing 6.10 that uses the class to create a stack, stores ten integers, and displays them in reverse order, as shown in Figure 6.23.

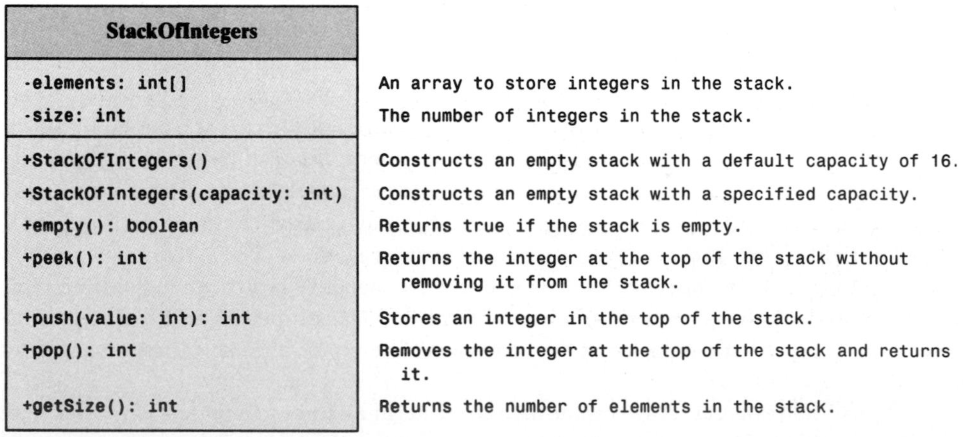

StackOfIntegers	
-elements: int[]	An array to store integers in the stack.
-size: int	The number of integers in the stack.
+StackOfIntegers()	Constructs an empty stack with a default capacity of 16.
+StackOfIntegers(capacity: int)	Constructs an empty stack with a specified capacity.
+empty(): boolean	Returns true if the stack is empty.
+peek(): int	Returns the integer at the top of the stack without removing it from the stack.
+push(value: int): int	Stores an integer in the top of the stack.
+pop(): int	Removes the integer at the top of the stack and returns it.
+getSize(): int	Returns the number of elements in the stack.

FIGURE 6.22 *The StackOfIntegers class encapsulates the stack storage and provides the operations for manipulating the stack.*

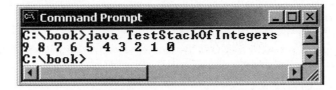

FIGURE 6.23   *You can store and retrieve integers from StackOfIntegers.*

LISTING 6.10   TestStackOfIntegers.java

```java
public class TestStackOfIntegers {
  public static void main(String[] args) {
    StackOfIntegers stack = new StackOfIntegers();

    for (int i = 0; i < 10; i++)
      stack.push(i);

    while (!stack.empty())
      System.out.print(stack.pop() + " ");
  }
}
```

How do you implement the StackOfIntegers class? The elements in the stack are stored in an array named elements. When you create a stack, the array is also created. The no-arg constructor creates an array with the default capacity of 16. The variable size counts the number of elements in the stack, and size - 1 is the index of the element at the top of the stack, as shown in Figure 6.24. For an empty stack, size is 0.

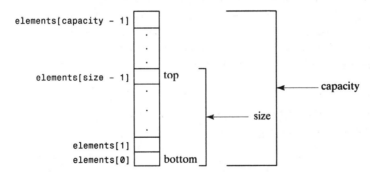

FIGURE 6.24   *The StackOfIntegers class encapsulates the stack storage and provides the operations for manipulating the stack.*

The StackOfIntegers class is implemented in Listing 6.11. The methods empty(), peek(), pop(), and getSize() are easy to implement. To implement push(int value), assign value to elements[size] if size < capacity (Line 23). If the stack is full (i.e., size >= capacity), create a new array of twice the current capacity (Line 18), copy the contents of the current array to the new array (Line 19), and assign the reference of the new array to the current array in the stack (Line 20). Now you can add the new value to the array (Line 23).

LISTING 6.11   StackOfIntegers.java (The StackOfIntegers Class)

```java
1 public class StackOfIntegers {
2   private int[] elements;
3   private int size;
4
5   /** Construct a stack with the default capacity 16 */
6   public StackOfIntegers() {
7     this(16);
8   }
```

default capacity 16

```java
 9
10    /** Construct a stack with the specified maximum capacity */
11    public StackOfIntegers(int capacity) {
12      elements = new int[capacity];
13    }
14
15    /** Push a new integer into the top of the stack */
16    public int push(int value) {
17      if (size >= elements.length) {
18        int[] temp = new int[elements.length * 2];
19        System.arraycopy(elements, 0, temp, 0, elements.length);
20        elements = temp;
21      }
22
23      return elements[size++] = value;
24    }
25
26    /** Return and remove the top element from the stack */
27    public int pop() {
28      return elements[--size];
29    }
30
31    /** Return the top element from the stack */
32    public int peek() {
33      return elements[size - 1];
34    }
35
36    /** Test whether the stack is empty */
37    public boolean empty() {
38      return size == 0;
39    }
40
41    /** Return the number of elements in the stack */
42    public int getSize() {
43      return size;
44    }
45  }
```

double the capacity (line 18)

add to stack (line 23)

NOTE

When you create a `StackOfIntegers` object, an array object is created. A `StackOfIntegers` object contains a reference to the array. For simplicity, you can say that the `StackOfIntegers` object contains the array.

NOTE

The user can create a stack and manipulate it through the public methods `push`, `pop`, `peek`, `empty`, and `getSize`. However, the user doesn't need to know how these methods are implemented. The `StackOfIntegers` class encapsulates the internal implementation of the stack. This example uses an array to implement a stack. You may use something other than an array to implement a stack. The program that uses `StackOfIntegers` does not need to change, since the contract of the public methods remains unchanged.

NOTE

Stacks are frequently used in programming. Java provides the `Stack` class in the `java.util` package, which will be introduced in Chapter 18, "Java Collections Framework."

6.17   Inner Classes

An *inner class*, or *nested class*, is a class defined within the scope of another class. Here is an example of an inner class:

inner class

```java
// ShowInnerClass.java: Demonstrate using inner classes
public class ShowInnerClass {
  private int data;

  /** A method in the outer class */
  public void m() {
    // Do something
    InnerClass instance = new InnerClass();
  }

  // An inner class
  class InnerClass {
    /** A method in the inner class */
    public void mi() {
      // Directly reference data and method defined in its outer class
      data++;
      m();
    }
  }
}
```

The class `InnerClass` is defined inside `ShowInnerClass`. An inner class is just like any regular class, with the following features:

✦ An inner class can reference the data and methods defined in the outer class in which it nests, so you do not need to pass the reference of an object of the outer class to the constructor of the inner class. For this reason, inner classes can make programs simple and concise.

✦ An inner class supports the work of its containing outer class and is compiled into a class named *OuterClassName$InnerClassName*.class. For example, the inner class `InnerClass` in `ShowInnerClass` is compiled into *ShowInnerClass$InnerClass*.class.

✦ An inner class can be declared `public`, `protected`, or `private` subject to the same visibility rules applied to a member of the class.

✦ An inner class can be declared `static`. A `static` inner class can be accessed using the outer class name. A `static` inner class cannot access nonstatic members of the outer class.

✦ Objects of an inner class are often created in the outer class. But you can also create an object of an inner class from another class. If the inner class is non-static, you must first create an instance of the outer class, then use the following syntax to create an object for the inner class:

```java
OuterClass.InnerClass innerObject = outerObject.new InnerClass();
```

✦ If the inner class is static, use the following syntax to create an object for it:

```java
OuterClass.InnerClass innerObject = new OuterClass.InnerClass();
```

KEY TERMS

KEY CLASSES AND METHODS

✦ **java.util.Date** is a class that encapsulates date and time. The no-arg constructor of Date creates an instance for the current date and time. Its toString() method returns the date and time as a string.

CHAPTER SUMMARY

✦ A class is a template for objects. It defines the generic properties of objects, and provides constructors for creating objects and methods for manipulating them.

✦ A class is also a data type. You can use it to declare object reference variables. An object reference variable that appears to hold an object actually contains a reference to that object. Strictly speaking, an object reference variable and an object are different, but most of the time the distinction between them can be ignored.

✦ An object is an instance of a class. You use the new operator to create an object, and the dot (.) operator to access members of that object through its reference variable.

✦ Modifiers specify how the class, method, and data are accessed. A public class, method, or data is accessible to all clients. A private method or data is only accessible inside the class. A static variable or a static method is defined using the keyword static.

✦ You can provide a get method or a set method to enable clients to see or modify the data. Colloquially, a get method is referred to as a *getter* (or *accessor*), and a set method is referred to as a *setter* (or *mutator*).

✦ A get method has the signature public returnType getPropertyName(). If the returnType is boolean, the get method should be defined as public boolean isPropertyName(). A set method has the signature public void setPropertyName-(dataType propertyValue).

✦ All parameters are passed to methods using pass by value. For a parameter of a primitive type, the actual value is passed; for a parameter of a reference type, the reference for the object is passed.

✦ An instance variable is a variable that belongs to an instance of a class. Its use is associated with individual instances. A static variable is a variable shared by all instances of the same class.

✦ An instance method is a method that belongs to an instance of a class. Its use is associated with individual instances. A static method is a method that can be invoked without using instances.

✦ Every instance of a class can access the class's static variables and methods. However, I recommend that you invoke static variables and methods using `ClassName.variable` and `ClassName.method`.

✦ The scope of instance and static variables is the entire class, regardless of where the variables are declared. The instance and static variables can be declared anywhere in the class.

✦ The object reference `this` inside an instance method serves as a pointer to the current instance of the class that invokes the instance method. The keyword `this` can also be used inside a constructor to invoke another constructor of the same class.

✦ A Java array is an object that can contain primitive type values or object type values. When an array is created, its elements are assigned the default value of `0` for the numeric primitive data types, `'\u0000'` for `char` types, `false` for `boolean` types, and `null` for object types.

✦ An *inner class*, or *nested class*, is a class defined within the scope of another class. An inner class can reference the data and methods defined in the outer class in which it nests, so you do not need to pass the reference of the outer class to the constructor of the inner class.

REVIEW QUESTIONS

Sections 6.2–6.4

6.1 Describe the relationship between an object and its defining class. How do you declare a class? How do you declare an object reference variable? How do you create an object? How do you declare and create an object in one statement?

6.2 What are the differences between constructors and methods?

6.3 What is wrong with the following program?

```
1 public class ShowErrors {
2   public static void main(String[] args) {
3     ShowErrors t = new ShowErrors(5);
4   }
5 }
```

6.4 Is an array an object or a primitive type value? Can an array contain elements of a primitive type as well as an object type? Describe the default value for the elements of an array.

6.5 What is wrong in the following code?

```
1 public class Foo {
2   public void method1() {
3     Circle c;
4     System.out.println("What is radius " + c.getRadius());
5     c = new Circle();
6   }
7 }
```

6.6 What is wrong in the following code?

```
1 class Test {
2   public static void main(String[] args) {
3     A a = new A();
4     a.print();
5   }
6 }
7
8 class A {
9   String s;
10
11   A(String s) {
12     this.s = s;
13   }
14
15   public void print() {
16     System.out.print(s);
17   }
18 }
```

6.7 What is wrong in the following code?

```
1 class Test {
2   public static void main(String[] args) {
3     C c = new C(5.0);
4     System.out.println(c.value);
5   }
6 }
7
8 class C {
9   int value = 2;
10 }
```

6.8 What is the printout of the following code?

```
public class Foo {
  private boolean x;

  public static void main(String[] args) {
    Foo foo = new Foo();
    System.out.println(foo.x);
  }
}
```

6.9 What is wrong with the following program?

```
1 public class ShowErrors {
2   public static void main(String[] args) {
3     ShowErrors t = new ShowErrors();
4     t.x();
5   }
6 }
```

Sections 6.6-6.8

6.10 What is an accessor method? What is a mutator method? What are the naming conventions for accessor methods and mutator methods?

6.11 What are the benefits of data field encapsulation?

6.12 In the following code, `radius` is private in the `Circle` class, and `myCircle` is an object of the `Circle` class. Can the following code compile and run? Explain why.

```
public class Circle {
  private double radius = 1.0;

  /** Find the area of this circle */
  double findArea() {
    return radius * radius * 3.14159;
  }

  public static void main(String[] args) {
    Circle myCircle = new Circle();
    System.out.println("Radius is " + myCircle.radius);
  }
}
```

6.13 If a class contains only private data fields and no set methods, is the class immutable?

6.14 If all the data fields in a class are private and primitive, and the class contains no **set** methods, is the class immutable?

Section 6.9 Passing Objects to Methods

6.15 Describe the difference between passing a parameter of a primitive type and passing a parameter of a reference type. Show the output of the following program:

```
public class Test {
  public static void main(String[] args) {
    Count myCount = new Count();
    int times = 0;

    for (int i = 0; i < 100; i++)
      increment(myCount, times);

    System.out.println("count is " + myCount.count);
    System.out.println("times is " + times);
  }

  public static void increment (Count c, int times) {
    c.count++;
    times++;
  }
}
```

```
class Count {
  public int count;

  Count(int c) {
    count = c;
  }

  Count() {
    count = 1;
  }
}
```

6.16 Show the output of the following program:

```
public class Test {
  public static void main(String[] args) {
    Circle circle1 = new Circle(1);
    Circle circle2 = new Circle(2);

    swap1(circle1, circle2);
    System.out.println("After swap1: circle1 = " +
      circle1.radius + " circle2 = " + circle2.radius);
    swap2(circle1, circle2);
    System.out.println("After swap2: circle1 = " +
      circle1.radius + " circle2 = " + circle2.radius);
  }

  public static void swap1(Circle x, Circle y) {
    Circle temp = x;
    x = y;
```

```
              y = temp;
          }

          public static void swap2(Circle x, Circle y) {
            double temp = x.radius;
            x.radius = y.radius;
            y.radius = temp;
          }
      }

      class Circle {
        double radius;

        Circle(double newRadius) {
          radius = newRadius;
        }
      }
```

6.17 Show the printout of the following code:

```
public class Test {
  public static void main(String[] args) {
    int[] a = {1, 2};
    swap(a[0], a[1]);
    System.out.println("a[0] = " + a[0]
      + " a[1] = " + a[1]);
  }

  public static void swap(int n1, int n2) {
    int temp = n1;
    n1 = n2;
    n2 = temp;
  }
}
```

(a)

```
public class Test {
  public static void main(String[] args) {
    int[] a = {1, 2};
    swap(a);
    System.out.println("a[0] = " + a[0]
      + " a[1] = " + a[1]);
  }

  public static void swap (int[] a) {
    int temp = a[0];
    a[0] = a[1];
    a[1] = temp;
  }
}
```

(b)

```
public class Test {
  public static void main(String[] args) {
    T t = new T();
    swap(t);
    System.out.println("e1 = " + t.e1
      + " e2 = " + t.e2);
  }

  public static void swap(T t) {
    int temp = t.e1;
    t.e1 = t.e2;
    t.e2 = temp;
  }
}

class T {
  int e1 = 1;
  int e2 = 2;
}
```

(c)

```
public class Test {
  public static void main(String[] args) {
    T t1 = new T();
    T t2 = new T();
    System.out.println("t1's i = " +
      t1.i + " and j = " + t1.j);
    System.out.println("t2's i = " +
      t2.i + " and j = " + t2.j);
  }
}

class T {
  static int i = 0;
  int j = 0;

  T() {
    i++;
    j = 1;
  }
}
```

(d)

Section 6.10 Static Variables, Constants, and Methods

6.18 Suppose that the class Foo is defined in (a). Let f be an instance of Foo. Which of the statements in (b) are correct?

```
public class Foo {
    int i;
    static String s;

    void imethod() {
    }

    static void smethod() {

    }
}
```

```
System.out.println(f.i);
System.out.println(f.s);
f.imethod();
f.smethod();
System.out.println(Foo.i);
System.out.println(Foo.s);
Foo.imethod();
Foo.smethod();
```

(a)   (b)

6.19 What is the output of the following program?

```
public class Foo {
  static int i = 0;
  static int j = 0;

  public static void main(String[] args) {
    int i = 2;
    int k = 3;

    {
      int j = 3;
      System.out.println("i + j is " + i + j);
    }

    k = i + j;
    System.out.println("k is " + k);
    System.out.println("j is " + j);
  }
}
```

6.20 Can you invoke an instance method or reference an instance variable from a static method? Can you invoke a static method or reference a static variable from an instance method? What is wrong in the following code?

```
1 public class Foo {
2   public static void main(String[] args) {
3     method1();
4   }
5
6   public void method1() {
7     method2();
8   }
9
10  public static void method2() {
11    System.out.println("What is radius " + c.getRadius());
12  }
13
14  Circle c = new Circle();
15 }
```

Sections 6.11–6.12

6.21 Describe the role of the this keyword.

6.22 What is wrong in the following code?

```
1 public class C {
2   int p;
3
4   public void setP(int p) {
5     p = p;
6   }
7 }
```

Sections 6.13-6.17

6.23 What is wrong in the following code?

```
1 public class Test {
2   public static void main(String[] args) {
3     java.util.Date[] dates = new java.util.Date[10];
4     System.out.println(dates[0]);
5     System.out.println(dates[0].toString());
6   }
7 }
```

6.24 The Loan class contains a private data field loanDate with a get method, but no set method. Is the Loan class immutable?

6.25 Is the StackOfIntegers class immutable?

6.26 Can an inner class be used in a class other than the class in which it nests?

6.27 Can the modifiers public, private, and static be used on inner classes?

PROGRAMMING EXERCISES

Sections 6.2–6.11

6.1 (*The* Rectangle *class*) Write a class named Rectangle to represent rectangles. The UML diagram for the class is shown in Figure 6.25. Suppose that all the rectangles are the same color. Use a static variable for color.

Write a client program to test the class Rectangle. In the client program, create two Rectangle objects. Assign width 4 and height 40 to each of the two objects. Assign color yellow. Display the properties of both objects and find their areas.

6.2 (*The* Fan *class*) Write a class named Fan to model fans. The properties, as shown in Figure 6.26, are speed, on, radius, and color. You need to provide the accessor and mutator methods for the properties, and the toString method for returning a string consisting of all the values of all the properties in this class. Suppose the fan has three fixed speeds. Use constants 1, 2, and 3 to denote slow, medium, and fast speed.

Rectangle	
-width: double	The width of this rectangle.
-height: double	The height of this rectangle.
-color: String	The color of this rectangle.
+Rectangle()	Constructs a rectangle with width 1 and height 1.
+Rectangle(width: double, height: double, color: String)	Constructs a rectangle with the specified width and height.
+getWidth(): double	Returns the width of this rectangle.
+setWidth(width: double): void	Sets a new width for this rectangle.
+getHeight(): double	Returns the height of this rectangle.
+setHeight(height: double): void	Sets a new height for this rectangle.
+getColor(): String	Returns the color of all rectangles.
+setColor(color: String): void	Sets a new color for all rectangles.
+findArea(): double	Returns the area of this rectangle.
+findPerimeter(): double	Returns the perimeter of this rectangle.

FIGURE 6.25 *The* Rectangle *class contains the properties* width, height, *and* color, *accessor and mutator methods, and the methods for computing area and perimeter.*

Fan	
-speed: int	The speed of this fan (default 1).
-on: boolean	Indicates whether the fan is on (default false).
-radius: double	The radius of this fan (default 5).
-color: String	The color of this fan (default white).
+Fan()	Constructs a fan with default values.
+getSpeed(): int	Returns the speed of this fan.
+setSpeed(speed: int): void	Sets a new speed for this fan.
+isOn(): boolean	Returns true if this fan is on.
+setOn(on: boolean): void	Sets this fan on to true or false.
+getRadius(): double	Returns the radius of this fan.
+setRadius(radius: double): void	Sets a new radius for this fan.
+getColor(): String	Returns the color of this fan.
+setColor(color: String): void	Sets a new color for this fan.
+toString(): String	Returns a string representation for this fan.

FIGURE 6.26 *The* Fan *class contains the properties* speed, on, radius, *and* color, *accessor and mutator methods, and the* toString *method for returning the values of the properties.*

Write a client program to test the Fan class. In the client program, create a Fan object. Assign maximum speed, radius 10, color yellow, and turn it on. Display the object by invoking its toString method.

6.3 (*The* Account *class*) Write a class named Account to model accounts. The UML diagram for the class is shown in Figure 6.27.

Write a client program to test the Account class. In the client program, create an Account object with an account ID of 1122, a balance of 20000, and an annual interest rate of 4.5%. Use the withdraw method to withdraw $2500, use the deposit method to deposit $3000, and print the balance and the monthly interest.

Account	
-id: int	The ID of this account.
-balance: double	The balance of this account.
-annualInterestRate: double	The interest rate of this account.
+Account()	Constructs a default account.
+Account(id: int, balance: double, annualInterestRate: double)	Constructs an account with the specified ID, balance, and interest rate.
+getId(): int	Returns the ID of this account.
+getBalance(): double	Returns the balance of this account.
+getAnnualInterestRate():double	Returns the interest rate of this account.
+setId(id: int): void	Sets a new ID for this account.
+setBalance(balance: double): void	Sets a new balance for this account.
+setAnnualInterestRate(annualInterestRate: double): void	Sets a new interest rate for this account.
+getMonthlyInterestRate(): double	Returns the monthly interest rate of this account.
+withdraw(amount: double): void	Withdraws the specified amount from this account.
+deposit(amount: double): void	Deposits the specified amount to this account.

FIGURE 6.27 *The* Account *class contains the properties ID, balance, annual interest rate, accessor and mutator methods, and the methods for computing interest, withdrawing money, and depositing money.*

Stock
-symbol: String
-name: String
-previousClosingPrice: double
-currentPrice: double
+Stock(symbol: String, name: String)
+getSymbol(): String
+getName(): String
+getPreviousClosingPrice(): double
+getCurrentPrice(): double
+setPreviousClosingPrice(price: double): void
+setCurrentPrice(price: double): void
+changePercent(): double

The symbol of this stock.
The name of this stock.
The previous closing price of this stock.
The current price of this stock.

Constructs a stock with a specified symbol and a name.
Returns the symbol of this stock.
Returns the name of this stock.
Returns the previous closing price of this stock.
Returns the current price of this stock.
Sets the previous closing price of this stock.
Sets the current price of this stock.
Returns the percentage of change of this stock.

FIGURE 6.28 *The* Stock *class contains the properties symbol, name, previous closing price, and current price, accessor and mutator methods, and the methods for computing price changes.*

6.4 (*The* Stock *class*) Write a class named Stock to model a stock. The UML diagram for the class is shown in Figure 6.28. The method changePercent computes the percentage of the change between the current price and the previous closing price.

Write a client program to test the Stock class. In the client program, create a Stock object with the stock symbol SUNW, the name Sun Microsystems Inc., and the previous closing price of 100. Set a new current price to 90 and display the price-change percentage.

6.5* (*Using the* GregorianCalendar *class*) Java API has the GregorianCalendar class in the java.util package that can be used to obtain the year, month, and day of a date. The no-arg constructor constructs an instance for the current date, and the methods get(GregorianCalendar.YEAR), get(GregorianCalendar.MONTH), and get(GregorianCalendar.DAY) return the year, month, and day. Write a program to test this class to display the current year, month, and day.

6.6** (*Displaying calendars*) Rewrite the PrintCalendar class in Section 4.10, "Stepwise Refinement," to display calendars in a message dialog box. Since the output is generated from several static methods in the class, you may define a static String variable output for storing the output and display it in a message dialog box.

6.7* (*The* Time *class*) Write a class named Time. The Time class contains the data fields hour, minute, and second with their respective get methods. The no-arg constructor sets the hour, minute, and second for the current time in GMT. The current time can be obtained using System.currentTime(), as shown in Example 2.5, "Displaying Current Time."

Write a client program to test the Time class. In the client program, create a Time object and display hour, minute, and second using the get methods.

6.8* (*The* Vote *and* Candidate *Classes*) Create two classes, Vote and Candidate. The Vote class has the data field count to count votes, and the methods getCount, setCount, clear, increment, and decrement for reading and handling the votes, as shown in Figure 6.29. The clear method sets the count to 0. The increment and decrement methods increase and decrease the count. The Candidate class has the data fields name (name of the candidate), vote (track the votes received by the candidate), and numberOfCandidates (track the total number of candidates), and the methods getName,

Vote
-count: int
+Count()
+getCount(): int
+setCount(count: int): void
+clear(): void
+increment(): void
+decrement(): void

Candidate
-name: String
-vote: Vote
-numberOfCandidates: int
+Candidate()
+Candidate(name: String, vote: Vote)
+getName(): String
+getVote(): Vote
+getNumberOfCandidates(): int

FIGURE 6.29 *The* Vote *class encapsulates the vote count, and the* Candidate *class encapsulates the candidates.*

getVote, and getNumberOfCandidates for reading the name, vote, and numberOf Candidates, as shown in Figure 6.29.

Write a test program that counts votes for two candidates for student body president. The votes are entered from the keyboard. Number 1 is a vote for Candidate 1, and number 2 is a vote for Candidate 2. Number −1 deducts a vote from Candidate 1, and −2 deducts a vote from Candidate 2. Number 0 signifies the end of the count.

Sections 6.12-6.16

6.9 (*The* Int *class*) Write a class named Int to represent an int value as an object. The UML diagram for the class is shown in Figure 6.30. Write a client program to test all the methods in the Int class.

Int	
-value: int	An int value for the object.
+Int(value: int)	Constructs an Int object with the specified int value.
+getValue(): int	Returns the value in this object.
+isPrime(): boolean	Returns true if the value in this object is prime.
+isPrime(value: int): boolean	Returns true if a specified int value is prime.
+isPrime(value: Int): boolean	Returns true if the value in a specified Int object is prime.
+isEven(): boolean	Returns true if the value in this object is even.
+isEven(value: int): boolean	Returns true if a specified int value is even.
+isEven(value: Int): boolean	Returns true if the value in a specified Int object is even.
+equals(anotherValue: int): boolean	Returns true if a specified int value is equal to the value in this object.
+equals(anotherValue: Int): boolean	Returns true if the value in a specified Int object is equal to the value in this object.

FIGURE 6.30 *The* Int *class represents an int value.*

6.10 (*Modifying the* Loan *class*) Rewrite the Loan class to add two static methods for computing monthly payment and total payment, as follows:

```
public static double monthlyPayment(double annualInterestRate,
   int numOfYears, double loanAmount)

public static double totalPayment(double annualInterestRate,
   int numOfYears, double loanAmount)
```

Write a client program to test these two methods.

MyPoint	
-x: double	x-coordinate of this point.
-y: double	y-coordinate of this point.
+MyPoint()	Constructs a default point object.
+MyPoint(double x, double y)	Constructs a point with specified x and y values.
+getX(): double	Returns x-coordinate value in this object.
+getY():double	Returns y-coordinate value in this object.
+distance(secondPoint: MyPoint): double	Returns the distance from this point to another point.
+distance(p1: Point, p2: MyPoint): double	Returns the distance between two points.

FIGURE 6.31   *The MyPoint class models a point.*

6.11   (*The MyPoint class*) Write a class named MyPoint to represent a point, as shown in Figure 6.31.

6.12*   (*Displaying the prime factors*) Write a program that receives a positive integer and displays all its smallest factors in decreasing order. For example, if the integer is 120, the smallest factors are displayed as 5, 3, 2, 2, 2. Use the StackOfIntegers class to store the factors (e.g., 2, 2, 2, 3, 5) and retrieve and display the factors in reverse order.

6.13**   (*Displaying the prime numbers*) Write a program that displays all the prime numbers less than 120 in decreasing order. Use the StackOfIntegers class to store the prime numbers (e.g., 2, 3, 5, . . .) and retrieve and display them in reverse order.

6.14***   (*The Tax class*) Write a class named Tax. The Tax class contains the following instance data fields:

✦   **int filingStatus**: One of the four tax filing statuses: 0 - single filer, 1 - married filing jointly, 2 - married filing separately, and 3 - head of household. Use the public static constants SINGLE_FILER (0), MARRIED_JOINTLY (1), MARRIED_SEPAR- ATELY (2), and HEAD_OF_HOUSEHOLD (3) to represent the status.

✦   **int[][] brackets**: Stores the tax brackets for each filing status (see Example 5.6).

✦   **double[] rates**: Stores tax rates for each bracket (see Example 5.6).

✦   **double taxableIncome**: Stores the taxable income.

Provide the get and set methods for each data field and the findTax() method that returns the tax. Also provide a no-arg constructor and the constructor Tax(filingStatus, brackets, rates, taxableIncome).

Use the Tax class to print the 2001 and 2002 tax tables for taxable income from $50,000 to $60,000 with intervals of $1,000 for all four statuses. The tax rates for the year 2002 were given in Table 3.1 on page 86. The tax rates for 2001 are shown in Table 6.1.

TABLE 6.1   2001 United States Federal Personal Tax Rates

Tax rate	Single filers	Married filing jointly or qualifying widow(er)	Married filing separately	Head of household
15%	Up to $27,050	Up to $45,200	Up to $22,600	Up to $36,250
27.5%	$27,051–$65,550	$45,201–$109,250	$22,601–$54,625	$36,251–$93,650
30.5%	$65,551–$136,750	$109,251–$166,500	$54,626–$83,250	$93,651–$151,650
35.5%	$136,751–$297,350	$166,501–$297,350	$83,251–$148,675	$151,651–$297,350
39.1%	$297,351 or more	$297,351 or more	$148,676 or more	$297,351 or more

chapter

7

Strings

Objectives

✦ To use the String class to process fixed strings (§7.2).

✦ To use the Character class to process a single character (§7.3).

✦ To use the StringBuffer class to process flexible strings (§7.4).

✦ To use the StringTokenizer class to extract tokens from a string (§7.5).

✦ To know the differences between the String, StringBuffer, and StringTokenizer classes (§§7.2–7.5).

✦ To use the JDK 1.5 Scanner class to scan tokens using words as delimiters (§7.6).

✦ To input primitive values and strings from the keyboard using the Scanner class (§7.7).

✦ To learn how to pass strings to the main method from the command line (§7.8).

7.1   Introduction

Strings are used often in programming. A *string* is sequence of characters. In many languages, strings are treated as arrays of characters, but in Java a string is an object. Java provides the `String` class, the `StringBuffer` class, and the `StringTokenizer` class for storing and processing strings.

In most cases, you use the `String` class to create strings. The `String` class is efficient for storing and processing strings, but strings created with the `String` class cannot be modified. The `StringBuffer` class enables you to create flexible strings that can be modified. `StringTokenizer` is a utility class that can be used to extract tokens from a string.

7.2   The `String` Class

The `java.lang.String` class models a sequence of characters as a string. You have already used string literals, such as the parameter in the `println(String s)` method. The Java compiler converts the string literal into a string object and passes it to `println`.

The `String` class has eleven constructors and more than forty methods for examining individual characters in a sequence, comparing strings, searching substrings, extracting substrings, and creating a copy of a string with all the characters translated to uppercase or lowercase. The most frequently used methods are listed in Figure 7.1.

7.2.1   Constructing a String

You can create a string from a string value or from an array of characters. To create a string from a string literal, use a syntax like this one:

```
String newString = new String(stringLiteral);
```

The argument `stringLiteral` is a sequence of characters enclosed inside double quotes. The following statement creates a `String` object `message` for the string literal `"Welcome to Java"`:

```
String message = new String("Welcome to Java");
```

shorthand initializer

Since strings are used frequently, Java provides a *shorthand initializer* for creating a string:

```
String message = "Welcome to Java";
```

You can also create a string from an array of characters. For example, the following statements create the string "Good Day".

```
char[] charArray = {'G', 'o', 'o', 'd', ' ', 'D', 'a', 'y'};
String message = new String(charArray);
```

 NOTE

string, string variable, string value

A `String` variable holds a reference to a `String` object that stores a string value. Strictly speaking, the terms *String variable*, *String object*, and *string value* are different, but the distinctions between them can be ignored most of the time. For simplicity, the term *string* will often be used to refer to `String` variable, `String` object, and string value.

---

java.lang.String	
+String()	Constructs an empty string.
+String(value: String)	Constructs a string with the specified string literal value.
+String(value: char[])	Constructs a string with the specified character array.
+charAt(index: int): char	Returns the character at the specified index from this string.
+compareTo(anotherString: String): int	Compares this string with another string.
+compareToIgnoreCase(anotherString: String): int	Compares this string with another string ignoring case.
+concat(anotherString: String): String	Concatenate this string with another string.
+endsWith(suffix: String): boolean	Returns true if this string ends with the specified suffix.
+equals(anotherString: String): boolean	Returns true if this string is equal to another string.
+equalsIgnoreCase(anotherString: String): boolean	Checks whether this string equals another string ignoring case.
+getChars(int srcBegin, int srcEnd, char[] dst, int dstBegin): void	Copies characters from this string into the destination character array.
+indexOf(ch: int): int	Returns the index of the first occurrence of ch.
+indexOf(ch: int, fromIndex: int): int	Returns the index of the first occurrence of ch after fromIndex.
+indexOf(str: String): int	Returns the index of the first occurrence of str.
+indexOf(str: String, fromIndex: int): int	Returns the index of the first occurrence of str after fromIndex.
+lastIndexOf(ch: int): int	Returns the index of the last occurrence of ch.
+lastIndexOf(ch: int, fromIndex: int): int	Returns the index of the last occurrence of ch before fromIndex.
+lastIndexOf(str: String): int	Returns the index of the last occurrence of str.
+lastIndexOf(str: String, fromIndex: int): int	Returns the index of the last occurrence of str before fromIndex.
+regionMatches(toffset: int, other: String, offset: int, len: int): boolean	Returns true if the specified subregion of this string exactly. matches the specified subregion of the string argument.
+length(): int	Returns the number of characters in this string.
+replace(oldChar: char, newChar: char): String	Returns a new string with oldChar replaced by newChar.
+startsWith(prefix: String): boolean	Returns true if this string starts with the specified prefix.
+subString(beginIndex: int): String	Returns the substring from beginIndex.
+subString(beginIndex: int, endIndex: int): String	Returns the substring from beginIndex to endIndex -1.
+toCharArray(): char[]	Returns a char array consisting of characters from this string.
+toLowerCase(): String	Returns a new string with all characters converted to lowercase.
+toString(): String	Returns a new string with itself.
+toUpperCase(): String	Returns a new string with all characters converted to uppercase.
+trim(): String	Returns a string with blank characters trimmed on both sides.
+copyValueOf(data: char[]): String	Returns a new string consisting of the char array data.
+valueOf(c: char): String	Returns a string consisting of the character c.
+valueOf(data: char[]): String	Same as copyValueOf(data: char[]): String.
+valueOf(d: double): String	Returns a string representing the double value.
+valueOf(f: float): String	Returns a string representing the float value.
+valueOf(i: int): String	Returns a string representing the int value.
+valueOf(l: long): String	Returns a string representing the long value.

FIGURE 7.1   *The String class provides the methods for processing a string.*

7.2.2   Immutable Strings and Canonical Strings

A String object is immutable; its contents cannot be changed. Does the following code change the contents of the string?   *immutable*

```
String s = "Java";
s = "HTML";
```

The answer is no. The first statement creates a String object with the content "Java" and assigns its reference to s. The second statement creates a new String object with the content "HTML" and

After executing

```
String s = "Java";
```

s ⟶ | **s: String** |
| String object for "Java" |

Contents cannot be changed

After executing s

```
s = "HTML";
```

This string object is
now unreferenced

| **:String** |
| String object for "Java" |

| **s: String** |
| String object for "HTML" |

FIGURE 7.2　*Strings are immutable; their contents cannot be changed once created.*

assigns its reference to s. The first String object still exists after the assignment, but it can no longer be accessed because variable s now points to the new object, as shown in Figure 7.2.

Since strings are immutable and are frequently used, JVM improves efficiency and saves memory by storing two String objects in the same object if they were created with the same string literal using the shorthand initializer. Such a string is called a *canonical string*. You can also use a String object's intern method to return a canonical string. A string of this kind is the same string that is created using the shorthand initializer. For example, the following statements:

canonical string

```
String s = "Welcome to Java";

String s1 = new String("Welcome to Java");

String s2 = s1.intern();

String s3 = "Welcome to Java";

System.out.println("s1 == s is " + (s1 == s));
System.out.println("s2 == s is " + (s2 == s));
System.out.println("s == s3 is " + (s == s3));
```

| **:String** |
| Canonical string object for "Welcome to Java" |

| **:String** |
| A string object for "Welcome to Java" |

display

```
s1 == s is false
s2 == s is true
s == s3 is true
```

In the preceding statements, s, s2, and s3 refer to the same canonical string "Welcome to Java"; therefore s2 == s and s == s3 are true. However, s1 == s is false, because s and s1 are two different string objects even though they have the same contents.

7.2.3　String Length and Retrieving Individual Characters

length()

You can get the length of a string by invoking its length() method. For example, message.length() returns the length of the string message.

charAt(index)

The s.charAt(index) method can be used to retrieve a specific character in a string s, where the index is between 0 and s.length()-1. For example, message.charAt(0) returns the character W, as shown in Figure 7.3.

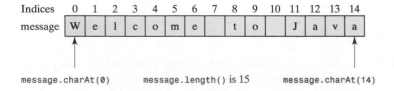

FIGURE 7.3　*A String object is represented using an array internally.*

NOTE

When you use a string, you often know its literal value. For convenience, Java allows you to use the string literal to refer directly to strings without creating new variables. Thus, `"Welcome to Java".charAt(0)` is correct and returns W.

 NOTE

A string value is represented using a private array variable internally. The array cannot be accessed outside of the `String` class. The `String` class provides many public methods, such as `length()` and `charAt(index)`, to retrieve the array information. This is a good example of encapsulation: the detailed data structure of the class is hidden from the user through the private modifier, and thus the user cannot directly manipulate the internal data structure. If the array were not private, the user would be able to change the string content by modifying the array. This would violate the tenet that the `String` class is immutable.

 CAUTION

Accessing characters in a string s out of bounds is a common programming error. To avoid it, make sure that you do not use an index beyond `s.length() - 1`. For example, `s.charAt(s.length())` would cause a `StringIndexOutOfBoundsException`.

CAUTION

`length` is a method in the `String` class, but `length` is a property in an array object. So you have to use `s.length()` to get the number of characters in string s, and `a.length` to get the number of elements in array a.

7.2.4 String Concatenation

You can use the concat method to concatenate two strings. The statement shown below, for example, concatenates strings s1 and s2 into s3:

```
String s3 = s1.concat(s2);
```

Since string concatenation is heavily used in programming, Java provides a convenient way to concatenate strings. You can use the plus (+) sign to concatenate two or more strings. The following code combines the strings message, `" and "`, and `"HTML"` into one string:

s1 + s2

```
String myString = message + " and " + "HTML";
```

Recall that you used the + sign to concatenate a number with a string in the `println` method. A number is converted into a string and then concatenated.

7.2.5 Extracting Substrings

`String` is an immutable class. After a string is created, its value cannot be modified. For example, you cannot change `"Java"` in message to `"HTML"`. So what can you do if you need to change the message string? You assign a completely new string to message. The following code illustrates this:

```
message = "Welcome to HTML";
```

As an alternative, you can use the substring method. You extract a substring from a string by using the substring method in the String class. The substring method has two versions:

`substring(int, int)`

✦ `public String substring(int beginIndex, int endIndex)`

Returns a new string that is a substring of the string. The substring begins at the specified `beginIndex` and extends to the character at index `endIndex - 1`, as shown in Figure 7.4. Thus the length of the substring is `endIndex-beginIndex`.

`substring(int)`

✦ `public String substring(int beginIndex)`

Returns a new string that is a substring of the string. The substring begins with the character at the specified index and extends to the end of the string, as shown in Figure 7.4.

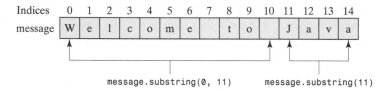

FIGURE 7.4 *The* substring *method extracts a substring from a string.*

For example,

```
String message = "Welcome to Java".substring(0, 11) + "HTML";
```

The string `message` now becomes `"Welcome to HTML"`.

7.2.6 String Comparisons

Often, in a program, you need to compare the contents of two strings. You might attempt to use the == operator, as follows:

`==`

```
if (string1 == string2)
  System.out.println("string1 and string2 are the same object");
else
  System.out.println("string1 and string2 are different objects");
```

However, the == operator only checks whether string1 and string2 refer to the same object; it does not tell you whether string1 and string2 contain the same contents when they are different objects. Therefore, you cannot use the == operator to find out whether two string variables have the same contents. Instead, you should use the equals() method for an equality comparison of the contents of objects. The code given below, for instance, can be used to compare two strings:

`s1.equals(s2)`

```
if (string1.equals(string2))
  System.out.println("string1 and string2 have the same contents");
else
  System.out.println("string1 and string2 are not equal");
```

 NOTE

Two String references are the same if they are created with the same literal value using the shorthand initializer. But strings with the same contents do not always share the same object. For example, the following two variables, s1 and s2, are different even though their contents are identical:

```
String s0 = " Java";
String s1 = "Welcome to" + s0;
String s2 = "Welcome to Java";

System.out.println("s1 == s2 is " + (s1 == s2));
System.out.println("s1.equals(s2) is " + (s1.equals(s2)));
```

In this case, s1 == s2 is false since they point to two different objects, but s1.equals(s2) is true since the objects have the same contents. For safety and clarity, you should always use the equals method to test whether two strings have the same contents, and the == operator to test whether the two strings have the same references (i.e., point to the same memory location).

NOTE

For two strings x and y, x.equals(y) if and only if x.intern() == y.intern().

The compareTo method can also be used to compare two strings. For example, consider the following code:

s1.compareTo(s2)

s1.compareTo(s2)

The method returns the value 0 if s1 is equal to s2, a value less than 0 if s1 is lexicographically less than s2, and a value greater than 0 if s1 is lexicographically greater than s2.

The actual value returned from the compareTo method depends on the offset of the first two distinct characters in s1 and s2 from left to right. For example, suppose s1 is "abc" and s2 is "abg", and s1.compareTo(s2) returns -4. The first two characters (a vs. a) from s1 and s2 are compared. Because they are equal, the second two characters (b vs. b) are compared. Because they are also equal, the third two characters (c vs. g) are compared. Since the character c is 4 less than g, the comparison returns -4.

CAUTION

Syntax errors will occur if you compare strings by using comparison operators, such as >, >=, <, or <=. Instead, you have to use s1.compareTo(s2).

NOTE

The equals method returns true if two strings are equal, and false if they are not equal. The compareTo method returns 0, a positive integer, or a negative integer, depending on whether one string is equal to, greater than, or less than the other string.

The String class also provides equalsIgnoreCase and regionMatches methods for comparing strings. The equalsIgnoreCase method ignores the case of the letters when determining whether two strings are equal. The regionMatches method compares portions of two strings for equality. You can also use str.startsWith(prefix) to check whether string str starts with a specified prefix, and str.endsWith(suffix) to check whether string str ends with a specified suffix.

7.2.7   String Conversions

The contents of a string cannot be changed once the string is created. But you can obtain a new string using the `toLowerCase`, `toUpperCase`, `trim`, and `replace` methods. The `toLowerCase` and `toUpperCase` methods return a new string by converting all the characters in the string to lowercase or uppercase. The `trim` method returns a new string by eliminating blank characters from both ends of the string. The `replace(oldChar, newChar)` method can be used to replace all occurrences of a character in the string with a new character.

For example,

`toLowerCase()`
`toUpperCase()`
`trim()`
`replace`

`"Welcome".toLowerCase()` returns a new string, `welcome`.

`"Welcome".toUpperCase()` returns a new string, `WELCOME`.

`" Welcome ".trime()` returns a new string, `Welcome`.

`"Welcome".replace('e', 'A')` returns a new string, `WAlcomA`.

`"Welcome".replaceFirst("e", "A")` returns a new string, `WAlcome`.

`"Welcome".replaceAll("e", "A")` returns a new string, `WAlcomA`.

7.2.8   Finding a Character or a Substring in a String

You can use the `indexOf` and `lastIndexOf` methods to find a character or a substring in a string. Four overloaded `indexOf` methods and four overloaded `lastIndexOf` methods are defined in the `String` class.

✦ `public int indexOf(int ch)`

  (*public int lastIndexOf(int ch)*)

  Returns the index of the first (*last*) character in the string that matches the specified character `ch`. Returns −1 if the specified character is not in the string. When you pass a character to `ch` (e.g., `indexOf('a')`), the character's Unicode value is passed to the parameter `ch` (e.g., the Unicode value for `'a'` is 97 in decimal).

✦ `public int indexOf(int ch, int fromIndex)`

  (*public int lastIndexOf(int ch, int endIndex)*)

  Returns the index of the first (*last*) character in the string starting from (*ending at*) the specified `fromIndex` (*endIndex*) that matches the specified character `ch`. Returns −1 if the specified character is not in the substring beginning at position `fromIndex` (*ending at position endIndex*).

✦ `public int indexOf(String str)`

  (*public int lastIndexOf(String str)*)

  Returns the index of the first (*last*) character of the substring in the string that matches the specified string `str`. Returns −1 if the `str` argument is not in the string.

✦ `public int indexOf(String str, int fromIndex)`

  (*public int lastIndexOf(String str, int endIndex)*)

  Returns the index of the first (*last*) character of the substring in the string starting from (*ending at*) the specified `fromIndex` (*endIndex*) that matches the specified string `str`. Returns −1 if the `str` argument is not in the substring.

For example,

`indexOf`

```
"Welcome to Java".indexOf('W') returns 0.
"Welcome to Java".indexOf('o') returns 4.
"Welcome to Java".indexOf('o', 5) returns 9.
```

```
"Welcome to Java".indexOf("come") returns 3.
"Welcome to Java".indexOf("Java", 5) returns 11.
"Welcome to Java".indexOf("java", 5) returns -1.
"Welcome to Java".lastIndexOf('W') returns 0.
"Welcome to Java".lastIndexOf('o') returns 9.
"Welcome to Java".lastIndexOf('o', 5) returns 4.
"Welcome to Java".lastIndexOf("come") returns 3.
"Welcome to Java".lastIndexOf("Java", 5) returns -1.
"Welcome to Java".lastIndexOf("java", 5) returns -1.
```

lastIndexOf

7.2.9 Conversion between Strings and Arrays

Strings are not arrays, but a string can be converted into an array, and vice versa. To convert a string to an array of characters, use the toCharArray method. For example, the following statement converts the string "Java" to an array:

```
char[] chars = "Java".toCharArray();
```

toCharArray

So chars[0] is 'J', chars[1] is 'a', chars[2] is 'v', and chars[3] is 'a'.

You can also use the getChars(int srcBegin, int srcEnd, char[] dst, int dstBegin) method to copy a substring of the string from index srcBegin to index srcEnd-1 into a character array dst starting from index dstBegin. For example, the following code copies a substring "3720" in "CS3720" from index 2 to index 6-1 into the character array dst starting from index 4.

```
char[] dst = {'J', 'A', 'V', 'A', '1', '3', '0', '1'};
"CS3720".getChars(2, 6, dst, 4);
```

getChars

Thus dst becomes {'J', 'A', 'V', 'A', '3', '7', '2', '0'}.

To convert an array of characters into a string, use the String(char[]) constructor or the valueOf(char[]) method. For example, the following statement constructs a string from an array using the String constructor:

```
String str = new String(new char[]{'J', 'a', 'v', 'a'});
```

The next statement constructs a string from an array using the valueOf method:

```
String str = String.valueOf(new char[]{'J', 'a', 'v', 'a'});
```

valueOf

7.2.10 Converting Characters and Numeric Values to Strings

The valueOf method can be used to convert an array of characters into a string. There are several overloaded versions of the valueOf method that can be used to convert a character and numeric values to strings with different parameter types, char, double, long, int, and float. For example, to convert a double value 5.44 to a string, use String.valueOf(5.44). The return value is a string consisting of the characters '5', '.', '4', and '4'.

overloaded valueOf

 NOTE

Use Double.parseDouble(str) or Integer.parseInt(str) to convert a string to a double value or an int value.

EXAMPLE 7.1 CHECKING PALINDROMES

Problem

Write a program that prompts the user to enter a string and reports whether the string is a palindrome, as shown in Figure 7.5. A string is a palindrome if it reads the same forward and backward. The words "mom," "dad," and "noon," for instance, are all palindromes.

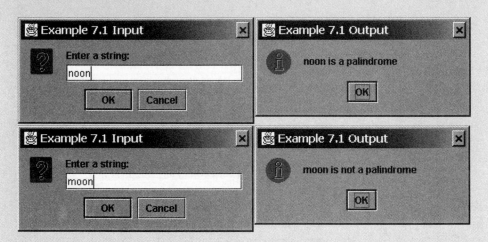

FIGURE 7.5   *The program checks whether a string is a palindrome.*

Solution

One solution is to check whether the first character in the string is the same as the last character. If so, check whether the second character is the same as the second-last character. This process continues until a mismatch is found or all the characters in the string are checked, except for the middle character if the string has an odd number of characters.

To implement this idea, use two variables, say low and high, to denote the position of two characters at the beginning and the end in a string s. Initially, low is 0 and high is s.length() - 1. If the two characters at these positions match, increment low by 1 and decrement high by 1. This process continues until (low >= high) or a mismatch is found.

LISTING 7.1   CheckPalindrome.java (Is a String Palindrome?)

input string

```
1 import javax.swing.JOptionPane;
2
3 public class CheckPalindrome {
4   /** Main method */
5   public static void main(String[] args) {
6     // Prompt the user to enter a string
7     String s = JOptionPane.showInputDialog(null,
8       "Enter a string:", "Example 7.1 Input",
9       JOptionPane.QUESTION_MESSAGE);
10
11     // Declare and initialize output string
12     String output = "";
13
14     if (isPalindrome(s))
15       output = s + " is a palindrome";
16     else
17       output = s + " is not a palindrome";
18
```

EXAMPLE 7.1 (CONTINUED)

```
19    // Display the result
20    JOptionPane.showMessageDialog(null, output,
21      "Example 7.1 Output", JOptionPane.INFORMATION_MESSAGE);
22  }
23
24  /** Check if a string is a palindrome */
25  public static boolean isPalindrome(String s) {
26    // The index of the first character in the string
27    int low = 0;
28
29    // The index of the last character in the string
30    int high = s.length() - 1;
31
32    while (low < high) {
33      if (s.charAt(low) != s.charAt(high))
34        return false; // Not a palindrome
35
36      low++;
37      high--;
38    }
39
40    return true; // The string is a palindrome
41  }
42 }
```

low index

high index

update indices

Review

The `isPalindrome` method uses a `while` loop (Lines 32–38) to compare characters and determine whether a string is a palindrome.

Alternatively, you can create a new string that is a reversal of the original string. If both strings have the same contents, the original string is a palindrome. The `String` class does not have a method for reversing a string. You can create a method of your own to return a reversed string (see Exercise 7.1) or you can use the `reverse` method provided in the `StringBuffer` class. Example 7.3 uses `StringBuffer` and the `reverse` method to determine whether a string is a palindrome.

7.3   The `Character` Class

Java provides a wrapper class for every primitive data type. These classes are `Character`, `Boolean`, `Byte`, `Short`, `Integer`, `Long`, `Float`, and `Double` for char, boolean, byte, short, int, long, float, and double. All these classes are in the `java.lang` package. They enable the primitive data values to be treated as objects. They also contain useful methods for processing primitive values. This section introduces the `Character` class. The other wrapper classes will be introduced in Chapter 9, "Abstract Classes and Interfaces."

The `Character` class has a constructor and more than thirty methods for manipulating characters. The most frequently used methods are shown in Figure 7.6.

You can create a `Character` object from a char value. For example, the following statement creates a `Character` object for the character 'a':

```
Character character = new Character('a');
```

The `charValue` method returns the character value wrapped in the `Character` object. The `compareTo` method compares this character with another character and returns an integer that is the difference between the Unicodes of this character and the other character. The `equals` method returns true if and only if the two characters are the same. For example, suppose `charObject` is new Character('b').

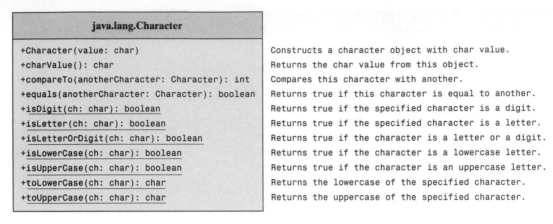

FIGURE 7.6   *The* Character *class provides the methods for manipulating a character.*

```
charObject.compareTo(new Character('a')) returns 1
charObject.compareTo(new Character('b')) returns 0
charObject.compareTo(new Character('c')) returns -1
charObject.compareTo(new Character('d') returns -2
charObject.equals(new Character('b')) returns true
charObject.equals(new Character('d')) returns false
```

Most of the methods in the Character class are static methods. The isDigit(char ch) method returns true if the character is a digit. The isLetter(char ch) method returns true if the character is a letter. The isLetterOrDigit(char ch) method is true if the character is a letter or a digit. The isLowerCase(char ch) method is true if the character is a lowercase letter. The isUpperCase(char ch) method is true if the character is an uppercase letter. The toLowerCase(char) method returns the lowercase letter for the character, and the toUpperCase(char ch) method returns the uppercase letter for the character.

EXAMPLE 7.2 COUNTING EACH LETTER IN A STRING

Problem

Write a program that prompts the user to enter a string and counts the number of occurrences of each letter in the string regardless of case, as shown in Figure 7.7.

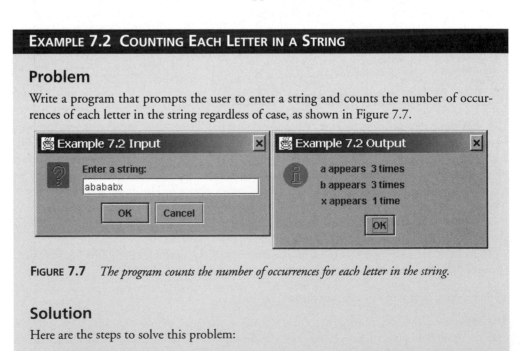

FIGURE 7.7   *The program counts the number of occurrences for each letter in the string.*

Solution

Here are the steps to solve this problem:

1. Convert all the uppercase letters in the string to lowercase using the toLowerCase method in the String class.

EXAMPLE 7.2 (CONTINUED)

2. Create an array, say counts of twenty-six int values, each of which counts the occurrences of a letter. That is, counts[0] counts the number of a's, counts[1] counts the number of b's, and so on.

3. For each character in the string, check whether it is a lowercase letter. If so, increment the corresponding count in the array.

LISTING 7.2   CountEachLetter.java (Counting Letters)

```
1 import javax.swing.JOptionPane;
2
3 public class CountEachLetter {
4   /** Main method */
5   public static void main(String[] args) {
6     // Prompt the user to enter a string
7     String s = JOptionPane.showInputDialog(null,
8       "Enter a string:", "Example 7.2 Input",
9       JOptionPane.QUESTION_MESSAGE);
10
11    // Invoke the countLetters method to count each letter
12    int[] counts = countLetters(s.toLowerCase());
13
14    // Declare and initialize output string
15    String output = "";
16
17    // Display results
18    for (int i = 0; i < counts.length; i++) {
19      if (counts[i] != 0)
20        output += (char)('a' + i) + " appears " +
21          counts[i] + ((counts[i] == 1) ? " time\n" : " times\n");
22    }
23
24    // Display the result
25    JOptionPane.showMessageDialog(null, output,
26      "Example 7.2 Output", JOptionPane.INFORMATION_MESSAGE);
27  }
28
29  // Count each letter in the string
30  public static int[] countLetters(String s) {
31    int[] counts = new int[26];
32
33    for (int i = 0; i < s.length(); i++) {
34      if (Character.isLetter(s.charAt(i)))
35        counts[s.charAt(i) - 'a']++;
36    }
37
38    return counts;
39  }
40 }
```

input string

count letters

count a letter

Review

The main method reads a string (Lines 7–9) and counts the number of occurrences of each letter in it by invoking the countLetters method (Line 12). Since the case of the letters is ignored, the program uses the toLowerCase method to convert the string into all lowercase and pass the new string to the countLetters method.

The `countLetters` method (Lines 30–39) returns an array of twenty-six elements. Each element counts the number of occurrences of a letter in the string s. The method processes each character in the string. If the character is a letter, its corresponding count is increased by 1. For example, if the character (`s.charAr(i)`) is `'a'`, the corresponding count is `counts['a' - 'a']` (i.e., `counts[0]`). If the character is `'b'`, the corresponding count is `counts['b' - 'a']` (i.e., `counts[1]`), since the Unicode of `'b'` is 1 more than that of `'a'`. If the character is `'z'`, the corresponding count is `counts['z' - 'a']` (i.e., `counts[25]`) since the Unicode of `'z'` is 25 more than that of `'a'`.

7.4   The `StringBuffer` Class

The `StringBuffer` class is an alternative to the `String` class. In general, a string buffer can be used wherever a string is used. `StringBuffer` is more flexible than `String`. You can add, insert, or append new contents into a string buffer, whereas the value of a string is fixed once the string is created.

The `StringBuffer` class has three constructors and more than thirty methods for managing the buffer and modifying strings in the buffer. The most frequently used methods are listed in Figure 7.8.

java.lang.StringBuffer	
+StringBuffer()	Constructs an empty string buffer with capacity 16.
+StringBuffer(capacity: int)	Constructs a string buffer with the specified capacity.
+StringBuffer(str: String)	Constructs a string buffer with the specified string.
+append(data: char[]): StringBuffer	Appends a char array into this string buffer.
+append(data: char[], offset: int, len: int): StringBuffer	Appends a subarray in data into this string buffer.
+append(v: *aPrimitiveType*): StringBuffer	Appends a primitive type value as a string to this buffer.
+append(str: String): StringBuffer	Appends a string to this string buffer.
+capacity(): int	Returns the capacity of this string buffer.
+charAt(index: int): char	Returns the character at the specified index.
+delete(startIndex: int, endIndex: int): StringBuffer	Deletes characters from startIndex to endIndex.
+deleteCharAt(index: int): StringBuffer	Deletes a character at the specified index.
+insert(index: int, data: char[], offset: int, len: int): StringBuffer	Inserts a subarray of the data in the array to the buffer a the specified index.
+insert(offset: int, data: char[]): StringBuffer	Inserts data into this buffer at the position offset.
+insert(offset: int, b: *aPrimitiveType*): StringBuffer	Inserts a value converted to a string into this buffer.
+insert(offset: int, str: String): StringBuffer	Inserts a string into this buffer at the position offset.
+length(): int	Returns the number of characters in this buffer.
+replace(startIndex: int, endIndex: int, str: String): StringBuffer	Replaces the characters in this buffer from startIndex to endIndex with the specified string.
+reverse(): StringBuffer	Reverses the characters in the buffer.
+setCharAt(index: int, ch: char): void	Sets a new character at the specified index in this buffer.
+setLength(newLength: int): void	Sets a new length in this buffer.
+substring(startIndex: int): String	Returns a substring starting at startIndex.
+substring(startIndex: int, endIndex: int): String	Returns a substring from startIndex to endIndex -1.

FIGURE 7.8   *The `StringBuffer` class provides the methods for processing a string buffer.*

7.4.1   Constructing a String Buffer

The `StringBuffer` class provides three constructors:

◆ `public StringBuffer()`

Constructs a string buffer with no characters in it and an initial capacity of sixteen characters.

◆ `public StringBuffer(int length)`

Constructs a string buffer with no characters in it and an initial capacity specified by the `length` argument.

◆ `public StringBuffer(String string)`

Constructs a string buffer for the string argument with an initial capacity of sixteen plus the length of the string argument.

7.4.2   Modifying Strings in the Buffer

You can append new contents at the end of a string buffer, insert new contents at a specified position in a string buffer, and delete or replace characters in a string buffer.

The `StringBuffer` class provides several overloaded methods to append `boolean`, `char`, `char` array, `double`, `float`, `int`, `long`, and `String` into a string buffer. For example, the following code appends strings and characters into `strBuf` to form a new string, `"Welcome to Java"`:

```
StringBuffer strBuf = new StringBuffer();
strBuf.append("Welcome");
strBuf.append(' ');
strBuf.append("to");
strBuf.append(' ');
strBuf.append("Java");
```

append

The `StringBuffer` class also contains overloaded methods to insert `boolean`, `char`, `char` array, `double`, `float`, `int`, `long`, and `String` into a string buffer. Consider the following code:

```
strBuf.insert(11, "HTML and ");
```

insert

Suppose `strBuf` contains `"Welcome to Java"` before the insert method is applied. This code inserts `"HTML and "` at position 11 in `strBuf` (just before J). The new `strBuf` is `"Welcome to HTML and Java"`.

You can also delete characters from a string in the buffer using the two `delete` methods, reverse the string using the `reverse` method, replace characters using the `replace` method, or set a new character in a string using the `setCharAt` method.

For example, suppose `strBuf` contains `"Welcome to Java"` before each of the following methods is applied:

`strBuf.delete(8, 11)` changes the buffer to `Welcome Java`.   delete
`strBuf.deleteCharAt(8)` changes the buffer to `Welcome o Java`.
`strBuf.reverse()` changes the buffer to `avaJ ot emocleW`.   reverse
`strBuf.replace(11, 15, "HTML")` changes the buffer to `Welcome to HTML`.   replace
`strBuf.setCharAt(0, 'w')` sets the buffer to `welcome to Java`.   setCharAt

> **NOTE**
>
> All these modification methods except `setCharAt` do two things: (1) change the contents of the string buffer, (2) return the reference of the string buffer. A method with nonvoid return value type can also be invoked as a statement in Java, if you are not interested in the return value of the method. In this case, the return value is simply ignored.

TIP

If a string does not require any change, use `String` rather than `StringBuffer`. Java can perform some optimizations for `String`, such as sharing canonical strings.

7.4.3 The `toString`, `capacity`, `length`, `setLength`, and `charAt` Methods

The `StringBuffer` class provides many other methods for manipulating string buffers.

`toString()`

◆ The `toString()` method returns the string from the string buffer.

`capacity()`

◆ The `capacity()` method returns the current capacity of the string buffer. The capacity is the number of new characters it is able to store without having to increase its size.

`length()`

◆ The `length()` method returns the number of characters actually stored in the string buffer.

`setLength(int)`

◆ The `setLength(newLength)` method sets the length of the string buffer. If the `newLength` argument is less than the current length of the string buffer, the string buffer is truncated to contain exactly the number of characters given by the `newLength` argument. If the `newLength` argument is greater than or equal to the current length, sufficient null characters (`'\u0000'`) are appended to the string buffer so that `length` becomes the `newLength` argument. The `newLength` argument must be greater than or equal to 0.

`charAt(int)`

◆ The `charAt(index)` method returns the character at a specific `index` in the string buffer. The first character of a string buffer is at index 0, the next at index 1, and so on. The `index` argument must be greater than or equal to 0, and less than the length of the string buffer.

NOTE

The length of the string is always less than or equal to the capacity of the buffer. The length is the actual size of the string stored in the buffer, and the capacity is the current size of the buffer. The buffer is dynamically increased if more characters are added to exceed its capacity. Internally, a string buffer is an array of characters, so the buffer's capacity is the size of the array. If the buffer's capacity is exceeded, the array is replaced by a new array. The new array size is 2 * (the previous array size + 1).

EXAMPLE 7.3 IGNORING NONALPHANUMERIC CHARACTERS WHEN CHECKING PALINDROMES

Problem

Example 7.1, "Checking Palindromes," considered all the characters in a string to check whether it was a palindrome. Write a new program that ignores nonalphanumeric characters in checking whether a string is a palindrome. A sample run of the program is shown in Figure 7.9.

EXAMPLE 7.3 (CONTINUED)

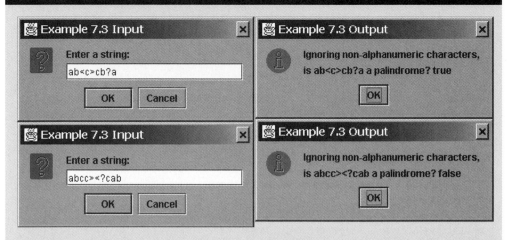

FIGURE **7.9** *The program checks whether a string is a palindrome, ignoring nonalphanumeric characters.*

Solution

Here are the steps to solve the problem:

1. Filter the string by removing the nonalphanumeric characters. This can be done by creating an empty string buffer, adding each alphanumeric character in the string to a string buffer, and returning the string from the string buffer. You can use the isLetterOrDigit(ch) method in the Character class to check whether character ch is a letter or a digit.

2. Obtain a new string that is the reversal of the filtered string. Compare the reversed string with the filtered string using the equals method.

LISTING 7.3 PalindromeIgnoreNonAlphanumeric.java

```
 1 import javax.swing.JOptionPane;
 2
 3 public class PalindromeIgnoreNonAlphanumeric {
 4   /** Main method */
 5   public static void main(String[] args) {
 6     // Prompt the user to enter a string
 7     String s = JOptionPane.showInputDialog(null,
 8       "Enter a string:", "Example 7.3 Input",
 9       JOptionPane.QUESTION_MESSAGE);
10
11     // Declare and initialize output string
12     String output = "Ignoring non-alphanumeric characters, \nis "
13       + s + " a palindrome? " + isPalindrome(s);
14
15     // Display the result
16     JOptionPane.showMessageDialog(null, output,
17       "Example 7.3 Output", JOptionPane.INFORMATION_MESSAGE);
18   }
19
20   /** Return true if a string is a palindrome */
21   public static boolean isPalindrome(String s) {
22     // Create a new string by eliminating non-alphanumeric chars
23     String s1 = filter(s);
24
```

EXAMPLE 7.3 (CONTINUED)

```
25      // Create a new string that is the reversal of s1
26      String s2 = reverse(s1);
27
28      // Compare if the reversal is the same as the original string
29      return s2.equals(s1);
30    }
31
32    /** Create a new string by eliminating non-alphanumeric chars */
33    public static String filter(String s) {
34      // Create a string buffer
35      StringBuffer strBuf = new StringBuffer();
36
37      // Examine each char in the string to skip alphanumeric char
38      for (int i = 0; i < s.length(); i++) {
39        if (Character.isLetterOrDigit(s.charAt(i))) {
40          strBuf.append(s.charAt(i));
41        }
42      }
43
44      // Return a new filtered string
45      return strBuf.toString();
46    }
47
48    /** Create a new string by reversing a specified string */
49    public static String reverse(String s) {
50      StringBuffer strBuf = new StringBuffer(s);
51      strBuf.reverse(); // Use the reverse method for StringBuffer object
52      return strBuf.toString();
53    }
54 }
```

add letter or digit

Review

The `filter(String s)` method (Lines 33–46) examines each character in string s and copies it to a string buffer if the character is a letter or a numeric character. The `filter` method returns the string in the buffer. The `reverse(String s)` method (Lines 49–53) creates a new string that reverses the specified string s. The `filter` and `reverse` methods both return a new string. The original string is not changed.

The program in Example 7.1 checks whether a string is a palindrome by comparing pairs of characters from both ends of the string. Example 7.3 uses the `reverse` method in the `StringBuffer` class to reverse the string, then compares whether the two strings are equal to determine whether the original string is a palindrome.

7.5   The `StringTokenizer` Class

Another useful class related to processing strings is the `java.util.StringTokenizer` class. This class is used to break a string into pieces so that information contained in it can be retrieved and processed. For example, to get all of the words in a string like `"I am learning Java now"`, you create an instance of the `StringTokenizer` class for the string and then retrieve individual words in the string by using the methods in the `StringTokenizer` class, as shown in Figure 7.10.

How does the `StringTokenizer` class recognize individual words? You can specify a set of characters as delimiters when constructing a `StringTokenizer` object. Each delimiters is a character. The delimiters break a string into pieces known as *tokens*. You can specify delimiters in the `StringTokenizer` constructors:

✦ `public StringTokenizer(String s, String delim, boolean returnDelims)`

Constructs a `StringTokenizer` for string s with specified delimiters. Each character in the string delim is a delimiter. If `returnDelims` is true, the delimiters are counted as tokens.

```
        java.util.StringTokenizer
+StringTokenizer(s: String)              Constructs a string tokenizer for the string
+StringTokenizer(s: String, delimiters:  Constructs a string tokenizer for the string
  String)                                   with the specified delimiters.
+StringTokenizer (s: String, delimiters: Constructs a string tokenizer for the string
  String, returnDelimiters: boolean)        with the delimiters and returnDelims.
+countTokens(): int                      Returns the number of remaining tokens.
+hasMoreTokens(): boolean                Returns true if there are more tokens left.
+nextToken(): String                     Returns the next token.
+nextToken(delimiters: String): String   Returns the next token using new delimiters.
```

FIGURE 7.10   *The* StringTokenizer *class provides the methods for processing tokens in a string.*

◆ public StringTokenizer(String s, String delim)

Constructs a StringTokenizer for string s with specified delimiters delim, and the delimiters are not counted as tokens.

◆ public StringTokenizer(String s)

Constructs a StringTokenizer for string s with default delimiters " \t\n\r" (a space, tab, new line, and carriage return), and the delimiters are not counted as tokens.

The following code creates a string tokenizer for a string using space as delimiters and extracts all the tokens:

```
1 String s = "Java is cool.";
2 StringTokenizer tokenizer = new StringTokenizer(s);          create a tokenizer
3
4 System.out.println("The total number of tokens is " +
5   tokenizer.countTokens());
6
7 while (tokenizer.hasMoreTokens())
8   System.out.println(tokenizer.nextToken());
```

The code displays

```
The total number of tokens is 3
Java
is
cool.
```

Line 2 creates a string tokenizer using the default delimiters. If you create it using delimiters "a" or "c" (new StringTokenizer(s, "ac")), the output would be

```
The total number of tokens is 4
J
v
 is
ool.
```

If you want the delimiters to be counted as tokens, create a string tokenizer using new String-Tokenizer(s, "ac", ture), the output would be

```
The total number of tokens is 7
J
a
v
a
 is
c
ool.
```

no no-arg constructor

NOTE

The StringTokenizer class does not have a no-arg constructor. Normally it is good programming practice to provide a no-arg constructor for each class. On rare occasions, however, a no-arg constructor does not make sense. StringTokenizer is such an example. A StringTokenizer object must be created for a string that is to be passed as an argument from a constructor.

7.6 The **Scanner** Class (JDK 1.5 Feature)

The delimiters are single characters in StringTokenizer. You can use the new JDK 1.5 java.util.Scanner class to specify a word as a delimiter. Here is an example that uses the word *Java* as a delimiter to scan tokens in a string:

create a scanner

```
1 String s = "Welcome to Java! Java is fun! Java is cool!";
2 Scanner scanner = new Scanner(s);
3 scanner.useDelimiter("Java");
4
5 while (scanner.hasNext())
6   System.out.println(scanner.next());
```

Line 2 creates an instance of Scanner for the string. Line 3 sets "Java" as a delimiter. Line 5, hasNext() returns true if there are still any tokens left. Line 6, the next() method returns a token as a string. So the output from this code is

```
Welcome to
!
 is fun!
 is cool!
```

If a token is a primitive data type value, you can use the methods nextByte(), nextShort(), nextInt(), nextLong(), nextFloat(), nextDouble(), or nextBoolean() to obtain it. For example, the following code adds all the numbers in the string. Note that the delimiter is space by default.

```
String s = "1 2 3 4";
Scanner scanner = new Scanner(s);

int sum = 0;
while (scanner.hasNext())
  sum += scanner.nextInt();

System.out.println("Sum is " + sum);
```

StringTokenizer vs. Scanner

NOTE

StringTokenizer can specify several single characters as delimiters. Scanner can use a single character or a word as the delimiter. If you need to scan a string with multiple single characters as delimiters, use StringTokenizer. If you need to use a word as the delimiter, use Scanner.

7.7 Implementing **MyInput** Using **Scanner**

Java uses System.out to refer to a standard output device and System.in to refer to a standard input device. By default the output device is the console and the input device is the keyboard. To perform console output, you simply use the print or println method to display a primitive value or a string to the console. Keyboard input is not directly supported in Java, but you can use the `Scanner` class to create an object to read input from `System.in` as follows:

```
Scanner scanner = new Scanner(System.in);
```

Now you can use `next()`, `nextByte()`, `nextShort()`, `nextInt()`, `nextLong()`, `nextFloat()`, `nextDouble()`, or `nextBoolean()` to obtain a string, byte, short, int, long, float, double, or boolean value. For convenience, let us create a class named `MyInput` for reading primitive data type values and strings from the keyboard, as shown in Figure 7.11.

MyInput	
+readByte(): byte	Reads an integer in the byte type from the keyboard.
+readShort(): short	Reads an integer in the short type from the keyboard.
+readInt(): int	Reads an integer in the int type from the keyboard.
+readLong(): int	Reads an integer in the long type from the keyboard.
+readFloat(): float	Reads a decimal value in the float type from the keyboard.
+readDouble(): double	Reads a decimal value in the double type from the keyboard.
+readChar(): char	Reads a character from the keyboard.
+readBoolean(): boolean	Reads a boolean value from the keyboard.
+readString(): String	Reads a string from the keyboard.

FIGURE 7.11 `MyInput` *provides static methods for reading primitive values and strings from the keyboard.*

This class was introduced in Section 2.16, "Getting Input from the Console." `TestMyInput`, a test program that uses `MyInput`, was also given in that section. Listing 7.4 implements `MyInput`.

LISTING 7.4 MyInput.java (Console Input)

```
 1 import java.util.*;
 2
 3 public class MyInput {
 4   static Scanner scanner = new Scanner(System.in);
 5
 6   /** Read a string from the keyboard */
 7   public static String readString() {
 8     return scanner.next();
 9   }
10
11   /** Read an int value from the keyboard */
12   public static int readInt() {
13     return scanner.nextInt();
14   }
15
16   /** Read a double value from the keyboard */
17   public static double readDouble() {
18     return scanner.nextDouble();
19   }
20
21   /** Read a byte value from the keyboard */
22   public static byte readByte() {
23     return scanner.nextByte();
24   }
25
26   /** Read a short value from the keyboard */
27   public static short readShort() {
28     return scanner.nextShort();
29   }
30
```

```
31   /** Read a long value from the keyboard */
32   public static long readLong() {
33     return scanner.nextLong();
34   }
35
36   /** Read a float value from the keyboard */
37   public static float readFloat() {
38     return scanner.nextFloat();
39   }
40
41   /** Read a character from the keyboard */
42   public static char readChar() {
43     return (scanner.next()).charAt(0);
44   }
45
46   /** Read a boolean value from the keyboard */
47   public static boolean readBoolean() {
48     return scanner.nextBoolean();
49   }
50 }
```

7.8   Command-Line Arguments

Perhaps you have already noticed the unusual declarations for the main method, which has parameter args of String[] type. It is clear that args is an array of strings. The main method is just like a regular method with a parameter. You can call a regular method by passing actual parameters. Can you pass arguments to main? This section will discuss how to pass and process arguments from the command line.

7.8.1   Passing Strings to the main Method

You can pass strings to a main method from the command line when you run the program. The following command line, for example, starts the program TestMain with three strings: arg0, arg1, and arg2:

```
java TestMain arg0 arg1 arg2
```

arg0, arg1, and arg2 are strings, but they don't have to appear in double quotes on the command line. The strings are separated by a space. A string that contains a space must be enclosed in double quotes. Consider the following command line:

```
java TestMain "First num" alpha 53
```

It starts the program with three strings: "First num" and alpha, and 53, a numeric string. Note that 53 is actually treated as a string. You can use "53" instead of 53 in the command line.

When the main method is invoked, the Java interpreter creates an array to hold the command-line arguments and pass the array reference to args. For example, if you invoke a program with n arguments, the Java interpreter creates an array like this:

```
args = new String[n];
```

The Java interpreter then passes args to invoke the main method.

 NOTE

If you run the program with no strings passed, the array is created with new String[0]. In this case, the array is empty with length 0. args references to this empty array. Therefore, args is not null, but args.length is 0.

7.8.2 Processing Command-Line Arguments

The strings passed to the main program are stored in args, which is an array of strings. The first string is stored in args[0], and args.length is the number of strings passed.

EXAMPLE 7.4 PASSING COMMAND-LINE ARGUMENTS

Problem

Write a program that performs binary operations on integers. The program receives three arguments: an integer followed by an operator and another integer. For example, to add two integers, use this command:

```
java Calculator 2 + 3
```

The program will display the following output:

```
2 + 3 = 5
```

Figure 7.12 shows sample runs of the program.

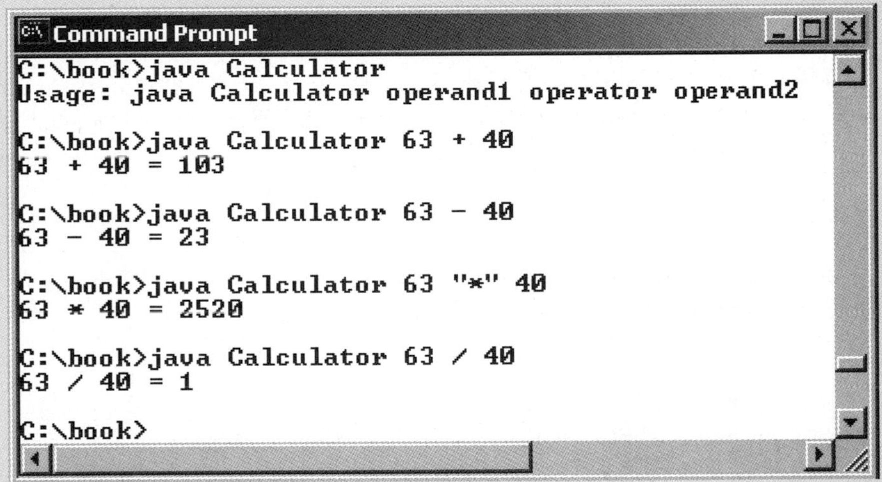

FIGURE 7.12 *The program takes three arguments (operand1, operator, operand2) from the command line and displays the expression and the result of the arithmetic operation.*

Solution

Here are the steps in the program:

1. Use args.length to determine whether three arguments have been provided in the command line. If not, terminate the program using System.exit(0).

2. Perform a binary arithmetic operation on the operands args[0] and args[2] using the operator specified in args[1].

LISTING 7.5 Calculator.java (Command-Line Arguments)

```
1 public class Calculator {
2   /** Main method */
3   public static void main(String[] args) {
```

EXAMPLE 7.4 (CONTINUED)

check operator

```
4     // Check number of strings passed
5     if (args.length != 3) {
6       System.out.println(
7         "Usage: java Calculator operand1 operator operand2");
8       System.exit(0);
9     }
10
11    // The result of the operation
12    int result = 0;
13
14    // Determine the operator
15    switch (args[1].charAt(0)) {
16      case '+': result = Integer.parseInt(args[0]) +
17                         Integer.parseInt(args[2]);
18            break;
19      case '-': result = Integer.parseInt(args[0]) -
20                         Integer.parseInt(args[2]);
21            break;
22      case '*': result = Integer.parseInt(args[0]) *
23                         Integer.parseInt(args[2]);
24            break;
25      case '/': result = Integer.parseInt(args[0]) /
26                         Integer.parseInt(args[2]);
27    }
28
29    // Display result
30    System.out.println(args[0] + ' ' + args[1] + ' ' + args[2]
31      + " = " + result);
32  }
33 }
```

Review

`Integer.parseInt(args[0])` (Line 16) converts a digital string into an integer. The string must consist of digits. If not, the program will terminate abnormally.

In the sample run, `"*"` had to be used instead of * for the command

```
java Calculator 63 "*" 40
```

In JDK 1.1 and above, the * symbol refers to all the files in the current directory when it is used on a command line. Therefore, in order to specify the multiplication operator, the * must be enclosed in quote marks in the command line. The following program displays all the files in the current directory when issuing the command java Test *:

```
public class Test {
  public static void main(String[] args) {
    for (int i = 0; i < args.length; i++)
      System.out.println(args[i]);
  }
}
```

KEY CLASSES AND METHODS

✦ `java.lang.String` is a class for creating an immutable string.

✦ `java.lang.Character` is a class for wrapping a character into an object.

✦ `java.lang.StringBuffer` is a class for creating a buffer to hold a modifiable string.

✦ `java.util.StringTokenizer` is a class for extracting tokens from a string.

✦ `java.util.Scanner` is a new JDK 1.5 class for scanning tokens.

CHAPTER SUMMARY

◆ Strings are objects encapsulated in the `String` class. A string can be constructed using one of the eleven constructors or using a string literal shorthand initializer.

◆ A `String` object is immutable; its contents cannot be changed. To improve efficiency and save memory, Java Virtual Machine stores two `String` objects in the same object if they were created with the same string literal using the shorthand initializer. Therefore, the shorthand initializer is preferred in creating strings.

◆ You can get the length of a string by invoking its `length()` method, and retrieve a character at the specified `index` in the string using the `charAt(index)` method.

◆ You can use the `concat` method to concatenate two strings, or the plus (+) sign to concatenate two or more strings.

◆ You can use the `substring` method to extract a substring from the string.

◆ You can use the `equals` and `compareTo` methods to compare strings. The `equals` method returns `true` if two strings are equal, and `false` if they are not equal. The `compareTo` method returns `0`, a positive integer, or a negative integer, depending on whether one string is equal to, greater than, or less than the other string.

◆ The `Character` class is a wrapper class for a single character. The `Character` class provides useful static methods to determine whether a character is a letter (`isLetter(char)`), a digit (`isDigit(char)`), uppercase (`isUpperCase(char)`), or lowercase (`isLowerCase(char)`).

◆ The `StringBuffer` class can be used to replace the `String` class. The `String` object is immutable, but you can add, insert, or append new contents into a `StringBuffer` object. Use `String` if the string contents do not require any change, and use `StringBuffer` if they change.

◆ The `StringTokenizer` class is used to retrieve and process tokens in a string. You learned the role of delimiters, how to create a `StringTokenizer` from a string, and how to use the `countTokens`, `hasMoreTokens`, and `nextToken` methods to process a string tokenizer.

◆ You can pass strings to the `main` method from the command line. Strings passed to the `main` program are stored in `args`, which is an array of strings. The first string is represented by `args[0]`, and `args.length` is the number of strings passed.

REVIEW QUESTIONS

Section 7.2 The `String` Class

7.1 Suppose that s1, s2, s3, and s4 are four strings, given as follows:

```
String s1 = "Welcome to Java";
String s2 = s1;
String s3 = new String("Welcome to Java");
String s4 = s3.intern();
```

What are the results of the following expressions?

```
(1)  s1 == s2                    (4) s2.equals(s3)
(2)  s2 == s3                    (5) s1.compareTo(s2)
(3)  s1.equals(s2)               (6) s2.compareTo(s3)
(7)  s1 == s4                    (16) s1.startsWith("Wel")
(8)  s1.charAt(0)                (17) s1.endsWith("Java")
(9)  s1.indexOf('j')             (18) s1.toLowerCase()
(10) s1.indexOf("to")            (19) s1.toUpperCase()
(11) s1.lastIndexOf('a')         (20) "  Welcome ".trim()
(12) s1.lastIndexOf("o", 15)     (21) s1.replace('o', "T")
(13) s1.length()                 (22) s1.replaceAll("o", "T")
(14) s1.substring(5)             (23) s1.replaceFirst("o", "T")
(15) s1.substring(5, 11)         (24) s1.toCharArray()
```

7.2   Suppose that s1 and s2 are two strings. Which of the following statements or expressions are incorrect?

```
String s = new String("new string");
String s3 = s1 + s2;
String s3 = s1 - s2;
s1 == s2;
s1 >= s2;
s1.compareTo(s2);
int i = s1.length();
char c = s1(0);
char c = s1.charAt(s1.length());
```

7.3   How do you compare whether two strings are equal without considering cases?

7.4   How do you convert all the letters in a string to uppercase? How do you convert all the letters in a string to lowercase? Do the conversion methods (toLowerCase, toUpperCase, trim, replace) change the contents of the string that invokes these methods?

7.5   Suppose string s is created using new String(); what is s.length()?

7.6   How do you convert a char, an array of characters, or a number to a string?

7.7   Why does the following code cause a NullPointerException?

```
1 public class Test {
2   private String text;
3
4   public Test(String s) {
5     String text = s;
6   }
7
8   public static void main(String[] args) {
9     Test test = new Test("ABC");
10    System.out.println(test.text.toLowerCase());
11  }
12 }
```

7.8   What is wrong in the following program?

```
1 public class Test {
2   String text;
3
4   public void Test(String s) {
5     this.text = s;
6   }
7
8   public static void main(String[] args) {
9     Test test = new Test("ABC");
10    System.out.println(test);
11  }
12 }
```

Section 7.3 The `Character` Class

7.9 How do you determine whether a character is in lowercase or uppercase?

7.10 How do you determine whether a character is alphanumeric?

Section 7.4 The `StringBuffer` Class

7.11 How do you create a string buffer for a string? How do you get the string from a string buffer?

7.12 Write three statements to reverse a string s using the `reverse` method in the `StringBuffer` class.

7.13 Write three statements to delete a substring from a string s of twenty characters, starting at index 4 and ending with index 10. Use the `delete` method in the `StringBuffer` class.

7.14 What is the internal structure of a string and a string buffer?

7.15 Suppose that s1 and s2 are given as follows:

```
StringBuffer s1 = new StringBuffer("Java");
StringBuffer s2 = new StringBuffer("HTML");
```

Show the results of the following expressions of s1 after each statement. Assume that the expressions are independent.

```
(1) s1.append(" is fun");        (7)  s1.deleteCharAt(3);
(2) s1.append(s2);               (8)  s1.delete(1, 3);
(3) s1.insert(2, "is fun");      (9)  s1.reverse();
(4) s1.insert(1, s2);            (10) s1.replace(1, 3, "Computer");
(5) s1charAt(2);                 (11) s1.substring(1, 3);
(6) s1.length();                 (12) s1.substring(2);
```

Section 7.5 The `StringTokenizer` Class

7.16 Declare a `StringTokenizer` for a string s with delimiters `"%$#"`.

7.17 What is the output of the following program?

```
1  import java.util.StringTokenizer;
2
3  public class TestStringTokenizer {
4    public static void main(String[] args) {
5      String s = "Java is cool.";
6      StringTokenizer tokenizer = new StringTokenizer(s, "v.");
7
8      System.out.println("The total number of tokens is " +
9        tokenizer.countTokens());
10
11     while (tokenizer.hasMoreTokens())
12         System.out.println(tokenizer.nextToken());
13
14     System.out.println("Any tokens left? " + tokenizer.countTokens());
15   }
16 }
```

What would be the output if Line 6 is replaced by the following code?

```
StringTokenizer tokenizer = new StringTokenizer(s, "v.", ture);
```

Section 7.6 The Scanner Class

7.18 Write the code to display all the tokens in a strings using the word "`to`" as the delimiter.

7.19 Write the code to read an int value from the console.

Section 7.7 Command-Line Arguments

7.19 Show the output of the following program when invoked using

1. java Test I have a dream
2. java Test "1 2 3"
3. java Test
4. java Test "*"
5. java Test *

```
public class Test {
  public static void main(String[] args) {
    System.out.println("Number of strings is " + args.length);
    for (int i = 0; i < args.length; i++)
      System.out.println(args[i]);
  }
}
```

PROGRAMMING EXERCISES

Section 7.2 The String Class

7.1* (*Revising Example 7.1 "Checking Palindromes"*) Rewrite Example 7.1 by creating a new string that is a reversal of the string and compare the two to determine whether the string is a palindrome. Write your own reverse method using the following header:

```
public static String reverse(String s)
```

7.2* (*Revising Example 7.1 "Checking Palindromes"*) Rewrite Example 7.1 to ignore cases.

7.3** (*Checking substrings*) You can check whether a string is a substring of another string by using the indexOf method in the String class. Write your own method for this function. Write a program that prompts the user to enter two strings, and check whether the first string is a substring of the second.

7.4* (*Occurrence of a specified character*) Write a method that finds the number of occurrences of a specified letter in the string using the following header:

```
public static int count(String str, char a)
```

For example, count("Welcome", 'e') returns 2.

Section 7.3 The Character Class

7.5** (*Occurrences of each digit in a string*) Write a method that counts the occurrences of each digit in a string using the following header:

```
public static int[] count(String s)
```

The method counts how many times a digit appears in the string. The return value is an array of ten elements, each of which holds the count for a digit.

Write a main method to display the count for "SSN is 343 32 4545 and ID is 434 34 4323".

7.6* (*Counting the letters in a string*) Write a method that counts the number of letters in the string using the following header:

```
public static int countLetters(String s)
```

Write a main method to invoke countLetters("Java in 2008") and display its return value.

7.7* (*Hex to decimal*) Write a method that parses a hex number as a string into a decimal integer. The method header is as follows:

```
public static int parseHex(String hexString)
```

For example, hexString A5 is $10 \times 16 + 5$ and FAA is $15 \times 16^2 + 10 \times 16 + 10$. Use hex strings ABC and 10A to test the method.

7.8* (*Binary to decimal*) Write a method that parses a binary number as a string into a decimal integer. The method header is as follows:

```
public static int parseBinary(String binaryString)
```

For example, binaryString 10001 is $1 \times 2^4 + 0 \times 2^3 + 0 \times 2^2 + 0 \times 2 + 1$. Use binary string 11111111 to test the method.

Section 7.4 The StringBuffer Class

7.9** (*Decimal to hex*) Write a method that parses a decimal number into a hex number as a string. The method header is as follows:

```
public static String convertDecimalToHex(int value)
```

See Section 1.5, "Number Systems," for converting a decimal into a hex. Use decimal 298 and 9123 to test the method.

7.10** (*Decimal to binary*) Write a method that parses a decimal number into a binary number as a string. The method header is as follows:

```
public static String convertDecimalToBinary(int value)
```

See Section 1.5, "Number Systems," for converting a decimal into a binary. Use decimal 298 and 9123 to test the method.

7.11** (*Sorting characters in a string*) Write a method that returns a sorted string using the following header:

```
public static String sort(String s)
```

For example, sort("acb") returns abc.

7.12** (*Anagrams*) Write a method that checks whether two words are anagrams. Two words are anagrams if they contain the same letters in any order. For example, "silent" and "listen" are anagrams. The header of the method is as follows:

```
public static boolean isAnagram(String s1, String s2)
```

Write a main method to invoke isAnagram("silent", "listen"), isAnagram("garden", "ranged"), and isAnagram("split", "lisp").

Section 7.5 The StringTokenizer Class

7.13* (*Monetary units*) Rewrite Example 2.3, "Monetary Units," to receive the input as a string, and extract the dollars and cents using the StringTokenizer class.

7.14* (*Extracting words*) Write a program that extracts words from a string using the spaces and punctuation marks as delimiters. Enter the string from an input dialog box.

Section 7.6 The Scanner Class

7.15* (*Revising Exercise 7.13 using* Scanner) Write a program that reads a string from an input dialog box. The string consists of double values separated by spaces. Display the sum of the values.

7.16* (*Console input*) Use the Scanner class to read numbers separated by spaces from the keyboard and displays their sum and average. Press CTRL+C to end the input.

Section 7.7 Command-Line Arguments

7.17* (*Passing a string to check palindromes*) Rewrite Example 7.1, "Checking Palindromes," by passing the string as a command-line argument.

7.18* (*Summing integers*) Write two programs. The first program passes an unspecified number of integers as separate strings to the main method and displays their total. The second program passes an unspecified number of integers in one string to the main method and displays their total. Name the two programs Exercise7_18a and Exercise7_18b, as shown in Figure 7.13.

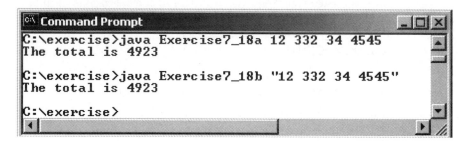

FIGURE 7.13 *The program adds all the numbers passed from the command line.*

7.19* (*Finding the number of uppercase letters in a string*) Write a program that passes a string to the main method and displays the number of uppercase letters in a string.

chapter

8

INHERITANCE AND POLYMORPHISM

Objectives

- ✦ To develop a subclass from a superclass through inheritance (§8.2).

- ✦ To invoke the superclass's constructors and methods using the super keyword (§8.3).

- ✦ To override methods in the subclass (§8.4).

- ✦ To explore the useful methods (equals(Object), hashCode(), toString(), finalize(), clone(), and getClass()) in the Object class (§8.5, §8.11 Optional).

- ✦ To comprehend polymorphism, dynamic binding, and generic programming (§8.6).

- ✦ To describe casting and explain why explicit downcasting is necessary (§8.7).

- ✦ To understand the effect of hiding data fields and static methods (§8.8 Optional).

- ✦ To restrict access to data and methods using the protected visibility modifier (§8.9).

- ✦ To declare constants, unmodifiable methods, and nonextendable classes using the final modifier (§8.10).

- ✦ To initialize data using initialization blocks and to distinguish between instance initialization and static initialization blocks (§8.12 Optional).

8.1   Introduction

inheritance

Object-oriented programming allows you to derive new classes from existing classes. This is called *inheritance*. Inheritance is an important and powerful concept in Java. In fact, every class you define in Java is inherited from an existing class, either explicitly or implicitly. The classes you created in the preceding chapters were all derived implicitly from the `java.lang.Object` class.

This chapter introduces the concept of inheritance. Specifically, it discusses superclasses and subclasses, the use of the keyword `super`, and the `Object` class, explores polymorphism and dynamic binding, generic programming, and casting objects, and introduces the modifiers `protected` and `final`.

8.2   Superclasses and Subclasses

subclass
superclass

In OOP terminology, a class `C1` derived from another class `C2` is called a *subclass*, and `C2` is called a *superclass*. A superclass is also referred to as a *parent class* or a *base class*, and a subclass as a *child class*, an *extended class*, or a *derived class*. A subclass inherits accessible data fields and methods from its superclass, and may also add new data fields and methods.

 NOTE

Contrary to the conventional interpretation, a subclass is not a subset of its superclass. In fact, a subclass is usually extended to contain more functions and more detailed information than its superclass.

Let us demonstrate inheritance by creating a new class, `Cylinder`, derived from the `Circle` class defined in Listing 6.3 on page 225. The `Cylinder` class inherits all accessible data fields and methods from the `Circle` class. In addition, it has a new data field, `length`, and a new method, `findVolume`. The relationship of these two classes is shown in Figure 8.1. An arrow pointing to the superclass is used to denote the inheritance relationship between the two classes involved. The `Cylinder` class is defined in Listing 8.1.

LISTING **8.1**   First Version of the `Cylinder` Class

```
1  // Cylinder.java: Class definition for describing Cylinder
2  public class Cylinder extends Circle {
3    private double length = 1;
4
5    /** Return length */
6    public double getLength() {
7      return length;
8    }
9
10   /** Set length */
11   public void setLength(double length) {
12     this.length = length;
13   }
14
15   /** Return the volume of this cylinder */
16   public double findVolume() {
17     return findArea() * length;
18   }
19 }
```

The reserved word `extends` (Line 2) tells the compiler that the `Cylinder` class is derived from the `Circle` class, thus inheriting the methods `getRadius`, `setRadius`, and `findArea` from `Circle`.

Superclass

Subclass

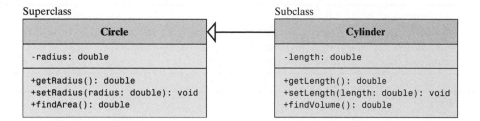

FIGURE **8.1**   *The* Cylinder *class inherits public methods from the* Circle *class and extends the* Circle *class with its own data and methods.*

The following code creates an instance of Cylinder and invokes the methods defined in Circle and Cylinder:

```
Cylinder cylinder = new Cylinder();
System.out.println("The length is " + cylinder.getLength());
System.out.println("The radius is " + cylinder.getRadius());
System.out.println("The volume of the cylinder is " +
  cylinder.findVolume());
System.out.println("The area of the circle is " +
  cylinder.findArea());
```

Since radius is 1 and length is 1 by default, the output is:

```
The length is 1.0
The radius is 1.0
The volume of the cylinder is 3.14159
The area of the circle is 3.14159
```

 NOTE

Private data fields and methods in a superclass are not accessible outside of the class. Therefore, they are not inherited in a subclass.

8.3   Using the Keyword **super**

Section 6.12, "The this keyword," introduced the use of the keyword this as a surrogate to refer to the calling object. The keyword super refers to the superclass of the class in which super appears. It can be used in two ways:

✦   To call a superclass constructor.

✦   To call a superclass method.

8.3.1   Calling Superclass Constructors

The syntax to call a superclass constructor is:

```
super(), or super(parameters);
```

The statement super() invokes the no-arg constructor of its superclass, and the statement super(arguments) invokes the superclass constructor that matches the arguments. The statement super() or super(arguments) must appear in the first line of the subclass constructor and is the only way to invoke a superclass constructor.

CAUTION

You must use the keyword `super` to call the superclass constructor, and the call must be the first statement in the constructor. Invoking a superclass constructor's name in a subclass causes a syntax error.

 NOTE

A constructor is used to construct an instance of a class. Unlike properties and methods, the constructors of a superclass are not inherited in the subclass. They can only be invoked from the constructors of the subclasses, using the keyword `super`.

8.3.2 Constructor Chaining

A constructor may invoke an overloaded constructor or its superclass's constructor. If neither of them is invoked explicitly, the compiler puts `super()` as the first statement in the constructor. For example,

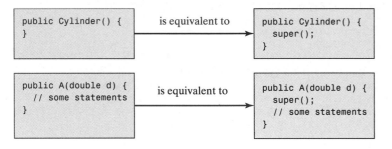

In any case, constructing an instance of a class invokes the constructors of all the superclasses along the inheritance chain. This is called *constructor chaining*. Consider the following code:

constructor chaining

```
1 public class Faculty extends Employee {
2   public static void main(String[] args) {
3     new Faculty();
4   }
5
6   public Faculty() {
7     System.out.println("Faculty's no-arg constructor is invoked");
8   }
9 }
10
11 class Employee extends Person {
12   public Employee() {
13     this("Invoke Employee's overloaded constructor");
14     System.out.println("Employee's no-arg constructor is invoked");
15   }
16
17   public Employee(String s) {
18     System.out.println(s);
19   }
20 }
21
22 class Person {
23   public Person() {
24     System.out.println("Person's no-arg constructor is invoked");
25   }
26 }
```

In Line 3, `new Faculty()` invokes Faculty's no-arg constructor. Since Faculty is a subclass of Employee, Employee's no-arg constructor is invoked before any statements in Faculty's constructor are executed. Employee's no-arg constructor invokes Employee's second constructor (Line 13). Since Employee is a subclass of Person, Person's no-arg constructor is invoked before any statements in Employee's second constructor are executed. Therefore, the output of creating an instance of Faculty is:

```
Person's no-arg constructor is invoked
Invoke Employee's overloaded constructor
Employee's no-arg constructor is invoked
Faculty's no-arg constructor is invoked
```

 CAUTION

If a class is designed to be extended, it is better to provide a no-arg constructor to avoid programming errors. Consider the following code:

no-arg constructor

```
1 public class Apple extends Fruit {
2 }
3
4 class Fruit {
5   public Fruit(String name) {
6     System.out.println("Fruit's constructor is invoked");
7   }
8 }
```

Since no constructor is explicitly defined in Apple, Apple's default no-arg constructor is declared implicitly. Since Apple is a subclass of Fruit, Apple's default constructor automatically invokes Fruit's no-arg constructor. However, Fruit does not have a no-arg constructor because Fruit has an explicit constructor defined. Therefore, the program cannot be compiled.

8.3.3 Calling Superclass Methods

The keyword super can also be used to reference a method other than the constructor in the superclass. The syntax is like this:

```
super.method(parameters);
```

You could rewrite the findVolume() method in the Cylinder class as follows:

```
double findVolume() {
  return super.findArea() * length;
}
```

It is not necessary to put super before findArea() in this case, however, because findArea is a method in the Circle class and is inherited by the Cylinder class. Nevertheless, in some cases, as shown in the next section, the keyword super is needed.

8.4 Overriding Methods

A subclass inherits methods from a superclass. Sometimes it is necessary for the subclass to modify the implementation of a method defined in the superclass. This is referred to as *method overriding*.

method overriding

The findArea method in the Circle class computes the area of a circle. This method should be overridden to compute the surface area of a cylinder in the Cylinder class. The new Cylinder class is given in Listing 8.2.

LISTING 8.2 Cylinder.java (An Improved Cylinder Class)

```java
1 public class Cylinder extends Circle {
2   /** length of this cylinder */
3   private double length;
4
5   /** Construct a cylinder with default radius and length */
6   public Cylinder() {
7     super(); // Default behavior and can be omitted
8     length = 1.0;
9   }
10
11   /** Construct a cylinder with specified radius and length */
12   public Cylinder(double radius, double length) {
13     super(radius);
14     this.length = length;
15   }
16
17   /** Return length */
18   public double getLength() {
19     return length;
20   }
21
22   /** Set length */
23   public void setLength(double length) {
24     this.length = length;
25   }
26
27   /** Return the surface area of this cylinder. The formula is
28    * 2 * circle area + cylinder body area
29    */
30   public double findArea() {
31     return 2 * super.findArea() + 2 * getRadius() * Math.PI * length;
32   }
33
34   /** Return the volume of this cylinder */
35   public double findVolume() {
36     return super.findArea() * length;
37   }
38 }
```

override findArea()

In Line 7, super() is used to invoke its superclass's no-arg constructor. This line can be omitted, since super() is invoked by default if no superclass constructor is invoked explicitly.

The findArea method is defined in the Circle class and modified in the Cylinder class. Both methods can be used in the Cylinder class. To invoke the findArea method defined in the Circle class, use super.findArea(). Can a subclass of Cylinder access the findArea method defined in the Circle class using a syntax such as super.super.findArea()? No. This is a syntax error. Can an instance of Cylinder invoke the findArea method defined in the Circle class? No, not any longer, since findArea in Circle has been overridden in Cylinder.

 NOTE

same signature
same return type

To override a method, the method must be defined in the subclass using the same signature and return type as in its superclass. You learned about overloading methods in Section 4.5, "Overloading Methods". Overloading a method is a way to provide more than one method with the same name but with different signatures to distinguish them. It is a compilation error if two methods differ only in return type.

NOTE

override accessible instance method

An instance method can be overridden only if it is accessible. Thus a private method cannot be overridden, because it is not accessible outside its own class. If a method defined in a subclass is private in its superclass, the two methods are completely unrelated.

NOTE

Like an instance method, a static method can be inherited. However, a static method cannot be overridden. If a static method defined in the superclass is redefined in a subclass, the method defined in the superclass is hidden. Hiding static methods will be further discussed in Section 8.8, "Hiding Data Fields and Static Methods."

cannot override static method

8.5   The `Object` class

Every class in Java is descended from the `java.lang.Object` class. If no inheritance is specified when a class is defined, the superclass of the class is `Object`. Classes like `String`, `StringBuffer`, `StringTokenizer`, `Loan`, and `Circle` are implicitly the subclasses of `Object` (as are all the main classes you have seen in this book so far). It is important to be familiar with the methods provided by the `Object` class so that you can use them in your classes. Three frequently used methods in the `Object` class are:

✦ `public boolean equals(Object object)`

✦ `public int hashCode()`

✦ `public String toString()`

8.5.1   The `equals` Method

The `equals` method tests whether two objects are equal. The syntax for invoking it is:

```
object1.equals(object2);
```

The default implementation of the `equals` method in the `Object` class is:

```
public boolean equals(Object obj) {
  return (this == obj);
}
```

Thus, using the `equals` method is equivalent to the `==` operator in the `Object` class, but it is really intended for the subclasses of the `Object` class to modify the `equals` method to test whether two distinct objects have the same content.

You have already used the `equals` method to compare two strings in Section 7.2, "The `String` Class." The `equals` method in the `String` class is inherited from the `Object` class and is modified in the `String` class to test whether two strings are identical in content.

 NOTE

The `==` comparison operator is used for comparing two primitive data type values or for determining whether two objects have the same references. The `equals` method is intended to test whether two objects have the same contents, provided that the method is modified in the defining class of the objects. The `==` operator is stronger than the `equals` method, in that the `==` operator checks whether the two reference variables refer to the same object.

== vs. equals

 CAUTION

Using the signature `equals(SomeClassName obj)` (e.g., `equals(Circle c)`) to override the `equals` method in a subclass is a common mistake. You should use `equals(Object obj)`. See Review Question 8.7.

equals(Object)

8.5.2 The hashCode Method

Invoking hashCode() on an object returns the object's hash code. *Hash code* is an integer that can be used to store the object in a hash set so that it can be located quickly. Hash sets will be introduced in Chapter 18, "Java Collections Framework." The hashCode implemented in the Object class returns the internal memory address of the object in hexadecimal. Your class should override the hashCode method whenever the equals method is overridden. By contract, if two objects are equal, their hash codes must be same. Two unequal objects may have the same hash code, but you should implement the hashCode method to avoid too many such cases. Additionally, it is required that invoking the hashCode method multiple times returns the same integer during one execution of the program. The integer need not be the same in different executions. For example, the hashCode method is overridden in the String class by returning $s_0 * 31^{(n-1)} + s_1 * 31^{(n-2)} + \cdots + s_{n-1}$ as the hash code, where s_i is s.charAt(i).

8.5.3 The toString method

Invoking toString() on an object returns a string that represents the object. By default, it returns a string consisting of a class name of which the object is an instance, an at sign (@), and the object's hash code in hexadecimal. For example, consider the following code:

```
Cylinder myCylinder = new Cylinder(5.0, 2.0);
System.out.println(myCylinder.toString());
```

The code displays something like Cylinder@15037e5. This message is not very helpful or informative. Usually you should override the toString method so that it returns a digestible string representation of the object. For example, you can override the toString method in the Cylinder class:

```
public String toString() {
  return "Cylinder length = " + length +
    " radius = " + getRadius();
}
```

Then System.out.println(myCylinder.toString()) will display the following:

```
Cylinder length = 2.0 radius = 5.0
```

> **✿ NOTE**
>
>
> You can also pass an object to invoke System.out.println(object) or System.out.print(object). This is equivalent to invoking System.out.println(object.toString()) or System.out.print(object.toString()). So you could replace System.out.println(myCylinder.toString()) with System.out.println(myCylinder).

8.6 Polymorphism, Dynamic Binding, and Generic Programming

The inheritance relationship enables a subclass to inherit features from its superclass with additional new features. A subclass is a specialization of its superclass; every instance of a subclass is an instance of its superclass, but not vice versa. For example, every circle is an object, but not every object is a circle. Therefore, you can always pass an instance of a subclass to a parameter of its superclass type. Consider the following code:

```
 1 public class Test {
 2   public static void main(String[] args) {
 3     m(new GraduateStudent());
 4     m(new Student());
 5     m(new Person());
 6     m(new Object());
 7   }
 8
 9   public static void m(Object x) {
10     System.out.println(x.toString());
11   }
12 }
13
14 class GraduateStudent extends Student {
15 }
16
17 class Student extends Person {
18   public String toString() {
19     return "Student";
20   }
21 }
22
23 class Person extends Object {
24   public String toString() {
25     return "Person";
26   }
27 }
```

It produces the following output:

```
Student
Student
Person
java.lang.Object@16f0472
```

Why? Let us discuss the reason. Method m (Line 9) takes a parameter of the Object type. You can invoke m with any object (e.g., new GraduateStudent(), new Student(), new Person(), and new Object()) in Lines 3-6. An object of a subclass can be used by any code designed to work with an object of its superclass. This feature is known as *polymorphism* (from a Greek word meaning "many forms").

polymorphism

When the method m(Object x) is executed, the argument x's toString method is invoked. x may be an instance of GraduateStudent, Student, Person, or Object. Classes GraduateStudent, Student, Person, and Object have their own implementations of the toString method. Which implementation is used will be determined dynamically by the Java Virtual Machine at runtime. This capability is known as *dynamic binding*.

dynamic binding

Dynamic binding works as follows: Suppose an object o is an instance of classes C_1, C_2, ..., C_{n-1}, and C_n, where C_1 is a subclass of C_2, C_2 is a subclass of C_3, ..., and C_{n-1} is a subclass of C_n, as shown in Figure 8.2. That is, C_n is the most general class, and C_1 is the most specific class. In Java, C_n is the Object class. If o invokes a method p, the JVM searches the implementation for

If o is an instance of C_1, o is also an instance of $C_2, C_3, ..., C_{n-1}$, and C_n

java.lang.Object

FIGURE 8.2 *The method to be invoked is dynamically bound at runtime.*

the method p in C_1, C_2, ..., C_{n-1}, and C_n, in this order, until it is found. Once an implementation is found, the search stops and the first-found implementation is invoked. For example, when m(new GraduateStudent()) is invoked in Line 3, the toString method defined in the Student class is used.

 NOTE

Matching a method signature and binding a method implementation are two separate issues. The compiler finds a matching method according to parameter type, number of parameters, and order of the parameters at compilation time. A method may be implemented in several subclasses. The Java Virtual Machine dynamically binds the implementation of the method at runtime. See Review Question 8.7.

---

generic programming

Polymorphism allows methods to be used generically for a wide range of object arguments. This is known as *generic programming*. If a method's parameter type is a superclass (e.g., Object), you may pass an object to this method of any of the parameter's subclasses (e.g., Student or String). When an object (e.g., a Student object or a String object) is used in the method, the particular implementation of the method of the object that is invoked (e.g., toString) is determined dynamically.

8.7 Casting Objects and the `instanceof` Operator

You have already used the casting operator to convert variables of one primitive type to another. Casting can also be used to convert an object of one class type to another within an inheritance hierarchy. In the preceding section, the statement

```
m(new Student());
```

assigns the object new Student() to a parameter of the Object type. This statement is equivalent to

```
Object o = new Student(); // Implicit casting
m(o);
```

implicit casting

The statement Object o = new Student(), known as *implicit casting*, is legal because an instance of Student is automatically an instance of Object.

Suppose you want to assign the object reference o to a variable of the Student type using the following statement:

```
Student b = o;
```

A compilation error would occur. Why does the statement Object o = new Student() work and the statement Student b = o doesn't? Because a Student object is always an instance of Object, but an Object is not necessarily an instance of Student. Even though you can see that o is really a Student object, the compiler is not clever enough to know it. To tell the compiler that o is a Student object, use an *explicit casting*. The syntax is similar to the one used for casting among primitive data types. Enclose the target object type in parentheses and place it before the object to be cast, as follows:

explicit casting

```
Student b = (Student)o; // Explicit casting
```

upcasting
downcasting

It is always possible to cast an instance of a subclass to a variable of a superclass (known as *upcasting*), because an instance of a subclass is *always* an instance of its superclass. When casting an instance of a superclass to a variable of its subclass (known as *downcasting*), explicit casting must be used to confirm your intention to the compiler with the (SubclassName) cast notation. For the casting to be successful, you must make sure that the object to be cast is an instance of the subclass. If the superclass object is not an instance of the subclass, a runtime *ClassCastException* occurs. For example, if an object is not an instance of Student, it cannot be cast into a variable of Student. It is a good practice, therefore, to ensure that the object is an instance of another object before attempting a casting. This can be accomplished by using the *instanceof* operator. Consider the following code:

`ClassCastException`

`instanceof`

```
/** Suppose myObject is declared as the Object type */
/** Perform casting if myObject is an instance of Cylinder */
if (myObject instanceof Cylinder) {
  Cylinder myCylinder = (Cylinder)myObject;
  System.out.println("The cylinder volume is " +
    myCylinder.findVolume());
  ...
}
```

You may be wondering why casting is necessary. The data type of a variable is determined at compile time. Suppose the variable myObject is declared as the Object type. Using myObject.findVolume() would cause a compilation error because the Object class does not have the findVolume method. So it is necessary to cast myObject into the Cylinder type to invoke the findVolume method. So why not declare myObject as a Cylinder type in the first place? To enable generic programming, it is a good practice to declare a variable with a superclass type, which can accept a value of any subclass type. This is shown in Example 8.1.

 NOTE

instanceof is a Java keyword. Every letter in a Java keyword is in lowercase.

 TIP

To help understand casting, consider the analogy of fruit, apple, and orange, with the Fruit class as the superclass for Apple and Orange. An apple is a fruit, so you can always safely assign an instance of Apple to a variable for Fruit. However, a fruit is not necessarily an apple, so you have to use explicit casting to assign an instance of Fruit to a variable of Apple.

EXAMPLE 8.1 DEMONSTRATING POLYMORPHISM AND CASTING

Problem

Write a program that creates two objects, a circle and a cylinder, and invokes the displayObject method to display them. The displayObject method displays area if the object is a circle, and area and volume if the object is a cylinder.

Solution

Listing 8.3 gives the solution to the problem. A sample run of the program is shown in Figure 8.3.

LISTING 8.3 TestPolymorphismCasting.java (Polymorphism and Casting)

```
1 public class TestPolymorphismCasting {
2   /** Main method */
3   public static void main(String[] args) {
```

EXAMPLE 8.1 (CONTINUED)

```
 4      // Declare and initialize two objects
 5      Object object1 = new Circle(1);
 6      Object object2 = new Cylinder(1, 1);
 7
 8      // Display circle and cylinder
 9      displayObject(object1);
10      displayObject(object2);
11   }
12
13   /** A method for displaying an object */
14   static void displayObject(Object object) {
15     if (object instanceof Cylinder) {
16       System.out.println("The cylinder area is " +
17         ((Cylinder)object).findArea());
18       System.out.println("The cylinder volume is " +
19         ((Cylinder)object).findVolume());
20     }
21     else if (object instanceof Circle) {
22       System.out.println("The circle area is " +
23         ((Circle)object).findArea());
24     }
25   }
26 }
```

FIGURE 8.3 *The program creates a* `Circle` *object and a* `Cylinder` *object, assigns them to variables of the* `Object` *type, and casts them to* `Circle` *and* `Cylinder` *in order to use the methods defined in* `Circle` *and* `Cylinder`.

Review

The `displayObject(Object object)` method is an example of generic programming. It can be invoked with any instance of `Object`.

The program uses implicit casting to assign a `Circle` object to `object1` and a `Cylinder` object to `object2` (Lines 5–6), and then invokes the `displayObject` method to display the information on these objects (Lines 9–10).

In the `displayObject` method (Lines 14–25), explicit casting is used to cast the object to `Cylinder` if the object is an instance of `Cylinder`, and the methods `findArea` and `findVolume` are used to display the area and volume of the cylinder.

Casting can only be done when the source object is an instance of the target class. The program uses the `instanceof` operator to ensure that the source object is an instance of the target class before performing a casting (Line 15).

Explicit casting to `Cylinder` (Lines 17, 19) and to `Circle` (Line 23) is necessary because the `findArea` and `findVolume` methods are not available in the `Object` class.

Note that the order in the `if` statement is significant. If it is reversed (i.e., testing whether the object is an instance of `Circle` first), then the cylinder will never be cast

EXAMPLE 8.1 (CONTINUED)

into `Cylinder` because `Cylinder` is an instance of `Circle`. Try to run the program with the following `if` statement and observe the effect:

```
if (object instanceof Circle) {
  System.out.println("The circle area is " +
    ((Circle)object).findArea());
}
else if (object instanceof Cylinder) {
  System.out.println("The cylinder area is " +
    ((Cylinder)object).findArea());
  System.out.println("The cylinder volume is " +
    ((Cylinder)object).findVolume());
}
```

CAUTION

The object member access operator (.) precedes the casting casting operator. Use parentheses to ensure that casting is done before the . operator, as in

```
((Cylinder)object).findArea());
```

. precedes casting

8.8 Hiding Data Fields and Static Methods (Optional)

This section is marked optional because hidden data fields and static methods are rarely useful, and in my view they should not be used, for the sake of simplicity and clarity. I recommend skipping this section now and consulting it for reference in the future.

You can override an instance method, but you cannot override a data field (instance or static) or a static method. If you declare a data field or a static method in a subclass with the same name as one in the superclass, the one in the superclass is hidden, but it still exists. The two data fields or static methods are independent. You can reference the hidden data field or static method using the keyword super in the subclass. The hidden field or method can also be accessed via a reference variable of the superclass's type.

When invoking an instance method from a reference variable, the *actual class of the object* referenced by the variable decides which implementation of the method is used *at runtime*. When accessing a data field or a static method, the *declared type* of the reference variable decides which field or static method is used *at compile time*. This is the key difference between invoking an instance method and accessing a data field or a static method.

Consider the following example:

```
1 public class Test {
2   public static void main(String[] args) {
3     Animal x = new Tiger();
4
5     // Access news
6     System.out.println("(1) x.news is " + x.news);
7     System.out.println("(2) ((Tiger)x).news is " + ((Tiger)x).news);
8
9     // Invoke static method smile
10    System.out.println("(3) x.smile() is " + x.smile());
11    System.out.println("(4) ((Tiger)x).smile() is " +
12      ((Tiger)x).smile());
13
14    // Invoke instance method getNews
15    System.out.println("(5) x.getNews() is " + x.getNews());
```

```
16      System.out.println("(6) x.getMessage() is " + x.getMessage());
17    }
18 }
19
20 class Animal {
21   public String news = "Animal's news";
22   public String message = "Animal's message";
23
24   public static String smile() {
25     return "smile from Animal";
26   }
27
28   public String getNews() {
29     return news;
30   }
31
32   public String getMessage() {
33     return message;
34   }
35 }
36
37 class Tiger extends Animal {
38   public String news = "Tiger's news";
39   public String message = "Tiger's message";
40
41   public static String smile() {
42     return "smile from Tiger";
43   }
44
45   /** Override getNews in Tiger */
46   public String getNews() {
47     return news;
48   }
49 }
```

The printout of the program is:

```
(1) x.news is Animal's news
(2) ((Tiger)x).news is Tiger's news
(3) x.smile() is smile from Animal
(4) ((Tiger)x).smile() is smile from Tiger
(5) x.getNews() is Tiger's news
(6) x.getMessage() is Animal's message
```

Here are the explanations:

1. x.news is "Animal's news" because x's declared type is the class Animal.

2. To use news in the class Tiger, you need to cast x to Tiger using ((Tiger)x).news.

3. x.smile() invokes the static smile method in Animal because x's declared type is Animal.

4. ((Tiger)x).smile() invokes the static smile method in Tiger because the type for (Tiger)x is Tiger.

5. x.getNews() invokes the getNews method in Tiger at runtime because x actually references to the object of the class Tiger.

6. x.getMessage() invokes the getMessage method in Animal at runtime because getMessage is implemented in Animal. Therefore, the message in Animal is returned.

 NOTE

A static method or a static field can always be accessed using its declared class name, regardless of whether it is hidden or not.

8.9 The protected Data and Methods

The modifier protected can be applied to data and methods in a class. A protected datum or a protected method in a public class can be accessed *by any class in the same package or its subclasses*, even if the subclasses are in different packages.

8.9.1 Using the Visibility Modifiers

The modifiers private, protected, and public are known as *visibility* or *accessibility modifiers* because they specify how class and class members are accessed. The visibility of these modifiers increases in this order:

```
            Visibility increases
      ────────────────────────────────▶
 private, none (if no modifier is used), protected, public
```

Figure 8.4 illustrates how a public, protected, default, and private data or method in class C1 can be accessed from a class C2 in the same package, from a subclass C3 in the same package, from a subclass C4 in a different package, and from a class C5 in a different package.

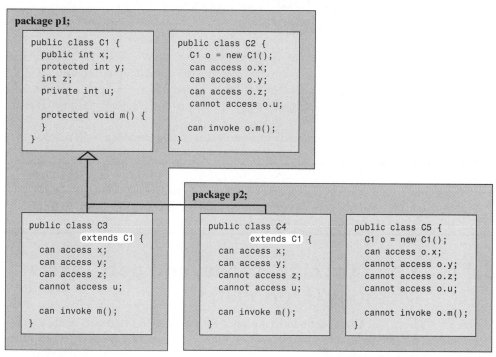

FIGURE 8.4 *Visibility modifiers are used to control how data and methods are accessed.*

Use the private modifier to hide the members of the class completely so that they cannot be accessed directly from outside the class. Use no modifiers to allow the members of the class to be accessed directly from any class within the same package but not from other packages. Use the protected modifier to enable the members of the class to be accessed by the subclasses in any package or classes in the same package. Use the public modifier to enable the members of the class to be accessed by any class.

Your class can be used in two ways: for creating instances of the class, and for creating subclasses by extending the class. Make the members private if they are not intended for use from outside the class. Make the members public if they are intended for the users of the class. Make the fields or methods protected if they are intended for the extenders of the class but not the users of the class.

The private and protected modifiers can only be used for members of the class. The public modifier and the default modifier (i.e., no modifier) can be used on members of the class as well on the class. A class with no modifier (i.e., not a public class) is not accessible by classes from other packages.

> **NOTE**
>
> In UML, the symbols -, #, and +, respectively, are used to denote private, protected, and public modifiers.

> **NOTE**
>
> A subclass may override a protected method in its superclass and change its visibility to public. However, a subclass cannot weaken the accessibility of a method defined in the superclass. For example, if a method is defined as public in the superclass, it must be defined as public in the subclass.

8.10 The `final` Classes, Methods, and Variables

You have already seen the `final` modifier used in declaring constants. You may occasionally want to prevent classes from being extended. In such cases, use the `final` modifier to indicate that a class is final and cannot be a parent class. The `Math` class, introduced in Chapter 4, "Methods," is a final class. The `String` and `StringBuffer` classes, introduced in Chapter 7, "Strings," are also final classes.

You also can define a method to be final; a final method cannot be overriden by its subclasses.

> **NOTE**
>
> The modifiers are used on classes and class members (data and methods), except that the `final` modifier can also be used on local variables in a method. A final local variable is a constant inside a method.

8.11 The `finalize`, `clone`, and `getClass` Methods (Optional)

Section 8.5, "The `Object` Class," introduces the `equals`, `hashCode`, and `toString` methods in the `Object` class. This section introduces the `finalize`, `clone`, and `getClass` methods. They are defined in the `Object` class as follows:

- ◆ `protected void finalize() throws Throwable`
- ◆ `protected native Object clone()`
     `throws CloneNotSupportedException`
- ◆ `public final native Class getClass()`

> **NOTE**
>
> The `native` modifier indicates that the method is implemented using a programming language other than Java. Some methods, such as `clone`, need to access hardware using the native machine language or the C language. These methods are marked `native`. A native method can be `final`, `public`, `private`, `protected`, overloaded, or overridden.

NOTE

The `finalize` method may throw `Throwable`, and the `clone` method may throw `CloneNotSupportedException`. Exception handling will be introduced in Chapter 15, "Exceptions and Assertions." (*Chapter 15 can be covered after Chapter 8.*) For now, you need to know that `throws Throwable` and `throws CloneNotSupported-Exception` are part of the method declarations for the `finalize` and `clone` methods.

8.11.1   The `finalize` Method

The `finalize` method is invoked by the garbage collector on an object when the object becomes garbage. An object becomes garbage if it is no longer accessed. By default, the `finalize` method does nothing. A subclass should override the `finalize` method to dispose of system resources or to perform other cleanup, if necessary.

 NOTE

The `finalize` method is invoked by the JVM. You should never write the code to invoke it in your program.

For an illustration, see the following code:

```
 1 public class Test {
 2   public static void main(String[] args) {
 3     Cake a1 = new Cake(1);
 4     Cake a2 = new Cake(2);
 5     Cake a3 = new Cake(3);
 6
 7     // To dispose the objects a2 and a3
 8     a2 = a3 = null;
 9     System.gc(); // Invoke the Java garbage collector
10   }
11 }
12
13 class Cake extends Object {
14   int id;
15
16   public Cake(int id) {
17     this.id = id;
18     System.out.println("Cake object " + id + " is created");
19   }
20
21   public void finalize() throws java.lang.Throwable {
22     System.out.println("Cake object " + id + " is disposed");
23   }
24 }
```

Here is the output of this program:

```
Cake object 1 is created
Cake object 2 is created
Cake object 3 is created
Cake object 2 is disposed
Cake object 3 is disposed
```

Line 8 assigns `null` to a2 and a3. The objects previously referenced by a2 and a3 are no longer accessible. Therefore, they are garbage. `System.gc()` in Line 9 requests the garbage collector to be invoked to reclaim space from all discarded objects. Normally you don't need to invoke this method explicitly, because the JVM automatically invokes it whenever the JVM determines it is necessary. The `finalize` method on the objects a2 and a3 are invoked by the garbage collector. When the program terminates, a1 also becomes garbage, and a1's `finalize` method is then invoked. Since the program has already exited, no message is displayed on the console.

8.11.2   The clone Method

Sometimes you need to make a copy of an object. Mistakenly, you might use the assignment statement, as follows:

```
newObject = someObject;
```

This statement does not create a duplicate object. It simply assigns the reference of someObject to newObject. To create a new object with separate memory space, use the clone() method:

```
newObject = someObject.clone();
```

This statement copies someObject to a new memory location and assigns the reference of the new object to newObject. For example,

```
java.util.Date date = new java.util.Date();
java.util.Date date1 = (java.util.Date)(date.clone());
```

creates a new Date object, date, and its clone, date1.

 NOTE

Not all objects can be cloned. For an object to be cloneable, its class must implement the java.lang.Cloneable interface, which is introduced in Section 9.4.4, "The Cloneable Interface."

 TIP

An array is treated as an object in Java and is an instance of the Object class. The clone method can also be used to copy arrays. The following statement uses the clone method to copy the sourceArray of the int[] type to the targetArray:

```
int[] targetArray = (int[])sourceArray.clone();
```

Since the return type of the clone method is Object, (int[]) is used to cast it to the int[] type.

8.11.3   The getClass Method

A class must be loaded in order to be used. When the JVM loads the class, it creates an object that contains the information about the class, such as class name, constructors, and methods. This object is an instance of java.lang.Class. It is referred to as a *meta-object* in this book because it describes the information about the class. Through the meta-object, you can discover the information about the class at runtime. Every object can use the getClass() method to return its meta-object. For example, the following code

meta-object

```
Object obj = new Object();
Class metaObject = obj.getClass();

System.out.println("Object obj's class is "
  + metaObject.getName());
```

displays

```
Object obj's class is java.lang.Object
```

 NOTE

There is only one meta-object for a class. Every object has a meta-object. If two objects were created from the same class, their meta-objects are the same.

8.12   Initialization Blocks (Optional)

Initialization blocks can be used to initialize objects along with the constructors. An *initialization block* is a block of statements enclosed inside a pair of braces. An initialization block appears within in the class declaration, but not inside methods or constructors. It is executed as if it were placed at the beginning of every constructor in the class.

Initialization blocks can simplify the classes if you have multiple constructors sharing a common code and none of the constructors can invoke other constructors. The common code can be placed in an initialization block, as shown in the example in Figure 8.5(a). In this example, none of the constructors can invoke any of the others using the syntax `this(...)`. When an instance is created using a constructor of the `Book` class, the initialization block is executed to increase the object count by 1. The program is equivalent to Figure 8.5(b):

```
public class Book {
  private static int numOfObjects;
  private String title
  private int id;

  public Book(String title) {
    this.title = title;
  }

  public Book(int id) {
    this.id = id;
  }

  {
    numOfObjects++;
  }
}
```

(a) A class with initialization blocks

Equivalent

```
public class Book {
  private static int numOfObjects;
  private String title;
  private int id;

  public Book(String title) {
    numOfObjects++;
    this.title = title;
  }

  public Book(int id) {
    numOfObjects++;
    this.id = id;
  }
}
```

(b) An equivalent class

FIGURE 8.5   *An initialization block can simplify coding for constructors.*

NOTE

A class may have multiple initialization blocks. In such cases, the blocks are executed in the order they appear in the class.

The initialization block in Figure 8.5(a) is referred to as an *instance initialization block* because it is invoked whenever an instance of the class is created. A *static initialization block* is much like an instance initialization block except that it is declared `static`, can only refer to static members of the class, and is invoked when the class is loaded. The JVM loads the class dynamically when it is needed. A superclass is loaded before its subclasses. The order of execution can be summarized as follows:

instatic initialization block
static initialization block

1. When a class is used for the first time, load the class, initialize static data fields, and execute the static initialization block of the class.

2. When an object of a class is created, a constructor of the class is invoked. The construction has three phases:

   2.1. Invoke a constructor of the superclass.
   2.2. Initialize instance data fields and execute instance initialization blocks.
   2.3. Execute the body of the constructor.

For an illustration, see the following code:

```
1 public class Test {
2   public static void main(String[] args) {
3     new Test();
4   }
5
6   public Test() {
7     new Parrot();
8   }
9
10    { // instance initialization block
11      System.out.println("(2) Test's instance initialization " +
12        "block is invoked");
13    }
14
15    static { // static initialization block
16      System.out.println("(1) Test's static initialization block " +
17        "is invoked");
18    }
19 }
20
21 class Parrot extends Bird {
22   Parrot() {
23     System.out.println("(8) Parrot's constructor is invoked");
24   }
25
26    { // instance initialization block
27      System.out.println("(7) Parrot's instance initialization block "
28        + "is invoked");
29    }
30
31    static { // static initialization block
32      System.out.println("(4) Parrot's static initialization block " +
33        "is invoked");
34    }
35 }
36
37 class Bird {
38   Bird() {
39     System.out.println("(6) Bird's constructor is invoked");
40   }
41
42    { // instance initialization block
43      System.out.println("(5) Bird's instance initialization block " +
44        "is invoked");
45    }
46
47    static { // static initialization block
48      System.out.println("(3) Bird's static initialization block " +
49        "is invoked");
50    }
51 }
```

Margin notes:
- (beside lines 10–13) instance initialization block
- (beside lines 15–18) static initialization block
- (beside lines 26–29) instance initialization block
- (beside lines 31–34) static initialization block
- (beside lines 42–45) instance initialization block
- (beside lines 47–50) static initialization block

The output of this program is:

```
(1) Test's static initialization block is invoked
(2) Test's instance initialization block is invoked
(3) Bird's static initialization block is invoked
(4) Parrot's static initialization block is invoked
(5) Bird's instance initialization block is invoked
(6) Bird's constructor is invoked
(7) Parrot's instance initialization block is invoked
(8) Parrot's constructor is invoked
```

The program is executed in the following order:

1. Class Test is loaded first, so Test's static initialization block is invoked.

2. Test's constructor is invoked (Line 3), so Test's instance initialization block is invoked.

3. When executing new Parrot() (Line 7), class Parrot needs to be loaded, which causes class Parrot's superclass (i.e., Bird) to be loaded first. So Bird's static instance initialization block is invoked.

4. Class Parrot is now loaded, so Parrot's static initialization block is invoked.

5. When invoking Parrot's constructor, the no-arg constructor of Parrot's superclass is invoked first; therefore, Bird's instance initialization block is invoked.

6. The regular code in Bird's no-arg constructor is invoked after Bird's instance initialization block is invoked.

7. After Bird's no-arg constructor is invoked, Parrot's no-arg constructor is invoked, which causes Parrot's instance initialization block to be invoked first.

8. The regular code in Parrot's no-arg constructor is invoked after Parrot's instance initialization block is invoked.

 NOTE

If an instance variable is declared with an initial value (e.g., double radius = 5), the variable is initialized just like in an initialization block. That is, it is initialized when the constructor of the class is executed.

If a static variable is declared with an initial value (e.g., static double radius = 5), the variable is initialized just like in a static initialization block. That is, it is initialized when the class is loaded.

KEY TERMS

casting objects 296	instanceof 297
constructor chaining 290	meta-object 304
dynamic binding 295	override 291
final 302	polymorphism 295
generic programming 296	protected 301
inheritance 288	subclass 288
initialization block 305	superclass 288

KEY CLASSES AND METHODS

✦ **java.lang.Object** is the root class of all Java classes. The Object class contains the useful methods toString, equals, hashCode, clone, finalize, and getClass. The toString() method returns a string that represents the object. The equals method tests whether two objects are equal. The hashCode method returns the hash code of the object. The hash code is an integer that can be used to store the object in a hash set so that it can be located quickly. The clone() method copies an object. The getClass method returns an instance of the java.lang.Class class, which contains the information about the class for the object. The finalize method is invoked by the garbage collector on an object when the object becomes garbage. An object becomes garbage if it is no longer accessed.

CHAPTER SUMMARY

✦ You can derive a new class from an existing class. This is known as *class inheritance*. The new class is called a *subclass*, *child class*, or *derived class*. The existing class is called a *super-class*, *parent class*, or *base class*.

✦ A constructor is used to construct an instance of a class. Unlike properties and methods, the constructors of a superclass are not inherited in the subclass. They can only be invoked from the constructors of the subclasses, using the keyword `super`.

✦ A constructor may invoke an overloaded constructor or its superclass's constructor. If none of them is invoked explicitly, the compiler puts `super()` as the first statement in the constructor.

✦ To override a method, the method must be defined in the subclass using the same signature as in its superclass.

✦ An instance method can be overridden only if it is accessible. Thus a private method cannot be overridden, because it is not accessible outside its own class. If a method defined in a subclass is private in its superclass, the two methods are completely unrelated.

✦ Like an instance method, a static method can be inherited. However, a static method cannot be overridden. If a static method defined in the superclass is redefined in a subclass, the method defined in the superclass is hidden.

✦ Every class in Java is descended from the `java.lang.Object` class. If no inheritance is specified when a class is defined, the superclass of the class is `Object`.

✦ If a method's parameter type is a superclass (e.g., `Object`), you may pass an object to this method of any of the parameter's subclasses (e.g., `Circle` or `String`). When an object (e.g., a `Circle` object or a `String` object) is used in the method, the particular implementation of the method of the object that is invoked (e.g., `toString`) is determined dynamically.

✦ It is always possible to cast an instance of a subclass to a variable of a superclass, because an instance of a subclass is *always* an instance of its superclass. When casting an instance of a superclass to a variable of its subclass, explicit casting must be used to confirm your intention to the compiler with the `(SubclassName)` cast notation.

✦ You can override an instance method, but you cannot override a field (instance or static) or a static method. If you declare a field or a static method in a subclass with the same name as one in the superclass, the one in the superclass is hidden, but it still exists. The two fields or static methods are independent. You can reference the hidden field or static method using the `super` keyword in the subclass. The hidden field or method can also be accessed via a reference variable of the superclass's type.

✦ When invoking an instance method from a reference variable, the *actual class of the object* referenced by the variable decides which implementation of the method is used *at run-time*. When accessing a field or a static method, the *declared type* of the reference variable decides which method is used *at compile time*.

✦ You can use `obj instanceof AClass` to check whether an object is an instance of a class.

✦ You can use the `protected` modifier to prevent the data and methods from being accessed by non-subclasses from a different package.

✦ You can use the `final` modifier to indicate that a class is final and cannot be a parent class.

REVIEW QUESTIONS

Sections 8.2–8.4

8.1   What is the printout of running the class C?

```
1 class A {
2   public A() {
3     System.out.println(
4       "The no-arg constructor of A is invoked");
5   }
6 }
7
8 class B extends A {
9   public B() {
10   }
11 }
12
13 public class C {
14   public static void main(String[] args) {
15     B b = new B();
16   }
17 }
```

8.2   What problem arises in compiling the following program?

```
1 class A {
2   public A(int x) {
3   }
4 }
5
6 class B extends A {
7   public B() {
8   }
9 }
10
11 public class C {
12   public static void main(String[] args) {
13     B b = new B();
14   }
15 }
```

8.3   Identify the problems in the following classes:

```
1 public class Circle {
2   private double radius;
3
4   public Circle(double radius) {
5     radius = radius;
6   }
7
8   public double getRadius() {
9     return radius;
10   }
11
12   public double findArea() {
13     return radius * radius * Math.PI;
14   }
15 }
16
17 class Cylinder extends Circle {
18   private double length;
19
20   Cylinder(double radius, double length) {
21     Circle(radius);
22     length = length;
23   }
24
```

```
25   /** Return the surface area for the cylinder */
26   public double findArea() {
27     return findArea() * length;
28   }
29 }
```

8.4   Explain the difference between method overloading and method overriding.

Section 8.5 The `Object` class

8.5   Does every class have a `toString` method and an `equals` method? Where do they come from? How are they used?

8.6   Show the output of the following program:

```
1 public class Test {
2   public static void main(String[] args) {
3     A a = new A(3);
4   }
5 }
6
7 class A extends B {
8   public A(int t) {
9     System.out.println("A's constructor is invoked");
10   }
11 }
12
13 class B {
14   public B() {
15     System.out.println("B's constructor is invoked");
16   }
17 }
```

Is the no-arg constructor of `Object` invoked when `new A(3)` is invoked?

Sections 8.6–8.7

8.7   When overriding the `equals` method, a common mistake is mistyping its signature in the subclass. For example, the `equals` method is incorrectly written as `equals(Circle circle)`, as shown in (a) in the following code; instead, it should be `equals(Object circle)`, as shown in (b). Show the output of running class `Test` with the `Circle` class in (a) and in (b).

```
public class Test {
  public static void main(String[] args) {
    Object circle1 = new Circle();
    Object circle2 = new Circle();
    System.out.println(circle1.equals(circle2));
  }
}
```

```
class Circle {
  double radius;

  public boolean equals(Circle circle) {
    return this.radius == circle.radius;
  }
}
```

```
class Circle {
  double radius;

  public boolean equals(Object circle) {
    return this.radius ==
      ((Circle)circle).radius;
  }
}
```

(a)   (b)

8.8   For the `Circle` and `Cylinder` class in Listing 8.2 on page 292 answer the following questions:

(a) Are the following Boolean expressions true or false?

```
Circle circle = new Circle(1);
Cylinder cylinder = new Cylinder(1, 1);
(circle instanceof Cylinder)
(cylinder instanceof Circle)
(circle instanceof Object)
(cylinder instanceof Object)
```

(b) Are the following statements correct?

```
Cylinder cylinder = new Cylinder(1, 1);
Circle circle = cylinder;
```

(c) Are the following statements correct?

```
Circle circle = new Circle(1);
Cylinder cylinder = (Cylinder)circle;
```

8.9 Suppose that `Fruit`, `Apple`, `Orange`, `Golden Delicious Apple`, and `Macintosh Apple` are declared, as shown in Figure 8.6.

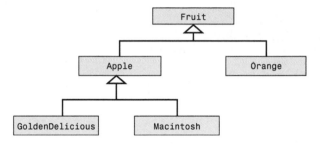

FIGURE 8.6 *`GoldenDelicious` and `Macintosh` are subclasses of `Apple`, `Apple` and `Orange` are subclasses of `Fruit`.*

Assume that the following declaration is given:

```
Fruit fruit = new GoldenDelicious();
Orange orange = new Orange();
```

Answer the following questions:

1. Is `fruit instanceof Orange`?
2. Is `fruit instanceof Apple`?
3. Is `fruit instanceof GoldenDelicious`?
4. Is `fruit instanceof Macintosh`?
5. Is `orange instanceof Orange`?
6. Is `orange instanceof Fruit`?
7. Is `orange instanceof Apple`?
8. Suppose the method `makeApple` is defined in the `Apple` class. Can `fruit` invoke this method? Can `orange` invoke this method?
9. Suppose the method `makeOrangeJuice` is defined in the `Orange` class. Can `orange` invoke this method? Can `fruit` invoke this method?

8.10 What is wrong in the following code?

```
1 public class Test {
2   public static void main(String[] args) {
3     Object fruit = new Fruit();
4     Object apple = (Apple)fruit;
5   }
6 }
7
8 class Apple extends Fruit {
9 }
```

```
10
11 class Fruit {
12 }
```

Section 8.8 Hiding Fields and Static Methods

8.11 Show the output of running class `Test`.

```
class A {
    int i = 1;
    static int j = 3;

    void m() {
        i = 5;
    }

    static void m1() {
        j = 7;
    }
}
```
(a)

```
class B extend A {
    int i = 2;
    static int j = 4;

    void m() {
        i = 6;
    }

    static void m1() {
        j = 8;
    }
}
```
(b)

```
public class Test {
    public static void main
        (String[] args) {
        B b = new B();
        System.out.println(b.i);
        System.out.println(b.j);

        A a = new B();
        System.out.println(a.i);
        System.out.println(a.j);

        a.m();
        a.m1();
        System.out.println(a.i);
        System.out.println(a.j);
    }
}
```
(c)

Section 8.9 The `protected` Data and Methods

8.12 What modifier should you use on a class so that a class in the same package can access it, but a class in a different package cannot access it?

8.13 What modifier should you use so that a class in a different package cannot access the class, but its subclasses in any package can access it?

8.14 In the following code, classes A and B are in the same package. Can class B be compiled?

```
package p1;

public class A {
    int i;
    void m() {
        ...
    }
}
```
(a)

```
package p1;

public class B extends A {
    public void m1(String[] args) {
        System.out.println(i);
        m();
    }
}
```
(b)

8.15 In the following code, classes A and B are in different packages. What modifier should you fill in to replace the question marks in class A in order to compile class B?

```
package p1;

public class A {
    ?    int i;

    ?    void m() {
        ...
    }
}
```
(a)

```
package p2;

public class B extends A {
    public void m1(String[] args) {
        System.out.println(i);
        m();
    }
}
```
(b)

Section 8.11 The `finalize`, `clone`, and `getClass` **Methods**

8.16 Where are the `finalize`, `clone`, and `getClass` methods defined? When is the `finalize` method invoked?

8.17 Since the `clone` method is defined in `Object`, every object can invoke this method. Is this true?

8.18 What is the return type of the `getClass` method?

Section 8.12 Initialization Blocks

8.19 Show the output of following program:

```
public class Test {
  public static void main(String[] args) {
    A a = new A();
  }
}

class A {
  int i = 1;
  static int j = 2;

  {
    System.out.println("i is " + i);
  }

  static {
    System.out.println("j is " + j);
  }
}
```

(a)

```
public class Test {
  public static void main(String[] args) {
    A a = new A();
  }
}

class A extends B {
    int i = 5;
    static int j = 4;

  A() {
    System.out.println("i is " + i);
    System.out.println("j is " + j);
  }

  void m() {
    System.out.println("i is " + i);
    System.out.println("j is " + j);
  }
}

class B {
  B() {
    m();
  }

  void m() {
  }
}
```

(b)

Comprehensive

8.20 Define the following terms: inheritance, superclass, subclass, the keywords `super` and `this`, casting objects, the modifiers `protected` and `final`.

8.21 Indicate true or false for the following statements:

✦ A protected datum or method can be accessed by any class in the same package.

✦ A protected datum or method can be accessed by any class in different packages.

✦ A protected datum or method can be accessed by its subclass in any package.

✦ A final class can have instances.

✦ A final class can be extended.

✦ A final method can be overridden.

✦ You can always successfully cast an instance of a subclass to a superclass.

✦ You can always successfully cast an instance of a superclass to a subclass.

✦ The order in which modifiers appear before a method is important.

PROGRAMMING EXERCISES

Sections 8.2–8.4

8.1 (*The* Triangle *class*) Write a class named Triangle defined as follows:

```
public class Triangle extends Object {
  private double side1, side2, side3;
  /** Construct a triangle with the specified sides */
  public Triangle(double side1, double side2, double side3) {
    // Implement it
  }

  /** Find the area of this triangle */
  public double findArea() {
    // Implement it
  }

  /** Find the perimeter of this triangle */
  public double findPerimeter() {
    // Implement it
  }

  /** Override the toString method */
  public String toString() {
    // Implement it to return the three sides
  }
}
```

For the formula to compute the area of a triangle, see Exercise 4.13.

Test the Triangle class by adding a main method in the class. Create a Triangle with sides 1, 1.5, 1, and display its area and perimeter.

Sections 8.5–8.9

8.2 (*The* Person, Student, Employee, *and* MyDate *classes*) Implement a class named Person and two subclasses of Person named Student and Employee. Make Faculty and Staff subclasses of Employee. A person has a name, address, phone number, and e-mail address. A student has a class status (freshman, sophomore, junior, or senior). Define the status as a constant. An employee has an office, salary, and date-hired. Define a class named MyDate that contains the fields year, month, and day. A faculty member has office hours and a rank. A staff member has a title. Override the toString method in each class to display the class name and the person's name.

8.3 (*Subclasses of* Account) In Exercise 6.3, the Account class was created to model a bank account. An account has the properties account number, balance, and annual interest rate, and methods to deposit and withdraw. Create two subclasses for checking and saving accounts. A checking account has an overdraft limit, but a savings account cannot go overdrawn.

8.4* (*The* StackOfObjects *class*) In Section 6.16, "Case Study: The StackOfIntegers Class," you created a stack class for storing integers. Modify the example to create a stack class to hold objects. Name the new class StackOfObjects and draw the UML diagram for the class. Write a test program that displays the first fifty prime numbers in decreasing order.

chapter

9

ABSTRACT CLASSES AND INTERFACES

Objectives

- ✦ To design and use abstract classes (§9.2).

- ✦ To process a calendar using the Calendar and GregorianCalendar classes (§9.3).

- ✦ To declare interfaces to model weak inheritance relationships (§9.4).

- ✦ To define a natural order using the Comparable interface (§9.4.1).

- ✦ To know the similarities and differences between an abstract class and an interface (§9.4.2).

- ✦ To declare custom interfaces (§9.4.3).

- ✦ To enable objects cloneable using the Cloneable interface (§9.4.4 Optional).

- ✦ To use wrapper classes (Byte, Short, Integer, Long, Float, Double, Character, and Boolean) to wrap primitive data values into objects (§9.5).

- ✦ To create a generic sort method (§9.5).

- ✦ To simplify programming using JDK 1.5 automatic conversion between primitive types and wrapper class types (§9.6).

9.1   Introduction

In the inheritance hierarchy, classes become more specific and concrete *with each new subclass*. If you move from a subclass back up to a superclass, the classes become more general and less specific. Class design should ensure that a superclass contains common features of its subclasses. Sometimes a superclass is so abstract that it cannot have any specific instances. Such a class is referred to as an *abstract class*.

abstract class

multiple inheritance
single inheritance

Sometimes it is necessary to derive a subclass from several classes. This capability is known as *multiple inheritance*. Java, however, does not allow multiple inheritance. Each Java class may inherit directly from one superclass. This restriction is known as *single inheritance*. If you use the extends keyword to define a subclass, it allows only one parent class. With interfaces, you can obtain the effect of multiple inheritance.

This chapter introduces abstract classes and interfaces, and discusses how to use wrapper classes for primitive data type values.

9.2   Abstract Classes

Consider geometric objects. Suppose you want to design the classes to model geometric objects like circles, cylinders, and rectangles. Geometric objects have many common properties and behaviors. They can be drawn in a certain color, filled or unfilled. Color and filled are examples of common properties. Common behaviors include the fact that the areas and perimeters of geometric objects can be computed. Thus a general class GeometricObject can be used to model all geometric objects. This class contains the properties color and filled, and the methods findArea and findPerimeter. Since a circle is a special type of geometric object, it shares common properties and methods with other geometric objects. Further, since a cylinder is a special type of circle, it shares common properties and behaviors with a circle. Thus it makes sense to define the Circle class that extends the GeometricObject class and the Cylinder class that extends the Circle class. Figure 9.1 illustrates the relationship of the classes for geometric objects.

The methods findArea and findPerimeter cannot be implemented in the GeometricObject class because their implementation is dependent on the specific type of geometric object. Such

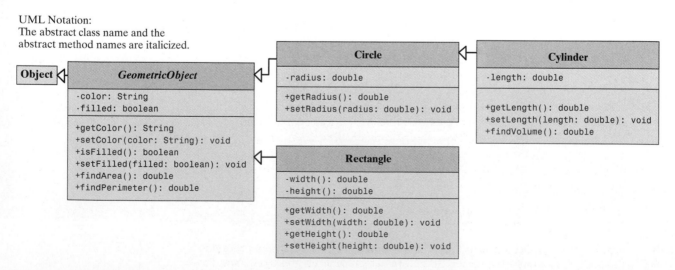

UML Notation:
The abstract class name and the abstract method names are italicized.

FIGURE 9.1   *The GeometricObject class models the common features of geometric objects.*

methods are referred to as *abstract methods*. In UML graphic notation, the names of abstract classes and their abstract methods are italicized. The GeometricObject class is shown in Listing 9.1.

abstract method

Listing 9.1   GeometricObject.java (The GeometricObject Class)

abstract class

```
 1  public abstract class GeometricObject {
 2    private String color = "white";
 3    private boolean filled;
 4
 5    /** Construct a default geometric object */
 6    protected GeometricObject() {
 7    }
 8
 9    /** Construct a geometric object with specified properties */
10    protected GeometricObject(String color, boolean filled) {
11      this.color = color;
12      this.filled = filled;
13    }
14
15    /** Return color */
16    public String getColor() {
17      return color;
18    }
19
20    /** Set a new color */
21    public void setColor(String color) {
22      this.color = color;
23    }
24
25    /** Return filled. Since filled is boolean,
26       so, the get method name is isFilled */
27    public boolean isFilled() {
28      return filled;
29    }
30
31    /** Set a new filled */
32    public void setFilled(boolean filled) {
33      this.filled = filled;
34    }
35
36    /** Abstract method findArea */
37    public abstract double findArea();
38
39    /** Abstract method findPerimeter */
40    public abstract double findPerimeter();
41  }
```

abstract method

abstract method

Abstract classes are like regular classes with data and methods, but you cannot create instances
of abstract classes using the new operator. An abstract method is a method signature without implementation. Its implementation is provided by the subclasses. A class that contains abstract
methods must be declared abstract.

The GeometricObject abstract class provides the common features (data and methods) for
geometric objects. Because you don't know how to compute areas and perimeters of geometric
objects, findArea and findPerimeter are defined as abstract methods. These methods are implemented in the subclasses. Listings 9.2, 9.3, and 9.4 give the implementation of the classes Circle,
Rectangle, and Cylinder.

 Note

To avoid naming conflicts with the Circle and Cylinder classes in the preceding
chapter, the Circle and Cylinder classes are named Circle9 and Cylinder9. For
convenience, they are still referred to as Circle and Cylinder classes.

LISTING 9.2 Circle9.java (The Circle Class)

```
 1  public class Circle9 extends GeometricObject {
 2    private double radius;
 3
 4    /** Construct a circle with default properties */
 5    public Circle9() {
 6      this(1.0);
 7    }
 8
 9    /** Construct a circle with a specified radius */
10    public Circle9(double radius) {
11      this(radius, "white", false);
12    }
13
14    /** Construct a circle with specified radius, filled, and color */
15    public Circle9(double radius, String color, boolean filled) {
16      super(color, filled);
17      this.radius = radius;
18    }
19
20    /** Return radius */
21    public double getRadius() {
22      return radius;
23    }
24
25    /** Set a new radius */
26    public void setRadius(double radius) {
27      this.radius = radius;
28    }
29
30    /** Implement the findArea method defined in GeometricObject */
31    public double findArea() {
32      return radius * radius * Math.PI;
33    }
34
35    /** Implement the findPerimeter method defined in GeometricObject*/
36    public double findPerimeter() {
37      return 2 * radius * Math.PI;
38    }
39
40    /** Override the toString() method defined in the Object class */
41    public String toString() {
42      return "[Circle] radius = " + radius;
43    }
44  }
```

override findArea (line 31)

override findPerimeter (line 36)

override toString (line 41)

LISTING 9.3 Rectangle.java (The Rectangle Class)

```
 1  public class Rectangle extends GeometricObject {
 2    private double width;
 3    private double height;
 4
 5    /** Construct a rectangle with default properties */
 6    public Rectangle() {
 7      this(1.0, 1.0);
 8    }
 9
10    /** Construct a rectangle with specified width and height */
11    public Rectangle(double width, double height) {
12      this(width, height, "white", false);
13    }
14
15    /** Construct a rectangle with specified width, height,
16      filled, and color */
17    public Rectangle(double width, double height,
18        String color, boolean filled) {
19      super(color, filled);
20      this.width = width;
```

```
21       this.height = height;
22     }
23
24     /** Return width */
25     public double getWidth() {
26       return width;
27     }
28
29     /** Set a new width */
30     public void setWidth(double width) {
31       this.width = width;
32     }
33
34     /** Return height */
35     public double getHeight() {
36       return height;
37     }
38
39     /** Set a new height */
40     public void setHeight(double height) {
41       this.height = height;
42     }
43
44     /** Implement the findArea method in GeometricObject */
45     public double findArea() {                                        override findArea
46       return width * height;
47     }
48
49     /** Implement the findPerimeter method in GeometricObject */
50     public double findPerimeter() {                                   override findPerimeter
51       return 2 * (width + height);
52     }
53
54     /** Override the toString method defined in the Object class */
55     public String toString() {                                       override toString
56       return "[Rectangle] width = " + width +
57         " and height = " + height;
58     }
59   }
60
```

LISTING 9.4   Cylinder9.java (The Cylinder9 Class)

```
1   public class Cylinder9 extends Circle9 {
2     private double length;
3
4     /** Construct a cylinder with default properties */
5     public Cylinder9() {
6       this(1.0, 1.0);
7     }
8
9     /** Construct a cylinder with specified radius, and length */
10    public Cylinder9(double radius, double length) {
11      this(radius, "white", false, length);
12    }
13
14    /** Construct a cylinder with specified radius, filled, color, and
15       length
16     */
17    public Cylinder9(double radius,
18        String color, boolean filled, double length) {
19      super(radius, color, filled);
20      this.length = length;
21    }
22
23    /** Return length */
24    public double getLength() {
25      return length;
26    }
```

```
27
28    /** Set a new length */
29    public void setLength(double length) {
30      this.length = length;
31    }
32
33    /** Return the surface area of this cylinder */
34    public double findArea() {
35      return 2 * super.findArea() + 2 * getRadius() * Math.PI * length;
36    }
37
38    /** Return the volume of this cylinder */
39    public double findVolume() {
40      return super.findArea() * length;
41    }
42
43    /** Override the toString method defined in the Object class */
44    public String toString() {
45      return "[Cylinder] radius = " + getRadius() + " and length "
46        + length;
47    }
48  }
```

override findArea (line 34)

override toString (line 44)

The method toString is defined in the Object class and modified in the Circle, Rectangle, and Cylinder classes. The abstract methods findArea and findPerimeter defined in the GeometricObject class are implemented in the Circle and Rectangle classes.

abstract method in abstract class

NOTE
An abstract method cannot be contained in a nonabstract class. If a subclass of an abstract superclass does not implement all the abstract methods, the subclass must be declared abstract. In other words, in a nonabstract subclass extended from an abstract class, all the abstract methods must be implemented, even if they are not used in the subclass.

object cannot be created from abstract class

NOTE
An abstract class cannot be instantiated using the new operator, but you can still define its constructors, which are invoked in the constructors of its subclasses. For instance, the constructors of GeometricObject are invoked in the Circle class and the Rectangle class.

abstract class without abstract method

NOTE
A class that contains abstract methods must be abstract. However, it is possible to declare an abstract class that contains no abstract methods. In this case, you cannot create instances of the class using the new operator. This class is used as a base class for defining a new subclass.

superclass of abstract class may be concrete

NOTE
A subclass can be abstract even if its superclass is concrete. For example, the Object class is concrete, but its subclasses, such as GeometricObject, may be abstract.

concrete method overridden to be abstract

NOTE
A subclass can override a method from its superclass to declare it abstract. This is *very unusual*, but is useful when the implementation of the method in the superclass becomes invalid in the subclass. In this case, the subclass must be declared abstract.

NOTE

You cannot create an instance from an abstract class using the new operator, but an abstract class can be used as a data type. Therefore, the following statement, which creates an array whose elements are of GeometricObject type, is correct:

```
GeometricObject[] geo = new GeometricObject[10];
```

abstract class as type

 NOTE

Cylinder inherits the findPerimeter method from Circle. If you invoke this method on a Cylinder object, the perimeter of a circle is returned. This method is not useful for Cylinder objects. Removing or disabling it from Cylinder would be helpful, but there is no good way to get rid of this method in a subclass once it is defined as public in its superclass. If you define the findPerimeter method as abstract in the Cylinder class, then the Cylinder class must be declared abstract.

You may be wondering whether the abstract methods findArea and findPerimeter should be removed from the GeometricObject class. The following example shows the benefits of retaining them in the GeometricObject class.

EXAMPLE 9.1 USING THE GeometricObject CLASS

Problem

Write a program that creates two geometric objects, a circle and a rectangle, invokes the equalArea method to check whether the two objects have equal areas, and invokes the displayGeometricObject method to display the objects.

Solution

Listing 9.5 gives the solution to the problem. A sample run of the program is shown in Figure 9.2.

```
Command Prompt                                    _ □ ×
C:\book>java TestGeometricObject
The two objects have the same area? false

[Circle] radius = 5.0
The area is 78.53981633974483
The perimeter is 31.41592653589793

[Rectangle] width = 5.0 and height = 3.0
The area is 15.0
The perimeter is 16.0

C:\book>_
```

FIGURE 9.2 *The program compares the areas of the objects and displays their properties.*

LISTING 9.5 TestGeometricObject.java

```
1 public class TestGeometricObject {
2   /** Main method */
```

EXAMPLE 9.1 (CONTINUED)

```
3  public static void main(String[] args) {
4    // Declare and initialize two geometric objects
5    GeometricObject geoObject1 = new Circle9(5);
6    GeometricObject geoObject2 = new Rectangle(5, 3);
7
8    System.out.println("The two objects have the same area? " +
9      equalArea(geoObject1, geoObject2));
10
11    // Display circle
12    displayGeometricObject(geoObject1);
13
14    // Display rectangle
15    displayGeometricObject(geoObject2);
16  }
17
18  /** A method for comparing the areas of two geometric objects */
19  static boolean equalArea(GeometricObject object1,
20      GeometricObject object2) {
21    return object1.findArea() == object2.findArea();
22  }
23
24  /** A method for displaying a geometric object */
25  static void displayGeometricObject(GeometricObject object) {
26    System.out.println();
27    System.out.println(object.toString());
28    System.out.println("The area is " + object.findArea());
29    System.out.println("The perimeter is " + object.findPerimeter());
30  }
31 }
```

Review

The methods `findArea()` and `findPerimeter()` defined in the `GeometricObject` class are overridden in the `Circle9` class and the `Rectangle` class. The statements (Lines 5–6)

```
GeometricObject geoObject1 = new Circle9(5);
GeometricObject geoObject2 = new Rectangle(5, 3);
```

create a new circle and rectangle, and assign them to the variables `geoObject1` and `geoObject2`. These two variables are of the `GeometricObject` type.

When invoking `equalArea(geoObject1, geoObject2)` (Line 9), the `findArea` method defined in the `Circle9` class is used for `object1.findArea()`, since `geoObject1` is a circle, and the `findArea` method defined in the `Rectangle` class is used for `object2.findArea()`, since `geoObject2` is a rectangle.

Similarly, when invoking `displayGeometricObject(geoObject1)` (Line 12), the methods `findArea`, `findPerimeter`, and `toString` defined in the `Circle` class are used, and when invoking `displayGeometricObject(geoObject2)` (Line 15), the methods `findArea`, `findPerimeter`, and `toString` defined in the `Rectangle` class are used. Which of these methods is invoked is dynamically determined at runtime, depending on the type of object.

9.3   The `Calendar` and `GregorianCalendar` classes

An instance of `java.util.Date` represents a specific instant in time with millisecond precision. `java.util.Calendar` is an abstract base class for extracting detailed calendar information, such as year, month, date, hour, minute, and second. Subclasses of `Calendar` can implement specific calendar systems, such as the Gregorian calendar, the lunar calendar, and the Jewish calendar. Currently, `java.util.GregorianCalendar` for the Gregorian calendar is supported in Java.

You can use `new GregorianCalendar( )` to construct a default `GregorianCalendar` with the current time and `new GregorianCalendar(year, month, date)` to construct a `GregorianCalendar` with the specified `year`, `month`, and `date`. The `month` parameter is 0-based, that is, 0 is for January.

The `get(int field)` method defined in the `Calendar` class is useful to extract the value for a given time field. The time fields are defined as constants, such as `YEAR`, `MONTH`, `DATE`, `HOUR` (for the twelve-hour clock), `HOUR_OF_DAY` (for the twenty-four-hour clock), `MINUTE`, `SECOND`, `DAY_OF_WEEK` (the day number within the current week, with 1 for Sunday), `DAY_OF_MONTH` (the day in the current month), `DAY_OF_YEAR` (the day number in the current year, with 1 for the first day of the year), `WEEK_OF_MONTH` (the week number within the current month), and `WEEK_OF_YEAR` (the week number within the current year). For example, the following code

```
// Construct a Gregorian calendar for the current date and time
java.util.Calendar calendar = new java.util.GregorianCalendar();
System.out.println("Year\tMonth\tDate\tHour\tHour24\tMinute\tSecond");
System.out.println(calendar.get(Calendar.YEAR) + "\t" +
  calendar.get(Calendar.MONTH) + "\t" + calendar.get(Calendar.DATE)
  + "\t" + calendar.get(Calendar.HOUR) + "\t" +
  calendar.get(Calendar.MINUTE) + "\t" +
  calendar.get(Calendar.SECOND));
System.out.print("Day of week: " +
  calendar.get(Calendar.DAY_OF_WEEK) + "\t");
System.out.print("Day of month: " +
  calendar.get(Calendar.DAY_OF_MONTH) + "\t");
System.out.println("Day of year: " +
  calendar.get(Calendar.DAY_OF_YEAR));
System.out.print("Week of month: " +
  calendar.get(Calendar.WEEK_OF_MONTH) + "\t");
System.out.print("Week of year: " +
  calendar.get(Calendar.WEEK_OF_YEAR));
```

displays the information for the current date and time, as follows:

```
Year Month  Date    Hour  Hour24   Minute   Second
2003 2      9       8     20       17       39
Day of week: 1      Day of month: 9         Day of year: 68
Week of month: 3    Week of year: 11
```

To obtain the number of days in a month, use `calendar.getActualMaximum(Calendar.DAY_OF_MONTH)`. For example, if the `calendar` were for March, this method would return 31.

The `set(int field, value)` method defined in the `Calendar` class can be used to set a field. For example, you can use `calendar.set(Calendar.DAY_OF_MONTH, 1)` to set the `calendar` to the first day of the month.

9.4   Interfaces

An *interface* is a classlike construct that contains only constants and abstract methods. In many ways, an interface is similar to an abstract class, but an abstract class can contain variables and concrete methods as well as constants and abstract methods.

interface

To distinguish an interface from a class, Java uses the following syntax to declare an interface:

```
modifier interface InterfaceName {
  /** Constant declarations */
  /** Method signatures */
}
```

An interface is treated like a special class in Java. Each interface is compiled into a separate byte-code file, just like a regular class. As with an abstract class, you cannot create an instance from an interface using the `new` operator, but in most cases you can use an interface more or less the same way you use an abstract class. For example, you can use an interface as a data type for a variable, as the result of casting, and so on.

Suppose you want to design a generic method to find the larger of two objects. The objects can be students, circles, or cylinders. Since compare methods are different for different types of objects, you need to define a generic compare method to determine the order of the two objects. Then you can tailor the method to compare students, circles, or cylinders. For example, you can use student ID as the key for comparing students, radius as the key for comparing circles, and volume as the key for comparing cylinders. You can use an interface to define a generic compareTo method, as follows:

java.lang.Comparable

```
// Interface for comparing objects, defined in java.lang
package java.lang;

public interface Comparable {
  public int compareTo(Object o);
}
```

The compareTo method determines the order of this object with the specified object o, and returns a negative integer, zero, or a positive integer if this object is less than, equal to, or greater than the specified object o.

 NOTE

The Comparable interface has been available since JDK 1.2, and is included in the java.lang package.

A generic max method for finding the larger of two objects can be declared in a class named Max, as follows:

```
// Max.java: Find a maximum object
public class Max {
  /** Return the maximum between two objects */
  public static Object max(Object o1, Object o2) {
    if (((Comparable)o1).compareTo(o2) > 0)
      return o1;
    else
      return o2;
  }
}
```

The Max class contains a static method named max. To use the max method to find the larger of two objects, implement the Comparable interface for the class of these objects. Since o1 is declared as Object, (Comparable)o1 tells the compiler to cast o1 into Comparable so that the compareTo method can be invoked from o1.

Many classes (e.g., String and Date) in the Java library implement Comparable to define a natural order for the objects. So you can use the max method in the Max class to find the larger of two instances of String or Date. Here is an example:

```
String s1 = "abcdef";
String s2 = "abcdee";
String s3 = (String)Max.max(s1, s2);
```

Since every object is automatically an instance of Object, s1 and s2 can be passed to the max method without explicit casting. However, an instance of Object is not necessarily an instance of String. Therefore, to assign the return value from the max method to a String type variable, you need to cast it to String explicitly. The string in s1 is larger than that in s2. So s3 is "abcdef".

9.4.1   Implementing Interfaces

You cannot use the max method to find the larger of two instances of Rectangle, because Rectangle does not implement Comparable. However, you can declare a new rectangle class that implements `Comparable`. The instances of this new class are comparable. Let this new class be named `ComparableRectangle`, as shown in Listing 9.6.

LISTING 9.6   ComparableRectangle.java (Comparable)

```
1 public class ComparableRectangle extends Rectangle
2     implements Comparable {
3   /** Construct a ComparableRectangle with specified properties */
4   public ComparableRectangle(double width, double height) {
5     super(width, height);
6   }
7
8   /** Implement the compareTo method defined in Comparable */
9   public int compareTo(Object o) {
10    if (findArea() > ((ComparableRectangle)o).findArea())
11      return 1;
12    else if (findArea() < ((ComparableRectangle)o).findArea())
13      return -1;
14    else
15      return 0;
16  }
17 }
```

`ComparableRectangle` extends `Rectangle` and implements `Comparable`, as shown in Figure 9.3. The keyword `implements` indicates that `ComparableRectangle` inherits all the constant from the `Comparable` interface and implements the methods in the interface. The `compareTo` method compares the areas of two rectangles. An instance of `CompareRectangle` is also an instance of `Rectangle`, `GeometricObject`, `Object`, and `Comparable`.

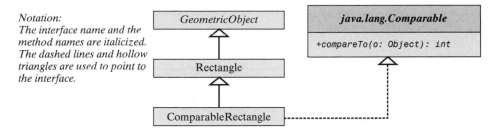

FIGURE 9.3   *ComparableRectangle extends Rectangle and implements Comparable.*

You can now use the `max` method to find the larger of two objects of `CompareRectangle`. Here is an example:

```
ComparableRectangle rectangle1 = new ComparableRectangle(4, 5);
ComparableRectangle rectangle2 = new ComparableRectangle(3, 6);
System.out.println(Max.max(rectangle1, rectangle2));
```

An interface provides another form of generic programming. It would be difficult to use a generic `max` method to find the maximum of the objects without using an interface in this example, because multiple inheritance would be necessary to inherit `Comparable` and another class, such as `Rectangle`, at the same time.

The `Object` class contains the `equals` method, which is intended for the subclasses of the `Object` class to override in order to compare whether the contents of the objects are the same. Suppose that the `Object` class contains the `compareTo` method, as defined in the `Comparable` interface; the new `max` method can be used to compare a list of *any* objects. Whether a `compareTo` method should be included in the `Object` class is debatable. Since the `compareTo` method is not defined in the `Object` class, the `Comparable` interface is created in Java 2 to enable objects to be compared if they are instances of the `Comparable` interface. It is strongly recommended (though not required) that `compareTo` should be consistent with `equals`. That is, for two objects `o1` and `o2`, `o1.compareTo(o2) == 0` if and only if `o1.equals(o2)` is true.

9.4.2 Interfaces vs. Abstract Classes

An interface can be used the same way as an abstract class, but defining an interface is different from defining an abstract class.

✦ In an interface, the data must be constants; an abstract class can have non-constant data fields.

✦ Each method in an interface has only a signature without implementation; an abstract class can have concrete methods.

omitting modifiers

 NOTE

All data fields are `public final static` and all methods are `public abstract` in an interface. For this reason, these modifiers can be omitted, as shown below:

```
public interface T1 {
   public static final int k = 1;
   public abstract void p ();
}
```
Equivalent
```
public interface T1 {
   int k = 1;
   void p ();
}
```

accessing constants

 TIP

A constant defined in an interface can be accessed using syntax `InterfaceName.CONSTANT_NAME` (e.g., `T1.K`).

Java allows only single inheritance for class extension, but multiple extensions for interfaces. For example,

```
public class NewClass extends BaseClass
      implements Interface1, ..., InterfaceN {
   ...
}
```

subinterface

An interface can inherit other interfaces using the `extends` keyword. Such an interface is called a *subinterface*. For example, `NewInterface` in the following code is a subinterface of `Interface1`, ..., and `InterfaceN`:

```
public interface NewInterface extends Interface1, ..., InterfaceN {
   // constants and abstract methods
}
```

A class implementing `NewInterface` must implement the abstract methods defined in `NewInterface`, `Interface1`, ..., and `InterfaceN`. An interface can only extend other interfaces, not classes. A class can extend its superclass and implement multiple interfaces.

All classes share a single root, the `Object` class, but there is no single root for interfaces. Like a class, an interface also defines a type. A variable of an interface type can reference any instance of the class that implements the interface. If a class implements an interface, the interface is like a superclass for the class. You can use an interface as a data type and cast a variable of an interface type to its subclass, and vice versa. For example, suppose that c is an instance of Class2 in Figure 9.4. c is also an instance of Object, Class1, Interface1, Interface1_1, Interface1_2, Interface2_1, and Interface2_2.

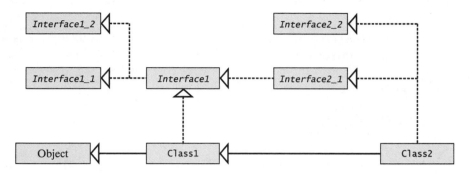

FIGURE 9.4 *Abstract class* Class1 *implements* Interface1. Interface1 *extends* Interface1_1 *and* Interface1_2. Class2 *extends* Class1 *and implements* Interface2_1 *and* Interface2_2.

Abstract classes and interfaces can both be used to model common features. How do you decide whether to use an interface or a class? In general, a *strong is-a relationship* that clearly describes a parent–child relationship should be modeled using classes. For example, a staff member is a person. So the relationship between them should be modeled using class inheritance. A *weak is-a relationship*, also known as an *is-kind-of relationship*, indicates that an object possesses a certain property. A weak is-a relationship can be modeled using interfaces. For example, all strings are comparable, so the String class implements the Comparable interface. You can also use interfaces to circumvent single inheritance restriction if multiple inheritance is desired. In the case of multiple inheritance, you have to design one as a superclass, and others as interfaces. See Chapter 10, "Object-Oriented Modeling," for more discussions.

strong is-a relationship

is-kind-of relationship

> **NOTE**
> Class names are nouns. Interface names may be adjectives or nouns. For example, both java.lang.Comparable and java.awt.event.ActionListener are interfaces. Comparable is an adjective, and ActionListener is a noun. ActionListener will be introduced in Chapter 12, "Event-Driven Programming."

9.4.3 Creating Custom Interfaces

Section 9.4.1, "Implementing Interfaces," gives an example of implementing an interface defined in the Java API. This section creates a custom interface. Suppose you want to describe whether an object is edible. You can declare the Edible interface as:

```
public interface Edible {
  /** Describe how to eat */
  public String howToEat();
}
```

To denote that an object is edible, the class for the object must implement Edible. Let us create the following two sets of classes:

◆ Create a class named Animal and its subclasses Tiger, Chicken, and Elephant. Since chicken is edible, implement the Edible interface for the Chicken class, as follows:

```
class Animal {
}

class Chicken extends Animal implements Edible {
  public String howToEat() {
```

```
          return "Fry it";
        }
      }

      class Tiger extends Animal {
      }
```

✦ Create a class named `Fruit` and its subclasses `Apple` and `Orange`. Since all fruits are edible, implement the `Edible` interface for the `Fruit` class. In the `Fruit` class, give a generic implementation of the `howToEat` method. In the `Apple` class and the `Orange` class, give a specific implementation of the `howToEat` method, as follows:

```
class Fruit implements Edible {
  public String howToEat() {
    return "Eat it fresh";
  }
}

class Apple extends Fruit {
  public String howToEat() {
    return "Make apple cider";
  }
}

class Orange extends Fruit {
  public String howToEat() {
    return "Make orange juice";
  }
}
```

To demonstrate how the `Edible` interface may be used, create the following program that creates an array with three objects. The `showObject` method invokes the `howToEat()` method if the object is edible.

```
public class TestEdible {
  public static void main(String[] args) {
    Object[] objects = {new Tiger(), new Chicken(), new Apple()};
    for (int i = 0; i < objects.length; i++)
      showObject(objects[i]);
  }

  public static void showObject(Object object) {
    if (object instanceof Edible)
      System.out.println(((Edible)object).howToEat());
  }
}
```

The program displays

```
Fry it
Make apple cider
```

9.4.4 The `Cloneable` Interface (Optional)

An interface contains constants and abstract methods, but the `Cloneable` interface is a special case. The `Cloneable` interface in the `java.lang` package is defined as follows:

java.lang.Cloneable

```
package java.lang;

public interface Cloneable {
}
```

marker interface

This interface is empty. An interface with an empty body is referred to as a *marker interface*. A marker interface does not contain constants or methods. It is used to denote that a class possesses certain desirable properties. A class that implements the `Cloneable` interface is marked cloneable, and its objects can be cloned using the `clone()` method defined in the `Object` class.

Many classes (e.g., `Date` and `Calendar`) in the Java library implement `Cloneable`. Thus, the instances of these classes can be cloned. For example, the following code

```
Calendar calendar = new GregorianCalendar(2003, 2, 1);
Calendar calendarCopy = (Calendar)calendar.clone();
System.out.println("calendar == calendarCopy is " +
  (calendar == calendarCopy));
System.out.println("calendar.equals(calendarCopy) is " +
  calendar.equals(calendarCopy));
```

displays

```
calendar == calendarCopy is false
calendar.equals(calendarCopy) is true
```

To declare a custom class that implements the `Cloneable` interface, the class must override the `clone()` method in the `Object` class. Listing 9.7 declares a class named `House` that implements `Cloneable` and `Comparable`.

how to implement Cloneable

LISTING 9.7 House.java (`Cloneable` and `Comparable`)

```
1  public class House implements Cloneable, Comparable {
2    private int id;
3    private double area;
4    private java.util.Date whenBuilt;
5
6    public House(int id, double area) {
7      this.id = id;
8      this.area = area;
9      whenBuilt = new java.util.Date();
10   }
11
12   public double getId() {
13     return id;
14   }
15
16   public double getArea() {
17     return area;
18   }
19
20   public java.util.Date getWhenBuilt() {
21     return whenBuilt;
22   }
23
24   /** Override the protected clone method defined in the Object
25     class, and strengthen its accessibility */
26   public Object clone() {
27     try {
28       return super.clone();
29     }
30     catch (CloneNotSupportedException ex) {
31       return null;
32     }
33   }
34
35   /** Implement the compareTo method defined in Comparable */
36   public int compareTo(Object o) {
37     if (area > ((House)o).area)
38       return 1;
39     else if (area < ((House)o).area)
40       return -1;
41     else
42       return 0;
43   }
44 }
```

The `House` class overrides the `clone` method (Lines 26–33) defined in the `Object` class. The `clone` method in the `Object` class is defined as follows:

```
protected native Object clone() throws CloneNotSupportedException;
```

The keyword `native` indicates that this method is not written in Java, but is implemented in the JVM for the native platform. The keyword `protected` restricts the method to be accessed in the same package or in a subclass. For this reason, the `Cloneable` class must override the method and change the visibility modifier to `public` so that the method can be used in any package. Since the `clone` method implemented for the native platform in the `Object` class performs the task of cloning objects, the `clone` method in the `House` class simply invokes `super.clone()`. The `clone` method defined in the `Object` class may throw `CloneNotSupportedException`. Thus, `super.clone()` must be placed in a `try-catch` block. Exceptions and the `try-catch` block are introduced in Chapter 15, "Exceptions and Assertions."

The `House` class overrides the `compareTo` method (Lines 36–43) defined in the `Comparable` interface. The method compares the areas of two houses.

You can now create an object of the `House` class and create an identical copy from it, as follows:

```
House house1 = new House(1, 1750.50);
House house2 = (House)house1.clone();
```

`house1` and `house2` are two different objects with identical contents. The `clone` method in the `Object` class copies each field from the original object to the target object. If the field is of a primitive type, its value is copied. For example, the value of `area` (`double` type) is copied from `house1` to `house2`. If the field is of an object, the reference of the field is copied. For example, the field `whenBuilt` is of the `Date` class, so its reference is copied into `house2`, as shown in Figure 9.5. Therefore, `house1.whenBuilt == house2.whenBuilt` is true, although `house1 == house2` is false. This is referred to as a *shallow copy* rather than a *deep copy*, meaning that if the field is of an object, the reference of the field is copied rather than its contents.

shallow copy
deep copy

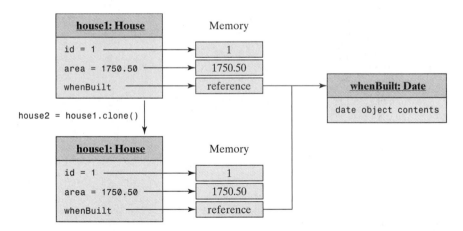

FIGURE 9.5 *The `clone` method copies the values of primitive type fields and the references of object type fields.*

If you want to perform a deep copy, you can override the `clone` method with custom cloning operations instead of invoking `super.clone()`. See Exercise 9.4.

🌱 **NOTE**

You learned how to use the `arraycopy` method to copy arrays in Chapter 5, "Arrays." This method provides shallow copies. It works fine for arrays of primitive data type elements, but not for arrays of object type elements. To support a deep copy, you have to deal with how to copy individual object elements in the array.

CAUTION
If the `House` class does not override the `clone()` method, the program will receive a syntax error because `clone()` is protected in `java.lang.Object`. If `House` does not implement `java.lang.Cloneable`, invoking `super.clone()` (Line 28) in House.java would cause a `CloneNotSupportedException`. Thus, to enable cloning an object, the class for the object must override the `clone()` method and implement `Cloneable`.

9.5   Processing Primitive Data Type Values as Objects

Primitive data types are not used as objects in Java due to performance considerations. Because of the overhead of processing objects, the language's performance would be adversely affected if primitive data types were treated as objects. However, many Java methods require the use of objects as arguments. Java offers a convenient way to incorporate, or wrap, a primitive data type into an object (e.g., wrapping int into the `Integer` class, and wrapping double into the `Double` class). The corresponding class is called a *wrapper class*. By using a wrapper object instead of a primitive data type variable, you can take advantage of generic programming.

wrapper class

Java provides `Boolean`, `Character`, `Double`, `Float`, `Byte`, `Short`, `Integer`, and `Long` wrapper classes for primitive data types. These classes are grouped in the `java.lang` package. Their inheritance hierarchy is shown in Figure 9.6.

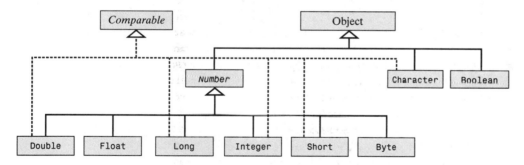

FIGURE 9.6   *The Number class is an abstract superclass for Double, Float, Long, Integer, Short, and Byte.*

 NOTE
The wrapper class name for a primitive type is the same as the primitive data type name with the first letter capitalized. The exceptions are `Integer` and `Character`.

Each numeric wrapper class extends the abstract `Number` class, which contains the methods `doubleValue()`, `floatValue()`, `intValue()`, `longValue()`, `shortValue()`, and `byteValue()`. These methods "convert" objects into primitive type values. The methods `doubleValue()`, `floatValue()`, `intValue()`, and `longValue()` are abstract. The methods `byteValue()` and `shortValue()` are not abstract; they simply return `(byte)intValue()` and `(short)intValue()`, respectively.

Each wrapper class overrides the `toString`, `equals`, and `hashCode` methods defined in the `Object` class. Since all the numeric wrapper classes and the `Character` class implement the `Comparable` interface, the `compareTo` method is implemented in these classes.

Wrapper classes are very similar. The `Character` class was introduced in Chapter 7, "Strings." The `Boolean` class is rarely used. The following sections use `Integer` and `Double` as examples to introduce the numeric wrapper classes. The key features of `Integer` and `Double` are shown in Figure 9.7.

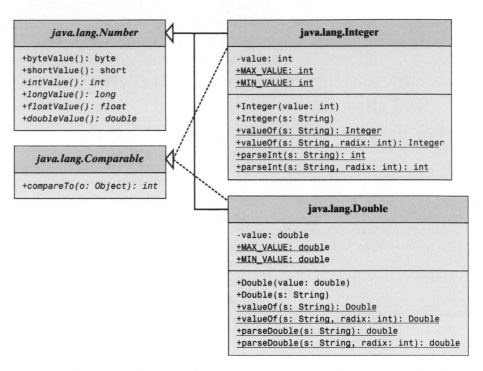

FIGURE 9.7 *The wrapper classes provide constructors, constants, and conversion methods for manipulating various data types.*

9.5.1 Numeric Wrapper Class Constructors

You can construct a wrapper object either from a primitive data type value or from a string representing the numeric value. The constructors for `Integer` and `Double` are:

```
public Integer(int value)
public Integer(String s)
public Double(double value)
public Double(String s)
```

For example, you can construct a wrapper object for `double` value `5.0` using either

```
Double doubleObject = new Double(5.0);
```

or

```
Double doubleObject = new Double("5.0");
```

You can construct a wrapper object for `int` value `5` using either

```
Integer integerObject = new Integer(5);
```

or

```
Integer integerObject = new Integer("5");
```

NOTE

(1) The wrapper classes do not have no-arg constructors. (2) The instances of all wrapper classes are immutable; this means that their internal values cannot be changed once the objects are created.

9.5.2   Numeric Wrapper Class Constants

Each numeric wrapper class has the constants MAX_VALUE and MIN_VALUE. MAX_VALUE represents the maximum value of the corresponding primitive data type. For Byte, Short, Integer, and Long, MIN_VALUE represents the minimum byte, short, int, and long values. For Float and Double, MIN_VALUE represents the minimum *positive* float and double values. The following statements display the maximum integer (2,147,483,647), the minimum positive float (1.4E-45), and the maximum double floating-point number (1.79769313486231570e + 308d):

```
System.out.println("The maximum integer is " + Integer.MAX_VALUE);
System.out.println("The minimum positive float is " +
  Float.MIN_VALUE);
System.out.println(
  "The maximum double precision floating-point number is " +
  Double.MAX_VALUE);
```

9.5.3   Conversion Methods

Each numeric wrapper class implements the abstract methods doubleValue, floatValue, intValue, longValue, and shortValue, which are defined in the Number class. These methods "convert" objects into primitive type values.

For example,

```
long l = doubleObject.longValue(); // Note it truncates
```

This converts doubleObject's double value to a long variable l.

```
int i = integerObject.intValue();
```

This assigns the int value of integerObject to i.

```
double d = 5.9;
Double doubleObject = new Double(d);
String s = doubleObject.toString();
```

This converts double d to a string s.

9.5.4   The Static valueOf Methods

The numeric wrapper classes have a useful class method, valueOf(String s). This method creates a new object initialized to the value represented by the specified string. For example,

```
Double doubleObject = Double.valueOf("12.4");
Integer integerObject = Integer.valueOf("12");
```

9.5.5   The Methods for Parsing Strings into Numbers

You have used the parseInt method in the Integer class to parse a numeric string into an int value and the parseDouble method in the Double class to parse a numeric string into a double value. Each numeric wrapper class has two overloaded parsing methods to parse a numeric string into an appropriate numeric value based on 10 (decimal) or any specified radix (e.g., 2 for binary, 8 for octal, and 16 for hexadecimal). These methods are shown below:

```
// These two methods are in the Byte class
public static byte parseByte(String s)
public static byte parseByte(String s, int radix)

// These two methods are in the Short class
public static short parseShort(String s)
public static short parseShort(String s, int radix)

// These two methods are in the Integer class
public static int parseInt(String s)
public static int parseInt(String s, int radix)

// These two methods are in the Long class
public static long parseLong(String s)
public static long parseLong(String s, int radix)

// These two methods are in the Float class
public static float parseFloat(String s)
public static float parseFloat(String s, int radix)

// These two methods are in the Double class
public static double parseDouble(String s)
public static double parseDouble(String s, int radix)
```

For example,

```
Integer.parseInt("11", 2) returns 3;
Integer.parseInt("12", 8) returns 10;
Integer.parseInt("13", 10) returns 13;
Integer.parseInt("1A", 16) returns 26;
```

`Integer.parseInt("12", 2)` would raise a runtime exception because 12 is not a binary number.

EXAMPLE 9.2 SORTING AN ARRAY OF OBJECTS

Problem

Write a static method for sorting an array of comparable objects. The objects are instances of the `Comparable` interface, and they are compared using the `compareTo` method. The method can be used to sort an array of any objects as long as their classes implement the `Comparable` interface.

Solution

A generic sort method is presented in the code in Listing 9.8. To test the method, the program sorts an array of integers, an array of double numbers, an array of characters, and an array of strings. Figure 9.8 shows a sample run of the code.

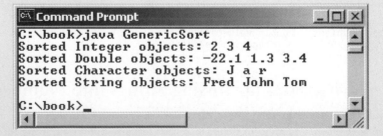

FIGURE 9.8 *The program uses a generic sort method to sort an array of comparable objects.*

EXAMPLE 9.2 (CONTINUED)

LISTING 9.8   GenericSort.java (Sorting an Array of Objects)

```java
1 public class GenericSort {
2   public static void main(String[] args) {
3     // Create an Integer array
4     Integer[] intArray = {new Integer(2), new Integer(4),
5       new Integer(3)};
6
7     // Create a Double array
8     Double[] doubleArray = {new Double(3.4), new Double(1.3),
9       new Double(-22.1)};
10
11     // Create a Character array
12     Character[] charArray = {new Character('a'),
13       new Character('J'), new Character('r')};
14
15     // Create a String array
16     String[] stringArray = {"Tom", "John", "Fred"};
17
18     // Sort the arrays
19     sort(intArray);
20     sort(doubleArray);
21     sort(charArray);
22     sort(stringArray);
23
24     // Display the sorted arrays
25     System.out.print("Sorted Integer objects: ");
26     printList(intArray);
27     System.out.print("Sorted Double objects: ");
28     printList(doubleArray);
29     System.out.print("Sorted Character objects: ");
30     printList(charArray);
31     System.out.print("Sorted String objects: ");
32     printList(stringArray);
33   }
34
35   /** Sort an array of comparable objects */
36   public static void sort(Object[] list) {
37     Object currentMax;
38     int currentMaxIndex;
39
40     for (int i = list.length - 1; i >= 1; i--) {
41       // Find the maximum in the list[0..i]
42       currentMax = list[i];
43       currentMaxIndex = i;
44
45       for (int j = i - 1; j >= 0; j--) {
46         if (((Comparable)currentMax).compareTo(list[j]) < 0) {
47           currentMax = list[j];
48           currentMaxIndex = j;
49         }
50       }
51
52       // Swap list[i] with list[currentMaxIndex] if necessary;
53       if (currentMaxIndex != i) {
54         list[currentMaxIndex] = list[i];
55         list[i] = currentMax;
56       }
57     }
58   }
59
60   /** Print an array of objects */
61   public static void printList(Object[] list) {
62     for (int i = 0; i < list.length; i++)
63       System.out.print(list[i] + " ");
64     System.out.println();
65   }
66 }
```

EXAMPLE 9.2 (CONTINUED)

Review

You will get a compilation warning "unchecked operation" in JDK 1.5. Ignore it. This warning can be fixed using generic types in Section 18.6.

The algorithm for the `sort` method is the same as in Section 5.6, "Sorting Arrays." The sort method in Section 5.6 sorts an array of double values. The sort method in this example can sort an array of any object type, provided that the objects are also instances of the `Comparable` interface. This is an example of *generic programming*. Generic programming enables a method to operate on arguments of generic types, making it reusable with multiple types.

`Integer`, `Double`, `Character`, and `String` implement `Comparable`, so the objects of these classes can be compared using the `compareTo` method. The sort method uses the `compareTo` method to determine the order of the objects in the array.

Arrays.sort method

 TIP

Java provides a static `sort` method for sorting an array of `Object` in the `java.util.Arrays` class, provided that the elements in the array are comparable. Thus you can use the following code to sort arrays in this example:

```
java.util.Arrays.sort(intArray);
java.util.Arrays.sort(doubleArray);
java.util.Arrays.sort(charArray);
java.util.Arrays.sort(stringArray);
```

 NOTE

Arrays are objects. An array is an instance of the `Object` class. Furthermore, if `A` is a subclass of `B`, every instance of `A[]` is an instance of `B[]`. Therefore, the following statements are all true:

```
new int[10] instanceof Object
new GregorianCalendar[10] instanceof Calendar[];
new Calendar[10] instanceof Object[]
new Calendar[10] instanceof Object
```

 CAUTION

Although an `int` value can be assigned to a `double` type variable, `int[]` and `double[]` are two incompatible types. Therefore, you cannot assign an `int[]` array to a variable of `double[]` or `Object[]` type.

9.6 Automatic Conversion Between Primitive Types and Wrapper Class Types (JDK 1.5 Feature)

JDK 1.5 allows primitive types and wrapper classes to be converted automatically. For example, the following statement in (a) can be simplified as in (b):

```
Integer intObject = new Integer(2);
```
Equivalent
```
Integer intObject = 2;
```
(a)   New JDK 1.5 boxing   (b)

Converting a primitive value to a wrapper object is called *boxing*. The reverse conversion is called *unboxing*. The JDK 1.5 compiler will automatically box a primitive value that appear in a context requiring an object, and will unbox an object that appears in a context requiring a primitive value. Consider the following example:

boxing
unboxing

```
Integer[] intArray = {1, 2, 3};
System.out.println(intArray[0] + intArray[1] + intArray[2]);
```

In Line 1, primitive values 1, 2, and 3 are automatically boxed into objects new Integer(1), new Integer(2), and new Integer(3). In Line 2, objects intArray[0], intArray[1], and intArray[2] are automatically converted into int values and these values are added together.

KEY TERMS

abstract class   316
abstract method   317
deep copy   330
interface   323
marker interface   328

multiple inheritance   316
subinterface   326
shallow copy   330
single inheritance   316
wrapper class   331

KEY CLASSES AND METHODS

✦ **java.util.Calendar** is an abstract base class for extracting detailed calendar information, such as year, month, date, hour, minute, and second. The get(int field) method can be used to extract such information, where field is a constant (e.g., Calendar.YEAR, Calendar.MONTH, Calendar.DATE) that specifies what information to get.

✦ **java.util.GregorianCalendar** is a subclass of java.util.Calendar that implements the Gregorian calendar system.

✦ **java.lang.Comparable** is an interface that imposes a total ordering on the objects of each class that implements it. The compareTo(anotherObject) method compares this object with anotherObject

✦ **java.lang.Cloneable** is a marker interface that enables the objects of each class to be able to be cloned.

✦ **java.lang.Number** is an abstract base class for numeric wrapper classes.

✦ **java.lang.Byte** is a wrapper class for the byte type.

✦ **java.lang.Short** is a wrapper class for the short type.

✦ **java.lang.Integer** is a wrapper class for the int type.

✦ **java.lang.Long** is a wrapper class for the long type.

✦ **java.lang.Float** is a wrapper class for the float type.

✦ **java.lang.Double** is a wrapper class for the double type.

✦ **java.lang.Character** is a wrapper class for the char type.

✦ **java.lang.Boolean** is a wrapper class for the boolean type.

✦ **java.util.Arrays.sort(Object[])**   sorts an array of comparable objects.

CHAPTER SUMMARY

◆ Abstract classes are like regular classes with data and methods, but you cannot create instances of abstract classes using the new operator.

◆ An abstract method cannot be contained in a nonabstract class. If a subclass of an abstract superclass does not implement all the abstract methods, the subclass must be declared abstract.

◆ A class that contains abstract methods must be abstract. However, it is possible to declare an abstract class that contains no abstract methods.

◆ A subclass can be abstract even if its superclass is concrete.

◆ An interface is a classlike construct that contains only constants and abstract methods. In many ways, an interface is similar to an abstract class, but an abstract class can contain constants and abstract methods as well as variables and concrete methods.

◆ An interface is treated like a special class in Java. Each interface is compiled into a separate bytecode file, just like a regular class.

◆ The `java.lang.Comparable` interface defines the `compareTo` method. Many classes in the Java library implement `Comparable`.

◆ The `java.lang.Cloneable` interface is a marker interface. An object of the class that implements the `Cloneable` interface is cloneable.

◆ A class can extend only one superclass, but a class can implement one or more interfaces.

◆ An interface can extend one or more interfaces.

◆ Many Java methods require the use of objects as arguments. Java offers a convenient way to incorporate, or wrap, a primitive data type into an object (e.g., wrapping `int` into the `Integer` class, and wrapping `double` into the `Double` class). The corresponding class is called a *wrapper class*. By using a wrapper object instead of a primitive data type variable, you can take advantage of generic programming.

◆ The wrapper class for `byte` is `Byte`, for `short` is `Short`, for `int` is `Integer`, for `long` is `Long`, for `float` is `Float`, for `double` is `Double`, for `char` is `Character`, and for `boolean` is `Boolean`.

◆ The numeric wrapper classes extend the abstract `java.lang.Number` class and implement the `java.lang.Comparable` interface. The `Character` class also implements `java.lang.Comparable`.

REVIEW QUESTIONS

Section 9.2 Abstract Classes

9.1   Which of the following class definitions defines a legal abstract class?

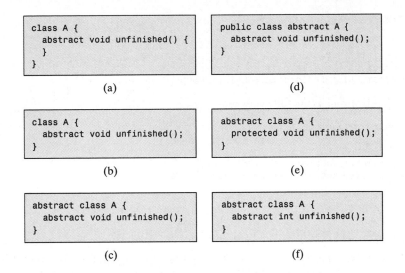

```
class A {                                public class abstract A {
  abstract void unfinished() {             abstract void unfinished();
  }                                      }
}
```
(a)   (d)

```
class A {                                abstract class A {
  abstract void unfinished();              protected void unfinished();
}                                        }
```
(b)   (e)

```
abstract class A {                       abstract class A {
  abstract void unfinished();              abstract int unfinished();
}                                        }
```
(c)   (f)

9.2 The `findArea` and `findPerimeter` methods may be removed from the `GeometricObject` class. What are the benefits of defining `findArea` and `findPerimeter` as abstract methods in the `GeometricObject` class?

Section 9.4 Interfaces

9.3 Which of the following is a correct interface?

```
interface A {                            abstract interface A extends I1, I2 {
  void print() { };                        abstract void print() { };
}                                        }
```
(a)   (c)

```
abstract interface A {                   interface A {
  print();                                 void print();
}                                        }
```
(b)   (d)

9.4 Consider redefining the `max` method in the `Max` class in Section 9.4 as follows:

```
public class Max {
  /** Return the maximum between two objects */
  public static Comparable max(Comparable o1, Comparable o2) {
    if (o1.compareTo(o2) > 0)
      return o1;
    else
      return o2;
  }
}
```

Are these statements correct?

```
String s = Max.max("abc", "efg");
Date date = Max.max(new Date(), new Date());
```

9.5 You can define the `compareTo` method in a class without implementing the `Comparable` interface. What are the benefits of implementing the `Comparable` interface?

9.6 What would happen if the `House` class (defined in Listing 9.7) does not override the `clone()` method or if `House` does not implement `java.lang.Cloneable`?

9.7 Show the printout of the following code:

```
java.util.Date date = new java.util.Date();
java.util.Date date1 = (java.util.Date)(date.clone());
System.out.println(date == date1);
System.out.println(date.equals(date1));
```

9.8 What is wrong in the following code?

```
public class Test {
  public static void main(String[] args) {
    GeometricObject x = new Circle(3);
    GeometricObject y = x.clone();
    System.out.println(x == y);
  }
}
```

Section 9.5 Processing Primitive Data Type Values as Objects

9.9 Can you assign new int[10], new String[100], new Object[50], or new Calendar[20] into a variable of Object[] type?

9.10 Describe primitive-type wrapper classes. Why do you need these wrapper classes?

9.11 Are the following statements correct?

```
Integer i = new Integer("23");
Integer i = new Integer(23);
Integer i = Integer.valueOf("23");
Integer i = Integer.parseInt("23",8);
Double d = new Double();
Double d = Double.valueOf("23.45");
int i = (Integer.valueOf("23")).intValue();
double d = (Double.valueOf("23.4")).doubleValue();
int i = (Double.valueOf("23.4")).intValue();
String s = (Double.valueOf("23.4")).toString();
```

9.12 How do you convert an integer into a string? How do you convert a numeric string into an integer? How do you convert a double number into a string? How do you convert a numeric string into a double value?

9.13 Why do the following two lines of code compile but cause a runtime error?

```
Number numberRef = new Integer(0);
Double doubleRef = (Double)numberRef;
```

9.14 Why do the following two lines of code compile but cause a runtime error?

```
Number[] numberArray = new Integer[2];
numberArray[0] = new Double(1.5);
```

9.15 What is wrong in the following code?

```
public class Test {
  public static void main(String[] args) {
    Number x = new Integer(3);
    System.out.println(x.intValue());
    System.out.println(x.compareTo(new Integer(4)));
  }
}
```

9.16 What is wrong in the following code?

```
public class Test {
  public static void main(String[] args) {
    Number x = new Integer(3);
    System.out.println(x.intValue());
    System.out.println((Integer)x.compareTo(new Integer(4)));
  }
}
```

9.17 Describe the boxing and unboxing features in JDK 1.5. Are the following statements correct in JDK 1.5?

```
Number x = 3;
Integer x = 3;
Double x = 3;
Double x = 3.0;
int x = new Integer(3);
int x = new Integer(3) + new Integer(4);
double y = 3.4;
y.intValue();
```

Comprehensive

9.18 Define the following terms: abstract classes, interfaces. What are the similarities and differences between abstract classes and interfaces?

9.19 Indicate true or false for the following statements:

◆ An abstract class can have instances created using the constructor of the abstract class.
◆ An abstract class can be extended.
◆ You can always successfully cast an instance of a subclass to a superclass.
◆ You can always successfully cast an instance of a superclass to a subclass.
◆ An interface is compiled into a separate bytecode file.
◆ A subclass of a nonabstract superclass cannot be abstract.
◆ A subclass cannot override a concrete method in a superclass to declare it abstract.

PROGRAMMING EXERCISES

Comprehensive

9.1* (*Enabling* GeometricObject *comparable*) Modify the GeometricObject class to implement the Comparable interface, and define the max method in the GeometricObject class. Write a test program that uses the max method to find the larger of two circles and the larger of two cylinders.

9.2* (*The* ComparableCylinder *class*) Create a class named ComparableCylinder that extends Cylinder and implements Comparable. Implement the compareTo method to compare the cylinders on the basis of volume. Write a test class to find the larger of two instances of ComparableCylinder objects.

9.3* (*The* Colorable *interface*) Create an interface named Colorable, as follows:

```
public interface Colorable {
  public void howToColor();
}
```

Every class of a colorable object must implement the Colorable interface. Create a class named Square that extends GeometricObject and implements Colorable. Implement howToColor to display a message on how to color the square.

9.4* (*Revising the* House *class*) Rewrite the House class in Listing 9.7 to perform a deep copy on the whenBuilt field.

9.5* (*Enabling* Circle *comparable*) Rewrite the Circle class on page 318 to extend GeometricObject and implement the Comparable interface. Override the equals and hashCode methods in the Object class. Two Circle objects are equal if their radii are the same.

9.6* (*Enabling* Rectangle *comparable*) Rewrite the Rectangle class on page 318 to extend GeometricObject and implement the Comparable interface. Override the equals and hashCode methods in the Object class. Two Rectangle objects are equal if their areas are the same.

9.7* (*The* Octagon *class*) Write a class named Octagon that extends GeometricObject and implements the Comparable and Cloneable interfaces. Assume that all eight sides of the octagon are of equal size. The area can be computed using the following formula:

$$area = (2 + 4/\sqrt{2})\ side * side$$

Write a test program that creates an Octagon object with side value 5 and displays its area and perimeter. Create a new object using the clone method and compare the two objects using the compareTo method.

9.8* (*Summing the areas of geometric objects*) Write a method that sums the areas of all the geometric objects in an array. The method header is:

```
public static double sumArea(GeometricObject[] a)
```

Write a test program that creates an array of three objects (a circle, a cylinder, and a rectangle) and computes their total area using the sumArea method.

9.9* (*Finding the largest object*) Write a method that returns the largest object in an array of objects. The method header is:

```
public static Object max(Object[] a)
```

All the objects are instances of the Comparable interface. The order of the objects in the array is determined using the compareTo method.

Write a test program that creates an array of ten strings, an array of ten integers, and an array of ten dates, and finds the largest string, integer, and date in the arrays.

9.10** (*Displaying calendars*) Rewrite the PrintCalendar class in Listing 4.7 on page 147 to display a calendar for a specified month using the Calendar and Gregorian Calendar classes. Your program receives the month and year from the command line. For example:

```
java Exercise9_10 3 2003
```

This displays the calendar shown in Figure 9.9.

You also can run the program without the year. In this case, the year is the current year. If you run the program without specifying a month and a year, the month is the current month.

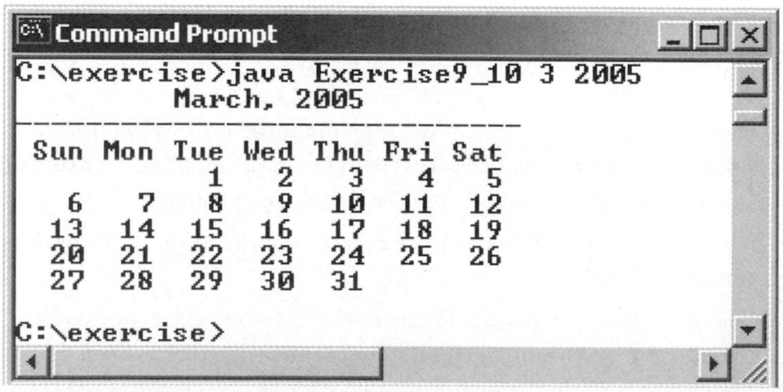

FIGURE 9.9   *The program displays a calendar for March 2005.*

chapter

10

OBJECT-ORIENTED MODELING

Objectives

- ✦ To become familiar with the process of program development (§10.2).

- ✦ To learn the relationship types: association, aggregation, composition, strong inheritance, and weak inheritance (§10.3).

- ✦ To declare classes to represent the relationships among the classes (§10.3).

- ✦ To design systems by identifying the classes and discovering the relationships among them (§10.4).

- ✦ To implement the `Rational` class and process rational numbers using this class (§10.5).

- ✦ To design classes that follow the class-design guidelines (§10.6).

- ✦ To model dynamic behavior using sequence diagrams and statechart diagrams (§10.7 Optional)

- ✦ To know the concept of framework-based programming using Java API (§10.8).

10.1   Introduction

The preceding chapters introduced objects, classes, class inheritance, and interfaces. You learned the concepts of object-oriented programming. This chapter focuses on the development of software systems using the object-oriented approach, and introduces class modeling using the Unified Modeling Language (UML). You will learn class-design guidelines, and the techniques for designing reusable classes through the `Rational` class.

10.2   The Software Development Process

Developing a software project is an engineering process. Software products, no matter how large or how small, have the same developmental phases: requirements specification, analysis, design, implementation, testing, deployment, and maintenance, as shown in Figure 10.1.

requirements specification

Requirements specification is a formal process that seeks to understand the problem and document in detail what the software system needs to do. This phase involves close interaction between users and designers. Most of the examples in this book are simple, and their requirements are clearly stated. In the real world, however, problems are not well defined. You need to study a problem carefully to identify its requirements.

system analysis

System analysis seeks to analyze the business process in terms of data flow, and to identify the system's input and output. Part of the analysis entails modeling the system's behavior. The model is intended to capture the essential elements of the system and to define services to the system.

system design

System design is the process of designing the system's components. This phase involves the use of many levels of abstraction to decompose the problem into manageable components, identify classes and interfaces, and establish relationships among the classes and interfaces.

implementation

Implementation is the process of translating the system design into programs. Separate programs are written for each component and put to work together. This phase requires the use of a programming language like Java. The implementation involves coding, testing, and debugging.

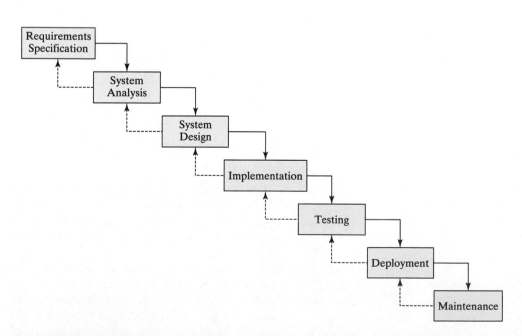

FIGURE 10.1 *Developing a project involves requirements specification, system analysis, system design, implementation, testing, deployment, and maintenance.*

Testing ensures that the code meets the requirements specification and weeds out bugs. An independent team of software engineers not involved in the design and implementation of the project usually conducts such testing.

Deployment makes the project available for use. For a Java applet, this means installing it on a Web server; for a Java application, installing it on the client's computer. A project usually consists of many classes. An effective approach for deployment is to package all the classes into a Java archive file, as will be introduced in Section 14.13, "Packaging and Deploying Java Projects."

Maintenance is concerned with changing and improving the product. A software product must continue to perform and improve in a changing environment. This requires periodic upgrades of the product to fix newly discovered bugs and incorporate changes.

The central task in object-oriented system development is to design classes to model the system. While there are many object-oriented methodologies, UML has become the industry-standard notation for object-oriented modeling, and itself leads to a methodology. The process of designing classes calls for identifying the classes and discovering the relationships among them. Class relationships are introduced in the next section.

testing

deployment

maintenance

10.3   Discovering Relationships Among Classes

The relationships among classes can be classified into three types: *association*, *aggregation*, and *inheritance*.

10.3.1   Association

Association is a general binary relationship that describes an activity between two classes. For example, a student taking a course is an association between the `Student` class and the `Course` class, and a faculty member teaching a course is an association between the `Faculty` class and the `Course` class. These associations can be represented in UML graphical notations, as shown in Figure 10.2.

association

FIGURE 10.2 *A student may take any number of courses, and a faculty member teaches at most three courses. A course may have from five to sixty students and is taught by only one faculty member.*

An association is illustrated using a solid line between two classes with an optional label that describes the relationship. In Figure 10.2, the labels are *Take* and *Teach*. Each relationship may have an optional small black triangle that indicates the direction of the relationship. In Figure 10.2, the direction indicates that a student takes a course, as opposed to a course taking a student.

Each class involved in the relationship may have a role name that describes the role played by the class in the relationship. In Figure 10.2, *teacher* is the role name for `Faculty`.

Each class involved in an association may specify a *multiplicity*. A multiplicity could be a number or an interval that specifies how many objects of the class are involved in the relationship. The character * means unlimited number of objects, and the interval m..n means that the number of objects should be between m and n, inclusive. In Figure 10.2, each student may take any number of courses, and each course must have at least five students and at most sixty students. Each course is taught by only one faculty member, and a faculty member may teach from zero to three courses per semester.

Association may exist between objects of the same class. For example, a person may have a supervisor. This is illustrated in Figure 10.3.

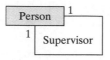

FIGURE 10.3 *A person may have a supervisor.*

An association is usually represented as a data field in the class. For example, the relationships in Figure 10.2 can be represented in the following classes:

```
public class Student {
   /** Data fields omitted */
   private Course[]
      courseList;


   /** Constructors omitted */
   /** Methods omitted */
}
```

```
public class Course {
   /** Data fields omitted */
   private Student[]
      classList;
   private Faculty faculty;


   /** Constructors */
   /** Methods */
}
```

```
public class Faculty {
   /** Data fields omitted */
   private Course[]
      courseList;


   /** Constructors omitted */
   /** Methods omitted */
}
```

> 🌸 **NOTE**
> If you don't need to know the courses a student takes or a faculty member teaches, the data field `courseList` in `Student` or `Faculty` can be omitted.

In the association "a person has a supervisor," as shown in Figure 10.3, a supervisor can be represented as a data field in the `Person` class, as follows:

```
public class Person {
   /** Data fields omitted*/
   private Person supervisor;

   /** Constructors omitted*/
   /** Methods omitted*/
}
```

10.3.2 Aggregation and Composition

aggregation

composition

Aggregation is a special form of association that represents an ownership relationship between two classes. Aggregation models *has-a* relationships. An object may be owned by several other aggregated objects. If an object is exclusively owned by an aggregated object, the relationship between the object and its aggregated object is referred to as *composition*. For example, "a person has a name" is a composition relationship between the `Person` class and the `Name` class, whereas "a person has an address" is an aggregation relationship between the `Person` class and the `Address` class, since an address may be shared by several persons. In UML, a filled diamond is attached to the `Person` class to denote the composition relationship with the `Name` class, and an empty diamond is attached to the `Person` class to denote the aggregation relationship with the `Address` class, as shown in Figure 10.4.

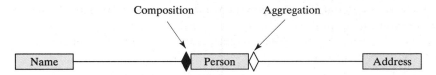

FIGURE 10.4 *A person has a name and an address.*

An aggregation relationship is usually represented as a data field in the aggregated class. For example, the relationship in Figure 10.4 can be represented as follows:

```
public class Name {
  /** Data fields omitted */
  /** Constructors omitted */
  /** Methods omitted */
}
```

```
public class Person {
  /** Data fields omitted */
  private Name name;
  private Address address;

  /** Constructors omitted */
  /** Methods omitted */
}
```

```
public class Address {
  /** Data fields omitted */
  /** Constructors omitted */
  /** Methods omitted */
}
```

🪶 **NOTE**

If `Name` or `Address` is used only in the `Person` class, it can be declared as an inner class in `Person`. For example,

```
public class Person {
  private Name name;
  private Address address;
  ...

  class Name {
  ...
  }

  class Address {
  ...
  }
}
```

10.3.3 Inheritance

Inheritance models the *is-a* relationship between two classes. A *strong is-a* relationship describes a direct inheritance relationship between two classes. A *weak is-a* relationship describes that a class has certain properties. A strong is-a relationship can be represented using class inheritance. For example, the relationship "a faculty member is a person," shown in Figure 10.5(a), is a strong is-a relationship and can be represented using the class in Figure 10.5(b).

strong is-a
weak is-a

```
public class Faculty extends Person {
  /** Data fields omitted */
  /** Constructors omitted */
  /** Methods omitted */
}
```

Person ◁── Faculty

(a)   (b)

FIGURE 10.5 `Faculty` *extends* `Person`.

A weak is-a relationship can be represented using interfaces. For example, the weak is-a relationship "students are comparable based on their grades," shown in Figure 10.6(a), can be represented by implementing the `Comparable` interface, as shown in Figure 10.6(b).

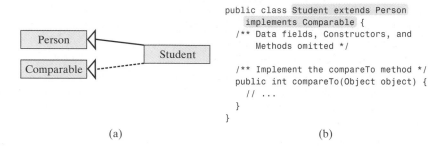

(a)   (b)

FIGURE 10.6 Student *extends* Person *and implements* Comparable.

10.4 CASE STUDY: A Class Design Example

The key to object-oriented programming is to model the application in terms of cooperative objects. Carefully designed classes are critical when a project is being developed. There are many levels of abstraction in system design. You have learned method abstraction and have applied it to the development of large programs. Methods are a means to group statements. Classes extend abstraction to a higher level and provide a means of grouping methods. Classes do more than just group methods, however; they also contain data fields. Methods and data fields together describe the properties and behaviors of classes.

The power of classes is further extended by inheritance. Inheritance enables a class to extend the contract and the implementation of an existing class without knowing the details of the existing class. In the development of a Java program, class abstraction is applied to decompose the problem into a set of related classes, and method abstraction is applied to design individual classes.

This case study models borrowing loans to demonstrate how to identify classes, discover the relationships between classes, and apply class abstraction in object-oriented program development.

For simplicity, the example does not attempt to build a complete system for storing, processing, and manipulating loans for borrowers; instead it focuses on modeling borrowers and the loans for the borrowers. The following steps are usually involved in building an object-oriented system:

1. Identify classes for the system.

2. Describe the attributes and methods in each class.

3. Establish relationships among classes.

4. Create classes.

identify classes

The first step is to *identify classes* for the system. There are many strategies for identifying classes in a system, one of which is to study how the system works and select a number of use cases, or scenarios. Since a borrower is a person who obtains a loan, and a person has a name and an address, you can identify the following classes: `Person`, `Name`, `Address`, `Borrower`, and `Loan`.

Identifying objects is not easy for novice programmers. How do you find the right objects? There is no unique solution even for simple problems. Software development is more an art than a science. The quality of a program ultimately depends on the programmer's intuition, experience, and knowledge. This example identifies five classes: `Name`, `Address`, `Person`, `Borrower`, and `Loan`. There are several alternatives. One would combine `Name`, `Address`, `Person`, and `Borrower` into one class. This design is not clear because it puts too many entities into one class.

The second step is to *describe the attributes* and methods in each of the classes you have identi- describe attributes
fied. The attributes and methods can be illustrated using UML, as shown in Figure 10.7. The `Name` class has the properties `firstName`, `mi`, and `lastName`, their associated `get` and `set` methods, and the `getFullName` method for returning the full name. The `Address` class has the properties `street`, `city`, `state`, and `zip`, their associated `get` and `set` methods, and the `getAddress` method for returning the full address. The `Loan` class, presented in Section 6.15, "Case Study: The `Loan` Class," has the properties `annualInterestRate`, `numberOfYears`, and `loanAmount`, property `get` and `set` methods, and `monthlyPayment` and `totalPayment` methods. The `Person` class has the properties `name` and `address`, their associated `get` and `set` methods, and the `toString` method for displaying complete information about the person. `Borrower` is a subclass of `Person`. Additionally, `Borrower` has the `loan` property and its associated `get` and `set` methods, and the `toString` method for displaying the person and the loan payments.

The third step is to *establish relationships* among the classes. The relationship is derived from establish relationships
the analysis in the preceding two steps. The first three steps are intertwined. When you identify classes, you also think about the relationships among them. Establishing relationships among objects helps you understand the interactions among objects. An object-oriented system consists of a collection of interrelated cooperative objects. The relationships for the classes in this example are illustrated in Figure 10.7.

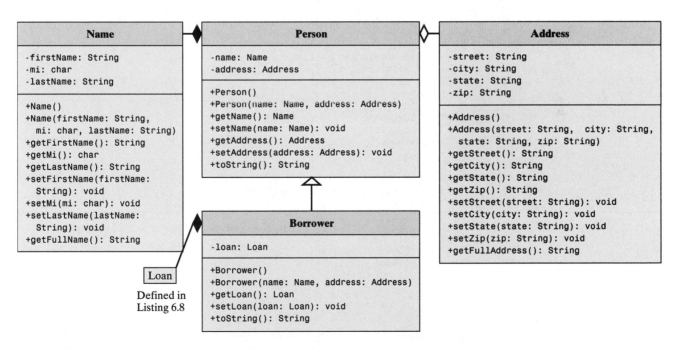

FIGURE 10.7 *A borrower has a name, an address, and a loan.*

The fourth step is to write the code for the classes. The program is long, but most of the *cod-* coding
ing is for the `get` and `set` methods. Once an object is identified, its properties and methods can be defined by analyzing the requirements and scenarios of the system. It is a good practice to provide complete `get` and `set` methods. These may not be needed for your current project, but will be useful in other projects, because your classes are designed for reuse in future projects. Listings 10.1, 10.2, 10.3, and 10.4 give the `Name`, `Address`, `Person`, and `Borrower` classes.

LISTING 10.1   **Name.java (The Name Class)**

```
 1 public class Name implements Cloneable {
 2   private String firstName;
 3   private char mi;
 4   private String lastName;
 5
 6   /** Construct a name with default properties */
 7   public Name() {
 8     this("Jill", 'S', "Barr");
 9   }
10
11   /** Construct a name with firstName, mi, and lastName */
12   public Name(String firstName, char mi, String lastName) {
13     this.firstName = firstName;
14     this.mi = mi;
15     this.lastName = lastName;
16   }
17
18   /** Return firstName */
19   public String getFirstName() {
20     return firstName;
21   }
22
23   /** Set a new firstName */
24   public void setFirstName(String firstName) {
25     this.firstName = firstName;
26   }
27
28   /** Return middle name initial */
29   public char getMi() {
30     return mi;
31   }
32
33   /** Set a new middlename initial */
34   public void setMi(char mi) {
35     this.mi = mi;
36   }
37
38   /** Return lastName */
39   public String getLastname() {
40     return lastName;
41   }
42
43   /** Set a new lastName */
44   public void setLastName(String lastName) {
45     this.lastName = lastName;
46   }
47
48   /** Obtain full name */
49   public String getFullName() {
50     return firstName + ' ' + mi + ' ' + lastName;
51   }
52 }
```

LISTING 10.2   **Address.java (The Address Class)**

```
 1 public class Address {
 2   private String street;
 3   private String city;
 4   private String state;
 5   private String zip;
 6
 7   /** Construct an address with default properties */
 8   public Address() {
 9     this("100 Main", "Savannah", "GA", "31411");
10   }
11
```

```
12   /** Create an address with street, city, state, and zip */
13   public Address(String street, String city,
14     String state, String zip) {
15     this.street = street;
16     this.city = city;
17     this.state = state;
18     this.zip = zip;
19   }
20
21   /** Return street */
22   public String getStreet() {
23     return street;
24   }
25
26   /** Set a new street */
27   public void setStreet(String street) {
28     this.street = street;
29   }
30
31   /** Return city */
32   public String getCity() {
33     return city;
34   }
35
36   /** Set a new city */
37   public void setCity(String city) {
38     this.city = city;
39   }
40
41   /** Return state */
42   public String getState() {
43     return state;
44   }
45
46   /** Set a new state */
47   public void setState(String state) {
48     this.state = state;
49   }
50
51   /** Return zip */
52   public String getZip() {
53     return zip;
54   }
55
56   /** Set a new zip */
57   public void setZip(String zip) {
58     this.zip = zip;
59   }
60
61   /** Get full address */
62   public String getFullAddress() {
63     return street + '\n' + city + ", " + state + ' ' + zip + '\n';
64   }
65 }
```

LISTING 10.3   **Person.java (The Person Class)**

```
1 public class Person {
2   private Name name;
3   private Address address;
4
5   /** Construct a person with default properties */
6   public Person() {
7     this(new Name("Jill", 'S', "Barr"),
8       new Address("100 Main", "Savannah", "GA", "31411"));
9   }
10
```

```
11    /** Construct a person with specified name and address */
12    public Person(Name name, Address address) {
13      this.name = name;
14      this.address = address;
15    }
16
17    /** Return name */
18    public Name getName() {
19      return name;
20    }
21
22    /** Set a new name */
23    public void setName(Name name) {
24      this.name = name;
25    }
26
27    /** Return address */
28    public Address getAddress() {
29      return address;
30    }
31
32    /** Set a new address */
33    public void setAddress(Address address) {
34      this.address = address;
35    }
36
37    /** Override the toString method */
38    public String toString() {
39      return '\n' + name.getFullName() + '\n' +
40        address.getFullAddress() + '\n';
41    }
42  }
```

LISTING 10.4   Borrower.java (The Borrower Class)

```
1 public class Borrower extends Person {
2    private Loan loan;
3
4    /** Construct a borrower with default properties */
5    public Borrower() {
6      super();
7    }
8
9    /** Create a borrower with specified name and address */
10   public Borrower(Name name, Address address) {
11     super(name, address);
12   }
13
14   /** Return loan */
15   public Loan getLoan() {
16     return loan;
17   }
18
19   /** Set a new loan */
20   public void setLoan(Loan loan) {
21     this.loan = loan;
22   }
23
24   /** String representation for borrower */
25   public String toString() {
26     return super.toString() +
27       "Monthly payment is " + loan.monthlyPayment() + '\n' +
28       "Total payment is " + loan.totalPayment();
29   }
30 }
```

Listing 10.5 is a test program that uses the classes Name, Address, Borrower, and Loan. The output of the program is shown in Figure 10.8.

LISTING 10.5   BorrowLoan.java

```
 1 import javax.swing.JOptionPane;
 2
 3 public class BorrowLoan {
 4   /** Main method */
 5   public static void main(String[] args) {
 6     // Create a name
 7     Name name = new Name("John", 'D', "Smith");
 8
 9     // Create an address
10     Address address = new Address("100 Main Street", "Savannah",
11       "GA", "31419");
12
13     // Create a loan
14     Loan loan = new Loan(5.5, 15, 250000);
15
16     // Create a borrower
17     Borrower borrower = new Borrower(name, address);
18
19     borrower.setLoan(loan);
20
21     // Display loan information
22     JOptionPane.showMessageDialog(null, borrower.toString());
23   }
24 }
```

FIGURE 10.8   *The program creates name, address, and loan, stores the information in a* Borrower *object, and displays the information with the loan payment.*

10.5   CASE STUDY: The Rational Class

A rational number is a number with a numerator and a denominator in the form a/b, where a is the numerator and b is the denominator. For example, 1/3, 3/4, and 10/4.

A rational number cannot have a denominator of 0, but a numerator of 0 is fine. Every integer a is equivalent to a rational number a/1. Rational numbers are used in exact computations involving fractions; for example, 1/3 = 0.33333. ... This number cannot be precisely represented in floating-point format using data type double or float. To obtain the exact result, it is necessary to use rational numbers.

Java provides data types for integers and floating-point numbers, but not for rational numbers. This section shows how to design a class to represent rational numbers.

Since rational numbers share many common features with integers and floating-point numbers, and Number is the root class for numeric wrapper classes, it is appropriate to define Rational as a subclass of Number. Since rational numbers are comparable, the Rational class should also implement the Comparable interface. Figure 10.9 illustrates the Rational class and its relationship to the Number class and the Comparable interface.

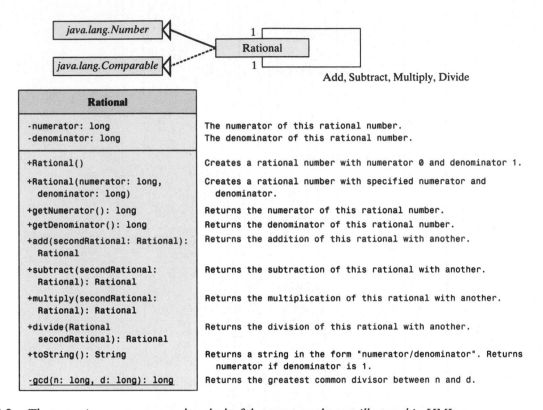

FIGURE 10.9 *The properties, constructors, and methods of the Rational class are illustrated in UML.*

A rational number consists of a numerator and a denominator. There are many equivalent rational numbers; for example, 1/3 = 2/6 = 3/9 = 4/12. For convenience, 1/3 is used in this example to represent all rational numbers that are equivalent to 1/3. The numerator and the denominator of 1/3 have no common divisor except 1, so 1/3 is said to be in lowest terms.

To reduce a rational number to its lowest terms, you need to find the greatest common divisor (GCD) of the absolute values of its numerator and denominator, and then divide both numerator and denominator by this value. You can use the method for computing the GCD of two integers n and d, as suggested in Example 3.7, "Finding Greatest Common Divisor". The numerator and denominator in a Rational object are reduced to their lowest terms.

As usual, I recommend that you first write a test program to create two Rational objects and test its methods (see the Important Pedagogical Tip on page 242). Listing 10.6 is a test program. Its output is shown in Figure 10.10.

LISTING 10.6 **TestRationalClass.java**

```
1 public class TestRationalClass {
2   /** Main method */
3   public static void main(String[] args) {
4     // Create and initialize two rational numbers r1 and r2.
5     Rational r1 = new Rational(4, 2);
6     Rational r2 = new Rational(2, 3);
7
```

```
8       // Display results
9       System.out.println(r1 + " + " + r2 + " = " + r1.add(r2));
10      System.out.println(r1 + " - " + r2 + " = " + r1.subtract(r2));
11      System.out.println(r1 + " * " + r2 + " = " + r1.multiply(r2));
12      System.out.println(r1 + " / " + r2 + " = " + r1.divide(r2));
13      System.out.println(r2 + " is " + r2.doubleValue());
14    }
15 }
```

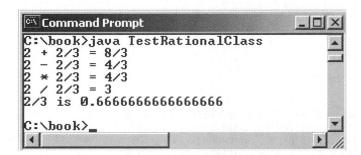

FIGURE 10.10 *The program creates two* Rational *objects and displays their addition, subtraction, multiplication, and division.*

The main method creates two rational numbers, r1 and r2 (Lines 5–6), and displays the results of r1 + r2, r1 - r2, r1 x r2, and r1 / r2 (Lines 9–12). To perform r1 + r2, invoke r1.add(r2) to return a new Rational object. Similarly, r1.subtract(r2) is for r1 - r2, r1.multiply(r2) for r1 x r2, and r1.divide(r2) for r1 / r2.

The doubleValue() method displays the double value of r2 (Line 13). The doubleValue() method is defined in java.lang.Number and overridden in Rational.

Note that when a string is concatenated with an object using the plus sign (+), the object's string representation from the toString() method is used to concatenate with the string. So r1 + " + " + r2 + " = " + r1.add(r2) is equivalent to r1.toString() + " + " + r2.toString() + " = " + r1.add(r2).toString().

The Rational class is implemented in Listing 10.7.

LISTING 10.7 Rational.java (The Rational Class)

```
1 public class Rational extends Number implements Comparable {
2    // Data fields for numerator and denominator
3    private long numerator = 0;
4    private long denominator = 1;
5
6    /** Construct a rational with default properties */
7    public Rational() {
8      this(0, 1);
9    }
10
11   /** Construct a rational with specified numerator and denominator */
12   public Rational(long numerator, long denominator) {
13     long gcd = gcd(numerator, denominator);
14     this.numerator = ((denominator > 0) ? 1 : -1) * numerator / gcd;
15     this.denominator = Math.abs(denominator) / gcd;
16   }
17
18   /** Find GCD of two numbers */
19   private static long gcd(long n, long d) {
20     long n1 = Math.abs(n);
21     long n2 = Math.abs(d);
22     int gcd = 1;
```

$$\frac{a}{b} + \frac{c}{d} = \frac{ad + bc}{bd}$$

$$\frac{a}{b} - \frac{c}{d} = \frac{ad - cb}{bd}$$

$$\frac{a}{b} \times \frac{c}{d} = \frac{ac}{bd}$$

$$\frac{a}{b} \div \frac{c}{d} = \frac{ad}{bc}$$

```java
23
24     for (int k = 1; k <= n1 && k <= n2; k++) {
25       if (n1 % k == 0 && n2 % k == 0)
26         gcd = k;
27     }
28
29     return gcd;
30   }
31
32   /** Return numerator */
33   public long getNumerator() {
34     return numerator;
35   }
36
37   /** Return denominator */
38   public long getDenominator() {
39     return denominator;
40   }
41
42   /** Add a rational number to this rational */
43   public Rational add(Rational secondRational) {
44     long n = numerator * secondRational.getDenominator() +
45       denominator * secondRational.getNumerator();
46     long d = denominator * secondRational.getDenominator();
47     return new Rational(n, d);
48   }
49
50   /** Subtract a rational number from this rational */
51   public Rational subtract(Rational secondRational) {
52     long n = numerator * secondRational.getDenominator()
53       - denominator * secondRational.getNumerator();
54     long d = denominator * secondRational.getDenominator();
55     return new Rational(n, d);
56   }
57
58   /** Multiply a rational number to this rational */
59   public Rational multiply(Rational secondRational) {
60     long n = numerator * secondRational.getNumerator();
61     long d = denominator * secondRational.getDenominator();
62     return new Rational(n, d);
63   }
64
65   /** Divide a rational number from this rational */
66   public Rational divide(Rational secondRational) {
67     long n = numerator * secondRational.getDenominator();
68     long d = denominator * secondRational.numerator;
69     return new Rational(n, d);
70   }
71
72   /** Override the toString() method */
73   public String toString() {
74     if (denominator == 1)
75       return numerator + "";
76     else
77       return numerator + "/" + denominator;
78   }
79
80   /** Override the equals method in the Object class */
81   public boolean equals(Object parm1) {
82     if ((this.subtract((Rational)(parm1))).getNumerator() == 0)
83       return true;
84     else
85       return false;
86   }
87
88   /** Override the hashCode method in the Object class */
89   public int hashCode() {
90     return new Double(this.doubleValue()).hashCode();
91   }
92
```

```
 93    /** Override the abstract intValue method in java.lang.Number */
 94    public int intValue() {
 95      return (int)doubleValue();
 96    }
 97
 98    /** Override the abstract floatValue method in java.lang.Number */
 99    public float floatValue() {
100      return (float)doubleValue();
101    }
102
103    /** Override the doubleValue method in java.lang.Number */
104    public double doubleValue() {
105      return numerator * 1.0 / denominator;
106    }
107
108    /** Override the abstract longValue method in java.lang.Number */
109    public long longValue() {
110      return (long)doubleValue();
111    }
112
113    /** Override the compareTo method in java.lang.Comparable */
114    public int compareTo(Object o) {
115      if ((this.subtract((Rational)o)).getNumerator() > 0)
116        return 1;
117      else if ((this.subtract((Rational)o)).getNumerator() < 0)
118        return -1;
119      else
120        return 0;
121    }
122  }
```

The rational number is encapsulated in a `Rational` object. Internally, a rational number is represented in its lowest terms (Line 13) and the numerator determines its sign (Line 14). The denominator is always positive (Line 15).

The `gcd()` method (Lines 19–30 in the `Rational` class) is private; it is not intended for use by clients. The `gcd()` method is only for internal use by the `Rational` class. The `gcd()` method is also static, since it is not dependent on any particular `Rational` object.

The `abs(x)` method (Lines 20–21 in the `Rational` class) is defined in the `Math` class that returns the absolute value of x.

Two `Rational` objects can interact with each other to perform add, subtract, multiply, and divide operations. These methods return a new `Rational` object (Lines 43–70).

The methods `toString`, `equals`, and `hashCode` in the `Object` class are overridden in the `Rational` class (Lines 73–91). The `toString()` method returns a string representation of a `Rational` object in the form numerator/denominator, or simply numerator if denominator is 1. The `equals(Object other)` method returns true if this rational number is equal to the other rational number. By contract, if two objects are equal, their hash codes must be same. For this reason, you should override `hashCode` whenever the `equals` method is overridden.

The abstract methods `intValue`, `longValue`, `floatValue`, and `doubleValue` in the `Number` class are implemented in the `Rational` class (Lines 94–111). These methods return int, long, float, and double value for this rational number.

The `compareTo(Object other)` method in the `Comparable` interface is implemented in the `Rational` class (Lines 114–121) to compare this rational number to the other rational number.

 TIP

The get methods for the properties `numerator` and `denominator` are provided in the `Rational` class, but the set methods are not provided, so the contents of a `Rational` object cannot be changed once the object is created. The `Rational` class is *immutable*. A well-known example of an immutable class is the `String` class. The wrapper classes that were introduced in Section 9.5, "Processing Primitive Data Type Values as Objects," are also immutable.

immutable

---

encapsulation

> **TIP**
>
> The numerator and denominator are represented using two variables. It is possible to use an array of two integers to represent the numerator and denominator. See Exercise 10.2. The signatures of the public methods in the `Rational` class are not changed, although the internal representation of a rational number is changed. This is a good example to illustrate the idea that the data fields of a class should be kept private so as to encapsulate the implementation of the class from the use of the class.

10.6   Class Design Guidelines

You have learned how to design classes from the preceding two examples and from many other examples in the preceding chapters. Here are some guidelines.

10.6.1   Designing a Class

A class should describe a single entity, and all the class operations should logically fit together to support a coherent purpose. You can use a class for students, for example, but you should not combine students and staff in the same class, because students and staff have different operations. Since the `Math` class provides mathematical operations, it is natural to group all mathematical methods in one class. A single entity with too many responsibilities can be broken into several classes to separate responsibilities. The `String` class, `StringBuffer` class, and `StringTokenizer` class all deal with strings, for example, but have different responsibilities.

Classes are usually designed for use by many different customers. In order to be useful in a wide range of applications, a class should provide a variety of ways for customization through properties and methods. For example, the `String` class contains many methods that are useful for a variety of applications.

Classes are designed for reuse. Users can incorporate classes in many different combinations, orders, and environments. Therefore, you should design a class that imposes no restrictions on what or when the user can do with it, design the properties in a way that lets the user set them in any order and with any combination of values, and design methods that function independently of their order of occurrence. For example, the `Loan` class contains the properties `loanAmount`, `numberOfYears`, and `annualInterestRate`. The values of these properties can be set in any order.

In general, you should provide a public no-arg constructor and override the methods `equals` and `toString` defined in the `Object` class whenever possible. Override the `hashCode` method whenever the `equals` method is overridden. By contract, two equal objects must have the same hash code. A public default no-arg constructor is assumed if no constructors are defined explicitly. If you want to prevent users from creating an object for a class, you may declare a private constructor in the class, as is the case for the `Math` class.

Follow standard Java programming style and naming conventions. Choose informative names for classes, data fields, and methods. I recommend that you place the data declaration before the constructor, and place constructors before methods.

10.6.2   Using the Visibility Modifiers `public`, `protected`, and `private`

A class can present two contracts: one for the users of the class, and one for the extenders of the class. Make the fields `private` and the accessor and mutator methods `public` if they are intended for the users of the class. Make the fields or methods protected if they are intended for extenders of the class. The contract for extenders encompasses the contract for users. The extended class may increase the visibility of an instance method from protected to public, or may change its implementation, but you should never change the implementation in a way that violates the contract.

A class should use the private modifier to hide its data from direct access by clients. Provide a get method only if you want the field to be readable, and provide a set method only if you want the field to be updateable. A class should also hide methods not intended for client use. The gcd method in the Rational class in the preceding section is private, for example, because it is only for internal use within the class.

10.6.3   Using the static Modifier

A property that is shared by all the instances of a class should be declared as a static property. For example, the variable numberOfObjects in the CircleWithStaticVariableAndMethod class in Section 6.10, "Static Variables, Constants, and Methods," is shared by all the objects of the Circle class, and therefore is declared as a static variable. A method that is not dependent on a specific instance should be declared as a static method. For instance, the getNumOfObjects method in CircleWithStaticVariableAndMethod and the gcd method in Rational are not tied to any specific instance, and therefore are declared as static methods. The static properties and methods are denoted using the static modifier.

10.6.4   Using Inheritance or Composition

The difference between inheritance and composition is the difference between an is-a relationship and a has-a relationship. For example, an apple is a fruit; thus, you would use inheritance to model the relationship between the classes Apple and Fruit. A person has a name; thus, you would use composition to model the relationship between the classes Person and Name. Sometimes the choice between inheritance and composition is not obvious. For example, you have used inheritance to model the relationship between the classes Circle and Cylinder, as shown in (a) in the following figure. One could argue that a cylinder consists of circles, and thus that you might use composition to define the Cylinder class, as shown in (b):

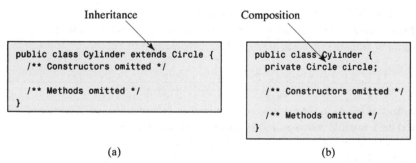

(a)   (b)

Both designs are fine. Which one is preferred? If polymorphism is desirable, use the inheritance design. If you don't care about polymorphism, the composition design gives more flexibility because the classes are less dependent when you use composition rather than inheritance.

10.6.5   Using Interfaces or Abstract Classes

Both interfaces and abstract classes can be used to generalize common features. How do you decide whether to use an interface or a class? In general, a *strong is-a relationship* that clearly describes a parent–child relationship should be modeled using classes. For example, since an orange is a fruit, their relationship should be modeled using class inheritance. A *weak is-a relationship*, also known as an *is-kind-of relationship*, indicates that an object possesses a certain property. A weak is-a relationship can be modeled using interfaces. For example, all strings are comparable, so the `String` class implements the `Comparable` interface. A circle or a rectangle is a geometric object, so `Circle` can be designed as a subclass of `GeometricObject`. Circles are different and comparable based on their radii, so `Circle` can implement the `Comparable` interface.

Interfaces are more flexible than abstract classes, because a subclass can extend only one superclass but can implement any number of interfaces. However, interfaces cannot contain concrete methods. The virtues of interfaces and abstract classes can be combined by creating an interface with an abstract class that implements it. Then you can use the interface or the abstract class, whichever is convenient. For this reason, such classes are known as *convenience classes*. For example, in the Java Collections Framework, which is introduced in Chapter 18, "Java Collections Framework," the `AbstractCollection` class is a convenience class for the `Collection` interface, and the `AbstractSet` class is a convenience class for the `Set` interface.

10.7 Modeling Dynamic Behavior Using Sequence Diagrams and Statecharts (Optional)

The UML diagrams presented so far describe the properties and methods of a class or the static relationships among classes. This section introduces the sequence diagrams and statechart diagrams that model the dynamic behaviors of objects.

10.7.1 Sequence Diagrams

Sequence diagrams describe interactions among objects by depicting the time-ordering of method invocations. A sequence diagram consists of the following elements, as shown in Figure 10.11:

✦ **Class role** represents the roles the object plays. The objects at the top of the diagram represent class roles.

✦ **Lifeline** represents the existence of an object over a period of time. A vertical dotted line extending from the object is used to denote a lifeline.

✦ **Activation** represents the time during which an object is performing an operation. Thin rectangles placed on lifelines are used to denote activations.

✦ **Method invocation** represents communication between objects. Horizontal arrows labeled with method calls are used to denote method invocations.

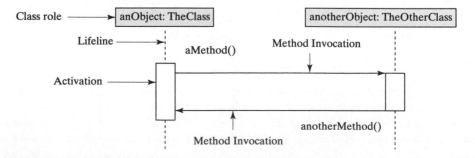

FIGURE 10.11 *Sequence diagrams describe interactions between objects.*

The interactions among the objects in the `BorrowLoan` class on page 353 are illustrated in Figure 10.12.

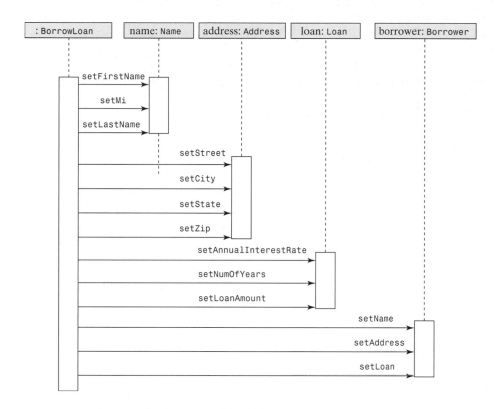

FIGURE 10.12   *The* `BorrowLoan` *object invokes the methods in the* `Name`, `Address`, `Loan`, *and* `Borrower` *objects.*

10.7.2   Statechart Diagrams

Statechart diagrams describe the flow of control of an object. A statechart diagram contains the following elements, as shown in Figure 10.13:

✦ **State** represents a situation during the life of an object in which it satisfies some condition, performs some action, or waits for some event to occur. All states have names. States are denoted by rectangles with rounded corners, except for the initial state, which is denoted by a small filled circle.

✦ **Transition** represents the relationship between two states, indicating that an object will perform some action to transfer from one state to the other. A solid arrow with appropriate method invocation denotes a transition.

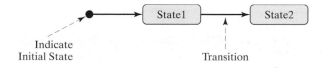

FIGURE 10.13   *Statechart diagrams describe the flow of control of an object.*

The life cycle of an object can be illustrated using a statechart diagram, as shown in Figure 10.14.

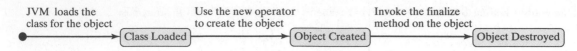

JVM loads the class for the object → Class Loaded → Use the new operator to create the object → Object Created → Invoke the finalize method on the object → Object Destroyed

FIGURE 10.14 *The life cycle of an object can be described using a statechart diagram.*

10.8 Framework-Based Programming Using Java API

API

The Java API (*Application Program Interface*) consists of numerous classes and interfaces grouped into more than a dozen packages. You have used classes and interfaces in the `java.lang`, `javax.swing`, and `java.util` packages.

✦ `java.lang` contains core Java classes (e.g., `System`, `Math`, `Object`, `String`, `StringBuffer`, `Number`, `Character`, `Boolean`, `Byte`, `Short`, `Integer`, `Long`, `Float`, `Double`, `Comparable`, and `Cloneable`). This package is implicitly imported to every Java program.

✦ `javax.swing` contains the lightweight graphical user interface components for developing Swing GUI programs.

✦ `java.util` contains many utilities, such as `StringTokenizer`, `Date`, `Calendar`, and `GregorianCalendar`.

These are just a few of the classes and interfaces you have learned. To create comprehensive projects, you have to use more classes and interfaces in the Java API. The classes and interfaces in the Java API establish a framework for programmers to develop applications using Java. For example, the classes and interfaces in the Java GUI API establish a framework for developing GUI programs. You have to use these classes and interfaces and follow their conventions and rules to create applications. This is referred to as *framework-based programming*.

framework-based programming

Once you understand the concept of Java and object-oriented programming, the most important lesson from now on is learning how to use the API to develop useful programs. The most effective way to achieve this is to imitate good examples. The book provides many carefully designed examples to demonstrate the concept of framework-based programming using the Java API. You will learn the Java GUI programming framework in Chapters 11, 12, 13, and 14, the Java exception handling framework in Chapter 15, and the Java IO framework in Chapter 16.

KEY TERMS

aggregation   346
Application Program Interface (API)   362
association   345
composition   346

framework-based programming   362
sequence diagram   360
statechart   361

CHAPTER SUMMARY

✦ Developing a project involves requirements *specification, system analysis, system design, implementation, testing, deployment,* and *maintenance.*

✦ The relationships among classes can be classified into three types: *association, aggregation,* and *inheritance.*

✦ Inheritance models the is-a relationship between two classes. A strong is-a relationship describes a direct inheritance relationship between two classes. A weak is-a relationship describes that a class has certain properties. A strong is-a relationship can be represented using class inheritance. A weak is-a relationship can be represented using interfaces.

✦ The `Rational` class extends `java.lang.Number` and implements `java.lang.Comparable`. A rational object represents a rational number.

✦ A class should describe a single entity or a set of similar operations. A single entity with too many responsibilities can be broken into several classes to separate responsibilities. The `String` class, `StringBuffer` class, and `StringTokenizer` class all deal with strings, for example, but have different responsibilities.

✦ Classes are usually designed for use by many different customers. In order to be useful in a wide range of applications, a class should provide a variety of ways for customization through properties and methods.

✦ Provide a public no-arg constructor and override the methods `equals` and `toString` defined in the `Object` class whenever possible. Override the `hashCode` method whenever the `equals` method is overridden.

✦ A class should use the `private` modifier to hide its data from direct access by clients. Provide a `get` method only if you want the field to be readable, and provide a `set` method only if you want the field to be updateable. A class should also hide methods not intended for client use.

✦ A property that is shared by all the instances of a class should be declared as a static property.

✦ The difference between inheritance and composition is the difference between an is-a relationship and a has-a relationship.

✦ Both interfaces and abstract classes can be used to generalize common features. How do you decide whether to use an interface or a class? In general, a *strong is-a relationship* that clearly describes a parent–child relationship should be modeled using classes.

✦ Interfaces are more flexible than abstract classes, because a subclass can extend only one superclass but can implement any number of interfaces. However, interfaces cannot contain concrete methods.

✦ Sequence diagrams describe interactions among objects by depicting the time-ordering of method invocations. A sequence diagram consists of class roles, lifelines, activation, and method invocations. *Class role* represents the roles the object plays. The objects at the top of the diagram represent class roles. *Lifeline* represents the existence of an object over a period of time. A vertical dotted line extending from the object is used to denote a lifeline. *Activation* represents the time during which an object is performing an operation. Thin rectangles placed on lifelines are used to denote activations. *Method invocation* represents communication between objects. Horizontal arrows labeled with method calls are used to denote method invocations.

✦ Statechart diagrams describe the flow of control of an object. A statechart diagram contains states and transitions. *State* represents a situation during the life of an object in which it satisfies some condition, performs some action, or waits for some event to occur.

Transition represents the relationship between two states, indicating that an object will perform some action to transfer from one state to the other.

REVIEW QUESTIONS

Section 10.3 Discovering Relationships Among Objects

10.1 What are the types of relationships among classes? Describe the graphical notations for modeling the relationships among classes.

10.2 What relationship is appropriate for the following classes? Draw the relationships using UML diagrams.

- ✦ Company and Employee
- ✦ Course and Faculty
- ✦ Student and Person
- ✦ House and Window
- ✦ Account and Savings Account

Section 10.5 The Rational Class

10.3 Show the output of the following code:

```java
public class Test {
  public static void main(String[] args) {
    Rational r1 = new Rational(1, 3);
    Rational r2 = new Rational(2, 4);
    System.out.println(r1 + " + " + r2 + " = " + r1.add(r2));
    System.out.println(r2 + " + " + r1 + " = " + r2.add(r1));
    System.out.println(r1 + " - " + r2 + " = " + r1.subtract(r2));
    System.out.println(r2 + " - " + r1 + " = " + r2.subtract(r1));
    System.out.println(r1 + " * " + r2 + " = " + r1.multiply(r2));
    System.out.println(r2 + " * " + r1 + " = " + r2.multiply(r1));
    System.out.println(r1 + " / " + r2 + " = " + r1.divide(r2));
    System.out.println(r2 + " / " + r1 + " = " + r2.divide(r1));
    System.out.println(r1 + " = " + r1.doubleValue());
    System.out.println(r2 + " = " + r2.doubleValue());
  }
}
```

10.4 What is wrong in the following code?

```java
Number r = new Rational();
System.out.println(r);
System.out.println(r.doubleValue());
System.out.println(r.add(new Rational()));
System.out.println((Rational)r.add(new Rational()));
System.out.println(((Rational)r).add(new Rational()));
```

10.5 What is wrong in the following code?

```java
Number r = new Number();
System.out.println(r);
```

10.6 Is the following code correct?

```java
Comparable r = new Rational();
System.out.println(r);
```

```java
Comparable r = new Rational();
System.out.println(
  r.compareTo(new Rational()));
```

(a)   (b)

PROGRAMMING EXERCISES

Section 10.5 The Rational Class

10.1 (*Using the* Rational *class*) Write a program that will compute the following summation series using the Rational class:

$$\frac{1}{2} + \frac{2}{3} + \frac{3}{4} + \cdots + \frac{98}{99} + \frac{99}{100}$$

10.2* (*Demonstrating the benefits of encapsulation*) Rewrite the Rational class in Section 10.5 using a new internal representation for numerator and denominator. Declare an array of two integers as follows:

```
private long[] r = new long[2];
```

Use r[0] to represent the numerator and r[1] to represent the denominator. The signatures of the methods in the Rational class are not changed, so a client application that uses the previous Rational class can continue to use this new Rational class without being recompiled.

10.3* (*Creating a rational number calculator*) Write a program similar to the Calculator class on page 279. Instead of using integers, use rationals, as shown in Figure 10.15. You will need to use the StringTokenizer class, introduced in Chapter 7, "Strings," to retrieve the numerator string and denominator string, and convert strings into integers using the Integer.parseInt method.

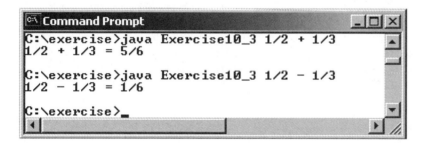

FIGURE 10.15 *The program takes three arguments (*operand1, operator, *and* operand2*) from the command line and displays the expression and the result of the arithmetic operation.*

Comprehensive

10.4** (*The* Person *and* Student *classes*) Create the classes as shown in Figure 10.16. Implement the compareTo method in the Person class to compare persons in alphabetical order of their last name, first name, and middle initial. Implement the compareTo method to compare students in alphabetical order of their major, last name, first name, and middle initial.

Write a test program with the following three methods:

```
/** Sort an array of comparable objects  */
public static void sort(Object[] list)

/** Return the max object in an array of comparable objects */
public static Object max(Object[] list)
```

main method: Test the sort and max methods using an array of four students, an array of four strings, an array of one hundred random rationals, and an array of one hundred random integers.

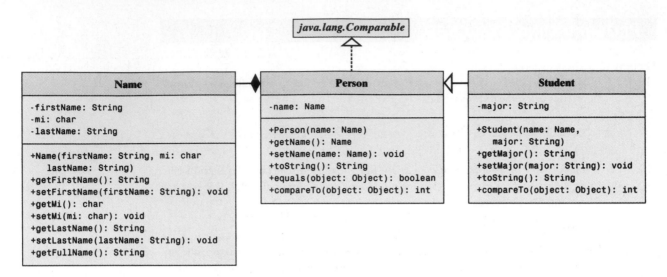

FIGURE **10.16** *A person has a name, a student is a person, and students are comparable.*

PART III

GUI PROGRAMMING

Part I, "Fundamentals of Programming," introduced basic programming concepts that are supported in all programming languages. Part II, "Object-Oriented Programming," introduced object-oriented programming concepts, principles, and practices that are common in the object-oriented programming languages. Java is not simply a programming language. It is also a development and deployment platform with an extensive set of classes and interfaces in the API. You have to use the classes and interfaces in the API and follow their conventions and rules to develop your own projects. The design of the API for Java GUI programming is an excellent example of how the object-oriented principle is applied. In the chapters that follow, you will learn the framework of Java GUI API and use the GUI components to develop user-friendly interfaces for applications and applets.

Chapter 11
Getting Started with GUI Programming

Chapter 12
Event-Driven Programming

Chapter 13
Creating User Interfaces

Chapter 14
Applets, Images, and Audio

Prerequisites for Part III

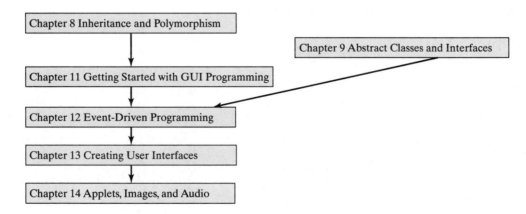

chapter

11

GETTING STARTED WITH GUI PROGRAMMING

Objectives

✦ To get a glimpse of simple GUI components (§11.2).

✦ To describe the Java GUI API hierarchy (§11.3).

✦ To create user interfaces using frames, panels, and simple GUI components (§11.4).

✦ To understand the role of layout managers (§11.5).

✦ To use the FlowLayout, GridLayout, and BorderLayout managers to layout components in a container (§11.5).

✦ To specify colors and fonts using the Color and Font classes (§§11.6–11.7).

✦ To use JPanels as subcontainers (§11.8).

✦ To paint graphics using the paintComponent method on a panel (§11.9).

✦ To draw strings, lines, rectangles, ovals, arcs, and polygons using the drawing methods in the Graphics class (§11.9).

✦ To center display using the FontMetrics Class (§11.10).

✦ To develop a reusable component, MessagePanel, to display a message on a panel (§11.11).

✦ To develop a reusable component, StillClock, to emulate an analog clock (§11.12 Optional).

11.1 Introduction

Until now, you have only used dialog boxes and the command window for input and output. You used `JOptionPane.showInputDialog` to obtain input, and `JOptionPane.showMessage-Dialog` and `System.out.println` to display results. These approaches have limitations and are inconvenient. For example, to read ten numbers, you have to open ten input dialog boxes. Starting with this chapter, you will learn Java GUI programming. You will create custom graphical user interfaces (GUI, pronounced *goo-ee*) to obtain input and display output in the same user interface.

This chapter introduces the basics of Java GUI programming. Specifically, it discusses GUI components and their relationships, containers and layout managers, colors, fonts, and drawing geometric figures, such as lines, rectangles, ovals, arcs, polygons, and polylines.

11.2 GUI Components

You create graphical user interfaces using GUI objects, such as buttons, labels, text fields, check boxes, radio buttons, and combo boxes. Each type of GUI object is defined in a class, such as `JButton`, `JLabel`, `JTextField`, `JCheckBox`, `JRadioButton`, and `JComboBox`. Each GUI component class provides several constructors that you can use to create GUI component objects. The following are the examples to create buttons, labels, text fields, check boxes, radio buttons, and combo boxes.

```
// Create a button with text OK
JButton jbtOK = new JButton("OK");

// Create a label with text "Enter your name: "
JLabel jlblName = new JLabel("Enter your name: ");

// Create a text field with text "Type Name Here"
JTextField jtfName = new JTextField("Type Name Here");

// Create a check box with text bold
JCheckBox jchkBold = new JCheckBox("Bold");

// Create a radio button with text red
JRadioButton jrbRed = new JRadioButton("Red");

// Create a combo box with choices red, green, and blue
JComboBox jcboColor = new JComboBox(new String[]{"Red",
  "Green", "Blue"});
```

Figure 11.1 shows these objects displayed in a frame. How to add the components into a frame will be introduced in Section 11.3.

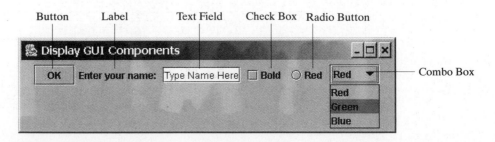

FIGURE 11.1 *The GUI component objects can be displayed.*

11.2.1 Swing vs. AWT

Why do the GUI component classes have the prefix *J*? Instead of JButton, why not name it simply Button? In fact, there is a class already named Button in the java.awt package.

When Java was introduced, the GUI classes were bundled in a library known as the Abstract Windows Toolkit (AWT). For every platform on which Java runs, the AWT components are automatically mapped to the platform-specific components through their respective agents, known as *peers*. AWT is fine for developing simple graphical user interfaces, but not for developing comprehensive GUI projects. Besides, AWT is prone to platform-specific bugs because its peer-based approach relies heavily on the underlying platform. With the release of Java 2, the AWT user-interface components were replaced by a more robust, versatile, and flexible library known as *Swing components*. Swing components are painted directly on canvases using Java code, except for components that are subclasses of java.awt.Window or java.awt.Panel, which must be drawn using native GUI on a specific platform. Swing components are less dependent on the target platform and use less of the native GUI resource. For this reason, Swing components that don't rely on native GUI are referred to as *lightweight components,* and AWT components are referred to as *heavyweight components.*

lightweight
heavyweight

To distinguish new Swing component classes from their AWT counterparts, the names of Swing GUI component classes begin with a prefixed *J*. Although AWT components are still supported in Java 2, it is better to learn how to program using Swing components, because the AWT user-interface components will eventually fade away. This book uses Swing GUI components exclusively.

11.3 The Java GUI API

The design of the Java API for GUI programming is an excellent example of the use of classes, inheritance, and interfaces. The API contains the essential classes listed below. Their hierarchical relationships are shown in Figures 11.2 and 11.3.

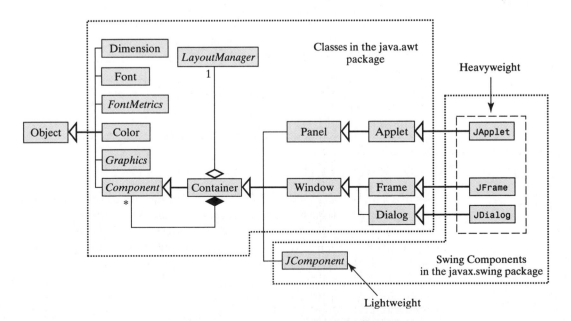

FIGURE 11.2 *Java GUI programming utilizes the classes shown in this hierarchical diagram.*

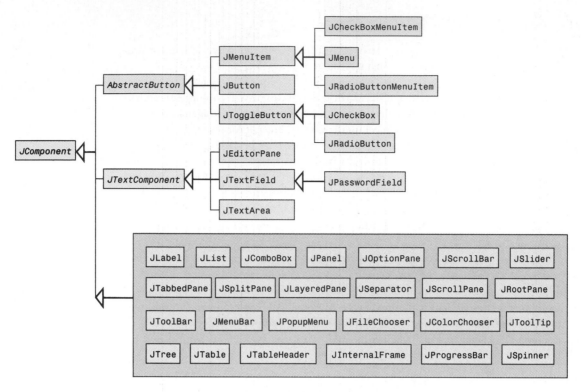

FIGURE 11.3 *JComponent and its subclasses are the basic elements for building graphical user interfaces.*

The GUI classes can be classified into three groups: *container classes*, *helper classes*, and *component classes*. The container classes, such as JFrame, JPanel, and JApplet, are used to contain other components. The helper classes, such as Graphics, Color, Font, FontMetrics, and Dimension, are used by components and containers to draw and place objects. The GUI component classes, such as JButton, JTextField, JTextArea, JComboBox, JList, JRadioButton, and JMenu, are subclasses of JComponent.

 NOTE

The JFrame, JApplet, JDialog, and JComponent classes and their subclasses are grouped in the javax.swing package. All the other classes in Figures 11.2 are grouped in the java.awt package.

11.3.1 Swing GUI Components

Component is a superclass of all the user-interface classes, and JComponent is a superclass of all the lightweight Swing components. Since JComponent is an abstract class, you cannot use new JComponent() to create an instance of JComponent. However, you can use the constructors of concrete subclasses of JComponent to create JComponent instances. It is important to become familiar with the class inheritance hierarchy. For example, the following statements all display true:

```java
JButton jbtOK = new JButton("OK");
System.out.println(jbtOK instanceof JButton);
System.out.println(jbtOK instanceof AbstractButton);
System.out.println(jbtOK instanceof JComponent);
System.out.println(jbtOK instanceof Container);
```

```
System.out.println(jbtOK instanceof Component);
System.out.println(jbtOK instanceof Object);
```

An instance of a subclass can invoke the accessible method defined in its superclass. For example, the getWidth() and getHeight() methods are defined in the Component class to return the component width and height. You can invoke the methods to find the width and height of a button.

11.3.2 Container Classes

Container classes are GUI components that are used as containers to contain other GUI components. Window, Panel, Applet, Frame, and Dialog are the container classes for AWT components. To work with Swing components, use Component, Container, JFrame, JDialog, JApplet, and JDialog.

◆ **Container** is used to group components. A layout manager is used to position and place components in a container in the desired location and style. Frames, panels, and applets are examples of containers.

◆ **JFrame** is a window not contained inside another window. It is the container that holds other Swing user-interface components in Java GUI applications.

◆ **JDialog** is a popup window or message box generally used as a temporary window to receive additional information from the user or to provide notification that an event has occurred.

◆ **JApplet** is a subclass of Applet. You must extend JApplet to create a Swing-based Java applet.

◆ **JPanel** is an invisible container that holds user-interface components. Panels can be nested. You can place panels inside a container that includes a panel. JPanel can also be used as a canvas to draw graphics.

11.3.3 GUI Helper Classes

The helper classes, such as Graphics, Color, Font, FontMetrics, Dimension, and LayoutManager, are not subclasses of Component. They are used to describe the properties of GUI components, such as graphics context, colors, fonts, and dimension.

◆ **Graphics** is an abstract class that provides a graphical context for drawing strings, lines, and simple shapes.

◆ **Color** deals with the colors of GUI components. For example, you can specify background or foreground colors in components like JFrame and JPanel, or you can specify colors of lines, shapes, and strings in drawings.

◆ **Font** specifies fonts for the text and drawings on GUI components. For example, you can specify the font type (e.g., SansSerif), style (e.g., bold), and size (e.g., 24 points) for the text on a button.

◆ **FontMetrics** is an abstract class used to get the properties of the fonts.

◆ **Dimension** encapsulates the width and height of a component (in integer precision) in a single object.

◆ **LayoutManager** is an interface, whose instances specify how components are arranged in a container.

NOTE

The helper classes are in the `java.awt` package. The Swing components do not replace all the classes in AWT, only the AWT GUI component classes (e.g., `Button`, `TextField`, `TextArea`). The AWT helper classes remain unchanged.

11.4 Frames

To create a user interface, you need to create either a frame or an applet to hold the user-interface components. Creating Java applets will be introduced in Chapter 14, "Applets, Images, and Audio." This section introduces the procedure for creating frames.

11.4.1 Creating a Frame

The following program creates a frame:

LISTING 11.1 **MyFrame.java (Creating a Frame)**

```
1 import javax.swing.*;
2
3 public class MyFrame {
4   public static void main(String[] args) {
5     JFrame frame = new JFrame("MyFrame");
6     frame.setSize(400, 300);
7     frame.setVisible(true);
8     frame.setDefaultCloseOperation(JFrame.EXIT_ON_CLOSE);
9   }
10 }
```

Because `JFrame` is in the `javax.swing` package, the statement `import javax.swing.*` (Line 1) makes available all the classes from the `javax.swing` package, including `JFrame`, so that they can be used in the `MyFrame` class.

The following two constructors are used to create a `JFrame` object:

✦ `public JFrame()`

Constructs an untitled `JFrame` object.

✦ `public JFrame(String title)`

Constructs a `JFrame` object with a specified title. The title appears in the title bar of the frame.

The frame is not displayed *until* the `frame.setVisible(true)` method is applied. `frame.setSize(400, 300)` specifies that the frame is 400 pixels wide and 300 pixels high. If the `setSize` method is not used, the frame will be sized to display just the title bar. Since the `setSize` and `setVisible` methods are both defined in the `Component` class, they are inherited by the `JFrame` class. Later you will see that these methods are also useful in many other subclasses of `Component`.

When you run the `MyFrame` program, a window will be displayed on-screen (see Figure 11.4).

`frame.setDefaultCloseOperation(JFrame.EXIT_ON_CLOSE)` (Line 8) tells the program to terminate when the frame is closed. If this statement is not used, the program does not terminate when the frame is closed. In that case, you have to stop the program by pressing `Ctrl+C` at the DOS prompt window in Windows or use the kill command to stop the process in Unix.

11.4.2 Adding Components to a Frame

The frame shown in Figure 11.4 is empty. Using the `add` method, you can add components into the frame's content pane, as in Listing 11.2.

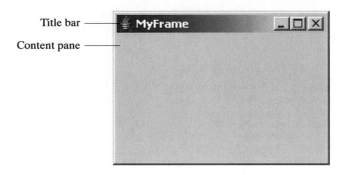

Title bar

Content pane

FIGURE **11.4**   *The program creates and displays a frame with the title* MyFrame.

LISTING 11.2   MyFrameWithComponents.java (Adding Components to a Frame)

```
 1 import javax.swing.*;
 2
 3 public class MyFrameWithComponents {
 4   public static void main(String[] args) {
 5     JFrame frame = new JFrame("Adding Components into the Frame");
 6
 7     // Add a button into the frame
 8     java.awt.Container container = frame.getContentPane();
 9     JButton jbtOK = new JButton("OK");
10     container.add(jbtOK);
11
12     frame.setSize(400, 300);
13     frame.setVisible(true);
14     frame.setDefaultCloseOperation(JFrame.EXIT_ON_CLOSE);
15   }
16 }
```

The getContentPane method (Line 8) in the JFrame class returns the content pane of the frame, which is an instance of java.awt.Container. The GUI components such as buttons are placed in the content pane. An object of JButton was created using new JButton("OK"), and this object was added to the content pane of the frame (Line 10).

You may be wondering how the content pane (a Container object) is created. The getContentPane method does not produce it. The content pane is created when a JFrame object is created. The getContentPane method simply returns a reference to the content pane, and you can use it to reference the content pane.

The add(Componentcomp) method defined in the Container class adds an instance of Component to the container. Since JButton is a subclass of Component, an instance of JButton is also an instance of Component. To remove a component from a container, use the remove method. The following statement removes the button from the container:

```
container.remove(jbtOK);
```

When you run the program MyFrameWithComponents, the following window will be displayed in Figure 11.5. The button is always centered in the frame and occupies the entire frame no matter how you resize it. This is because components are put in the frame by the content pane's layout manager, and the default layout manager for the content pane places the button in the center. In the next section, you will use several different layout managers to place components in other locations as desired.

11.4.3   Centering a Frame (Optional)

By default, a frame is displayed in the upper-left corner of the screen. The coordinates at the upper-left corner of the screen are (0, 0). The *x* coordinate increases rightward, and the

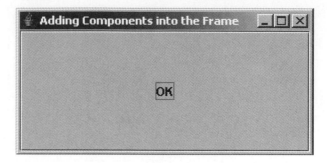

FIGURE **11.5**   *An OK button is added to the frame.*

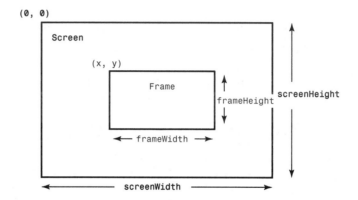

FIGURE **11.6**   *The frame is centered on the screen.*

y coordinate increases downward. To display a frame at a specified location, use the setLocation(x, y) method in the JFrame class. This method places the upper-left corner of the frame at location (x, y) on the screen.

To center a frame on the screen, you need to know the width and height of the screen and the frame in order to determine the frame's upper-left coordinates. The screen's width and height can be obtained using the java.awt.Toolkit class:

```
Dimension screenSize = Toolkit.getDefaultToolkit().getScreenSize();
int screenWidth = screenSize.width;
int screenHeight = screenSize.height;
```

Therefore, as shown in Figure 11.6, the upper-left x and y coordinates of the centered frame frame are:

```
// Locate the upper-left corner (x, y) of the centered frame
int x = (screenWidth - frame.getWidth()) / 2;
int y = (screenHeight - frame.getHeight()) / 2;
```

The java.awt.Dimension class encapsulates the width and height of a component (in integer precision) in a single object. The methods getWidth() and getHeight() are defined in the Component class. You can apply these methods to get the width and height of any component.

Listing 11.3 displays a frame centered on the screen.

LISTING **11.3**   **CenterFrame.java (Centering a Frame)**

```
1 import javax.swing.*;
2 import java.awt.*;
3
```

```
 4 public class CenterFrame {
 5   public static void main(String[] args) {
 6     JFrame frame = new JFrame("CenterFrame");
 7     frame.setSize(400, 300);
 8     frame.setDefaultCloseOperation(JFrame.EXIT_ON_CLOSE);
 9
10     // Get the dimension of the screen
11     Dimension screenSize =
12       Toolkit.getDefaultToolkit().getScreenSize();
13     int screenWidth = screenSize.width;
14     int screenHeight = screenSize.height;
15
16     // Locate the upper-left corner (x, y) of the centered frame
17     int x = (screenWidth - frame.getWidth()) / 2;
18     int y = (screenHeight - frame.getHeight()) / 2;
19
20     // Set the location of the frame
21     frame.setLocation(x, y);
22     frame.setVisible(true);
23   }
24 }
```

11.5   Layout Managers

In many other window systems, the user-interface components are arranged by using hard-coded pixel measurements. For example, put a button at location (10, 10) in the window. Using hard-coded pixel measurements, the user interface might look fine on one system but be unusable on another. Java's layout managers provide a level of abstraction that automatically maps your user interface on all window systems.

 NOTE

Java also supports hard-coded fixed layout, which will be covered in Chapter 22, "Containers, Layout Managers, and Borders." Since it is platform-dependent, it is rarely used in practice.

The Java GUI components are placed in containers, where they are arranged by the container's layout manager. In the preceding program, you did not specify where to place the OK button in the frame, but Java knows where to place it because the layout manager works behind the scenes to place components in the correct locations. A layout manager is created using a layout manager class. Every layout manager class implements the LayoutManager interface.

Layout managers are set in containers using the setLayout(LayoutManager) method. For example, you can use the following statements to create an instance of XLayout and set it in a container:

```
LayoutManager layoutManager = new XLayout();
container.setLayout(layoutManager);
```

This section introduces three basic layout managers: FlowLayout, GridLayout, and BorderLayout. More layout managers will be introduced in Chapter 22, "Containers, Layout Managers, and Borders."

11.5.1   FlowLayout

FlowLayout is the simplest layout manager. The components are arranged in the container from left to right in the order in which they were added. When one row is filled, a new row is started. You can specify the way the components are aligned by using one of three constants:

`FlowLayout.RIGHT`, `FlowLayout.CENTER`, or `FlowLayout.LEFT`. You can also specify the gap between components in pixels. `FlowLayout` has three constructors:

✦ `public FlowLayout(int align, int hGap, int vGap)`

   Constructs a new `FlowLayout` with the specified alignment, horizontal gap, and vertical gap. The gaps are the distances in pixels between components.

✦ `public FlowLayout(int alignment)`

   Constructs a new `FlowLayout` with a specified alignment and a default gap of 5 pixels horizontally and vertically.

✦ `public FlowLayout()`

   Constructs a new `FlowLayout` with a default center alignment and a default gap of 5 pixels horizontally and vertically.

EXAMPLE 11.1 TESTING THE `FlowLayout` MANAGER

Problem

Write a program that adds ten buttons labeled `Component 1`, ..., and `Component 10` into the content pane of a frame with a `FlowLayout` manager, as shown in Figure 11.7.

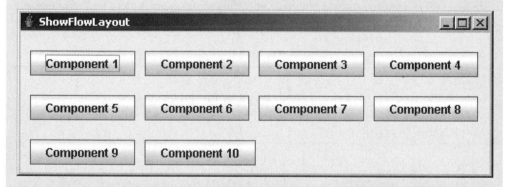

FIGURE **11.7** *The components are added with the `FlowLayout` manager to fill in the rows in the container one after another.*

Solution

Create a subclass of `JFrame`, set the layout manager of the content pane to a `FlowLayout`, and add ten buttons into the content pane using a loop.

LISTING **11.4**   ShowFlowLayout.java (Using `FlowLayout`)

```
1 import javax.swing.JButton;
2 import javax.swing.JFrame;
3 import java.awt.Container;
4 import java.awt.FlowLayout;
5
6 public class ShowFlowLayout extends JFrame {
7   public ShowFlowLayout() {
```

EXAMPLE 11.1 (CONTINUED)

```
8      // Get the content pane of the frame
9      Container container = getContentPane();                          contentPane
10
11     // Set FlowLayout, aligned left with horizontal gap 10
12     // and vertical gap 20 between components
13     container.setLayout(new FlowLayout(FlowLayout.LEFT, 10, 20));     set layout
14
15     // Add buttons to the frame
16     for (int i = 1; i <= 10; i++)
17       container.add(new JButton("Component " + i));                   add buttons
18   }
19
20   /** Main method */
21   public static void main(String[] args) {
22     ShowFlowLayout frame = new ShowFlowLayout();
23     frame.setTitle("ShowFlowLayout");                                 create frame
24     frame.setDefaultCloseOperation(JFrame.EXIT_ON_CLOSE);
25     frame.setSize(200, 200);
26     frame.setVisible(true);                                           set visible
27   }
28 }
```

Review

This example creates a program using a style different from the programs in the preceding section, where frames were created using the JFrame class. This example creates a class named ShowFlowLayout that extends the JFrame class (Line 6). The main method in this program creates an instance of ShowFlowLayout (Line 22). The constructor of ShowFlowLayout constructs and places the components in the frame. This is the preferred style of creating GUI applications for two reasons: (1) creating a GUI application means creating a frame, so it is natural to define a frame to extend JFrame; (2) the new class can be reused if desirable. Using one style consistently makes programs easy to read. From now on, all the GUI main classes will extend the JFrame class. The constructor of the main class constructs the user interface. The main method creates an instance of the main class and then displays the frame.

In this example, the FlowLayout manager is used to place components in a frame. If you resize the frame, the components are automatically rearranged to fit in it.

If you replace the setLayout statement (Line 13) with setLayout(newFlowLayout (FlowLayout.RIGHT, 0, 0)), all the rows of buttons will be right-aligned with no gaps.

An anonymous FlowLayout object was created in the statement (Line 13):

```
container.setLayout(new FlowLayout(FlowLayout.LEFT, 10, 20));
```

which is equivalent to:

```
FlowLayout layout = new FlowLayout(FlowLayout.LEFT, 10, 20);
container.setLayout(layout);
```

This code creates an explicit reference to the object layout of the FlowLayout class. The explicit reference is not necessary, because the object is not directly referenced in the ShowFlowLayout class.

The setTitle method (Line 23) is defined in the java.awt.Frame class. Since JFrame is a subclass of Frame, you can use it to set a title for an object of JFrame.

Suppose you add the same button into the container ten times, will ten buttons appear in the container? No, only the last one will be displayed.

CAUTION

Do not forget to put the `new` operator before a layout manager class when setting a layout style; for example, `setLayout(new FlowLayout())`.

 NOTE

The constructor `ShowFlowLayout()` does not explicitly invoke the constructor `JFrame()`, but the constructor `JFrame()` is invoked implicitly. See Section 8.3.2, "Constructor Chaining".

11.5.2 GridLayout

The `GridLayout` manager arranges components in a grid (matrix) formation with the number of rows and columns defined by the constructor. The components are placed in the grid from left to right, starting with the first row, then the second, and so on, in the order in which they are added. The `GridLayout` manager has three constructors:

✦ `public GridLayout(int rows, int columns, int hGap, int vGap)`

Constructs a new `GridLayout` with the specified number of rows and columns, along with specified horizontal and vertical gaps between components in the container.

✦ `public GridLayout(int rows, int columns)`

Constructs a new `GridLayout` with the specified number of rows and columns. The horizontal and vertical gaps are zero.

✦ `public GridLayout()`

Constructs a new `GridLayout` with one row.

You can specify the number of rows and columns in the grid. The basic rule is as follows:

✦ The number of rows or the number of columns can be zero, but not both. If one is zero and the other is nonzero, the nonzero dimension is fixed, while the zero dimension is determined dynamically by the layout manager. For example, if you specify zero rows and three columns for a grid that has ten components, `GridLayout` creates three fixed columns of four rows, with the last row containing one component. If you specify three rows and zero columns for a grid that has ten components, `GridLayout` creates three fixed rows of four columns, with the last row containing two components.

✦ If both the number of rows and the number of columns are nonzero, the number of rows is the dominating parameter; that is, the number of rows is fixed, and the layout manager dynamically calculates the number of columns. For example, if you specify three rows and three columns for a grid that has ten components, `GridLayout` creates three fixed rows of four columns, with the last row containing two components.

EXAMPLE 11.2 TESTING THE `GridLayout` MANAGER

Problem

Write a program that adds ten buttons labeled `Component 1`, ..., and `Component 10` into the content pane of a frame with a `GridLayout` manager, as shown in Figure 11.8.

EXAMPLE 11.2 (CONTINUED)

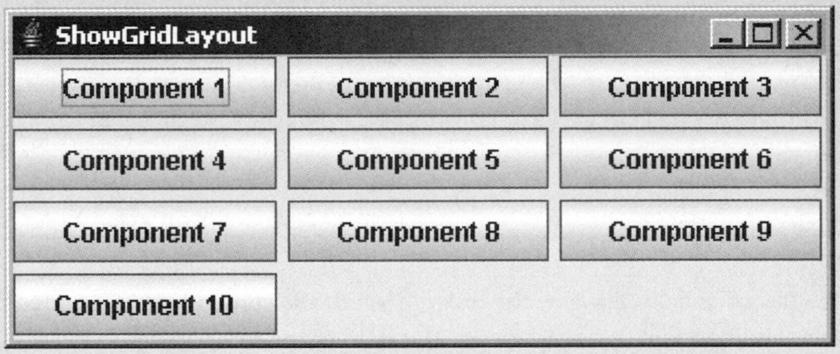

FIGURE **11.8**   *The* GridLayout *manager divides the container into grids, then the components are added to fill in the cells row by row.*

Solution

Create a subclass of JFrame, set the layout manager of the content pane to a GridLayout with four rows and three columns, and add ten buttons into the content pane using a loop.

LISTING 11.5   ShowGridLayout.java (Using GridLayout)

```
 1 import javax.swing.JButton;
 2 import javax.swing.JFrame;
 3 import java.awt.GridLayout;
 4 import java.awt.Container;
 5
 6 public class ShowGridLayout extends JFrame {
 7   public ShowGridLayout() {
 8     // Get the content pane of the frame
 9     Container container = getContentPane();                   contentPane
10
11     // Set GridLayout, 4 rows, 3 columns, and gaps 5 between
12     // components horizontally and vertically
13     container.setLayout(new GridLayout(4, 3, 5, 5));          set layout
14
15     // Add buttons to the frame
16     for (int i = 1; i <= 10; i++)
17       container.add(new JButton("Component " + i));           add buttons
18   }
19
20   /** Main method */
21   public static void main(String[] args) {
22     ShowGridLayout frame = new ShowGridLayout();
23     frame.setTitle("ShowGridLayout");
24     frame.setDefaultCloseOperation(JFrame.EXIT_ON_CLOSE);
25     frame.setSize(200, 200);
26     frame.setVisible(true);
27   }
28 }
```

Review

If you resize the frame, the layout of the buttons remains unchanged (i.e., the number of rows and columns does not change, and the gaps don't change either).

All components are given equal size in the container of GridLayout.

Replacing the setLayout statement (Line 13) with setLayout(new GridLayout(3, 10)) would yield three rows and *four* columns, with the last row containing two

EXAMPLE 11.2 (CONTINUED)

components. The columns parameter is ignored because the rows parameter is nonzero. The actual number of columns is calculated by the layout manager.

What would happen if the `setLayout` statement (Line 13) is replaced with `setLayout(new GridLayout(3, 2))` or with `setLayout(new GridLayout(2, 2))`? Please try it yourself.

 NOTE

In `FlowLayout` and `GridLayout`, the order in which the components are added to the container is important. It determines the location of the components in the container.

11.5.3   BorderLayout

The `BorderLayout` manager divides the window into five areas: East, South, West, North, and Center. Components are added to a `BorderLayout` by using `add(Component, index)`, where index is a constant `BorderLayout.EAST`, `BorderLayout.SOUTH`, `BorderLayout.WEST`, `BorderLayout.NORTH`, or `BorderLayout.CENTER`. You can use one of the following two constructors to create a new `BorderLayout`:

◆   `public BorderLayout(int hGap, int vGap)`

Constructs a new `BorderLayout` with the specified horizontal and vertical gaps between the components.

◆   `public BorderLayout()`

Constructs a new `BorderLayout` without horizontal or vertical gaps.

The components are laid out according to their preferred sizes and where they are placed in the container. The North and South components can stretch horizontally; the East and West components can stretch vertically; the Center component can stretch both horizontally and vertically to fill any empty space.

EXAMPLE 11.3 TESTING THE BorderLayout MANAGER

Problem

Write a program that adds five buttons labeled `East`, `South`, `West`, `North`, and `Center` into the content pane of a frame with a `BorderLayout` manager, as shown in Figure 11.9.

FIGURE 11.9   *BorderLayout divides the container into five areas, each of which can hold a component.*

EXAMPLE 11.3 (CONTINUED)

Solution

Create a subclass of JFrame, set the layout manager of the content pane to a BorderLayout, and add five buttons into the content pane.

LISTING 11.6   ShowBorderLayout.java (Using BorderLayout)

```
 1 import javax.swing.JButton;
 2 import javax.swing.JFrame;
 3 import java.awt.Container;
 4 import java.awt.BorderLayout;
 5
 6 public class ShowBorderLayout extends JFrame {
 7   public ShowBorderLayout() {
 8     // Get the content pane of the frame
 9     Container container = getContentPane();                              contentPane
10
11     // Set BorderLayout with horizontal gap 5 and vertical gap 10
12     container.setLayout(new BorderLayout(5, 10));                        set layout
13
14     // Add buttons to the frame
15     container.add(new JButton("East"), BorderLayout.EAST);              add buttons
16     container.add(new JButton("South"), BorderLayout.SOUTH);
17     container.add(new JButton("West"), BorderLayout.WEST);
18     container.add(new JButton("North"), BorderLayout.NORTH);
19     container.add(new JButton("Center"), BorderLayout.CENTER);
20   }
21
22   /** Main method */
23   public static void main(String[] args) {
24     ShowBorderLayout frame = new ShowBorderLayout();
25     frame.setTitle("ShowBorderLayout");
26     frame.setDefaultCloseOperation(JFrame.EXIT_ON_CLOSE);
27     frame.setSize(300, 200);
28     frame.setVisible(true);
29   }
30 }
```

Review

The buttons are added to the frame (Lines 15-19). Note that the **add** method for BorderLayout is different from the one for FlowLayout and GridLayout. With BorderLayout you specify where to put the components.

It is unnecessary to place components to occupy all the areas. If you remove the East button from the program and rerun it, you will see that the center stretches rightward to occupy the East area.

NOTE

For convenience, BorderLayout interprets the absence of an index specification as BorderLayout.CENTER. For example, add(component) is the same as add(Component, BorderLayout.CENTER). If you add two components into a container of BorderLayout, as follows,

```
    container.add(component1);
    container.add(component2);
```

only the last component is displayed.

JDK 1.5 Feature

 TIP
You can use a new JDK 1.5 feature to directly import static constants from a class. The imported constants can be referenced without specifying a class. For example, you can use EAST, instead of BorderLayout.EAST, if you have the following import statement in the class:

```
import static java.awt.BorderLayout.*;
```

11.5.4   Properties of Layout Managers (Optional)

Layout managers have properties that can be changed dynamically. FlowLayout has alignment, hGap, and vGap properties. You can use the setAlignment, setHGap, and setVGap methods to specify the alignment and the horizontal and vertical gaps. GridLayout has the rows, columns, hGap, and vGap properties. You can use the setRows, setColumns, setHGap, and setVGap methods to specify the number of rows, the number of columns, and the horizontal and vertical gaps. BorderLayout has the hGap and vGap properties. You can use the setHGap and setVGap methods to specify the horizontal and vertical gaps.

In the preceding sections, an anonymous layout manager is used because the properties of a layout manager do not change once it is created. If you have to change the properties of a layout manager dynamically, the layout manager must be explicitly referenced by a variable. You can then change the properties of the layout manager through the variable. For example, the following code creates a layout manager and sets its properties:

```
// Create a layout manager
FlowLayout flowLayout = new FlowLayout();

// Set layout properties
flowLayout.setAlignment(FlowLayout.RIGHT);
flowLayout.setHGap(10);
flowLayout.setVGap(20);
```

11.5.5   The validate and doLayout Methods (Optional)

validate()

doLayout()

A container can have only one layout manager at a time. You can change its layout manager by using the setLayout(aNewLayout) method and then use the validate() method to force the container to again layout the components in the container using the new layout manager.

If you use the same layout manager but change its properties, you need to use the doLayout() method to force the container to re-layout the components using the new properties of the layout manager.

11.6   The Color Class

You can set colors for GUI components by using the java.awt.Color class. Colors are made of red, green, and blue components, each of which is represented by a byte value that describes its intensity, ranging from 0 (darkest shade) to 255 (lightest shade). This is known as the *RGB model*.

You can create a color using the following constructor:

```
public Color(int r, int g, int b);
```

in which r, g, and b specify a color by its red, green, and blue components. For example,

```
Color color = new Color(128, 100, 100);
```

You can use the `setBackground(Color c)` and `setForeground(Color c)` methods defined in the `java.awt.Component` class to set a component's background and foreground colors. Here is an example of setting the background of a panel using a color:

```
JButton jbtOK = new JButton();
jbtOK.setBackground(color);
jbtOK.setForeground(new Color(100, 1, 1));
```

Alternatively, you can use one of the thirteen standard colors (`black`, `blue`, `cyan`, `darkGray`, `gray`, `green`, `lightGray`, `magenta`, `orange`, `pink`, `red`, `white`, `yellow`) defined as constants in `java.awt.Color`. The following code, for instance, sets the background color of a panel to yellow:

```
jbtOK.setForeground(Color.red);
```

color constants

 NOTE

The standard color names are constants, but they are named as variables with low-ercase for the first word and uppercase for the first letters of subsequent words. Thus the color names violate the Java naming convention. Since JDK 1.4, you can also use the new constants BLACK, BLUE, CYAN, DARK_GRAY, GRAY, GREEN, LIGHT_GRAY, MAGENTA, ORANGE, PINK, RED, WHITE, and YELLOW.

11.7 The Font Class

You can create a font using the `java.awt.Font` class and set fonts for the components using the `setFont` method in the `Component` class.

The constructor for `Font` is:

```
public Font(String name, int style, int size);
```

You can choose a font name from `SansSerif`, `Serif`, `Monospaced`, `Dialog`, or `DialogInput`, choose a style from `Font.PLAIN` (0), `Font.BOLD` (1), `Font.ITALIC` (2), and `Font.BOLD + Font.ITALIC` (3), and specify a font size of any positive integer. For example, the following statements create two fonts and set one font to a button:

```
Font font1 = new Font("SansSerif", Font.BOLD, 16);
Font font2 = new Font("Serif", Font.BOLD + Font.ITALIC, 12);

JButton jbtOK = new JButton("OK");
jbtOK.setFont(font1);
```

 TIP (OPTIONAL)

If your system supports other fonts, such as "Times New Roman," you can use it to create a `Font` object. To find the fonts available on your system, you need to create an instance of `java.awt.GraphicsEnvironment` using its static method `getLocalGraphicsEnvironment()`. `GraphicsEnvironment` is an abstract class that describes the graphics environment on a particular system. You can use its `getAllFonts()` method to obtain all the available fonts on the system, and its `getAvailableFontFamilyNames()` method to obtain the names of all the available fonts. For example, the following statements print all the available font names in the system:

```
GraphicsEnvironment e =
  GraphicsEnvironment.getLocalGraphicsEnvironment();
String[] fontnames = e.getAvailableFontFamilyNames();

for (int i = 0; i < fontnames.length; i++)
  System.out.println(fontnames[i]);
```

find available fonts

11.8 Using Panels as Subcontainers

Suppose that you want to place ten buttons and a text field on a frame. The buttons are placed in grid formation, but the text field is placed on a separate row. It is difficult to achieve the desired look by placing all the components in a single container. With Java GUI programming, you can divide a window into panels. Panels act as subcontainers to group user-interface components. You add the buttons in one panel, and then add the panel into the frame.

The Swing version of panel is `JPanel`. You can use `new JPanel()` to create a panel with a default `FlowLayout` manager or `new JPanel(LayoutManager)` to create a panel with the specified layout manager. Use the `add(Component)` method to add a component to the panel. For example, the following code creates a panel and adds a button to it:

```
JPanel p = new JPanel();
p.add(new JButton("OK"));
```

Panels can be placed inside a frame or inside another panel. The following statement places panel p into frame f:

```
f.getContentPane().add(p);
```

 NOTE

To add a component to `JFrame`, you actually add it to the content pane of `JFrame`. To add a component to a panel, you add it directly to the panel using the `add` method.

EXAMPLE 11.4 TESTING PANELS

Problem

Write a program that uses panels to organize components. The program creates a user interface for a microwave oven, as shown in Figure 11.10.

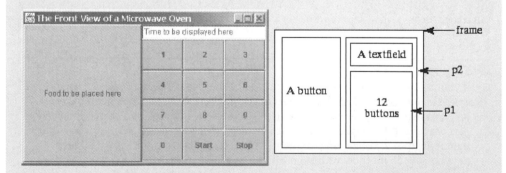

FIGURE **11.10** *The program uses panels to organize components.*

Solution

The program is given in Listing 11.7.

EXAMPLE **11.4** (CONTINUED)

LISTING 11.7   **TestPanels.java (Using Panels as Subcontainers)**

```
1 import java.awt.*;
2 import javax.swing.*;
3
4 public class TestPanels extends JFrame {
5   public TestPanels() {
6     // Get the content pane of the frame
7     Container container = getContentPane();
8
9     // Set BorderLayout for the frame
10    container.setLayout(new BorderLayout());
11
12    // Create panel p1 for the buttons and set GridLayout
13    JPanel p1 = new JPanel();
14    p1.setLayout(new GridLayout(4, 3));
15
16    // Add buttons to the panel
17    for (int i = 1; i <= 9; i++) {
18      p1.add(new JButton("" + i));
19    }
20
21    p1.add(new JButton("" + 0));
22    p1.add(new JButton("Start"));
23    p1.add(new JButton("Stop"));
24
25    // Create panel p2 to hold a text field and p1
26    JPanel p2 = new JPanel(new BorderLayout());
27    p2.add(new JTextField("Time to be displayed here"),
28      BorderLayout.NORTH);
29    p2.add(p1, BorderLayout.CENTER);
30
31    // Add p2 and a button to the frame
32    container.add(p2, BorderLayout.EAST);
33    container.add(new JButton("Food to be placed here"),
34      BorderLayout.CENTER);
35  }
36
37  /** Main method */
38  public static void main(String[] args) {
39    TestPanels frame = new TestPanels();
40    frame.setTitle("The Front View of a Microwave Oven");
41    frame.setDefaultCloseOperation(JFrame.EXIT_ON_CLOSE);
42    frame.setSize(400, 250);
43    frame.setVisible(true);
44  }
45 }
```

panel p1

panel p2

Review

The setLayout method is defined in java.awt.Container. Since JPanel is a subclass of Container, you can use setLayout to set a new layout manager in the panel (Line 14). Lines 13–14 can be replaced by JPanel p1 = new JPanel(new GridLayout(4, 3)).

To achieve the desired layout, the program uses panel p1 of GridLayout to group the number buttons, the Stop button, and the Start button, and panel p2 of BorderLayout to hold a text field in the north and p1 in the center. The button representing the food is placed in the center of the frame, and p2 is placed in the east of the frame.

The statement (Lines 27–28)

```
p2.add(new JTextField("Time to be displayed here"),
  BorderLayout.NORTH);
```

creates an instance of JTextField and adds it to p2.

Text field is a GUI component that can be used for user input as well as to display values. More detail on using text fields will be introduced in Chapter 13, "Creating User Interfaces."

11.9   Drawing Graphics on Panels

Panels are invisible and are used as small containers that group components to achieve a desired layout. Another important use of JPanel is for drawing.

To draw in a JPanel, you create a new class that extends JPanel and overrides the paintComponent method to tell the panel how to draw things. Although you can draw things directly in a frame or an applet using the paint method, it is better to use JPanel to draw strings and shapes and to show images; this way your drawing will not interfere with other components.

The paintComponent method is defined in JComponent, and its signature is as follows:

```
protected void paintComponent(Graphics g)
```

The Graphics object g is created automatically by the JVM for every visible GUI component. This object controls how information is drawn. You can use various drawing methods defined in the Graphics class to draw strings and geometric figures. For example, you can draw a string using the following method in the Graphics class:

```
public void drawString(String string, int x, int y)
```

The program given in Listing 11.8 draws the message "Welcome to Java" on the panel, as shown in Figure 11.11.

LISTING 11.8   DrawMessage.java (Using Panels as Canvases)

```
 1 import javax.swing.*;
 2 import java.awt.*;
 3
 4 public class DrawMessage extends JPanel {
 5   /** Main method */
 6   public static void main(String[] args) {
 7     JFrame frame = new JFrame("DrawMessage");
 8     frame.getContentPane().add(new DrawMessage());
 9     frame.setDefaultCloseOperation(JFrame.EXIT_ON_CLOSE);
10     frame.setSize(300, 200);
11     frame.setVisible(true);
12   }
13
14   /** Paint the message */
15   protected void paintComponent(Graphics g) {
16     super.paintComponent(g);
17
18     g.drawString("Welcome to Java!", 40, 40);
19   }
20 }
```

override paintComponent

draw string

All the drawing methods have parameters that specify the locations of the subjects to be drawn. All measurements in Java are made in pixels. Each component has its own coordinate system with the origin (0, 0) at the upper-left corner of the component. The x coordinate increases to the right, and the y coordinate increases downward. Note that the Java coordinate system is different from the traditional coordinate system, as shown in Figure 11.12.

FIGURE **11.11**   *The message is drawn on a panel, and the panel is placed inside the frame.*

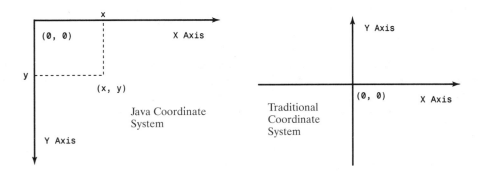

FIGURE **11.12**   *The Java graphics coordinate system is measured in pixels, with* (0, 0) *at its upper-left corner.*

 NOTE

The Graphics class is an abstract class that provides a device-independent graphics interface for displaying figures and images on the screen on different platforms. The Graphics class is implemented on the native platform in the JVM. When you use the paintComponent method to draw things in a graphics context g, this g is an instance of a concrete subclass of the abstract Graphics class for the specific platform. The Graphics class encapsulates the platform details and enables you to draw things uniformly without having to be concerned about the specific platform.

Graphics class

 NOTE

Whenever a component is displayed, a Graphics object is created for it. The Swing components use the paintComponent method to draw things. The paintComponent method is automatically invoked to paint the graphics context when the component is first displayed or whenever the component needs to be redisplayed. Invoking super.paintComponent(g) is necessary to ensure that the viewing area is cleared before a new drawing is displayed. The user can request the component to be redisplayed by invoking the repaint() method defined in the Component class. Invoking repaint() causes paintComponent to be invoked by the JVM. The user should never invoke paintComponent directly. For this reason, the protected visibility is sufficient for paintComponent.

repaint()

 NOTE

To draw things, normally you create a subclass of JPanel and override its paintComponent method to tell the system how to draw. In fact, you can draw things on any GUI component. See Exercise 11.6 for a custom button class that displays a figure instead of a text in the button.

You can not only draw strings, but also lines, rectangles, ovals, arcs, polygons, and polylines.

11.9.1 Drawing Lines

You can use the method shown below to draw a straight line:

```
drawLine(int x1, int y1, int x2, int y2);
```

The parameters x1, y1, x2, and y2 represent the starting point (x1, y1) and the ending point (x2, y2) of the line, as shown in Figure 11.13.

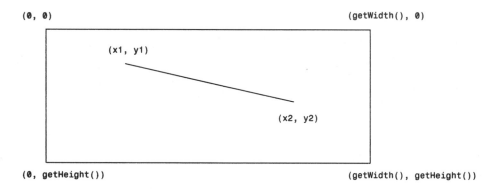

FIGURE **11.13** *The* `drawLine` *method draws a line between two specified points.*

11.9.2 Drawing Rectangles

Java provides six methods for drawing rectangles in outline or filled with color. You can draw plain rectangles, rounded rectangles, or three-dimensional rectangles.

To draw a plain rectangle, use the following code:

```
drawRect(int x, int y, int w, int h);
```

To draw a rectangle filled with color, use:

```
fillRect(int x, int y, int w, int h);
```

The parameters x and y represent the upper-left corner of the rectangle, and w and h are its width and height (see Figure 11.14).

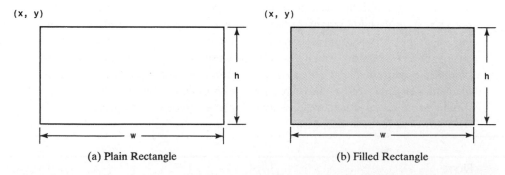

(a) Plain Rectangle   (b) Filled Rectangle

FIGURE **11.14** *The* `drawRect` *method draws a rectangle with specified upper-left corner* `(x, y)`, *width, and height.*

To draw a rounded rectangle, use the following method:

```
drawRoundRect(int x, int y, int w, int h, int aw, int ah);
```

To draw a rounded rectangle filled with color, use this method:

```
fillRoundRect(int x, int y, int w, int h, int aw, int ah);
```

Parameters x, y, w, and h are the same as in the drawRect method, parameter aw is the horizontal diameter of the arcs at the corner, and ah is the vertical diameter of the arcs at the corner (see Figure 11.15). In other words, aw and ah are the width and the height of the oval that produces a quarter-circle at each corner.

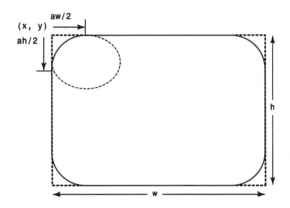

FIGURE 11.15 *The drawRoundRect method draws a rounded rectangle.*

To draw a 3D rectangle, use

```
draw3DRect(int x, int y, int w, int h, int raised);
```

in which x, y, w, and h are the same as in the drawRect method. The last parameter, a Boolean value, indicates whether the rectangle is raised above the surface or etched into the surface.

The example given in Listing 11.9 demonstrates these methods. The output is shown in Figure 11.16.

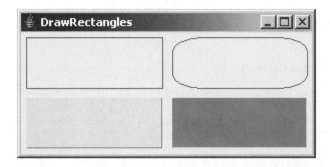

FIGURE 11.16 *The program draws a rectangle, a rounded rectangle, a raised 3D rectangle, and a plain 3D rectangle.*

LISTING 11.9   DrawRectangles.java (Drawing Rectangles)

add a panel

override paintComponent

```
 1 import java.awt.Graphics;
 2 import java.awt.Color;
 3 import javax.swing.JPanel;
 4 import javax.swing.JFrame;
 5
 6 public class DrawRectangles extends JFrame {
 7   public DrawRectangles() {
 8     setTitle("DrawRectangles");
 9     getContentPane().add(new RectPanel());
10   }
11
12   /** Main method */
13   public static void main(String[] args) {
14     DrawRectangles frame = new DrawRectangles();
15     frame.setDefaultCloseOperation(JFrame.EXIT_ON_CLOSE);
16     frame.setSize(300, 250);
17     frame.setVisible(true);
18   }
19 }
20
21 class RectPanel extends JPanel {
22   protected void paintComponent(Graphics g) {
23     super.paintComponent(g);
24
25     // Set new color
26     g.setColor(Color.red);
27
28     // Draw a rectangle
29     g.drawRect(5, 5, getWidth() / 2 - 10, getHeight() / 2 - 10);
30
31     // Draw a rounded rectangle
32     g.drawRoundRect(getWidth() / 2 + 5, 5,
33       getWidth() / 2 - 10, getHeight() / 2 - 10, 60, 30);
34
35     // Change the color to cyan
36     g.setColor(Color.cyan);
37
38     // Draw a 3D rectangle
39     g.fill3DRect(5, getHeight() / 2 + 5, getWidth() / 2 - 10,
40       getHeight() / 2 - 10, true);
41
42     // Draw a raised 3D rectangle
43     g.fill3DRect(getWidth() / 2 + 5, getHeight() / 2 + 5,
44       getWidth() / 2 - 10, getHeight() / 2 - 10, false);
45   }
46 }
```

🌴 **NOTE**

You can draw things using appropriate colors and fonts using the `setColor` method and `setFont` method in the `Graphics` class.

11.9.3   Drawing Ovals

Depending on whether you wish to draw an oval in outline or filled solid, you can use either the `drawOval` method or the `fillOval` method. Since an oval in Java is drawn based on its bounding rectangle, give the parameters as if you were drawing a rectangle.

Here is the method for drawing an oval:

```
drawOval(int x, int y, int w, int h);
```

To draw a filled oval, use the following method:

```
fillOval(int x, int y, int w, int h);
```

Parameters x and y indicate the top-left corner of the bounding rectangle, and w and h indicate the width and height, respectively, of the bounding rectangle, as shown in Figure 11.17(a).

Listing 11.10 is an example of how to draw ovals, with the output in Figure 11.17(b).

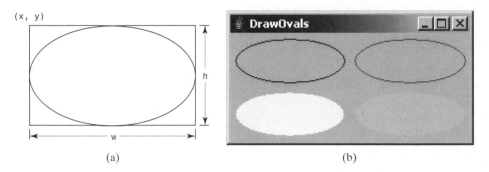

(a)   (b)

FIGURE 11.17   *(a) The* drawOval *method draws an oval based on its bounding rectangle. (b) The DrawOvals program draws four ovals.*

LISTING **11.10**   DrawOvals.java (Drawing Ovals)

```
 1 import javax.swing.JFrame;
 2 import javax.swing.JPanel;
 3 import java.awt.Color;
 4 import java.awt.Graphics;
 5
 6 public class DrawOvals extends JFrame {
 7   public DrawOvals() {
 8     setTitle("DrawOvals");
 9     getContentPane().add(new OvalsPanel());          add a panel
10   }
11
12   /** Main method */
13   public static void main(String[] args) {
14     DrawOvals frame = new DrawOvals();
15     frame.setDefaultCloseOperation(JFrame.EXIT_ON_CLOSE);
16     frame.setSize(250, 250);
17     frame.setVisible(true);
18   }
19 }
20
21 // The class for drawing the ovals on a panel
22 class OvalsPanel extends JPanel {
23   protected void paintComponent(Graphics g) {        override paintComponent
24     super.paintComponent(g);
25
26     g.drawOval(5, 5, getWidth() / 2 - 10, getHeight() / 2 - 10);
27     g.setColor(Color.red);
28     g.drawOval(getWidth() / 2 + 5, 5, getWidth() / 2 - 10,
29       getHeight() / 2 - 10);
30     g.setColor(Color.yellow);
31     g.fillOval(5, getHeight() / 2 + 5, getWidth() / 2 - 10,
32       getHeight() / 2 - 10);
33     g.setColor(Color.orange);
```

```
34      g.fillOval(getWidth() / 2 + 5, getHeight() / 2 + 5,
35        getWidth() / 2 - 10, getHeight() / 2 - 10);
36    }
37 }
```

11.9.4 Drawing Arcs

An arc is conceived as part of an oval. Like an oval, an arc is drawn based on its bounding rectangle. The methods to draw or fill an arc are as follows:

```
drawArc(int x, int y, int w, int h, int startAngle, int arcAngle);
fillArc(int x, int y, int w, int h, int startAngle, int arcAngle);
```

Parameters x, y, w, and h are the same as in the drawOval method; parameter startAngle is the starting angle; arcAngle is the spanning angle (i.e., the angle covered by the arc). Angles are measured in degrees and follow the usual mathematical conventions (i.e., 0 degrees is in the easterly direction), and positive angles indicate counterclockwise rotation from the easterly direction; see Figure 11.18.

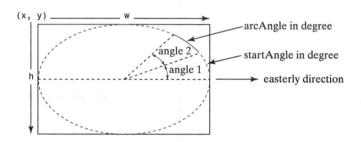

FIGURE 11.18 *The drawArc method draws an arc based on an oval with specified angles.*

Listing 11.11 is an example of how to draw arcs; the output is shown in Figure 11.19.

LISTING 11.11 DrawArcs.java (Drawing Arcs)

```
1 import javax.swing.JFrame;
2 import javax.swing.JPanel;
3 import java.awt.Graphics;
4
5 public class DrawArcs extends JFrame {
6   public DrawArcs() {
7     setTitle("DrawArcs");
8     getContentPane().add(new ArcsPanel());
9   }
10
11   /** Main method */
12   public static void main(String[] args) {
13     DrawArcs frame = new DrawArcs();
14     frame.setDefaultCloseOperation(JFrame.EXIT_ON_CLOSE);
15     frame.setSize(250, 300);
16     frame.setVisible(true);
17   }
18 }
19
20 // The class for drawing arcs on a panel
21 class ArcsPanel extends JPanel {
22   // Draw four blazes of a fan
23   protected void paintComponent(Graphics g) {
24     super.paintComponent(g);
25
```

add a panel

override paintComponent

```
26      int xCenter = getWidth() / 2;
27      int yCenter = getHeight() / 2;
28      int radius =
29        (int)(Math.min(getWidth(), getHeight()) * 0.4);
30
31      int x = xCenter - radius;
32      int y = yCenter - radius;
33
34      g.fillArc(x, y, 2 * radius, 2 * radius, 0, 30);
35      g.fillArc(x, y, 2 * radius, 2 * radius, 90, 30);
36      g.fillArc(x, y, 2 * radius, 2 * radius, 180, 30);
37      g.fillArc(x, y, 2 * radius, 2 * radius, 270, 30);
38    }
39 }
```

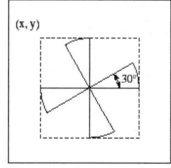

FIGURE 11.19   *The program draws four filled arcs.*

11.9.5   The `Polygon` class and Drawing Polygons and Polylines

The `Polygon` class encapsulates a description of a closed two-dimensional region within a coordinate space. This region is bounded by an arbitrary number of line segments, each of which is one side (or edge) of the polygon. Internally, a polygon comprises a list of (x, y) coordinate pairs in which each pair defines a vertex of the polygon, and two successive pairs are the endpoints of a line that is a side of the polygon. The first and final pairs of (x, y) points are joined by a line segment that closes the polygon.

The two constructors given below are used to create a `Polygon` object.

✦ `public Polygon()`

Constructs an empty polygon.

✦ `Polygon(int[] xpoints, int[] ypoints, int npoints)`

Constructs and initializes a `Polygon` with specified points. Parameters `xpoints` and `ypoints` are arrays representing x-coordinates and y-coordinates, and `npoints` indicates the number of points.

To append a point to the polygon, use the `addPoint(int x, int y)` method. The `Polygon` class has the public data fields `xpoints`, `ypoints`, and `npoints`, which represent the array of x-coordinates and y-coordinates, and the total number of points.

Here is an example of creating a polygon and adding points into it:

```
Polygon polygon = new Polygon();
polygon.addPoint(40, 20);
polygon.addPoint(70, 40);
polygon.addPoint(60, 80);
polygon.addPoint(45, 45);
polygon.addPoint(20, 60);
```

To draw or fill a polygon, use one of the following methods:

```
drawPolygon(Polygon polygon);
```

```
fillPolygon(Polygon polygon);
```

```
drawPolygon(int[] xpoints, int[] ypoints, int npoints);
```

```
fillPolygon(int[] xpoints, int[] ypoints, int npoints);
```

For example:

```
int x[] = {40, 70, 60, 45, 20};
int y[] = {20, 40, 80, 45, 60};
g.drawPolygon(x, y, x.length);
```

The drawing method opens the polygon by drawing lines between point (x[i], y[i]) and point (x[i+1], y[i+1]) for i = 0, ... , x.length - 1; it closes the polygon by drawing a line between the first and last points (see Figure 11.20(a)).

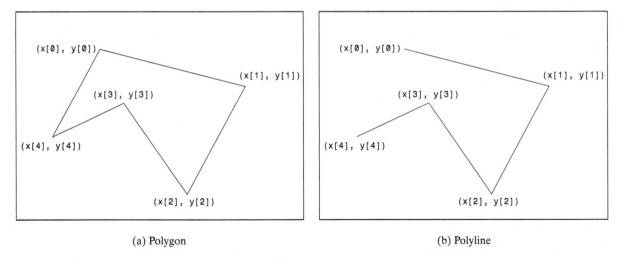

(a) Polygon   (b) Polyline

FIGURE 11.20 *The drawPolygon method draws a polygon, and the polyLine method draws a polyline.*

To draw a polyline, use the drawPolyline(int[] x, int[] y, int nPoints) method, which draws a sequence of connected lines defined by arrays of x and y coordinates. For example, the following code draws the polyline shown in Figure 11.20(b):

```
int x[] = {40, 70, 60, 45, 20};
int y[] = {20, 40, 80, 45, 60};
g.drawPolygon(x, y, x.length);
```

Listing 11.12 is an example of how to draw a hexagon, with the output shown in Figure 11.21.

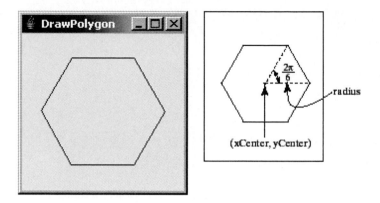

FIGURE 11.21   *The program uses the* drawPolygon *method to draw a polygon.*

LISTING **11.12**   DrawPolygon.java (Drawing Polygons)

```
1 import javax.swing.JFrame;
2 import javax.swing.JPanel;
3 import java.awt.Graphics;
4 import java.awt.Polygon;
5
6 public class DrawPolygon extends JFrame {
7   public DrawPolygon() {
8     setTitle("DrawPolygon");
9     getContentPane().add(new PolygonsPanel());                          add a panel
10   }
11
12   /** Main method */
13   public static void main(String[] args) {
14     DrawPolygon frame = new DrawPolygon();
15     frame.setDefaultCloseOperation(JFrame.EXIT_ON_CLOSE);
16     frame.setSize(200, 250);
17     frame.setVisible(true);
18   }
19 }
20
21 // Draw a polygon in the panel
22 class PolygonsPanel extends JPanel {
23   protected void paintComponent(Graphics g) {                          override paintComponent
24     super.paintComponent(g);
25
26     int xCenter = getWidth() / 2;
27     int yCenter = getHeight() / 2;
28     int radius =
29       (int)(Math.min(getWidth(), getHeight()) * 0.4);
30
31     // Create a Polygon object
32     Polygon polygon = new Polygon();
33
34     // Add points to the polygon
35     polygon.addPoint(xCenter + radius, yCenter);
36     polygon.addPoint((int)(xCenter + radius *
37       Math.cos(2 * Math.PI / 6)), (int)(yCenter - radius *
38       Math.sin(2 * Math.PI / 6)));
39     polygon.addPoint((int)(xCenter + radius *
40       Math.cos(2 * 2 * Math.PI / 6)), (int)(yCenter - radius *
41       Math.sin(2 * 2 * Math.PI / 6)));
42     polygon.addPoint((int)(xCenter + radius *
43       Math.cos(3 * 2 * Math.PI / 6)), (int)(yCenter - radius *
44       Math.sin(3 * 2 * Math.PI / 6)));
45     polygon.addPoint((int)(xCenter + radius *
46       Math.cos(4 * 2 * Math.PI / 6)), (int)(yCenter - radius *
47       Math.sin(4 * 2 * Math.PI / 6)));
```

```
48      polygon.addPoint((int)(xCenter + radius *
49        Math.cos(5 * 2 * Math.PI / 6)), (int)(yCenter - radius *
50        Math.sin(5 * 2 * Math.PI / 6)));
51
52      // Draw the polygon
53      g.drawPolygon(polygon);
54    }
55  }
```

11.10 Centering a Display Using the **FontMetrics** Class

You can display a string at any location in a panel. Can you display it centered? To do so, you need to use the FontMetrics class to measure the exact width and height of the string for a particular font. FontMetrics can measure the following attributes (see Figure 11.22):

✦ **Leading,** pronounced *ledding*, is the amount of space between lines of text.

✦ **Ascent** is the height of a character, from the baseline to the top.

✦ **Descent** is the distance from the baseline to the bottom of a descending character, such as *j*, *y*, and *g*.

✦ **Height** is the sum of leading, ascent, and descent.

FIGURE 11.22 *The FontMetrics class can be used to determine the font properties of characters.*

FontMetrics is an abstract class. To get a FontMetrics object for a specific font, use the following getFontMetrics methods defined in the Graphics class:

✦ **public FontMetrics getFontMetrics(Font font)**

Returns the font metrics of the specified font.

✦ **public FontMetrics getFontMetrics()**

Returns the font metrics of the current font.

You can use the following instance methods in the FontMetrics class to obtain the attributes of a font and the width of a string when it is drawn using the font:

```
public int getAscent() // Return the ascent
public int getDescent() // Return the descent
public int getLeading() // Return the leading
public int getHeight() // Return the hight
public int stringWidth(String str) // Return the width of the sting
```

Now you can modify the DrawMessage class to display a message in the center of the panel, as shown in Figure 11.23.

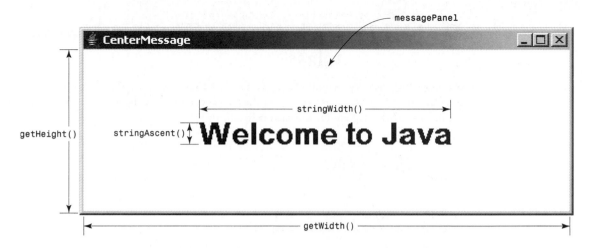

FIGURE 11.23 *The program uses the* FontMetrics *class to measure the string width and height, and displays it at the center of the frame.*

LISTING 11.13 **CenterMessage.java (Centering a Message)**

```
 1 import javax.swing.*;
 2 import java.awt.*;
 3
 4 public class CenterMessage extends JPanel {
 5   /** Main method */
 6   public static void main(String[] args) {
 7     JFrame frame = new JFrame("CenterMessage");
 8     CenterMessage m = new CenterMessage();                       a message panel
 9     m.setBackground(Color.white);                                set background
10     m.setFont(new Font("Californian FB", Font.BOLD, 30));        set font
11     frame.getContentPane().add(m);
12     frame.setDefaultCloseOperation(JFrame.EXIT_ON_CLOSE);
13     frame.setSize(300, 200);
14     frame.setVisible(true);
15   }
16
17   /** Paint the message */
18   protected void paintComponent(Graphics g) {                   override paintComponent
19     super.paintComponent(g);
20
21     // Get font metrics for the current font
22     FontMetrics fm = g.getFontMetrics();                        get FontMetrics
23
24     // Find the center location to display
25     int stringWidth = fm.stringWidth("Welcome to Java");
26     int stringAscent = fm.getAscent();
27
28     // Get the position of the leftmost character in the baseline
29     int xCoordinate = getWidth() / 2 - stringWidth / 2;
30     int yCoordinate = getHeight() / 2 + stringAscent / 2;
31
32     g.drawString("Welcome to Java", xCoordinate, yCoordinate);
33   }
34 }
```

The methods getWidth() and getHeight(), defined in the Component class, return the component's width and height, respectively.

yCoordinate is the height of the baseline for the first character of the string to be displayed. When centered is true, yCoordinate should be getHeight() / 2 + stringAscent / 2.

xCoordinate is the width of the baseline for the first character of the string to be displayed. When centered is true, xCoordinate should be getWidth() / 2 - stringWidth / 2.

✺ 11.11   CASE STUDY: The MessagePanel Class

This case study develops a useful class that displays a message in a panel. The class enables the user to set the location of the message, center the message, and move the message with the specified interval. The UML diagram for the class is shown in Figure 11.24.

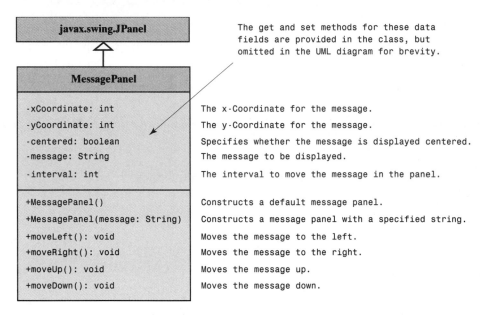

The get and set methods for these data fields are provided in the class, but omitted in the UML diagram for brevity.

The x-Coordinate for the message.

The y-Coordinate for the message.

Specifies whether the message is displayed centered.

The message to be displayed.

The interval to move the message in the panel.

Constructs a default message panel.

Constructs a message panel with a specified string.

Moves the message to the left.

Moves the message to the right.

Moves the message up.

Moves the message down.

FIGURE 11.24   *MessagePanel displays a message on the panel.*

The UML diagram serves as the contract for the MessagePanel class. The user can use the class without knowing how the class is implemented. Let us begin by writing a program in Listing 11.14 that uses the class to display four message panels, as shown in Figure 11.25.

LISTING 11.14   TestMessagePanel.java (Using MessagePanel)

```
1  import java.awt.*;
2  import javax.swing.*;
3
4  public class TestMessagePanel extends JFrame {
5    public TestMessagePanel() {
6      MessagePanel messagePanel1 = new MessagePanel("Wecome to Java");
7      MessagePanel messagePanel2 = new MessagePanel("Java is fun");
8      MessagePanel messagePanel3 = new MessagePanel("Java is cool");
9      MessagePanel messagePanel4 = new MessagePanel("I love Java");
10     messagePanel1.setFont(new Font("SansSerif", Font.ITALIC, 20));
11     messagePanel2.setFont(new Font("Courier", Font.BOLD, 20));
12     messagePanel3.setFont(new Font("Times", Font.ITALIC, 20));
13     messagePanel4.setFont(new Font("Californian FB", Font.PLAIN, 20));
14     messagePanel1.setBackground(Color.red);
15     messagePanel2.setBackground(Color.cyan);
16     messagePanel3.setBackground(Color.green);
17     messagePanel4.setBackground(Color.white);
18     messagePanel1.setCentered(true);
19
20     getContentPane().setLayout(new GridLayout(2, 2));
21     getContentPane().add(messagePanel1);
22     getContentPane().add(messagePanel2);
```

create message panel

set font

set background

add message panel

```
23      getContentPane().add(messagePanel3);
24      getContentPane().add(messagePanel4);
25    }
26
27    public static void main(String[] args) {
28      TestMessagePanel frame = new TestMessagePanel();
29      frame.setSize(300, 200);
30      frame.setTitle("TestMessagePanel");
31      frame.setDefaultCloseOperation(JFrame.EXIT_ON_CLOSE);
32      frame.setVisible(true);
33    }
34 }
```

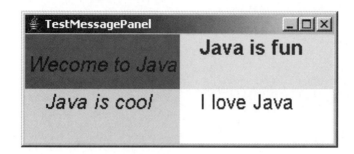

FIGURE 11.25   *TestMessagePanel uses* MessagePanel *to display four message panels.*

The MessagePanel class is implemented in Listing 11.15. The program seems long but is actually simple, because most of the methods are get and set methods, and each method is relatively short and easy to read.

LISTING **11.15**   MessagePanel.java (The MessagePanel Class)

```
 1 import java.awt.Font;
 2 import java.awt.FontMetrics;
 3 import java.awt.Dimension;
 4 import java.awt.Graphics;
 5 import javax.swing.JPanel;
 6
 7 public class MessagePanel extends JPanel {
 8   /** The message to be displayed */
 9   private String message = "Welcome to Java";
10
11   /** The x coordinate where the message is displayed */
12   private int xCoordinate = 20;
13
14   /** The y coordinate where the message is displayed */
15   private int yCoordinate = 20;
16
17   /** Indicate whether the message is displayed in the center */
18   private boolean centered;
19
20   /** The interval for moving the message horizontally and vertically */
21   private int interval = 10;
22
23   /** Construct with default properties */
24   public MessagePanel() {
25   }
26
27   /** Construct a message panel with a specified message */
28   public MessagePanel(String message) {
29     this.message = message;
30   }
31
32   /** Return message */
33   public String getMessage() {
```

```
34    return message;
35  }
36
37  /** Set a new message */
38  public void setMessage(String message) {
39    this.message = message;
40    repaint();
41  }
42
43  /** Return xCoordinator */
44  public int getXCoordinate() {
45    return xCoordinate;
46  }
47
48  /** Set a new xCoordinator */
49  public void setXCoordinate(int x) {
50    this.xCoordinate = x;
51    repaint();
52  }
53
54  /** Return yCoordinator */
55  public int getYCoordinate() {
56    return yCoordinate;
57  }
58
59  /** Set a new yCoordinator */
60  public void setYCoordinate(int y) {
61    this.yCoordinate = y;
62    repaint();
63  }
64
65  /** Return centered */
66  public boolean isCentered() {
67    return centered;
68  }
69
70  /** Set a new centered */
71  public void setCentered(boolean centered) {
72    this.centered = centered;
73    repaint();
74  }
75
76  /** Return interval */
77  public int getInterval() {
78    return interval;
79  }
80
81  /** Set a new interval */
82  public void setInterval(int interval) {
83    this.interval = interval;
84    repaint();
85  }
86
87  /** Paint the message */
88  protected void paintComponent(Graphics g) {
89    super.paintComponent(g);
90
91    if (centered) {
92      // Get font metrics for the current font
93      FontMetrics fm = g.getFontMetrics();
94
95      // Find the center location to display
96      int stringWidth = fm.stringWidth(message);
97      int stringAscent = fm.getAscent();
98      // Get the position of the leftmost character in the baseline
99      xCoordinate = getWidth() / 2 - stringWidth / 2;
100     yCoordinate = getHeight() / 2 + stringAscent / 2;
101   }
102
```

override paintComponent

```
103        g.drawString(message, xCoordinate, yCoordinate);
104      }
105
106      /** Move the message left */
107      public void moveLeft() {
108        xCoordinate -= interval;
109        repaint();
110      }
111
112      /** Move the message right */
113      public void moveRight() {
114        xCoordinate += interval;
115        repaint();
116      }
117
118      /** Move the message up */
119      public void moveUp() {
120        yCoordinate -= interval;
121        repaint();
122      }
123
124      /** Move the message down */
125      public void moveDown() {
126        yCoordinate += interval;
127        repaint();
128      }
129
130      /** Override get method for preferredSize */              override getPreferredSize
131      public Dimension getPreferredSize() {
132        return new Dimension(200, 30);
133      }
134    }
```

The getPreferredSize() method (Lines 131–133), defined in Component, is overridden in MessagePanel to specify the preferred size for the layout manager to consider when laying out a MessagePanel object. This property may or may not be considered by the layout manager, depending on its rules. For example, a component uses its preferred size in a container with a FlowLayout manager, but its preferred size may be ignored if it is placed in a container with a GridLayout manager.

The repaint method is defined in the Component class. Invoking repaint causes the paintComponent method to be called. The repaint method is invoked to refresh the viewing area. Typically, you call it if you have new things to display.

 CAUTION

The paintComponent method should never be invoked directly. It is invoked either by the JVM whenever the viewing area changes or by the repaint method. You should override the paintComponent method to tell the system how to paint the viewing area, but never override the repaint method.

don't invoke
paintComponent

 NOTE

The repaint method lodges a request to update the viewing area and returns immediately. Its effect is asynchronous, and if several requests are outstanding, it is likely that only the last paintComponent will be done.

request repaint using
repaint()

 CAUTION

The MessagePanel class uses the properties xCoordinate and yCoordinate to specify the position of the message displayed on the panel. Do not use the property names x and y, because they are already defined in the Component class to specify the position of the component in the parent's coordinate system.

 NOTE

The Component class has the setBackground, setForeground, and setFont methods. These methods are for setting colors and fonts for the entire component. Suppose you want to draw several messages in a panel with different colors and fonts; you have to use the setColor and setFont methods in the Graphics class to set the color and font for the current drawing.

---

design classes for reuse

 NOTE

One of the key features of Java programming is the reuse of classes. Throughout the book, you will develop reusable classes and later reuse them. MessagePanel is an example of this. It can be reused whenever you need to display a message on a panel. To make your class reusable in a wide range of applications, you should provide a variety of ways to use it. MessagePanel provides many properties and methods that will be used in several examples in the book.

✦ 11.12 Case Study: The StillClock Class (Optional)

This case study develops a class that displays a clock in a panel. The contract of the class is shown in Figure 11.26.

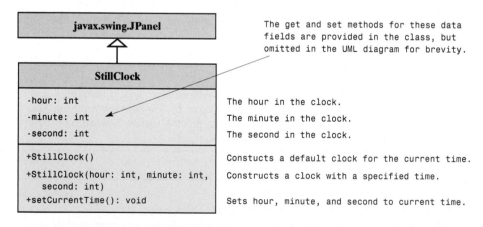

FIGURE 11.26 *StillClock displays an analog clock.*

Let us first write a test program in Listing 11.16 that uses the StillClock class to display an analog clock and the MessagePanel class to display the hour, minute, and second in a panel, as shown in Figure 11.26.

LISTING **11.16**   DisplayClock.java (Using StillClock)

```
1 import java.awt.*;
2 import javax.swing.*;
3 import java.util.*;
4
5 public class DisplayClock extends JFrame {
6   public DisplayClock() {
7     // Create an analog clock for the current time
8     StillClock clock = new StillClock();                                    create a clock
9
10    // Display hour, minute, and hour in the message panel
11    MessagePanel messagePanel = new MessagePanel(clock.getHour() +          create a message panel
12      ":" + clock.getMinute() + ":" + clock.getSecond());
13    messagePanel.setCentered(true);
14    messagePanel.setForeground(Color.blue);
15    messagePanel.setFont(new Font("Courier", Font.BOLD, 16));
16
17    // Add the clock and message panel to the frame
18    getContentPane().add(clock);                                            add a clock
19    getContentPane().add(messagePanel, BorderLayout.SOUTH);                 add a message panel
20  }
21
22  public static void main(String[] args) {
23    DisplayClock frame = new DisplayClock();
24    frame.setTitle("DisplayClock");
25    frame.setDefaultCloseOperation(JFrame.EXIT_ON_CLOSE);
26    frame.setSize(300, 350);
27    frame.setVisible(true);
28  }
29 }
```

Now we turn our attention to implementing the StillClock class. To draw a clock, you need to draw a circle and three hands for second, minute, and hour. To draw a hand, you need to specify the two ends of the line. As shown in Figure 11.27(a), one end is the center of the clock at (xCenter, yCenter); the other end, at (xEnd, yEnd), is determined by the following formula:

```
xEnd = xCenter + handLength × sin(θ)
yEnd = yCenter - handLength × cos(θ)
```

Since there are sixty seconds in one minute, the angle for the second hand is

```
second × (2π/60)
```

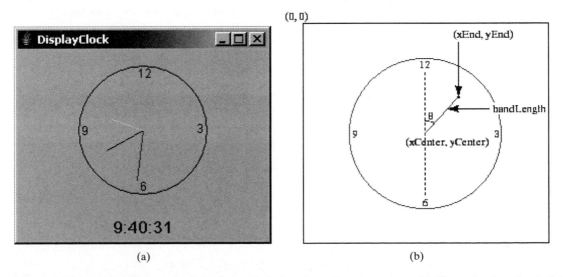

(a)   (b)

FIGURE **11.27**   *(a) The DisplayClock program displays a clock that shows the current time. (b) The end point of a clock hand can be determined given the spanning angle, the hand length, and the center point.*

The position of the minute hand is determined by the minute and second. The exact minute value combined with seconds is `minute + second/60`. For example, if the time is 3 minutes and 30 seconds, the total minutes are 3.5. Since there are sixty minutes in one hour, the angle for the minute hand is

```
(minute + second/60) × (2π/60)
```

Since one circle is divided into twelve hours, the angle for the hour hand is

```
(hour + minute/60 + second/(60 × 60))) × (2π/12)
```

For simplicity, you can omit the seconds in computing the angles of the minute hand and the hour hand, because they are very small and can be neglected. Therefore, the end points for the second hand, minute hand, and hour hand can be computed as:

```
xSecond = xCenter + secondHandLength × sin(second × (2π/60))
ySecond = yCenter - secondHandLength × cos(second × (2π/60))
xMinute = xCenter + minuteHandLength × sin(minute × (2π/60))
yMinute = yCenter - minuteHandLength × cos(minute × (2π/60))
xHour = xCenter + hourHandLength × sin((hour + minute/60) × (2π/60)))
yHour = yCenter - hourHandLength × cos((hour + minute/60) × (2π/60)))
```

The `StillClock` class is implemented in Listing 11.17.

LISTING 11.17 StillClock.java (Displaying a Still Clock)

```
1 import java.awt.*;
2 import javax.swing.*;
3 import java.util.*;
4
5 public class StillClock extends JPanel {
6   private int hour;
7   private int minute;
8   private int second;
9
10   /** Construct a default clock with the current time*/
11   public StillClock() {
12     setCurrentTime();
13   }
14
15   /** Construct a clock with specified hour, minute, and second */
16   public StillClock(int hour, int minute, int second) {
17     this.hour = hour;
18     this.minute = minute;
19     this.second = second;
20   }
21
22   /** Return hour */
23   public int getHour() {
24     return hour;
25   }
26
27   /** Set a new hour */
28   public void setHour(int hour) {
29     this.hour = hour;
30     repaint();
31   }
32
33   /** Return minute */
34   public int getMinute() {
35     return minute;
36   }
37
38   /** Set a new minute */
39   public void setMinute(int minute) {
40     this.minute = minute;
```

```
41      repaint();
42    }
43
44    /** Return second */
45    public int getSecond() {
46      return second;
47    }
48
49    /** Set a new second */
50    public void setSecond(int second) {
51      this.second = second;
52      repaint();
53    }
54
55    /** Draw the clock */
56    protected void paintComponent(Graphics g) {
57      super.paintComponent(g);
58
59      // Initialize clock parameters
60      int clockRadius =
61        (int)(Math.min(getWidth(), getHeight()) * 0.8 * 0.5);
62      int xCenter = getWidth() / 2;
63      int yCenter = getHeight() / 2;
64
65      // Draw circle
66      g.setColor(Color.black);
67      g.drawOval(xCenter - clockRadius, yCenter - clockRadius,
68        2 * clockRadius, 2 * clockRadius);
69      g.drawString("12", xCenter - 5, yCenter - clockRadius + 12);
70      g.drawString("9", xCenter - clockRadius + 3, yCenter + 5);
71      g.drawString("3", xCenter + clockRadius - 10, yCenter + 3);
72      g.drawString("6", xCenter - 3, yCenter + clockRadius - 3);
73
74      // Draw second hand
75      int sLength = (int)(clockRadius * 0.8);
76      int xSecond = (int)(xCenter + sLength *
77        Math.sin(second * (2 * Math.PI / 60)));
78      int ySecond = (int)(yCenter - sLength *
79        Math.cos(second * (2 * Math.PI / 60)));
80      g.setColor(Color.red);
81      g.drawLine(xCenter, yCenter, xSecond, ySecond);
82
83      // Draw minute hand
84      int mLength = (int)(clockRadius * 0.65);
85      int xMinute = (int)(xCenter + mLength *
86        Math.sin(minute * (2 * Math.PI / 60)));
87      int yMinute = (int)(yCenter - mLength *
88        Math.cos(minute * (2 * Math.PI / 60)));
89      g.setColor(Color.blue);
90      g.drawLine(xCenter, yCenter, xMinute, yMinute);
91
92      // Draw hour hand
93      int hLength = (int)(clockRadius * 0.5);
94      int xHour = (int)(xCenter + hLength *
95        Math.sin((hour % 12 + minute / 60.0) * (2 * Math.PI / 12)));
96      int yHour = (int)(yCenter - hLength *
97        Math.cos((hour % 12 + minute / 60.0) * (2 * Math.PI / 12)));
98      g.setColor(Color.green);
99      g.drawLine(xCenter, yCenter, xHour, yHour);
100   }
101
102   public void setCurrentTime() {
103     // Construct a calendar for the current date and time
104     Calendar calendar = new GregorianCalendar();
105
106     // Set current hour, minute and second
107     this.hour = calendar.get(Calendar.HOUR_OF_DAY);
108     this.minute = calendar.get(Calendar.MINUTE);
109     this.second = calendar.get(Calendar.SECOND);
110   }
111
```

override paintComponent

get current time

override getPreferredSize

```
112    public Dimension getPreferredSize() {
113      return new Dimension(200, 200);
114    }
115  }
```

The program enables the clock size to adjust as the frame resizes. Every time you resize the frame, the `paintComponent` method is automatically invoked to paint the new frame. The `paintComponent` method displays the clock in proportion to the panel width (`getWidth()`) and height (`getHeight()`) (Lines 60–63 in `StillClock`).

🌿 **NOTE**

Like the `MessagePanel` class, the `StillClock` class is an example of a reusable class. `StillClock` will be used throughout the book. `StillClock` provides many properties and methods that enable it to be used in a wide range of applications.

KEY CLASSES AND METHODS

✦ **java.awt.Component** is the root class for GUI components.

✦ **java.awt.Container** is the root class for all container classes. The container classes (e.g., JFrame, JPanel, JApplet) are used to contain other GUI components.

✦ **javax.swing.JFrame** is a class for creating a frame as a top-level container.

✦ **javax.swing.JComponent** is the root class for Swing GUI components such as JButton, JLabel, JTextField, and JPanel.

✦ **java.awt.FlowLayout** is the flow layout manager for a container. In a container with FlowLayout, the components are arranged from left to right in the order in which they were added. When one row is filled, a new row is started.

✦ **java.awt.GridLayout** is the grid layout manager for a container. The GridLayout manager arranges components in a grid (matrix) formation with the number of rows and columns defined by the constructor. The components are placed in the grid from left to right, starting with the first row, then the second, and so on, in the order in which they are added.

✦ **java.awt.BorderLayout** is the border layout manager for a container. The BorderLayout manager divides the window into five areas: East, South, West, North, and Center. Components are added to a BorderLayout by using add(Component,index), where index is a constant BorderLayout.EAST, BorderLayout.SOUTH, BorderLayout.WEST, BorderLayout.NORTH, or BorderLayout.CENTER.

✦ **javax.swing.JPanel** is a class for holding components or for displaying drawings.

✦ **java.awt.Color** is a class for specifying a color.

✦ **java.awt.Font** is a class for specifying a font. To set a font, you need to create a Font object from the Font class. The syntax is Font myFont = new Font(name, style, size).

✦ **java.awt.FontMetrics** is a class for measuring font properties: leading, ascent, descent, and height. Leading is the amount of space between lines of text. Ascent is the height of a character, from the baseline to the top. Descent is the distance from the baseline to the bottom of a descending character, such as *j*, *y*, and *g*. Height is the sum of leading, ascent, and descent.

✦ **java.awt.Dimension** is a class for measuring the dimensions of a GUI component.

✦ **java.awt.Graphics** is a class for drawing strings and geometrical figures.

CHAPTER SUMMARY

✦ Each container uses a layout manager to position and place components in a container in the desired location. Three simple and useful layout managers are `FlowLayout`, `GridLayout`, and `BorderLayout`.

✦ Panels are invisible and are used as small containers that group components to achieve a desired layout. Another important use of `JPanel` is for drawing. To draw in a `JPanel`, you create a new class that extends `JPanel` and overrides the `paintComponent` method to tell the panel how to draw things.

✦ To add components to a `JFrame`, you need to add them into the `JFrame`'s content pane. You can add components directly into a `JPanel`. By default, the content pane's layout is `BorderLayout`, and the `JPanel`'s layout is `FlowLayout`.

✦ The `paintComponent` method is defined in `JComponent`, and its signature is `protected void paintComponent(Graphics g)`. The `Graphics` object g is created automatically by the JVM for every visible GUI component. This object controls how information is drawn. You can use various drawing methods defined in the `Graphics` class to draw figures.

✦ The `Graphics` class is an abstract class for displaying figures and images on the screen on different platforms. The `Graphics` class is implemented on the native platform in the JVM. When you use the `paintComponent` method to draw things on a graphics context g, this g is an instance of a concrete subclass of the abstract `Graphics` class for the specific platform. The `Graphics` class encapsulates the platform details and enables you to draw things uniformly without concern for the specific platform.

✦ Invoking `super.paintComponent(g)` is necessary to ensure that the viewing area is cleared before a new drawing is displayed. The user can request the component to be redisplayed by invoking the `repaint()` method defined in the `Component` class. Invoking `repaint()` causes `paintComponent` to be invoked by the JVM. The user should never invoke `paintComponent` directly. For this reason, the protected visibility is sufficient for `paint-Component`.

✦ Each component has its own coordinate system with the origin (`0, 0`) at the upper-left corner of the window. The x coordinate increases to the right, and the y coordinate increases downward.

✦ You can set colors for GUI components by using the `java.awt.Color` class. Colors are made of red, green, and blue components, each of which is represented by a byte value that describes its intensity, ranging from 0 (darkest shade) to 255 (lightest shade). This is known as the *RGB model*.

✦ The syntax to create a `Color` object is `Color color = new Color(r, g, b)`, in which r, g, and b specify a color by its red, green, and blue components. Alternatively, you can use one of the thirteen standard colors (`black`, `blue`, `cyan`, `darkGray`, `gray`, `green`, `lightGray`, `magenta`, `orange`, `pink`, `red`, `white`, `yellow`) defined as constants in `java.awt.Color`.

✦ You can use the `setBackground(Color c)` and `setForeground(Color c)` methods defined in the `Component` class to set a component's background and foreground colors.

✦ You can set fonts for the components or subjects you draw, and use font metrics to measure font size. Fonts and font metrics are encapsulated in the classes `Font` and `FontMetrics`. `FontMetrics` can be used to compute the exact length and width of a string, which is helpful for measuring the size of a string in order to display it in the right position.

◆ The Component class has the setBackground, setForeground, and setFont methods. These methods are used to set colors and fonts for the entire component. Suppose you want to draw several messages in a panel with different colors and fonts; you have to use the setColor and setFont methods in the Graphics class to set the color and font for the current drawing.

◆ The method for drawing a string is drawString(string, x, y). To draw a line, use drawLine(x1, y1, x2, y2). To draw a plain rectangle, use drawRect(x, y, w, h). To draw a filled rectangle, use fillRect(x, y, w, h). To draw a rounded rectangle, use drawRoundRect(x, y, w, h, aw, ah). To draw a 3D rectangle, use draw3DRect(x, y, w, h, raised). To draw an oval, use drawOval(x, y, w, h). To draw a filled oval, use fillOval(x, y, w, h). To draw an arc, use drawArc(x, y, w, h, startAngle, arcAngle). To draw a filled arc, use fillArc(x, y, w, h, startAngle, arcAngle). To draw a polygon, use drawPolygon(Polygon polygon) or drawPolygon(int[] xpoints, int[] ypoints, int npoints). To draw a filled polygon, use fillPolygon(Polygon polygon) or fillPolygon(int[] xpoints, int[] ypoints, int npoints).

REVIEW QUESTIONS

Sections 11.3–11.4

11.1 Which class is the root of the Java GUI component classes? Is a container class a subclass of Component? Which class is the root of the Swing GUI component classes? Since a GUI component class such as JButton is a subclass of Container, can you add components into a button?

11.2 Explain the difference between AWT GUI components, such as java.awt.Button, and Swing GUI components, such as javax.swing.JButton.

11.3 How do you create a frame? How do you set the size for a frame? How do you get the size of a frame? How do you add components to a frame? What would happen if the statements frame.setSize(400, 300) and frame.setVisible(true) were swapped in the MyFrameWithComponents class in Section 11.4.2, "Adding Components to a Frame"?

11.4 Determine whether the following statements are true or false:

◆ You can add a button to a frame.

◆ You can add a frame to a panel.

◆ You can add a panel to a frame.

◆ You can add any number of components to a panel, a frame, or an applet.

◆ You can derive a class from JPanel, JFrame, or JApplet.

11.5 The following program is supposed to display a button in a frame, but nothing is displayed. What is the problem?

```
1 public class Test extends javax.swing.JFrame {
2   public Test() {
3     getContentPane().add(new javax.swing.JButton("OK"));
4   }
5
6   public static void main(String[] args) {
7     javax.swing.JFrame frame = new javax.swing.JFrame();
8     frame.setSize(100, 200);
9     frame.setVisible(true);
10  }
11 }
```

11.6 The following program is supposed to display a message on the panel, but nothing is displayed. There are problems in Lines 2 and 14. Identify them.

```
1 public class TestDrawMessage extends javax.swing.JFrame {
2   public void TestDrawMessage() {
3     getContentPane().add(new DrawMessage());
4   }
5
6   public static void main(String[] args) {
7     javax.swing.JFrame frame = new TestDrawMessage();
8     frame.setSize(100, 200);
9     frame.setVisible(true);
10  }
11 }
12
13 class DrawMessage extends javax.swing.JPanel {
14   protected void PaintComponent(java.awt.Graphics g) {
15     super.paintComponent(g);
16     g.drawString("Welcome to Java", 20, 20);
17   }
18 }
```

Section 11.5 Layout Managers

11.7 Why do you need to use layout managers? What is the default layout manager for the content pane of a frame? How do you add a component to a frame?

11.8 Describe FlowLayout. How do you create a FlowLayout manager? How do you add a component to a FlowLayout container? Is there a limit to the number of components that can be added to a FlowLayout container?

11.9 Describe GridLayout. How do you create a GridLayout manager? How do you add a component to a GridLayout container? Is there a limit to the number of components that can be added to a GridLayout container?

11.10 Describe BorderLayout. How do you create a BorderLayout manager? How do you add a component to a BorderLayout container? Can you add multiple components in the same section?

Sections 11.6–11.7

11.11 How do you get and set background color, foreground color, and font for a component? How do you get and set colors and fonts in a graphics context?

11.12 How do you create a color? How do you create a font?

Section 11.8 Using Panels as Subcontainers

11.13 How do you create a panel with a specified layout manager?

11.14 What is the default layout manager for a JPanel? How do you add a component to a JPanel?

11.15 Can you use the setTitle method in a panel? What is the purpose of using a panel?

Section 11.9 Drawing Graphics on Panels

11.16 Suppose that you want to draw a new message below an existing message. Should the x, y coordinate increase or decrease?

11.17 Describe the paintComponent method. Where is it defined? How is it invoked? Can you use the paintComponent method to draw things directly on a frame?

11.18 Describe the methods for drawing lines, rectangles, ovals, arcs, and polygons.

11.19 Write a statement to draw the following shapes:

✦ Draw a thick line from (10, 10) to (70, 30). You can draw several lines next to each other to create the effect of one thick line.

✦ Draw a rectangle of width 100 and height 50 with the upper-left corner at (10, 10).

✦ Draw a rounded rectangle with width 100, height 200, corner horizontal diameter 40, and corner vertical diameter 20.

✦ Draw a circle with radius 30.

✦ Draw an oval with width 50 and height 100.

✦ Draw the upper half of a circle with radius 50.

✦ Draw a polygon connecting the following points: (20, 40), (30, 50), (40, 90), (90, 10), (10, 30).

✦ Draw a 3D cube like the one in Figure 11.28.

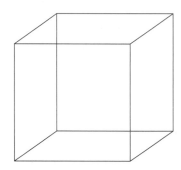

FIGURE 11.28 *Use the drawLine method to draw a 3D cube.*

PROGRAMMING EXERCISES

Section 11.5 Layout Managers

11.1 (*Using the* FlowLayout *manager*) Write a program that meets the following requirements (see Figure 11.29):

✦ Create a frame and set its content pane's layout to FlowLayout.
✦ Create two panels and add them to the frame.
✦ Each panel contains three buttons. The panel uses FlowLayout.

FIGURE 11.29 *Exercise 11.1 places the first three buttons in one panel and the remaining three buttons in another panel.*

11.2 (*Using the* BorderLayout *manager*) Rewrite the preceding program to create the same user interface, but instead of using FlowLayout for the frame's content pane, use BorderLayout. Place one panel in the south of the content pane, and the other panel in the center of the content pane.

11.3   (*Using the* GridLayout *manager*) Rewrite the preceding program to create the same user interface. Instead of using FlowLayout for the panels, use a GridLayout of two rows and three columns.

11.4   (*Creating a subclass of* JPanel *to group buttons*) Rewrite the preceding program to create the same user interface. Instead of creating buttons and panels separately, define a class that extends the JPanel class. Place three buttons in your panel class, and create two panels from the user-defined panel class.

Sections 11.6–11.9

11.5*   (*Displaying a 3 by 3 grid*) Write a program that displays a 3 by 3 grid, as shown in Figure 11.30(a). Use red color for vertical lines and blue color for horizontal lines.

11.6**   (*Creating a custom button class*) Develop a custom button class named OvalButton that extends JButton and displays the button text inside an oval. Figure 11.30(b) shows two buttons created using the OvalButton class.

11.7*   (*Displaying a checker board*) Write a program that displays a checkerboard, as shown in Figure 11.30(c).

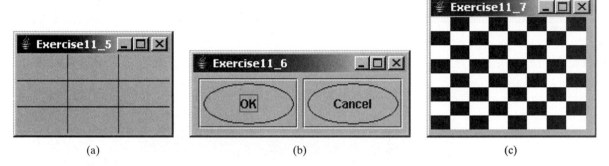

(a)   (b)   (c)

FIGURE **11.30**   *(a) Exercise 11.5 displays a grid. (b) Exercise 11.6 displays two objects of* OvalButton. *(c) Exercise 11.7 displays a checkerboard.*

11.8*   (*Displaying a multiplication table*) Write a program that displays a multiplication table in a panel using the drawing methods, as shown in Figure 11.31(a).

11.9**   (*Displaying numbers in a triangular pattern*) Write a program that displays numbers in a triangular pattern, as shown in Figure 11.31(b). The number of lines in the display changes to fit the window as the window resizes.

11.10**   (*Creating four panels of various shapes*) Write a program that creates four panels using the classes RectPanel, OvalsPanel, ArcsPanel, and PolygonsPanel presented in Section 11.9, "Drawing Graphics on Panels," and places the panels in the content pane of the frame using a GridLayout, as shown in Figure 11.32.

11.11**   (*Displaying a pie chart*) Write a program that uses a pie chart to display the percentages of the overall grade represented by projects, quizzes, midterm exams, and the final exam, as shown in Figure 11.33(a). Suppose that projects take 20 percent and are displayed in red, quizzes take 10 percent and are displayed in blue, midterm exams take 30 percent and are displayed in green, and the final exam takes 40 percent and is displayed in orange.

11.12**   (*Drawing an octagon*) Write a program that draws an octagon, as shown in Figure 11.33(b).

11.13*   (*Creating four fans*) Write a program that places four fans in a frame of GridLayout with two rows and two columns, as shown in Figure 11.34(a).

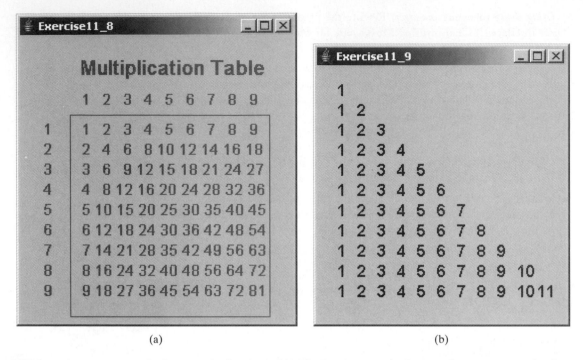

FIGURE 11.31 *(a) Exercise 11.8 displays a multiplication table. (b) Exercise 11.9 displays numbers in a triangular formation.*

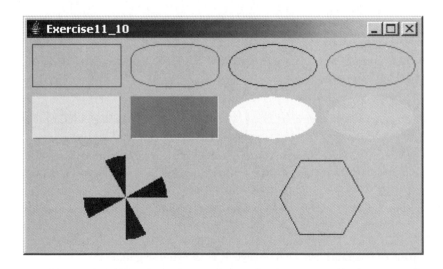

FIGURE 11.32 *Four panels of geometric figures are displayed in a frame of* GridLayout.

Comprehensive

11.14 *(Drawing a detailed clock)* Modify the StillClock class in Section 11.12, "Case Study: The StillClock class," to draw the clock with more details on the hours and minutes, as shown in Figure 11.34(b).

11.15** *(Plotting the square function)* Write a program that draws a diagram for the function $f(x) = x^2$ (see Figure 11.35).

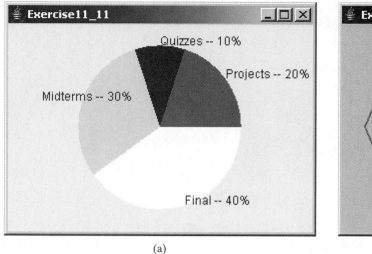
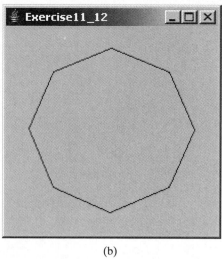

(a)   (b)

FIGURE 11.33   *(a) Exercise 11.11 uses a pie chart to show the percentages of projects, quizzes, midterm exams, and the final exam in the overall grade. (b) Exercise 11.12 draws an octagon.*

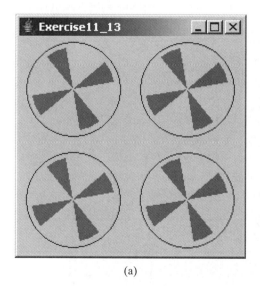
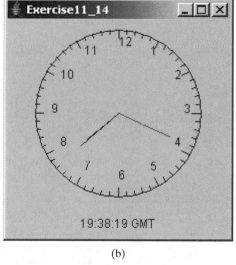

(a)   (b)

FIGURE 11.34   *(a) Exercise 11.13 draws four fans. (b) Exercise 11.14 displays a detailed clock.*

🌸 HINT

Add points to a polygon p using the following loop:

```
double scaleFactor = 0.1;
for (int x = -100; x <= 100; x++) {
  p.addPoint(x + 200, 200 - (int)(scaleFactor * x * x));
}
```

Connect the points using `g.drawPolyline(p.xpoints,p.ypoints, p.npoints)` for a `Graphics` object g. `p.xpoints` returns an array of x coordinates, `p.ypoints` returns an array of y coordinates, and `p.npoints` returns the number of points in `Polygon` object p.

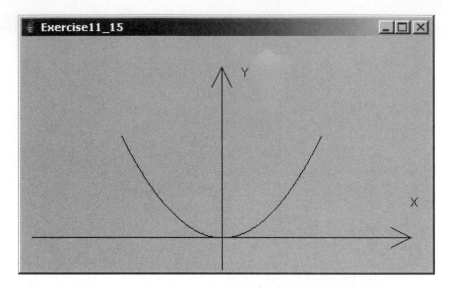

FIGURE 11.35 *Exercise 11.15 draws a diagram for function f(x) = x²*

11.16** (*Plotting the sine function*) Write a program that draws a diagram for the sine function, as shown in Figure 11.36.

🌻 **HINT**

The Unicode for π is \u03c0. To display -2π, use g.drawString ("-2\u03c0", x, y). For a trigonometric function like sin(x), x is in radians. Use the following loop to add the points to a polygon p:

```
for (int x = -100; x <= 100; x++) {
  p.addPoint(x + 200,
    100 - (int)(50 * Math.sin((x / 100.0) * 2 * Math.PI)));
}
```

-2π is at (100, 100), the center of the axis is at (200, 100), and 2π is at (300, 100). Use the drawPolyline method in the Graphics class to connect the points.

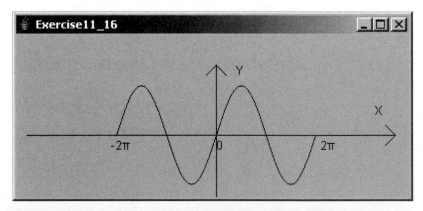

FIGURE 11.36 *Exercise 11.16 draws a diagram for function f(x) = sin(x)*

11.17** (*Plotting functions using generic methods*) Write a generic class that draws the diagram for a function. The class is defined as follows:

```
public abstract class AbstractDrawFunction extends JPanel {
  /** Polygon to hold the points */
  private Polygon p = new Polygon();

  protected AbstractDrawFunction () {
    drawFunction();
  }

  /** Return the y coordinate */
  abstract double f(double x);

  /** Obtain points for x coordinates 100, 101, ..., 300 */
  public void drawFunction() {
    for (int x = -100; x <= 100; x++) {
      p.addPoint(x + 200, 200 - (int)f(x));
    }
  }

  /** Implement paintComponent to draw axes, labels, and
   *  connecting points
   */
  protected void paintComponent(Graphics g) {
    // To be completed by you
  }
}
```

Test the class with the following functions:

```
f(x) = x²;
f(x) = sin(x);
f(x) = cos(x);
f(x) = tan(x);
f(x) = cos(x) + 5sin(x);
f(x) = cos(x) + 5sin(x);
f(x) = log(x) + x²;
```

For each function, create a class that extends the AbstractDrawFunction class and implements the f method. Figure 11.37 displays the drawings for the sine function and the cosine function.

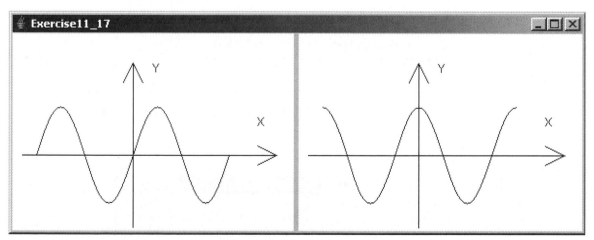

FIGURE 11.37   *Exercise 11.17 draws the sine and cosine functions.*

11.18** (*Displaying a bar chart*) Write a program that uses a bar chart to display the percentages of the overall grade represented by projects, quizzes, midterm exams, and the final exam, as shown in Figure 11.38. Suppose that projects take 20 percent and are displayed in red, quizzes take 10 percent and are displayed in blue, midterm exams take 30 percent and are displayed in green, and the final exam takes 40 percent and is displayed in orange.

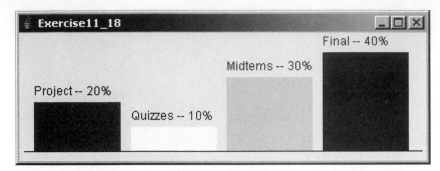

FIGURE 11.38 *Exercise 11.18 uses a bar chart to show the percentages of projects, quizzes, midterm exams, and the final exam in the overall grade.*

11.19 (*Using the* MessagePanel *class*) Write a program that displays four messages, as shown in Figure 11.39(a).

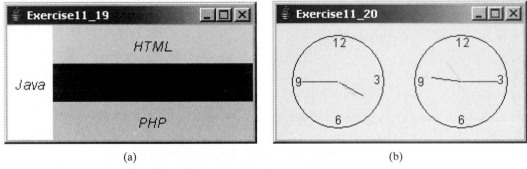

(a)   (b)

FIGURE 11.39 *(a) Exercise 11.19 uses* MessagePanel *to display four strings. (b) Exercise 11.20 displays two clocks.*

11.20 (*Using the* StillClock *class*) Write a program that displays two clocks. The hour, minute, and second values are 4, 20, 45 for the first clock, and 22, 46, 15 for the second clock, as shown in Figure11.39(b).

11.21** (*Displaying a TicTacToe board*) Create a custom panel that displays X, O, or nothing. What to display is randomly decided whenever a panel is repainted. Use the Math.random() method to generate an integer 0, 1, or 2, which corresponds to displaying X, O, or nothing. Create a frame that contains nine custom panels, as shown in Figure 11.40.

FIGURE 11.40 *TicTacToe cells display X, O, or nothing randomly.*

EVENT-DRIVEN PROGRAMMING

Objectives

- ◆ To explain the concept of event-driven programming (§12.2).

- ◆ To understand events, event sources, and event classes (§12.2).

- ◆ To declare listener classes and write the code to handle events (§12.3).

- ◆ To register listener objects in the source object (§12.3).

- ◆ To understand how an event is handled (§12.3).

- ◆ To write programs to deal with ActionEvent (§12.3).

- ◆ To write programs to deal with MouseEvent (§12.4).

- ◆ To write programs to deal with KeyEvent (§12.5).

- ◆ To use the Timer class to control animations (§12.6 Optional).

12.1   Introduction

event-driven programming

All non-GUI programs execute in a procedural order. Java GUI programming is event-driven. In *event-driven programming*, code is executed when an event occurs—a button click, perhaps, or a mouse movement. This chapter introduces the concepts and techniques for Java event-driven programming

12.2   Event and Event Source

event

When you run Java GUI programs, the program interacts with the user and the events drive its execution. An *event* can be defined as a signal to the program that something has happened. Events are triggered either by external user actions, such as mouse movements, button clicks, and keystrokes, or by the operating system, such as a timer. The program can choose to respond to or ignore an event.

source object

The component on which an event is generated is called the *source object*. For example, a button is the source object for a button-clicking action event. An event is an instance of an event class. The root class of the event classes is `java.util.EventObject`. The hierarchical relationships of some event classes are shown in Figure 12.1.

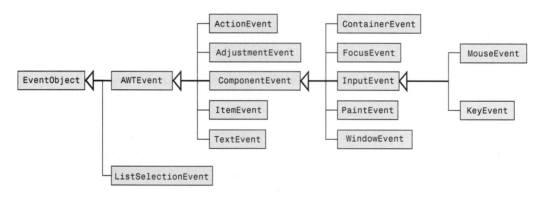

FIGURE 12.1 *An event is an object of the* `EventObject` *class.*

getSource()

An event object contains whatever properties are pertinent to the event. You can identify the source object of an event using the `getSource()` instance method in the `EventObject` class. The subclasses of `EventObject` deal with special types of events, such as action events, window events, component events, mouse movements, and keystrokes. Table 12.1 lists external user actions, source objects, and event types generated.

 NOTE

If a component can generate an event, any subclass of the component can generate the same type of event. For example, every GUI component can generate `MouseEvent`, `KeyEvent`, `FocusEvent`, and `ComponentEvent`, since `Component` is the superclass of all GUI components.

 NOTE

All the event classes in Figure 12.1 are included in the `java.awt.event` package except `ListSelectionEvent`, which is in the `javax.swing.event` package. The AWT events were originally designed for AWT components, but many Swing components fire them.

TABLE 12.1 User Action, Source Object, and Event Type

User action	Source object	Event type generated
Click a button	JButton	ActionEvent
Press return on a text field	JTextField	ActionEvent
Select a new item	JComboBox	ItemEvent, ActionEvent
Select item(s)	JList	ListSelectionEvent
Click a check box	JCheckBox	ItemEvent, ActionEvent
Click a radio button	JRadioButton	ItemEvent, ActionEvent
Select a menu item	JMenuItem	ActionEvent
Move the scroll bar	JScrollBar	AdjustmentEvent
Window opened, closed, iconified, deiconified, or closing	Window	WindowEvent
Component added or removed from the container	Container	ContainerEvent
Component moved, resized, hidden, or shown	Component	ComponentEvent
Component gained or lost focus	Component	FocusEvent
Key released or pressed	Component	KeyEvent
Mouse pressed, released, clicked, entered, or exited	Component	MouseEvent
Mouse moved or dragged	Component	MouseEvent

12.3 Listeners, Registrations, and Handling Events

Java uses a delegation-based model for event handling: an external user action on a source object triggers an event, and an object interested in the event receives the event. The latter object is called a *listener*. Two things are needed for an object to be a listener for an event on a source object:

listener

♦ The listener object's class must implement the corresponding event-listener interface. Java provides a listener interface for every type of GUI event. The listener interface is usually named *X*Listener for *X*Event, with the exception of MouseMotionListener. For example, the corresponding listener interface for ActionEvent is ActionListener; each listener for ActionEvent should implement the ActionListener interface. Table 12.2 lists event types, the corresponding listener interfaces, and the methods defined in the listener interfaces. The listener interface contains the method(s), known as the *handler(s)*, which process the events.

listener interface

handler

♦ The listener object must be registered by the source object. Registration methods are dependent on the event type. For ActionEvent, the method is addActionListener. In

TABLE 12.2   Events, Event Listeners, and Listener Methods

Event class	Listener interface	Listener methods (Handlers)
ActionEvent	ActionListener	actionPerformed(ActionEvent)
ItemEvent	ItemListener	itemStateChanged(ItemEvent)
WindowEvent	WindowListener	windowClosing(WindowEvent)
		windowOpened(WindowEvent)
		windowIconified(WindowEvent)
		windowDeiconified(WindowEvent)
		windowClosed(WindowEvent)
		windowActivated(WindowEvent)
		windowDeactivated(WindowEvent)
ContainerEvent	ContainerListener	componentAdded(ContainerEvent)
		componentRemoved(ContainerEvent)
ComponentEvent	ComponentListener	componentMoved(ComponentEvent)
		componentHidden(ComponentEvent)
		componentResized(ComponentEvent)
		componentShown(ComponentEvent)
FocusEvent	FocusListener	focusGained(FocusEvent)
		focusLost(FocusEvent)
KeyEvent	KeyListener	keyPressed(KeyEvent)
		keyReleased(KeyEvent)
		keyTyped(KeyEvent)
MouseEvent	MouseListener	mousePressed(MouseEvent)
		mouseReleased(MouseEvent)
		mouseEntered(MouseEvent)
		mouseExited(MouseEvent)
		mouseClicked(MouseEvent)
	MouseMotionListener	mouseDragged(MouseEvent)
		mouseMoved(MouseEvent)
AdjustmentEvent	AdjustmentListener	adjustmentValueChanged(AdjustmentEvent)

general, the method is named add*X*Listener for *X*Event. A source object may fire several types of events. For each event, the source object maintains a list of listeners and notifies all the *registered listeners* by invoking the *handler* on the listener object to respond to the event, as shown in Figure 12.2.

register listener

For example, if an object is interested in listening to an action event on a JButton source object, its defining class must implement the ActionListener interface and the actionPerformed method, as shown in Figure 12.3.

The listener object must also register with the JButton object. The registration is done by invoking the addActionListener method in the JButton object, as follows:

create listener object
create source object
register listener

```
ListenerClass listener = new ListenerClass();
JButton jbt = new JButton("OK");
jbt.addActionListener(listener);
```

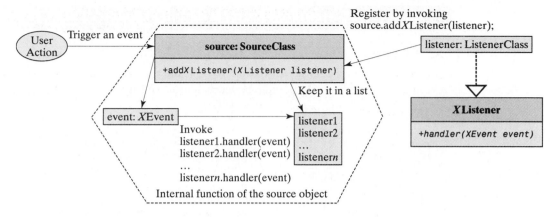

FIGURE 12.2 *An event is triggered by user actions on the source object; the source object generates the event object and invokes the handler of the listener object to process the event.*

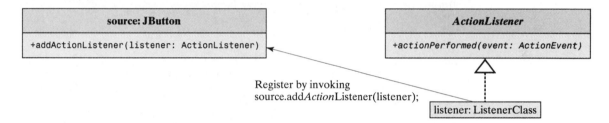

FIGURE 12.3 *An* `ActionListener` *is registered with a* `JButton`.

When you click the button, the `JButton` object generates an `ActionEvent` and passes it to invoke the `actionPerformed` method to handle the event.

The event object contains information pertinent to the event type, which can be obtained using the methods, as shown in Figure 12.4. For example, you can use `e.getSource()` to obtain the source object in order to determine whether it is a button, a check box, or a radio button. For an action event, you can use the `e.getWhen()` to obtain the time when the event occurs.

Three examples of the use of event handling are given below. The first is for `ActionEvent`, the second for `WindowEvent`, and the third involves multiple listeners for a source.

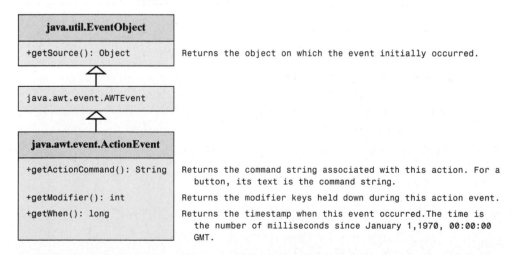

FIGURE 12.4 *You can obtain useful information from an event object.*

EXAMPLE 12.1 HANDLING SIMPLE ACTION EVENTS

Problem

Write a program that displays two buttons, OK and Cancel, in the window. A message is displayed on the console to indicate which button and when it is clicked, as shown in Figure 12.5.

FIGURE 12.5 *The program responds to the button action events.*

Solution

Here are the steps in the program:

1. Create a listener class named `ButtonListener` for handling `ActionEvent` on the buttons. This class implements the `ActionListener` interface.

2. Create a test program named `TestActionEvent` that extends `JFrame`. Add two buttons to the frame, and create a listener object from `ButtonListener`. Register the listener with the buttons.

LISTING 12.1 TestActionEvent.java (Handling an `ActionEvent`)

```
 1  import javax.swing.*;
 2  import java.awt.*;
 3  import java.awt.event.*;
 4
 5  public class TestActionEvent extends JFrame {
 6    // Create two buttons
 7    private JButton jbtOk = new JButton("OK");
 8    private JButton jbtCancel = new JButton("Cancel");
 9
10    public TestActionEvent() {
11      // Set the window title
12      setTitle("TestActionEvent");
13
14      // Set FlowLayout manager to arrange the components
15      // inside the frame
16      getContentPane().setLayout(new FlowLayout());
17
18      // Add buttons to the frame
19      getContentPane().add(jbtOk);
20      getContentPane().add(jbtCancel);
21
22      // Create a listener object
23      ButtonListener btListener = new ButtonListener();
24
25      // Register listeners
26      jbtOk.addActionListener(btListener);
27      jbtCancel.addActionListener(btListener);
28    }
29
30    /** Main method */
31    public static void main(String[] args) {
```

listener

register

EXAMPLE 12.1 (CONTINUED)

```
32      TestActionEvent frame = new TestActionEvent();
33      frame.setDefaultCloseOperation(JFrame.EXIT_ON_CLOSE);
34      frame.setSize(100, 80);
35      frame.setVisible(true);
36   }
37 }
38
39 class ButtonListener implements ActionListener {                              listener class
40   /** This method will be invoked when a button is clicked */
41   public void actionPerformed(ActionEvent e) {
42     System.out.println("The " + e.getActionCommand() + " button is "
43       + "clicked at\n   " + new java.util.Date(e.getWhen()));
44   }
45 }
```

Review

The button objects `jbtOk` and `jbtCancel` are the source of `ActionEvent`. The `ButtonListener` class defines the listeners for the buttons, and its instance `btListener` is registered with the buttons (Lines 26–27).

Clicking a button causes the `actionPerformed` method in `btListener` to be invoked. The `e.getActionCommand()` method returns the action command from the button (Line 42). By default, a button's action command is the text of the button.

The `e.getWhen()` method returns the time in milliseconds since January 1, 1970, 00:00:00 GMT. The `Date` class converts the time to year, month, date, hours, minutes, and seconds (Line 43).

The `TestActionEvent` class itself can be a listener class if you rewrite the program as follows:

```
 1 import javax.swing.*;
 2 import java.awt.*;
 3 import java.awt.event.*;
 4
 5 public class TestActionEvent extends JFrame
 6     implements ActionListener {
 7   // Create two buttons
 8   private JButton jbtOk = new JButton("OK");
 9   private JButton jbtCancel = new JButton("Cancel");
10
11   public TestActionEvent() {
12     // Set the window title
13     setTitle("TestActionEvent");
14
15     // Set FlowLayout manager to arrange the components
16     // inside the frame
17     getContentPane().setLayout(new FlowLayout());
18
19     // Add buttons to the frame
20     getContentPane().add(jbtOk);
21     getContentPane().add(jbtCancel);
22
23     // Register listeners
24     jbtOk.addActionListener(this);
25     jbtCancel.addActionListener(this);
26   }
27
28   /** Main method */
29   public static void main(String[] args) {
30     TestActionEvent frame = new TestActionEvent();
31     frame.setDefaultCloseOperation(JFrame.EXIT_ON_CLOSE);
32     frame.setSize(100, 80);
33     frame.setVisible(true);
34   }
```

EXAMPLE 12.1 (CONTINUED)

```
35
36   /** This method will be invoked when a button is clicked */
37   public void actionPerformed(ActionEvent e) {
38     System.out.println("The " + e.getActionCommand() + " button is "
39       + "clicked at\n   " + new java.util.Date(e.getWhen()));
40   }
41 }
```

The statements (Lines 24–25)

```
jbtOk.addActionListener(this);
jbtCancel.addActionListener(this);
```

register this (referring to the object of TestActionEvent, which is being constructed. See Section 6.12, "The this Keyword,") to listen to ActionEvent on jbtOk and jbtCancel.

listener registration

 CAUTION

Missing *listener registration* is a common mistake in event handling. If the source object doesn't notify the listener, the listener cannot act on the event.

 NOTE

If a listener is registered with a source twice, the handler of the listener will be invoked twice when an event occurs.

EXAMPLE 12.2 HANDLING WINDOW EVENTS

Problem

Write a program that demonstrates handling window events.

Solution

Any subclass of the Window class can generate the following window events: window opened, closing, closed, activated, deactivated, iconified, and deiconified. The program in Listing 12.2 creates a frame, listens to the window events, and displays a message to indicate the occurring event. Figure 12.6 shows a sample run of the program.

FIGURE 12.6 *The window events are displayed on the console when you run the program from a DOS prompt.*

LISTING 12.2 TestWindowEvent.java (Handling a WindowEvent)

```
1 import java.awt.*;
2 import java.awt.event.*;
3 import javax.swing.JFrame;
```

EXAMPLE 12.2 (CONTINUED)

```
 4
 5 public class TestWindowEvent extends JFrame
 6     implements WindowListener {
 7   // Main method
 8   public static void main(String[] args) {
 9     TestWindowEvent frame = new TestWindowEvent();
10     frame.setDefaultCloseOperation(JFrame.EXIT_ON_CLOSE);
11     frame.setTitle("TestWindowEvent");
12     frame.setSize(100, 80);
13     frame.setVisible(true);
14   }
15
16   public TestWindowEvent() {
17     addWindowListener(this);   // Register listener
18   }
19
20   /**
21    * Handler for window deiconified event
22    * Invoked when a window is changed from a minimized
23    * to a normal state.
24    */
25   public void windowDeiconified(WindowEvent event) {          override handler
26     System.out.println("Window deiconified");
27   }
28
29   /**
30    * Handler for window iconified event
31    * Invoked when a window is changed from a normal to a
32    * minimized state. For many platforms, a minimized window
33    * is displayed as the icon specified in the window's
34    * iconImage property.
35    */
36   public void windowIconified(WindowEvent event) {            override handler
37     System.out.println("Window iconified");
38   }
39
40   /**
41    * Handler for window activated event
42    * Invoked when the window is set to be the user's
43    * active window, which means the window (or one of its
44    * subcomponents) will receive keyboard events.
45    */
46   public void windowActivated(WindowEvent event) {            override handler
47     System.out.println("Window activated");
48   }
49
50   /**
51    * Handler for window deactivated event
52    * Invoked when a window is no longer the user's active
53    * window, which means that keyboard events will no longer
54    * be delivered to the window or its subcomponents.
55    */
56   public void windowDeactivated(WindowEvent event) {          override handler
57     System.out.println("Window deactivated");
58   }
59
60   /**
61    * Handler for window opened event
62    * Invoked the first time a window is made visible.
63    */
64   public void windowOpened(WindowEvent event) {               override handler
65     System.out.println("Window opened");
66   }
67
68   /**
69    * Handler for window closing event
70    * Invoked when the user attempts to close the window
```

EXAMPLE 12.2 (CONTINUED)

```
71    * from the window's system menu.  If the program does not
72    * explicitly hide or dispose the window while processing
73    * this event, the window close operation will be cancelled.
74    */
75   public void windowClosing(WindowEvent event) {
76     System.out.println("Window closing");
77   }
78
79   /**
80    * Handler for window closed event
81    * Invoked when a window has been closed as the result
82    * of calling dispose on the window.
83    */
84   public void windowClosed(WindowEvent event) {
85     System.out.println("Window closed");
86   }
87 }
```

override handler *(line 75)*

override handler *(line 84)*

Review

The WindowEvent can be generated by the Window class or any subclass of Window. Since JFrame is a subclass of Window, it can generate WindowEvent.

TestWindowEvent extends JFrame and implements WindowListener. The Window-Listener interface defines several abstract methods (windowActivated, windowClosed, windowClosing, windowDeactivated, windowDeiconified, windowIconified, window-Opened) for handling window events when the window is activated, closed, closing, deactivated, deiconified, iconified, or opened.

When a window event, such as activation, occurs, the windowActivated method is triggered. Implement the windowActivated method with a concrete response if you want the event to be processed.

Because the methods in the WindowListener interface are abstract, you must implement all of them even if your program does not care about some of the events.

For an object to receive event notification, it must register as an event listener. addWindowListener(this) (Line 17) registers the object of TestWindowEvent as a window-event listener so that it can receive notification about the window event. TestWindowEvent is both a listener and a source object.

 NOTE
As demonstrated in this example, a source object and a listener object may be the same.

EXAMPLE 12.3 MULTIPLE LISTENERS FOR A SINGLE SOURCE

Problem

Write a program that modifies Example 12.1, "Handling Simple Action Events," to add a new listener for the OK and Cancel buttons. This example creates a new listener class as an additional listener for the action events on the buttons. When a button is clicked, both listeners respond to the action event.

Solution

Listing 12.3 gives the solution to the problem. Figure 12.7 shows a sample run of the program.

EXAMPLE 12.2 (CONTINUED)

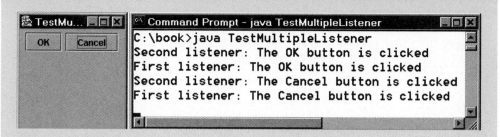

FIGURE 12.7 *Both listeners respond to the button action events.*

LISTING 12.3 TestMultipleListener.java (Multiple Listeners on a Source)

```
1  import javax.swing.*;
2  import java.awt.*;
3  import java.awt.event.*;
4
5  public class TestMultipleListener extends JFrame
6      implements ActionListener {
7    // Create two buttons
8    private JButton jbtOk = new JButton("OK");
9    private JButton jbtCancel = new JButton("Cancel");
10
11   public TestMultipleListener() {
12     // Set the window title
13     setTitle("TestMultipleListener");
14
15     // Set FlowLayout manager to arrange the components
16     // inside the frame
17     getContentPane().setLayout(new FlowLayout());
18
19     // Add buttons to the frame
20     getContentPane().add(jbtOk);
21     getContentPane().add(jbtCancel);
22
23     // Register the frame as listeners
24     jbtOk.addActionListener(this);                      register listener
25     jbtCancel.addActionListener(this);
26
27     // Register a second listener for buttons
28     SecondListener secondListener = new SecondListener();   create listener
29     jbtOk.addActionListener(secondListener);                register listener
30     jbtCancel.addActionListener(secondListener);
31   }
32
33   /** Main method */
34   public static void main(String[] args) {
35     TestMultipleListener frame = new TestMultipleListener();
36     frame.setDefaultCloseOperation(JFrame.EXIT_ON_CLOSE);
37     frame.setSize(100, 80);
38     frame.setVisible(true);
39   }
40
41   /** This method will be invoked when a button is clicked */
42   public void actionPerformed(ActionEvent e) {            override handler
43     System.out.print("First listener: ");
44
45     if (e.getSource() == jbtOk) {
46       System.out.println("The OK button is clicked");
47     }
48     else if (e.getSource() == jbtCancel) {
49       System.out.println("The Cancel button is clicked");
50     }
```

EXAMPLE 12.3 (CONTINUED)

```
51   }
52 }
53
54 /** The class for the second listener */
55 class SecondListener implements ActionListener {
56   /** Handle ActionEvent */
57   public void actionPerformed(ActionEvent e) {
58     System.out.print("Second listener: ");
59
60     // A button has an actionCommand property, which is same as the
61     // text of the button by default.
62     if (e.getActionCommand().equals("OK")) {
63       System.out.println("The OK button is clicked");
64     }
65     else if (e.getActionCommand().equals("Cancel")) {
66       System.out.println("The Cancel button is clicked");
67     }
68   }
69 }
```

Review

Each source object in the preceding two examples has a single listener. Each button in this example has two listeners: one is an instance of TestMultipleListener, and the other is an instance of SecondListener.

When a button is clicked, both listeners are notified and their respective actionPerformed methods are invoked. Using this method can detect which button is clicked. If you want to use the getSource method to detect which button is clicked, see Exercise 12.2.

The source object maintains a list of all its listeners. When a listener is registered with the source object, it is added at the top of the list. When an event occurs, the source object notifies the listener objects on the list by invoking each listener's handler. In this case, the handler is the actionPerformed method.

What would happen if you replaced Lines 27-30 in the example with the following code?

```
// Register a second listener for buttons
jbtOk.addActionListener(new SecondListener());
jbtCancel.addActionListener(new SecondListener());
```

Two instances of SecondListener would be created. The program would run just as before the change, but the change is obviously not good.

12.4   Mouse Events

A mouse event is generated whenever a mouse is pressed, released, clicked, moved, or dragged on a component. The mouse event object captures the event, such as the number of clicks associated with it or the location (x and y coordinates) of the mouse, as shown in Figure 12.8.

Since the MouseEvent class inherits InputEvent, you can use the methods defined in the InputEvent class on a MouseEvent object.

The java.awt.Point class encapsulates a point in a plane. The class contains two instance variables, x and y, for coordinates. To create a point object, use the following constructor:

```
Point(int x, int y)
```

This constructs a Point object with the specified x-and y-coordinates.

```
java.awt.event.InputEvent
```

+getWhen(): long	Returns the timestamp when this event occurred.
+isAltDown(): boolean	Returns whether or not the Alt modifier is down on this event.
+isControlDown(): boolean	Returns whether or not the Control modifier is down on this event.
+isMetaDown(): boolean	Returns whether or not the Meta modifier is down on this event
+isShiftDown(): boolean	Returns whether or not the Shift modifier is down on this event.

```
java.awt.event.MouseEvent
```

+getButton(): int	Indicates which mouse button has been clicked.
+getClickCount(): int	Returns the number of mouse clicks associated with this event.
+getPoint():java.awt.Point	Returns a Point object containing the x and y coordinates.
+getX(): int	Returns the x-coordinate of the mouse point.
+getY(): int	Returns the y-coordinate of the mouse point.

FIGURE 12.8 *The MouseEvent class encapsulates information for mouse events.*

```
java.awt.event.MouseListener
```

+mousePressed(e: MouseEvent): void	Invoked when the mouse button has been pressed on the source component.
+mouseReleased(e: MouseEvent): void	Invoked when the mouse button has been released on the source component.
+mouseClicked(e: MouseEvent): void	Invoked when the mouse button has been clicked (pressed and released) on the source component.
+mouseEntered(e: MouseEvent): void	Invoked when the mouse enters the source component.
+mouseExited(e: MouseEvent): void	Invoked when the mouse exits the source component.

```
java.awt.event.MouseMotionListener
```

+mouseDragged(e: MouseEvent): void	Invoked when a mouse button is moved with a button pressed.
+mouseMoved(e: MouseEvent): void	Invoked when a mouse button is moved without a button pressed.

FIGURE 12.9 *The MouseListener interface handles mouse pressed, released, clicked, entered, and exited events. The MouseMotionListener interface handles mouse dragged and moved events.*

Java provides two listener interfaces, MouseListener and MouseMotionListener, to handle mouse events, as shown in Figure 12.9. Implement the MouseListener interface to listen for such actions as pressing, releasing, entering, exiting, or clicking the mouse, and implement the MouseMotionListener interface to listen for such actions as dragging or moving the mouse.

EXAMPLE 12.4 MOVING A MESSAGE ON A PANEL USING A MOUSE

Problem

Write a program that displays a message in a panel. You can use the mouse to move the message. The message moves as the mouse drags and is always displayed at the mouse point. A sample run of the program is shown in Figure 12.10.

EXAMPLE 12.4 (CONTINUED)

FIGURE **12.10**   *You can move the message by dragging the mouse.*

Solution

Listing 12.4 gives the solution to the problem.

LISTING **12.4**   MoveMessageDemo.java (Handling a MouseEvent)

```
 1 import java.awt.*;
 2 import java.awt.event.*;
 3 import javax.swing.*;
 4
 5 public class MoveMessageDemo extends JFrame {
 6   public MoveMessageDemo() {
 7     // Create a MoveMessagePanel instance for drawing a message
 8     MoveMessagePanel p = new MoveMessagePanel("Welcome to Java");
 9
10     // Place the message panel in the frame
11     getContentPane().setLayout(new BorderLayout());
12     getContentPane().add(p);
13   }
14
15   /** Main method */
16   public static void main(String[] args) {
17     MoveMessageDemo frame = new MoveMessageDemo();
18     frame.setTitle("MoveMessageDemo");
19     frame.setDefaultCloseOperation(JFrame.EXIT_ON_CLOSE);
20     frame.setSize(100, 80);
21     frame.setVisible(true);
22   }
23 }
24
25 // MoveMessagePanel draws a message
26  class MoveMessagePanel extends MessagePanel
27      implements MouseMotionListener {
28    /** Construct a panel to draw string s */
29    public MoveMessagePanel(String s) {
30      super(s); // What if this line is omitted?
31      this.addMouseMotionListener(this);
32    }
33
34    /** Handle mouse moved event */
35    public void mouseMoved(MouseEvent e) {
36    }
37
38    /** Handle mouse dragged event */
39    public void mouseDragged(MouseEvent e) {
40      // Get the new location and repaint the screen
41      setXCoordinate(e.getX());
42      setYCoordinate(e.getY());
43    }
44  }
```

listener class

register listener

override handler

override handler

EXAMPLE 12.4 (CONTINUED)

Review

The class MoveMessagePanel extends MessagePanel and implements MouseMotionListener. The MessagePanel class was presented Section 11.11, "Case Study: The MessagePanel Class" to display a message in a panel. The MoveMessagePanel class inherits all the features from MessagePanel. Additionally, it handles redisplaying the message when the mouse is dragged.

The MouseMotionListener interface contains two handlers, mouseMoved and mouseDragged, for handling mouse-motion events. When you move the mouse with the button pressed, the mouseDragged method is invoked to repaint the viewing area and display the message at the mouse point. When you move the mouse without pressing the button, the mouseMoved method is invoked.

Because the methods in the MouseMotionListener interface are abstract, you must implement all of them even if your program does not care about some of the events. In MoveMessagePanel, the mouseMoved and mouseDragged event handlers are both implemented, although only the mouseDragged handler is needed.

For an object to receive event notification, it must register as an event listener. addMouseMotionListener(this) (Line 31) registers the object of MoveMessagePanel as a mouse motion event listener so that the object can receive notification about the mouse-motion event. MoveMessagePanel is both a listener and a source object.

The mouseDragged method is invoked when you move the mouse with a button pressed. This method obtains the mouse location using getX and getY methods (Lines 41–42) in the MouseEvent class. This becomes the new location for the message, which is set using the MessagePanel's setXCoordinate and setYCoordinate methods.

EXAMPLE 12.5 SCRIBBLING WITH A MOUSE (OPTIONAL)

Problem

Write a program that uses a mouse for scribbling. It can be used to draw things on a panel by dragging with the left mouse button pressed. The drawing can be erased by dragging with the right button pressed. A sample run of the program is shown in Figure 12.11.

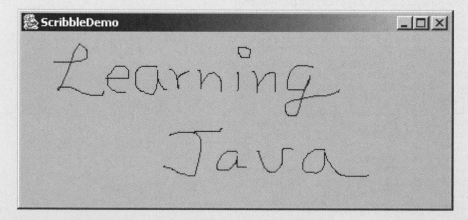

FIGURE 12.11 *The program enables you to scribble using the mouse.*

EXAMPLE 12.5 (CONTINUED)

Solution

Listing 12.5 gives the solution to the problem.

LISTING 12.5 ScribbleDemo.java (Scribble Using Mouse)

```
1 import java.awt.*;
2 import javax.swing.*;
3 import java.awt.event.*;
4
5 public class ScribbleDemo extends JFrame {
6   public ScribbleDemo() {
7     // Create a ScribblePanel and add it to the content pane
8     getContentPane().add(new ScribblePanel(), BorderLayout.CENTER);
9   }
10
11   /** Main method */
12   public static void main(String[] args) {
13     ScribbleDemo frame = new ScribbleDemo();
14     frame.setTitle("ScribbleDemo");
15     frame.setDefaultCloseOperation(JFrame.EXIT_ON_CLOSE);
16     frame.setSize(300, 300);
17     frame.setVisible(true);
18   }
19 }
20
21 // ScribblePanel for scribbling using the mouse
22 class ScribblePanel extends JPanel
23     implements MouseListener, MouseMotionListener {
24   final int CIRCLESIZE = 20; // Circle diameter used for erasing
25   private Point lineStart = new Point(0, 0); // Line start point
26   private Graphics g; // Create a Graphics object for drawing
27
28   public ScribblePanel() {
29     // Register listener for the mouse event
30     addMouseListener(this);
31     addMouseMotionListener(this);
32   }
33
34   public void mouseClicked(MouseEvent e) {
35   }
36
37   public void mouseEntered(MouseEvent e) {
38   }
39
40   public void mouseExited(MouseEvent e) {
41   }
42
43   public void mouseReleased(MouseEvent e) {
44   }
45
46   public void mousePressed(MouseEvent e) {
47     lineStart.move(e.getX(), e.getY());
48   }
49
50   public void mouseDragged(MouseEvent e) {
51     g = getGraphics(); // Get graphics context
52
53     if (e.isMetaDown()) { // Detect right button pressed
54       // Erase the drawing using an oval
55       g.setColor(getBackground());
56       g.fillOval(e.getX() - (CIRCLESIZE / 2),
57         e.getY() - (CIRCLESIZE / 2), CIRCLESIZE, CIRCLESIZE);
58     }
59     else {
60       g.setColor(Color.black);
```

listener class (line 22)

add mouse listener (line 30)
add mouse motion listener (line 31)

override handler (line 46)

override handler (line 50)

EXAMPLE 12.5 (CONTINUED)

```
61        g.drawLine(lineStart.x, lineStart.y,
62          e.getX(), e.getY());
63      }
64
65      lineStart.move(e.getX(), e.getY());
66
67      // Dispose this graphics context
68      g.dispose();
69    }
70
71    public void mouseMoved(MouseEvent e) {
72    }
73  }
```

Review

The program creates a `ScribblePanel` instance to capture mouse movements on the panel. Lines are created or erased by dragging the mouse with the left or right button pressed.

When a button is pressed, the `mousePressed` handler is invoked. This handler sets the `lineStart` to the current mouse point as the starting point. Drawing begins when the mouse is dragged with the left button pressed. In this case, the `mouseDragged` handler sets the foreground color to black, and draws a line along the path of the mouse movement.

When the mouse is dragged with the right button pressed, erasing occurs. In this case, the `mouseDragged` handler sets the foreground color to the background color and draws an oval filled with the background color at the mouse pointer to erase the area covered by the oval.

The program does not use the `paintComponent(Graphics g)` method. Instead, it uses `getGraphics()` to obtain a `Graphics` instance and draws on this.

Because the `mousePressed` handler is defined in the `MouseListener` interface, and the `mouseDragged` handler is defined in the `MouseMotionListener` interface, the program implements both interfaces (Line 23).

The `dispose` method (Line 68) disposes of this graphics context and releases any system resources it is using. Although the finalization process of the JVM automatically disposes of an object after it is no longer in use, it is better to manually free the associated resources by calling this method rather than rely on a finalization process that may take a long time to run to completion. In this program, a large number of `Graphics` objects can be created within a short time. The program would run fine if these objects were not disposed of manually, but they would consume a lot of memory.

12.5   Keyboard Events

Keyboard events enable the use of the keys to control and perform actions or get input from the keyboard. A key event is generated whenever a key is pressed, released, or typed on a component. The keyboard event object describes the nature of the event (namely, that a key has been pressed, released, or typed) and the value of the key, as shown in Figure 12.12.

The keys captured in an event are integers representing Unicode character values, which include alphanumeric characters, function keys, the Tab key, the Enter key, and so on. Every keyboard event has an associated key character or key code that is returned by the `getKeyChar()` or `getKeyCode()` method in `KeyEvent`.

Java defines many constants for keys, including function keys in the `KeyEvent` class. Table 12.3 shows the most commonly used ones.

Java provides the `KeyListener` to handle key events, as shown in Figure 12.13.

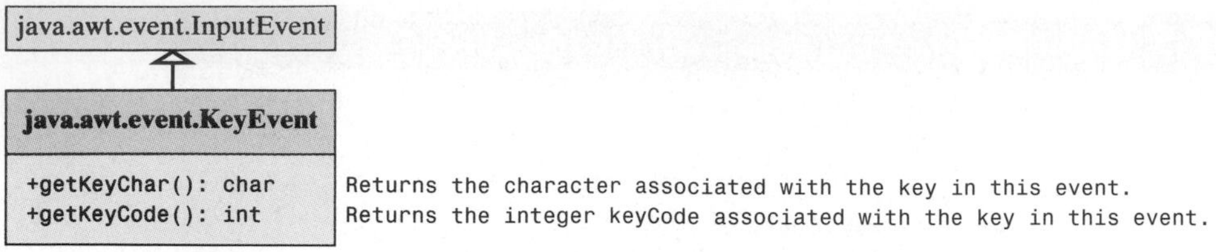

```
java.awt.event.InputEvent
```
⬆
```
java.awt.event.KeyEvent
```

+getKeyChar(): char	Returns the character associated with the key in this event.
+getKeyCode(): int	Returns the integer keyCode associated with the key in this event.

FIGURE **12.12** *The KeyEvent class encapsulates information about key events.*

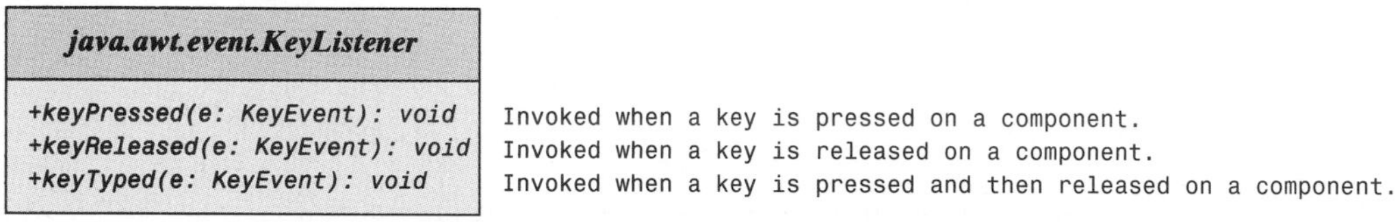

```
java.awt.event.KeyListener
```

+keyPressed(e: KeyEvent): void	Invoked when a key is pressed on a component.
+keyReleased(e: KeyEvent): void	Invoked when a key is released on a component.
+keyTyped(e: KeyEvent): void	Invoked when a key is pressed and then released on a component.

FIGURE **12.13** *The KeyListener handles key pressed, released, and typed events.*

TABLE **12.3** Key Constants

Constant	Description
VK_HOME	The Home key
VK_End	The End key
VK_PGUP	The Page Up key
VK_PGDN	The Page Down key
VK_UP	The up-arrow key
VK_DOWN	The down-arrow key
VK_LEFT	The left-arrow key
VK_RIGHT	The right-arrow key
VK_ESCAPE	The Esc key
VK_TAB	The Tab key
VK_CONTROL	The Control key
VK_SHIFT	The Shift key
VK_BACK_SPACE	The Backspace key
VK_CAPS_LOCK	The Caps Lock key
VK_NUM_LOCK	The Num Lock key
VK_ENTER	The Enter key
VK_F1 to VK_F12	The function keys from F1 to F12
VK_0 to VK_9	The number keys from 0 to 9
VK_A to VK_Z	The letter keys from A to Z

The keyPressed handler is invoked when a key is pressed, the keyReleased handler is invoked when a key is released, and the keyTyped handler is invoked when a Unicode character is entered. If a key does not have a Unicode (e.g., function keys, modifier keys, action keys, and control keys), the keyTyped handler will be not be invoked.

EXAMPLE 12.6 HANDLING KEY EVENTS

Problem

Write a program that displays a user-input character. The user can move the character up, down, left, and right, using the arrow keys VK_UP, VK_DOWN, VK_LEFT, and VK_RIGHT. Figure 12.14 contains a sample run of the program.

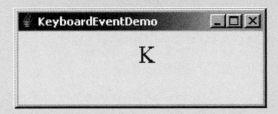

FIGURE **12.14** *The program responds to keyboard events by displaying a character and moving it up, down, left, or right.*

Solution

The following code gives the solution to the problem.

LISTING **12.6** KeyboardEventDemo.java (Handling a KeyEvent)

```
1 import java.awt.*;
2 import java.awt.event.*;
3 import javax.swing.*;
4
5 public class KeyboardEventDemo extends JFrame {
6   private KeyboardPanel keyboardPanel = new KeyboardPanel();
7
8   /** Initialize UI */
9   public KeyboardEventDemo() {
10     // Add the keyboard panel to accept and display user input
11     getContentPane().add(keyboardPanel);
12
13     // Set focus
14     keyboardPanel.setFocusable(true);
15   }
16
17   /** Main method */
18   public static void main(String[] args) {
19     KeyboardEventDemo frame = new KeyboardEventDemo();
20     frame.setTitle("KeyboardEventDemo");
21     frame.setDefaultCloseOperation(JFrame.EXIT_ON_CLOSE);
22     frame.setSize(300, 300);
23     frame.setVisible(true);
24   }
25 }
26
27 // KeyboardPanel for receiving key input
28 class KeyboardPanel extends JPanel implements KeyListener {          listener class
29   private int x = 100;
30   private int y = 100;
31   private char keyChar = 'A'; // Default key
32
33   public KeyboardPanel() {
34     addKeyListener(this); // Register listener                      register listener
35   }
```

EXAMPLE 12.6 (CONTINUED)

```
36
37    public void keyReleased(KeyEvent e) {
38    }
39
40    public void keyTyped(KeyEvent e) {
41    }
42
43    public void keyPressed(KeyEvent e) {
44      switch (e.getKeyCode()) {
45        case KeyEvent.VK_DOWN: y += 10; break;
46        case KeyEvent.VK_UP: y -= 10; break;
47        case KeyEvent.VK_LEFT: x -= 10; break;
48        case KeyEvent.VK_RIGHT: x += 10; break;
49        default: keyChar = e.getKeyChar();
50      }
51
52      repaint();
53    }
54
55    /** Draw the character */
56    protected void paintComponent(Graphics g) {
57      super.paintComponent(g);
58
59      g.setFont(new Font("TimesRoman", Font.PLAIN, 24));
60      g.drawString(String.valueOf(keyChar), x, y);
61    }
62  }
```

override handler

Review

When a non-arrow key is pressed, the key is displayed. When an arrow key is pressed, the character moves in the direction indicated by the arrow key.

Because the program gets input from the keyboard, it listens for `KeyEvent` and implements `KeyListener` to handle key input.

When a key is pressed, the `keyPressed` handler is invoked. The program uses `e.getKeyCode()` to obtain the int value for the key and `e.getKeyChar()` to get the character for the key. In fact, `(int)e.getKeyChar()` is the same as `e.getKeyCode()`.

Only a focused component can receive `KeyEvent`. To make a component focusable, set its `isFocusable` property to `true` (Line 14). This new property was introduced in JDK 1.4.

12.6   The `Timer` Class (Optional)

Not all source objects are GUI components. The `javax.swing.Timer` class is a source component that fires an `ActionEvent` at a predefined rate. Figure 12.15 lists some of the methods in the class.

A `Timer` object serves as the source of an `ActionEvent`. The listeners must be instances of `ActionListener` and registered with the `Timer` object. You create a `Timer` object using its sole constructor with a delay and a listener, where `delay` specifies the number of milliseconds between two action events. You can add additional listeners using the `addActionListener` method, and adjust the delay using the `setDelay` method. To start the timer, invoke the `start()` method. To stop the timer, invoke the `stop()` method.

javax.swing.Timer	
+Timer(delay: int,listener: ActionListener)	Creates a Timer with a specified delay in milliseconds and an ActionListener.
+addActionListener(listener: ActionListener): void	Adds an ActionListener to the timer.
+start(): void	Starts this timer.
+stop(): void	Stops this timer.
+setDelay(delay: int): void	Sets a new delay value for this timer.

FIGURE 12.15   *A* Timer *object fires an* ActionEvent *at a fixed rate.*

FIGURE 12.16   *A message moves in the panel.*

The Timer class can be used to control animations. For example, you can use it to display a moving message with the code in Listing 12.7.

LISTING 12.7   AnimationDemo.java (Moving a Message)

```
 1 import java.awt.*;
 2 import java.awt.event.*;
 3 import javax.swing.*;
 4
 5 public class AnimationDemo extends JFrame {
 6   public AnimationDemo() {
 7     // Create a MovingMessagePanel for displaying a moving message
 8     MovingMessagePanel p = new MovingMessagePanel("message moving?");
 9     getContentPane().add(p);
10
11     // Create a timer for the listener p
12     Timer timer = new Timer(1000, p);                                    create timer
13     timer.start();                                                       start timer
14   }
15
16   /** Main method */
17   public static void main(String[] args) {
18     AnimationDemo frame = new AnimationDemo();
19     frame.setTitle("AnimationDemo");
20     frame.setDefaultCloseOperation(JFrame.EXIT_ON_CLOSE);
21     frame.setSize(100, 80);
22     frame.setVisible(true);
23   }
24 }
25
26 // Displaying a moving message
27 class MovingMessagePanel extends JPanel implements ActionListener {
28   private String message = "Welcome to Java";
29   private int xCoordinate = 20;
30   private int yCoordinate = 20;
31
32   public MovingMessagePanel(String message) {
33     this.message = message;                                              set message
34   }
```

```
35
36   /** Handle ActionEvent */
37   public void actionPerformed(ActionEvent e) {
38     repaint();
39   }
40
41   /** Paint message */
42   public void paintComponent(Graphics g) {
43     super.paintComponent(g);
44
45     if (xCoordinate > getWidth()) xCoordinate = -20;
46     xCoordinate += 5;
47     g.drawString(message, xCoordinate, yCoordinate);
48   }
49 }
```

handler
repaint

move message

The program displays a moving message, as shown in Figure 12.16. `MovingMessagePanel` implements `ActionListener` (Line 27) so that it can listen for `ActionEvent`. Line 12 creates a `Timer` for a `MovingMessagePanel`. The timer is started in Line 13. The timer fires an `ActionEvent`, every second, and the listener responds in Line 38 to repaint the panel. When a panel is painted, its *x* coordinate is increased (Line 46), so the message is displayed to the right.

In Section 11.12, "Case Study: The `StillClock` Class", you drew a `StillClock` to show the current time. The clock does not tick after it is displayed. What can you do to make the clock display a new current time every second? The key to making the clock tick is to repaint it every second with a new current time. You can use a timer to control the repainting of the clock with the code in listing 12.8.

LISTING **12.8** ClockAnimation.java (Animating a Clock)

```
1 import java.awt.*;
2 import java.awt.event.*;
3 import javax.swing.*;
4
5 public class ClockAnimation extends StillClock
6     implements ActionListener {
7   // Create a timer with delay 1000 ms
8   protected Timer timer = new Timer(1000, this);
9
10   public ClockAnimation() {
11     timer.start();
12   }
13
14   /** Handle the action event */
15   public void actionPerformed(ActionEvent e) {
16     // Set new time and repaint the clock to display current time
17     setCurrentTime();
18     repaint();
19   }
20
21   /** Main method */
22   public static void main(String[] args) {
23     JFrame frame = new JFrame("ClockAnimation");
24     ClockAnimation clock = new ClockAnimation();
25     frame.getContentPane().add(clock);
26     frame.setDefaultCloseOperation(JFrame.EXIT_ON_CLOSE);
27     frame.setSize(200, 200);
28     frame.setVisible(true);
29   }
30 }
```

create timer

set new time

repaint
start timer

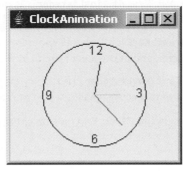

FIGURE **12.17**   *A clock is displayed in the panel.*

The program displays a running clock, as shown in Figure 12.17. `ClockAnimation` extends `StillClock` and implements `ActionListener` (Line 6) so that it can listen for `ActionEvent`. Line 8 creates a `Timer` for a `ClockAnimation`. The timer is started in Line 11 when a `ClockAnimation` is constructed. The timer fires an `ActionEvent` every second, and the listener responds in Line 15 to set a new time and repaint the clock. The `setCurrentTime()` method defined in `StillClock` sets the current time in the clock.

KEY TERMS

event 420	event listener interface 421
event delegation 421	event object 420
event-driven programming 420	event registration 421
event handler 421	event source (source object) 420
event listener 421	

KEY CLASSES AND METHODS

✦ **java.util.EventObject**   is the root class for all event classes. The `getSource()` method returns the source object for the event.

✦ **java.awt.ActionEvent**   is the action event class. The `getActionCommand()` method returns the action command for the event, and `getWhen()` returns the timestamp for the event.

✦ **java.awt.ActionListener**   is the action event listener interface that contains the `actionPerformed(ActionEvent)` handler.

✦ **java.awt.InputEvent**   is the base class for `MouseEvent` and `KeyEvent`. The key methods are `getWhen()`, `isAltDown()`, `isControlDown()`, `isMetaDown()`, and `isShiftDown()`.

✦ **java.awt.MouseEvent**   is the mouse event class. The `getButton()` method indicates which button has been clicked, `getClickCount()` returns the click count, `getX()` returns the x-coordinate of the mouse, and `getY()` returns the y-coordinate of the mouse.

✦ **java.awt.MouseListener**   is the mouse event listener interface that contains the `mousePressed(MouseEvent)`, `mouseReleased(MouseEvent)`, `mouseClicked(MouseEvent)`, `mouseEntered(MouseEvent)`, and `mouseExited(MouseEvent)` handlers.

◆ **java.awt.MouseMotionListener** is the mouse motion event listener interface that contains the mouseMoved(MouseEvent) and mouseDragged(MouseEvent) handlers.

◆ **java.awt.KeyEvent** is the mouse event class. The getKeyChar() method returns the character, and getKeyCode() returns the code for the character.

◆ **java.awt.KeyListener** is the key event listener interface that contains the keyPressed (KeyEvent), keyReleased(KeyEvent), and keyTyped(KeyEvent) handlers.

◆ **javax.swing.Timer** sets a timer that fires one or more action events after a specified delay.

Chapter Summary

◆ The root class of the event classes is java.util.EventObject. The subclasses of EventObject deal with special types of events, such as button actions, window events, component events, mouse movements, and keystrokes. You can identify the source object of an event using the getSource() instance method in the EventObject class. If a component can generate an event, any subclass of the component can generate the same type of event.

◆ The listener object's class must implement the corresponding event-listener interface. Java provides a listener interface for every type of GUI event. The listener interface is usually named XListener for XEvent, with the exception of MouseMotionListener. For example, the corresponding listener interface for ActionEvent is ActionListener; each listener for ActionEvent should implement the ActionListener interface. The listener interface contains the method(s), known as the *handler(s)*, which process the events.

◆ The listener object must be registered by the source object. Registration methods are dependent on the event type. For ActionEvent, the method is addActionListener. In general, the method is named addXListener for XEvent.

◆ A source object may fire several types of events. For each event, the source object maintains a list of listeners and notifies all the registered listeners by invoking the *handler* on the listener object to respond to the event.

◆ A mouse event is generated whenever a mouse is clicked, released, moved, or dragged on a component. The mouse event object captures the event, such as the number of clicks associated with it or the location (x-and y-coordinates) of the mouse.

◆ Java provides two listener interfaces, MouseListener and MouseMotionListener, to handle mouse events, implement the MouseListener interface to listen for such actions as pressing, releasing, entering, exiting, or clicking the mouse, and implement the MouseMotionListener interface to listen for such actions as dragging or moving the mouse.

◆ The Point class is often used for handling mouse events. The Point class encapsulates a point on a plane. The class contains two instance variables, x and y, for coordinates.

◆ The keyboard event object describes the nature of the event (namely, that a key has been pressed, released, or typed) and the value of the key.

✦ The keyPressed handler is invoked when a key is pressed, the keyReleased handler is invoked when a key is released, and the keyTyped handler is invoked when a Unicode character is entered. If a key does not have a Unicode (e.g., function keys, modifier keys, action keys, and control keys), the keyTyped handler will not be involved.

✦ Java defines many constants for keys, including function keys in the KeyEvent class. For example, the number keys from 0 to 9 are VK_0 to VK_9. The letter keys from A to Z are VK_A to VK_Z, and the up-arrow key is VK_UP.

✦ You can use the Timer class to control Java animations. The timer fires an ActionEvent at a fixed rate. The listener updates the painting to simulate an animation.

REVIEW QUESTIONS

Sections 12.2–12.3

12.1   Can a button generate a WindowEvent? Can a button generate a MouseEvent? Can a button generate an ActionEvent?

12.2   Explain how to register a listener object and how to implement a listener interface.

12.3   What information is contained in an AWTEvent object and the objects of its subclasses? Find the variables, constants, and methods defined in these event classes.

12.4   How do you override a method defined in the listener interface? Do you need to override all the methods defined in the listener interface?

12.5   What is wrong in the following code?

```
1 import java.awt.*;
2 import java.swing.*;
3
4 public class Test extends JFrame implements ActionListener {
5   public Test() {
6     JButton jbtOK = new JButton("OK");
7     getContentPane().add(jbtOK);
8   }
9
10  public void actionPerform(ActionEvent e) {
11    if (e.getSource() == jbtOK)
12      System.out.println("OK button is clicked");
13  }
14 }
```

Sections 12.4–12.5

12.6   What is the event type for a mouse movement? What is the event type for getting key input?

12.7   What is the listener interface for mouse pressed, released, clicked, entered, and exited? What is the listener interface for mouse moved and dragged?

12.8   What method is used to process a key event?

12.9   What methods are used in responding to a mouse-motion event?

12.10   How do you use the Timer class to control Java animations?

PROGRAMMING EXERCISES

Sections 12.2–12.3

12.1 (*Displaying which button is clicked on the console*) Add the code to Exercise 11.1 that will display a message on the console indicating which button has been clicked.

12.2 (*Multiple listeners*) Rewrite Example 12.3 "Multiple Listeners for a Single Source," as follows:

◆ Create a method in `TestMultipleListener`:

```
public void processButtons(ActionEvent e) {
  if (e.getSource() == jbtOk) {
    System.out.println("The OK button is clicked");
  }
  else if (e.getSource() == jbtCancel) {
    System.out.println("The Cancel button is clicked");
  }
}
```

◆ Invoke `processButtons(e)` from the `actionPerformed(e)` method in `TestMultipleListener`.

◆ Modify `SecondListener` to invoke `processButtons(e)` defined in `TestMultipleListener` from the `actionPerformed` method in `SecondListener`. For the action `Performed` method in the `SecondListener` class to invoke the `processButtons(e)` method in the `TestMultipleListener` class, you may pass a reference of a `TestMultipleListener` object to `SecondListener` through the constructor of `SecondListener`.

12.3* (*Displaying which button is clicked on a message panel*) Write a program that creates a user interface with two buttons named OK and Cancel and a message panel for displaying a message. When you click the OK button, a message "OK button is clicked" is displayed. When you click the Cancel button, a message "Cancel button is clicked" is displayed, as shown in Figure 12.18(a).

(a)   (b)

FIGURE 12.18 *(a) Exercise 12.3 displays which button is clicked on a message panel. (b) Exercise 12.4 displays the mouse position.*

Section 12.4

12.4* (*Displaying the mouse position*) Write a program that displays the mouse position when the mouse is pressed (see Figure 12.18(b)).

12.5* (*Setting background color using a mouse*) Write a program that displays the background color of a panel as black when the mouse is pressed and as white when the mouse is released. You need to create a custom panel class that implements `MouseListener`.

Section 12.5

12.6* (*Using* KeyboardEvent) Write a program to get character input from the keyboard and put the characters where the mouse points.

12.7* (*Drawing lines using the arrow keys*) Write a program that draws line segments using the arrow keys. The line starts from the center of the frame and draws toward east, north, west, or south when the right-arrow key, up-arrow key, left-arrow key, or down-arrow key is clicked, as shown in Figure 12.19.

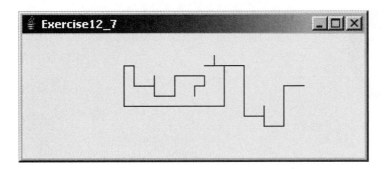

FIGURE 12.19 *You use the arrow keys to draw the lines.*

Section 12.6

12.8* (*Displaying a flashing label*) Write a program that displays a flashing label. Enable it to run standalone.

 HINT

To make the label flash, you need to repaint the panel alternately with the label and without the label (blank screen) at a fixed rate. Use a boolean variable to control the alternation.

12.9* (*Controlling a moving label*) Modify Listing 12.7 to control a moving label using the mouse. The label freezes when the mouse is pressed, and moves again when the button is released.

12.10** (*Displaying a running fan*) Listing 11.11 on page 394 displays a motionless fan. Write a program that displays a running fan.

chapter

13

CREATING USER INTERFACES

Objectives

✦ To create graphical user interfaces with various user-interface components: JButton, JCheckBox, JRadioButton, JLabel, JTextField, JTextArea, JComboBox, JList, JScrollBar, and JSlider (§§13.2–13.12).

✦ To create listeners for various types of events (§§13.2–13.12).

✦ To use borders to visually group user-interface components (§13.2).

✦ To create image icons using the ImageIcon class (§13.3).

✦ To display multiple windows in an application (§13.13).

13.1   Introduction

A *graphical user interface* (GUI) makes a system user-friendly and easy to use. Creating a GUI requires creativity and knowledge of how GUI components work. Since the GUI components in Java are very flexible and versatile, you can create a wide assortment of useful user interfaces.

GUI

Many Java IDEs provide tools for visually designing and programming Java classes. This enables you to rapidly assemble the elements of a user interface (UI) for a Java application or applet with minimum coding. Tools, however, cannot do everything. You have to modify the programs they produce. Consequently, before you begin to use the visual tools, it is imperative that you understand the basic concepts of Java GUI programming.

This chapter introduces the frequently used GUI components highlighted in Figure 13.1.

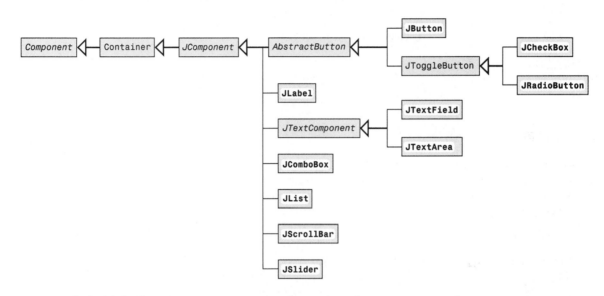

FIGURE **13.1**   *The highlighted Swing GUI components are frequently used to create user interfaces.*

13.2   Common Features of Swing GUI Components

Once you understand the basics of Java GUI programming, such as containers, layout managers, and event handling, you will be able to learn new components and explore their properties. The `Component` class is the root for all UI components and containers. All but a few Swing components, such as `JFrame`, `JApplet`, and `JDialog`, are subclasses of `JComponent`. Figure 13.2 lists some frequently used methods in `Component`, `Container`, and `JComponent` for manipulating properties like font, color, size, tool tip text, and border.

Component
Container
JComponent

You can set a border on any object of the `JComponent` class. Swing has several types of borders. To create a titled border, use new `TitleBorder(String title)`. To create a line border, use new `LineBorder(Color color, int width)`, where `width` specifies the thickness of the line. For example, Listing 13.1 displays a titled border on a message panel, as shown in Figure 13.3:

LISTING **13.1**   TestSwingCommonFeatures.java (Swing Common Features)

```
1 import java.awt.*;
2 import javax.swing.*;
3 import javax.swing.border.*;
4
5 public class TestSwingCommonFeatures {
6   public static void main(String[] args) {
```

message panel
set properties

```
 7      // Create a message panel and set its properties
 8      MessagePanel messagePanel = new MessagePanel();
 9      messagePanel.setFont(new Font("timesRoman", Font.BOLD, 20));
10      messagePanel.setBackground(Color.white);
11      messagePanel.setForeground(Color.red);
12      messagePanel.setBorder(new TitledBorder("Display Message"));
13      messagePanel.setCentered(true);
14
15      // Create a frame and set its properties
16      JFrame frame = new JFrame("TestSwingCommonFeatures");
17      frame.getContentPane().add(messagePanel);
18      frame.setSize(300, 200);
19      frame.setDefaultCloseOperation(JFrame.EXIT_ON_CLOSE);
20      frame.setVisible(true);
21
22      // Set message panel width and height as its tool tip text
23      messagePanel.setToolTipText("Width " +
24        messagePanel.getWidth() + " and height " +
25        messagePanel.getHeight());
26    }
27 }
```

frame
add panel

---

java.awt.Component

+getFont(): java.awt.Font	Returns the font of this component.
+setFont(f: java.awt.Font): void	Sets the font of this component.
+getBackground(): java.awt.Color	Returns the background color of this component.
+setBackground(c: Color): void	Sets the background color of this component.
+getForeground(): java.awt.Color	Returns the foreground color of this component.
+setForeground(c: Color): void	Sets the foreground color of this component.
+getWidth(): int	Returns the width of this component.
+getHeight(): int	Returns the height of this component.
+getPreferredSize(): Dimension	Returns the preferred size of this component.
+setPreferredSize(d: Dimension): void	Sets the preferred size of this component.
+isVisible(): boolean	Indicates whether this component is visible.
+setVisible(b: boolean): void	Shows or hides this component.

java.awt.Container

+add(comp: Component): Component	Adds a component to the container.
+add(comp: Component, index: int): Component	Adds a component to the container with the specified index.
+remove(comp: Component): void	Removes the component from the container.
+getLayout(): LayoutManager	Returns the layout manager for this container.
+setLayout(l: LayoutManager): void	Sets the layout manager for this container.
+paintComponents(g: Graphics): void	Paints each of the components in this container.

javax.swing.JComponent

+getToolTipText(): String	Returns the tool tip text for this component. Tool tip text is displayed when the mouse points on the component without clicking.
+setToolTipText(text: String): void	Sets a new tool tip text for this component.
+getBorder(): javax.swing.border.Border	Returns the border for this component.
+setBorder(border: Border): void	Sets a new border for this component.

FIGURE 13.2 *All the Swing GUI components inherit the public methods from* Component, Container, *and* JComponent.

FIGURE 13.3 *The font, color, border, and tool tip text are set in the message panel.*

Since the `MessagePanel` class (introduced on page 400) is a subclass of `JPanel`, `MessagePanel` is a Swing GUI component. Therefore, you can apply the methods `setFont`, `setBackground`, `setForeground`, `setBorder`, and `setToolTipText` to an object of `MessagePanel`. Lines 23–25 sets a tool tip on `messagePanel`. The tool tip indicates the height and width of `messagePanel`. If frame were not displayed (Line 20), the width and height of `messagePanel` would be 0.

 NOTE

The `Container` class is the superclass for Swing GUI component classes, such as `JButton`. In theory, you could use the `setLayout` method to set the layout in a button and add components into a button, because all the public methods in the `Container` class are inherited into `JButton`, but for practical reasons you should not use buttons as containers.

 NOTE

Throughout this book, the prefixes `jbt`, `jchk`, `jrb`, `jlbl`, `jtf`, `jta`, `jcbo`, `jlst`, `jscb`, and `jsld` are used to name objects of `JButton`, `JCheckBox`, `JRadioButton`, `JLabel`, `JTextField`, `JTextArea`, `JComboBox`, `JList`, `JScrollBar`, and `JSlider`.

naming convention for components

13.3   Buttons

A *button* is a component that triggers an action event when clicked. Swing provides regular buttons, toggle buttons, check box buttons, and radio buttons. The common features of these buttons are represented in `javax.swing.AbstractButton`, as shown in Figure 13.4.

AbstractButton
JButton

This section introduces the regular buttons defined in the `JButton` class. `JButton` inherits `AbstractButton` and provides several constructors to create buttons, as shown in Figure 13.5.

13.3.1   Icons

An icon is a fixed-size picture; typically it is small and used to decorate components. `javax.swing.Icon` is an interface. To create an image, use its concrete class `javax.swing.ImageIcon`. For example, the following statement creates an icon from an image file:

```
Icon icon = new ImageIcon("photo.gif");
```

 NOTE

Java currently supports three image formats: GIF (Graphics Interchange Format), JPEG (Joint Photographic Experts Group), and PNG (Portable Network Graphics). The image filenames for these types end with .gif, .jpg, and .png, respectively. If you have a bitmap file or image files in other formats, you can use image-processing utilities to convert them into GIF, JPEG, or PNG format for use in Java.

image file format

javax.swing.JComponent	

↑

javax.swing.AbstractButton	
+getActionCommand(): String	Returns the action command of this button.
+setActionCommand(s: String): void	Sets a new action command for this button.
+getText(): String	Returns the button's text (i.e., the text label on the button).
+setText(text: String): void	Sets the button's text.
+getIcon(): javax.swing.Icon	Returns the button's default icon.
+setIcon(icon: Icon): void	Sets the button's default icon. This icon is also used as the "pressed" and "disabled" icon if there is no explicitly set pressed icon.
+getPressedIcon(): javax.swing.Icon	Returns the pressed icon (displayed when the button is pressed).
+setPressedIcon(pressedIcon: Icon): void	Sets a pressed icon for the button.
+getRolloverIcon(): javax.swing.Icon	Returns the rollover icon (displayed when the mouse is over the button).
+setRolloverIcon(pressedIcon: Icon): void	Sets a rollover icon for the button.
+getMnemonic(): int	Returns the mnemonic key value of this button. You can select the button by pressing the ALT key and the mnemonic key at the same time.
+setMnemonic(mnemonic: int): void	Sets a mnemonic key value of this button.
+getHorizontalAlignment(): int	Returns the horizontal alignment of the icon and text on the button.
+setHorizontalAlignment(alignment: int): void	Sets the horizontal alignment of the icon and text (default: CENTER).
+getHorizontalTextPosition(): int	Returns the horizontal text position relative to the icon on the button.
+setHorizontalTextPosition(position: int): void	Sets the horizontal text position of the text relative to the icon (default: RIGHT).
+getVerticalAlignment(): int	Returns the vertical alignment of the icon and text on the button.
+setVerticalAlignment(vAlignment: int): void	Sets the vertical alignment of the icon and text (default: CENTER).
+getVerticalTextPosition(): int	Returns the vertical text position relative to the icon on the button.
+setVerticalTextPosition(position: int): void	Sets the vertical text position of the text relative to the icon (default: CENTER).
+isBorderPainted(): Boolean	Indicates whether the border of the button is painted.
+setBorderPainted(b: boolean): void	Draws or hides the border of the button. By default, a regular button's border is painted, but the borders for a check box and a radio button are not painted.
+getIconTextGap(): int	Returns the gap between the text and the icon on the button (JDK 1.4).
+setIconTextGap(iconTextGap: int): void	Sets a gap between the text and the icon on the button (JDK 1.4).
+isSelected(): Boolean	Returns the state of the button. True if the check box or radio button is selected, false if it's not.
+setSelected(b: boolean): void	Sets the state for the check box or radio button.

FIGURE 13.4 *AbstractButton defines common features of different types of buttons.*

naming files consistently

 NOTE

File names are not case-sensitive on Windows, but are case-sensitive on Unix. To enable your programs to run on all platforms, name all the image files consistently.

A regular button has a default icon, pressed icon, and rollover icon. Normally, you use the default icon. The other icons are for special effects. A pressed icon is displayed when a button is pressed, and a rollover icon is displayed when the mouse is over the button but pressed. For

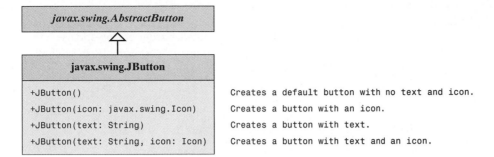

```
┌─────────────────────────────────────┐
│     javax.swing.AbstractButton        │
└─────────────────────────────────────┘
                    △
                    │
┌─────────────────────────────────────┐
│        javax.swing.JButton            │
├─────────────────────────────────────┤
│ +JButton()                            │   Creates a default button with no text and icon.
│ +JButton(icon: javax.swing.Icon)      │   Creates a button with an icon.
│ +JButton(text: String)                │   Creates a button with text.
│ +JButton(text: String, icon: Icon)    │   Creates a button with text and an icon.
└─────────────────────────────────────┘
```

FIGURE 13.5 *JButton defines a regular push button.*

example, Listing 13.2 displays the American flag as a regular icon, the Canadian flag as a pressed icon, and the British flag as a rollover icon, as shown in Figure 13.6.

LISTING 13.2 TestButtonIcons.java (Using Icons)

```java
1 import javax.swing.*;
2
3 public class TestButtonIcons extends JFrame {
4   public static void main(String[] args) {
5     // Create a frame and set its properties
6     JFrame frame = new TestButtonIcons();
7     frame.setTitle("ButtonIcons");
8     frame.setSize(200, 100);
9     frame.setDefaultCloseOperation(JFrame.EXIT_ON_CLOSE);
10    frame.setVisible(true);
11  }
12
13  public TestButtonIcons() {
14    ImageIcon usIcon = new ImageIcon("image/usIcon.gif");
15    ImageIcon caIcon = new ImageIcon("image/caIcon.gif");
16    ImageIcon ukIcon = new ImageIcon("image/ukIcon.gif");
17
18    JButton jbt = new JButton("Click it", usIcon);
19    jbt.setPressedIcon(caIcon);
20    jbt.setRolloverIcon(ukIcon);
21
22    getContentPane().add(jbt);
23  }
24 }
```

icon

(a) Default icon (b) Pressed icon

(c) Rollover icon

FIGURE 13.6 *A button can have several types of icons.*

NOTE

Borders and icons can be shared. Thus you can create a border or icon and use it to set the `border` or `icon` property for any GUI component. For example, the following statements set a border b for two panels p1 and p2:

```
p1.setBorder(b);
p2.setBorder(b);
```

The following statements set an icon in two buttons jbt1 and jbt2:

```
jbt1.setIcon(icon);
jbt2.setIcon(icon);
```

13.3.2 Alignments

horizontal alignment

Horizontal alignment specifies how the icon and text are placed horizontally on a button. You can set the horizontal alignment using `setHorizontalAlignment(int)` with one of the five constants `LEADING`, `LEFT`, `CENTER`, `RIGHT`, `TRAILING`, as shown in Figure 13.7. At present, `LEADING` and `LEFT` are the same, and `TRAILING` and `RIGHT` are the same. Future implementation may distinquish them. The default horizontal alignment is `SwingConstants.TRAILING`.

left-aligned ——  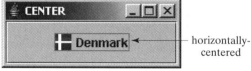 —— horizontally-centered

(a) Text and icon are left-aligned.   (b) Text and icon are center-aligned.

 —— right-aligned

(c) Text and icon are right-aligned.

FIGURE 13.7 *You can specify how the icon and text are placed on a button horizontally.*

vertical alignment

Vertical alignment specifies how the icon and text are placed vertically on a button. You can set the vertical alignment using `setVerticalAlignment(int)` with one of the three constants `TOP`, `CENTER`, `BOTTOM`, as shown in Figure 13.8. The default vertical alignment is `SwingConstants.CENTER`.

13.3.3 Text Positions

horizontal text position

Horizontal text position specifies the horizontal position of the text relative to the icon. You can set the horizontal text position using `setHorizontalTextPosition(int)` with one of the five constants `LEADING`, `LEFT`, `CENTER`, `RIGHT`, `TRAILING`, as shown in Figure 13.9. At present, `LEADING` and `LEFT` are the same, and `TRAILING` and `RIGHT` are the same. Future implementations may distinquish them. The default horizontal text position is `SwingConstants.RIGHT`.

vertical text position

Vertical text position specifies the vertical position of the text relative to the icon. You can set the vertical text position using `setVerticalTextPosition(int)` with one of the three constants

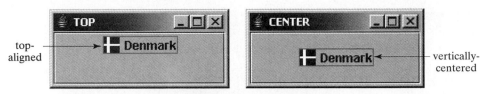

top-aligned →

(a) Text and icon are top-aligned.

vertically-centered

(b) Text and icon are centered vertically.

bottom-aligned

(c) Text and icon are bottom-aligned.

FIGURE 13.8 *You can specify how the icon and text are placed on a button vertically.*

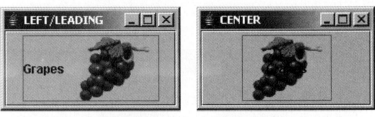

(a) Text is on the left of the icon.

(b) Text is centered on the icon.

(c) Text is on the right of the icon.

FIGURE 13.9 *You can specify the horizontal position of the text relative to the icon.*

TOP, CENTER, BOTTOM, as shown in Figure 13.10. The default vertical text position is SwingConstants.CENTER.

 NOTE

The constants LEFT, CENTER, RIGHT, LEADING, TRAILING, TOP, BOTTOM used in AbstractButton are also used in many other Swing components. These constants are centrally defined in the javax.swing.SwingConstants interface. Since all Swing GUI components implement SwingConstants, you can reference the constants through SwingConstants or a GUI component. For example, SwingConstants.CENTER is the same as JButton.CENTER.

JButton can generate many types of events, but often you need to respond to an ActionEvent. When a button is pressed, it generates an ActionEvent.

(a) Text appears top relative to the icon.   (b) Text appears centered relative to the icon.

(c) Text appears bottom relative to the icon.

FIGURE 13.10 *You can specify the vertical position of the text relative to the icon.*

EXAMPLE 13.1 USING BUTTONS

Problem

Write a program that displays a message on a panel and uses two buttons, $<=$ and $=>$, to move the message on the panel to the left or right. The layout of the UI and the output of the program are shown in Figure 13.11.

FIGURE 13.11 *Clicking the $<=$ and $=>$ buttons causes the message on the panel to move to the left and right, respectively.*

Solution

Here are the major steps in the program:

1. Create the user interface.

   Create a `MessagePanel` object to display the message. The `MessagePanel` class was created in Listing 11.15. Place it in the center of the frame. Create two buttons, $<=$ and $=>$, on a panel. Place the panel in the south of the frame.

EXAMPLE **13.1** (CONTINUED)

2. Process the event.

   Implement the actionPerformed handler to move the message left or right according to whether the left or right button was clicked.

LISTING 13.3 ButtonDemo.java (Using Buttons)

```java
1 import java.awt.*;
2 import java.awt.event.ActionListener;
3 import java.awt.event.ActionEvent;
4 import javax.swing.*;
5
6 public class ButtonDemo extends JFrame implements ActionListener {
7   // Create a panel for displaying message
8   protected MessagePanel messagePanel
9     = new MessagePanel("Welcome to Java");
10
11   // Declare two buttons to move the message left and right
12   private JButton jbtLeft = new JButton("Left");
13   private JButton jbtRight = new JButton("Right");
14
15   public static void main(String[] args) {
16     ButtonDemo frame = new ButtonDemo();
17     frame.setTitle("ButtonDemo");
18     frame.setDefaultCloseOperation(JFrame.EXIT_ON_CLOSE);
19     frame.setSize(500, 200);
20     frame.setVisible(true);
21   }
22
23   public ButtonDemo() {
24     // Set the background color of messagePanel
25     messagePanel.setBackground(Color.yellow);
26
27     // Create Panel jpButtons to hold two Buttons "<=" and "right =>"
28     JPanel jpButtons = new JPanel();
29     jpButtons.setLayout(new FlowLayout());
30     jpButtons.add(jbtLeft);
31     jpButtons.add(jbtRight);
32
33     // Set keyboard mnemonics
34     jbtLeft.setMnemonic('L');
35     jbtRight.setMnemonic('R');
36
37     // Set icons and remove text
38 //      jbtLeft.setIcon(new ImageIcon("image/left.gif"));
39 //      jbtRight.setIcon(new ImageIcon("image/right.gif"));
40 //      jbtLeft.setText(null);
41 //      jbtRight.setText(null);
42
43     // Set tool tip text on the buttons
44     jbtLeft.setToolTipText("Move message to left");
45     jbtRight.setToolTipText("Move message to right");
46
47     // Place panels in the frame
48     getContentPane().setLayout(new BorderLayout());
49     getContentPane().add(messagePanel, BorderLayout.CENTER);
50     getContentPane().add(jpButtons, BorderLayout.SOUTH);
51
52     // Register listeners with the buttons
53     jbtLeft.addActionListener(this);
54     jbtRight.addActionListener(this);
55   }
```

create frame

create UI

mnemonic

tool tip

register listener

EXAMPLE 13.1 (CONTINUED)

```
56
57   /** Handle ActionEvent */
58   public void actionPerformed(ActionEvent e) {
59     if (e.getSource() == jbtLeft) {
60       messagePanel.moveLeft();
61     }
62     else if (e.getSource() == jbtRight) {
63       messagePanel.moveRight();
64     }
65   }
66 }
```

Review

messagePanel (Line 8) is deliberately declared protected so that it can be referenced by a subclass in future examples.

You can set an icon image on the button by using the setIcon method. If you uncomment the following code in Lines 38–41:

```
//   jbtLeft.setIcon(new ImageIcon("image/left.gif"));
//   jbtRight.setIcon(new ImageIcon("image/right.gif"));
//   jbtLeft.setText(null);
//   jbtRight.setText(null);
```

the texts are replaced by the icons, as shown in Figure 13.12(a) . "image/left.gif" is located in "c:\book\image\left.gif."

(a)　　　　　　　　　　　　　(b)

FIGURE 13.12 *(a) You can set an icon on a JButton. (b) You can set a text and icon on a button at the same time.*

 NOTE

The back slash (\) is the Windows file path notation. On Unix, the forward slash (/) should be used. In Java, you should use the forward slash (/) to denote a relative file path under the Java classpath (e.g., image/left.gif, as in this example).

You can set text and an icon on a button at the same time, if you wish, as shown in Figure 13.12(b) . By default, the text and icon are centered horizontally and vertically.

Each button has a tool-tip text (Lines 44–45), which appears when the mouse is set on the button without clicking, as shown in Figure 13.13(a) .

The button can also be accessed by using the keyboard mnemonics. Pressing ALT+L is equivalent to clicking the <= button, since you set the mnemonic property to 'L' in the left button (Line 34). If you change the left button text to "Left" and the right button to "Right", the L and R in the captions of these buttons will be underlined, as shown in Figure 13.13(b) .

EXAMPLE 13.1 (CONTINUED)

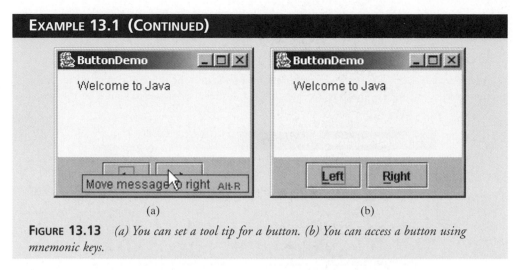

(a)   (b)

FIGURE 13.13 *(a) You can set a tool tip for a button. (b) You can access a button using mnemonic keys.*

13.4 Check Boxes

A *toggle button* is a two-state button like a light switch. JToggleButton inherits AbstractButton and implements a toggle button. Often JToggleButton's subclasses JCheckBox and JRadioButton are used to enable the user to toggle a choice on or off. This section introduces JCheckBox. JRadioButton will be introduced in the next section.

toggle button

JCheckBox inherits all the properties, such as text, icon, mnemonic, verticalAlignment, horizontalAlignment, horizontalTextPosition, verticalTextPosition, and selected, from AbstractButton, and provides several constructors to create check boxes, as shown in Figure 13.14.

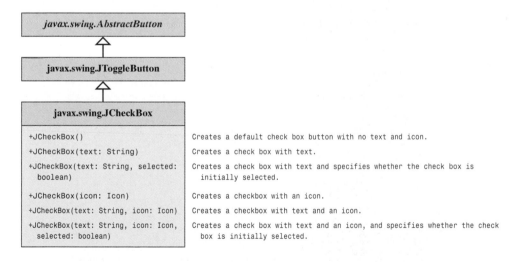

FIGURE 13.14 *JCheckBox defines a check box button.*

Here is an example of a check box with text "Student", red foreground, white background, mnemonic key 'S', and initially selected:

```
JCheckBox jchk = new JCheckBox("Student", true);
jchk.setForeground(Color.red);
jchk.setBackground(Color.white);
jchk.setMnemonic('S');
```

When a check box is clicked (checked or unchecked), it fires an ItemEvent and then an ActionEvent. To see if a check box is selected, use the isSelected() method.

EXAMPLE 13.2 USING CHECK BOXES

Problem

Add three check boxes named *Centered*, *Bold*, and *Italic* into the preceding example to let the user specify whether the message is centered, bold, or italic, as shown in Figure 13.15.

FIGURE 13.15 *Three check boxes are added to specify how the message is displayed.*

Solution

There are at least two approaches to writing this program. The first is to revise the preceding ButtonDemo class to insert the code for adding the check boxes and processing their events. The second is to create a subclass that extends ButtonDemo. Please implement the first approach as an exercise. Below is the code to implement the second approach.

LISTING 13.4 CheckBoxDemo.java (Using Check Boxes)

```
 1 import java.awt.*;
 2 import java.awt.event.ActionEvent;
 3 import javax.swing.*;
 4
 5 public class CheckBoxDemo extends ButtonDemo {
 6   // Create three check boxes to control the display of message
 7   private JCheckBox jchkCentered = new JCheckBox("Centered");
 8   private JCheckBox jchkBold = new JCheckBox("Bold");
 9   private JCheckBox jchkItalic = new JCheckBox("Italic");
10
11   public static void main(String[] args) {
12     CheckBoxDemo frame = new CheckBoxDemo();
13     frame.setTitle("CheckBoxDemo");
14     frame.setDefaultCloseOperation(JFrame.EXIT_ON_CLOSE);
15     frame.setSize(500, 200);
16     frame.setVisible(true);
17   }
18
19   public CheckBoxDemo() {
20     // Set mnemonic keys
21     jchkCentered.setMnemonic('C');
22     jchkBold.setMnemonic('B');
23     jchkItalic.setMnemonic('I');
24
25     // Create a new panel to hold check boxes
26     JPanel jpCheckBoxes = new JPanel();
27     jpCheckBoxes.setLayout(new GridLayout(3, 0));
28     jpCheckBoxes.add(jchkCentered);
29     jpCheckBoxes.add(jchkBold);
30     jpCheckBoxes.add(jchkItalic);
31     getContentPane().add(jpCheckBoxes, BorderLayout.EAST);
32
33     // Register listeners with the check boxes
34     jchkCentered.addActionListener(this);
```

create frame

create UI

register listener

EXAMPLE 13.2 (CONTINUED)

```
35      jchkBold.addActionListener(this);
36      jchkItalic.addActionListener(this);
37    }
38
39    /** Handle ActionEvent */
40    public void actionPerformed(ActionEvent e) {                        handler
41      super.actionPerformed(e); // Invoke the handler for buttons
42
43      if (e.getSource() == jchkCentered) {
44        messagePanel.setCentered(jchkCentered.isSelected());
45      }
46      else if ((e.getSource() == jchkBold) ||
47        (e.getSource() == jchkItalic)) {
48        // Determine a font style
49        int fontStyle = Font.PLAIN;
50        fontStyle += (jchkBold.isSelected() ? Font.BOLD : 0);
51        fontStyle += (jchkItalic.isSelected() ? Font.ITALIC : 0);
52
53        // Set font for the message
54        Font font = messagePanel.getFont();
55        messagePanel.setFont(
56          new Font(font.getName(), fontStyle, font.getSize()));
57      }
58    }
59  }
```

Review

CheckBoxDemo extends ButtonDemo and adds three check boxes to control how the message is displayed. When a CheckBoxDemo is constructed (Line 12), its superclass's no-arg constructor is invoked, so you don't have to rewrite the code that is already in the constructor of ButtonDemo.

Since ButtonDemo implements ActionListener, an instance of CheckBoxDemo can also be a listener for ActionEvent, which is registered with the check boxes in Lines 34–36. An ActionEvent may be fired from a button or a check box. super.actionPerformed(e) (Line 41) invokes the actionPerformed method defined in ButtonDemo class to process ActionEvent fired from the Left or the Right button.

When a check box is checked or unchecked, the actionPerformed method is invoked to process the event. When the Centered check box is checked or unchecked, the centered property of the MessagePanel class is set to true or false.

The current font name and size used in MessagePanel are obtained from messagePanel.getFont() using the getName() and getSize() methods. The font styles (Font.BOLD and Font.ITALIC) are specified in the check boxes. If no font style is selected, the font style is Font.PLAIN. Font styles are combined by adding together the selected integers representing the fonts.

The keyboard mnemonics 'C', 'B', and 'I' are set on the check boxes "Centered", "Bold", and "Italic", respectively (Lines 21–23). You can use a mouse gesture or a shortcut key to select a check box.

The setFont method (Line 55) defined in the Component class is inherited in the MessagePanel class. This method automatically invokes the repaint method. Invoking setFont in messagePanel automatically repaints the message.

A check box fires an ActionEvent or an ItemEvent when it is clicked. You could process either the ActionEvent or the ItemEvent to redisplay the message. The example processes the ActionEvent. If you wish to process the ItemEvent, you could create a listener for ItemEvent and register it with a check box, as shown below:

```
public class CheckBoxDemoUsingItemEvent extends ButtonDemo
    implements ItemListener {
      ... // Same as in CheckBoxDemo.java, so omitted
```

EXAMPLE 13.2 (CONTINUED)

```
public CheckBoxDemoUsingItemEvent() {
  ... // Same as in CheckBoxDemo.java, so omitted

  // TO listen for ItemEvent
  jchkCentered.addItemListener(this);
  jchkBold.addItemListener(this);
  jchkItalic.addItemListener(this);
}

/** Handle ItemEvent */
public void itemStateChanged(ItemEvent e) {
  ... // Same as Lines 46-60 in CheckBoxDemo.java, so omitted
}
}
```

13.5   Radio Buttons

Radio buttons, also known as *option buttons*, enable you to choose a single item from a group of choices. In appearance radio buttons resemble check boxes, but check boxes display a square that is either checked or blank, whereas radio buttons display a circle that is either filled (if selected) or blank (if not selected).

JRadioButton inherits AbstractButton, and provides several constructors to create radio buttons, as shown in Figure 13.16. These constructors are similar to the constructors for JCheckBox.

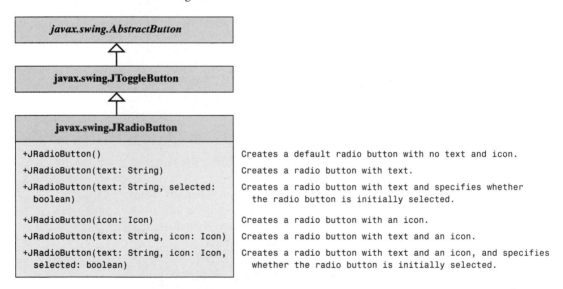

+JRadioButton()	Creates a default radio button with no text and icon.
+JRadioButton(text: String)	Creates a radio button with text.
+JRadioButton(text: String, selected: boolean)	Creates a radio button with text and specifies whether the radio button is initially selected.
+JRadioButton(icon: Icon)	Creates a radio button with an icon.
+JRadioButton(text: String, icon: Icon)	Creates a radio button with text and an icon.
+JRadioButton(text: String, icon: Icon, selected: boolean)	Creates a radio button with text and an icon, and specifies whether the radio button is initially selected.

FIGURE 13.16   *JRadioButton defines a radio button.*

Here is an example of a radio button with text "Student", red foreground, white background, mnemonic key 'S', and initially selected:

```
JRadioButton jrb = new JRadioButton("Student", true);
jrb.setForeground(Color.red);
jrb.setBackground(Color.white);
jrb.setMnemonic('S');
```

To group radio buttons, you need to create an instance of java.swing.ButtonGroup and use the add method to add them to it, as follows:

```
ButtonGroup group = new ButtonGroup();
group.add(jrb1);
group.add(jrb2);
```

This code creates a radio button group for radio buttons jrb1 and jrb2 so that jrb1 and jrb2 are selected mutually exclusively. Without grouping, jrb1 and jrb2 would be independent.

🌸 NOTE

ButtonGroup is not a subclass of java.awt.Component, so a ButtonGroup object cannot be added to a container.

When a radio button is clicked (selected or deselected), it fires an ItemEvent and then an ActionEvent. To see if a radio button is selected, use the isSelected() method.

EXAMPLE 13.3 USING RADIO BUTTONS

Problem

Add three radio buttons named *Red*, *Green*, and *Blue* into the preceding example to let the user choose the color of the message, as shown in Figure 13.17.

FIGURE 13.17 *Three radio buttons are added to specify the color of the message.*

Solution

Again there are at least two approaches to writing this program. The first is to revise the preceding CheckBoxDemo class to insert the code for adding the radio buttons and processing their events. The second is to create a subclass that extends CheckBoxDemo. Below is the code to implement the second approach.

LISTING 13.5 RadioButtonDemo.java (Using Radio Buttons)

```
1  import java.awt.*;
2  import java.awt.event.*;
3  import javax.swing.*;
4
5  public class RadioButtonDemo extends CheckBoxDemo {
6    // Declare radio buttons
7    private JRadioButton jrbRed, jrbGreen, jrbBlue;
8
9    public static void main(String[] args) {
10     RadioButtonDemo frame = new RadioButtonDemo();
11     frame.setDefaultCloseOperation(JFrame.EXIT_ON_CLOSE);
12     frame.setTitle("RadioButtonDemo");
13     frame.setSize(500, 200);
14     frame.setVisible(true);
15   }
16
17   public RadioButtonDemo() {
18     // Create a new panel to hold check boxes
```

create frame

create UI

EXAMPLE 13.3 (CONTINUED)

```
19      JPanel jpRadioButtons = new JPanel();
20      jpRadioButtons.setLayout(new GridLayout(3, 1));
21      jpRadioButtons.add(jrbRed = new JRadioButton("Red"));
22      jpRadioButtons.add(jrbGreen = new JRadioButton("Green"));
23      jpRadioButtons.add(jrbBlue = new JRadioButton("Blue"));
24      getContentPane().add(jpRadioButtons, BorderLayout.WEST);
25
26      // Create a radio button group to group three buttons
27      ButtonGroup group = new ButtonGroup();
28      group.add(jrbRed);
29      group.add(jrbGreen);
30      group.add(jrbBlue);
31
32      // Set keyboard mnemonics
33      jrbRed.setMnemonic('E');
34      jrbGreen.setMnemonic('G');
35      jrbBlue.setMnemonic('U');
36
37      // Register listeners for check boxes
38      jrbRed.addActionListener(this);
39      jrbGreen.addActionListener(this);
40      jrbBlue.addActionListener(this);
41
42      // Set initial message color to blue
43      jrbBlue.setSelected(true);
44      messagePanel.setForeground(Color.blue);
45    }
46
47    /** Handle ActionEvent */
48    public void actionPerformed(ActionEvent e) {
49      super.actionPerformed(e); // Invoke the handler in the superclass
50
51      if (e.getSource() == jrbRed)
52        messagePanel.setForeground(Color.red);
53      else if (e.getSource() == jrbGreen)
54        messagePanel.setForeground(Color.green);
55      else if (e.getSource() == jrbBlue)
56        messagePanel.setForeground(Color.blue);
57    }
58 }
```

group buttons

handler

Review

`RadioButtonDemo` extends `CheckBoxDemo` and adds three radio buttons to specify the message color. Since `CheckBoxDemo` extends `ButtonDemo`, and `ButtonDemo` implements `ActionListener`, an instance of `RadioButtonDemo` can also be a listener for `ActionEvent`, which is registered with the radio buttons in Lines 38–40.

When an `ActionEvent` occurs, the `actionPerformed` method is invoked to process the event. If it is fired from a button or a check box, it is processed by the `actionPerformed` method defined in the superclass of `RadioButtonDemo` (Line 49). When a radio button is clicked, the corresponding foreground color in `messagePanel` is set.

The keyboard mnemonics `'R'` and `'B'` are already set for the Right button and Bold check box. To avoid conflict, the keyboard mnemonics `'E'`, `'G'`, and `'U'` are set on the radio buttons `"Red"`, `"Green"`, and `"Blue"`, respectively (Lines 33–35).

The program creates a `ButtonGroup` group and puts three `JRadioButton` instances (`jrbRed`, `jrbGreen`, and `jrbBlue`) in the group (Lines 27–30).

A radio button fires an `ActionEvent` or an `ItemEvent` when it is selected or deselected. You could process either the `ActionEvent` or the `ItemEvent` to choose a color. The example processes the `ActionEvent`. Please rewrite the code using the `ItemEvent` as an exercise.

13.6 Labels

A *label* is a display area for a short text, an image, or both. It is often used to label other components (usually text fields). Figure 13.18 lists the constructors and methods in JLabel.

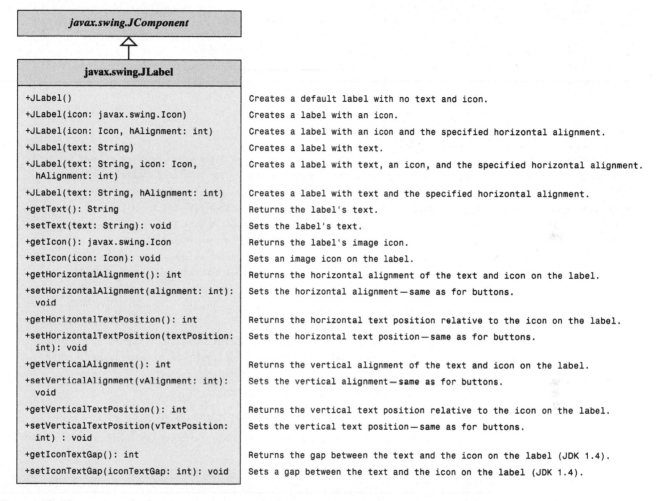

javax.swing.JComponent	

javax.swing.JLabel	
+JLabel()	Creates a default label with no text and icon.
+JLabel(icon: javax.swing.Icon)	Creates a label with an icon.
+JLabel(icon: Icon, hAlignment: int)	Creates a label with an icon and the specified horizontal alignment.
+JLabel(text: String)	Creates a label with text.
+JLabel(text: String, icon: Icon, hAlignment: int)	Creates a label with text, an icon, and the specified horizontal alignment.
+JLabel(text: String, hAlignment: int)	Creates a label with text and the specified horizontal alignment.
+getText(): String	Returns the label's text.
+setText(text: String): void	Sets the label's text.
+getIcon(): javax.swing.Icon	Returns the label's image icon.
+setIcon(icon: Icon): void	Sets an image icon on the label.
+getHorizontalAlignment(): int	Returns the horizontal alignment of the text and icon on the label.
+setHorizontalAlignment(alignment: int): void	Sets the horizontal alignment—same as for buttons.
+getHorizontalTextPosition(): int	Returns the horizontal text position relative to the icon on the label.
+setHorizontalTextPosition(textPosition: int): void	Sets the horizontal text position—same as for buttons.
+getVerticalAlignment(): int	Returns the vertical alignment of the text and icon on the label.
+setVerticalAlignment(vAlignment: int): void	Sets the vertical alignment—same as for buttons.
+getVerticalTextPosition(): int	Returns the vertical text position relative to the icon on the label.
+setVerticalTextPosition(vTextPosition: int) : void	Sets the vertical text position—same as for buttons.
+getIconTextGap(): int	Returns the gap between the text and the icon on the label (JDK 1.4).
+setIconTextGap(iconTextGap: int): void	Sets a gap between the text and the icon on the label (JDK 1.4).

FIGURE 13.18 *JLabel displays text or an icon, or both.*

JLabel inherits all the properties from JComponent and has many properties similar to the ones in JButton, such as text, icon, horizontalAlignment, verticalAlignment, horizontalTextPosition, verticalTextPosition, and iconTextGap. For example, the following code displays a label with text and an icon:

```
// Create an image icon from an image file
ImageIcon icon = new ImageIcon("image/grapes.gif");

// Create a label with text, an icon,
// with centered horizontal alignment
JLabel jlbl = new JLabel("Grapes", icon, SwingConstants.CENTER);

// Set label's text alignment and gap between text and icon
jlbl.setHorizontalTextPosition(SwingConstants.CENTER);
jlbl.setVerticalTextPosition(SwingConstants.BOTTOM);
jlbl.setIconTextGap(5);
```

13.7   Text Fields

A *text field* can be used to enter or display a string. JTextField is a subclass of JTextComponent. Figure 13.19 lists the constructors and methods in JTextField.

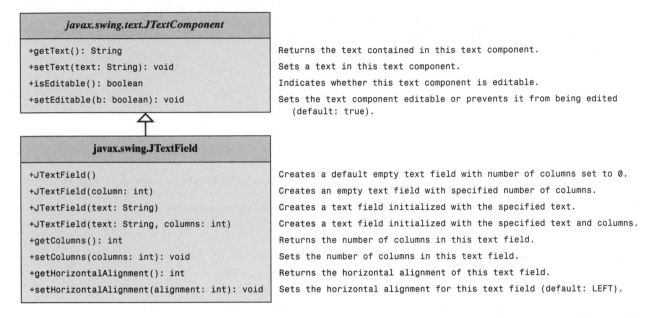

javax.swing.text.JTextComponent	
+getText(): String	Returns the text contained in this text component.
+setText(text: String): void	Sets a text in this text component.
+isEditable(): boolean	Indicates whether this text component is editable.
+setEditable(b: boolean): void	Sets the text component editable or prevents it from being edited (default: true).

javax.swing.JTextField	
+JTextField()	Creates a default empty text field with number of columns set to 0.
+JTextField(column: int)	Creates an empty text field with specified number of columns.
+JTextField(text: String)	Creates a text field initialized with the specified text.
+JTextField(text: String, columns: int)	Creates a text field initialized with the specified text and columns.
+getColumns(): int	Returns the number of columns in this text field.
+setColumns(columns: int): void	Sets the number of columns in this text field.
+getHorizontalAlignment(): int	Returns the horizontal alignment of this text field.
+setHorizontalAlignment(alignment: int): void	Sets the horizontal alignment for this text field (default: LEFT).

FIGURE 13.19   *JTextField enables you to enter or display a string.*

JTextField inherits JTextComponent, which inherits JComponent. Here is an example of creating a non-editable text field with red foreground color and right horizontal alignment:

```
JTextField jtfMessage = new JTextField("T-Strom");
jtfMessage.setEditable(false);
jtfMessage.setForeground(Color.red);
jtfMessage.setHorizontalAlignment(SwingConstants.RIGHT);
```

When you move the cursor in the text field and press the Enter key, it fires an ActionEvent.

EXAMPLE 13.4 USING TEXT FIELDS

Problem

Add a text field to the preceding example to let the user set a new message, as shown in Figure 13.20.

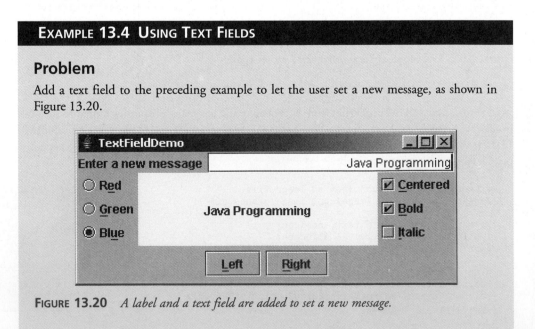

FIGURE 13.20   *A label and a text field are added to set a new message.*

EXAMPLE 13.4 (CONTINUED)

Solution

Listing 13.6 creates a subclass that extends `RadioButtonDemo`.

LISTING 13.6   TextFieldDemo.java (Using Text Fields)

```
1 import java.awt.*;
2 import java.awt.event.*;
3 import javax.swing.*;
4
5 public class TextFieldDemo extends RadioButtonDemo {
6   private JTextField jtfMessage = new JTextField(10);
7
8   /** Main method */
9   public static void main(String[] args) {
10    TextFieldDemo frame = new TextFieldDemo();
11    frame.pack();
12    frame.setTitle("TextFieldDemo");
13    frame.setDefaultCloseOperation(JFrame.EXIT_ON_CLOSE);
14    frame.setVisible(true);
15  }
16
17  public TextFieldDemo() {
18    // Create a new panel to hold label and text field
19    JPanel jpTextField = new JPanel();
20    jpTextField.setLayout(new BorderLayout(5, 0));
21    jpTextField.add(
22      new JLabel("Enter a new message"), BorderLayout.WEST);
23    jpTextField.add(jtfMessage, BorderLayout.CENTER);
24    getContentPane().add(jpTextField, BorderLayout.NORTH);
25
26    jtfMessage.setHorizontalAlignment(JTextField.RIGHT);
27
28    // Register listener
29    jtfMessage.addActionListener(this);
30  }
31
32  /** Handle ActionEvent */
33  public void actionPerformed(ActionEvent e) {
34    super.actionPerformed(e);
35
36    if (e.getSource() == jtfMessage)
37      messagePanel.setMessage(jtfMessage.getText());
38
39    jtfMessage.requestFocusInWindow();
40  }
41 }
```

create frame (lines 10–11)

create UI (line 18)

handler (line 33)

Review

`TextFieldDemo` extends `RadioButtonDemo` and adds a label and a text field to let the user enter a new message. Since `RadioButtonDemo` extends `CheckBoxDemo`, `CheckBoxDemo` extends `ButtonDemo`, and `ButtonDemo` implements `ActionListener`, an instance of `TextFieldDemo` can also be a listener for `ActionEvent`, which is registered with the radio buttons in Line 29, as shown in Figure 13.21.

FIGURE 13.21 *TextFieldDemo builds upon* RadioButtonDemo, CheckBoxDemo, *and* ButtonDemo.

When an `ActionEvent` occurs, the `actionPerformed` method is invoked to process the event. If it is fired from a button, a check box, or a radio button, it is processed by

EXAMPLE 13.4 (CONTINUED)

the `actionPerformed` method defined in the superclass of `TextFieldDemo` (Line 34). After you set a new message in the text field and press the Enter key, a new message is set in `messagePanel` (Line 37).

Instead of using the `setSize` method to set the size for the frame, the program uses the `pack()` method (Line 11), which automatically sizes up the frame according to the size of the components placed in it.

The `requestFocusInWindow()` method (Line 39) defined in the `Component` class requests the component to receive input focus. Thus, `jtfMessage.requestFocusInWindow()` (Line 39) requests the input focus on `jtfMessage`. So you will see the cursor on `jtfMessage` after the `actionPerformed` method is invoked.

13.8 Text Areas

If you want to let the user enter multiple lines of text, you have to create several instances of `JTextField`. A better alternative is to use `JTextArea`, which enables the user to enter multiple lines of text. Figure 13.22 lists the constructors and methods in `JTextArea`.

javax.swing.text.JTextComponent	

javax.swing.JTextArea	
+JTextArea()	Creates a default empty text area.
+JTextArea(rows: int, columns: int)	Creates an empty text area with the specified number of rows and columns.
+JTextArea(text: String)	Creates a new text area with the specified text displayed.
+JTextArea(text: String, rows: int, columns: int)	Creates a new text area with the specified text and number of rows and columns.
+append(s: String): void	Appends the string to text in the text area.
+insert(s: String, pos: int): void	Inserts string s in the specified position in the text area.
+replaceRange(s: String, start: int, end: int): void	Replaces partial text in the range from position start to end with string s.
+getColumns(): int	Returns the number of columns in this text area.
+setColumns(columns: int): void	Sets the number of columns in this text area.
+getRows(): int	Returns the number of rows in this text area.
+setRows(rows: int): void	Sets the number of rows in this text area.
+getLineCount(): int	Returns the actual number of lines contained in the text area.
+getTabSize(): int	Returns the number of characters used to expand tabs in this text area.
+setTabSize(size: int): void	Sets the number of characters to expand tabs to (default: 8).
+getLineWrap(): boolean	Indicates whether the line in the text area is automatically wrapped.
+setLineWrap(wrap: boolean): void	Sets the line-wrapping policy of the text area (default: false).
+getWrapStyleWord(): boolean	Indicates whether the line is wrapped on words or characters.
+setWrapStyleWord(word: boolean): void	Sets the style of wrapping used if the text area is wrapping lines. The default value is false, which indicates that the line is wrapped on characters.

FIGURE 13.22 *JTextArea enables you to enter or display multiple lines of character.*

Like `JTextField`, `JTextArea` inherits `JTextComponent`, which contains the methods `getText`, `setText`, `isEditable`, and `setEditable`. Here is an example of creating a text area with five rows and twenty columns, line-wrapped on words, red foreground color, and courier font, bold, 20 pixels.

```
JTextArea jtaNote = new JTextArea("This is a text area", 5, 20);
jtaNote.setLineWrap(true);
jtaNote.setWrapStyleWord(true);
```

```
jtaNote.setForeground(Color.red);
jtaNote.setFont(new Font("Courier", Font.BOLD, 20));
```

JTextArea does not handle scrolling, but you can create a JScrollPane object to hold an instance of JTextArea and let JScrollPane handle scrolling for JTextArea, as follows:

```
// Create a scroll pane to hold text area
JScrollPane scrollPane = new JScrollPane(jta = new JTextArea());
getContentPane().add(scrollPane, BorderLayout.CENTER);
```

EXAMPLE 13.5 USING TEXT AREAS

Problem

Write a program that displays an image in a label, a title in a label, and a text in a text area. A sample run of the program is shown in Figure 13.23.

FIGURE 13.23 *The program displays an image in a label, a title in a label, and a text in the text area.*

Solution

Here are the major steps in the program:

1. Create a class named DescriptionPanel that extends JPanel. This class contains a text area inside a scroll pane, a label for displaying an image icon, and a label for displaying a title. This class is used in the present example and will be reused in later examples.

2. Create a class named TextAreaDemo that extends JFrame. Create an instance of DescriptionPanel and add it to the center of the frame. The relationship between DescriptionPanel and TextAreaDemo is shown in Figure 13.24.

LISTING 13.7 TextAreaDemo.java (Using Text Area)

```
 1 import java.awt.*;
 2 import javax.swing.*;
 3
 4 public class TextAreaDemo extends JFrame {
 5   // Declare and create a description panel
 6   private DescriptionPanel descriptionPanel = new DescriptionPanel();
 7
 8   public static void main(String[] args) {
 9     TextAreaDemo frame = new TextAreaDemo();               create frame
10     frame.pack();
11     frame.setDefaultCloseOperation(JFrame.EXIT_ON_CLOSE);
12     frame.setTitle("TextAreaDemo");
13     frame.setVisible(true);
14   }
```

EXAMPLE 13.5 (CONTINUED)

create UI

scroll pane
text area

create panel

```
15
16    public TextAreaDemo() {
17      // Set title, text and image in the description panel
18      descriptionPanel.setTitle("Canada");
19      String description = "The Maple Leaf flag \n\n" +
20        "The Canadian National Flag was adopted by the Canadian " +
21        "Parliament on October 22, 1964 and was proclaimed into law " +
22        "by Her Majesty Queen Elizabeth II (the Queen of Canada) on " +
23        "February 15, 1965. The Canadian Flag (colloquially known " +
24        "as The Maple Leaf Flag) is a red flag of the proportions " +
25        "two by length and one by width, containing in its center a " +
26        "white square, with a single red stylized eleven-point " +
27        "mapleleaf centered in the white square.";
28      descriptionPanel.setDescription(description);
29      descriptionPanel.setImageIcon(new ImageIcon("image/ca.gif"));
30
31      // Add the description panel to the frame
32      getContentPane().setLayout(new BorderLayout());
33      getContentPane().add(descriptionPanel, BorderLayout.CENTER);
34    }
35  }
36
37  // Define a panel for displaying image and text
38  class DescriptionPanel extends JPanel {
39    /** Label for displaying an image icon */
40    private JLabel jlblImage = new JLabel();
41
42    /** Label for displaying a title */
43    private JLabel jlblTitle = new JLabel();
44
45    /** Text area for displaying text */
46    private JTextArea jtaDescription;
47
48    public DescriptionPanel() {
49      // Group image label and title label in a panel
50      JPanel panel = new JPanel();
51      panel.setLayout(new BorderLayout());
52      panel.add(jlblImage, BorderLayout.CENTER);
53      panel.add(jlblTitle, BorderLayout.SOUTH);
54
55      // Create a scroll pane to hold text area
56      JScrollPane scrollPane = new JScrollPane
57        (jtaDescription = new JTextArea());
58
59      // Center the title on the label
60      jlblTitle.setHorizontalAlignment(JLabel.CENTER);
61
62      // Set the font for the title and text
63      jlblTitle.setFont(new Font("SansSerif", Font.BOLD, 16));
64      jtaDescription.setFont(new Font("Serif", Font.PLAIN, 14));
65
66      // Set lineWrap and wrapStyleWord true for text area
67      jtaDescription.setLineWrap(true);
68      jtaDescription.setWrapStyleWord(true);
69      jtaDescription.setEditable(false);
70
71      // Set preferred size for the scroll pane
72      scrollPane.setPreferredSize(new Dimension(200, 100));
73
74      // Set BorderLayout for the whole panel, add panel and scrollpane
75      setLayout(new BorderLayout(5, 5));
76      add(scrollPane, BorderLayout.CENTER);
77      add(panel, BorderLayout.WEST);
78    }
79
```

EXAMPLE 13.5 (CONTINUED)

```
80   /** Set the title */
81   public void setTitle(String title) {
82     jlblTitle.setText(title);
83   }
84
85   /** Set the image icon */
86   public void setImageIcon(ImageIcon icon) {
87     jlblImage.setIcon(icon);
88     Dimension dimension = new Dimension(icon.getIconWidth(),
89       icon.getIconHeight());
90     jlblImage.setPreferredSize(dimension);
91   }
92
93   /** Set the text description */
94   public void setDescription(String text) {
95     jtaDescription.setText(text);
96   }
97 }
```

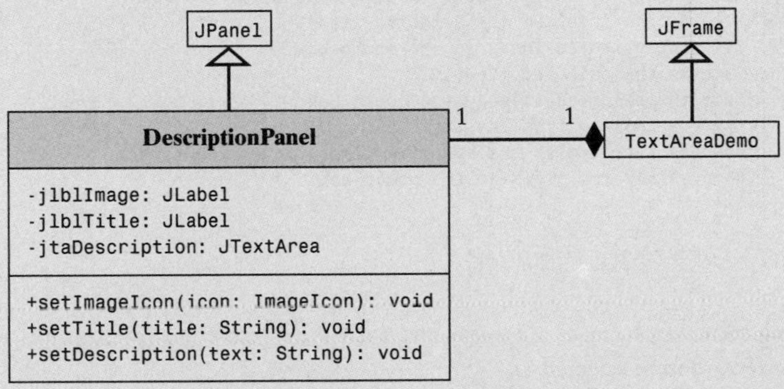

FIGURE 13.24   *TextAreaDemo uses DescriptionPanel to display an image, title, and text description of a national flag.*

Review

TextAreaDemo simply creates an instance of DescriptionPanel (Line 6), and sets the title (Line 18), image (Line 29), and text in the description panel (Line 28). DescriptionPanel is a subclass of JPanel. DescriptionPanel contains a label for displaying the image icon, a label for displaying title, and a text area for displaying a description of the image.

It is not necessary to create a separate class for DescriptionPanel in this example. Nevertheless, this class was created for reuse in the next example, where you will use it to display a description panel for various images.

The text area is inside a JScrollPane, which provides scrolling functions for the text area. Scroll bars automatically appear if there is more text than the physical size of the text area, and disappear if the text is deleted and the remaining text does not exceed the text area size.

The lineWrap property is set to true (Line 67) so that the line is automatically wrapped when the text cannot fit in one line. The wrapStyleWord property is set to true (Line 68) so that the line is wrapped on words rather than characters.

The text area is set non-editable (Line 69), so you cannot edit the description in the text area.

The preferredSize property in jlblImage is set to the size of the image icon (Line 90). The getIconWidth() and getIconHeight() methods (Lines 88–89) obtain the width and height of the icon. The preferredSize property (Line 72) in scrollPane is set to 200 in width and 100 in height. The BorderLayout manager respects the preferred size of the components.

13.9 Combo Boxes

A *combo box*, also known as a *choice list* or *drop-down list*, contains a list of items from which the user can choose. It is useful in limiting a user's range of choices and avoids the cumbersome validation of data input. Figure 13.25 lists several frequently used constructors and methods in JComboBox.

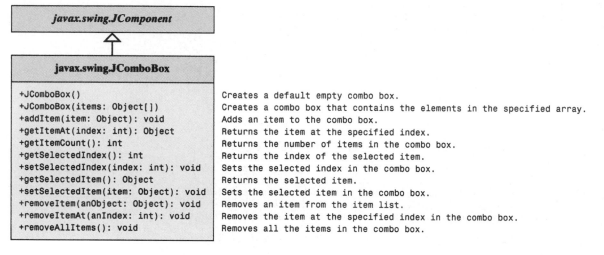

FIGURE **13.25** *JComboBox enables you to select an item from a set of items.*

The following statements create a combo box with four items, red foreground, white background, and the second item selected:

```
JComboBox jcb = new JComboBox(new Object[]
  {"Item 1", "Item 2", "Item 3", "Item 4"});
jcb.setForeground(Color.red);
jcb.setBackground(Color.white);
jcb.setSelectedItem("Item 2");
```

JComboBox can generate ActionEvent and ItemEvent, among many other events. Whenever a new item is selected, JComboBox generates ItemEvent twice, once for deselecting the previously selected item, and the other for selecting the currently selected item. JComboBox generates an ActionEvent after generating ItemEvent. To respond to an ItemEvent, you need to implement the itemStateChanged(ItemEvent e) handler for processing a choice. To get data from a JComboBox menu, you can use getSelectedItem() to return the currently selected item, or e.getItem() method to get the item from the itemStateChanged(ItemEvent e) handler.

EXAMPLE 13.6 USING COMBO BOXES

Problem

Write a program that lets users view an image and a description of a country's flag by selecting the country from a combo box. Figure 13.26 shows a sample run of the program.

Solution

Here are the major steps in the program:

1. Create the user interface.
   Create a combo box with country names as its selection values. Create a DescriptionPanel object. The DescriptionPanel class was introduced in the preceding

EXAMPLE 13.6 (CONTINUED)

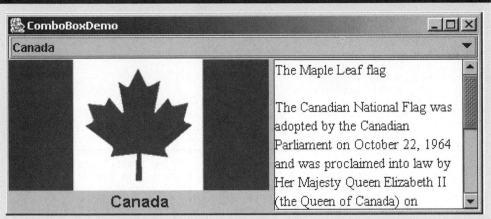

FIGURE 13.26 *A country's info, including a flag image and a description of the flag, is displayed when the country is selected in the combo box.*

example. Place the combo box in the north of the frame and the description panel in the center of the frame.

2. Process the event.
   Implement the `itemStateChanged` handler to set the flag title, image, and text in the description panel for the selected country name.

LISTING 13.8   ComboBoxDemo.java (Using Combo Boxes)

```
1 import java.awt.*;
2 import java.awt.event.*;
3 import javax.swing.*;
4
5 public class ComboBoxDemo extends JFrame implements ItemListener {
6   // Declare an array of Strings for flag titles
7   private String[] flagTitles = {"Canada", "China", "Denmark",
8     "France", "Germany", "India", "Norway", "United Kingdom",
9     "United States of America"};
10
11   // Declare an ImageIcon array for the national flags of 9 countries
12   private ImageIcon[] flagImage = {
13     new ImageIcon("image/ca.gif"),
14     new ImageIcon("image/china.gif"),
15     new ImageIcon("image/denmark.gif"),
16     new ImageIcon("image/fr.gif"),
17     new ImageIcon("image/germany.gif"),
18     new ImageIcon("image/india.gif"),
19     new ImageIcon("image/norway.gif"),
20     new ImageIcon("image/uk.gif"),
21     new ImageIcon("image/us.gif")
22   };
23
24   // Declare an array of strings for flag descriptions
25   private String[] flagDescription = new String[9];
26
27   // Declare and create a description panel
28   private DescriptionPanel descriptionPanel = new DescriptionPanel();
29
30   // Create a combo box for selecting countries
31   private JComboBox jcbo = new JComboBox(flagTitles);
32
33   public static void main(String[] args) {
34     ComboBoxDemo frame = new ComboBoxDemo();
35     frame.pack();
```

country

image icon

description

combo box

create frame

EXAMPLE 13.6 (CONTINUED)

create UI

```
36       frame.setTitle("ComboBoxDemo");
37       frame.setDefaultCloseOperation(JFrame.EXIT_ON_CLOSE);
38       frame.setVisible(true);
39     }
40
41     public ComboBoxDemo() {
42       // Set text description
43       flagDescription[0] = "The Maple Leaf flag \n\n" +
44         "The Canadian National Flag was adopted by the Canadian " +
45         "Parliament on October 22, 1964 and was proclaimed into law " +
46         "by Her Majesty Queen Elizabeth II (the Queen of Canada) on " +
47         "February 15, 1965. The Canadian Flag (colloquially known " +
48         "as The Maple Leaf Flag) is a red flag of the proportions " +
49         "two by length and one by width, containing in its center a " +
50         "white square, with a single red stylized eleven-point " +
51         "mapleleaf centered in the white square.";
52       flagDescription[1] = "Description for China ... ";
53       flagDescription[2] = "Description for Denmark ... ";
54       flagDescription[3] = "Description for France ... ";
55       flagDescription[4] = "Description for Germany ... ";
56       flagDescription[5] = "Description for India ... ";
57       flagDescription[6] = "Description for Norway ... ";
58       flagDescription[7] = "Description for UK ... ";
59       flagDescription[8] = "Description for US ... ";
60
61       // Set the first country (Canada) for display
62       setDisplay(0);
63
64       // Add combo box and description panel to the list
65       getContentPane().add(jcbo, BorderLayout.NORTH);
66       getContentPane().add(descriptionPanel, BorderLayout.CENTER);
67
68       // Register listener
69       jcbo.addItemListener(this);
70     }
71
72     /** Handle item selection */
73     public void itemStateChanged(ItemEvent e) {
74       setDisplay(jcbo.getSelectedIndex());
75     }
76
77     /** Set display information on the description panel */
78     public void setDisplay(int index) {
79       descriptionPanel.setTitle(flagTitles[index]);
80       descriptionPanel.setImageIcon(flagImage[index]);
81       descriptionPanel.setDescription(flagDescription[index]);
82     }
83   }
```

handler

Review

The frame listens to ItemEvent from the combo box and implements ItemListener (Lines 73–75). Instead of using ItemEvent, you may rewrite the program to use ActionEvent for handling combo box item selection.

The program stores the flag information in three arrays: flagTitles, flagImage, and flagDescription (Lines 7–25). The array flagTitles contains the names of nine countries, the array flagImage contains images of the nine countries' flags, and the array flagDescription contains descriptions of the flags.

The program creates an instance of DescriptionPanel (Line 28), which was presented in Example 13.5, "Using Text Areas." The program creates a combo box with initial values from flagTitles (Line 31). When the user selects an item in the combo box, the ItemStateChanged handler is executed, finds the selected index, and sets its corresponding flag title, flag image, and flag description on the panel.

13.10 Lists

A *list* is a component that basically performs the same function as a combo box but enables the user to choose a single value or multiple values. The Swing JList is very versatile. Figure 13.27 lists several frequently used constructors and methods in JList.

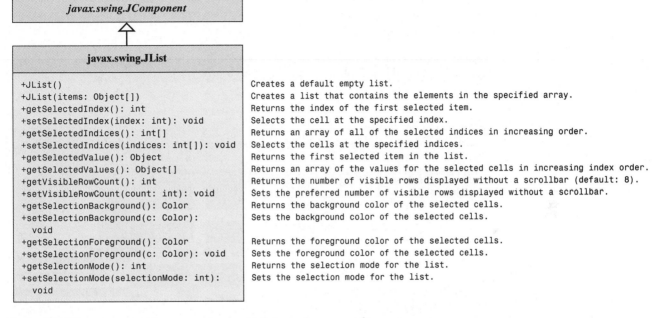

javax.swing.JComponent	

javax.swing.JList	
+JList()	Creates a default empty list.
+JList(items: Object[])	Creates a list that contains the elements in the specified array.
+getSelectedIndex(): int	Returns the index of the first selected item.
+setSelectedIndex(index: int): void	Selects the cell at the specified index.
+getSelectedIndices(): int[]	Returns an array of all of the selected indices in increasing order.
+setSelectedIndices(indices: int[]): void	Selects the cells at the specified indices.
+getSelectedValue(): Object	Returns the first selected item in the list.
+getSelectedValues(): Object[]	Returns an array of the values for the selected cells in increasing index order.
+getVisibleRowCount(): int	Returns the number of visible rows displayed without a scrollbar (default: 8).
+setVisibleRowCount(count: int): void	Sets the preferred number of visible rows displayed without a scrollbar.
+getSelectionBackground(): Color	Returns the background color of the selected cells.
+setSelectionBackground(c: Color): void	Sets the background color of the selected cells.
+getSelectionForeground(): Color	Returns the foreground color of the selected cells.
+setSelectionForeground(c: Color): void	Sets the foreground color of the selected cells.
+getSelectionMode(): int	Returns the selection mode for the list.
+setSelectionMode(selectionMode: int): void	Sets the selection mode for the list.

FIGURE 13.27 *JList enables you to select multiple items from a set of items.*

selectionMode is one of the three values (SINGLE_SELECTION, SINGLE_INTERVAL_SELECTION, MULTIPLE_INTERVAL_SELECTION) defined in javax.swing.SelectionModel that indicate whether a single item, single-interval item, or multiple-interval item can be selected. Single selection allows only one item to be selected. Single-interval selection allows multiple selections, but the selected items must be contiguous. Multiple-interval selection allows selections of multiple contiguous items without restrictions, as shown in Figure 13.28. The default value is MULTIPLE_INTERVAL_SELECTION.

(a) Single selection   (b) Single-interval selection   (c) Multiple-interval selection

FIGURE 13.28 *JList has three selection modes: single selection, single-interval selection, and multiple-interval selection.*

The following statements create a list with six items, red foreground, white background, pink selection foreground, black selection background, and visible row count 4:

```
JList jlst = new JList(new Object[]
  {"Item 1", "Item 2", "Item 3", "Item 4", "Item 5", "Item 6"});
```

```
jlst.setForeground(Color.red);
jlst.setBackground(Color.white);
jlst.setSelectionForeground(Color.pink);
jlst.setSelectionBackground(Color.black);
jlst.setVisibleRowCount(4);
```

Lists do not scroll automatically. To make a list scrollable, create a scroll pane and add the list to it. Text areas are made scrollable in the same way.

JList generates javax.swing.event.ListSelectionEvent to notify the listeners of the selections. The listener must implement the valueChanged handler in the javax.swing.event. ListSelectionListener interface to process the event.

EXAMPLE 13.7 USING LISTS

Problem

Write a program that lets users select countries in a list and display the flags of the selected countries in the labels. Figure 13.29 shows a sample run of the program.

FIGURE 13.29 *When the countries in the list are selected, corresponding images of their flags are displayed in the labels.*

Solution

Here are the major steps in the program:

1. Create the user interface.
   Create a list with nine country names as selection values, and place the list inside a scroll pane. Place the scroll pane in the west of the frame. Create nine labels to be used to display the countries' flag images. Place the labels in the panel, and place the panel in the center of the frame.

2. Process the event.
   Implement the valueChanged method in the ListSelectionListener interface to set the selected countries' flag images in the labels.

LISTING 13.9   ListDemo.java (Using Lists)

```
1 import java.awt.*;
2 import javax.swing.*;
3 import javax.swing.event.*;
4
5 public class ListDemo extends JFrame
6     implements ListSelectionListener {
7   final int NUMBER_OF_FLAGS = 9;
8
```

EXAMPLE **13.7** (CONTINUED)

```
 9    // Declare an array of Strings for flag titles
10    private String[] flagTitles = {"Canada", "China", "Denmark",
11      "France", "Germany", "India", "Norway", "United Kingdom",
12      "United States of America"};
13
14    // The list for selecting countries
15    private JList jlst = new JList(flagTitles);
16
17    // Declare an ImageIcon array for the national flags of 9 countries
18    private ImageIcon[] imageIcons = {
19      new ImageIcon("image/ca.gif"),
20      new ImageIcon("image/china.gif"),
21      new ImageIcon("image/denmark.gif"),
22      new ImageIcon("image/fr.gif"),
23      new ImageIcon("image/germany.gif"),
24      new ImageIcon("image/india.gif"),
25      new ImageIcon("image/norway.gif"),
26      new ImageIcon("image/uk.gif"),
27      new ImageIcon("image/us.gif")
28    };
29
30    // Arrays of labels for displaying images
31    private JLabel[] jlblImageViewer = new JLabel[NUMBER_OF_FLAGS];
32
33    public static void main(String[] args) {
34      ListDemo frame = new ListDemo();                        create frame
35      frame.setSize(650, 500);
36      frame.setTitle("ListDemo");
37      frame.setDefaultCloseOperation(JFrame.EXIT_ON_CLOSE);
38      frame.setVisible(true);
39    }
40
41    public ListDemo() {
42      // Create a panel to hold nine labels                   create UI
43      JPanel p = new JPanel();
44      p.setLayout(new GridLayout(3, 3, 5, 5));
45
46      for (int i = 0; i < NUMBER_OF_FLAGS; i++) {
47        p.add(jlblImageViewer[i] = new JLabel());
48        jlblImageViewer[i].setHorizontalAlignment
49          (SwingConstants.CENTER);
50      }
51
52      // Add p and the list to the frame
53      getContentPane().add(p, BorderLayout.CENTER);
54      getContentPane().add(new JScrollPane(jlst), BorderLayout.WEST);
55
56      // Register listeners
57      jlst.addListSelectionListener(this);
58    }
59
60    /** Handle list selection */                              handler
61    public void valueChanged(ListSelectionEvent e) {
62      // Get selected indices
63      int[] indices = jlst.getSelectedIndices();
64
65      int i;
66      // Set icons in the labels
67      for (i = 0; i < indices.length; i++) {
68        jlblImageViewer[i].setIcon(imageIcons[indices[i]]);
69      }
70
71      // Remove icons from the rest of the labels
72      for ( ; i < NUMBER_OF_FLAGS; i++) {
73        jlblImageViewer[i].setIcon(null);
74      }
75    }
76  }
```

EXAMPLE 13.7 (CONTINUED)

Review

The frame listens to `ListSelectionEvent` for handling the selection of country names in the list, so it implements `ListSelectionListener` (Line 6). `ListSelectionEvent` and `ListSelectionListener` are defined in the `javax.swing.event` package, so this package is imported in the program (Line 3).

The program creates an array of nine labels for displaying flag images for nine countries. The program loads the images of the nine countries into an image array (Lines 18–28) and creates a list of the nine countries in the same order as in the image array (Lines 10–12). Thus the index 0 of the image array corresponds to the first country in the list.

The list is placed in a scroll pane (Line 54) so that it can be scrolled when the number of items in the list extends beyond the viewing area.

By default, the selection mode of the list is multiple-interval, which allows the user to select multiple items from different blocks in the list. When the user selects countries in the list, the `valueChanged` handler (Lines 61–75) is executed, gets the indices of the selected item, and sets their corresponding image icons in the label to display the flags.

13.11 Scroll Bars

`JScrollBar` is a control that enables the user to select from a range of values. `JScrollBar` has the following properties, as pictured in Figure 13.30:

◆ **orientation** specifies horizontal or vertical style, with `JScrollBar.HORIZONTAL` (0) for horizontal and `JScrollBar.VERTICAL` (1) for vertical.

◆ **maximum** specifies the maximum value the scroll bar represents when the bubble reaches the right end of the scroll bar for horizontal style or the bottom of the scroll bar for vertical style.

◆ **minimum** specifies the minimum value the scroll bar represents when the bubble reaches the left end of the scroll bar for horizontal style or the top of the scroll bar for vertical style.

◆ **visibleAmount** (also called extent) specifies the relative width of the scroll bar's bubble. The actual width appearing on the screen is determined by the maximum value and the value of `visibleAmount`.

◆ **value** represents the current value of the scroll bar. Normally, a program changes a scroll bar's value by calling the `setValue` method. The `setValue` method simultaneously and

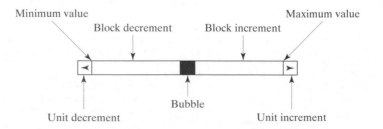

FIGURE 13.30 *A scroll bar represents a range of values graphically.*

synchronously sets the minimum, maximum, visible amount, and value properties of a scroll bar, so that they are mutually consistent.

✦ **blockIncrement** is the value added (subtracted) when the user activates the block-increment (decrement) area of the scroll bar, as shown in Figure 13.30. The `blockIncrement` property, which is new in JDK 1.1, supersedes the `pageIncrement` property used in JDK 1.02.

✦ **unitIncrement** is the value added (subtracted) when the user activates the unit-increment (decrement) area of the scroll bar, as shown in Figure 13.30. The `unitIncrement` property, which is new in JDK 1.1, supersedes the `lineIncrement` property used in JDK 1.02.

 NOTE

The width of the scroll bar's track corresponds to `maximum + visibleAmount`. When a scroll bar is set to its maximum value, the left side of the bubble is at `maximum`, and the right side is at `maximum + visibleAmount`.

Figure 13.31 lists several frequently used constructors and methods in `JScrollBar`.

Normally, the user changes the value of the scroll bar by making a gesture with the mouse. For example, the user can drag the scroll bar's bubble up and down, or click in the scroll bar's unit-increment or block-increment areas. Keyboard gestures can also be mapped to the scroll bar. By convention, the Page Up and Page Down keys are equivalent to clicking in the scroll bar's block-increment and block-decrement areas.

When the user changes the value of the scroll bar, the scroll bar generates an instance of `AdjustmentEvent`, which is passed to every registered listener. An object that wishes to be notified of changes to the scroll bar's value must implement the `adjustmentValueChanged` method in the `AdjustmentListener` interface defined in the package `java.awt.event`.

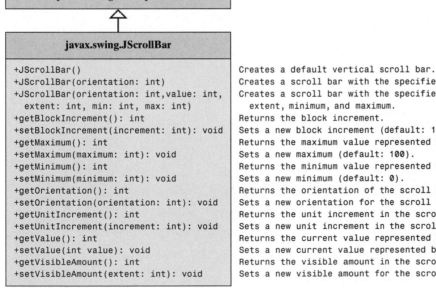

FIGURE 13.31 *JScrollBar enables you to select from a range of values.*

EXAMPLE 13.8 USING SCROLL BARS

Problem

Write a program that uses horizontal and vertical scroll bars to control a message displayed on a panel. The horizontal scroll bar is used to move the message to the left or the right, and the vertical scroll bar to move it up and down. A sample run of the program is shown in Figure 13.32.

FIGURE 13.32 *The scroll bars move the message on a panel horizontally and vertically.*

Solution

Here are the major steps in the program:

1. Create the user interface.
   Create a MessagePanel object and place it in the center of the frame. Create a vertical scroll bar and place it in the east of the frame. Create a horizontal scroll bar and place it in the south of the frame.

2. Process the event.
   Implement the adjustmentValueChanged handler to move the message according to the bar movement in the scroll bars.

LISTING 13.10 ScrollBarDemo.java (Using Scroll Bars)

```
 1 import java.awt.*;
 2 import java.awt.event.*;
 3 import javax.swing.*;
 4
 5 public class ScrollBarDemo extends JFrame
 6     implements AdjustmentListener {
 7   // Create horizontal and vertical scroll bars
 8   private JScrollBar jscbHort =
 9     new JScrollBar(JScrollBar.HORIZONTAL);
10   private JScrollBar jscbVert =
11     new JScrollBar(JScrollBar.VERTICAL);
12
13   // Create a MessagePanel
14   private MessagePanel messagePanel =
15     new MessagePanel("Welcome to Java");
16
17   public static void main(String[] args) {
18     ScrollBarDemo frame = new ScrollBarDemo();
19     frame.setTitle("ScrollBarDemo");
20     frame.setDefaultCloseOperation(JFrame.EXIT_ON_CLOSE);
21     frame.pack();
22     frame.setVisible(true);
23   }
24
25   public ScrollBarDemo() {
26     // Add scroll bars and message panel to the frame
```

scroll bar

create frame

create UI

EXAMPLE 13.8 (CONTINUED)

```
27        getContentPane().setLayout(new BorderLayout());
28        getContentPane().add(messagePanel, BorderLayout.CENTER);
29        getContentPane().add(jscbVert, BorderLayout.EAST);
30        getContentPane().add(jscbHort, BorderLayout.SOUTH);
31
32        // Register listener for the scroll bars
33        jscbHort.addAdjustmentListener(this);
34        jscbVert.addAdjustmentListener(this);
35    }
36
37    /** Handle scroll bar adjustment actions */
38    public void adjustmentValueChanged(AdjustmentEvent e) {
39      if (e.getSource() == jscbHort) {
40        // getValue() and getMaximumValue() return int, but for better
41        // precision, use double
42        double value = jscbHort.getValue();
43        double maximumValue = jscbHort.getMaximum();
44        double newX = (value * messagePanel.getWidth() / maximumValue);
45        messagePanel.setXCoordinate((int)newX);
46      }
47      else if (e.getSource() == jscbVert) {
48        // getValue() and getMaximumValue() return int, but for better
49        // precision, use double
50        double value = jscbVert.getValue();
51        double maximumValue = jscbVert.getMaximum();
52        double newY = (value * messagePanel.getHeight() / maximumValue);
53        messagePanel.setYCoordinate((int)newY);
54      }
55    }
56 }
```

vertical
horizontal

handler

Review

The program creates two scroll bars (jscbVert and jscbHort) (Lines 8–11) and an instance of MessagePanel (messagePanel) (Lines 14–15). messagePanel is placed in the center of the frame; jscbVert and jscbHort are placed in the east and south sections of the frame (Lines 29–30), respectively.

You can specify the orientation of the scroll bar in the constructor or use the setOrientation method. By default, the property value is 100 for maximum, 0 for minimum, 10 for blockIncrement, and 10 for visibleAmount.

When the user drags the bubble, or clicks the increment or decrement unit, the value of the scroll bar changes. An instance of AdjustmentEvent is generated and passed to the listener by invoking the adjustmentValueChanged handler (Lines 38–55). Since there are two scroll bars in the frame, the e.getSource() method is used to determine the source of the event. The vertical scroll bar moves the message up and down, and the horizontal bar moves the message to right and left.

The maximum value of the vertical scroll bar corresponds to the height of the panel, and the maximum value of the horizontal scroll bar corresponds to the width of the panel. The ratio between the current and maximum values of the horizontal scroll bar is the same as the ratio between the x value and the width of the message panel. Similarly, the ratio between the current and maximum values of the vertical scroll bar is the same as the ratio between the y value and the height of the message panel. The x-coordinate and y-coordinate are set in response to the scroll bar adjustments (Lines 45, 53).

13.12   Sliders

JSlider is similar to JScrollBar, but JSlider has more properties and can appear in many forms. Figure 13.33 lists several frequently used constructors and methods in JSlider.

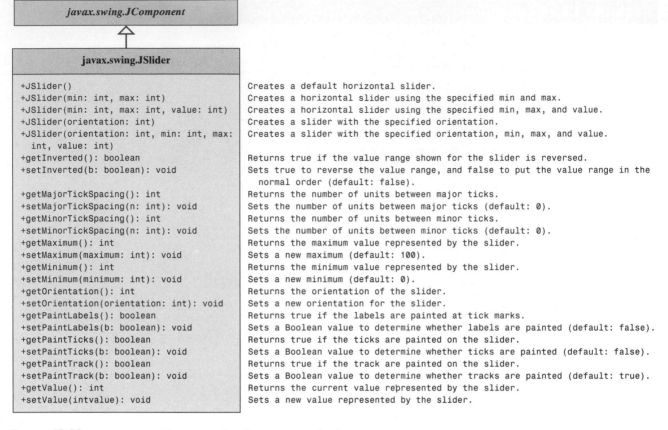

FIGURE 13.33 *JSlider enables you to select from a range of values.*

JSlider lets the user graphically select a value by sliding a knob within a bounded interval. The slider can show both major tick marks and minor tick marks between them. The number of pixels between the tick marks is controlled with setMajorTickSpacing and setMinorTickSpacing. Sliders can be displayed horizontally or vertically, with or without ticks, and with or without labels.

 NOTE
The values of a vertical scroll bar increase from top to bottom, but the values of a vertical slider decrease from top to bottom.

 NOTE
The names of the getPaintLabels(), getPaintTicks(), and getPaintTrack() methods violate the naming pattern. Since paintLabels, paintTicks, and paintTracks are boolean properties, they should be named isPaintLabels(), isPaintTicks(), and isPaintTrack().

When the user changes the value of the slider, the slider generates an instance of javax.swing.event.ChangeEvent, which is passed to any registered listeners. Any object that wishes to be notified of changes to the slider's value must implement stateChanged method in the ChangeListener interface defined in the package javax.swing.event.

Example 13.9 Using Sliders

Problem

Rewrite the preceding program using the sliders to control a message displayed on a panel instead of using scroll bars, as shown in Figure 13.34.

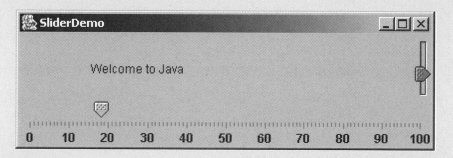

Figure 13.34 *The sliders move the message on a panel horizontally and vertically.*

Solution

Here are the major steps in the program:

1. Create the user interface.
   Create a `MessagePanel` object and place it in the center of the frame. Create a vertical slider and place it in the east of the frame. Create a horizontal slider and place it in the south of the frame.

2. Process the event.
   Implement the `stateChanged` handler in the `ChangeListener` interface to move the message according to the knot movement in the slider.

Listing 13.11   SliderBarDemo.java (Using Sliders)

```
1  import java.awt.*;
2  import javax.swing.*;
3  import javax.swing.event.*;
4
5  public class SliderDemo extends JFrame implements ChangeListener {
6    // Create horizontal and vertical sliders
7    private JSlider jsldHort = new JSlider(JSlider.HORIZONTAL);        slider
8    private JSlider jsldVert = new JSlider(JSlider.VERTICAL);
9
10   // Create a MessagePanel
11   private MessagePanel messagePanel =
12     new MessagePanel("Welcome to Java");
13
14   public static void main(String[] args) {
15     SliderDemo frame = new SliderDemo();                             create frame
16     frame.setTitle("SliderDemo");
17     frame.setDefaultCloseOperation(JFrame.EXIT_ON_CLOSE);
18     frame.pack();
19     frame.setVisible(true);
20   }
21
22   public SliderDemo() {
23     // Add sliders and message panel to the frame                    create UI
24     getContentPane().setLayout(new BorderLayout());
25     getContentPane().add(messagePanel, BorderLayout.CENTER);
26     getContentPane().add(jsldVert, BorderLayout.EAST);
27     getContentPane().add(jsldHort, BorderLayout.SOUTH);
```

EXAMPLE 13.9 (CONTINUED)

slider properties

```
28
29      // Set properties for sliders
30      jsldHort.setPaintLabels(true);
31      jsldHort.setPaintTicks(true);
32      jsldHort.setMajorTickSpacing(10);
33      jsldHort.setMinorTickSpacing(1);
34      jsldHort.setPaintTrack(false);
35      jsldVert.setInverted(true);
36
37      // Register listener for the sliders
38      jsldHort.addChangeListener(this);
39      jsldVert.addChangeListener(this);
40    }
41
42    /** Handle scroll bar adjustment actions */
43    public void stateChanged(ChangeEvent e) {
44      if (e.getSource() == jsldHort) {
45        // getValue() and getMaximumValue() return int, but for better
46        // precision, use double
47        double value = jsldHort.getValue();
48        double maximumValue = jsldHort.getMaximum();
49        double newX = (value * messagePanel.getWidth() / maximumValue);
50        messagePanel.setXCoordinate((int)newX);
51      }
52      else if (e.getSource() == jsldVert) {
53        // getValue() and getMaximumValue() return int, but for better
54        // precision, use double
55        double value = jsldVert.getValue();
56        double maximumValue = jsldVert.getMaximum();
57        double newY = (value * messagePanel.getHeight() / maximumValue);
58        messagePanel.setYCoordinate((int)newY);
59      }
60    }
61 }
```

handler (marginal note, beside lines 42-43)

Review

JSlider is similar to JScrollBar, but JSlider has more features. As shown in this example, you can specify labels, major ticks, and minor ticks on a JSlider (Lines 30–33). You can also choose to hide the track (Line 34). Since the values of a vertical slider decrease from top to bottom, the setInverted method reverses the order (Line 35).

JSlider fires ChangeEvent when the slider is changed. The listener needs to implement the stateChanged handler in the ChangeListener (Lines 43–60). Note that JScrollBar fires AdjustmentEvent when the scroll bar is adjusted.

13.13 Creating Multiple Windows

Occasionally, you may want to create multiple windows in an application. The application opens a new window to perform the specified task. The new windows are called *subwindows,* and the main frame is called the *main window.*

To create a subwindow from an application, you need to create a subclass of JFrame that defines the task and tells the new window what to do. You can then create an instance of this subclass in the application and launch the new window by setting the frame instance to be visible.

EXAMPLE 13.10 CREATING MULTIPLE WINDOWS

Problem

Write a program that creates a main window with a text area in the scroll pane and a button named "Show Histogram". When the user clicks the button, a new window appears that displays a histogram to show the occurrences of the letters in the text area. Figure 13.35 contains a sample run of the program.

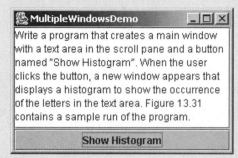
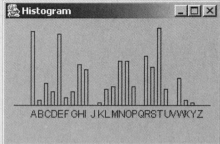

FIGURE 13.35   *The histogram is displayed in a separate frame.*

Solution

Here are the major steps in the program:

1. Create a main class for the frame named `MultipleWindowsDemo` in Listing 13.12. Add a text area inside a scroll pane, and place the scroll pane in the center of the frame. Create a button "Show Histogram" and place it in the south of the frame.

2. Create a subclass of `JPanel` named `Histogram` in Listing 13.13. The class contains a data field named `count` of the `int[]` type, which counts the occurrences of twenty-six letters. The values in `count` are displayed in the histogram.

3. Implement the `actionPerformed` handler in `MultipleWindowsDemo`, as follows:

   ♦ Create an instance of `Histogram`. Count the letters in the text area and pass the count to the `Histogram` object.

   ♦ Create a new frame and place the `Histogram` object in the center of frame. Display the frame.

LISTING 13.12   MultipleWindowsDemo.java (Creating Multiple Windows)

```
 1 import java.awt.*;
 2 import java.awt.event.*;
 3 import javax.swing.*;
 4
 5 public class MultipleWindowsDemo extends JFrame
 6     implements ActionListener {
 7   private JTextArea jta;
 8   private JButton jbtShowHistogram = new JButton("Show Histogram");
 9   private Histogram histogram = new Histogram();
10
11   // Create a new frame to hold the histogram panel
12   private JFrame histogramFrame = new JFrame();
13
14   public MultipleWindowsDemo() {
15     // Store text area in a scroll pane
```

create subframe

create UI

EXAMPLE **13.10** (CONTINUED)

```
16      JScrollPane scrollPane = new JScrollPane(jta = new JTextArea());
17      scrollPane.setPreferredSize(new Dimension(300, 200));
18      jta.setWrapStyleWord(true);
19      jta.setLineWrap(true);
20
21      // Place scroll pane and button in the frame
22      getContentPane().add(scrollPane, BorderLayout.CENTER);
23      getContentPane().add(jbtShowHistogram, BorderLayout.SOUTH);
24
25      // Register listener
26      jbtShowHistogram.addActionListener(this);
27
28      // Create a new frame to hold the histogram panel
29      histogramFrame.getContentPane().add(histogram);
30      histogramFrame.pack();
31      histogramFrame.setTitle("Histogram");
32    }
33
34    /** Handle the button action */
35    public void actionPerformed(ActionEvent e) {
36      // Count the letters in the text area
37      int[] count = countLetters();
38
39      // Set the letter count to histogram for display
40      histogram.showHistogram(count);
41
42      // Show the frame
43      histogramFrame.setVisible(true);
44    }
45
46    /** Count the letters in the text area */
47    private int[] countLetters() {
48      // Count for 26 letters
49      int[] count = new int[26];
50
51      // Get contents from the text area
52      String text = jta.getText();
53
54      // Count occurrence of each letter (case insensitive)
55      for (int i = 0; i < text.length(); i++) {
56        char character = text.charAt(i);
57
58        if ((character >= 'A') && (character <= 'Z')) {
59          count[(int)character - 65]++; // The ASCII for 'A' is 65
60        }
61        else if ((character >= 'a') && (character <= 'z')) {
62          count[(int)character - 97]++; // The ASCII for 'a' is 97
63        }
64      }
65
66      return count; // Return the count array
67    }
68
69    public static void main(String[] args) {
70      MultipleWindowsDemo frame = new MultipleWindowsDemo();
71      frame.setDefaultCloseOperation(JFrame.EXIT_ON_CLOSE);
72      frame.setTitle("MultipleWindowsDemo");
73      frame.pack();
74      frame.setVisible(true);
75    }
76 }
```

display subframe is marked at lines 40–43.

create main frame is marked at lines 69–74.

LISTING **13.13**   Histogram.java (Displaying a Histogram)

```
1 import javax.swing.*;
2 import java.awt.*;
```

Example **13.10** (Continued)

```
 3
 4 public class Histogram extends JPanel {
 5   // Count the occurrence of 26 letters
 6   private int[] count;
 7
 8   /** Set the count and display histogram */
 9   public void showHistogram(int[] count) {
10     this.count = count;
11     repaint();
12   }
13
14   /** Paint the histogram */
15   protected void paintComponent(Graphics g) {
16     if (count == null) return; // No display if count is null
17
18     super.paintComponent(g);
19
20     // Find the panel size and bar width and interval dynamically
21     int width = getWidth();
22     int height = getHeight();
23     int interval = (width - 40) / count.length;
24     int individualWidth = (int)(((width - 40) / 24) * 0.60);
25
26     // Find the maximum count. The maximum count has the highest bar
27     int maxCount = 0;
28     for (int i = 0; i < count.length; i++) {
29       if (maxCount < count[i])
30         maxCount = count[i];
31     }
32
33     // x is the start position for the first bar in the histogram
34     int x = 30;
35
36     // Draw a horizontal base line
37     g.drawLine(10, height - 45, width - 10, height - 45);
38     for (int i = 0; i < count.length; i++) {
39       // Find the bar height
40       int barHeight =
41         (int)(((double)count[i] / (double)maxCount) * (height - 55));
42
43       // Display a bar (i.e., rectangle)
44       g.drawRect(x, height - 45 - barHeight, individualWidth,
45         barHeight);
46
47       // Display a letter under the base line
48       g.drawString((char)(65 + i) + "", x, height - 30);
49
50       // Move x for displaying the next character
51       x += interval;
52     }
53   }
54
55   /** Override getPreferredSize */
56   public Dimension getPreferredSize() {
57     return new Dimension(300, 300);
58   }
59 }
```

paint histogram

preferredSize

Review

The program contains two classes: MultipleWindowsDemo and Histogram. Their relationship is shown in Figure 13.36.

EXAMPLE 13.10 (CONTINUED)

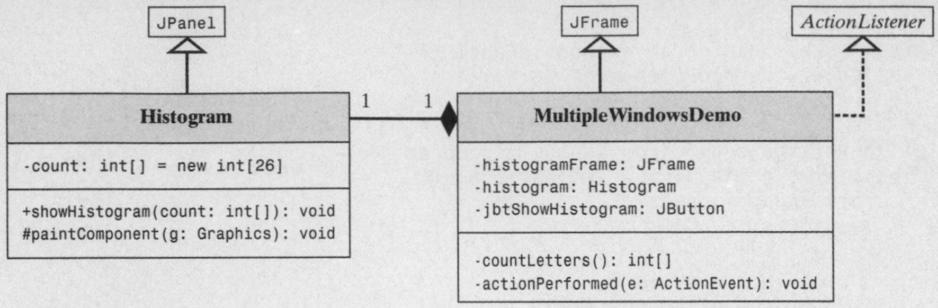

FIGURE 13.36 *MultipleWindowsDemo uses* `Histogram` *to display a histogram of the occurrences of the letters in a text area in the frame.*

`MultipleWindowsDemo` is a frame that holds a text area in a scroll pane and a button. `Histogram` is a subclass of `JPanel` that displays a histogram for the occurrences of letters in the text area.

When the user clicks the "Show Histogram" button, the handler counts the occurrences of letters in the text area. Letters are counted regardless of their case. Nonletter characters are not counted. The count is stored in an `int` array of twenty-six elements. The first element stores the count for letter `'a'` or `'A'`, and the last element in the array stores the count for letter `'z'` or `'Z'`. The count array is passed to the histogram for display.

The `MultipleWindowsDemo` class contains a `main` method. The `main` method creates an instance of `MultipleWindowsDemo` and displays the frame. The `MultipleWindowsDemo` class also contains an instance of `JFrame`, named `histogramFrame`, which holds an instance of `Histogram`. When the user clicks the "Show Histogram" button, `histogramFrame` is set visible to display the histogram.

The height and width of the bars in the histogram are determined dynamically according to the window size of the histogram.

You cannot add an instance of `JFrame` to a container. For example, adding `histogramFrame` to the main frame would cause a runtime exception. However, you can create a frame instance and set it visible to launch a new window.

KEY CLASSES AND METHODS

✦ **java.awt.Component** is the root class for GUI components. Commonly used properties in Component are `font`, `background`, `foreground`, `height`, `width`, and `preferredSize`.

✦ **javax.swing.JComponent** is the root class for Swing GUI components such as `JButton`, `JLabel`, `JTextField`, and `JPanel`. Commonly used properties in JComponent are `toolTipText` and `border`.

✦ **javax.swing.AbstractButton** is an abstract base class for `JButton`, `JToggleButton`, `JCheckBox`, and `JRadioButton`. Commonly used properties defined in AbstractButton are `text`, `icon`, `mnemonic`, `horizontalAlignment`, `verticalAlignment`, `horizontalTextPosition`, and `verticalTextPosition`.

✦ **javax.swing.JButton** is a push button that triggers an action event when clicked. All the properties in JButton are inherited from AbstractButton.

✦ **javax.swing.ImageIcon** is a class to create image icons. For example, `new ImagIcon("photo.gif")` creates an icon from image file photo.gif.

◆ **javax.swing.border.TitledBorder** is a class to create titled borders. For example, new TitledBorder("Message Panel") creates a border with the title Message Panel.

◆ **javax.swing.border.LineBorder** is a class to create line borders. For example, new LineBorder(Color.YELLOW, 5) creates a line border of yellow color and 5 pixels thickness.

◆ **javax.swing.JCheckBox** is a button that enables the user to toggle a choice on or off, like a light switch. All the properties in JCheckBox are inherited from AbstractButton. JCheckBox can generate ActionEvent and ItemEvent.

◆ **javax.swing.JRadioButton** is a button that enables you to choose a single item from a group of choices. JRadioButton is similar to JCheckBox, but is generally used to select a value exclusively. All the properties in JRadioButton are inherited from AbstractButton. To group radio buttons, use ButtonGroup. JRadioButton can generate ActionEvent and ItemEvent, among many other events.

◆ **javax.swing.ButtonGroup** is a class to group buttons (usually radio buttons).

◆ **javax.swing.JLabel** is a component for displaying texts or images, or both. Commonly used properties in JLabel are text, icon, horizontalAlignment, and verticalAlignment.

◆ **javax.swing.JTextField** is a component used to accept user input into a string. Commonly used properties in JTextField are text, horizontalAlignment, editable, and columns. JTextField can generate ActionEvent among many other events. Pressing Enter in a text field triggers ActionEvent.

◆ **javax.swing.JTextArea** is a component used to enter multiple lines of strings. Commonly used properties in JTextArea are text, editable, columns, lineWrap, wrapStyleWord, rows, lineCount, and tabSize.

◆ **javax.swing.JComboBox** is a component that displays a simple list of items from which the user can choose. It is useful in limiting a user's range of choices and avoids the cumbersome validation of data input. JComboBox can generate ActionEvent and ItemEvent, among many other events. Commonly used properties in JComboBox are selectedIndex and selectedItem. Commonly used methods are addItem(Object), getItemAt(index), removeItem(Object), and removeAllItems().

◆ **javax.swing.JList** is a component that basically performs the same function as a combo box but enables the user to choose a single value or multiple values. Commonly used properties in JComboBox are selectedIndex, selectedIndices, selectedValue, selectedValues, selectionMode, and visibleRowCount. JList generates javax.swing.event.ListSelectionEvent to notify the listeners of the selections. The listener must implement the valueChanged handler in the ListSelectionListener interface to process the event.

◆ **javax.swing.JScrollBar** is a control for selecting from a range of values. You can create scroll bars using the JScrollBar class and specify horizontal or vertical scroll bars using the setOrientation method. JScrollBar generates java.awt.event.AdjustmentEvent to notify the listeners of the value changes. The listener must implement the adjustment-ValueChanged(AdjustmentEvent) method in the java.awt.event.AdjustmentListener interface.

◆ **javax.swing.JSlider** is similar to JScrollBar but has more properties and can appear in many forms. JSlider generates javax.swing.event.ChangeEvent to notify the listeners of value changes. The listener must implement the stateChanged(ChangeEvent) method in the javax.swing.event.ChangeEvent interface.

CHAPTER SUMMARY

✦ You learned how to create graphical user interfaces using Swing GUI components `JButton`, `JCheckBox`, `JRadioButton`, `JLabel`, `JTextField`, `JTextArea`, `JComboBox`, `JList`, `JScrollBar`, and `JSlider`. You also learned how to handle events on these components.

✦ Every Swing GUI component is a subclass of `javax.swing.JComponent`, and `JComponent` is a subclass of `java.awt.Component`. The properties `font`, `background`, `foreground`, `height`, `width`, and `preferredSize` in `Component` are inherited in these subclasses, as are `toolTipText` and `border` in `JComponent`.

✦ You can display icons on buttons (`JButton`, `JCheckBox`, `JRadioButton`) and labels. You can use borders on any Swing components. Icons and borders can be shared.

REVIEW QUESTIONS

Sections 13.2–13.5

13.1   How do you set background color, foreground color, and font on a Swing GUI component?

13.2   How do you create a button labeled "OK"? How do you change the text on a button? How do you set an icon in a button?

13.3   Can you have a border for any subclass of `JComponent`? How do you set a titled border for a panel?

13.4   Which of the following statements have syntax errors?

```
Component c1 = new Component();
JComponent c2 = new JComponent();
Component c3 = new JButton();
JComponent c4 = new JButton();
Container c5 = new JButton();
c5.add(c4);
Object c6 = new JButton();
c5.add(c6);
```

13.5   What happens if you add a button to a container several times, as follows?

```
JButton jbt = new JButton();
JPanel panel = new JPanel();
panel.add(jbt);
panel.add(jbt);
panel.add(jbt);
```

13.6   Will the following code display three buttons? Will the buttons display the same icon?

```
import javax.swing.*;
import java.awt.*;

public class Test extends JFrame {
  public static void main(String[] args) {
    // Create a frame and set its properties
    JFrame frame = new Test();
    frame.setTitle("ButtonIcons");
    frame.setSize(200, 100);
    frame.setDefaultCloseOperation(JFrame.EXIT_ON_CLOSE);
    frame.setVisible(true);
  }

  public Test() {
    ImageIcon usIcon = new ImageIcon("image/usIcon.gif");
```

```
            JButton jbt1 = new JButton(usIcon);
            JButton jbt2 = new JButton(usIcon);

            JPanel p1 = new JPanel();
            p1.add(jbt1);

            JPanel p2 = new JPanel();
            p2.add(jbt2);

            JPanel p3 = new JPanel();
            p2.add(jbt1);

            getContentPane().add(p1, BorderLayout.NORTH);
            getContentPane().add(p2, BorderLayout.SOUTH);
            getContentPane().add(p3, BorderLayout.CENTER);
        }
    }
```

13.7   Can you share a border or icon for GUI components?

13.8   How do you create a check box? How do you determine whether a check box is selected?

13.9   What is wrong if the statement super.actionPerformed(e) in CheckBoxDemo in Listing 13.4 is omitted?

13.10   How do you create a radio button? How do you group the radio buttons together? How do you determine whether a radio button is selected?

Sections 13.6–13.10

13.11   How do you create a label named "Address"? How do you change the name on a label? How do you set an icon in a label?

13.12   How do you create a text field with ten columns and the default text "Welcome to Java"? How do you write the code to check whether a text field is empty?

13.13   How do you create a text area with ten rows and twenty columns? How do you insert three lines into the text area? How do you create a scrollable text area?

13.14   How do you create a combo box, add three items to it, and retrieve a selected item?

13.15   How do you create a list with an array of strings?

Sections 13.11–13.13

13.16   How do you create a horizontal scroll bar? What event can a scroll bar generate?

13.17   How do you create a vertical slider? What event can a slider generate?

13.18   Explain how to create and show multiple frames in an application.

PROGRAMMING EXERCISES

Sections 13.2–13.5

13.1*   (*Revising Example 13.1 "Using Buttons"*) Rewrite Example 13.1 to add a group of radio buttons to select background colors. The available colors are red, yellow, white, gray, and green (see Figure 13.37).

13.2*   (*Selecting geometric figures*) Write a program that draws various figures on a panel. The user selects a figure from a radio button. The selected figure is then displayed on the panel (see Figure 13.38).

13.3**   (*Traffic lights*) Write a program that simulates a traffic light. The program lets the user select one of three lights: red, yellow, or green. When a radio button is selected, the light is turned on, and only one light can be on at a time (see Figure 13.39). No light is on when the program starts.

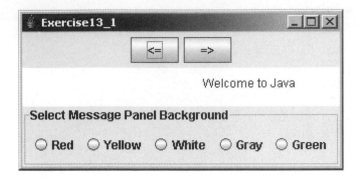

FIGURE 13.37 *The <= and => buttons move the message on the panel, and you can also set the color for the message.*

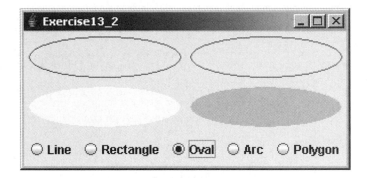

FIGURE 13.38 *The program displays lines, rectangles, ovals, arcs, or polygons when you select a shape type.*

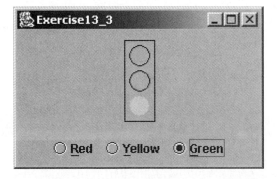

FIGURE 13.39 *The radio buttons are grouped to let you select only one color in the group to control a traffic light.*

Sections 13.6–13.10

13.4* (*Creating a simple calculator*) Write a program to perform add, subtract, multiply, and divide operations (see Figure 13.40).

13.5* (*Creating a miles/kilometers converter*) Write a program that converts miles and kilometers, as shown in Figure 13.41. If you enter a value in the Mile text field and press the Enter key, the corresponding kilometer is displayed in the Kilometer text field.

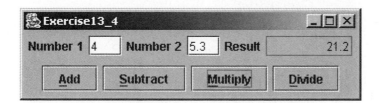

FIGURE 13.40   *The program does addition, subtraction, multiplication, and division on double numbers.*

FIGURE 13.41   *The program converts miles to kilometers, and vice versa.*

Likewise, if you enter a value in the Kilometer text field and press the Enter key, the corresponding mile is displayed in the Mile text field.

13.6*   (*Creating an investment value calculator*) Write a program that calculates the future value of an investment at a given interest rate for a specified number of years. The formula for the calculation is as follows:

```
futureValue = investmentAmount * (1 + monthlyInterestRate)^years*12
```

Use text fields for interest rate, investment amount, and years. Display the future amount in a text field when the user clicks the Calculate button, as shown in Figure 13.42.

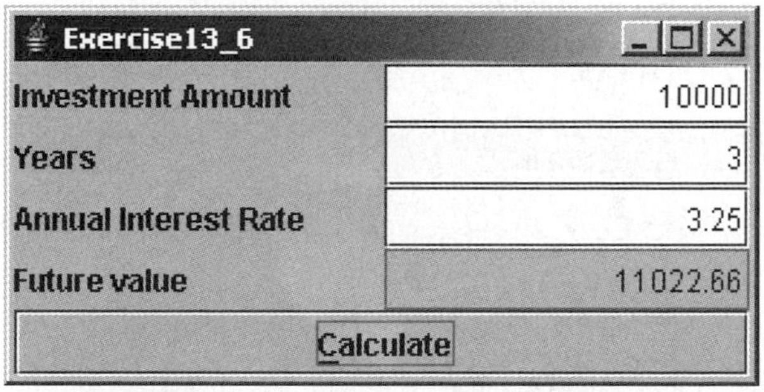

FIGURE 13.42   *The user enters the investment amount, years, and interest rate to compute future value.*

13.7*   (*Setting clock time*) Write a program that displays a clock time and sets the clock time with three text fields to give the time for the clock, as shown in Figure 13.43. Use the `StillClock` in Section 11.12, "Case Study: The `StillClock` Class."

13.8**   (*Selecting a font*) Write a program that can dynamically change the font of a message to be displayed on a panel. The message can be displayed in bold and italic at the same time, or can be displayed in the center of the panel. You can select the font name or font size from combo boxes, as shown in Figure 13.44. The available font names can be obtained using `getAvailableFontFamilyNames()` in `GraphicsEnvironment` (see page 385). The combo box for font size is initialized with numbers from 1 to 100.

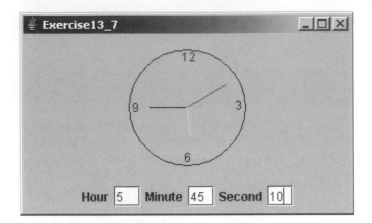

FIGURE 13.43 *The program displays the time specified in the text fields.*

FIGURE 13.44 *You can dynamically set the font for the message.*

13.9** (*Demonstrating* JLabel *properties*) Write a program to let the user dynamically set the properties horizontalAlignment, verticalAlignment, horizontalTextAlignment, and verticalTextAlignment, as shown in Figure 13.45.

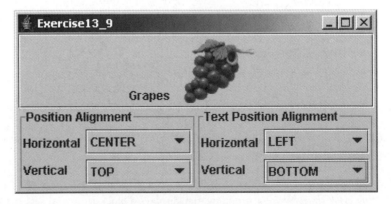

FIGURE 13.45 *You can set the alignment and text-position properties of a button dynamically.*

13.10* (*Adding new features into Example 13.1, "Using Buttons," incrementally*) Improve Example 13.1 incrementally as follows (see Figure 13.46):

1. Add a text field labeled "Enter a new message" in the same panel with the buttons. Upon typing a new message in the text field and pressing the Enter key, the new message is displayed in the message panel.

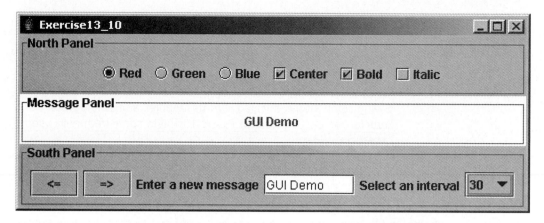

2. Add a combo box labeled "Select an interval" in the same panel with the buttons. The combo box enables the user to select a new interval for moving the message. The selection values range from 5 to 100 with interval 5. The user can also type a new interval in the combo box.

3. Add three radio buttons that enable the user to select the foreground color for the message as Red, Green, and Blue. The radio buttons are grouped in a panel, and the panel is placed in the north of the frame's content pane.

4. Add three check boxes that enable the user to center the message and display it in italic or bold. Place the check boxes in the same panel with the radio buttons.

5. Add a border titled "Message Panel" on the message panel, add a border titled "South Panel" on the panel for buttons, and add a border titled "North Panel" on the panel for radio buttons and check boxes.

13.11* (*Demonstrating* `JTextField` *properties*) Write a program that sets the horizontal-alignment and column-size properties of a text field dynamically, as shown in Figure 13.47.

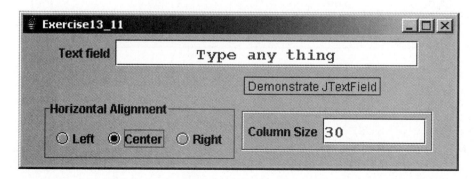

FIGURE **13.47** *You can set the horizontal-alignment and column-size properties of a text field dynamically.*

13.12* (*Demonstrating* `JTextArea` *properties*) Write a program that demonstrates the wrapping styles of the text area. The program uses a check box to indicate whether the text area is wrapped. In the case where the text area is wrapped, you need to specify whether it is wrapped by characters or by words, as shown in Figure 13.48.

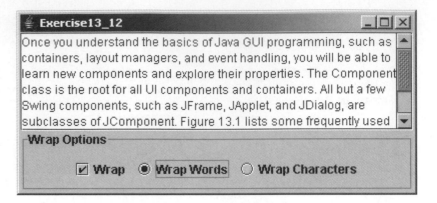

FIGURE **13.48** *You can set the options to wrap a text area by characters or by words dynamically.*

13.13* (*Comparing loans with various interest rates*) Rewrite Exercise 3.26 to create a user interface, as shown in Figure 13.49. Your program should let the user enter the loan amount and loan period in number of years from a text field, and should display the monthly and total payments for each interest rate starting from 5 percent to 8 percent, with increments of one-eighth, in a text area.

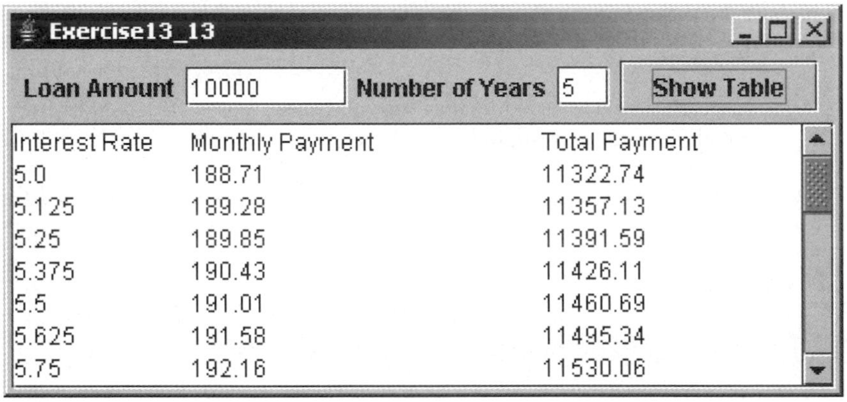

FIGURE **13.49** *The program displays a table for monthly payments and total payments on a given loan based on various interest rates.*

13.14* (*Using* JComboBox *and* JList) Write a program that demonstrates selecting items in a list. The program uses a combo box to specify a selection mode, as shown in Figure 13.50. When you select items, they are displayed in a label below the list.

Sections 13.11–13.13

13.15** (*Creating a color selector*) Write a program that uses scroll bars to select the foreground color for a label, as shown in Figure 13.51. Three horizontal scroll bars are used for selecting the red, green, and blue components of the color. Use a title border on the panel that holds the scroll bars.

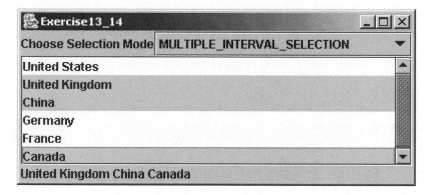

FIGURE **13.50** *You can choose single selection, single-interval selection, or multiple-interval selection in a list.*

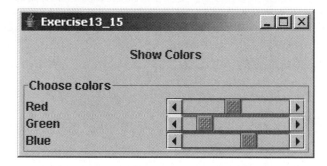

FIGURE **13.51** *The foreground color changes in the label as you adjust the scroll bars.*

13.16* (*Revising Example 13.10, "Creating Multiple Windows"*) Instead of displaying the occurrences of the letters using the Histogram component in Example 13.10, use a bar chart, so that the display is as shown in Figure 13.52.

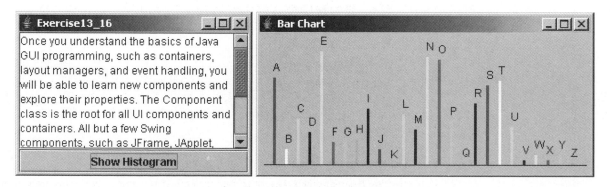

FIGURE **13.52** *The number of occurrences of each letter is displayed in a bar chart.*

13.17*** (*Displaying a calendar*) Write a program that displays the calendar for the current month, as shown in Figure 13.53. Use labels, and set texts on the labels to display the calendar. Use the `GregorianCalendar` class on page 322 to obtain the information about month, year, first day of the month, and number of days in the month.

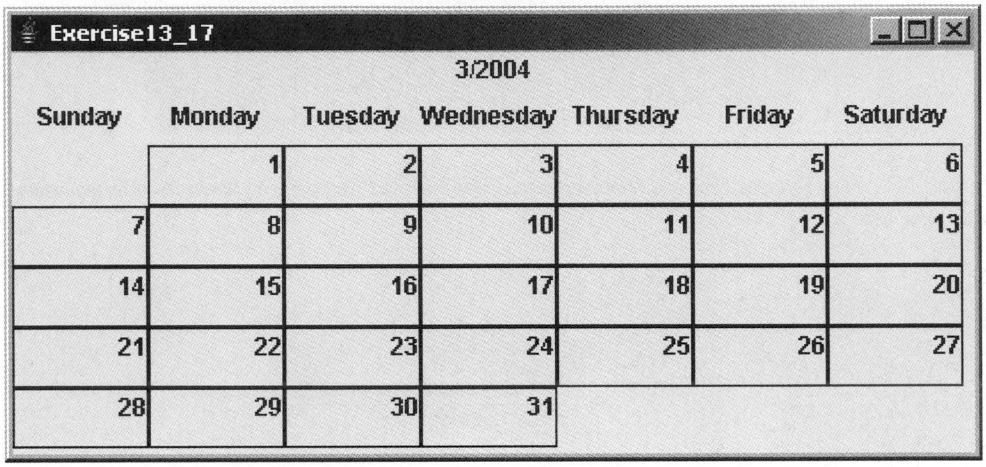
Exercise13_17
3/2004
Sunday
Monday
Tuesday
Wednesday
Thursday
Friday
Saturday
1 2 3 4 5 6
7 8 9 10 11 12 13
14 15 16 17 18 19 20
21 22 23 24 25 26 27
28 29 30 31

FIGURE 13.53 *The program displays the calendar for the current month.*

chapter

14

APPLETS, IMAGES, AND AUDIO

Objectives

- ✦ To explain how the Web browser controls and executes applets (§14.2).

- ✦ To describe the init, start, stop, and destroy methods in the Applet class (§§14.2.1-14.4).

- ✦ To develop Swing applets using the JApplet class (§14.3).

- ✦ To know how to embed applets in Web pages (§14.4).

- ✦ To run applets from the appletviewer and from Web browsers (§14.4).

- ✦ To pass string values to applets from HTML (§14.5).

- ✦ To write a Java program that can run as both an application and an applet (§14.6).

- ✦ To get image files using the URL class and display images in the panel (§14.9 Optional).

- ✦ To develop a reusable component ImageViewer to display images (§14.10 Optional).

- ✦ To get audio files and play sound (§14.12 Optional).

- ✦ To package and deploy Java projects using Java archive files (§14.13 Optional).

- ✦ To use Swing pluggable look-and-feel (§14.14 Optional).

14.1 Introduction

Java's early success has been attributed to applets. Running from a Java-enabled Web browser, applets bring dynamic interaction and live animation to an otherwise static HTML page. It is safe to say that Java would be nowhere today without applets. They made Java instantly appealing, attractive, and popular during its infancy. Java is now used not only for applets, but also for standalone applications and as a programming language for developing server-side applications and for mobile devices.

In this book so far, you have only used Java applications. Everything you have learned about writing applications, however, also applies to writing applets. Applications and applets share many common programming features, although they differ slightly in some respects. For example, every application must have a main method , which is invoked by the Java interpreter. Java applets, on the other hand, do not need a main method. They run in the Web browser environment. Because applets are invoked from a Web page, Java provides special features that enable applets to run from a Web browser.

In this chapter, you will learn how to write Java applets, discover the relationship between applets and the Web browser, and explore the similarities and differences between applications and applets. You will also learn how to display images and play audio.

14.2 The `Applet` Class

The `Applet` class provides the essential framework that enables applets to be run by a Web browser. While every Java application has a main method that is executed when the application starts, applets do not have a main method. Instead they depend on the browser to call the methods in the `Applet` class. Every applet is a subclass of `java.applet.Applet` as outlined below:

```
public class MyApplet extends java.applet.Applet {
  ...
  /** The no-arg constructor is called by the browser when the Web
   *  page containing this applet is initially loaded, or reloaded
   */
  public MyApplet() {
    ...
  }

  /** Called by the browser after the applet is loaded
   */
  public void init() {
    ...
  }

  /** Called by the browser after the init() method, or
   *  every time the Web page is visited
   */
  public void start() {
    ...
  }

  /** Called by the browser when the page containing this
   *  applet becomes inactive
   */
  public void stop() {
    ...
  }

  /** Called by the browser when the Web browser exits */
  public void destroy() {
    ...
  }

  /** Other methods if necessary... */
}
```

When the applet is loaded, the Web browser creates an instance of the applet by invoking the applet's no-arg constructor. The browser uses the init, start, stop, and destroy methods to control the applet. By default, these methods do nothing. To perform specific functions, they need to be modified in the user's applet so that the browser can call your code properly. Figure 14.1(a) shows how the browser calls these methods, and Figure 14.1(b) illustrates the flow of control of an applet using a statechart diagram.

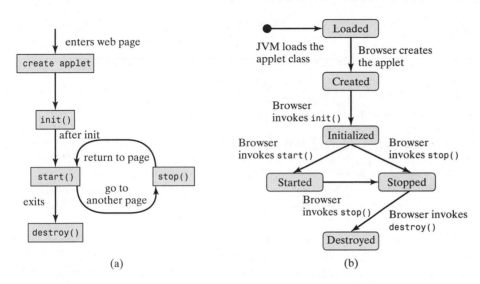

(a)   (b)

FIGURE 14.1 *The Web browser uses the init, start, stop, and destroy methods to control the applet.*

14.2.1 The init Method

The init method is invoked after the applet is created or recreated.

A subclass of Applet should override this method if the subclass has an initialization to perform. The functions usually implemented in this method include creating new threads, loading images, setting up user-interface components, and getting string parameter values from the <applet> tag in the HTML page. Chapter 19, "Multithreading," discusses threads in more detail; passing strings to applets is discussed in Section 14.5, "Passing Strings to Applets."

14.2.2 The start Method

The start method is invoked after the init method. It is also called whenever the applet becomes active again after the page containing the applet is revisited. The start method is called, for example, when the user returns to the Web page containing the applet after surfing other pages.

A subclass of Applet overrides this method if it has any operation that needs to be performed whenever the Web page containing the applet is visited. An applet with animation, for example, might use the start method to resume animation.

14.2.3 The stop Method

The stop method is the opposite of the start method. The start method is called when the user moves back to the page that contains the applet. The stop method is invoked when the user leaves the page.

A subclass of `Applet` overrides this method if it has any operation that needs to be performed each time the Web page containing the applet is no longer visible. When the user leaves the page, any threads the applet has started but not completed will continue to run. You should override the `stop` method to suspend the running threads so that the applet does not take up system resources when it is inactive.

14.2.4 The `destroy` Method

The `destroy` method is invoked when the browser exits normally to inform the applet that it is no longer needed and should release any resources it has allocated. The `stop` method is always called before the `destroy` method.

A subclass of `Applet` overrides this method if it has any operation that needs to be performed before it is destroyed. Usually, you won't need to override this method unless you wish to release specific resources, such as threads that the applet created.

14.3 The `JApplet` Class

The `Applet` class is an AWT class and is not designed to work with Swing components. To use Swing components in Java applets, it is necessary to create a Java applet that extends `javax.swing.JApplet`, which is a subclass of `java.applet.Applet`. `JApplet` inherits all the methods from the `Applet` class. In addition, it provides support for laying out Swing components.

To add a component to a `JApplet`, you add it to the content pane of a `JApplet` instance, which is the same as adding a component to a `JFrame` instance. By default, the content pane of `JApplet` uses `BorderLayout`. Here is an example of a simple applet that uses `JLabel` to display a message:

```
// WelcomeApplet.java: Applet for displaying a message
import javax.swing.*;

public class WelcomeApplet extends JApplet {
  /** Initialize the applet */
  public void init() {
    getContentPane().add(
      new JLabel("Welcome to Java", JLabel.CENTER));
  }
}
```

You cannot run this applet standalone, because it does not have a `main` method. To run this applet, you have to create an HTML file with the applet tag that references the applet. When you write Java GUI applications, you must create a frame to hold graphical components, set the frame size, and make the frame visible. Applets are run from the Web browser. The Web browser automatically places the applet inside it and makes it visible. The following section shows how to create HTML files for applets.

NOTE

You could rewrite the `WelcomeApplet` by moving the code in the `init` method to the no-arg constructor, as follows:

```
// WelcomeApplet.java: Applet for displaying a message
import javax.swing.*;

public class WelcomeApplet extends JApplet {
  /** Construct the applet */
  public WelcomeApplet() {
    getContentPane().add(
      new JLabel("Welcome to Java", JLabel.CENTER));
  }
}
```

14.4 The HTML File and the <applet> Tag

HTML is a markup language that presents static documents on the Web. It uses tags to instruct the Web browser how to render a Web page and contains a tag called <applet> that incorporates applets into a Web page.

The following HTML file named WelcomeApplet.html invokes the **WelcomeApplet.class**:

```
<html>
<head>
<title>Welcome Java Applet</title>
</head>
<body>
<applet
  code = "WelcomeApplet.class"
  width = 350
  height = 200>
</applet>
</body>
</html>
```

A *tag* is an instruction to the Web browser. The browser interprets the tag and decides how to display or otherwise treat the subsequent contents of the HTML document. Tags are enclosed inside brackets. The first word in a tag, called the *tag name*, describes tag functions. Tags can have additional attributes, sometimes with values after an equals sign, which further define the tag's action. For example, in the preceding HTML file, <applet> is the tag name, and code, width, and height are the attributes. The width and height attributes specify the rectangular viewing area of the applet.

Most tags have a *start tag* and a corresponding *end tag*. The tag has a specific effect on the region between the start tag and the end tag. For example, <applet...>...</applet> tells the browser to display an applet. An end tag is always the start tag's name preceded by a slash.

An HTML document begins with the <html> tag, which declares that the document is written in HTML. Each document has two parts, a *head* and a *body*, defined by <head> and <body> tags, respectively. The head part contains the document title, using the <title> tag and other information the browser can use when rendering the document, and the body part contains the actual contents of the document. The header is optional. For more information, refer to Supplement E, "An HTML Tutorial."

The complete syntax of the <applet> tag is as follows:

```
<applet
  [codebase=applet_url]
  code=classfilename.class
  width=applet_viewing_width_in_pixels
  height=applet_viewing_height_in_pixels
  [archive=archivefile]
  [vspace=vertical_margin]
  [hspace=horizontal_margin]
  [align=applet_alignment]
  [alt=alternative_text]
>
<param name=param_name1 value=param_value1>
<param name=param_name2 value=param_value2>
...
<param name=param_name3 value=param_value3>
</applet>
```

The code, width, and height attributes are required; all the others are optional. The <param> tag is introduced in Section 14.5, "Passing Strings to Applets." The meanings of the other attributes are explained below.

- **codebase** specifies a base where your classes are loaded. If this attribute is not used, the Web browser loads the applet from the directory in which the HTML page is located. If your applet is located in a different directory from the HTML page, you must specify the `applet_url` for the browser to load the applet. This attribute enables you to load the class from anywhere on the Internet. The classes used by the applet are dynamically loaded when needed.
- **archive** instructs the browser to load an archive file that contains all the class files needed to run the applet. Archiving allows the Web browser to load all the classes from a single compressed file at one time, thus reducing loading time and improving performance. To create archives, see Section 14.13, "Packaging and Deploying Java Projects."
- **vspace** and **hspace** specify the size, in pixels, of the blank margin to pad around the applet vertically and horizontally.
- **align** specifies how the applet will be aligned in the browser. One of nine values is used: `left`, `right`, `top`, `texttop`, `middle`, `absmiddle`, `baseline`, `bottom`, or `absbottom`.
- **alt** attribute specifies the text to be displayed in case the browser cannot run Java.

14.4.1 Viewing Applets Using the Applet Viewer Utility

You can test the applet using the applet viewer utility, which can be invoked from the DOS prompt using the **appletviewer** command from **c:\book**, as shown in Figure 14.2. Its output is shown in Figure 14.3.

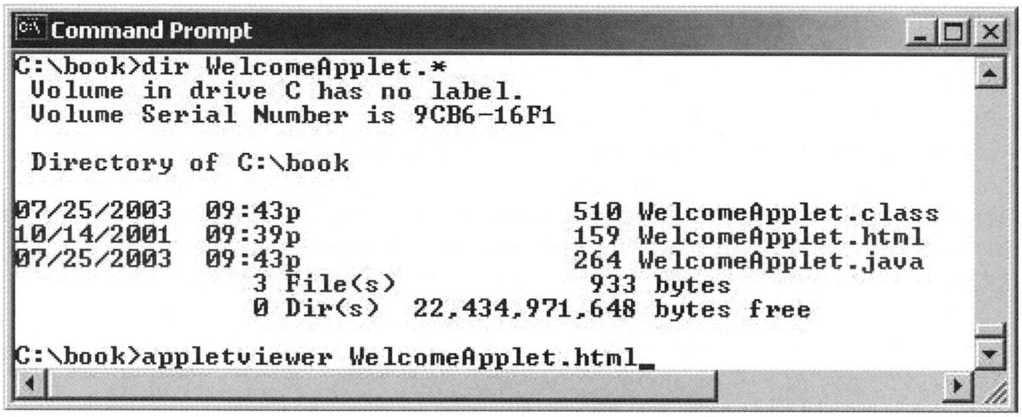

Command Prompt
C:\book>dir WelcomeApplet.*
Volume in drive C has no label.
Volume Serial Number is 9CB6-16F1
Directory of C:\book
07/25/2003 09:43p 510 WelcomeApplet.class
10/14/2001 09:39p 159 WelcomeApplet.html
07/25/2003 09:43p 264 WelcomeApplet.java
3 File(s) 933 bytes
0 Dir(s) 22,434,971,648 bytes free
C:\book>appletviewer WelcomeApplet.html

FIGURE 14.2 *The appletviewer command runs a Java applet in the applet viewer utility.*

Applet Viewer: WelcomeApplet.class
Applet
Welcome to Java
Applet started.

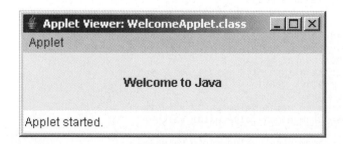

FIGURE 14.3 *The WelcomeApplet program is running from the applet viewer.*

14.4.2   Viewing Applets from a Web Browser

Applets are eventually displayed in a Web browser. Using the applet viewer, you do not need to start a Web browser. The applet viewer functions as a browser. It is convenient for testing applets during development. However, you should also test the applets from a Web browser before deploying them on a Web site. To display an applet from a Web browser, open the applet's HTML file (e.g., WelcomeApplet.html). Its output is shown in Figure 14.4.

FIGURE 14.4   *The WelcomeApplet program is displayed in Internet Explorer.*

To make your applet accessible on the Web, you need to store the WelcomeApplet.class and WelcomeApplet.html on a Web server. You can view the applet from an appropriate URL. For example, I have uploaded these two files on Web server `www.cs.armstrong.edu`. As shown in Figure 14.5, you can access the applet from `www.cs.armstrong.edu/liang/intro5e/book/WelcomeApplet.html`.

FIGURE 14.5   *The* `WelcomeApplet` *program is downloaded from the Web server.*

EXAMPLE 14.1 USING APPLETS

Problem

Write an applet that computes loan payments. The applet enables the user to enter the interest rate, the number of years, and the loan amount. Clicking the Compute Payment button displays the monthly payment and the total payment.

Solution

The applet and the HTML code containing the applet are provided in Listings 14.1 and 14.2. Figure 14.6 contains a sample run of the applet.

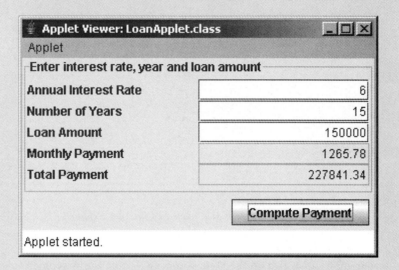

FIGURE 14.6 *The applet computes the monthly payment and the total payment when provided with the interest rate, number of years, and loan amount.*

LISTING 14.1   LoanApplet.java (Computing Loans)

```
 1 import java.awt.*;
 2 import java.awt.event.*;
 3 import javax.swing.*;
 4 import javax.swing.border.TitledBorder;
 5
 6 public class LoanApplet extends JApplet
 7     implements ActionListener {
 8   // Declare and create text fields for interest rate
 9   // year, loan amount, monthly payment, and total payment
10   private JTextField jtfAnnualInterestRate = new JTextField();
11   private JTextField jtfNumberOfYears = new JTextField();
12   private JTextField jtfLoanAmount = new JTextField();
13   private JTextField jtfMonthlyPayment = new JTextField();
14   private JTextField jtfTotalPayment = new JTextField();
15
16   // Declare and create a Compute Payment button
17   private JButton jbtComputeLoan = new JButton("Compute Payment");
18
19   /** Initialize user interface */
20   public void init() {
21     // Set properties on the text fields
22     jtfMonthlyPayment.setEditable(false);
23     jtfTotalPayment.setEditable(false);
24
```

text field

create UI

EXAMPLE 14.1 (CONTINUED)

```
25        // Right align text fields
26        jtfAnnualInterestRate.setHorizontalAlignment(JTextField.RIGHT);
27        jtfNumberOfYears.setHorizontalAlignment(JTextField.RIGHT);
28        jtfLoanAmount.setHorizontalAlignment(JTextField.RIGHT);
29        jtfMonthlyPayment.setHorizontalAlignment(JTextField.RIGHT);
30        jtfTotalPayment.setHorizontalAlignment(JTextField.RIGHT);
31
32        // Panel p1 to hold labels and text fields
33        JPanel p1 = new JPanel();
34        p1.setLayout(new GridLayout(5, 2));
35        p1.add(new JLabel("Annual Interest Rate"));
36        p1.add(jtfAnnualInterestRate);
37        p1.add(new JLabel("Number of Years"));
38        p1.add(jtfNumberOfYears);
39        p1.add(new JLabel("Loan Amount"));
40        p1.add(jtfLoanAmount);
41        p1.add(new JLabel("Monthly Payment"));
42        p1.add(jtfMonthlyPayment);
43        p1.add(new JLabel("Total Payment"));
44        p1.add(jtfTotalPayment);
45        p1.setBorder(new
46          TitledBorder("Enter interest rate, year and loan amount"));
47
48        // Panel p2 to hold the button
49        JPanel p2 = new JPanel();
50        p2.setLayout(new FlowLayout(FlowLayout.RIGHT));
51        p2.add(jbtComputeLoan);
52
53        // Add the components to the applet
54        getContentPane().add(p1, BorderLayout.CENTER);                    contentPane
55        getContentPane().add(p2, BorderLayout.SOUTH);
56
57        // Register listener
58        jbtComputeLoan.addActionListener(this);
59      }
60
61      /** Handle the Compute Payment button */
62      public void actionPerformed(ActionEvent e) {                        handler
63        if (e.getSource() == jbtComputeLoan) {
64          // Get values from text fields
65          double interest =
66            Double.parseDouble(jtfAnnualInterestRate.getText());
67          int year =
68            Integer.parseInt(jtfNumberOfYears.getText());
69          double loanAmount =
70            Double.parseDouble(jtfLoanAmount.getText());
71
72          // Create a loan object
73          Loan loan = new Loan(interest, year, loanAmount);            create Loan
74
75          // Display monthly payment and total payment
76          jtfMonthlyPayment.setText("" +
77            (int)(loan.monthlyPayment() * 100) / 100.0);
78          jtfTotalPayment.setText("" +
79            (int)(loan.totalPayment() * 100) / 100.0);
80        }
81      }
82    }
```

LISTING 14.2 LoanApplet.html (HTML File for LOANAPPLET)

```
1  <!--HTML code, this code is separated from the preceding Java code-->
2  <html>
3  <head>
4  <title>Loan Applet</title>
5  </head>
6  <body>
```

EXAMPLE **14.1** (CONTINUED)

```
 7  This is a loan calculator. Enter your input for interest, year, and
 8  loan amount.
 9  Click the "Compute Payment" button, you will get the payment
10  information.<p>
11  <applet
12    code = "LoanApplet.class"
13    width = 300
14    height = 150
15    alt="You must have a Java 2-enabled browser to view the applet">
16  </applet>
17  </body>
18  </html>
```

Review

You need to use the `public` modifier for the `LoanApplet`; otherwise, the Web browser cannot load it.

`LoanApplet` implements `ActionListener` because it listens for button actions.

The `init` method initializes the user interface. The program overrides this method to create user-interface components (labels, text fields, and a button), and places them in the applet.

The only event handled is the Compute Payment button. When this button is clicked, the `actionPerformed` method gets the interest rate, number of years, and loan amount from the text fields. It then creates a `Loan` object (Line 73) to obtain the monthly payment and the total payment. Finally, it displays the monthly and total payments in their respective text fields.

The `Loan` class is responsible for computing the payments. This class was introduced in Section 6.15, "Case Study: The `Loan` Class."

14.5   Passing Strings to Applets

In Chapter 7, "Strings," you learned how to pass strings to Java applications from a command line. Strings are passed to the `main` method as an array of strings. When the application starts, the `main` method can use these strings. There is no `main` method in an applet, however, and applets are not run from the command line by the Java interpreter.

How, then, can applets accept arguments? In this section, you will learn how to pass strings to Java applets.

To be passed to an applet, a parameter must be declared in the HTML file, and must be read by the applet when it is initialized. Parameters are declared using the <param> tag. The <param> tag must be embedded in the <applet> tag and has no end tag. The syntax for the <param> tag is given below:

```
<param name=parametername value=stringvalue>
```

This tag specifies a parameter and its corresponding string value.

 NOTE

There is no comma separating the parameter name from the parameter value in the HTML code. The HTML parameter names are not case-sensitive.

Suppose you want to write an applet to display a message. The message is passed as a parameter. In addition, you want the message to be displayed at a specific location with x-coordinate and y-coordinate, which are passed as two parameters. The parameters and their values are listed in Table 14.1.

TABLE **14.1**   Parameter Names and Values for the DisplayMessage Applet

Parameter name	Parameter value
MESSAGE	"Welcome to Java"
X	20
Y	30

The HTML source file is given in Listing 14.3:

LISTING **14.3**   LoanApplet.html (HTML File for LoanApplet)

```
<html>
<head>
<title>Passing Strings to Java Applets</title>
</head>
<body>
This applet gets a message from the HTML page and displays it.
<p>
<applet
  code = "DisplayMessage.class"
  width = 200
  height = 50
  alt="You must have a Java 2-enabled browser to view the applet"
>
<param name = MESSAGE value = "Welcome to Java">
<param name = X value = 20>
<param name = Y value = 30>
</applet>
</body>
</html>
```

To read the parameter from the applet, use the following method defined in the Applet class:

```
public String getParameter("parametername");
```

This returns the value of the specified parameter.

EXAMPLE 14.2 PASSING STRINGS TO JAVA APPLETS

Problem

Write an applet that displays a message at a specified location. The message and the location (x, y) are obtained from the HTML source.

Solution

The program creates a Java source file named **DisplayMessage.java**, as shown below. The output of a sample run is shown in Figure 14.7.

LISTING **14.4**   DisplayMessage.java (Displaying a Message)

```
1 import javax.swing.*;
2
3 public class DisplayMessage extends JApplet {
4   /** Initialize the applet */
5   public void init() {
6     // Get parameter values from the HTML file
7     String message = getParameter("MESSAGE");
```

getParameter

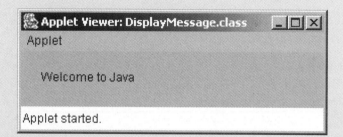

EXAMPLE 14.2 (CONTINUED)

```
 8       int x = Integer.parseInt(getParameter("X"));
 9       int y = Integer.parseInt(getParameter("Y"));
10
11       // Create a message panel
12       MessagePanel messagePanel = new MessagePanel(message);
13       messagePanel.setXCoordinate(x);
14       messagePanel.setYCoordinate(y);
15
16       // Add the message panel to the applet
17       getContentPane().add(messagePanel);
18     }
19 }
```

contentPane

FIGURE 14.7 *The applet displays the message Welcome to Java passed from the HTML page.*

Review

The program gets the parameter values from the HTML in the init method. The values are strings obtained using the getParameter method (Lines 7–9). Because x and y are int, the program uses Integer.parseInt(string) to parse a digital string into an int value.

If you change *Welcome to Java* in the HTML file to *Welcome to HTML*, and reload the HTML file in the Web browser, you should see *Welcome to HTML* displayed. Similarly, the x and y values can be changed to display the message in a desired location.

CAUTION

The Applet's getParameter method can be invoked only after an instance of the applet is created. Therefore, this method cannot be invoked in the constructor of the applet class. You should invoke it from the init method.

14.6 Enabling Applets to Run as Applications

The JFrame class and the JApplet class have a lot in common despite some differences. Since they both are subclasses of the Container class, all their user-interface components, layout managers, and event-handling features are the same. Applications, however, are invoked from the static `main` method by the Java interpreter, and applets are run by the Web browser. The Web browser creates an instance of the applet using the applet's no-arg constructor and controls and executes the applet through the `init`, `start`, `stop`, and `destroy` methods .

For security reasons, the restrictions listed below are imposed on applets to prevent destructive programs from damaging the system on which the browser is running:

✦ Applets are not allowed to read from, or write to, the file system of the computer. Otherwise, they could damage the files and spread viruses.

✦ Applets are not allowed to run programs on the browser's computer. Otherwise, they might call destructive local programs and damage the local system on the user's computer.

✦ Applets are not allowed to establish connections between the user's computer and any other computer, except for the server where the applets are stored. This restriction prevents the applet from connecting the user's computer to another computer without the user's knowledge.

 NOTE
A new security protocol was introduced in Java 2. You can use a security policy file to grant applets access to local files.

In general, an applet can be converted to an application without loss of functionality. An application can be converted to an applet as long as it does not violate the security restrictions imposed on applets. You can implement a `main` method in an applet to enable the applet to run as an application. This feature has both theoretical and practical implications. Theoretically, it blurs the difference between applets and applications. You can write a class that is both an applet and an application. From the standpoint of practicality, it is convenient to be able to run a program in two ways.

It is not difficult to write such programs on your own. Suppose you have an applet named `TestApplet`. To enable it to run as an application, all you need to do is add a `main` method in the applet with the implementation, as follows:

```
public static void main(String[] args) {
  // Create a frame
  JFrame frame = new JFrame (                      create frame
    "Running a program as applet and frame");

  // Create an instance of TestApplet
  TestApplet applet = new TestApplet();            create applet

  // Add the applet instance to the frame
  frame.getContentPane().add(applet, BorderLayout.CENTER);   add applet

  // Invoke init and start
  applet.init();                                   init()
  applet.start();                                  start()

  // Display the frame
  frame.setSize(300, 300);
  frame.setVisible(true);                          show frame
}
```

Since the `JApplet` class is a subclass of `Component`, it can be placed in a frame. You can invoke the `init` and `start` methods of the applet to run a `JApplet` object in an application.

EXAMPLE 14.3 RUNNING A PROGRAM AS AN APPLET AND AS AN APPLICATION

Problem

Write a program that modifies the `DisplayMessage` applet in Example 14.2, "Passing Strings to Java Applets," to enable it to run both as an applet and as an application.

Solution

The program is identical to `DisplayMessage` except for the addition of a new `main` method and of a variable named `isStandalone` to indicate whether it is running as an applet or as an application. Listing 14.5 gives the solution to the problem.

LISTING 14.5 DisplayMessageApp.java (Running Applets Standalone)

```java
1  import javax.swing.*;
2  import java.awt.Font;
3  import java.awt.BorderLayout;
4
5  public class DisplayMessageApp extends JApplet {
6    private String message = "A default message"; // Message to display
7    private int x = 20; // Default x coordinate
8    private int y = 20; // Default y coordinate
9
10   /** Determine if it is application */
11   private boolean isStandalone = false;
12
13   /** Initialize the applet */
14   public void init() {
15     if (!isStandalone) {
16       // Get parameter values from the HTML file
17       message = getParameter("MESSAGE");
18       x = Integer.parseInt(getParameter("X"));
19       y = Integer.parseInt(getParameter("Y"));
20     }
21
22     // Create a message panel
23     MessagePanel messagePanel = new MessagePanel(message);
24     messagePanel.setFont(new Font("SansSerif", Font.BOLD, 20));
25     messagePanel.setXCoordinate(x);
26     messagePanel.setYCoordinate(y);
27
28     // Add the message panel to the applet
29     getContentPane().add(messagePanel);
30   }
31
32   /** Main method to display a message
33      @param args[0] x coordinate
34      @param args[1] y coordinate
35      @param args[2] message
36   */
37   public static void main(String[] args) {
38     // Create a frame
39     JFrame frame = new JFrame("DisplayMessageApp");
40
41     // Create an instance of the applet
42     DisplayMessageApp applet = new DisplayMessageApp();
43
44     // It runs as an application
45     applet.isStandalone = true;
46
47     // Get parameters from the command line
48     applet.getCommandLineParameters(args);
49
50     // Add the applet instance to the frame
51     frame.getContentPane().add(applet, BorderLayout.CENTER);
```

(margin annotations)

isStandalone

applet params

standalone

command params

EXAMPLE 14.3 (CONTINUED)

```
52
53     // Invoke init() and start()
54     applet.init();
55     applet.start();
56
57     // Display the frame
58     frame.setSize(300, 300);
59     frame.setDefaultCloseOperation(JFrame.EXIT_ON_CLOSE);
60     frame.setVisible(true);
61   }
62
63   /** Get command line parameters */
64   private void getCommandLineParameters(String[] args) {
65     // Check usage and get x, y and message
66     if (args.length != 3) {
67       System.out.println(
68         "Usage: java DisplayMessageApp x y message");
69       System.exit(0);
70     }
71     else {
72       x = Integer.parseInt(args[0]);
73       y = Integer.parseInt(args[1]);
74       message = args[2];
75     }
76   }
77 }
```

Review

When you run the program as an applet, the main method is ignored. When you run it as an application, the main method is invoked. A sample run of the program as an application and as an applet is shown in Figure 14.8.

FIGURE 14.8 *The* DisplayMessageApp *class can run as an application and as an applet.*

The main method creates a JFrame object frame and creates a JApplet object applet, then places the applet applet into the frame frame and invokes its init method. The application runs just like an applet.

The main method sets isStandalone true (Line 45) so that it does not attempt to retrieve HTML parameters when the init method is invoked.

The setVisible(true) method (Line 60) is invoked *after* the components are added to the applet, and the applet is added to the frame to ensure that the components will be visible. Otherwise, the components are not shown when the frame starts.

🌿 **NOTE**   omitting main method

From now on, all the GUI examples will be created as applets with a main method. Thus you will be able to run the program either as an applet or as an application. For brevity, the main method is not listed in the text.

14.7 CASE STUDY: TicTacToe (Optional)

You have learned about objects, classes, arrays, class inheritance, GUI, event-driven programming, and applets from the many examples in this chapter and the preceding chapters. Now it is time to put what you have learned to work in developing comprehensive projects. In this section, you will develop a Java applet with which to play the popular game of TicTacToe.

In a game of TicTacToe, two players take turns marking an available cell in a 3 × 3 grid with their respective tokens (either X or O). When one player has placed three tokens in a horizontal, vertical, or diagonal row on the grid, the game is over and that player has won. A draw (no winner) occurs when all the cells on the grid have been filled with tokens and neither player has achieved a win. Figure 14.9 shows two representative sample runs of the example.

(a) X player won the game

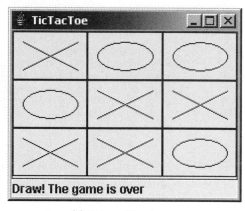
(b) Draw -- No winners

FIGURE 14.9 *Two players play a TicTacToe game.*

All the examples you have seen so far show simple behaviors that are easy to model with classes. The behavior of the TicTacToe game is somewhat more complex. To create classes that model the behavior, you need to study and understand the game.

Assume that all the cells are initially empty, and that the first player takes the X token, and the second player takes the O token. To mark a cell, the player points the mouse to the cell and clicks it. If the cell is empty, the token (X or O) is displayed. If the cell is already filled, the player's action is ignored.

From the preceding description, it is obvious that a cell is a GUI object that handles the mouse-click event and displays tokens. Such an object could be either a button or a panel. Drawing on panels is more flexible than on buttons, because the token (X or O) can be drawn on a panel in any size, but on a button it can only be displayed as a text label. Therefore, a panel should be used to model a cell. How do you know the state of the cell (empty, X, or O)? You use a property named token of char type in the Cell class. The Cell class is responsible for drawing the token when an empty cell is clicked. So you need to write the code for listening to the MouseEvent and for painting the shapes for tokens X and O. The Cell class can be defined as shown in Figure 14.10.

The TicTacToe board consists of nine cells, declared using new Cell[3][3]. To determine which player's turn it is, you can introduce a variable named whoseTurn of char type. whoseTurn is initially X, then changes to O, and subsequently changes between X and O whenever a new cell is occupied. When the game is over, set whoseTurn to ' '.

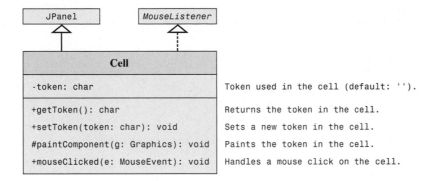

FIGURE 14.10 *The* Cell *class paints the token on a cell.*

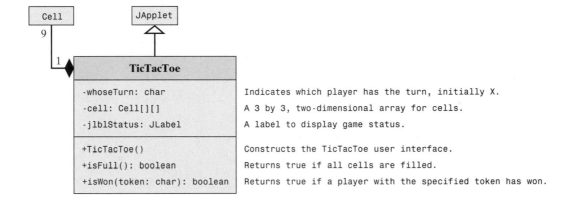

FIGURE 14.11 *The* TicTacToe *class contains nine cells.*

How do you know whether the game is over, whether there is a winner, and who the winner, if any, is? You can create a method named isWon(char token) to check whether a specified token has won and a method named isFull() to check whether all the cells are occupied.

Clearly, two classes emerge from the foregoing analysis. One is the Cell class, which handles operations for a single cell; and the other is the TicTacToe class, which plays the whole game and deals with all the cells. The relationship between these two classes is shown in Figure 14.11.

Since the Cell class is only to support the TicTacToe class, it can be defined as an inner class in TicTacToe. The complete program is given as follows:

LISTING 14.6 TicTacToe.java (TicTacToe Game)

```
1 import java.awt.*;
2 import java.awt.event.*;
3 import javax.swing.*;
4 import javax.swing.border.LineBorder;
5
6 public class TicTacToe extends JApplet {
7   // Indicate which player has a turn, initially it is the X player
8   private char whoseTurn = 'X';
9
10  // Create and initialize cells
11  private Cell[][] cells =  new Cell[3][3];
12
```

```
13   // Create and initialize a status label
14   private JLabel jlblStatus = new JLabel("X's turn to play");
15
16   /** Initialize UI */
17   public TicTacToe() {
18     // Panel p to hold cells
19     JPanel p = new JPanel(new GridLayout(3, 3, 0, 0));
20     for (int i = 0; i < 3; i++)
21       for (int j = 0; j < 3; j++)
22         p.add(cells[i][j] = new Cell());
23
24     // Set line borders on the cells panel and the status label
25     p.setBorder(new LineBorder(Color.red, 1));
26     jlblStatus.setBorder(new LineBorder(Color.yellow, 1));
27
28     // Place the panel and the label to the applet
29     this.getContentPane().add(p, BorderLayout.CENTER);
30     this.getContentPane().add(jlblStatus, BorderLayout.SOUTH);
31   }
32
33   /** Determine if the cells are all occupied */
34   public boolean isFull() {
35     for (int i = 0; i < 3; i++)
36       for (int j = 0; j < 3; j++)
37         if (cells[i][j].getToken() == ' ')
38           return false;
39
40     return true;
41   }
42
43   /** Determine if the player with the specified token wins */
44   public boolean isWon(char token) {
45     for (int i = 0; i < 3; i++)
46       if ((cells[i][0].getToken() == token)
47           && (cells[i][1].getToken() == token)
48           && (cells[i][2].getToken() == token)) {
49         return true;
50       }
51
52     for (int j = 0; j < 3; j++)
53       if ((cells[0][j].getToken() ==  token)
54           && (cells[1][j].getToken() == token)
55           && (cells[2][j].getToken() == token)) {
56         return true;
57       }
58
59     if ((cells[0][0].getToken() == token)
60         && (cells[1][1].getToken() == token)
61         && (cells[2][2].getToken() == token)) {
62       return true;
63     }
64
65     if ((cells[0][2].getToken() == token)
66         && (cells[1][1].getToken() == token)
67         && (cells[2][0].getToken() == token)) {
68       return true;
69     }
70
71     return false;
72   }
73
74   // An inner class for a cell
75   public class Cell extends JPanel implements MouseListener {
76     // Token used for this cell
77     private char token = ' ';
78
79     public Cell() {
80       setBorder(new LineBorder(Color.black, 1)); // Set cell's border
81       addMouseListener(this);  // Register listener
82     }
```

check rows

check columns

check major diagonal

check subdiagonal

inner class

```
83
84      /** Return token */
85      public char getToken() {
86        return token;
87      }
88
89      /** Set a new token */
90      public void setToken(char c) {
91        token = c;
92        repaint();
93      }
94
95      /** Paint the cell */
96      protected void paintComponent(Graphics g) {                    paint cell
97        super.paintComponent(g);
98
99        if (token == 'X') {
100          g.drawLine(10, 10, getWidth() - 10, getHeight() - 10);
101          g.drawLine(getWidth() - 10, 10, 10, getHeight() - 10);
102        }
103        else if (token == 'O') {
104          g.drawOval(10, 10, getWidth() - 20, getHeight() - 20);
105        }
106      }
107
108      /** Handle mouse click on a cell */
109      public void mouseClicked(MouseEvent e) {                       handler
110        // If cell is empty and game is not over
111        if (token == ' ' && whoseTurn != ' ') {
112          setToken(whoseTurn); // Set token in the cell
113
114          // Check game status
115          if (isWon(whoseTurn)) {
116            jlblStatus.setText(whoseTurn + " won! The game is over");
117            whoseTurn = ' '; // Game is over
118          }
119          else if (isFull()) {
120            jlblStatus.setText("Draw! The game is over");
121            whoseTurn = ' '; // Game is over
122          }
123          else {
124            whoseTurn = (whoseTurn == 'X') ? 'O': 'X'; // Change the turn
125            jlblStatus.setText(whoseTurn + "'s turn");  // Display whose turn
126          }
127        }
128      }
129
130      public void mousePressed(MouseEvent e) {
131        // TODO: implement this java.awt.event.MouseListener method;
132      }
133
134      public void mouseReleased(MouseEvent e) {
135        // TODO: implement this java.awt.event.MouseListener method;
136      }
137
138      public void mouseEntered(MouseEvent e) {
139        // TODO: implement this java.awt.event.MouseListener method;
140      }
141
142      public void mouseExited(MouseEvent e) {
143        // TODO: implement this java.awt.event.MouseListener method;
144      }
145    }
146 }                                                                  main method omitted
```

The TicTacToe class initializes the user interface with nine cells placed in a panel of GridLayout (Lines 19–22). A label named jlblStatus is used to show the status of the game (Line 14). The variable whoseTurn (Line 8) is used to track the next type of token to be placed in a cell. The methods `isFull` (Lines 34–41) and `isWon` (Lines 44–72) are for checking the status of the game.

Since `Cell` is an inner class in `TicTacToe`, the variable (`whoseTurn`) and methods (`isFull` and `isWon`) defined in `TicTacToe` can be referenced from the `Cell` class. The inner class makes programs simple and concise. If `Cell` were not declared as an inner class of `TicTacToe`, you would have to pass an object of `TicTacToe` to `Cell` in order for the variables and methods in `TicTacToe` to be used in `Cell`. You will rewrite the program without using an inner class in Exercise 14.6.

The `Cell` class implements `MouseListener` to listen for `MouseEvent`. If an empty cell is clicked and the game is not over, a token is set in the cell (Line 112). If the game is over, `whoseTurn` is set to ' ' (Lines 117, 121). Otherwise, `whoseTurn` is alternated to a new turn (Line 124).

 TIP

Use an incremental approach in developing a Java project of this kind, working one step at a time. The foregoing program can be divided into five steps:

1. Lay out the user interface and display a fixed token X on a cell.

2. Enable the cell to display a fixed token X upon a mouse click.

3. Coordinate between the two players so as to display tokens X and O alternately.

4. Check whether a player wins, or whether all the cells are occupied without a winner.

5. Implement displaying a message on the label upon each move by a player.

 14.8   CASE STUDY: Bouncing Ball (Optional)

Write an applet that displays a ball bouncing in a panel. Use two buttons to suspend and resume the movement, and use a scroll bar to control the bouncing speed, as shown in Figure 14.12.

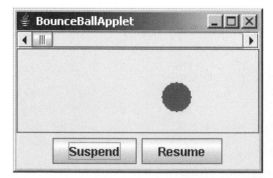 

FIGURE 14.12   *The ball's movement is controlled by the Suspend and Resume buttons and the scroll bar.*

Here are the major steps to complete this example:

1. Create a subclass of `JPanel` named `Ball` to display a ball bouncing, as shown in Listing 14.7.

2. Create a subclass of `JPanel` named `BallControl` to contain the ball with a scroll bar and two control buttons *Suspend* and *Resume*, as shown in Listing 14.8.

3. Create an applet named `BounceBallApp` to contain an instance of `BallControl` and enable the applet to run standalone, as shown in Listing 14.9.

The relationship among these classes is shown in Figure 14.13.

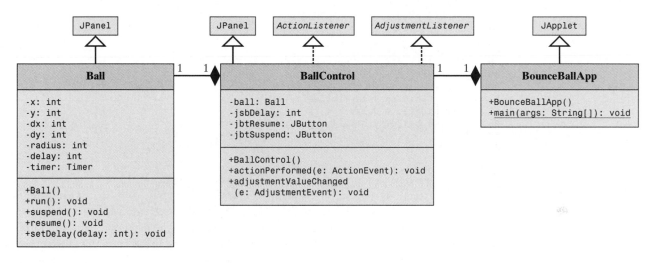

FIGURE 14.13   *BounceBallApp contains* `BallControl`, *and* `BallControl` *contains* `Ball`.

LISTING 14.7   Ball.java (Displaying a Moving Ball)

```
 1 import java.awt.event.*;
 2 import javax.swing.Timer;
 3 import java.awt.*;
 4 import javax.swing.*;
 5
 6 public class Ball extends JPanel implements ActionListener {
 7   private int delay = 10;                                          timer delay
 8
 9   // Create a timer with delay 1000 ms
10   protected Timer timer = new Timer(delay, this);                  create timer
11
12   private int x = 0; private int y = 0; // Current ball position
13   private int radius = 15; // Ball radius
14   private int dx = 2; // Increment on ball's x-coordinate
15   private int dy = 2; // Increment on ball's y-coordinate
16
17   public Ball() {
18     timer.start();                                                 start timer
19   }
20
21   /** Handle the action event */
22   public void actionPerformed(ActionEvent e) {
23     repaint();                                                     repaint ball
24   }
25
26   protected void paintComponent(Graphics g) {                      paint ball
27     super.paintComponent(g);
28
29     g.setColor(Color.red);
30
31     // Check boundaries
32     if (x < radius) dx = Math.abs(dx);
33     if (x > getWidth() - radius) dx = -Math.abs(dx);
```

```
34     if (y < radius) dy = Math.abs(dy);
35     if (y > getHeight() - radius) dy = -Math.abs(dy);
36
37     // Adjust ball position
38     x += dx;
39     y += dy;
40     g.fillOval(x - radius, y - radius, radius * 2, radius * 2);
41   }
42
43   public void suspend() {
44     timer.stop(); // Suspend clock
45   }
46
47   public void resume() {
48     timer.start(); // Resume clock
49   }
50
51   public void setDelay(int delay) {
52     this.delay = delay;
53     timer.setDelay(delay);
54   }
55 }
```

Using Timer class to control animation was introduced in Section 12.6, "The Timer Class" name. Ball extends JPanel and implements ActionListener (Line 6) so that it can listen for ActionEvent. Line 10 creates a Timer for a Ball. The timer is started in Line 18 when a Ball is constructed. The timer fires an ActionEvent at a fixed rate. The listener responds in Line 23 to repaint the ball to animate ball movement. The center of the ball is at (x, y), which changes to (x + dx, y + dy) on the next display. The suspend and resume methods (Lines 43–49) can be used to stop and start the timer. The setDelay(int) method (Lines 51–54) sets a new delay.

LISTING 14.8 BallControl.java (Controlling Ball Movement)

```
1 import javax.swing.*;
2 import java.awt.event.*;
3 import java.awt.*;
4
5 public class BallControl extends JPanel
6     implements ActionListener, AdjustmentListener {
7   private Ball ball = new Ball();
8   private JButton jbtSuspend = new JButton("Suspend");
9   private JButton jbtResume = new JButton("Resume");
10  private JScrollBar jsbDelay = new JScrollBar();
11
12  public BallControl() {
13    // Group buttons in a panel
14    JPanel panel = new JPanel();
15    panel.add(jbtSuspend);
16    panel.add(jbtResume);
17
18    // Add ball and buttons to the panel
19    ball.setBorder(new javax.swing.border.LineBorder(Color.red));
20    jsbDelay.setOrientation(JScrollBar.HORIZONTAL);
21    ball.setDelay(jsbDelay.getMaximum());
22    setLayout(new BorderLayout());
23    add(jsbDelay, BorderLayout.NORTH);
24    add(ball, BorderLayout.CENTER);
25    add(panel, BorderLayout.SOUTH);
26
27    // Register listeners
28    jbtSuspend.addActionListener(this);
29    jbtResume.addActionListener(this);
30    jsbDelay.addAdjustmentListener(this);
31  }
32
```

```
25   /** Construct an image viewer for a specified Image
26   public ImageViewer(Image image) {
27     this.image = image;
28     repaint();
29   }
30
31   /** Create an image icon from a local file name */
32   public static ImageIcon createImageIcon(String image
33       Object object) {
34     URL url = object.getClass().getResource(imageFile
35     return new ImageIcon(url);
36   }
37
38   /** Create an image from a local file name */
39   public static Image createImage(String imageFilenam
40       Object object) {
41     ImageIcon imageIcon = createImageIcon(imageFilena
42     if (imageIcon != null)
43       return imageIcon.getImage();
44     else
45       return null;
46   }
47
48   /** Create an image icon from an Internet URL stri
49   public static ImageIcon createImageIcon(String url
50     return new ImageIcon(getURL(urlString));
51   }
52
53   /** Create an image from an URL string */
54   public static Image createImage(String urlString)
55     return new ImageIcon(getURL(urlString)).getImage
56   }
57
58   private static URL getURL(String urlString) {
59     URL url = null;
60     try {
61       url = new URL(urlString);
62     }
63     catch (java.net.MalformedURLException ex) {
64       ex.printStackTrace();
65     }
66
67     return url;
68   }
69
70   protected void paintComponent(Graphics g) {
71     super.paintComponent(g);
72
73     if (image != null)
74       if (isStretched())
75         g.drawImage(image, xCoordinate, yCoordinat
76             getSize().width, getSize().height, this
77       else
78         g.drawImage(image, xCoordinate, yCoordinat
79   }
80
81   /** Return value of property image */
82   public java.awt.Image getImage() {
83     return image;
84   }
85
86   /** Set a new value for property image */
87   public void setImage(java.awt.Image image) {
88     this.image = image;
89     repaint();
90   }
91
92   /** Return value of property imageFilename */
93   public String getImageFilename() {
94     return imageFilename;
95   }
```

```
33   public void actionPerformed(ActionEvent e) {
34     if (e.getSource() == jbtSuspend)
35       ball.suspend();                                    suspend
36     else if (e.getSource() == jbtResume)
37       ball.resume();                                     resume
38   }
39
40   public void adjustmentValueChanged(AdjustmentEvent e) {
41     ball.setDelay(jsbDelay.getMaximum() - e.getValue());   new delay
42   }
43 }
```

The `BallControl` class extends `JPanel` to display the ball with a scroll bar and two control buttons, implements the `ActionListener` to handle action events from the buttons, and implements the `AdjustmentListener` to handle value change events from the scroll bar. When the *Suspend* button is clicked, the ball's `suspend()` method is invoked to suspend the ball movement (Line 35). When the *Resume* button is clicked, the ball's `resume()` method is invoked to resume the ball movement (Line 37). The bouncing speed can be changed using the scroll bar.

LISTING 14.9   BounceBallApp.java

```
1 import java.awt.*;
2 import java.awt.event.*;
3 import java.applet.*;
4 import javax.swing.*;
5
6 public class BounceBallApp extends JApplet {
7   public BounceBallApp() {
8     getContentPane().add(new BallControl());              add BallControl
9   }
10 }                                                         main method omitted
```

The `BounceBallApp` class simply places an instance of `BallControl` in the applet's content pane. The main method is provided in the applet (not displayed in the listing for brevity) so that you can also run it standalone.

14.8   The `URL` Class (Optional)

Images and audio are stored in files. The `java.net.URL` class can be used to identify files on the Internet. In general, a URL (Uniform Resource Locator) is a pointer to a "resource" on the World Wide Web. A resource can be something as simple as a file or a directory. You can create a URL object using the following constructor:

```
public URL(String spec) throws MalformedURLException
```

For example, the following statement creates a URL object for `http://www.sun.com`:

```
try {
  URL url = new URL("http://www.sun.com");
}
catch (MalformedURLException ex) {
}
```

A `MalformedURLException` is thrown if the URL string has a syntax error. For example, the URL string `"http:/www.sun.com"` would cause a `MalformedURLException` runtime error because two slashes (`//`) are required.

The following statement creates a URL object for the file c:\book\image\us.gif:

```
try {
  URL url = new URL("c:\\book\\image\\us.gif");
}
catch (MalformedURLException ex) {
}
```

◈ 14.10   CASE S[TUDY]
Comp[onent]

Displaying an image is a frequent task [...]
component named ImageViewer that d[...]

The ImageViewer class given in Lis[...]
stretched, xCoordinate, and yCoordi[...]

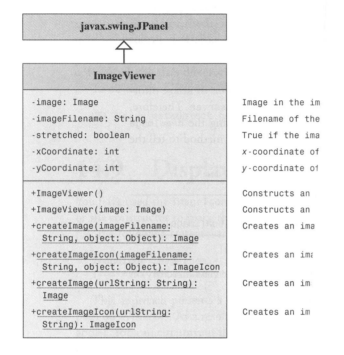

FIGURE 14.14   *The* ImageViewer *component displays an image [...]*

LISTING 14.11   ImageViewer[...]

```
 1 import java.awt.*;
 2 import java.net.URL;
 3 import javax.swing.*;
 4
 5 public class ImageViewer
 6   /** Hold value of prop
 7   private java.awt.Image
 8
 9   /** Hold value of prop
10   private String imageFi
11
12   /** Hold value of prop
13   private boolean stret
14
15   /** Hold value of pro
16   private int xCoordina
17
18   /** Hold value of pro
19   private int yCoordina
20
21   /** Construct an empt
22   public ImageViewer()
23   }
24
```

properties

no-arg constructor

```
 96
 97   /** Set a new value for property imageFilename */
 98   public void setImageFilename(String imageFilename) {
 99     this.imageFilename = imageFilename;
109     image = createImage(imageFilename, this);
101     repaint();
102   }
103
104   /** Return value of property stretched */
105   public boolean isStretched() {
106     return stretched;
107   }
108
109   /** Set a new value for property stretched */
110   public void setStretched(boolean stretched) {
111     this.stretched = stretched;
112     repaint();
113   }
114
115   /** Return value of property xCoordinate */
116   public int getXCoordinate() {
117     return xCoordinate;
118   }
119
120   /** Set a new value for property xCoordinate */
121   public void setXCoordinate(int xCoordinate) {
122     this.xCoordinate = xCoordinate;
123     repaint();
124   }
125
126   /** Return value of property yCoordinate */
127   public int getYCoordinate() {
128     return yCoordinate;
129   }
130
131   /** Set a new value for property yCoordinate */
132   public void setYCoordinate(int yCoordinate) {
133     this.yCoordinate = yCoordinate;
134     repaint();
135   }
136 }
```

The ImageViewer class provides two overloaded static methods, createImageIcon (imageFilename, object) (Lines 32–36) and createImageIcon(urlString) (Lines 49–51). The createImageIcon(imageFilename, object) method returns an ImageIcon from the image file name through the resource of the object, and createImageIcon(urlString) returns an ImageIcon from the specified URL.

Two other overloaded static methods are createImage(imageFilename, object) (Lines 39–46) and createImage(urlString) (Lines 54–56). The createImage(imageFilename, object) method returns an Image from the image file name through the resource of the object, and createImage (urlString) returns an Image from the specified URL.

The imageFilename property enables you to set a filename for the image. The setImageFilename method sets the imageFilename and creates the image for the file.

The ImageViewer component also provides the image property. You can set the image directly using the setImage method. This is convenient if your program knows the image but not the file-name for the image. This is another good example of class design that provides many ways to use the class. You can use the imageFilename property or the image property to set the image for ImageViewer, whichever is convenient.

 NOTE

The createImageIcon method and createImage method could have been eliminated and combined with the setImageFilename method. The purpose of creating these two static methods is for use by other programs. You can now use these two methods as well as other methods to create image icons and images.

 NOTE

You can use images in Swing components like `JLabel` and `JButton`, but the images are not stretchable and their filenames cannot be used directly with these components. The `ImageViewer` component provides better support for displaying images.

Now let us use the `ImageViewer` class to create six images in Listing 14.12. Figure 14.15 shows a sample run of the program.

LISTING 14.12 SixFlags.java

```
1  import javax.swing.*;
2  import java.awt.*;
3
4  public class SixFlags extends javax.swing.JApplet {
5    public SixFlags() {
6      ImageViewer imageViewer1 = new ImageViewer();        image viewer
7      ImageViewer imageViewer2 = new ImageViewer();
8      ImageViewer imageViewer3 = new ImageViewer();
9      ImageViewer imageViewer4 = new ImageViewer();
10     ImageViewer imageViewer5 = new ImageViewer();
11     ImageViewer imageViewer6 = new ImageViewer();
12
13     getContentPane().setLayout(new java.awt.GridLayout(2, 0, 5, 5));
14     imageViewer1.setImageFilename("/image/us.gif");      image file
15     getContentPane().add(imageViewer1);
16     imageViewer2.setImageFilename("/image/ca.gif");
17     getContentPane().add(imageViewer2);
18     imageViewer3.setImageFilename("/image/india.gif");
19     getContentPane().add(imageViewer3);
20     imageViewer4.setImageFilename("/image/uk.gif");
21     getContentPane().add(imageViewer4);
22     imageViewer5.setImageFilename("/image/china.gif");
23     getContentPane().add(imageViewer5);
24     imageViewer6.setImageFilename("/image/norway.gif");
25     getContentPane().add(imageViewer6);
26   }
27 }                                                        main method omitted
```

FIGURE 14.15 *Six images are displayed in six `ImageViewer` components.*

You can use files from your local machine or from any Internet site. For example, you may replace Line 14 with the following statement to use a file from www.cs.armstrong.edu:

```
imageViewer1.setImage(ImageViewer.createImage(
  "http://www.cs.armstrong.edu/liang/image/uk.gif"));
```

The image icon in the `createImageIcon(imageFilename, object)` method is created using `new ImageIcon(url)` (Line 35 in ImageViewer.java), where `url` is obtained using the `getResource` method in a `Class` instance of the object. You may create an image icon directly from the absolute path of the image file, as follows:

```
new ImageIcon("c:\\book\image\\someimage.gif");
```

This approach is simple, but it works only with standalone applications. To load images in Java applets, you have to obtain the URL of the image and load the image through it. This approach works for both Java applications and applets.

✦ 14.11   CASE STUDY: Image Animations (Optional)

This case study gives an example of how to display a sequence of images that simulates a movie. You can use a timer to trigger repainting of the viewing area with different images. The `Timer` class was introduced in Section 12.6, "The `Timer` Class."

Let us write a program in Listing 14.13 that displays a sequence of images in order to create a movie. The images are files stored in the **image** directory that are named **L1.gif**, **L2.gif**, and so on, to **L52.gif**. When you run the program, you will see a phrase entitled "Learning Java" rotate, as shown in Figure 14.16.

 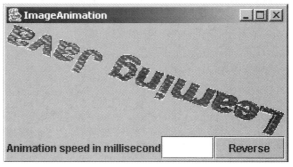

FIGURE 14.16   *The applet displays a sequence of images.*

LISTING 14.13   ImageAnimation.java

```
 1 import java.awt.*;
 2 import java.awt.event.*;
 3 import javax.swing.*;
 4
 5 public class ImageAnimation extends JApplet
 6     implements ActionListener {
 7   // Total number of images
 8   public final static int NUM_OF_IMAGES = 52;
 9   protected Image[] images = new Image[NUM_OF_IMAGES]; // Hold images
10   protected int currentImageIndex = 0, // Current image subscript
11             sleepTime = 100; // Milliseconds to sleep
12   protected int direction = 1; // Image rotating direction
```

image number

```
13
14    // Image viewer to display an image
15    private ImageViewer imageViewer = new ImageViewer();
16
17    // Text field for setting animation speed
18    protected JTextField jtfSpeed = new JTextField(5);
19
20    // Button for reversing direction
21    private JButton jbtReverse = new JButton("Reverse");
22
23    // Create a timer with delay 1000 ms and listener Clock
24    private Timer timer = new Timer(1000, this);                          create timer
25
26    /** Initialize the applet */
27    public void init() {
28      // Load the image, the image files are named
29      // L1 - L52 in image directory
30      for (int i = 0; i < images.length; i++ ) {
31        images[i] = ImageViewer.createImage(                              create image
32          "image/L" + (i + 1) + ".gif", this );
33      }
34
35      // Panel p to hold animation control
36      JPanel p = new JPanel();                                           create UI
37      p.setLayout(new BorderLayout());
38      p.add(new JLabel("Animation speed in millisecond"),
39        BorderLayout.WEST);
40      p.add(jtfSpeed, BorderLayout.CENTER);
41      p.add(jbtReverse, BorderLayout.EAST);
42
43      // Add the image panel and p to the applet
44      getContentPane().add(imageViewer, BorderLayout.CENTER);
45      getContentPane().add(p, BorderLayout.SOUTH);
46
47      // Register listener
48      jtfSpeed.addActionListener(this);
49      jbtReverse.addActionListener(this);
50
51      // Start the timer
52      timer.start();                                                     start timer
53    }
54
55    /** Handle ActionEvent */
56    public void actionPerformed(ActionEvent e) {
57      if (e.getSource() == jtfSpeed) {
58        sleepTime = Integer.parseInt(jtfSpeed.getText());
59        timer.setDelay(sleepTime);
60      }
61      else if (e.getSource() == jbtReverse) {
62        direction = -direction;
63      }
64      else if (e.getSource() == timer) {
65        imageViewer.setImage(                                            change image
66          images[currentImageIndex % NUM_OF_IMAGES]);
67
68        // Make sure currentImageIndex is nonnegative
69        if (currentImageIndex == 0) currentImageIndex = NUM_OF_IMAGES;
70        currentImageIndex = currentImageIndex + direction;
71      }
72    }
73 }                                                                       main method omitted
```

Fifty-two image files are located in the **image** directory, which is a subdirectory of the code base directory. The images in these files are loaded to images (Lines 30–33) and then painted continuously on the applet at a fixed rate using a timer.

The image is drawn to occupy the entire applet viewing area in a rectangle. It is scaled to fill in the area.

The timer is created in Line 24 and started in the init method in Line 52. You can adjust sleepTime to control animation speed by entering a value in milliseconds and pressing the Enter key for the change to take place.

The display sequence can be reversed by clicking the Reverse button.

You can add a simple function to suspend a timer when the mouse is pressed. You can resume a suspended timer when the mouse is released.

 NOTE

The JComponent class has a property named doubleBuffered. By default, this property is set to true. Double buffering is a technique for reducing animation flickering. It creates a graphics context off-screen and does all the drawings in the off-screen context. When the drawing is complete, it displays the whole context on the real screen. Thus, there is no flickering within an image because all the drawings are displayed at the same time. To see the effect of double buffering, set the doubleBuffered property to false. You will be stunned by the difference.

14.12   Playing Audio

There are several formats for audio files. Prior to Java 2, sound files in the AU format used on the UNIX operating system were the only ones Java was able to play. With Java 2, you can play sound files in the WAV, AIFF, MIDI, AU, and RMF formats, with better sound quality.

To play an audio file in an applet, first create an *audio clip object* for the audio file. The audio clip is created once and can be played repeatedly without reloading the file. To create an audio clip, use the static method newAudioClip() in the java.applet.Applet class:

```
AudioClip audioClip = Applet.newAudioClip(url);
```

Audio was originally used with Java applets. For this reason, the AudioClip interface is in the java.applet package.

The following statements, for example, create an AudioClip for the beep.au audio file in the class directory:

```
Class metaObject = this.getClass();
URL url = metaObject.getResource("beep.au");
AudioClip audioClip = Applet.newAudioClip(url);
```

To manipulate a sound for an audio clip, use the play(), loop(), and stop() methods in java.applet.AudioClip, as shown in Figure 14.17.

Let us write a program that displays national flags and plays national anthems. The program enables you to select a country from a combo box and then displays the country's flag. You can play the selected country's national anthem by clicking the Play Anthem button, as shown in Figure 14.18. Listing 14.14 gives the solution.

java.applet.AudioClip	
+play()	Starts playing this audio clip. Each time this method is called, the clip is restarted from the beginning.
+loop()	Plays the clip repeatedly.
+stop()	Stops playing the clip.

FIGURE **14.17**   *The AudioClip interface provides the methods for playing sound.*

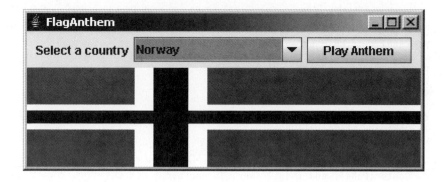

FIGURE 14.18 *The program displays the flag of the selected country and plays its national anthem.*

LISTING 14.14 FlagAnthem.java (Playing Audio)

```
1  import java.awt.*;
2  import java.awt.event.*;
3  import javax.swing.*;
4  import java.applet.*;
5
6  public class FlagAnthem extends JApplet implements ActionListener {
7    // Image viewer for displaying an image
8    private ImageViewer imageViewer = new ImageViewer();                          image viewer
9
10   // Combo box for selecting a country
11   private JComboBox jcboCountry = new JComboBox(new String[] {
12     "United States of America", "United Kingdom", "Denmark",
13     "Norway", "China", "India", "Germany"});
14
15   // Create flag images
16   private Image[] images = {
17     ImageViewer.createImage("image/us.gif", this),                             images
18     ImageViewer.createImage("image/uk.gif", this),
19     ImageViewer.createImage("image/denmark.gif", this),
20     ImageViewer.createImage("image/norway.gif", this),
21     ImageViewer.createImage("image/china.gif", this),
22     ImageViewer.createImage("image/india.gif", this),
23     ImageViewer.createImage("image/germany.gif", this)};
24
25   // Create audio clips
26   private AudioClip[] audioClips = {
27     Applet.newAudioClip(                                                        audio clips
28       this.getClass().getResource("anthem/us.mid")),
29     Applet.newAudioClip(
30       this.getClass().getResource("anthem/uk.mid")),
31     Applet.newAudioClip(
32       this.getClass().getResource("anthem/denmark.mid")),
33     Applet.newAudioClip(
34       this.getClass().getResource("anthem/norway.mid")),
35     Applet.newAudioClip(
36       this.getClass().getResource("anthem/china.mid")),
37     Applet.newAudioClip(
38       this.getClass().getResource("anthem/india.mid")),
39     Applet.newAudioClip(
40       this.getClass().getResource("anthem/germany.mid"))
41   };
42
43   private int currentIndex = 0; // Denote the current selected index
44
45   // Button to play an audio
46   private JButton jbtPlayAnthem = new JButton("Play Anthem");
```


create UI

```
47
48   /** Initialize the applet */
49   public void init() {
50     // Panel p to hold a label combo box and a button for play audio
51     JPanel p = new JPanel();
52     p.add(new JLabel("Select a country"));
53     p.add(jcboCountry);
54     p.add(jbtPlayAnthem);
55
56     // By default, the US flag is displayed
57     imageViewer.setImage(images[0]);
58
59     // Place p and an image panel in the applet
60     getContentPane().add(p, BorderLayout.NORTH);
61     getContentPane().add(imageViewer, BorderLayout.CENTER);
62
63     // Register listener
64     jbtPlayAnthem.addActionListener(this);
65     jcboCountry.addActionListener(this);
66   }
67
68   /** Handle ActionEvent */
69   public void actionPerformed(ActionEvent e) {
70     if (e.getSource() == jcboCountry)
71       imageViewer.setImage(images[jcboCountry.getSelectedIndex()]);
72     else if (e.getSource() == jbtPlayAnthem) {
73       audioClips[currentIndex].stop(); // Stop current audio clip
74       currentIndex = jcboCountry.getSelectedIndex();
75       audioClips[currentIndex].play();
76     }
77   }
78 }
```

event handler — line 69

main method omitted — line 78

An image viewer is created in Line 8 to display a flag image. An array of flag images for seven nations is created in Lines 16–23. Each image is created using the static `createImage` method in the `ImageViewer` class.

An array of audio clips is created in Lines 26–41. Each audio clip is created for an audio file through the URL of the current class. The audio files are stored in the same directory with class file `FlagAnthem`.

The combo box for country names is created in Lines 11–13. When a new country name in the combo box is selected, a new image is set in the image viewer (Line 71).

When the *Play Anthem* button is clicked, the current audio is stopped and a new audio for the current selected country is played.

14.13 Packaging and Deploying Java Projects (Optional)

Your project may consist of many classes and supporting files, such as image files and audio files. To make your programs run on the end-user side, you need to provide end-users with all these files. For convenience, Java supports an archive file that can be used to group all the project files in a compressed file.

The Java archive file format (JAR) is based on the popular ZIP file format. Although JAR can be used as a general archiving tool, the primary motivation for its development was to make it possible for Java applications, applets, and their requisite components (.class files, images, and sounds) to be transported in a single file.

This single file can be deployed on an end-user's machine as an application. It also can be downloaded to a browser in a single HTTP transaction, rather than opening a new connection for each piece. This greatly simplifies application deployment and improves the speed with which an applet can be loaded onto a web page and begin functioning. The JAR format also supports compression, which reduces the size of the file and improves download time still further. Additionally, individual entries in a JAR file can be digitally signed by the applet author to authenticate their origin.

You can use the JDK **jar** command to create an archive file. The following command creates an archive file named TicTacToe.jar for classes TicTacToe.class and TicTacToe$Cell.class (inner class):

```
jar -cf TicTacToe.jar TicTacToe.class TicTacToe$Cell.class
```

The **-c** option is for creating a new archive file, and the **-f** option specifies the archive file's name.

✿ NOTE

You can view the contents of a .jar file using WinZip, a popular compression utility for Windows, as shown in Figure 14.19.   view .jar contents

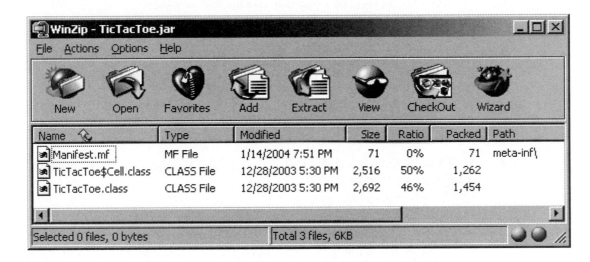

FIGURE 14.19   *You can view the files contained in the archive file using the WinZip utility.*

14.13.1   The Manifest File

As shown in Figure 14.19, a manifest file was created with the path name meta-inf\. The manifest is a special file that contains information about the files packaged in a JAR file. For instance, the manifest file in Figure 14.19 contains the following information:

```
Manifest-Version: 1.0

Name: TicTacToe.class
Java-Bean: True

Name: TioTacToe$Cell.class
Java-Bean: True
```

You can modify the information contained in the manifest file to enable the JAR file to be used for a variety of purposes. For instance, you can add information to specify a main class to run an application using the .jar file.

14.13.2 Running Archived Projects

You can package all the class files and dependent resource files in an archive file for distribution to the end-user. If the project is a Java application, the user should have a Java-running environment already installed. If it is not installed, the user can download the Java Runtime Environment (JRE) from JavaSoft at `http://www.javasoft.com/` and install it.

JRE

 NOTE

The Java Runtime Environment is the minimum standard Java platform for running Java programs. It contains the Java interpreter, Java core classes, and supporting files. The JRE does not contain any development tools (such as Applet Viewer or javac) or classes that pertain only to a development environment. The JRE is a subset of JDK.

To run `TicTacToe` as an application, take the following steps:

1. Update the manifest file to insert an entry for the main class. You need to create a text file containing the following two lines:

```
Main-Class: TicTacToe
Sealed: true
```

The first line specifies the main class. The second line is necessary to ensure that the first line can be inserted into an existing manifest file in a jar. Assume that these two lines are contained in the file temp.mf.

2. Execute the `jar` command to insert the main class line into the manifest file in TicTac-Toe.jar, as follows:

```
jar -uvmf temp.mf TicTacToe.jar
```

The **-u** option is for updating an existing jar file, the **-v** option is for displaying command output, and the **-m** option is for appending the contents in temp.mf to the manifest file in the archive.

3. Run the .jar file using the java command from the directory that contains TicTacToe.jar, as follows:

```
java -jar TicTacToe.jar
```

 NOTE

You can write an installation procedure that creates the necessary directories and subdirectories on the end-user's computer. The installation can also create an icon that the end-user can double-click on to start the program. For information on creating Windows desktop icons, please see Supplement O, "Creating Shortcuts for Java Applications on Windows."

To run `TicTacToe` as an applet, modify the <applet> tag in the HTML file to include an archive attribute. The archive attribute specifies the archive file in which the applet is contained. For example, the HTML file for running `TicTacToe` can be modified as shown below:

```
<applet
  code     = "TicTacToe.class"
```

```
    archive  = "TicTacToe.jar"
    width    = 400
    height   = 300
    hspace   = 0
    vspace   = 0
    align    = middle
>
</applet>
```

14.14   Pluggable Look-and-Feel (Optional)

Lightweight components consume fewer resources and can be transparent, but they lack the AWT's platform-specific look-and-feel advantage. To address this problem, a new pluggable look-and-feel feature was introduced in Java.

The pluggable look-and-feel feature lets you design a single set of GUI components that automatically has the look-and-feel of any OS platform. The implementation of this feature is independent of the underlying native GUI, yet it can imitate the native behavior of the native GUI.

Currently, Java supports the following three look-and-feel styles:

✦ Metal

✦ Motif

✦ Windows

To see an example that demonstrates these three styles, change the directory to c:\ book, and type the following command at the DOS prompt: **java -jar SimpleExample.jar**.

Figure 14.20 shows a sample run of the program.

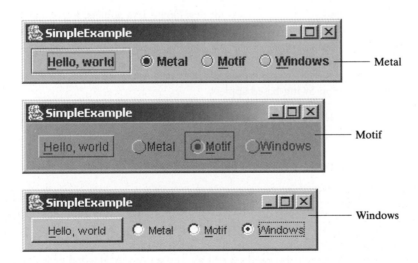

FIGURE **14.20**   *The* SimpleExample *demonstrates three look-and-feel styles.*

The Metal style, also known as the *Java style*, gives you a consistent look regardless of operating system. The Windows style is currently only available on Windows due to Windows copyright restrictions. The Motif style is used on Unix operating systems.

The `javax.swing.UIManager` class manages the look-and-feel of the user interface. You can use one of the following three methods to set the look-and-feel for Metal, Motif, or Windows:

```
UIManager.setLookAndFeel
  (UIManager.getCrossPlatformLookAndFeelClassName());
UIManager.setLookAndFeel
  (new com.sun.java.swing.plaf.motif.MotifLookAndFeel());
UIManager.setLookAndFeel
  (new com.sun.java.swing.plaf.windows.WindowsLookAndFeel());
```

The `setLookAndFeel` method throws `UnsupportedLookAndFeelException`, so you have to put the method inside a `try-catch` block for it to compile. To ensure that the setting takes effect, the `setLookAndFeel` method should be executed before any of the components are instantiated. Thus, you can put the code in a static block, as shown below:

```
static {
  try {
    // Set a look-and-feel, e.g.,
    //UIManager.setLookAndFeel
    //   (UIManager.getCrossPlatformLookAndFeelClassName());
  }
  catch (UnsupportedLookAndFeelException ex) {}
}
```

Static initialization blocks are executed when the class is loaded. For more information on static initialization blocks, please refer to Section 8.12, "Initialization Blocks."

KEY CLASSES AND METHODS

✦ **java.applet.Applet** is a base class for developing Java applets. Every applet must be a subclass of `Applet`. The `Applet` class provides the essential framework that enables applets to be run by a Web browser.

✦ **javax.swing.JApplet** is a subclass of `java.applet.Applet`. An applet must extend `JApplet` to develop Swing-based applets.

✦ **java.net.URL** is a class that represents a URL resource, such as audio files and image files. To load an audio or an image file in a platform-independent way for applications and applets, place the files in the same directory with the class file and use the class's `getResource(filename)` method to load the files.

✦ **java.awt.Image** is an abstract class that represents graphical images. An image can be created in many ways. You can create an `Image` object from an `ImageIcon` using the `getImage()` method. You can create an `ImageIcon` from an `Image` instance using new `ImageIcon(Image)`. To display an image in a Swing GUI component, override the `paintComponent(Graphics)` method and use the various overloaded `drawImage` methods to draw images in the `Graphics` class.

✦ **java.applet.AudioClip** is an interface that provides a simple abstraction for playing a sound clip. Use the `Applet`'s static method `newAudioClip(url)` to create an instance of `AudioClip`. To manipulate a sound for an audio clip, use the following instance methods of `AudioClip`: `play()`, `loop()`, and `stop()`.

CHAPTER SUMMARY

✦ The Web browser controls and executes applets through the `init`, `start`, `stop`, and `destroy` methods in the `Applet` class. Applets always extend the `Applet` class and implement these methods, if applicable, so that they can be run by a Web browser.

✦ `JApplet` is a subclass of `Applet`. It should be used for developing Java applets with Swing components.

✦ The applet bytecode must be specified, using the `<applet>` tag in an HTML file to tell the Web browser where to find the applet. The applet can accept string parameters from HTML using the `<param>` tag.

✦ When an applet is loaded, the Web browser creates an instance of the applet by invoking its no-arg constructor.

✦ The `init` method is invoked after the applet is created or recreated.

✦ The `start` method is invoked after the `init` method. It is also called whenever the applet becomes active again after the page containing the applet is revisited.

✦ The `stop` method is invoked when the user leaves the page for the applet.

✦ The `destroy` method is invoked when the browser exits normally to inform the applet that it is no longer needed and should release any resources it has allocated. The `stop` method is always called before the `destroy` method.

✦ The procedures for writing applications and writing applets are very similar. An applet can easily be converted into an application, and vice versa. Moreover, an applet can be written with the additional capability of running as an application.

✦ You can pass arguments to an applet using the `param` attribute in the applet's tag in HTML. To retrieve the value of the parameter, invoke the `getParameter(paramName)` method.

✦ The `Applet`'s `getParameter` method can be invoked only after an instance of the applet is created. Therefore, this method cannot be invoked in the constructor of the applet class. You should invoke this method from the `init` method.

✦ You learned how to incorporate images and audio in Java applications and applets. To load audio and images for Java applications and applets, you have to create a URL for the audio and image. You can create a URL from a file under the class directory or from an Internet source.

✦ To display an image, first create an image icon from the URL for the image source. You can then use `ImageIcon`'s `getImage()` method to get an `Image` object for the image and draw the image using the `drawImage` method in the `java.awt.Graphics` class.

✦ To play an audio, create an audio clip from the URL for the audio source. You can use the `AudioClip`'s `play()` method to play it once, the `loop()` method to play it repeatedly, and the `stop()` method to stop it.

REVIEW QUESTIONS

Sections 14.2–14.4

14.1 How do you write a Web page that will contain an applet?

14.2 Describe the `init()`, `start()`, `stop()`, and `destroy()` methods in the `Applet` class.

14.3 How do you add components to a `JApplet`? What is the default layout manager of the content pane of `JApplet`?

14.4 Why does the following applet have a runtime `NullPointerException` error on Line 9?

```
 1 public class WelcomeApplet extends JApplet {
 2   private MessagePanel messagePanel;
 3
 4   public WelcomeApplet() {
 5     MessagePanel messagePanel = new MessagePanel("Welcome to Java!");
 6   }
 7
 8   public void init() {
 9     getContentPane().add(messagePanel);
10   }
11 }
```

Sections 14.5–14.6

14.5 Describe the `<applet>` HTML tag. How do you pass parameters to an applet?

14.6 Where is the `getParameter` method defined?

14.7 What is wrong if the `DisplayMessage` applet is revised as follows?

Revision 1

```
public class DisplayMessage extends JApplet {
  /** Initialize the applet */
  public DisplayMessage() {
    // Get parameter values from the HTML file
    String message = getParameter("MESSAGE");
    int x =
      Integer.parseInt(getParameter("X"));
    int y =
      Integer.parseInt(getParameter("Y"));

    // Create a message panel
    MessagePanel messagePanel =
      new MessagePanel(message);
    messagePanel.setXCoordinate(x);
    messagePanel.setYCoordinate(y);

    // Add the message panel to the applet
    getContentPane().add(messagePanel);
  }
}
```

Revision 2

```
public class DisplayMessage extends JApplet {
  private String message;
  private int x;
  private int y;

  /** Initialize the applet */
  public void init() {
    // Get parameter values from the HTML file
    message = getParameter("MESSAGE");
    x = Integer.parseInt(getParameter("X"));
    y = Integer.parseInt(getParameter("Y"));
  }

  public DisplayMessage() {
    // Create a message panel
    MessagePanel messagePanel =
      new  MessagePanel(message);
    messagePanel.setXCoordinate(x);
    messagePanel.setYCoordinate(y);

    // Add the message panel to the applet
    getContentPane().add(messagePanel);
  }
}
```

14.8 What are the differences between applications and applets? How do you run an application, and how do you run an applet? Is the compilation process different for applications and applets? List some security restrictions on applets.

14.9 Can you place a frame in an applet?

14.10 Can you place an applet in a frame?

14.11 Delete super.paintComponent(g) on Line 99 in TicTacToe.java in Listing 14.6 and run the program to see what happens.

Sections 14.8–14.11

14.12 How do you create a URL object for the file www.cs.armstrong.edu/liang/ anthem/us.gif on the Internet? How do you create a URL object for the file image/us.gif in the class directory?

14.13 How do you create an ImageIcon from the file image/us.gif in the class directory? How do you create an ImageIcon from www.cs.armstrong.edu/liang/image/us.gif?

14.14 How do you create an Image object from the ImageIcon object?

14.15 How do you create an ImageIcon object from an Image object?

14.16 Explain the differences between displaying images in a JLabel and in a JPanel.

14.17 Describe the drawImage method in the Graphics class.

14.18 Which package contains ImageIcon and which contains Image?

Section 14.12 Playing Audio

14.19 What types of audio files are used in Java?

14.20 How do you create an audio clip from a file anthem/us.mid in the class directory? How do you create an audio clip from www.cs.armstrong.edu/liang/anthem/us.mid?

14.21 How do you play, repeatedly play, and stop an audio clip?

PROGRAMMING EXERCISES

Sections 14.2–14.4

14.1 (*Converting applications to applets*) Convert Example 13.1, "Using Buttons," into an applet.

Sections 14.5–14.6

14.2* (*Passing strings to applets*) Rewrite Example 14.2, "Passing Strings to Java applets," to display a message with a standard color, font, and size. The message, x, y, color, fontname, and fontsize are parameters in the <applet> tag, as shown below:

```
<applet
  code = "Exercise14_2.class"
  width = 200
  height = 50>
  <param name=MESSAGE value="Welcome to Java">
  <param name=X value=40>
  <param name=Y value=50>
  <param name=COLOR value="red">
  <param name=FONTNAME value="Monospaced">
  <param name=FONTSIZE value=20>
You must have a Java-enabled browser to view the applet
</applet>
```

14.3 (*Enabling applets to run standalone*) Rewrite the LoanApplet in Example 14.1, "Using Applets," to enable it to run as an application as well as an applet.

14.4* (*Creating multiple windows from an applet*) Write an applet that contains two buttons called *Investment Calculator* and *Loan Calculator*. When you click Investment Calculator, a frame appears in a new window for calculating future investment values. When you click *Loan Calculator*, a frame appears in a separate new window for computing loan payments (see Figure 14.21).

FIGURE 14.21 *You can show frames in the applets.*

14.5** (*Creating a maze*) Write an applet that will find a path in a maze, as shown in Figure 14.22(a). The applet should also run as an application. The maze is represented by an 8 × 8 board. The path must meet the following conditions:

✦ The path is between the upper-left corner cell and the lower-right corner cell in the maze.

(a) Correct path   (b) Illegal path

FIGURE 14.22 *The program finds a path from the upper-left corner to the bottom-right corner.*

✦ The applet enables the user to insert or remove a mark on a cell. A path consists of adjacent unmarked cells. Two cells are said to be adjacent if they are horizontal or vertical neighbors, but not if they are diagonal neighbors.

✦ The path does not contain cells that form a square. The path in Figure 14.22(b), for example, does not meet this condition. (The condition makes a path easy to identify on the board.)

14.6** (*TicTacToe*) Rewrite the program in Section 14.7, "Case Study: TicTacToe," with the following modifications:

✦ Declare `Cell` as a separate class rather than an inner class.

✦ Add a button named *New Game*, as shown in Figure 14.23. The New Game button starts a new game.

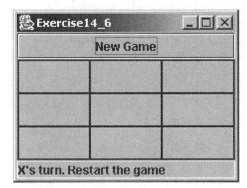

FIGURE 14.23 *The New Game button starts a new game.*

14.7** (*Tax calculator*) Create an applet to compute tax, as shown in Figure 14.24. The applet lets the user select the tax status and enter the taxable income to compute the tax based on the 2001 federal tax rates, as shown in Exercise 6.14 on page 256. Enable it to run standalone.

Exercise14_7

Select Tax Status

⦿ **Single filers**

○ **Married filing jointly**

○ **Married filing separately**

○ **Head of household**

Single Filers	
Taxable Income	Rate
Up to $27,050	15%
$27,051 - $65,550	27.5%
$65,551 - $136,750	30.5%
$136,751 - $297,350	35.5%
$297,351 or more	39.1%

Taxable income 100000

Tax   21850.0

Compute Tax

FIGURE 14.24 *The tax calculator computes the tax for the specified taxable income and tax status.*

14.8*** (*Creating a calculator*) Use various panels of FlowLayout, GridLayout, and BorderLayout to lay out the following calculator and to implement addition (+), subtraction (−), division (/), square root (sqrt), and modulus (%) functions (see Figure 14.25(a)). Enable it to run standalone.

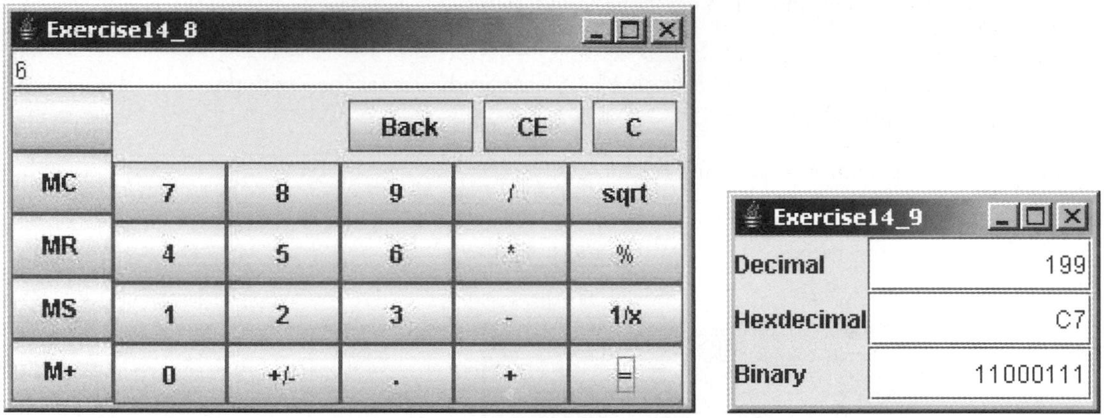

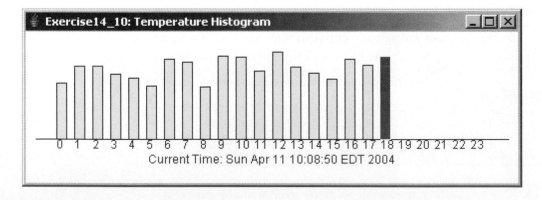

(a)   (b)

FIGURE 14.25 *(a) Exercise 14.8 is a Java implementation of a popular calculator. (b) Exercise 14.9 converts between decimal, hex, and binary numbers.*

14.9* (*Converting numbers*) Write an applet that converts between decimal, hex, and binary numbers, as shown in Figure 14.25(b). When you enter a decimal value on the decimal value text field and press the Enter key, its corresponding hex and binary numbers are displayed in the other two text fields. Likewise, you can enter values in the other fields and convert them accordingly. Enable it to run standalone.

14.10** (*Repainting a partial area*) When you repaint the entire viewing area of a panel, sometimes only a tiny portion of the viewing area is changed. You can improve the performance by only repainting the affected area, but do not invoke super.paintComponent(g) when repainting the panel, because this will cause the entire viewing area to be cleared. Use this approach to write an applet to display the temperatures of each hour during the last twenty-four hours in a histogram. Suppose that the temperatures between 50 and 90 degrees Fahrenheit are obtained randomly and are updated every hour. The temperature of the current hour needs to be redisplayed, while the others remain unchanged. Use a unique color to highlight the temperature for the current hour (see Figure 14.26).

FIGURE 14.26 *The histogram displays the average temperature of every hour in the last twenty-four hours.*

14.11** (*Showing a running fan*) Write a Java applet that simulates a running fan, as shown in Figure 14.27. The buttons Start, Stop, and Reverse control the fan. The scrollbar controls the fan's speed. Create a class named Fan, a subclass of JPanel, to display the fan. This class also contains the methods to suspend and resume the fan, set its speed, and reverse its direction. Create a class named FanControl that contains a fan, and three buttons and a scroll bar to control the fan. Create a Java applet that contains an instance of FanControl. Enable the applet to run standalone.

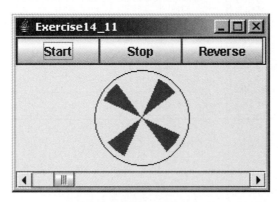

FIGURE **14.27** *The program simulates a running fan.*

14.12** (*Controlling a group of fans*) Write a Java applet that displays three fans in a group, with control buttons to start and stop all of them, as shown in Figure 14.28. Use the FanControl to control and display a single fan. Enable the applet to run standalone.

FIGURE **14.28** *The program runs and controls a group of fans.*

14.13*** (*Creating an elevator simulator*) Write an applet that simulates an elevator going up and down (see Figure 14.29). The buttons on the left indicate the floor where the passenger is now located. The passenger must click a button on the left to request that the elevator come to his or her floor. On entering the elevator, the passenger clicks a button on the right to request that it go to the specified floor. Enable the applet to run standalone.

14.14* (*Controlling a group of clocks*) Write a Java applet that displays three clocks in a group, with control buttons to start and stop all of them, as shown in Figure 14.30. Use the ClockControl to control and display a single clock. Enable the applet to run standalone.

Section 14.9 Displaying Images

14.15* (*Enlarging and shrinking an image*) Write an applet that will display a sequence of images from a single image file in different sizes. Initially, the viewing area for this

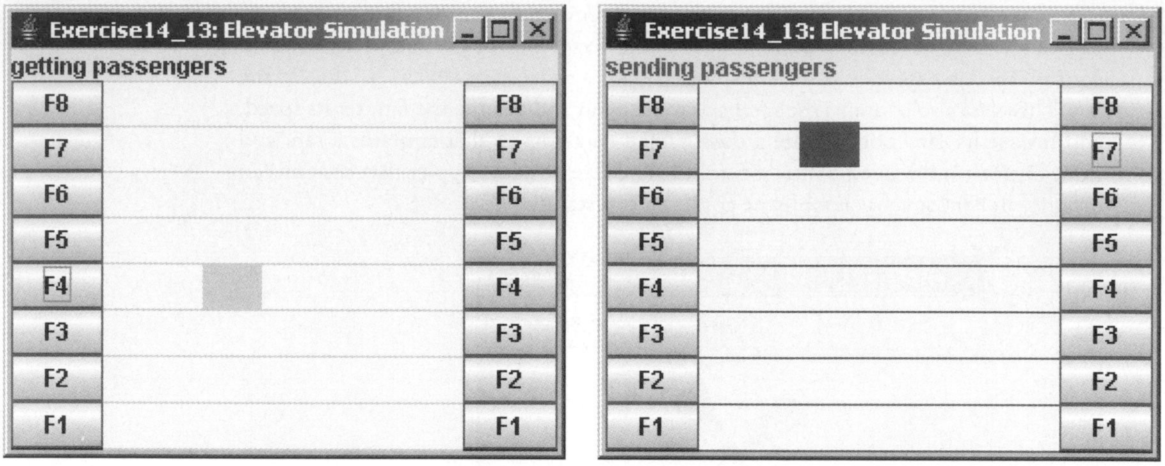

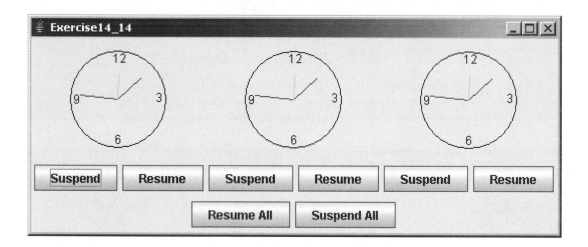

FIGURE 14.29   *The program simulates elevator operations.*

FIGURE 14.30   *Three clocks run independently with individual control and group control.*

image has a width of 300 and a height of 300. Your program should continuously shrink the viewing area by 1 in width and 1 in height until it reaches a width of 50 and a height of 50. At that point, the viewing area should continuously enlarge by 1 in width and 1 in height until it reaches a width of 300 and a height of 300. The viewing area should shrink and enlarge (alternately) to create animation for the single image. Enable the applet to run standalone.

14.16*** (*Simulating a stock ticker*) Write a Java applet that displays a stock index ticker (see Figure 14.31). The stock index information is passed from the <param> tag in the HTML file. Each index has four parameters: Index Name (e.g., S&P 500), Current Time (e.g., 15:54), the index from the previous day (e.g., 919.01), and Change (e.g., 4.54). Enable the applet to run standalone.

Use at least five indexes, such as Dow Jones, S&P 500, NASDAQ, NIKKEI, and Gold & Silver Index. Display positive changes in green, and negative changes in red. The indexes move from right to left in the applet's viewing area. The applet freezes the ticker when the mouse button is pressed; it moves again when the mouse button is released.

FIGURE 14.31 *The program displays a stock index ticker.*

14.17** (*Showing national flags*) Write an applet that introduces national flags, one after the other, by presenting each one's photo, name, and description (see Figure 14.32) along with audio that reads the description.

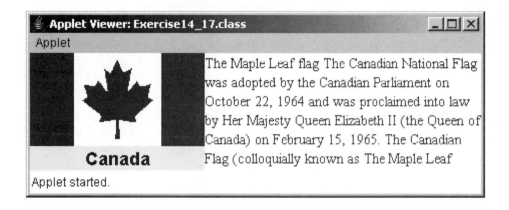

FIGURE 14.32 *This applet shows each country's flag, name, and description, one after another, and reads the description that is currently shown.*

Suppose your applet displays the flags of eight countries. Assume that the photo image files, named **photo0.gif**, **photo1.gif**, and so on, up to **photo7.gif**, are stored in a subdirectory named **photo** in the applet's directory. The length of each audio is less than 10 seconds. Assume that the name and description of each country's flag are passed from the HTML using the parameter name0, name1, ..., name7, and description0, description1, ..., and description7. Pass the number of countries as an HTML parameter using numberOfCountries. Here is an example:

```
<param name="numberOfCountries" value=8>
<param name="name0" value="Canada">
<param name="description0" value=
"The Maple Leaf flag
The Canadian National Flag was adopted by the Canadian
Parliament on October 22, 1964 and was proclaimed into law
by Her Majesty Queen Elizabeth II (the Queen of Canada) on
February 15, 1965. The Canadian Flag (colloquially known
as The Maple Leaf Flag) is a red flag of the proportions
two by length and one by width, containing in its center a
```

```
white square, with a single red stylized eleven-point
mapleleaf centered in the white square.">
```

 HINT

Use the DescriptionPanel class to display the image, name, and text. The DescriptionPanel class was introduced in Example 13.5, "Using Text Area."

Section 14.12 Playing Audio

14.18* (*Playing, looping, and stopping a sound clip*) Write an applet that meets the following requirements:

✦ Get an audio file. The file is in the class directory.

✦ Place three buttons labeled Play, Loop, and Stop, as shown in Figure 14.33.

FIGURE 14.33 *Click Play to play an audio clip once, click Loop to play an audio repeatedly, and click Stop to terminate playing.*

✦ If you click the Play button, the audio file is played once. If you click the Loop button, the audio file keeps playing repeatedly. If you click the Stop button, the playing stops.

✦ The applet can run as an application.

14.19** (*Creating an alarm clock*) Write an applet that will display a digital clock with a large display panel that shows hour, minute, and second. This clock should allow the user to set an alarm. Figure 14.34(a) shows an example of such a clock. To turn on the alarm, check the Alarm check box. To specify the alarm time, click the "Set alarm" button to display a new frame, as shown in Figure 14.34(b). You can set the alarm time in the frame. Enable the applet to run standalone.

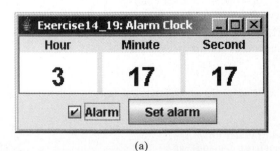
(a)

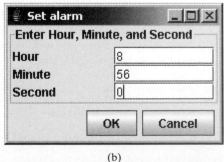
(b)

FIGURE 14.34 *The program displays current hour, minute, and second, and enables you to set an alarm.*

14.20**   (*Creating an image animator with audio*) Create animation using the applet (see Figure 14.35) to meet the following requirements:

◆ Allow the user to specify the animation speed. The user can enter the speed in a text field.

◆ Get the number of frames and the image filename prefix from the user. For example, if the user enters **n** for the number of frames and **L** for the image prefix, then the files are **L1**, **L2**, and so on, to **L*n***. Assume that the images are stored in the **image** directory, a subdirectory of the applet's directory.

◆ Allow the user to specify an audio filename. The audio file is stored in the same directory as the applet. The sound is played while the animation runs.

◆ Enable the applet to run standalone.

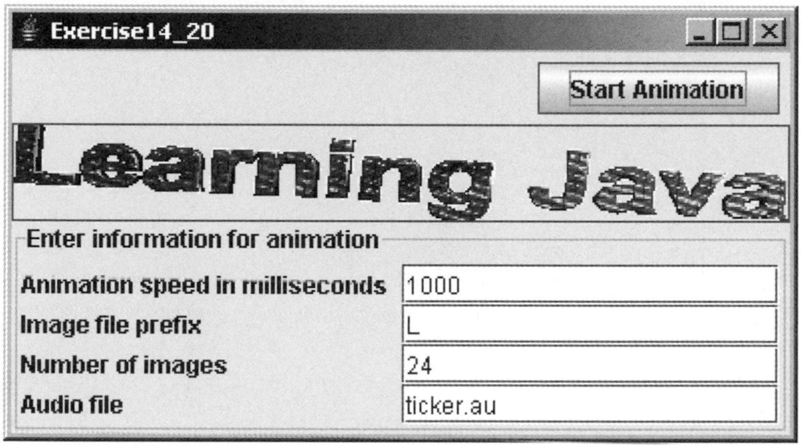

FIGURE 14.35   *This applet lets the user select image files, audio file, and animation speed.*

PART IV

EXCEPTION HANDLING AND IO

This part introduces the use of exception handling and assertions to make programs robust and correct, and the use of input and output to manage and process a large quantity of data.

Chapter 15
Exceptions and Assertions

Chapter 16
Simple Input and Output

Prerequisites for Part IV

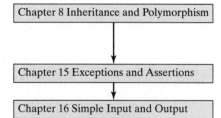

Chapter 8 Inheritance and Polymorphism

Chapter 15 Exceptions and Assertions

Chapter 16 Simple Input and Output

EXCEPTIONS AND ASSERTIONS

Objectives

- ✦ To understand exceptions and exception handling (§15.2).

- ✦ To distinguish exception types: `Error` (fatal) vs. `Exception` (non-fatal), and checked vs. uncheck exceptions (§§15.2.1–15.2.2).

- ✦ To declare exceptions in the method header (§15.3.1).

- ✦ To throw exceptions out of a method (§15.3.2).

- ✦ To write a `try-catch` block to handle exceptions (§15.3.3).

- ✦ To explain how an exception is propagated (§15.3.3).

- ✦ To rethrow exceptions in a `try-catch` block (§15.4).

- ✦ To use the `finally` clause in a `try-catch` block (§15.5).

- ✦ To know when to use exceptions (§15.6).

- ✦ To declare custom exception classes (§15.7 Optional).

- ✦ To apply assertions to help ensure program correctness (§15.8 Optional).

15.1 Introduction

Section 2.19, "Programming Errors," introduced three categories of errors: syntax errors, runtime errors, and logic errors. *Syntax errors* arise because the rules of the language have not been followed. They are detected by the compiler. *Runtime errors* occur while the program is running if the environment detects an operation that is impossible to carry out. *Logic errors* occur when a program doesn't perform the way it was intended to. In general, syntax errors are easy to find and easy to correct because the compiler indicates where they came from and why they occurred. You can use the debugging techniques introduced in Section 2.20, "Debugging," to find logic errors. This chapter introduces using exception handling to deal with runtime errors and using assertions to help ensure program correctness.

15.2 Exceptions and Exception Types

Runtime errors cause *exceptions*, which are events that occur during the execution of a program and disrupt the normal flow of control. A program that does not provide code for handling exceptions may terminate abnormally, causing serious problems. For example, if your program attempts to transfer money from a savings account to a checking account, but because of a runtime error is terminated *after* the money is drawn from the savings account and *before* the money is deposited in the checking account, the customer will lose money.

Runtime errors occur for various reasons. The user may enter an invalid input, for example, or the program may attempt to open a file that doesn't exist, or the network connection may hang up, or the program may attempt to access an out-of-bounds array element. When a runtime error occurs, Java raises an exception.

Exceptions are handled differently from the events of GUI programming. (In Chapter 12, "Event-Driven Programming," you learned the events used in GUI programming.) An *event* may be ignored in GUI programming, but an *exception* cannot be ignored. In GUI programming, a listener must register with the source object. External user action on the source object generates an event, and the source object notifies the listener by invoking the handlers implemented by the listener. If no listener is registered with the source object, the event is ignored. When an exception occurs, however, the program will terminate if the exception is not caught by the program.

exception handling

Java provides programmers with the capability to elegantly handle runtime errors. With this capability, referred to as *exception handling*, you can develop robust programs for mission-critical computing.

Here is an example. The following program terminates abnormally if you entered a floating-point value instead of an integer.

```java
import javax.swing.JOptionPane;

public class Test {
  public static void main(String[] args) {
    String input = JOptionPane.showInputDialog(null,
      "Please enter an integer");
    int number = Integer.parseInt(input);

    // Display the result
    JOptionPane.showMessageDialog(null,
      "The number entered is " + number);
  }
}
```

If an exception occurs on this line, the rest of the lines in the method are skipped and the program is terminated.

▼ Terminated.

Java allows the programmer to catch this error when it occurs and perform some specific actions, including choosing whether to halt the program or not. You can handle this error in the following code, using a new construct called the *try-catch block* to enable the program to catch the error and continue to execute:

try-catch block

```
import javax.swing.JOptionPane;

public class Test {
  public static void main(String[] args) {
    try {
      String input = JOptionPane.showInputDialog(null,
        "Please enter an integer");
      int number = Integer.parseInt(input);

      // Display the result
      JOptionPane.showMessageDialog(null,
        "The number entered is " + number);
    }
    catch (Exception ex) {
      JOptionPane.showMessageDialog(null,
        "Incorrect input: an integer is required");
    }

    System.out.println("Execution continues ...");
  }
}
```

If an exception occurs on this line, the rest of the lines in the try clause are skipped and the control is transferred to the catch clause.

After the exception is caught and processed, the control is transferred to the next statement after the try-catch block.

15.2.1 Exception Classes

A Java exception is an instance of a class derived from `Throwable`. The `Throwable` class is contained in the `java.lang` package, and subclasses of `Throwable` are contained in various packages. Errors related to GUI components are included in the `java.awt` package; numeric exceptions are included in the `java.lang` package because they are related to the `java.lang.Number` class. You can create your own exception classes by extending `Throwable` or a subclass of `Throwable`. Figure 15.1 shows some of Java's predefined exception classes.

 NOTE

The class names `Error`, `Exception`, and `RuntimeException` are somewhat confusing. All three of these classes are exceptions, and all of the errors discussed here occur at runtime.

The exception classes can be classified into three major types: system errors, exceptions, and runtime exceptions.

✦ *System errors* are thrown by the JVM and represented in the `Error` class. The `Error` class describes internal system errors. Such errors rarely occur. If one does, there is little you can do beyond notifying the user and trying to terminate the program gracefully. Examples of subclasses of `Error` are listed in Table 15.1.

system error

✦ *Exceptions* are represented in the `Exception` class, which describes errors caused by your program and by external circumstances. These errors can be caught and handled by your program. Examples of subclasses of `Exception` are listed in Table 15.2.

exception

✦ *Runtime exceptions* are represented in the `RuntimeException` class, which describes programming errors, such as bad casting, accessing an out-of-bounds array, and numeric

runtime exception

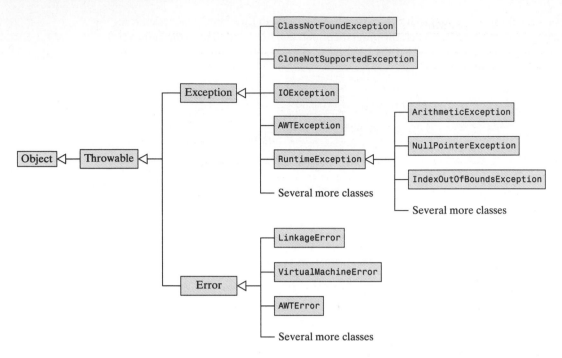

FIGURE 15.1 *Exceptions thrown are instances of the classes shown in this diagram, or of subclasses of one of these classes.*

TABLE **15.1** **Examples of Subclasses of Error**

Class	Possible Reason for Exception
LinkageError	A class has some dependency on another class, but the latter class has changed incompatibly after the compilation of the former class.
VirtualMachineError	The JVM is broken or has run out of the resources necessary for it to continue operating.
AWTError	A fatal error in the GUI runtime system.
AssertionError	An assertion has failed. Assertions will be introduced in Section 15.8, "Assertions."

errors. Runtime exceptions are generally thrown by the JVM. Examples of subclasses are listed in Table 15.3.

15.2.2 Checked and Unchecked Exceptions

unchecked exception
checked exception

RuntimeException, Error, and their subclasses are known as *unchecked exceptions*. All other exceptions are known as *checked exceptions*, meaning that the compiler forces the programmer to check and deal with them.

In most cases, unchecked exceptions reflect programming logic errors that are not recoverable. For example, a NullPointerException is thrown if you access an object through a reference variable before an object is assigned to it; an IndexOutOfBoundsException is thrown if you access an element in an array outside the bounds of the array. These are logic errors that should be corrected in the program. Unchecked exceptions can occur anywhere in a program. To avoid

TABLE 15.2 Examples of Subclasses of Exception

Class	Possible reason for exception
ClassNotFoundException	Attempt to use a class that does not exist. This exception would occur, for example, if you tried to run a nonexistent class using the **java** command, or if your program was composed of, say, three class files, only two of which could be found.
CloneNotSupportedException	Attempt to clone an object whose defining class does not implement the Cloneable interface. Cloning objects were introduced in Chapter 9, "Abstract Classes and Interfaces."
IOException	Related to input/output operations, such as invalid input, reading past the end of a file, and opening a nonexistent file. Examples of subclasses of IOException are InterruptedIOException, EOFException (EOF is short for End Of File), and FileNotFoundException.
AWTException	Exceptions in GUI components.

TABLE 15.3 Examples of Subclasses of RuntimeException

Class	Possible Reason for Exception
ArithmeticException	Dividing an integer by zero. Note that floating-point arithmetic does not throw exceptions.
NullPointerException	Attempt to access an object through a null reference variable.
IndexOutOfBoundsException	Index to an array is out of range.
IllegalArgumentException	A method is passed an argument that is illegal or inappropriate.

cumbersome overuse of try-catch blocks, Java does not mandate that you write code to catch or declare unchecked exceptions.

15.3 Understanding Exception Handling

Java's exception-handling model is based on three operations: *declaring an exception*, *throwing an exception*, and *catching an exception*, as shown in Figure 15.2.

15.3.1 Declaring Exceptions

In Java, the statement currently being executed belongs to a method. The Java interpreter invokes the main method for a Java application, and the Web browser invokes the applet's no-arg constructor and then the init method for a Java applet. Every method must state the types of checked exceptions it might throw. This is known as *declaring exceptions*. Because system errors and runtime errors can happen to any code, Java does not require that you declare Error and RuntimeException (unchecked exceptions) explicitly in the method. However, all other exceptions thrown by the

declare exception

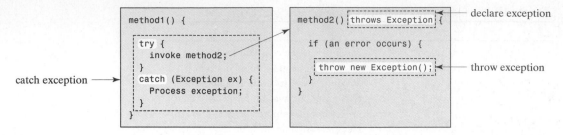

FIGURE 15.2 *Exception handling in Java consists of declaring exceptions, throwing exceptions, and catching and processing exceptions.*

method must be explicitly declared in the method declaration so that the caller of the method is informed of the exception.

To declare an exception in a method, use the `throws` keyword in the method declaration, as in this example:

```
public void myMethod() throws IOException
```

The `throws` keyword indicates that `myMethod` might throw an `IOException`. If the method might throw multiple exceptions, add a list of the exceptions, separated by commas, after `throws`:

```
public void myMethod()
  throws Exception1, Exception2, ..., ExceptionN
```

15.3.2   Throwing Exceptions

throw exception

A program that detects an error can create an instance of an appropriate exception type and throw it. This is known as *throwing an exception*. Here is an example: Suppose the program detected that an argument passed to the method violates the method contract (e.g., the argument must be non-negative, but a negative argument is passed); the program can create an instance of `IllegalArgumentException` and throw it, as follows:

```
IllegalArgumentException ex =
  new IllegalArgumentException("Wrong Argument");
throw ex;
```

Or if you prefer, you can use the following:

```
throw new IllegalArgumentException("Wrong Argument");
```

> **NOTE**
> The keyword to declare an exception is `throws`, and the keyword to throw an exception is `throw`. A method can always throw an unchecked exception. If a method throws a checked exception, the exception must be declared in the method declaration.

15.3.3   Catching Exceptions

catch exception

You now know how to declare an exception and how to throw an exception. When an exception is thrown, it can be caught and handled in a try-catch block, as follows:

```
try {
  statements; // Statements that may throw exceptions
}
```

```
catch (Exception1 exVar1) {
  handler for exception1;
}
catch (Exception2 exVar2) {
  handler for exception2;
}
...
catch (ExceptionN exVar3) {
  handler for exceptionN;
}
```

If no exceptions arise during the execution of the try clause, the catch clauses are skipped.

If one of the statements inside the try block throws an exception, Java skips the remaining statements in the try block and starts the process of finding the code to handle the exception. The code that handles the exception is called the *exception handler*; it is found by propagating the exception backward through a chain of method calls, starting from the current method. Each catch clause is examined in turn, from first to last, to see whether the type of the exception object is an instance of the exception class in the catch clause. If so, the exception object is assigned to the variable declared and the code in the catch clause is executed. If no handler is found, Java exits this method, passes the exception to the method that invoked the method, and continues the same process to find a handler. If no handler is found in the chain of methods being invoked, the program terminates and prints an error message on the console. The process of finding a handler is called *catching an exception*.

exception handler

Suppose the main method invokes method1, method1 invokes method2, method2 invokes method3, and an exception occurs in method3, as shown in Figure 15.3. Consider the following scenario:

◆ If method3 cannot handle the exception, method3 is aborted and the control is returned to method2. If the exception type is Exception3, it is caught by the catch clause for handling exception ex3 in method2. statement5 is skipped, and statement6 is executed.

◆ If the exception type is Exception2, method2 is aborted, the control is returned to method1, and the exception is caught by the catch clause for handling exception ex2 in method1. statement3 is skipped, and statement4 is executed.

◆ If the exception type is Exception1, method1 is aborted, the control is returned to the main method, and the exception is caught by the catch clause for handling exception ex1 in the main method. statement1 is skipped, and statement2 is executed.

◆ If the exception type is not Exception1, Exception2, or Exception3, the exception is not caught and the program terminates. statement1 and statement2 are not executed.

```
main method {                method1 {                    method2 {                           An exception
  ...                          ...                          ...                               is thrown in
  try {                        try {                        try {                             method3
    ...                          ...                          ...
    invoke method1;              invoke method2;              invoke method3;
    statement1;                  statement3;                  statement5;
  }                            }                            }
  catch (Exception1 ex1) {     catch (Exception2 ex2) {     catch (Exception3 ex3) {
    Process ex1;                 Process ex2;                 Process ex3;
  }                            }                            }
  statement2;                  statement4;                  statement6;
}                            }                            }
```

FIGURE 15.3   *If an exception is not caught in the current method, it is passed to its caller. The process is repeated until the exception is caught or passed to the main method.*

An exception object contains valuable information about the exception. You may use the following instance methods in the `java.lang.Throwable` class to get information regarding the exception:

✦ `public String getMessage()`
Returns the detailed message of the `Throwable` object.

✦ `public String toString()`
Returns the concatenation of three strings: (1) the full name of the exception class; (2) `":"` (a colon and a space); (3) the `getMessage()` method.

✦ `public void printStackTrace()`
Prints the `Throwable` object and its trace information on the console.

catch clause

  NOTE

Various exception classes can be derived from a common superclass. If a `catch` clause catches exception objects of a superclass, it can catch all the exception objects of the subclasses of that superclass.

order of exception handlers

  NOTE

The order in which exceptions are specified in `catch` clauses is important. A compilation error will result if a catch clause for a superclass type appears before a catch clause for a subclass type. For example, the ordering in (a) is erroneous, because `RuntimeException` is a subclass of `Exception`. The correct ordering should be as shown in (b).

```
try {
    ...
}
catch (Exception ex) {
    ...
}
catch (RuntimeException ex) {
    ...
}
```

```
try {
    ...
}
catch (RuntimeException ex) {
    ...
}
catch (Exception ex) {
    ...
}
```

(a) Wrong   (b) Correct

catch or declare exceptions

  NOTE

Java forces you to deal with checked exceptions. If a method declares a checked exception (i.e., an exception other than `Error` or `RuntimeException`), you must invoke it in a `try-catch` block or declare to throw the exception in the calling method.

EXAMPLE 15.1 DECLARING, THROWING, AND CATCHING EXCEPTIONS

Problem

This example demonstrates declaring, throwing, and catching exceptions by modifying the `setRadius` method in the `CircleWithStaticVariableAndMethod` class in Section 6.10, "Static Variables, Constants, and Methods." The new `setRadius` method throws an exception if the radius is negative.

Solution

Rename the circle class given in Listing 15.1 as `CircleWithException`, which is the same as `CircleWithStaticVariableAndMethod` except that the `setRadius(double newRadius)` method throws an `IllegalArgumentException` if the argument `newRadius` is negative.

LISTING 15.1 CircleWithException.java (Throwing Exceptions)

```
1 public class CircleWithException {
2   /** The radius of the circle */
3   private double radius;
4
5   /** The number of the objects created */
6   private static int numberOfObjects = 0;
7
8   /** Construct a circle with radius 1 */
9   public CircleWithException() {
10     this(1.0);
11   }
12
13   /** Construct a circle with a specified radius */
14   public CircleWithException(double newRadius) {
15     setRadius(newRadius);
16     numberOfObjects++;
17   }
18
19   /** Return radius */
20   public double getRadius() {
21     return radius;
22   }
23
24   /** Set a new radius */
25   public void setRadius(double newRadius)
26       throws IllegalArgumentException {                  declare exception
27     if (newRadius >= 0)
28       radius = newRadius;
29     else
30       throw new IllegalArgumentException(                throw exception
31         "Radius cannot be negative");
32   }
33
34   /** Return numberOfObjects */
35   public static int getNumberOfObjects() {
36     return numberOfObjects;
37   }
38
39   /** Return the area of this circle */
40   public double findArea() {
41     return radius * radius * 3.14159;
42   }
43 }
```

A test program that uses the new `Circle` class is given in Listing 15.2. Figure 15.4 shows a sample run of the test program.

LISTING 15.2 TestCircleWithException.java (Catching Exceptions)

```
1 public class TestCircleWithException {
2   /** Main method */
3   public static void main(String[] args) {
4     try {                                                try
5       CircleWithException c1 = new CircleWithException(5);
6       CircleWithException c2 = new CircleWithException(-5);
```

EXAMPLE 15.1 (CONTINUED)

```
7        CircleWithException c3 = new CircleWithException(0);
8      }
9      catch (IllegalArgumentException ex) {
10       System.out.println(ex);
11     }
12
13     System.out.println("Number of objects created: " +
14       CircleWithException.getNumberOfObjects());
15   }
16 }
```

catch

```
Command Prompt                                          _ □ X
C:\book>java TestCircleWithException
java.lang.IllegalArgumentException: Radius cannot be negative
Number of objects created: 1

C:\book>
```

FIGURE 15.4   *The exception is thrown when the radius is negative.*

Review

The original `CircleWithStaticVariableAndMethod` class remains intact except that the class name is changed to `CircleWithException`, a new constructor `CircleWithException-`(newRadius) is added, and the `setRadius` method now declares an exception and throws it if the radius is negative.

The `setRadius` method declares to throw `IllegalArgumentException` in the method declaration (Lines 25–26 in CircleWithException.java). The `CircleWithException` class would still compile if the `throws IllegalArgumentException` clause were removed from the method declaration, since it is a subclass of `RuntimeException` and every method can throw `RuntimeException` (unchecked exception) regardless of whether it is declared in the method header.

The test program creates three `CircleWithException` objects, c1, c2, and c3, to test how to handle exceptions. Invoking new `CircleWithException(-5)` (Line 6 in Test CircleWithException) causes the `setRadius` method to be invoked, which throws an `IllegalArgumentException`, because the radius is negative. In the `catch` clause, the type of the object ex is `IllegalArgumentException`, which matches the exception object thrown by the `setRadius` method. So this exception is caught by the `catch` clause.

The exception handler prints a short message, `ex.toString()` (Line 10), about the exception, using `System.out.println(ex)`.

Note that the execution continues in the event of the exception. If the handlers had not caught the exception, the program would have abruptly terminated.

The test program would still compile if the `try` statement were not used, because the method throws an instance of `IllegalArgumentException`, a subclass of `Runtime Exception` (unchecked exception). If a method throws an exception other than `RuntimeException` and `Error`, the method must be invoked within a `try-catch` block.

Methods are executed on threads. If an exception occurs on a thread, the thread is terminated if the exception is not handled. However, the other threads in the application are not affected. There are several threads running to support a GUI application. A thread is launched to execute an event handler (e.g., the `actionPerformed` method for the `ActionEvent`). If an exception occurs during the execution of a GUI event handler, the thread is terminated if the exception is not handled. Interestingly, Java prints the error message on the console, but does not terminate the application. The program goes back to its user-interface-processing loop to run continuously. The next example demonstrates this.

EXAMPLE 15.2 EXCEPTIONS IN GUI APPLICATIONS

Problem

Write a program that creates a user interface to perform integer divisions, as shown in Figure 15.5. The user enters two numbers in the text fields Number 1 and Number 2. The division of Number 1 and Number 2 is displayed in the Result field when the Divide button is clicked.

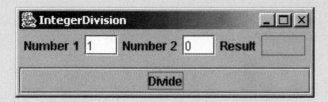

FIGURE 15.5 *Since the divisor is 0 in the Number 2 field, a* RuntimeException *is thrown when the Divide button is clicked.*

Solution

Listing 15.3 gives the program.

LISTING 15.3   IntegerDivision.java (Exceptions in GUI Programs)

```
1  import java.awt.*;
2  import java.awt.event.*;
3  import javax.swing.*;
4
5  public class IntegerDivision extends JApplet
6      implements ActionListener {
7    // Text fields for Number 1, Number 2, and Result
8    private JTextField jtfNum1, jtfNum2, jtfResult;
9
10   // Create the "Divide" button
11   private JButton jbtDiv = new JButton("Divide");
12
13   public IntegerDivision() {
14     // Panel p1 to hold text fields and labels
15     JPanel p1 = new JPanel();
16     p1.setLayout(new FlowLayout());
17     p1.add(new JLabel("Number 1"));
18     p1.add(jtfNum1 = new JTextField(3));
19     p1.add(new JLabel("Number 2"));
20     p1.add(jtfNum2 = new JTextField(3));
21     p1.add(new JLabel("Result"));
22     p1.add(jtfResult = new JTextField(4));
23     jtfResult.setEditable(false);
24     jtfResult.setHorizontalAlignment(SwingConstants.RIGHT);
25
26     getContentPane().add(p1, BorderLayout.CENTER);
27     getContentPane().add(jbtDiv, BorderLayout.SOUTH);
28
29     // Register listener
30     jbtDiv.addActionListener(this);
31   }
```

EXAMPLE 15.2 (CONTINUED)

```
32
33    /** Handle ActionEvent from the Divide button */
34    public void actionPerformed(ActionEvent e) {
35      if (e.getSource() == jbtDiv) {
36        // Get numbers
37        int num1 = Integer.parseInt(jtfNum1.getText().trim());
38        int num2 = Integer.parseInt(jtfNum2.getText().trim());
39
40        int result = num1 / num2;
41
42        // Set result in jtfResult
43        jtfResult.setText(String.valueOf(result));
44      }
45    }
46  }
```

main method omitted

Run the program and enter any number in the Number 1 field and 0 in the Number 2 field; then click the Divide button (see Figure 15.5). You will see nothing in the Result field, but an error message will appear in the Output window, as shown in Figure 15.6. The GUI application continues.

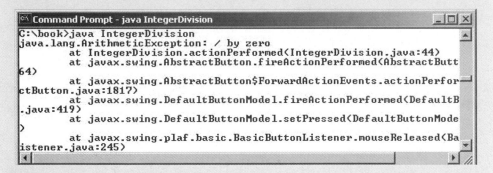

FIGURE 15.6   *In GUI programs, if an exception is not caught, an error message appears in the console window.*

Review

An `ArithmeticException` occurred during the execution of the `actionPerformed` method. The thread on which the method is executed is terminated, but the program continues to run.

If you add a try-catch block around the code in Lines 40–43, as shown below, the program will display a message dialog box in the case of a numerical error, as shown in Figure 15.7. No errors are reported because they are handled in the program.

FIGURE 15.7   *When you click the Divide button to divide a number by 0, a numerical exception occurs. The exception is displayed in the message dialog box.*

EXAMPLE 15.2 (CONTINUED)

```
 1 try {
 2   int result = num1 / num2;
 3
 4   // Set result in jtfResult
 5   jtfResult.setText(String.valueOf(result));
 6 }
 7 catch (RuntimeException ex) {
 8   JOptionPane.showMessageDialog(this, ex.getMessage(),
 9     "Operation error", JOptionPane.ERROR_MESSAGE);
10 }
```

15.4 Rethrowing Exceptions

When an exception occurs in a method, the method exits immediately if it does not catch the exception. If the method is required to perform some task before exiting, you can catch the exception in the method and then rethrow it to the calling method in a structure like the one given below:

```
try {
  statements;
}
catch (TheException ex) {
  perform operations before exits;
  throw ex;
}
```

The statement `throw ex` rethrows the exception so that other handlers get a chance to process the exception `ex`.

15.5 The `finally` Clause

Occasionally, you may want some code to be executed regardless of whether an exception occurs or is caught. Java has a `finally` clause that can be used to accomplish this objective. The syntax for the `finally` clause might look like this:

```
try {
  statements;
}
catch (TheException ex) {
  handling ex;
}
finally {
  finalStatements;
}
```

The code in the `finally` block is executed under all circumstances, regardless of whether an exception occurs in the try block or is caught. Consider three possible cases:

✦ If no exception arises in the `try` block, `finalStatements` is executed, and the next statement after the `try` statement is executed.

✦ If one of the statements causes an exception in the `try` block that is caught in a `catch` clause, the other statements in the `try` block are skipped, the `catch` clause is executed, and the `finally` clause is executed. If the `catch` clause does not rethrow an exception, the next statement after the `try` statement is executed. If it does, the exception is passed to the caller of this method.

✦ If one of the statements causes an exception that is not caught in any `catch` clause, the other statements in the `try` block are skipped, the `finally` clause is executed, and the exception is passed to the caller of this method.

omitting catch clause

 NOTE

The catch clause may be omitted when the finally clause is used.

15.6 When to Use Exceptions

Exception handling separates error-handling code from normal programming tasks, thus making programs easier to read and to modify. Be aware, however, that exception handling usually requires more time and resources because it requires instantiating a new exception object, rolling back the call stack, and propagating the exception through the chain of methods invoked to search for the handler.

An exception occurs in a method. If you want the exception to be processed by its caller, you should create an exception object and throw it. If you can handle the exception in the method where it occurs, there is no need to throw it.

In general, common exceptions that may occur in multiple classes in a project are candidates for exception classes. Simple errors that may occur in individual methods are best handled locally without throwing exceptions.

When should you use a try-catch block in the code? Use it when you have to deal with unexpected error conditions. Do not use a try-catch block to deal with simple, expected situations. For example, the following code

```
try {
  System.out.println(refVar.toString());
}
catch (NullPointerException ex) {
  System.out.println("refVar is null");
}
```

is better replaced by

```
if (refVar != null)
  System.out.println(refVar.toString());
else
  System.out.println("refVar is null");
```

Which situations are exceptional and which are expected is sometimes difficult to decide. The point is not to abuse exception handling as a way to deal with a simple logic test.

15.7 Creating Custom Exception Classes (Optional)

Java provides quite a few exception classes. Use them whenever possible instead of creating your own exception classes. However, if you run into a problem that cannot be adequately described by the predefined exception classes, you can create your own exception class, derived from Exception or from a subclass of Exception, such as IOException.

In Example 15.1, "Declaring, Throwing, and Catching Exceptions," the setRadius method throws an exception if the radius is negative. Suppose you wish to pass the radius to the handler. In that case you have to create a custom exception class. The class may be created as follows:

```
// RadiusException.java: An exception class for describing
// invalid radius exception
public class RadiusException extends Exception {
  /** Information to be passed to the handlers */
  private double radius;

  /** Construct an exception */
  public RadiusException(double radius) {
```

```
      this.radius = radius;
    }

    /** Return the radius */
    public double getRadius() {
      return radius;
    }

    /** Override the "toString" method */
    public String toString() {
      return "Radius is " + radius;
    }
  }
```

The java.lang.Exception class has a no-arg constructor and three other constructors. To create a RadiusException, you have to pass a radius. So the setRadius method in Example 15.1 can be modified as follows:

```
/** Set a new radius */
public void setRadius(double newRadius)
    throws RadiusException {
  if (newRadius >= 0)
    radius = newRadius;
  else
    throw new RadiusException(newRadius);
}
```

The following code creates a circle object and sets its radius to −5:

```
try {
  CircleWithException1 c = new CircleWithException1(4);
  c.setRadius(-5);
}
catch (RadiusException ex) {
  System.out.println("The invalid radius is " + ex.getRadius());
}
```

Invoking setRadius(-5) throws a RadiusException, which is caught by the handler. The handler displays the radius in the exception object ex.

15.8 Assertions (Optional)

An *assertion* is a Java statement that enables you to assert an assumption about your program. An assertion contains a Boolean expression that should be true during program execution. Assertions can be used to ensure program correctness and avoid logic errors.

assertion

15.8.1 Declaring Assertions

An *assertion* is declared using the new Java keyword assert in JDK 1.4, as follows:

```
assert assertion;
```

or

```
assert assertion : detailMessage;
```

where *assertion* is a Boolean expression and *detailMessage* is a primitive-type or an Object value.

When an assertion statement is executed, Java evaluates the assertion. If it is false, an AssertionError will be thrown. The AssertionError class has a no-arg constructor and seven overloaded single-parameter constructors of type int, long, float, double, boolean, char, and Object. For the first assert statement with no detailed message, the no-arg constructor of AssertionError is used. For the second assert statement with a detailed message, an appropriate AssertionError constructor is used to match the data type of the message. `AssertionError` is a subclass of `Error`, so when an assertion becomes false, the program displays a message on the console and exits.

Here is an example of using assertions:

```
 1 public class AssertionDemo {
 2   public static void main(String[] args) {
 3     int i; int sum = 0;
 4     for (i = 0; i < 10; i++) {
 5       sum += i;
 6     }
 7     assert i == 10;
 8     assert sum > 10 && sum < 5 * 10 : "sum is " + sum;
 9   }
10 }
```

The statement `assert i == 10` asserts that `i` is 10 when the statement is executed. If `i` is not 10, an `AssertionError` is thrown. The statement `assert sum > 10 && sum < 5 * 10 : "sum is " + sum` asserts that `sum > 10` and `sum < 5 * 10`. If false, an `AssertionError` with message `"sum is " + sum` is thrown.

Suppose you typed `i < 100` instead of `i < 10` by mistake in Line 4, the following `AssertionError` would be thrown:

```
Exception in thread "main" java.lang.AssertionError
        at AssertionDemo.main(AssertionDemo.java:7)
```

Suppose you typed `sum += 1` instead of `sum += i` by mistake in Line 5, the following `AssertionError` would be thrown:

```
Exception in thread "main" java.lang.AssertionError: sum is 10
        at AssertionDemo.main(AssertionDemo.java:8)
```

15.8.2 Running Programs with Assertions

By default, assertions are disabled at runtime. To enable them, use the switch `-enableassertions`, or `-ea` for short, as follows:

`java -ea AssertionDemo`

Assertions can be selectively enabled or disabled at the class level or the package level. The disable switch is `-disableassertions`, or `-da` for short. For example, the following command enables assertions in package `package1` and disables assertions in class `Class1`.

```
java -ea:package1 -da:Class1 AssertionDemo
```

15.8.3 Using Exception Handling or Assertions

Assertion should not be used to replace exception handling. Exception handling deals with unusual circumstances during program execution. Assertions are intended to ensure the correctness of the program. Exception handling addresses robustness, whereas assertion addresses correctness. Like exception handling, assertions are not used for normal tests, but for internal consistency and validity checks. Assertions are checked at runtime and can be turned on or off at startup time.

Do not use assertions for argument checking in public methods. Valid arguments that may be passed to a public method are considered to be part of the method's contract. The contract must always be obeyed whether assertions are enabled or disabled. For example, the following code should be rewritten using exception handling, as shown in Lines 27–31 in CircleWithException.java in Example 15.1, "Declaring, Throwing, and Catching Exceptions":

```
public void setRadius(double newRadius) {
  assert newRadius >= 0;
  radius = newRadius;
}
```

Use assertions to reaffirm assumptions. This will increase your confidence in the program's correctness. A common use of assertions is to replace assumptions with assertions in the code. For example, the following code in (a) can be replaced by (b):

```
if (even) {
  ...
}
else { // even is false
  ...
}
```
(a)

```
if (even) {
  ...
}
else {
  assert !even;
  ...
}
```
(b)

Similarly, the following code in (a) can also be replaced by (b):

```
if (numberOfDollars > 1) {
  ...
}
else if (numberOfDollars == 1) {
  ...
}
```
(a)

```
if (numberOfDollars > 1) {
  ...
}
else if (numberOfDollars == 1) {
  ...
}
else
 assert false : numberOfDollars;
```
(b)

Another good use of assertions is to place them in a `switch` statement without a default case. For example,

```
switch (month) {
  case 1: ... ; break;
  case 2: ... ; break;
  ...
  case 12: ... ; break;
  default: assert false : "Invalid month: " + month
}
```

KEY TERMS

assertion 563
checked exception   552

exception   551
unchecked exception   552

KEY CLASSES AND METHODS

◆ **java.lang.Throwable** is the root class for exceptions. The `getMessage()` method returns the detailed message of the exception, `toString()` returns the combination of the exception class name, colon (:), and `getMessage()`, and `printStackTrace()` displays track information on the console.

◆ **java.lang.Error** is the base class for internal system errors.

◆ **`java.lang.AssertionError`** is a subclass of `Error` thrown when an assertion fails.

◆ **`java.lang.Exception`** is the base class for errors caused by the program and external circumstances.

◆ **`java.lang.ClassNotFoundException`** is thrown when a dependent class is not found at runtime.

◆ **`java.lang.CloneNotSupportedException`** is thrown if the object being cloned is not an instance of `java.lang.Cloneable`.

◆ **`java.lang.RuntimeException`** is the base class for programming errors, such as bad casting, array index errors, and numeric errors.

◆ **`java.lang.NullPointerException`** is a runtime exception thrown when accessing an object through a null reference.

◆ **`java.lang.IndexOutOfBoundsException`** is a runtime exception thrown when accessing an array object through a `null` reference.

CHAPTER SUMMARY

◆ When an exception occurs, Java creates an object that contains the information for the exception. You can use the information to handle the exception.

◆ A Java exception is an instance of a class derived from `java.lang.Throwable`. Java provides a number of predefined exception classes, such as `Error`, `Exception`, `RuntimeException`, `ClassNotFoundException`, `NullPointerException`, and `ArithmeticException`. You can also define your own exception class by extending `Exception`.

◆ Exceptions occur during the execution of a method. `RuntimeException` and `Error` are unchecked exceptions; all other exceptions are checked exceptions.

◆ When declaring a method, you have to declare a checked exception if the method might throw that checked exception, thus telling the compiler what can go wrong.

◆ The keyword for declaring an exception is `throws`, and the keyword for throwing an exception is `throw`.

◆ To invoke the method that declares checked exceptions, you must enclose the method call in a `try` statement. When an exception occurs during the execution of the method, the `catch` clause catches and handles the exception.

◆ If an exception is not caught in the current method, it is passed to its caller. The process is repeated until the exception is caught or passed to the `main` method.

◆ If an exception of a subclass of `Exception` occurs in a GUI component, Java prints the error message on the console, but the program goes back to its user-interface-processing loop to run continuously. The exception is ignored.

◆ Various exception classes can be derived from a common superclass. If a `catch` clause catches the exception objects of a superclass, it can also catch all the exception objects of the subclasses of that superclass.

◆ The order in which exceptions are specified in a `catch` clause is important. A compilation error will result if you do not specify an exception object of a class before an exception object of the superclass of that class.

✦ When an exception occurs in a method, the method exits immediately if it does not catch the exception. If the method is required to perform some task before exiting, you can catch the exception in the method and then rethrow it to the caller.

✦ The code in the `finally` block is executed under all circumstances, regardless of whether an exception occurs in the `try` block or is caught.

✦ Exception handling separates error-handling code from normal programming tasks, thus making programs easier to read and to modify.

✦ Exception handling should not be used to replace simple tests. You should test simple exceptions whenever possible, and reserve exception handling for dealing with situations that cannot be handled with `if` statements.

✦ Exceptions address robustness, whereas assertions address correctness. Exceptions and assertions are not meant to substitute for simple tests. Avoid using exception handling if a simple `if` statement is sufficient. Never use assertions to check normal conditions.

REVIEW QUESTIONS

 NOTE

In the following questions, assume that the `divide` method in `Rational` in Section 10.5, "Case Study: The `Rational` Class," is modified as follows:

```
public Rational divide(Rational secondRational) throws Exception {
  if (secondRational.getNumerator() == 0)
    throw new Exception("Divisor cannot be zero");

  long n = numerator * secondRational.getDenominator();
  long d = denominator * secondRational.getNumerator();
  return new Rational(n, d);
}
```

The `divide` method in the `Rational` class throws `Exception` if the divisor is 0.

Sections 15.2–15.3

15.1 Describe the Java `Throwable` class, its subclasses, and the types of exceptions.

15.2 What is the purpose of declaring exceptions? How do you declare an exception, and where? Can you declare multiple exceptions in a method declaration?

15.3 What is a checked exception, and what is an unchecked exception?

15.4 How do you throw an exception? Can you throw multiple exceptions in one `throw` statement?

15.5 What is the keyword `throw` used for? What is the keyword `throws` used for?

15.6 What does the JVM do when an exception occurs?

15.7 How do you catch an exception?

15.8 Suppose that `statement2` causes an exception in the following `try-catch` block:

```
try {
  statement1;
  statement2;
  statement3;
}
catch (Exception1 ex1) {
}
catch (Exception2 ex2) {
}

statement4;
```

Answer the following questions:

✦ Will statement3 be executed?

✦ If the exception is not caught, will statement4 be executed?

✦ If the exception is caught in the catch clause, will statement4 be executed?

✦ If the exception is passed to the caller, will statement4 be executed?

15.9 What is displayed when the following program is run?

```java
public class Test {
  public static void main(String[] args) {
    try {
      Rational r1 = new Rational(3, 4);
      Rational r2 = new Rational(0, 1);
      Rational x = r1.divide(r2);

      int i = 0;
      int y = 2 / i;
      System.out.println("Welcome to Java");
    }
    catch (RuntimeException ex) {
      System.out.println("Integer operation error");
    }
    catch (Exception ex) {
      System.out.println("Rational operation error");
    }
  }
}
```

15.10 What is displayed when the following program is run?

```java
public class Test {
  public static void main(String[] args) {
    try {
      method();
      System.out.println("After the method call");
    }
    catch (RuntimeException ex) {
      System.out.println("Integer operation error");
    }
    catch (Exception e) {
      System.out.println("Rational operation error");
    }
  }

  static void method() throws Exception {
    Rational r1 = new Rational(3, 4);
    Rational r2 = new Rational(0, 1);
    Rational x = r1.divide(r2);
    int i = 0;
    int y = 2 / i;
    System.out.println("Welcome to Java");
  }
}
```

15.11 What is displayed when the following program is run?

```java
public class Test {
  public static void main(String[] args) {
    try {
      method();
      System.out.println("After the method call");
    }
    catch (RuntimeException ex) {
      System.out.println("Integer operation error");
    }
```

```
      catch (Exception ex) {
        System.out.println("Rational operation error");
      }
    }

    static void method() throws Exception {
      try {
        Rational r1 = new Rational(3, 4);
        Rational r2 = new Rational(0, 1);
        Rational x = r1.divide(r2);

        int i = 0;
        int y = 2 / i;
        System.out.println("Welcome to Java");
      }
      catch (RuntimeException ex) {
        System.out.println("Integer operation error");
      }
      catch (Exception ex) {
        System.out.println("Rational operation error");
      }
    }
  }
```

15.12 If an exception is not caught in a non-GUI application, what will happen? If an exception is not caught in a GUI application, what will happen?

15.13 What does the method `printStackTrace` do?

15.14 Does the presence of a `try-catch` block impose overhead when no exception occurs?

Sections 15.4–15.5

15.15 Suppose that `statement2` causes an exception in the following statement:

```
try {
  statement1;
  statement2;
  statement3;
}
catch (Exception1 ex1) {
}
catch (Exception2 ex2) {
}
catch (Exception3 ex3) {
  throw ex3;
}
finally {
  statement4;
};
statement5;
```

Answer the following questions:

✦ Will `statement5` be executed if the exception is not caught?

✦ If the exception is of type `Exception3`, will `statement4` be executed, and will `statement5` be executed?

15.16 What is displayed when the following program is run?

```
public class Test {
  public static void main(String[] args) {
    try {
      method();
      System.out.println("After the method call");
    }
    catch (RuntimeException ex) {
      System.out.println("Integer operation error");
    }
```

```
          catch (Exception ex) {
            System.out.println("Rational operation error");
          }
        }

        static void method() throws Exception {
          try {
            Rational r1 = new Rational(3, 4);
            Rational r2 = new Rational(0, 1);
            Rational x = r1.divide(r2);

            int i = 0;
            int y = 2 / i;
            System.out.println("Welcome to Java");
          }
          catch (RuntimeException ex) {
            System.out.println("Integer operation error");
          }
          catch (Exception ex) {
            System.out.println("Rational operation error");
            throw ex;
          }
        }
      }
```

Section 15.8 Assertions

15.17 What is assertion for? How do you declare assertions? How do you compile code with assertions? How do you run programs with assertions?

15.18 What happens when you run the following code?

```
public class Test {
  public static void main(String[] args) {
    int i; int sum = 0;
    for (i = 0; i < 11; i++) {
      sum += i;
    }
    assert i == 10: "i is " + i;
  }
}
```

PROGRAMMING EXERCISES

Sections 15.2–15.3

15.1* (*NumberFormatException*) Example 7.4, "Passing Command-Line Arguments," is a simple command-line calculator. Note that the program terminates if any operand is non-numeric. Write a program with an exception handler that deals with non-numeric operands; then write another program without using an exception handler to achieve the same objective. Your program should display a message that informs the user of the wrong operand type before exiting (see Figure 15.8).

15.2* (*ArithmeticException and NumberFormatException*) Example 15.2, "Exceptions in GUI Applications," is a GUI calculator. Note that if Number 1 or Number 2 were a non-numeric string, the program would report exceptions. Modify the program with an exception handler to catch ArithmeticException (e.g., divided by 0) and NumberFormatException (e.g., input is not an integer), and display the errors in a message dialog box, as shown in Figure 15.9.

15.3* (*ArrayIndexOutBoundsException*) Write a program that meets the following requirements:

✦ Create an array with one hundred randomly chosen integers.

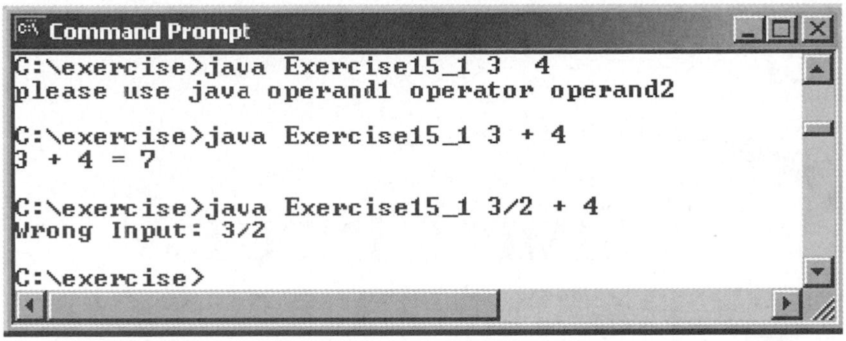

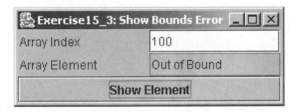

FIGURE 15.8 *The program performs arithmetic operations and detects input errors.*

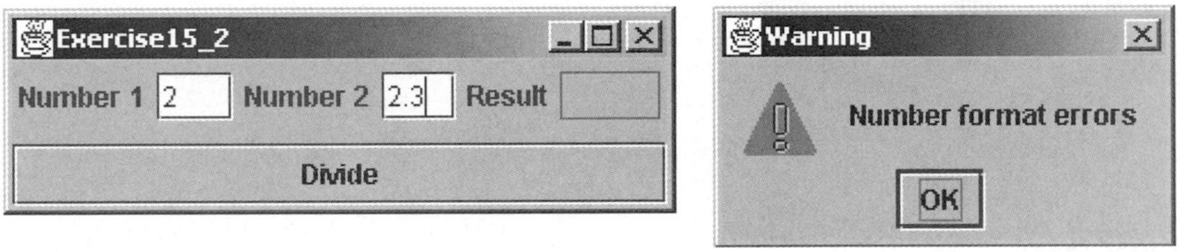

FIGURE 15.9 *The program displays an error message in the dialog box if the number is not well formatted.*

♦ Create a text field to enter an array index and another text field to display the array element at the specified index (see Figure 15.10).

FIGURE 15.10 *The program displays the array element at the specified index or displays the message* Out of Bound *if the index is out of bounds.*

♦ Create a Show Element button to cause the array element to be displayed. If the specified index is out of bounds, display the message Out of Bound.

15.4* (*IllegalArgumentException*) Modify the Loan class in Section 6.15, "Case Study: The Loan Class," to throw IllegalArgumentException if the loan amount, interest rate, or number of years is less than or equal to zero.

15.5* (*IllegalTriangleException*) Exercise 8.1 defined the Triangle class with three sides. In a triangle, the sum of any two sides is greater than the other side. The Triangle class must adhere to this rule. Create the IllegalTriangleException class, and modify the constructor of the Triangle class to throw an IllegalTriangleException object if a triangle is created with sides that violate the rule, as follows:

```
/** Construct a triangle with the specified sides */
public Triangle(double side1, double side2, double side3)
  throws IllegalTriangleException {
  // Implement it
}
```

chapter

16

SIMPLE INPUT AND OUTPUT

Objectives

✦ To discover file properties, delete and rename files using the `File` class (§16.2).

✦ To understand how I/O is processed in Java (§16.3).

✦ To distinguish between text I/O and binary I/O (§16.3.1).

✦ To read and write characters using `FileReader` and `FileWriter` (§16.4.1).

✦ To improve the performance of text I/O using `BufferedReader` and `BufferedWriter` (§16.4.3).

✦ To write primitive values, strings, and objects as text using `PrintWriter` and `PrintStream` (§16.4.4).

✦ To read and write bytes using `FileInputStream` and `FileOutputStream` (§16.6.1).

✦ To read and write primitive values and strings using `DataInputStream`/`DataOutputStream` (§16.6.3).

✦ To store and restore objects using `ObjectOutputStream` and `ObjectInputStream`, and to understand how objects are serialized and what kind of objects can be serialized (§16.9 Optional).

✦ To use the `Serializable` interface to enable objects to be serializable (§16.9.1 Optional).

✦ To use `RandomAccessFile` for both read and write (§16.10 Optional).

16.1   Introduction

Data stored in variables, arrays, and objects are temporary; they are lost when the program terminates. To permanently store the data created in a program, you need to save them in a file on a disk or a CD. The file can be transported and can be read later by other programs. In this chapter, you will learn how to read/write data from/to a file, and how to store/restore objects to/from a file. Since data are stored in files, the following section introduces how to use the File class to obtain file properties and to delete and rename files.

16.2   The **File** Class

Every file is placed in a directory in the file system. The complete file name consists of the directory path and the file name. For example, **c:\book\Welcome.java** is the complete file name for the file **Welcome.java** on the Windows operating system. Here **c:\book** is referred to as the *directory path*   directory path
for the file. The directory path and complete file name are machine-dependent. On Unix, the complete file name may be **/home/liang/book/Welcome.java**, where **/home/liang/book** is the directory path for the file **Welcome.java.**

The File class is intended to provide an abstraction that deals with most of the machine-dependent complexities of files and path names in a machine-independent fashion. The File class contains the methods for obtaining file properties and for renaming and deleting files, as shown in Figure 16.1. However, the File class does not contain the methods for reading and writing file contents

The filename is a string. The File class is a wrapper class for the file name and its directory path. For example, new File("c:\\book") creates a File object for the directory **c:\book**, and new File("c:\\book\\test.dat") creates a File object for the file **c:\\book\\test.dat**, both on Windows. You can use the File class's isDirectory() method to check whether the object represents a directory, and the isFile() method to check whether the object represents a file name.

 CAUTION
The directory separator for Windows is a backslash (\). The backslash is a special   directory separator
character in Java and should be written as \\ (see Table 2.4 on page 46).

The File class has four constants: pathSeparator, pathSeparatorChar, separator, and separatorChar. These constants are platform-dependent path separators and name separators. separatorChar is '\' on Windows and '/' on Unix. separatorChar is a char, and separator is a string representation of separatorChar. Likewise, pathSeparator is a string representation for pathSeparatorChar. pathSeparator is ';' on Windows and ':' on Unix.

 NOTE
pathSeparator, pathSeparatorChar, separator, and separatorChar are constants, but they are named as variables with lowercase for the first word and uppercase for the first letters of subsequent words. Thus these names violate the Java naming convention.

An *absolute path* name is system-dependent. For example, if you create a File object using new   absolute path
File("c:\\book\\test.dat"), it is an absolute path name. If you create a File object using new
File("test.dat"), it refers to the file in the current class path directory. This path is not absolute because no system-specific path separators are used.

java.io.File	
+File(pathname: String)	Creates a File object for the specified pathname. The pathname may be a directory or a file.
+File(parent: String, child: String)	Creates a File object for the child under the directory parent. The child may be a filename or a subdirectory.
+File(parent: File, child: String)	Creates a File object for the child under the directory parent. The parent is a File object. In the preceding constructor, the parent is a string.
+exists(): boolean	Returns true if the file or the directory represented by the File object exists.
+canRead(): boolean	Returns true if the file represented by the File object exists and can be read.
+canWrite(): boolean	Returns true if the file represented by the File object exists and can be written.
+isDirectory(): boolean	Returns true if the File object represents a directory.
+isFile(): boolean	Returns true if the File object represents a file.
+isAbsolute(): boolean	Returns true if the File object is created using an absolute path name.
+isHidden(): boolean	Returns true if the file represented in the File object is hidden. The exact definition of *hidden* is system-dependent. On Windows, you can mark a file hidden in the File Properties dialog box. On Unix systems, a file is hidden if its name begins with a period character '.'.
+getAbsolutePath(): String	Returns the complete absolute file or directory name represented by the File object.
+getCanonicalPath(): String	Returns the same as getAbsolutePath() except that it removes redundant names, such as "." and "..", from the pathname, resolves symbolic links (on Unix platforms), and converts drive letters to standard uppercase (on Win32 platforms).
+getName(): String	Returns the last name of the complete directory and file name represented by the File object. For example, new File("c:\\book\\test.dat").getName() returns test.dat.
+getPath(): String	Returns the complete directory and file name represented by the File object. For example, new File("c:\\book\\test.dat").getPath() returns c:\book\test.dat.
+getParent(): String	Returns the complete parent directory of the current directory or the file represented by the File object. For example, new File("c:\\book\\test.dat").getParent() returns c:\book.
+lastModified(): long	Returns the time that the file was last modified.
+delete(): boolean	Deletes this file. The method returns true if the deletion succeeds.
+renameTo(dest: File): boolean	Renames this file. The method returns true if the operation succeeds.

FIGURE 16.1 *The* File *class can be used to obtain file and directory properties and to delete and rename files.*

Do not use the absolute directory and file name literals in your program. If you use a literal such as "c:\\book\\test.dat", it will work on Windows but not on other platforms. To enable the program to run correctly on different platforms, use the following string to replace "c:\\book\\test.dat":

```
new File(".").getCanonicalPath() + "book" + File.separator
  + "test.dat";
```

current directory

Here "." denotes the current directory. If you run the Java program from the command line, the current directory is where the java command is issued. If you run the program from an IDE, the current directory is dependent on the IDE settings.

Listing 16.1 demonstrates how to create a File object in a platform-independent way and use the methods in the File class to obtain its properties. The program creates a File object for the file **us.gif.** This file is stored under the **image** directory in the current directory. The statement in Line 8 creates the object in a platform-independent fashion without using the platform-specific name separator and drive letter.

LISTING **16.1**   TestFileClass.java (Using the File Class)

```
1 import java.io.*;
2 import java.util.*;
3
4 public class TestFileClass {
5   public static void main(String[] args) {
6     // Create a File object
7     File file = new File(".", "image" + File.separator + "us.gif");
8     System.out.println("Does it exist? " + file.exists());
9     System.out.println("Can it be read? " + file.canRead());
10    System.out.println("Can it be written? " + file.canWrite());
11    System.out.println("Is it a directory? " + file.isDirectory());
12    System.out.println("Is it a file? " + file.isFile());
13    System.out.println("Is it absolute? " + file.isAbsolute());
14    System.out.println("Is it hidden? " + file.isHidden());
15    System.out.println("What is its absolute path? " +
16      file.getAbsolutePath());
17
18    try {
19      System.out.println("What is its canonical path? " +
20        file.getCanonicalPath());
21    }
22    catch (IOException ex) { }
23
24    System.out.println("What is its name? " + file.getName());
25    System.out.println("What is its path? " + file.getPath());
26    System.out.println("When was it last modified? " +
27      new Date(file.lastModified()));
28
29    System.out.println("What is the path separator? " +
30      File.pathSeparatorChar);
31    System.out.println("What is the name separator? " +
32      File.separatorChar);
33  }
34 }
```

file exist?

All the Java I/O classes introduced in this chapter are in the java.io package, so it is imported in Line 1.

The getCanonicalPath() method can throw an IOException, so it is put in a try-catch block in Lines 18–22.

The lastModified() method returns the date and time when the file was last modified, measured in milliseconds since the epoch (00:00:00 GMT, January 1, 1970). The Date class is used to display it in a readable format in Lines 26–27.

Figure 16.2 shows a sample run of the program on Windows, and Figure 16.3 a sample run on Unix. As shown in the figures, the path name and separator on Windows are different from those on Unix.

 TIP
To develop platform-independent applications, it is imperative not to use absolute directory and file names.

16.3   How is I/O Handled in Java?

A File object encapsulates the properties of a file or a path, but does not contain the methods for reading/writing data from/to a file. In order to perform I/O, you need to create objects using appropriate Java I/O classes. The objects contain the methods for reading/writing data from/to a file. For example, to write text to a file named temp.txt, you may create an object using the java.io.FileWriter class as follows:

```
FileWriter output = new FileWriter("temp.txt");
```

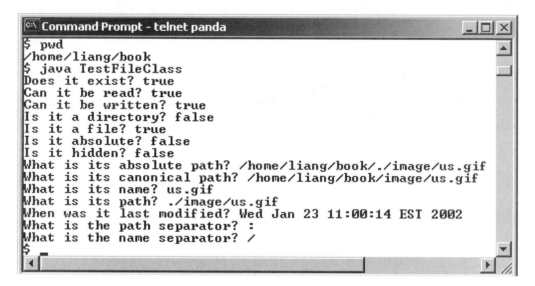

FIGURE 16.2 *The program creates a* File *object and displays file properties on Windows.*

```
Command Prompt - telnet panda                    _ □ ×
$ pwd
/home/liang/book
$ java TestFileClass
Does it exist? true
Can it be read? true
Can it be written? true
Is it a directory? false
Is it a file? true
Is it absolute? false
Is it hidden? false
What is its absolute path? /home/liang/book/./image/us.gif
What is its canonical path? /home/liang/book/image/us.gif
What is its name? us.gif
What is its path? ./image/us.gif
When was it last modified? Wed Jan 23 11:00:14 EST 2002
What is the path separator? :
What is the name separator? /
$
```

FIGURE 16.3 *The program creates a* File *object and displays file properties on Unix.*

You can now invoke write(String) from the object to write a string into the file. For example, the following statement writes "Java 101" to the file:

```
output.write("Java 101");
```

The next statement closes the file:

```
output.close();
```

There are many I/O classes for various purposes. In general, these can be classified as input classes and output classes. An input class contains the methods to read data, and an output class contains the methods to write data. FileWriter is an example of an output class and FileReader is an example of an input class. The following code shows an example of creating an input object for the file temp.txt and reading data from the file:

```
FileReader input = new FileReader("temp.txt");
int code = input.read();
System.out.println((char)code);
```

If temp.txt contains "Java 101", input.read() returns the Unicode for 'J'. So the printout is J.

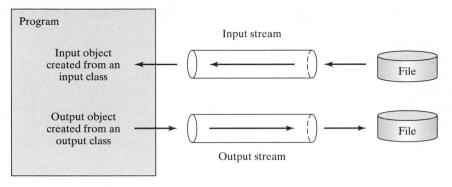

FIGURE 16.4 *The program receives data through an input object and sends data through an output object.*

Figure 16.4 illustrates Java I/O programming. An input object reads a stream of data from a file, and an output object writes a stream of data to a file. You will learn how to use I/O classes to create objects and use the methods in the objects to read/write data from/to files in this chapter.

Almost all the methods in the I/O classes throw java.io.IOException. Therefore you have to declare to throw java.io.IOException in the method or place the code in a try-catch block, as shown below:

IOException

Declaring exception in the method

```
public static void main(String[] args)
    throws IOException {
  FileWriter output =
    new FileWriter("temp.txt");
  output.write("Java 101");
  output.close();

  FileReader input =
    new FileReader("temp.txt");
  int code = input.read();
  System.out.println((char)code);
  input.close();
}
```

Using try-catch block

```
public static void main(String[] args) {
  try {
    FileWriter output =
      new FileWriter("temp.txt");
    output.write("Java 101");
    output.close();

    FileReader input =
      new FileReader("temp.txt");
    int code = input.read();
    System.out.println((char)code);
    input.close();
  }
  catch (IOException ex) {
    ex.printStackTrace();
  }
}
```

 NOTE

An input object reads a stream of data. For convenience, an input object is also called an *input stream*. For the same reason, an output object is called an *output stream*.

input stream
output stream

 TIP

When a stream is no longer needed, always close it using the close() method. Not closing streams may cause programming errors.

close stream

16.3.1 Text Files and Binary Files

Java offers many classes for performing file input and output. These classes can be categorized as *text I/O classes* and *binary I/O classes.*

text I/O
binary I/O

Data stored in a text file are represented in human-readable form. Data stored in a binary file are represented in binary form. You cannot read binary files. They are designed to be read by programs. For example, the Java source programs are stored in text files and can be read by a text editor, but the Java classes are stored in binary files and are read by the JVM. The advantage of binary files is that they are more efficient to process than text files.

Although it is not technically precise and correct, you can envision a text file as consisting of a sequence of characters and a binary file as consisting of a sequence of bits. For example, the decimal integer 199 is stored as the sequence of three characters, '1', '9', '9', in a text file, and the same integer is stored as a byte-type value C7 in a binary file, because decimal 199 equals hex C7 ($199 = 12 \times 16^1 + 7$).

16.4 Text I/O

The design of the Java I/O classes is a good example of applying inheritance, where common operations are generalized in superclasses, and subclasses provide specialized operations. Figure 16.5 lists some of the classes for performing text I/O.

Reader is the root for text input classes, and Writer is the root for text output classes. Figures 16.6 and 16.7 list all the methods in Reader and Writer.

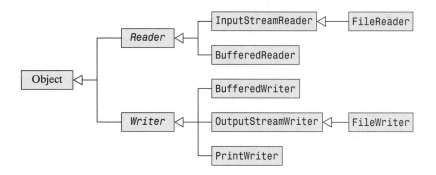

FIGURE **16.5** *Reader,* *Writer,* *and their subclasses are for text I/O.*

java.io.Reader	
+read(): int	Reads the next character from the input stream. The value returned is an int in the range from 0 to 65535, which represents a Unicode character. Returns –1 at the end of the stream.
+read(cbuf: char[]): int	Reads characters from the input stream into an array. Returns the actual number of characters read. Returns –1 at the end of the stream.
+read(cbuf: char[], off: int, len: int): int	Reads characters from the input stream and stores them in cbuf[off], cbuf[off+1], ..., cbuf[off+len–1]. The actual number of bytes read is returned. Returns –1 at the end of the stream.
+close(): void	Closes this input stream and releases any system resources associated with it.
+skip(n: long): long	Skips over and discards n characters of data from this input stream. The actual number of characters skipped is returned.
+markSupported(): boolean	Tests whether this input stream supports the mark and reset methods.
+mark(readAheadLimit: int): void	Marks the current position in this input stream.
+ready(): boolean	Returns true if this input stream is ready to be read.
+reset(): void	Repositions this stream to the position at the time the mark method was last called on this input stream.

FIGURE **16.6** *The abstract* Reader *class defines the methods for reading a stream of characters.*

java.io.Writer	
+write(int c): void	Writes the specified character to this output stream. The parameter c is the Unicode for a character
+write(cbuf: byte[]): void	Writes all the characters in array cbuf to the output stream.
+write(cbuf: char[], off: int, len: int): void	Writes cbuf[off], cbuf[off+1], …, cbuf[off+len-1] into the output stream.
+write(str: String): void	Writes the characters from the string into the output stream.
+write(str: String, off: int, len: int): void	Writes a portion of the string characters into the output stream.
+close(): void	Closes this input stream and releases any system resources associated with it.
+flush(): void	Flushes this output stream and forces any buffered output characters to be written out.

FIGURE 16.7 *The abstract* Writer *class defines the methods for writing a stream of characters.*

NOTE

The read() method reads a character. If no data are available, it blocks the thread from executing the next statement. The thread that invokes the read() method is suspended until the data become available.

NOTE

All the methods in the text I/O classes except PrintWriter are declared to throw java.io.IOException.

16.4.1 FileReader/FileWriter

FileReader/FileWriter are convenience classes for reading/writing characters from/to files using the default character encoding on the host computer. FileReader/FileWriter associates an input/output stream with an external file.

All the methods in FileReader/FileWriter are inherited from their superclasses. To construct a FileReader, use the following constructors:

```
public FileReader(String filename)
public FileReader(File file)
```

A java.io.FileNotFoundException would occur if you attempt to create a FileReader with a nonexistent file. For example, Listing 16.2 reads and displays all the characters from the file temp.txt.

FileNotFoundException

LISTING 16.2 TestFileReader.java (Input Using FileReader)

```
 1 import java.io.*;
 2
 3 public class TestFileReader {
 4   public static void main(String[] args) {
 5     FileReader input = null;
 6     try {
 7       // Create an input stream
 8       input = new FileReader("temp.txt");
 9
10       int code;
11       // Repeatedly read a character and display it on the console
12       while ((code = input.read()) != -1)
13         System.out.print((char)code);
14     }
```

import

input object

read character

```
15     catch (FileNotFoundException ex) {
16       System.out.println("File temp.txt does not exist");
17     }
18     catch (IOException ex) {
19       ex.printStackTrace();
20     }
21     finally {
22       try {
23         input.close(); // Close the stream
24       }
25       catch (IOException ex) {
26         ex.printStackTrace();
27       }
28     }
29   }
30 }
```

close file

The constructors and methods in `FileReader` may throw `IOException`, so they are invoked from a try-catch block. Since `java.io.FileNotFoundException` is a subclass of `IOException`, the catch clause for `FileNotFoundException` (Line 15) is put before the `catch` clause for `IOException` (Line 18). Closing files in the `finally` class ensures that the files are always closed in any case (Line 23).

test end of a file

Recall that Java allows the assignment operator in an expression (see page 37). The expression `((code = input.read()) != -1)` (Line 12) reads a byte from `input.read()`, assigns it to `code`, and checks whether it is −1. The input value of −1 signifies the end of a file.

 NOTE

EOFException

Attempting to read data after the end of a file is reached would cause `java.io.EOFException`.

To construct a `FileWriter`, use the following constructors:

```
public FileWriter(String filename)
public FileWriter(File file)
public FileWriter(String filename, boolean append)
public FileWriter(File file, boolean append)
```

If the file does not exist, a new file will be created. If the file already exists, the first two constructors will delete the current contents of the file. To retain the current content and append new data into the file, use the last two constructors by passing true to the `append` parameter. For example, suppose the file temp.txt exists, Listing 16.3 appends a new string, "Introduction to Java," to the file.

LISTING 16.3 TestFileWriter.java (Output Using `FileWriter`)

append to file

```
1 import java.io.*;
2
3 public class TestFileWriter {
4   public static void main(String[] args) throws IOException {
5     // Create an output stream to the file
6     FileWriter output = new FileWriter("temp.txt", true);
7
8     // Output a string to the file
9     output.write("Introduction to Java");
10
11     // Close the stream
12     output.close();
13   }
14 }
```

If you replace Line 6 with the following statement,

```
FileWriter output = new FileWriter("temp.txt");
```

the current contents of the file are lost. To avoid this, use the `File` class's `exists()` method to   file exists?
check whether a file exists before creating it, as follows:

```
File file = new File("temp.txt");
if (!file.exists()) {
  FileWriter output = new FileWriter(file);
}
```

16.4.2 `InputStreamReader/OutputStreamWriter` (Optional)

`InputStreamReader/OutputStreamWriter` are used to convert between bytes and characters. Characters written to an `OutputStreamWriter` are encoded into bytes using a specified encoding scheme. Bytes read from an `InputStreamReader` are decoded into characters using a specified encoding scheme. You can specify an encoding scheme using a constructor of `InputStreamReader/OutputStreamWriter`. If no encoding scheme is specified, the system's default encoding scheme is used.

All the methods in `InputStreamReader/OutputStreamWriter` are inherited from `Reader/Writer` except `getEncoding()`, which returns the name of the encoding being used by this stream. Since `FileReader` is a subclass of `InputStreamReader`, you can also invoke `getEncoding()` from a `FileReader` object. For example, the following code

```
public static void main(String[] args) throws IOException {
  FileReader input = new FileReader("temp.txt");
  System.out.println("Default encoding is " + input.getEncoding());
}
```

displays the default encoding for the host machine. For a list of encoding schemes supported in Java, please see `http://java.sun.com/j2se/1.5.0/docs/guide/intl/encoding.doc.html` and `http://mindprod.com/jgloss/encoding.html`.

 NOTE

Java programs use Unicode. When you read a character from a `FileReader` stream, the Unicode code of the character is returned. The encoding of the character in the file may be different from the Unicode encoding. Java automatically converts it to the Unicode. When you write a character to a `FileWriter` stream, Java automatically converts the Unicode of the character to the encoding specified for the file. This is pictured in Figure 16.8.

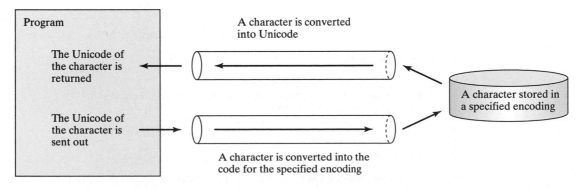

FIGURE **16.8** *The encoding of the file may be different from the encoding used in the program.*

16.4.3 BufferedReader/BufferedWriter

BufferedReader/BufferedWriter can be used to speed up input and output by reducing the number of reads and writes. Buffered streams employ a buffered array of characters that acts as a cache. In the case of input, the array reads a chunk of characters into the buffer before the individual characters are read. In the case of output, the array accumulates a block of characters before writing the entire block to the output stream.

The use of buffered streams enables you to read and write a chunk of characters at once instead of reading or writing the bytes one at a time. You can wrap a BufferedReader/BufferedWriter around any Reader/Writer streams. The following constructors are used to create a BufferedReader/BufferedWriter:

```
// Create a BufferedReader
public BufferedReader(Reader in)
public BufferedReader(Reader in, int bufferSize)

// Create a BufferedWriter
public BufferedWriter(Writer out)
public BufferedWriter(Writer out, int bufferSize)
```

If no buffer size is specified, the default size is 8192 characters. A buffered input stream reads as many data as possible into its buffer in a single read call. By contrast, a buffered output stream calls the write method only when its buffer fills up or when the flush() method is called.

The buffered stream classes inherit methods from their superclasses. In addition to using the methods from their superclasses, BufferedReader has a readLine() method to read a line, and BufferedWriter has a newLine() method to write a line separator. If the end of stream is reached, readLine() returns null.

🌸 NOTE

The readLine() method return a line without the line separator. The newLine() method writes a system-dependent line separator to a file. The line separator string is defined by the system and is not necessarily a single ('\n') character. To get the system line separator, use

```
static String lineSeparator = (String)java.security.
  AccessController.doPrivileged(
    new sun.security.action.GetPropertyAction("line.separator"));
```

Listing 16.4 uses BufferedReader to read text from the file "Welcome.java", displays the text on the console, and copies the text to a file named "Welcome.java~".

LISTING 16.4 TestBufferedReaderWriter.java (Using Buffers)

```
 1 import java.io.*;
 2
 3 public class TestBufferedReaderWriter {
 4   public static void main(String[] args) throws IOException {
 5     // Create an input stream
 6     BufferedReader input =
 7       new BufferedReader(new FileReader("Welcome.java"));
 8
 9     // Create an output stream
10     BufferedWriter output =
11       new BufferedWriter(new FileWriter("Welcome.java~"));
12
13     // Repeatedly read a line and display it on the console
14     String line;
```

input stream

output stream

```
15     while ((line = input.readLine()) != null) {
16       System.out.println(line);
17       output.write(line);
18       output.newLine(); // Write a line separator
19     }
20
21     // Close the stream
22     input.close();
23     output.close();
24   }
25 }
```

read line

close stream

A `BufferedReader` is created on top of a `FileReader` (Lines 6–7), and a `BufferedWriter` on top of a `FileWriter` (Lines 10–11). Data from the file are read repeatedly, one line at a time (Line 15). Each line is displayed in Line 16, and output to a new file (Line 17) with a line separator (Line 18).

You are encouraged to rewrite the program without using buffers and then compare the performance of the two programs. This will show you the improvement in performance obtained by using buffers when reading from a large file.

 TIP

Since physical input and output involving I/O devices are typically very slow compared with CPU processing speeds, you should use buffered input/output streams to improve performance.

16.4.4   `PrintWriter` and `PrintStream`

`BufferedWriter` is used to output characters and strings. `PrintWriter` and `PrintStream` can be used to output objects, strings, and numeric values as text. `PrintWriter` was introduced in JDK 1.2 to replace `PrintStream`. Both classes are almost identical in the sense that they provide the same function and the same methods for outputting strings and numeric values as text. `PrintWriter` is more efficient than `PrintStream` and therefore is the class you ought to use.

`PrintWriter` and `PrintStream` contain the following overloaded `print` and `println` methods:

```
public void print(Object o)          public void println(Object o)
public void print(String s)          public void println(String s)
public void print(char c)            public void println(char c)
public void print(char[] cArray)     public void println(char[] cArray)
public void print(int i)             public void println(int i)
public void print(long l)            public void println(long l)
public void print(float f)           public void println(float f)
public void print(double d)          public void println(double d)
public void print(boolean b)         public void println(boolean b)
```

A numeric value, character, or boolean value is converted into a string and printed to the output stream. To print an object is to print the object's string representation returned from the `toString()` method. `PrintWriter` and `PrintStream` also contain the `printf` method for printing formatted output, which was introduced in Section 2.17, "Formatting Output."

You have already used these methods in `System.out`. `out` is declared as a static variable of the `PrintStream` type in the `System` class. By default, `out` refers to the standard output device, that is, the screen console. You can use the `System.setOut(PrintStream)` to set a new `out`. Since `System` was introduced before `PrintWriter`, `out` is declared in `PrintStream` and not `PrintWriter`.

This section introduces `PrintWriter`, but `PrintStream` can be used in the same way. To construct a `PrintWriter`, use the following constructors:

```
public PrintWriter(Writer out)
public PrintWriter(Writer out, boolean autoFlush)
```

If `autoFlush` is `true`, the `println` methods will cause the buffer to be flushed.

NOTE

The constructors and methods in `PrintWriter` and `PrintStream` do not throw an `IOException`. So you don't need to invoke them from a `try-catch` block.

Listing 16.5 is an example of generating ten integers and storing them in a text file using `PrintWriter`. The example later writes the data back from the file and computes the total.

LISTING 16.5   TestPrintWriter.java (Output Data and Strings)

```
 1 import java.io.*;
 2 import java.util.*;
 3
 4 public class TestPrintWriter {
 5   public static void main(String[] args) throws IOException {
 6     // Check if file temp.txt already exists
 7     File file = new File("temp.txt");
 8     if (file.exists()) {
 9       System.out.println("File temp.txt already exists");
10       System.exit(0);
11     }
12
13     // Create an output stream
14     PrintWriter output = new PrintWriter(new FileWriter(file));
15
16     // Generate ten integers and write them to a file
17     for (int i = 0; i < 10; i++) {
18       output.print((int)(Math.random() * 100) + " ");
19     }
20
21     // Close the output stream
22     output.close();
23
24     // Open an input stream
25     BufferedReader input =
26       new BufferedReader(new FileReader("temp.txt"));
27
28     int total = 0;  // Store total
29     String line;
30     while ((line = input.readLine()) != null) {
31       // Extract numbers using string tokenizer
32       StringTokenizer tokens = new StringTokenizer(line);
33       while (tokens.hasMoreTokens())
34         total += Integer.parseInt(tokens.nextToken());
35     }
36
37     System.out.println("Total is " + total);
38
39     // Close input stream
40     input.close();
41   }
42 }
```

check file

output stream

output to file

close stream

input stream

read line

close stream

Lines 7–11 check whether the file exists. If so, exit the program. Line 14 creates a `PrintWriter` stream for the file. Lines 17–19 generate ten random integers and output the integers separated by a space.

Line 25 opens the file for input. Lines 30–35 read all the lines from the file and use `StringTokenizer` to extract tokens from the line. Each token is converted to a number and added to the total (Line 34).

JDK 1.5 Scanner class

TIP

You can also use the `Scanner` class to extract tokens from a file and then use `next-Token()` to read a string, `nextInt()` to read an `int`, `nextDouble()` to read a `double`, and so on, as introduced in Section 7.6. "The `Scanner` Class." To create a `Scanner` for a file, use

```
Scanner scanner = new Scanner(File file);
```

 # 16.5 Case Study: Text Viewer

This case study writes a program that views a text file in a text area. The user enters a filename in a text field and clicks the View button; the file is then displayed in a text area, as shown in Figure 16.9.

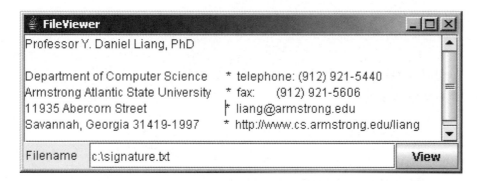

FIGURE 16.9 *The program displays the specified file in the text area.*

Clearly, you need to use text input to read a text file. Normally, you should use `BufferedReader` wrapped on a `FileReader` to improve performance. When the View button is pressed, the program gets the input filename from the text field; it then creates a text input stream. The data are read one line at a time and appended to the text area for display. Listing 16.6 displays the source code for the program.

LISTING 16.6 FileViewer.java (View Text Files)

```java
1 import java.awt.*;
2 import java.awt.event.*;
3 import java.io.*;
4 import javax.swing.*;
5
6 public class FileViewer extends JFrame implements ActionListener {
7   // Button to view a file
8   private JButton jbtView = new JButton("View");
9
10   // Text field to the receive file name
11   private JTextField jtfFilename = new JTextField(12);
12
13   // Text area to display the file
14   private JTextArea jtaFile = new JTextArea();
15
16   public FileViewer() {
17     // Panel p to hold a label, a text field, and a button
18     Panel p = new Panel();
19     p.setLayout(new BorderLayout());
20     p.add(new Label("Filename"), BorderLayout.WEST);
21     p.add(jtfFilename, BorderLayout.CENTER);
22     p.add(jbtView, BorderLayout.EAST);
```
create UI

```
23
24      // Add jtaFile to a scroll pane
25      JScrollPane jsp = new JScrollPane(jtaFile);
26
27      // Add jsp and p to the frame
28      getContentPane().add(jsp, BorderLayout.CENTER);
29      getContentPane().add(p, BorderLayout.SOUTH);
30
31      // Register listener
32      jbtView.addActionListener(this);
33   }
34
35   /** Handle the View button */
36   public void actionPerformed(ActionEvent e) {
37     if (e.getSource() == jbtView)
38       showFile();
39   }
40
41   /** Display the file in the text area */
42   private void showFile() {
43     // Use a BufferedReader to read text from the file
44     BufferedReader input = null;
45
46     // Get file name from the text field
47     String filename = jtfFilename.getText().trim();
48
49     String inLine;
50
51     try {
52       // Create a buffered stream
53       input = new BufferedReader(new FileReader(filename));
54
55       // Read a line and append the line to the text area
56       while ((inLine = input.readLine()) != null) {
57         jtaFile.append(inLine + '\n');
58       }
59     }
60     catch (FileNotFoundException ex) {
61       System.out.println("File not found: " + filename);
62     }
63     catch (IOException ex) {
64       System.out.println(ex.getMessage());
65     }
66     finally {
67       try {
68         if (input != null) input.close();
69       }
70       catch (IOException ex) {
71         System.out.println(ex.getMessage());
72       }
73     }
74   }
75
76   public static void main(String[] args) {
77     FileViewer frame = new FileViewer();
78     frame.setTitle("FileViewer");
79     frame.setSize(400, 300);
80     frame.setDefaultCloseOperation(JFrame.EXIT_ON_CLOSE);
81     frame.setVisible(true);
82   }
83 }
```

display file

input stream

read line
display line

A `BufferedReader` is created on top of a `FileReader` (Line 53). Data from the file are read repeatedly, one line at a time, and appended to the text area (Line 57). If the file does not exist, the catch clause in Lines 60–62 catches and processes it. All other I/O errors are caught and processed in Lines 63–65. Whether the program runs with or without errors, the input stream is closed in Lines 66–73.

16.6   Binary I/O

Text I/O requires encoding and decoding. The JVM converts a Unicode to a file-specific encoding when writing a character and converts a file-specific encoding to a Unicode when reading a character. Binary I/O does not require conversions. When you write a byte to a file, the original byte is copied into the file. When you read a byte from a file, the exact byte in the file is returned, as shown in Figure 16.10.

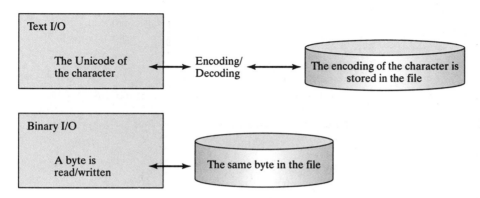

FIGURE 16.10   *Text I/O requires encoding and decoding, whereas binary I/O does not.*

For example, suppose you write character '9' using text I/O to a file. Since the Unicode for '9' is 0x0039, the Unicode 0x0039 is converted to a code that depends on the encoding scheme for the file. (Note that the prefix 0x denotes a hex number.) If you write an integer value to a file using binary I/O, the exact integer value in the memory is copied into the file.

Binary I/O is more efficient than text I/O, because binary I/O does not require encoding and decoding. Binary files are independent of the encoding scheme on the host machine and thus are portable. Java programs on any machine can read a binary file created by a Java program. This is why Java class files are binary files. Java class files can run on a JVM on any machine.

Figure 16.11 lists some of the classes for performing binary I/O. InputStream is the root for binary input classes, and OutputStream is the root for binary output classes. Figures 16.12 and 16.13 list all the methods in InputStream and OutputStream. The methods in InputStream/OutputStream are very similar to the methods in Reader/Writer. The difference is that InputStream/OutputStream reads bytes and Reader/Writer reads characters.

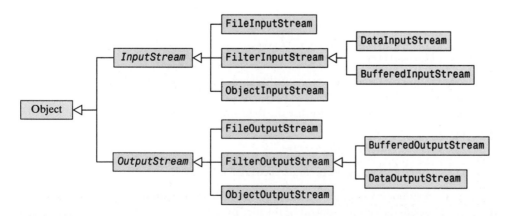

FIGURE 16.11   *InputStream, OutputStream, and their subclasses are for binary I/O.*

java.io.InputStream	
+read(): int	Reads the next byte of data from the input stream. The value byte is returned as an int value in the range 0 to 255. If no byte is available because the end of the stream has been reached, the value -1 is returned.
+read(b: byte[]): int	Reads up to b.length bytes into array b from the input stream and returns the actual number of bytes read. Returns -1 at the end of the stream.
+read(b: byte[], off: int, len: int): int	Reads bytes from the input stream and stores them in b[off], b[off+1], ..., b[off+len-1]. The actual number of bytes read is returned. Returns -1 at the end of the stream.
+available(): int	Returns the number of bytes that can be read from the input stream.
+close(): void	Closes this input stream and releases any system resources associated with the stream.
+skip(n: long): long	Skips over and discards n bytes of data from this input stream. The actual number of bytes skipped is returned.
+markSupported(): boolean	Tests whether this input stream supports the mark and reset methods.
+mark(readlimit: int): void	Marks the current position in this input stream.
+reset(): void	Repositions this stream to the position at the time the mark method was last called on this input stream.

FIGURE 16.12   *The abstract* InputStream *class defines the methods for the input stream of bytes.*

java.io.OutputStream	
+write(int b): void	Writes the specified byte to this output stream. The parameter b is an int value. (byte)b is written to the output stream.
+write(b: byte[]): void	Writes all the bytes in array b to the output stream.
+write(b: byte[], off: int, len: int): void	Writes b[off], b[off+1], ..., b[off+len-1] into the output stream.
+close(): void	Closes this input stream and releases any system resources associated with the stream.
+flush(): void	Flushes this output stream and forces any buffered output bytes to be written out.

FIGURE 16.13   *The abstract* OutputStream *class defines the methods for the output stream of bytes.*

16.6.1   FileInputStream/FileOutputStream

FileInputStream/FileOutputStream is for reading/writing bytes from/to files. All the methods in these classes are inherited from InputStream and OutputStream. FileInputStream/FileOutputStream does not introduce new methods. To construct a FileInputStream, use the following constructors:

```
public FileInputStream(String filename)
public FileInputStream(File file)
```

A java.io.FileNotFoundException would occur if you attempt to create a FileInputStream with a nonexistent file.

To construct a FileOutputStream, use the following constructors:

```
public FileOutputStream(String filename)
public FileOutputStream(File file)
public FileOutputStream(String filename, boolean append)
public FileOutputStream(File file, boolean append)
```

If the file does not exist, a new file will be created. If the file already exists, the first two constructors will delete the current content of the file. To retain the current content and append new data into the file, use the last two constructors by passing true to the append parameter.

Listing 16.7 uses binary I/O to write ten byte values from 1 to 10 to a file named temp.dat and reads them back from the file.

LISTING 16.7   TestFileStream.java (Binary I/O)

```
1 import java.io.*;
2
3 public class TestFileStream {
4   public static void main(String[] args) throws IOException {
5     // Create an output stream to the file
6     FileOutputStream output = new FileOutputStream("temp.dat");          output stream
7
8     // Output values to the file
9     for (int i = 1; i <= 10; i++)
10      output.write(i);                                                   output
11
12    // Close the output stream
13    output.close();
14
15    // Create an input stream for the file
16    FileInputStream input = new FileInputStream("temp.dat");             input stream
17
18    // Read values from the file
19    int value;
20    while ((value = input.read()) != -1)                                 input
21      System.out.print(value + " ");
22
23    // Close the output stream
24    input.close();
25  }
26 }
```

A FileOutputStream is created for file temp.dat in Line 6. The for loop writes ten byte values into the file (Lines 9–10). Invoking write(i) is the same as invoking write((byte)i). Line 13 closes the output stream. Line 16 creates a FileInputStream for file temp.dat. Values are read from the file and displayed on the console in Lines 19–21. The expression ((value = input.read()) != -1) (Line 20) reads a byte from input.read(), assigns it to value, and checks whether it is −1. The input value of −1 signifies the end of a file.

end of a file

The file temp.dat created in this example is a binary file. It can be read from a Java program but not from a text editor, as shown in Figure 16.14.

binary data —

FIGURE **16.14**   *A binary file cannot be displayed in text mode.*

16.6.2   FilterInputStream/FilterOutputStream

Filter streams are streams that filter bytes for some purpose. The basic byte input stream provides a read method that can only be used for reading bytes. If you want to read integers, doubles, or strings, you need a filter class to wrap the byte input stream. Using a filter class enables you to read integers, doubles, and strings instead of bytes and characters. FilterInputStream and FilterOutputStream are the base classes for filtering data. When you need to process primitive numeric types, use DataInputStream and DataOutputStream to filter bytes.

16.6.3 `DataInputStream/DataOutputStream`

`DataInputStream` reads bytes from the stream and converts them into appropriate primitive type values or strings. `DataOutputStream` converts primitive type values or strings into bytes and outputs the bytes to the stream.

`DataInputStream` extends `FilterInputStream` and implements the `DataInput` interface, as shown in Figure 16.15. `DataOutputStream` extends `FilterOutputStream` and implements the `DataOutput` interface, as shown in Figure 16.16.

`DataInputStream` implements the methods defined in the `DataInput` interface to read primitive data type values and strings. `DataOutputStream` implements the methods defined in the `DataOutput` interface to write primitive data type values and strings. Primitive values are copied from memory to the output without any conversions. Characters in a string may be written in several ways, as discussed in the next section.

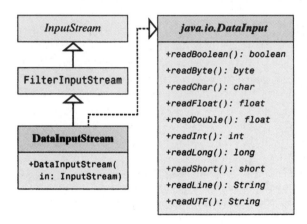

FIGURE 16.15 *`DataInputStream` filters input stream of bytes into primitive data type values and strings.*

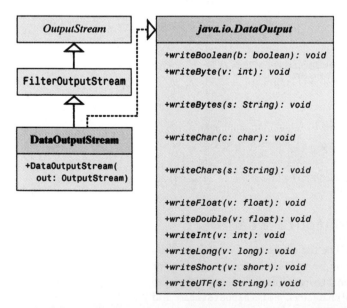

FIGURE 16.16 *`DataOutputStream` enables you to write primitive data type values and strings into an output stream.*

16.6.3.1 Characters and Strings in Binary I/O

A Unicode consists of two bytes. The `writeChar(char c)` method writes the Unicode of character `c` to the output. The `writeChars(String s)` method writes the Unicode for each character in the string `s` to the output. The `writeBytes(String s)` method writes the lower byte of the Unicode for each character in the string `s` to the output. The high byte of the Unicode is discarded. The `writeBytes` method is suitable for strings that consist of ASCII characters, since an ASCII code is stored only in the lower byte of a Unicode. If a string consists of non-ASCII characters, you have to use the `writeChars` method to write the string.

UTF is a coding scheme that allows systems to operate efficiently with both ASCII and Unicode. Most operating systems use ASCII. Java uses Unicode. The ASCII character set is a subset of the Unicode character set. Since most applications need only the ASCII character set, it is a waste to represent an 8-bit ASCII character as a 16-bit Unicode character. The UTF scheme stores a character using one, two, or three bytes. ASCII values less than 0x7F are coded in one byte. Unicode values less than 0x7FF are coded in two bytes. Other Unicode values are coded in three bytes.

The initial bits of a UTF character indicate whether a character is stored in one byte, two bytes, or three bytes. If the first bit is 0, it is a one-byte character. If the first bits are 110, it is the first byte of a two-byte sequence. If the first bits are 1110, it is the first byte of a three-byte sequence. The information that indicates the number of characters in a string is stored in the first two bytes preceding the UTF characters. For example, `writeUTF("ABCDEF")` actually writes eight bytes to the file because the first two bytes store the number of characters in the string.

The `writeUTF(String s)` method converts a string into a series of bytes in the UTF format and writes them into a binary stream. The `readUTF()` method reads a string that has been written using the `writeUTF` method.

The UTF format has the advantage of saving a byte for each ASCII character, because a Unicode character takes up two bytes and an ASCII character in UTF takes up only one byte. If most characters in a string are regular ASCII characters, using UTF is more efficient.

16.6.3.2 Using `DataInputStream`/`DataOutputStream`

Data streams are used as wrappers on existing input and output streams to filter data in the original stream. They are created using the following constructors:

```
public DataInputStream(InputStream instream)
public DataOutputStream(OutputStream outstream)
```

The statements given below create data streams. The first statement creates an input stream for file **in.dat**; the second statement creates an output stream for file **out.dat**:

```
DataInputStream infile =
  new DataInputStream(new FileInputStream("in.dat"));
DataOutputStream outfile =
  new DataOutputStream(new FileOutputStream("out.dat"));
```

Listing 16.8 writes student names and scores to a file named `temp.dat` and reads the data back from the file.

LISTING 16.8 **TestDataStream.java (Binary I/O of Data and Strings)**

```
1 import java.io.*;
2
3 public class TestDataStream {
4   public static void main(String[] args) throws IOException {
5     // Create an output stream for file temp.dat
6     DataOutputStream output =
7       new DataOutputStream(new FileOutputStream("temp.dat"));
```

output stream

```
 8
 9      // Write student test scores to the file
10      output.writeUTF("John");
11      output.writeDouble(85.5);
12      output.writeUTF("Jim");
13      output.writeDouble(185.5);
14      output.writeUTF("George");
15      output.writeDouble(105.25);
16
17      // Close output stream
18      output.close();
19
20      // Create an input stream for file temp.dat
21      DataInputStream input =
22        new DataInputStream(new FileInputStream("temp.dat"));
23
24      // Read student test scores from the file
25      System.out.println(input.readUTF() + " " + input.readDouble());
26      System.out.println(input.readUTF() + " " + input.readDouble());
27      System.out.println(input.readUTF() + " " + input.readDouble());
28    }
29  }
```

output

close stream

input stream

input

A `DataOutputStream` is created for file temp.dat in Lines 6–7. Student names and scores are written to the file in Lines 10–15. Line 18 closes the output stream. A `DataInputStream` is created for the same file in Lines 21–22. Student names and scores are read back from the file and displayed on the console in Lines 25–27.

`DataInputStream` and `DataOutputStream` read and write Java primitive type values and strings in a machine-independent fashion, thereby enabling you to write a data file on one machine and read it on another machine that has a different operating system or file structure. An application uses a data output stream to write data that can later be read by a program using a data input stream.

 CAUTION

You have been reading data in the same order and format in which they are stored. For example, since names are written in UTF using `writeUTF`, you must read names using `readUTF`.

 TIP

If you keep reading data at the end of a `DataInputStream`, an `EOFException` will occur. How, then, do you check the end of a file? Use `input.available()` to check it. `input.available() == 0` indicates the end of a file.

16.6.4 `BufferedInputStream/BufferedOutputStream`

`BufferedInputStream/BufferedOutputStream` can be used to speed up input and output by reducing the number of reads and writes, just like `BufferedReader/BufferedWriter`. `BufferedReader/BufferedWriter` is for reading/writing characters, and `BufferedInputStream/BufferedOutputStream` is for bytes.

`BufferedInputStream/BufferedOutputStream` does not contain new methods. All the methods in `BufferedInputStream/BufferedOutputStream` are inherited from the `InputStream/OutputStream` classes. `BufferedInputStream/BufferedOutputStream` adds a buffer in the stream for storing bytes for efficient processing.

You may wrap a `BufferedInputStream/BufferedOutputStream` on any `InputStream/OutputStream` using the following constructors:

```
// Create a BufferedInputStream
public BufferedInputStream(InputStream in)
public BufferedInputStream(InputStream in, int bufferSize)
```

```
// Create a BufferedOutputStream
public BufferedOutputStream(OutputStream out)
public BufferedOutputStream(OutputStream out, int bufferSize)
```

If no buffer size is specified, the default size is 512 bytes. A buffered input stream reads as many data as possible into its buffer in a single read call. By contrast, a buffered output stream calls the write method only when its buffer fills up or when the `flush()` method is called.

You can improve the performance of the `TestDataStream` program in the preceding example by adding buffers in the stream in Lines 6–7 and 21–22 as follows:

```
DataOutputStream output = new DataOutputStream(
  new BufferedOutputStream(new FileOutputStream("temp.dat")));
```

```
DataInputStream input = new DataInputStream(
  new BufferedInputStream(new FileInputStream("temp.dat")));
```

16.7   Case Study: Copying Files

This case study develops a program that copies files. The user needs to provide a source file and a target file as command-line arguments using the following command:

`java Copy source target`

The program copies a source file to a target file and displays the number of bytes in the file. If the source does not exist, tell the user that the file has not been found. If the target file already exists, tell the user that the file exists. A sample run of the program is shown in Figure 16.17.

FIGURE 16.17   *The program copies a file.*

To copy the contents from a source to a target file, it is appropriate to use a binary input stream to read bytes from the source file and a binary output stream to send bytes to the target file, regardless of the contents of the file. The source file and the target file are specified from the command line. Create an `InputFileStream` for the source file and an `OutputFileStream` for the target file. Use the `read()` method to read a byte from the input stream, and then use the `write(b)` method to write the byte to the output stream. Use `BufferedInputStream` and `BufferedOutputStream` to improve the performance. Listing 16.9 gives the solution to the problem.

LISTING 16.9   Copy.java (Copy a File)

```
1  import java.io.*;
2
3  public class Copy {
4    /** Main method
5        @param args[0] for sourcefile
6        @param args[1] for target file
7    */
8    public static void main(String[] args) throws IOException {
9      // Check command-line parameter usage
10     if (args.length != 2) {
11       System.out.println(
12         "Usage: java CopyFile sourceFile targetfile");
13       System.exit(0);
14     }
15
16     // Check if source file exists
17     File sourceFile = new File(args[0]);
18     if (!sourceFile.exists()) {
19       System.out.println("Source file " + args[0] + " not exist");
20       System.exit(0);
21     }
22
23     // Check if target file exists
24     File targetFile = new File(args[1]);
25     if (targetFile.exists()) {
26       System.out.println("Target file " + args[1] + " already exists");
27       System.exit(0);
28     }
29
30     // Create an input stream
31     BufferedInputStream input =
32       new BufferedInputStream(new FileInputStream(sourceFile));
33
34     // Create an output stream
35     BufferedOutputStream output =
36       new BufferedOutputStream(new FileOutputStream(targetFile));
37
38     // Display the file size
39     System.out.println("The file " + args[0] + " has "+
40       input.available() + " bytes");
41
42     // Continuously read a byte from input and write it to output
43     int r;
44     while ((r = input.read()) != -1)
45       output.write((byte)r);
46
47     // Close streams
48     input.close();
49     output.close();
50
51     System.out.println("Copy done!");
52   }
53 }
```

check usage *(Line 10)*

source file *(Line 17)*

target file *(Line 24)*

input stream *(Lines 31–32)*

output stream *(Lines 35–36)*

read *(Line 44)*
write *(Line 45)*

close stream *(Lines 47–49)*

✦ The program first checks whether the user has passed two required arguments from the command line in Lines 10–14.

✦ The program uses the File class to check whether the source file and target file exist. If the source file does not exist (Lines 18–21) or if the target file already exists, exit the program.

✦ An input stream is created using BufferedInputStream wrapped on FileInputStream in Lines 31–32, and an output stream is created using BufferedOutputStream wrapped on FileOutputStream in Lines 35–36.

✦ The available() method (Line 40) defined in the InputStream class returns the number of bytes remaining in the input stream.

✦ The expression ((r = input.read()) != -1) (Line 44) reads a byte from input.read(), assigns it to r, and checks whether it is −1. The input value of −1 signifies the end of a file. The program continuously reads bytes from the input stream and sends them to the output stream until all of the bytes have been read.

16.8 More on Text Files and Binary Files

Now it is time to tell the whole story and set the record straight. Computers do not differentiate binary files and text files. All files are stored in binary format, and thus all files are essentially binary files. Text I/O is built upon binary I/O to provide a level of abstraction for character encoding and decoding. Encoding and decoding are automatically performed by text I/O. In general, you should use text input to read a file created by a text editor or a text output program, and use binary input to read a file created by a Java binary output program. For binary input, you need to know exactly how data were written in order to read them in correct type and order. Binary I/O also contains methods to read and write strings.

The example below shows how to write 199 as a numeric value to the file out.dat and read it back from the same file:

```
1 import java.io.*;
2
3 public class Test {
4   public static void main(String[] args) throws IOException {
5     FileOutputStream output = new FileOutputStream("out.dat");        binary stream
6     output.write(199); // Output byte 199 to the stream
7     output.close();
8
9     FileInputStream input = new FileInputStream("out.dat");
10    System.out.println(input.read()); // Read and display a byte
11    input.close();
12  }
13 }
```

The next example shows how to write 199 as three characters to the file **out.txt** and read it back from the same file:

```
1 import java.io.*;
2
3 public class Test {
4   public static void main(String[] args) throws IOException {
5     FileWriter output = new FileWriter("out.txt");                    text stream
6     output.write("199"); // Output string "199" to the stream
7     output.close();
8
9     // Read and display three characters
10    FileReader input = new FileReader("out.txt");
11    System.out.print((char)input.read());
12    System.out.print((char)input.read());
13    System.out.println((char)input.read());
14    input.close();
15  }
16 }
```

When you write a byte to a byte stream, the exact byte value is sent to the output, as shown in Figure 16.18(a). When you write a character to a character stream, the character is converted to a numeric representation of the character using an encoding scheme. If you don't specify an encoding scheme, the default encoding scheme of the machine is used. In the United States, the default encoding for Windows is ASCII. The ASCII code for character 1 is 49 (31 in hex) and for character 9 is 57 (39 in hex). So to write the characters 199, three bytes, 49, 57, and 57, are sent to the output, as shown in Figure 16.18(b).

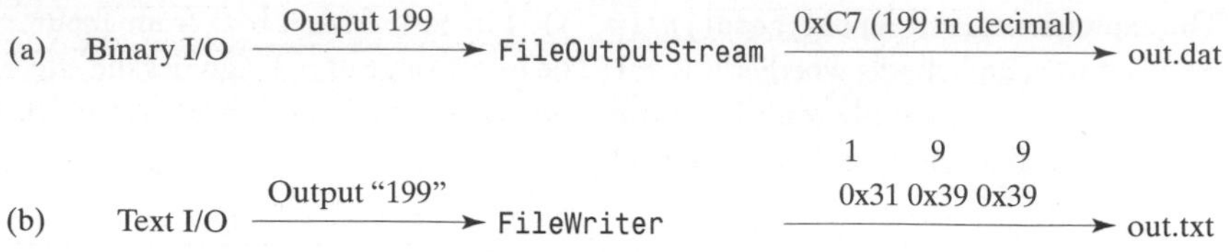

(a) Binary I/O $\xrightarrow{\text{Output 199}}$ FileOutputStream $\xrightarrow{\text{0xC7 (199 in decimal)}}$ out.dat

(b) Text I/O $\xrightarrow{\text{Output "199"}}$ FileWriter $\xrightarrow[\text{0x31 0x39 0x39}]{1 \quad 9 \quad 9}$ out.txt

FIGURE 16.18 *Binary I/O outputs the exact value, and text I/O outputs the encoding of the characters.*

When you read a byte from a byte stream, one byte value is read from the input. When you read a character from a character stream, how many bytes are read is dependent on the encoding system. On an ASCII system, one byte is read and promoted to a Unicode character. On a Unicode system, two bytes are read to form a Unicode.

✿ CAUTION

ASCII code uses 8 bits. Java uses the 16-bit Unicode. If a Unicode cannot be converted to an ASCII code, the character '?' is used. For example, if you attempt to write Unicode '\u03b1' to a character stream, the numeric value 63 (representing character '?') would be sent to the stream. Text files are dependent on the encoding used by the host machine. Moving a text file from one computer to another may cause problems if the computers use different encodings.

16.9 Object I/O (Optional)

`DataInputStream/DataOutputStream` enables you to perform I/O for primitive type values and strings. `ObjectInputStream/ObjectOutputStream` enables you to perform I/O for objects in addition to primitive type values and strings. Since `ObjectInputStream/ObjectOutputStream` contains all the functions of `DataInputStream/DataOutputStream`, you can replace `DataInputStream/DataOutputStream` completely with `ObjectInputStream/ObjectOutputStream`.

`ObjectInputStream` extends `InputStream` and implements `ObjectInput` and `ObjectStreamConstants`, as shown in Figure 16.19. `ObjectInput` is a subinterface of `DataInput`. `DataInput` is shown in Figure 16.15. `ObjectStreamConstants` contains the constants to support `ObjectInputStream/ObjectOutputStream`.

`ObjectOutputStream` extends `OutputStream` and implements `ObjectOutput` and `ObjectStreamConstants`, as shown in Figure 16.20. `ObjectOutput` is a subinterface of `DataOutput`. `DataOutput` is shown in Figure 16.16.

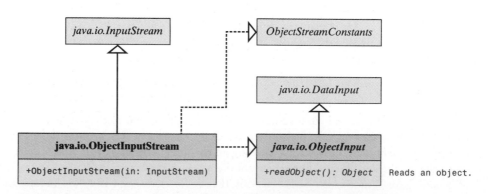

FIGURE 16.19 *ObjectInputStream can read objects, primitive type values, and strings.*

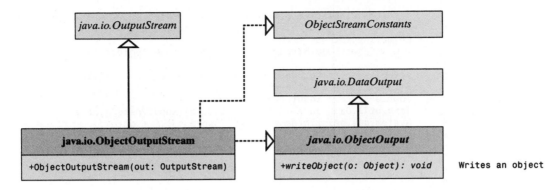

FIGURE 16.20 *ObjectOutputStream can write objects, primitive type values, and strings.*

You may wrap an ObjectInputStream/ObjectOutputStream on any InputStream/OutputStream using the following constructors:

```
// Create an ObjectInputStream
public ObjectInputStream(InputStream in)

// Create an ObjectOutputStream
public ObjectOutputStream(OutputStream out)
```

Listing 16.10 writes student names, scores, and current date to a file named object.dat.

LISTING 16.10 TestObjectOutputStream.java (Object Output)

```
 1 import java.io.*;
 2
 3 public class TestObjectOutputStream {
 4   public static void main(String[] args) throws IOException {
 5     // Create an output stream for file object.dat
 6     ObjectOutputStream output =
 7       new ObjectOutputStream(new FileOutputStream("object.dat"));
 8
 9     // Write a string, double value, and object to the file
10     output.writeUTF("John");
11     output.writeDouble(85.5);
12     output.writeObject(new java.util.Date());
13
14     // Close output stream
15     output.close();
16   }
17 }
```

output stream

output

An ObjectOutputStream is created to write data into file object.dat in Lines 6–7. A string, a double value, and an object are written to the file in Lines 10–12. To improve performance, you may add a buffer in the stream using the following statement to replace Lines 6–7:

```
ObjectOutputStream output = new ObjectOutputStream(
  new BufferedOutputStream(new FileOutputStream("object.dat")));
```

Multiple objects or primitives can be written to the stream. The objects must be read back from the corresponding ObjectInputStream with the same types and in the same order as they were written. Java's safe casting should be used to get the desired type. Listing 16.11 reads data back from object.dat.

LISTING 16.11 TestObjectInputStream.java (Object Input)

```
1 import java.io.*;
2
3 public class TestObjectInputStream {
4   public static void main(String[] args)
```

```
 5          throws ClassNotFoundException, IOException {
 6      // Create an input stream for file object.dat
 7      ObjectInputStream input =
 8        new ObjectInputStream(new FileInputStream("object.dat"));
 9
10      // Write a string, double value, and object to the file
11      String name = input.readUTF();
12      double score = input.readDouble();
13      java.util.Date date = (java.util.Date)(input.readObject());
14      System.out.println(name + " " + score + " " + date);
15
16      // Close output stream
17      input.close();
18    }
19 }
```

input stream appears beside lines 7–8.
input appears beside lines 11–14.

ClassNotFoundException (margin note)

The `readObject()` method may throw `java.lang.ClassNotFoundException`. The reason is that when the JVM restores an object, it first loads the class for the object if the class has not been loaded. Since `ClassNotFoundException` is a checked exception, the `main` method declares to throw it in Line 5. An `ObjectInputStream` is created to read input from object.dat in Lines 7–8. You have to read the data from the file in the same order and format as they were written to the file. A string, a double value, and an object are read in Lines 11–13. Since `readObject()` returns an `Object`, it is cast into `Date` and assigned to a `Date` variable in Line 13.

16.9.1 The `Serializable` Interface

serializable (margin note)

Not every object can be written to an output stream. Objects that can be written to an object stream are said to be *serializable*. A serializable object is an instance of the `java.io.Serializable` interface, so the class of a serializable object must implement `Serializable`.

The `Serializable` interface is a marker interface. Since it has no methods, you don't need to add additional code in your class that implements `Serializable`. Implementing this interface enables the Java serialization mechanism to automate the process of storing objects and arrays.

To appreciate this automation feature and understand how an object is stored, consider what you need to do in order to store an object without using this feature. Suppose you want to store a `JButton` object. To do this you need to store all the current values of the properties (e.g., color, font, text, alignment) in the object. Since `JButton` is a subclass of `AbstractButton`, the property values of `AbstractButton` have to be stored as well as the properties of all the superclasses of `AbstractButton`. If a property is of an object type (e.g., `background` of the `Color` type), storing it requires storing all the property values inside this object. As you can see, this is a very tedious process.

serialization (margin note)

Fortunately, you don't have to go through it manually. Java provides a built-in mechanism to automate the process of writing objects. This process is referred to as *object serialization*, which is implemented in `ObjectOutputStream`. In contrast, the process of reading objects is referred to as *object deserialization*, which is implemented in `ObjectInputStream`.

deserialization (margin note)

NotSerializable-Exception (margin note)

Many classes in the Java API implement `Serializable`. The utility classes, such as `java.util.Date`, and all the Swing GUI component classes implement `Serializable`. Attempting to store an object that does not support the `Serializable` interface would cause a `NotSerializableException`.

When a serializable object is stored, the class of the object is encoded; this includes the class name and the signature of the class, the values of the object's instance variables, and the closure of any other objects referenced from the initial object. The values of the object's static variables are not stored.

---

nonserializable fields (margin note)

🌿 **NOTE**

If an object is an instance of `Serializable` but contains nonserializable instance data fields, can it be serialized? The answer is no. To enable the object to be serialized, mark these data fields with the `transient` keyword to tell the JVM to ignore them when writing the object to an object stream. Consider the following class:

transient

```
public class Foo implements java.io.Serializable {
  private int v1;
  private static double v2;
  private transient A v3 = new A();
}

class A { } // A is not serializable
```

When an object of the `Foo` class is serialized, only variable `v1` is serialized. Variable `v2` is not serialized because it is a static variable, and variable `v3` is not serialized because it is marked `transient`. If `v3` were not marked `transient`, a `java.io.NotSerializableException` would occur.

 NOTE

If an object is written to an object stream more than once, will it be stored in multiple copies? The answer is no. When an object is written for the first time, a serial number is created for it. The JVM writes the complete content of the object along with the serial number into the object stream. After the first time, only the serial number is stored if the same object is written again. When the objects are read back, their references are the same, since only one object is actually created in memory.

duplicate objects

16.9.2 Serializing Arrays

An array is serializable if all its elements are serializable. An entire array can be saved using `writeObject` into a file and later can be restored using `readObject`. Listing 16.12 stores an array of five `int` values, an array of three strings, and an array of two `JButton` objects, and reads them back to display on the console.

LISTING 16.12 **TestObjectStreamForArray.java (Array Object I/O)**

```
 1 import java.io.*;
 2 import javax.swing.*;
 3
 4 public class TestObjectStreamForArray {
 5   public static void main(String[] args)
 6       throws ClassNotFoundException, IOException {
 7     int[] numbers = {1, 2, 3, 4, 5};
 8     String[] strings = {"John", "Jim", "Jake"};
 9     JButton[] buttons = {new JButton("OK"), new JButton("Cancel")};
10
11     // Create an output stream for file array.dat
12     ObjectOutputStream output =
13       new ObjectOutputStream(new FileOutputStream("array.dat", true));
14
15     // Write arrays to the object output stream
16     output.writeObject(numbers);
17     output.writeObject(strings);
18     output.writeObject(buttons);
19
20     // Close the stream
21     output.close();
22
23     // Create an input stream for file array.dat
24     ObjectInputStream input =
25       new ObjectInputStream(new FileInputStream("array.dat"));
```

output stream

store array

input stream

restore array

```
26
27    int[] newNumbers = (int[])(input.readObject());
28    String[] newStrings = (String[])(input.readObject());
29    JButton[] newButtons = (JButton[])(input.readObject());
30
31    // Display arrays
32    for (int i = 0; i < newNumbers.length; i++)
33      System.out.print(newNumbers[i] + " ");
34    System.out.println();
35
36    for (int i = 0; i < newStrings.length; i++)
37      System.out.print(newStrings[i] + " ");
38    System.out.println();
39
40    for (int i = 0; i < newButtons.length; i++)
41      System.out.print(newButtons[i].getText() + " ");
42  }
43 }
```

Lines 16–18 write three arrays into file array.dat. Lines 27–29 read three arrays back in the same order they were written. Since readObject() returns Object, casting is used to cast the objects into int[], String[], and JButton[].

16.10 Random Access Files (Optional)

read-only
write-only
sequential

All of the streams you have used so far are known as *read-only* or *write-only* streams. The external files of these streams are *sequential* files that cannot be updated without creating a new file. It is often necessary to modify files or to insert new records into files. Java provides the RandomAccessFile class to allow a file to be read from and written to at random locations.

The RandomAccessFile class implements the DataInput and DataOutput interfaces, as shown in Figure 16.21. The DataInput interface shown in Figure 16.15 defines the methods (e.g., readInt, readDouble, readChar, readBoolean, readUTF) for reading primitive type values and strings, and the DataOutput interface shown in Figure 16.16 defines the methods (e.g., writeInt, writeDouble, writeChar, writeBoolean, writeUTF) for writing primitive type values and strings.

When creating a RandomAccessFile, you can specify one of two modes ("r" or "rw"). Mode "r" means that the stream is read-only, and mode "rw" indicates that the stream allows both read and write. For example, the following statement creates a new stream, raf, that allows the program to read from and write to the file **test.dat**:

```
RandomAccessFile raf = new RandomAccessFile("test.dat", "rw");
```

If **test.dat** already exists, raf is created to access it; if **test.dat** does not exist, a new file named **test.dat** is created, and raf is created to access the new file. The method raf.length() returns the number of bytes in **test.dat** at any given time. If you append new data into the file, raf.length() increases.

🌱 **TIP**

Open the file with the "r" mode if the file is not intended to be modified. This prevents unintentional modification of the file.

---

file pointer

A random access file consists of a sequence of bytes. There is a special marker called *file pointer* positioned at one of these bytes. A read or write operation takes place at the location of the file pointer. When a file is opened, the file pointer is set at the beginning of the file. When you read or write data to the file, the file pointer moves forward to the next data item. For example, if you read an int value using readInt(), the JVM reads four bytes from the file pointer and now the file pointer is four bytes ahead of the previous location, as shown in Figure 16.22.

For a RandomAccessFile raf, you can use raf.seek(position) method to move the file pointer to a specified position. raf.seek(0) moves it to the beginning of the file, and raf.seek(raf.length()) moves it to the end of the file. Listing 16.13 demonstrates RandomAccessFile.

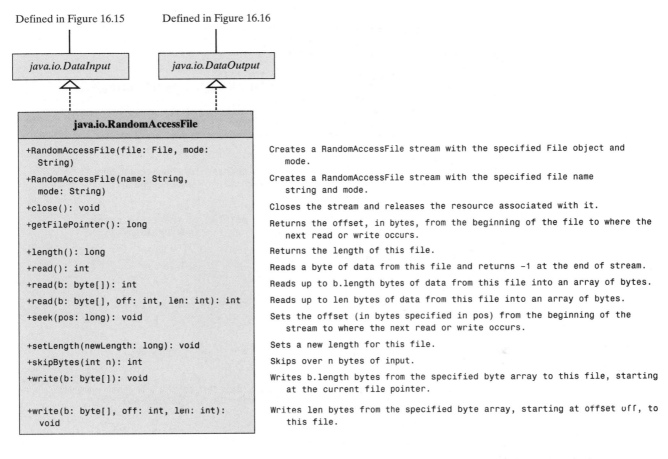

FIGURE **16.21**   *RandomAccessFile implements the* DataInput *and* DataOutput *interfaces with additional methods to support random access.*

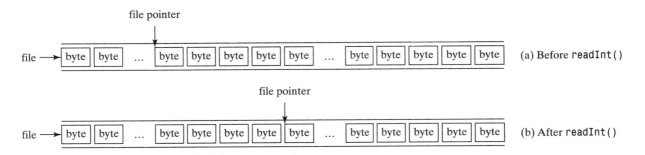

FIGURE **16.22**   *After reading an* int *value, the file pointer is moved four bytes ahead.*

LISTING 16.13   TestRandomAccessFile.java (Random Access of File)

```
1 import java.io.*;
2
3 public class TestRandomAccessFile {
4   public static void main(String[] args) throws IOException {
5     // Create a random access file
6     RandomAccessFile inout = new RandomAccessFile("inout.dat", "rw");
7
8     // Clear the file to destroy the old contents if exists
9     inout.setLength(0);
```

RandomAccessFile

empty file

write

move pointer
read

close file

```
10
11      // Write new integers to the file
12      for (int i = 0; i < 200; i++)
13        inout.writeInt(i);
14
15      // Display the current length of the file
16      System.out.println("Current file length is " + inout.length());
17
18      // Retrieve the first number
19      inout.seek(0); // Move the file pointer to the beginning
20      System.out.println("The first number is " + inout.readInt());
21
22      // Retrieve the second number
23      inout.seek(1 * 4); // Move the file pointer to the second number
24      System.out.println("The second number is " + inout.readInt());
25
26      // Retrieve the tenth number
27      inout.seek(9 * 4); // Move the file pointer to the tenth number
28      System.out.println("The tenth number is " + inout.readInt());
29
30      // Modify the eleventh number
31      inout.writeInt(555);
32
33      // Append a new number
34      inout.seek(inout.length()); // Move the file pointer to the end
35      inout.writeInt(999);
36
37      // Display the new length
38      System.out.println("The new length is " + inout.length());
39
40      // Retrieve the new eleventh number
41      inout.seek(10 * 4); // Move the file pointer to the eleventh number
42      System.out.println("The eleventh number is " + inout.readInt());
43
44      inout.close();
45    }
46  }
```

◆ A `RandomAccessFile` is created for the file named inout.dat with mode `"rw"` to allow both read and write operations in Line 6.

◆ `inout.setLength(0)` sets the length to 0 in Line 9. This, in effect, destroys the old contents of the file.

◆ The `for` loop writes 200 `int` values from 0 to 199 into the file in Lines 12–13. Since each `int` value takes four bytes, the total length of the file returned from `inout.length()` is now 800 (Line 16), as shown in Figure 16.23.

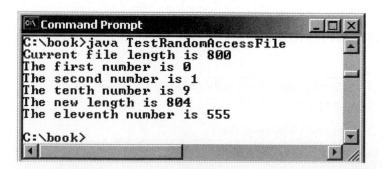

FIGURE **16.23** *TestRandomAccessFile manipulates a RandomAccessFile.*

✦ Invoking `inout.seek(0)` in Line 19 sets the file pointer to the beginning of the file. `inout.readInt()` reads the first value in Line 20 and moves the file pointer to the next number. The second number is read in Line 23.

✦ `inout.seek(9 * 4)` (Line 26) moves the file pointer to the tenth number. `inout.readInt()` reads the tenth number and moves the file pointer to the eleventh number in Line 27. `inout.write(555)` writes a new eleventh number at the current position (Line 31). The previous eleventh number is destroyed.

✦ `inout.seek(inout.length())` moves the file pointer to the end of the file (Line 34). `inout.writeInt(999)` writes a 999 to the file. Now the length of the file is increased by 4, so `inout.length()` returns 804 (Line 38).

✦ `inout.seek(10 * 4)` moves the file pointer to the eleventh number in Line 41. The new eleventh number, 555, is displayed in Line 42.

✦ 16.11 Case Study: Address Book (Optional)

Now let us use `RandomAccessFile` to create a useful project for storing and viewing an address book. The user interface of the program is shown in Figure 16.24. The *Add* button stores a new address at the end of the file. The *First*, *Next*, *Previous*, and *Last* buttons retrieve the first, next, previous, and last addresses from the file, respectively.

Random access files are often used to process files of records. For convenience, *fixed-length records*   fixed-length record
are used in random access files so that a record can be located easily, as shown in Figure 16.25. A record consists of a fixed number of fields. A field can be a string or a primitive data type. A string in a fixed-length record has a maximum size. If a string is smaller than the maximum size, the rest of the string is padded with blanks.

Let **address.dat** be the file to store addresses. A `RandomAccessFile` for both read and write can be created using

```
RandomAccessFile raf = new RandomAccessFile("address.dat", "rw");
```

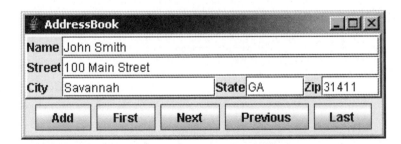

FIGURE 16.24 *AddressBook stores and retrieves addresses from a file.*

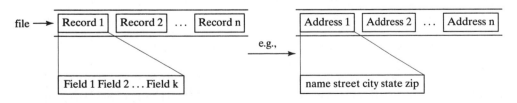

FIGURE 16.25 *Random access files are often used to process files of fixed-length records.*

Let each address consist of a name (32 characters), street (32 characters), city (20 characters), state (2 characters), and zip (5 characters). If the actual size of a field (e.g., name) is less than the fixed maximum size, fill it in with blank characters. If the actual size of a field is greater than the fixed maximum size, truncate the string. Thus the total size of an address is $32 + 32 + 20 + 2 + 5 = 91$ characters. Since each character occupies two bytes, one address takes $2 * 91 = 182$ bytes. After an address record is read, the file pointer is 182 bytes ahead of the previous file pointer.

For convenience, Listing 16.14 contains two methods for reading and writing a fixed-length string.

LISTING 16.14 FixedLengthStringIO.java (Fixed-Length String Binary I/O)

```
1 import java.io.*;
2
3 public class FixedLengthStringIO {
4   /** Read fixed number of characters from a DataInput stream */
5   public static String readFixedLengthString(int size,
6       DataInput in) throws IOException {
7     // Declare an array of characters
8     char[] chars = new char[size];
9
10    // Read fixed number of characters to the array
11    for (int i = 0; i < size; i++)
12      chars[i] = in.readChar();
13
14    return new String(chars);
15  }
16
17  /** Write fixed number of characters to a DataOutput stream */
18  public static void writeFixedLengthString(String s, int size,
19      DataOutput out) throws IOException {
20    char[] chars = new char[size];
21
22    // Fill in string with characters
23    s.getChars(0, s.length(), chars, 0);
24
25    // Fill in blank characters in the rest of the array
26    for (int i = Math.min(s.length(), size); i < chars.length; i++)
27      chars[i] = ' ';
28
29    // Create and write a new string padded with blank characters
30    out.writeChars(new String(chars));
31  }
32 }
```

read characters

fill string

fill blank

write string

The writeFixedLengthString(String s, int size, DataOutput out) method writes a string in a fixed size to a DataOutput stream. If the string is longer than the specified size, it is truncated; if it is shorter than the specified size, blanks are padded into it (Lines 26–27). In any case, a new fixed-length string is written to a specified output stream. Since RandomAccessFile implements DataOutput, this method can be used to write a string to a RandomAccessFile. For example, invoking writeFixedLengthString("John", 2, raf) actually writes "Jo" to the RandomAccessFile raf, since the size is 2. Invoking writeFixedLengthString("John", 6, raf) actually writes "John " to the RandomAccessFile raf, since the size is 6.

The readFixedLengthString(int size, InputOutput in) method reads a fixed number of characters from an InputStream and returns as a string. Since RandomAccessFile implements InputOutput, this method can be used to read a string from a writeFixedLengthString(String s, int size, DataOutput out).

The rest of the work can be summarized in the following steps:

1. Create the user interface.

2. Add a record to the file.

3. Read a record from the file.

4. Write the code to implement the button actions.

The program is shown in Listing 16.15.

LISTING 16.15 AddressBook.java (Write/View Address)

```
 1 import java.io.*;
 2 import java.awt.*;
 3 import java.awt.event.*;
 4 import javax.swing.*;
 5 import javax.swing.border.*;
 6
 7 public class AddressBook extends JFrame implements ActionListener {
 8   // Specify the size of five string fields in the record
 9   final static int NAME_SIZE = 32;                                          constant
10   final static int STREET_SIZE = 32;
11   final static int CITY_SIZE = 20;
12   final static int STATE_SIZE = 2;
13   final static int ZIP_SIZE = 5;
14   final static int RECORD_SIZE =
15     (NAME_SIZE + STREET_SIZE + CITY_SIZE + STATE_SIZE + ZIP_SIZE);
16
17   // Access address.dat using RandomAccessFile
18   private RandomAccessFile raf;                                             raf
19
20   // Text fields
21   private JTextField jtfName = new JTextField(NAME_SIZE);                   GUI component
22   private JTextField jtfStreet = new JTextField(STREET_SIZE);
23   private JTextField jtfCity = new JTextField(CITY_SIZE);
24   private JTextField jtfState = new JTextField(ZIP_SIZE);
25   private JTextField jtfZip = new JTextField(ZIP_SIZE);
26
27   // Buttons
28   private JButton jbtAdd = new JButton("Add");
29   private JButton jbtFirst = new JButton("First");
30   private JButton jbtNext = new JButton("Next");
31   private JButton jbtPrevious = new JButton("Previous");
32   private JButton jbtLast = new JButton("Last");
33
34   public AddressBook() {
35     // Open or create a random access file
36     try {
37       raf = new RandomAccessFile("address.dat", "rw");                      open file
38     }
39     catch(IOException ex) {
40       System.out.print("Error: " + ex);
41       System.exit(0);
42     }
43
44     // Panel p1 for holding labels Name, Street, and City
45     JPanel p1 = new JPanel();                                               create UI
46     p1.setLayout(new GridLayout(3, 1));
47     p1.add(new JLabel("Name"));
48     p1.add(new JLabel("Street"));
49     p1.add(new JLabel("City"));
50
51     // Panel jpState for holding state
52     JPanel jpState = new JPanel();
53     jpState.setLayout(new BorderLayout());
54     jpState.add(new JLabel("State"), BorderLayout.WEST);
55     jpState.add(jtfState, BorderLayout.CENTER);
```

```
56
57      // Panel jpZip for holding zip
58      JPanel jpZip = new JPanel();
59      jpZip.setLayout(new BorderLayout());
60      jpZip.add(new JLabel("Zip"), BorderLayout.WEST);
61      jpZip.add(jtfZip, BorderLayout.CENTER);
62
63      // Panel p2 for holding jpState and jpZip
64      JPanel p2 = new JPanel();
65      p2.setLayout(new BorderLayout());
66      p2.add(jpState, BorderLayout.WEST);
67      p2.add(jpZip, BorderLayout.CENTER);
68
69      // Panel p3 for holding jtfCity and p2
70      JPanel p3 = new JPanel();
71      p3.setLayout(new BorderLayout());
72      p3.add(jtfCity, BorderLayout.CENTER);
73      p3.add(p2, BorderLayout.EAST);
74
75      // Panel p4 for holding jtfName, jtfStreet, and p3
76      JPanel p4 = new JPanel();
77      p4.setLayout(new GridLayout(3, 1));
78      p4.add(jtfName);
79      p4.add(jtfStreet);
80      p4.add(p3);
81
82      // Place p1 and p4 into jpAddress
83      JPanel jpAddress = new JPanel(new BorderLayout());
84      jpAddress.add(p1, BorderLayout.WEST);
85      jpAddress.add(p4, BorderLayout.CENTER);
86
87      // Set the panel with line border
88      jpAddress.setBorder(new BevelBorder(BevelBorder.RAISED));
89
90      // Add buttons to a panel
91      JPanel jpButton = new JPanel();
92      jpButton.add(jbtAdd);
93      jpButton.add(jbtFirst);
94      jpButton.add(jbtNext);
95      jpButton.add(jbtPrevious);
96      jpButton.add(jbtLast);
97
98      // Add jpAddress and jpButton to the frame
99      getContentPane().add(jpAddress, BorderLayout.CENTER);
100     getContentPane().add(jpButton, BorderLayout.SOUTH);
101
102     jbtAdd.addActionListener(this);
103     jbtFirst.addActionListener(this);
104     jbtNext.addActionListener(this);
105     jbtPrevious.addActionListener(this);
106     jbtLast.addActionListener(this);
107
108     // Display the first record if it exists
109     try {
110       if (raf.length() > 0) readAddress(0);
111     }
112     catch (IOException ex) {
113       ex.printStackTrace();
114     }
115   }
116
117   /** Write a record at the end of the file */
118   public void writeAddress() throws IOException {
119     raf.seek(raf.length());
120     FixedLengthStringIO.writeFixedLengthString(
121       jtfName.getText(), NAME_SIZE, raf);
122     FixedLengthStringIO.writeFixedLengthString(
123       jtfStreet.getText(), STREET_SIZE, raf);
124     FixedLengthStringIO.writeFixedLengthString(
125       jtfCity.getText(), CITY_SIZE, raf);
```

register listener

first record

```
126     FixedLengthStringIO.writeFixedLengthString(
127       jtfState.getText(), STATE_SIZE, raf);
128     FixedLengthStringIO.writeFixedLengthString(
129       jtfZip.getText(), ZIP_SIZE, raf);
130   }
131
132   /** Read a record at the specified position */
133   public void readAddress(long position) throws IOException {
134     raf.seek(position);
135     String name = FixedLengthStringIO.readFixedLengthString(
136       NAME_SIZE, raf);
137     String street = FixedLengthStringIO.readFixedLengthString(
138       STREET_SIZE, raf);
139     String city = FixedLengthStringIO.readFixedLengthString(
140       CITY_SIZE, raf);
141     String state = FixedLengthStringIO.readFixedLengthString(
142       STATE_SIZE, raf);
143     String zip = FixedLengthStringIO.readFixedLengthString(
144       ZIP_SIZE, raf);
145
146     jtfName.setText(name);
147     jtfStreet.setText(street);
148     jtfCity.setText(city);
149     jtfState.setText(state);
150     jtfZip.setText(zip);
151   }
152
153   /** Handle button actions */
154   public void actionPerformed(ActionEvent e) {
155     try {
156       if (e.getSource() == jbtAdd) {                                  add address
157         writeAddress();
158       }
159       else if (e.getSource() == jbtFirst) {                          first address
160         if (raf.length() > 0) readAddress(0);
161       }
162       else if (e.getSource() == jbtNext) {                           next address
163         long currentPosition = raf.getFilePointer();
164         if (currentPosition < raf.length())
165           readAddress(currentPosition);
166       }
167       else if (e.getSource() == jbtPrevious) {                       previous address
168         long currentPosition = raf.getFilePointer();
169         if (currentPosition - 2 * RECORD_SIZE > 0)
170           // Why 2 * 2 * RECORD_SIZE? See the follow-up remarks
171           readAddress(currentPosition - 2 * 2 * RECORD_SIZE);
172         else
173           readAddress(0);
174       }
175       else if (e.getSource() == jbtLast) {                           last address
176         long lastPosition = raf.length();
177         if (lastPosition > 0)
178           // Why 2 * RECORD_SIZE? See the follow-up remarks
179           readAddress(lastPosition - 2 * RECORD_SIZE);
180       }
181     }
182     catch(IOException ex) {
183       System.out.print("Error: " + ex);
184     }
185   }
186
187   public static void main(String[] args) {
188     AddressBook frame = new AddressBook();
189     frame.pack();
190     frame.setTitle("AddressBook");
191     frame.setDefaultCloseOperation(JFrame.EXIT_ON_CLOSE);
192     frame.setVisible(true);
193   }
194 }
```

✦ A random access file, **address.dat**, is created to store address information if the file does not yet exist (Line 37). If it already exists, the file is opened. A random file object, `raf`, is used for both write and read operations. The size of each field in the record is fixed and therefore defined as constants in Lines 9–15.

✦ The user interface is created in Lines 44–100. The listeners are registered in Lines 102–106. When the program starts, it displays the first record, if it exists, in Lines 109–114.

✦ The `writeAddress()` method sets the file pointer to the end of the file (Line 119) and writes a new record to the file (Lines 120–129).

✦ The `readAddress()` method sets the file pointer at the specified position (Line 134) and reads a record from the file (Lines 135–144). The record is displayed in Lines 146–150.

✦ To add a record, you need to collect the address information from the user interface and write the address into the file (Line 157).

✦ The code to process button events is implemented in Lines 156–180. For the *First* button, read the record from position 0 (Line 160). For the *Next* button, read the record from the current file pointer (Line 165). When a record is read, the file pointer is moved `2 *` `RECORD_SIZE` number of bytes ahead of the previous file pointer. For the *Previous* button, you need to display the record prior to the one being displayed now. So, you have to move the file pointer two records before the current file pointer (Line 179). For the *Last* button, read the record from the position at `raf.length() - 2 * RECORD_SIZE`.

KEY TERMS

binary I/O 577	sequential access file 600
deserialization 598	serialization 598
file pointer 600	stream 577
random access file 600	text I/O 577

KEY CLASSES AND METHODS

✦ `java.io.File` is a wrapper class for the filename and its directory path. A `File` object contains the meta-information about a file, but it does not have the methods for reading/writing the file contents. You can use the `exist()` method to check whether a file exists.

✦ `java.io.Reader` is an abstract base class for reading characters.

✦ `java.io.Writer` is an abstract base class for writing characters.

✦ `java.io.FileReader` is a class for reading characters from a file.

✦ `java.io.FileWriter` is a class for writing characters to a file.

✦ `java.io.BufferedReader` is a class for reading characters from a buffer.

✦ `java.io.BufferedWriter` is a class for writing characters to a buffer.

✦ `java.io.PrintWriter` is a class for writing primitive values, strings, and strings as text.

✦ `java.io.PrintStream` is a class similar to `PrintWriter`, used for console output.

◆ `java.io.InputStream` is an abstract base class for a byte input stream.

◆ `java.io.OutputStream` is an abstract base class for a byte output stream.

◆ `java.io.FileInputStream` is a class for reading bytes from a file.

◆ `java.io.FileOutputStream` is a class for writing bytes to a file.

◆ `java.io.DataInputStream` is a class for reading primitive data values and strings.

◆ `java.io.DataOutputStream` is a class for writing primitive data values and strings.

◆ `java.io.BufferedInputStream` is a class for reading bytes from a buffer.

◆ `java.io.BufferedOutputStream` is class for writing bytes to a buffer.

◆ `java.io.ObjectInputStream` is a class for reading objects.

◆ `java.io.ObjectOutputStream` is a class for writing objects.

◆ `java.io.Seriablizable` is a marker interface that enables objects to be serializable.

◆ `java.io.RandomAccessFile` is a class for reading/writing from/to random access files.

CHAPTER SUMMARY

◆ The `File` class is used to obtain file properties and manipulate files. To read/write data from/to files, you have to use I/O classes.

◆ I/O can be classified into text I/O and binary I/O. Text I/O interprets data in sequences of characters. Binary I/O interprets data as raw binary values. How text is stored in a file is dependent on the encoding scheme for the file. Java automatically performs encoding and decoding for text I/O.

◆ The `Reader` and `Writer` classes are the roots of all text I/O classes. `FileReader`/`FileWriter` associates a file for text input/output. `BufferedReader`/`BufferedWriter` can be used to wrap on any text I/O stream to improve performance.

◆ The `PrintWriter` and `PrintStream` classes can be used to write primitive values, strings, and objects as text.

◆ The `InputStream` and `OutputStream` classes are the roots of all binary I/O classes. `FileInputStream`/`FileOutputStream` associates a file for binary input/output. `BufferedInputStream`/`BufferedOutputStream` can be used to wrap on any binary I/O stream to improve performance. `DataInputStream`/`DataOutputStream` can be used to read/write primitive values and strings.

◆ `ObjectInputStream`/`ObjectOutputStream` can be used to read/write objects in addition to primitive values and strings. To enable object serialization, the object's defining class must implement the `java.io.Serializable` marker interface.

◆ The `RandomAccessFile` class enables you to read and write data to a file. You can open a file with the `"r"` mode to indicate that it is read-only, or with the `"rw"` mode to indicate that it is updateable. Since the `RandomAccessFile` class implements `DataInput` and `DataOutput` interfaces, many methods in `RandomAccessFile` are the same as those in `DataInputStream` and `DataOutputStream`.

REVIEW QUESTIONS

Section 16.2 The *File* Class

16.1 What is wrong about creating a File object using the following statement?

```
new File("c:\book\test.dat");
```

16.2 How do you check whether a file already exists? How do you delete a file? How do you rename a file? Can you find the file size (the number of bytes) using the File class?

16.3 How do you obtain the file separator and path separator for the current system?

Section 16.3 How Is I/O Handled in Java?

16.4 Can you use the File class for I/O?

16.5 How do you read or write data in Java? What is a stream?

16.6 What is a text file, and what is a binary file? Can you view a text file or a binary file using a text editor?

Section 16.4 Text I/O

16.7 How is a Java character represented in the memory, and how is a character represented in a text file?

16.8 What value is returned from read() for text input? Is this the exact value stored in the file?

16.9 Is the exact Unicode value written into the file using write(int) for text output?

16.10 How do you create an input stream using FileReader? What happens if a file does not exist? How do you create an output stream using FileWriter? What happens if a file already exists? Can you append data to an existing file?

16.11 Why do you have to declare to throw IOException in the method or use a try-catch block to handle IOException for Java IO programs?

16.12 What is written to a file using write("91") on a FileWriter?

16.13 Why should you always close streams?

16.14 Is the line separator the same on all systems? How do you obtain a system-specific line separator?

16.15 Why should you use BufferedReader/BufferedWriter? How do you create a buffer stream for text I/O. Are the following the valid statements?

```
PrintWriter output1 = new PrintWriter(
   new BufferedWriter(new FileWriter("out1.txt")));

BufferedWriter output2 = new BufferedWriter(
   new PrintWriter(new FileWriter("out2.txt")));
```

Is the line separator the same on all systems? How do you obtain a system-specific line separator?

16.16 When should you use PrintWriter and PrintStream? How do you create a PrintWriter? What are the data types for System.in, System.out, and System.err? When you invoke System.out.println(), you don't have to place it in a try-catch block. Why?

16.17 How do you write a primitive value in BufferedWriter and in PrintWriter?

Section 16.6 Binary I/O

16.18   What are the differences between byte streams and character streams?

16.19   InputStream reads bytes. Why does the read() method return an int instead of a byte? Find the abstract methods in InputSteam and OutputStream?

16.20   Does FileInputStream/FileOutputStream introduce any new methods? How do you create a FileInputStream/FileOutputStream?

16.21   What will happen if you attempt to create an input stream on a nonexistent file? What will happen if you attempt to create an output stream on an existing file? Can you append data to an existing file?

16.22   Suppose input is a DataInputStream, input.available() returns 100. After invoking read(), what is input.available()? After invoking readInt(), what is input.available()? After invoking readChar(), what is input.available()? After invoking readDouble(), what is input.available()?

16.23   What is written to a file using writeByte(91) on a FileOutputStream?

16.24   How do you check the end of a file in a binary input stream (FileInputStream, DataInputStream)?

16.25   What is wrong in the following code?

```
import java.io.*;

public class Test {
  public static void main(String[] args) {
    try {
      FileInputStream fis = new FileInputStream("test.dat");
    }
    catch(IOException ex) {
      ex.printStackTrace();
    }
    catch(FileNotFoundException ex) {
      ex.printStackTrace();
    }
  }
}
```

16.26   Suppose you run the program on Windows using the default ASCII encoding. After the program is finished, how many bytes are in the file t.txt? Show the contents of each byte.

```
import java.io.*;

public class Test {
  public static void main(String[] args) throws IOException {
    FileWriter output = new FileWriter("t.txt");
    output.write("1234");
    output.write("5678");
    output.close();
  }
}
```

16.27   After the program is finished, how many bytes are in the file t.dat? Show the contents of each byte.

```
import java.io.*;

public class Test {
  public static void main(String[] args) throws IOException {
    DataOutputStream output = new DataOutputStream(
      new FileOutputStream("t.dat"));
    output.writeInt(1234);
    output.writeInt(5678);
    output.close();
  }
}
```

16.28 For each of the following statements on a DataOutputStream out, how many bytes are sent to the output?

```
output.writeChar('A');
output.writeChars("BC");
output.writeUTF("DEF");
```

16.29 What are the advantages of using buffered streams? Are the following statements correct?

```
BufferedInputStream input1 =
  new BufferedInputStream(new FileInputStream("t.dat"));

DataInputStream input2 = new DataInputStream(
  new BufferedInputStream(new FileInputStream("t.dat")));

ObjectInputStream input3 = new ObjectInputStream(
  new BufferedInputStream(new FileInputStream("t.dat")));
```

Section 16.9 Object I/O

16.30 What types of objects can be stored using the ObjectOutputStream? What is the method for writing an object? What is the method for reading an object? What is the return type of the method that reads an object from ObjectInputStream?

16.31 Is it true that any instance of java.io.Serializable can be successfully serialized? Are the static variables in an object serialized? How do you mark an instance variable not to be serialized?

16.32 Can you write an array to an ObjectOutputStream?

16.33 Is it true that DataInputStream/DataOutputStream can always be replaced by ObjectInputStream/ObjectOutputStream?

16.34 What will happen when you attempt to run the following code?

```
import java.io.*;

public class Test {
  public static void main(String[] args) throws IOException {
    ObjectOutputStream output =
      new ObjectOutputStream(new FileOutputStream("object.dat"));

    output.writeObject(new A());
  }
}

class A implements Serializable {
  B b = new B();
}

class B {
}
```

Section 16.10 Random Access Files (Optional)

16.35 Can RandomAccessFile streams read and write a data file created by DataOutputStream? Can RandomAccessFile streams read and write objects?

16.36 Create a RandomAccessFile stream for the file **address.dat** to allow the updating of student information in the file. Create a DataOutputStream for the file **address.dat**. Explain the differences between these two statements.

16.37 What happens if the file **test.dat** does not exist when you attempt to compile and run the following code?

```
import java.io.*;

public class Test {
  public static void main(String[] args) {
```

```
      try {
        RandomAccessFile raf =
          new RandomAccessFile("test.dat", "r");
        int i = raf.readInt();
      }
      catch(IOException ex) {
        System.out.println("IO exception");
      }
    }
  }
```

PROGRAMMING EXERCISES

Section 16.4 Text I/O

16.1* (*Counting characters, words, and lines in a file*) Write a program that will count the number of characters, including blanks, words, and lines, in a file. The filename should be passed as a command-line argument, as shown in Figure 16.26.

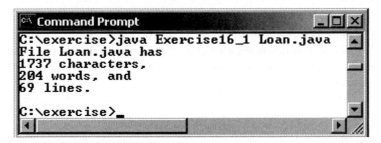

```
Command Prompt                              _ □ ×
C:\exercise>java Exercise16_1 Loan.java
File Loan.java has
1737 characters,
204 words, and
69 lines.

C:\exercise>_
```

FIGURE 16.26 *The program displays the number of characters, words, and lines in the given file.*

16.2 (*Processing scores in a text file*) Suppose that a text file **Exercise16_2.txt** contains an unspecified number of scores. Write a program that reads the scores from the file and displays their total and average. Scores are separated by blanks.

 HINT
Read the scores one line at a time until all the lines are read. For each line, use `StringTokenizer` or `Scanner` to extract the scores, and convert them into double values using the `Double.parseDouble` method.

16.3* (*Displaying country flag and flag description*) Example 13.6, "Using Combo Boxes," gives a program that lets users view a country's flag image and description by selecting the country from a combo box. The description is a string coded in the program. Rewrite the program to read the text description from a file. Suppose that the descriptions are stored in the file **description0.txt**, ..., and **description8.txt** for the nine countries Canada, China, Denmark, France, Germany, India, Norway, the United Kingdom, and the United States, in this order.

16.4** (*Reformatting Java source code*) Write a program that converts the Java source code from the next-line brace style to the end-of-line brace style. For example, the following Java source uses the next-line brace style:

```
public class Test
{
  public static void main(String[] args)
  {
    System.out.println("Welcome to Java!");
  }
}
```

Your program converts it to the end-of-line brace style, as follows:

```
public class Test {
  public static void main(String[] args) {
    System.out.println("Welcome to Java!");
  }
}
```

Your program can be invoked from the command line with the Java source code file as the argument. It converts the Java source code to a new format. For example, the following command converts the Java source code file **Test.java** to the end-of-line brace style.

java Exercise16_4 Test.java

16.5* (*Removing a given string from a text file*) Write a program that removes a specified string from a text file. Your program reads the file and generates a new file without the specified string, copies the new file to the original file, and passes the string and the file name from the command line, as follows:

java Exercise16_5 John Exercise16_5.txt

This command removes string John from **Exercise16_5.txt.**

16.6** (*Creating a histogram for occurrences of letters*) In Example 13.10, "Creating Multiple Windows," you developed a program that displays a histogram to show the occurrences of each letter in a text area. Reuse the Histogram class created in Example 13.10 to write a program that will display a histogram on a panel. The histogram should show the occurrences of each letter in a text file, as shown in Figure 16.27. Assume that the letters are not case-sensitive.

✦ Place a panel that will display the histogram in the center of the frame.

✦ Place a label and a text field in a panel, and put the panel in the south side of the frame. The text file will be entered from this text field.

✦ Pressing the Enter key on the text field causes the program to count the occurrences of each letter and display the count in a histogram.

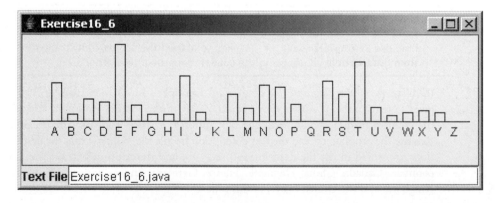

FIGURE 16.27 *The program displays a histogram that shows the occurrences of each letter in the file.*

16.7* (*Scanning data from a file*) Write a program to create a file named **Exercise16_7.txt** if it does not exist. Write one hundred integers created randomly into the file using text I/O. Integers are separated by spaces in the file. Use StringTokenizer or Scanner to read the data back from the file and display the sorted data.

Section 16.6 Binary I/O

16.8*   (*Creating a binary data file*) Write a program to create a file named **Exercise16_8.dat** if it does not exist. If it exists, append new data to it. Write one hundred integers created randomly into the file using binary I/O.

16.9*   (*Summing all the integers in a binary data file*) Suppose a binary data file named **Exercise16_9.dat** has been created using writeInt(int) in DataOutputStream. The file contains an unspecified number of integers. Write a program to find the total of the integers.

16.10*   (*Converting a text file into UTF*) Write a program that reads lines of characters from a text and writes each line as a UTF string into a binary file. Display the sizes of both text file and binary file. Use the following command to run the program:

```
java Exercise16_10 Welcome.java Welcome.utf
```

Section 16.9 Object I/O

16.11*   (*Storing objects and arrays into a file*) Write a program that stores an array of five int values 1, 2, 3, 4 and 5, a Date object for current time, and the double value 5.5 into the file named **Exercise16_11.dat**.

16.12*   (*Storing Loan objects*) The Loan class, introduced in Section 6.15, "Case Study: The Loan Class," does not implement Serializable. Rewrite the Loan class to implement Serializable. Write a program that creates five Loan objects and stores them in a file named **Exercise16_12.dat**.

16.13*   (*Restoring objects from a file*) Suppose a file named **Exercise16_13.dat** has been created using the ObjectOutputStream. The file contains Loan objects. The Loan class, introduced in Section 6.15, "Case Study: The Loan Class," does not implement Serializable. Rewrite the Loan class to implement Serializable. Write a program that reads the Loan objects from the file and computes the total of the loan amount. Suppose you don't know how many Loan objects are in the file. Use EOFException to end the loop.

Section 16.10 Random Access Files (Optional)

16.14*   (*Updating count*) Suppose you want to track how many times a program has been executed. You may store an int to count the file. Increase the count by 1 each time this program is executed. Let the program be **Exercise16_14** and store the count in **Exercise16_14.dat**.

16.15**   (*Updating address*) Modify AddressBook in Listing 16.15 on page 605 to add an *Update* button, as shown in Figure 16.28, to enable the user to modify an address that is being displayed.

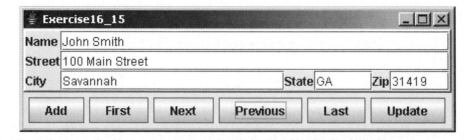

FIGURE 16.28   *You can update the address record that is currently displayed.*

PART V

DATA STRUCTURES
AND COLLECTIONS FRAMEWORK

The design and implementation of efficient data structures is an important subject in computer science. Data structures such as lists, stacks, queues, sets, maps, and binary trees have many applications in compiler construction, computer operating systems, and file management. Java provides the data structures for lists, stacks, sets, and maps in the collections framework. This part of the book introduces data structure concepts and implementation techniques in Chapter 17, "Object-Oriented Data Structures," and introduces how to use the classes and interfaces in the Java collections framework in Chapter 18, "Java Collections Framework." These two chapters are designed to be independent. You can skip Chapter 17 if you are only interested in learning how to use the predefined data structures in the Java collections framework.

Chapter 17
Object-Oriented Data Structures

Chapter 18
Java Collections Framework

Prerequisites for Part V

Chapter 9 Abstract Classes and Interfaces

Chapter 17 Object-Oriented Data Structures

Chapter 18 Java Collections Framework

chapter

17

OBJECT-ORIENTED DATA STRUCTURES

Objectives

- ✦ To describe what a data structure is (§17.1).

- ✦ To explain the limitations of arrays (§17.1).

- ✦ To implement a dynamic list using an array (§17.2.1).

- ✦ To implement a dynamic list using a linked structure (§17.2.2 Optional).

- ✦ To implement a stack using an array list (§17.3).

- ✦ To implement a queue using a linked list (§17.3).

- ✦ To implement a binary search tree (§17.4 Optional).

17.1   Introduction

A data structure is a collection of data organized in some fashion. A data structure not only stores data, but also supports the operations for manipulating data in the structure. For example, an array is a data structure that holds a collection of data in sequential order. You can find the size of the array, and store, retrieve, and modify data in the array. Arrays are simple and easy to use, but they have two limitations: (1) once an array is created, its size cannot be altered; (2) an array does not provide adequate support for insertion and deletion operations. This chapter introduces dynamic data structures that grow and shrink at runtime.

array limitation

Four classic dynamic data structures are introduced in this chapter: lists, stacks, queues, and binary trees. A *list* is a collection of data stored sequentially. It supports insertion and deletion anywhere in the list. A *stack* can be perceived as a special type of list where insertions and deletions take place only at one end, referred to as the *top* of the stack. A *queue* represents a waiting list, where insertions take place at the back (also referred to as the tail) of the queue, and deletions take place from the front (also referred to as the head) of the queue. A *binary tree* is a data structure that supports searching, sorting, inserting, and deleting data efficiently.

list
stack
queue

binary tree

In object-oriented thinking, a data structure is an object that stores other objects, referred to as data or elements. Some people refer to data structures as *container objects* or *collection objects*. To define a data structure is essentially to declare a class. The class for a data structure should use data fields to store data and provide methods to support such operations as insertion and deletion. To create a data structure is therefore to create an instance from the class. You can then apply the methods on the instance to manipulate the data structure, such as inserting an element into the data structure or deleting an element from the data structure.

collection object

This chapter introduces the design and implementation of the classes for data structures: lists, stacks, queues, and binary trees. *The whole chapter is optional and can be skipped.*

17.2   Lists

A list is a popular data structure for storing data in sequential order. For example, a list of students, a list of available rooms, a list of cities, and a list of books can all be stored using lists. The operations listed below are typical of most lists:

✦   Retrieve an element from a list.

✦   Insert a new element to a list.

✦   Delete an element from a list.

✦   Find how many elements are in a list.

✦   Find whether an element is in a list.

✦   Find whether a list is empty.

There are two ways to implement a list. One is to use an *array* to store the elements. Arrays are dynamically created. If the capacity of the array is exceeded, create a new, larger array and copy all the elements from the current array to the new array. The other approach is to use a *linked structure*. A linked structure consists of nodes. Each node is dynamically created to hold an element. All the nodes are linked together to form a list. Thus you can declare two classes for lists. For convenience, let's name these two classes `MyArrayList` and `MyLinkedList`. These two classes have common operations but different data fields. The common operations can be generalized in an interface or an abstract class. As discussed in Section 10.6.5, "Using Interfaces or Abstract Classes," a good strategy is to combine the virtues of interfaces and abstract classes by providing both an interface and an abstract class in the design so that the user can use either of them, whichever is convenient. Such an abstract class is known as a *convenience class*.

Let us name the interface `MyList` and the convenience class `MyAbstractList`. Figure 17.1 shows the relationship of `MyList`, `MyAbstractList`, `MyArrayList`, and `MyLinkedList`. The methods in

FIGURE 17.1 MyList *defines a common interface for* MyAbstractList, MyArrayList, *and* MyLinkedList.

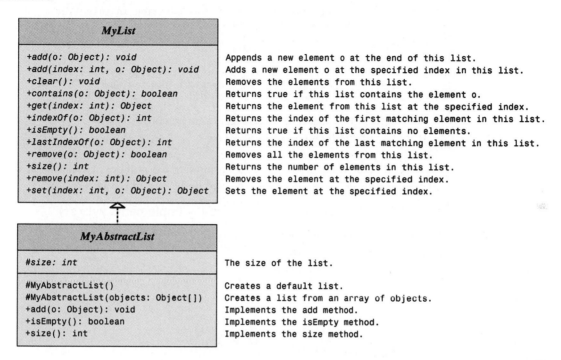

FIGURE 17.2 *List supports many methods for manipulating a list.* MyAbstractList *provides a partial implementation of the* List *interface.*

MyList and the methods implemented in MyAbstractList are shown in Figure 17.2. Listing 17.1 gives the source code for MyList.

LISTING 17.1   MyList.java (The Interface for Lists)

```java
 1 public interface MyList {
 2   /** Add a new element o at the end of this list */
 3   public void add(Object o);
 4
 5   /** Add a new element o at the specified index in this list */
 6   public void add(int index, Object o);
 7
 8   /** Clear the list */
 9   public void clear();
10
11   /** Return true if this list contains the element o */
12   public boolean contains(Object o);
13
14   /** Return the element from this list at the specified index */
15   public Object get(int index);
16
17   /** Return the index of the first matching element in this list.
18    *  Return -1 if no match. */
19   public int indexOf(Object o);
20
21   /** Return true if this list contains no elements */
22   public boolean isEmpty();
```

```
23
24   /** Return the index of the last matching element in this list
25    *  Return -1 if no match. */
26   public int lastIndexOf(Object o);
27
28   /** Remove the first occurrence of the element o from this list.
29    *  Shift any subsequent elements to the left.
30    *  Return true if the element is removed. */
31   public boolean remove(Object o);
32
33   /** Remove the element at the specified position in this list
34    *  Shift any subsequent elements to the left.
35    *  Return the element that was removed from the list. */
36   public Object remove(int index);
37
38   /** Replace the element at the specified position in this list
39    *  with the specified element and return the new set. */
40   public Object set(int index, Object o);
41
42   /** Return the number of elements in this list */
43   public int size();
44 }
```

`MyAbstractList` declares variable `size` to indicate the number of elements in the list. The methods `isEmpty` and `size` can be implemented in the class in Listing 17.2.

LISTING 17.2 **MyAbstractList.java (Partially Implements `MyList`)**

size

no-arg constructor

constructor

```
1 public abstract class MyAbstractList implements MyList {
2   protected int size; // The size of the list
3
4   /** Create a default list */
5   protected MyAbstractList() {
6   }
7
8   /** Create a list from an array of objects */
9   protected MyAbstractList(Object[] objects) {
10    for (int i = 0; i < objects.length; i++)
11      this.add(objects[i]);
12  }
13
14  /** Add a new element o at the end of this list */
15  public void add(Object o) {
16    add(size, o);
17  }
18
19  /** Return true if this list contains no elements */
20  public boolean isEmpty() {
21    return size == 0;
22  }
23
24  /** Return the number of elements in this list */
25  public int size() {
26    return size;
27  }
28 }
```

The following sections give the implementation for `MyArrayList` and `MyLinkedList`, respectively.

17.2.1 Array Lists

An array is a fixed-size data structure. Once an array is created, its size cannot be changed. Nevertheless, you can still use arrays to implement dynamic data structures. The trick is to create a larger new array to replace the current array if the current array cannot hold new elements in the list. This section shows how to use arrays to implement `MyArrayList`.

Initially, an array, say data of `Object[]` type, is created with a default size. When inserting a new element into the array, first make sure that there is enough room in the array. If not, create a new array twice as large as the current one. Copy the elements from the current array to the new array. The new array now becomes the current array. Before inserting a new element at a specified index, shift all the elements after the index to the right and increase the list size by 1, as shown in Figure 17.3.

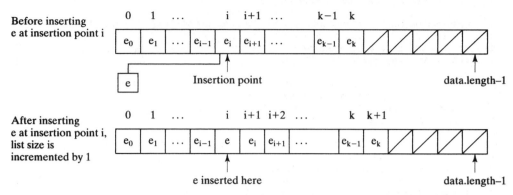

FIGURE 17.3   *Inserting a new element to the array requires that all the elements after the insertion point be shifted one position to the right so that the new element can be inserted at the insertion point.*

 NOTE

The data array is of type `Object[]`. Each cell in the array actually stores the reference of an object.

To remove an element at a specified index, shift all the elements after the index to the left by one position and decrease the list size by 1, as shown in Figure 17.4.

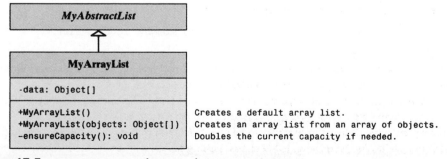

FIGURE 17.4   *Deleting an element from the array requires that all the elements after the deletion point be shifted one position to the left.*

`MyArrayList` uses an array to implement `MyAbstractList`, as shown in Figure 17.5. Its implementation is given in Listing 17.3.

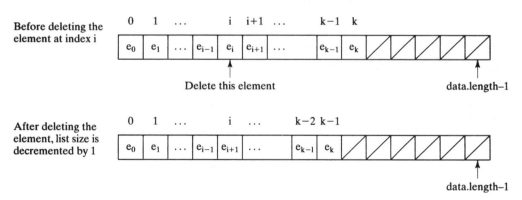

FIGURE 17.5   *`MyArrayList` implements a list using an array.*

LISTING 17.3   MyArrayList.java (Implementing List Using Array)

initial capacity
array

double capacity

```java
1  public class MyArrayList extends MyAbstractList {
2    public static final int INITIAL_CAPACITY = 16;
3    private Object[] data = new Object[INITIAL_CAPACITY];
4
5    /** Create a default list */
6    public MyArrayList() {
7    }
8
9    /** Create a list from an array of objects */
10   public MyArrayList(Object[] objects) {
11     data = objects;
12     size = objects.length;
13   }
14
15   /** Add a new element o at the specified index in this list */
16   public void add(int index, Object o) {
17     ensureCapacity();
18
19     // Move the elements to the right after the specified index
20     for (int i = size - 1; i >= index; i--)
21       data[i + 1] = data[i];
22
23     // Insert new element to data[index]
24     data[index] = o;
25
26     // Increase size by 1
27     size++;
28   }
29
30   /** Create a new larger array, double the current size */
31   private void ensureCapacity() {
32     if (size >= data.length) {
33       Object[] newData = new Object[data.length * 2];
34       System.arraycopy(data, 0, newData, 0, data.length);
35       data = newData;
36     }
37   }
38
39   /** Clear the list */
40   public void clear() {
41     data = new Object[INITIAL_CAPACITY];
42   }
43
44   /** Return true if this list contains the element o */
45   public boolean contains(Object o) {
46     for (int i = 0; i < size; i++)
47       if (o.equals(data[i])) return true;
48
49     return false;
50   }
51
52   /** Return the element from this list at the specified index */
53   public Object get(int index) {
54     return data[index];
55   }
56
57   /** Return the index of the first matching element in this list.
58    *  Return -1 if no match. */
59   public int indexOf(Object o) {
60     for (int i = 0; i < size; i++)
61       if (o.equals(data[i])) return i;
62
63     return -1;
64   }
```

```
65
66    /** Return the index of the last matching element in this list
67     *   Return -1 if no match. */
68    public int lastIndexOf(Object o) {
69      for (int i = size - 1; i >= 0; i--)
70        if (o.equals(data[i])) return i;
71
72      return -1;
73    }
74
75    /** Remove the first occurrence of the element o from this list.
76     *   Shift any subsequent elements to the left.
77     *   Return true if the element is removed. */
78    public boolean remove(Object o) {
79      for (int i = 0; i < size; i++)
80        if (o.equals(data[i])) {
81          remove(i);
82          return true;
83        }
84
85      return false;
86    }
87
88    /** Remove the element at the specified position in this list
89     *   Shift any subsequent elements to the left.
90     *   Return the element that was removed from the list. */
91    public Object remove(int index) {
92      Object o = data[index];
93
94      // Shift data to the left
95      for (int j = index; j < size - 1; j++)
96        data[j] = data[j + 1];
97
98      // Decrement size
99      size--;
100
101      return o;
102   }
103
104   /** Replace the element at the specified position in this list
105    *   with the specified element. */
106   public Object set(int index, Object o) {
107     data[index] = o;
108     return o;
109   }
110
111   /** Override toString() to return elements in the list */
112   public String toString() {
113     StringBuffer result = new StringBuffer("[");
114
115     for (int i = 0; i < size; i++) {
116       result.append(data[i]);
117       if (i < size - 1) result.append(", ");
118     }
119
120     return result.toString() + "]";
121   }
122 }
```

The constant INITIAL_CAPACITY (Line 2) is used to create an initial array data of type Object (Line 3).

The add(int index, Object o) method (Lines 16–28) adds element o at the specified index in the array. This method first invokes ensureCapacity() (Line 17), which ensures that there is a space in the array for the new element. It then shifts all the elements after the index one position to the right before inserting the element (Lines 20–21). After the element is added, `size` is incremented by 1 (Line 27). Note that variable `size` is defined as `protected` in `MyAbstractList`, so it can be accessed in `MyArrayList`.

The `ensureCapacity()` method (Lines 31–37) checks whether the array is full. If so, create a new array that doubles the current array size, copy the current array to the new array using the `System.arraycopy` method, and set the new array as the current array.

The `clear()` method (Lines 40–42) creates a brand-new array with initial capacity.

The `contains(Object o)` method (Lines 45–50) checks whether element o is contained in the array by comparing o with each element in the array using the `equals` method.

The `get(int index)` method (Lines 53–55) simply returns `data[index]`. The implementation of this method is simple and efficient.

The `indexOf(Object o)` method (Lines 59–64) compares element o with the elements in the array starting from the first one. If a match is found, the index of the element is returned; otherwise, it returns –1.

The `lastIndexOf(Object o)` method (Lines 68–73) compares element o with the elements in the array starting from the last one. If a match is found, the index of the element is returned; otherwise, it returns –1.

The `remove(Object o)` method (Lines 78–86) compares element o with the elements in the array. If a match is found, the first matching element in the list is deleted.

The `remove(int index)` method (Lines 91–102) shifts all the elements before the index one position to the left and decrements `size` by 1.

The `set(int index, Object o)` method (Lines 106–109) simply assigns o to `data[index]` to replace the element at the specified index with element o

The `toString()` method (Lines 112–121) overrides the `toString` method in the `Object` class to return a string representing all the elements in the list.

EXAMPLE 17.1 USING ARRAY LISTS

Problem

Write a program that creates a list using `MyArrayList`. It then uses the `add` method to add strings to the list and the `remove` method to remove strings from the list.

Solution

Listing 17.4 gives the solution to the problem. A sample run of the program is shown in Figure 17.6.

```
Command Prompt                                              _ |□| x
C:\book>java TestList
(1) [Tom]
(2) [John, Tom]
(3) [John, Tom, George]
(4) [John, Tom, George, Michael]
(5) [John, Tom, Michelle, George, Michael]
(6) [John, Tom, Michelle, George, Michael, Samantha]
(7) [Daniel, John, Tom, Michelle, George, Michael, Samantha]
(8) [John, Tom, Michelle, George, Michael, Samantha]
(9) [John, Tom, George, Michael, Samantha]
(10) [John, Tom, George, Michael]

C:\book>_
```

FIGURE 17.6   *The program uses a list to store and process strings.*

EXAMPLE 17.1 (CONTINUED)

LISTING 17.4   TestList.java (Using Lists)

```
 1 public class TestList {
 2   public static void main(String[] args) {
 3     // Create a list
 4     MyList list = new MyArrayList();
 5
 6     // Add elements to the list
 7     list.add("Tom"); // Add it to the list
 8     System.out.println("(1) " + list);
 9
10     list.add(0, "John"); // Add it to the beginning of the list
11     System.out.println("(2) " + list);
12
13     list.add("George"); // Add it to the end of the list
14     System.out.println("(3) " + list);
15
16     list.add("Michael"); // Add it to the end of the list
17     System.out.println("(4) " + list);
18
19     list.add(2, "Michelle"); // Add it to the list at index 2
20     System.out.println("(5) " + list);
21
22     list.add(5, "Samantha"); // Add it to the list at index 5
23     System.out.println("(6) " + list);
24
25     list.add(0, "Daniel"); // Same as list.addFirst("Daniel")
26     System.out.println("(7) " + list);
27
28     // Remove elements from the list
29     list.remove("Daniel"); // Same as list.remove(0) in this case
30     System.out.println("(8) " + list);
31
32     list.remove(2); // Remove the element at index 2
33     System.out.println("(9) " + list);
34
35     list.remove(list.size() - 1); // Remove the last element
36     System.out.println("(10) " + list);
37   }
38 }
```

Review

MyArrayList is implemented using arrays. Although an array is a fixed-size data structure, MyArrayList is a dynamic data structure. The user can create an instance of MyArrayList to store any number of elements. The internal array in MyArrayList is encapsulated. The user manipulates the list through the public methods in MyArrayList.

The list can hold any objects. A primitive data type value cannot be directly stored in a list. However, you can create an object for a primitive data type value using the corresponding wrapper class. For example, to store number 10, use the following method:

```
list.add(new Integer(10));
```

17.2.2   Linked Lists (Optional)

Since MyArrayList is implemented using an array, the methods get(int index) and set(int index, Object o) for accessing and modifying an element through an index and the add(Object o) for adding an element at the end of the list are efficient. However, the methods add(int index,

`Object o)` and `remove(int index)` are inefficient because they require shifting a potentially large number of elements. You can use a linked structure to implement a list to improve efficiency for adding and removing an element anywhere in a list.

A linked list consists of nodes, as shown in Figure 17.7. Each node contains an element, and each node is linked to its next neighbor. Thus a node can be defined as a class, as follows:

```
class Node {
  Object element;
  Node next;

  public Node(Object o) {
    element = o;
  }
}
```

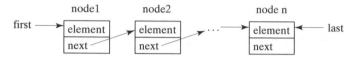

FIGURE 17.7 *A linked list consists of any number of nodes chained together.*

The variable `first` refers to the first node in the list, and the variable `last` refers to the last node in the list. If the list is empty, both are `null`. For example, you can create three nodes to store three circle objects (radius 1, 2, and 3) in a list:

```
Node first, last;

// Create a node to store the first circle object
first = new Node(new Circle(1));
last = first;

// Create a node to store the second circle object
last.next = new Node(new Circle(2));
last = last.next;

// Create a node to store the third circle object
last.next = new Node(new Circle(3));
last = last.next;
```

The process of creating a new linked list and adding three nodes is shown in Figure 17.8.

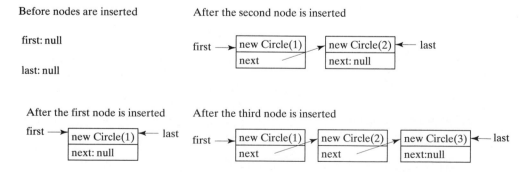

FIGURE 17.8 *Three nodes are added to a new linked list.*

`MyLinkedList` uses a linked structure to implement a dynamic list. It extends `MyAbstractList`. In addition, it provides the methods `addFirst`, `addLast`, `removeFirst`, `removeLast`, `getFirst`, and `getLast`, as shown in Figure 17.9. Its implementation is given in Listing 17.5.

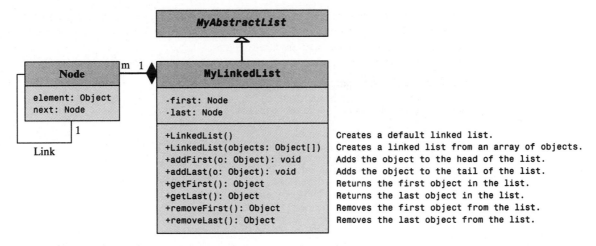

FIGURE 17.9   *MyLinkedList implements a list using a linked list of nodes.*

LISTING **17.5   MyLinkedList.java (Implementing Lists Using Linked Structures)**

```
 1  public class MyLinkedList extends MyAbstractList {
 2    private Node first, last;
 3
 4    /** Create a default list */
 5    public MyLinkedList() {
 6    }
 7
 8    /** Create a list from an array of objects */
 9    public MyLinkedList(Object[] objects) {
10      super(objects);
11    }
12
13    /** Return the first element in the list */
14    public Object getFirst() {
15      if (size == 0) return null;
16      else return first.element;
17    }
18
19    /** Return the last element in the list */
20    public Object getLast() {
21      if (size == 0) return null;
22      else return last.element;
23    }
24
25    /** Add an element to the beginning of the list */
26    public void addFirst(Object o) {                        addFirst
27      Node newNode = new Node(o);                           create node
28      newNode.next = first;
29      first = newNode;
30      size++;
31
32      if (last == null)
33        last = first;
34    }
35
36    /** Add an element to the end of the list */
37    public void addLast(Object o) {                         addLast
38      if (last == null) {
39        first = last = new Node(o);
40      }
41      else {
42        last.next = new Node(o);
43        last = last.next;
44      }
```

```
45
46     size++;
47   }
48
49   /** Adds a new element o at the specified index in this list
50    * The index of the first element is 0 */
51   public void add(int index, Object o) {
52     if (index == 0) addFirst(o);
53     else if (index >= size) addLast(o);
54     else {
55       Node current = first;
56       for (int i = 1; i < index; i++)
57         current = current.next;
58       Node temp = current.next;
59       current.next = new Node(o);
60       (current.next).next = temp;
61       size++;
62     }
63   }
64
65   /** Remove the first node and
66    *  return the object that is contained in the removed node. */
67   public Object removeFirst() {
68     if (size == 0) return null;
69     else {
70       Node temp = first;
71       first = first.next;
72       size--;
73       return temp.element;
74     }
75   }
76
77   /** Remove the last node and
78    * return the object that is contained in the removed node. */
79   public Object removeLast() {
80     // Implementation left as an exercise
81     return null;
82   }
83
84   /** Removes the element at the specified position in this list
85    *  Returns the element that was removed from the list. */
86   public Object remove(int index) {
87     if ((index < 0) || (index >= size)) return null;
88     else if (index == 0) return removeFirst();
89     else if (index == size - 1) return removeLast();
90     else {
91       Node previous = first;
92
93       for (int i = 1; i < index; i++) {
94         previous = previous.next;
95       }
96
97       Node current = previous .next;
98       previous.next = current.next;
99       size--;
100      return current.element;
101    }
102  }
103
104  /** Override toString() to return elements in the list */
105  public String toString() {
106    StringBuffer result = new StringBuffer("[");
107
108    Node current = first;
109    for (int i = 0; i < size; i++) {
110      result.append(current.element);
```

add

removeFirst

removeLast

remove

```
111      current = current.next;
112      if (current != null)
113        result.append(", "); // Seperate two elements with a comma
114      else
115        result.append("]"); // Insert the closing ] in the string
116    }
117
118    return result.toString();
119  }
120
121  /** Clear the list */
122  public void clear() {
123    first = last = null;
124  }
125
126  /** Return true if this list contains the element o */
127  public boolean contains(Object o) {
128    // Implementation left as an exercise
129    return true;
130  }
131
132  /** Return the element from this list at the specified index */
133  public Object get(int index) {
134    // Implementation left as an exercise
135    return null;
136  }
137
138  /** Returns the index of the first matching element in this list.
139   *  Returns -1 if no match. */
140  public int indexOf(Object o) {
141    // Implementation left as an exercise
142    return 0;
143  }
144
145  /** Returns the index of the last matching element in this list
146   *  Returns -1 if no match. */
147  public int lastIndexOf(Object o) {
148    // Implementation left as an exercise
149    return 0;
150  }
151
152  /** Remove the first node that contains the specified element
153   * Return true if the element is removed
154   * Return false if no element is removed
155   */
156  public boolean remove(Object o) {
157    // Implementation left as an exercise
158    // return true;
159  }
160
161  /** Replace the element at the specified position in this list
162   *  with the specified element. */
163  public Object set(int index, Object o) {
164    // Implementation left as an exercise
165    return null;
166  }
167
168  private static class Node {
169    Object element;
170    Node next;
171
172    public Node(Object o) {
173      element = o;
174    }
175  }
176 }
```

The variables `first` and `last` (Line 2) refer to the first and last nodes in the list, respectively. The `getFirst()` and `getLast()` methods (Lines 14–23) return the first and last elements in the list, respectively.

Since variable `size` is defined as `protected` in `MyAbstractList`, it can be accessed in `MyLinkedList`. When a new element is added to the list, `size` is incremented by 1, and when an element is removed from the list, `size` is decremented by 1. The `addFirst(Object o)` method (Lines 26–34) creates a new node to store the element and insert the node to the beginning of the list. After the insertion, `first` should refer to this new element node (Line 29), as shown in Figure 17.10.

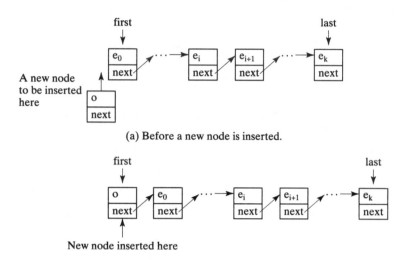

(a) Before a new node is inserted.

(b) After a new node is inserted.

FIGURE 17.10 *A new element* o *is added to the beginning of the list.*

The `addLast(Object o)` method (Lines 37–47) creates a node to hold element o and inserts the node at the end of the list. After the insertion, `last` should refer to this new element node (Line 43), as shown in Figure 17.11.

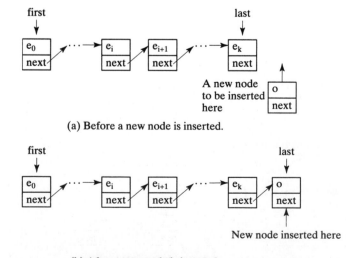

(a) Before a new node is inserted.

(b) After a new node is inserted.

FIGURE 17.11 *A new element* o *is added at the end of the list.*

The add(int index, Object o) method (Lines 51–63) adds an element o to the list at the specified index. Consider three cases: (1) if index is 0, invoke addFirst(o) to insert the element at the beginning of the list; (2) if index is greater than or equal to size, invoke addLast(o) to insert the element at the end of the list; (3) create a new node to store the new element and locate where to insert it. As shown in Figure 17.12, the new node is to be inserted between the nodes current and temp. The method assigns the new node to current.next and assigns temp to the new node's next.

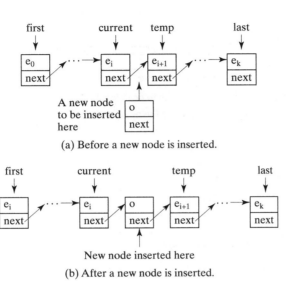

(a) Before a new node is inserted.

(b) After a new node is inserted.

FIGURE 17.12 *A new element is inserted in the middle of the list.*

The removeFirst() method (Lines 67–75) removes the first node from the list by pointing first to the second node, as shown in Figure 17.13. The removeLast() method (Lines 79–82) removes the last node from the list. Afterwards, last should refer to the former second-last node.

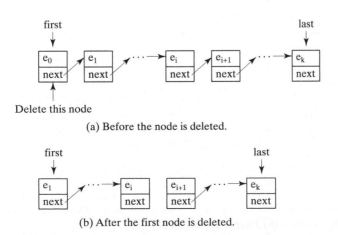

(a) Before the node is deleted.

(b) After the first node is deleted.

FIGURE 17.13 *The first node is deleted from the list.*

The `remove(int index)` method (Lines 86–102) finds the node at the specified index and then removes it. Consider four cases: (1) if `index` is beyond the range of the list (i.e., index < 0 ||index >= size), return null; (2) if `index` is 0, invoke `removeFirst()` to remove the first node; (3) if `index` is `size - 1`, invoke `removeLast()` to remove the last node; (4) locate the node at the specified `index`. Let `current` denote this node and `previous` denote the node before this node, as shown in Figure 17.14. Assign `current.next` to `previous.next` to eliminate the current node.

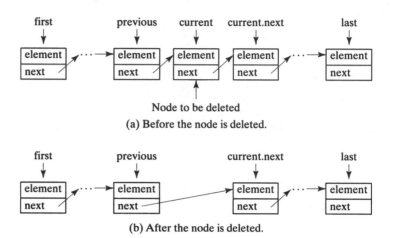

(a) Before the node is deleted.

(b) After the node is deleted.

FIGURE 17.14 *A node is deleted from the list.*

The implementation of methods `removeLast()`, `clear()`, `contains(Objecto)`, `get(int index)`, `indexOf(Object o)`, `lastIndexOf(Object o)`, `remove(Object o)`, and `set(int index, Object o)` is omitted and left as an exercise.

To test `MyLinkedList`, simply replace `MyArrayList` on Line 7 by `MyLinkedList` in `TestList` in Example 17.1. The output should be the same as shown in Figure 17.6.

17.3 Stacks and Queues

A stack can be viewed as a special type of list whose elements are accessed, inserted, and deleted only from the end (top), of the stack. A queue represents a waiting list. A queue can be viewed as a special type of list whose elements are inserted into the end (tail) of the queue, and are accessed and deleted from the beginning (head) of the queue.

Since the insertion and deletion operations on a stack are made only at the end of the stack, it is more efficient to implement a stack with an array list than with a linked list. Since deletions are made at the beginning of the list, it is more efficient to implement a queue using a linked list than an array list. This section implements a stack class using an array list and a queue using a linked list.

There are two ways to design stack and queue classes:

inheritance

✦ Using *inheritance*: You can declare a stack class by extending the array list class, and a queue class by extending the linked list class.

composition

✦ Using *composition*: You can declare an array list as a data field in the stack class, and a linked list as a data field in the queue class.

Both designs are fine, but using composition is better because it enables you to declare a completely new stack class and queue class without inheriting unnecessary and inappropriate methods from the array list and linked list. The stack class named MyStack is shown in Figure 17.15. Its implementation is given in Listing 17.6.

```
┌──────────────────────────────┐
│           MyStack            │
├──────────────────────────────┤
│ -list: MyArrayList           │
├──────────────────────────────┤
│ +isEmpty(): boolean          │   Returns true if this stack is empty.
│ +getSize(): int              │   Returns the number of elements in this stack.
│ +peek(): Object              │   Returns the top element in this stack.
│ +pop(): Object               │   Returns and removes the top element in this stack.
│ +push(o: Object): Object     │   Adds a new element to the top of this stack.
│ +search(o: Object): int      │   Returns the position of the first element in the stack from
└──────────────────────────────┘          the top that matches the specified element.
```

FIGURE 17.15 *MyStack uses an array list to provide a last-in/first-out data structure.*

LISTING 17.6   **MyStack.java (Implementing Stack)**

```java
 1 public class MyStack {
 2   private MyArrayList list = new MyArrayList();          array list
 3
 4   public boolean isEmpty() {
 5     return list.isEmpty();
 6   }
 7
 8   public int getSize() {
 9     return list.size();
10   }
11
12   public Object peek() {
13     return list.get(getSize() - 1);
14   }
15
16   public Object pop() {
17     Object o = list.get(getSize() - 1);
18     list.remove(getSize() - 1);
19     return o;
20   }
21
22   public Object push(Object o) {
23     list.add(o);
24     return o;
25   }
26
27   public int search(Object o) {
28     return list.lastIndexOf(o);
29   }
30
31   public String toString() {
32     return "stack: " + list.toString();
33   }
34 }
```

An array list is created to store the elements in a stack (Line 2). The isEmpty() method (Lines 4–6) is the same as list.isEmpty(). The getSize() method (Lines 8–10) is the same as list.size(). The peek() method (Lines 12–14) looks at the element at the top of the stack without removing it. The pop() method (Lines 16–20) removes the top element from the stack and returns it.

The push(Object element) method (Lines 22–24) adds the specified element to the stack. The search(Object element) method checks whether the specified element is in the stack.

The queue class named MyQueue is shown in Figure 17.16. Its implementation is given in Listing 17.7.

MyQueue
-list: MyLinkedList
+enqueue(element: Object): void   Adds an element to this queue. +dequeue(): Object   Removes an element from this queue. +getSize(): int   Returns the number of elements from this queue.

FIGURE 17.16 *MyQueue uses a linked list to provide a first-in/first-out data structure.*

LISTING 17.7   MyQueue.java (Implementing Queue)

linked list

```
1 public class MyQueue {
2   private MyLinkedList list = new MyLinkedList();
3
4   public void enqueue(Object o) {
5     list.addLast(o);
6   }
7
8   public Object dequeue() {
9     return list.removeFirst();
10  }
11
12  public int getSize() {
13    return list.size();
14  }
15
16  public String toString() {
17    return "Queue: " + list.toString();
18  }
19 }
```

A linked list is created to store the elements in a queue (Line 2). The enqueue(Object o) method (Lines 4–6) adds element o into the tail of the queue. The dequeue() method (Lines 8–10) removes an element from the head of the queue and returns the removed element. The getSize() method (Lines 12–14) returns the number of elements in the queue.

EXAMPLE 17.2 USING STACKS AND QUEUES

Problem

Write a program that creates a stack using MyStack and a queue using MyQueue. It then uses the push (enqueue) method to add strings to the stack (queue) and the pop (dequeue) method to remove strings from the stack (queue).

Solution

Listing 17.8 gives the solution to the problem. A sample run of the program is shown in Figure 17.17.

EXAMPLE 17.2 (CONTINUED)

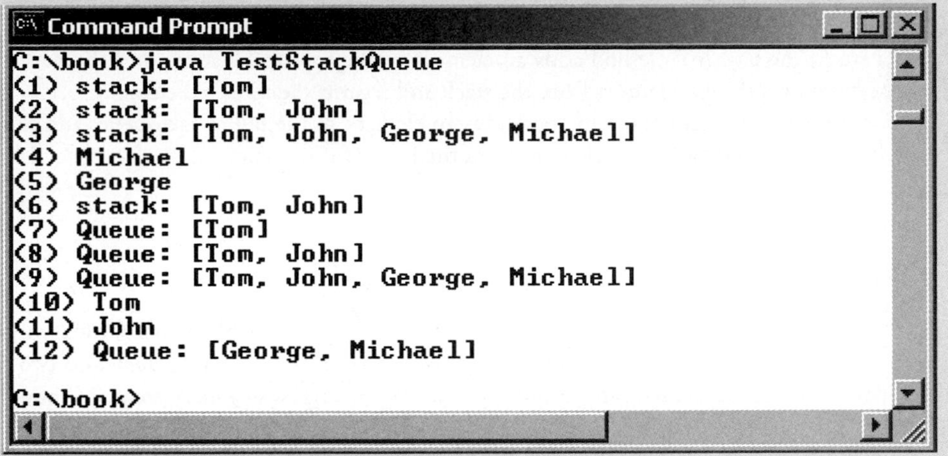

```
Command Prompt                                            _ □ X
C:\book>java TestStackQueue
(1) stack: [Tom]
(2) stack: [Tom, John]
(3) stack: [Tom, John, George, Michael]
(4) Michael
(5) George
(6) stack: [Tom, John]
(7) Queue: [Tom]
(8) Queue: [Tom, John]
(9) Queue: [Tom, John, George, Michael]
(10) Tom
(11) John
(12) Queue: [George, Michael]

C:\book>
```

FIGURE **17.17**   *The program uses a stack and a queue to store and process strings.*

LISTING **17.8**   TestStackQueue.java (Using Stack and Queue)

```java
 1 public class TestStackQueue {
 2   public static void main(String[] args) {
 3     // Create a stack
 4     MyStack stack = new MyStack();
 5
 6     // Add elements to the stack
 7     stack.push("Tom"); // Push it to the stack
 8     System.out.println("(1) " + stack);
 9
10     stack.push("John"); // Push it to the stack
11     System.out.println("(2) " + stack);
12
13     stack.push("George"); // Push it to the stack
14     stack.push("Michael"); // Push it to the stack
15     System.out.println("(3) " + stack);
16
17     // Remove elements from the stack
18     System.out.println("(4) " + stack.pop());
19     System.out.println("(5) " + stack.pop());
20     System.out.println("(6) " + stack);
21
22     // Create a queue
23     MyQueue queue = new MyQueue();
24
25     // Add elements to the queue
26     queue.enqueue("Tom"); // Add it to the queue
27     System.out.println("(7) " + queue);
28
29     queue.enqueue("John"); // Add it to the queue
30     System.out.println("(8) " + queue);
31
32     queue.enqueue("George"); // Add it to the queue
33     queue.enqueue("Michael"); // Add it to the queue
34     System.out.println("(9) " + queue);
35
36     // Remove elements from the queue
37     System.out.println("(10) " + queue.dequeue());
38     System.out.println("(11) " + queue.dequeue());
39     System.out.println("(12) " + queue);
40   }
41 }
```

EXAMPLE 17.2 (CONTINUED)

Review

For a stack, the push(o) method adds an element to the top of the stack, and the pop() method removes the top element from the stack and returns the removed element.

For a queue, the enqueue(o) method adds an element to the tail of the queue, and the dequeue() method removes the element from the head of the queue.

17.4 Binary Trees (Optional)

root
left subtree
right subtree

A list, stack, or queue is a linear structure that consists of a sequence of elements. A binary tree is a hierarchical structure. It is either empty or consists of an element, called the *root*, and two distinct binary trees, called the *left subtree* and *right subtree*. Examples of binary trees are shown in Figure 17.18.

binary search tree

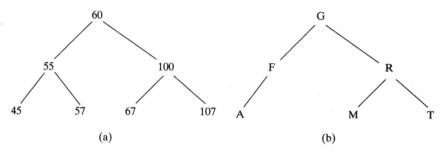

      (a)   (b)

FIGURE 17.18 *Each node in a binary tree has zero, one, or two branches.*

leaf
binary search tree

The root of a left (right) subtree of a node is called a *left (right) child* of the node. A node without children is called a *leaf*. A special type of binary tree called a *binary search tree* is often useful. A binary search tree (with no duplicate elements) has the property that for every node in the tree, the value of any node in its left subtree is less than the value of the node, and the value of any node in its right subtree is greater than the value of the node. The binary trees in Figure 17.18 are all binary search trees. This section is concerned with binary search trees.

17.4.1 Representing Binary Trees

A binary tree can be represented using a set of linked nodes. Each node contains a value and two links named *left* and *right* that reference the left child and right child, respectively, as shown in Figure 17.19.

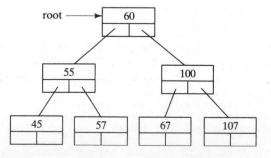

FIGURE 17.19 *A binary tree can be represented using a set of linked nodes.*

A node can be defined as a class, as follows:

```
class TreeNode {
  Object element;
  TreeNode left;
  TreeNode right;

  public TreeNode(Object o) {
    element = o;
  }
}
```

The variable root refers to the root node of the tree. If the tree is empty, root is null. The following code creates the first three nodes of the tree in Figure 17.19:

```
// Create the root node
TreeNode root = new TreeNode(new Integer(60));

// Create the left child node
root.left = new TreeNode(new Integer(55));

// Create the right child node
root.right = new TreeNode(new Integer(100));
```

17.4.2   Inserting an Element into a Binary Search Tree

If a binary tree is empty, create a root node with the new element. Otherwise, locate the parent node for the new element node. If the new element is less than the parent element, the node for the new element becomes the left child of the parent. If the new element is greater than the parent element, the node for the new element becomes the right child of the parent. Here is the algorithm:

```
if (root == null)
  root = new TreeNode(element);
else {
  // Locate the parent node
  current = root;
  while (current != null)
    if (element value < the value in current.element) {
      parent = current;
      current = current.left;
    }
    else if (element value > the value in current.element) {
      parent = current;
      current = current.right;
    }
    else
      return false; // Duplicate node not inserted

  // Create the new node and attach it to the parent node
  if (element < parent.element)
    parent.left = new TreeNode(elemenet);
  else
    parent.right = new TreeNode(elemenet);

  return true; // Element inserted
}
```

For example, to insert 101 into the tree in Figure 17.19, the parent is the node for 107. The new node for 101 becomes the left child of the parent. To insert 59 into the tree, the parent is the node for 57. The new node for 59 becomes the right child of the parent. Both of these insertions are shown in Figure 17.20.

17.4.3   Tree Traversal

Tree traversal is the process of visiting each node in the tree exactly once. There are several ways to traverse a tree. This section presents *inorder*, *preorder*, *postorder*, *depth-first*, and *breadth-first* traversals.

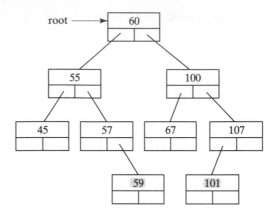

FIGURE 17.20 *Two new elements are inserted into the tree.*

inorder

With *inorder traversal*, the left subtree of the current node is visited first, then the current node, and finally the right subtree of the current node.

postorder

With *postorder traversal*, the left subtree of the current node is visited first, then the right subtree of the current node, and finally the current node itself.

preorder
depth-first

With *preorder traversal*, the current node is visited first, then the left subtree of the current node, and finally the right subtree of the current node. *Depth-first traversal* is the same as preorder traversal.

breadth-first

With *breadth-first traversal*, the nodes are visited level by level. First the root is visited, then all the children of the root from left to right, then the grandchildren of the root from left to right, and so on.

For example, in the tree in Figure 17.20, the inorder is 45 55 57 59 60 67 100 101 107. The postorder is 45 59 57 55 67 101 107 100 60. The preorder is 60 55 45 57 59 100 67 107 101. The breadth-first traversal is 60 55 100 45 57 67 107 59 101.

17.4.4 The Binary Tree Class

Let us define a binary tree class named `BinaryTree` with insert, inorder traversal, postorder traversal, and preorder traversal, as shown in Figure 17.21. Its implementation is given in Listing 17.9.

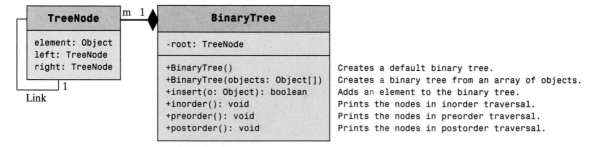

FIGURE 17.21 `BinaryTree` *implements a binary tree with operations* `insert`, `inorder`, `preorder`, *and* `postorder`.

LISTING 17.9 BinaryTree.java (Implementing Binary Tree)

no-arg constructor

```
1 public class BinaryTree {
2   private TreeNode root;
3
4   /** Create a default binary tree */
5   public BinaryTree() {
6   }
7
```

```
 8   /** Create a binary tree from an array of objects */
 9   public BinaryTree(Object[] objects) {                              constructor
10     for (int i = 0; i < objects.length; i++)
11       insert(objects[i]);
12   }
13
14   /** Insert element o into the binary tree
15    * Return true if the element is inserted successfully */
16   public boolean insert(Object o) {                                  insert
17     if (root == null)
18       root = new TreeNode(o); // Create a new root
19     else {
20       // Locate the parent node
21       TreeNode parent = null;
22       TreeNode current = root;
23       while (current != null)
24         if (((Comparable)o).compareTo(current.element) < 0) {
25           parent = current;
26           current = current.left;
27         }
28         else if (((Comparable)o).compareTo(current.element) > 0) {
29           parent = current;
30           current = current.right;
31         }
32         else
33           return false; // Duplicate node not inserted
34
35       // Create the new node and attach it to the parent node
36       if (((Comparable)o).compareTo(parent.element) < 0)
37         parent.left = new TreeNode(o);
38       else
39         parent.right = new TreeNode(o);
40     }
41
42     return true; // Element inserted
43   }
44
45   /** Inorder traversal */
46   public void inorder() {
47     inorder(root);
48   }
49
50   /** Inorder traversal from a subtree */
51   private void inorder(TreeNode root) {                              inorder
52     if (root == null) return;
53     inorder(root.left);
54     System.out.print(root.element + " ");
55     inorder(root.right);
56   }
57
58   /** Postorder traversal */
59   public void postorder() {
60     postorder(root);
61   }
62
63   /** Postorder traversal from a subtree */
64   private void postorder(TreeNode root) {                            postorder
65     if (root == null) return;
66     postorder(root.left);
67     postorder(root.right);
68     System.out.print(root.element + " ");
69   }
70
71   /** Preorder traversal */
72   public void preorder() {
73     preorder(root);
74   }
75
76   /** Preorder traversal from a subtree */
77   private void preorder(TreeNode root) {                             preorder
78     if (root == null) return;
```

```
79      System.out.print(root.element + " ");
80      preorder(root.left);
81      preorder(root.right);
82    }
83
84    /** Inner class tree node */
85    private static class TreeNode {
86      Object element;
87      TreeNode left;
88      TreeNode right;
89
90      public TreeNode(Object o) {
91        element = o;
92      }
93    }
94  }
```

tree node

The insert(Object o) method (Lines 16–43) creates a node for element o and inserts it into the tree. If the tree is empty, the node becomes the root. Otherwise, the method finds an appropriate parent for the node to maintain the order of the tree. If the element is already in the tree, the method returns false; otherwise it returns true.

The inorder() method (Lines 46–48) invokes inorder(root) to traverse the entire tree. The method inorder(TreeNode root) traverses the tree with the specified root. This is a recursive method. It recursively traverses the left subtree, then the root, and finally the right subtree. The traversal ends when the tree is empty.

The postorder() method (Lines 59–61) and the preorder() method (Lines 72–74) are implemented similarly using recursion.

EXAMPLE 17.3 USING BINARY TREES

Problem

Write a program that creates a binary tree using BinaryTree. Add strings into the binary tree and traverse the tree in inorder, postorder, and preorder.

Solution

Listing 17.10 gives the solution to the problem. A sample run of the program is shown in Figure 17.22.

```
C:\book>java TestBinaryTree
Inorder: Adam Daniel George Jones Michael Peter Tom
Postorder: Daniel Adam Jones Peter Tom Michael George
Preorder: George Adam Daniel Michael Jones Tom Peter
C:\book>
```

FIGURE 17.22 *The program creates a tree, inserts elements into it, and displays them in inorder, postorder, and preorder.*

LISTING 17.10 **TestBinaryTree.java (Using BinaryTree)**

```
1 public class TestBinaryTree {
2   public static void main(String[] args) {
3     BinaryTree tree = new BinaryTree();
4     tree.insert("George");
5     tree.insert("Michael");
6     tree.insert("Tom");
7     tree.insert("Adam");
8     tree.insert("Jones");
9     tree.insert("Peter");
```

create tree
insert

EXAMPLE 17.3 (CONTINUED)

```
10      tree.insert("Daniel");
11      System.out.print("Inorder: ");
12      tree.inorder();
13      System.out.print("\nPostorder: ");
14      tree.postorder();
15      System.out.print("\nPreorder: ");
16      tree.preorder();
17    }
18 }
```

inorder

postorder

preorder

Review

After all the elements are inserted, the tree should appear as shown in Figure 17.23.

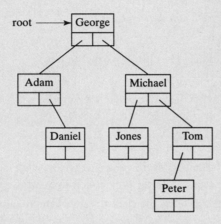

FIGURE 17.23 *A binary search tree is pictured here after Line 10 is executed.*

If the elements are inserted in a different order (e.g., Daniel, Adam, Jones, Peter, Tom, Michael, George), the tree will look different. However, the inorder is the same as long as the set of elements is the same.

KEY TERMS

binary search tree   638
binary tree   638
data structure   620
dynamic data structure   620
inorder traversal   640
list   620

object-oriented data structure   620
postorder traversal   640
preorder traversal   640
queue   620
stack   620
tree traversal   639

CHAPTER SUMMARY

✦ You have learned the concept of object-oriented data structures and how to create lists, stacks, queues, and binary trees using object-oriented approach.

✦ To define a data structure is essentially to declare a class. The class for a data structure should use data fields to store data and provide methods to support such operations as insertion and deletion.

✦ To create a data structure is to create an instance from the class. You can then apply the methods on the instance to manipulate the data structure, such as inserting an element to the data structure or deleting an element from the data structure.

REVIEW QUESTIONS

Sections 17.1–17.2

17.1 What is a data structure? What is an object-oriented data structure?

17.2 What are the limitations of the array data type?

17.3 MyArrayList is implemented using an array, and an array is a fixed-size data structure. Why is MyArrayList considered as a dynamic data structure?

17.4 What are the benefits of defining both the MyList interface and the MyAbstractList class? What is a convenience class?

17.5 What is wrong in the following code?

```
MyArrayList list = new MyArrayList();
list.add(100);
```

17.6 What is wrong if Lines 11–12 in MyArrayList.java

```
data = objects;
size = objects.length;
```

are replaced by

```
super(objects);
```

17.7 If the number of elements in the program is fixed, what data structure should you use? If the number of elements in the program changes, what data structure should you use?

17.8 If you have to add or delete the elements anywhere in a list, should you use ArrayList or LinkedList?

Section 17.3 Stacks and Queues

17.9 You can use inheritance or composition to design the data structures for stacks and queues. Discuss the pros and cons of these two approaches.

17.10 Which lines of the following code are wrong?

```
MyList list = new MyArrayList();
list.add("Tom");
list = new MyLinkedList();
list.add("Tom");
list = new MyStack();
list.add("Tom");
```

Section 17.4 Binary Trees

17.11 If a set of the same elements is inserted into a binary tree in two different orders, will the two corresponding binary trees look the same? Will the inorder traversal be the same? Will the postorder traversal be the same? Will the preorder traversal be the same?

PROGRAMMING EXERCISES

Section 17.2 Lists

17.1 (*Adding set operations in* MyAbstractList) Add and implement the following methods in MyAbstractList:

```
/** Add the elements in otherList to this list.
  * Returns true if this list changed as a result of the call */
public boolean addAll(MyList otherList)
```

```
/** Remove all the elements in otherList from this list
  * Returns true if this list changed as a result of the call */
public boolean removeAll(MyList otherList)

/** Retain the elements in this list if they are also in otherList
  * Returns true if this list changed as a result of the call */
public boolean retainAll(MyList otherList)
```

Write a test program that creates two MyArrayLists, list1 and list2, with the initial values {"Tom", "George", "Peter", "Jean", "Jane"} and {"Tom", "George", "Michael", "Michelle", "Daniel"}, then invokes list1.addAll(list2), list1.removeAll(list2), and list1.retainAll(list2), and displays the resulting new list1.

17.2* (*Completing the implementation of MyLinkedList*) The implementations of methods removeLast(), contains(Object o), get(int index), indexOf(Object o), lastIndex-Of(Object o), remove(Object o), and set(int index, Object o) are omitted in the text. Implement these methods.

17.3* (*Creating a two-way linked list*) The MyLinkedList class in Listing 17.5 is a one-way directional linked list that enables one-way traversal of the list. Modify the Node class to add the new field name previous to refer to the previous node in the list, as follows:

```
public class TreeNode {
  Object element;
  TreeNode next;
  TreeNode previous;

  public TreeNode(Object o) {
    element = o;
  }
}
```

Simplify the implementation of the add(Object element, int index) method and the remove(int index) and remove(Object element) to take advantage of the bi-directional linked list.

Section 17.3 Stacks and Queues

17.4 (*Implementing MyStack using inheritance*) In Section 17.3, "Stacks and Queues," MyStack is implemented using composition. Create a new stack class that extends MyArrayList.

17.5 (*Implementing MyQueue using inheritance*) In Section 17.3, "Stacks and Queues," MyQueue is implemented using composition. Create a new queue class that extends MyLinkedList.

Section 17.4 Binary Trees

17.6* (*Adding new methods in BinaryTree*) Add the following new methods in BinaryTree.

```
/** Search element o in this binary tree */
public boolean search(Object o)

/** Return the number of nodes in this binary tree */
public int size()

/** Return the depth of this binary tree. Depth is the
  * number of the nodes in the longest path of the tree */
public int depth()
```

17.7* * (*Implementing inorder traversal using a stack*) Implement the inorder method in BinaryTree using a stack instead of recursion.

chapter

18

JAVA COLLECTIONS FRAMEWORK

Objectives

+ To describe the Java Collections Framework hierarchy (§18.1).

+ To use the common methods defined in the `Collection` interface for operating sets and lists (§18.2).

+ To use the `Iterator` interface to traverse a collection (§18.3).

+ To use the JDK 1.5 enhanced `for` loop to replace an iterator for traversing a collection (§18.3).

+ To discover the `Set` interface, and know how and when to use `HashSet`, `LinkedHashSet`, or `TreeSet` to store elements (§18.3).

+ To compare elements using the `Comparator` interface (§18.4).

+ To explore the `List` interface, and know how and when to use `ArrayList` or `LinkedList` to store elements (§18.5).

+ To distinguish `Vector` and `ArrayList`, and know how to use `Vector` and `Stack` (§18.5).

+ To simplify programming using JDK 1.5 generic types (§18.6).

+ To understand the differences between `Collection` and `Map`, and know how and when to use `HashMap`, `LinkedHashMap`, and `TreeMap` to store values associated with keys (§18.7).

+ To use the static methods in the `Collections` class (§18.8).

+ To use the static methods in the `Arrays` classes (§18.9).

18.1 Introduction

The preceding chapter introduced data structures and the techniques for implementing dynamic data structures using array lists, linked lists, and binary trees. Array lists and linked lists are predefined in Java. Java introduced several interfaces and classes that can be used to organize and manipulate data efficiently. These interfaces and classes form the *Java Collections Framework*. This chapter introduces the data structures in the Java collections framework. The focus is on how to use the classes and interfaces in the collections framework. Since knowledge of implementing data structures is not required for learning the Java collections framework, this chapter is designed independently from the preceding chapter.

    A *collection* is a container object that stores a group of objects, often referred to as *elements*. The Java Collections Framework supports three types of collections: *set*, *list*, and *map*. They are defined in the interfaces `Set`, `List`, and `Map`. An instance of `Set` stores a group of nonduplicate elements. An instance of `List` stores an ordered collection of elements. An instance of `Map` stores a group of objects, each of which is associated with a key. The relationships of the interfaces and classes in the Java Collections Framework are shown in Figures 18.1 and 18.2. These interfaces and classes provide a unified API for efficiently storing and processing a collection of objects. You will learn how to use these interfaces and classes in this chapter.

Java Collection Framework

collection

set
list
map

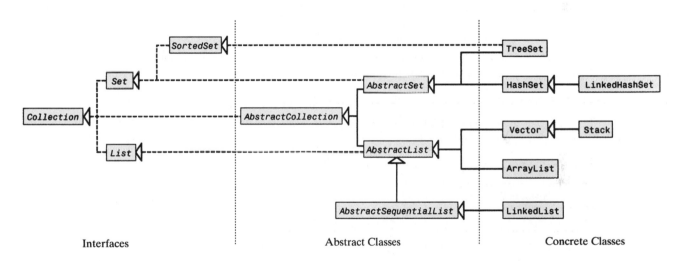

FIGURE **18.1** *Set and List are subinterfaces of* Collection.

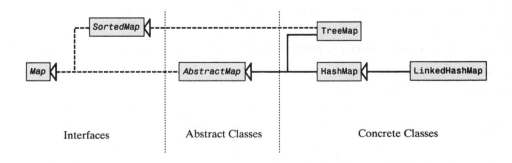

FIGURE **18.2** *An instance of* Map *stores a group of objects and their associated keys.*

NOTE

All the interfaces and classes defined in the Java Collections Framework are grouped in the `java.util` package.

 NOTE

The design of the Java Collections Framework is a good example of using interfaces, abstract classes, and concrete classes. The interfaces define the framework. The abstract classes provide partial implementation for convenience. The concrete classes implement the interfaces with concrete data structures.

Cloneable
Serializable

 NOTE

All the concrete classes in the Java Collections Framework implement the `Cloneable` and `Serializable` interfaces. Thus their instances can be cloned and serialized.

18.2 The `Collection` Interface and the `AbstractCollection` Class

The `Collection` interface is the root interface for manipulating a collection of objects. Its public methods are listed in Figure 18.3. The `AbstractCollection` class is a convenience class that provides partial implementation for the `Collection` interface. It implements all the methods in `Collection` except the `size` and `iterator` methods. These are implemented in appropriate subclasses.

The `Collection` interface provides the basic operations for adding and removing elements in a collection. The `add` method adds an element to the collection. The `addAll` method adds all the elements in the specified collection to this collection. The `remove` method removes an element from the collection. The `removeAll` method removes the elements from this collection that are present in the specified collection. The `retainAll` method retains the elements in this collection that are also present in the specified collection. All these methods return `boolean`. The return

---

java.util.Collection

+add(o: Object): boolean	Adds a new element o to this collection.
+addAll(c: Collection): boolean	Adds all the elements in the collection c to this collection.
+clear(): void	Removes all the elements from this collection.
+contains(o: Object): boolean	Returns true if this collection contains the element o.
+containsAll(c: Collection): boolean	Returns true if this collection contains all the elements in c.
+equals(o: Object): boolean	Returns true if this collection is equal to another collection o.
+hashCode(): int	Returns the hash code for this collection.
+isEmpty(): boolean	Returns true if this collection contains no elements.
+iterator(): Iterator	Returns an iterator for the elements in this collection.
+remove(o: Object): boolean	Removes the element o from this collection.
+removeAll(c: Collection): boolean	Removes all the elements in c from this collection.
+retainAll(c: Collection): boolean	Returns the elements that are both in c and in this collection.
+size(): int	Returns the number of elements in this collection.
+toArray(): Object[]	Returns an array of Object for the elements in this collection.
+toArray(array: Object[]): Object[]	Returns an array for the elements with the specified type.

java.util.Iterator

+hasNext(): boolean	Returns true if this iterator has more elements to traverse.
+next(): Object	Returns the next element from this iterator.
+remove(): void	Removes the last element obtained using the next method.

FIGURE 18.3 *The `Collection` interface contains the methods for manipulating the elements in a collection, and each collection object contains an iterator for traversing elements in the collection.*

value is true if the collection is changed as a result of the method execution. The clear() method simply removes all the elements from the collection.

 NOTE

The methods addAll, removeAll, and retainAll are similar to the set union, difference, and intersection operations.

The Collection interface provides various query operations. The size method returns the number of elements in the collection. The contains method checks whether the collection contains the specified element. The containsAll method checks whether the collection contains all the elements in the specified collection. The isEmpty method returns true if the collection is empty.

The Collection interface provides two overloaded methods to convert the collection into an array. The toArray() method returns an array representation for the collection. The toArray(Object[] a) method returns an array containing all of the elements in this collection whose runtime type matches the element type of array a.

The iterator method in the Collection interface returns an instance of the Iterator interface, as shown in Figure 18.3, which provides sequential access to the elements in the collection using the next() method. You can also use the hasNext() method to check whether there are more elements in the iterator, and the remove() method to remove the last element returned by the iterator.

 NOTE

Some of the methods in the Collection interface cannot be implemented in the concrete subclass. In this case, the method would throw java.lang.Unsupported-OperationException, a subclass of RuntimeException. This is a good design that you can use in your project. Recall that Cylinder inherits the findPerimeter method from Circle in Figure 9.1. The findPerimeter method has no meaning in the Cylinder class. Therefore, you can implement it in the Cylinder class:

```
public double findPerimeter() {
    throw new UnsupportedOperationException("Method not supported");
}
```

18.3 Sets

The Set interface extends the Collection interface. It does not introduce new methods or constants, but it stipulates that an instance of Set contains no duplicate elements. The concrete classes that implement Set must ensure that no duplicate elements can be added to the set. That is, no two elements e1 and e2 can be in the set such that e1.equals(e2) is true.

no duplicates

The AbstractSet class is a convenience class that extends AbstractCollection and implements Set. The AbstractSet class provides concrete implementations for the equals method and the hashCode method. The hash code of a set is the sum of the hash codes of all the elements in the set. Since the size method and iterator method are not implemented in the AbstractSet class, AbstractSet is an abstract class.

Three concrete classes of Set are HashSet, LinkedHashSet, and TreeSet.

18.3.1 HashSet

The HashSet class is a concrete class that implements Set. You can create a HashSet using its no-arg constructor. A HashSet can be used to store duplicate-free elements. For efficiency, objects added to a hash set need to implement the hashCode method in a manner that properly disperses the hash code. Most of the classes in the Java API implement the hashCode method. For example, the hashCode in the Integer class returns its int value. The hashCode in the Character class returns the Unicode of the character. The hashCode in the String class returns $s_0*31^{(n-1)} + s_1*31^{(n-2)} + \ldots + s_{n-1}$, where s_i is s.charAt(i).

Recall that the hash codes of two objects must be same if two objects are equal. Two unequal objects may have the same hash code, but you should implement the hashCode method to avoid too many such cases. Additionally, it is required that invoking the hashCode method multiple times returns the same integer during one execution of the program.

 NOTE

You will get a compilation warning "unchecked operation" in JDK 1.5. Ignore it. This warning can be fixed using generic types in Section 18.6.

EXAMPLE 18.1 USING HashSet AND Iterator

Problem

Write a program that finds all the words used in a text. The program creates a hash set to store the words extracted from the text, and uses an iterator to traverse the elements in the set.

Solution

Listing 18.1 gives the solution to the problem. The output of the program is shown in Figure 18.4.

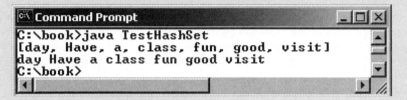

FIGURE 18.4 *The program adds string elements to a hash set, displays the elements using the* toString *method, and traverses the elements using an iterator.*

LISTING 18.1 TestHashSet.java (Using HashSet and Iterator)

```
 1 import java.util.*;
 2
 3 public class TestHashSet {
 4   public static void main(String[] args) {
 5     // Create a hash set
 6     Set set = new HashSet();
 7
 8     // Text in a string
 9     String text = "Have a good day. Have a good class. " +
10       "Have a good visit. Have fun!";
11
12     // Extract words from text
13     StringTokenizer st = new StringTokenizer(text, " .!?");
14     while (st.hasMoreTokens())
15       set.add(st.nextToken());
16
17     System.out.println(set);
18
19     // Obtain an iterator for the hash set
20     Iterator iterator = set.iterator();
21
22     // Display the elements in the hash set
23     while (iterator.hasNext()) {
24       System.out.print(iterator.next() + " ");
25     }
26   }
27 }
```

create set

get iterator

EXAMPLE 18.1 (CONTINUED)

Review

The words are extracted using StringTokenizer and are added to the set (Lines 13–15). If a word like "good" is added to the set more than once, only one is stored, because a set does not allow duplicates.

As shown in Figure 18.4, the words are not stored in the order in which they are inserted into the set. There is no particular order for the elements in a hash set. To impose an order on them, you need to use the LinkedHashSet class, which is introduced in the next section.

 TIP

You can simplify the code in Lines 20–25 using a JDK 1.5 enhanced for loop without using an iterator, as follows:

```
for (Object element: set)
    System.out.print(element.toString() + " ");
```

JDK 1.5 enhanced for loop

18.3.2   LinkedHashSet

LinkedHashSet was added in JDK 1.4. It extends HashSet with a linked list implementation that supports an ordering of the elements in the set. The elements in a HashSet are not ordered, but the elements in a LinkedHashSet can be retrieved in the order in which they were inserted into the set. A LinkedHashSet can be created by using its no-arg constructor.

EXAMPLE 18.2 USING LinkedHashSet

Problem

Rewrite the preceding example using LinkedHashSet.

Solution

Simply replace HashSet by LinkedHashSet. Listing 18.2 gives the solution to the problem. The output of the program is shown in Figure 18.5.

```
Command Prompt                                    _ □ ×
C:\book>java TestLinkedHashSet
[Have, a, good, day, class, visit, fun]
Have a good day class visit fun
C:\book>_
```

FIGURE 18.5   *The program adds string elements to a linked hash set, displays the elements using the toString method, and traverses the elements using an iterator.*

LISTING 18.2   TestLinkedHashSet.java (Using LinkedHashSet)

```
1 import java.util.*;
2
3 public class TestLinkedHashSet {
4   public static void main(String[] args) {
```

EXAMPLE **18.2** (CONTINUED)

create set

```
 5      // Create a hash set
 6      Set set = new LinkedHashSet();
 7
 8      // Text in a string
 9      String text = "Have a good day. Have a good class. " +
10        "Have a good visit. Have fun!";
11
12      // Extract words from text
13      StringTokenizer st = new StringTokenizer(text, " .!?");
14      while (st.hasMoreTokens())
15        set.add(st.nextToken());
16
17      System.out.println(set);
18
19      // Obtain an iterator for the hash set
20      Iterator iterator = set.iterator();
21
22      // Display the elements in the hash set
23      while (iterator.hasNext()) {
24        System.out.print(iterator.next() + " ");
25      }
26    }
27 }
```

get iterator

Review

A `LinkedHashSet` is created in Line 6. As shown in Figure 18.5, the words are stored in the order in which they are inserted. Since `LinkedHashSet` is a set, it does not store duplicate elements.

The `LinkedHashSet` maintains the order in which the elements are inserted. To impose a different order (e.g., increasing or decreasing order), you can use the `TreeSet` class introduced in the next section.

 TIP

If you don't need to maintain the order in which the elements are inserted, use `HashSet`, which is more efficient than `LinkedHashSet`.

18.3.3 `TreeSet`

`SortedSet` is a subinterface of `Set`, which guarantees that the elements in the set are sorted. `TreeSet` is a concrete class that implements the `SortedSet` interface. To create a `TreeSet`, use its no-arg constructor or use `new TreeSet(Collection)`. You can add objects into a tree set as long as they can be compared with each other. There are two ways to compare objects.

Comparable

◆ Use the `Comparable` interface. Since the objects added to the set are instances of `Comparable`, they can be compared using the `compareTo` method. The `Comparable` interface was introduced in Section 9.4, "Interfaces." Several classes in the Java API, such as the `String` class and all the wrapper classes for the primitive types, implement the `Comparable` interface. This approach is referred to as *natural order*.

natural order

◆ If the class for the elements does not implement the `Comparable` interface or if you don't want to use the `compareTo` method in the class that implements the `Comparable` interface, specify a comparator for the elements in the set. This approach is referred to as *order by comparator*. It will be introduced in Section 18.4, "The `Comparator` Interface."

Comparator

EXAMPLE 18.3 USING TreeSet TO SORT ELEMENTS IN A SET

Problem

The preceding example displays all the words used in a text. The words are displayed in their insertion order. This example rewrites the preceding example to display the words in alphabetical order using the TreeSet class.

Solution

Listing 18.3 gives the solution to the problem. Figure 18.6 shows a sample run of the program.

```
Command Prompt                                    _ □ ×
C:\book>java TestTreeSet
[Have, a, class, day, fun, good, visit]
Have a class day fun good visit
C:\book>
```

FIGURE 18.6 *The program demonstrates the differences between hash sets and tree sets.*

LISTING 18.3 TestTreeSet.java (Using TreeSet)

```java
1 import java.util.*;
2
3 public class TestTreeSet {
4   public static void main(String[] args) {
5     // Create a hash set
6     Set set = new HashSet();                              create hash set
7
8     // Text in a string
9     String text = "Have a good day. Have a good class. " +
10      "Have a good visit. Have fun!";
11
12    // Extract words from text
13    StringTokenizer st = new StringTokenizer(text, " .!?");
14    while (st.hasMoreTokens())
15      set.add(st.nextToken());
16
17    TreeSet treeSet = new TreeSet(set);                   create tree set
18    System.out.println(treeSet);
19
20    // Obtain an iterator for the hash set
21    Iterator iterator = treeSet.iterator();               get iterator
22
23    // Display the elements in the hash set
24    while (iterator.hasNext()) {
25      System.out.print(iterator.next() + " ");
26    }
27  }
28 }
```

Review

The example creates a hash set filled with strings, and then creates a tree set for the same strings. The strings are sorted in the tree set using the compareTo method in the Comparable interface.

EXAMPLE 18.3 (CONTINUED)

The elements in the set are sorted once you create a `TreeSet` object from a `HashSet` object using `new TreeSet(hashSet)` (Line 17). You may rewrite the program to create an instance of `TreeSet` using its no-arg constructor, and add the strings into the `TreeSet` object. Then, every time a string is added to the `TreeSet` object, the elements in it will be reordered. The approach used in the example is generally more efficient because it requires only a one-time sorting.

 NOTE

All the classes in Figure 18.1 have at least two constructors. One is the no-arg constructor that constructs an empty collection. The other constructs instances from a collection. Thus the `TreeSet` class has the constructor `TreeSet(Collection c)` for constructing a `TreeSet` from a collection c. In this example, `new TreeSet(hashSet)` creates an instance of `TreeSet` from the collection `hashSet`.

 TIP

If you don't need to maintain a sorted set when updating a set, you can use a hash set, because it takes less time to insert and remove elements in a hash set. When you need a set to be sorted, you can convert it into a tree set.

 CAUTION

All the elements added to the tree set must be comparable, such as all `String` objects. A runtime error will occur if you add an object that is not comparable with the existing objects in the tree set. For example, a `ClassCastException` will occur if you add an `Integer` object to a tree set of strings.

18.4   The `Comparator` Interface

Sometimes you want to insert elements of different types into a tree set. The elements may not be instances of `java.lang.Comparable` or are not comparable. You can define a comparator to compare these elements. To do so, create a class that implements the `java.util.Comparator` interface. The `Comparator` interface has two methods, `compare` and `equals`.

✦ `public int compare(Object element1, Object element2)`
Returns a negative value if `element1` is less than `element2`, a positive value if `element1` is greater than `element2`, and zero if they are equal.

✦ `public boolean equals(Object element)`
Returns true if the specified object is also a comparator and imposes the same ordering as this comparator.

 NOTE

The equals method is also defined in the `Object` class. Therefore, you will not get a compilation error even if you don't implement the `equals` method in your custom comparator class. However, in some cases implementing this method may improve performance by allowing programs to determine quickly whether two distinct comparators impose the same order.

For example, you can provide the following comparator to compare two elements of the
GeometricObject class, defined in Section 9.2, "Abstract Classes":

```
import java.util.Comparator;

public class GeometricObjectComparator implements Comparator {
  public int compare(Object o1, Object o2) {
    double area1 = ((GeometricObject)o1).findArea();
    double area2 = ((GeometricObject)o2).findArea();

    if (area1 < area2)
      return -1;
    else if (area1 == area2)
      return 0;
    else
      return 1;
  }
}
```

If you create a TreeSet using its no-arg constructor, the compareTo method is used to compare
the elements in the set, assuming that the class of the elements implements the Comparable interface. To use a comparator, you have to use the constructor TreeSet(Comparator comparator) to
create a sorted set that uses the compare method in the comparator to order the elements in the set.

EXAMPLE 18.4 USING Comparator TO SORT ELEMENTS IN A SET

Problem

Write a program that demonstrates how to sort elements in a tree set using the Comparator
interface. The example creates a tree set of geometric objects. The geometric objects are
sorted using the compare method in the Comparator interface.

Solution

Listing 18.4 gives the solution to the problem. The output of the program is shown in
Figure 18.7.

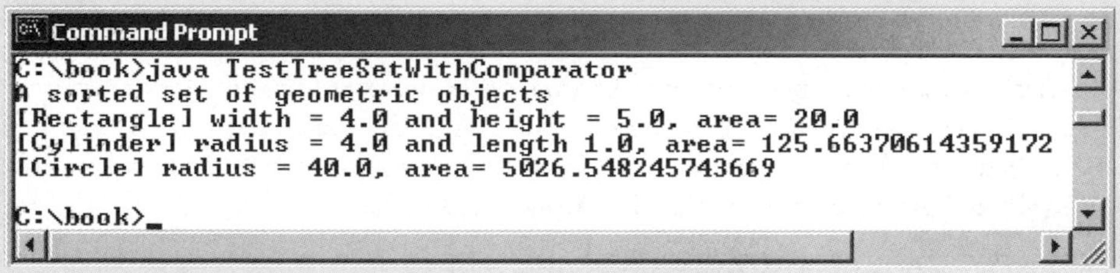

```
Command Prompt                                                    _ □ ×
C:\book>java TestTreeSetWithComparator
A sorted set of geometric objects
[Rectangle] width = 4.0 and height = 5.0, area= 20.0
[Cylinder] radius = 4.0 and length 1.0, area= 125.66370614359172
[Circle] radius = 40.0, area= 5026.548245743669

C:\book>_
```

FIGURE 18.7   *The program demonstrates the use of the Comparator interface.*

LISTING 18.4   TestTreeSetWithComparator.java

```
 1 import java.util.*;
 2
 3 public class TestTreeSetWithComparator {
 4   public static void main(String[] args) {
 5     // Create a tree set for geometric objects using a comparator
 6     Set geometricObjectSet =
 7       new TreeSet(new GeometricObjectComparator());          tree set
 8     geometricObjectSet.add(new Rectangle(4, 5));
 9     geometricObjectSet.add(new Circle9(40));
10     geometricObjectSet.add(new Circle9(40));
11     geometricObjectSet.add(new Cylinder9(4, 1));
```

EXAMPLE **18.4** (CONTINUED)

```
12
13      // Obtain an iterator for the tree set of geometric objects
14      Iterator iterator = geometricObjectSet.iterator();
15
16      // Display geometric objects in the tree set
17      System.out.println("A sorted set of geometric objects");
18      while (iterator.hasNext()) {
19        GeometricObject object = (GeometricObject)iterator.next();
20        System.out.println(object + ", area= " + object.findArea());
21      }
22    }
23 }
```

Review

The Circle9, Cylinder9, and Rectangle classes were defined in Section 9.2, "Abstract Classes." They are all subclasses of GeometricObject.

Two circles of the same radius are added to the set in the tree set (Lines 9–10), but only one is stored, because the two circles are equal and the set does not allow duplicates.

18.5   Lists

A set stores nonduplicate elements. To allow duplicate elements to be stored in a collection, you need to use a list. A list can not only store duplicate elements, but also allows the user to specify where they are stored. The user can access elements by an index. The List interface extends Collection to define an ordered collection with duplicates allowed. The List interface adds position-oriented operations, as well as a new list iterator that enables the user to traverse the list bi-directionally. The new methods in the List interface are shown in Figure 18.8.

The add(index, element) method is used to insert an element at a specified index, and the addAll(index, collection) method to insert all the elements in a collection at a specified index. The remove(index) method is used to remove an element at the specified index from the list. A new element can be set at the specified index using the set(index, element) method.

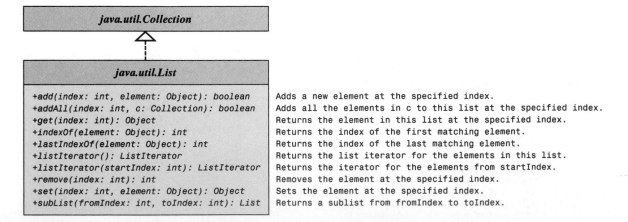

FIGURE 18.8   *The List interface stores elements in sequence, permitting duplicates.*

The `indexOf(element)` method is used to obtain the index of the first occurrence of the specified element in the list, and the `lastIndexOf(element)` method to obtain the index of the last occurrence of the specified element in the list. A sublist can be obtained by using the `subList(fromIndex, toIndex)` method.

The `listIterator()` or `listIterator(startIndex)` method returns an instance of `List-Iterator`. The `ListIterator` interface extends the `Iterator` interface to add bi-directional traversal of the list. The methods in `ListIterator` are listed in Figure 18.9.

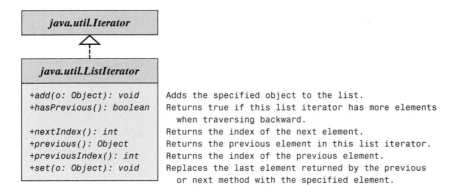

FIGURE 18.9 `ListIterator` *enables traversal of a list bi-directionally.*

The `add(element)` method inserts the specified element into the list. The element is inserted immediately before the next element that would be returned by the `next()` method defined in the `Iterator` interface, if any, and after the element that would be returned by the `previous()` method, if any. If the list contains no elements, the new element becomes the sole element on the list. The `set(element)` method can be used to replace the last element returned by the `next` method or the `previous` method with the specified element.

The `hasNext()` method defined in the `Iterator` interface is used to check whether the iterator has more elements when traversed in the forward direction, and the `hasPrevious()` method to check whether the iterator has more elements when traversed in the backward direction.

The `next()` method defined in the `Iterator` interface returns the next element in the iterator, and the `previous()` method returns the previous element in the iterator. The `nextIndex()` method returns the index of the next element in the iterator, and the `previousIndex()` returns the index of the previous element in the iterator.

The `AbstractList` class provides a partial implementation for the `List` interface. The `Abstract-SequentialList` class extends `AbstractList` to provide support for linked lists.

18.5.1 The `ArrayList` and `LinkedList` Classes

The `ArrayList` class and the `LinkedList` class are two concrete implementations of the `List` interface. `ArrayList` stores elements in an array. The array is dynamically created. If the capacity of the array is exceeded, create a larger new array and copy all the elements from the current array to the new array. `LinkedList` stores elements in a linked list. Which of the two classes you use depends on your specific needs. If you need to support random access through an index without inserting or removing elements except at the end, `ArrayList` offers the most efficient collection. If, however, your application requires the insertion or deletion of elements anywhere in the list, you should choose `LinkedList`. A list can grow or shrink dynamically. An array is fixed once it is created. If your application does not require the insertion or deletion of elements, an array is the most efficient data structure.

`ArrayList` is a resizable-array implementation of the `List` interface. In addition to implementing the `List` interface, this class provides methods for manipulating the size of the array that is used internally to store the list. Each `ArrayList` instance has a capacity. The capacity is the size of the array used to store the elements in the list. It is always at least as large as the list size. As elements are added to an `ArrayList`, its capacity grows automatically. An `ArrayList` can be constructed using its no-arg constructor, `ArrayList(Collection)`, or `ArrayList(intialCapacity)`.

`LinkedList` is a linked list implementation of the `List` interface. In addition to implementing the `List` interface, this class provides the methods for retrieving, inserting, and removing elements from both ends of the list, as shown in Figure 18.10. A `LinkedList` can be constructed using its no-arg constructor or `LinkedList(Collection)`.

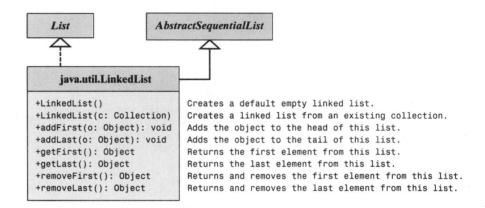

java.util.LinkedList	
+LinkedList()	Creates a default empty linked list.
+LinkedList(c: Collection)	Creates a linked list from an existing collection.
+addFirst(o: Object): void	Adds the object to the head of this list.
+addLast(o: Object): void	Adds the object to the tail of this list.
+getFirst(): Object	Returns the first element from this list.
+getLast(): Object	Returns the last element from this list.
+removeFirst(): Object	Returns and removes the first element from this list.
+removeLast(): Object	Returns and removes the last element from this list.

FIGURE 18.10 *`LinkedList` provides methods for adding and inserting elements at both ends of the list.*

EXAMPLE 18.5 USING `ArrayList` AND `LinkedList`

Problem

Write a program that creates an array list filled with numbers and inserts new elements into specified locations in the list. The example also creates a linked list from the array list, and inserts and removes elements from the list. Finally, the example traverses the list forward and backward.

Solution

Listing 18.5 gives the solution to the problem. The output of the program is shown in Figure 18.11.

```
C:\book>java TestArrayAndLinkedList
A list of integers in the array list:
[10, 1, 2, 30, 3, 1, 4]
Display the linked list forward:
green 10 red 1 2 30 3 1
Display the linked list backward:
1 3 30 2 1 red 10 green
C:\book>
```

FIGURE 18.11 *The program uses an array list and linked lists.*

EXAMPLE 18.5 (CONTINUED)

LISTING 18.5 TestArrayAndLinkedList.java

```
1 import java.util.*;
2
3 public class TestArrayAndLinkedList {
4   public static void main(String[] args) {
5     List arrayList = new ArrayList();
6     arrayList.add(new Integer(1));
7     arrayList.add(new Integer(2));
8     arrayList.add(new Integer(3));
9     arrayList.add(new Integer(1));
10    arrayList.add(new Integer(4));
11    arrayList.add(0, new Integer(10));
12    arrayList.add(3, new Integer(30));
13
14    System.out.println("A list of integers in the array list:");
15    System.out.println(arrayList);
16
17    LinkedList linkedList = new LinkedList(arrayList);
18    linkedList.add(1, "red");
19    linkedList.removeLast();
20    linkedList.addFirst("green");
21
22    System.out.println("Display the linked list forward:");
23    ListIterator listIterator = linkedList.listIterator();
24    while (listIterator.hasNext()) {
25      System.out.print(listIterator.next() + " ");
26    }
27    System.out.println();
28
29    System.out.println("Display the linked list backward:");
30    listIterator = linkedList.listIterator(linkedList.size());
31    while (listIterator.hasPrevious()) {
32      System.out.print(listIterator.previous() + " ");
33    }
34  }
35 }
```

array list

linked list

list iterator

list iterator

Review

A list can hold identical elements. Integer 1 is stored twice in the list (Lines 6, 9). `ArrayList` and `LinkedList` are operated similarly. The critical difference between them pertains to internal implementation, which affects their performance. `ArrayList` is efficient for retrieving elements, and for inserting and removing elements from the end of the list. `LinkedList` is efficient for inserting and removing elements anywhere in the list.

You can use `TreeSet` to store sorted elements. But there is no sorted list. However, the Java Collections Framework provides static methods in the `Collections` class that can be used to sort a list. The `Collections` class is introduced in Section 18.8, "The Collections Class."

18.5.2 The `Vector` Class

The Java Collections Framework was introduced with Java 2. Several data structures were supported prior to Java 2. Among them were the `Vector` class and the `Stack` class. These classes were redesigned to fit into the Java Collections Framework, but all their methods are retained for compatibility. This section introduces the Vector class, and the next section introduces the Stack class.

In Java 2, Vector is the same as ArrayList, except that it contains synchronized methods for accessing and modifying the vector. Synchronized methods can prevent data corruption when a vector is accessed and modified by two or more threads concurrently. Synchronization will be introduced in Chapter 19, "Multithreading." None of the new data collection structures introduced so far are synchronized. If synchronization is required, you can use the synchronized versions of the collection classes. These classes are introduced in Section 18.8, "The Collections Class."

The Vector class implements the List interface. It also has the methods contained in the original Vector class defined prior to Java 2, as shown in Figure 18.12.

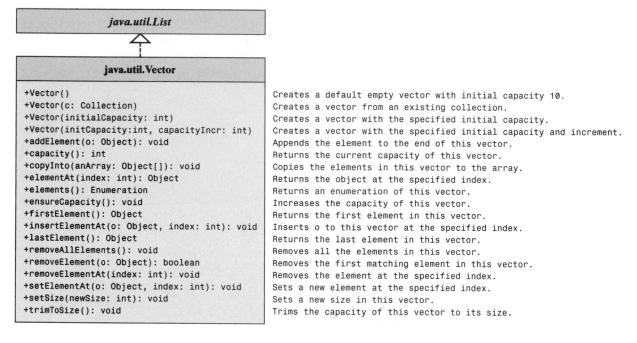

java.util.List

java.util.Vector	
+Vector()	Creates a default empty vector with initial capacity 10.
+Vector(c: Collection)	Creates a vector from an existing collection.
+Vector(initialCapacity: int)	Creates a vector with the specified initial capacity.
+Vector(initCapacity:int, capacityIncr: int)	Creates a vector with the specified initial capacity and increment.
+addElement(o: Object): void	Appends the element to the end of this vector.
+capacity(): int	Returns the current capacity of this vector.
+copyInto(anArray: Object[]): void	Copies the elements in this vector to the array.
+elementAt(index: int): Object	Returns the object at the specified index.
+elements(): Enumeration	Returns an enumeration of this vector.
+ensureCapacity(): void	Increases the capacity of this vector.
+firstElement(): Object	Returns the first element in this vector.
+insertElementAt(o: Object, index: int): void	Inserts o to this vector at the specified index.
+lastElement(): Object	Returns the last element in this vector.
+removeAllElements(): void	Removes all the elements in this vector.
+removeElement(o: Object): boolean	Removes the first matching element in this vector.
+removeElementAt(index: int): void	Removes the element at the specified index.
+setElementAt(o: Object, index: int): void	Sets a new element at the specified index.
+setSize(newSize: int): void	Sets a new size in this vector.
+trimToSize(): void	Trims the capacity of this vector to its size.

FIGURE 18.12 *The Vector class in Java 2 implements List and also retains all the methods in the original Vector class.*

Most of the additional methods in the Vector class listed in the UML diagram in Figure 18.12 are similar to the methods in the List interface. These methods were introduced before the Java Collections Framework. For example, addElement(Object element) is the same as the add(Object element) method, except that addElement method is synchronized. Use the ArrayList class if you don't need synchronization. It works much faster than Vector.

 NOTE

The elements() method returns an Enumeration. The Enumeration interface was introduced prior to Java 2 and was superseded by the Iterator interface.

 NOTE

Vector is widely used in Java programming because it was the Java resizable array implementation before Java 2. Many of the Swing data models use vectors.

EXAMPLE 18.6 USING THE Vector CLASS

Problem

Example 3.10, "Displaying Prime Numbers," determines whether a number n is prime by checking whether 2, 3, 4, 5, 6, . . . , n/2 is a divisor. If a divisor is found, n is not prime. A more efficient approach to determine whether n is prime is to check whether any of the prime numbers less than or equal to $\sqrt{n}$ can divide n evenly. If not, n is prime. Write a program that finds all the prime numbers less than 250.

Solution

The program stores the prime numbers in a vector. Initially, the vector is empty. For n = 2, 3, 4, 5, . . . , 250, the program determines whether n is prime by checking whether any prime number less than or equal to $\sqrt{n}$ in the vector is a divisor for n. If not, n is prime, so add n to the vector. The program that uses a vector is given in Listing 18.6. Figure 18.13 shows a sample run of the program.

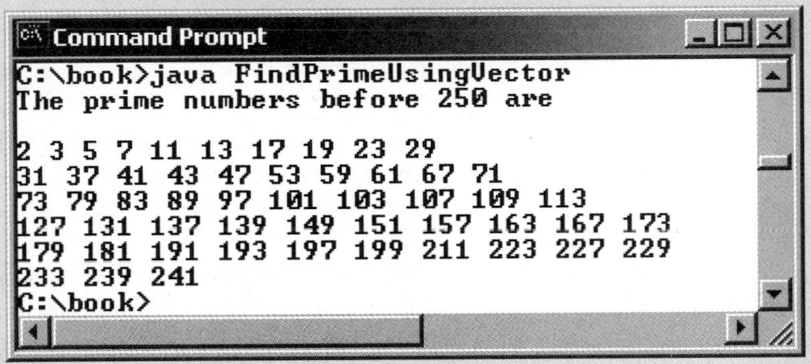

```
Command Prompt

C:\book>java FindPrimeUsingVector
The prime numbers before 250 are

2 3 5 7 11 13 17 19 23 29
31 37 41 43 47 53 59 61 67 71
73 79 83 89 97 101 103 107 109 113
127 131 137 139 149 151 157 163 167 173
179 181 191 193 197 199 211 223 227 229
233 239 241
C:\book>
```

FIGURE 18.13 *The program displays all the prime numbers before 250.*

LISTING 18.6 FindPrimeUsingVector.java

```
1 public class FindPrimeUsingVector {
2   public static void main(String[] args) {
3     // Print 10 numbers per line
4     final int NUMBER_PER_LINE = 10;
5
6     // Count the number of primes found
7     int count = 0;
8
9     // Create a vector to store prime numbers
10    java.util.Vector vector = new java.util.Vector();          create vector
11
12    System.out.println("The prime numbers before 250 are \n");
13
14    for (int n = 2; n < 250; n++) {
15      // Test if n is prime
16      boolean isPrime = true;
17      for (int i = 0; i < vector.size(); i++) {
18        int primeNumber =
19          ((Integer)(vector.elementAt(i))).intValue();
20
21        if (primeNumber > Math.sqrt(n)) break;
22
23        if (n % primeNumber == 0) {
24          // Set isPrime to false, if the number is not prime
```

EXAMPLE 18.6 (CONTINUED)

```
25              isPrime = false;
26              break; // Exit the for loop
27          }
28      }
29
30      // Print the prime number and increase the count
31      if (isPrime) {
32        count++; // Increase prime number count
33
34        // Add the prime number to the vector
35        vector.addElement(new Integer(n));
36
37        if (count % NUMBER_PER_LINE == 0) {
38          // Print the number and advance to the new line
39          System.out.println(n);
40        }
41        else
42          System.out.print(n + " ");
43      }
44    }
45  }
46 }
```

Review

The program needs to store the prime numbers and later uses them to check whether they are possible divisors for n. Since one cannot know in advance how many prime numbers are to be stored, using an array to store the prime numbers is not appropriate. So a vector is used to store the prime numbers.

Line 10 creates a vector. The `size` method (Line 17) returns the number of elements in the vector. The `addElement` method (Line 35) appends an element to the vector. Since vector elements are of the `Object` type, an integer is stored as an `Integer` object in the vector (Line 35).

 TIP

The size of an array is fixed once the array is created. Use array lists, linked lists, or vectors to store an unspecified number of elements.

 CAUTION

The element type in an array can be a primitive type value or an object, but the element type in the Java Collections Framework must be the `Object` type.

18.5.3   The `Stack` Class

In the Java Collections Framework, `Stack` is implemented as an extension of `Vector`, as illustrated in Figure 18.14.

The `Stack` class was introduced prior to Java 2. The methods shown in Figure 18.14 were used before Java 2. The `empty()` method is the same as `isEmpty()`. The `peek()` method looks at the element at the top of the stack without removing it. The `pop()` method removes the top element from the stack and returns it. The `push(Object element)` method adds the specified element to the stack. The `search(Object element)` method checks whether the specified element is in the stack.

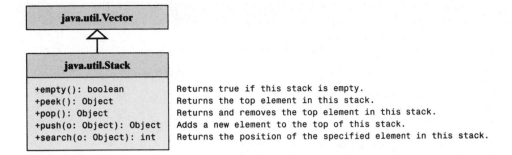

FIGURE **18.14** *The* Stack *class extends* Vector *to provide a last-in/first-out data structure.*

EXAMPLE **18.7** USING THE Stack CLASS

Problem

Write a program that reads a positive integer and displays all its distinct prime factors in decreasing order. For example, if the input integer is 6, its distinct prime factors displayed are 3, and 2; if the input integer is 12, the distinct prime factors are also 3 and 2.

Solution

The program uses a stack to store all the distinct prime factors. Initially, the stack is empty. To find all the distinct prime factors for an integer *n*, use the following algorithm:

```
int factor = 2;
while (factor <= n) {
  if (n % factor == 0) {
    n = n / factor;
    if (stack is empty or factor is not in the stack)
      push factor to the stack;
  }
  else {
    factor++;
  }
}
```

To display all the prime factors in decreasing order, pop the factor from the stack and display them. Listing 18.7 gives the solution to the problem. Figure 18.15 shows a sample run of the program.

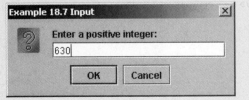
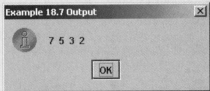

FIGURE **18.15** *The program receives a positive integer and displays its distinct prime factors.*

LISTING **18.7** FindPrimeFactorUsingStack.java

```
1 import javax.swing.JOptionPane;
2
3 public class FindPrimeFactorUsingStack {
4   public static void main(String[] args) {
```

EXAMPLE 18.7 (CONTINUED)

create stack

```
5    // Prompt the user to enter a positive integer
6    String intString = JOptionPane.showInputDialog(null,
7      "Enter a positive integer:",
8      "Example 18.7 Input", JOptionPane.QUESTION_MESSAGE);
9
10   // Convert string to int
11   int n = Integer.parseInt(intString);
12
13   // Create a stack to store prime factors
14   java.util.Stack stack = new java.util.Stack();
15
16   // Find all prime factors of the integer
17   int factor = 2;
18   while (factor <= n) {
19     if (n % factor == 0) {
20       n = n / factor;
21       if (stack.isEmpty() ||
22         ((Integer)stack.peek()).intValue() != factor)
23         stack.push(new Integer(factor));
24     }
25     else {
26       factor++;
27     }
28   }
29
30   // Prepare the output
31   String outString = "";
32   while (!stack.isEmpty()) {
33     outString += stack.pop() + "  ";
34   }
35
36   // Display the output
37   JOptionPane.showMessageDialog(null, outString,
38     "Example 18.7 Output", JOptionPane.INFORMATION_MESSAGE);
39   }
40 }
```

Review

Line 14 creates a stack to store the prime factors. The program searches for all possible factors starting with 2. If a factor is found (Line 19), push it to the stack if it is not in the stack (Lines 21–23), and remove the factor from the number (Line 20) continuously until the number does not contain this factor.

The factor to be considered is initially 2, then 3, 4, 5, 6, ..., until the factor is greater than the number (Line 18). Ideally, you should consider only next prime numbers 3, 5, 7, 11, ..., as possible factors. But it would take more time to find these prime numbers than is needed to simply consider 2, 3, 4, 5, 6, ..., as possible factors.

The prime factors are pushed into the stack (Line 23) in increasing order. The factors are popped in decreasing order (Line 33).

18.6 Using Generic Types (JDK 1.5 Feature)

You can add any object into a collection (e.g., set, list, vector, or stack). Sometimes, you wish only one type of object to be in a collection. The new JDK 1.5 generic types provide a mechanism that supports type checking at compile time. For example, the following statement creates a set for strings:

```
HashSet<String> set = new HashSet<String>();
```

You can now add only strings into the set. For example,

```
set.add("Red");
```

If you attempt to add a non-string, a compile time error would occur. For example, the following statement is now illegal, because set can only contain strings:

```
set.add(new Integer(1));
```

To retrieve a value from a collection with a specified element type, no casting is needed because the compiler already knows the element type. For example, the following statements create a list that contains only double values, add elements to the list, and retrieve elements from the list:

```
1    ArrayList<Double> list = new ArrayList<Double>();
2    list.add(5.5); // 5.5 is automatically converted to new Double(5.5)
3    list.add(3.0); // 3.0 is automatically converted to new Double(3.0)
4    Double doubleObject = list.get(0); // No casting is needed
5    double d = list.get(1); // Automatically converted to double
```

In Lines 2 and 3, 5.5 and 3.0 are automatically converted into Double objects and added to list. Automatic conversion, a new feature in JDK 1.5, was introduced in Section 9.6, "Automatic Conversion Between Primitive Types and Wrapper Class Types." In Line 4, the first element in list is assigned to a Double variable. No casting is necessary because list is declared for Double objects. In Line 5, the second element in list is assigned to a double variable. The object in list.get(1) is automatically converted into a primitive type value.

 NOTE

All the collection classes support generic types, so you can use the <> notation to specify a particular type for the elements in a collection. To enable a class to support generic types, a class has to be declared using a special syntax. Supplement Q, "Creating Generic Types," discusses how to create generic types.

18.7 Maps

The Collection interface represents a collection of elements stored in a set or a list. The Map interface maps keys to the elements. The keys are like indexes. In List, the indexes are integers. In Map, the keys can be any objects. A map cannot contain duplicate keys. Each key maps to one value. The Map interface provides the methods for querying, updating, and obtaining a collection of values and a set of keys, as shown in Figure 18.16.

java.util.Map	
+clear(): void	Removes all mappings from this map.
+containsKey(key: Object): boolean	Returns true if this map contains a mapping for the specified key.
+containsValue(value: Object): boolean	Returns true if this map maps one or more keys to the specified value.
+entrySet(): Set	Returns a set consisting of the entries in this map.
+get(key: Object): Object	Returns the value for the specified key in this map.
+isEmpty(): boolean	Returns true if this map contains no mappings.
+keySet(): Set	Returns a set consisting of the keys in this map.
+put(key: Object, value: Object): Object	Puts a mapping in this map.
+putAll(m: Map): void	Adds all the mappings from m to this map.
+remove(key: Object): Object	Removes the mapping for the specified key.
+size(): int	Returns the number of mappings in this map.
+values(): Collection	Returns a collection consisting of the values in this map.

FIGURE 18.16 *The Map interface maps keys to values.*

The update methods include clear, put, putAll, and remove. The clear() method removes all the mappings from the map. The put(Object key, Object value) method associates the specified value with the specified key in the map. If the map formerly contained a mapping for this key, the old value associated with the key is returned. The putAll(Map m) method adds the specified map to this map. The remove(Object key) method removes the map elements for the specified key from the map.

The query methods include containsKey, containsValue, isEmpty, and size. The containsKey(Object key) method checks whether the map contains a mapping for the specified key. The containsValue(Object value) method checks whether the map contains a mapping for this value. The isEmpty() method checks whether the map contains any mappings. The size() method returns the number of mappings in the map.

You can obtain a set of the keys in the map using the keySet() method, and a collection of the values in the map using the values() method. The entrySet() method returns a collection of objects that implement the Map.Entry interface, where Entry is an inner interface for the Map interface. Each object in the collection is a specific key-value pair in the underlying map.

The AbstractMap class is a convenience class that implements all the methods in the Map interface except the entrySet() method. The SortedMap interface extends the Map interface to maintain the mapping in ascending order of keys.

The HashMap, LinkedHashMap, and TreeMap classes are three concrete implementations of the Map interface. The HashMap class is efficient for locating a value, inserting a mapping, and deleting a mapping.

LinkedHashMap was introduced in JDK 1.4. It extends HashMap with a linked list implementation that supports an ordering of the entries in the map. The entries in a HashMap are not ordered, but the entries in a LinkedHashMap can be retrieved either in the order in which they were inserted into the map (known as the *insertion order*) or in the order in which they were last accessed, from least recently accessed to most recently accessed (*access order*). The no-arg constructor constructs a LinkedHashMap with the insertion order. To construct a LinkedHashMap with the access order, use the LinkedHashMap(initialCapacity, loadFactor, true).

insertion order
access order

The TreeMap class, implementing SortedMap, is efficient for traversing the keys in a sorted order. The keys can be sorted using the Comparable interface or the Comparator interface. If you create a TreeMap using its no-arg constructor, the compareTo method in the Comparable interface is used to compare the elements in the set, assuming that the class of the elements implements the Comparable interface. To use a comparator, you have to use the TreeMap(Comparator comparator) constructor to create a sorted map that uses the compare method in the comparator to order the elements in the map based on the keys.

 NOTE

Prior to JDK 1.2, Map was supported in java.util.Hashtable. Hashtable was redesigned to fit into the Java Collections Framework with all its methods retained for compatibility. Hashtable implements the Map interface and is used in the same way as HashMap except that Hashtable is synchronized.

EXAMPLE 18.8 USING HashMap, LinkedHashMap, AND TreeMap

Problem

This example creates a hash map, a linked hash map, and a tree map that map borrowers to loans. The Loan class, introduced in Section 6.15, "Case Study: The Loan Class," was used to model loans. Recall that you can create a loan using the following constructor:

```
public Loan(double annualInterestRate, int numberOfYears,
    double loanAmount)
```

EXAMPLE 18.8 (CONTINUED)

The program first creates a hash map with the borrower's name as its key and the loan as its value. The program then creates a tree map from the hash map and displays the mappings in ascending order of the keys. Finally, the program creates a linked hash map, adds the same entries to the map, and displays the entries.

Solution

Listing 18.8 gives the solution to the problem. The output of the program is shown in Figure 18.17.

```
C:\book>javac TestMap.java

C:\book>java TestMap
Display entries in HashMap
Cook=Loan@360be0
Smith=Loan@45a877
Lewis=Loan@1372a1a
Anderson=Loan@ad3ba4

Display entries in ascending order of key
Anderson=Loan@ad3ba4
Cook=Loan@360be0
Lewis=Loan@1372a1a
Smith=Loan@45a877
The loan amount for Lewis is 20000.0

Display entries in LinkedHashMap
Smith=Loan@f6a746
Anderson=Loan@15ff48b
Cook=Loan@affc70
Lewis=Loan@1e63e3d

C:\book>
```

FIGURE 18.17 *The program demonstrates the use of* HashMap, LinkedHashMap, *and* TreeMap.

LISTING 18.8 **TestMap.java (Using various maps)**

```
1  import java.util.*;
2
3  public class TestMap {
4    public static void main(String[] args) {
5      // Create a HashMap
6      HashMap hashMap = new HashMap();                              create map
7      hashMap.put("Smith", new Loan(7, 15, 150000));               add entry
8      hashMap.put("Anderson", new Loan(7.5, 30, 150000));
9      hashMap.put("Lewis", new Loan(7.85, 30, 20000));
10     hashMap.put("Cook", new Loan(7, 15, 100000));
11
12     System.out.println("Display entries in HashMap");
13     displayMapEntries(hashMap);
14
15     // Create a TreeMap from the previous HashMap
16     Map treeMap = new TreeMap(hashMap);                          tree map
17     System.out.println("\nDisplay entries in ascending order of key");
18     displayMapEntries(treeMap);
19
20     // Create a LinkedHashMap
21     HashMap linkedHashMap = new LinkedHashMap(16, 0.75f, true);  linked hash map
22     linkedHashMap.put("Smith", new Loan(7, 15, 150000));
```

EXAMPLE 18.8 (CONTINUED)

```
23      linkedHashMap.put("Anderson", new Loan(7.5, 30, 150000));
24      linkedHashMap.put("Lewis", new Loan(7.85, 30, 20000));
25      linkedHashMap.put("Cook", new Loan(7, 15, 100000));
26
27      // Display the loan amount for Gerry K Lewis
28      System.out.println("The loan amount for " + "Lewis is " +
29        ((Loan)(linkedHashMap.get("Lewis"))).getLoanAmount());
30
31      System.out.println("\nDisplay entries in LinkedHashMap");
32      displayMapEntries(linkedHashMap);
33    }
34
35    public static void displayMapEntries(Map map) {
36      // Get an entry set for the map
37      Set entrySet = map.entrySet();
38
39      // Get an iterator for the entry set
40      Iterator iterator = entrySet.iterator();
41
42      // Display mappings
43      while (iterator.hasNext()) {
44        System.out.println(iterator.next());
45      }
46    }
47 }
```

get iterator

Review

As shown in Figure 18.17, the entries in the `HashMap` are in random order. The entries in the `TreeMap` are in increasing order of the keys. The entries in the `LinkedHashMap` are in the order of their access, from least recently accessed to most recently.

All the concrete classes that implement the `Map` interface have at least two constructors. One is the no-arg constructor that constructs an empty map, and the other constructs a map from an instance of `Map`. So new `TreeMap(hashMap)` (Line 16) constructs a tree map from a hash map.

Unlike the `Collection` interface, the `Map` interface does not provide an iterator. To traverse the map, you create an entry set of the mappings using the `entrySet()` method (Line 37) in the `Map` interface. Each element in the entry set is a string that consists of the string representation of the key object and its counterpart connected by the = sign. As shown in Figure 18.17, the first element in the entry set is `Cook=Loan@f4a2a4`.

> **TIP**
>
> If you don't need to maintain an order in a map when updating it, use a `HashMap`, because less time is needed to insert and remove mappings in a `HashMap`. When you need to maintain the insertion order or access order in the map, use a `LinkedHashMap`. When you need the map to be sorted on keys, convert it to a tree map.

EXAMPLE 18.9 COUNTING THE OCCURRENCES OF WORDS IN A TEXT

Problem

Write a program that counts the occurrences of words in a text and displays the words and their occurrences in ascending order of word frequency. The program uses a hash map to store a pair consisting of a word and its count. For each word, check whether it is already a key in the map. If not, add the key and value 1 to the map. Otherwise, increase the value for the word (key) by 1 in the map. To sort the map, convert it to a tree map.

EXAMPLE 18.9 (CONTINUED)

Solution

Listing 18.9 gives the solution to the problem. The output of the program is shown in Figure 18.18.

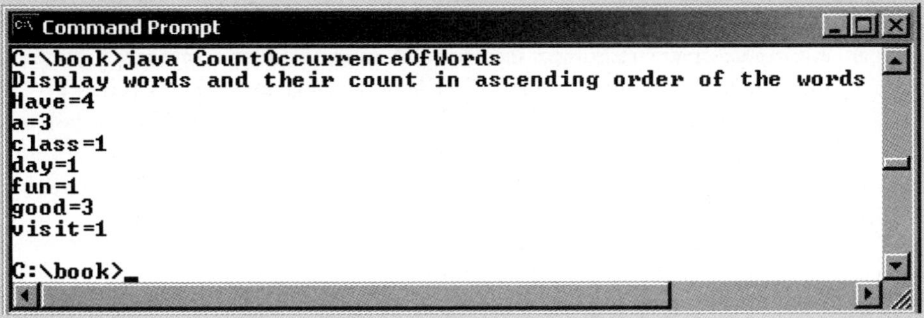

```
Command Prompt                                           _ □ ×
C:\book>java CountOccurrenceOfWords
Display words and their count in ascending order of the words
Have=4
a=3
class=1
day=1
fun=1
good=3
visit=1

C:\book>_
```

FIGURE **18.18** *The program finds the occurrences of each word in a text.*

LISTING **18.9** CountOccurrenceOfWords.java

```java
 1 import java.util.*;
 2
 3 public class CountOccurrenceOfWords {
 4   public static void main(String[] args) {
 5     // Text in a string
 6     String text = "Have a good day. Have a good class. " +
 7       "Have a good visit. Have fun!";
 8
 9     // Create a hash map to hold words as key and count as value
10     Map hashMap = new HashMap();                              hash map
11
12     StringTokenizer st = new StringTokenizer(text, " .!?");
13     while (st.hasMoreTokens()) {
14       String key = st.nextToken();
15
16       if (hashMap.get(key) != null) {
17         int value = ((Integer)hashMap.get(key)).intValue();
18         value++;
19         hashMap.put(key, new Integer(value));                add entry
20       }
21       else {
22         hashMap.put(key, new Integer(1));                    add entry
23       }
24     }
25
26     // Create a tree map from the hash map
27     Map treeMap = new TreeMap(hashMap);                       tree map
28
29     // Get an entry set for the tree map
30     Set entrySet = treeMap.entrySet();                        entry set
31
32     // Get an iterator for the entry set
33     Iterator iterator = entrySet.iterator();                  get iterator
34
35     // Display mappings
36     System.out.println("Display words and their count in " +
37       "ascending order of the words");
38     while (iterator.hasNext()) {
39       System.out.println(iterator.next());
40     }
41   }
42 }
```

EXAMPLE 18.9 (CONTINUED)

Review

The pairs of words and their occurrence counts are stored in the map. The words serve as the keys. Since all elements in the map must be stored as objects, the count is wrapped in an Integer object.

The program extracts a word from a text and checks whether it is already stored as a key in the map. If not, a new pair consisting of the word and a zero count (new Integer(1)) is stored to the map (Lines 22). Otherwise, the count for the word is incremented by 1 (Lines 17–19).

The program first stores the pairs in a hash map, then creates a tree map from the hash map (Line 27). It then creates an entry set (Line 30) and displays all the entries in the set. Each entry consists of a word and its count connected by the = sign in ascending order of word frequency. To display them in ascending order of the occurrence counts, see Exercise 18.7.

18.8   The Collections Class

The Collections class contains static methods for operating on collections and maps, creating synchronized collection classes, and creating read-only collection classes, as shown in Figure 18.19.

Most of the methods in the Collections class deal with lists. The sort methods can be used to sort a list using the Comparable interface or the Comparator interface. The binarySearch methods

java.util.Collections	
+binarySearch(list: List, key: Object): int	Searches the key in the sorted list using binary search.
+binarySearch(list: List, key: Object, c: Comparator): int	Searches the key in the sorted list using binary search with the comparator.
+copy(src: List, des: List): void	Copies from the source list to the destination list.
+enumeration(c: final Collection): Enumeration	Returns the enumeration for the specified collection.
+fill(list: List, o: Object): void	Fills the list with the object.
+max(c: Collection): Object	Returns the max object in the collection.
+max(c: Collection, c: Comparator): Object	Returns the max object using the comparator.
+min(c: Collection): Object	Returns the min object in the collection.
+min(c: Collection, c: Comparator): Object	Returns the min object using the comparator.
+nCopies(n: int, o: Object): List	Returns a list consisting of n copies of the object.
+reverse(list: List): void	Reverses the specified list.
+reverseOrder(): Comparator	Returns a comparator with the reverse ordering.
+shuffle(list: List): void	Shuffles the specified list randomly.
+shuffle(list: List, rnd: Random): void	Shuffles the specified list with a random object.
+singleton(o: Object): Set	Returns a singleton set containing the specified object.
+singletonList(o: Object): List	Returns a singleton list containing the specified object.
+singletonMap(key: Object, value: Object): Map	Returns a singleton map with the key and value pair.
+sort(list: List): void	Sorts the specified list.
+sort(list: List, c: Comparator): void	Sorts the specified list with the comparator.
+synchronizedCollection(c: Collection): Collection	Returns a synchronized collection.
+synchronizedList(list: List): List	Returns a synchronized list from the specified list.
+synchronizedMap(m: Map): Map	Returns a synchronized map from the specified map.
+synchronizedSet(s: Set): Set	Returns a synchronized set from the specified set.
+synchronizedSortedMap(s: SortedMap): SortedMap	Returns a synchronized sorted map from the specified sorted map.
+synchronizedSortedSet(s: SortedSet): SortedSet	Returns a synchronized sorted set.
+unmodifiedCollection(c: Collection): Collection	Returns an unmodified collection.
+unmodifiableList(list: List): List	Returns an unmodified list.
+unmodifiableMap(m: Map): Map	Returns an unmodified map.
+unmodifiableSet(s: Set): Set	Returns an unmodified set.
+unmodifiableSortedMap(s: SortedMap): SortedMap	Returns an unmodified sorted map.
+unmodifiableSortedSet(s: SortedSet): SortedSet	Returns an unmodified sorted set.

FIGURE 18.19 *The Collections class contains static methods for supporting the Java Collections Framework.*

can be used to find an element in a presorted list. In order to use the `binarySearch(list, key)` method, the list must first be sorted through the `Comparable` interface. To use the `binarySearch` `(list, key, comparator)` method, the list must first be sorted through the `Comparator` interface. The `binarySearch` method returns the index of the search key if it is contained in the list. Otherwise, it returns –(insertion point) −1. The insertion point is the point at which the key would be inserted into the list.

Use the `copy(src, des)` method to copy a source list to a destination list. Use the `fill(list, object)` method to fill a list with a specified object. Use the `nCopy(n, object)` method to create a list of the specified `object` for *n* times.

The `min` and `max` methods are generic for all collections. You can use them to find the minimum and maximum elements in a collection.

The `Collections` class defines three constants: one for an empty set, one for an empty list, and one for an empty map (`EMPTY_SET`, `EMPTY_LIST`, and `EMPTY_MAP`). The class also provides the `singleton(Object o)` method for creating an immutable set containing only a single item, the `singletonList(Object o)` method for creating an immutable list containing only a single item, and the `singletonMap(Object key, Object value)` method for creating an immutable map containing only a single mapping.

The methods in the `Collection` and `Map` interfaces are not thread-safe; in other words, the contents may be corrupted if they are processed concurrently by multiple threads. The `Collections` class provides six static methods for wrapping a collection into a synchronized version: `synchronized-Collection(Collection c)`, `synchronizedList(List list)`, `synchronizedMap(Map m)`, `synchronizedSet(Set set)`, `synchronizedSortedMap(SortedMap m)`, and `synchronizedSortedSet(SortedSet s)`. The synchronized collections can be safely accessed and modified by multiple threads concurrently.

The `Collections` class also provides six static methods for creating read-only collections: `unmodifiableCollection(Collection c)`, `unmodifiableList(List list)`, `unmodifiableMap(Map m)`, `unmodifiableSet(Set set)`, `unmodifiableSortedMap(SortedMap m)`, and `unmodifiableSortedSet(SortedSet s)`. The read-only collections prevent the data in the collections from being modified, and, as well, offer better performance for read-only operations.

EXAMPLE 18.10 USING THE Collections CLASS

Problem

Write a program that demonstrates the use of the methods in the `Collections` class. The example creates a list, sorts it, and searches for an element. The example wraps the list into a synchronized and read-only list.

Solution

Listing 18.10 gives the solution to the problem. The output of the program is shown in Figure 18.20.

LISTING 18.10   **TestCollections.java**

```
1 import java.util.*;
2
3 public class TestCollections {
4   public static void main(String[] args) {
5     // Create a list of three strings
6     List list = Collections.nCopies(3, "red");
7
8     // Create an array list
9     ArrayList arrayList = new ArrayList(list);
10    System.out.println("The initial list is " + arrayList);
11    list = null; // Release list
12
```
list

array list

EXAMPLE 18.10 (CONTINUED)

fill

shuffle

sort

binary search

```
13      // Fill in "yellow" to the list
14      Collections.fill(arrayList, "yellow");
15      System.out.println("After filling yellow, the list is " +
16        arrayList);
17
18      // Add three new elements to the list
19      arrayList.add("white");
20      arrayList.add("black");
21      arrayList.add("orange");
22      System.out.println("After adding new elements, the list is\n"
23        + arrayList);
24
25      // Shuffle the list
26      Collections.shuffle(arrayList);
27      System.out.println("After shuffling, the list is\n"
28        + arrayList);
29
30      // Find the minimum and maximum elements in the list
31      System.out.println("The minimum element in the list is "
32        + Collections.min(arrayList));
33      System.out.println("The maximum element in the list is "
34        + Collections.max(arrayList));
35
36      // Sort the list
37      Collections.sort(arrayList);
38      System.out.println("The sorted list is\n" + arrayList);
39
40      // Find an element in the list
41      System.out.println("The search result for gray is " +
42        Collections.binarySearch(arrayList, "gray"));
43
44      // Create a synchronized list
45      List syncList = Collections.synchronizedList(arrayList);
46
47      // Create a synchronized read-only list
48      List unmodifiableList = Collections.unmodifiableList(syncList);
49      arrayList = null; // Release arrayList
50      syncList = null; // Release syncList
51
52      try {
53        unmodifiableList.add("black");
54      }
55      catch (Exception ex) {
56        System.out.println(ex);
57      }
58    }
59 }
```

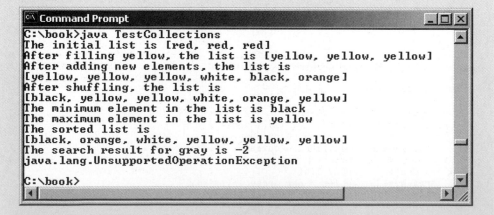

```
C:\book>java TestCollections
The initial list is [red, red, red]
After filling yellow, the list is [yellow, yellow, yellow]
After adding new elements, the list is
[yellow, yellow, yellow, white, black, orange]
After shuffling, the list is
[black, yellow, yellow, white, orange, yellow]
The minimum element in the list is black
The maximum element in the list is yellow
The sorted list is
[black, orange, white, yellow, yellow, yellow]
The search result for gray is -2
java.lang.UnsupportedOperationException

C:\book>
```

FIGURE 18.20   *The program demonstrates the use of* Collections.

EXAMPLE 18.10 (CONTINUED)

Review

The program first creates a list filled with the same elements three times using nCopies(3, "red") (Line 6). This list is an instance of List, but it is not an array list or a linked list. The program creates an array list from the list (Line 9).

The program uses Collections.fill(arrayList, "yellow") (Line 14) to replace each element in the list with "yellow".

After adding three new elements into arrayList, Collections.shuffle(arrayList) (Line 26) rearranges them in arrayList.

The program uses Collections.min(arrayList) (Line 32) to find the minimum element in arrayList, and Collections.max(arrayList) (Line 34) to find the maximum element in arrayList.

Collections.sort(arrayList) (Line 37) is invoked to sort arrayList. Collections.binarySearch(arrayList, "gray") (Line 42) is invoked to find "gray" in arrayList. This method returns -2 because $-(\text{insertion point}) - 1 = -2$.

The program finally uses Collections.synchronizedList(arrayList) (Line 45) to create a synchronized list for arrayList, and then creates a synchronized read-only list by wrapping the synchronized list using unmodifiableList. As shown in Figure 18.20, an UnsupportedOperationException is thrown when the program attempts to add a new element to the read-only list.

18.9   The Arrays Class

The Arrays class contains various static methods for sorting and searching arrays, comparing arrays, and filling array elements. It also contains a method for converting an array to a list. Figure 18.21 shows the methods in Arrays.

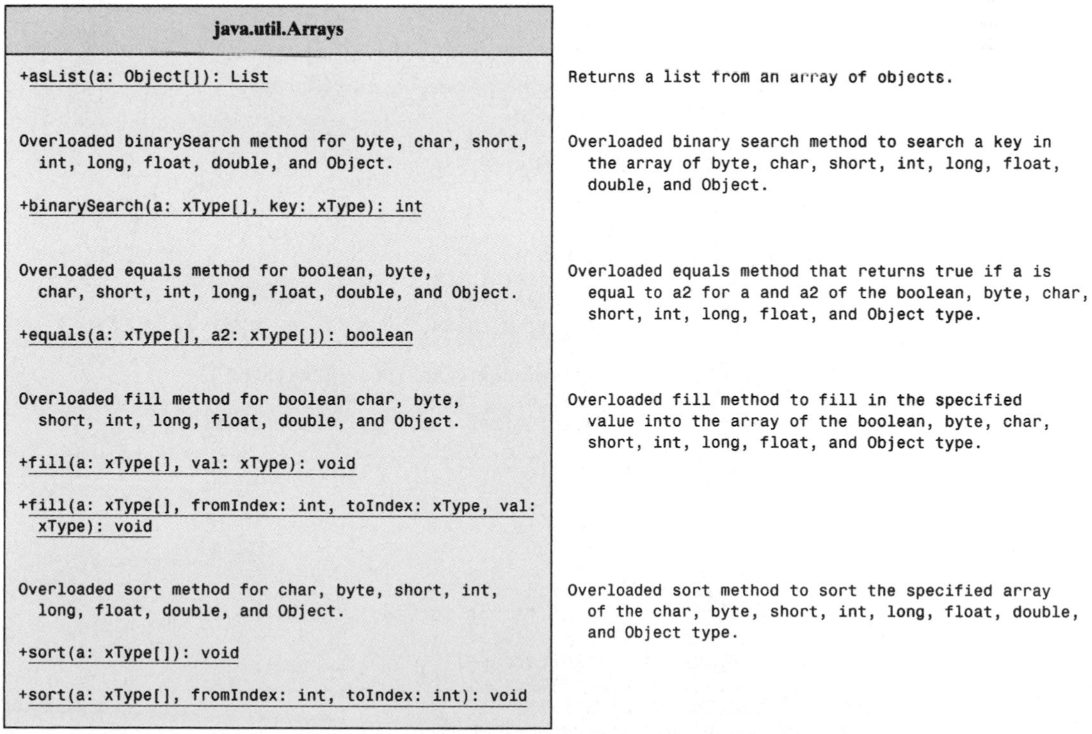

java.util.Arrays	
+asList(a: Object[]): List	Returns a list from an array of objects.
Overloaded binarySearch method for byte, char, short, int, long, float, double, and Object. +binarySearch(a: xType[], key: xType): int	Overloaded binary search method to search a key in the array of byte, char, short, int, long, float, double, and Object.
Overloaded equals method for boolean, byte, char, short, int, long, float, double, and Object. +equals(a: xType[], a2: xType[]): boolean	Overloaded equals method that returns true if a is equal to a2 for a and a2 of the boolean, byte, char, short, int, long, float, and Object type.
Overloaded fill method for boolean char, byte, short, int, long, float, double, and Object. +fill(a: xType[], val: xType): void +fill(a: xType[], fromIndex: int, toIndex: xType, val: xType): void	Overloaded fill method to fill in the specified value into the array of the boolean, byte, char, short, int, long, float, and Object type.
Overloaded sort method for char, byte, short, int, long, float, double, and Object. +sort(a: xType[]): void +sort(a: xType[], fromIndex: int, toIndex: int): void	Overloaded sort method to sort the specified array of the char, byte, short, int, long, float, double, and Object type.

FIGURE 18.21 *The Arrays class contains static methods for arrays.*

An array must be sorted before the `binarySearch` method is used. The `fill` method can be used to fill part of the array or the whole array with the same value. The `sort` method can be used to sort part of the array or the whole array. `fill(a, fromIndex, toIndex, val)` fills `val` into `a[fromIndex],..., a[toIndex - 1]`, and `sort(a, fromIndex, toIndex, val)` sorts `a[from-Index],..., a[toIndex - 1]`.

EXAMPLE 18.11 USING THE Arrays CLASS

Problem

Write a program that demonstrates how to use the methods in the `Arrays` class. The example creates an array of `int` values, fills part of the array with 50, sorts it, searches for an element, and compares the array with another one.

Solution

Listing 18.11 gives the solution to the problem. The output of the program is shown in Figure 18.22.

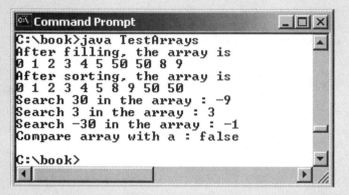

```
C:\book>java TestArrays
After filling, the array is
0 1 2 3 4 5 50 50 8 9
After sorting, the array is
0 1 2 3 4 5 8 9 50 50
Search 30 in the array : -9
Search 3 in the array : 3
Search -30 in the array : -1
Compare array with a : false

C:\book>
```

FIGURE **18.22** *The program demonstrates the use of Arrays.*

LISTING **18.11** TestArrays.java

```java
1 import java.util.*;
2
3 public class TestArrays {
4   public static void main(String[] args) {
5     // Create an array of 10 int values
6     int[] array = {0, 1, 2, 3, 4, 5, 6, 7, 8, 9};
7
8     // Fill array from index 6 to index 8 with 50
9     Arrays.fill(array, 6, 8, 50);
10    System.out.println("After filling, the array is");
11    for (int i = 0; i < 10; i++) {
12      System.out.print(array[i] + " ");
13    }
14    System.out.println();
15
16    // Sort the array
17    Arrays.sort(array);
18    System.out.println("After sorting, the array is");
19    for (int i = 0; i < 10; i++) {
20      System.out.print(array[i] + " ");
21    }
22    System.out.println();
23
```

fill

sort

EXAMPLE 18.11 (CONTINUED)

```
24      // Search for 30 in the array
25      System.out.println("Search 30 in the array : " +
26        Arrays.binarySearch(array, 30));
27
28      // Search for 3 in the array
29      System.out.println("Search 3 in the array : " +
30        Arrays.binarySearch(array, 3));
31
32      // Search for -30 in the array
33      System.out.println("Search -30 in the array : " +
34        Arrays.binarySearch(array, -30));
35
36      // Test if two arrays are the same
37      int[] a = new int[10];
38      System.out.println("Compare array with a : " +
39        Arrays.equals(array, a));
40    }
41 }
```

binary search

Review

The program first creates an array of ten int values (Line 6), then fills 50 in the array at index 6 and 7 (Line 9). The sort method is used to sort the entire array (Line 17).

The program uses the binarySearch method to search for 30, 3, and −30 in the array (Lines 26, 30, 34). The return value is −9 for searching 30, because 30 is not in the list and the insertion point for 30 is at 8. The return value is 3 for searching 3, because 3 is in the list and its index is 3. The return value is −1 for searching −30, because −30 is not in the list and the insertion point for −30 is at 0.

The program also uses the equals method (Line 39) to compare two arrays.

KEY TERMS

KEY CLASSES AND METHODS

✦ **java.util.Collection** is the root interface for the Set and List interfaces. It provides the basic operations for adding and removing elements in a collection, and for querying the elements in a collection.

✦ **java.util.Set** is a subinterface that extends the Collection interface. It does not introduce new methods or constants, but it stipulates that an instance of Set contains no duplicate elements.

✦ **java.util.HashSet** is a concrete class that implements Set. There is no guarantee that the elements are stored in any order.

✦ **java.util.LinkedHashSet** is a class that extends HashSet with a linked list implementation that supports an ordering in which the elements were inserted.

✦ **java.util.TreeSet** is a set in which the elements are sorted.

✦ **java.util.Iterator** is an interface for traversing elements in a collection. The iterator() method in the Collection interface returns an instance of the Iterator interface. You can use the next() method to return the next object in the collection, the hasNext() method to check whether there are more elements in the iterator, and the remove() method to remove the last element returned by the iterator.

◆ **java.util.List** is a subinterface that extends the Collection interface. It defines an ordered collection with duplicates allowed. The List interface adds position-oriented operations, as well as a new list iterator that enables the user to traverse the list bi-directionally.

◆ **java.util.ListIterator** is a subinterface of java.util.Iterator that supports bi-directional traversal.

◆ **java.util.ArrayList** is a concrete class that implements java.util.List as a resizable array.

◆ **java.util.LinkedList** is a concrete class that implements java.util.List as a linked list.

◆ **java.util.Vector** is an implementation of java.util.List as a vector. It is the same as ArrayList, except that it contains synchronized methods for accessing and modifying the vector.

◆ **java.util.Stack** is a stack that is implemented by extending java.util.Vector.

◆ **java.util.Map** is an interface that maps keys to elements.

◆ **java.util.HashMap** is a concrete implementation of java.util.Map. There is no guarantee that the entries in the map are ordered.

◆ **java.util.LinkedHashMap** is a class that extends HashMap with a linked list implementation that supports ordering of the entries in the map.

◆ **java.util.TreeMap** is a map in which the entries are sorted on the keys.

◆ **java.util.Collections** is a class that provides static methods for operating on collections and maps, creating synchronized collection classes, and creating read-only collection classes.

◆ **java.util.Arrays** is a class that contains static methods for sorting and searching arrays, comparing arrays, and filling array elements.

CHAPTER SUMMARY

◆ The Java Collections Framework supports three types of collections: sets, lists, and maps. They are defined in the interfaces Set, List, and Map. A *set* stores a group of nonduplicate elements. A *list* stores an ordered collection of elements. A *map* stores a group of objects, each of which is associated with a key.

◆ A set stores nonduplicate elements. To allow duplicate elements to be stored in a collection, you need to use a list. A list can not only store duplicate elements, it also allows the user to specify where they are stored. The user can access elements by an index.

◆ Three types of sets are supported: HashSet, LinkedHashSet, and TreeSet. HashSet stores elements in an unpredictable order. LinkedHashSet stores elements in the order they were inserted. TreeSet stores the elements sorted. All the methods in HashSet, LinkedHashSet, and TreeSet are inherited from the Collection interface.

✦ Two types of lists are supported: `ArrayList` and `LinkedList`. `ArrayList` is a resizable-array implementation of the `List` interface. All the methods in `ArrayList` are defined in `List`. `LinkedList` is a linked list implementation of the `List` interface. In addition to implementing the `List` interface, this class provides the methods for retrieving, inserting, and removing elements from both ends of the list.

✦ The `Vector` class implements the `List` interface. In Java 2, `Vector` is the same as `ArrayList`, except that it contains synchronized methods for accessing and modifying the vector. The `Stack` class extends the `Vector` class and provides several methods for manipulating the stack.

✦ The `Collection` interface represents a collection of elements stored in a set or a list. The `Map` interface maps keys to the elements. The keys are like indexes. In `List`, the indexes are integers. In `Map`, the keys can be any objects. A map cannot contain duplicate keys. Each key can map to at most one value. The `Map` interface provides the methods for querying, updating, and obtaining a collection of values and a set of keys.

✦ Three types of maps are supported: `HashMap`, `LinkedHashMap`, and `TreeMap`. `HashMap` is efficient for locating a value, inserting a mapping, and deleting a mapping. `LinkedHashMap` supports ordering of the entries in the map. The entries in a `HashMap` are not ordered, but the entries in a `LinkedHashMap` can be retrieved either in the order in which they were inserted into the map (known as the *insertion order*) or in the order in which they were last accessed, from least recently accessed to most recently (*access order*). `TreeMap` is efficient for traversing the keys in a sorted order. The keys can be sorted using the `Comparable` interface or the `Comparator` interface.

✦ The `Collections` class provides static methods for operating on collections and maps, creating synchronized collection classes, and creating read-only collection classes.

✦ The `Arrays` class contains static methods for sorting and searching arrays, comparing arrays, and filling array elements.

REVIEW QUESTIONS

Sections 18.1–18.2

18.1 Describe the Java Collections Framework. List the interfaces, convenience abstract classes, and concrete classes.

18.2 Can a collection object be cloned and serialized?

18.3 The `hashCode` method and the `equals` method are defined in the `Object` class. Why are they redefined in the `Collection` interface?

18.4 Find the default implementation for the `equals` method and the `hashCode` method in the `Object` class from the source code of Object.java.

Section 18.3 Sets

18.5 How do you create an instance of `Set`? How do you insert a new element in a set? How do you remove an element from a set? How do you find the size of a set?

18.6 What are the differences between `HashSet`, `LinkedHashSet`, and `TreeSet`?

18.7 How do you traverse the elements in a set? Can you traverse the elements in a set in an arbitrary order?

18.8 How do you sort the elements in a set using the compareTo method in the Comparable interface? How do you sort the elements in a set using the Comparator interface? What would happen if you added an element that cannot be compared with the existing elements in a tree set?

18.9 Suppose that set1 is a set that contains the strings "red", "yellow", "green", and that set2 is another set that contains the strings "red", "yellow", "blue". Answer the following questions:

✦ What are set1 and set2 after executing set1.addAll(set2)?

✦ What are set1 and set2 after executing set1.add(set2)?

✦ What are set1 and set2 after executing set1.removeAll(set2)?

✦ What are set1 and set2 after executing set1.remove(set2)?

✦ What are set1 and set2 after executing set1.retainAll(set2)?

✦ What is set1 after executing set1.clear()?

Section 18.4 The Comparator Interface

18.10 What are the differences between the Comparable interface and the Comparator interface? Which package is Comparable in, and which package is Comparator in?

18.11 The Comparator interface contains the equals method. Why is the method not implemented in the GeometricObjectComparator class in this section?

Section 18.5 Lists

18.12 How do you add and remove elements from a list? How do you traverse a list in both directions?

18.13 Suppose that list1 is a list that contains the strings "red", "yellow", "green," and that list2 is another list that contains the strings "red", "yellow", "blue". Answer the following questions:

✦ What are list1 and list2 after executing list1.addAll(list2)?

✦ What are list1 and list2 after executing list1.add(list2)?

✦ What are list1 and list2 after executing list1.removeAll(list2)?

✦ What are list1 and list2 after executing list1.remove(list2)?

✦ What are list1 and list2 after executing list1.retainAll(list2)?

✦ What is list1 after executing list1.clear()?

18.14 What are the differences between ArrayList and LinkedList? Are all the methods in ArrayList also in LinkedList? What methods are in LinkedList but not in ArrayList?

18.15 How do you create an instance of Vector? How do you add or insert a new element into a vector? How do you remove an element from a vector? How do you find the size of a vector?

18.16 How do you create an instance of Stack? How do you add a new element into a stack? How do you remove an element from a stack? How do you find the size of a stack?

18.17 Does Example 18.1, "Using HashSet and Iterator," compile and run if Line 7 (Set set = new HashSet()) is replaced by one of the following statements?

```
Collection set = new LinkedHashSet();
Collection set = new TreeSet();
Collection set = new ArrayList();
```

```
Collection set = new LinkedList();
Collection set = new Vector();
Collection set = new Stack();
```

Section 18.6 Maps

18.18 How do you create an instance of Map? How do you add a pair consisting of an element and a key into a map? How do you remove an entry from a map? How do you find the size of a map? How do you traverse entries in a map?

18.19 Describe and compare HashMap, LinkedHashMap, and TreeMap.

18.20 Show the printout of the following code:

```
public class Test {
  public static void main(String[] args) {
    Map map = new LinkedHashMap();
    map.put("123", "John Smith");
    map.put("111", "George Smith");
    map.put("123", "Steve Yao");
    map.put("222", "Steve Yao");
    System.out.println("(1) " + map);
    System.out.println("(2) " + new TreeMap(map));
  }
}
```

Sections 18.7–18.8

18.21 Are all the methods in the Collections class and the Arrays class static?

18.22 How do you create a set or a list from an array of objects?

18.23 Which method can you use to sort the elements in an ArrayList or a LinkedList? Which method can you use to sort an array of strings?

18.24 Which method can you use to perform binary search for elements in an ArrayList or a LinkedList? Which method can you use to perform binary search for an array of strings?

18.25 Write a statement to find the largest element in an array of comparable objects?

PROGRAMMING EXERCISES

Section 18.3 Sets

18.1 (*Performing set operations on hash sets*) Create two hash sets {"George", "Jim", "John", "Blake", "Kevin", "Michael"} and {"George", "Katie", "Kevin", "Michelle", "Ryan"}, and find their union, difference, and intersection. (You may clone the sets to preserve the original sets from being changed by these set methods.)

18.2 (*Displaying nonduplicate words in ascending order*) Write a program that reads words from a text file and displays all the nonduplicate words in ascending order. The text file is passed as a command-line argument.

18.3** (*Counting the keywords in Java source code*) Write a program that reads a Java source code file and reports the number of keywords in the file. Pass the Java file name from the command line.

 HINT
Create a set to store all the Java keywords.

Section 18.4 Lists

18.4 (*Performing set operations on array lists*) Create two array lists {"George", "Jim", "John", "Blake", "Kevin", "Michael"} and {"George", "Katie", "Kevin", "Michelle", "Ryan"}, and find their union, difference, and intersection. (You may clone the lists to preserve the original lists from being changed by these methods.)

18.5* (*Displaying words in ascending alphabetical order*) Write a program that reads words from a text file and displays all the words (duplicates allowed) in ascending alphabetical order. The text file is passed as a command-line argument.

Section 18.6 Maps

18.6* (*Counting the occurrences of numbers entered*) Write a program that reads an unspecified number of integers and finds the one that has the most occurrences. Your input ends when the input is 0. For example, if you entered 2 3 40 3 5 4 −3 3 3 2 0, the number 3 occurred most often. Please enter one number at a time. If not one but several numbers have the most occurrences, all of them should be reported. For example, since 9 and 3 appear twice in the list 9 30 3 9 3 2 4, both should be reported.

18.7** (*Revising Example 18.9 "Counting the Occurrences of Words in a Text"*) Rewrite Example 18.9 to display the words in ascending order of occurrence counts.

 Hint

Create a class named `WordOccurrence` that implements the `Comparable` interface. The class contains two fields, `word` and `count`. The `compareTo` method compares the counts. For each pair in the hash set in Example 18.9, create an instance of `WordOccurrence` and store it in an array list. Sort the array list using the `Collections.sort` method. What would be wrong if you stored the instances of `WordOccurrence` in a tree set?

18.8* (*Counting the occurrences of words in a text file*) Rewrite Example 18.9 to read the text from a text file. The text file name is passed as a command-line argument.

Section 18.7 The `Collections` Class

18.9* (*Storing numbers in a linked list*) Write a program that lets the user enter numbers from a graphical user interface and display them in a text area, as shown in Figure 18.23. Use a linked list to store the numbers. Do not store duplicate numbers. Add the buttons Sort, Shuffle, and Reverse to sort, shuffle, and reverse the list.

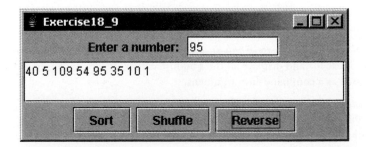

FIGURE 18.23 *The program stores numbers in a list.*

PART VI

THREADS AND INTERNATIONALIZATION

This part of the book is devoted to two unique and useful features of Java. Chapter 19 treats the use of multithreading to make programs more responsive and interactive. Chapter 20 covers the use of internationalization support to develop projects for international audiences.

Chapter 19
Multithreading

Chapter 20
Internationalization

Prerequisites for Part VI

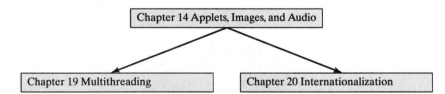

Chapter 14 Applets, Images, and Audio

Chapter 19 Multithreading

Chapter 20 Internationalization

MULTITHREADING

Objectives

- ✦ To understand the concept of multithreading and apply it to develop concurrent programs (§19.2).

- ✦ To develop thread classes by extending the Thread class (§19.3).

- ✦ To develop thread classes by implementing the Runnable interface in cases of multiple inheritance (§19.4).

- ✦ To know how to control threads and how to interact among threads (§19.5).

- ✦ To describe the life cycle of thread states and set thread priorities (§§19.5.1–19.5.2).

- ✦ To group threads using the ThreadGroup class (§19.6).

- ✦ To use synchronized methods or blocks to synchronize threads to avoid race conditions (§§19.7.1–19.7.2).

- ✦ To use wait(), notify(), and notifyAll() to facilitate thread cooperation (§19.7.3).

- ✦ To use the resource-ordering technique to avoid deadlocks (§19.7.4).

- ✦ To control animation using threads (§19.8 Optional).

- ✦ To play audio clips on separate threads (§19.9 Optional).

- ✦ To display the completion status of a task using JProgressBar (§19.10 Optional).

19.1   Introduction

multithreading

One of the important features of Java is its built-in support for multithreading. *Multithreading* is the capability of running multiple tasks concurrently within a program. In many programming languages, you have to invoke system-dependent procedures and functions to implement multithreading. This chapter introduces the concepts of threads and how to develop multithreading programs in Java.

19.2   Thread Concepts

thread

A *thread* is the flow of execution, from beginning to end, of a task in a program. With Java, you can launch multiple threads from a program concurrently. These threads can be executed simultaneously in multiprocessor systems, as shown in Figure 19.1.

FIGURE 19.1   *Here multiple threads are running on multiple CPUs.*

In single-processor systems, as shown in Figure 19.2, the multiple threads share CPU time, and the operating system is responsible for scheduling and allocating resources to them. This arrangement is practical because most of the time the CPU is idle. It does nothing, for example, while waiting for the user to enter data.

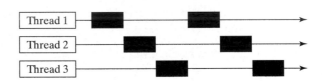

FIGURE 19.2   *Here multiple threads share a single CPU.*

Multithreading can make your program more responsive and interactive, as well as enhance performance. For example, a good word processor lets you print or save a file while you are typing. In some cases, multithreaded programs run faster than single-threaded programs even on single-processor systems. Java provides exceptionally good support for creating and running threads and for locking resources to prevent conflicts.

When your program executes as an application, the Java interpreter starts a thread for the `main` method. When your program executes as an applet, the Web browser starts a thread to run the applet. You can create additional threads to run concurrent tasks in the program. Each new thread is an object of a class that implements the `Runnable` interface or extends a class that implements the `Runnable` interface. This new object is referred to as a *runnable object*.

You can create threads either by extending the `Thread` class or by implementing the `Runnable` interface. Both `Thread` and `Runnable` are defined in the `java.lang` package. `Thread` actually implements `Runnable`. In the following sections, you will learn how to use the `Thread` class and the `Runnable` interface to write multithreaded programs.

19.3 Creating Threads by Extending the **Thread** Class

The Thread class contains the constructors for creating threads and many useful methods for controlling threads. To create and run a thread, first define a class that extends the Thread class. Your thread class must override the run() method, which tells the system how the thread will be executed when it runs. You can then create an object running on the thread.

Thread class

A template for developing a custom thread class that extends the Thread class and for creating threads from the custom thread class is shown in Figure 19.3. thread1 and thread2 are runnable objects created from the CustomThread class. The start method tells the system that the thread is ready to run.

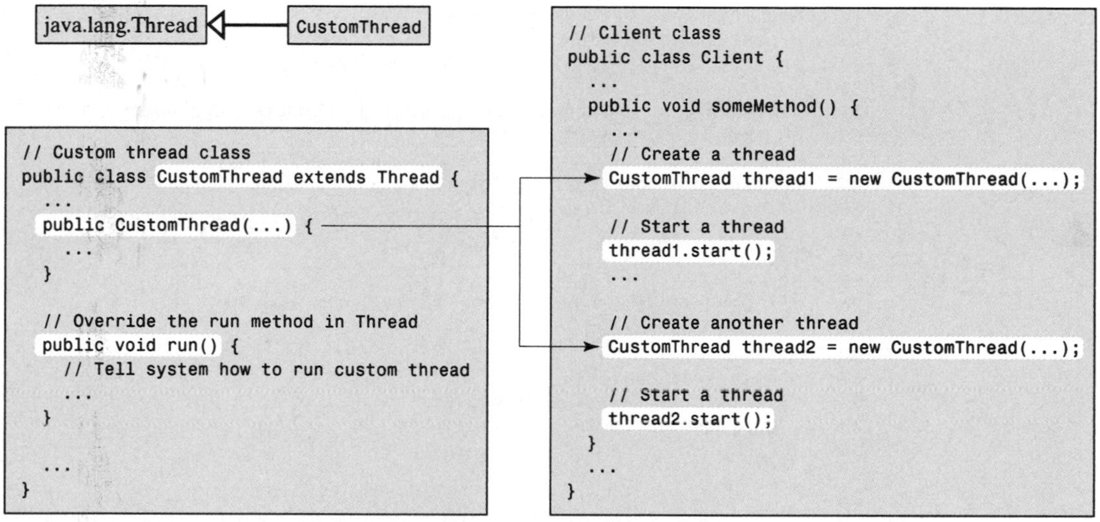

```
java.lang.Thread  <|————  CustomThread
```

```
// Custom thread class
public class CustomThread extends Thread {
  ...
  public CustomThread(...) {
    ...
  }

  // Override the run method in Thread
  public void run() {
    // Tell system how to run custom thread
    ...
  }

  ...
}
```

```
// Client class
public class Client {
  ...
  public void someMethod() {
    ...
    // Create a thread
    CustomThread thread1 = new CustomThread(...);

    // Start a thread
    thread1.start();
    ...

    // Create another thread
    CustomThread thread2 = new CustomThread(...);

    // Start a thread
    thread2.start();
  }
  ...
}
```

FIGURE 19.3 *Define a thread class by extending the* Thread *class.*

EXAMPLE 19.1 USING THE **Thread** CLASS TO CREATE AND LAUNCH THREADS

Problem

Write a program that creates and runs three threads:

♦ The first thread prints the letter *a* one hundred times.
♦ The second thread prints the letter *b* one hundred times.
♦ The third thread prints the integers 1 through 100.

Solution

The program has three independent threads. To run them concurrently, it needs to create a runnable object for each thread. Because the first two threads have similar functionality, they can be defined in one thread class.

The program is given in Listing 19.1, and its output is shown in Figure 19.4.

LISTING 19.1 TestThread.java (Using **Thread**)

```
1 public class TestThread {
2   /** Main method */
3   public static void main(String[] args) {
```

EXAMPLE 19.1 (CONTINUED)

create thread

start thread

extend Thread class

run thread

extend Thread class

run thread

```
4       // Create threads
5       PrintChar printA = new PrintChar('a', 100);
6       PrintChar printB = new PrintChar('b', 100);
7       PrintNum  print100 = new PrintNum(100);
8
9       // Start threads
10      print100.start();
11      printA.start();
12      printB.start();
13    }
14  }
15
16  // The thread class for printing a specified character
17  // in specified times
18  class PrintChar extends Thread {
19    private char charToPrint;  // The character to print
20    private int times;  // The times to repeat
21
22    /** Construct a thread with specified character and number of
23       times to print the character
24     */
25    public PrintChar(char c, int t) {
26      charToPrint = c;
27      times = t;
28    }
29
30    /** Override the run() method to tell the system
31       what the thread will do
32     */
33    public void run() {
34      for (int i = 0; i < times; i++)
35        System.out.print(charToPrint);
36    }
37  }
38
39  // The thread class for printing number from 1 to n for a given n
40  class PrintNum extends Thread {
41    private int lastNum;
42
43    /** Construct a thread for print 1, 2, ... i */
44    public PrintNum(int n) {
45      lastNum = n;
46    }
47
48    /** Tell the thread how to run */
49    public void run() {
50      for (int i = 1; i <= lastNum; i++) {
51        System.out.print(" " + i);
52      }
53    }
54  }
```

```
Command Prompt                                          _ □ ×
C:\book>java TestThread
 1 2 3 4 5 6 7 8 9 10 11 12 13 14 15 16abababababababababaaaaa
aaaaaaaaaaaaabbbbbbbbbbbbbbbbbbaaaaaaaaaaaaaaaaaaabbbbbbbbbbbbbbb
bbbaaaaaaaaaaaaaaabbbbbbbbbbbbbbbbbbaaaaaaaaaaaaaaaaaaabbbbbbbbbb
bbbbbbbbbaaaaaaaaaaaaaaabbbbbbbbbbbbbbbbbbaaaaaaaaaaaaaaaaaaabbbbbbbbbb
17 18 19 20 21 22 23 24 25 26 27 28 29 30 31 32 33 34 35 36
37 38 39 40 41 42 43 44 45 46 47 48 49 50 51 52 53 54 55 56
57 58 59 60 61 62 63 64 65 66 67 68 69 70 71 72 73 74 75 76
77 78 79 80 81 82 83 84 85 86 87 88 89 90 91 92 93 94 95 96
97 98 99 100
C:\book>
```

FIGURE 19.4 *Threads printA, printB, and print100 are executed simultaneously to display the letter a one hundred times, the letter b one hundred times, and the numbers from 1 to 100.*

EXAMPLE 19.1 (CONTINUED)

Review

If you run this program on a multiple-CPU system, all three threads will execute simultaneously. If you run the program on a single-CPU system, the three threads will share the CPU and take turns printing letters and numbers on the console. This is known as *time-sharing*.

time-sharing

The program defines thread classes by extending the Thread class. The PrintChar class (Lines 18–37), derived from the Thread class, overrides the run() method (Lines 33–36) with the print-character action. This class provides a framework for printing any single character a given number of times. The runnable objects printA and printB are instances of the user-defined thread class PrintChar.

The PrintNum class (Lines 40–54) overrides the run() method (Lines 49–53) with the print-number action. This class provides a framework for printing numbers from *1* to *n* for any integer *n*. The runnable object print100 is an instance of the user-defined thread class printNum.

In the client program, the program creates a thread, printA, for printing the letter *a*, and a thread, printB, for printing the letter *b*. Both are objects of the PrintChar class. The print100 thread object is created from the PrintNum class.

The start() method (Lines 10–12) is invoked to start a thread that causes the run() method to execute. When the run() method completes, the threads terminate.

19.4   Creating Threads by Implementing the **Runnable** Interface

In the preceding section, you created and ran a thread by declaring a user thread class that extends the Thread class. This approach works well if the user thread class inherits only from the Thread class. But if it already inherits a classes, you have to implement the Runnable interface.

Runnable interface

The Runnable interface is rather simple. All it contains is the run method. You need to implement this method to tell the system how your thread is going to run. A template for developing a custom thread class that implements the Runnable interface and for creating threads from the custom thread class is shown in Figure 19.5.

```
java.lang.Runnable  <-------  CustomThread

// Custom thread class
public class CustomThread
    implements Runnable {
  ...
  public CustomThread(...) {
    ...
  }

  // Implement the run method in Runnable
  public void run() {
    // Tell system how to run custom thread
    ...
  }
  ...
}
```

```
// Client class
public class Client {
  ...
  public void someMethod() {
    ...
    // Create an instance of CustomThread
    CustomThread customThread
        = new CustomThread(...);

    // Create a thread
    Thread thread = new Thread(customThread);

    // Start a thread
    thread.start();
    ...
  }
  ...
}
```

FIGURE 19.5 *Define a thread class by implementing the* Runnable *interface.*

To start a new thread with the `Runnable` interface, you must first create an instance of the class that implements the `Runnable` interface, then use the `Thread` class constructor to construct a thread. The following example demonstrates how to create threads using the `Runnable` interface.

EXAMPLE 19.2 USING THE Runnable INTERFACE TO CREATE AND LAUNCH THREADS

Problem

Modify Example 19.1, "Using the `Thread` Class to Create and Launch Threads," to create and run the same threads using the `Runnable` interface.

Solution

Listing 19.2 gives the solution to the problem.

LISTING 19.2   TestRunnable.java (Using Runnable)

```
 1 public class TestRunnable {
 2   // Create threads
 3   Thread printA = new Thread(new PrintChar('a', 100));
 4   Thread printB = new Thread(new PrintChar('b', 100));
 5   Thread print100 = new Thread(new PrintNum(100));
 6
 7   public static void main(String[] args) {
 8     new TestRunnable();
 9   }
10
11   public TestRunnable() {
12     // Start threads
13     print100.start();
14     printA.start();
15     printB.start();
16   }
17
18   // The thread class for printing a specified character
19   // in specified times
20   class PrintChar implements Runnable {
21     private char charToPrint;  // The character to print
22     private int times;  // The times to repeat
23
24     /** Construct a thread with specified character and number of
25        times to print the character
26      */
27     public PrintChar(char c, int t) {
28       charToPrint = c;
29       times = t;
30     }
31
32     /** Override the run() method to tell the system
33        what the thread will do
34      */
35     public void run() {
36       for (int i = 0; i < times; i++)
37         System.out.print(charToPrint);
38     }
39   }
40
41   // The thread class for printing number from 1 to n for a given n
42   class PrintNum implements Runnable {
43     private int lastNum;
44
45     /** Construct a thread for print 1, 2, ... i */
46     public PrintNum(int n) {
47       lastNum = n;
48     }
```

Margin notes: create thread (lines 3–5); start thread (lines 13–15); implement Runnable (line 20); run thread (line 35); implement Runnable (line 42).

EXAMPLE 19.2 (CONTINUED)

```
49
50      /** Tell the thread how to run */
51      public void run() {
52        for (int i = 1; i <= lastNum; i++)
53          System.out.print(" " + i);
54      }
55    }
56 }
```

run thread

Review

This example performs the same task as Example 19.1. The classes PrintChar and PrintNum are the same as in Example 19.1 except that they implement the Runnable interface rather than extend the Thread class.

The PrintChar and PrintNum classes are implemented as inner classes to avoid naming conflicts with the PrintChar and PrintNum classes in Example 19.1. Threads printA, printB, and print100 are created in the constructor (Lines 3–5) instead of directly in the main method. This is because the main method is static and the inner classes PrintChar and PrintNum are nonstatic; you cannot reference nonstatic members of a class in a static method.

An instance of the class that extends the Thread class is a thread, which can be started using the start() method in the Thread class. But an instance of the class that implements the Runnable interface is not yet a thread. You have to wrap it, using the Thread class, to construct a thread for the instance, such as

```
Thread printA = new Thread(new PrintChar('a', 100));
```

19.5   Thread Controls and Communications

The Thread class contains the methods for controlling threads, as shown in Figure 19.6.

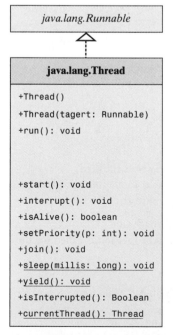

java.lang.Runnable	
java.lang.Thread	
+Thread()	Creates a default thread.
+Thread(tagert: Runnable)	Creates a new thread to run the target object.
+run(): void	Invoked by the JVM to execute the thread. You must override this method and provide the code you want your thread to execute in your thread class. This method is never directly invoked by the runnable object in a program, although it is an instance method of a runnable object.
+start(): void	Starts the thread that causes the run() method to be invoked by the JVM.
+interrupt(): void	Interrupts this thread. If the thread is blocked, it is ready to run again.
+isAlive(): boolean	Tests whether the thread is currently running.
+setPriority(p: int): void	Sets priority p (ranging from 1 to 10) for this thread.
+join(): void	Waits for this thread to finish.
+sleep(millis: long): void	Puts the runnable object to sleep for a specified time in milliseconds.
+yield(): void	Causes this thread to temporarily pause and allow other threads to execute.
+isInterrupted(): Boolean	Tests whether the current thread has been interrupted.
+currentThread(): Thread	Returns a reference to the currently executing thread object.

FIGURE 19.6   *The Thread class contains the methods for controlling threads.*

deprecated method

> ### 🌿 NOTE
> The Thread class also contains the stop(), suspend(), and resume() methods. As of Java 2, these methods are *deprecated* (or *outdated*) because they are known to be inherently unsafe. Instead of using the stop() method, you should assign null to a Thread variable to indicate that it is stopped.

yield

You can use the yield() method to temporarily release time for other threads. For example, suppose you modify the code in the run() method (Lines 52–53 in PrintNum in TestRunnable.java) in Example 19.2 as follows:

```
public void run() {
  for (int i = 1; i <= lastNum; i++) {
    System.out.print(" " + i);
    Thread.yield();
  }
}
```

Every time a number is printed, the print100 thread is yielded. So each number is followed by some characters.

sleep

The sleep(long mills) method puts the thread to sleep for the specified time in milliseconds. For example, suppose you modify the code in the run() mehod (Lines 52–53 in PrintNum in TestRunnable.java) in Example 19.2 as follows:

```
public void run() {
  for (int i = 1; i <= lastNum; i++) {
    System.out.print(" " + i);
    try {
      if (i >= 50) Thread.sleep(1);
    }
    catch (InterruptedException ex) {
    }
  }
}
```

Every time a number ($>= 50$) is printed, the print100 thread is put to sleep for 1 millisecond.

join

You can use the join() method to force one thread to wait for another thread to finish. For example, suppose you modify the code in the run() method (Lines 52–53 in PrintNum in TestRunnable.java) in Example 19.2 as follows:

```
public void run() {
  for (int i = 1; i <= lastNum; i++) {
    System.out.print(" " + i);
    try {
      if (i == 50) printA.join();
    }
    catch (InterruptedException ex) {
    }
  }
}
```

The numbers from 50 to 100 are printed after thread printA is finished.

The wait(), notify(), and notifyAll() methods defined in the Object class are also used with threads to facilitate communications among the active threads.

wait

♦ public final void wait() throws InterruptedException
Forces the thread to wait until the notify or notifyAll method is called for the object to which wait is called.

notify

♦ public final void notify()
Awakens one of the threads that are waiting on this object. Which one is notified depends on the system implementation.

notifyAll

♦ public final void notifyAll()
Awakens all the threads that are waiting on this object.

While the join() method forces one thread to wait for another thread to finish, the wait(), notify(), and notifyAll() are used to synchronize the active threads, as shown in Figure 19.7. These methods are discussed in more detail in Section 19.7.3, "Cooperation Among Threads."

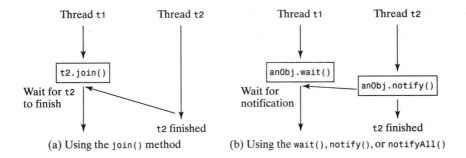

FIGURE 19.7 *The join(), wait(), notify(), and notifyAll() are used to communicate among threads.*

19.5.1 Thread States

Threads can be in one of five states: New, Ready, Running, Blocked, or Finished (see Figure 19.8).

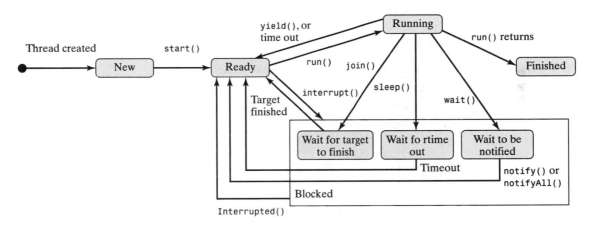

FIGURE 19.8 *A thread can be in one of five states: New, Ready, Running, Blocked, or Finished.*

When a thread is newly created, it enters the ***New*** state. After a thread is started by calling its start() method, it enters the ***Ready*** state. A ready thread is runnable but may not be running yet. The operating system has to allocate CPU time to it.

When a ready thread begins executing, it enters the ***Running*** state. A running thread may enter the Ready state if its given CPU time expires or its yield() method is called.

A thread can enter the ***Blocked*** state (i.e., become inactive) for several reasons. It may have invoked the join(), sleep(), or wait() method, or some other thread may have invoked these methods. It may be waiting for an I/O operation to finish. A blocked thread may be reactivated when the action inactivating it is reversed. For example, if a thread has been put to sleep and the sleep time has expired, the thread is reactivated and enters the Ready state.

Finally, a thread is *finished* if it completes the execution of its run() method.

The isAlive() method is used to find out the state of a thread. It returns true if a thread is in the **Ready**, **Blocked**, or **Running** state; it returns false if a thread is new and has not started or if it is finished.

The interrupt() method interrupts a thread in the following way: If a thread is currently in the **Ready** or **Running** state, its interrupted flag is set; if a thread is currently blocked, it is awakened and enters the **Ready** state, and a java.lang.InterruptedException is thrown.

19.5.2   Thread Priorities

Java assigns every thread a priority. By default, a thread inherits the priority of the thread that spawned it. You can increase or decrease the priority of any thread by using the setPriority method, and you can get the thread's priority by using the getPriority method. Priorities are numbers ranging from 1 to 10. The Thread class has the int constants MIN_PRIORITY, NORM_PRIORITY, and MAX_PRIORITY, representing 1, 5, and 10, respectively. The priority of the main thread is Thread.NORM_PRIORITY.

The JVM always picks the currently runnable thread with the highest priority. If several runnable threads have equally high priorities, the CPU is allocated to all of them in round-robin fashion. A lower-priority thread can run only when no higher-priority threads are running. For example, suppose you insert the following code in Line 16 in TestRunnable.java in Example 19.2:

```
print100.setPriority(Thread.MAX_PRIORITY);
```

The print100 thread will be finished first.

 TIP

The priority numbers may be changed in a future version of Java. To minimize the impact of any changes, use the constants in the Thread class to specify thread priorities.

 TIP

A thread may never get a chance to run if there is always a higher-priority thread running or a same-priority thread that never yields. This situation is known as *contention* or *starvation*. To avoid contention, the thread with high priority must periodically invoke the sleep or yield method to give a thread with a lower or the same priority a chance to run.

19.6   Thread Groups

A *thread group* is a set of threads. Some programs contain quite a few threads with similar functionality. For convenience, you can group them together and perform operations on the entire group. For example, you can suspend or resume all of the threads in a group at the same time.

Listed below are the guidelines for using thread groups:

1. Use the ThreadGroup constructor to construct a thread group:

   ```
   ThreadGroup g = new ThreadGroup("thread group");
   ```

   This creates a thread group g named "thread group". The name is a string and must be unique.

2. Using the Thread constructor, place a thread in a thread group:

   ```
   Thread t = new Thread(g, new ThreadClass(), "label for the thread");
   ```

This statement creates a thread and places it in the thread group g. You can add a thread group under another thread group to form a tree in which every thread group except the initial one has a parent.

3. To find out how many threads in a group are currently running, use the `activeCount()` method. The following statement displays the active number of threads in group g:

```
System.out.println("The number of runnable threads in the group "
  + g.activeCount());
```

4. Each thread belongs to a thread group. By default, a newly created thread becomes a member of the current thread group that spawned it. To find which group a thread belongs to, use the `getThreadGroup()` method.

 NOTE

You have to start each thread individually. There is no `start()` method in `ThreadGroup`.

In the next section, you will see an example that uses the `ThreadGroup` class.

19.7 Synchronization and Cooperation Among Threads

A shared resource may be corrupted if it is accessed simultaneously by multiple threads. The following example demonstrates the problem.

EXAMPLE 19.3 SHOWING RESOURCE CONFLICT

Problem

Write a program that demonstrates the problem of resource conflict. Suppose that you create and launch one hundred threads, each of which adds a penny to an account. Assume that the account is initially empty. A sample run of the program is shown in Figure 19.9.

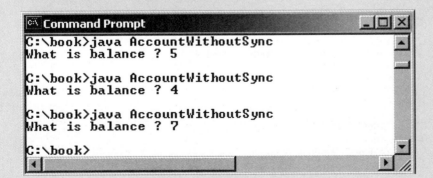

FIGURE 19.9 *The `AccountWithoutSync` program causes data inconsistency.*

Solution

Create a class named `Account` to model the account, a class named `AddAPennyThread` to add a penny to the account, and a main class that creates and launches threads. The relationships of these classes are shown in Figure 19.10. The program is given in Listing 19.3.

EXAMPLE 19.3 (CONTINUED)

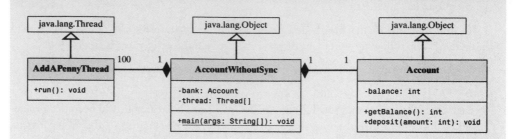

FIGURE **19.10**   *AccountWithoutSync contains an instance of* Account *and one hundred threads of* AddAPennyThread.

LISTING **19.3   AccountWithoutSync.java (Resource Conflict)**

```
1  public class AccountWithoutSync {
2    private Account account = new Account();
3    private Thread[] thread = new Thread[100];
4
5    public static void main(String[] args) {
6      AccountWithoutSync test = new AccountWithoutSync();
7      System.out.println("What is balance ? " +
8        test.account.getBalance());
9    }
10
11   public AccountWithoutSync() {
12     ThreadGroup g = new ThreadGroup("group");
13     boolean done = false;
14
15     // Create and launch 100 threads
16     for (int i = 0; i < 100; i++) {
17       thread[i] = new Thread(g, new AddAPennyThread(), "t");
18       thread[i].start();
19     }
20
21     // Check if all the threads are finished
22     while (!done)
23       if (g.activeCount() == 0)
24         done = true;
25   }
26
27   // A thread for adding a penny to the account
28   class AddAPennyThread extends Thread {
29     public void run() {
30       account.deposit(1);
31     }
32   }
33
34   // An inner class for account
35   class Account {
36     private int balance = 0;
37
38     public int getBalance() {
39       return balance;
40     }
41
42     public void deposit(int amount) {
43       int newBalance = balance + amount;
44
45       // This delay is deliberately added to magnify the
46       // data-corruption problem and make it easy to see.
47       try {
```

100 threads

group thread
start thread

run thread

Account class

EXAMPLE 19.3 (CONTINUED)

```
48        Thread.sleep(5);
49      }
50      catch (InterruptedException ex) {
51      }
52
53      balance = newBalance;
54    }
55  }
56 }
```

Review

The program creates one hundred threads in the array `thread` and groups them in a thread group `g` (Lines 16–19). The `activeCount()` method (Line 23) is used to count the active threads. When all the threads are finished, it returns 0.

The balance of the account is initially 0 (Line 36). When all the threads are finished, the balance should be 100, but the output is unpredictable. As can be seen in Figure 19.9, the answers are wrong in the sample run. This demonstrates the data-corruption problem that occurs when all the threads have access to the same data source simultaneously.

Lines 43–53 could be replaced by one statement:

```
balance = balance + amount;
```

However, it is highly unlikely, although plausible, that the problem can be replicated using this single statement. The statements in Lines 43–53 are deliberately designed to magnify the data-corruption problem and make it easy to see. If you run the program several times but still do not see the problem, increase the sleep time (Line 48). This will increase the chances for showing the problem of data inconsistency.

What, then, caused the error in Example 19.3? Here is a possible scenario, as shown in Figure 19.11.

Step	balance	thread[i]	thread[j]
1	0	newBalance = balance + 1;	
2	0		newBalance = balance + 1;
3	1	balance = newBalance;	
4	1		balance = newBalance;

FIGURE 19.11 `thread[i]` and `thread[j]` both add 1 to the same balance.

In Step 1, `thread[i]`, for some `i`, gets the balances from the account. In Step 2, `thread[j]`, for some `j`, gets the same balances from the account. In Step 3, `thread[i]` writes a new balance to the account. In Step 4, `thread[j]` writes a new balance to the account.

The effect of this scenario is that thread `thread[i]` does nothing, because in Step 4 thread `thread[j]` overrides `thread[i]`'s result. Obviously, the problem is that `thread[i]` and `thread[j]` are accessing a common resource in a way that causes conflict. This is a common problem, known as a *race condition,* in multithreaded programs. A class is said to be *thread-safe* if an object of the class does not cause a race condition in the presence of multiple threads. As demonstrated in the preceding example, the `Account` class is not thread-safe.

race condition

thread-safe

19.7.1 Synchronizing Instance and Static Methods

critical region

To avoid race conditions, it is necessary to prevent more than one thread from simultaneously entering a certain part of the program, known as the *critical region*. The critical region in Example 19.3 is the entire deposit method. You can use the keyword synchronized to synchronize the method so that only one thread can access the method at a time. There are several ways to correct the problem in Example 19.3. One approach is to make Account thread-safe by adding the keyword synchronized in the deposit method in Line 42, as follows:

```
public synchronized void deposit(double amount)
```

A synchronized method acquires a lock before it executes. In the case of an instance method, the lock is on the object for which the method was invoked. In the case of a static method, the lock is on the class. If one thread invokes a synchronized instance method (respectively, static method) on an object, the lock of that object (respectively, class) is acquired first, then the method is executed, and finally the lock is released. Another thread invoking the same method of that object (respectively, class) is blocked until the lock is released.

With the deposit method synchronized, the preceding scenario cannot happen. If thread thread[j] starts to enter the method, and thread thread[i] is already in the method, thread thread[j] is blocked until thread thread[i] finishes the method, as shown in Figure 19.12.

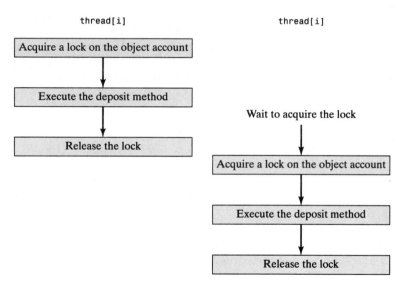

FIGURE 19.12 *thread[i] and thread[j] are synchronized.*

Suppose you are not allowed to modify Account. You could add a new, synchronized method that invokes deposit(1) and invoke this new method from the run() method. See Exercise 19.3.

19.7.2 Synchronizing Statements

Invoking a synchronized instance method of an object acquires a lock on the object, and invoking a synchronized static method of a class acquires a lock on the class. A synchronized statement can be used to acquire a lock on any object, not just *this* object, when executing a block of the code in a method. This block is referred to as a *synchronized block*. The general form of a synchronized statement is as follows:

synchronized block

```
synchronized (expr) {
  statements;
}
```

The expression expr must evaluate to an object reference. If the object is already locked by another thread, the thread is blocked until the lock is released. When a lock is obtained on the object, the statements in the synchronized block are executed, and then the lock is released.

Synchronized statements enable you to synchronize part of the code in a method instead of the entire method. This increases concurrency. Synchronized statements enable you to acquire a lock on any object so that you can synchronize the access to an object instead of to a method. You can make Example 19.3 thread-safe by placing the statement in Line 30 inside a synchronized block:

```
synchronized (account) {
  account.deposit(1);
}
```

 NOTE

Any synchronized instance method can be converted into a synchronized statement. Suppose that the following is a synchronized instance method:

```
public synchronized void xMethod() {
  // method body
}
```

This method is equivalent to

```
public void xMethod() {
  synchronized (this) {
    // method body
  }
}
```

19.7.3   Cooperation Among Threads

Thread synchronization suffices to avoid race conditions by ensuring mutual exclusion of multiple threads in the critical region, but sometimes you also need a way for threads to cooperate. The wait(), notify(), and notifyAll() methods can be used to facilitate communication among threads. The wait() method lets the thread wait until some condition occurs. When it occurs, you can use the notify() or notifyAll() methods to notify the waiting threads to resume normal execution. The notifyAll() method wakes up all the waiting threads, while notify() picks up only one thread from a waiting queue.

The wait(), notify(), and notifyAll() methods must be called in a synchronized method or a synchronized block on the receiving object of these methods. Otherwise, an Illegal-MonitorStateException will occur. The template for invoking these methods is shown in Figure 19.13.

Thread 1

```
synchronized (anObject) {
  try {
    // Wait for the condition to become true
    while (!condition)
      anObject.wait();            resume

    // Do something when condition is true
  }
  catch (InterruptedException ex) {
    ex.printStackTrace();
  }
}
```

Thread 2

```
synchronized (anObject) {
  // When condition becomes true
  anObject.notify(); or  anObject.notifyAll();
  ...
}
```

FIGURE 19.13   *The* wait(), notify(), *and* notifyAll() *methods coordinate thread communication.*

NOTE

A synchronization lock must be obtained on the object to be waited or notified. When wait() is invoked, it pauses the thread and simultaneously releases the lock on the object. When the thread is restarted after being notified, the lock is automatically reacquired.

EXAMPLE 19.4 THREAD COOPERATION

Problem

Write a program that demonstrates thread cooperation. Suppose that you create and launch two threads, one that deposits to an account, and one that withdraws from the same account. The second thread has to wait if the amount to be withdrawn is more than the current balance in the account. Whenever new funds are deposited to the account, the first thread notifies the second thread to resume. If the amount is still not enough for a withdrawal, the second thread has to continue to wait for more funds in the account. Assume that the initial balance is 0 and the amounts to deposit and withdraw are randomly generated. A sample run of the program is shown in Figure 19.14.

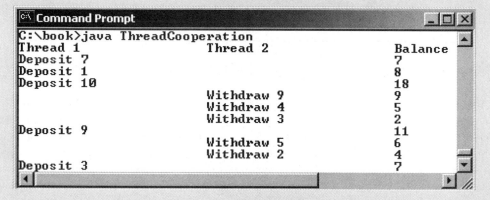

FIGURE 19.14   *Thread 2 waits if there are not sufficient funds to withdraw.*

Solution

Create a new inner class named Account to model the account with two synchronized methods deposit(int) and withdraw(int), a class named DepositThread to add an amount to the balance and a class named WithdrawThread to withdraw an amount from the balance, and a main class that creates and launches two threads. Listing 19.4 gives the program.

LISTING 19.4   ThreadCooperation.java

```
1 public class ThreadCooperation {
2   private Account account = new Account();
3   private Thread thread1 = new DepositThread();
4   private Thread thread2 = new WithdrawThread();
5
6   public static void main(String[] args) {
7     ThreadCooperation test = new ThreadCooperation();
8     System.out.println("Thread 1\t\tThread 2\t\tBalance");
9   }
10
11  public ThreadCooperation() {
12    thread1.start();
```

account
thread

start thread

EXAMPLE 19.4 (CONTINUED)

```
13    thread2.start();
14  }
15
16  // A thread for adding an amount to the account
17  class DepositThread extends Thread {
18    public void run() {
19      while (true) {
20        account.deposit((int)(Math.random() * 10) + 1);
21        try { // Purposely delay it to let the withdraw method proceed
22          Thread.sleep(1000);
23        }
24        catch (InterruptedException ex) {
25          ex.printStackTrace();
26        }
27      }
28    }
29  }
30
31  // A thread for subtracting an amount from the account
32  class WithdrawThread extends Thread {
33    public void run() {
34      while (true) {
35        account.withdraw((int)(Math.random() * 10) + 1);
36      }
37    }
38  }
39
40  // An inner class for account
41  class Account {
42    private int balance = 0;
43
44    public int getBalance() {
45      return balance;
46    }
47
48    public synchronized void deposit(int amount) {
49      balance += amount;
50      System.out.println("Deposit " + amount +
51        "\t\t\t\t\t" + account.getBalance());
52      notifyAll();
53    }
54
55    public synchronized void withdraw(int amount) {
56      try {
57        while (balance < amount)
58          wait();
59      }
60      catch (InterruptedException ex) {
61        ex.printStackTrace();
62      }
63
64      balance -= amount;
65      System.out.println("\t\t\tWithdraw " + amount +
66        "\t\t" + account.getBalance());
67    }
68  }
69 }
```

inner class
run thread

inner class
run thread

inner class

synchronized method

notifyAll()

synchronized method

wait()

Review

The program creates thread1 for deposit (Line 3) and thread2 for withdrawal (Line 4). thread1 is purposely put to sleep (Line 22) to let thread2 run. When there are not enough funds to withdraw, thread2 waits (Line 58) for notification of the balance change from thread1 (Line 52).

> ### EXAMPLE 19.4 (CONTINUED)
>
> What will happen if you replace the `while` loop in Lines 57–58 with the following `if` statement?
>
> ```
> if (balance < amount)
>   wait();
> ```
>
> `thread1` will notify `thread2` whenever the balance changes. (`balance < amount`) may be still true when `thread2` is awakened. Using the `if` statement, `thread2` may wait forever. Using the loop statement, `thread2` will have chance to recheck the condition. Thus you should always test the condition in a loop.

19.7.4 Deadlock

deadlock

Sometimes two or more threads need to acquire the locks on several shared objects. This could cause a *deadlock*, in which each thread has the lock on one of the objects and is waiting for the lock on the other object. Consider the scenario with two threads and two objects, as shown in Figure 19.15. Thread 1 has acquired a lock on `object1`, and Thread 2 has acquired a lock on `object2`. Now Thread 1 is waiting for the lock on `object2`, and Thread 2 for the lock on `object1`. Each thread waits for the other to release the lock it needs, and until that happens neither can continue to run.

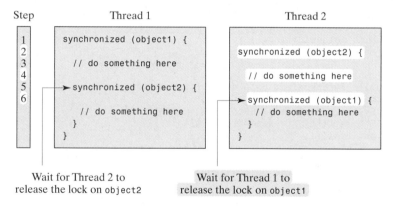

FIGURE 19.15 *Thread 1 and Thread 2 are deadlocked.*

resource ordering

Deadlock is easily avoided by using a simple technique known as *resource ordering*. With this technique, you assign an order on all the objects whose locks must be acquired and ensure that each thread acquires the locks in that order. For the example in Figure 19.15, suppose that the objects are ordered as `object1` and `object2`. Using the resource ordering technique, Thread 2 must acquire a lock on `object1` first, then on `object2`. Once Thread 1 acquires a lock on `object1`, Thread 2 has to wait for a lock on `object1`. So Thread 1 will be able to acquire a lock on `object2` and no deadlock will occur.

19.8 Controlling Animation Using Threads (Optional)

Section 12.6, "The `Timer` Class," introduced the use of the `Timer` class to control animations. You can also use a thread to control animations. Let us write an applet that displays a running clock. Use two buttons to suspend and resume the clock, as shown in Figure 19.16.

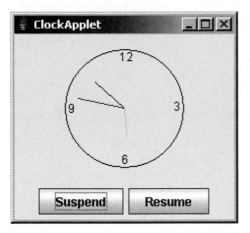

FIGURE 19.16 *You can click the Suspend button to suspend the clock and the Resume button to resume the clock.*

Here are the major steps to complete this example:

1. Create a subclass of StillClock named Clock to enable the clock to run, as shown in Listing 19.5.

2. Create a subclass of JPanel named ClockControl to contain the clock with two control buttons, *Suspend* and *Resume*, as shown in Listing 19.6.

3. Create an applet named ClockApp to contain an instance of ClockControl, and enable the applet to run standalone, as shown in Listing 19.7.

The relationships among these classes are shown in Figure 19.17.

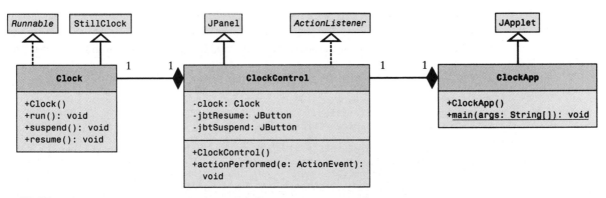

FIGURE 19.17 ClockApp *contains* ClockControl, *and* ClockControl *contains* Clock.

LISTING 19.5 Clock.java (Animating a Clock)

```
1 public class Clock extends StillClock implements Runnable {
2   private boolean suspended;
3
4   public Clock() {
5     new Thread(this).start();
6   }
7
```

suspended?

start thread

```
       8    public void run() {
       9      while (true) {
set new time   10      setCurrentTime();
repaint     11      repaint();
            12
sleep       13      try {
            14        Thread.sleep(1000);
            15        waitIfSuspended();
            16      }
            17      catch(InterruptedException ex) {
            18      }
            19    }
            20  }
            21
            22  public synchronized void suspend() {
suspended   23    suspended = true;
            24  }
            25
            26  public synchronized void resume() {
            27    if (suspended) {
not suspended 28      suspended = false;
notifyAll   29      notifyAll();
            30    }
            31  }
            32
            33  private synchronized void waitIfSuspended()
            34    throws InterruptedException {
            35    while (suspended)
wait        36      wait();
            37  }
            38 }
```

The Clock class extends StillClock to display the clock and implements the Runnable interface to enable the clock to run. Since the suspend() and resume() methods in the Thread class are deprecated, you must create new methods for resuming and suspending threads. The variable suspended is declared as a data member of the class (Line 2), which indicates the state of the thread. The keyword synchronized ensures that the resume() and suspend() methods are synchronized to avoid race conditions that could result in an inconsistent value for the variable suspended.

Line 5 creates and starts the thread. The run method (Lines 8–20) is implemented to set a new time and repaint the clock every one second continuously. In the while loop body, the thread is blocked if suspended is true. The waitIfSuspended() (Line 15) method causes the thread to suspend and wait for notification by the notifyAll() method (Line 29) invoked from the resume() method.

LISTING 19.6 ClockControl.java (Controlling a Clock)

```
 1 import javax.swing.*;
 2 import java.awt.event.*;
 3 import java.awt.BorderLayout;
 4
 5 public class ClockControl extends JPanel implements ActionListener {
clock    6   private Clock clock = new Clock();
 7   private JButton jbtSuspend = new JButton("Suspend");
 8   private JButton jbtResume = new JButton("Resume");
 9
create UI 10  public ClockControl() {
11    // Group buttons in a panel
12    JPanel panel = new JPanel();
13    panel.add(jbtSuspend);
14    panel.add(jbtResume);
15
16    // Add clock and buttons to the panel
17    setLayout(new BorderLayout());
18    add(clock, BorderLayout.CENTER);
19    add(panel, BorderLayout.SOUTH);
20
21    // Register listeners
22    jbtSuspend.addActionListener(this);
```

```
23     jbtResume.addActionListener(this);
24   }
25
26   public void actionPerformed(ActionEvent e) {
27     if (e.getSource() == jbtSuspend)
28       clock.suspend();
29     else if (e.getSource() == jbtResume)
30       clock.resume();
31   }
32 }
```

suspend

resume

The `ClockControl` class extends `JPanel` to display the clock and two control buttons and implements the `ActionListener` to handle action events from the buttons. When the *Suspend* button is clicked, the clock's `suspend()` method is invoked to suspend the clock. When the *Resume* button is clicked, the clock's `resume()` method is invoked to resume the clock.

LISTING 19.7 ClockApp.java

```
1 public class ClockApp extends JApplet {
2   public ClockApp() {
3     getContentPane().add(new ClockControl());
4   }
5 }
```

main method omitted

The `ClockApp` class simply places an instance of `ClockControl` in the applet's content pane.

19.9 Running Audio on a Separate Thread (Optional)

When developing animation programs with audio, run the audio on a separate thread to avoid animation delays. To illustrate the problem, let us first write a program without playing the audio on a separate thread.

The program creates an applet that displays a running clock and announces the time at one-minute intervals. For example, if the current time is 6:30:00, the applet announces, "six o'clock thirty minutes A.M." If the current time is 20:20:00, the applet announces, "eight o'clock twenty minutes P.M." Also add a label to display the digital time, as shown in Figure 19.18.

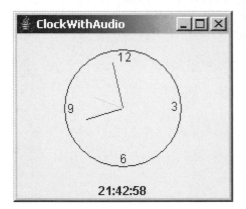

FIGURE **19.18** *The applet displays a clock and announces the time.*

In Section 11.12, "Case Study: The `StillClock` Class," the `StillClock` class was developed to draw a still clock to show the current time. Create an applet named `ClockWithAudio` (Listing 19.8) that contains an instance of `StillClock` to display an analog clock, and an instance of `JLabel` to display the digital time. Override the `init` method to load the audio files. Use a `Timer` object to set and display the current time continuously at a fixed rate. When the second is zero, announce the current time.

LISTING 19.8   ClockWithAudio.java (Announcing Time)

```
 1 import java.applet.*;
 2 import javax.swing.*;
 3 import java.awt.event.*;
 4 import java.awt.*;
 5
 6 public class ClockWithAudio extends JApplet
 7    implements ActionListener {
 8   // Declare audio files
 9   protected AudioClip[] hourAudio = new AudioClip[12];
10   protected AudioClip minuteAudio;
11   protected AudioClip amAudio;
12   protected AudioClip pmAudio;
13
14   // Create a clock
15   private StillClock clock = new StillClock();
16
17   // Create a timer
18   private Timer timer = new Timer(1000, this);
19
20   // Create a label to display time
21   private JLabel jlblDigitTime = new JLabel("", JLabel.CENTER);
22
23   /** Initialize the applet */
24   public void init() {
25     Class metaObject = this.getClass();
26
27     // Create audio clips for pronouncing hours
28     for (int i = 0; i < 12; i++)
29       hourAudio[i] = Applet.newAudioClip(
30         metaObject.getResource("timeaudio/hour" + i + ".au"));
31
32     // Create audio clips for pronouncing am and pm
33     amAudio =
34       Applet.newAudioClip(metaObject.getResource("timeaudio/am.au"));
35     pmAudio =
36       Applet.newAudioClip(metaObject.getResource("timeaudio/pm.au"));
37
38     // Add clock and time label to the content pane of the applet
39     getContentPane().add(clock, BorderLayout.CENTER);
40     getContentPane().add(jlblDigitTime, BorderLayout.SOUTH);
41   }
42
43   /** Override the applet's start method */
44   public void start() {
45     timer.start(); // Resume clock
46   }
47
48   /** Override the applet's stop method */
49   public void stop() {
50     timer.stop(); // Suspend clock
51   }
52
53   public void actionPerformed(ActionEvent e) {
54     clock.setCurrentTime();
55     clock.repaint();
56     jlblDigitTime.setText(clock.getHour() + ":" + clock.getMinute()
57       + ":" + clock.getSecond());
58     if (clock.getSecond() == 0)
59       announceTime(clock.getMinute(), clock.getHour());
60   }
61
62   /** Announce the current time at every minute */
63   public void announceTime(int m, int h) {
64     // Announce hour
65     hourAudio[h % 12].play();
66
67     // Load the minute file
68     minuteAudio = Applet.newAudioClip(this.getClass().getResource(
69       "timeaudio/minute" + m + ".au"));
```

The following labels appear in the left margin, aligned to the code lines:

- audio clip (line 9)
- still clock (line 15)
- timer (line 18)
- hour clip (line 29)
- am clip (line 33)
- pm clip (line 35)
- start timer (line 45)
- stop timer (line 50)
- new time (line 54)
- announce time (line 59)
- announce hour (line 65)

```
70
71      // Time delay to allow hourAudio play to finish
72      try {
73        Thread.sleep(1500);
74      }
75      catch(InterruptedException ex) {
76      }
77
78      // Announce minute
79      minuteAudio.play();
80
81      // Time delay to allow minuteAudio play to finish
82      try {
83        Thread.sleep(1500);
84      }
85      catch(InterruptedException ex) {
86      }
87
88      // Announce am or pm
89      if (h < 12)
90        amAudio.play();
91      else
92        pmAudio.play();
93    }
94  }
```

announce minute

announce am

announce pm

main method omitted

The hourAudio is an array of twelve audio clips that are used to announce the twelve hours of the day (Line 9); the minuteAudio is an audio clip that is used to announce the minutes in an hour (Line 10). The amAudio announces A.M. (Line 11); the pmAudio announces P.M (Line 12).

The init() method creates audio clips for announcing the time (Lines 24–41) and places a clock and a label in the applet (Lines 39–40).

All of the audio files are stored in the directory timeaudio, a subdirectory of the applet's directory. The twelve audio clips that are used to announce the hours are stored in the files **hour0.au**, **hour1.au**, and so on, to **hour11.au**. They are loaded using the following loop (Lines 29–30):

```
for (int i = 0; i < 12; i++)
  hourAudio[i] = Applet.newAudioClip(
    metaObject.getResource("timeaudio/hour" + i + ".au"));
```

Similarly, the amAudio clip is stored in the file **am.au**, and the pmAudio clip is stored in the file **pm.au**; they are loaded along with the hour clips in the init() method (Lines 33–36).

The program creates an array of twelve audio clips to announce each of the twelve hours, but does not create sixty audio clips to announce each of the minutes. Instead, it creates and loads the minute audio clip (Lines 68–69) when needed in the announceTime method. The audio files are very large. Loading all sixty audio clips at once may cause an OutOfMemoryError exception.

In the announceTime method (Lines 63–93), the sleep() method (Lines 73, 83) is purposely invoked to ensure that one clip finishes before the next clip starts, so that the clips do not interfere with each other.

An ActionEvent is fired by the timer every second. In the actionPerformed method (Lines 53–60), the clock is repainted with the new current time, and the digital time is displayed in the label.

The applet's start() and stop() methods (Lines 44–51) are overridden to ensure that the timer starts or stops when the applet is restarted or stopped.

When you run the preceding program, you will notice that the second hand does not display at the first, second, and third seconds of the minute. This is because sleep(1500) is invoked twice in the announceTime() method, which takes three seconds to announce the time at the beginning of each minute. Thus, the actionPerformed method is delayed for three seconds during the first three seconds of each minute. As a result of this delay, the time is not updated and the clock is not repainted for these three seconds. To avoid this conflict, you should announce the time on a separate thread. This problem is fixed in Listing 19.9.

LISTING 19.9 ClockWithAudioOnSeparateThread.java

```
1  import java.applet.*;
2  import java.awt.*;
3  import javax.swing.*;
4
5  public class ClockWithAudioOnSeparateThread
6      extends ClockAppletWithAudio {
7    /** Override this method defined in ClockAppletWithAudio
8       to announce the current time at every minute */
9    public void announceTime(int m, int h) {
10     // Load the minute file
11     minuteAudio = Applet.newAudioClip(this.getClass().getResource(
12       "timeaudio/minute" + m + ".au"));
13
14     // Announce current time
15     AnnounceTime announceTime;
16     if (h < 12)
17       announceTime = new AnnounceTime(hourAudio[h],
18         minuteAudio, amAudio);
19     else
20       announceTime = new AnnounceTime(hourAudio[h % 12],
21         minuteAudio, pmAudio);
22     announceTime.start();
23   }
24
25   // Define a thread class for announcing time
26   class AnnounceTime extends Thread {
27     private AudioClip hourAudio, minuteAudio, amPM;
28
29     /** Get Audio clips */
30     public AnnounceTime(AudioClip hourAudio,
31                         AudioClip minuteAudio,
32                         AudioClip amPM) {
33       this.hourAudio = hourAudio;
34       this.minuteAudio = minuteAudio;
35       this.amPM = amPM;
36     }
37
38     public void run() {
39       // Announce hour
40       hourAudio.play();
41
42       // Time delay to allow hourAudio play to finish
43       // before playing the clip
44       try {
45         Thread.sleep(1500);
46       }
47       catch (InterruptedException ex) {
48       }
49
50       // Announce minute
51       minuteAudio.play();
52
53       // Time delay to allow minuteAudio play to finish
54       try {
55         Thread.sleep(1500);
56       }
57       catch (InterruptedException ex) {
58       }
59
60       // Announce am or pm
61       amPM.play();
62     }
63   }
64 }
```

Margin notes:

minute clip — (Line 11)

create thread — (Line 17)

create thread — (Line 20)

start thread — (Line 22)

extend Thread class — (Line 26)

main method omitted — (Line 64)

The program extends ClockAppletWithAudio (Line 6) with the capability to announce time without delaying the actionPerformed method. The program defines a new thread class, AnnounceTime (Lines 26–63), which is derived from the Thread class. This new class plays audio.

To create an instance of the AnnounceTime class, you need to pass the three audio clips used to announce the hour, the minute, and A.M. or P.M. (Lines 15–21).

When running this program, you will discover that the audio does not interfere with the clock animation because an instance of AnnounceTime starts on a separate thread to announce the current time. This thread is independent of the thread on which the actionPerformed method runs.

An object of AnnounceTime is created every minute to announce the current time. The program can be improved to run more efficiently by creating one such object in advance and passing hour audio, minute audio, and A.M./P.M. audio to the object when it is time to announce the current time. See Exercise 19.10.

19.10   `JProgressBar` (Optional)

JProgressBar is a component that displays a value graphically within a bounded interval. A progress bar is typically used to show the percentage of completion of a lengthy operation; it comprises a rectangular bar that is "filled in" from left to right horizontally or from bottom to top vertically as the operation is performed. It provides the user with feedback on the progress of the operation. For example, when a file is being read, it alerts the user to the progress of the operation, thereby keeping the user attentive.

JProgressBar is often implemented using a thread to monitor the completion status of other threads. The progress bar can be displayed horizontally or vertically, as determined by its orientation property. The minimum, value, and maximum properties determine the minimum, current, and maximum lengths on the progress bar, as shown in Figure 19.19. Figure 19.20 lists frequently used features of JProgressBar.

$$percentComplete = \frac{value}{maximum}$$

FIGURE **19.19**   *JProgressBar displays the progress of a task.*

javax.swing.JComponent	
↑	

javax.swing.JProgressBar	
+JProgressBar()	Creates a horizontal progress bar with min 0 and max 100.
+JProgressBar(min: int, max: int)	Creates a horizontal progress bar with specified min and max.
+JProgressBar(orient: int)	Creates a progress bar with min 0 and max 100 and a specified orientation.
+JProgressBar(orient: int, min: int, max: int)	Creates a progress bar with a specified orientation, min, and max.
+getMaximum(): int	Gets the maximum value (default: 100).
+setMaximum(n: int): void	Sets a new maximum value.
+getMinimum(): int	Gets the minimum value (default: 0).
+setMinimum(n: int): void	Sets a new minimum value.
+getOrientation(): int	Gets the orientation value (default: HORIZONTAL).
+setOrientation(orient: int): void	Sets a new orientation.
+getPercentComplete(): double	Returns the percent complete for the progress bar.
+getValue(): int	Returns the progress bar's current value.
+setValue(n: int): void	Sets the progress bar's current value.
+getString(): String	Returns the current value of the progress string.
+setString(s: String): void	Sets the value of the progress string.
+isStringPainted(): boolean	Returns the value of the stringPainted property.
+setStringPainted(b: boolean): void	Sets the value of the stringPainted property, which determines whether the progress bar should render a progress percentage string (default: false).

FIGURE **19.20**   *JProgressBar is a Swing component with many properties that enable you to customize a progress bar.*

EXAMPLE 19.5 JProgressBar Demo

Problem

Write a GUI application that lets you copy files. A progress bar is used to show the progress of the copying operation, as shown in Figure 19.21.

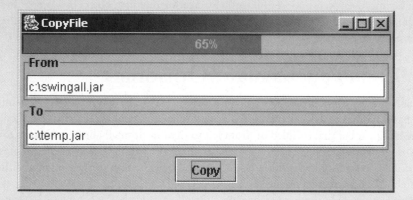

FIGURE 19.21 *The user enters the files in the text fields and clicks the Copy button to start copying files.*

Solution

Place a JProgressBar in the north of the frame. Place a button in a panel, and place the panel in the source of the frame. Place the two text fields in two panels, set the titles on the borders of the panels, and place the panels in another panel of the GridLayout with two rows. Place the panel in the center of the frame.

While copying date from a source file to a destination file on one thread, the progress bar is updated on another thread. You need to create a thread that copies a file and another thread that updates the progress bar. Every time some bytes of the file are copied, the current value in the progress bar is updated to show the progress.

Create a main class named CopyFile that lays out the user interface. Create an inner class named CopyFileThread that extends Thread to copy files when the Copy button is pressed. Update the progress bar as a file is being copied. The complete program is given in Listing 19.10.

LISTING 19.10 CopyFile.java

progress bar

UI

```
 1 import java.awt.*;
 2 import java.awt.event.*;
 3 import javax.swing.*;
 4 import javax.swing.border.*;
 5 import java.io.*;
 6
 7 public class CopyFile extends JFrame implements ActionListener {
 8   private JProgressBar jpb = new JProgressBar();
 9   private JButton jbtCopy = new JButton("Copy");
10   private JTextField jtfFrom = new JTextField();
11   private JTextField jtfTo = new JTextField();
12
13   public CopyFile() {
14     JPanel jPanel2 = new JPanel();
15     jPanel2.setLayout(new BorderLayout());
16     jPanel2.setBorder(new TitledBorder("From"));
17     jPanel2.add(jtfFrom, BorderLayout.CENTER);
18
```

EXAMPLE 19.5 (CONTINUED)

```
19      JPanel jPanel3 = new JPanel();
20      jPanel3.setLayout(new BorderLayout());
21      jPanel3.setBorder(new TitledBorder("To"));
22      jPanel3.add(jtfTo, BorderLayout.CENTER);
23
24      JPanel jPanel1 = new JPanel();
25      jPanel1.setLayout(new GridLayout(2, 1));
26      jPanel1.add(jPanel2);
27      jPanel1.add(jPanel3);
28
29      JPanel jPanel4 = new JPanel();
30      jPanel4.add(jbtCopy);
31
32      this.getContentPane().add(jpb, BorderLayout.NORTH);
33      this.getContentPane().add(jPanel1, BorderLayout.CENTER);
34      this.getContentPane().add(jPanel4, BorderLayout.SOUTH);
35
36      jpb.setStringPainted(true); // Paint the percent in a string
37
38      jbtCopy.addActionListener(this);
39    }
40
41    public void actionPerformed(ActionEvent e) {
42      // Create a thread for copying files
43      new CopyFileThread().start();
44    }
45
46    public static void main(String[] args) {
47      CopyFile frame = new CopyFile();
48      frame.setDefaultCloseOperation(JFrame.EXIT_ON_CLOSE);
49      frame.setTitle("CopyFile");
50      frame.setSize(400, 180);
51      frame.setVisible(true);
52    }
53
54    // Copy file and update progress bar in a separate thread
55    class CopyFileThread extends Thread {                          extend Thread class
56      private int currentValue;
57
58      public void run() {
59        BufferedInputStream in = null;
60        BufferedOutputStream out = null;
61        try {
62          // Create file input stream
63          File inFile = new File(jtfFrom.getText().trim());
64          in = new BufferedInputStream(new FileInputStream(inFile));
65
66          // Create file output stream
67          File outFile = new File(jtfTo.getText());
68          out = new BufferedOutputStream(new FileOutputStream(outFile));
69
70          // Get total bytes in the file
71          long totalBytes = in.available();
72
73          // Start progress meter bar
74          jpb.setValue(0);
75          jpb.setMaximum(100);
76
77          int r;
78          long bytesRead = 0;
79          // You may increase buffer size to improve IO speed
80          byte[] b = new byte[10];
81          while ((r = in.read(b, 0, b.length)) != -1) {
82            out.write(b, 0, r);
83            bytesRead += r;
84            currentValue = (int)(bytesRead * 100 / totalBytes);
85
```

progress bar value

EXAMPLE 19.5 (CONTINUED)

```
86              // Update the progress bar
87              jpb.setValue(currentValue);
88            }
89          }
90          catch (FileNotFoundException ex) {
91            ex.printStackTrace();
92          }
93          catch (IOException ex) {
94            ex.printStackTrace();
95          }
96          finally {
97            try {
98              if (in != null) in.close();
99              if (out != null) out.close();
100           }
101           catch (Exception ex) {}
102         }
103       }
104     }
105 }
```

Review

The `CopyFile` class lays out the user interface and responds to the Copy button event. When the Copy button is pressed, it creates and starts a thread of `CopyFileThread` (Line 43).

The class `CopyFileThread` is a subclass of `Thread`. This class is for copying a file on a separate thread. What would happen if copying a file is not run on a separate thread? The progress bar will not be updated until the copy ends. This is because the `paint` method for repainting the progress bar runs on the thread with the `actionPerformed` method. As long as the copy operation continues, the progress bar never gets a chance to be repainted. Running the copy operation on a separate thread will enable the progress bar to be repainted simultaneously with the copy operations.

KEY TERMS

deadlock   700
multithreading   684
race condition   695

synchronized   696
thread   684
thread-safe   695

KEY CLASSES AND METHODS

✦ `java.lang.Thread` is a class that contains the constructors for creating threads, as well as many useful methods for controlling threads.

✦ `java.lang.Runnable` is an interface that provides a common protocol for runnable objects. It contains the `run()` method.

✦ `javax.swing.JProgressBar` is a Swing component that can be used to graphically display the completion status of a thread.

CHAPTER SUMMARY

✦ You can derive your thread class from the `Thread` class and create a thread instance to run a task on a separate thread. If your class needs to inherit multiple classes, implement the `Runnable` interface to run multiple tasks in the program simultaneously.

✦ After a thread object is created, use the start() method to start a thread, and the sleep(long) method to put a thread to sleep so that other threads get a chance to run. Since the stop, suspend, and resume methods are deprecated in Java 2, you need to implement these methods to stop, suspend, and resume a thread, if necessary.

✦ A thread object never directly invokes the run method. The JVM invokes the run method when it is time to execute the thread. Your class must override the run method to tell the system what the thread will do when it runs.

✦ A thread can be in one of five states: **New**, **Ready**, **Running**, **Blocked**, or **Finished**. When a thread is newly created, it enters the *New state*. After a thread is started by calling its start() method, it enters the *Ready state*. A **Ready** thread is runnable but may not be running yet. The operating system has to allocate CPU time to it.

✦ When a ready thread begins executing, it enters the *Running state*. A running thread may reenter the **Ready** state if its given CPU time expires or its yield() method is called.

✦ A thread can enter the *Blocked* state (i.e., become inactive) for several reasons. It may have invoked the sleep(long), wait(), or interrup() method, or some other thread may have invoked its sleep or interrupt() method. It may be waiting for an I/O operation to finish. A **Blocked** thread may be reactivated when the action inactivating it is reversed. For example, if a thread has been put to sleep and the sleep time has expired, the thread is reactivated and enters the **Ready** state.

✦ A thread is *Finished* if it completes the execution of its run() method.

✦ Threads can be assigned priorities. The JVM always executes the **Ready** thread with the highest priority. You can use a thread group to put relevant threads together for group control.

✦ To prevent threads from corrupting a shared resource, use synchronized methods or blocks. A synchronized method acquires a lock before it executes. In the case of an instance method, the lock is on the object for which the method was invoked. In the case of a static (class) method, the lock is on the class.

✦ A synchronized statement can be used to acquire a lock on any object, not just *this* object, when executing a block of the code in a method. This block is referred to as a *synchronized block*.

✦ *Deadlock* occurs when two or more threads acquire locks on multiple objects and each has a lock on one object and is waiting for the lock on the other object. The *resource ordering technique* can be used to avoid deadlock.

✦ You can use a JProgressBar to track progress of a thread.

REVIEW QUESTIONS

Sections 19.1–19.4

19.1   Why do you need multithreading? How can multiple threads run simultaneously in a single-processor system?

19.2 Name two ways to create threads. When do you use the `Thread` class? When do you use the `Runnable` interface? What are the differences between the `Thread` class and the `Runnable` interface?

19.3 How do you create a thread and launch a thread object? What would happen if you replace the `start()` method by the `run()` method in Lines 10–12 in Example 19.1?

```
print100.start();                 print100.run();
printA.start();    Replaced by    printA.run();
printB.start();                    printB.run();
```

Section 19.5 Thread Controls and Communications

19.4 Why does the following class have a runtime error?

```
1 public class Test extends Thread {
2   public static void main(String[] args) {
3     Test t = new Test();
4     t.start();
5     t.start();
6   }
7
8   public void run() {
9     System.out.println("test");
10   }
11 }
```

19.5 Which of the following methods are instance methods in `java.lang.Thread`? Which method may throw an `InterruptedException`? Which of them are deprecated in Java 2?

`run`, `start`, `stop`, `suspend`, `resume`, `sleep`, `interrupt`, `isInterrupted`, `yield`, `join`

19.6 Can `wait()`, `notify()`, and `notifyAll()` be invoked from any object? What is the purpose of these methods?

19.7 Explain the life cycle of a thread object. How do you set a priority for a thread? What is the default priority?

Section 19.6 Thread Groups

19.8 Describe a thread group. How do you create a thread group?

19.9 How do you start the threads in a group? How do you find the number of active threads in a group of threads?

Section 19.7 Synchronization and Cooperation Among Threads

19.10 Give some examples of possible resource corruption when running multiple threads. How do you synchronize conflicting threads?

19.11 Suppose you place the statement in Line 30 of Listing 19.3, AccountWithoutSync.java inside a synchronized block to avoid race conditions, as follows:

```
synchronized (this) {
  account.deposit(1);
}
```

Does it work?

19.12 What is wrong in the following code?

```
synchronized (object1) {
  try {
    while (!condition) object2.wait();
```

```
    }
    catch (InterruptedException ex) {
    }
  }
```

19.13 What would happen if the `while` loop in Lines 57–58 of Listing 19.4, ThreadCoopera-tion.java, is changed to an `if` statement?

```
while (balance < amount)     Replaced by      if (balance < amount)
  wait();                                         wait();
```

19.14 Why does the following class have a syntax error?

```
1 import javax.swing.*;
2
3 public class Test extends JApplet implements Runnable {
4   public void init() throws InterruptedException {
5     Thread thread = new Thread(this);
6     thread.sleep(1000);
7   }
8
9   public synchronized void run() {
10  }
11 }
```

19.15 What is deadlock? How can you avoid deadlock?

Sections 19.8–19.9

19.16 How do you override the methods `init`, `start`, `stop`, and `destroy` in the `Applet` class to work well with the threads in the applets?

19.17 Will the program behave differently if `Thread.sleep(1000)` is replaced by `thread.sleep(1000)` in Listing 19.5, clock.java?

19.18 For a `JProgressBar`, what is the property that displays the percentage of work complet-ed? How do you set its orientation?

PROGRAMMING EXERCISES

Sections 19.1–19.4

19.1* (*Revising Example 19.1 "Using the `Thread` Class to Create and Launch Threads"*) Rewrite Example 19.1 to display the output in a text area, as shown in Figure 19.22.

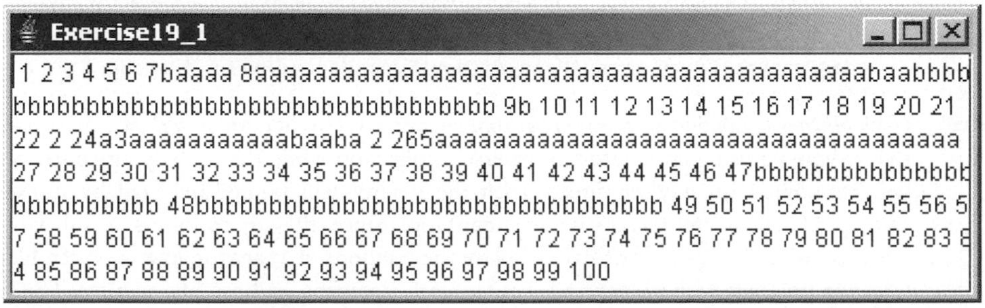

FIGURE 19.22 *The output from three threads is displayed in a text area.*

Section 19.7 Synchronization and Cooperation Among Threads

19.2* (*Synchronizing threads*) Write a program that launches one hundred threads. Each thread adds 1 to a variable sum that initially is zero. You need to pass sum by reference to each thread. In order to pass it by reference, define an Integer wrapper object to hold sum. Run the program with and without synchronization to see its effect.

19.3 (*Modifying Example 19.3 "Showing Resource Conflict"*) Suppose you are not allowed to modify Account. Add a new synchronized method that invokes deposit(1), and invoke this new method from the run() method.

19.4 (*Using synchronized statements*) Modify Example 19.3, "Showing Resource Conflict," using a synchronized statement to synchronize access to the Account object in the run() method.

19.5* (*Revising Example 19.3 "Showing Resource Conflict"*) Modify Example 19.3 as follows:

✦ Create two panels with the titles "Synchronized Threads" and "Unsynchronized Threads", as shown in Figure 19.23. The Synchronized Threads panel displays an account balance after a penny has been added one hundred times using synchronized threads. The Unsynchronized Threads panel displays an account balance after a penny has been added one hundred times using unsynchronized threads.

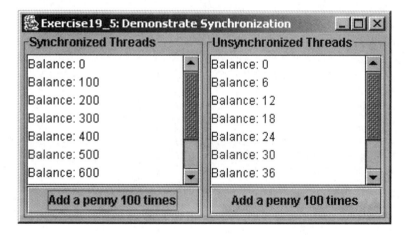

FIGURE 19.23 *The program shows the effect of executing the threads with and without synchronization.*

✦ Since the two panels are very similar, you can create a class to model them uniformly, as shown in Figure 19.24. Use a variable named mode to indicate whether synchronized threads or unsynchronized threads are used in the panel. Invoke the method addAPennyWithSync or addAPennyWithoutSync, depending on the mode.

19.6* (*Demonstrating ConcurrentModificationException*) The iterator is *fail-fast*. This means that if you are using an iterator to traverse a collection while the underlying collection is being modified by another thread, then the iterator will immediately fail by throwing java.util.ConcurrentModificationException. Since this exception is a subclass of RuntimeException, you don't have to place the methods of Iterator in a try-catch block. Create a program with two threads concurrently accessing and modifying a set. The first thread creates a hash set filled with numbers, and adds a new number to the set every second. The second thread obtains an iterator for the set and traverses the set back and forth

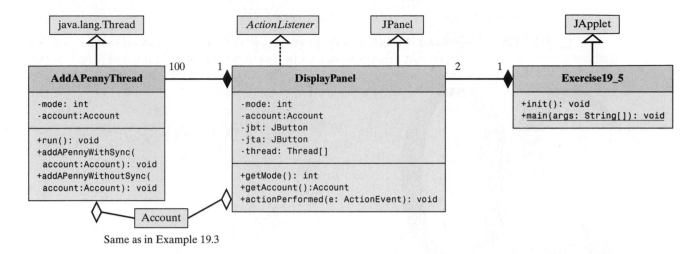

FIGURE 19.24 `DisplayPanel` *displays the balance in the text area after a penny is added to the balance one hundred times.*

through the iterator every second. You will receive a `ConcurrentModificationException`, because the underlying set is being modified in the first thread while the set in the second thread is being traversed.

19.7* (*Using synchronized sets*) Using synchronization, correct the problem in the preceding exercise so that the second thread does not throw `ConcurrentModificationException`. You will have to use the `Collections.synchronizedSet(set)` method to obtain a synchronized set and acquire a lock on the returned set when traversing it. It is, however, imperative for a thread to acquire a lock on the synchronized list, set, or map when traversing it through an iterator, as shown in the following code:

```
Set hashSet = Collections.synchronizedSet(new HashSet());

synchronized (hashSet) { // Must synchronize it
  Iterator iterator = hashSet.iterator();

  while (iterator.hasNext()) {
    System.out.println(iterator.next());
  }
}
```

Failure to do so may result in nondeterministic behavior, such as `ConcurrentModific-ationException`.

19.8** (*Producer and consumer*) A classic exercise in the use of thread communication is the producer and consumer type of program. Write a program with two threads named producer and consumer. The producer produces data and the consumer consumes the data. Assume that the data are stored in a stack. When the stack is empty, the consumer waits. Whenever the producer adds data to the stack, it notifies the consumer.

19.9* (*Demonstrating deadlock*) Write a program that demonstrates deadlock.

19.10 (*Revising Listing 19.9*) In Listing 19.9, ClockWithAudioOnSeparateThread.java, an object of `AnnounceTime` is created every minute to announce the current time. Rewrite the program by creating one such object in advance and passing hour audio, minute audio, and am/pm audio to the object when it is time to announce the current time.

Section 19.10 `JProgressBar`

19.11* (*Using `JProgressBar`*) Create a program that displays an instance of `JProgressBar` and sets its `value` property randomly every 500 milliseconds infinitely.

chapter

20

INTERNATIONALIZATION

Objectives

- ✦ To describe Java's internationalization features (§20.1).

- ✦ To construct a locale with language, country, and variant (§20.2).

- ✦ To process date and time based on locale (§20.3).

- ✦ To display numbers, currencies, and percentages based on locale (§20.4).

- ✦ To develop applications for international audiences using resource bundles (§20.5).

20.1   Introduction

Java is an Internet programming language. Since the Internet has no boundaries, your applets may be viewed by people who don't understand English. What is useful for those who can read English may be unusable for those who can only read French. Many Web sites maintain several versions of HTML pages so that readers can choose one written in a language they understand. Because there are so many languages in the world, it would be highly problematic to create and maintain enough different versions to meet the needs of all clients everywhere. Java comes to the rescue. Java is the first language designed from the ground up to support internationalization. In consequence, it allows your programs to be customized for any number of countries or languages without requiring cumbersome changes in the code.

Here are the major Java features that support internationalization:

✦ Java characters use *Unicode*, a 16-bit encoding scheme established by the Unicode Consortium to support the interchange, processing, and display of written texts in the world's diverse languages. The use of Unicode encoding makes it easy to write Java programs that can manipulate strings in any international language.   Unicode

✦ Java provides the `Locale` class to encapsulate information about a specific locale. A `Locale`   Locale class
object determines how locale-sensitive information, such as date, time, and number, is displayed, and how locale-sensitive operations, such as sorting strings, are performed. The classes for formatting date, time, and numbers, and for sorting strings are grouped in the `java.text` package.

✦ Java uses the `ResourceBundle` class to separate locale-specific information, such as status   ResourceBundle
messages and GUI component labels, from the program. The information is stored outside the source code and can be accessed and loaded dynamically at runtime from a `ResourceBundle`, rather than hard-coded into the program.

In this chapter, you will learn how to format dates, numbers, currencies, and percentages for different regions, countries, and languages. You will also learn how to use resource bundles to define which images and strings are used by a component, depending on the user's locale and preferences.

20.2   The `Locale` Class

A `Locale` object represents a geographical, political, or cultural region in which a specific language or custom is used. For example, Americans speak English, and the Chinese speak Chinese. The conventions for formatting dates, numbers, currencies, and percentages may differ from one country to another. The Chinese, for instance, use year/month/day to represent the date, while Americans use month/day/year. It is important to realize that locale is not defined only by country. For example, Canadians speak either Canadian English or Canadian French, depending on which region of Canada they reside in.

 NOTE
Every Swing user-interface class has a `locale` property inherited from the `java.awt Component` class.

To create a `Locale` object, use the following constructors in the `java.util.Locale` class:

```
Locale(String language)
Locale(String language, String country)
Locale(String language, String country, String variant)
```

language

The `language` should be a valid language code, that is to say, one of the lowercase two-letter codes defined by ISO-639. For example, zh stands for Chinese, da for Danish, en for English, de for German, and ko for Korean. A complete list can be found at a number of sites, among them:

```
http://www.ics.uci.edu/pub/ietf/http/related/iso639.txt
```

country

The *country* should be a valid ISO country code, that is to say, one of the uppercase, two-letter codes defined by ISO-3166. For example, CA stands for Canada, CN for China, DK for Denmark, DE for Germany, and US for the United States. A complete list can be found at a number of sites, including:

```
http://userpage.chemie.fu-berlin.de/diverse/doc/ISO_3166.html
```

variant

The argument *variant* is rarely used and is needed only for exceptional or system-dependent situations to designate information specific to a browser or vendor. For example, the Norwegian language has two sets of spelling rules, a traditional one called *bokmål* and a new one called *nynorsk*. The locale for traditional spelling would be created as follows:

```
new Locale("no", "NO", "B");
```

For convenience, the `Locale` class contains many predefined locale constants. `Locale.CANADA` is for the country Canada and language English; `Locale.CANADA_FRENCH` is for the country Canada and language French.

At present Java supports the locales shown in Table 20.1.

Several useful methods contained in the `Locale` class are listed in Figure 20.1.

java.util.Local	
+Locale(language: String)	Constructs a locale from a language code.
+Locale(language: String, country: String)	Constructs a locale from language and country codes.
+Locale(language: String, country: String, variant: String)	Constructs a locale from language, country, and variant codes.
+getCountry(): String	Returns the country/region code for this locale.
+getLanguage(): String	Returns the language code for this locale.
+getVariant(): String	Returns the variant code for this locale.
+getDefault(): Locale	Gets the default locale on the machine.
+getDisplayCountry(): String	Returns the name of the country as expressed in the current locale.
+getDisplayLanguage(): String	Returns the name of the language as expressed in the current locale.
+getDisplayName(): String	Returns the name for the locale. For example, the name is Chinese (China) for the locale Locale.CHINA.
+getDisplayVariant(): String	Returns the name for the locale's variant if it exists.

FIGURE 20.1 *The `Locale` class encapsulates a locale.*

locale-sensitive

An operation that requires a `Locale` to perform its task is called *locale-sensitive*. Displaying a number as a date or time, for example, is a locale-sensitive operation; the number should be formatted according to the customs and conventions of the user's locale.

Several classes in the Java class libraries contain locale-sensitive methods. `Date`, `Calendar`, `DateFormat`, and `NumberFormat`, for example, are locale-sensitive. All the locale-sensitive classes contain a static method, `getAvailableLocales()`, which returns an array of the locales they support. For example,

```
Locale[] availableLocales = Calendar.getAvailableLocales();
```

returns all the locales for which calendars are installed.

TABLE 20.1   A List of Supported Locales

Locale	Language	Country
da_DK	Danish	Denmark
de_AT	German	Austria
de_CH	German	Switzerland
de_DE	German	Germany
el_GR	Greek	Greece
en_CA	English	Canada
en_GB	English	United Kingdom
en_IE	English	Ireland
en_US	English	United States
es_ES	Spanish	Spain
fi_FI	Finnish	Finland
fr_BE	French	Belgium
fr_CA	French	Canada
fr_CH	French	Switzerland
fr_FR	French	France
it_CH	Italian	Switzerland
it_IT	Italian	Italy
ja_JP	Japanese	Japan
ko_KR	Korean	Korea
nl_BE	Dutch	Belgium
nl_NL	Dutch	Netherlands
no_NO	Norwegian (*nynorsk*)	Norway
no_NO_B	Norwegian (*bokmål*)	Norway
pt_PT	Portuguese	Portugal
sv_SE	Swedish	Sweden
tr_TR	Turkish	Turkey
zh_CN	Chinese (Simplified)	China
zh_TW	Chinese (Traditional)	Taiwan

20.3   Processing Date and Time

Applications often need to obtain date and time. Java provides a system-independent encapsulation of date and time in the `java.util.Date` class; it also provides `java.util.TimeZone` for dealing with time zones, and `java.util.Calendar` for extracting detailed information from `Date`. Different locales have different conventions for displaying date and time. Should the year, month, or day be displayed first? Should slashes, periods, or colons be used to separate fields of the date? What are the names of the months in the language? The `java.text.DateFormat` class can be used to format date and time in a locale-sensitive way for display to the user. The `Date` class was introduced in Section 6.5, "Using Classes from the Java Library," and the `Calendar` class and its subclass `GregorianCalendar` were introduced in Section 9.3, "The `Calendar` and `GregorianCalendar` classes."

TimeZone

20.3.1 The `TimeZone` Class

`TimeZone` represents a time zone offset and also figures out daylight savings. To get a `TimeZone` object for a specified time zone ID, use `TimeZone.getTimeZone(id)`. To set a time zone in a `Calendar` object, use the `setTimeZone` method with a time zone ID. For example, `cal.setTimeZone(TimeZone.getTimeZone("CST"))` sets the time zone to Central Standard Time. To find all the available time zones supported in Java, use the static method `getAvailableIDs()` in the `TimeZone` class. In general, the international time zone ID is a string in the form of continent/city like Europe/Berlin, Asia/Taipei, and America/Washington. You can also use the static method `getDefault()` in the `TimeZone` class to obtain the default time zone on the host machine.

DateFormat

20.3.2 The `DateFormat` Class

The `DateFormat` class can be used to format date and time in a number of styles. The `DateFormat` class supports several standard formatting styles. To format date and time, simply create an instance of `DateFormat` using one of the three static methods `getDateInstance`, `getTimeInstance`, and `getDateTimeInstance` and apply the `format(Date)` method on the instance, as shown in Figure 20.2.

java.text.DateFormat	
+format(date: Date): String	Formats a date into a date/time string.
+getDateInstance(): DateFormat	Gets the date formatter with the default formatting style for the default locale.
+getDateInstance(dateStyle: int): DateFormat	Gets the date formatter with the given formatting style for the default locale.
+getDateInstance(dateStyle: int, aLocale: Locale): DateFormat	Gets the date formatter with the given formatting style for the given locale.
+getDateTimeInstance(): DateFormat	Gets the date and time formatter with the default formatting style for the default locale.
+getDateTimeInstance(dateStyle: int, timeStyle: int): DateFormat	Gets the date and time formatter with the given date and time formatting styles for the default locale.
+getDateTimeInstance(dateStyle: int, timeStyle: int, aLocale: Locale): DateFormat	Gets the date and time formatter with the given formatting styles for the given locale.
+getInstance(): DateFormat	Get a default date and time formatter that uses the SHORT style for both the date and the time.

FIGURE 20.2 *The `DateFormat` class formats date and time.*

The `dateStyle` and `timeStyle` are one of the following constants: `DateFormat.SHORT`, `DateFormat.MEDIUM`, `DateFormat.LONG`, `DateFormat.FULL`. The exact result depends on the locale, but generally,

✦ SHORT is completely numeric, such as 7/24/98 (for date) and 4:49 PM (for time).

✦ MEDIUM is longer, such as 24-Jul-98 (for date) and 4:52:09 PM (for time).

✦ LONG is even longer, such as July 24, 1998 (for date) and 4:53:16 PM EST (for time).

✦ FULL is completely specified, such as Friday, July 24, 1998 (for date) and 4:54:13 o'clock PM EST (for time).

The statements given below display current time with a specified time zone (CST), formatting style (full date and full time), and locale (US):

```
GregorianCalendar calendar = new GregorianCalendar();
DateFormat formatter = DateFormat.getDateTimeInstance(
  DateFormat.FULL, DateFormat.FULL, Locale.US);
TimeZone timeZone = TimeZone.getTimeZone("CST");
formatter.setTimeZone(timeZone);
System.out.println("The local time is "+
  formatter.format(calendar.getTime()));
```

20.3.3 The `SimpleDateFormat` Class

The date and time formatting subclass, `SimpleDateFormat`, enables you to choose any user-defined pattern for date and time formatting. The constructor shown below can be used to create a `SimpleDateFormat` object, and the object can be used to convert a `Date` object into a string with the desired format:

SimpleDateFormat

```
public SimpleDateFormat(String pattern)
```

The parameter `pattern` is a string consisting of characters with special meanings. For example, y means year, M means month, d means day of the month, G is for era designator, h means hour, m means minute of the hour, s means second of the minute, and z means time zone. Therefore, the following code will display a string like "Current time is 1997.11.12 AD at 04:10:18 PST" because the pattern is `"yyyy.MM.dd G 'at' hh:mm:ss z"`:

```
SimpleDateFormat formatter
  = new SimpleDateFormat("yyyy.MM.dd G 'at' hh:mm:ss z");
date currentTime = new Date();
String dateString = formatter.format(currentTime);
System.out.println("Current time is " + dateString);
```

20.3.4 The `DateFormatSymbols` Class

The `DateFormatSymbols` class encapsulates localizable date-time formatting data, such as the names of the months, and the names of the days of the week, as shown in Figure 20.3.

DateFormatSymbols

java.text.DateFormatSymbols	
+DateFormatSymbols()	Constructs a DateFormatSymbols object for the default locale.
+DateFormatSymbols(Locale locale)	Constructs a DateFormatSymbols object by for the given locale.
+getAmPmStrings(): String[]	Gets AM/PM strings. For example: "AM" and "PM".
+getEras(): String[]	Gets era strings. For example: "AD" and "BC".
+getMonths(): String[]	Gets month strings. For example: "January", "February", etc.
+setMonths(newMonths: String[]): void	Sets month strings for this locale.
+getShortMonths(): String[]	Gets short month strings. For example: "Jan", "Feb", etc.
+setShortMonths(newShortMonths: String[]): void	Sets short month strings for this locale.
+getWeekdays(): String[]	Gets weekday strings. For example: "Sunday", "Monday", etc.
+setWeekdays(newWeekdays: String[]): void	Sets weekday strings.
+getShotWeekdays(): String[]	Gets short weekday strings. For example: "Sun", "Mon", etc.
+setShortWeekdays(newWeekdays: String[]): void	Sets short weekday strings. For example: "Sun", "Mon", etc.

FIGURE 20.3 *The `DateFormatSymbols` class encapsulates localizable date-time formatting data.*

For example, the following statement displays the month names and weekday names for the default locale:

```
DateFormatSymbols symbols = new DateFormatSymbols();
String[] monthNames = symbols.getMonths();
for (int i = 0; i < monthNames.length; i++) {
  System.out.println(monthNames[i]);
}

String[] weekdayNames = symbols.getWeekdays();
for (int i = 0; i < weekdayNames.length; i++) {
  System.out.println(weekdayNames[i]);
}
```

The following two examples demonstrate how to display date, time, and calendar based on locale. The first example creates a clock and displays date and time in locale-sensitive format. The second example displays several different calendars with the names of the days shown in the appropriate local language.

EXAMPLE 20.1 DISPLAYING AN INTERNATIONAL CLOCK

Problem

Write a program that displays a clock to show the current time based on the specified locale and time zone. The locale and time zone are selected from the combo boxes that contain the available locales and time zones in the system, as shown in Figure 20.4.

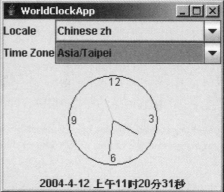

FIGURE **20.4** *The program displays a clock that shows the current time with the specified locale and time zone.*

Solution

Here are the major steps in the program:

1. Create a subclass of `JPanel` named `WorldClock` (Listing 20.1) to contain an instance of the `StillClock` class (developed in Section 11.12, "Case Study: The `StillClock` Class"), and place it in the center. Create a `JLabel` to display the digit time, and place it in the south. Use the `GregorianCalendar` class to obtain the current time for a specific locale and time zone.

2. Create a subclass of `JPanel` named `WorldClockControl` (Listing 20.2) to contain an instance of `WorldClock` and two instances of `JComboBox` for selecting locales and time zones.

3. Create an applet named `WorldClockApp` (Listing 20.3) to contain an instance of `World-ClockControl`, and enable the applet to run standalone.

The relationship among these classes is shown in Figure 20.5.

LISTING **20.1** WorldClock.java

```
1 import javax.swing.*;
2 import java.awt.*;
3 import java.awt.event.*;
4 import java.util.Calendar;
5 import java.util.TimeZone;
6 import java.util.GregorianCalendar;
7 import java.text.*;
8
9 public class WorldClock extends JPanel implements ActionListener {
10    private TimeZone timeZone = TimeZone.getTimeZone("EST");
11    private Timer timer = new Timer(1000, this);
12    private StillClock clock = new StillClock();
```

create timer
create clock

EXAMPLE 20.1 (CONTINUED)

```
13   private JLabel jlblDigitTime = new JLabel("", JLabel.CENTER);
14
15   public WorldClock() {
16     setLayout(new BorderLayout());
17     add(clock, BorderLayout.CENTER);
18     add(jlblDigitTime, BorderLayout.SOUTH);
19     timer.start();
20   }
21
22   public void setTimeZone(TimeZone timeZone) {
23     this.timeZone = timeZone;
24   }
25
26   public void actionPerformed(ActionEvent e) {
27     Calendar calendar = new GregorianCalendar(timeZone, getLocale());
28     clock.setHour(calendar.get(Calendar.HOUR));
29     clock.setMinute(calendar.get(Calendar.MINUTE));
30     clock.setSecond(calendar.get(Calendar.SECOND));
31
32     // Display digit time on the label
33     DateFormat formatter = DateFormat.getDateTimeInstance
34       (DateFormat.MEDIUM, DateFormat.LONG, getLocale());
35     formatter.setTimeZone(timeZone);
36     jlblDigitTime.setText(formatter.format(calendar.getTime()));
37   }
38 }
```

start timer

new time

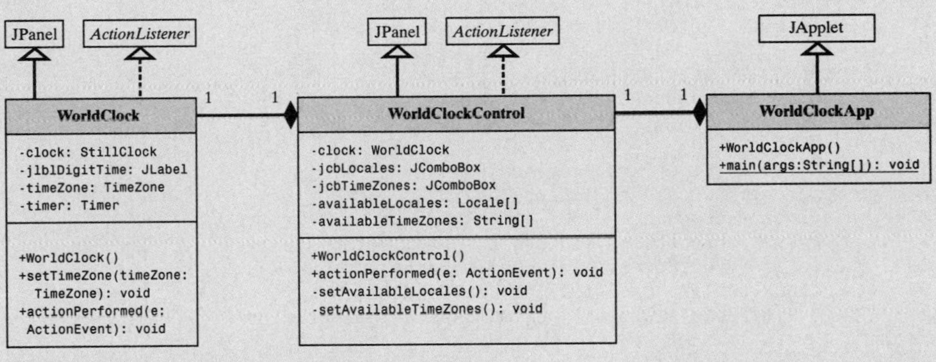

FIGURE 20.5   *WorldClockApp contains WorldClockControl, and WorldClockControl contains WorldClock.*

LISTING 20.2   WorldClockControl.java

```
1 import javax.swing.*;
2 import java.awt.*;
3 import java.awt.event.*;
4 import java.util.*;
5
6 public class WorldClockControl extends JPanel
7     implements ActionListener {
8   // Obtain all available locales and time zone ids
9   private Locale[] availableLocales = Locale.getAvailableLocales();
10  private String[] availableTimeZones = TimeZone.getAvailableIDs();
11
12  // Comboxes to display available locales and time zones
13  private JComboBox jcbLocales = new JComboBox();
14  private JComboBox jcbTimeZones = new JComboBox();
15
16  // Create a clock
17  private WorldClock clock = new WorldClock();
18
19  public WorldClockControl() {
20    // Initialize jcbLocales with all available locales
21    setAvailableLocales();
```

locales
time zones

combo boxes

create clock

create UI

EXAMPLE 20.1 (CONTINUED)

```
22
23     // Initialize jcbTimeZones with all available time zones
24     setAvailableTimeZones();
25
26     // Initialize locale and time zone
27     clock.setLocale(
28       availableLocales[jcbLocales.getSelectedIndex()]);
29     clock.setTimeZone(TimeZone.getTimeZone(
30       availableTimeZones[jcbTimeZones.getSelectedIndex()]));
31
32     JPanel panel1 = new JPanel();
33     panel1.setLayout(new GridLayout(2, 1));
34     panel1.add(new JLabel("Locale"));
35     panel1.add(new JLabel("Time Zone"));
36     JPanel panel2 = new JPanel();
37
38     panel2.setLayout(new GridLayout(2, 1));
39     panel2.add(jcbLocales, BorderLayout.CENTER);
40     panel2.add(jcbTimeZones, BorderLayout.CENTER);
41
42     JPanel panel3 = new JPanel();
43     panel3.setLayout(new BorderLayout());
44     panel3.add(panel1, BorderLayout.WEST);
45     panel3.add(panel2, BorderLayout.CENTER);
46
47     setLayout(new BorderLayout());
48     add(panel3, BorderLayout.NORTH);
49     add(clock, BorderLayout.CENTER);
50
51     jcbLocales.addActionListener(this);
52     jcbTimeZones.addActionListener(this);
53   }
54
55   public void actionPerformed(ActionEvent e) {
56     if (e.getSource() == jcbLocales)
57       clock.setLocale(
58         availableLocales[jcbLocales.getSelectedIndex()]);
59     else if (e.getSource() == jcbTimeZones)
60       clock.setTimeZone(TimeZone.getTimeZone(
61         availableTimeZones[jcbTimeZones.getSelectedIndex()]));
62   }
63
64   private void setAvailableLocales() {
65     for (int i = 0; i < availableLocales.length; i++) {
66       jcbLocales.addItem(availableLocales[i].getDisplayName() + " "
67         + availableLocales[i].toString());
68     }
69   }
70
71   private void setAvailableTimeZones() {
72     // Sort time zones
73     Arrays.sort(availableTimeZones);
74     for (int i = 0; i < availableTimeZones.length; i++) {
75       jcbTimeZones.addItem(availableTimeZones[i]);
76     }
77   }
78 }
```

new locale (margin note at line 57)

new time zone (margin note at line 60)

LISTING 20.3   WorldClockApp.java

```
1 import javax.swing.*;
2
3 public class WorldClockApp extends JApplet {
4   /** Construct the applet */
5   public WorldClockApp() {
6     getContentPane().add(new WorldClockControl());
7   }
8 }
```

main method omitted (margin note)

EXAMPLE 20.1 (CONTINUED)

Review

The WorldClock class uses GregorianCalendar to obtain a Calendar object for the specified locale and time zone (Line 27). Since WorldClock extends JPanel, and every GUI component has the locale property, the locale for the calendar is obtained from the WorldClock using getLocale() (Line 27).

An instance of StillClock is created (Line 12) and placed in the panel (Line 17). The clock time is updated every one second using the current Calendar object in Lines 27–30.

An instance of DateFormat is created (Lines 33–34) and is used to format the date in accordance with the locale (Line 36).

The WorldClockControl class contains an instance of WorldClock and two combo boxes. The combo boxes store all the available locales and time zones (Lines 64–77). The newly selected locale and time zone are set in the clock (Lines 55–62) and used to display a new time based on the current locale and time zone.

EXAMPLE 20.2 DISPLAYING A CALENDAR

Problem

Write a program that displays a calendar based on the specified locale, as shown in Figure 20.6. The user can specify a locale from a combo box that consists of a list of all the available locales supported by the system. When the program starts, the calendar for the current month of the year is displayed. The user can use the *Prior* and *Next* buttons to browse the calendar.

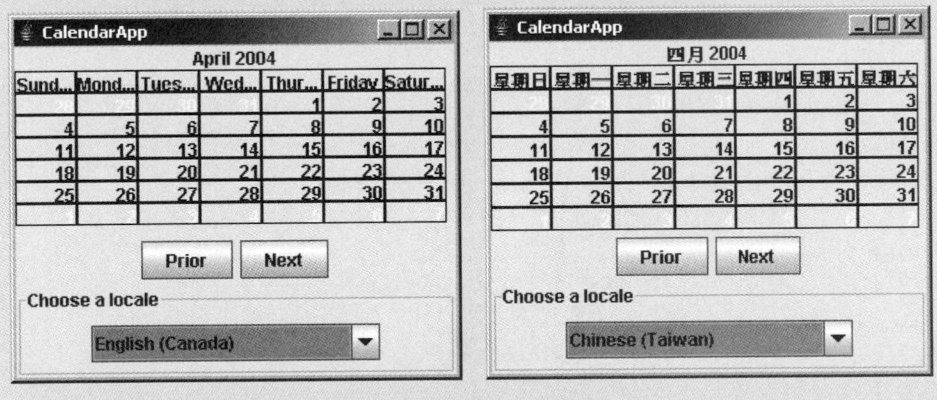

FIGURE 20.6 *The calendar applet displays a calendar with a specified locale.*

Solution

Here are the major steps in the program:

1. Create a subclass of JPanel named CalendarPanel (Listing 20.4) to display the calendar for the given year and month based on the specified locale and time zone.

2. Create an applet named CalendarApp (Listing 20.5). Create a panel to hold an instance of CalendarPanel and two buttons, *Prior* and *Next*. Place the panel in the center of the applet. Create a combo box and place it in the south of the applet. The relationships among these classes are shown in Figure 20.7.

EXAMPLE 20.2 (CONTINUED)

```
  JPanel                              JApplet          ┈┈┈▷ ItemListener
    △                                   △              ┊
    │                                   │              ┈┈┈▷ ActionListener

┌─────────────────────────┐      ┌──────────────────────────────────────────┐
│       CalenderPanel     │ 1  1 │                CalenderApp                 │
├─────────────────────────┤◆─────┼────────────────────────────────────────────┤
│ -month: int             │      │ -calenderPanel: CalenderPanel              │
│ -year: int              │      │ -jboLocale: JComboBox                      │
│ -locale: Locale         │      │ -jbtPrior: JButton                         │
│ -calender: Calender     │      │ -jbtNext: JButton                          │
├─────────────────────────┤      │ -locales: Locale[]                         │
│ +getMonth(): int        │      ├────────────────────────────────────────────┤
│ +setMonth(newMonth: int): void │ +int(): void                               │
│ +getYear(): int         │      │ +main(args: Strings[]): void               │
│ +setYear(newYear: int): void   │ +actionPerformed(e: ActionEvent): void     │
│ +setLocale(newLocale: Locale): void │ +itemStateChanged(e: ItemEvent): void │
│ +showHeader(): void     │      └────────────────────────────────────────────┘
│ +showDayNames(): void   │
│ +showDays(): void       │
└─────────────────────────┘
```

FIGURE 20.7 *CalendarApp contains* CalendarPanel.

LISTING 20.4 CalendarPanel.java

```
 1 import java.awt.*;
 2 import javax.swing.*;
 3 import javax.swing.border.LineBorder;
 4 import java.util.*;
 5 import java.text.*;
 6
 7 public class CalendarPanel extends JPanel {
 8   // The header label
 9   private JLabel jlblHeader = new JLabel(" ", JLabel.CENTER);
10
11   // Labels to display day names and days
12   private JLabel[] jlblDay = new JLabel[49];
13
14   private Calendar calendar;
15   private int month;  // The specified month
16   private int year;  // The specified year
17
18   public CalendarPanel() {
19     // Panel jpDays to hold day names and days
20     JPanel jpDays = new JPanel();
21     jpDays.setLayout(new GridLayout(7, 1));
22     for (int i = 0; i < 49; i++) {
23       jpDays.add(jlblDay[i] = new JLabel());
24       jlblDay[i].setBorder(new LineBorder(Color.black, 1));
25       jlblDay[i].setHorizontalAlignment(JLabel.RIGHT);
26       jlblDay[i].setVerticalAlignment(JLabel.TOP);
27     }
28
29     // Place header and calendar body in the panel
30     this.setLayout(new BorderLayout());
31     this.add(jlblHeader, BorderLayout.NORTH);
32     this.add(jpDays, BorderLayout.CENTER);
33
34     // Set current month, and year
35     calendar = new GregorianCalendar();
36     month = calendar.get(Calendar.MONTH) + 1;
37     year = calendar.get(Calendar.YEAR);
38
39     // Show calendar
40     showHeader();
41     showDayNames();
42     showDays();
43   }
```

header

days

calendar

create UI

EXAMPLE 20.2 (CONTINUED)

```
44
45   /** Update the header based on locale */
46   private void showHeader() {
47     SimpleDateFormat sdf =
48       new SimpleDateFormat("MMMM yyyy", getLocale());
49     String header = sdf.format(calendar.getTime());
50     jlblHeader.setText(header);
51   }
52
53   /** Update the day names based on locale */
54   private void showDayNames() {
55     DateFormatSymbols dfs = new DateFormatSymbols(getLocale());
56     String dayNames[] = dfs.getWeekdays();
57
58     // Set calendar days
59     for (int i = 0; i < 7; i++) {
60       jlblDay[i].setText(dayNames[i + 1]);
61       jlblDay[i].setHorizontalAlignment(JLabel.CENTER);
62     }
63   }
64
65   /** Display days */
66   public void showDays() {
67     // Set the calendar to the first day of the
68     // specified month and year
69     calendar.set(Calendar.YEAR, year);
70     calendar.set(Calendar.MONTH, month - 1);
71     calendar.set(Calendar.DATE, 1);
72
73     // Get the day of the first day in a month
74     int startingDayOfMonth = calendar.get(Calendar.DAY_OF_WEEK);
75
76     // Fill the calendar with the days before this month
77     Calendar cloneCalendar = (Calendar)calendar.clone();
78     cloneCalendar.add(Calendar.DATE, -1);
79     int daysInMonth = cloneCalendar.getActualMaximum(
80         Calendar.DAY_OF_MONTH);
81
82     for (int i = 0; i < startingDayOfMonth - 1; i++) {
83       jlblDay[i + 7].setForeground(Color.yellow);
84       jlblDay[i + 7].setText(daysInMonth -
85         startingDayOfMonth + 2 + i + "");
86     }
87
88     // Display days of this month
89     for (int i = 1; i <= daysInMonth; i++) {
90       jlblDay[i - 2 + startingDayOfMonth + 7].
91         setForeground(Color.black);
92       jlblDay[i - 2 + startingDayOfMonth + 7].setText(i + "");
93     }
94
95     // Fill the calendar with the days after this month
96     int j = 1;
97     for (int i = daysInMonth - 1 + startingDayOfMonth + 7;
98       i < 49; i++) {
99       jlblDay[i].setForeground(Color.yellow);
100      jlblDay[i].setText(j++ + "");
101    }
102
103    showHeader();
104  }
105
106  /** Return month */
107  public int getMonth() {
108    return month;
109  }
110
```

header

day names

days

EXAMPLE 20.2 (CONTINUED)

```
111    /** Set a new month */
112    public void setMonth(int newMonth) {
113      month = newMonth;
114      showDays();
115    }
116
117    /** Return year */
118    public int getYear() {
119      return year;
120    }
121
122    /** Set a new year */
123    public void setYear(int newYear) {
124      year = newYear;
125      showDays();
126    }
127
128    /** Set a new locale */
129    public void changeLocale(Locale newLocale) {
130      setLocale(newLocale);
131      showHeader();
132      showDayNames();
133    }
134  }
```

LISTING 20.5   CalendarApp.java

```
 1 import java.awt.*;
 2 import java.awt.event.*;
 3 import javax.swing.*;
 4 import javax.swing.border.*;
 5 import java.util.*;
 6
 7 public class CalendarApp extends JApplet implements ActionListener {
 8   // Create a CalendarPanel for showing calendars
 9   private CalendarPanel calendarPanel = new CalendarPanel();
10
11   // Combo box for selecting available locales
12   private JComboBox jcboLocale = new JComboBox();
13
14   // Declare locales to store available locales
15   private Locale locales[] = Calendar.getAvailableLocales();
16
17   // Buttons Prior and Next to displaying prior and next month
18   private JButton jbtPrior = new JButton("Prior");
19   private JButton jbtNext = new JButton("Next");
20
21   /** Initialize the applet */
22   public void init() {
23     // Panel jpLocale to hold the combo box for selecting locales
24     JPanel jpLocale = new JPanel();
25     jpLocale.setBorder(new TitledBorder("Choose a locale"));
26     jpLocale.setLayout(new FlowLayout());
27     jpLocale.add(jcboLocale);
28
29     // Initialize the combo box to add locale names
30     for (int i = 0; i < locales.length; i++)
31       jcboLocale.addItem(locales[i].getDisplayName());
32
33     // Panel jpButtons to hold buttons
34     JPanel jpButtons = new JPanel();
35     jpButtons.setLayout(new FlowLayout());
36     jpButtons.add(jbtPrior);
37     jpButtons.add(jbtNext);
38
```

calendar panel

locales

create UI

EXAMPLE 20.2 (CONTINUED)

```
39     // Panel jpCalendar to hold calendarPanel and buttons
40     JPanel jpCalendar = new JPanel();
41     jpCalendar.setLayout(new BorderLayout());
42     jpCalendar.add(calendarPanel, BorderLayout.CENTER);
43     jpCalendar.add(jpButtons, BorderLayout.SOUTH);
44
45     // Place jpCalendar and jpLocale to the applet
46     this.getContentPane().add(jpCalendar, BorderLayout.CENTER);
47     this.getContentPane().add(jpLocale, BorderLayout.SOUTH);
48
49     // Register listeners
50     jcboLocale.addActionListener(this);
51     jbtPrior.addActionListener(this);
52     jbtNext.addActionListener(this);
53
54     calendarPanel.changeLocale(
55       locales[jcboLocale.getSelectedIndex()]);
56   }
57
58   /** Handle the Prior and Next buttons */
59   public void actionPerformed(ActionEvent e) {
60     int currentMonth = calendarPanel.getMonth();
61
62     if (e.getSource() == jbtPrior) {                        previous month
63       if (currentMonth == 1) {
64         calendarPanel.setMonth(12);
65         calendarPanel.setYear(calendarPanel.getYear() - 1);
66       }
67       else
68         calendarPanel.setMonth(currentMonth - 1);
69     }
70     else if (e.getSource() == jbtNext) {                    next month
71       if (currentMonth == 12) {
72         calendarPanel.setMonth(1);
73         calendarPanel.setYear(calendarPanel.getYear() + 1);
74       }
75       else
76         calendarPanel.setMonth(currentMonth + 1);
77     }
78     else if (e.getSource() == jcboLocale)                   new locale
79       calendarPanel.changeLocale(
80         locales[jcboLocale.getSelectedIndex()]);
81   }
82
83   /** Main method */
84   public static void main(String[] args) {
85     // Create a frame
86     JFrame frame = new JFrame("CalendarApp");
87
88     // Create an instance of the applet
89     CalendarApp applet = new CalendarApp();
90
91     // Add the applet instance to the frame
92     frame.getContentPane().add(applet, BorderLayout.CENTER);
93
94     // Invoke init() and start()
95     applet.init();
96     applet.start();
97
98     // Display the frame
99     frame.pack();
100    frame.setDefaultCloseOperation(JFrame.EXIT_ON_CLOSE);
101    frame.setVisible(true);
102  }
103 }
```

EXAMPLE 20.2 (CONTINUED)

Review

`CalendarApp` creates the user interface and handles the button actions and combo box item selections for locales. The `Calendar.getAvailableLocales()` method (Line 15) is used to find all the available locales that have calendars. Its `getDisplayName()` method returns the name of each locale and adds the name to the combo box (Line 31). When the user selects a locale name in the combo box, a new locale is passed to `calendarPanel`, and a new calendar is displayed based on the new locale (Lines 79–80).

`CalendarPanel` is created to control and display the calendar. It displays the month and year in the header, and the day names and days in the calendar body. The header and day names are locale-sensitive.

showHeader

The `showHeader` method (Lines 46–51) displays the calendar title in a form like `"MMMM yyyy"`. The `SimpleDateFormat` class used in the `showHeader` method is a subclass of `DateFormat`. `SimpleDateFormat` allows you to customize the date format to display the date in various nonstandard styles.

showDayNames

The `showDayNames` method (Lines 54–63) displays the day names in the calendar. The `DateFormatSymbols` class used in the `showDayNames` method is a class for encapsulating localizable date-time formatting data, such as the names of the months, the names of the days of the week, and the time zone data. The `getWeekdays` method is used to get an array of day names.

showDays

The `showDays` method (Lines 66–104) displays the days for the specified month of the year. As you can see in Figure 20.6, the labels before the current month are filled with the last few days of the preceding month, and the labels after the current month are filled with the first few days of the next month.

To fill the calendar with the days before the current month, a clone of `calendar`, named `cloneCalendar`, is created to obtain the days for the preceding month (Line 77). `cloneCalendar` is a copy of `calendar` with separate memory space. Thus you can change the properties of `cloneCalendar` without corrupting the `calendar` object. The `clone()` method is defined in the `Object` class, which was introduced in Section 8.11.4, "The `clone` Method." You can clone any object as long as its defining class implements the `Cloneable` interface. The `Calendar` class implements `Cloneable`.

The `cloneCalendar.getActualMaximum(Calendar.DAY_OF_MONTH)` method (Lines 79–80) returns the number of days in the month for the specified calendar.

20.4   Formatting Numbers

Formatting numbers is highly locale-dependent. For example, number 5000.555 is displayed as 5,000.555 in the United States, but as 5 000,555 in France and as 5.000,555 in Germany.

Numbers are formatted using the `java.text.NumberFormat` class, an abstract base class that provides the methods for formatting and parsing numbers, as shown in Figure 20.8.

With `NumberFormat`, you can format and parse numbers for any locale. Your code will be completely independent of locale conventions for decimal points, thousands-separators, currency format, and percentage formats.

20.4.1   Plain Number Format

You can get an instance of `NumberFormat` for the current locale using `NumberFormat.getInstance()` or `NumberFormat.getNumberInstance` and for the specified locale using `NumberFormat.getInstance(Locale)` or `NumberFormat.getNumberInstance(Locale)`. You can then invoke `format(number)` on the `NumberFormat` instance to return a formatted number as a string.

java.text.NumberFormat	
+getInstance(): NumberFormat	Returns the default number format for the default locale.
+getInstance(locale:Locale): NumberFormat	Returns the default number format for the specified locale.
+getIntegerInstance(): NumberFormat	Returns an integer number format for the default locale.
+getIntegerInstance(locale: Locale): NumberFormat	Returns an integer number format for the specified locale.
+getCurrencyInstance(): NumberFormat	Returns a currency format for the current default locale.
+getNumberInstance(): NumberFormat	Returns a general-purpose number format for the default locale.
+getNumberInstance(locale: Locale): NumberFormat	Returns a general-purpose number format for the specified locale.
+getPercentInstance(): NumberFormat	Returns a percentage format for the default locale.
+getPercentInstance(locale: Locale): NumberFormat	Returns a percentage format for the specified locale.
+format(number: double): String	Formats a floating-point number.
+format(number: long): String	Formats an integer.
+getMaximumFractionDigits(): int	Returns the maximum number of allowed fraction digits.
+setMaximumFractionDigits(newValue: int): void	Sets the maximum number of allowed fraction digits.
+getMinimumFractionDigits(): int	Returns the minimum number of allowed fraction digits.
+setMinimumFractionDigits(newValue: int): void	Sets the minimum number of allowed fraction digits.
+getMaximumIntegerDigits(): int	Returns the maximum number of allowed integer digits in a fraction number.
+setMaximumIntegerDigits(newValue: int): void	Sets the maximum number of allowed integer digits in a fraction number.
+getMinimumIntegerDigits(): int	Returns the minimum number of allowed integer digits in a fraction number.
+setMinimumIntegerDigits(newValue: int): void	Sets the minimum number of allowed integer digits in a fraction number.
+isGroupingUsed(): boolean	Returns true if grouping is used in this format. For example, in the English locale, with grouping on, the number 1234567 is formatted as "1,234,567".
+setGroupingUsed(newValue: boolean): void	Sets whether or not grouping will be used in this format.
+parse(source: String): Number	Parses string into a number.
+getAvailableLocales(): Locale[]	Gets the set of locales for which NumberFormats are installed.

FIGURE 20.8 *The* NumberFormat *class provides the methods for formatting and parsing numbers.*

For example, to display number 5000.555 in France, use the following code:

```
NumberFormat numberFormat = NumberFormat.getInstance(Locale.FRANCE);
System.out.println(numberFormat.format(5000.555));
```

You can control the display of numbers with such methods as setMaximumFractionDigits and setMinimumFractionDigits. For example, 5000.555 would be displayed as 5000.6 if you use numberFormat.setMaximumFractionDigits(1).

20.4.2   Currency Format

To format a number in a currency, use NumberFormat.getCurrencyInstance to get the currency number format for the current locale or NumberFormat.getCurrencyInstance(Locale) to get the currency number for the specified locale.

For example, to display number 5000.555 as currency in the United States, use the following code:

```
NumberFormat currencyFormat =
  NumberFormat.getCurrencyInstance(Locale.US);
System.out.println(currencyFormat.format(5000.555));
```

5000.555 is formatted into $5,000,56. If the locale is set to France, the number would be formatted into 5 000,56€.

20.4.3 Percent Format

To format a number in a percent, use `NumberFormat.getPercentInstance()` or `NumberFormat.getPercentInstance(Locale)` to get the percent number format for the current locale or the specified locale.

For example, to display number 0.555367 as a percent in the United States, use the following code:

```
NumberFormat percentFormat =
  NumberFormat.getPercentInstance(Locale.US);
System.out.println(percentFormat.format(0.555367));
```

0.555367 is formatted into 56%. By default, the format truncates the fraction part in a percent number. If you want to keep three digits after the decimal point, use `percentFormat.setMinimumFraction Digits(3)`. So 0.555367 would be displayed as 55.537%.

20.4.4 Parsing Numbers

You can format a number into a string using the `format(numericalValue)` method. You can also use the `parse(String)` method to convert a formatted plain number, currency value, or percent number with the conventions of a certain locale into an instance of `java.lang.Number`. The parse method throws a `java.text.ParseException` if parsing fails. For example, U.S. $5,000.56 can be parsed into a number using the following statements:

```
NumberFormat currencyFormat =
  NumberFormat.getCurrencyInstance(Locale.US);
try {
  Number number = currencyFormat.parse("$5,000.56");
  System.out.println(number.doubleValue());
}
catch (java.text.ParseException ex) {
  System.out.println("Parse failed");
}
```

20.4.5 The `DecimalFormat` Class

If you want even more control over the format or parsing, or want to give your users more control, cast the `NumberFormat` you get from the factory methods to a `java.text.DecimalFormat`, which is a subclass of `NumberFormat`. You can then use the `applyPattern(String pattern)` method of the `DecimalFormat` class to specify the patterns for displaying the number.

A pattern can specify the minimum number of digits before the decimal point and the maximum number of digits after the decimal point. The characters `'0'` and `'#'` are used to specify a required digit and an optional digit, respectively. The optional digit is not displayed if it is zero. For example, the pattern `"00.0##"` indicates minimum two digits before the decimal point and maximum three digits after the decimal point. If there are more actual digits before the decimal point, all of them are displayed. If there are more than three digits after the decimal point, the number of digits is rounded. Applying the pattern `"00.0##"`, number 111.2226 is formatted to 111.223, number 1111.2226 to 1111.223, number 1.22 to 01.22, and number 1 to 01.0. Here is the code:

```
NumberFormat numberFormat = NumberFormat.getInstance(Locale.US);
DecimalFormat decimalFormat = (DecimalFormat)numberFormat;
decimalFormat.applyPattern("00.0##");
System.out.println(decimalFormat.format(111.2226));
System.out.println(decimalFormat.format(1111.2226));
System.out.println(decimalFormat.format(1.22));
System.out.println(decimalFormat.format(1));
```

The character `'%'` can be put at the end of a pattern to indicate that a number is formatted as a percentage. This causes the number to be multiplied by 100 and appends a percent sign %.

EXAMPLE 20.3   FORMATTING NUMBERS

Problem

Create a loan calculator similar to the one in Example 14.1, "Using Applets." This new loan calculator allows the user to choose locales, and displays numbers in locale-sensitive format. As shown in Figure 20.9, the user enters interest rate, number of years, and loan amount, then clicks the Compute button to display the interest rate in percentage format, the number of years in normal number format, and the loan amount, total payment, and monthly payment in currency format.

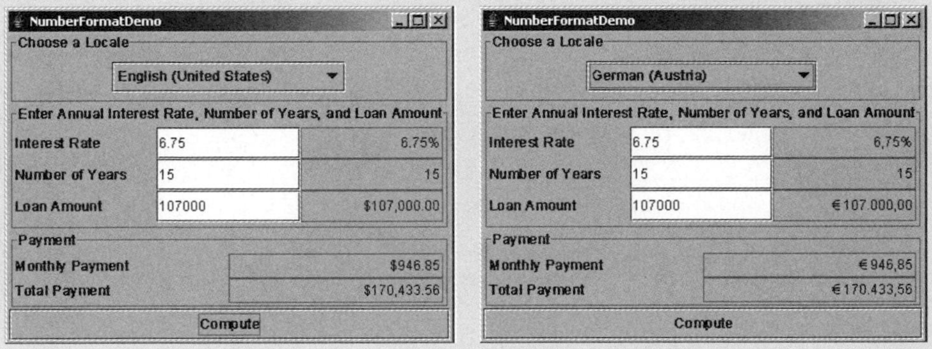

FIGURE 20.9   *The locale determines the format of the numbers displayed in the loan calculator.*

Solution

Listing 20.6 gives the solution to the problem.

LISTING 20.6   NumberFormatDemo.java (Formatting Numbers)

```
1 import java.awt.*;
2 import java.awt.event.*;
3 import javax.swing.*;
4 import javax.swing.border.*;
5 import java.util.*;
6 import java.text.NumberFormat;
7
8 public class NumberFormatDemo extends JApplet implements ActionListener {
9    // Combo box for selecting available locales
10   private JComboBox jcboLocale = new JComboBox();
11
12   // Text fields for interest rate, year, loan amount,
13   private JTextField jtfInterestRate = new JTextField(10);
14   private JTextField jtfNumberOfYears = new JTextField(10);
15   private JTextField jtfLoanAmount = new JTextField(10);
16   private JTextField jtfFormattedInterestRate = new JTextField(10);
17   private JTextField jtfFormattedNumberOfYears = new JTextField(10);
18   private JTextField jtfFormattedLoanAmount = new JTextField(10);
19
20   // Text fields for monthly payment and total payment
21   private JTextField jtfTotalPayment = new JTextField();
22   private JTextField jtfMonthlyPayment = new JTextField();
23
24   // Compute button
25   private JButton jbtCompute = new JButton("Compute");
26
27   // Current locale
28   private Locale locale = Locale.getDefault();
29
30   // Declare locales to store available locales
31   private Locale locales[] = Calendar.getAvailableLocales();
```

UI components

EXAMPLE 20.3 (CONTINUED)

create UI

```
32
33    /** Initialize the combo box */
34    public void initializeComboBox() {
35      // Add locale names to the combo box
36      for (int i = 0; i < locales.length; i++)
37        jcboLocale.addItem(locales[i].getDisplayName());
38    }
39
40    /** Initialize the applet */
41    public void init() {
42      // Panel p1 to hold the combo box for selecting locales
43      JPanel p1 = new JPanel();
44      p1.setLayout(new FlowLayout());
45      p1.add(jcboLocale);
46      initializeComboBox();
47      p1.setBorder(new TitledBorder("Choose a Locale"));
48
49      // Panel p2 to hold the input
50      JPanel p2 = new JPanel();
51      p2.setLayout(new GridLayout(3, 3));
52      p2.add(new JLabel("Interest Rate"));
53      p2.add(jtfInterestRate);
54      p2.add(jtfFormattedInterestRate);
55      p2.add(new JLabel("Number of Years"));
56      p2.add(jtfNumberOfYears);
57      p2.add(jtfFormattedNumberOfYears);
58      p2.add(new JLabel("Loan Amount"));
59      p2.add(jtfLoanAmount);
60      p2.add(jtfFormattedLoanAmount);
61      p2.setBorder(new TitledBorder("Enter Annual Interest Rate, " +
62        "Number of Years, and Loan Amount"));
63
64      // Panel p3 to hold the result
65      JPanel p3 = new JPanel();
66      p3.setLayout(new GridLayout(2, 2));
67      p3.setBorder(new TitledBorder("Payment"));
68      p3.add(new JLabel("Monthly Payment"));
69      p3.add(jtfMonthlyPayment);
70      p3.add(new JLabel("Total Payment"));
71      p3.add(jtfTotalPayment);
72
73      // Set text field alignment
74      jtfFormattedInterestRate.setHorizontalAlignment(JTextField.RIGHT);
75      jtfFormattedNumberOfYears.setHorizontalAlignment(JTextField.RIGHT);
76      jtfFormattedLoanAmount.setHorizontalAlignment(JTextField.RIGHT);
77      jtfTotalPayment.setHorizontalAlignment(JTextField.RIGHT);
78      jtfMonthlyPayment.setHorizontalAlignment(JTextField.RIGHT);
79
80      // Set editable false
81      jtfFormattedInterestRate.setEditable(false);
82      jtfFormattedNumberOfYears.setEditable(false);
83      jtfFormattedLoanAmount.setEditable(false);
84      jtfTotalPayment.setEditable(false);
85      jtfMonthlyPayment.setEditable(false);
86
87      // Panel p4 to hold result payments and a button
88      JPanel p4 = new JPanel();
89      p4.setLayout(new BorderLayout());
90      p4.add(p3, BorderLayout.CENTER);
91      p4.add(jbtCompute, BorderLayout.SOUTH);
92
93      // Place panels to the applet
94      getContentPane().add(p1, BorderLayout.NORTH);
95      getContentPane().add(p2, BorderLayout.CENTER);
96      getContentPane().add(p4, BorderLayout.SOUTH);
97
98      // Register listeners
99      jcboLocale.addActionListener(this);
```

EXAMPLE 20.3 (CONTINUED)

```
100      jbtCompute.addActionListener(this);
101    }
102
103    /** Handle button action */
104    public void actionPerformed(ActionEvent e) {
105      if (e.getSource() == jbtCompute)
106        computeLoan();
107      else if (e.getSource() == jcboLocale) {
108        locale = locales[jcboLocale.getSelectedIndex()];
109        computeLoan();
110      }
111    }
112
113    /** Compute payments and display results locale-sensitive format */
114    private void computeLoan() {
115      // Retrieve input from user
116      double loan = new Double(jtfLoanAmount.getText()).doubleValue();
117      double interestRate =
118        new Double(jtfInterestRate.getText()).doubleValue() / 1200;
119      int numberOfYears =
120        new Integer(jtfNumberOfYears.getText()).intValue();
121
122      // Calculate payments
123      double monthlyPayment = loan * interestRate/
124        (1 - (Math.pow(1 / (1 + interestRate), numberOfYears * 12)));
125      double totalPayment = monthlyPayment * numberOfYears * 12;
126
127      // Get formatters
128      NumberFormat percentFormatter =
129        NumberFormat.getPercentInstance(locale);
130      NumberFormat currencyForm =
131        NumberFormat.getCurrencyInstance(locale);
132      NumberFormat numberForm = NumberFormat.getNumberInstance(locale);
133      percentFormatter.setMinimumFractionDigits(2);
134
135      // Display formatted input
136      jtfFormattedInterestRate.setText(
137        percentFormatter.format(interestRate * 12));
138      jtfFormattedNumberOfYears.setText(numberForm.format(numberOfYears));
139      jtfFormattedLoanAmount.setText(currencyForm.format(loan));
140
141      // Display results in currency format
142      jtfMonthlyPayment.setText(currencyForm.format(monthlyPayment));
143      jtfTotalPayment.setText(currencyForm.format(totalPayment));
144    }
145  }
```

compute loan

new locale

format numbers

main method omitted

Review

The computeLoan method (Lines 114–144) gets the input on interest rate, number of years, and loan amount from the user, computes monthly payment and total payment, and displays annual interest rate in percentage format, number of years in normal number format, and loan amount, monthly payment, and total payment in locale-sensitive format.

The statement percentFormatter.setMinimumFractionDigits(2) (Line 133) sets the minimum number of fractional parts to 2. Without this statement, 0.075 would be displayed as 7% rather than 7.5%.

20.5 Resource Bundles (Optional)

The NumberFormatDemo in Example 20.3, "Formatting Numbers," displays the numbers, currencies, and percentages in accordance with local customs, but displays all the message strings, titles, and button labels in English. In this section, you will learn how to use resource bundles to localize message strings, titles, button labels, and so on.

resource bundle

A *resource bundle* is a Java class file or text file that provides locale-specific information. This information can be accessed by Java programs dynamically. When a locale-specific resource is needed—a message string, for example—your program can load it from the resource bundle appropriate for the desired locale. In this way, you can write program code that is largely independent of the user's locale, isolating most, if not all, of the locale-specific information in resource bundles.

With resource bundles, you can write programs that separate the locale-sensitive part of your code from the locale-independent part. The programs can easily handle multiple locales, and can easily be modified later to support even more locales.

The resources are placed inside the classes that extend the `ResourceBundle` class or a subclass of `ResourceBundle`. Resource bundles contain *key/value* pairs. Each key uniquely identifies a locale-specific object in the bundle. You can use the key to retrieve the object. `ListResourceBundle` is a convenient subclass of `ResourceBundle` that is often used to simplify the creation of resource bundles. Here is an example of a resource bundle that contains four keys using `ListResourceBundle`:

```
// MyResource.java: resource file
public class MyResource extends java.util.ListResourceBundle {
  static final Object[][] contents = {
    {"nationalFlag", "us.gif"},
    {"nationalAnthem", "us.au"},
    {"nationalColor", Color.red},
    {"annualGrowthRate", new Double(7.8)}
  };

  public Object[][] getContents() {
    return contents;
  }
}
```

Keys are case-sensitive strings. In this example, the keys are `nationalFlag`, `nationalAnthem`, `nationalColor`, and `annualGrowthRate`. The values can be any type of `Object`.

If all the resources are strings, they can be placed in a convenient text file with the extension .properties. A typical property file would look like this:

```
#Wed Jul 01 07:23:24 EST 1998
nationalFlag=us.gif
nationalAnthem=us.au
```

To retrieve values from a `ResourceBundle` in a program, you first need to create an instance of `ResourceBundle` using one of the following two static methods:

```
public static final ResourceBundle getBundle(String baseName)
  throws MissingResourceException

public static final ResourceBundle getBundle
  (String baseName, Locale locale) throws MissingResourceException
```

The first method returns a `ResourceBundle` for the default locale, and the second method returns a `ResourceBundle` for the specified locale. `baseName` is the base name for a set of classes, each of which describes the information for a given locale. These classes are named in Table 20.2.

TABLE 20.2   Resource Bundle Naming Conventions

1. BaseName_language_country_variant.class

2. BaseName_language_country.class

3. BaseName_language.class

4. BaseName.class

5. BaseName_language_country_variant.properties

6. BaseName_language_country.properties

7. BaseName_language.properties

8. BaseName.properties

For example, MyResource_en_BR.class stores resources specific to the United Kingdom, MyResource_en_US.class stores resources specific to the United States, and MyResource_en.class stores resources specific to all the English-speaking countries.

The getBundle method attempts to load the class that matches the specified locale by language, country, and variant by searching the file names in the order shown in Table 20.2. The files searched in this order form a *resource chain*. If no file is found in the resource chain, the getBundle method raises a MissingResourceException, a subclass of RuntimeException.

Once a resource bundle object is created, you can use the getObject method to retrieve the value according to the key. For example,

```
ResourceBundle res = ResourceBundle.getBundle("MyResource");
String flagFile = (String)res.getObject("nationalFlag");
String anthemFile = (String)res.getObject("nationalAnthem");
Color color = (Color)res.getObject("nationalColor");
double growthRate =
  (Double)res.getObject("annualGrowthRate").doubleValue();
```

 TIP

If the resource value is a string, the convenient getString method can be used to replace the getObject method. The getString method simply casts the value returned by getObject to a string.

What happens if a resource object you are looking for is not defined in the resource bundle? Java employs an intelligent look-up scheme that searches the object in the parent file along the resource chain. This search is repeated until the object is found or all the parent files in the resource chain have been searched. A MissingResourceException is raised if the search is unsuccessful.

EXAMPLE 20.4 USING RESOURCE BUNDLES

Problem

Modify the NumberFormatDemo program in Example 20.3, "Formatting Numbers," so that it displays messages, title, and button labels in multiple languages, as shown in Figure 20.10.

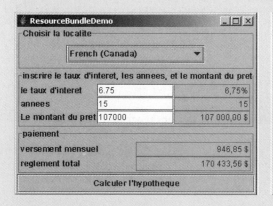

FIGURE 20.10 *The program displays the strings in multiple languages.*

Solution

Listing 20.7 gives the solution to the problem.

EXAMPLE 20.4 (CONTINUED)

LISTING 20.7   ResourceBundleDemo.java (Resource Bundle)

get resource

create UI

```
1 import java.awt.*;
2 import java.awt.event.*;
3 import javax.swing.*;
4 import javax.swing.border.*;
5 import java.util.*;
6 import java.text.NumberFormat;
7
8 public class ResourceBundleDemo extends JApplet implements ActionListener {
9   // Combo box for selecting available locales
10   private JComboBox jcboLocale = new JComboBox();
11   private ResourceBundle res = ResourceBundle.getBundle("MyResource");
12
13   // Create labels
14   private JLabel jlblInterestRate =
15     new JLabel(res.getString("Annual_Interest_Rate"));
16   private JLabel jlblNumberOfYears =
17     new JLabel(res.getString("Number_Of_Years"));
18   private JLabel jlblLoanAmount = new JLabel(res.getString("Loan_Amount"));
19   private JLabel jlblMonthlyPayment =
20     new JLabel(res.getString("Monthly_Payment"));
21   private JLabel jlblTotalPayment = new JLabel
22     (res.getString("Total_Payment"));
23
24   // Create titled borders
25   private TitledBorder comboBoxTitle =
26     new TitledBorder(res.getString("Choose_a_Locale"));
27   private TitledBorder inputTitle = new TitledBorder
28     (res.getString("Enter_Interest_Rate"));
29   private TitledBorder paymentTitle =
30     new TitledBorder(res.getString("Payment"));
31
32   // Text fields for interest rate, year, loan amount,
33   private JTextField jtfInterestRate = new JTextField(10);
34   private JTextField jtfNumberOfYears = new JTextField(10);
35   private JTextField jtfLoanAmount = new JTextField(10);
36   private JTextField jtfFormattedInterestRate = new JTextField(10);
37   private JTextField jtfFormattedNumberOfYears = new JTextField(10);
38   private JTextField jtfFormattedLoanAmount = new JTextField(10);
39
40   // Text fields for monthly payment and total payment
41   private JTextField jtfTotalPayment = new JTextField();
42   private JTextField jtfMonthlyPayment = new JTextField();
43
44   // Compute button
45   private JButton jbtCompute = new JButton(res.getString("Compute"));
46
47   // Current locale
48   private Locale locale = Locale.getDefault();
49
50   // Declare locales to store available locales
51   private Locale locales[] = Calendar.getAvailableLocales();
52
53   /** Initialize the combo box */
54   public void initializeComboBox() {
55     // Add locale names to the combo box
56     for (int i = 0; i < locales.length; i++)
57       jcboLocale.addItem(locales[i].getDisplayName());
58   }
59
60   /** Initialize the applet */
61   public void init() {
62     // Panel p1 to hold the combo box for selecting locales
63     JPanel p1 = new JPanel();
64     p1.setLayout(new FlowLayout());
65     p1.add(jcboLocale);
```

EXAMPLE 20.4 (CONTINUED)

```
66      initializeComboBox();
67      p1.setBorder(comboBoxTitle);
68
69      // Panel p2 to hold the input for annual interest rate,
70      // number of years and loan amount
71      JPanel p2 = new JPanel();
72      p2.setLayout(new GridLayout(3, 3));
73      p2.add(jlblInterestRate);
74      p2.add(jtfInterestRate);
75      p2.add(jtfFormattedInterestRate);
76      p2.add(jlblNumberOfYears);
77      p2.add(jtfNumberOfYears);
78      p2.add(jtfFormattedNumberOfYears);
79      p2.add(jlblLoanAmount);
80      p2.add(jtfLoanAmount);
81      p2.add(jtfFormattedLoanAmount);
82      p2.setBorder(inputTitle);
83
84      // Panel p3 to hold the payment
85      JPanel p3 = new JPanel();
86      p3.setLayout(new GridLayout(2, 2));
87      p3.setBorder(paymentTitle);
88      p3.add(jlblMonthlyPayment);
89      p3.add(jtfMonthlyPayment);
90      p3.add(jlblTotalPayment);
91      p3.add(jtfTotalPayment);
92
93      // Set text field alignment
94      jtfFormattedInterestRate.setHorizontalAlignment
95        (JTextField.RIGHT);
96      jtfFormattedNumberOfYears.setHorizontalAlignment(JTextField.RIGHT);
97      jtfFormattedLoanAmount.setHorizontalAlignment(JTextField.RIGHT);
98      jtfTotalPayment.setHorizontalAlignment(JTextField.RIGHT);
99      jtfMonthlyPayment.setHorizontalAlignment(JTextField.RIGHT);
100
101     // Set editable false
102     jtfFormattedInterestRate.setEditable(false);
103     jtfFormattedNumberOfYears.setEditable(false);
104     jtfFormattedLoanAmount.setEditable(false);
105     jtfTotalPayment.setEditable(false);
106     jtfMonthlyPayment.setEditable(false);
107
108     // Panel p4 to hold result payments and a button
109     JPanel p4 = new JPanel();
110     p4.setLayout(new BorderLayout());
111     p4.add(p3, BorderLayout.CENTER);
112     p4.add(jbtCompute, BorderLayout.SOUTH);
113
114     // Place panels to the applet
115     getContentPane().add(p1, BorderLayout.NORTH);
116     getContentPane().add(p2, BorderLayout.CENTER);
117     getContentPane().add(p4, BorderLayout.SOUTH);
118
119     // Register listeners
120     jcboLocale.addActionListener(this);
121     jbtCompute.addActionListener(this);
122   }
123
124   /** Handle button action */
125   public void actionPerformed(ActionEvent e) {
126     if (e.getSource() == jbtCompute)
127       computeLoan();
128     else if (e.getSource() == jcboLocale) {
129       locale = locales[jcboLocale.getSelectedIndex()];
130       updateStrings();                                      // update resource
131       computeLoan();
132     }
133   }
```

EXAMPLE 20.4 (CONTINUED)

```
134
135     /** Compute payments and display results locale-sensitive format */
136     private void computeLoan() {
137       // Retrieve input from user
138       double loan = new Double(jtfLoanAmount.getText()).doubleValue();
139       double interestRate =
140         new Double(jtfInterestRate.getText()).doubleValue() / 1200;
141       int numberOfYears =
142         new Integer(jtfNumberOfYears.getText()).intValue();
143
144       // Calculate payments
145       double monthlyPayment = loan * interestRate/
146         (1 - (Math.pow(1 / (1 + interestRate), numberOfYears * 12)));
147       double totalPayment = monthlyPayment * numberOfYears * 12;
148
149       // Get formatters
150       NumberFormat percentFormatter =
151         NumberFormat.getPercentInstance(locale);
152       NumberFormat currencyForm =
153         NumberFormat.getCurrencyInstance(locale);
154       NumberFormat numberForm = NumberFormat.getNumberInstance(locale);
155       percentFormatter.setMinimumFractionDigits(2);
156
157       // Display formatted input
158       jtfFormattedInterestRate.setText(
159         percentFormatter.format(interestRate * 12));
160       jtfFormattedNumberOfYears.setText(numberForm.format(numberOfYears));
161       jtfFormattedLoanAmount.setText(currencyForm.format(loan));
162
163       // Display results in currency format
164       jtfMonthlyPayment.setText(currencyForm.format(monthlyPayment));
165       jtfTotalPayment.setText(currencyForm.format(totalPayment));
166     }
167
168     /** Update resource strings */
169     private void updateStrings() {
170       res = ResourceBundle.getBundle("MyResource", locale);
171       jlblInterestRate.setText(res.getString("Annual_Interest_Rate"));
172       jlblNumberOfYears.setText(res.getString("Number_Of_Years"));
173       jlblLoanAmount.setText(res.getString("Loan_Amount"));
174       jlblTotalPayment.setText(res.getString("Total_Payment"));
175       jlblMonthlyPayment.setText(res.getString("Monthly_Payment"));
176       jbtCompute.setText(res.getString("Compute"));
177       comboBoxTitle.setTitle(res.getString("Choose_a_Locale"));
178       inputTitle.setTitle(res.getString("Enter_Interest_Rate"));
179       paymentTitle.setTitle(res.getString("Payment"));
180
181       // Make sure the new labels are displayed
182       repaint();
183     }
184 }
```

new resource — line 170
main method omitted — line 184

The resource bundle for the English language is given as follows:

```
#MyResource.properties for English language
Number_Of_Years=Years
Total_Payment=French Total\ Payment
Enter_Interest_Rate=Enter\ Interest\ Rate,\ Years,\ and\ Loan\ Amount
Payment=Payment
Compute=Compute
Annual_Interest_Rate=Interest\ Rate
Number_Formatting=Number\ Formatting\ Demo
Loan_Amount=Loan\ Amount
Choose_a_Locale=Choose\ a\ Locale
Monthly_Payment=Monthly\ Payment
```

The resource bundle for the Chinese language is given as follows:

```
#MyResource_zh.properties for Chinese language
Choose_a_Locale    = \u9078\u64c7\u570b\u5bb6
```

EXAMPLE 20.4 (CONTINUED)

```
Enter_Interest_Rate =
    \u8f38\u5165\u5229\u7387,\u5e74\u9650,\u8cb8\u6b3e\u7e3d\u984d
Annual_Interest_Rate  =  \u5229\u7387
Number_Of_Years       =  \u5e74\u9650
Loan_Amount           =  \u8cb8\u6b3e\u984d\u5ea6
Payment               =  \u4ed8\u606f
Monthly_Payment       =  \u6708\u4ed8
Total_Payment         =  \u7e3d\u984d
Compute               =  \u8a08\u7b97\u8cb8\u6b3e\u5229\u606f
```

The resource bundle for the French language is given as follows:

```
#MyResourse_fr.properties for French language
Number_Of_Years=annees
Annual_Interest_Rate=le taux d'interet
Loan_Amount=Le montant du pret
Enter_Interest_Rate=inscrire le taux d'interet, les annees, et le montant
du pret
Payment=paiement
Compute=Calculer l'hypotheque
Number_Formatting=demonstration du formatting des chiffres
Choose_a_Locale=Choisir la localite
Monthly_Payment=versement mensuel
Total_Payment=reglement total
```

The resource bundle files MyResource.properties, MyResource_zh.properties, and MyResource_fr.properties should all be placed under the classpath.

Review

Property resource bundles are implemented as text files with a .properties extension, and are placed in the same location as the class files for the application or applet. List-ResourceBundles are provided as Java class files. Because they are implemented using Java source code, new and modified ListResourceBundles need to be recompiled for deployment. With PropertyResourceBundles, there is no need for recompilation when translations are modified or added to the application. Nevertheless, ListResourceBundles provide considerably better performance than PropertyResourceBundles.

If the resource bundle is not found or a resource object is not found in the resource bundle, a MissingResourceException is raised. Since MissingResourceException is a subclass of RuntimeException, you do not need to catch the exception explicitly in the code.

This example is the same as Example 20.3, "Formatting Numbers," except that the program contains the code for handling resource strings. The updateString method (Lines 169–183) is responsible for displaying the locale-sensitive strings. This method is invoked when a new locale is selected in the combo box. Since the variable res of the ResourceBundle class is an instance variable in ResourceBundleDemo, it cannot be directly used in the main method, because the main method is static. To fix the problem, create applet as an instance of ResourceBundleDemo and you will then be able to reference res using applet.res.

KEY TERMS

locale 717	resource bundle 736

KEY CLASSES AND METHODS

✦ **java.util.Locale** is a class that represents locale. Locale is dependent on country and language. It determines how locale-sensitive information (e.g., date, time, number, currency) is displayed. The classes Date, Calendar, DateFormat, and NumberFormat are locale-sensitive and contain the static method getAvailableLocales() to return an array of the supported locales.

◆ **java.util.TimeZone**   is a class that represents a time zone offset and also figures out daylight savings. You can set a time zone in `Calendar` and `DateFormat` using the `setTimeZone(TimeZone)` method.

◆ **java.text.DateFormat**   is a class that is used to format date and time.

◆ **java.text.SimpleDateFormat**   is a subclass of `DateFormat` that enables you to use a user-defined pattern for date and time formatting.

◆ **java.text.SimpleDateSymbols**   is a class that encapsulates localizable date-time formatting data, such as the names of the months, the names of the days of the week, and the time zone data.

◆ **java.text.NumberFormat**   is an abstract base class that provides the methods for formatting and parsing numbers.

CHAPTER SUMMARY

◆ Java is the first language designed from the ground up to support internationalization. In consequence, it allows your programs to be customized for any number of countries or languages without requiring cumbersome changes in the code.

◆ Java characters use *Unicode*, a 16-bit encoding scheme established by the Unicode Consortium to support the interchange, processing, and display of written texts in the world's diverse languages. The use of Unicode encoding makes it easy to write Java programs that can manipulate strings in any international language.

◆ Java provides the `Locale` class to encapsulate information about a specific locale. A `Locale` object determines how locale-sensitive information, such as date, time, and number, is displayed, and how locale-sensitive operations, such as sorting strings, are performed. The classes for formatting date, time, and numbers, and for sorting strings are grouped in the `java.text` package.

◆ Java uses the `ResourceBundle` class to separate locale-specific information, such as status messages and GUI component labels, from the program. The information is stored outside the source code and can be accessed and loaded dynamically at runtime from a `ResourceBundle`, rather than hard-coded into the program.

◆ A `Locale` object represents a geographical, political, or cultural region in which a specific language or custom is used. To create a `Locale` object, use the constructor `Locale(String language, String country)` or `Locale(String language, String country, String variant)`. The `language` should be a valid language code. For example, zh stands for Chinese and en for English. The country should be a valid country code. For example, CA stands for Canada and CN for China.

◆ Java provides a system-independent encapsulation of date and time in the `java.util.Date` class; it also provides `java.util.TimeZone` for dealing with time zones, and `java.util.Calendar` for extracting detailed information from `Date`. Different locales have different conventions for displaying date and time. The `java.text.DateFormat` class can be used to format date and time in a locale-sensitive way for display to the user.

◆ Formatting numbers as currency or percentages is highly locale-dependent. You can format numbers using the `java.text.NumberFormat` class, an abstract base class that provides the methods for formatting and parsing numbers. With NumberFormat, you can format and parse numbers for any locale. Your code will be completely independent of locale conventions for decimal points, thousands-separators, or the particular decimal digits used, and even for whether the number format is decimal.

✦ To format a number for the current locale, use one of the factory class methods to get a formatter. Use getInstance or getNumberInstance to get the normal number format. Use getCurrencyInstance to get the currency number format. And use getPercentInstance to get a format for displaying percentages.

✦ When a locale-specific resource is needed—a message string, for example—your program can load it from the resource bundle appropriate for the desired locale. In this way, you can write programs that are largely independent of the user's locale, isolating most, if not all, of the locale-specific information in resource bundles.

✦ Resources are placed inside classes that extend the ResourceBundle class or a subclass of ResourceBundle. Resource bundles contain *key/value* pairs. Each key uniquely identifies a locale-specific object in the bundle. You can use the key to retrieve the object. ListResourceBundle is a convenient subclass of ResourceBundle that is often used to simplify the creation of resource bundles. If all the resources are strings, they can be placed in a convenient text file with the extension .properties.

REVIEW QUESTIONS

Sections 20.1–20.2

20.1 How does Java support international characters in languages like Chinese and Arabic?

20.2 How do you construct a Locale object? How do you get all the available locales from a Calendar object?

20.3 How do you set a locale for the French-speaking region of Canada in a Swing JButton? How do you set a locale for the Netherlands in a Swing JLabel?

Section 20.3 Processing Date and Time

20.4 How do you set the time zone "PST" for a Calendar object?

20.5 How do you display current date and time in German?

20.6 How do you use the SimpleDateFormat class to display date and time using the pattern "yyyy.MM.dd hh:mm:ss"?

20.7 In Line 73 of WorldClockControl.java, Arrays.sort(availableTimeZones) is used to sort available time zones. What happens if you attempt to sort the available locales using Arrays.sort(availableLocales)?

Section 20.4 Formatting Numbers

20.8 Write the code to format number 12345.678 in the United Kingdom locale. Keep two digits after the decimal point.

20.9 Write the code to format number 12345.678 in U.S. currency.

20.10 Write the code to format number 0.345678 as percentage with at least three digits after the decimal point.

20.11 Write the code to parse 3,456.78 into a number.

20.12 Write the code that uses the DecimalFormat class to format number 12345.678 using the pattern "0.0000#".

Section 20.5 Resource Bundles

20.13 How does the getBundle method locate a resource bundle?

20.14 How does the getObject method locate a resource?

PROGRAMMING EXERCISES

Sections 20.1–20.2

20.1* (*Unicode viewer*) Develop an applet that displays Unicode characters, as shown in Figure 20.11. The user specifies a Unicode in the text field and presses the Enter key to display a sequence of Unicode characters starting with the specified Unicode. The Unicode characters are displayed in a scrollable text area of twenty lines. Each line contains sixteen characters preceded by the Unicode that is the code for the first character on the line.

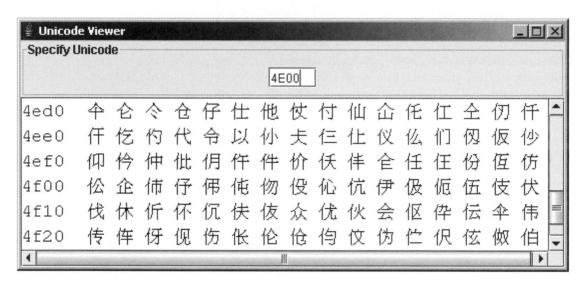

FIGURE 20.11 *The applet displays the Unicode characters.*

20.2** (*Processing Unicode files*) Write a program named Exercise20_2Writer that writes 1307 × 16 Chinese Unicode characters starting from \u0E00 to a file named Exercise20_2.gb using the GBK encoding scheme. Output sixteen characters per line, and separate the characters with spaces. Write a program named Exercise20_2Reader that reads all the characters from a file using a specified encoding. Figure 20.12 displays the file using the GBK encoding scheme.

 HINT

Use new BufferedWriter(new OutputStreamWriter(new FileOutputStream("Exercise20_2.gb"), "GBK")) to create an output stream to write data to the file, and use new BufferedReader(new InputStreamReader(new FileInputStream("Exercise20_2.gb"), "GBK")) to read the file.

Section 20.3 Processing Date and Time

20.3 (*Placing the calendar and clock in a panel*) Write an applet that displays the current date in a calendar and current time in a clock, as shown in Figure 20.13. Enable the applet to run standalone.

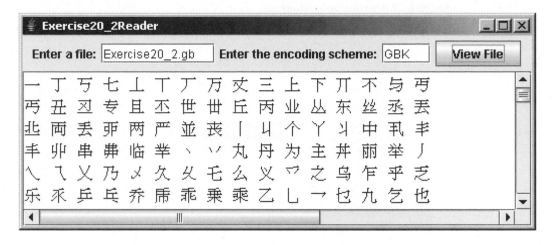

FIGURE 20.12   *The program displays the file using the specified encoding scheme.*

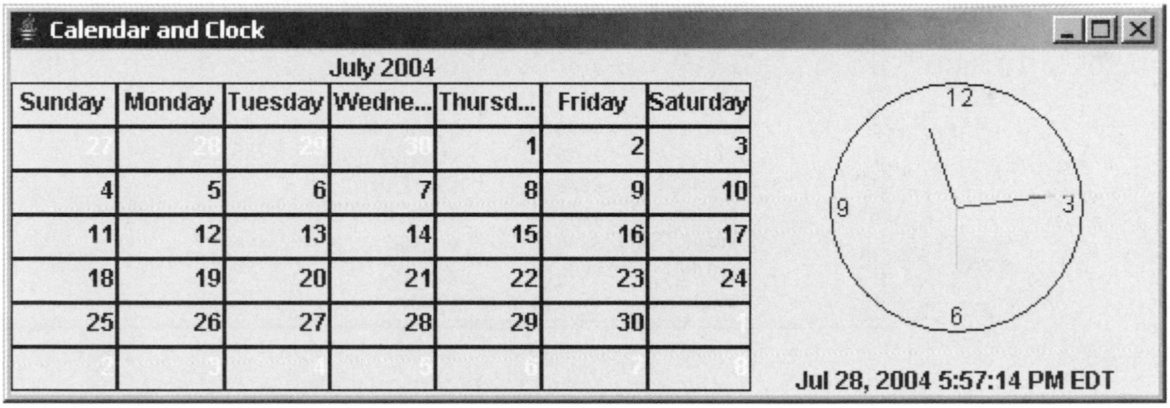

FIGURE 20.13   *The calendar and clock displays the current date and time.*

20.4   (*Finding the available locales and time zone IDs*) Write two programs to display the available locales and time zone IDs. One uses buttons, as shown in Figure 20.14.

FIGURE 20.14   *The program displays available locales and time zones using buttons.*

Section 20.4 Formatting Numbers

20.5* (*Computing loan amortization schedule*) Rewrite Exercise 3.27 using an applet, as shown in Figure 20.15. The applet allows the user to set the loan amount, loan period, and interest rate, and displays the corresponding interest, principal, and balance in the currency format.

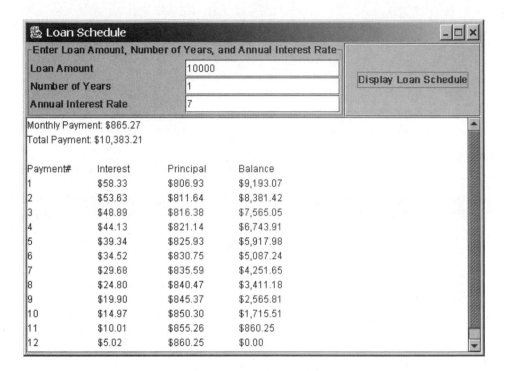

FIGURE 20.15 *The program displays the loan payment schedule.*

20.6 (*Converting dollars to other currencies*) Write a program that converts U.S. dollars to Canadian dollars, German marks, and British pounds, as shown in Figure 20.16. The user enters the U.S. dollar amount and the conversion rate, and clicks the Convert button to display the converted amount.

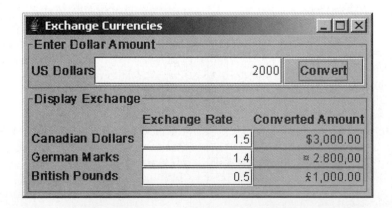

FIGURE 20.16 *The program converts U.S. dollars to Canadian dollars, German marks, and British pounds.*

20.7   (*Revising Example 2.3 "Computing Loan Payments"*) Rewrite Example 2.3 to display the monthly payment and total payment in currency.

20.8   (*Using the* `DecimalFormat` *class*) Rewrite Exercise 4.4 to display at most two digits after the decimal point for the temperature using the `DecimalFormat` class.

Section 20.5 Resource Bundles

20.9*   (*Revising Example 20.2 "Displaying a Calendar"*) Modify Example 20.2 to localize the labels "Choose a locale" and "Calendar Demo" in French, German, Chinese, or a language of your choice.

20.10** (*Flag and anthem*) Rewrite Listing 14.14 FlagAnthem.java on page 529 to use the resource bundle to retrieve image and audio files.

 HINT

When a new country is selected, set an appropriate locale for it. Have your program look for the flag and audio file from the resource file for the locale.

PART VII

ADVANCED GUI PROGRAMMING

In Part III, "GUI Programming," you learned how to develop GUI programs, event-driven programming, creating user interfaces, and applets. This part introduces Java GUI programming in more depth and breadth. You will delve into JavaBeans and will learn how to develop custom events and how to develop components using the MVC approach in Chapter 21, review and explore new containers, layout managers, and borders in Chapter 22, learn how to create GUI with menus, popup menus, toolbars, dialogs, and internal frames in Chapter 23, and explore the advanced Swing components JSpinner, JList, JComboBox, JSpinner, JTable, and JTree in Chapter 24.

Chapter 21
JavaBeans, Bean Events, and MVC

Chapter 22
Containers, Layout Managers, and Borders

Chapter 23
Menus, Toolbars, Dialogs, and Internal Frames

Chapter 24
Advanced Swing Components

Prerequisites for Part VII

```
                    ┌─────────────────────────────────────────┐
                    │   Chapter 14 Applets, Images, and Audio   │
                    └─────────────────────────────────────────┘
                     /                    │                   \
                    /                     │                    \
   ┌────────────────────────┐  ┌────────────────────────┐  ┌────────────────────────┐
   │ Chapter 21 JavaBeans,  │  │ Chapter 22 Containers, │  │ Chapter 23 Menus,      │
   │ Bean Events, and MVC   │  │ Layout Managers, and   │  │ Toolbars, Dialogs, and │
   │                        │  │ Borders                │  │ Internal Frames        │
   └────────────────────────┘  └────────────────────────┘  └────────────────────────┘
               │
               ↓
   ┌────────────────────────┐
   │ Chapter 24 Advanced    │
   │ Swing Components        │
   └────────────────────────┘
```

chapter

21

JavaBeans, Bean Events, and MVC

Objectives

- ✦ To know what a JavaBeans component is (§21.2).

- ✦ To discover the similarities and differences between beans and regular objects (§21.2).

- ✦ To understand JavaBeans properties and naming patterns (§21.3).

- ✦ To review the Java event delegation model (§21.4).

- ✦ To create custom event classes and listener interfaces (§21.5).

- ✦ To develop source components using custom event sets or event sets from the Java API (§21.6).

- ✦ To utilize existing events for creating source components (§21.7).

- ✦ To distinguish standard adapters, inner classes, and anonymous classes (§21.8).

- ✦ To use the model-view-controller approach to separate data and logic from the presentation of data (§21.9).

- ✦ To implement the model-view-controller components using the JavaBeans event model (§21.9).

21.1   Introduction

Every Java user interface class is a JavaBeans component. Understanding JavaBeans will help you to learn GUI components. In Chapter 12, "Event-Driven Programming," you learned how to handle the events fired from source components such as `JButton`, `JTextField`, `JRadioButton`, and `JComboBox`. In this chapter, you will learn how to create custom events and develop your own source components that can fire events. By developing your own events and source components, you will gain a better understanding of the Java event model and apply the techniques to implementing the model-view-controller components.

21.2   JavaBeans

JavaBeans

JavaBeans is a software component architecture that extends the power of the Java language by enabling well-formed objects to be manipulated visually at design time in a pure Java builder tool, such as JBuilder, NetBeans, or Eclipse. Such well-formed objects are referred to as *JavaBeans* or simply *beans*. The classes that define the beans, referred to as *JavaBeans components* or *bean components*, or simply *components*, conform to the JavaBeans component model with the following requirements:

✦ A bean must be a public class.

✦ A bean must have a public no-arg constructor, though it can have other constructors if needed. For example, a bean named `MyBean` must either have a constructor with the signature

```
public MyBean();
```

or have no constructor if its superclass has a no-arg constructor.

Serializable

✦ A bean must implement the `java.io.Serializable` interface to ensure a persistent state.

accessor
mutator

✦ A bean usually has properties with correctly constructed public *accessor* (get) methods and *mutator* (set) methods that enable the properties to be seen and updated visually by a builder tool.

event registration

✦ A bean may have events with correctly constructed public registration and deregistration methods that enable the bean to add and remove listeners. If the bean plays a role as the source of events, it must provide registration methods for registering listeners. For example, you can register a listener for `ActionEvent` using the `addActionListener` method of a `JButton` bean.

The first three requirements must be observed, and therefore are referred to as *minimum JavaBeans component requirements*. The last two requirements are dependent on implementations. It is possible to write a bean without get/set methods and event registration/deregistration methods.

A JavaBeans component is a special kind of Java class. The relationship between JavaBeans components and Java classes is illustrated in Figure 21.1.

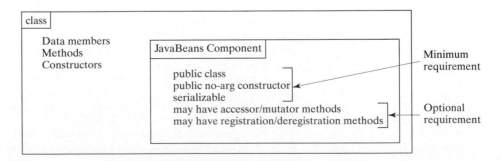

FIGURE 21.1   *A JavaBeans component is a serializable public class with a public no-arg constructor.*

Every GUI class is a JavaBeans component, because (1) it is a public class, (2) it has a public no-arg constructor, and (3) it is an extension of java.awt.Component, which implements java.io.Serializable.

 NOTE

This chapter does not require the use of builder tools. If you are interested in learning how to use JavaBeans in rapid Java application development using JBuilder or NetBeans, please refer to one of my books on the subject, *Rapid Java Application Development Using JBuilder* and *Rapid Java Application Development Using Sun ONE Studio.*

Rapid Java

21.3 Bean Properties

Properties are discrete, named attributes of a Java bean that can affect its appearance or behavior. They are often data fields of a bean. For example, the JButton component has a property named text that represents the text to be displayed on the button. Private data fields are often used to hide specific implementations from the user and prevent the user from accidentally corrupting the properties. Accessor and mutator methods are provided instead to let the user read and write the properties.

21.3.1 Property-Naming Patterns

The bean property-naming pattern is a convention of the JavaBeans component model that simplifies the bean developer's task of presenting properties. A property can be a primitive data type or an object type. The property type dictates the signature of the accessor and mutator methods.

In general, the accessor method is named get<PropertyName>(), which takes no parameters and returns a primitive type value or an object of a type identical to the property type. For example,

```
public String getMessage() { }
public int getXCoordinate() { }
public int getYCoordinate() { }
```

For a property of boolean type, the accessor method should be named is<PropertyName>(), which returns a boolean value. For example,

```
public boolean isCentered() { }
```

The mutator method should be named set<PropertyName>(dataType p), which takes a single parameter identical to the property type and returns void. For example,

```
public void setMessage(String s) { }
public void setXCoordinate(int x) { }
public void setYCoordinate(int y) { }
public void setCentered(boolean centered) { }
```

 NOTE

You may have multiple get and set methods, but there must be one get or set method with a signature conforming to the naming patterns.

21.3.2 Properties and Data Fields

Properties describe the state of the bean. Naturally, data fields are used to store properties. However, a bean property is not necessarily a data field. For example, in the MessagePanel class in Section 11.11, "Case Study: The MessagePanel Class," you may create a new property named messageLength that represents the number of characters in message. The get method for the property may be defined as follows:

```
public int getMessageLength() {
  return message.length();
}
```

 NOTE

A property may be *read-only* with a get method but no set method, or *write-only* with a set method but no get method. However, both the get and set methods must be provided to enable the property to be seen in a builder tool.

21.4   Bean Events

A bean may communicate with other beans. The Java event delegation model provides the foundation for beans to send, receive, and handle events. When something happens to a bean, such as a mouse click on a `javax.swing.JButton` bean, an event object is created that encapsulates information pertaining to the event. The bean passes the event object to the listeners for processing the event.

Events are typically generated by Java GUI components, such as `javax.swing.JButton`, but are not limited to GUI components. This section introduces the development of custom events and the beans that can generate events.

21.4.1   Java Event Model

Let us review the Java event model that was introduced in Chapter 12, "Event-Driven Programming." The Java event model consists of the following three types of elements, as shown in Figure 12.12:

✦ The event object

✦ The source object

✦ The event listener object

event

source object

listener

An *event* is a signal to the program that something has happened. It can be triggered by external user actions, such as mouse movements, mouse button clicks, and keystrokes, or by the operating system, such as a timer. An *event object* contains the information that describes the event. A *source object* is where the event originates. When an event occurs on a source object, an event object is created. An object interested in the event receives the event. Such an object is called a *listener*. Not all objects can receive events. To become a listener, an object must be registered as a listener by the source object. The source object maintains a list of listeners and notifies all the registered listeners by invoking the event-handling method implemented on the listener object. The handlers are defined in the class known as the *event listener interface*. Each class of an event object has a corresponding event listener interface. The Java event model is referred to as a *delegation-based model* because the source object delegates the event to the listeners for processing.

21.4.2   Event Classes and Event Listener Interfaces

An event object is created using an event class, such as `ActionEvent`, `MouseEvent`, and `ItemEvent` as shown in Figure 12.1. All the event classes extend `java.util.EventObject`. The event class contains whatever data values and methods are pertinent to the particular event type. For example, the `KeyEvent` class describes the data values related to a key event and contains the methods, such as `getKeyChar()`, for retrieving the key associated with the event.

handler

Every event class is associated with an event listener interface that defines one or more methods referred to as *handlers*. An event listener interface is a subinterface of `java.util.EventListener`. The handlers are implemented by the listener components. The source component invokes the listeners' handlers when an event is detected.

Since an event class and its listener interface are coexistent, they are often referred to as an *event set* or *event pair*. The event listener interface must be named as *X*Listener for the *X*Event. For example, the listener interface for ActionEvent is ActionListener. The parameter list of a handler always consists of an argument of the event class type. Figure 21.2 shows the pair of ActionEvent and ActionListener.

event set

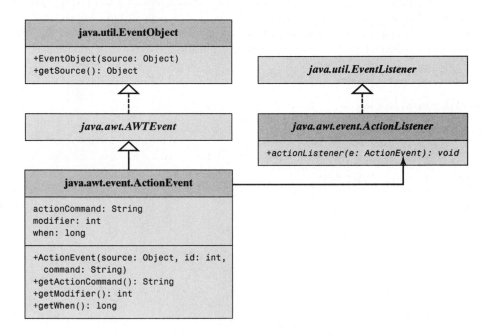

FIGURE 21.2   *ActionEvent and ActionListener are examples of an event pair.*

21.4.3   Source Components

The component on which an event is generated is referred to as an *event source*. Every Java GUI component is an *event source* for one or more events. For example, JComboBox is an event source for ActionEvent and ItemEvent. A JComboBox object fires a java.awt.event.ActionEvent and a java.awt.event.ItemEvent when a new item is selected in the combo box.

The source component contains the code that detects an external or internal action that triggers the event. Upon detecting the action, the source should fire an event to the listeners by invoking the event handler defined by the listeners. The source component must also contain methods for registering and deregistering listeners, as shown in Figure 21.3.

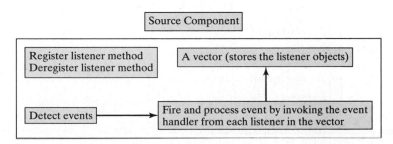

FIGURE 21.3   *The source component detects events and processes them by invoking the event listener's handlers.*

21.4.4 Listener Components

A listener component for an event must implement the event listener interface. The object of the listener component cannot receive event notifications from a source component unless the object is registered as a listener of the source.

A listener component may implement any number of listener interfaces to listen to several types of events. A source component may register many listeners. A source component may register itself as a listener.

Here is an example that creates a source object and a listener object, and registers the listener with the source object. Figure 21.4 highlights the relationship between source and listener.

```java
import javax.swing.*;
import java.awt.event.*;

public class Test {
  public static void main(String[] args) {
    JFrame frame = new JFrame("Test");
    // Create a source object
    JButton jbt = new JButton("OK");
    frame.getContentPane().add(jbt);
    frame.setSize(200, 200);
    frame.setVisible(true);

    // Create listeners
    MyListener listener = new MyListener();

    // Register listeners
    jbt.addActionListener(listener);
  }
}

/** MyListener class */
class MyListener implements ActionListener {
  public void actionPerformed(ActionEvent e) {
    System.out.println("I will process it!");
  }
}
```

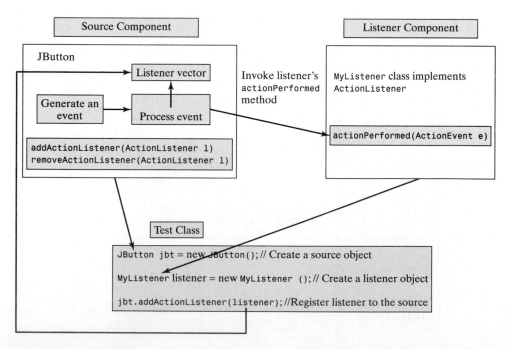

FIGURE 21.4 *The listener is registered with the source, and the source invokes the listener's handler to process the event.*

21.5 Creating Custom Event Sets

You have already used event sets and event source components in Java GUI programming, since certain event sets and source components are provided as part of the Java API. You can also create custom event sets and source components.

A custom event class must extend `java.util.EventObject` or one of its subclasses. Additionally, it may provide constructors to create events, data members, and methods to describe events.

A custom event listener interface must extend `java.util.EventListener` or a subinterface of `java.util.EventListener`, and define the signature of the handlers for the event. By convention, the listener interface should be named *<Event>*Listener for the corresponding event class named *<Event>*. For example, `ActionListener` is the listener interface for `ActionEvent`.

EXAMPLE 21.1 CREATING A CUSTOM EVENT SET

Problem

This example creates a custom event named `TickEvent` (Listing 21.1) for describing tick events, and its corresponding listener interface `TickListener` (Listing 21.2) for defining a tick handler.

Solution

The event class contains the information on tick count and tick interval, and the tick listener interface defines the handler for the event, as shown in Figure 21.5.

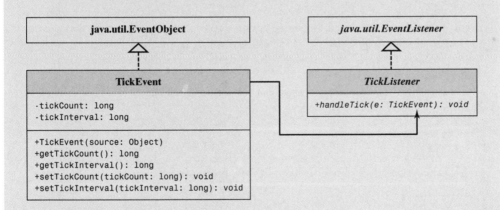

FIGURE 21.5 *`TickEvent` and `TickListener` comprise an event set for tick event.*

LISTING 21.1 TickEvent.java (Event Class)

```
1 public class TickEvent extends java.util.EventObject {
2   /** tickCount counts the number of ticks for the event */
3   private long tickCount;
4
5   /** tickInterval is the interval between ticks in milliseconds */
6   private long tickInterval;
7
8   /** Construct a TickEvent */
9   public TickEvent(Object source) {
10     super(source);
11   }
12
13   /** Return tickCount */
14   public long getTickCount() {
```

invoke superclass
constructor

EXAMPLE 21.1 (CONTINUED)

```
15      return tickCount;
16   }
17
18   /** Set a new tickCount */
19   public void setTickCount(long tickCount) {
20      this.tickCount = tickCount;
21   }
22
23   /** Return tickInterval */
24   public long getTickInterval() {
25      return tickInterval;
26   }
27
28   /** Set a new tickInterval */
29   public void setTickInterval(long milliseconds) {
30      tickInterval = milliseconds;
31   }
32 }
```

LISTING 21.2   TickListener.java (Listener Interface)

```
1 public interface TickListener extends java.util.EventListener {
2    /** Handle a TickEvent, to be implemented by a listener */
3    public void handleTick(TickEvent e);
4 }
```

Review

The event pair `TickEvent` and `TickListener` will be used to create a source component that generates `TickEvent` in Example 21.2.

An event class is an extension of `EventObject`. To construct an event, the constructor of `EventObject` must be invoked by passing a source object as the argument. In the constructor for `TickEvent`, `super(source)` (Line 10) invokes the superclass's constructor with the source object as the argument. `TickEvent` contains the information pertaining to the event, such as tick count and tick interval.

`TickListener` simply extends `EventListener` and defines the `handleTick` method for handling tick events.

 TIP

An event class does not have a no-arg constructor, because you must always specify a source for the event when creating an event.

---

specifying a source for an
event

21.6   Creating Custom Source Components

A source component must have the appropriate registration and deregistration methods for adding and removing listeners. Events can be unicasted (only one listener object is notified of the event) or multicasted (each object in a list of listeners is notified of the event). The naming pattern for adding a unicast listener is

```
public void add<Event>Listener(<Event>Listener l) throws
   TooManyListenersException;
```

The naming pattern for adding a multicast listener is the same, except that it does not throw the `TooManyListenersException`:

```
public void add<Event>Listener(<Event>Listener l)
```

The naming pattern for removing a listener (either unicast or multicast) is:

```
public void remove<Event>Listener(<Event>Listener l)
```

A source component contains the code that creates an event object and passes it to the listening components by calling a method in the listener's event listener interface. You may use a standard Java event class like ActionEvent to create event objects or may define your own event classes if necessary.

EXAMPLE 21.2 CREATING A SOURCE COMPONENT

Problem

Create a custom source component that is capable of generating tick events at variant time intervals. The component contains the properties tickCount, tickInterval, maxInterval, minInterval, and step. The component adjusts the tickInterval by adding step to it after a tick event occurs. If step is 0, tickInterval is unchanged. If step > 0, tickInterval is increased. If step < 0, tickInterval is decreased. If tickInterval > maxInterval or tickInterval < minInterval, the component will no longer generate tick events.

 NOTE

You learned to use javax.swing.Timer to control animation in Section 12.6, "The Timer Class." The Timer class generates a timer at fixed time intervals. This new component can generate tick events at variant time intervals as well as at fixed time intervals.

Solution

The source component is responsible for registering listeners, creating events, and notifying listeners by invoking the methods defined in the listeners' interfaces. The Tick component shown in Figure 21.6 is capable of registering multiple listeners, generating TickEvent objects at variant time intervals, and notifying the listeners by invoking the listeners' handleTick method. The source code of Tick is given as follows:

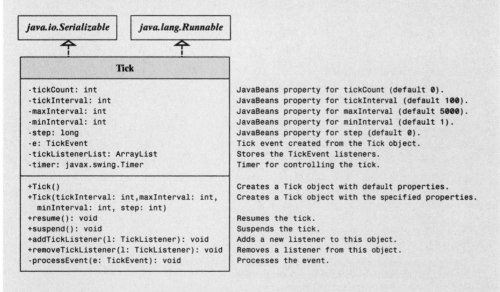

FIGURE 21.6 *Tick is a component that generates TickEvent.*

EXAMPLE 21.2 (CONTINUED)

 NOTE

From this chapter on, for brevity, the get and set methods of JavaBeans properties are not listed in the UML diagrams.

LISTING 21.3   Tick.java (Source Component)

bean properties

tick event

store listeners

no-arg constructor

constructor

start timer

```
 1 import java.util.ArrayList;
 2 import javax.swing.Timer;
 3 import java.awt.event.*;
 4
 5 public class Tick implements java.io.Serializable, ActionListener {
 6   /** Tick properties */
 7   private int tickCount = 0;
 8   private int tickInterval = 100;
 9   private int maxInterval = 5000;
10   private int minInterval = 1;
11   private int step = 0;
12
13   /** Tick event */
14   private TickEvent tickEvent = new TickEvent(this);
15
16   /** Store Tick listeners in a list */
17   private ArrayList tickListenerList;
18
19   // Control tick using a timer
20   private Timer timer = new Timer(tickInterval, this);
21
22   /** Construct a tick with the default properties */
23   public Tick() {
24     this(100, 5000, 1, 0);
25   }
26
27   /** Construct a tick with the specified properties */
28   public Tick(int tickInterval, int maxInterval,
29       int minInterval, int step) {
30     this.tickInterval = tickInterval;
31     this.maxInterval = maxInterval;
32     this.minInterval = minInterval;
33     this.step = step;
34
35     // Start the thread
36     timer.start();
37   }
38
39   /** Return tickCount */
40   public long getTickCount() {
41     return tickInterval;
42   }
43
44   /** Set a tickCount */
45   public void setTickCount(int tickCount) {
46     this.tickCount = tickCount;
47   }
48
49   /** Return tickInterval */
50   public long getTickInterval() {
51     return tickInterval;
52   }
53
54   /** Set tickInterval */
55   public void setTickInterval(int tickInterval) {
56     this.tickInterval = tickInterval;
57     timer.setDelay(tickInterval);
58   }
```

EXAMPLE 21.2 (CONTINUED)

```
59
60    /** Return maxInterval */
61    public long getMaxInterval() {
62      return maxInterval;
63    }
64
65    /** Set maxInterval */
66    public void setMaxInterval(int maxInterval) {
67      this.maxInterval = maxInterval;
68    }
69
70    /** Return minInterval */
71    public long getMinInterval() {
72      return minInterval;
73    }
74
75    /** Set minInterval */
76    public void setMinInterval(int minInterval) {
77      this.minInterval = minInterval;
78    }
79
80    /** Return step */
81    public long getStep() {
82      return step;
83    }
84
85    /** Set step */
86    public void setStep(int step) {
87      this.step = step;
88    }
89
90    /** Handle timer */
91    public void actionPerformed(ActionEvent e) {
92      if (tickInterval > maxInterval ||
93          tickInterval < minInterval) {
94        return;
95      }
96
97      // Adjust Tick count and interval
98      tickEvent.setTickCount(tickCount++);
99      tickInterval += step;
100     tickEvent.setTickInterval(tickInterval);
101
102     // Process event
103     processEvent(tickEvent);
104   }
105
106   /** Suspend the tick */
107   public synchronized void suspend() {
108     timer.stop();
109   }
110
111   /** Resume the tick */
112   public synchronized void resume() {
113     timer.start();
114   }
115
116   /** Register a tick event listener */
117   public synchronized void addTickListener(TickListener l) {          register listener
118     if (tickListenerList == null)
119       tickListenerList = new ArrayList(2);
120
121     if (!tickListenerList.contains(l))
122       tickListenerList.add(l);
123   }
124
```

remove listener

process event

storing listeners

EXAMPLE 21.2 (CONTINUED)

```
125   /** Remove a tick event listener */
126   public synchronized void removeTickListener(TickListener l) {
127     if (tickListenerList != null && tickListenerList.contains(l)) {
128       tickListenerList.remove(l);
129     }
130   }
131
132   /** Fire TickEvent */
133   private void processEvent(TickEvent e) {
134     ArrayList list;
135
136     synchronized (this) {
137       list = (ArrayList)tickListenerList.clone();
138     }
139
140     for (int i = 0; i < list.size(); i++) {
141       TickListener listener = (TickListener)list.get(i);
142       listener.handleTick(e);
143     }
144   }
145 }
```

Review

A TickEvent object is created in Line 14. A timer is created to generate a TickEvent at a variant time interval (Line 20). When a TickEvent is generated, the listeners' handleTick method is invoked at every specified interval (Line 142).

The suspend() (Lines 107–109) and resume() (Lines 112–114) methods defined in the Tick class are for suspending and resuming ticking.

Since the source component Tick is designed for multiple listeners, a java.util.ArrayList instance tickListenerList is used to hold all the listeners for the source component. The data type of the elements in the array list is Object. To add a listener, listener, to tickListenerList, use

tickListenerList.add(listener); (Line 122)

To remove a listener, listener, from tickListenerList, use

tickListenerList.remove(listener); (Line 128)

The if statement (Lines 121–122) ensures that the addTickListener method does not add the listener twice if it is already in the list. The removeTickListener method removes a listener if it is in list. tickListenerList is an instance of ArrayList, which functions as a flexible array that can grow or shrink dynamically. Initially, tickListenerList is new ArrayList(2), which implies that the capacity of the list is 2, but the capacity can be changed dynamically. If more than two listeners are added to tickListenerList, the list size will be automatically increased.

❧ NOTE

Instead of using ArrayList, you can also use javax.swing.event. EventListenerList to store listeners. Using EventListenerList is preferred, since it provides the support for synchronization and it is efficient in the case of no listeners.

The addTickListener and removeTickListener methods are synchronized to prevent data corruption on tickListenerList when attempting to register multiple listeners concurrently.

EXAMPLE 21.2 (CONTINUED)

The processEvent method (Lines 133–144) is invoked when a TickEvent is generated. This notifies the listeners in tickListenerList by calling each listener's handleTick method to process the event. It is possible that a new listener may be added or an existing listener may be removed when processEvent is running. To avoid corruption on tickListenerList, a clone list of tickListenerList is created for use to notify listeners. To avoid corruption when creating the clone, invoke it in a synchronized block, as in Lines 136–138:

```
synchronized (this) {
    list = (ArrayList)tickListenerList.clone();
}
```

The Tick component is created from scratch. If you build a new component that extends a component capable of generating events, the new component inherits the ability to generate the same type of events. For example, since JButton is a subclass of java.awt. Component that can fire MouseEvent, JButton can also detect and generate mouse events. You don't need to write the code to generate these events and register listeners for them, since the code is already given in the superclass. However, you still need to write the code to make your component capable of firing events not supported in the superclass.

EXAMPLE 21.3 USING THE TickEvent CLASS

Problem

Write a program that displays a moving message, as shown in Figure 21.7. The message continuously moves from left to right in the applet at a decreasing pace. When the message disappears at the far right of the view area, it reappears again on the left-hand side. Display the TickEvent count and interval in the message.

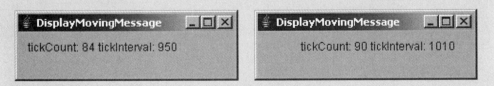

FIGURE 21.7 *A moving message is displayed in the applet.*

Solution

Create an applet named DisplayMovingMessage, and create a panel named MovingMessage to display the message (Listing 21.4). Place an instance of the panel in the applet. To enable the message to move rightward, redraw the message with a new incremental *x*-coordinate. You can use a Tick object to generate a tick event and invoke the repaint method to redraw the message when a tick event occurs. To move the message at a decreasing pace, use a positive step (e.g., 10) when constructing a Tick object. The relationship of the classes is shown in Figure 21.8.

LISTING 21.4 DisplayMovingMessage.java (Using Source Component)

```
1 import javax.swing.*;
2 import java.awt.*;
```

EXAMPLE 21.3 (CONTINUED)

```
 3
 4  public class DisplayMovingMessage extends JApplet {
 5    public DisplayMovingMessage() {
 6      MovingMessage messagePanel = new MovingMessage();
 7      getContentPane().add(messagePanel);
 8      Tick tick = new Tick(100, 1000, 100, 10);
 9      tick.addTickListener(messagePanel);
10    }
11
12    class MovingMessage extends JPanel implements TickListener {
13      private int xCoordinate = 20;
14      private int yCoordinate = 20;
15      private String message = "I am moving";
16
17      public void paintComponent(Graphics g) {
18        super.paintComponent(g);
19        if (xCoordinate > getWidth())
20          xCoordinate = -20;
21        else
22          xCoordinate += 5;
23        g.drawString(message, xCoordinate, yCoordinate);
24      }
25
26      public void setMessage(String message) {
27        this.message = message;
28      }
29
30      public void handleTick(TickEvent e) {
31        setMessage("tickCount: " + e.getTickCount() +
32                   " tickInterval: " + e.getTickInterval());
33        repaint();
34      }
35    }
36  }
```

tick listener (Lines 6)

create tick (Line 8)
register listener (Line 9)

listener class (Line 12)

handler (Line 30)

main method omitted

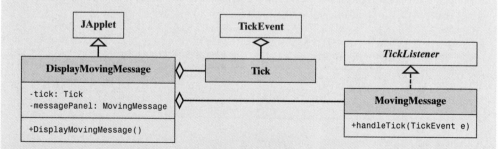

FIGURE 21.8   *A* Tick *object is used to control animation.*

Review

The constructor of the applet creates an instance of MovingMessage (Line 6) called messagePanel and places it in the applet (Line 7). It also creates an instance of Tick (Line 8) and registers messagePanel with it (Line 9).

The MovingMessage class implements TickListener and displays the message every time a tick event occurs. The handleTick method invokes repaint() to redisplay the message (Line 33). The flow of event processing from the source to the listener is shown in Figure 21.9.

EXAMPLE 21.3 (CONTINUED)

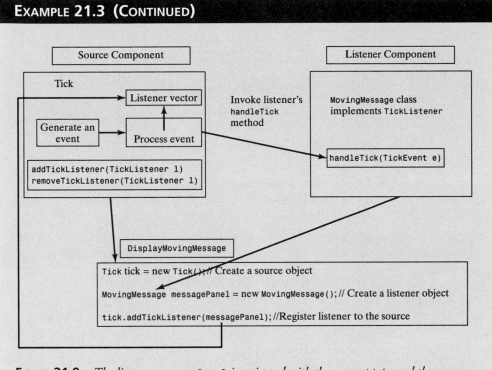

FIGURE 21.9 *The listener* messagePanel *is registered with the source* tick, *and the source invokes the listener's handler* handleTick *to process the event.*

21.7   Working with Existing Event Sets

TickEvent and TickListener constitute a new event pair. Most of the time you don't need to create your own event pairs unless you want to encapsulate information not available in the existing event classes, as in the case of the TickEvent class that contains tick count and tick interval. If you don't need the tick count and tick interval contained in a tick event, there is no need to create a TickEvent class; instead you can use java.awt.ActionEvent and let the Tick class generate an ActionEvent instance when a tick event occurs.

EXAMPLE 21.4 DEVELOPING A SOURCE COMPONENT
                USING EXISTING EVENT SETS

Problem

This example presents a new component that generates an ActionEvent when a tick event occurs rather than use a TickEvent. Use this new component to rewrite the preceding example to display a moving message.

Solution

Name the new source component TickUsingActionEvent (Listing 21.5), the new applet DisplayMovingMessageUsingActionEvent (Listing 21.6), and the panel MovingMessageNew for displaying the message. The relationship of the classes is shown in Figure 21.10.

EXAMPLE 21.4 (CONTINUED)

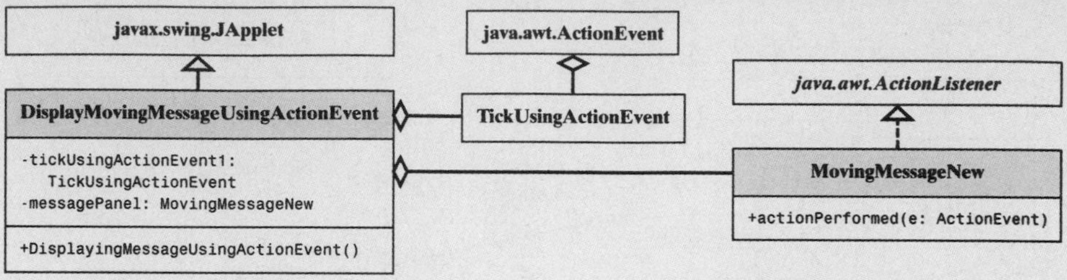

FIGURE 21.10 *The* `DisplayMovingMessageUsingActionEvent` *class uses* `TickUsingActionEvent` *and* `MessagePanelNew` *to control and display a message.*

The new source component `TickUsingActionEvent` is very similar to `Tick`, except that it generates `ActionEvent` rather than `TickEvent`. Its source code is shown as follows:

LISTING 21.5 TickUsingActionEvent.java (Source Component)

```
 1 import java.util.ArrayList;
 2 import javax.swing.Timer;
 3 import java.awt.event.*;
 4
 5 public class TickUsingActionEvent
 6     implements java.io.Serializable, ActionListener {
 7   /** TickUsingActionEvent properties */
 8   private int tickCount = 0;
 9   private int tickInterval = 100;
10   private int maxInterval = 5000;
11   private int minInterval = 1;
12   private int step = 0;
13
14   /** Store listeners in a list */
15   private ArrayList actionListenerList;
16
17   // Control tick using a timer
18   private Timer timer = new Timer(tickInterval, this);
19
20   /** Construct a tick with the default properties */
21   public TickUsingActionEvent() {
22     this(100, 5000, 1, 0);
23   }
24
25   /** Construct a tick with the specified properties */
26   public TickUsingActionEvent(int tickInterval, int maxInterval,
27       int minInterval, int step) {
28     this.tickInterval = tickInterval;
29     this.maxInterval = maxInterval;
30     this.minInterval = minInterval;
31     this.step = step;
32
33     // Start the thread
34     timer.start();
35   }
36
37   /** Return tickCount */
38   public long getTickCount() {
39     return tickInterval;
40   }
41
42   /** Set a tickCount */
43   public void setTickCount(int tickCount) {
44     this.tickCount = tickCount;
45   }
```

bean properties

store listeners

no-arg constructor

constructor

start timer

accessor

mutator

EXAMPLE **21.4** (CONTINUED)

```
46
47   /** Return tickInterval */
48   public long getTickInterval() {
49     return tickInterval;
50   }
51
52   /** Set tickInterval */
53   public void setTickInterval(int tickInterval) {
54     this.tickInterval = tickInterval;
55     timer.setDelay(tickInterval);
56   }
57
58   /** Return maxInterval */
59   public long getMaxInterval() {
60     return maxInterval;
61   }
62
63   /** Set maxInterval */
64   public void setMaxInterval(int maxInterval) {
65     this.maxInterval = maxInterval;
66   }
67
68   /** Return minInterval */
69   public long getMinInterval() {
70     return minInterval;
71   }
72
73   /** Set minInterval */
74   public void setMinInterval(int minInterval) {
75     this.minInterval = minInterval;
76   }
77
78   /** Return step */
79   public long getStep() {
80     return step;
81   }
82
83   /** Set step */
84   public void setStep(int step) {
85     this.step = step;
86   }
87
88   /** Handle timer */
89   public void actionPerformed(ActionEvent e) {
90     if (tickInterval > maxInterval ||
91         tickInterval < minInterval) {
92       return;
93     }
94
95     // Increase the tick count and interval
96     tickCount++;
97     tickInterval += step;
98
99     // Set new delay
100    timer.setDelay(tickInterval);
101
102    // Fire ActionEvent
103    processEvent(new ActionEvent(this,
104      ActionEvent.ACTION_PERFORMED, null));
105  }
106
107  /** Suspend the tick */
108  public synchronized void suspend() {
109    timer.stop();
110  }
111
```

fire ActionEvent

EXAMPLE 21.4 (CONTINUED)

```
112   /** Resume the tick */
113   public synchronized void resume() {
114     timer.start();
115   }
116
117   /** Register an action event listener */
118   public synchronized void addActionListener(ActionListener l) {
119     if (actionListenerList == null)
120       actionListenerList = new ArrayList(2);
121
122     if (!actionListenerList.contains(l))
123       actionListenerList.add(l);
124   }
125
126   /** Remove an action event listener */
127   public synchronized void removeActionListener(ActionListener l) {
128     if (actionListenerList != null && actionListenerList.contains(l))
129       actionListenerList.remove(l);
130   }
131
132   /** Fire ActionEvent */
133   private void processEvent(ActionEvent e) {
134     ArrayList list;
135
136     synchronized (this) {
137       list = (ArrayList)actionListenerList.clone();
138     }
139
140     for (int i = 0; i < list.size(); i++) {
141       ActionListener listener = (ActionListener)list.get(i);
142       listener.actionPerformed(e);
143     }
144   }
145 }
```

register listener

remove listener

process event

LISTING 21.6   DisplayMovingMessageUsingActionEvent.java

```
1 import javax.swing.*;
2 import java.awt.*;
3 import java.awt.event.*;
4
5 public class DisplayMovingMessageUsingActionEvent extends JApplet {
6   private TickUsingActionEvent tick =
7     new TickUsingActionEvent(100, 1000, 100, 10);
8
9   public DisplayMovingMessageUsingActionEvent() {
10     MovingMessageNew messagePanel = new MovingMessageNew();
11     getContentPane().add(messagePanel);
12     tick.addActionListener(messagePanel);
13   }
14
15   class MovingMessageNew extends JPanel implements ActionListener {
16     private int xCoordinate = 20;
17     private int yCoordinate = 20;
18     private String message = "I am moving";
19
20     public void paintComponent(Graphics g) {
21       super.paintComponent(g);
22       if (xCoordinate > getWidth())
23         xCoordinate = -20;
24       else
25         xCoordinate += 5;
26       g.drawString(message, xCoordinate, yCoordinate);
27     }
28
```

create tick

register listener

listener class

EXAMPLE 21.4 (CONTINUED)

```
29      public void setMessage(String message) {
30        this.message = message;
31      }
32
33      public void actionPerformed(ActionEvent e) {          handler
34        setMessage("tickCount: " + tick.getTickCount()
35                   + " tickInterval: " + tick.getTickInterval());
36        repaint();
37      }
38    }
39 }                                                          main method omitted
```

Review

The UML diagram for `ActionEvent` is shown in Figure 21.2. To create an `ActionEvent`, use the constructor

```
ActionEvent(Object source, int id, String command)
```

where `source` specifies the source component, `id` identifies the event, and `command` specifies a command associated with the event. Use `ActionEvent.ACTION_PERFORMED` for the id. If you don't want to associate a command with the event, use `null`.

The `TickUsingActionEvent` class creates an `ActionEvent` when a tick occurs (Lines 103–104) and invokes the listener's `actionPerformed` handler to process the events (Line 142). The `addActionListener(ActionListener l)` registers an action listener, and `remove-ActionListener(ActionListener l)` deregisters an action listener.

The inner class `MovingMessageNew` implements `ActionListener` and displays the message every time an `ActionEvent` occurs. The `actionPerformed` method invokes `repaint()` to redisplay the message (Line 36). The `tickCount` and `tickInterval` are obtained from the `TickUsingActionEvent` object, whereas they were obtained from the `TickEvent` class in the preceding example. The flow of event processing from the source to the listener is shown in Figure 21.11.

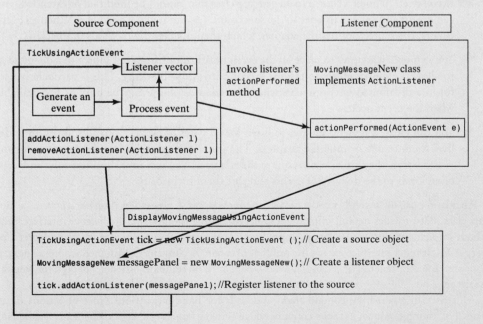

FIGURE 21.11 *The listener* `messagePanel` *is registered with the source* `tick`, *and the source invokes the listener's handler* `actionPerformed` *to process the event.*

21.8   Event Adapters

The Java event model shown in Figure 12.2 is flexible, allowing modifications and variations. One useful variation of the model is the addition of adapters, as shown in Figure 21.12. When an event occurs, the source object notifies the adapter. The adapter then delegates the handling of the event to the actual processing object, which is referred to as an *adaptee*.

adaptee

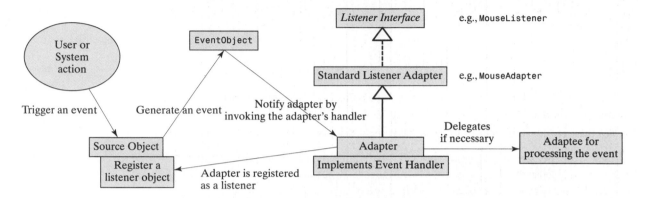

FIGURE 21.12   *The adapter listens for events and delegates handling to the actual listener (adaptee).*

The adapter is a service object that provides a level of indirection between the source and the adaptee. It is registered as a listener for the source event. Instead of passing the event object to the adaptee directly, the source passes the event object to the adapter and lets it delegate to the actual handler in the adaptee.

At first glance, the advantages of using adapters are not apparent. Adapters seem to make things more complex, but they are valuable in many situations. Here are some examples:

why using adapter?

◆ If you need to hook a source to an existing class that cannot be modified or extended, you can use an adapter as a listener to the source and register it with the source. When an event occurs, the source notifies the adapter, which then invokes the methods in the class.

◆ You can use an adapter to place all the event notifications from the source in a queue so as to allow the source object to resume execution without blocking. This is particularly useful in a distributed environment, where the adaptee object may be busy or not available when the event occurs.

◆ You can create a generic adapter to listen for all types of events from all sources, then deliver them to one or multiple adaptees. The generic adapter can be used as a filter for the events before they are delegated out to the adaptees. You can apply business rules and logic of all kinds to the delivery of events and sort them by priority.

convenience listener adapter

An adapter usually extends a convenience listener adapter. A *convenience listener adapter* is a support class that provides default implementations for all the methods in the listener interface. The default implementation is usually an empty body. Java provides convenience listener adapters for every AWT listener interface except the `ActionListener`. A convenience listener adapter is named *X*Adapter for *X*Listener. For example, `MouseAdapter` is a standard listener adapter for `Mouse-Listener`.

A listener interface may contain many methods for handling various types of actions of an event. For example, `MouseListener` contains `mouseClicked`, `mousePressed`, `mouseReleased`, `mouse-Entered`, and `mouseExited`. The convenience listener adapter is convenient because a listener class may simply extend the adapter and implement only the method for the intended type of action instead of all the methods of the listener interface.

Adapters are an important addition to the Java event model. They are used in the Java IDE tools to automatically generate the code for processing events. Three types of event adapters—standard adapters, inner class adapters, and anonymous adapters—are introduced in the following sections.

21.8.1 Standard Adapters

A *standard adapter* is a named class that extends a convenience listener adapter or implements a listener interface. Typically, adaptee is passed to the constructor of the standard adapter and the adaptee is a data field in the standard adapter. The following example demonstrates the use of standard adapters.

standard adapter

EXAMPLE 21.5 HANDLING EVENTS USING STANDARD ADAPTERS

Problem

Rewrite the preceding example with two new features: (1) the message freezes when the mouse button is pressed on the message panel, and moves when the mouse button is released; (2) use standard adapters.

Solution

The program in Listing 21.7 creates two standard adapters: one for handling the action event from `TickEventUsingAction`, and another for handling the mouse-pressed and mouse-release events from `MouseEvent`.

LISTING 21.7 **StandardAdapterDemo.java**

```
 1 import javax.swing.*;
 2 import java.awt.*;
 3 import java.awt.event.*;
 4
 5 public class StandardAdapterDemo extends JApplet {
 6   public StandardAdapterDemo() {
 7     ControlMovingMessage messagePanel = new ControlMovingMessage();
 8     getContentPane().add(messagePanel);
 9   }
10 }
11
12 class ControlMovingMessage extends JPanel {
13   private int xCoordinate = 20;
14   private int yCoordinate = 20;
15   private TickUsingActionEvent tick = new TickUsingActionEvent();
16
17   ControlMovingMessage() {
18     tick.setTickInterval(100);
19     tick.addActionListener(new MyActionListenerAdapter(this));
20     this.addMouseListener(new MyMouseListenerAdapter(this));
21   }
22
23   public void paintComponent(Graphics g) {
24     super.paintComponent(g);
25     if (xCoordinate > getWidth())
26       xCoordinate = -20;
27     else
28       xCoordinate += 5;
29     g.drawString("I am moving", xCoordinate, yCoordinate);
30   }
31
32   public void actionPerformed(ActionEvent e) {
33     repaint();
34   }
35
36   public void mousePressed(MouseEvent e) {
37     tick.suspend();
38   }
```

main method omitted

register adapter
register adapter

action handler

mouse pressed

EXAMPLE **21.5** (CONTINUED)

mouse released

```
39
40   public void mouseReleased(MouseEvent e) {
41     tick.resume();
42   }
43 }
44
45 /** Adapter class for action event */
46 class MyActionListenerAdapter implements ActionListener {
47   ControlMovingMessage adaptee;
48
49   MyActionListenerAdapter(ControlMovingMessage adaptee) {
50     this.adaptee = adaptee;
51   }
52
53   public void actionPerformed(ActionEvent e) {
54     adaptee.actionPerformed(e);
55   }
56 }
57
58 /** Adapter class for mouse event */
59 class MyMouseListenerAdapter extends MouseAdapter {
60   ControlMovingMessage adaptee;
61
62   MyMouseListenerAdapter(ControlMovingMessage adaptee) {
63     this.adaptee = adaptee;
64   }
65
66   public void mousePressed(MouseEvent e) {
67     adaptee.mousePressed(e);
68   }
69
70   public void mouseReleased(MouseEvent e) {
71     adaptee.mouseReleased(e);
72   }
73 }
```

adapter class (line 46)

adapter class (line 59)

Review

MyActionListenerAdapter implements ActionListener (Line 46). An instance of MyActionListenerAdapter is registered as a listener for action events with tick (an instance of TickUsingActionEvent) in the constructor of ControlMovingMessage using the following statement (Line 19):

```
tick.addMouseListener(new MyActionListenerAdapter(this));
```

this is the current instance of ControlMovingMessage, which is passed to the constructor of MyActionListenerAdapter as adaptee. The purpose is to enable the adapter to invoke the adaptee's actionPerformed method (Line 54) to actually process an action event (i.e., repaint the message in Line 33). The flow of event processing from the source to the adapter, and from the adapter to the actual handler is shown in Figure 21.13.

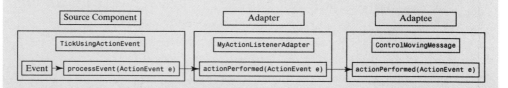

FIGURE 21.13 *When a tick occurs, the source object creates an action event and invokes the* actionPerformed *method in the adapter, which in turn invokes the actual handler in the adaptee.*

EXAMPLE 21.5 (CONTINUED)

MyMouseListenerAdapter extends MouseAdapter (Line 59), which is a convenience listener adapter that implements MouseListener. An instance of MyMouseListenerAdapter is registered as a listener for mouse events in ControlMovingMessage using the following statement (Line 20):

```
this.addMouseListener(new MyMouseListenerAdapter(this));
```

The source and the adaptee are the same object, this is, the current object (this) of ControlMovingMessage. When the source detects a mouse button pressed, it creates a MouseEvent and invokes the adapter's mousePressed method (Line 66), which then invokes the mousePressed method (Line 36) in the adaptee to suspend the tick (tick.suspend()). When the source detects a mouse button released, it creates a MouseEvent and invokes the adapter's mouseReleased method (Line 70), which then invokes the mouseReleased method (Line 40) in the adaptee to resume the tick (tick.resume()). The flow of event processing from the source to the adapter, and from the adapter to the actual handler is shown in Figure 21.14.

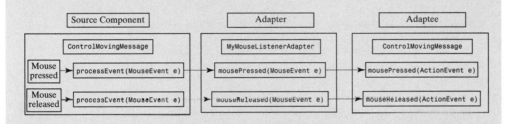

FIGURE 21.14 *When a mouse event occurs, the source object creates a mouse event and invokes the corresponding handler in the adapter, which in turn invokes the actual handler in the adaptee.*

21.8.2   Inner Class Adapters

Standard adapters can be shortened using inner classes. Listing 21.8 rewrites the preceding example using inner classes. The inner classes are italicized.

LISTING 21.8   InnerClassAdapterDemo.java

```
 1 import javax.swing.*;
 2 import java.awt.*;
 3 import java.awt.event.*;
 4
 5 public class InnerClassAdapterDemo extends JApplet {
 6   public InnerClassAdapterDemo() {
 7     ControlMovingMessage1 messagePanel = new ControlMovingMessage1();
 8     getContentPane().add(messagePanel);
 9   }
10 }                                                          main method omitted
11
12 class ControlMovingMessage1 extends JPanel {
13   private int xCoordinate = 20;
14   private int yCoordinate = 20;
15   private TickUsingActionEvent tick = new TickUsingActionEvent();
16
17   ControlMovingMessage1() {
18     tick.setTickInterval(100);
```

register adapter
register adapter

```
19    tick.addActionListener(new MyActionListenerAdapter());
20    this.addMouseListener(new MyMouseListenerAdapter());
21  }
22
23  public void paintComponent(Graphics g) {
24    super.paintComponent(g);
25    if (xCoordinate > getWidth())
26      xCoordinate = -20;
27    else
28      xCoordinate += 5;
29    g.drawString("I am moving", xCoordinate, yCoordinate);
30  }
31
32  public void actionPerformed(ActionEvent e) {
33    repaint();
34  }
35
36  public void mousePressed(MouseEvent e) {
37    tick.suspend();
38  }
39
40  public void mouseReleased(MouseEvent e) {
41    tick.resume();
42  }
43
44  /** Adapter class for action event */
45  class MyActionListenerAdapter implements ActionListener {
46    public void actionPerformed(ActionEvent e) {
47      ControlMovingMessage1.this.actionPerformed(e);
48    }
49  }
50
51  /** Adapter class for mouse event */
52  class MyMouseListenerAdapter extends MouseAdapter {
53    public void mousePressed(MouseEvent e) {
54      ControlMovingMessage1.this.mousePressed(e);
55    }
56
57    public void mouseReleased(MouseEvent e) {
58      ControlMovingMessage1.this.mouseReleased(e);
59    }
60  }
61 }
```

adapter class (line 45)

adapter class (line 52)

The adapter classes `MyActionListenerAdapter` and `MyMouseListenerAdapter` become inner classes of the adaptee class `ControlMovingMessage1`. Since an inner class can reference the data and methods defined in its outer class, you do not need to pass the reference of the adaptee class (outer class) to the constructor of the adapter class (inner class). Therefore, the constructors of the adapters are eliminated. The handlers `actionPerformed`, `mousePressed`, and `mouseReleased` in the adapters directly invoke the actual handlers `actionPerformed`, `mousePressed`, and `mouse-Released` in the adaptee.

An inner class can reference the methods defined in its outer class. The `mousePressed` method is defined in both the inner class and the outer class. To reference the `mousePressed` method defined in the outer class from the inner class, use the following statement (Line 54):

```
ControlMovingMessage1.this.mousePressed(e);
```

Inner classes are compiled into `OuterClassName$InnerClassName.class`. In this example, two inner classes are compiled into `ControlMovingMessage1$MyActionListenerAdapter.class` and `ControlMovingMessage1$MyMouseListenerAdapter.class`.

21.8.3 Anonymous Inner Class Adapters

Inner classes make programs simple and concise. As you can see, the new class is shorter and lean-

anonymous inner class

er. Inner class adapters can be further shortened using anonymous inner classes. An *anonymous inner class* is an inner class without a name. It combines declaring an inner class and creating an instance of the class in one step. An anonymous inner class is declared as follows:

```
new SuperClassName/InterfaceName() {
  // Implement or override methods in superclass or interface

  // Other methods if necessary
}
```

Since an anonymous inner class is a special kind of inner class, it is treated like an inner class in many ways. In addition, it has the following features:

✦ An anonymous inner class must always extend a superclass or implement an interface, but it cannot have an explicit extends or implements clause.

✦ An anonymous inner class must implement all the abstract methods in the superclass and the interface.

✦ An anonymous inner class always uses the no-arg constructor from its superclass to create an instance. If an anonymous inner class implements an interface, the constructor is Object().

✦ An anonymous inner class is compiled into a class named OuterClassName+*n*.class. For example, if the outer class Test has two anonymous inner classes, these two classes are compiled into Test+1.class and Test+2.class.

Adapters implemented with anonymous inner classes are referred to as *anonymous adapters*. Listing 21.9 is an example of rewriting the preceding example using anonymous inner classes. The anonymous inner classes are italicized.

anonymous adapter

LISTING 21.9 AnonymousInnerClassAdapterDemo.java

```
1 import javax.swing.*;
2 import java.awt.*;
3 import java.awt.event.*;
4
5 public class AnonymousInnerClassAdapterDemo extends JApplet {
6   public AnonymousInnerClassAdapterDemo() {
7     ControlMovingMessage2 messagePanel = new ControlMovingMessage2();
8     getContentPane().add(messagePanel);
9   }
10 }
11
12 class ControlMovingMessage2 extends JPanel {
13   private int xCoordinate = 20;
14   private int yCoordinate = 20;
15   private TickUsingActionEvent tick = new TickUsingActionEvent();
16
17   ControlMovingMessage2() {
18     tick.setTickInterval(100);
19     tick.addActionListener(new ActionListener() {
20       public void actionPerformed(ActionEvent e) {
21         ControlMovingMessage2.this.actionPerformed(e);
22       }
23     });
24
25     this.addMouseListener(new MouseAdapter() {
26       public void mousePressed(MouseEvent e) {
27         ControlMovingMessage2.this.mousePressed(e);
28       }
29       public void mouseReleased(MouseEvent e) {
30         ControlMovingMessage2.this.mouseReleased(e);
31       }
32     });
33   }
34
35   public void paintComponent(Graphics g) {
36     super.paintComponent(g);
```

main method omitted

register listener

register listener

```
37       if (xCoordinate > getWidth())
38         xCoordinate = -20;
39       else
40         xCoordinate += 5;
41       g.drawString("I am moving", xCoordinate, yCoordinate);
42     }
43
44     public void actionPerformed(ActionEvent e) {
45       repaint();
46     }
47
48     public void mousePressed(MouseEvent e) {
49       tick.suspend();
50     }
51
52     public void mouseReleased(MouseEvent e) {
53       tick.resume();
54     }
55 }
```

The anonymous adapters (Lines 19–23 and 25–32) in this example work the same way as the inner class adapters in the preceding example. The program is condensed using anonymous adapters.

Anonymous inner classes are compiled into `OuterClassName$#.class`, where # starts at 1 and is incremented for each anonymous class encountered by the compiler. In this example, two anonymous inner classes are compiled into `ControlMovingMessage2$1.class` and `Control-MovingMessage2$2.class`.

21.9 MVC

The model-view-controller (MVC) approach is a way of developing components by separating data storage and handling from the visual representation of the data. The component for storing and handling data, known as a *model*, contains the actual contents of the component. The component for presenting the data, known as a *view*, handles all essential component behaviors. It is the view that comes to mind when you think of the component. It does all the displaying of the components. The *controller* is a component that is usually responsible for obtaining data, as shown in Figure 21.15.

model
view

controller

FIGURE 21.15 *The controller obtains data and stores it in a model. The view displays the data stored in the model.*

MVC benefits

Separating a component into a model and a view has two major benefits:

✦ It makes multiple views possible so that data can be shared through the same model. For example, a model storing student names can simultaneously be displayed in a combo box and a list box.

✦ It simplifies the task of writing complex applications and makes the components scalable and easy to maintain. Changes can be made to the view without affecting the model, and vice versa.

A model contains data, whereas a view makes the data visible. Once a view is associated with a model, it is synchronized with the model. This ensures that all of the model's views display the same data consistently. To achieve consistency and synchronization with its dependent views, the model should notify the views when there is a change in any of its properties that are used in the view. In response to a change notification, the view is responsible for redisplaying the viewing area affected by the property change.

Prior to JDK 1.1, you would create a model by extending the `java.util.Observable` class, and would create a view by implementing the `java.util.Observer` interface. `Observable` and `Observer` were introduced in JDK 1.0, and their use is not consistent with the JDK 1.1 event model. With the arrival of the new Java event delegation model, using `Observable` and `Observer` is obsolete. The JDK event delegation model provides a superior architecture for supporting MVC component development. The model can be implemented as a source with appropriate event and event listener registration methods. The view can be implemented as a listener. Thus, if data are changed in the model, the view will be notified. To enable the selection of the model from the view, simply add the model as a property in the view with a set method.

This example demonstrates the development of components using the MVC approach with the event delegation model.

EXAMPLE 21.6 DEVELOPING MODEL-VIEW-CONTROLLER COMPONENTS

Problem

The example creates a model named `CircleModel`, a view named `CircleView`, and a controller named `CircleControl`. `CircleModel` stores the properties (`radius`, `filled`, and `color`) that describe a circle. `filled` is a boolean value that indicates whether a circle is filled. `CircleView` draws a circle according to the properties of the circle. `CircleControl` enables the user to enter circle properties from a graphical user interface. Create an applet with two buttons named *Show Controller* and *Show View*. When you click the Show Controller button, the controller is displayed in a frame. When you click the Show View button, the view is displayed in a separate frame, as shown in Figure 21.16.

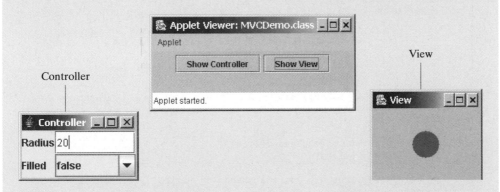

FIGURE 21.16 *The controller obtains circle properties and stores them in a circle model. The view displays the circle specified by the circle model.*

Solution

The circle model contains the properties `radius`, `filled`, and `color`, as well as the registration/deregistration methods for action event, as shown in Figure 21.17.

EXAMPLE 21.6 (CONTINUED)

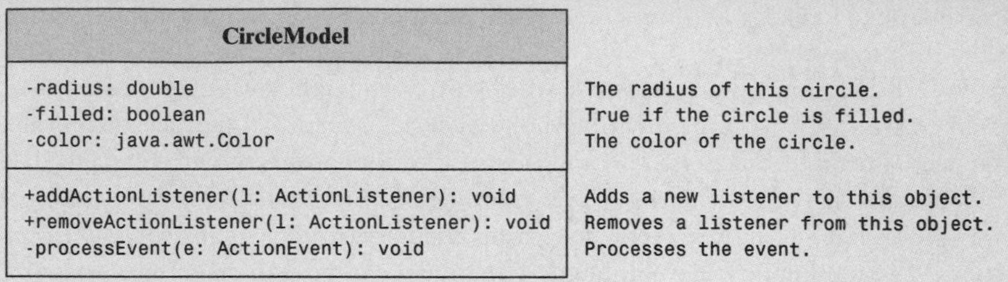

CircleModel
-radius: double
-filled: boolean
-color: java.awt.Color
+addActionListener(l: ActionListener): void
+removeActionListener(l: ActionListener): void
-processEvent(e: ActionEvent): void

The radius of this circle.
True if the circle is filled.
The color of the circle.

Adds a new listener to this object.
Removes a listener from this object.
Processes the event.

FIGURE 21.17 *The circle model stores the data and notifies the listeners if any of the data change.*

When a property value is changed, the listeners are notified. The complete source code for `CircleModel` is given in Listing 21.10.

LISTING 21.10   CircleModel.java (Model)

```
1  import java.awt.event.*;
2  import java.util.*;
3
4  public class CircleModel {
5    /** Property radius. */
6    private double radius = 20;
7
8    /** Property filled. */
9    private boolean filled;
10
11   /** Property color. */
12   private java.awt.Color color;
13
14   /** Utility field used by event firing mechanism. */
15   private ArrayList actionListenerList;
16
17   public double getRadius() {
18     return radius;
19   }
20
21   public void setRadius(double radius) {
22     this.radius = radius;
23
24     // Notify the listener for the change on radius
25     processEvent(
26       new ActionEvent(this, ActionEvent.ACTION_PERFORMED, "radius"));
27   }
28
29   public boolean isFilled() {
30     return filled;
31   }
32
33   public void setFilled(boolean filled) {
34     this.filled = filled;
35
36     // Notify the listener for the change on filled
37     processEvent(
38       new ActionEvent(this, ActionEvent.ACTION_PERFORMED, "filled"));
39   }
40
41   public java.awt.Color getColor() {
42     return color;
43   }
44
45   public void setColor(java.awt.Color color) {
46     this.color = color;
```

properties (line 6)

fire event (line 25)

fire event (line 37)

EXAMPLE 21.6 (CONTINUED)

```
47
48     // Notify the listener for the change on color
49     processEvent(                                                    fire event
50       new ActionEvent(this, ActionEvent.ACTION_PERFORMED, "color"));
51   }
52
53   /** Register an action event listener */
54   public synchronized void addActionListener(ActionListener l) {       standard code
55     ArrayList list = actionListenerList == null ?
56       new ArrayList(2) : (ArrayList)actionListenerList.clone();
57     if (!list.contains(l)) {
58       list.add(l);
59       actionListenerList = list;
60     }
61   }
62
63   /** Remove an action event listener */
64   public synchronized void removeActionListener(ActionListener l) {    standard code
65     if (actionListenerList != null && actionListenerList.contains(l))
66       actionListenerList.remove(l);
67   }
68
69   /** Fire TickEvent */
70   private void processEvent(ActionEvent e) {                           standard code
71     ArrayList list;
72
73     synchronized (this) {
74       list = (ArrayList)actionListenerList.clone();
75     }
76
77     for (int i = 0; i < list.size(); i++) {
78       ActionListener listener = (ActionListener)list.get(i);
79       listener.actionPerformed(e);
80     }
81   }
82 }
```

> **NOTE**
> The registration/deregistration/processEvent methods (Lines 53–81) are
> the same as in Example 21.4. If you use a builder tool, the code can be
> generated automatically.

The view implements ActionListener to listen for notifications from the model. It
contains the model as its property. When a model is set in the view, the view is registered
with the model. The view extends JPanel and overrides the paintComponent method to
draw the circle according to the property values specified in the mode. The UML diagram
for CircleView is shown in Figure 21.18 and its source code is given in Listing 21.11.

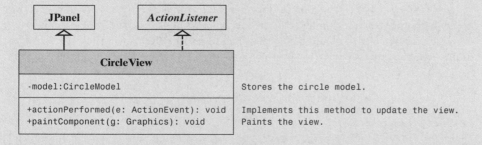

FIGURE 21.18   *The view displays the circle according to the model.*

EXAMPLE 21.6 (CONTINUED)

LISTING 21.11 CircleView.java (View)

model

set model

paint view

```
 1 import java.awt.*;
 2 import java.awt.event.*;
 3
 4 public class CircleView extends javax.swing.JPanel
 5     implements ActionListener {
 6   private CircleModel model;
 7
 8   public void actionPerformed(ActionEvent actionEvent) {
 9     repaint();
10   }
11
12   /** Set a model */
13   public void setModel(CircleModel newModel) {
14     model = newModel;
15
16     if (model != null)
17       // Register the view as listener for the model
18       model.addActionListener(this);
19
20     repaint();
21   }
22
23   public CircleModel getModel() {
24     return model;
25   }
26
27   public void paintComponent(Graphics g) {
28     super.paintComponent(g);
29
30     if (model == null) return;
31
32     g.setColor(model.getColor());
33
34     int xCenter = getWidth() / 2;
35     int yCenter = getHeight() / 2;
36     int radius = (int)model.getRadius();
37
38     if (model.isFilled()) {
39       g.fillOval(xCenter - radius, yCenter - radius,
40         2 * radius, 2 * radius);
41     }
42     else {
43       g.drawOval(xCenter - radius, yCenter - radius,
44         2 * radius, 2 * radius);
45     }
46   }
47 }
```

The controller presents a GUI interface that enables the user to enter circle properties radius, filled, and color. It contains the model as its property. You can use the setModel method to associate a circle model with the controller. It uses a text field to obtain a new radius and a combo box to obtain a boolean value to specify whether the circle is filled. The source code for CircleController is given in Listing 21.12.

LISTING 21.12 CircleController.java (Controller)

```
1 import java.awt.event.*;
2 import java.awt.*;
3 import javax.swing.*;
```

EXAMPLE 21.6 (CONTINUED)

```
4
5  public class CircleController extends JPanel
6      implements ActionListener {
7    private CircleModel model;                                          model
8    private JTextField jtfRadius = new JTextField();
9    private JComboBox jcboFilled = new JComboBox(new Boolean[]{
10     new Boolean(false), new Boolean(true)});
11
12   /** Creates new form CircleController */
13   public CircleController() {
14     // Panel to group labels                                          create UI
15     JPanel panel1 = new JPanel();
16     panel1.setLayout(new GridLayout(3, 1));
17     panel1.add(new JLabel("Radius"));
18     panel1.add(new JLabel("Filled"));
19
20     // Panel to group text field, combo box, and another panel
21     JPanel panel2 = new JPanel();
22     panel2.setLayout(new GridLayout(3, 1));
23     panel2.add(jtfRadius);
24     panel2.add(jcboFilled);
25
26     setLayout(new BorderLayout());
27     add(panel1, BorderLayout.WEST);
28     add(panel2, BorderLayout.CENTER);
29
30     // Register listeners
31     jtfRadius.addActionListener(this);
32     jcboFilled.addActionListener(this);
33   }
34
35   public void actionPerformed(ActionEvent e) {
36     if (model == null) return; // No model associated yet. Do nothing
37
38     if (e.getSource() == jtfRadius)
39       model.setRadius(new Double(jtfRadius.getText()).doubleValue());
40     else if (e.getSource() == jcboFilled)
41       model.setFilled(
42         ((Boolean)jcboFilled.getSelectedItem()).booleanValue());
43   }
44
45   public void setModel(CircleModel newModel) {                        set model
46     model = newModel;
47   }
48
49   public CircleModel getModel() {
50     return model;
51   }
52 }
```

Finally, let us create an applet named MVCDemo with two buttons, *Show Controller* and *Show View*. The Show Controller button displays a controller in a frame, and the Show View button displays a view in a separate frame. The program is shown in Listing 21.13.

LISTING 21.13   **MVCDemo.java**

```
1 import java.awt.*;
2 import java.awt.event.*;
3 import javax.swing.*;
4
5 public class MVCDemo extends JApplet  {
6   private JButton jbtController = new JButton("Show Controller");
```

EXAMPLE 21.6 (CONTINUED)

create model

create UI

set model

set model

```
 7    private JButton jbtView = new JButton("Show View");
 8    private CircleModel model = new CircleModel();
 9
10    public MVCDemo() {
11      getContentPane().setLayout(new FlowLayout());
12      getContentPane().add(jbtController);
13      getContentPane().add(jbtView);
14
15      jbtController.addActionListener(new ActionListener() {
16        public void actionPerformed(ActionEvent e) {
17          JFrame frame = new JFrame("Controller");
18          CircleController controller = new CircleController();
19          controller.setModel(model);
20          frame.getContentPane().add(controller);
21          frame.setSize(200, 200);
22          frame.setLocation(200, 200);
23          frame.setVisible(true);
24        }
25      });
26
27      jbtView.addActionListener(new ActionListener() {
28        public void actionPerformed(ActionEvent e) {
29          JFrame frame = new JFrame("View");
30          CircleView view = new CircleView();
31          view.setModel(model);
32          frame.getContentPane().add(view);
33          frame.setSize(500, 200);
34          frame.setLocation(200, 200);
35          frame.setVisible(true);
36        }
37      });
38    }
39  }
```

Review

The model stores and handles data, and the views are responsible for presenting data. The fundamental issue in the model-view approach is to ensure consistency between the views and the model. Any change in the model should be notified to the dependent views, and all the views should display the same data consistently. The data in the model are changed through the controller.

The methods setRadius, setFilled, and setColor (Lines 21, 33, 45) in CircleModel invoke the processEvent method to notify the listeners of any change in the properties. The setModel method in CircleView sets a new model and registers the view with the model by invoking the model's addActionListener method (Line 18). When the data in the model are changed, the view's actionPerformed method is invoked to repaint the circle (Line 9).

The controller CircleController presents a GUI. You can enter the radius from the radius text field. You can specify whether the circle is filled from the combo box that contains two Boolean objects, new Boolean(false) and new Boolean(true) (Lines 9–10).

Several controllers or views can share a model. Every time you click the Show Controller button in MVCDemo, a new controller is created (Line 18). Every time you click the Show View button, a new view is created (Line 30). All the controllers and views share the same model.

21.9.1 MVC Variations

A variation of the model-view-controller architecture combines the controller with the view. In this case, a view not only presents the data, but is also used as an interface to interact with the user and accept user input, as shown in Figure 21.19.

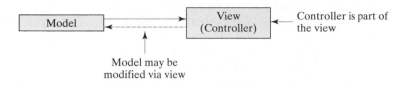

FIGURE 21.19 *The view can interact with the user as well as display data.*

For example, you can modify the view in the preceding example to enable the user to change the circle's radius using the mouse. When the left mouse button is clicked, the radius is increased by 5 pixels. When the right mouse button is clicked, the radius is decreased by 5 pixels. The new view, named `ViewController`, can be implemented by extending `CircleView`, as follows:

```java
public class ViewController extends CircleView {
  public ViewController() {
    // Register mouse listener
    addMouseListener(new java.awt.event.MouseAdapter() {
      public void mousePressed(java.awt.event.MouseEvent e) {
        CircleModel model = getModel(); // Get model

        if (model == null) return;

        if (e.isMetaDown())
          model.setRadius(model.getRadius() - 5); // Right button
        else
          model.setRadius(model.getRadius() + 5); // Left button
      }
    });
  }
}
```

Another variation of the model-view-controller architecture adds some of the data from the model to the view so that frequently used data can be accessed directly from the view.

 NOTE

Swing components are designed using the MVC architecture. Each Swing GUI component is a view that uses a model to store data. A Swing GUI component contains some data in the model so that they can be accessed directly from the component. Swing MVC architecture will be further discussed in Chapter 24, "Advanced Swing Components."

KEY TERMS

anonymous adapter   775
convenience listener adapter   770
event adapter   770
inner class adapter   773
JavaBeans component   752

JavaBeans events   754
JavaBeans properties   753
MVC architecture   776
standard adapter   771

KEY CLASSES AND METHODS

✦ `java.util.EventObject` is the root class for all event classes.

✦ `java.util.EventListener` is the root interface for event listener interfaces.

CHAPTER SUMMARY

✦ JavaBeans is a software component architecture that extends the power of the Java language for building reusable software components. JavaBeans properties describe the state of the bean. Naturally, data fields are used to store properties. However, a bean property is not necessarily a data field.

✦ An event object is created using an event class, such as `ActionEvent`, `MouseEvent`, and `ItemEvent`. All event classes extend `java.util.EventObject`. Every event class is associated with an event listener interface that defines one or more methods referred to as *handlers*. An event listener interface is a subinterface of `java.util.EventListener`. Since an event class and its listener interface are coexistent, they are often referred to as an *event set* or *event pair*.

✦ A source component must have the appropriate registration and deregistration methods for adding and removing listeners. Events can be unicasted (only one object is notified of the event) or multicasted (each object in a list of listeners is notified of the event).

✦ The fundamental issue in the model-view approach is to ensure consistency between the views and the model. Any change in the model should be notified to the dependent views, and all the views should display the same data consistently. The model can be implemented as a source with appropriate event and event listener registration methods. The view can be implemented as a listener. Thus, if data are changed in the model, the view will be notified.

REVIEW QUESTIONS

Sections 21.1–21.4

21.1 What is a JavaBeans component? Is every GUI class a JavaBeans component? Is every GUI user interface component a JavaBeans component? Is it true that a JavaBeans component must be a GUI user interface component?

21.2 Describe the naming conventions for accessor and mutator methods in a JavaBeans component.

21.3 Describe the naming conventions for JavaBeans registration and deregistration methods.

21.4 What is an event pair? How do you declare an event class? How do you declare an event listener interface?

Section 21.8 Event Adapters

21.5 Describe the extended Java event model with adapters?

21.6 What are the advantages of using adapters?

21.7   What is a standard adapter? What is an inner class adapter? What is an anonymous inner class adapter?

Section 21.9 MVC

21.8   What is model-view-controller architecture?

21.9   How do you do implement models, views, and controllers?

21.10   What are variations of MVC architecture?

PROGRAMMING EXERCISES

Sections 21.1–21.8

21.1*   (*Enabling* `MessagePanel` *to fire* `ActionEvent`) The `MessagePanel` class in Section 11.11, "Case Study: The `MessagePanel` Class," is a subclass of `JPanel`; it can fire a `MouseEvent`, `KeyEvent`, and `ComponentEvent`, but not an `ActionEvent`. Modify the `MessagePanel` class so that it can fire an `ActionEvent` when an instance of the `MessagePanel` class is clicked. Name the new class `MessagePanelWithActionEvent`. Test it with a Java applet that displays the current time in a message panel whenever the message panel is clicked, as shown in Figure 21.20.

FIGURE 21.20   *The current time is displayed whenever you click on the message panel.*

21.2*   (*Creating custom event sets and source components*) Develop a project that meets the following requirements:

✦   Create a source component named `MemoryWatch` for monitoring memory. The component generates a `MemoryEvent` when the free memory space exceeds a specified `highLimit` or is below a specified `lowLimit`. The `highLimit` and `lowLimit` are customizable properties in `MemoryWatch`.

✦   Create an event set named `MemoryEvent` and `MemoryListener`. The `MemoryEvent` simply extends `java.util.EventObject` and contains two methods, `freeMemory` and `totalMemory`, which return the free memory and total memory of the system. The `MemoryListener` interface contains two handlers, `sufficientMemory` and `insufficientMemory`. The `sufficientMemory` method is invoked when the free memory space exceeds the specified high limit, and `insufficientMemory` is invoked when the free memory space is less than the specified low limit. The free memory and total memory in the JVM can be obtained by using

```
Runtime runtime = Runtime.getRuntime();
runtime.freeMemory();
runtime.totalMemory();
```

✦ Develop a listener component that displays free memory, total memory, and whether the memory is sufficient or insufficient when a MemoryEvent occurs. Make the listener an applet with a main method to run standalone.

21.3** (*The* Hurricane *source component*) Create a class named Hurricane with properties name and category and its accessor methods. The Hurricane component generates an ActionEvent whenever its category property is changed. Write a listener that displays the hurricane category. If the category is 2 or greater, a message "Hurricane Warning!!!" is displayed, as shown in Figure 21.21.

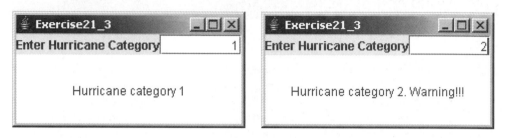

FIGURE 21.21 *Whenever the hurricane category is changed, an appropriate message is displayed in the message panel.*

21.4** (*The* Clock *source component*) Create a JavaBeans component for displaying an analog clock. This bean allows the user to customize a clock through the properties, as shown in Figure 21.22. Write a test program that displays four clocks, as shown in Figure 21.23.

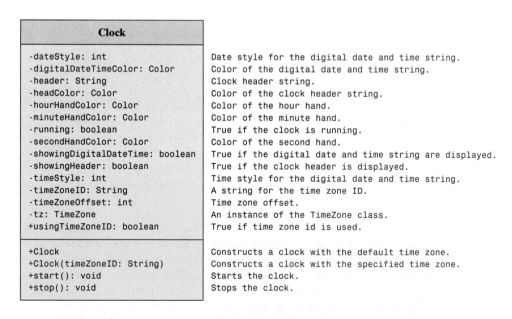

Clock
-dateStyle: int   Date style for the digital date and time string.

-dateStyle: int — Date style for the digital date and time string.
-digitalDateTimeColor: Color — Color of the digital date and time string.
-header: String — Clock header string.
-headColor: Color — Color of the clock header string.
-hourHandColor: Color — Color of the hour hand.
-minuteHandColor: Color — Color of the minute hand.
-running: boolean — True if the clock is running.
-secondHandColor: Color — Color of the second hand.
-showingDigitalDateTime: boolean — True if the digital date and time string are displayed.
-showingHeader: boolean — True if the clock header is displayed.
-timeStyle: int — Time style for the digital date and time string.
-timeZoneID: String — A string for the time zone ID.
-timeZoneOffset: int — Time zone offset.
-tz: TimeZone — An instance of the TimeZone class.
+usingTimeZoneID: boolean — True if time zone id is used.

+Clock — Constructs a clock with the default time zone.
+Clock(timeZoneID: String) — Constructs a clock with the specified time zone.
+start(): void — Starts the clock.
+stop(): void — Stops the clock.

FIGURE 21.22 *The* Clock *component displays an analog clock.*

21.5* (*Creating* ClockWithAlarm *from* Clock) Create an alarm clock, named ClockWithAlarm, which extends the Clock component built in the preceding exercise, as shown in

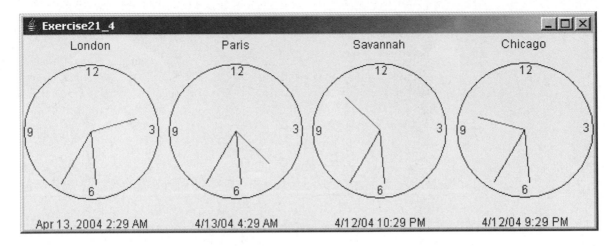

FIGURE 21.23   *The program displays four clocks using the* `Clock` *component.*

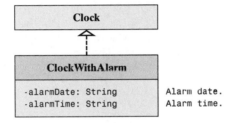

FIGURE 21.24   *The* `ClockWithAlarm` *component extends* `Clock` *with alarm functions.*

Figure 21.24. This component contains two new properties, `alarmDate` and `alarmTime`. `alarmDate` is a string consisting of year, month, and day, separated by commas. For example, 1998,5,13 represents the year 1998, month 5, and day 13. `alarmTime` is a string consisting of hour, minute, and second, separated by commas. For example, 10,45,2 represents 10 hours, 45 minutes, and 2 seconds. When the clock time matches the alarm time, `ClockWithAlarm` fires an `ActionEvent`. Write a test program that displays the alert message `"You have an appointment now"` on a dialog box at a specified time (e.g., date: 2004,1,1 and time: 10,30,0).

Section 21.9 MVC

21.6*** (*Creating MVC components*) Create a model, named `Exercise21_6ChartModel`, which holds data in an array of double elements named `data`, and the names for the data in an array of strings named `dataName`. For example, the enrollment data {200, 40, 50, 100, 40} stored in the array `data` are for {`"CS"`, `"Math"`, `"Chem"`, `"Biol"`, `"Phys"`} in the array `dataName`. These two properties have their respective get methods, but not individual set methods. Both properties are set together in the `setChartData(String[] newDataName, double[] newData)` method so that they can be displayed properly. Create a view named `Exercise21_6PieChart` to present the data in a pie chart, and create a view named `Exercise21_6BarChart` to present the data in a bar chart, as shown in Figure 21.25. In Exercise 24.13, you will create a controller that enables the user to insert, delete, and update data interactively using a table.

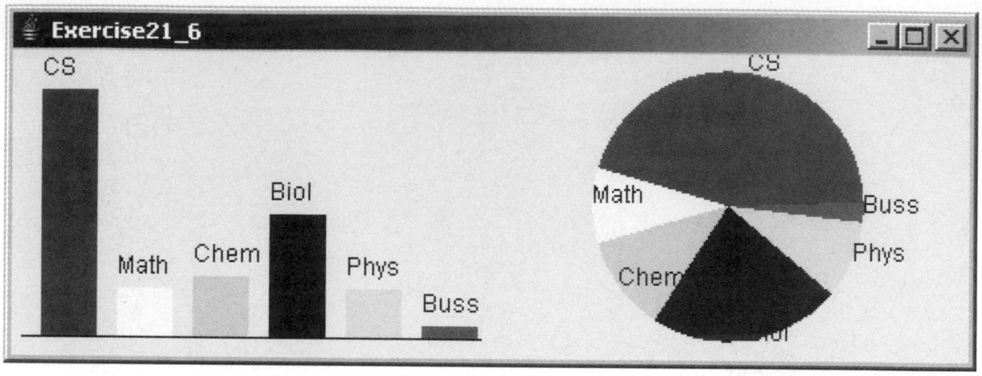

FIGURE 21.25 *The two views,* PieChart *and* BarChart, *receive data from the* ChartModel.

🌿 **HINT**

Each pie represents a percentage of the total data. Color the pie using the colors from an array named colors, which is {Color.red, Color.yellow, Color.green, Color.blue, Color.cyan, Color.magenta, Color.orange, Color.pink, Color.darkGray}. Use colors[i%colors.length] for the *i*th pie. Use black color to display the data names.

chapter

22

CONTAINERS, LAYOUT MANAGERS, AND BORDERS

Objectives

✦ To know the internal structures of the Swing container (§22.2).

✦ To understand how a layout manager works in Java (§22.3).

✦ To know how to use CardLayout, GridBagLayout, BoxLayout, OverlayLayout, and SpringLayout (§22.3).

✦ To create custom layout managers (§22.4).

✦ To use JScrollPane to create scroll panes (§22.5).

✦ To use JTabbedPane to create tabbed panes (§22.6).

✦ To use JSplitPane to create split panes (§22.7).

✦ To use various borders for Swing components (§22.8).

22.1 Introduction

container
layout manager

Chapter 11, "Getting Started with GUI Programming," introduced the concept of containers and the role of layout managers. You learned how to add components into a container and how to use FlowLayout, BorderLayout, and GridLayout to arrange components in a container. A *container* is an object that holds and groups components. A *layout manager* is a special object used to place components in a container. Containers and layout managers play a crucial role in creating user interfaces. This chapter presents a conceptual overview of containers, reviews the layout managers in Java, and introduces several new containers and layout managers. You will also learn how to create custom layout managers and use various borders.

22.2 Swing Container Structures

User interface components like JButton cannot be displayed without being placed in a container. A container is a component that is capable of containing other components. You do not display a user interface component; you place it in a container, and the container displays the components it contains.

The base class for all containers is java.awt.Container, which is a subclass of java.awt.Component. The Container class has the following essential functions:

◆ It adds and removes components using various add and remove methods.

◆ It maintains a layout property for specifying a layout manager that is used to lay out components in the container. Every container has a default layout manager.

◆ It provides registration methods for the java.awt.event.ContainerEvent.

In AWT programming, the java.awt.Frame class is used as a top-level container for Java applications, the java.awt.Applet class is used for all Java applets, and java.awt.Dialog is used for dialog windows. These classes do not work properly with Swing lightweight components. Special versions of Frame, Applet, and Dialog named JFrame, JApplet, and JDialog have been developed to accommodate Swing components. JFrame is a subclass of Frame, JApplet is a subclass of Applet, and JDialog is a subclass of Dialog. JFrame and JApplet inherit all the functions of their heavyweight counterparts, but they have a more complex internal structure with several layered panes, as shown in Figure 22.1.

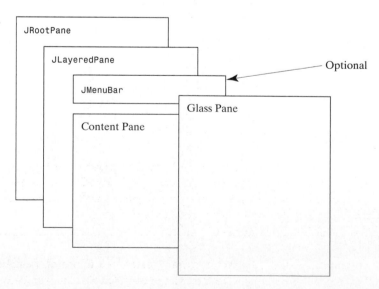

FIGURE 22.1 *Swing top-level containers use layers of panes to group lightweight components and make them work properly.*

javax.swing.JRootPane is a lightweight container used behind the scenes by Swing's top-level containers, such as JFrame, JApplet, and JDialog. javax.swing.JLayeredPane is a container that manages the optional menu bar and the content pane. The content pane is an instance of Container. By default, it is a JPanel with BorderLayout. This is the container where the user interface components are added. To obtain the content pane in a JFrame or in a JApplet, use the getContentPane() method. If you wish to set an instance of Container to be a new content pane, use the setContentPane method. The glass pane floats on top of everything. javax.swing.JGlassPane is a hidden pane by default. If you make the glass pane visible, then it's like a sheet of glass over all the other parts of the root pane. It's completely transparent unless you implement the glass pane's paint method so that it does something, and it intercepts input events for the root pane. In general, JRootPane, JLayeredPane, and JGlassPane are not used directly.

Now let us review the three most frequently used Swing containers: JFrame, JApplet, and JPanel.

22.2.1 JFrame

JFrame, a Swing version of Frame, is a top-level container for Java graphics applications. Like Frame, JFrame is displayed as a standalone window with a title bar and a border. The following properties are often useful in JFrame:

+ contentPane is the content pane of the frame.

+ iconImage is the image that represents the frame. This image replaces the default Java image on the frame's title bar and is also displayed when the frame is minimized. This property type is Image. You can get an image using the ImageIcon class, as follows:

  ```
  Image image = (new ImageIcon(filename)).getImage();
  ```

+ jMenuBar is the optional menu bar for the frame.

+ resizable is a boolean value indicating whether the frame is resizable. The default value is true.

+ title specifies the title of the frame.

22.2.2 JApplet

JApplet is a Swing version of Applet. Since it is a subclass of Applet, it has all the functions required by the Web browser. Here are the four essential methods defined in Applet:

```
// Called by the browser after an applet is constructed
public void init()

// Called by the browser after the init() method and
// every time the Web page is visited.
public void start()

// Called by the browser when the page containing this
// applet becomes inactive.
public void stop()

// Called by the browser when the Web browser exits.
public void destroy()
```

Additionally, JApplet has the contentPane and jMenuBar properties, among others. As with JFrame, you do not place components directly into JApplet; instead you place them into the content pane of the applet. The Applet class cannot have a menu bar, but the JApplet class allows you to set a menu bar using the setJMenuBar method.

NOTE

When an applet is loaded, the Web browser creates an instance of the applet by invoking the applet's no-arg constructor. So the constructor is invoked before the init method.

22.2.3 `JPanel`

Panels act as subcontainers for grouping user interface components. `javax.swing.JPanel` is different from `JFrame` and `JApplet`. First, `JPanel` is not a top-level container; it must be placed inside another container, and it can be placed inside another `JPanel`. Second, since `JPanel` is a subclass of `JComponent`, it is a lightweight component, but `JFrame` and `JApplet` are heavyweight components.

`JPanel` is a Swing version of `Panel`, but it is not a subclass of `Panel`. Nevertheless, you can use `JPanel` the same way you use `Panel`. As a subclass of `JComponent`, `JPanel` can take advantage of `JComponent`, such as double buffering and borders. You should draw figures on `JPanel` rather than `JFrame` or `JApplet`, because `JPanel` supports double buffering, which is a technique for eliminating flickers.

22.3 Layout Managers

Every container has a layout manager that is responsible for arranging its components. The container's `setLayout` method can be used to set a layout manager. Certain types of containers have default layout managers. For instance, the content pane of `JFrame` or `JApplet` uses `BorderLayout`, and `JPanel` uses `FlowLayout`.

The layout manager places the components in accordance with its own rules and property settings, and with the constraints associated with each component. Every layout manager has its own specific set of rules. For example, the `FlowLayout` manager places components in rows from left to right and starts a new row when the previous row is filled. The `BorderLayout` manager places components in the north, south, east, west, or center of the container. The `GridLayout` manager places components in a grid of cells in rows and columns from left to right in order.

Some layout managers have properties that can affect the sizing and location of the components in the container. For example, `BorderLayout` has properties called `hgap` (horizontal gap) and `vgap` (vertical gap) that determine the distance between components horizontally and vertically. `FlowLayout` has properties that can be used to specify the alignment (left, center, right) of the components and properties for specifying the horizontal or vertical gap between the components. `GridLayout` has properties that can be used to specify the horizontal or vertical gap between columns and rows and properties for specifying the number of rows and columns. These properties can be retrieved and set using their accessor and mutator methods

The size of a component in a container is determined by many factors, such as:

✦ The type of layout manager used by the container.

✦ The layout constraints associated with each component.

✦ The size of the container.

✦ Certain properties common to all components (such as `preferredSize`, `minimumSize`, `maximumSize`, `alignmentX`, and `alignmentY`).

preferredSize

The `preferredSize` property indicates the ideal size at which the component looks best. Depending on the rules of the particular layout manager, this property may or may not be considered. For example, the preferred size of a component is used in a container with a `FlowLayout` manager, but ignored if it is placed in a container with a `GridLayout` manager.

minimumSize

The `minimumSize` property specifies the minimum size at which the component is useful. For most GUI components, `minimumSize` is the same as `preferredSize`. Layout managers generally respect `minimumSize` more than `preferredSize`.

maximumSize

The `maximumSize` property specifies the maximum size needed by a component, so that the layout manager won't wastefully give space to a component that does not need it. For instance,

BorderLayout limits the center component's size to its maximum size, and gives the space to edge components.

The alignmentX (alignmentY) property specifies how the component would like to be aligned relative to other components along the x-axis (y-axis). This value should be a number between 0 and 1, where 0 represents alignment along the origin, 1 is aligned the farthest away from the origin, 0.5 is centered, and so on. These two properties are used in the BoxLayout and OverlayLayout.

Java provides a variety of layout managers. You have learned how to use BorderLayout, FlowLayout, and GridLayout. The following sections will introduce CardLayout, GridBagLayout, Null layout, BoxLayout, OverlayLayout, and SpringLayout.

 TIP

If you set a new layout manager in a container, invoke the container's validate() method to force the container to again lay out the components. If you change the properties of a layout manager in a JFrame or JApplet, invoke the doLayout() method to force the container to again lay out the components using the new layout properties. If you change the properties of a layout manager in a JPanel, invoke either the doLayout() or revalidate() method to force it to again lay out the components using the new layout properties, but it is better to use revalidate(). Note that validate() is a public method defined in java.awt.Container, revalidate() is a public method defined in javax.swing.JComponent, and doLayout() is a public method defined in java.awt.Container.

22.3.1   CardLayout

CardLayout places components in the container as cards. Only one card is visible at a time, and the container acts as a stack of cards. The ordering of cards is determined by the container's own internal ordering of its component objects. You can specify the size of the horizontal and vertical gaps surrounding a stack of components in a CardLayout manager, as shown in Figure 22.2.

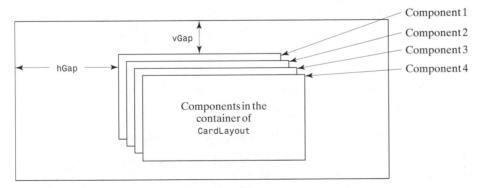

FIGURE 22.2   *The CardLayout places components in the container as a stack of cards.*

CardLayout defines a set of methods that allow an application to flip through the cards sequentially or to show a specified card directly, as shown in Figure 22.3.

To add a component into a container, use the add(Component c, String name) method defined in the LayoutManager interface. The String parameter, name, gives an explicit identity to the component in the container.

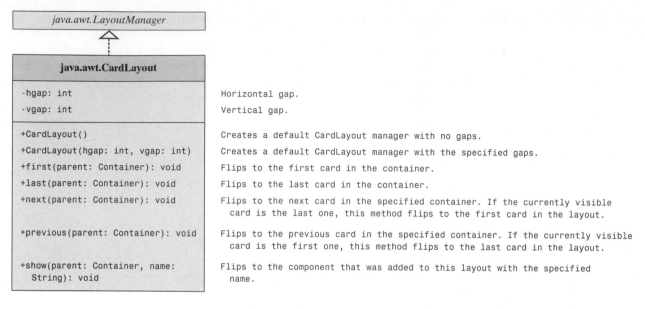

FIGURE 22.3 *CardLayout contains the methods to flip the card.*

EXAMPLE 22.1 USING CardLayout

Problem

Write a program that creates two panels in a frame. The first panel uses CardLayout to hold nine labels for displaying images. The second panel uses FlowLayout to group four buttons named First, Next, Previous, and Last, and a combo box labeled Image, as shown in Figure 22.4.

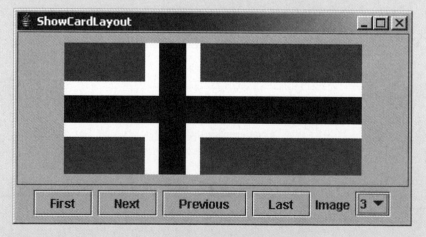

FIGURE 22.4 *The program shows images in a panel of CardLayout.*

These buttons control which image will be shown in the CardLayout panel. When the user clicks the button named First, for example, the first image in the CardLayout panel appears. The combo box enables the user to directly select an image.

Solution

Listing 22.1 gives the solution to the program.

EXAMPLE 22.1 (CONTINUED)

LISTING 22.1 ShowCardLayout.java

```
1  import java.awt.*;
2  import java.awt.event.*;
3  import javax.swing.*;
4  import javax.swing.border.*;
5
6  public class ShowCardLayout extends JApplet
7      implements ActionListener, ItemListener {
8    private CardLayout cardLayout = new CardLayout(20, 10);
9    private JPanel cardPanel = new JPanel(cardLayout);
10   private JButton jbtFirst, jbtNext, jbtPrevious, jbtLast;
11   private JComboBox jcboImage;
12   private final int NUM_OF_FLAGS = 9;
13
14   public ShowCardLayout() {
15     cardPanel.setBorder(
16       new javax.swing.border.LineBorder(Color.red));
17
18     // Add 9 labels for displaying images into cardPanel
19     for (int i = 1; i <= NUM_OF_FLAGS; i++) {
20       JLabel label =
21         new JLabel(new ImageIcon("image/flag" + i + ".gif"));
22       cardPanel.add(label, String.valueOf(i));
23     }
24
25     // Panel p to hold buttons and a combo box
26     JPanel p = new JPanel();
27     p.add(jbtFirst = new JButton("First"));
28     p.add(jbtNext = new JButton("Next"));
29     p.add(jbtPrevious = new JButton("Previous"));
30     p.add(jbtLast = new JButton("Last"));
31     p.add(new JLabel("Image"));
32     p.add(jcboImage = new JComboBox());
33
34     // Initialize combo box items
35     for (int i = 1; i <= NUM_OF_FLAGS; i++)
36       jcboImage.addItem(String.valueOf(i));
37
38     // Place panels in the frame
39     getContentPane().add(cardPanel, BorderLayout.CENTER);
40     getContentPane().add(p, BorderLayout.SOUTH);
41
42     // Register listeners with the source objects
43     jbtFirst.addActionListener(this);
44     jbtNext.addActionListener(this);
45     jbtPrevious.addActionListener(this);
46     jbtLast.addActionListener(this);
47     jcboImage.addItemListener(this);
48   }
49
50   /** Handle button actions */
51   public void actionPerformed(ActionEvent e) {
52     String actionCommand = e.getActionCommand();
53     if (e.getSource() instanceof JButton)
54       if ("First".equals(actionCommand))
55         // Show the first component in cardPanel
56         cardLayout.first(cardPanel);
57       else if ("Last".equals(actionCommand))
58         // Show the last component in cardPanel
59         cardLayout.last(cardPanel);
60       else if ("Previous".equals(actionCommand))
61         // Show the previous component in cardPanel
62         cardLayout.previous(cardPanel);
63       else if ("Next".equals(actionCommand))
64         // Show the next component in cardPanel
65         cardLayout.next(cardPanel);
66   }
```

card layout

create UI

register listener

EXAMPLE 22.1 (CONTINUED)

```
67
68   /** Handle selection of combo box item */
69   public void itemStateChanged(ItemEvent e) {
70     if (e.getSource() == jcboImage)
71       // Show the component at specified index
72       cardLayout.show(cardPanel, (String)e.getItem());
73   }
74 }
```

main method omitted

Review

An instance of `CardLayout` is created in Line 8, and a panel of `CardLayout` is created in Line 9. You have already used such statements as `setLayout(new FlowLayout())` to create an anonymous layout object and set the layout for a container, instead of declaring and creating a separate instance of the layout manager, as in this program. The `cardLayout` object, however, is useful later in the program to show components in `cardPanel`. You have to use `cardLayout.first(cardPanel)` (Line 56), for example, to view the first component in `cardPanel`.

The statement in Lines 20–22 adds the image label with the identity `String.valueOf(i)`. Later, when the user selects an image with number `i`, the identity `String.valueOf(i)` is used in the `cardLayout.show()` method (Line 72) to view the image with the specified identity.

22.3.2 The `GridBagLayout` Manager (Optional)

The `GridBagLayout` manager is the most flexible and the most complex. It is similar to the `GridLayout` manager in the sense that both layout managers arrange components in a grid. The components of `GridBagLayout` can vary in size, however, and can be added in any order. For example, with `GridBagLayout` you can create the layout shown in Figure 22.5.

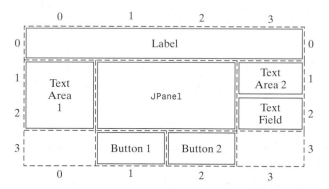

FIGURE 22.5 *A* `GridBagLayout` *manager divides the container into cells. A component can occupy several cells.*

The constructor `GridBagLayout()` is used to create a new `GridBagLayout`. In `GridLayout`, the grid size (the number of rows and columns) may be specified in the constructor. It is not specified in `GridBagLayout`. The actual size is dynamically determined by the constraints associated with the components added to the container of `GridBagLayout`.

Each `GridBagLayout` uses a dynamic rectangular grid of cells, with each component occupying one or more cells called its *display area*. Each component managed by a `GridBagLayout` is associated with a `GridBagConstraints` instance that specifies how the component is laid out within its display area. How a `GridBagLayout` places a set of components depends on the `GridBagConstraints` and minimum size of each component, as well as the preferred size of the component's container.

To use `GridBagLayout` effectively, you must customize the `GridBagConstraints` of one or more of its components. You customize a `GridBagConstraints` object by setting one or more of its public instance variables. These variables specify the component's location, size, growth factor, anchor, inset, filling, and padding.

22.3.2.1 Location

The variables `gridx` and `gridy` specify the cell at the upper left of the component's display area, where the upper-leftmost cell has the address `gridx=0`, `gridy=0`. Note that `gridx` specifies the column in which the component will be placed, and `gridy` specifies the row in which it will be placed. In Figure 22.5, Button 1 has a `gridx` value of 1 and a `gridy` value of 3, and Label has a `gridx` value of 0 and a `gridy` value of 0.

You can assign `GridBagConstraints.RELATIVE` to `gridx` to specify that the component be placed immediately after the component that was just added to the container. You can assign `GridBagConstraints.RELATIVE` to `gridy` to specify that the component be placed immediately below the component that was just added to the container.

22.3.2.2 Size

The variables `gridwidth` and `gridheight` specify the number of cells in a row (for `gridheight`) or column (for `gridwidth`) in the component's display area. The default value is 1. In Figure 22.5, the `JPanel` in the center occupies two columns and two rows, so its `gridwidth` is 2, and its `gridheight` is 2. Text Area 2 occupies one row and one column; therefore its `gridwidth` is 1, and its `gridheight` is 1.

You can assign `GridBagConstraints.RELATIVE.REMAINDER` to `gridwidth` to specify that the component is to be the last one in its row, and assign `GridBagConstraints.RELATIVE` to `gridheight` to specify that the component is to be the next-to-last one in its column.

22.3.2.3 Growth Weight

The variables `weightx` and `weighty` specify the extra horizontal and vertical space to allocate for the component when the resulting layout is smaller horizontally than the area it needs to fill.

The `GridBagLayout` manager calculates the weight of a column to be the maximum `weightx` (`weighty`) of all the components in a column (row). The extra space is distributed to each column (row) in proportion to its weight.

Unless you specify a weight for at least one component in a row (`weightx`) and a column (`weighty`), all the components clump together in the center of their container. This is because, when the weight is zero (the default), the `GridBagLayout` puts any extra space between its grid of cells and the edges of the container. You will see the effect of these parameters in Example 22.2.

22.3.2.4 Anchor

The variable `anchor` specifies where in the area the component is placed when it does not fill the entire area. Valid values are:

```
GridBagConstraints.CENTER (the default)
GridBagConstraints.NORTH
GridBagConstraints.NORTHEAST
GridBagConstraints.EAST
GridBagConstraints.SOUTHEAST
GridBagConstraints.SOUTH
GridBagConstraints.SOUTHWEST
GridBagConstraints.WEST
GridBagConstraints.NORTHWEST
```

22.3.2.5 Filling

The variable `fill` specifies how the component should be resized if its viewing area is larger than its current size. Valid values are `GridBagConstraints.NONE` (the default), `GridBagConstraints.HORIZONTAL` (makes the component wide enough to fill its display area horizontally, but doesn't change its height), `GridBagConstraints.VERTICAL` (makes the component tall enough to fill its display area vertically, but doesn't change its width), and GridBagConstraints.BOTH (makes the component totally fill its display area).

22.3.2.6 Insets

The variable insets specifies the external padding of the component, the minimum amount of space between the component and the edges of its display area. The default value is new Insets(0, 0, 0, 0).

22.3.2.7 Padding

The variables ipadx and ipady specify the internal padding of the component: how much space to add to its minimum width and height. The width of the component is at least its minimum width plus (ipadx * 2) pixels, and the height of the component is at least its minimum height plus (ipady * 2) pixels. The default value of these variables is 0. The insets variable specifies the external padding, while the ipadx and ipady variables specify the internal padding, as shown in Figure 22.6.

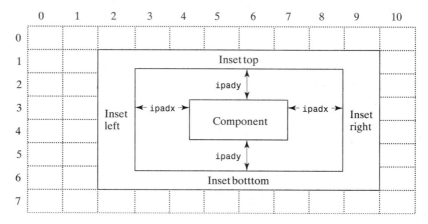

FIGURE 22.6 *You can specify the external insets and internal padding for a component in the container of the* GridBadLayout *manager.*

22.3.2.8 Constructing a GridBagConstraints Object

There are two constructors for creating a GridBagConstraints object:

✦ public GridBagConstraints()

Constructs a GridBagConstraints object with all of its fields set to their default values.

✦ public GridBagConstraints(int gridx, int gridy, int gridwidth,
    int gridheight, double weightx,
    double weighty, int anchor, int fill,
    Insets insets, int ipadx, int ipady)

Constructs a GridBagConstraints object with the specified field values.

22.3.2.9 Adding a Component to the Container of GridBagLayout

To add a component to the container of GridBagLayout, use the following method in the container:

public void add(Component comp, Object gbConstraints)

This adds a component to the container with the specified GridBagConstraints.

EXAMPLE 22.2 USING `GridBagLayout`

Problem

Write a program that uses the `GridBagLayout` manager to create a layout for Figure 22.5. The output of the program is shown in Figure 22.7.

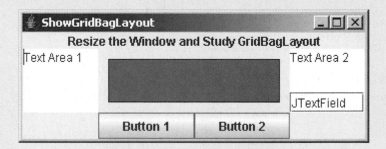

FIGURE 22.7 *The components are placed in the frame of* `GridBagLayout`.

Solution

Listing 22.2 gives the solution to the problem.

LISTING 22.2 ShowGridBagLayout.java

```
1 import java.awt.*;
2 import javax.swing.*;
3
4 public class ShowGridBagLayout extends JApplet {
5   private JLabel jlbl = new JLabel(                                    UI components
6     "Resize the Window and Study GridBagLayout", JLabel.CENTER);
7   private JTextArea jta1 = new JTextArea("Text Area1", 5, 15 );
8   private JTextArea jta2 = new JTextArea("Text Area2", 5, 15 );
9   private JTextField jtf = new JTextField("JTextField");
10  private JPanel jp = new JPanel();
11  private JButton jbt1 = new JButton("Button 1");
12  private JButton jbt2 = new JButton("Button 2");
13
14  public ShowGridBagLayout() {
15    // Set GridBagLayout in the container                              create UI
16    Container container = getContentPane();
17    container.setLayout(new GridBagLayout());
18
19    // Create a GridBagConstraints object
20    GridBagConstraints gbConstraints = new GridBagConstraints();
21
22    gbConstraints.fill = GridBagConstraints.BOTH;
23    gbConstraints.anchor = GridBagConstraints.CENTER;
24
25    // Place JLabel to occupy row 0 (the first row)
26    addComp(jlbl, container, gbConstraints, 0, 0, 1, 4, 0, 0);
27
28    // Place text area 1 in row 1 and 2, and column 0
29    addComp(jta1, container, gbConstraints, 1, 0, 2, 1, 5, 1);
30
31    // Place text area 2 in row 1 and column 3
32    addComp(jta2, container, gbConstraints, 1, 3, 1, 1, 5, 1);
33
34    // Place text field in row 2 and column 3
35    addComp(jtf, container, gbConstraints, 2, 3, 1, 1, 5, 0);
```

EXAMPLE 22.2 (CONTINUED)

```
36
37        // Place JButton 1 in row 3 and column 1
38        addComp(jbt1, container, gbConstraints, 3, 1, 1, 1, 5, 0);
39
40        // Place JButton 2 in row 3 and column 2
41        addComp(jbt2, container, gbConstraints, 3, 2, 1, 1, 5, 0);
42
43        // Place Panel in row 1 and 2, and column 1 and 2
44        jp.setBackground(Color.red);
45        jp.setBorder(new javax.swing.border.LineBorder(Color.black));
46        gbConstraints.insets = new Insets(10, 10, 10, 10);
47        addComp(jp, container, gbConstraints, 1, 1, 2, 2, 10, 1);
48      }
49
50      /** Add a component to the container of GridBagLayout */
51      private void addComp(Component c, Container container,
52                           GridBagConstraints gbConstraints,
53                           int row, int column,
54                           int numberOfRows,  int numberOfColumns,
55                           double weightx, double weighty) {
56        // Set parameters
57        gbConstraints.gridx = column;
58        gbConstraints.gridy = row;
59        gbConstraints.gridwidth = numberOfColumns;
60        gbConstraints.gridheight = numberOfRows;
61        gbConstraints.weightx = weightx;
62        gbConstraints.weighty = weighty;
63
64        // Add component to the container with the specified layout
65        container.add(c, gbConstraints);
66      }
67    }
```

set constraints

main method omitted

Review

The program defines the addComp method (Lines 51–66) to add a component to the container of GridBagLayout with the specified constraints. The GridBagConstraints object gbConstraints created in Line 20 is used to specify the layout constraints for each component. Before adding a component to the container, set the constraints in gbConstraints and then use container.add(c, gbConstraints) (Line 65) to add the component to the container.

What would happen if you change the weightx parameter for jbt2 to 10 in Line 41? Now jbt2's weightx is larger than jbt1's. When you enlarge the window, jbt2 will get larger horizontally than jbt1.

The weightx and weighty for all the other components are 0. Whether the size of these components grows or shrinks depends on the fill parameter. The program defines fill = BOTH for all the components added to the container (Line 22).

Consider this scenario: Suppose that you enlarge the window. The display area for text area jta1 will increase. Because fill is BOTH for jta1, jta1 fills in its new display area. If you set fill to NONE for jta1, jta1 will not expand or shrink when you resize the window.

The insets parameter is (0, 0, 0, 0) by default. For the panel jp, insets is set to (10, 10, 10, 10) (Line 46).

22.3.3 Using No Layout Manager

If you have used a Windows-based RAD tool like Visual Basic, you know that it is easier to create user interfaces with Visual Basic than in Java. This is mainly because the components are placed in absolute positions and sizes in Visual Basic, whereas they are placed in containers using a variety of layout managers in Java. Absolute positions and sizes are fine if the application is developed and deployed on the same platform, but what looks fine on a development system may not look right on a deployment system. To solve this problem, Java provides a set of layout managers that place components in containers in a way that is independent of fonts, screen resolutions, and platform differences.

For convenience, Java also supports absolute layout that enables you to place components at a fixed location. In this case, the component must be placed using the component's instance method setBounds() (defined in java.awt.Component), as follows:

```
public void setBounds(int x, int y, int width, int height);
```

This sets the location and size for the component, as in the next example:

```
JButton jbt = new JButton("Help");
jbt.setBounds(10, 10, 40, 20);
```

The upper-left corner of the Help button is placed at (10, 10); the button width is 40, and the height is 20.

You perform the following steps in order not to use a layout manager:

1. Use this statement to specify no layout manager:

   ```
   setLayout(null);
   ```

2. Add the component to the container:

   ```
   add(component);
   ```

3. Specify the location where the component is to be placed, using the setBounds() method:

   ```
   JButton jbt = new JButton("Help");
   jbt.setBounds(10, 10, 40, 20);
   ```

EXAMPLE 22.3 USING NO LAYOUT MANAGER

Problem

Write a program that places the same components in the same layout as in the preceding example but without using a layout manager. Figure 22.8 contains the sample output.

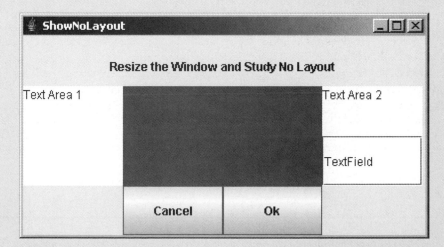

FIGURE 22.8 *The components are placed in the frame without using a layout manager.*

EXAMPLE 22.3 (CONTINUED)

Solution

Listing 22.3 gives the solution to the problem.

LISTING 22.3   ShowNoLayout.java

UI components

create UI

```
 1 import java.awt.*;
 2 import java.awt.event.*;
 3 import javax.swing.*;
 4
 5 public class ShowNoLayout extends JApplet {
 6   private JLabel jlbl =
 7     new JLabel("Resize the Window and Study No Layout",
 8       JLabel.CENTER);
 9   private JTextArea jta1 = new JTextArea("Text Area 1", 5, 10 );
10   private JTextArea jta2 = new JTextArea("Text Area 2", 5, 10 );
11   private JTextField jtf = new JTextField("TextField");
12   private JPanel jp = new JPanel();
13   private JButton jbt1 = new JButton("Cancel" );
14   private JButton jbt2 = new JButton("Ok" );
15   private GridBagLayout gbLayout;
16   private GridBagConstraints gbConstraints;
17
18   public ShowNoLayout() {
19     // Set background color for the panel
20     jp.setBackground(Color.red);
21
22     // Specify no layout manager
23     getContentPane().setLayout(null);
24
25     // Add components to frame
26     getContentPane().add(jlbl);
27     getContentPane().add(jp);
28     getContentPane().add(jta1);
29     getContentPane().add(jta2);
30     getContentPane().add(jtf);
31     getContentPane().add(jbt1);
32     getContentPane().add(jbt2);
33
34     // Put components in the right place
35     jlbl.setBounds(0, 10, 400, 40);
36     jta1.setBounds(0, 50, 100, 100);
37     jp.setBounds(100, 50, 200, 100);
38     jta2.setBounds(300, 50, 100, 50);
39     jtf.setBounds(300, 100, 100, 50);
40     jbt1.setBounds(100, 150, 100, 50);
41     jbt2.setBounds(200, 150, 100, 50);
42   }
43 }
```

main method omitted

Review

If you run this program on Windows with 640 × 480 resolution, the layout size is just right. When the program is run on Windows with a higher resolution, the components appear very small and clump together. When it is run on Windows with a lower resolution, they cannot be shown in their entirety.

If you resize the window, you will see that the location and size of the components are not changed, as shown in Figure 22.9.

 TIP

Do not use the no-layout-manager option to develop platform-independent applications.

EXAMPLE 22.3 (CONTINUED)

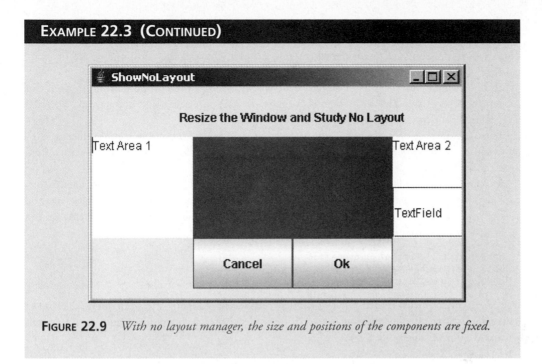

FIGURE 22.9   *With no layout manager, the size and positions of the components are fixed.*

22.3.3 BoxLayout

javax.swing.BoxLayout is a Swing layout manager that arranges components in a row or a column. To create a BoxLayout, use the following constructor:

```
public BoxLayout(Container target, int axis)
```

This constructor is different from other layout constructors. It creates a layout manager that is dedicated to the given target container. The axis parameter is BoxLayout.X_AXIS or BoxLayout.Y_AXIS, which specifies whether the components are laid out horizontally or vertically. For example, the following code creates a horizontal BoxLayout for panel p1:

```
JPanel p1 = new JPanel();
BoxLayout boxLayout = new BoxLayout(p1, BoxLayout.X_AXIS);
p1.setLayout(boxLayout);
```

You still need to invoke the setLayout method on p1 to set the layout manager.

You can use BoxLayout in any container, but it is simpler to use the Box class, which is a container of BoxLayout. To create a Box container, use one of the following two static methods:

```
Box box1 = Box.createHorizontalBox();
Box box2 = Box.createVerticalBox();
```

The former creates a box that contains components horizontally, and the latter creates a box that contains components vertically.

You can add components to a box in the same way that you add them to the containers of FlowLayout or GridLayout using the add method, as follows:

```
box1.add(new JButton("A Button"));
```

You can remove components from a box in the same way that you drop components to a container. The components are laid left to right in a horizontal box, and top to bottom in a vertical box.

BoxLayout is similar to GridLayout but has many unique features.

First, BoxLayout respects a component's preferred size, maximum size, and minimum size. If the total preferred size of all the components in the box is less than the box size, then the components are expanded up to their maximum size. If the total preferred size of all the components in the box is greater than the box size, then the components are shrunk down to their minimum size. If the components do not fit at their minimum width, some of them will not be shown. In GridLayout, the container is divided into cells of equal size, and the components are fit in regardless of their preferred maximum or minimum size.

Second, unlike other layout managers, BoxLayout considers the component's alignmentX or alignmentY property. The alignmentX property is used in a vertical box layout, and the alignmentY property is used in a horizontal box layout.

Third, BoxLayout does not have gaps between the components, but you can use fillers to separate components. A filler is an invisible component. There are three kinds of fillers: struts, rigid areas, and glues.

strut

A *strut* simply adds some space between components. The static method createHorizontalStrut(int) in the Box class is used to create a horizontal strut, and the static method createVerticalStrut(int) to create a vertical strut. For example, the code shown below adds a vertical strut of 8 pixels between two buttons in a vertical box:

```
box2.add(new JButton("Button 1"));
box2.add(Box.createVerticalStrut(8));
box2.add(new JButton("Button 2"));
```

rigid area

A *rigid area* is a two-dimensional space that can be created using the static method createRigidArea(dimension) in the Box class. For example, the next code adds a rigid area 10 pixels wide and 20 pixels high into a box:

```
box2.add(Box.createRigidArea(new Dimension(10, 20)));
```

glue

A *glue* separates components as much as possible. For example, by adding a glue between two components in a horizontal box, you place one component at the left end and the other at the right end. A glue can be created using the Box.createGlue() method.

EXAMPLE 22.4 USING THE BoxLayout MANAGER

Problem

Write a program that creates a horizontal box and a vertical box. The horizontal box holds two buttons with print and save icons. The horizontal box holds four buttons for selecting flags. When a button in the vertical box is clicked, a corresponding flag icon is displayed in the label centered in the applet, as shown in Figure 22.10.

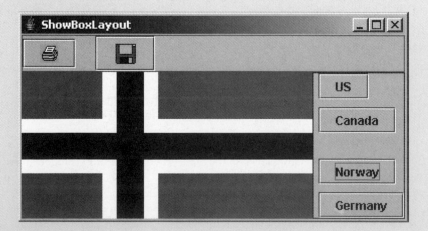

FIGURE 22.10   *The components are placed in the containers of BoxLayout.*

EXAMPLE 22.4 (CONTINUED)

Solution

Listing 22.4 gives the solution to the problem.

LISTING 22.4 **ShowBoxLayout.java**

```
1 import java.awt.*;
2 import java.awt.event.*;
3 import javax.swing.*;
4
5 public class ShowBoxLayout extends JApplet
6     implements ActionListener {
7   // Create two box containers
8   private Box box1 = Box.createHorizontalBox();
9   private Box box2 = Box.createVerticalBox();
10
11  // Create a label to display flags
12  private JLabel jlblFlag = new JLabel();
13
14  // Create image icons for flags
15  private ImageIcon imageIconUS = ImageViewer.createImageIcon(
16    "/image/us.gif", this);
17  private ImageIcon imageIconCanada = ImageViewer.createImageIcon(
18    "/image/ca.gif", this);
19  private ImageIcon imageIconNorway = ImageViewer.createImageIcon(
20    "/image/norway.gif", this);
21  private ImageIcon imageIconGermany = ImageViewer.createImageIcon(
22    "/image/germany.gif", this);
23  private ImageIcon imageIconPrint = ImageViewer.createImageIcon(
24    "/image/print.gif", this);
25  private ImageIcon imageIconSave = ImageViewer.createImageIcon(
26    "/image/save.gif", this);
27
28  // Create buttons to select images
29  private JButton jbtUS = new JButton("US");
30  private JButton jbtCanada = new JButton("Canada");
31  private JButton jbtNorway = new JButton("Norway");
32  private JButton jbtGermany = new JButton("Germany");
33
34  public ShowBoxLayout() {
35    box1.add(new JButton(imageIconPrint));
36    box1.add(Box.createHorizontalStrut(20));
37    box1.add(new JButton(imageIconSave));
38
39    box2.add(jbtUS);
40    box2.add(Box.createVerticalStrut(8));
41    box2.add(jbtCanada);
42    box2.add(Box.createGlue());
43    box2.add(jbtNorway);
44    box2.add(Box.createRigidArea(new Dimension(10, 8)));
45    box2.add(jbtGermany);
46
47    box1.setBorder(new javax.swing.border.LineBorder(Color.red));
48    box2.setBorder(new javax.swing.border.LineBorder(Color.black));
49
50    getContentPane().add(box1, BorderLayout.NORTH);
51    getContentPane().add(box2, BorderLayout.EAST);
52    getContentPane().add(jlblFlag, BorderLayout.CENTER);
53
54    // Register listeners
55    jbtUS.addActionListener(this);
56    jbtCanada.addActionListener(this);
57    jbtNorway.addActionListener(this);
58    jbtGermany.addActionListener(this);
59  }
60
61  public void actionPerformed(ActionEvent e) {
62    if (e.getSource() == jbtUS)
63      jlblFlag.setIcon(imageIconUS);
64    else if (e.getSource() == jbtCanada)
```

UI components

create icons

buttons

create UI

Example 22.4 (Continued)

```
65        jlblFlag.setIcon(imageIconCanada);
66     if (e.getSource() == jbtNorway)
67        jlblFlag.setIcon(imageIconNorway);
68     if (e.getSource() == jbtGermany)
69        jlblFlag.setIcon(imageIconGermany);
70   }
71 }
```

main method omitted

Review

Two containers of the Box class are created in Lines 8–9 using the convenient static methods createHorizontalBox() and createVerticalBox(). You could also create it using the constructor Box(int axis). The box containers always use the BoxLayout manager. You cannot reset the layout manager for the box containers.

The image icons are created using the static createImageIcon method in ImageViewer, which was introduced in Section 14.10, "Case Study: The ImageViewer Component."

Two buttons with the print and save icons are added into the horizontal box (Line 35–37). A horizontal strut with size 20 is added between these two buttons (Line 36).

Four buttons with texts US, Canada, Norway, and Germany are added into the vertical box (Line 39–45). A horizontal strut with size 8 is added to separate the US button and the Canada button (Line 40). A rigid area is inserted between the Norway button and the Germany button (Line 44). A glue is inserted to separate the Canada button and the Norway button as far as possible in the vertical box.

The strut, rigid area, and glue are instances of Component, so they can be added to the box container. In theory, you can add them to a container other than the box container. But they may be ignored and have no effect in other containers.

22.3.4 OverlayLayout

OverlayLayout is a Swing layout manager that arranges components on top of each other. To create an OverlayLayout, use the following constructor:

```
public OverlayLayout(Container target)
```

The constructor creates a layout manager that is dedicated to the given target container. For example, the following code creates an OverlayLayout for panel p1:

```
JPanel p1 = new JPanel();
OverlayLayout overlayLayout = new OverlayLayout(p1);
p1.setLayout(overlayLayout);
```

You still need to invoke the setLayout method on p1 to set the layout manager.

A component is on top of another component if it is added to the container before the other one. Suppose components p1, p2, and p3 are added to a container of the OverlayLayout in this order, then p1 is on top of p2, and p2 is on top of p3.

Example 22.5 Using the OverlayLayout Manager

Problem

Write a program that overlays two buttons in a panel of OverlayLayout, as shown in Figure 22.11. The first button is on top of the second button. The program enables the user to set the alignmentX and alignmentY properties of the two buttons dynamically. You can also set the opaque (blocked) property of the first button. When the opaque property is set to true, the first button blocks the scene of the second button, as shown in Figure 22.11(a). When the opaque property is set to false, the first button becomes transparent, allowing the second button to be seen through the first button, as shown in Figure 22.11(b).

EXAMPLE 22.5 (CONTINUED)

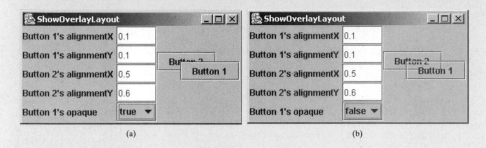

(a)   (b)

FIGURE **22.11**   *The components are overlaid in the container of* OverlayLayout.

Solution

Listing 22.5 gives the solution to the problem.

LISTING **22.5**   ShowOverLayLayout.java

```
1  import java.awt.*;
2  import java.awt.event.*;
3  import javax.swing.*;
4
5  public class ShowOverlayLayout extends JApplet
6      implements ActionListener {
7    private JButton jbt1 = new JButton("Button 1");
8    private JButton jbt2 = new JButton("Button 2");
9
10   private JTextField jtfButton1AlignmentX = new JTextField(4);
11   private JTextField jtfButton1AlignmentY = new JTextField(4);
12   private JTextField jtfButton2AlignmentX = new JTextField(4);
13   private JTextField jtfButton2AlignmentY = new JTextField(4);
14   private JComboBox jcboButton1Opaque = new JComboBox(
15     new Object[]{new Boolean(true), new Boolean(false)});
16
17   // Panel p1 to hold two buttons
18   private JPanel p1 = new JPanel();
19
20   public ShowOverlayLayout() {
21     // Add two buttons to p1 of OverlayLayout
22     p1.setLayout(new OverlayLayout(p1));
23     p1.add(jbt1);
24     p1.add(jbt2);
25
26     JPanel p2 = new JPanel();
27     p2.setLayout(new GridLayout(5, 1));
28     p2.add(new JLabel("Button 1's alignmentX"));
29     p2.add(new JLabel("Button 1's alignmentY"));
30     p2.add(new JLabel("Button 2's alignmentX"));
31     p2.add(new JLabel("Button 2's alignmentY"));
32     p2.add(new JLabel("Button 1's opaque"));
33
34     JPanel p3 = new JPanel();
35     p3.setLayout(new GridLayout(5, 1));
36     p3.add(jtfButton1AlignmentX);
37     p3.add(jtfButton1AlignmentY);
38     p3.add(jtfButton2AlignmentX);
39     p3.add(jtfButton2AlignmentY);
40     p3.add(jcboButton1Opaque);
41
42     JPanel p4 = new JPanel();
43     p4.setLayout(new BorderLayout(4, 4));
44     p4.add(p2, BorderLayout.WEST);
45     p4.add(p3, BorderLayout.CENTER);
```

overlay layout

EXAMPLE 22.5 (CONTINUED)

```
46
47      getContentPane().add(p1, BorderLayout.CENTER);
48      getContentPane().add(p4, BorderLayout.WEST);
49
50      jtfButton1AlignmentX.addActionListener(this);
51      jtfButton1AlignmentY.addActionListener(this);
51      jtfButton2AlignmentX.addActionListener(this);
53      jtfButton2AlignmentY.addActionListener(this);
54      jcboButton1Opaque.addActionListener(this);
55    }
56
57    public void actionPerformed(ActionEvent e) {
58      if (e.getSource() == jtfButton1AlignmentX)
59        jbt1.setAlignmentX(
60          Float.parseFloat(jtfButton1AlignmentX.getText()));
61      else if (e.getSource() == jtfButton1AlignmentY)
62        jbt1.setAlignmentY(
63          Float.parseFloat(jtfButton1AlignmentY.getText()));
64      else if (e.getSource() == jtfButton2AlignmentX)
65        jbt2.setAlignmentX(
66          Float.parseFloat(jtfButton2AlignmentX.getText()));
67      else if (e.getSource() == jtfButton2AlignmentY)
68        jbt2.setAlignmentY(
69          Float.parseFloat(jtfButton2AlignmentY.getText()));
70      else if (e.getSource() == jcboButton1Opaque)
71        jbt1.setOpaque(((Boolean)(jcboButton1Opaque.
72          getSelectedItem())).booleanValue());
73
74      p1.revalidate(); // Cause the components to be rearranged
75      p1.repaint(); // Cause the viewing area to be repainted
76    }
77 }
```

main method omitted

Review

A panel p1 of OverlayLayout is created (Line 18) to hold two buttons (Lines 22–24). Since Button 1 is added before Button 2, Button 1 is on top of Button 2.

The alignmentX and alignmentY properties specify how the two buttons are aligned relative to each other along the x-axis and y-axis (Lines 58–69). These two properties are used in BoxLayout and OverlayLayout, but are ignored by other layout managers. Note that the alignment is a float type number between 0 and 1.

The opaque property is defined in JComponent for all Swing lightweight components. By default, it is true for JButton, which means that the button is nontransparent. So if Button 1's opaque is true, you cannot see any other components behind Button 1. To enable the components behind Button 1 to be seen, set Button 1's opaque property to false (Lines 71–72).

22.3.5 SpringLayout

SpringLayout is a new Swing layout manager introduced in JDK 1.4. The idea of SpringLayout is to put a flexible spring around a component. The spring may compress or expand to place the components in desired locations.

To create a SpringLayout, use its no-arg constructor:

```
public SpringLayout()
```

A spring is an instance of the Spring class that can be created using one of the following two static methods:

◆ public static Spring constant(int pref)

   Returns a spring whose minimum, preferred, and maximum values each have the value pref.

◆ `public static Spring constant(int min, int pref, int max)`

Returns a spring with the specified minimum, preferred, and maximum values.

Each spring has a preferred value, minimum value, maximum value, and actual value. The `getPreferredValue()`, `getMinimumValue()`, `getMaximumValue()`, and `getValue()` methods retrieve these values. The `setValue(int value)` method can be used to set an actual value.

The `Spring` class defines the static `sum(Spring s1, Spring s2)` to produce a combined new spring, the static `minus(Spring s)` to produce a new spring running in the opposite direction, and the static `max(Spring s1, Spring s2)` to produce a new spring with larger values from `s1` and `s2`.

To add a spring or a fixed space to separate components in the container, use one of the following two methods in the `SpringLayout` class:

◆ `public void putConstraint(String e1, Component c1, Spring s, String e2, Component c2)`

Places a spring between edge `e1` of component `c1` and edge `e2` of component `c2`, anchored on `c2`. Each edge must have one of the following values: `SpringLayout.NORTH`, `SpringLayout.SOUTH`, `SpringLayout.EAST`, `SpringLayout.WEST`.

◆ `public void putConstraint(String e1, Component c1, int pad, String e2, Component c2)`

Places a fixed pad between edge `e1` of component `c1` and edge `e2` of component `c2`, anchored on `c2`.

In the preceding methods, `e2` and `c2` are referred to as the *anchor edge* and *anchor component*, and `e1` and `c1` as the *dependent edge* and *dependent component*.

anchor edge
dependent edge

EXAMPLE 22.6 USING THE `SpringLayout` MANAGER

Problem

Write a program that places a button in the center of the container, as shown in Figure 22.12.

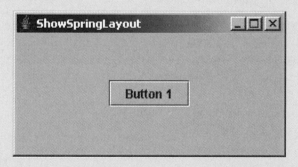

FIGURE 22.12 *The button is centered in the container of* `SpringLayout`.

Solution

Listing 22.6 gives the solution to the problem.

LISTING 22.6 ShowSpringLayout.java

```
1 import java.awt.*;
2 import javax.swing.*;
3
4 public class ShowSpringLayout extends JApplet {
5   public ShowSpringLayout() {
6     SpringLayout springLayout = new SpringLayout();
7     JPanel p1 = new JPanel(springLayout);
```

spring layout

EXAMPLE 22.6 (CONTINUED)

```
8      JButton jbt1 = new JButton("Button 1");
9      p1.add(jbt1);
10
11     Spring spring = Spring.constant(0, 1000, 2000);
12     springLayout.putConstraint(SpringLayout.WEST, jbt1, spring,
13                                SpringLayout.WEST, p1);
14     springLayout.putConstraint(SpringLayout.EAST, p1, spring,
15                                SpringLayout.EAST, jbt1);
16     springLayout.putConstraint(SpringLayout.NORTH, jbt1, spring,
17                                SpringLayout.NORTH, p1);
18     springLayout.putConstraint(SpringLayout.SOUTH, p1, spring,
19                                SpringLayout.SOUTH, jbt1);
20
21     getContentPane().add(p1, BorderLayout.CENTER);
22   }
23 }
```

spring
spring constraints

main method omitted

Review

A `SpringLayout` named `springLayout` is created in Line 6 and is set in `JPanel` `p1` (Line 7). An instance of `Spring` is created using the static `constant` method with minimum value 0, preferred value 1000, and maximum value 2000 (Line 11).

Like icons and borders, an instance of `Spring` can be shared. The `putConstraint` method in `SpringLayout` put a spring between two components. In Lines 12–13, the spring is padded between the west of the button and the west of the panel `p1`, anchored at `p1`. In Lines 14–15, the same spring is padded between the east of the panel and the east of the button, anchored at the button. The selection of the anchor components is important. For example, if Lines 12–13 were replaced by the following code,

```
springLayout.putConstraint(SpringLayout.WEST, p1, spring,
                           SpringLayout.WEST, jbt1);
```

the button would be pushed all the way to the east, as shown in Figure 22.13(a). If Lines 12–13 were replaced by the following code,

```
springLayout.putConstraint(SpringLayout.NORTH, p1, spring,
                           SpringLayout.NORTH, jbt1);
```

the button would be pushed all the way to the top, as shown in Figure 22.13(b).

If Lines 14–15 were replaced by the following code,

```
springLayout.putConstraint(SpringLayout.EAST, p1,
    Spring.sum(spring, spring), SpringLayout.EAST, jbt1);
```

the spring on the right of the button is twice strong as the left spring of the button, as shown in Figure 22.13(c).

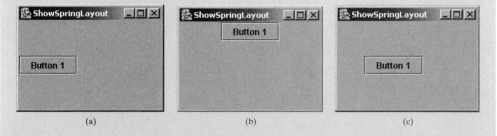

| (a) | (b) | (c) |

FIGURE 22.13 *The selection of the anchor component can affect the layout.*

22.4   Creating Custom Layout Managers

In addition to the layout managers provided in Java, you can create your own layout managers. To do so, you need to understand how a layout manager lays out components. A container's setLayout method specifies a layout manager for the container. The layout manager is responsible for laying out the components and displaying them in a desired location with an appropriate size. Every layout manager must directly or indirectly implement the LayoutManager interface. For instance, FlowLayout directly implements LayoutManager, and BorderLayout implements LayoutManager2, a subinterface of LayoutManager. The LayoutManager interface provides the following methods for laying out components in a container:

✦ `public void addLayoutComponent(String name, Component comp)`

Adds the specified component with the specified name to the container.

✦ `public void layoutContainer(Container parent)`

Lays out the components in the specified container. In this method, you should provide concrete instructions that specify where the components are to be placed.

✦ `public Dimension minimumLayoutSize(Container parent)`

Calculates the minimum size dimensions for the specified panel, given the components in the specified parent container.

✦ `public Dimension preferredLayoutSize(Container parent)`

Calculates the preferred size dimensions for the specified panel, given the components in the specified parent container.

✦ `public void removeLayoutComponent(Component comp)`

Removes the specified component from the layout.

These methods in LayoutManager are invoked by the methods in the java.awt.Container class through the layout manager in the container. Container contains a property named layout (an instance of LayoutManager) and the methods for adding and removing components from the container. There are five overloading add methods defined in Container for adding components with various options. The remove method removes a component from the container. The add method invokes the addLayoutComponent method defined in the LayoutManager interface. The layoutContainer method in the LayoutManager interface is indirectly invoked by validate through several calls. The remove method invokes removeLayoutComponent in LayoutManager. The validate method is invoked to refresh the container after the components it contains have been added to or modified. The relationship of Container and LayoutManager is shown in Figure 22.14.

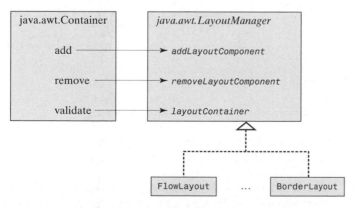

FIGURE 22.14   *The* add, remove, *and* validate *methods in* Container *invoke the methods defined in the* LayoutManager *interface.*

EXAMPLE 22.7 CREATING A CUSTOM LAYOUT MANAGER

Problem

This example creates a layout manager named DiagonalLayout that places the components in a diagonal. To test DiagonalLayout, the example creates an applet with radio buttons named "FlowLayout," "GridLayout," and "DiagonalLayout," as shown in Figure 22.15. You can dynamically select one of these three layouts in the panel.

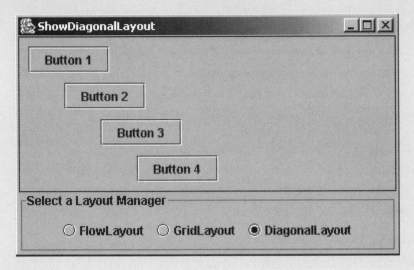

FIGURE 22.15 *The DiagonalLayout manager places the components in a diagonal in the container.*

Solution

The DiagonalLayout class is similar to FlowLayout. DiagonalLayout arranges components along a diagonal using each component's natural preferredSize. It contains three constraints, gap, lastFill, and majorDiagonal, as shown in Figure 22.16.

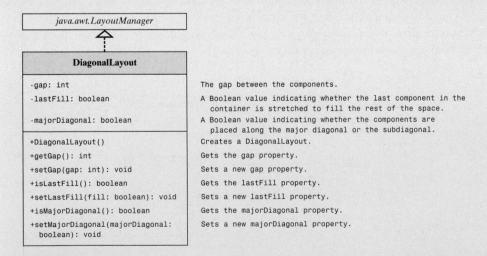

FIGURE 22.16 *The DiagonalLayout manager has three properties with the supporting accessor and mutator methods.*

The source code for DiagonalLayout is given in Listing 22.7.

EXAMPLE 22.7 (CONTINUED)

LISTING 22.7   DiagonalLayout.java

```
 1 import java.awt.*;
 2
 3 public class DiagonalLayout implements LayoutManager,
 4     java.io.Serializable {
 5   /** Vertical gap between the components */
 6   private int gap = 10;
 7
 8   /** True if components are placed along the major diagonal */
 9   private boolean majorDiagonal = true;
10
11   /*True if the last component is stretched to fill the space */
12   private boolean lastFill = false;
13
14   /** Constructor */
15   public DiagonalLayout() {
16   }
17
18   public void addLayoutComponent(String name, Component comp) {
19     //TODO: implement this java.awt.LayoutManager method;
20   }
21
22   public void removeLayoutComponent(Component comp) {
23     //TODO: implement this java.awt.LayoutManager method;
24   }
25
26   public Dimension preferredLayoutSize(Container parent) {
27     //TODO: implement this java.awt.LayoutManager method;
28     return minimumLayoutSize(parent);
29   }
30
31   public Dimension minimumLayoutSize(Container parent) {
32     //TODO: implement this java.awt.LayoutManager method;
33     return new Dimension(0, 0);
34   }
35
36   public void layoutContainer(Container parent) {
37     //TODO: implement this java.awt.LayoutManager method;
38     int numberOfComponents = parent.getComponentCount();
39
40     Insets insets = parent.getInsets();
41     int w = parent.getSize().width - insets.left - insets.right;
42     int h = parent.getSize().height - insets.bottom - insets.top;
43
44     if (majorDiagonal) {
45       int x = 10, y = 10;
46
47       for (int j = 0; j < numberOfComponents; j++) {
48         Component c = parent.getComponent(j);
49         Dimension d = c.getPreferredSize();
50
51         if (c.isVisible())
52           if (lastFill && (j == numberOfComponents - 1))
53             c.setBounds(x, y, w - x, h - y);
54           else
55             c.setBounds(x, y, d.width, d.height);
56         x += d.height + gap;
57         y += d.height + gap;
58       }
59     }
60     else { // It is subdiagonal
61       int x = w - 10, y = 10;
62
63       for (int j = 0; j < numberOfComponents; j++) {
64         Component c = parent.getComponent(j);
65         Dimension d = c.getPreferredSize();
```

properties

layout container

EXAMPLE 22.7 (CONTINUED)

```
66
67              if (c.isVisible())
68                if (lastFill & (j == numberOfComponents - 1))
69                  c.setBounds(0, y, x, h - y);
70                else
71                  c.setBounds(x, d.width, y, d.height);
72
73            x -= (d.height + gap);
74            y += d.height + gap;
75          }
76        }
77    }
78
79    public int getGap() {
80      return gap;
81    }
82
83    public void setGap(int gap) {
84      this.gap = gap;
85    }
86
87    public void setMajorDiagonal(boolean newMajorDiagonal) {
88      majorDiagonal = newMajorDiagonal;
89    }
90
91    public boolean isMajorDiagonal() {
92      return majorDiagonal;
93    }
94
95    public void setLastFill(boolean newLastFill) {
96      lastFill = newLastFill;
97    }
98
99    public boolean isLastFill() {
100     return lastFill;
101   }
102 }
```

The program in Listing 22.8 tests DiagonalLayout.

LISTING 22.8   ShowDiagonalLayout.java

```
1 import javax.swing.*;
2 import javax.swing.border.*;
3 import java.awt.*;
4 import java.awt.event.*;
5
6 public class ShowDiagonalLayout extends JApplet
7     implements ActionListener {
8   private FlowLayout flowLayout = new FlowLayout();
9   private GridLayout gridLayout = new GridLayout(2, 2);
10  private DiagonalLayout diagonalLayout = new DiagonalLayout();
11
12  private JButton jbt1 = new JButton("Button 1");
13  private JButton jbt2 = new JButton("Button 2");
14  private JButton jbt3 = new JButton("Button 3");
15  private JButton jbt4 = new JButton("Button 4");
16
17  private JRadioButton jrbFlowLayout =
18    new JRadioButton("FlowLayout");
19  private JRadioButton jrbGridLayout =
20    new JRadioButton("GridLayout");
21  private JRadioButton jrbDiagonalLayout =
22    new JRadioButton("DiagonalLayout", true);
23
24  private JPanel jPanel2 = new JPanel();
```

diagonal layout

EXAMPLE 22.7 (CONTINUED)

```
25
26    public ShowDiagonalLayout() {
27      // Set default layout in jPanel2                          create UI
28      jPanel2.setLayout(diagonalLayout);
29      jPanel2.add(jbt1);
30      jPanel2.add(jbt2);
31      jPanel2.add(jbt3);
32      jPanel2.add(jbt4);
33      jPanel2.setBorder(new LineBorder(Color.black));
34
35      JPanel jPanel1 = new JPanel();
36      jPanel1.setBorder(new TitledBorder("Select a Layout Manager"));
37      jPanel1.add(jrbFlowLayout);
38      jPanel1.add(jrbGridLayout);
39      jPanel1.add(jrbDiagonalLayout);
40
41      ButtonGroup buttonGroup1 = new ButtonGroup();
42      buttonGroup1.add(jrbFlowLayout);
43      buttonGroup1.add(jrbGridLayout);
44      buttonGroup1.add(jrbDiagonalLayout);
45
46      getContentPane().add(jPanel1, BorderLayout.SOUTH);
47      getContentPane().add(jPanel2, BorderLayout.CENTER);
48
49      jrbFlowLayout.addActionListener(this);
50      jrbGridLayout.addActionListener(this);
51      jrbDiagonalLayout.addActionListener(this);
52    }
53
54    public void actionPerformed(ActionEvent e) {
55      if (e.getSource() == jrbFlowLayout) {
56        jPanel2.setLayout(flowLayout);
57        jPanel2.validate();
58      }
59      else if (e.getSource() == jrbGridLayout) {
60        jPanel2.setLayout(gridLayout);
61        jPanel2.validate();
62      }
63      else if (e.getSource() == jrbDiagonalLayout) {
64        jPanel2.setLayout(diagonalLayout);
65        jPanel2.validate();
66      }
67    }
68  }                                                            main method omitted
```

Review

The `DiagonalLayout` class implements the `LayoutManger` and `Serializable` interfaces (Lines 3–4). The reason to implement `Serializable` is to make it a JavaBeans component.

The `Insets` class describes the size of the borders of a container. It contains the variables `left`, `right`, `bottom`, and `top`, which correspond to the measurements for the *left border*, *right border*, *top border*, and *bottom border* (Lines 40–42).

The `Dimension` class used in `DiagonalLayout` encapsulates the width and height of a component in a single object. The class is associated with certain properties of components. Several methods defined by the `Component` class and the `LayoutManager` interface return a `Dimension` object.

The `ShowDiagonalLayout` class enables you to dynamically set the layout in `jPanel2`. When you select a new layout, the layout manager is set in `jPanel2`, and the `validate()` method is invoked (Lines 57, 61, 65), which in turn invokes the `layoutContainer` method in the `LayoutManager` interface to display the components in the container.

22.5   `JScrollPane`

Often you need to use a scrollbar to scroll the contents of an object that does not fit completely into the viewing area. `JScrollBar` and `JSlider` can be used for this purpose, but you have to *manually* write the code to implement scrolling with them. `JScrollPane` is a component that supports *automatic* scrolling without coding. It was used to scroll the text area in Example 13.4, "Using Text Areas," and to scroll a list in Example 13.6, "Using Lists." In fact, it can be used to scroll any subclass of `JComponent`.

A `JScrollPane` can be viewed as a specialized container with a view port for displaying the contained component. In addition to horizontal and vertical scrollbars, a `JScrollPane` can have a column header, a row header, and corners, as shown in Figure 22.17.

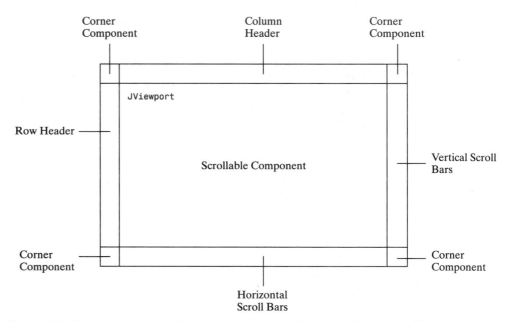

FIGURE 22.17   *A* `JScrollPane` *has a view port, optional horizontal and vertical bars, optional column and row headers, and optional corners.*

view port

The *view port* is an instance of `JViewport` through which a scrollable component is displayed. When you add a component to a scroll pane, you are actually placing it in the scroll pane's view port. Figure 22.18 shows the frequently used properties, constructors, and methods in `JScrollPane`.

The constructor always creates a view port regardless of whether the viewing component is specified. Normally, you have the component and you want to place it in a scroll pane. A convenient way to create a scroll pane for a component is to use the `JScrollPane(component)` constructor.

The `vsbPolicy` parameter can be one of the following three values:

```
JScrollPane.VERTICAL_SCROLLBAR_AS_NEEDED
JScrollPane.VERTICAL_SCROLLBAR_NEVER
JScrollPane.VERTICAL_SCROLLBAR_ALWAYS
```

The `hsbPolicy` parameter can be one of the following three values:

```
JScrollPane.HORIZONTAL_SCROLLBAR_AS_NEEDED
JScrollPane.HORIZONTAL_SCROLLBAR_NEVER
JScrollPane.HORIZONTAL_SCROLLBAR_ALWAYS
```

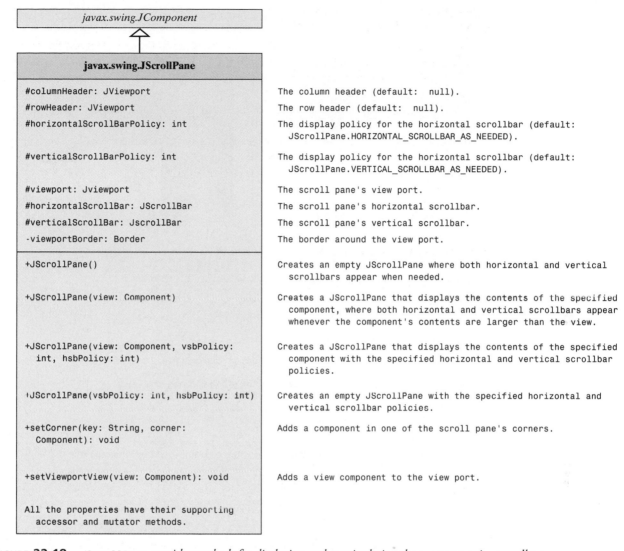

FIGURE 22.18 *JScrollPane provides methods for displaying and manipulating the components in a scroll pane.*

To set a corner component, you can use the setCorner(String key, Component corner) method. The legal values for the key are:

```
JScrollPane.LOWER_LEFT_CORNER
JScrollPane.LOWER_RIGHT_CORNER
JScrollPane.UPPER_LEFT_CORNER
JScrollPane.UPPER_RIGHT_CORNER
```

EXAMPLE 22.8 USING SCROLL PANES

Problem

Write a program that uses a scroll pane to browse a large map. The program lets you choose a map from a combo box and display it in the scroll pane, as shown in Figure 22.19.

Solution

Listing 22.9 displays a map in a label and places the label in a scroll pane so that a large map can be scrolled.

EXAMPLE 22.8 (CONTINUED)

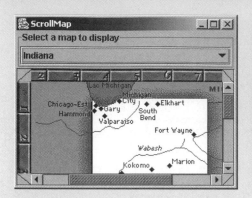 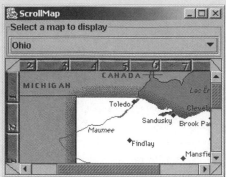

FIGURE 22.19 *The scroll pane can be used to scroll contents automatically.*

LISTING 22.9 ScrollMap.java

```
1  import java.awt.*;
2  import java.awt.event.*;
3  import javax.swing.*;
4  import javax.swing.border.*;
5
6  public class ScrollMap extends JApplet implements ItemListener {
7    // Create images in labels
8    private JLabel lblIndianaMap = new JLabel(ImageViewer.
9      createImageIcon("image/indianaMap.gif", this));
10   private JLabel lblOhioMap = new JLabel(ImageViewer.
11    createImageIcon("image/ohioMap.gif", this));
12
13   // Create a scroll pane to scroll map in the labels
14   private JScrollPane jspMap = new JScrollPane(lblIndianaMap);
15
16   public ScrollMap() {
17     // Create a combo box for selecting maps
18     JComboBox jcboMap = new JComboBox(new String[]{"Indiana",
19       "Ohio"});
20
21     // Panel p to hold combo box
22     JPanel p = new JPanel();
23     p.setLayout(new BorderLayout());
24     p.add(jcboMap);
25     p.setBorder(new TitledBorder("Select a map to display"));
26
27     // Set row header, column header and corner header
28     jspMap.setColumnHeaderView(new JLabel(ImageViewer.
29       createImageIcon("image/horizontalRuler.gif", this)));
30     jspMap.setRowHeaderView(new JLabel(ImageViewer.
31       createImageIcon("image/verticalRuler.gif", this)));
32     jspMap.setCorner(JScrollPane.UPPER_LEFT_CORNER,
33       new CornerPanel(JScrollPane.UPPER_LEFT_CORNER));
34     jspMap.setCorner(ScrollPaneConstants.UPPER_RIGHT_CORNER,
35       new CornerPanel(JScrollPane.UPPER_RIGHT_CORNER));
36     jspMap.setCorner(JScrollPane.LOWER_RIGHT_CORNER,
37       new CornerPanel(JScrollPane.LOWER_RIGHT_CORNER));
38     jspMap.setCorner(JScrollPane.LOWER_LEFT_CORNER,
39       new CornerPanel(JScrollPane.LOWER_LEFT_CORNER));
40
41     // Add the scroll pane and combo box panel to the frame
42     getContentPane().add(jspMap, BorderLayout.CENTER);
43     getContentPane().add(p, BorderLayout.NORTH);
44
45     // Register listener
46     jcboMap.addItemListener(this);
47   }
```

labels

create UI

scroll pane

EXAMPLE 22.8 (CONTINUED)

```
48
49    /** Show the selected map */
50    public void itemStateChanged(ItemEvent e) {
51      String selectedItem = (String)e.getItem();
52      if (selectedItem.equals("Indiana")) {
53        // Set a new view in the view port
54        jspMap.setViewportView(lblIndianaMap);
55      }
56      else if (selectedItem.equals("Ohio")) {
57        // Set a new view in the view port
58        jspMap.setViewportView(lblOhioMap);
59      }
60
61      // Revalidate the scroll pane
62      jspMap.revalidate();
63    }
64  }
65
66  // A panel displaying a line used for scroll pane corner
67  class CornerPanel extends JPanel {
68    // Line location
69    private String location;
70
71    public CornerPanel(String location) {
72      this.location = location;
73    }
74
75    /** Draw a line depending on the location */
76    protected void paintComponent(Graphics g) {
77      super.paintComponents(g);
78
79      if (location == "UPPER_LEFT_CORNER")
80        g.drawLine(0, getHeight(), getWidth(), 0);
81      else if (location == "UPPER_RIGHT_CORNER")
82        g.drawLine(0, 0, getWidth(), getHeight());
83      else if (location == "LOWER_RIGHT_CORNER")
84        g.drawLine(0, getHeight(), getWidth(), 0);
85      else if (location == "LOWER_LEFT_CORNER")
86        g.drawLine(0, 0, getWidth(), getHeight());
87    }
88  }
```

main method omitted

Review

The program creates a scroll pane to view image maps. The image maps are created using the static `createImageIcon` method in the `ImageViewer` class (Lines 8–11). The `createImageIcon` method can load image file for both applets and standalone applications. To view an image, the label that contains the image is placed in the scroll pane's view port (Line 14).

The scroll pane has a main view, a header view, a column view, and four corner views. Each view is a subclass of `Component`. Since `ImageIcon` is not a subclass of `Component`, it cannot be directly used as a view in the scroll pane. Instead the program places an `ImageIcon` to a label and uses the label as a view.

The `CornerPanel` (Lines 67–88) is a subclass of `JPanel` that is used to display a line. How the line is drawn depends on the `location` of the corner. The `location` is a string passed in as a parameter in the `CornerPanel`'s constructor.

Whenever a new map is selected, the label for displaying the map image is set to the scroll pane's view port. The `revalidate()` method (Line 62) must be invoked to cause the new image to be displayed. The `revalidate()` method causes a container to lay out its sub-components again after the components it contains have been added to or modified.

22.6 JTabbedPane

JTabbedPane is a useful Swing container that provides a set of mutually exclusive tabs for accessing multiple components, as shown in Figure 22.20.

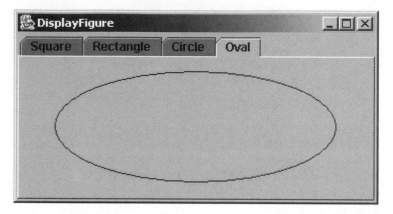

FIGURE 22.20 *JTabbedPane displays components through the tabs.*

Usually you place the panels inside a JTabbedPane and associate a tab with each panel. JTabbedPane is easy to use, because the selection of the panel is handled automatically by clicking the corresponding tab. You can switch between a group of panels by clicking on a tab with a given title and/or icon. Figure 22.21 shows the frequently used properties, constructors, and methods in JTabbedPane.

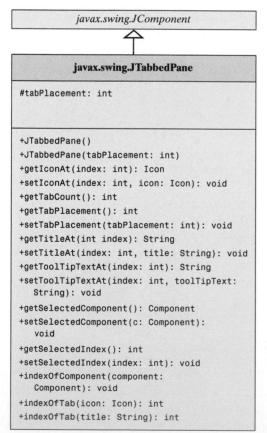

javax.swing.JComponent	

javax.swing.JTabbedPane	

#tabPlacement: int	The tab placement for this tabbed pane. Possible values are: JTabbedPane.TOP, JTabbedPane.BOTTOM, JTabbedPane.LEFT, and JTabbedPane.RIGHT (default: JTabbedPane.TOP).
+JTabbedPane()	Constructs a JTabbedPane with default tab placement.
+JTabbedPane(tabPlacement: int)	Constructs a JTabbedPane with the specified tab placement.
+getIconAt(index: int): Icon	Returns the icon at the specified tab index.
+setIconAt(index: int, icon: Icon): void	Sets the icon at the specified tab index.
+getTabCount(): int	Returns the number of tabs in this tabbed pane.
+getTabPlacement(): int	Returns the placement of the tabs for this tabbed pane.
+setTabPlacement(tabPlacement: int): void	Sets the placement of the tabs for this tabbed pane.
+getTitleAt(int index): String	Returns the tab title at the specified tab index.
+setTitleAt(index: int, title: String): void	Sets the tab title at the specified tab index.
+getToolTipTextAt(index: int): String	Returns the tool tip text at the specified tab index.
+setToolTipTextAt(index: int, toolTipText: String): void	Sets the tool tip text at the specified tab index.
+getSelectedComponent(): Component	Returns the currently selected component for this tabbed pane.
+setSelectedComponent(c: Component): void	Sets the currently selected component for this tabbed pane.
+getSelectedIndex(): int	Returns the currently selected index for this tabbed pane.
+setSelectedIndex(index: int): void	Sets the currently selected index for this tabbed pane.
+indexOfComponent(component: Component): void	Returns the index of the tab for the specified component.
+indexOfTab(icon: Icon): int	Returns the index of the tab for the specified icon.
+indexOfTab(title: String): int	Returns the index of the tab for the specified title.

FIGURE 22.21 *JTabbedPane provides methods for displaying and manipulating the components in the tabbed pane.*

EXAMPLE 22.9 USING JTabbedPane

Problem

This example uses a tabbed pane with four tabs to display four types of figures: square, rectangle, circle, and oval. You can select a figure to display by clicking the corresponding tab, as shown in Figure 22.20.

Solution

First let us create a class named `FigurePanel` for displaying the figures. The class has the property `figureType` of the `int` type to specify a figure type, as shown in Listing 22.10.

LISTING 22.10 **FigurePanel.java**

```
1 import java.awt.*;
2 import javax.swing.JPanel;
3
4 public class FigurePanel extends JPanel {
5   private int figureType = 1;
6
7   // Define constants
8   public static final int SQUARE = 1;
9   public static final int RECTANGLE = 2;
10   public static final int CIRCLE = 3;
11   public static final int OVAL = 4;
12
13   /** Constructor */
14   public FigurePanel() {
15   }
16
17   /** Constructs a FigurePanel with the specified type */
18   public FigurePanel(int type) {
19     this.figureType = type;
20     repaint();
21   }
22
23   /** Draw a figure on the panel */
24   public void paintComponent(Graphics g) {
25     super.paintComponent(g);
26
27     // Get the appropriate size for the figure
28     int width = getSize().width;
29     int height = getSize().height;
30     int side = (int)(0.80 * Math.min(width, height));
31
32     switch (figureType) {
33       case SQUARE: // Display a square
34         g.drawRect((width-side) / 2, (height-side) / 2, side, side);
35         break;
36       case RECTANGLE: // Display a rectangle
37         g.drawRect((int)(0.1 * width), (int)(0.1 * height),
38           (int)(0.8 * width), (int)(0.8 * height));
39         break;
40       case CIRCLE: // Display a circle
41         g.drawOval((width-side) / 2, (height-side) / 2, side, side);
42         break;
43       case OVAL: // Display an oval
44         g.drawOval((int)(0.1 * width), (int)(0.1 * height),
45           (int)(0.8 * width), (int)(0.8 * height));
46         break;
47     }
48   }
49
50   /** Setter figureType */
51   public void setFigureType(int newFigureType) {
52     figureType = newFigureType;
53   }
```

constants

select a type

EXAMPLE 22.9 (CONTINUED)

```
54
55   /** Return figureType */
56   public int getFigureType() {
57     return figureType;
58   }
59
60   /** Specify preferred size */
61   public Dimension getPreferredSize() {
62     return new Dimension(80, 80);
63   }
64 }
```

Now let us create a test class that displays four figures in a tabbed pane, as shown in Listing 22.11.

LISTING 22.11   DisplayFigure.java

```
 1 import java.awt.*;
 2 import javax.swing.*;
 3
 4 public class DisplayFigure extends JApplet {
 5   private JTabbedPane jtpFigures = new JTabbedPane();
 6   private FigurePanel squarePanel = new FigurePanel();
 7   private FigurePanel rectanglePanel = new FigurePanel();
 8   private FigurePanel circlePanel = new FigurePanel();
 9   private FigurePanel ovalPanel = new FigurePanel();
10
11   public DisplayFigure() {
12     squarePanel.setFigureType(FigurePanel.SQUARE);
13     rectanglePanel.setFigureType(FigurePanel.RECTANGLE);
14     circlePanel.setFigureType(FigurePanel.CIRCLE);
15     ovalPanel.setFigureType(FigurePanel.OVAL);
16
17     getContentPane().add(jtpFigures, BorderLayout.CENTER);
18     jtpFigures.add(squarePanel, "Square");
19     jtpFigures.add(rectanglePanel, "Rectangle");
20     jtpFigures.add(circlePanel, "Circle");
21     jtpFigures.add(ovalPanel, "Oval");
22
23     jtpFigures.setToolTipTextAt(0, "Square");
24     jtpFigures.setToolTipTextAt(1, "Rectangle");
25     jtpFigures.setToolTipTextAt(2, "Circle");
26     jtpFigures.setToolTipTextAt(3, "Oval");
27   }
28 }
```

tabbed pane

set type

add tabs

main method omitted

Review

The program creates a tabbed pane to hold four panels, each of which displays a figure. A panel is associated with a tab. The tabs are titled Square, Rectangle, Circle, and Oval.

By default, the tabs are placed at the top of the tabbed pane. You can select a different placement using the tabPlacement property.

22.7   JSplitPane

JSplitPane is a convenient Swing container that contains two components with a separate bar known as a *divider*, as shown in Figure 22.22.

The bar can divide the container horizontally or vertically, and can be dragged to change the amount of space occupied by each component. Figure 22.23 shows the frequently used properties, constructors, and methods in JSplitPane.

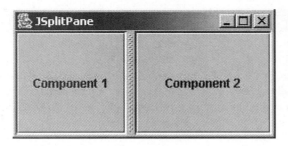 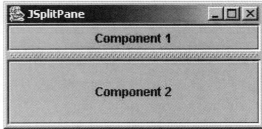

FIGURE 22.22 *JSplitPane divides a container into two parts.*

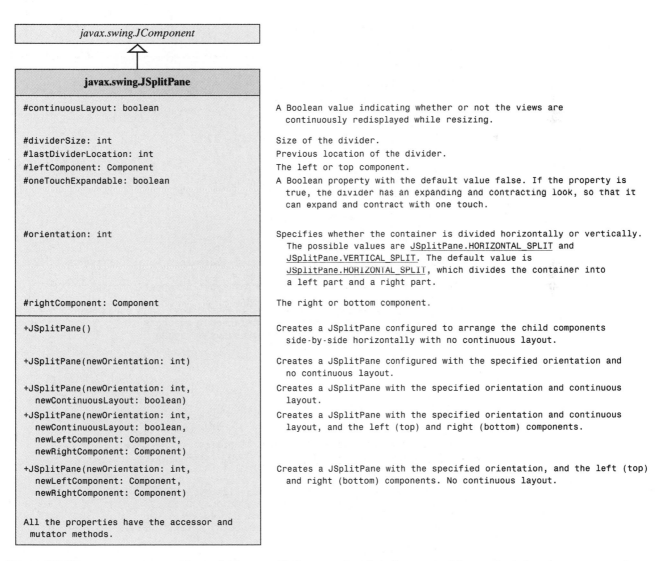

FIGURE 22.23 *JSplitPane provides methods to specify the properties of a split pane and for manipulating the components in a split pane.*

EXAMPLE 22.10 USING JSplitPane

Problem

Write a program that uses radio buttons to let the user select a `FlowLayout`, `GridLayout`, or `BoxLayout` manager dynamically for a panel. The panel contains four buttons, as shown in Figure 22.24. The description of the currently selected layout manager is displayed in a text area. The radio buttons, buttons, and text area are placed in two split panes.

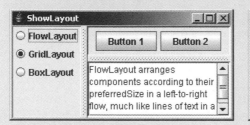 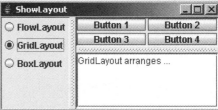

FIGURE 22.24 *The split pane lets you adjust the component size in the split panes.*

Solution

The source code for the program is given in Listing 22.12.

LISTING 22.12 **ShowLayout.java**

```
 1  import java.awt.*;
 2  import java.awt.event.*;
 3  import java.net.*;
 4  import javax.swing.*;
 5
 6  public class ShowLayout extends JApplet implements ActionListener {
 7    // Get the url for HTML files
 8    private String flowLayoutDesc = "FlowLayout arranges components " +
 9      "according to their preferredSize in " +
10      "a left-to-right flow, much like lines of text in a paragraph.";
11    private String gridLayoutDesc = "GridLayout arranges ...";
12    private String boxLayoutDesc = "BoxLayout arranges ...";
13
14    private JRadioButton jrbFlowLayout =
15      new JRadioButton("FlowLayout");
16    private JRadioButton jrbGridLayout =
17      new JRadioButton("GridLayout", true);
18    private JRadioButton jrbBoxLayout =
19      new JRadioButton("BoxLayout");
20
21    private JPanel jpComponents = new JPanel();
22    private JTextArea jtfDescription = new JTextArea();
23
24    // Create layout managers
25    private FlowLayout flowLayout = new FlowLayout();
26    private GridLayout gridLayout = new GridLayout(2, 2, 3, 3);
27    private BoxLayout boxLayout =
28      new BoxLayout(jpComponents, BoxLayout.X_AXIS);
29
30    public ShowLayout() {
31      // Create a box to hold radio buttons
32      Box jpChooseLayout = Box.createVerticalBox();
33      jpChooseLayout.add(jrbFlowLayout);
34      jpChooseLayout.add(jrbGridLayout);
35      jpChooseLayout.add(jrbBoxLayout);
36
```

descriptions (margin note, lines 8–12)

radio buttons (margin note, lines 14–19)

layout managers (margin note, lines 24–28)

EXAMPLE 22.10 (CONTINUED)

```
37      // Group radio buttons
38      ButtonGroup btg = new ButtonGroup();
39      btg.add(jrbFlowLayout);
40      btg.add(jrbGridLayout);
41      btg.add(jrbBoxLayout);
42
43      // Wrap lines and words
44      jtfDescription.setLineWrap(true);
45      jtfDescription.setWrapStyleWord(true);
46
47      // Add fours buttons to jpComponents
48      jpComponents.add(new JButton("Button 1"));
49      jpComponents.add(new JButton("Button 2"));
50      jpComponents.add(new JButton("Button 3"));
51      jpComponents.add(new JButton("Button 4"));
52
53      // Create two split panes to hold jpChooseLayout, jpComponents,
54      // and jtfDescription
55      JSplitPane jSplitPane2 = new JSplitPane(                        split pane
56        JSplitPane.VERTICAL_SPLIT, jpComponents,
57        new JScrollPane(jtfDescription));
58      JSplitPane jSplitPane1 = new JSplitPane(                        split pane
59        JSplitPane.HORIZONTAL_SPLIT, jpChooseLayout, jSplitPane2);
60
61      // Set FlowLayout as default
62      jpComponents.setLayout(flowLayout);
63      jpComponents.validate();
64      jtfDescription.setText(flowLayoutDesc);
65
66      getContentPane().add(jSplitPane1, BorderLayout.CENTER);
67
68      // Register listeners
69      jrbFlowLayout.addActionListener(this);
70      jrbGridLayout.addActionListener(this);
71      jrbBoxLayout.addActionListener(this);
72    }
73
74    public void actionPerformed(ActionEvent e) {
75      if (e.getSource() == jrbFlowLayout) {
76        jpComponents.setLayout(flowLayout);
77        jtfDescription.setText(flowLayoutDesc);
78      }
79      else if (e.getSource() == jrbGridLayout) {
80        jpComponents.setLayout(gridLayout);
81        jtfDescription.setText(gridLayoutDesc);
82      }
83      else if (e.getSource() == jrbBoxLayout) {
84        jpComponents.setLayout(boxLayout);
85        jtfDescription.setText(boxLayoutDesc);
86      }
87
88      jpComponents.revalidate();                                      validate
89    }
90 }                                                                    main method omitted
```

Review

Split panes can be embedded. Adding a split pane to an existing split results in three split panes. The program creates two split panes (Lines 55–59) to hold a panel for radio buttons, a panel for buttons, and a scroll pane.

The radio buttons are used to select layout managers. A selected layout manager is used in the panel for laying out the buttons (Lines 75–87). The scroll pane contains a JTextField for displaying the text that describes the selected layout manager (Line 57).

22.8   Swing Borders

Swing provides a variety of borders that you can use to decorate components. You learned how to create titled borders and line borders in Chapter 13, "Creating User Interfaces." This section introduces borders in more detail.

A Swing border is defined in the `Border` interface. Every instance of `JComponent` can set a border through the `border` property defined in `JComponent`. If a border is present, it replaces the inset. The `AbstractBorder` class implements an empty border with no size. This provides a convenient base class from which other border classes can easily be derived. There are eight concrete border classes, `BevelBorder`, `SoftBevelBorder`, `CompoundBorder`, `EmptyBorder`, `EtchedBorder`, `LineBorder`, `MatteBorder`, and `TitledBorder`, as shown in Figure 22.25.

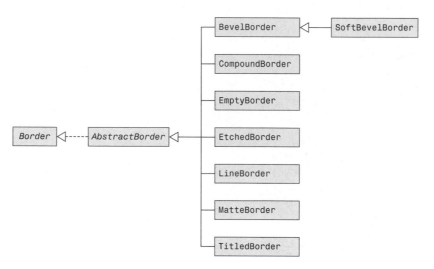

FIGURE 22.25   *Every instance of `JComponent` can have a border derived from the `Border` interface.*

◆ **BevelBorder** is a 3D-look border that can be lowered or raised. `BevelBorder` has the following constructors, which create a `BevelBorder` with the specified `bevelType` (`BevelBorder.LOWERED` or `BevelBorder.RAISED`) and colors:

```
BevelBorder(int bevelType)
BevelBorder(int bevelType, Color highlight, Color shadow)
BevelBorder(int bevelType, Color highlightOuterColor,
        Color highlightInnerColor, Color shadowOuterColor,
        Color shadowInnerColor)
```

◆ **SoftBevelBorder** is a raised or lowered bevel with softened corners. `SoftBevelBorder` has the following constructors:

```
SoftBevelBorder(int bevelType)
SoftBevelBorder(int bevelType, Color highlight, Color shadow)
SoftBevelBorder(int bevelType, Color highlightOuterColor,
            Color highlightInnerColor, Color shadowOuterColor,
            Color shadowInnerColor)
```

◆ **EmptyBorder** is a border with border space but no drawings. `EmptyBorder` has the following constructors:

```
EmptyBorder(Insets borderInsets)
EmptyBorder(int top, int left, int bottom, int right)
```

◆ **EtchedBorder** is an etched border that can be etched-in or etched-out. EtchedBorder has the property etchType with the value LOWERED or RAISED. EtchedBorder has the following constructors:

```
EtchedBorder() // default constructor with a lowered border
EtchedBorder(Color highlight, Color shadow)
EtchedBorder(int etchType)
EtchedBorder(int etchType, Color highlight, Color shadow)
```

◆ **LineBorder** draws a line of arbitrary thickness and a single color around the border. LineBorder has the following constructors:

```
LineBorder(Color color) // Thickness 1
LineBorder(Color color, int thickness)
LineBorder(Color color, int thickness, boolean roundedCorners)
```

◆ **MatteBorder** is a matte-like border padded with the icon images. MatteBorder has the following constructors:

```
MatteBorder(Icon tileIcon)
MatteBorder(Insets borderInsets, Color matteColor)
MatteBorder(Insets borderInsets, Icon tileIcon)
MatteBorder(int top, int left, int bottom, int right, Color matteColor)
MatteBorder(int top, int left, int bottom, int right, Icon tileIcon)
```

◆ **CompoundBorder** is used to compose two Border objects into a single border by nesting an inside Border object within the insets of an outside Border object using the following constructor:

```
CompoundBorder(Border outsideBorder, Border insideBorder)
```

◆ **TitledBorder** is a border with a string title in a specified position. Titled border can be composed with other borders. TitledBorder has the following constructors:

```
TitledBorder(String title)
TitledBorder(Border border) // Empty title on another border
TitledBorder(Border border, String title)
TitledBorder(Border border, String title,
             int titleJustification, int titlePosition)
TitledBorder(Border border, String title,
             int titleJustification, int titlePosition,
             Font titleFont)
TitledBorder(Border border, String title, int titleJustification,
             int titlePosition, Font titleFont, Color titleColor)
```

For convenience, Java also provides the javax.swing.BorderFactory class, which contains the following static methods for creating borders:

```
public static Border createBevelBorder(int type)

public static Border createBevelBorder(int type,
  Color highlight, Color shadow)

public static Border createBevelBorder(int type,
  Color highlightOuter, Color highlightInner,
  Color shadowOuter, Color shadowInner)

public static CompoundBorder createCompoundBorder()

public static CompoundBorder createCompoundBorder(
  Border outsideBorder, Border insideBorder)

public static Border createEmptyBorder()
```

```
public static Border createEmptyBorder(int top, int left,
  int bottom, int right)

public static Border createEtchedBorder()

public static Border createEtchedBorder(
  Color highlight, Color shadow)

public static Border createEtchedBorder(int type)

public static Border createEtchedBorder(
  int type, Color highlight, Color shadow)

public static Border createLineBorder(Color color)

public static Border createLineBorder(Color color, int thickness)

public static Border createLoweredBevelBorder()

public static MatteBorder createMatteBorder(
  int top, int left, int bottom, int right, Color color)

public static MatteBorder createMatteBorder(
  int top, int left, int bottom, int right, Icon tileIcon)

public static Border createRaisedBevelBorder()

public static TitledBorder createTitledBorder(Border border)

public static TitledBorder createTitledBorder(Border border,
  String title)

public static TitledBorder createTitledBorder(Border border,
  String title, int titleJustification, int titlePosition)

public static TitledBorder createTitledBorder(Border border,
  String title, int titleJustification, int titlePosition,
  Font titleFont)

public static TitledBorder createTitledBorder(Border border,
  String title, int titleJustification, int titlePosition,
  Font titleFont, Color titleColor)

public static TitledBorder createTitledBorder(String title)
```

For example, to create an etched border, use the following statement:

```
Border border = BorderFactory.createEtchedBorder();
```

 NOTE

All the border classes and interfaces are grouped in the package javax.swing.
border except javax.swing.BorderFactory.

 NOTE

Borders and icons can be shared. Thus you can create a border or icon and use it to
set the border or icon property for any GUI component. For example, the following statements set a border b for two panels p1 and p2:

```
p1.setBorder(b);
p2.setBorder(b);
```

EXAMPLE 22.11 USING BORDERS

Problem

Write a program that creates and displays various types of borders. You can select a border with a title or without a title. For a border without a title, you can choose a border style from Lowered Bevel, Raised Bevel, Etched, Line, Matte, or Empty. For a border with a title, you can specify the title position and justification. You can also embed another border into a titled border. Figure 22.26 displays a sample run of the program.

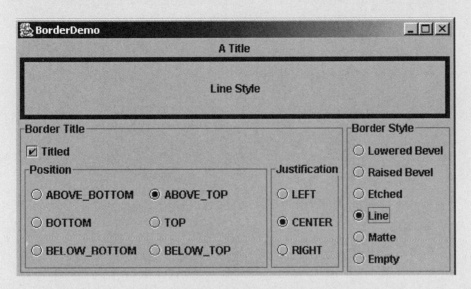

FIGURE **22.26**   *The program demonstrates various types of borders.*

Solution

The program is shown in Listing 22.13. Here are the major steps in the program:

1. Create the user interface.

   a. Create a JLabel object and place it in the center of the frame.

   b. Create a panel named jpPosition to group the radio buttons for selecting the border title position. Set the border of this panel in the titled border with the title "Position".

   c. Create a panel named jpJustification to group the radio buttons for selecting the border title justification. Set the border of this panel in the titled border with the title "Justification".

   d. Create a panel named jpTitleOptions to hold the jpPosition panel and the jpJustification panel.

   e. Create a panel named jpTitle to hold a check box named "Titled" and the jpTitleOptions panel.

   f. Create a panel named jpBorderStyle to group the radio buttons for selecting border styles.

   g. Create a panel named jpAllChoices to hold the panels jpTitle and jpBorderStyle. Place jpAllChoices in the south of the frame.

2. Process the event.
   Implement the actionPerformed handler to set the border for the label according to the events from the check box, and from all the radio buttons.

EXAMPLE 22.11 (CONTINUED)

LISTING 22.13   BorderDemo.java

```java
1  import java.awt.*;
2  import java.awt.event.ActionListener;
3  import java.awt.event.ActionEvent;
4  import javax.swing.*;
5  import javax.swing.border.*;
6
7  public class BorderDemo extends JApplet implements ActionListener {
8    // Declare a label for displaying message
9    private JLabel jLabel1 = new JLabel("Display the border type",
10     JLabel.CENTER);
11
12   // A check box for selecting a border with or without a title
13   private JCheckBox jchkTitled;
14
15   // Radio buttons for border styles
16   private JRadioButton jrbLoweredBevel, jrbRaisedBevel,
17     jrbEtched, jrbLine, jrbMatte, jrbEmpty;
18
19   // Radio buttons for titled border options
20   private JRadioButton jrbAboveBottom, jrbBottom,
21     jrbBelowBottom, jrbAboveTop, jrbTop, jrbBelowTop,
22     jrbLeft, jrbCenter, jrbRight;
23
24   // TitledBorder for the label
25   private TitledBorder jLabel1Border;
26
27   /** Constructor */
28   public BorderDemo() {
29     // Create a JLabel instance and set colors
30     jLabel1.setBackground(Color.yellow);
31     jLabel1.setBorder(jLabel1Border);
32
33     // Place title position radio buttons
34     JPanel jpPosition = new JPanel();
35     jpPosition.setLayout(new GridLayout(3, 2));
36     jpPosition.add(
37       jrbAboveBottom = new JRadioButton("ABOVE_BOTTOM"));
38     jpPosition.add(jrbAboveTop = new JRadioButton("ABOVE_TOP"));
39     jpPosition.add(jrbBottom = new JRadioButton("BOTTOM"));
40     jpPosition.add(jrbTop = new JRadioButton("TOP"));
41     jpPosition.add(
42       jrbBelowBottom = new JRadioButton("BELOW_BOTTOM"));
43     jpPosition.add(jrbBelowTop = new JRadioButton("BELOW_TOP"));
44     jpPosition.setBorder(new TitledBorder("Position"));
45
46     // Place title justification radio buttons
47     JPanel jpJustification = new JPanel();
48     jpJustification.setLayout(new GridLayout(3,1));
49     jpJustification.add(jrbLeft = new JRadioButton("LEFT"));
50     jpJustification.add(jrbCenter = new JRadioButton("CENTER"));
51     jpJustification.add(jrbRight = new JRadioButton("RIGHT"));
52     jpJustification.setBorder(new TitledBorder("Justification"));
53
54     // Create panel jpTitleOptions to hold jpPosition and
55     // jpJustification
56     JPanel jpTitleOptions = new JPanel();
57     jpTitleOptions.setLayout(new BorderLayout());
58     jpTitleOptions.add(jpPosition, BorderLayout.CENTER);
59     jpTitleOptions.add(jpJustification, BorderLayout.EAST);
60
61     // Create Panel jpTitle to hold a check box and title position
62     // radio buttons, and title justification radio buttons
63     JPanel jpTitle = new JPanel();
64     jpTitle.setBorder(new TitledBorder("Border Title"));
65     jpTitle.setLayout(new BorderLayout());
66     jpTitle.add(jchkTitled = new JCheckBox("Titled"),
```

create UI

EXAMPLE 22.11 (CONTINUED)

```
67          BorderLayout.NORTH);
68      jpTitle.add(jpTitleOptions, BorderLayout.CENTER);
69
70      // Group radio buttons for title position
71      ButtonGroup btgTitlePosition = new ButtonGroup();
72      btgTitlePosition.add(jrbAboveBottom);
73      btgTitlePosition.add(jrbBottom);
74      btgTitlePosition.add(jrbBelowBottom);
75      btgTitlePosition.add(jrbAboveTop);
76      btgTitlePosition.add(jrbTop);
77      btgTitlePosition.add(jrbBelowTop);
78
79      // Group radio buttons for title justification
80      ButtonGroup btgTitleJustification = new ButtonGroup();
81      btgTitleJustification.add(jrbLeft);
82      btgTitleJustification.add(jrbCenter);
83      btgTitleJustification.add(jrbRight);
84
85      // Create Panel jpBorderStyle to hold border style radio buttons
86      JPanel jpBorderStyle = new JPanel();
87      jpBorderStyle.setBorder(new TitledBorder("Border Style"));
88      jpBorderStyle.setLayout(new GridLayout(6, 1));
89      jpBorderStyle.add(jrbLoweredBevel =
90        new JRadioButton("Lowered Bevel"));
91      jpBorderStyle.add(jrbRaisedBevel =
92        new JRadioButton("Raised Bevel"));
93      jpBorderStyle.add(jrbEtched = new JRadioButton("Etched"));
94      jpBorderStyle.add(jrbLine = new JRadioButton("Line"));
95      jpBorderStyle.add(jrbMatte = new JRadioButton("Matte"));
96      jpBorderStyle.add(jrbEmpty = new JRadioButton("Empty"));
97
98      // Group radio buttons for border styles
99      ButtonGroup btgBorderStyle = new ButtonGroup();
100     btgBorderStyle.add(jrbLoweredBevel);
101     btgBorderStyle.add(jrbRaisedBevel);
102     btgBorderStyle.add(jrbEtched);
103     btgBorderStyle.add(jrbLine);
104     btgBorderStyle.add(jrbMatte);
105     btgBorderStyle.add(jrbEmpty);
106
107     // Create Panel jpAllChoices to place jpTitle and jpBorderStyle
108     JPanel jpAllChoices = new JPanel();
109     jpAllChoices.setLayout(new BorderLayout());
110     jpAllChoices.add(jpTitle, BorderLayout.CENTER);
111     jpAllChoices.add(jpBorderStyle, BorderLayout.EAST);
112
113     // Place panels in the frame
114     getContentPane().setLayout(new BorderLayout());
115     getContentPane().add(jLabel1, BorderLayout.CENTER);
116     getContentPane().add(jpAllChoices, BorderLayout.SOUTH);
117
118     // Register listeners
119     jchkTitled.addActionListener(this);
120     jrbAboveBottom.addActionListener(this);
121     jrbBottom.addActionListener(this);
122     jrbBelowBottom.addActionListener(this);
123     jrbAboveTop.addActionListener(this);
124     jrbTop.addActionListener(this);
125     jrbBelowTop.addActionListener(this);
126     jrbLeft.addActionListener(this);
127     jrbCenter.addActionListener(this);
128     jrbRight.addActionListener(this);
129     jrbLoweredBevel.addActionListener(this);
130     jrbRaisedBevel.addActionListener(this);
131     jrbLine.addActionListener(this);
132     jrbEtched.addActionListener(this);
133     jrbMatte.addActionListener(this);
134     jrbEmpty.addActionListener(this);
135   }
136
```

EXAMPLE 22.11 (CONTINUED)

```
137    /** Handle ActionEvents on check box and radio buttons */
138    public void actionPerformed(ActionEvent e) {
139      // Get border style
140      Border border = new EmptyBorder(2, 2, 2, 2);
141
142      if (jrbLoweredBevel.isSelected()) {
143        border = new BevelBorder(BevelBorder.LOWERED);
144        jLabel1.setText("Lowered Bevel Style");
145      }
146      else if (jrbRaisedBevel.isSelected()) {
147        border = new BevelBorder(BevelBorder.RAISED);
148        jLabel1.setText("Raised Bevel Style");
149      }
150      else if (jrbEtched.isSelected()) {
151        border = new EtchedBorder();
152        jLabel1.setText("Etched Style");
153      }
154      else if (jrbLine.isSelected()) {
155        border = new LineBorder(Color.black, 5);
156        jLabel1.setText("Line Style");
157      }
158      else if (jrbMatte.isSelected()) {
159        border = new MatteBorder(15, 15, 15, 15,
160          ImageViewer.createImageIcon("image/caIcon.gif", this));
161        jLabel1.setText("Matte Style");
162      }
163      else if (jrbEmpty.isSelected()) {
164        border = new EmptyBorder(2, 2, 2, 2);
165        jLabel1.setText("Empty Style");
166      }
167
168      if (jchkTitled.isSelected()) {
169        // Get the title position and justification
170        int titlePosition = TitledBorder.DEFAULT_POSITION;
171        int titleJustification = TitledBorder.DEFAULT_JUSTIFICATION;
172
173        if (jrbAboveBottom.isSelected())
174          titlePosition = TitledBorder.ABOVE_BOTTOM;
175        else if (jrbBottom.isSelected())
176          titlePosition = TitledBorder.BOTTOM;
177        else if (jrbBelowBottom.isSelected())
178          titlePosition = TitledBorder.BELOW_BOTTOM;
179        else if (jrbAboveTop.isSelected())
180          titlePosition = TitledBorder.ABOVE_TOP;
181        else if (jrbTop.isSelected())
182          titlePosition = TitledBorder.TOP;
183        else if (jrbBelowTop.isSelected())
184          titlePosition = TitledBorder.BELOW_TOP;
185
186        if (jrbLeft.isSelected())
187          titleJustification = TitledBorder.LEFT;
188        else if (jrbCenter.isSelected())
189          titleJustification = TitledBorder.CENTER;
190        else if (jrbRight.isSelected())
191          titleJustification = TitledBorder.RIGHT;
192
193        jLabel1Border = new TitledBorder("A Title");
194        jLabel1Border.setBorder(border);
195        jLabel1Border.setTitlePosition(titlePosition);
196        jLabel1Border.setTitleJustification(titleJustification);
197        jLabel1.setBorder(jLabel1Border);
198      }
199      else {
200        jLabel1.setBorder(border);
201      }
202    }
203  }
```

empty border

lowered bevel border

raised bevel border

etched border

line border

matte border

empty border

border on border

main method omitted

EXAMPLE 22.11 (CONTINUED)

Review

This example uses many panels to group UI components to achieve the desired look. Figure 22.26 illustrates the relationship of the panels. The Border Title panel groups all the options for setting title properties. The position options are grouped in the Position panel. The justification options are grouped in the Justification panel. The Border Style panel groups the radio buttons for choosing Lowered Bevel, Raised Bevel, Etched, Line, Matte, and Empty borders.

The label displays the selected border with or without a title, depending on the selection of the title check box. The label also displays a text indicating which type of border is being used, depending on the selection of the radio button in the Border Style panel.

The `TitledBorder` can be mixed with other borders. To do so, simply create an instance of `TitledBorder`, and use the `setBorder` method to embed a new border in `TitledBorder`.

The `MatteBorder` can be used to display icons on the border, as shown in Figure 22.27.

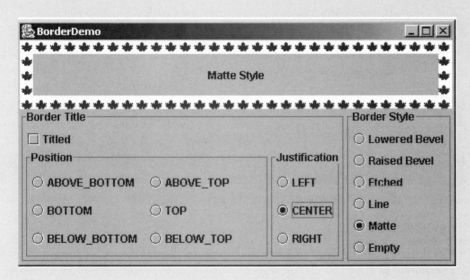

FIGURE 22.27 *MatteBorder can display icons on the border.*

KEY CLASSES AND METHODS

✦ `java.awt.CardLayout` is a layout manager that places components as cards in a container.

✦ `java.awt.GridBagLayout` is a layout manager that is similar to the `GridLayout` manager in the sense that both layout managers arrange components in a grid. The components of `GridBagLayout` can vary in size, however, and can be added in any order.

✦ `java.awt.GridBagConstraints` is a constraint object used to specify the constraints (component location, size, growth factor, anchor, inset, filling, and padding) in a `GridBagLayout`.

✦ `javax.swing.BoxLayout` is a Swing layout manager that arranges components in a row or a column. You can use `BoxLayout` in any container, but it is simpler to use the `Box` class.

✦ `javax.swing.Box` is a container class with a built-in `BoxLayout`.

◆ **javax.swing.OverlayLayout** is a Swing layout manager that arranges components on top of each other. A component is on top of another component if it is added to the container before the other one.

◆ **javax.swing.SpringLayout** is a Swing layout manager that puts a flexible spring around a component. The spring may compress or expand to place the components in desired locations.

◆ **javax.swing.Spring** is a class to create springs. Each spring has a preferred value, minimum value, maximum value, and actual value. The getPreferredValue(), getMinimumValue(), getMaximumValue(), and getValue() methods retrieve these values. The setValue(int value) method can be used to set an actual value. The Spring class defines the static sum(Spring s1, Spring s2) to produce a combined new spring, the static minus(Spring s) to produce a new spring running in the opposite direction, and the static max(Spring s1, Spring s2) to produce a new spring with larger values from s1 and s2.

◆ **javax.swing.JScrollPane** is a specialized container with a view port for displaying the contained component. In addition to horizontal and vertical scrollbars, a JScrollPane can have a column header, a row header, and corners. You can place any instance of JComponent into a JScrollPane.

◆ **javax.swing.JTabbedPane** is a specialized container that provides a set of mutually exclusive tabs for accessing multiple components. JTabbedPane is easy to use, because the selection of the panel is handled automatically by clicking the corresponding tab. You can switch between a group of panels by clicking on a tab with a given title and/or icon.

◆ **javax.swing.JSplitPane** is a specialized container that contains two components with a bar that divides the container horizontally or vertically. The bar can be dragged to change the amount of space occupied by each component.

◆ **javax.swing.border.Border** is a root interface for Swing borders. Every instance of JComponent can set a border through the border property defined in JComponent. If a border is present, it replaces the inset. There are eight concrete border classes: BevelBorder, SoftBevelBorder, CompoundBorder, EmptyBorder, EtchedBorder, LineBorder, MatteBorder, and TitledBorder.

◆ **javax.swing.BorderFactory** is a utility class for creating various borders using static methods.

Chapter Summary

◆ javax.swing.JRootPane is a lightweight container used behind the scenes by Swing's top-level containers, such as JFrame, JApplet, and JDialog. javax.swing.JLayeredPane is a container that manages the optional menu bar and the content pane. The content pane is an instance of Container. By default, it is a JPanel with BorderLayout. This is the container where the user interface components are added. To obtain the content pane in a JFrame or in a JApplet, use the getContentPane() method. You can set any instance of Container to be a new content pane using the setContentPane method.

◆ Every container has a layout manager that is responsible for arranging its components. The container's setLayout method can be used to set a layout manager. Certain types of containers have default layout managers.

◆ Java provides FlowLayout, GridLayout, BorderLayout, CardLayout, GridBagLayout, BoxLayout, OverlayLayout, and SpringLayout. The layout manager places the components in accordance with its own rules and property settings, and with the constraints associated with each component. Every layout manager has its own specific set of rules. Some layout managers have properties that can affect the sizing and location of the components in the container.

♦ Java also supports absolute layout that enables you to place components at a fixed location. In this case, the component must be placed using the component's instance method `setBounds()` (defined in `java.awt.Component`). Absolute positions and sizes are fine if the application is developed and deployed on the same platform, but what looks fine on a development system may not look right on a deployment system on a different platform. To solve this problem, Java provides a set of layout managers that place components in containers in a way that is independent of fonts, screen resolutions, and operating systems.

♦ In addition to the layout managers provided in Java, you can create custom layout managers by implementing the `LayoutManager` interface.

♦ Java provides specialized containers `Box`, `JScrollPane`, `JTabbedPane`, and `JSplitPane` with fixed layout managers.

♦ A Swing border is defined in the `Border` interface. Every instance of `JComponent` can set a border through the `border` property defined in `JComponent`. If a border is present, it replaces the inset. There are eight concrete border classes: `BevelBorder`, `SoftBevelBorder`, `CompoundBorder`, `EmptyBorder`, `EtchedBorder`, `LineBorder`, `MatteBorder`, and `TitledBorder`. You can use the constructors of these classes or the static methods in `javax.swing.BorderFactory` to create borders.

REVIEW QUESTIONS

Section 22.2 Swing Container Structures

22.1 Since `JButton` is a subclass of `Container`, can you add a button inside a button?

22.2 How do you set an image icon in a `JFrame`'s title bar? Can you set an image icon in a `JApplet`'s title bar?

22.3 Which of the following are the properties in `JFrame`, `JApplet`, and `JPanel`?

contentPane, iconImage, jMenuBar, resizable, title

Section 22.3 Layout Managers

22.4 How does the layout in Java differ from the ones in Visual Basic and Delphi?

22.5 Discuss the factors that determine the size of the components in a container.

22.6 Discuss the properties `preferredSize`, `minimumSize`, and `maximumSize`.

22.7 Discuss the properties `alignmentX` and `alignmentY`.

22.8 What is a `CardLayout` manager? How do you create a `CardLayout` manager?

22.9 What is a `GridBagLayout` manager? How do you create a `GridBagLayout` manager?

22.10 Can you use absolute positioning in Java? How do you use absolute positioning? Why should you avoid using absolute positioning?

22.11 What is `BoxLayout`? How do you use `BoxLayout`? How do you use fillers to separate the components?

22.12 What is `OverlayLayout`? How do you use `OverlayLayout`?

22.13 What is `SpringLayout`? How do you use `SpringLayout`?

Sections 22.4–22.8

22.14 How do you create a custom layout manager?

22.15 What is JScrollPane? How do you use JScrollPane?

22.16 What is JTabbedPane? How do you use JTabbedPane?

22.17 What is JSplitPane? How do you use JSplitPane?

22.18 Can you specify a layout manager in Box, JScrollPane, JTabbedPane, and JSplitPane?

Section 22.9 Swing Borders

22.19 How do you create a titled border, a line border, a bevel border, and an etched border?

22.20 Can you set a border for every Swing GUI component? Can a border object be shared by different GUI components?

22.21 What package contains Border, BevelBorder, CompoundBorder, EmptyBorder, EtchedBorder, LineBorder, MatteBorder, TitledBorder, and BorderFactory?

PROGRAMMING EXERCISES

Section 22.3 Layout Managers

22.1* (*Demonstrating* FlowLayout *properties*) Create a program that enables the user to set the properties of a FlowLayout manager dynamically, as shown in Figure 22.28. The FlowLayout manager is used to place fifteen components in a panel. You can set the alignment, hgap, and vgap properties of the FlowLayout dynamically.

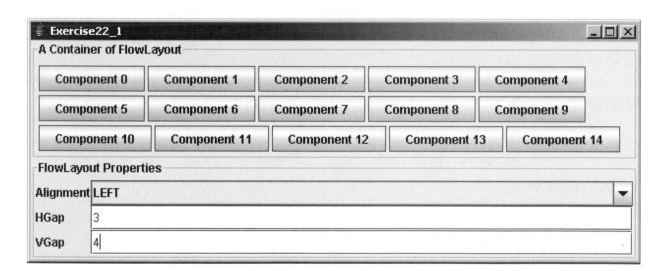

FIGURE 22.28 *The program enables you to set the properties of a* FlowLayout *manager dynamically.*

22.2* (*Demonstrating* GridLayout *properties*) Create a program that enables the user to set the properties of a GridLayout manager dynamically, as shown in Figure 22.29. The GridLayout manager is used to place fifteen components in a panel. You can set the rows, columns, hgap, and vgap properties of the GridLayout dynamically.

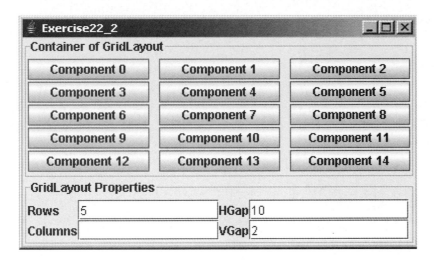

FIGURE 22.29 *The program enables you to set the properties of a* GridLayout *manager dynamically.*

22.3* (*Demonstrating* BorderLayout *properties*) Create a program that enables the user to set the properties of a BorderLayout manager dynamically, as shown in Figure 22.30. The BorderLayout manager is used to place five components in a panel. You can set the hgap and vgap properties of the BorderLayout dynamically.

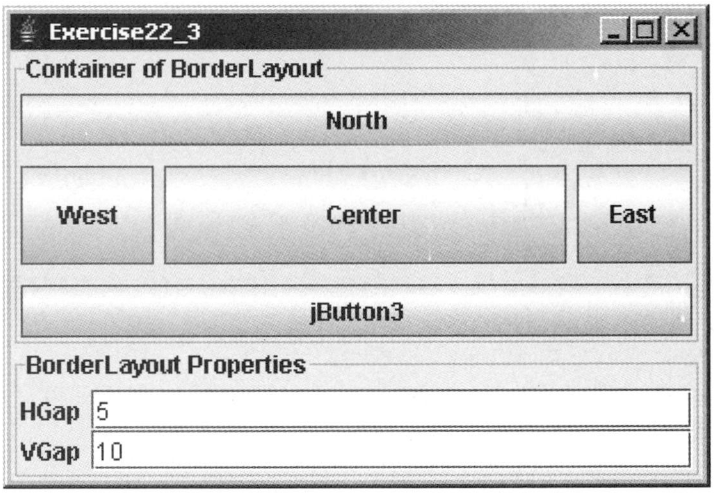

FIGURE 22.30 *The program enables you to set the properties of a* BorderLayout *manager dynamically.*

22.4* (*Using* CardLayout) Write an applet that does arithmetic on integers and rationals. The program uses two panels in a CardLayout manager, one for integer arithmetic and the other for rational arithmetic.

The program provides a combo box with two items, Integer and Rational. When the user chooses the Integer item, the integer panel is activated. When the user chooses the rational item, the rational panel is activated (see Figure 22.31).

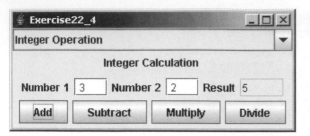
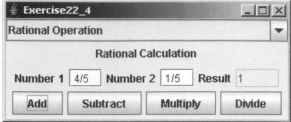

FIGURE 22.31 *CardLayout is used to select panels that perform integer operations and rational number operations.*

22.5* (*Using* GridBagLayout)

Use GridBagLayout to lay out a calculator as shown in Figure 14.25(a) on page 540.

Sections 22.4–22.8

22.6* (*Modifying Example 22.9, "Using* JTabbedPane*"*) Modify Example 22.9 to add a panel of radio buttons for specifying the tab placement of the tabbed pane, as shown in Figure 22.32.

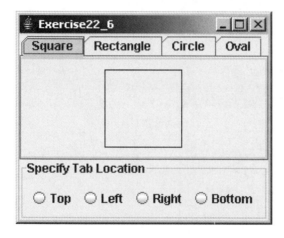
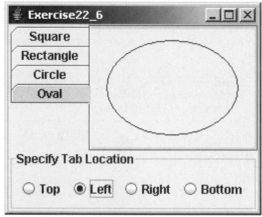

FIGURE 22.32 *The radio buttons let you choose the tab placement of the tabbed pane.*

22.7* (*Using tabbed pane*) Rewrite Exercise 22.4 using tabbed panes instead of CardLayout (see Figure 22.33).

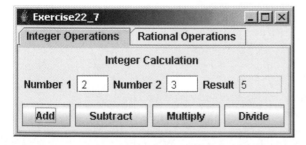
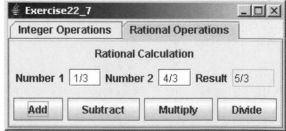

FIGURE 22.33 *A tabbed pane is used to select panels that perform integer operations and rational number operations.*

22.8* (*Using* JSplitPane) Create a program that displays four figures in split panes, as shown in Figure 22.34. Use the FigurePanel class defined in Example 22.9, "Using JTabbedPane," to display figures.

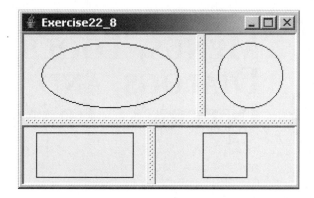

FIGURE **22.34** *Four figures are displayed in split panes.*

22.9* (*Demonstrating* JSplitPane *properties*) Create a program that enables the user to set the properties of a split pane dynamically, as shown in Figure 22.35.

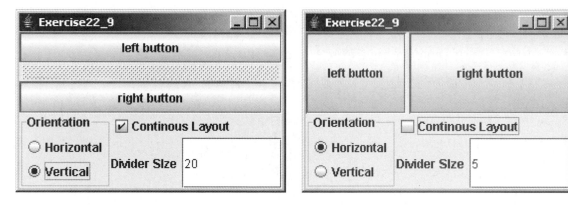

FIGURE **22.35** *The program enables you to set the properties of a split pane dynamically.*

chapter

23

Menus, Toolbars, Dialogs, and Internal Frames

Objectives

✦ To create menus using components JMenuBar, JMenu, JMenuItem, JCheckBoxMenuItem, and JRadioButtonMenuItem (§23.2).

✦ To create popup menus using components JPopupMenu, JMenuItem, JCheckBoxMenuItem, and JRadioButtonMenuItem (§23.3).

✦ To use JToolBar to create tool bars (§23.4).

✦ To use the Action objects to generalize the code for processing actions (§23.5).

✦ To create standard dialogs using the JOptionPane class (§23.6).

✦ To extend the JDialog class to create custom dialogs (§23.7).

✦ To select colors using JColorChooser (§23.8).

✦ To use JFileChooser to display Open and Save File dialogs (§23.9).

✦ To create internal frames using JInternalFrame (§23.10 Optional).

23.1 Introduction

Java provides a comprehensive solution for building graphical user interfaces. This chapter introduces menus, popup menus, tool bars, dialogs, and internal frames. You will also learn how to use the Action objects to generalize the code for processing actions.

23.2 Menus

Menus make selection easier and are widely used in window applications. Java provides   menu
five classes that implement menus: JMenuBar, JMenu, JMenuItem, JCheckBoxMenuItem, and
JRadioButtonMenuItem.

    JMenuBar is a top-level menu component used to hold the menus. A menu consists of *menu*   menu item
items that the user can select (or toggle on or off). A menu item can be an instance of JMenuItem,
JCheckBoxMenuItem, or JRadioButtonMenuItem. Menu items can be associated with icons, keyboard mnemonics, and keyboard accelerators. Menu items can be separated using separators.

23.2.1 Creating Menus

The sequence of implementing menus in Java is as follows:

1. Create a menu bar and associate it with a frame or an applet by using the setJMenuBar method. For example, the following code creates a frame and a menu bar, and sets the menu bar in the frame:

```
JFrame frame = new JFrame();
frame.setSize(300, 200);
frame.setVisible(true);
JMenuBar jmb = new JMenuBar();
frame.setJMenuBar(jmb);  // Attach a menu bar to a frame
```

2. Create menus and associate them with the menu bar. You can use the following constructor to create a menu:

```
public JMenu(String label)
```

Here is an example of creating menus:

```
JMenu fileMenu = new JMenu("File");
JMenu helpMenu = new JMenu("Help");
```

This creates two menus labeled File and Help, as shown in Figure 23.1(a). The menus will not be seen until they are added to an instance of JMenuBar, as follows:

```
jmb.add(fileMenu);
jmb.add(helpMenu);
```

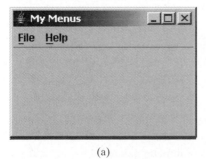
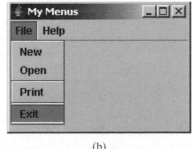
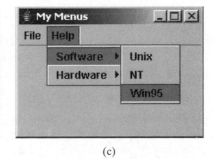

(a)   (b)   (c)

Figure 23.1 *The menu bar appears below the title bar on the frame in (a). Clicking a menu on the menu bar reveals the items under the menu in (b). Clicking a menu item reveals the submenu items under the menu item in (c).*

3. Create menu items and add them to the menus.

```
fileMenu.add(new JMenuItem("New"));
fileMenu.add(new JMenuItem("Open"));
fileMenu.addSeparator();
fileMenu.add(new JMenuItem("Print"));
fileMenu.addSeparator();
fileMenu.add(new JMenuItem("Exit"));
```

This code adds the menu items New, Open, a separator bar, Print, another separator bar, and Exit, in this order, to the File menu, as shown in Figure 23.1(b). The addSeparator() method adds a separator bar in the menu.

3.1. Creating submenu items.

You can also embed menus inside menus so that the embedded menus become submenus. Here is an example:

```
JMenu softwareHelpSubMenu = new JMenu("Software");
JMenu hardwareHelpSubMenu = new JMenu("Hardware");
helpMenu.add(softwareHelpSubMenu);
helpMenu.add(hardwareHelpSubMenu);
softwareHelpSubMenu.add(new JMenuItem("Unix"));
softwareHelpSubMenu.add(new JMenuItem("NT"));
softwareHelpSubMenu.add(new JMenuItem("Win95"));
```

This code adds two submenus, softwareHelpSubMenu and hardwareHelpSubMenu, in helpMenu. The menu items Unix, NT, and Win95 are added to softwareHelpSubMenu (see Figure 23.1(c)).

3.2. Creating check box menu items.

You can also add a JCheckBoxMenuItem to a JMenu. JCheckBoxMenuItem is a subclass of JMenuItem that adds a Boolean state to the JMenuItem, and displays a check when its state is true. You can click a menu item to turn it on or off. For example, the following statement adds the check box menu item Check it (see Figure 23.2(a)):

```
helpMenu.add(new JCheckBoxMenuItem("Check it"));
```

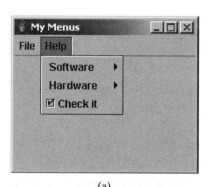
(a)

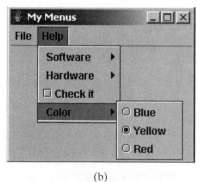
(b)

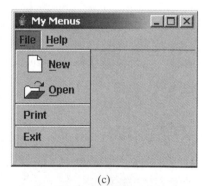
(c)

FIGURE 23.2 *A check box menu item in (a) lets you check or uncheck a menu item just like a check box. You can use* JRadioButtonMenuItem *to choose among mutually exclusive menu choices in (b). You can set image icons, keyboard mnemonics, and keyboard accelerators in menus in (c).*

3.3 Creating radio button menu items.

You can also add radio buttons to a menu, using the JRadioButtonMenuItem class. This is often useful when you have a group of mutually exclusive choices in the menu. For example, the following statements add a submenu named Color and a set of radio buttons for choosing a color (see Figure 23.2(b)):

```
JMenu colorHelpSubMenu = new JMenu("Color");
helpMenu.add(colorHelpSubMenu);
```

```
JRadioButtonMenuItem jrbmiBlue, jrbmiYellow, jrbmiRed;
colorHelpSubMenu.add(jrbmiBlue =
  new JRadioButtonMenuItem("Blue"));
colorHelpSubMenu.add(jrbmiYellow =
  new JRadioButtonMenuItem("Yellow"));
colorHelpSubMenu.add(jrbmiRed =
  new JRadioButtonMenuItem("Red"));

ButtonGroup btg = new ButtonGroup();
btg.add(jrbmiBlue);
btg.add(jrbmiYellow);
btg.add(jrbmiRed);
```

4. The menu items generate `ActionEvent`. Your program must implement the `ActionListener` and the `actionPerformed` handler to respond to the menu selection. The following is an example:

```
public void actionPerformed(ActionEvent e) {
  String actionCommand = e.getActionCommand();

  // Make sure the source is JMenuItem
  if (e.getSource() instanceof JMenuItem)
    if ("New".equals(actionCommand))
      respondToNew();
}
```

This code executes the method `respondToNew()` when the menu item labeled New is selected.

23.2.2   Image Icons, Keyboard Mnemonics, and Keyboard Accelerators

The menu components `JMenu`, `JMenuItem`, `JCheckBoxMenuItem`, and `JRadioButtonMenuItem` have the `icon` and `mnemonic` properties. For example, using the following code, you can set icons for the New and Open menu items, and set keyboard mnemonics for File, Help, New, and Open:

```
JMenuItem jmiNew, jmiOpen;
fileMenu.add(jmiNew = new JMenuItem("New"));
fileMenu.add(jmiOpen = new JMenuItem("Open"));
jmiNew.setIcon(new ImageIcon("image/new.gif"));
jmiOpen.setIcon(new ImageIcon("image/open.gif"));
helpMenu.setMnemonic('H');
fileMenu.setMnemonic('F');
jmiNew.setMnemonic('N');
jmiOpen.setMnemonic('O');
```

The new icons and mnemonics are shown in Figure 23.2(c). You can also use `JMenuItem` constructors like the ones that follow to construct and set an icon or mnemonic in one statement:

```
public JMenuItem(String label, Icon icon);
public JMenuItem(String label, int mnemonic);
```

By default, the text is at the right of the icon. Use `setHorizontalTextPosition` (`SwingConstants.LEFT`) to set the text to the left of the icon.

To select a menu, press the ALT key and the mnemonic key. For example, press ALT+F to select the File menu, and then press ALT+O to select the Open menu item. Keyboard mnemonics are useful, but only let you select menu items from the currently open menu. Key *accelerators*, however, let you select a menu item directly by pressing the CTRL and accelerator keys. For example, by using the following code, you can attach the accelerator key CTRL+O to the Open menu item:

accelerator

```
jmiOpen.setAccelerator(KeyStroke.getKeyStroke
  (KeyEvent.VK_O, ActionEvent.CTRL_MASK));
```

The `setAccelerator` method takes a `KeyStroke` object. The static method `getKeyStroke` in the `KeyStroke` class creates an instance of the keystroke. `VK_O` is a constant representing the O key, and `CTRL_MASK` is a constant indicating that the CTRL key is associated with the keystroke.

NOTE

As shown in Figure 11.3 on page 372, `AbstractButton` is the superclass for `JButton` and `JMenuItem`, and `JMenuItem` is a superclass for `JCheckBoxMenuItem`, `JMenu`, and `JRadioButtonMenuItem`. The menu components are very similar to buttons.

EXAMPLE 23.1 USING MENUS

Problem

Write a program that creates a user interface to perform arithmetic. The interface contains labels and text fields for Number 1, Number 2, and Result. The Result text field displays the result of the arithmetic operation between Number 1 and Number 2. Figure 23.3 contains a sample run of the program.

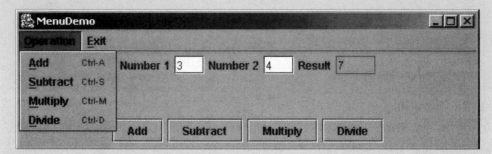

FIGURE 23.3   *Arithmetic operations can be performed by clicking buttons or by choosing menu items from the Operation menu.*

Solution

Here are the major steps in the program (Listing 23.1):

1. Create a menu bar and set it in the applet. Create the menus Operation and Exit, and add them to the menu bar. Add the menu items Add, Subtract, Multiply, and Divide under the Operation menu, and add the menu item Close under the Exit menu.

2. Create a panel to hold labels and text fields, and place the panel in the center of the applet.

3. Create a panel to hold the four buttons labeled Add, Subtract, Multiply, and Divide. Place the panel in the south of the applet.

4. Implement the `actionPerformed` handler to process the events from the menu items and the buttons.

LISTING 23.1   MenuDemo.java (Using Menus)

```
 1 import java.awt.*;
 2 import java.awt.event.*;
 3 import javax.swing.*;
 4
 5 public class MenuDemo extends JApplet implements ActionListener {
 6   // Text fields for Number 1, Number 2, and Result
 7   private JTextField jtfNum1, jtfNum2, jtfResult;
 8
 9   // Buttons "Add", "Subtract", "Multiply" and "Divide"
10   private JButton jbtAdd, jbtSub, jbtMul, jbtDiv;
11
12   // Menu items "Add", "Subtract", "Multiply","Divide" and "Close"
13   private JMenuItem jmiAdd, jmiSub, jmiMul, jmiDiv, jmiClose;
```

EXAMPLE 23.1 (CONTINUED)

```
14
15   public MenuDemo() {
16     // Create menu bar
17     JMenuBar jmb = new JMenuBar();                                    menu bar
18
19     // Set menu bar to the applet
20     setJMenuBar(jmb);                                                 set menu bar
21
22     // Add menu "Operation" to menu bar
23     JMenu operationMenu = new JMenu("Operation");                     add menus
24     operationMenu.setMnemonic('O');
25     jmb.add(operationMenu);
26
27     // Add menu "Exit" to menu bar
28     JMenu exitMenu = new JMenu("Exit");
29     exitMenu.setMnemonic('E');
30     jmb.add(exitMenu);
31
32     // Add menu items with mnemonics to menu "Operation"
33     operationMenu.add(jmiAdd = new JMenuItem("Add", 'A'));            add menu items
34     operationMenu.add(jmiSub = new JMenuItem("Subtract", 'S'));
35     operationMenu.add(jmiMul = new JMenuItem("Multiply", 'M'));
36     operationMenu.add(jmiDiv = new JMenuItem("Divide", 'D'));
37     exitMenu.add(jmiClose = new JMenuItem("Close", 'C'));
38
39     // Set keyboard accelerators
40     jmiAdd.setAccelerator(                                            accelerator
41       KeyStroke.getKeyStroke(KeyEvent.VK_A, ActionEvent.CTRL_MASK));
42     jmiSub.setAccelerator(
43       KeyStroke.getKeyStroke(KeyEvent.VK_S, ActionEvent.CTRL_MASK));
44     jmiMul.setAccelerator(
45       KeyStroke.getKeyStroke(KeyEvent.VK_M, ActionEvent.CTRL_MASK));
46     jmiDiv.setAccelerator(
47       KeyStroke.getKeyStroke(KeyEvent.VK_D, ActionEvent.CTRL_MASK));
48
49     // Panel p1 to hold text fields and labels
50     JPanel p1 = new JPanel(new FlowLayout());
51     p1.add(new JLabel("Number 1"));
52     p1.add(jtfNum1 = new JTextField(3));
53     p1.add(new JLabel("Number 2"));
54     p1.add(jtfNum2 = new JTextField(3));
55     p1.add(new JLabel("Result"));
56     p1.add(jtfResult = new JTextField(4));
57     jtfResult.setEditable(false);
58
59     // Panel p2 to hold buttons
60     JPanel p2 = new JPanel(new FlowLayout());
61     p2.add(jbtAdd = new JButton("Add"));                             buttons
62     p2.add(jbtSub = new JButton("Subtract"));
63     p2.add(jbtMul = new JButton("Multiply"));
64     p2.add(jbtDiv = new JButton("Divide"));
65
66     // Add panels to the frame
67     getContentPane().setLayout(new BorderLayout());
68     getContentPane().add(p1, BorderLayout.CENTER);
69     getContentPane().add(p2, BorderLayout.SOUTH);
70
71     // Register listeners
72     jbtAdd.addActionListener(this);                                 register listeners
73     jbtSub.addActionListener(this);
74     jbtMul.addActionListener(this);
75     jbtDiv.addActionListener(this);
76     jmiAdd.addActionListener(this);
77     jmiSub.addActionListener(this);
78     jmiMul.addActionListener(this);
79     jmiDiv.addActionListener(this);
```

EXAMPLE 23.1 (CONTINUED)

handler

```
 80        jmiClose.addActionListener(this);
 81    }
 82
 83    /** Handle ActionEvent from buttons and menu items */
 84    public void actionPerformed(ActionEvent e) {
 85      String actionCommand = e.getActionCommand();
 86
 87      // Handle button events
 88      if (e.getSource() instanceof JButton) {
 89        if ("Add".equals(actionCommand))
 90          calculate('+');
 91        else if ("Subtract".equals(actionCommand))
 92          calculate('-');
 93        else if ("Multiply".equals(actionCommand))
 94          calculate('*');
 95        else if ("Divide".equals(actionCommand))
 96          calculate('/');
 97      }
 98      else if (e.getSource() instanceof JMenuItem) {
 99        // Handle menu item events
100        if ("Add".equals(actionCommand))
101          calculate('+');
102        else if ("Subtract".equals(actionCommand))
103          calculate('-');
104        else if ("Multiply".equals(actionCommand))
105          calculate('*');
106        else if ("Divide".equals(actionCommand))
107          calculate('/');
108        else if ("Close".equals(actionCommand))
109          System.exit(0);
110      }
111    }
112
113    /** Calculate and show the result in jtfResult */
114    private void calculate(char operator) {
115      // Obtain Number 1 and Number 2
116      int num1 = (Integer.parseInt(jtfNum1.getText().trim()));
117      int num2 = (Integer.parseInt(jtfNum2.getText().trim()));
118      int result = 0;
119
120      // Perform selected operation
121      switch (operator) {
122        case '+': result = num1 + num2;
123                  break;
124        case '-': result = num1 - num2;
125                  break;
126        case '*': result = num1 * num2;
127                  break;
128        case '/': result = num1 / num2;
129      }
130
131      // Set result in jtfResult
132      jtfResult.setText(String.valueOf(result));
133    }
134 }
```

main method omitted

Review

The program creates a menu bar, jmb, which holds two menus: operationMenu and exitMenu (Lines 17–30). The operationMenu contains four menu items for doing arithmetic: Add, Subtract, Multiply, and Divide. The exitMenu contains the menu item Close for exiting the program. The menu items in the Operation menu are created with keyboard mnemonics and accelerators.

The user enters two numbers in the number fields. When an operation is chosen from the menu, its result, involving two numbers, is displayed in the Result field. The user can also click the buttons to perform the same operation.

EXAMPLE 23.1 (CONTINUED)

The private method `calculate(char operator)` (Lines 114–133) retrieves operands from the text fields in Number 1 and Number 2, applies the binary operator on the operands, and sets the result in the Result text field.

 NOTE

The menu bar is usually attached to the window using the `setJMenuBar` method. However, like any other component, it can be placed in a container. For instance, you can place a menu bar in the south of the container with `BorderLayout`.

23.3 Popup Menus

A *popup menu*, also known as *a context menu*, is like a regular menu, but does not have a menu bar and can float anywhere on the screen. Creating a popup menu is similar to creating a regular menu. First, you create an instance of `JPopupMenu`, then you can add `JMenuItem`, `JCheckBoxMenuItem`, `JRadioButtonMenuItem`, and separators to the popup menu. For example, the following code creates a `JPopupMenu` and adds `JMenuItems` into it:

popup menu

```
JPopupMenu jPopupMenu = new JPopupMenu();
JPopupMenu(new JMenuItem("New"));
JPopupMenu(new JMenuItem("Open"));
```

A regular menu is always attached to a menu bar using the `setJMenuBar` method, but a popup menu is associated with a parent component and is displayed using the `show` method in the `JPopupMenu` class. You specify the parent component and the location of the popup menu, using the coordinate system of the parent like this:

```
jPopupMenu.show(component, x, y);
```

The popup menu usually contains the commands for an object. Customarily, you display a popup menu by pointing to the object and clicking a certain mouse button, the so-called *popup trigger*. Popup triggers are system-dependent. In Windows, the popup menu is displayed when the right mouse button is released. In Motif, the popup menu is displayed when the third mouse button is pressed and held down.

popup trigger

EXAMPLE 23.2 USING POPUP MENUS

Problem

The program creates a text area in a scroll pane. When the mouse points to the text area, it triggers the popup menu display, as shown in Figure 23.4.

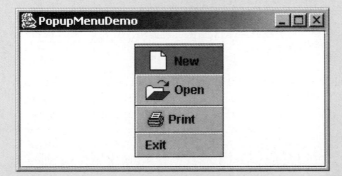

FIGURE 23.4 *A popup menu is displayed when the popup trigger is issued on the text area.*

EXAMPLE 23.2 (CONTINUED)

Solution

Here are the major steps in the program (Listing 23.2):

1. Create a popup menu using JPopupMenu. Create menu items for New, Open, Print, and Exit using JMenuItem. For the menu items with both labels and icons, it is convenient to use the JMenuItem(label, icon) constructor.

2. Add the menu items into the popup menu.

3. Create a scroll pane and add a text area into the scroll pane. Place the scroll pane in the center of the applet.

4. Implement the actionPerformed handler to process the events from the menu items.

5. Implement the mousePressed and mouseReleased methods to process the events for handling popup triggers.

LISTING 23.2   PopupMenuDemo.java

```
 1  import javax.swing.*;
 2  import java.awt.*;
 3  import java.awt.event.*;
 4
 5  public class PopupMenuDemo extends JApplet
 6        implements ActionListener {
 7    private JPopupMenu jPopupMenu1 = new JPopupMenu();
 8    private JMenuItem jmiNew = new JMenuItem("New",
 9      ImageViewer.createImageIcon("image/new.gif", this));
10    private JMenuItem jmiOpen = new JMenuItem("Open",
11      ImageViewer.createImageIcon("image/open.gif", this));
12    private JMenuItem jmiPrint = new JMenuItem("Print",
13      ImageViewer.createImageIcon("image/print.gif", this));
14    private JMenuItem jmiExit = new JMenuItem("Exit");
15    private JTextArea jTextArea1 = new JTextArea();
16
17    public PopupMenuDemo() {
18      jPopupMenu1.add(jmiNew);
19      jPopupMenu1.add(jmiOpen);
20      jPopupMenu1.addSeparator();
21      jPopupMenu1.add(jmiPrint);
22      jPopupMenu1.addSeparator();
23      jPopupMenu1.add(jmiExit);
24      jPopupMenu1.add(jmiExit);
25
26      getContentPane().add(new JScrollPane(jTextArea1),
27        BorderLayout.CENTER);
28
29      jmiNew.addActionListener(this);
30      jmiOpen.addActionListener(this);
31      jmiPrint.addActionListener(this);
32      jmiExit.addActionListener(this);
33      jTextArea1.addMouseListener(new MouseAdapter() {
34        public void mousePressed(MouseEvent e) { // For Motif
35          showPopup(e);
36        }
37
38        public void mouseReleased(MouseEvent e) { // For Windows
39          showPopup(e);
40        }
41      });
42    }
43
44    /** Display popup menu when triggered */
45    private void showPopup(java.awt.event.MouseEvent evt) {
46      if (evt.isPopupTrigger())
```

popup menu

add menu items

show popup menu

show popup menu

EXAMPLE 23.2 (CONTINUED)

```
47          jPopupMenu1.show(evt.getComponent(), evt.getX(), evt.getY());
48    }
49
50    public void actionPerformed(ActionEvent e) {
51      if (e.getSource() == jmiNew)
52        System.out.println("Process New");
53      else if (e.getSource() == jmiOpen)
54        System.out.println("Process Open");
55      else if (e.getSource() == jmiPrint)
56        System.out.println("Process Print");
57      else if (e.getSource() == jmiExit)
58        System.exit(0);
59    }
60  }
```

main method omitted

Review

The process of creating popup menus is similar to the process for creating regular menus. To create a popup menu, create a JPopupMenu as the basis (Line 7), and add JmenuItems to the popup menu (Lines 18–24).

To show a popup menu, the applet uses the show method by specifying the parent component and the location for the popup menu (Line 47). The show method is invoked when the popup menu is triggered by a particular mouse click on the text area. Popup triggers are system-dependent. This program implements the mouseReleased handler for displaying the popup menu in Windows (Lines 34–36) and the mousePressed handler for displaying the popup menu in Motif (Lines 38–40).

23.4   JToolBar

In user interfaces, a *toolbar* is often used to hold commands that also appear in the menus. Frequently used commands are placed in a toolbar for quick access. Clicking a command in the toolbar is faster than choosing it from the menu.

toolbar

Swing provides the JToolBar class as the container to hold tool bar components. JToolBar uses BoxLayout to manage components by default. You can set a different layout manager if desired. The components usually appear as icons. Since icons are not components, they cannot be placed into a tool bar directly. Instead you place buttons into the tool bar and set the icons on the buttons. An instance of JToolBar is like a regular container. Often it is placed in the north, west, or east of a container of BorderLayout.

The following properties in the JToolBar class are often useful:

✦ **orientation** specifies whether the items in the tool bar appear horizontally or vertically. The possible values are JToolBar.HORIZONTAL and JToolBar.VERTICAL. The default value is JToolBar.HORIZONTAL.

✦ **floatable** is a boolean value that specifies whether the tool bar can be floated. By default, a tool bar is floatable.

EXAMPLE 23.3 CREATING TOOL BARS

Problem

Create a JToolBar that contains three buttons with the icons representing the commands New, Open, and Print icons, as shown in Figure 23.5.

EXAMPLE **23.3** (CONTINUED)

FIGURE **23.5** *The tool bar contains the icons representing the commands New, Open, and Print.*

Solution

Listing 23.3 shows the program.

LISTING **23.3** ToolBarDemo.java

```
 1 import javax.swing.*;
 2 import java.awt.*;
 3
 4 public class ToolBarDemo extends JApplet {
 5   private JButton jbtNew = new JButton(
 6     ImageViewer.createImageIcon("image/new.gif", this));
 7   private JButton jbtOpen = new JButton(
 8     ImageViewer.createImageIcon("image/open.gif", this));
 9   private JButton jbPrint = new JButton(
10     ImageViewer.createImageIcon("image/print.gif", this));
11
12   public ToolBarDemo() {
13     JToolBar jToolBar1 = new JToolBar("My Tool Bar");
14     jToolBar1.setFloatable(true);
15     jToolBar1.add(jbtNew);
16     jToolBar1.add(jbtOpen);
17     jToolBar1.add(jbPrint);
18
19     jbtNew.setToolTipText("New");
20     jbtOpen.setToolTipText("Open");
21     jbPrint.setToolTipText("Print");
22
23     jbtNew.setBorderPainted(false);
24     jbtOpen.setBorderPainted(false);
25     jbPrint.setBorderPainted(false);
26
27     getContentPane().add(jToolBar1, BorderLayout.NORTH);
28   }
29 }
```

buttons — (lines 5–10)

tool bar — (line 13)

add tool bar — (line 27)

main method omitted — (line 29)

Review

A JToolBar is created in Line 13. The tool bar is a container with BoxLayout by default. Using the orientation property, you can specify whether components in the tool bar are organized horizontally or vertically. By default, it is horizontal.

By default, the tool bar is floatable, and a floatable controller is displayed in front of its components. You can drag the floatable controller to move the tool bar to different locations of the window or can show the tool bar in a separate window, as shown in Figure 23.6.

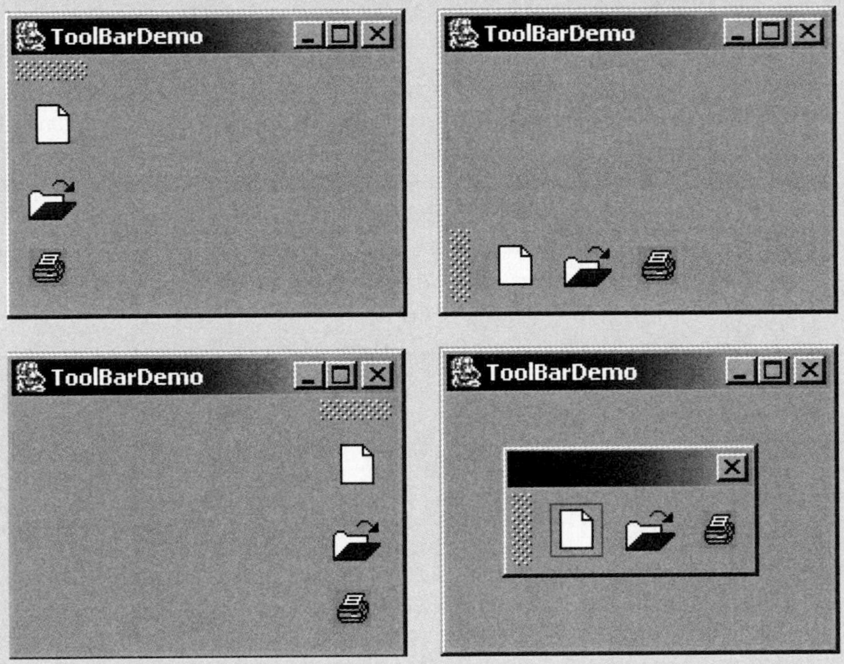

FIGURE 23.6   *The toolbar buttons are floatable.*

You can also set a title for the floatable tool bar, as shown in Figure 23.7(a). To do so, create a tool bar using the `JToolBar(String title)` constructor. If you set `floatable` false, the floatable controller is not displayed, as shown in Figure 23.7(b). If you set a border (e.g., a line border), as shown in Figure 23.7(c), the line border is displayed and the floatable controller is not displayed.

    (a)   (b)   (c)

FIGURE 23.7   *The toolbar buttons can be customized in many forms.*

TIP

For the floatable feature to work properly, do the following: (1) place a tool bar to one side of the container of `BorderLayout` and add no component to the other sides; (2) don't set border on a tool bar. Setting a border would make it non-floatable.

23.5   Processing Actions Using the **Action** Interface

Often menus and tool bars contain some common actions. For example, you can save a file by choosing *File, Save*, or by clicking the save button in the tool bar. Swing provides the Action interface, which can be used to create action objects for processing actions. Using Action objects, common action processing can be centralized and separated from the other application code.

The Action interface is a subinterface of ActionListener, as shown in Figure 23.8. Additionally, it defines several methods for checking whether the action is enabled, for enabling and disabling the action, and for retrieving and setting the associated action value using a key. The key can be any string, but four keys have predefined meanings:

Key	Description
Action.NAME	A name for the action
Action.SMALL_ICON	A small icon for the action
Action.SHORT_DESCRIPTION	A tool tip for the action
Action.LONG_DESCRIPTION	A description for online help

AbstractAction is a default implementation of the Action interface, as shown in Figure 23.9. It implements all the methods in the Action interface except the actionPerformed method. Additionally, it defines the getKeys() method.

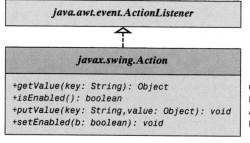

```
java.awt.event.ActionListener
              △
              ┆
javax.swing.Action

+getValue(key: String): Object          Gets one of this object's properties using the associated key.
+isEnabled(): boolean                    Returns true if action is enabled.
+putValue(key: String,value: Object): void   Associates a key/value pair with the action.
+setEnabled(b: boolean): void            Enables or disables the action.
```

FIGURE 23.8   *The* Action *interface provides a useful extension to the* ActionListener *interface in cases where the same functionality may be accessed by several controls.*

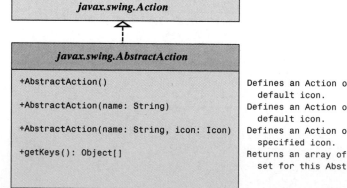

```
javax.swing.Action
              △
              ┆
javax.swing.AbstractAction

+AbstractAction()                                   Defines an Action object with a default description string and
                                                        default icon.
+AbstractAction(name: String)                       Defines an Action object with the specified description string and a
                                                        default icon.
+AbstractAction(name: String, icon: Icon)           Defines an Action object with the specified description string and the
                                                        specified icon.
+getKeys(): Object[]                                Returns an array of objects which are keys for which values have been
                                                        set for this AbstractAction, or null if no keys have values set.
```

FIGURE 23.9   *The* AbstractAction *class provides a default implementation for* Action.

Since `AbstractAction` is an abstract class, you cannot create an instance using its constructor. However, you can create a concrete subclass of `AbstractAction` and implement the `actionPerformed` method. This subclass can be conveniently defined as an anonymous inner class. For example, the following code creates an `Action` object for terminating a program:

```
Action exitAction = new AbstractAction("Exit") {
  public void actionPerformed(ActionEvent e) {
    System.exit(0);
  }
};
```

Certain containers, such as `JMenu` and `JToolBar`, know how to add an `Action` object. When an `Action` object is added to such a container, the container automatically creates an appropriate component for the `Action` object, and registers a listener with the `Action` object. Here is an example of adding an `Action` object to a menu and a tool bar:

```
jMenu.add(exitAction);
jToolBar.add(exitAction);
```

Several Swing components, such as `JButton`, `JRadioButton`, and `JCheckBox`, contain constructors to create instances from `Action` objects. For example, you can create a `JButton` from an `Action` object, as follows:

```
JButton jbt = new JButton(exitAction);
```

`Action` objects can also be associated with mnemonic and accelerator keys. To associate actions with a mnemonic key (e.g., ALT+E), use the following statement:

```
exitAction.putValue(Action.MNEMONIC_KEY, new Integer(KeyEvent.VK_E));
```

To associate actions with an accelerator key (e.g., CTRL+E), use the following statement:

```
KeyStroke exitKey =
  KeyStroke.getKeyStroke(KeyEvent.VK_E, KeyEvent.CTRL_MASK);
exitAction.putValue(Action.ACCELERATOR_KEY, exitKey);
```

EXAMPLE 23.4 USING ACTIONS

Problem

Write a program that creates three menu items, Left, Center, and Right, three tool bar buttons, Left, Center, and Right, and three regular buttons, Left, Center, and Right, in a panel, as shown in Figure 23.10. The panel that holds the buttons uses the `FlowLayout`. The actions of the left, center, and right buttons set the alignment of the `FlowLayout` to left, right, and center, respectively.

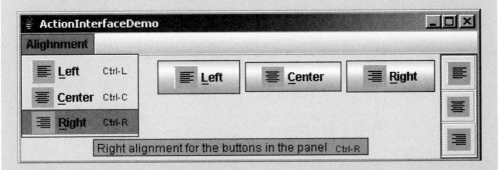

FIGURE 23.10 *Left, Center, and Right appear in the menu, in the toolbar, and in regular buttons.*

Example 23.4 (Continued)

Solution

The actions of the menu items, the tool bar buttons, and the buttons in the panel can be processed through common action handlers using the Action interface. The source code for the program is given in Listing 23.4:

LISTING 23.4   ActionInterfaceDemo.java

```
 1  import java.awt.*;
 2  import java.awt.event.*;
 3  import javax.swing.*;
 4
 5  public class ActionInterfaceDemo extends JApplet {
 6    private JPanel buttonPanel = new JPanel();
 7    private FlowLayout flowLayout = new FlowLayout();
 8
 9    public ActionInterfaceDemo() {
10      // Create image icons
11      ImageIcon leftImageIcon = ImageViewer.createImageIcon(
12        "image/leftAlignment.png", this);
13      ImageIcon centerImageIcon = ImageViewer.createImageIcon(
14        "image/centerAlignment.png", this);
15      ImageIcon rightImageIcon = ImageViewer.createImageIcon(
16        "image/rightAlignment.png", this);
17
18      // Create actions
19      Action leftAction = new MyAction("Left", leftImageIcon,
20        "Left alignment for the buttons in the panel",
21        new Integer(KeyEvent.VK_L),
22        KeyStroke.getKeyStroke(KeyEvent.VK_L, ActionEvent.CTRL_MASK));
23      Action centerAction = new MyAction("Center", centerImageIcon,
24        "Center alignment for the buttons in the panel",
25        new Integer(KeyEvent.VK_C),
26        KeyStroke.getKeyStroke(KeyEvent.VK_C, ActionEvent.CTRL_MASK));
27      Action rightAction = new MyAction("Right", rightImageIcon,
28        "Right alignment for the buttons in the panel",
29        new Integer(KeyEvent.VK_R),
30        KeyStroke.getKeyStroke(KeyEvent.VK_R, ActionEvent.CTRL_MASK));
31
32      // Create menus
33      JMenuBar jMenuBar1 = new JMenuBar();
34      JMenu jmenuAlignment = new JMenu("Alignment");
35      setJMenuBar(jMenuBar1);
36      jMenuBar1.add(jmenuAlignment);
37
38      // Add actions to the menu
39      jmenuAlignment.add(leftAction);
40      jmenuAlignment.add(centerAction);
41      jmenuAlignment.add(rightAction);
42
43      // Add actions to the toolbar
44      JToolBar jToolBar1 = new JToolBar(JToolBar.VERTICAL);
45      jToolBar1.setBorder(BorderFactory.createLineBorder(Color.red));
46      jToolBar1.add(leftAction);
47      jToolBar1.add(centerAction);
48      jToolBar1.add(rightAction);
49
50      // Add buttons to the button panel
51      buttonPanel.setLayout(flowLayout);
52      JButton jbtLeft = new JButton(leftAction);
53      JButton jbtCenter = new JButton(centerAction);
54      JButton jbtRight = new JButton(rightAction);
55      buttonPanel.add(jbtLeft);
56      buttonPanel.add(jbtCenter);
57      buttonPanel.add(jbtRight);
```

image icon

create action

menu

tool bar

button

EXAMPLE 23.4 (CONTINUED)

```
58
59      // Add tool bar to the east and panel to the center
60      getContentPane().add(jToolBar1, BorderLayout.EAST);
61      getContentPane().add(buttonPanel, BorderLayout.CENTER);
62    }
63
64    private class MyAction extends AbstractAction {          custom action
65      String name;
66
67      MyAction(String name, Icon icon) {                     constructor
68        super(name, icon);
69        this.name = name;
70      }
71
72      MyAction(String name, Icon icon, String desc, Integer mnemonic,    constructor
73          KeyStroke accelerator) {
74        super(name, icon);
75        putValue(Action.SHORT_DESCRIPTION, desc);
76        putValue(Action.MNEMONIC_KEY, mnemonic);
77        putValue(Action.ACCELERATOR_KEY, accelerator);
78        this.name = name;
79      }
80
81      public void actionPerformed(ActionEvent e) {           handler
82        if (name.equals("Left"))
83          flowLayout.setAlignment(FlowLayout.LEFT);
84        else if (name.equals("Center"))
85          flowLayout.setAlignment(FlowLayout.CENTER);
86        else if (name.equals("Right"))
87          flowLayout.setAlignment(FlowLayout.RIGHT);
88
89        buttonPanel.revalidate();
90      }
91    }
92 }                                                            main method omitted
```

Review

The inner class `MyAction` extends `AbstractAction` with a constructor to construct an action with a name and an icon (Lines 67–70) and another constructor to construct an action with a name, icon, description, mnemonic, and accelerator (Lines 72–79). The constructors invoke the `putValue` method to associate the name, icon, description, mnemonic, and accelerator. It implements the `actionPerformed` method to set a new alignment in the panel of the `FlowLayout` (Line 81–90). The `revalidate()` method validates the new alignment (Line 89).

Three actions, `leftAction`, `centerAction`, and `rightAction`, were created from the `MyAction` class (Lines 19–30). Each action has a name, icon, description, mnemonic, and accelerator. The actions are for the menu items and the buttons in the tool bar and in the panel. The menu and toolbar know how to add these objects automatically (Lines 39–41, 46–48). Three regular buttons are created with the properties taken from the actions (Lines 51–54).

23.6   JOptionPane Dialogs

You have used `JOptionPane` to create input and output dialog boxes. This section provides a comprehensive introduction to `JOptionPane` and other dialog boxes. A *dialog box* is normally used as a temporary window to receive additional information from the user or to provide notification that some event has occurred. Java provides the `JOptionPane` class, which can be used to create standard dialogs. You can also build custom dialogs by extending the `JDialog` class.

The JOptionPane class can be used to create four kinds of standard dialogs:

✦ **Message dialog** shows a message and waits for the user to click OK.

✦ **Confirmation dialog** shows a question and asks for confirmation, such as OK or Cancel.

✦ **Input dialog** shows a question and gets the user's input from a text field, combo box, or list.

✦ **Option dialog** shows a question and gets the user's answer from a set of options.

These dialogs are created using the static methods show*Xxx*Dialog and generally appear as shown in Figure 23.11(a).

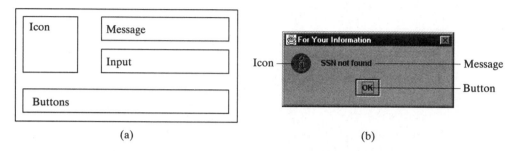

(a)   (b)

FIGURE 23.11 *A JOptionPane dialog can display an icon, a message, an input, and option buttons in (a). The message dialog displays a message and waits for the user to click OK in (b).*

For example, you can use the following method to create a message dialog box, as shown in Figure 23.11(b):

```
JOptionPane.showMessageDialog(null, "SSN not found",
  "For Your Information", JOptionPane.INFORMATION_MESSAGE);
```

23.6.1 Message Dialogs

A *message dialog* box displays a message that alerts the user and waits for the user to click the OK button to close the dialog. The methods for creating message dialogs are:

```
public static void showMessageDialog(Component parentComponent,
                                     Object message)
public static void showMessageDialog(Component parentComponent,
                                     Object message,
                                     String title,
                                     int messageType)
public static void showMessageDialog(Component parentComponent,
                                     Object message,
                                     String title,
                                     int messageType,
                                     Icon icon)
```

The parentComponent can be any component or null. The message is an object, but often a string is used. These two parameters must always be specified. The title is a string displayed in the title bar of the dialog with the default value "Message".

The messageType is one of the following constants:

```
JOptionPane.ERROR_MESSAGE
JOptionPane.INFORMATION_MESSAGE
JOptionPane.PLAIN_MESSAGE
JOptionPane.WARNING_MESSAGE
JOptionPane.QUESTION_MESSAGE
```

By default, messageType is JOptionPane.INFORMATION_MESSAGE. Each type has an associated icon except the PLAIN_MESSAGE type, as shown in Figure 23.12. You can also supply your own icon in the icon parameter.

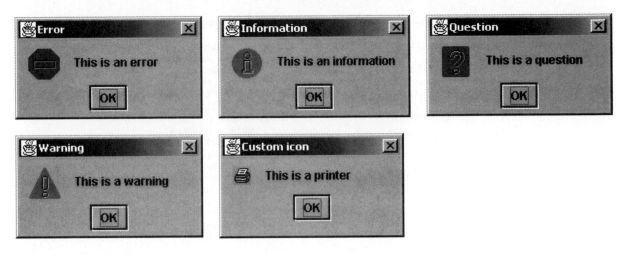

FIGURE 23.12 *There are five types of message dialog boxes.*

The `message` parameter is an object. If it is a GUI component, the component is displayed. If it is a non-GUI component, the string representation of the object is displayed. For example, the following statement displays a clock in a message dialog, as shown in Figure 23.13:

```
JOptionPane.showMessageDialog(null, new StillClock(),
    "Current Time", JOptionPane.PLAIN_MESSAGE);
```

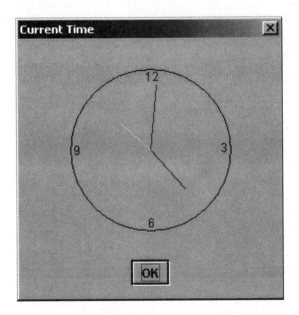

FIGURE 23.13 *A clock is displayed in a message dialog.*

23.6.2 Confirmation Dialogs

A message dialog box displays a message and waits for the user to click the OK button to dismiss the dialog. The message dialog does not return any value. A *confirmation dialog* asks a question and requires the user to respond with an appropriate button. The confirmation dialog returns a value that corresponds to a selected button.

The methods for creating confirmation dialogs are:

```
public static int showConfirmDialog(Component parentComponent,
                                    Object message)
public static int showConfirmDialog(Component parentComponent,
                                    Object message,
                                    String title,
                                    int optionType)
public static int showConfirmDialog(Component parentComponent,
                                    Object message,
                                    String title,
                                    int optionType,
                                    int messageType)
public static int showConfirmDialog(Component parentComponent,
                                    Object message,
                                    String title,
                                    int optionType,
                                    int messageType,
                                    Icon icon)
```

The parameters parentComponent, message, title, icon, and messageType are the same as in the showMessageDialog method. The default value for title is "Select an Option" and for messageType is QUESTION_MESSAGE. The optionType determines which buttons are displayed in the dialog. The possible values are:

```
JOptionPane.YES_NO_OPTION
JOptionPane.YES_NO_CANCEL_OPTION
JOptionPane.OK_CANCEL_OPTION
```

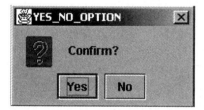 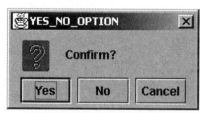 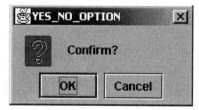

FIGURE 23.14 *The confirmation dialog displays a question and three types of option buttons, and requires responses from the user.*

Figure 23.14 shows the confirmation dialogs with these options.

The showConfirmDialog method returns one of the following int values corresponding to the selected option:

```
JOptionPane.YES_OPTION
JOptionPane.NO_OPTION
JOptionPane.CANCEL_OPTION
JOptionPane.OK_OPTION
JOptionPane.CLOSED_OPTION
```

These options correspond to the button that was activated, except for the CLOSED_OPTION, which implies that the dialog box is closed without buttons activated.

23.6.3 Input Dialogs

An *input dialog* box is used to receive input from the user. The input can be entered from a text field or selected from a combo box or a list. Selectable values can be specified in an array, and one of them can be designated as the initial selected value. If no selectable value is specified when an input dialog is created, a text field is used for entering input. If fewer than twenty selection values are specified, a combo box is displayed in the input dialog. If twenty or more selection values are specified, a list is used in the input dialog.

The methods for creating input dialogs are shown below:

```
public static String showInputDialog(Object message)
public static String showInputDialog(Component parentComponent,
                                     Object message)
public static String showInputDialog(Component parentComponent,
                                     Object message,
                                     String title,
                                     int messageType)
public static Object showInputDialog(Component parentComponent,
                                     Object message,
                                     int messageType,
                                     Icon icon,
                                     Object[] selectionValues,
                                     Object initialSelectionValue)
```

The first three methods listed above use a text field for input, as shown in Figure 23.15(a). The last method listed above specifies an array of `Object` type as selection values in addition to an object specified as an initial selection. The first three methods return a `String` that is entered from the text field in the input dialog. The last method returns an `Object` selected from a combo box or a list. The input dialog displays a combo box if there are fewer than twenty selection values, as shown in Figure 23.15(b); it displays a list if there are twenty or more selection values, as shown in Figure 23.15(c).

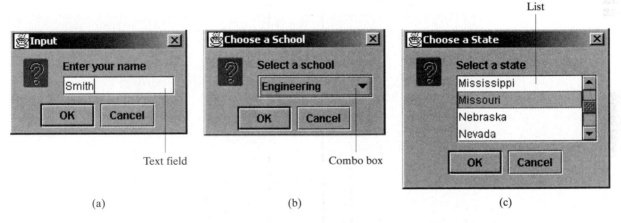

(a)   (b)   (c)

FIGURE 23.15 *(a) When creating an input dialog without specifying selection values, the input dialog displays a text field for data entry. (b) When creating an input dialog with selection values, the input dialog displays a combo box if there are fewer than twenty selection values. (c) When creating an input dialog with selection values, the input dialog displays a list if there are twenty or more selection values.*

 NOTE

The `showInputDialog` method does not have the `optionType` parameter. The buttons for input dialog are not configurable. The OK and Cancel buttons are always used.

23.6.4 Option Dialogs

An *option dialog* allows you to create custom buttons. You can create an option dialog using the following method:

```
public static int showOptionDialog(Component parentComponent,
                                   Object message,
                                   String title,
                                   int optionType,
```

```
                        int messageType,
                        Icon icon,
                        Object[] options,
                        Object initialValue)
```

The buttons are specified using the `options` parameter. The `initialValue` parameter allows you to specify a button to receive initial focus. The `showOptionDialog` method returns an `int` value indicating the button that was activated. For example, here is the code that creates an option dialog, as shown in Figure 23.16:

```
int value =
  JOptionPane.showOptionDialog(null, "Select a button",
    "Option Dialog", JOptionPane.DEFAULT_OPTION,
    JOptionPane.PLAIN_MESSAGE, null,
     new Object[]{"Button 0", "Button 1", "Button 2"}, "Button 1");
```

FIGURE 23.16 *The option dialog displays the custom buttons.*

EXAMPLE 23.5 CREATING `JOptionPane` DIALOGS

Problem

Write a program that demonstrates the use of `JOptionPane` dialogs. The program prompts the user to select the annual interest rate from a list in an input dialog, the number of years from a combo box in an input dialog, and the loan amount from an input dialog, and it displays the loan payment schedule in a text area inside a `JScrollPane` in a message dialog, as shown in Figure 23.17.

Solution

Here are the major steps in the program (Listing 23.5):

1. Display an input dialog box to let the user select an annual interest rate from a list.

2. Display an input dialog box to let the user select the number of years from a combo box.

3. Display an input dialog box to let the user enter the loan amount.

4. Compute the monthly payment, total payment, and loan payment schedule, and display the result in a text area in a message dialog box.

LISTING 23.5 JOptionPaneDemo.java (Using Standard Dialog)

```
1 import javax.swing.*;
2
3 public class JOptionPaneDemo {
4   public static void main(String args[]) {
5     // Create an array for annual interest rates
6     Object[] rateList = new Object[25];
7     int i = 0;
8     for (double rate = 5; rate <= 8; rate += 1.0 / 8)
9       rateList[i++] = new Double(rate);
```

EXAMPLE 23.5 (CONTINUED)

```
10
11       // Prompt the user to select an annual interest rate
12       Object annualInterestRateObject = JOptionPane.showInputDialog(
13         null, "Select annual interest rate:", "JOptionPaneDemo",
14         JOptionPane.QUESTION_MESSAGE, null, rateList, null);
15       double annualInterestRate =
16         ((Double)annualInterestRateObject).doubleValue();
17
18       // Create an array for number of years
19       Object[] yearList = {new Integer(7), new Integer(15),
20         new Integer(30)};
21
22       // Prompt the user to enter number of years
23       Object numberOfYearsObject = JOptionPane.showInputDialog(null,
24         "Select number of years:", "JOptionPaneDemo",
25         JOptionPane.QUESTION_MESSAGE, null, yearList, null);
26       int numberOfYears = ((Integer)numberOfYearsObject).intValue();
27
28       // Prompt the user to enter loan amount
29       String loanAmountString = JOptionPane.showInputDialog(null,
30         "Enter loan amount,\nfor example, 150000 for $150000",
31         "JOptionPaneDemo", JOptionPane.QUESTION_MESSAGE);
32       double loanAmount = Double.parseDouble(loanAmountString);
33
34       // Obtain monthly payment and total payment
35       Loan loan = new Loan(
36         annualInterestRate, numberOfYears, loanAmount);
37       double monthlyPayment = loan.monthlyPayment();
38       double totalPayment = loan.totalPayment();
39
40       // Prepare output string
41       String output = "Interest Rate: " + annualInterestRate + "%" +
42         " Number of Years: " + numberOfYears + " Loan Amount: $"
43         + loanAmount;
44       output += "\nMonthly Payment: " + "$" +
45         (int)(monthlyPayment * 100) / 100.0;
46       output += "\nTotal Payment: $" +
47         (int)(monthlyPayment * 12 * numberOfYears * 100) / 100.0 + "\n";
48
49       // Obtain monthly interest rate
50       double monthlyInterestRate = annualInterestRate / 1200;
51
52       double balance = loanAmount;
53       double interest;
54       double principal;
55
56       // Display the header
57       output += "\nPayment#\tInterest\tPrincipal\tBalance\n";
58
59       for (i = 1; i <= numberOfYears * 12; i++) {
60         interest = (int)(monthlyInterestRate * balance * 100) / 100.0;
61         principal = (int)((monthlyPayment - interest) * 100) / 100.0;
62         balance = (int)((balance - principal) * 100) / 100.0;
63         output += i + "\t" + interest + "\t" + principal + "\t" +
64           balance + "\n";
65       }
66
67       // Display monthly payment and total payment
68       JScrollPane jsp = new JScrollPane(new JTextArea(output));
69       jsp.setPreferredSize(new java.awt.Dimension(400, 200));
70       JOptionPane.showMessageDialog(null, jsp,
71         "JOptionPaneDemo", JOptionPane.INFORMATION_MESSAGE, null);
72   }
73 }
```

input dialog

input dialog

input dialog

message dialog

EXAMPLE 23.5 (CONTINUED)

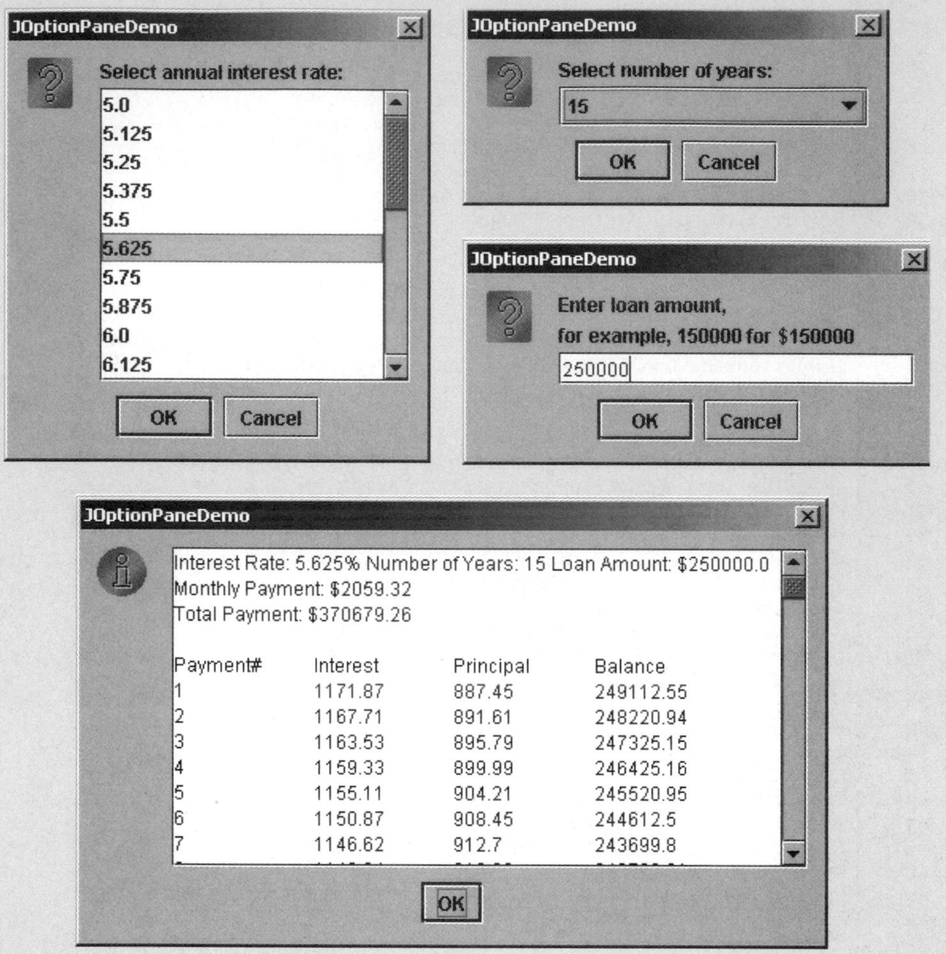

FIGURE 23.17 *The input dialogs can contain a list or a combo box for selecting input, and the message dialogs can contain GUI objects like* JScrollPane.

Review

The JOptionPane dialog boxes are *modal*, which means that no other window can be accessed until a dialog box is dismissed.

You have used the input dialog box to enter input from a text field. This example shows that input dialog boxes can also contain a list (Lines 12–14) or a combo box (Lines 23–25) to list input options. The elements of the list are objects. The return value from these input dialog boxes is of the Object type. To obtain a double value or an int value, you have to cast the return object into Double or Integer, then use the doubleValue or intValue method to get the double or int value (Lines 15–16 and 26).

You have already used the message dialog box to display a string. This example shows that the message dialog box can also contain GUI objects. The output string is contained in a text area, the text area is inside a scroll pane, and the scroll pane is placed in the message dialog box (Lines 68–71).

23.7 Creating Custom Dialogs

Standard `JOptionPane` dialogs are sufficient in most cases. Occasionally, you need to create custom dialogs. In Swing, the `JDialog` class can be extended to create custom dialogs.

As with `JFrame`, components are added to the `contentPane` of `JDialog`. Creating a custom dialog usually involves laying out user interface components in the dialog, adding buttons for dismissing the dialog, and installing listeners that respond to button actions.

The standard dialog is *modal*, which means that no other window can be accessed before the dialog is dismissed. However, the custom dialogs derived from `JDialog` are not modal by default. To make a dialog modal, set its `modal` property to `true`. To display an instance of `JDialog`, set its `visible` property to `true`.

EXAMPLE 23.6 CREATING CUSTOM DIALOGS

Problem

Create a custom dialog box for choosing colors, as shown in Figure 23.18(a). Use this dialog to choose the color for the foreground for the button, as shown in Figure 23.18(b). When the user clicks the Change Button Text Color button, the Choose Color dialog box is displayed.

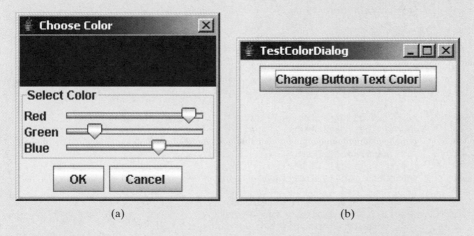

(a)   (b)

FIGURE 23.18 *The custom dialog allows you to choose a color for the label's foreground.*

Solution

Create a custom dialog component named `ColorDialog` for choosing colors by extending `JDialog`. Use three sliders to specify red, green, and blue components of a color. The program is given in Listing 23.6.

LISTING 23.6 ColorDialog.java (Custom Dialog)

```
1 import java.awt.*;
2 import java.awt.event.*;
3 import javax.swing.*;
4 import javax.swing.event.*;
5
6 public class ColorDialog extends JDialog {
7   // Declare color component values and selected color
8   private int redValue, greenValue, blueValue;
9   private Color color = null;
```

color value

EXAMPLE 23.6 (CONTINUED)

```
10
11    // Create sliders
12    private JSlider jslRed = new JSlider(0, 128);
13    private JSlider jslGreen = new JSlider(0, 128);
14    private JSlider jslBlue = new JSlider(0, 128);
15
16    // Create two buttons
17    private JButton jbtOK = new JButton("OK");
18    private JButton jbtCancel = new JButton("Cancel");
19
20    // Create a panel to display the selected color
21    private JPanel jpSelectedColor = new JPanel();
22
23    public ColorDialog() {
24      this(null, true);
25    }
26
27    public ColorDialog(java.awt.Frame parent, boolean modal) {
28      super(parent, modal);
29      setTitle("Choose Color");
30
31      // Group two buttons OK and Cancel
32      JPanel jpButtons = new JPanel();
33      jpButtons.add(jbtOK);
34      jpButtons.add(jbtCancel);
35
36      // Group labels
37      JPanel jpLabels = new JPanel();
38      jpLabels.setLayout(new GridLayout(3, 0));
39      jpLabels.add(new JLabel("Red"));
40      jpLabels.add(new JLabel("Green"));
41      jpLabels.add(new JLabel("Blue"));
42
43      // Group sliders for selecting red, green, and blue colors
44      JPanel jpSliders = new JPanel();
45      jpSliders.setLayout(new GridLayout(3, 0));
46      jpSliders.add(jslRed);
47      jpSliders.add(jslGreen);
48      jpSliders.add(jslBlue);
49
50      // Group jpLabels and jpSliders
51      JPanel jpSelectColor = new JPanel();
52      jpSelectColor.setLayout(new BorderLayout());
53      jpSelectColor.setBorder(
54        BorderFactory.createTitledBorder("Select Color"));
55      jpSelectColor.add(jpLabels, BorderLayout.WEST);
56      jpSelectColor.add(jpSliders, BorderLayout.CENTER);
57
58      // Group jpSelectColor and jpSelectedColor
59      JPanel jpColor = new JPanel();
60      jpColor.setLayout(new BorderLayout());
61      jpColor.add(jpSelectColor, BorderLayout.SOUTH);
62      jpColor.add(jpSelectedColor, BorderLayout.CENTER);
63
64      // Place jpButtons and jpColor into the dialog box
65      getContentPane().add(jpButtons, BorderLayout.SOUTH);
66      getContentPane().add(jpColor, BorderLayout.CENTER);
67      pack();
68
69      jbtOK.addActionListener(new ActionListener() {
70        public void actionPerformed(ActionEvent e) {
71          setVisible(false);
72        }
73      });
74
75      jbtCancel.addActionListener(new ActionListener() {
76        public void actionPerformed(ActionEvent e) {
```

sliders

buttons

constructor

constructor
create UI

listeners

EXAMPLE 23.6 (CONTINUED)

```
77            color = null;
78            setVisible(false);
79        }
80      });
81
82      jslRed.addChangeListener(new ChangeListener() {
83        public void stateChanged(ChangeEvent e) {
84          redValue = jslRed.getValue();
85          color = new Color(redValue, greenValue, blueValue);
86          jpSelectedColor.setBackground(color);
87        }
88      });
89
90      jslGreen.addChangeListener(new ChangeListener() {
91        public void stateChanged(ChangeEvent e) {
92          greenValue = jslGreen.getValue();
93          color = new Color(redValue, greenValue, blueValue);
94          jpSelectedColor.setBackground(color);
95        }
96      });
97
98      jslBlue.addChangeListener(new ChangeListener() {
99        public void stateChanged(ChangeEvent e) {
100          blueValue = jslBlue.getValue();
101          color = new Color(redValue, greenValue, blueValue);
102          jpSelectedColor.setBackground(color);
103        }
104      });
105    }
106
107    public Dimension getPreferredSize() {
108      return new java.awt.Dimension(200, 200);
109    }
110
111    /** Return color */
112    public Color getColor() {
113      return color;
114    }
115 }
```

Let us create a test class to use the color dialog to select the color for the foreground color of the button in Listing 23.7.

LISTING 23.7 TestColorDialog.java

```
1 import javax.swing.*;
2 import java.awt.*;
3 import java.awt.event.*;
4
5 public class TestColorDialog extends JApplet {
6   private ColorDialog colorDialog1 = new ColorDialog();
7   private JButton jbtChangeColor = new JButton("Choose color");
8
9   public TestColorDialog() {
10     getContentPane().setLayout(new java.awt.FlowLayout());
11     jbtChangeColor.setText("Change Button Text Color");
12     jbtChangeColor.addActionListener(new ActionListener() {          listener
13       public void actionPerformed(ActionEvent e) {
14         colorDialog1.setVisible(true);
15
16         if (colorDialog1.getColor() != null)
17           jbtChangeColor.setForeground(colorDialog1.getColor());
18       }
19     });
20     getContentPane().add(jbtChangeColor);
21   }
22 }                                                                   main method omitted
```

EXAMPLE 23.6 (CONTINUED)

Review

The custom dialog box allows the user to use the sliders to select colors. The selected color is stored in the color variable. When the user clicks the *Cancel* button, color becomes null, which implies that no selection has been made.

The dialog box is displayed when the user clicks the "Change Button Text Color" button and is closed when the OK button or the Cancel button is clicked.

TIP

Not setting the dialog modal when needed is a common mistake. In this example, the dialog is set modal in Line 24 in ColorDialog.java. If the dialog is not modal, all the statements in the "Change Button Text Color" button handler are executed before the color is selected from the dialog box.

23.8   JColorChooser

You created a color dialog in the preceding example as a subclass of JDialog, which is a subclass of java.awt.Dialog (a top-level heavy-weight component). Therefore, it cannot be added to a container as a component. Color dialogs are commonly used in GUI programming. Swing provides a convenient and versatile color dialog named javax.swing.JColorChooser. Like JOptionPane, JColorChooser is a lightweight component inherited from JComponent. It can be added to any container. Figure 23.19 shows a JColor-Chooser in an applet.

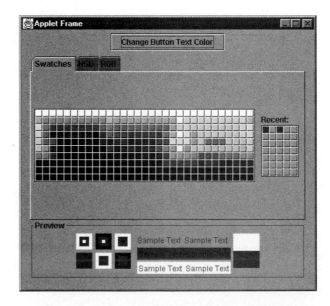

FIGURE 23.19   *An instance of JColorChooser is displayed in an applet.*

Often an instance of JColorChooser is added to a dialog window to display a color dialog. To display color chooser in a dialog box, use JColorChooser's static showDialog method:

```
public static Color showDialog(Component parentComponent,
                               String title,
                               Color initialColor)
```

This method creates an instance of `JDialog` with three buttons, OK, Cancel, and Reset, to hold a `JColorChooser` object, as shown in Figure 23.20. The method displays a modal dialog. If the user clicks the *OK* button, the method dismisses the dialog and returns the selected color. If the user clicks the *Cancel* button or closes the dialog, the method dismisses the dialog and returns null.

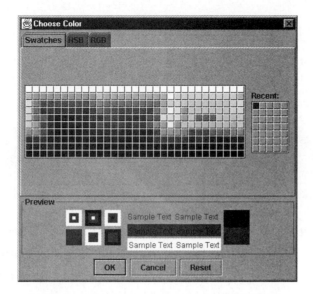

FIGURE 23.20   *An instance of `JColorChooser` is displayed in a dialog box with the OK, Cancel, and Reset buttons.*

`JColorChooser` consists of a tabbed pane and a color preview panel. The tabbed pane has three tabs for choosing colors using Swatches, HSB, and RGB, as shown in Figure 23.21. The preview panel shows the effect of the selected color.

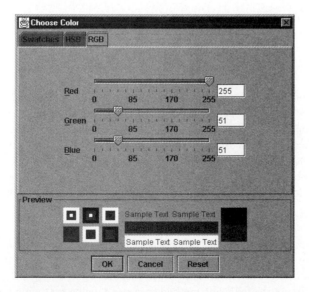

FIGURE 23.21   *The `JColorChooser` class contains a tabbed pane with three tabs for selecting colors using Swatches, HSB, and RGB.*

NOTE

JColorChooser is very flexible. It allows you to replace the tabbed pane or the color preview panel with custom components. The default tabbed pane and the color preview panel are sufficient. You rarely need to use custom components.

23.9 JFileChooser

The `javax.swing.JFileChooser` class displays a dialog box from which the user can navigate through the file system and select files for loading or saving, as shown in Figure 23.22.

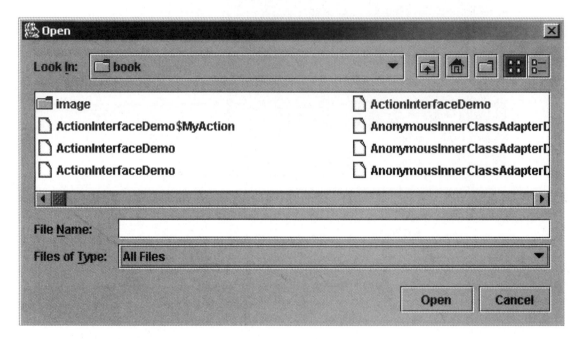

FIGURE 23.22 *The Swing JFileChooser shows files and directories, and enables the user to navigate through the file system visually.*

Like `JColorChooser`, `JFileChooser` is a lightweight component inherited from `JComponent`. It can be added to any container if desired, but often you create an instance of `JFileChooser` and display it standalone.

`JFileChooser` is a subclass of `JComponent`. There are several ways to construct a file dialog box. The simplest is to use `JFileChooser`'s no-arg constructor.

The file dialog box can appear in two types: open and save. The *open type* is for opening a file, and the *save type* is for storing a file. To create an open file dialog, use the following method:

```
public int showOpenDialog(Component parent)
```

This method creates a dialog box that contains an instance of `JFileChooser` for opening a file. The method returns an `int` value, either `APPROVE_OPTION` or `CANCEL_OPTION`, which indicates whether the OK button or the Cancel button was clicked.

Similarly, you can use the following method to create a dialog for saving files:

```
public int showSaveDialog(Component parent)
```

The file dialog box created with showOpenDialog or showSaveDialog is modal. The JFileChooser class has the properties inherited from JComponent. It also has the following useful properties:

✦ **dialogType** specifies the type of this dialog. Use OPEN_DIALOG when you want to bring up a file chooser that the user can use to open a file. Likewise, use SAVE_DIALOG to let the user choose a file for saving.

✦ **dialogTitle** is the string that is displayed in the title bar of the dialog box.

✦ **currentDirectory** is the current directory of the file. The type of this property is java.io.File. If you want the current directory to be used, use setCurrentDirectory(new File(".")).

✦ **selectedFile** is the file you have selected. You can use getSelectedFile() to return the selected file from the dialog box. The type of this property is java.io.File. If you have a default file name that you expect to use, use setSelectedFile(new File(filename)).

✦ **selectedFiles** is a list of the files selected if the file chooser is set to allow multi-selection. The type of this property is File[].

✦ **multiSelectionEnabled** is a boolean value indicating whether multiple files can be selected. By default, it is false.

EXAMPLE 23.7 CREATING A TEXT EDITOR

Problem

This example uses Swing menus, tool bar, file chooser, and color chooser to create a simple text editor, as shown in Figure 23.23, which allows the user to open and save text files, clear text, and change the color and font of the text.

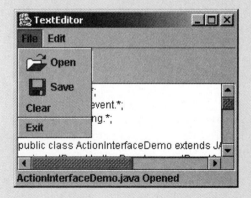
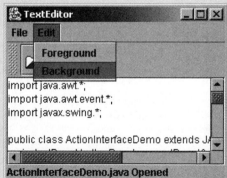

FIGURE 23.23 *The editor enables you to open and save text files from the File menu or from the tool bar, and to change the color and font of the text from the Edit menu.*

Solution

Listing 23.8 shows the program.

EXAMPLE 23.7 (CONTINUED)

LISTING 23.8 TextEditor.java

```java
1  import java.io.*;
2  import java.awt.*;
3  import java.awt.event.*;
4  import javax.swing.*;
5
6  public class TextEditor extends JApplet {
7    // Declare and create image icons
8    private ImageIcon openImageIcon = ImageViewer.createImageIcon(
9      "image/open.gif", this);
10   private ImageIcon saveImageIcon = ImageViewer.createImageIcon(
11     "image/save.gif", this);
12
13   // Create menu items
14   private JMenuItem jmiOpen = new JMenuItem("Open", openImageIcon);
15   private JMenuItem jmiSave = new JMenuItem("Save", saveImageIcon);
16   private JMenuItem jmiClear = new JMenuItem("Clear");
17   private JMenuItem jmiExit = new JMenuItem("Exit");
18   private JMenuItem jmiForeground = new JMenuItem("Foreground");
19   private JMenuItem jmiBackground = new JMenuItem("Background");
20
21   // Create buttons to be placed in a tool bar
22   private JButton jbtOpen = new JButton(openImageIcon);
23   private JButton jbtSave = new JButton(saveImageIcon);
24   private JLabel jlblStatus = new JLabel();
25
26   // Create a JFileChooser with the current directory
27   private JFileChooser jFileChooser1
28     = new JFileChooser(new File("."));
29
30   // Create a text area
31   private JTextArea jta = new JTextArea();
32
33   public TextEditor() {
34     // Add menu items to the menu
35     JMenu jMenu1 = new JMenu("File");
36     jMenu1.add(jmiOpen);
37     jMenu1.add(jmiSave);
38     jMenu1.add(jmiClear);
39     jMenu1.addSeparator();
40     jMenu1.add(jmiExit);
41
42     // Add menu items to the menu
43     JMenu jMenu2 = new JMenu("Edit");
44     jMenu2.add(jmiForeground);
45     jMenu2.add(jmiBackground);
46
47     // Add menus to the menu bar
48     JMenuBar jMenuBar1 = new JMenuBar();
49     jMenuBar1.add(jMenu1);
50     jMenuBar1.add(jMenu2);
51
52     // Set the menu bar
53     setJMenuBar(jMenuBar1);
54
55     // Create tool bar
56     JToolBar jToolBar1 = new JToolBar();
57     jToolBar1.add(jbtOpen);
58     jToolBar1.add(jbtSave);
59
60     jmiOpen.addActionListener(new ActionListener() {
61       public void actionPerformed(ActionEvent e) {
62         open();
63       }
64     });
```

create UI

EXAMPLE 23.7 (CONTINUED)

```
65
66     jmiSave.addActionListener(new ActionListener() {
67       public void actionPerformed(ActionEvent evt) {
68         save();
69       }
70     });
71
72     jmiClear.addActionListener(new ActionListener() {
73       public void actionPerformed(ActionEvent evt) {
74         jta.setText(null);
75       }
76     });
77
78     jmiExit.addActionListener(new ActionListener() {
79       public void actionPerformed(ActionEvent evt) {
80         System.exit(0);
81       }
82     });
83
84     jmiForeground.addActionListener(new ActionListener() {
85       public void actionPerformed(ActionEvent evt) {
86         Color selectedColor =
87           JColorChooser.showDialog(null, "Choose Foreground Color",
88             jta.getForeground());
89
90         if (selectedColor != null)
91           jta.setForeground(selectedColor);
92       }
93     });
94
95     jmiBackground.addActionListener(new ActionListener() {
96       public void actionPerformed(ActionEvent evt) {
97         Color selectedColor =
98           JColorChooser.showDialog(null, "Choose Background Color",
99             jta.getForeground());
100
101         if (selectedColor != null)
102           jta.setBackground(selectedColor);
103       }
104     });
105
106    jbtOpen.addActionListener(new ActionListener() {
107      public void actionPerformed(ActionEvent evt) {
108        open();
109      }
110    });
111
112    jbtSave.addActionListener(new ActionListener() {
113      public void actionPerformed(ActionEvent evt) {
114        save();
115      }
116    });
117
118    getContentPane().add(jToolBar1, BorderLayout.NORTH);
119    getContentPane().add(jlblStatus, BorderLayout.SOUTH);
120    getContentPane().add(new JScrollPane(jta), BorderLayout.CENTER);
121  }
122
123  /** Open file */
124  private void open() {
125    if (jFileChooser1.showOpenDialog(this) ==
126      JFileChooser.APPROVE_OPTION)
127      open(jFileChooser1.getSelectedFile());
128  }
129
130  /** Open file with the specified File instance */
131  private void open(File file) {
```

color chooser

color chooser

file chooser

EXAMPLE 23.7 (CONTINUED)

```
132      try {
133        // Read from the specified file and store it in jta
134        BufferedInputStream in = new BufferedInputStream(
135          new FileInputStream(file));
136        byte[] b = new byte[in.available()];
137        in.read(b, 0, b.length);
138        jta.append(new String(b, 0, b.length));
139        in.close();
140
141        // Display the status of the Open file operation in jlblStatus
142        jlblStatus.setText(file.getName() + " Opened");
143      }
144      catch (IOException ex) {
145        jlblStatus.setText("Error opening " + file.getName());
146      }
147    }
148
149    /** Save file */
150    private void save() {
151      if (jFileChooser1.showSaveDialog(this) ==
152        JFileChooser.APPROVE_OPTION) {
153          save(jFileChooser1.getSelectedFile());
154      }
155    }
156
157    /** Save file with specified File instance */
158    private void save(File file) {
159      try {
160        // Write the text in jta to the specified file
161        BufferedOutputStream out = new BufferedOutputStream(
162          new FileOutputStream(file));
163        byte[] b = (jta.getText()).getBytes();
164        out.write(b, 0, b.length);
165        out.close();
166
167        // Display the status of the save file operation in jlblStatus
168        jlblStatus.setText(file.getName()  + " Saved ");
169      }
170      catch (IOException ex) {
171        jlblStatus.setText("Error saving " + file.getName());
172      }
173    }
174 }
```

main method omitted

Review

The program creates the File and Edit menus (Lines 34–45). The File menu contains the menu commands Open for loading a file, Save for saving a file, Clear for clearing the text editor, and Exit for terminating the program. The Edit menu contains the menu commands Foreground Color and Background Color for setting foreground color and background color in the text. The Open and Save menu commands can also be accessed from the tool bar, which is created in Lines 56–58. The status of executing Open and Save is displayed in the status label, which is created in Line 23.

jFileChooser1, an instance of JFileChooser, is created for displaying the file dialog box to open and save files (Lines 27–28). new File(".") is used to set the current directory to the directory where the class is stored.

The open method is invoked when the user clicks the Open menu command or the Open tool bar button (Lines 62, 108). The showOpenDialog method (Line 125) displays an Open dialog box, as shown in Figure 23.22. Upon receiving the selected file, the method open(file) (Line 127) is invoked to load the file to the text area using a BufferedInputStream wrapped on a FileInputStream.

EXAMPLE 23.7 (CONTINUED)

The save method is invoked when the user clicks the Save menu command or the Save tool bar button (Lines 68, 114). The showSaveDialog method (Line 151) displays a Save dialog box. Upon receiving the selected file, the method save(file) (Line 153) is invoked to save the contents from the text area to the file using a BufferedOutputStream wrapped on a FileOutputStream.

The color dialog is displayed using the static method showDialog (Lines 87, 98) of JColorChooser. Thus you don't need to create an instance of JFileChooser. The showDialog method returns the selected color if the OK button is clicked after a color is selected.

23.10   Creating Internal Frames (Optional)

You can create multiple windows as shown in Example 13.10, "Creating Multiple Windows." Java also allows you to use the JInternalFrame class to create windows within a window. This user interface is commonly known as a *multiple document interface* or *MDI*. It was once quite popular and was used in the earlier versions of many popular Windows software programs. Now, however, MDI is rarely used. That is why this section is marked optional.

MDI

The JInternalFrame class is almost the same as the external JFrame class. The components are added to the internal frame in the same way as they are added to the external frame. An internal frame can have menus, title, Close icon, Minimize icon, and Maximize icon just like an external frame. The following are the major differences:

✦ JInternalFrame extends JComponent, and JFrame extends the AWT Frame class. Therefore, JInternalFrame is a Swing lightweight component, and JFrame is a Swing heavyweight component.

✦ Both JInternalFrame and JFrame are used to hold other components. JFrame is a top-level window component, and JInternalFrame must be contained inside a JDesktopPane of a JFrame or a JApplet.

Here are the steps to create an internal frame inside another window:

1. Use a JFrame or a JApplet as the outer window.

2. Create a JDesktopPane and add it to the content pane of a JFrame or JApplet. Usually, the JDesktopPane is added to the center of the content pane.

3. Create a JInternalFrame and add it to the JDesktopPane using the add method.

4. Use the setVisible(true) method to display the internal frame.

EXAMPLE 23.8 CREATING INTERNAL FRAMES

Problem

This example creates internal frames to display flags in an applet. You can select flags from the Flags menu. Clicking a menu item causes a flag to be displayed in an internal frame, as shown in Figure 23.24.

EXAMPLE 23.8 (CONTINUED)

FIGURE 23.24   *The flag image is displayed in an internal frame.*

Solution

Listing 23.9 shows the program.

LISTING 23.9   ShowInternalFrame.java

```
1  import java.awt.*;
2  import java.awt.event.*;
3  import java.applet.*;
4  import javax.swing.*;
5
6  public class ShowInternalFrame extends JApplet {
7    private JMenuBar jMenuBar1 = new JMenuBar();
8    private JMenuItem jmiUS = new JMenuItem("US");
9    private JMenuItem jmiCanada = new JMenuItem("Canada");
10   private ImageViewer imageViewer = new ImageViewer();
11
12   // Create JDesktopPane to hold the internal frame
13   private JDesktopPane desktop = new JDesktopPane();
14   private JInternalFrame internalFrame =
15     new JInternalFrame("US", true, true, true, true);
16
17   // Create images
18   private Image imageUS = ImageViewer.createImage(
19     "image/us.gif", this);
20   private Image imageCanada = ImageViewer.createImage(
21     "image/ca.gif", this);
22
23   // Create image icons
24   private ImageIcon imageUSIcon = ImageViewer.createImageIcon(
25     "image/usIcon.gif", this);
26   private ImageIcon imageCanadaIcon = ImageViewer.createImageIcon(
27     "image/caIcon.gif", this);
28
29   public ShowInternalFrame() {
30     desktop.add(internalFrame);
31
32     this.setSize(new Dimension(400,300));
33     this.getContentPane().add(desktop, BorderLayout.CENTER);
34
35     imageViewer.setImage(imageUS);
36     internalFrame.setFrameIcon(imageUSIcon);
37
38     internalFrame.getContentPane().add(imageViewer);
39     internalFrame.setLocation(20, 20);
```

desktop pane
internal frame

add frame

EXAMPLE 23.8 (CONTINUED)

```
40        internalFrame.setSize(100, 100);
41        internalFrame.setVisible(true);
42
43        JMenu jMenu1 = new JMenu("Flags");
44        jMenuBar1.add(jMenu1);
45        jMenu1.add(jmiUS);
46        jMenu1.add(jmiCanada);
47
48        this.setJMenuBar(jMenuBar1);
49
50        jmiUS.addActionListener(new ActionListener() {
51          public void actionPerformed(ActionEvent e) {
52            imageViewer.setImage(imageUS);
53            internalFrame.setFrameIcon(imageUSIcon);
54            internalFrame.setTitle("US");
55          }
56        });
57
58        jmiCanada.addActionListener(new ActionListener() {
59          public void actionPerformed(ActionEvent e) {
60            imageViewer.setImage(imageCanada);
61            internalFrame.setFrameIcon(imageCanadaIcon);
62            internalFrame.setTitle("Canada");
63          }
64        });
65    }
66 }
```

main method omitted

Review

As shown in Figure 23.24, an internal frame looks like an external frame. Internal frames can be used much the same way as external frames, except that internal frames are always placed inside a JDesktopPane. JDesktopPane is a subclass of JLayeredPane. Since JDesktopPane is also a subclass of JComponent, it can be placed into the content pane of a JFrame or a JApplet.

The properties of the JInternalFrame and JFrame are very similar. You can set a title, an internal frame icon, size, and visible for an internal frame. You may modify this example to add menus to the internal frame too.

KEY CLASSES AND METHODS

✦ **javax.swing.JMenuBar** is a top-level menu bar component used to hold the menus.

✦ **javax.swing.JMenu** is a component to hold the menu items.

✦ **javax.swing.JMenuItem** is a component to represent a menu item.

✦ **javax.swing.JCheckBoxMenuItem** is a component to represent a check box menu item.

✦ **javax.swing.JRadioButtonMenuItem** is a component to represent a radio button menu item.

✦ **javax.swing.JPopupMenu** is a component to represent a popup menu.

✦ **javax.swing.JToolBar** is a Swing container to hold tool bar components (usually buttons). JToolBar uses BoxLayout to manage components.

◆ **javax.swing.Action** is a subinterface of java.awt.event.ActionListener that enables actions to be accessed by several controls.

◆ **javax.swing.AbstractAction** is a default implementation of the Action interface. It implements all the methods in the Action interface except actionPerformed.

◆ **javax.swing.JOptionPane** is a class that provides static methods to create message dialogs, confirmation dialogs, input dialogs, and option dialogs. Use static method showMessageDialog to display a message dialog, showConfirmDialog to display a confirmation dialog, showInputDialog to display an input dialog, and showOptionDialog to display an option dialog.

◆ **javax.swing.JColorChooser** is a lightweight component inherited from javax.swing. JComponent for selecting a color. To display a JColorChooser, invoke its static method showDialog.

◆ **javax.swing.JFileChooser** is a lightweight component inherited from javax.swing. JComponent to display Open and Save File dialogs. To display an Open File dialog, use showOpenDialog(Component) method. To display a Save File dialog, use showSaveDialog(Component) method.

◆ **javax.swing.JInternalFrame** is a class for creating an internal frame.

CHAPTER SUMMARY

◆ Menus make selection easier and are widely used in window applications. Java provides five classes that implement menus: JMenuBar, JMenu, JMenuItem, JCheckBoxMenuItem, and JRadioButtonMenuItem. These classes are subclasses of AbstractButton. They are very similar to buttons.

◆ JMenuBar, is a top-level menu component used to hold menus. A menu consists of *menu items* that the user can select (or toggle on or off). A menu item can be an instance of JMenuItem, JCheckBoxMenuItem, or JRadioButtonMenuItem. Menu items can be associated with icons, keyboard mnemonics, and keyboard accelerators. Menu items can be separated using separators.

◆ A *popup menu*, also known as *a context menu*, is like a regular menu, but does not have a menu bar and can float anywhere on the screen. Creating a popup menu is similar to creating a regular menu. First, you create an instance of JPopupMenu, then you can add JMenuItem, JCheckBoxMenuItem, JradioButtonMenuItem, and separators to the popup menu.

◆ A popup menu usually contains the commands for an object. Customarily, you display a popup menu by pointing to the object and clicking a certain mouse button, the so-called *popup trigger*. Popup triggers are system-dependent. In Windows, the popup menu is displayed when the right mouse button is released. In Motif, the popup menu is displayed when the third mouse button is pressed and held down.

◆ Swing provides the JToolBar class as the container to hold tool bar components. JToolBar uses BoxLayout to manage components. The components usually appear as icons. Since icons are not components, they cannot be placed into a tool bar directly. Instead you may place buttons into the tool bar and set the icons on the buttons. An instance of JToolBar is like a regular container. Often it is placed in the north, west, or east of a container of BorderLayout.

✦ Swing provides the Action interface, which can be used to create action objects for processing actions. Using Action objects, common action processing for menu items and tool bar buttons can be centralized and separated from the other application code.

✦ The JOptionPane class contains the static methods for creating message dialogs, confirmation dialogs, input dialogs, and option dialogs. You can also create custom dialogs by extending the JDialog class.

✦ Swing provides a convenient and versatile color dialog named javax.swing.JColorChooser. Like JOptionPane, JColorChooser is a lightweight component inherited from JComponent. It can be added to any container.

✦ Swing provides the javax.swing.JFileChooser class that displays a dialog box from which the user can navigate through the file system and select files for loading or saving.

✦ You can create internal frames using the JInternalFrame class. This user interface is commonly known as a *multiple document interface* or *MDI*. The JInternalFrame class is almost the same as the external JFrame class. The components are added to the internal frame in the same way as they are added to the external frame. An internal frame can have menus, a title, a Close icon, a Minimize icon, and a Maximize icon just like an external frame.

REVIEW QUESTIONS

Section 23.2 Menus

23.1   How do you create a menu bar?

23.2   How do you create a submenu? How do you create a check box menu item? How do you create a radio button menu item?

23.3   How do you add a separator in a menu?

23.4   How do you set an icon and text in a menu item? How do you associate keyboard mnemonics and accelerators in a menu item?

Section 23.3 Popup Menus

23.5   How do you create a popup menu? How do you show a popup menu?

23.6   Describe a popup trigger.

Section 23.4 JToolBar

23.7   What is the layout manager used in JToolBar? Can you change the layout manager?

23.8   How do you add buttons into a JToolBar? How do you add a JToolBar into a frame or an applet?

Section 23.5 Processing Actions Using the Action Interface

23.9   What is the Action interface for?

23.10   How do you add an Action object to a JToolBar, JMenu, JButton, JRadioButton, and JCheckBox?

Section 23.6 `JOptionPane` Dialogs

23.11   Describe the standard dialog boxes created using the `JOptionPane` class.

23.12   How do you create a message dialog? What are the message types? What is the button in the message dialog?

23.13   How do you create a confirmation dialog? What are the button option types?

23.14   How do you create an input dialog with a text field for entering input? How do you create a combo box dialog for selecting values as input? How do you create a list dialog for selecting values as input?

Sections 23.7–23.10

23.15   How do you show an instance of `JDialog`? Is a standard dialog box created using the static methods in `JOptionPane` modal? Is an instance of `JDialog` modal?

23.16   How do you display an instance of `JColorChooser`? Is an instance of `JColorChooser` modal? How do you obtain the selected color?

23.17   How do you display an instance of `JFileChooser`? Is an instance of `JFileChooser` modal? How do you obtain the selected file? What is the return type for `getSelectedFile()` and `getSelectedDirectory()`? How do you set the current directory as the default directory for a `JFileChooser` dialog?

23.18   How do you create an internal frame?

PROGRAMMING EXERCISES

Sections 23.2–23.3

23.1*   (*Creating an investment value calculator*) Write a program that calculates the future value of an investment at a given interest rate for a specified number of years. The formula for the calculation is as follows:

`futureValue = investmentAmount * (1 + monthlyInterestRate)`^{years*12}

Use text fields for interest rate, investment amount, and years. Display the future amount in a text field when the user clicks the Calculate button or chooses Calculate from the Operation menu (see Figure 23.25). Show a message dialog box when the user clicks the About menu item from the Help menu.

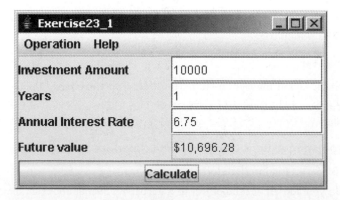

FIGURE 23.25   *The user enters the investment amount, years, and interest rate to compute future value.*

23.2* (*Using popup menus*) Modify Example 23.1, "Using Menus," to create a popup menu that contains the menus Operations and Exit, as shown in Figure 23.26. The popup is displayed when you click the right mouse button on the panel that contains the labels and the text fields.

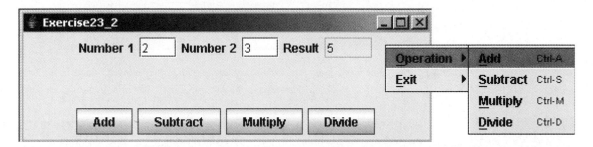

FIGURE 23.26 *The popup menu contains the commands to perform arithmetic operations.*

Sections 23.4–23.5

23.3** (*A paint utility*) Write a program that emulates a paint utility. Your program should enable the user to choose options and draw shapes or get characters from the keyboard based on the selected options (see Figure 23.27). The options are displayed in a tool bar. To draw a line, the user first clicks the line icon in the tool bar and then uses the mouse to draw a line in the same way you would draw using Microsoft Paint.

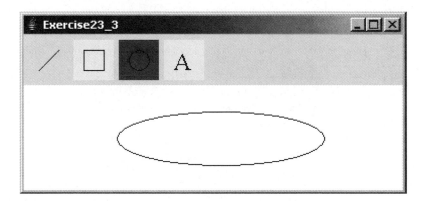

FIGURE 23.27 *This exercise produces a prototype drawing utility that enables you to draw lines, rectangles, ovals, and characters.*

23.4* (*Using action*) Write a program that contains the menu items and tool bar buttons that can be used to select flags to be displayed in an `ImageViewer`, as shown in Figure 23.28. Use the `Action` interface to centralize the processing for the actions.

Sections 23.6–23.10

23.5* (*Demonstrating `JOptionPane`*) Write a program that creates option panes of all types, as shown in Figure 23.29. Each menu item invokes a static `showXxxDialog` method to display a dialog box.

FIGURE 23.28 *The menu items and tool buttons are used to display selected images in the* ImageViewer.

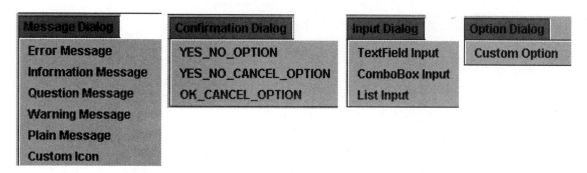

FIGURE 23.29 *You can display a dialog box by clicking a menu item.*

23.6* (*Creating custom dialog*) Write a program that creates a custom dialog box to gather user information, as shown in Figure 23.30.

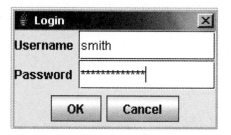

FIGURE 23.30 *The custom dialog box prompts the user to enter username and password.*

23.7* (*Using* JFileChooser) Write a program that enables the user to select a file from a file open dialog box. A file open dialog box is displayed when the Browse button is clicked, as shown in Figure 23.31. The file is displayed in the text area, and the filename is displayed in the text field when the OK button is clicked in the file open dialog box. You can also enter the filename in the text field and press the Enter key to display the file in the text area.

FIGURE 23.31   *The program enables the user to view a file by selecting it from a file open dialog box.*

23.8*   (*Selecting an audio file*) Write a program that selects an audio file using the file dialog box, and use three buttons, Play, Loop, and Stop, to control the audio, as shown in Figure 23.32. If you click the Play button, the audio file is played once. If you click the Loop button, the audio file keeps playing repeatedly. If you click the Stop button, the playing stops. The selected audio files are stored in the folder named anthems under the exercise directory. The exercise directory contains the class file for this exercise.

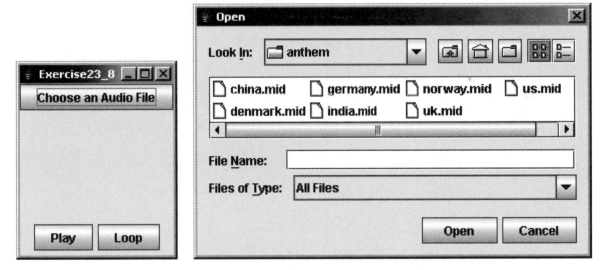

FIGURE 23.32   *The program allows you to choose an audio file from a dialog box and use the buttons to play, repeatedly play, or stop the audio.*

23.9**   (*Playing TicTacToe with a computer*) Section 14.7, "Case Study: TicTacToe," facilitates two players. Write a new game that enables a player to play against the computer. Add a File menu with two items, New Game and Exit, as shown in Figure 23.33. When you click New Game, it displays a dialog box. From this dialog box, you can decide whether to let the computer go first.

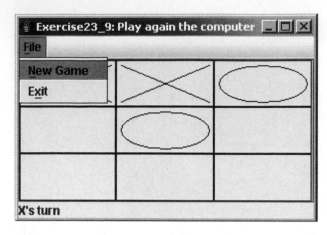

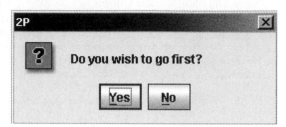

FIGURE 23.33   *The new TicTacToe game enables you to play against the computer.*

ADVANCED SWING COMPONENTS

Objectives

- ✦ To understand the Swing model-view-controller architecture (§24.2).

- ✦ To use JSpinner to scroll the next and previous values (§24.3).

- ✦ To use JList to select single or multiple items in a list (§24.4).

- ✦ To use JComboBox to select or edit a single item from a combo box (§24.5).

- ✦ To use JTable to display and process tables (§24.6).

- ✦ To use JTree to display data in a tree hierarchy (§24.7).

- ✦ To create custom renderers for JSpinner, JList, JComboBox, JTable, and JTree (§§24.2–24.7).

24.1   Introduction

In Chapter 21, "JavaBeans, Bean Events, and MVC," you learned how to use the model-view architecture in developing models and views that separate data storage and management from the visual representation of data. The Swing user interface components are implemented using variations of the MVC architecture. You have used simple Swing components without concern for their supporting models, but in order to use advanced Swing components, you have to use their models to store, access, and modify data. This chapter introduces the models for Swing components and how to use the components JSpinner, JList, JComboBox, JTable, and JTree.

24.2   Swing Model-View-Controller Architecture

Every Swing user interface component (except some containers and dialog boxes, such as JPanel, JSplitPane, JFileChooser, and JColorChooser) has a property named model that refers to its data model. The data model is defined in an interface whose name ends with Model. For example, the model for button component is ButtonModel. Most model interfaces have a default implementation class that is commonly named DefaultX, where X is its model interface name. For example, the default implementation class for ButtonModel is DefaultButtonModel. The relationship of a Swing component, its model interface, and its default model implementation class is illustrated in Figure 24.1.

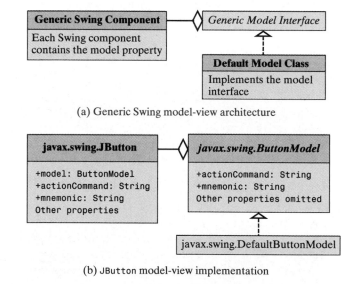

(a) Generic Swing model-view architecture

(b) JButton model-view implementation

FIGURE 24.1   *Swing components are implemented using the MVC architecture.*

For convenience, most Swing components contain some properties of their models, and these properties can be accessed and modified directly from the component without knowing the existence of the model. For example, the properties actionCommand and mnemonic are defined in both ButtonModel and JButton. Actually, these properties are in the AbstractButton class. Since JButton is a subclass of AbstractButton, it inherits all the properties from AbstractButton.

When you create a Swing component without specifying a model, a default data model is assigned to the model property. For example, the following code sets the actionCommand and mnemonic properties of a button through its model:

```
public class Test {
  public static void main(String[] args) {
    javax.swing.JButton jbt = new javax.swing.JButton();

    // Obtain the default model from the component
    javax.swing.ButtonModel model = jbt.getModel();

    // Set properties in the model
    model.setActionCommand("OK");
    model.setMnemonic('O');

    // Display the property values from the component
    System.out.println("actionCommand is " + jbt.getActionCommand());
    System.out.println("mnemonic is " + (char)(jbt.getMnemonic()));
  }
}
```

The output is

```
actionCommand is OK
mnemonic is O
```

You can also create a new model and assign it to a Swing component. For example, the following code creates an instance of `ButtonModel` and assigns it to an instance of `JButton`:

```
public class Test {
  public static void main(String[] args) {
    javax.swing.JButton jbt = new javax.swing.JButton();

    // Create a new button model
    javax.swing.ButtonModel model =
      new javax.swing.DefaultButtonModel();

    // Set properties in the model
    model.setActionCommand("OK");
    model.setMnemonic('O');

    // Assign the model to the button
    jbt.setModel(model);

    // Display the property values from the component
    System.out.println("actionCommand is " + jbt.getActionCommand());
    System.out.println("mnemonic is " + jbt.getMnemonic());
  }
}
```

It is unnecessary to use the models for simple Swing components, such as `JButton`, `JToggleButton`, `JCheckBox`, `JRadioButton`, `JTextField`, and `JTextArea`, because the frequently used properties in their models are also in these components. You can access and modify these properties directly through the components. For advanced components, such as `JSpinner`, `JList`, `JComboBox`, `JTable`, and `JTree`, you have to work with their models to store, access, and modify data.

24.3 JSpinner

A spinner is a text field with a pair of tiny arrow buttons on its right side that enable the user to select numbers, dates, or values from an ordered sequence, as shown in Figure 24.2. The keyboard up/down arrow keys also cycle through the elements. The user may also be allowed to type a (legal) value directly into the spinner. A spinner is similar to a combo box, but a spinner is sometimes preferred because it doesn't require a drop-down list that can obscure important data.

Figure 24.3 shows the constructors and commonly used methods in `JSpinner`. A `JSpinner`'s sequence value is defined by the `SpinnerModel` interface, which manages a potentially unbounded

Spinner   Spinner

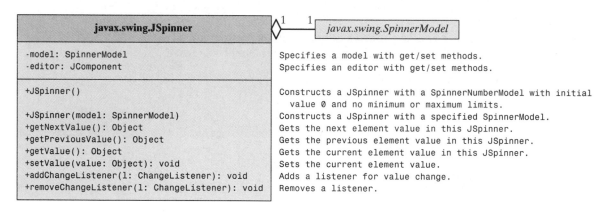

FIGURE 24.2 *Two JSpinner components enable the user to select a month and a year for the calendar.*

javax.swing.JSpinner	
-model: SpinnerModel -editor: JComponent	Specifies a model with get/set methods. Specifies an editor with get/set methods.
+JSpinner()	Constructs a JSpinner with a SpinnerNumberModel with initial value 0 and no minimum or maximum limits.
+JSpinner(model: SpinnerModel) +getNextValue(): Object +getPreviousValue(): Object +getValue(): Object +setValue(value: Object): void +addChangeListener(l: ChangeListener): void +removeChangeListener(l: ChangeListener): void	Constructs a JSpinner with a specified SpinnerModel. Gets the next element value in this JSpinner. Gets the previous element value in this JSpinner. Gets the current element value in this JSpinner. Sets the current element value. Adds a listener for value change. Removes a listener.

1   1   *javax.swing.SpinnerModel*

FIGURE 24.3 *JSpinner uses a spinner model to store data.*

sequence of elements. The model doesn't support indexed random access to sequence elements. Only three sequence elements are accessible at a time, current, next, and previous, using the methods getValue(), getNextValue(), and getPreviousValue(), respectively. The current sequence element can be modified using the setValue method. When the current value in a spinner is changed, the model invokes the stateChanged(javax.swing.event.ChangeEvent e) method of the registered listeners. The listeners must implement javax.swing.event.ChangeListener. All these methods in SpinnerModel are also defined in JSpinner for convenience. So you can access the data in the model from JSpinner directly.

 NOTE

If you create a JSpinner object without specifying a model, the spinner displays a sequence of integers.

EXAMPLE 24.1 A SIMPLE JSpinner DEMO

Problem

This example creates a JSpinner object for a sequence of numbers and displays the previous, current, and next numbers from the spinner on a label, as shown in Figure 24.4.

EXAMPLE 24.1 (CONTINUED)

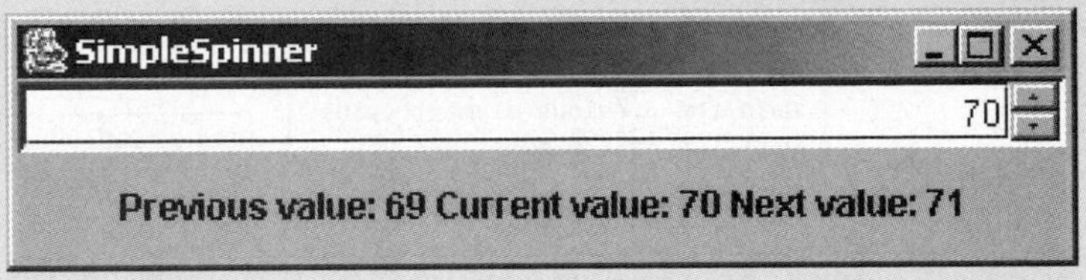

```
SimpleSpinner                              _ □ ×
                                        70
        Previous value: 69 Current value: 70 Next value: 71
```

FIGURE 24.4 *The previous, current, and next values in the spinner are displayed on the label.*

Solution

The source code of the example is given in Listing 24.1.

LISTING 24.1 SimpleSpinner.java

```
 1 import javax.swing.*;
 2 import javax.swing.event.*;
 3 import java.awt.BorderLayout;
 4
 5 public class SimpleSpinner extends JApplet {
 6   // Create a JSpinner
 7   private JSpinner spinner = new JSpinner();                      spinner
 8
 9   // Create a JLabel
10   private JLabel label = new JLabel("", JLabel.CENTER);
11
12   public SimpleSpinner() {
13     // Add spinner and label to the UI
14     getContentPane().add(spinner, BorderLayout.NORTH);
15     getContentPane().add(label, BorderLayout.CENTER);
16
17     // Register and create a listener
18     spinner.addChangeListener(new ChangeListener() {             spinner listener
19       public void stateChanged(javax.swing.event.ChangeEvent e) {
20         label.setText("Previous value: " + spinner.getPreviousValue()
21           + " Current value: " + spinner.getValue()
22           + " Next value: " + spinner.getNextValue());
23       }
24     });
25   }
26 }                                                               main method omitted
```

Review

A JSpinner object is created using its no-arg constructor (Line 7). By default, a spinner displays a sequence of integers.

An anonymous inner class event adapter is created to process the value change event on the spinner (Lines 18–24). The previous, current, and next values in a spinner can be obtained using the JSpinner's instance methods getPreviousValue(), getValue(), and getNextValue().

To display a sequence of values other than integers, you have to use spinner models.

24.3.1 Spinner Models

SpinnerModel is an interface for all spinner models. AbstractSpinnerModel is a convenience abstract class that implements SpinnerModel and provides the implementation for its registration/deregistration methods. SpinnerListModel, SpinnerNumberModel, and SpinnerDateModel are concrete

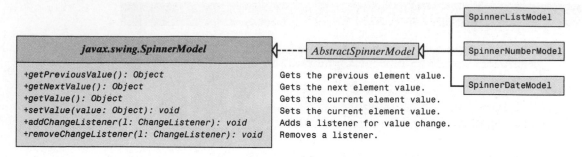

FIGURE 24.5 *SpinnerListModel, SpinnerNumberModel, and SpinnerDateModel are concrete implementations for SpinnerModel.*

implementations of SpinnerModel. The relationship among them is illustrated in Figure 24.5. Besides these models, you can create a custom spinner model that extends AbstractSpinnerModel or directly implements SpinnerModel.

24.3.1.1 SpinnerListModel

SpinnerListModel (see Figure 24.6) is a simple implementation of SpinnerModel whose values are stored in a java.util.List.

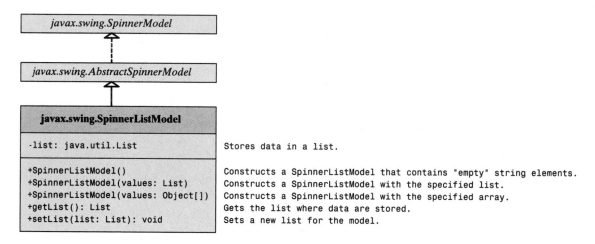

FIGURE 24.6 *SpinnerListModel uses a java.util.List to store a sequence of data in the model.*

You can create a SpinnerListModel using an array or a list. For example, the following code creates a model that consists of the values Freshman, Sophomore, Junior, Senior, and Graduate in an array:

```
// Create an array
String[] grades = {"Freshman", "Sophomore", "Junior",
  "Senior", "Graduate"};

// Create a model from an array
model = new SpinnerListModel(grades);
```

Alternatively, the following code creates a model using a list:

```
// Create an array
String[] grades = {"Freshman", "Sophomore", "Junior",
  "Senior", "Graduate"};
```

```
// Create an array list from the array
list = new ArrayList(Arrays.asList(grades));

// Create a model from list
model = new SpinnerListModel(list);
```

The alternative code seems unnecessary. However, it is useful if you need to add or remove elements from the model. The size of the array is fixed once the array is created. The list is a flexible data structure that enables you to add or remove elements dynamically.

24.3.1.2 SpinnerNumberModel

SpinnerNumberModel (see Figure 24.7) is a concrete implementation of SpinnerModel that represents a sequence of numbers. It contains the properties maximum, minimum, and stepSize. The maximum and minimum properties specify the upper and lower bounds of the sequence. The stepSize specifies the size of the increase or decrease computed by the nextValue and previousValue methods defined in SpinnerModel. The minimum and maximum properties can be null to indicate that the sequence has no lower or upper limit. All of the properties in this class are defined in terms of two generic types, Number and Comparable, so that all Java numeric types may be accommodated. Internally, only the values with type Double, Float, Long, Integer, Short, or Byte are supported.

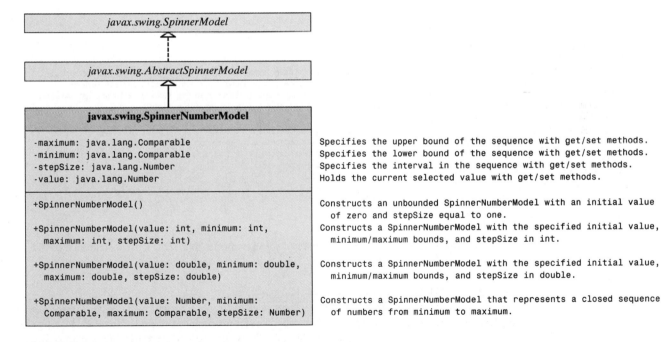

FIGURE 24.7 *SpinnerNumberModel represents a sequence of numbers.*

You can create a SpinnerNumberModel with integers or double. For example, the following code creates a model that represents a sequence of numbers from 0 to 3000 with initial value 2004 and interval 1:

```
// Create a spinner number model
SpinnerNumberModel model = new SpinnerNumberModel(2004, 0, 3000, 1);
```

The following code creates a model that represents a sequence of numbers from 0 to 120 with initial value 50 and interval 0.1:

```
// Create a spinner number model
SpinnerNumberModel model = new SpinnerNumberModel(50, 0, 120, 0.1);
```

24.3.1.3   SpinnerDateModel

SpinnerDateModel (see Figure 24.8) is a concrete implementation of SpinnerModel that represents a sequence of dates. The upper and lower bounds of the sequence are defined by properties called start and end, and the size of the increase or decrease computed by the nextValue and previousValue methods is defined by a property called calendarField. The start and end properties can be null to indicate that the sequence has no lower or upper limit. The value of the calendarField property must be one of the java.util.Calendar constants that specify a field within a Calendar. The getNextValue and getPreviousValue methods change the date forward or backward by this amount. For example, if calendarField is Calendar.DAY_OF_WEEK, then nextValue produces a date that is twenty-four hours after the current value, and previousValue produces a date that is twenty-four hours earlier.

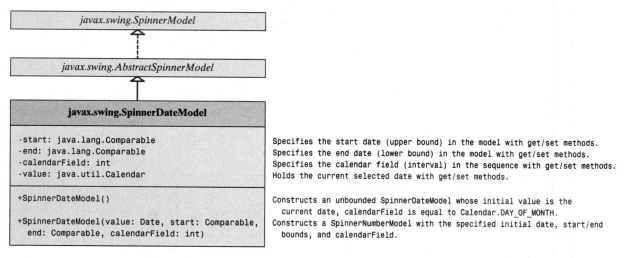

FIGURE 24.8   *SpinnerDateModel represents a sequence of dates.*

For example, the following code creates a spinner model that represents a sequence of dates, starting from the current date, without an upper limit and with calendar field on month.

24.3.2   The JSpinner Editors

A JSpinner has a single child component, called the *editor*, which is responsible for displaying the current element or value of the model. Four editors are defined as static inner classes inside JSpinner.

✦ **JSpinner.DefaultEditor** is a simple base class for all other specialized editors to display a read-only view of the model's current value with a JFormattedTextField. JFormattedTextField extends JTextField adding support for formatting arbitrary values, as well as retrieving a particular object once the user has edited the text.

✦ **JSpinner.NumberEditor** is a specialized editor for a JSpinner whose model is a SpinnerNumberModel. The value of the editor is displayed with a JFormattedTextField whose format is defined by a NumberFormatter instance.

◆ **JSpinner.DateEditor** is a specialized editor for a JSpinner whose model is a SpinnerDateModel. The value of the editor is displayed with a JFormattedTextField whose format is defined by a DateFormatter instance.

◆ **JSpinner.ListEditor** is a specialized editor for a JSpinner whose model is a SpinnerListModel. The value of the editor is displayed with a JFormattedTextField.

The JSpinner's constructor creates a NumberEditor for SpinnerNumberModel, a DateEditor for SpinnerDateModel, a ListEditor for SpinnerListModel, a DefaultEditor for all other models. The editor can also be changed using the setEditor method. The JSpinner's editor stays in sync with the model by listening for ChangeEvents. The commitEdit() method should be used to commit the currently edited value to the model.

EXAMPLE 24.2 USING SPINNER MODELS AND EDITORS

Problem

This example uses a JSpinner component to display the date and three separate JSpinner components to display the day in a sequence of numbers, the month in a sequence of strings, and the year in a sequence of numbers, as shown in Figure 24.9. All four components are synchronized. For example, if you change the year in the spinner for year, the date value in the date spinner is updated accordingly.

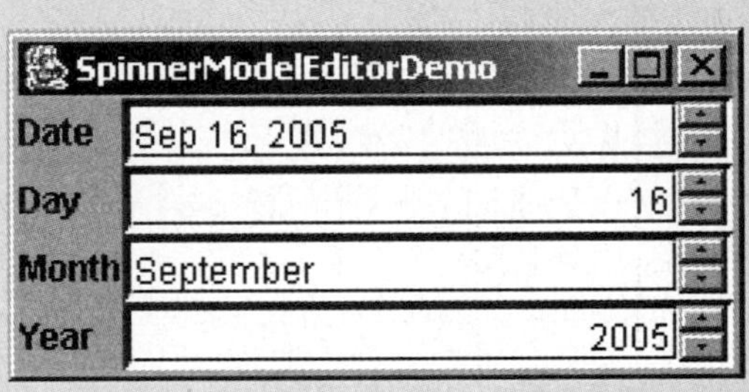

FIGURE 24.9 *The four spinner components are synchronized to display the date in one field and the day, month, and year in three separate fields.*

Solution

The source code of the example is given in Listing 24.2.

LISTING 24.2 SpinnerModelEditorDemo.java

```
1  import javax.swing.*;
2  import javax.swing.event.*;
3  import java.util.*;
4  import java.text.*;
5  import java.awt.*;
6
7  public class SpinnerModelEditorDemo extends JApplet {
8    // Create four spinners for date, day, month, and year
9    private JSpinner spinnerDate =
10     new JSpinner(new SpinnerDateModel());
11   private JSpinner spinnerDay =
12     new JSpinner(new SpinnerNumberModel(1, 1, 31, 1));
13   private String[] monthNames = new DateFormatSymbols().getMonths();
```

spinners

EXAMPLE 24.2 (CONTINUED)

create UI

```
14   private JSpinner spinnerMonth = new JSpinner
15     (new SpinnerListModel(Arrays.asList(monthNames).subList(0, 12)));
16   private JSpinner spinnerYear =
17     new JSpinner(new SpinnerNumberModel(2004, 1, 3000, 1));
18
19   public SpinnerModelEditorDemo() {
20     // Group labels
21     JPanel panel1 = new JPanel();
22     panel1.setLayout(new GridLayout(4, 1));
23     panel1.add(new JLabel("Date"));
24     panel1.add(new JLabel("Day"));
25     panel1.add(new JLabel("Month"));
26     panel1.add(new JLabel("Year"));
27
28     // Group spinners
29     JPanel panel2 = new JPanel();
30     panel2.setLayout(new GridLayout(4, 1));
31     panel2.add(spinnerDate);
32     panel2.add(spinnerDay);
33     panel2.add(spinnerMonth);
34     panel2.add(spinnerYear);
35
36     // Add spinner and label to the UI
37     getContentPane().add(panel1, BorderLayout.WEST);
38     getContentPane().add(panel2, BorderLayout.CENTER);
39
40     // Set editor for date
41     JSpinner.DateEditor dateEditor =
42       new JSpinner.DateEditor(spinnerDate, "MMM dd, yyyy");
43     spinnerDate.setEditor(dateEditor);
44
45     // Set editor for year
46     JSpinner.NumberEditor yearEditor =
47       new JSpinner.NumberEditor(spinnerYear, "####");
48     spinnerYear.setEditor(yearEditor);
49
50     // Update date to synchronize with the day, month, and year
51     updateDate();
52
53     // Register and create a listener for spinnerDay
```

spinner listener

```
54     spinnerDay.addChangeListener(new ChangeListener() {
55       public void stateChanged(javax.swing.event.ChangeEvent e) {
56         updateDate();
57       }
58     });
59
60     // Register and create a listener for spinnerMonth
```

spinner listener

```
61     spinnerMonth.addChangeListener(new ChangeListener() {
62       public void stateChanged(javax.swing.event.ChangeEvent e) {
63         updateDate();
64       }
65     });
66
67     // Register and create a listener for spinnerYear
```

spinner listener

```
68     spinnerYear.addChangeListener(new ChangeListener() {
69       public void stateChanged(javax.swing.event.ChangeEvent e) {
70         updateDate();
71       }
72     });
73   }
74
75   // Update date spinner to synchronize with the other three spinners
76   private void updateDate() {
77     // Get current month and year in int
78     int month = ((SpinnerListModel)spinnerMonth.getModel()).
79       getList().indexOf(spinnerMonth.getValue());
80     int year = ((Integer)spinnerYear.getValue()).intValue();
```

EXAMPLE 24.2 (CONTINUED)

```
81
82    // Set a new maximum number of days for the new month and year
83    SpinnerNumberModel numberModel =
84      (SpinnerNumberModel)spinnerDay.getModel();
85    numberModel.setMaximum(new Integer(maxDaysInMonth(year, month)));
86
87    // Set a new current day if it exceeds the maximum
88    if (((Integer)(numberModel.getValue())).intValue() >
89        maxDaysInMonth(year, month))
90      numberModel.setValue(new Integer(maxDaysInMonth(year, month)));
91
92    // Get the current day
93    int day = ((Integer)spinnerDay.getValue()).intValue();
94
95    // Set a new date in the date spinner
96    spinnerDate.setValue(
97      new GregorianCalendar(year, month, day).getTime());
98  }
99
100  /** Return the maximum number of days in a month. For example,
101     Feb 2004 has 29 days. */
102  private int maxDaysInMonth(int year, int month) {
103    Calendar calendar = new GregorianCalendar(year, month, 1);
104    return calendar.getActualMaximum(Calendar.DAY_OF_MONTH);
105  }
106 }
```

main method omitted

Review

A `JSpinner` object for dates, `spinnerDate`, is created with a default `SpinnerDateModel` (Lines 9–10). The format of the date displayed in the spinner is MMM dd, yyyy (e.g., Feb 01, 2006). This format is created using the `JSpinner`'s inner class constructor `DateEditor` (Lines 41–42) and is set as `spinnerDate`'s editor (Line 43).

A `JSpinner` object for days, `spinnerDay`, is created with a `SpinnerNumberModel` with a sequence of integers between 1 and 31 in which the initial value is 1 and the interval is 1 (Lines 11–12). The maximum number is reset in the `updateDate()` method based on the current month and year (Lines 88–90). For example, February 2004 has twenty-nine days, so the maximum in `spinnerDay` is set to 29 for February 2004.

A `JSpinner` object for months, `spinnerMonth`, is created with a `SpinnerListModel` with a list of month names (Lines 14–15). Month names are locale-specific and can be obtained using the new `DateFormatSymbols().getMonths()` (Line 13). Some calendars can have thirteen months. `Arrays.asList(monthNames)` creates a list from an array of strings, and `subList(0, 12)` returns the first twelve elements in the list.

A `JSpinner` object for years, `spinnerYear`, is created with a `SpinnerNumberModel` with a sequence of integers between 1 and 3000 in which the initial value is 2004 and the interval is 1 (Lines 16–17). By default, locale-specific number separators are used. For example, 2004 would be displayed as 2,004 in the spinner. To display the number without separators, the number pattern `####` is specified to construct a new `NumberEditor` for `spinnerYear` (Lines 46–47). The editor is set as `spinnerYear`'s editor (Line 48).

The `updateDate()` method synchronizes the date spinner with the day, month, and year spinners. Whenever a new value is selected in the day, month, or year spinner, a new date is set in the date spinner. The `maxDaysInMonth` method (Lines 102–105) returns the maximum number of days in a month. For example, February 2004 has 29 days.

A `JSpinner` object can fire `javax.swing.event.ChangeEvent` to notify the listeners of the state change in the spinner. The anonymous event adapters are created to process spinner state changes for the day, month, and year spinners (Lines 53–72). Whenever a new

EXAMPLE 24.2 (CONTINUED)

value is selected in one of these three spinners, the date spinner value is updated accordingly. In Exercise 24.1, you will improve the example to synchronize the day, month, and year
spinners with the date spinner. Then, when a new value is selected in the date spinner, the
values in the day, month, and year spinners will be updated accordingly.

This example uses `SpinnerNumberModel`, `SpinnerDateModel`, and `SpinnerListModel`.
They are predefined concrete spinner models in the API. You can also create custom spinner models (see Exercise 24.2).

24.4 JList

Section 13.10, "Lists," introduced the basic features of `JList` without using list models. You
learned how to create a list and how to respond to list selections. However, you cannot add or remove elements from a list without using list models. This section introduces list models and gives
a detailed discussion on how to use `JList`.

`JList` has two supporting models: a list model and a list-selection model. The *list model* is for storing and processing data. The *list-selection model* is for selecting items. By default, items are rendered as
strings or icons. You can also create a custom renderer implementing the `ListCellRenderer` interface. The relationship of these interfaces and classes is shown in Figure 24.10.

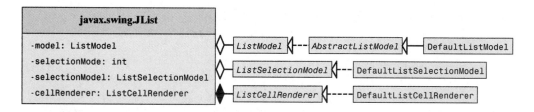

FIGURE 24.10 *JList contains several supporting interfaces and classes.*

24.4.1 JList Constructors, Properties, and Methods

Figure 24.11 shows the properties and constructors of `JList`. You can create a list from a list
model, an array of objects, or a vector.

24.4.2 List Layout Orientations

The `layoutOrientation` property, introduced in JDK 1.4, specifies the layout of the items using
one of the following three values:

✦ `JList.VERTICAL` specifies that the cells should be laid out vertically in one column. This is
the default value.

✦ `JList.HORIZONTAL_WRAP` specifies that the cells should be laid out horizontally, wrapping
to a new row as necessary. The number of rows to use is determined by the
`visibleRowCount` property if its value is greater than 0; otherwise the number of rows is
determined by the width of the `JList`.

✦ `JList.VERTICAL_WRAP` specifies that the cells should be laid out vertically, wrapping to a
new column as necessary. The number of rows to use is determined by the

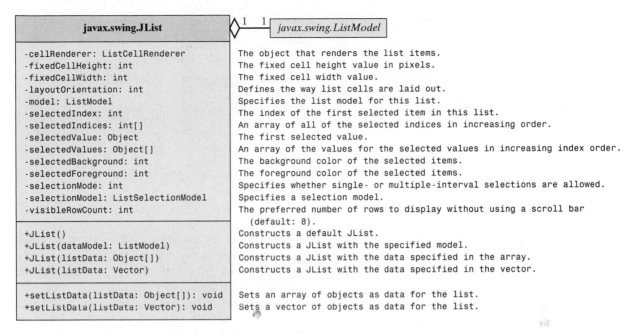

FIGURE 24.11 *JList displays elements in a list.*

visibleRowCount property if its value is greater than 0; otherwise the number of rows is determined by the height of the JList.

For example, suppose there are five elements (item1, item2, item3, item4, and item5) in the list and the visibleRowCount is 2. Figure 24.12 shows the layout in these three cases.

(a) JList.VERTICAL   (b) JList.HORIZONTAL_WRAP   (c) JList.VERTICAL_WRAP

FIGURE 24.12 *Layout orientation specifies how elements are laid out in a list.*

24.4.3 List-Selection Modes and List Selection Models

The selectionMode property is one of the three values (SINGLE_SELECTION, SINGLE_ INTERVAL_SELECTION, MULTIPLE_INTERVAL_SELECTION) that indicate whether a single item, single-interval item, or multiple-interval item can be selected. Single selection allows only one item to be selected. Single-interval selection allows multiple selections, but the selected items must be contiguous. Multiple-interval selection allows selections of multiple contiguous items without restrictions, as shown in Figure 24.13. The default value is MULTIPLE_ INTERVAL_SELECTION.

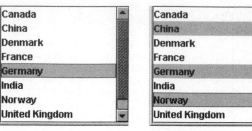

(a) Single Selection	(b) Single-Interval Selection	(c) Multiple-Interval Selection

FIGURE 24.13   *A list has three selection modes.*

The `selectionModel` property specifies an object that tracks list selection. `JList` has two models: a list model and a list-selection model. *List models* handle data management, and *list-selection models* deal with data selection. A list-selection model must implement the `ListSelectionModel` interface, which defines constants for three selection modes (`SINGLE_SELECTION`, `SINGLE_INTERVAL_SELECTION`, and `MULTIPLE_INTERVAL_SELECTION`) and registration methods for `ListSectionListener`. It also defines the methods for adding and removing selection intervals, and the access methods for the properties, such as `selectionMode`, `anchorSelectionIndex`, `leadSelectionIndex`, and `valueIsAdjusting`.

By default, an instance of `JList` uses `DefaultListSelectionModel`, which is a concrete implementation of `ListSelectionModel`. Usually, you do not need to provide a custom list-selection model, because the `DefaultListSelectionModel` class is sufficient in most cases. List-selection models are rarely used explicitly, because you can set the selection mode directly in `JList`.

EXAMPLE 24.3   LIST PROPERTIES DEMO

Problem

This example creates a list of a fixed number of items displayed as strings. The example enables you to dynamically set `visibleRowCount` from a spinner, `layoutOrientation` from a combo box, and `selectionMode` from a combo box, as shown in Figure 24.14. When you select one or more items, their values are displayed in a status label below the list.

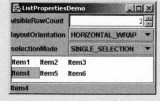
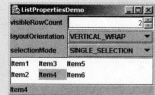
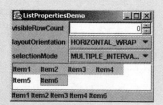

FIGURE 24.14   *You can dynamically set the properties for* `visibleRowCount`, `layoutOrientation`, *and* `selectionMode` *in a list.*

Solution

The source code of the example is given in Listing 24.3.

EXAMPLE 24.3 (CONTINUED)

LISTING 24.3 ListPropertiesDemo.java

```
1  import java.awt.*;
2  import java.awt.event.*;
3  import javax.swing.*;
4  import javax.swing.event.*;
5
6  public class ListPropertiesDemo extends JApplet {
7    private JList jlst = new JList(new String[] {"Item1",
8      "Item2", "Item3", "Item4", "Item5", "Item6"});
9    private JSpinner jspinnerVisibleRowCount =
10     new JSpinner(new SpinnerNumberModel(8, -1, 20, 1));
11   private JComboBox jcboLayoutOrientation =
12     new JComboBox(new String[]{"VERTICAL", "HORIZONTAL_WRAP",
13       "VERTICAL_WRAP"});
14   private JComboBox jcboSelectionMode =
15     new JComboBox(new String[]{"SINGLE_SELECTION",
16       "SINGLE_INTERVAL_SELECTION", "MULTIPLE_INTERVAL_SELECTION"});
17   private JLabel jlblStatus = new JLabel();
18
19   /** Construct the applet */
20   public ListPropertiesDemo() {
21     // Place labels in a panel
22     JPanel panel1 = new JPanel();
23     panel1.setLayout(new GridLayout(3, 1));
24     panel1.add(new JLabel("visibleRowCount"));
25     panel1.add(new JLabel("layoutOrientation"));
26     panel1.add(new JLabel("selectionMode"));
27
28     // Place text fields in a panel
29     JPanel panel2 = new JPanel();
30     panel2.setLayout(new GridLayout(3, 1));
31     panel2.add(jspinnerVisibleRowCount);
32     panel2.add(jcboLayoutOrientation);
33     panel2.add(jcboSelectionMode);
34
35     // Place panel1 and panel2
36     JPanel panel3 = new JPanel();
37     panel3.setLayout(new BorderLayout(5, 5));
38     panel3.add(panel1, BorderLayout.WEST);
39     panel3.add(panel2, BorderLayout.CENTER);
40
41     // Place elements in the applet
42     getContentPane().add(panel3, BorderLayout.NORTH);
43     getContentPane().add(new JScrollPane(jlst), BorderLayout.CENTER);
44     getContentPane().add(jlblStatus, BorderLayout.SOUTH);
45
46     // Set initial property values
47     jlst.setFixedCellWidth(50);
48     jlst.setFixedCellHeight(20);
49     jlst.setSelectionMode(ListSelectionModel.SINGLE_SELECTION);
50
51     // Register listeners
52     jspinnerVisibleRowCount.addChangeListener(new ChangeListener() {
53       public void stateChanged(ChangeEvent e) {
54         jlst.setVisibleRowCount(
55           ((Integer)jspinnerVisibleRowCount.getValue()).intValue());
56       }
57     });
58
59     jcboLayoutOrientation.addActionListener(new ActionListener() {
60       public void actionPerformed(ActionEvent e) {
61         if ((jcboLayoutOrientation.getSelectedItem()).
62             equals("VERTICAL"))
63           jlst.setLayoutOrientation(JList.VERTICAL);
64         else if ((jcboLayoutOrientation.getSelectedItem()).
65             equals("HORIZONTAL_WRAP"))
```

list

spinner

combo boxes

create UI

spinner listener

combo box listener

EXAMPLE 24.3 (CONTINUED)

combo box listener

```
66              jlst.setLayoutOrientation(JList.HORIZONTAL_WRAP);
67          else if ((jcboLayoutOrientation.getSelectedItem()).
68              equals("VERTICAL_WRAP"))
69              jlst.setLayoutOrientation(JList.VERTICAL_WRAP);
70        }
71      });
72
73      jcboSelectionMode.addActionListener(new ActionListener() {
74        public void actionPerformed(ActionEvent e) {
75          if ((jcboSelectionMode.getSelectedItem()).
76              equals("SINGLE_SELECTION"))
77            jlst.setSelectionMode(
78            ListSelectionModel.SINGLE_SELECTION);
79          else if ((jcboSelectionMode.getSelectedItem()).
80                equals("SINGLE_INTERVAL_SELECTION"))
81            jlst.setSelectionMode(
82            ListSelectionModel.SINGLE_INTERVAL_SELECTION);
83          else if ((jcboSelectionMode.getSelectedItem()).
84                equals("MULTIPLE_INTERVAL_SELECTION"))
85            jlst.setSelectionMode(
86            ListSelectionModel.MULTIPLE_INTERVAL_SELECTION);
87        }
88      });
89
```

list listener

```
90      jlst.addListSelectionListener(new ListSelectionListener() {
91        public void valueChanged(ListSelectionEvent e) {
92          Object[] values = jlst.getSelectedValues();
93          String display = "";
94
95          for (int i = 0; i < values.length; i++) {
96            display += (String)values[i] + " ";
97          }
98
99          jlblStatus.setText(display);
100        }
101      });
102    }
```

main method omitted

```
103 }
```

Review

A JList is created with six string values (Lines 7–8). A JSpinner is created using a Spinner-NumberModel with initial value 8, minimum value −1, maximum value 20, and step 1 (Lines 9–10). A JComboBox is created with string values VERTICAL, HORIZONTAL_WRAP, and VERTICAL_WRAP for choosing layout orientation (Lines 11–13). A JComboBox is created with string values SINGLE_SELECTION, INTERVAL_SELECTION, and MULTIPLE_INTERVAL_SELECTION for choosing a selection mode (Lines 14–16). A JLabel is created to display the selected elements in the list (Lines 17).

A JList does not support scrolling. To create a scrollable list, create a JScrollPane and add an instance of JList to it (Line 43).

The fixed list cell width and height are specified in Lines 47–48. The default selection mode is multiple-interval selection. Line 49 sets the selection mode to single selection.

When a new visible row count is selected from the spinner, the setVisibleRowCount method is used to set the count (Lines 52–57). When a new layout orientation is selected from the jcboLayoutOrientation combo box, the setLayoutOrientation method is used to set the layout orientation (Lines 59–71). When a new selection mode is selected from the jcboSelectionMode combo box, the setSelectionMode method is used to set the selection mode (Lines 73–88).

JList generates javax.swing.event.ListSelectionEvent to notify the listeners of the selections. The listener must implement the valueChanged handler to process the event. When the user selects an item in the list, the valueChanged handler is executed, which gets the selected items and displays all the items in the label (90–101).

The example enables you to specify selection mode from a combo box. When you choose SINGLE_SELECTION, only one item can be selected at a given time. When you choose SINGLE_INTERVAL_SELECTION, multiple consecutive items can be selected all together by holding down the SHIFT key. When you choose MULTIPLE_INTERVAL_SELECTION, you can choose any number of items anywhere in the list by holding down the CTRL key.

24.4.4 List Models

The preceding example constructs a list with a fixed set of strings. If you want to add new items to the list or delete existing items, you have to use a list model. This section introduces list models.

The JList class delegates the responsibilities of storing and maintaining data to its data model. The JList class itself does not have methods for adding or removing items from the list. These methods are supported in ListModel, as shown in Figure 24.15.

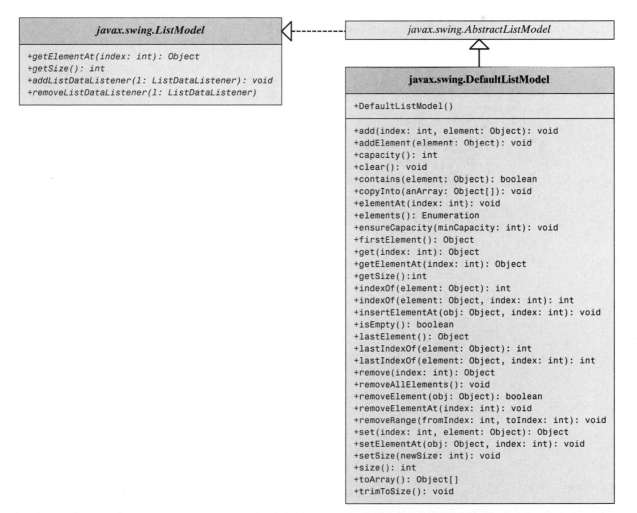

FIGURE 24.15 *ListModel stores and manages data in a list.*

All list models implement the `ListModel` interface, which defines the registration methods for `ListDataEvent`. The instances of `ListDataListener` are notified when the items in the list are modified. `ListModel` also defines the methods `getSize` and `getElementAt`. The `getSize` method returns the length of the list, and the `getElementAt` method returns the element at the specified index.

`AbstractListModel` implements the `ListModel` and `Serializable` interfaces. `Abstract-ListModel` implements the registration methods in the `ListModel`, but does not implement the `getSize` and `getElementAt` methods.

`DefaultListModel` extends `AbstractListModel` and implements the two methods `getSize` and `getElementAt`, which are not implemented by `AbstractListModel`.

The methods in `DefaultListModel` are similar to those in the `java.util.Vector` class. You use the `add` method to insert an element to the list, the `remove` method to remove an element from the list, the `clear` method to clear the list, the `getSize` method to return the number of elements in the list, and the `getElementAt` method to retrieve an element. In fact, the `DefaultListModel` stores data in an instance of `Vector`, which is essentially a resizable array. Swing components were developed before the Java Collections Framework. In future implementations, `Vector` may be replaced by `java.util.ArrayList`.

 NOTE

In most cases, if you create a Swing GUI object without specifying a model, an instance of the default model class is created. But this is not true for `JList`. By default, the `model` property in `JList` is not an instance of `DefaultListModel`.

EXAMPLE 24.4 LIST MODEL DEMO

Problem

This example creates a list using a list model and allows the user to add and delete items in the list, as shown in Figure 24.16. When the user clicks the *Add new item* button, an input dialog box is displayed to receive a new item.

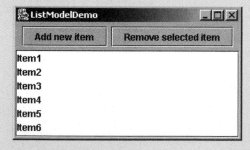 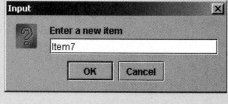

FIGURE 24.16 *You can add elements and remove elements in a list using list models.*

Solution

The source code of the example is given in Listing 24.4.

LISTING 24.4   ListModelDemo.java

```
1 import java.awt.*;
2 import java.awt.event.*;
3 import java.applet.*;
4 import javax.swing.*;
```

EXAMPLE 24.4 (CONTINUED)

```
5
6  public class ListModelDemo extends JApplet {
7    private DefaultListModel listModel = new DefaultListModel();
8    private JList jlst = new JList(listModel);
9    private JButton jbtAdd = new JButton("Add new item");
10   private JButton jbtRemove = new JButton("Remove selected item");
11
12   /** Construct the applet */
13   public ListModelDemo() {
14     // Add items to the list model
15     listModel.addElement("Item1");
16     listModel.addElement("Item2");
17     listModel.addElement("Item3");
18     listModel.addElement("Item4");
19     listModel.addElement("Item5");
20     listModel.addElement("Item6");
21
22     JPanel panel = new JPanel();
23     panel.add(jbtAdd);
24     panel.add(jbtRemove);
25
26     getContentPane().add(panel, BorderLayout.NORTH);
27     getContentPane().add(new JScrollPane(jlst), BorderLayout.CENTER);
28
29     // Register listeners
30     jbtAdd.addActionListener(new ActionListener() {
31       public void actionPerformed(ActionEvent e) {
32         String newItem =
33           JOptionPane.showInputDialog("Enter a new item");
34
35         if (newItem != null)
36           if (jlst.getSelectedIndex() == -1)
37             listModel.addElement(newItem);
38           else
39             listModel.add(jlst.getSelectedIndex(), newItem);
40       }
41     });
42
43     jbtRemove.addActionListener(new ActionListener() {
44       public void actionPerformed(ActionEvent e) {
45         listModel.remove(jlst.getSelectedIndex());
46       }
47     });
48   }
49 }
```

list model
list

add items

button listener

button listener

main method omitted

Review

The program creates listModel (Line 7), which is an instance of DefaultListModel, and uses it to manipulate data in the list. The model enables you to add and remove items in the list.

A list is created from the list model (Line 8). The initial elements are added into the model using the addElement method (Lines 14–20).

To add an element, the user clicks the *Add new item* button to display an input dialog box. Type a new item in the dialog box. The new item is inserted before the currently selected element in the list (Line 39). If no element is selected, the new element is appended to the list (Line 37).

To remove an element, the user has to select the element and then click the *Remove selected item* button. Note that only the first selected item is removed. You can modify the program to remove all the selected items (see Exercise 24.4).

What would happen if you click the *Remove selected item* button but no items are currently selected? This would cause an error. To fix it, see Exercise 24.4.

24.4.5 List Cell Renderer

The preceding example displays items as strings in a list. JList is very flexible and versatile, and it can be used to display images and GUI components in addition to simple text. This section introduces list cell renderers for displaying graphics.

In addition to delegating data storage and processing to list models, JList delegates the rendering of list cells to list cell renderers. All list cell renderers implement the ListCellRenderer interface, which defines a single method, getListCellRendererComponent, as follows:

```
public Component getListCellRendererComponent
   (JList list, Object value, int index, boolean isSelected,
   boolean cellHasFocus)
```

This method is passed with a list, the value associated with the cell, the index of the value, and information regarding whether the value is selected and the cell has the focus. The component returned from the method is painted on the cell in the list. By default, JList uses DefaultListCellRenderer to render its cells. The DefaultListCellRenderer class implements ListCellRenderer, extends JLabel, and can display either a string or an icon, but not both in the same cell. You can create a custom renderer by implementing ListCellRenderer, as shown in Figure 24.17.

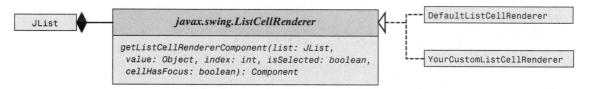

FIGURE 24.17 *ListCellRenderer defines how cells are rendered in a list.*

EXAMPLE 24.5 LIST CELL RENDERER DEMO

Problem

This example creates a list of countries and displays the country flags and country names in the list, as shown in Figure 24.18. When a country is selected in the list, its flag is displayed in a panel next to the list.

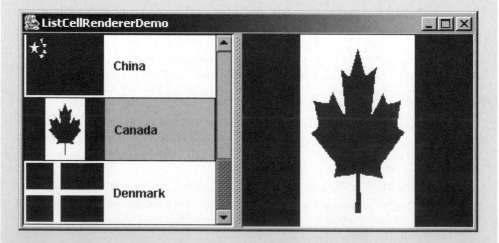

FIGURE 24.18 *The image and the text are displayed in the list cell.*

EXAMPLE 24.5 (CONTINUED)

Solution

Each cell in the list contains an image for the country flag and a string for the country name. Intuitively, you can store both image and string as a single item in the list model. Each item is an array consisting of two elements. The first element is for the image, and the second is for the string. An image can be created using the static `createImage` method in the `ImageViewer` class. For example, you can add the item for Canada to the list model, as follows:

```
Image imageCanada = ImageViewer.createImage(
  "/image/ca.gif", this);
listModel.addElement(new Object[]{imageCanada, "Canada"});
```

To render the image and string in the cell, create a custom list cell renderer, `MyListCellRenderer`, in Listing 24.5.

LISTING 24.5   MyListCellRenderer.java

```
1 import java.awt.*;
2 import javax.swing.*;
3 import javax.swing.border.*;
4
5 public class MyListCellRenderer implements ListCellRenderer {
6   private JPanel listCellPanel = new JPanel();
7   private ImageViewer imageViewer = new ImageViewer();
8   private JLabel jlbl = new JLabel(" ", JLabel.LEFT);
9   private Border lineBorder =
10    BorderFactory.createLineBorder(Color.black, 1);
11  private Border emptyBorder =
12    BorderFactory.createEmptyBorder(2, 2, 2, 2);
13
14  public MyListCellRenderer() {
15    listCellPanel.setOpaque(true);
16    jlbl.setPreferredSize(new Dimension(100, 60));
17    listCellPanel.setLayout(new BorderLayout(10, 5));
18    listCellPanel.add(imageViewer, BorderLayout.CENTER);
19    listCellPanel.add(jlbl, BorderLayout.EAST);
20  }
21
22  /** Implement this method in ListCellRenderer */
23  public Component getListCellRendererComponent
24     (JList list, Object value, int index, boolean isSelected,
25       boolean cellHasFocus) {
26    Object[] pair = (Object[])value; // Cast value into an array
27    imageViewer.setImage((Image)pair[0]);
28    jlbl.setText(pair[1].toString());
29
30    if (isSelected) {
31      listCellPanel.setForeground(list.getSelectionForeground());
32      listCellPanel.setBackground(list.getSelectionBackground());
33    }
34    else {
35      listCellPanel.setForeground(list.getForeground());
36      listCellPanel.setBackground(list.getBackground());
37    }
38
39    listCellPanel.setBorder(cellHasFocus ? lineBorder : emptyBorder);
40
41    return listCellPanel;
42  }
43 }
```

cell component
image viewer

image viewer
label

cell component

cell selected

cell component

The main program that utilizes the custom list cell renderer is given in Listing 24.6.

EXAMPLE 24.5 (CONTINUED)

LISTING 24.6 ListCellRendererDemo.java

images

list model

list

list cell renderer

split pane

image viewer

add elements

set renderer

list listener

```java
 1 import javax.swing.*;
 2 import javax.swing.event.*;
 3 import java.awt.*;
 4
 5 public class ListCellRendererDemo extends JApplet {
 6   // Create images
 7   private Image imageUS = ImageViewer.createImage(
 8     "/image/us.gif", this);
 9   private Image imageFrance = ImageViewer.createImage(
10     "/image/fr.gif", this);
11   private Image imageUK = ImageViewer.createImage(
12     "/image/uk.gif", this);
13   private Image imageGermany = ImageViewer.createImage(
14     "/image/germany.gif", this);
15   private Image imageIndia = ImageViewer.createImage(
16     "/image/india.gif", this);
17   private Image imageNorway = ImageViewer.createImage(
18     "/image/norway.gif", this);
19   private Image imageChina = ImageViewer.createImage(
20     "/image/china.gif", this);
21   private Image imageCanada = ImageViewer.createImage(
22     "/image/ca.gif", this);
23   private Image imageDenmark = ImageViewer.createImage(
24     "/image/denmark.gif", this);
25
26   // Create a list model
27   private DefaultListModel listModel = new DefaultListModel();
28
29   // Create a list using the list model
30   private JList jlst = new JList(listModel);
31
32   // Create a list cell renderer
33   private ListCellRenderer renderer = new MyListCellRenderer();
34
35   // Create a split pane
36   private JSplitPane jSplitPane1 = new JSplitPane();
37
38   // Create an image viewer
39   private ImageViewer imageViewer1 = new ImageViewer(imageUS);
40
41   /** Construct ListCellRenderer */
42   public ListCellRendererDemo() {
43     listModel.addElement(new Object[]{imageUS, "United States"});
44     listModel.addElement(new Object[]{imageFrance, "France"});
45     listModel.addElement(new Object[]{imageUK, "United Kingdom"});
46     listModel.addElement(new Object[]{imageGermany, "Germany"});
47     listModel.addElement(new Object[]{imageIndia, "India"});
48     listModel.addElement(new Object[]{imageNorway, "Norway"});
49     listModel.addElement(new Object[]{imageChina, "China"});
50     listModel.addElement(new Object[]{imageCanada, "Canada"});
51     listModel.addElement(new Object[]{imageDenmark, "Denmark"});
52
53     // Set list cell renderer
54     jlst.setCellRenderer(renderer);
55     jSplitPane1.setLeftComponent(new JScrollPane(jlst));
56     jSplitPane1.setRightComponent(imageViewer1);
57     getContentPane().add(jSplitPane1, BorderLayout.CENTER);
58
59     // Register listener
60     jlst.addListSelectionListener(new ListSelectionListener() {
61       public void valueChanged(ListSelectionEvent evt) {
62         Object[] pair = (Object[])(jlst.getSelectedValue());
```

```
63              imageViewer1.setImage((Image)pair[0]);
64        }
65      });
66    }
67 }
```

main method omitted

Review

The example uses two classes: `MyListCellRenderer` and `ListCellRendererDemo`. The `MyListCellRenderer` class is responsible for rendering the cell with image and text. The `ListCellRendererDemo` class tests the list with the custom list cell renderer.

The `ListCellRendererDemo` class creates a list model (Line 27) and adds the items to the model (Lines 43–51). Each item is an array of two elements (image and string). The list is created using the list model (Line 30). The list cell renderer is created (Line 33) and associated with the list (Line 54).

The `ListCellRendererDemo` class creates a split pane (Line 36) and places the list on the left (Line 55) and an image viewer on the right (Line 56).

When you choose a country in the list, the list-selection event handler is invoked (Lines 62–63). This handler obtains the selected value (Line 62), retrieves the country's flag image (Line 63), and displays the image in the image viewer on the right side of the split pane.

The `MyListCellRenderer` class implements the `getListCellRendererComponent` method in the `ListCellRenderer` interface. This method is passed with the parameters `list`, `value`, `index`, `isSelected`, and `isFocused` (Lines 23–25). The `value` represents the current item value. In this case, it is an array consisting of two elements. The first element is an image (Line 27) displayed in an image viewer. The second element is a string (Line 28) displayed in a label. The image viewer and the label are contained in a panel. The `getListCellRendererComponent` method returns the panel (Line 41), which is painted on the cell in the list.

The label's preferred size is set to 100 by 60 in the `MyListCellRenderer` class (Line 16), so it will be limited to 100 by 60 and the rest of the space in the cell renderer is allocated to the image.

If a cell is selected, the background and foreground of the cell are set to the list's selection background and foreground (Lines 31–32). If the cell is focused, the cell's border is set to the line border (Line 39); otherwise, it is set to the empty border (Line 39). The empty border serves as a divider between the cells.

24.5 JComboBox

Section 13.9, "Combo Boxes," introduced the basic features of `JComboBox` without using combo box models. This section introduces combo models and discusses the use of `JComboBox` in some detail.

A combo box is similar to a list. Combo boxes and lists are both used for selecting items from a list. A combo box allows the user to select one item at a time, whereas a list permits multiple selections. A combo box displays a drop-down list contained in a popup menu when the combo box is selected. The selected item can be edited in the cell as if it were a text field. Figure 24.19 shows the properties and constructors of `JComboBox`. The data for a combo box are stored in `ComboBoxModel`. You can create a combo box from a combo box model, an array of objects, or a vector.

`JComboBox` delegates the responsibilities of storing and maintaining data to its data model. All combo box models implement the `ComboBoxModel` interface, which extends the `ListModel` interface

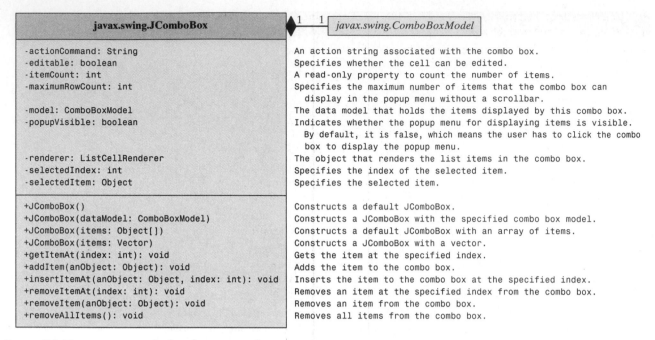

FIGURE 24.19   *JComboBox displays elements in a list.*

and defines the getSelectedItem and setSelectedItem methods for retrieving and setting a select-ed item. The methods for adding and removing items are defined in the MutableComboBoxModel in-terface, which extends ComboBoxModel. When an instance of JComboBox is created without explicitly specifying a model, an instance of DefaultComboBoxModel is used. The DefaultComboBoxModel class extends AbstractListModel and implements MutableComboBoxModel, as shown in Figure 24.20.

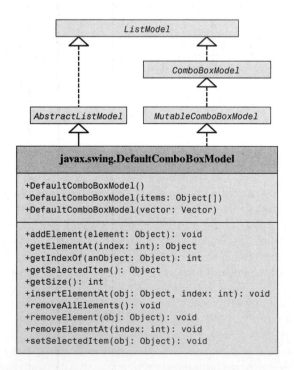

FIGURE 24.20   *ComboBoxModel stores and manages data in a combo box.*

Usually you don't need to use combo box models explicitly, because `JComboBox` contains the methods for retrieving (`getItemAt`, `getSelectedItem`, and `getSelectedIndex`), adding (`addItem` and `insertItemAt`), and removing (`removeItem`, `removeItemAt`, and `removeAllItems`) items from the list.

Combo boxes render cells exactly like lists, because the combo box items are displayed in a list contained in a popup menu. Therefore, a combo box cell renderer can be created exactly like a list cell renderer by implementing the `ListCellRenderer` interface.

`JComboBox` can generate `ActionEvent` and `ItemEvent`, among many other events. Whenever a new item is selected, `JComboBox` generates `ItemEvent` twice, once for deselecting the previously selected item, and the other for selecting the currently selected item. `JComboBox` generates an `ActionEvent` after generating an `ItemEvent`.

EXAMPLE 24.6 COMBO BOX CELL RENDERER DEMO

Problem

This example creates a combo box that contains a list of countries and displays the country flags and country names in the list cell, as shown in Figure 24.21. When a country is selected in the list, its flag is displayed in a panel below the combo box.

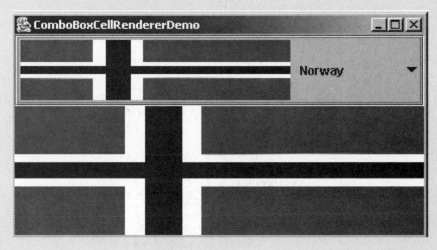

FIGURE 24.21   *The image and the text are displayed in the list cell of a combo box.*

Solution

Each combo box has a default cell renderer that displays a string or an icon, but not both at the same time. To display a combination of a string and an icon, you need to create a custom renderer. The custom list cell renderer `MyListCellRenderer`, developed in Example 24.5, "List Cell Renderer Demo," can be used as the combo box cell renderer in this example without any modification. Each item in the combo box consists of an image viewer and a string in an array. The array is stored in the combo box model. `DefaultComboBoxModel` is sufficient for storing and handling items for this example. The source code for the program is given in Listing 24.7.

LISTING 24.7   ComboBoxCellRendererDemo.java

```
1 import java.awt.*;
2 import java.awt.event.*;
3 import javax.swing.*;
4
```

EXAMPLE 24.6 (CONTINUED)

images

```java
 5  public class ComboBoxCellRendererDemo extends JApplet {
 6    // Create images
 7    private Image imageUS = ImageViewer.createImage(
 8      "/image/us.gif", this);
 9    private Image imageFrance = ImageViewer.createImage(
10      "/image/fr.gif", this);
11    private Image imageUK = ImageViewer.createImage(
12      "/image/uk.gif", this);
13    private Image imageGermany = ImageViewer.createImage(
14      "/image/germany.gif", this);
15    private Image imageIndia = ImageViewer.createImage(
16      "/image/india.gif", this);
17    private Image imageNorway = ImageViewer.createImage(
18      "/image/norway.gif", this);
19    private Image imageChina = ImageViewer.createImage(
20      "/image/china.gif", this);
21    private Image imageCanada = ImageViewer.createImage(
22      "/image/ca.gif", this);
23    private Image imageDenmark = ImageViewer.createImage(
24      "/image/denmark.gif", this);
25
26    // Create a combo box model
27    private DefaultComboBoxModel model = new DefaultComboBoxModel();
28
29    // Create a combo box with the specified model
30    private JComboBox jcboCountries = new JComboBox(model);
31
32    // Create a list cell renderer
33    private MyListCellRenderer renderer = new MyListCellRenderer();
34
35    // Create an image viewer
36    private ImageViewer imageViewer1 = new ImageViewer(imageUS);
37
38    /** Construct the applet */
39    public ComboBoxCellRendererDemo() {
40      model.addElement(new Object[]{imageUS, "United States"});
41      model.addElement(new Object[]{imageFrance, "France"});
42      model.addElement(new Object[]{imageUK, "United Kingdom"});
43      model.addElement(new Object[]{imageGermany, "Germany"});
44      model.addElement(new Object[]{imageIndia, "India"});
45      model.addElement(new Object[]{imageNorway, "Norway"});
46      model.addElement(new Object[]{imageChina, "China"});
47      model.addElement(new Object[]{imageCanada, "Canada"});
48      model.addElement(new Object[]{imageDenmark, "Denmark"});
49
50      // Set list cell renderer for the combo box
51      jcboCountries.setRenderer(renderer);
52
53      getContentPane().add(jcboCountries, java.awt.BorderLayout.NORTH);
54      getContentPane().add(imageViewer1, java.awt.BorderLayout.CENTER);
55
56      // Register listener
57      jcboCountries.addActionListener(new ActionListener() {
58        public void actionPerformed(java.awt.event.ActionEvent evt) {
59          Object[] pair = (Object[])(jcboCountries.getSelectedItem());
60          imageViewer1.setImage((Image)pair[0]);
61        }
62      });
63    }
64  }
```

combo box model

combo box

list cell renderer

image viewer

add elements

set renderer

combo box listener

main method omitted

Review

The images are created using the static createImage method in ImageViewer (Lines 7–24). A default combo box model is created (Line 27) and is used for the combo box (Line 30). Items are added to the combo box model (Lines 40–48). Each item is an array of two elements (image and string).

EXAMPLE 24.6 (CONTINUED)

`MyListCellRenderer`, defined in the preceding example, is used to create a cell renderer in Line 33. The cell renderer is plugged into the combo box in Line 51.

When you choose a country from the combo box, the action event handler is invoked (Lines 57–62). This handler obtains the selected value (Line 59), retrieves the country's flag image (Line 60), and displays the image in the image viewer.

24.6 JTable

`JTable` is a Swing component that displays data in rows and columns in a two-dimensional grid, as shown in Figure 24.22.

Country	Capital	Population in Millions	Democracy
USA	Washington DC	280	true
Canada	Ottawa	32	true
United Kingdom	London	60	true
Germany	Berlin	83	true
France	Paris	60	true
Norway	Oslo	4.5	true

FIGURE 24.22 *JTable displays data in a table.*

`JTable` doesn't directly support scrolling. To create a scrollable table, you need to create a `JScrollPane` and add an instance of `JTable` to the scroll pane. If a table is not placed in a scroll pane, its column header will not be visible, because the column header is placed in the header of the view port of a scroll pane.

`JTable` has three supporting models: a table model, a column model, and a list-selection model. The *table model* is for storing and processing data. The *column model* represents all the columns in the table. The *list-selection model* is the same as the one used by `JList` for selecting rows, columns, and cells in a table. `JTable` also has two useful supporting classes, `TableColumn` and `JTableHeader`. `TableColumn` contains the information on a particular column. `JTableHeader` contains the information on the header of a `JTable`. Each column has a default editor and renderer. You can also create a custom editor by implementing the `TableCellEditor` interface, and create a custom renderer by implementing the `TableCellRenderer` interface. The relationship of these interfaces and classes is shown in Figure 24.23.

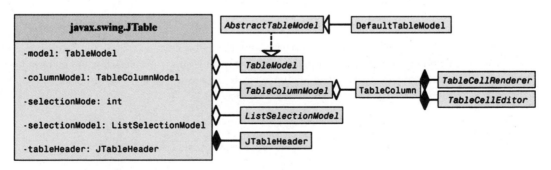

FIGURE 24.23 *JTable contains many supporting interfaces and classes.*

NOTE

All the supporting interfaces and classes for `JTable` are grouped in the `javax.swing.table` package.

24.6.1   JTable Constructors, Properties, and Methods

Figure 24.24 shows the constructors, properties, and methods of JTable.

javax.swing.JTable	
-autoCreateColumnsFromModel: boolean	Indicates whether the columns are created in the table (default: true).
-autoResizeMode: int	Specifies how columns are resized (default: SUBSEQUENT_COLUMNS).
-cellEditor: TableCellEditor	Specifies a cell editor.
-columnModel: TableColumnModel	Maintains the table column data.
-columnSelectionAllowed: boolean	Specifies whether the rows can be selected (default: false).
-editingColumn: int	Specifies the column of the cell that is currently being edited.
-editingRow: int	Specifies the row of the cell that is currently being edited.
-gridColor: java.awt.Color	The color used to draw grid lines (default: GRAY).
-intercellSpacing: Dimension	Specifies the horizontal and vertical margins between cells (default: 1, 1).
-model: TableModel	Maintains the table model.
-rowCount: int	Read-only property that counts the number of rows in the table.
-rowHeight: int	Specifies the row height of the table (default: 16 pixels).
-rowMargin: int	Specifies the vertical margin between rows (default: 1 pixel).
-rowSelectionAllowed: boolean	Specifies whether the rows can be selected (default: true).
-selectionBackground: java.awt.Color	The background color of selected cells.
-selectionForeground: java.awt.Color	The foreground color of selected cells.
-showGrid: boolean	Specify whether the grid lines are displayed (write-only, default: true).
-selectionMode: int	Specifies a selection mode (write-only).
-selectionModel: ListSelectionModel	Specifies a selection model.
-showHorizontalLines: boolean	Specifies whether the horizontal grid lines are displayed (default: true).
-showVerticalLines: boolean	Specifies whether the vertical grid lines are displayed (default: true).
-tableHeader: JTableHeader	Specifies a table header.
+JTable()	Creates a default JTable with all the default models.
+JTable(numRows: int, numColumns: int)	Creates a JTable with the specified number of empty rows and columns.
+JTable(rowData: Object[][], columnData: Object[])	Creates a JTable with the specified row data and column header names.
+JTable(dm: TableModel)	Creates a JTable with the specified table model.
+JTable(dm: TableModel, cm: TableColumnModel)	Creates a JTable with the specified table model and table column model.
+JTable(dm: TableModel, cm: TableColumnModel, sm: ListSelectionModel)	Creates a JTable with the specified table model, table column model, and selection model.
+JTable(rowData: Vector, columnNames: Vector)	Creates a JTable with the specified row data and column data in vectors.
+addColumn(aColumn: TableColumn): void	Adds a new column to the table.
+clearSelection(): void	Deselects all selected columns and rows.
+editCellAt(row: int, column: int): void	Edits the cell if it is editable.
+getDefaultEditor(column: Class): TableCellEditor	Returns the default editor for the column.
+getDefaultRenderer(col: Class): TableCellRenderer	Returns the default renderer for the column.
+setDefaultEditor(column: Class, editor: TableCellEditor): void	Sets the default editor for the column.
+setDefaultRenderer(column: Class, editor:	Sets the default renderer for the column.

FIGURE 24.24   *The* JTable *class is for creating, customizing, and manipulating tables.*

The JTable class contains seven constructors for creating tables. You can create a table using its no-arg constructor, its models, row data in a two-dimensional array, and column header names in an array, or row data and column header names in vectors. For instance, the following statements construct a table, as shown in Figure 24.22:

```
// Create table column names
String[] columnNames =
  {"Country", "Capital", "Population in Millions", "Democracy"};

// Create table data
Object[][] data = {
  {"USA", "Washington DC", new Integer(280), new Boolean(true)},
  {"Canada", "Ottawa", new Integer(32), new Boolean(true)},
  {"United Kingdom", "London", new Integer(60), new Boolean(true)},
  {"Germany", "Berlin", new Integer(83), new Boolean(true)},
  {"France", "Paris", new Integer(60), new Boolean(true)},
```

```
    {"Norway", "Oslo", new Double(4.5), new Boolean(true)},
    {"India", "New Deli", new Integer(1046), new Boolean(true)}
};

// Create a table
JTable jTable1 = new JTable(data, columnNames);
```

JTable is a powerful control with a variety of properties that provide many ways to customize tables. All the frequently used properties are documented in Figure 24.23. The autoResizeMode property specifies how columns are resized (you can resize table columns but not rows). Possible values are:

```
JTable.AUTO_RESIZE_OFF
JTable.AUTO_RESIZE_LAST_COLUMN
JTable.AUTO_RESIZE_SUBSEQUENT_COLUMNS
JTable.AUTO_RESIZE_NEXT_COLUMN
JTable.AUTO_RESIZE_ALL_COLUMNS
```

The default mode is JTable.AUTO_RESIZE_SUBSEQUENT_COLUMNS. Initially, each column in the table occupies the same width (75 pixels). With AUTO_RESIZE_OFF, resizing a column does not affect the widths of the other columns. With AUTO_RESIZE_LAST_COLUMN, resizing a column affects the width of the last column. With AUTO_RESIZE_SUBSEQUENT_COLUMNS, resizing a column affects the widths of all the subsequent columns. With AUTO_RESIZE_NEXT_COLUMN, resizing a column affects the widths of the next columns. With AUTO_RESIZE_ALL_COLUMNS, resizing a column affects the widths of all the columns.

EXAMPLE 24.7 TABLE PROPERTIES DEMO

Problem

This example demonstrates the use of several JTable properties. The example creates a table and allows the user to choose an Auto Resize Mode, specify the row height and margin, and indicate whether the grid is shown. A sample run of the program is shown in Figure 24.25.

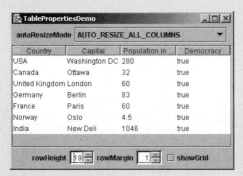

FIGURE 24.25   *You can specify an auto-resizing mode, the table's row height and row margin, and whether to show the grid in the table.*

Solution

Listing 24.8 gives the program.

EXAMPLE 24.7 (CONTINUED)

LISTING 24.8   TablePropertiesDemo.java

```
1 import java.awt.*;
2 import java.awt.event.*;
3 import java.applet.*;
4 import javax.swing.*;
5 import javax.swing.event.*;
6
7 public class TablePropertiesDemo extends JApplet {
8   // Create table column names
9   String[] columnNames =
10    {"Country", "Capital", "Population in Millions", "Democracy"};
11
12   // Create table data
13   Object[][] rowData = {
14     {"USA", "Washington DC", new Integer(280), new Boolean(true)},
15     {"Canada", "Ottawa", new Integer(32), new Boolean(true)},
16     {"United Kingdom", "London", new Integer(60), new Boolean(true)},
17     {"Germany", "Berlin", new Integer(83), new Boolean(true)},
18     {"France", "Paris", new Integer(60), new Boolean(true)},
19     {"Norway", "Oslo", new Double(4.5), new Boolean(true)},
20     {"India", "New Deli", new Integer(1046), new Boolean(true)}
21   };
22
23   // Create a table
24   JTable jTable1 = new JTable(rowData, columnNames);
25
26   // Create two spinners
27   JSpinner jspiRowHeight =
28     new JSpinner(new SpinnerNumberModel(16, 1, 50, 1));
29   JSpinner jspiRowMargin =
30     new JSpinner(new SpinnerNumberModel(1, 1, 50, 1));
31
32   // Create a checkbox
33   JCheckBox jchkShowGrid = new JCheckBox("showGrid", true);
34
35   // Create a combo box
36   JComboBox jcboAutoResizeMode = new JComboBox(new String[]{
37     "AUTO_RESIZE_OFF", "AUTO_RESIZE_LAST_COLUMN",
38     "AUTO_RESIZE_SUBSEQUENT_COLUMNS", "AUTO_RESIZE_NEXT_COLUMN",
39     "AUTO_RESIZE_ALL_COLUMNS"});
40
41   public TablePropertiesDemo() {
42     JPanel panel1 = new JPanel();
43     panel1.add(new JLabel("rowHeight"));
44     panel1.add(jspiRowHeight);
45     panel1.add(new JLabel("rowMargin"));
46     panel1.add(jspiRowMargin);
47     panel1.add(jchkShowGrid);
48
49     JPanel panel2 = new JPanel();
50     panel2.add(new JLabel("autoResizeMode"));
51     panel2.add(jcboAutoResizeMode);
52
53     getContentPane().add(panel1, BorderLayout.SOUTH);
54     getContentPane().add(panel2, BorderLayout.NORTH);
55     getContentPane().add(new JScrollPane(jTable1));
56
57     // Initialize jTable1
58     jTable1.setAutoResizeMode(JTable.AUTO_RESIZE_OFF);
59     jTable1.setGridColor(Color.BLUE);
60     jTable1.setSelectionMode(ListSelectionModel.SINGLE_SELECTION);
61     jTable1.setSelectionBackground(Color.RED);
62     jTable1.setSelectionForeground(Color.WHITE);
63
```

column names

table data

table

spinners

combo box

create UI

table properties

EXAMPLE 24.7 (CONTINUED)

```
64       // Register and create a listener for jspiRowHeight
65       jspiRowHeight.addChangeListener(new ChangeListener() {
66         public void stateChanged(ChangeEvent e) {
67           jTable1.setRowHeight(
68             ((Integer)(jspiRowHeight.getValue())).intValue());
69         }
70       });
71
72       // Register and create a listener for jspiRowMargin
73       jspiRowMargin.addChangeListener(new ChangeListener() {
74         public void stateChanged(ChangeEvent e) {
75           jTable1.setRowMargin(
76             ((Integer)(jspiRowMargin.getValue())).intValue());
77         }
78       });
79
80       // Register and create a listener for jchkShowGrid
81       jchkShowGrid.addActionListener(new ActionListener() {
82         public void actionPerformed(ActionEvent e) {
83           jTable1.setShowGrid(jchkShowGrid.isSelected());
84         }
85       });
86
87       // Register and create a listener for jcboAutoResizeMode
88       jcboAutoResizeMode.addActionListener(new ActionListener() {
89         public void actionPerformed(ActionEvent e) {
90           String selectedItem =
91             (String)jcboAutoResizeMode.getSelectedItem();
92
93           if (selectedItem.equals("AUTO_RESIZE_OFF"))
94             jTable1.setAutoResizeMode(JTable.AUTO_RESIZE_OFF);
95           else if (selectedItem.equals("AUTO_RESIZE_LAST_COLUMN"))
96             jTable1.setAutoResizeMode(JTable.AUTO_RESIZE_LAST_COLUMN);
97           else if (selectedItem.equals
98                  ("AUTO_RESIZE_SUBSEQUENT_COLUMNS"))
99             jTable1.setAutoResizeMode(
100              JTable.AUTO_RESIZE_SUBSEQUENT_COLUMNS);
101          else if (selectedItem.equals("AUTO_RESIZE_NEXT_COLUMN"))
102            jTable1.setAutoResizeMode(JTable.AUTO_RESIZE_NEXT_COLUMN);
103          else if (selectedItem.equals("AUTO_RESIZE_ALL_COLUMNS"))
104            jTable1.setAutoResizeMode(JTable.AUTO_RESIZE_ALL_COLUMNS);
105        }
106      });
107    }
108 }
```

spinner listener

spinner listener

check box listener

combo box listener

main method omitted

Review

If you know the row data in advance, creating a table using the constructor `JTable(Object[][] rowData, Object[] columnNames)` is convenient. As shown in Line 24, a `JTable` is created using this constructor.

Two `JSpinner` objects (`jspiRowHeight`, `jspiRowMargin`) for selecting row height and row margin are created in Lines 27–30. The initial value for `jspiRowHeight` is set to 16, which is the default property value for `rowHeight`. The initial value for `jspiRowMargin` is set to 1, which is the default property value for `rowMargin`. A check box (`jchkShowGrid`) is created with label showGrid and initially selected in Line 33. A combo box for selecting `autoResizeMode` is created in Lines 36–39.

The values of the `JTable` properties (`autoResizeMode`, `gridColor`, `selectionMode`, `selectionBackground`, and `selectionForeground`) are set in Lines 58–62.

The code for processing spinners, check box, and combo box are given in Lines 65–106.

24.6.2 Table Models

JTable delegates data storing and processing to its table data model. A table data model must implement the TableModel interface, which defines the methods for registering table model listeners, manipulating cells, and obtaining row count, column count, column class, and column name.

The AbstractTableModel class provides partial implementations for most of the methods in TableModel. It takes care of the management of listeners and provides some conveniences for generating TableModelEvents and dispatching them to the listeners. To create a concrete TableModel, you simply extend AbstractTableModel and implement at least the following three methods:

♦ public int getRowCount()

♦ public int getColumnCount()

♦ public Object getValueAt(int row, int column)

The DefaultTableModel class extends AbstractTableModel and implements these three methods. Additionally, DefaultTableModel provides concrete storage for data. The data are stored in a vector. The elements in the vector are arrays of objects, each of which represents an individual cell value. The methods in DefaultTableModel for accessing and modifying data are shown in Figure 24.26.

javax.swing.table.TableModel

+getColumnClass(columnIndex: int): Class
+getColumnName(columnIndex: int): String
+getColumnCount(): int
+getRowCount(): int
+getValueAt(rowIndex: int, columnIndex: int):
  Object
+setValueAt(aValue: Object, rowIndex:
  int, columnIndex: int): void
+isCellEditable(rowIndex: int, columnIndex:
  int): boolean
+addTableModelListener(l:
  TableModelListener): void
+removeTableModelListener(l:
  TableModelListener): void

javax.swing.table.AbstractTableModel

javax.swing.table.DefaultTableModel

+DefaultTableModel()
+DefaultTableModel(rowCount: int, columnCount: int)
+DefaultTableModel(columnNames: Object[], rowCount: int)
+DefaultTableModel(data: Object[][], columnNames: Object[])
+DefaultTableModel(columnNames: Vector, rowCount: int)
+DefaultTableModel(data: Vector, columnNames: Vector)
+DefaultTableModel(rowData: Vector, columnNames: Vector)
+addColumn(columnName: Object): void
+addColumn(columnName: Object, columnData: Vector)
+addRow(rowData: Object[]): void
+addRow(rowData: Vector): void
+getColumnCount(): int
+getDataVector(): Vector
+getRowCount(): int
+insertRow(row: int, rowData: Object[]): void
+insertRow(row: int, rowData: Vector): void
+setColumnCount(columnCount: int): void
+setColumnIdentifiers(newIdentifiers: Object[]): void
+setColumnIdentifiers(columnIdentifiers: Vector): void
+setDataVector(dataVector: Object[][], columnIdentifiers:
  Object[]): void
+setDataVector(dataVector: Vector, columnIdentifiers: Vector):
  void
+setRowCount(rowCount: int): void

FIGURE 24.26 *TableModel stores and manages data in a table.*

24.6.3   Table Column Models

TableModel manages table data. You can add and remove rows through a TableModel. You can also add a column through a TableModel. However, you cannot remove a column through a TableModel. To remove a column from a JTable, you have to use a table column model.

Table column models manage columns in a table. They can be used to select, add, move, and remove table columns. A table column model must implement the TableColumnModel interface, which defines the methods for registering table column model listeners, and for accessing and manipulating columns, as shown in Figure 24.27.

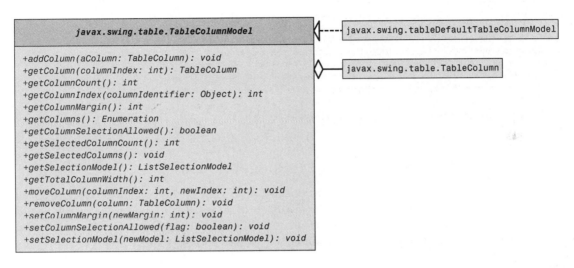

FIGURE 24.27   *TableColumnModel manages columns in a table.*

DefaultTableColumnModel is a concrete class that implements TableColumnModel and PropertyChangeListener. The DefaultTableColumnModel class stores its columns in a vector and contains an instance of ListSelectionModel for selecting columns.

24.6.4   The TableColumn Class

The column model deals with all the columns in a table. The TableColumn class is used to model an individual column in the table. An instance of TableColumn for a specified column can be obtained using the getColumn(index) method in TableColumnModel or the getColumn(columnIdentifier) method in JTable.

Figure 24.28 shows the properties, constructors, and methods in TableColumn for manipulating column width and specifying cell renderer, cell editor, and header renderer.

🌸 **NOTE**

Some of the methods defined in the table model and the table column model are also defined in the JTable class for convenience. For instance, the getColumnCount() method is defined in JTable, TableModel, and TableColumnModel, the addColumn method defined in the column model is also defined in the table model, and the getColumn() method defined in the column model is also defined in the JTable class.

```
┌─────────────────────────────────────────┐
│      javax.swing.table.TableColumn        │
├─────────────────────────────────────────┤
│ #cellEditor: TableCellEditor              │
│ #cellRenderer: TableCellRenderer          │
│ #headerRenderer: TableCellRenderer        │
│ #headerValue: Object                      │
│ #identifier: Object                       │
│ #maxWidth: int                            │
│ #minWidth: int                            │
│ #modelIndex: int                          │
│ #preferredWidth: int                      │
│ #resizable: boolean                       │
│ #width: int                               │
├─────────────────────────────────────────┤
│ +TableColumn()                            │
│ +TableColumn(modelIndex: int)             │
│ +TableColumn(modelIndex: int, width: int) │
│ +TableColumn(modelIndex: int, width: int, │
│   cellRenderer: TableCellRenderer)        │
│ +sizeWidthToFit(): void                   │
└─────────────────────────────────────────┘
```

The editor for editing a cell in this column.
The renderer for displaying a cell in this column.
The renderer for displaying the header of this column.
The header value of this column.
The identifier for this column.
The maximum width of this column.
The minimum width of this column (default: 15 pixels).
The index of the column in the table model (default: 0).
The preferred width of this column (default: 75 pixels).
Indicates whether this column can be resized (default: true).
Specifies the width of this column (default: 75 pixels).

Constructs a default table column.
Constructs a table column for the specified column.
Constructs a table column with the specified column and width.
Constructs a table column with the specified column, width, and
   cell renderer.
Resizes the column to fit the width of its header cell.

FIGURE 24.28   *The* TableColumn *class models a single column.*

24.6.5   The JTableHeader Class

JTableHeader is a GUI component that manages the header of the JTable (see Figure 24.29). When you create a JTable, an instance of JTableHeader is automatically created and stored in the tableHeader property. By default, you can reorder the columns by dragging the header of the column. To disable it, set the reorderingAllowed property to false.

```
┌─────────────────────────────────────────┐
│      javax.swing.table.JTableHeader       │
├─────────────────────────────────────────┤
│ #columnModel: TableColumnModel            │
│ #draggedColumn: TableColumn               │
│ #draggedDistance: TableCellRenderer       │
│ #reorderingAllowed: boolean               │
│ #resizingAllowed: boolean                 │
│ #resizingColumn: TableColumn              │
│ #table: JTable                            │
├─────────────────────────────────────────┤
│ +JTableHeader()                           │
│ +JTableHeader(cmTableColumnModel)         │
└─────────────────────────────────────────┘
```

The Table ColumnModel of the table header.
The column being dragged.
The distance from its original position to the dragged position.
Whether reordering of columns is allowed (default: true).
Whether resizing of columns is allowed (default: true).
The column being resized.
The table for which this object is the header.

Constructs a JTableHeader with a default TableColumnModel.
Constructs a JTableHeader with a TableColumnModel.

FIGURE 24.29   *The* JTableHeader *class manages the header of the* JTable.

EXAMPLE 24.8 MODIFYING ROWS AND COLUMNS

Problem

This example demonstrates the use of table models, table column models, list-selection models, and the TableColumn class. The program allows the user to choose selection mode and selection type, to add or remove rows and columns, and to save, clear, and restore the table, as shown in Figure 24.30.

EXAMPLE 24.8 (CONTINUED)

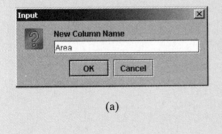

FIGURE 24.30   *You can add or remove rows and columns in a table.*

The *Add New Row* button adds a new empty row before the currently selected row, as shown in Figure 24.30(b). If no row is currently selected, a new empty row is appended to the end of the table.

When you click the *Add New Column* button, an input dialog box is displayed to receive the title of the column, as shown in Figure 24.31(a). The new column is appended in the table, as shown in Figure 24.31(b).

FIGURE 24.31   *You can add a new column in a table.*

The *Delete Selected Row* button deletes the first selected row. The *Delete Selected Column* button deletes the first selected column.

The *Save* button saves the current table data and column names. The *Clear* button clears the row data in the table. The *Restore* button restores the save table.

Solution

Listing 24.9 gives the program.

EXAMPLE 24.8 (CONTINUED)

LISTING 24.9 TableModelDemo.java

```
 1  import java.awt.*;
 2  import java.awt.event.*;
 3  import java.applet.*;
 4  import javax.swing.*;
 5  import javax.swing.table.*;
 6  import java.io.*;
 7  import java.util.Vector;
 8
 9  public class TableModelDemo extends JApplet {
10    // Create table column names
11    private String[] columnNames =
12      {"Country", "Capital", "Population in Millions", "Democracy"};
13
14    // Create table data
15    private Object[][] rowData = {
16      {"USA", "Washington DC", new Integer(280), new Boolean(true)},
17      {"Canada", "Ottawa", new Integer(32), new Boolean(true)},
18      {"United Kingdom", "London", new Integer(60), new Boolean(true)},
19      {"Germany", "Berlin", new Integer(83), new Boolean(true)},
20      {"France", "Paris", new Integer(60), new Boolean(true)},
21      {"Norway", "Oslo", new Double(4.5), new Boolean(true)},
22      {"India", "New Deli", new Integer(1046), new Boolean(true)}
23    };
24
25    // Create a table model
26    private DefaultTableModel tableModel = new DefaultTableModel(
27      rowData, columnNames);
28
29    // Create a table
30    private JTable jTable1 = new JTable(tableModel);
31
32    // Create buttons
33    private JButton jbtAddRow = new JButton("Add New Row");
34    private JButton jbtAddColumn = new JButton("Add New Column");
35    private JButton jbtDeleteRow = new JButton("Delete Selected Row");
36    private JButton jbtDeleteColumn = new JButton(
37      "Delete Selected Column");
38    private JButton jbtSave = new JButton("Save");
39    private JButton jbtClear = new JButton("Clear");
40    private JButton jbtRestore = new JButton("Restore");
41
42    // Create a combo box for selection modes
43    private JComboBox jcboSelectionMode =
44      new JComboBox(new String[] {"SINGLE_SELECTION",
45        "SINGLE_INTERVAL_SELECTION", "MULTIPLE_INTERVAL_SELECTION"});
46
47    // Create check boxes
48    private JCheckBox jchkRowSelectionAllowed =
49      new JCheckBox("RowSelectionAllowed", true);
50    private JCheckBox jchkColumnSelectionAllowed =
51      new JCheckBox("ColumnSelectionAllowed", false);
52
53    public TableModelDemo() {
54      JPanel panel1 = new JPanel();
55      panel1.setLayout(new GridLayout(2, 2));
56      panel1.add(jbtAddRow);
57      panel1.add(jbtAddColumn);
58      panel1.add(jbtDeleteRow);
59      panel1.add(jbtDeleteColumn);
60
61      JPanel panel2 = new JPanel();
62      panel2.add(jbtSave);
63      panel2.add(jbtClear);
64      panel2.add(jbtRestore);
65
```

Margin annotations:
- column names (line 11)
- table data (line 15)
- table model (line 26)
- table (line 30)
- buttons (line 33)
- combo box (line 43)
- check boxes (line 48)
- create UI (line 53)

EXAMPLE 24.8 (CONTINUED)

```
66    JPanel panel3 = new JPanel();
67    panel3.setLayout(new BorderLayout(5, 0));
68    panel3.add(new JLabel("Selection Mode"), BorderLayout.WEST);
69    panel3.add(jcboSelectionMode, BorderLayout.CENTER);
70
71    JPanel panel4 = new JPanel();
72    panel4.setLayout(new FlowLayout(FlowLayout.LEFT));
73    panel4.add(jchkRowSelectionAllowed);
74    panel4.add(jchkColumnSelectionAllowed);
75
76    JPanel panel5 = new JPanel();
77    panel5.setLayout(new GridLayout(2, 1));
78    panel5.add(panel3);
79    panel5.add(panel4);
80
81    JPanel panel6 = new JPanel();
82    panel6.setLayout(new BorderLayout());
83    panel6.add(panel1, BorderLayout.SOUTH);
84    panel6.add(panel2, BorderLayout.CENTER);
85
86    getContentPane().add(panel5, BorderLayout.NORTH);
87    getContentPane().add(new JScrollPane(jTable1),
88      BorderLayout.CENTER);
89    getContentPane().add(panel6, BorderLayout.SOUTH);
90
91    jTable1.setSelectionMode(ListSelectionModel.SINGLE_SELECTION);
92
93    jbtAddRow.addActionListener(new ActionListener() {        button listener
94      public void actionPerformed(ActionEvent e) {
95        if (jTable1.getSelectedRow() >= 0)
96          tableModel.insertRow(jTable1.getSelectedRow(),
97            new java.util.Vector());
98        else
99          tableModel.addRow(new java.util.Vector());
100      }
101    });
102
103    jbtAddColumn.addActionListener(new ActionListener() {
104      public void actionPerformed(ActionEvent e) {
105        String name = JOptionPane.showInputDialog("New Column Name");
106        tableModel.addColumn(name, new java.util.Vector());
107      }
108    });
109
110    jbtDeleteRow.addActionListener(new ActionListener() {
111      public void actionPerformed(ActionEvent e) {
112        if (jTable1.getSelectedRow() >= 0)
113          tableModel.removeRow(jTable1.getSelectedRow());
114      }
115    });
116
117    jbtDeleteColumn.addActionListener(new ActionListener() {
118      public void actionPerformed(ActionEvent e) {
119        if (jTable1.getSelectedColumn() >= 0) {
120        TableColumnModel columnModel = jTable1.getColumnModel();
121        TableColumn tableColumn =
122            columnModel.getColumn(jTable1.getSelectedColumn());
123        columnModel.removeColumn(tableColumn);
124      }
125    }
126    });
127
128    jbtSave.addActionListener(new ActionListener() {
129      public void actionPerformed(ActionEvent e) {
130        try {
131          ObjectOutputStream out = new ObjectOutputStream(
132            new FileOutputStream("tablemodel.dat"));
133          out.writeObject(tableModel.getDataVector());
```

EXAMPLE 24.8 (CONTINUED)

```
134              out.writeObject(getColumnNames());
135              out.close();
136            }
137          catch (Exception ex) {
138            ex.printStackTrace();
139          }
140        }
141      });
142
143      jbtClear.addActionListener(new ActionListener() {
144        public void actionPerformed(ActionEvent e) {
145         tableModel.setRowCount(0);
146        }
147      });
148
149      jbtRestore.addActionListener(new ActionListener() {
150        public void actionPerformed(ActionEvent e) {
151          try {
152            ObjectInputStream in = new ObjectInputStream(
153              new FileInputStream("tablemodel.dat"));
154            Vector rowData = (Vector)in.readObject();
155            Vector columnNames = (Vector)in.readObject();
156            tableModel.setDataVector(rowData, columnNames);
157            in.close();
158          }
159          catch (Exception ex) {
160            ex.printStackTrace();
161          }
162        }
163      });
164
165      jchkRowSelectionAllowed.addActionListener(new ActionListener() {
166        public void actionPerformed(ActionEvent e) {
167          jTable1.setRowSelectionAllowed(
168            jchkRowSelectionAllowed.isSelected());
169        }
170      });
171
172      jchkColumnSelectionAllowed.addActionListener(
173        new ActionListener() {
174        public void actionPerformed(ActionEvent e) {
175          jTable1.setColumnSelectionAllowed(
176            jchkColumnSelectionAllowed.isSelected());
177        }
178      });
179
180      jcboSelectionMode.addActionListener(new ActionListener() {
181        public void actionPerformed(ActionEvent e) {
182          String selectedItem =
183            (String) jcboSelectionMode.getSelectedItem();
184
185          if (selectedItem.equals("SINGLE_SELECTION"))
186            jTable1.setSelectionMode(
187              ListSelectionModel.SINGLE_SELECTION);
188          else if (selectedItem.equals("SINGLE_INTERVAL_SELECTION"))
189            jTable1.setSelectionMode(
190              ListSelectionModel.SINGLE_INTERVAL_SELECTION);
191          else if (selectedItem.equals("MULTIPLE_INTERVAL_SELECTION"))
192            jTable1.setSelectionMode(
193              ListSelectionModel.MULTIPLE_INTERVAL_SELECTION);
194        }
195      });
196  }
197
198  private Vector getColumnNames() {
199    Vector columnNames = new Vector();
200
```

check box listener

combo box listener

EXAMPLE 24.8 (CONTINUED)

```
201      for (int i = 0; i < jTable1.getColumnCount(); i++)
202        columnNames.add(jTable1.getColumnName(i));
203
204      return columnNames;
205    }
206  }
```

main method omitted

Review

A table model is created using `DefaultTableModel` with row data and column names (Lines 26–27). This model is used to create a `JTable` (Line 30).

The GUI objects (buttons, combo box, check boxes) are created in Lines 33–51 and are placed in the UI in Lines 54–89.

The table-selection mode is the same as the list-selection mode. By default, the selection mode is `MULTIPLE_INTERVAL_SELECTION`. To match the initial value in the selection combo box (`jcboSelectionMode`), the table's selection mode is set to `SINGLE_SELECTION`.

The *Add New Row* button action is processed in Lines 93–101. The `insertRow` method inserts a new row before the selected row (Lines 96–97). If no row is currently selected, the `addRow` method appends a new row into the table model (Line 99).

The *Add New Column* button action is processed in Lines 103–108. The `addColumn` method appends a new column into the table model (Line 106).

The *Delete Selected Row* button action is processed in Lines 110–115. The `removeRow` `(rowIndex)` method removes the selected row from the table model (Line 113).

The *Delete Selected Column* button action is processed in Lines 117–126. To remove a column, you have to use the `removeColumn` method in `TableColumnModel` (Line 123).

The *Save* button action is processed in Lines 128–141. It writes row data and column names to an output file using object stream (Lines 133–134). The column names are obtained using the `getColumnNames()` method (Lines 198–205). You may attempt to save `tableModel`, because `tableModel` is an instance of `DefaultTableModel` (Lines 26–27) and `DefaultTableModel` is serializable. However, `tableModel` may contain non-serializable listeners for the `TableModel` event.

The *Clear* button action is processed in Lines 143–147. It clears the table by setting the row count to 0 (Line 145).

The *Restore* button action is processed in Lines 149–163. It reads row data and column names from the file using object stream (Lines 154–155), and sets the new data and column names to the table model (Line 156).

24.6 .6 Table Renderers and Editors

Table cells are painted by cell renderers. By default, a cell object's string representation (`toString()`) is displayed and the string can be edited as it was in a text field. `JTable` maintains a set of predefined renderers and editors, listed in Table 24.1, which can be specified to replace default string renderers and editors.

The predefined renderers and editors are automatically located and loaded to match the class returned from the `getColumnClass()` method in the table model. To use a predefined renderer or editor for a class other than `String`, you need to create your own table model by extending a subclass of `TableModel`. In your table model class, you need to override the `getColumnClass()` method to return the class of the column, as follows:

```
public Class getColumnClass(int column) {
  return getValueAt(0, column).getClass();
}
```

TABLE 24.1 Predefined Renderers and Editors for Tables

Class	Renderer	Editor
Object	JLabel (left aligned)	JTextField
Date	JLabel (right aligned)	JTextField
Number	JLabel (right aligned)	JTextField
ImageIcon	JLabel (center aligned)	
Boolean	JCheckBox (center aligned)	JCheckBox (center aligned)

By default, all cells are editable. To prohibit a cell from being edited, override the isCellEditable(int rowIndex, int columnIndx) method in TableModel to return false. By default, this method returns true in AbstractTableModel.

EXAMPLE 24.9 USING PREDEFINED TABLE RENDERERS AND EDITORS

Problem

Write a program that displays a table for books. The table consists of three rows with the column names Title, Copies Needed, Publisher, Date Published, In-Stock, and Book Photo, as shown in Figure 24.32. Display all the columns using the predefined renderers and editors. Assume that dates and icons are not editable, and prohibit users from editing these two columns.

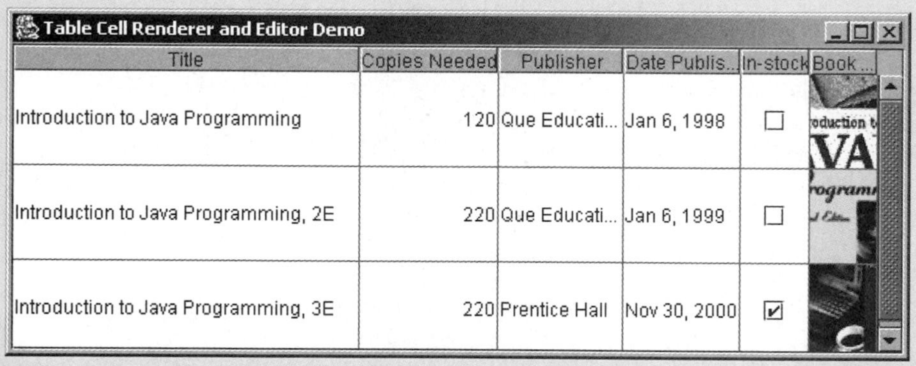

FIGURE 24.32 JTable uses predefined renderers and editors for numbers, boolean values, dates, and image icons.

Solution

To use the predefined renderers and editors to render and edit numbers, date, Boolean values, and icons, create a new data model named MyTableModel that extends DefaultTableModel and overrides the getColumnClass(int columnIndex) method. Since dates and icons are not editable, override the isCellEditable(int rowIndex, int columnIndex) method to return false on the Date Published and Book Photo columns. The MyTableModel class is given in Listing 24.10.

EXAMPLE 24.9 (CONTINUED)

LISTING 24.10   MyTableModel.java

```
1 import javax.swing.*;
2 import javax.swing.table.*;
3 import java.util.*;
4
5 public class MyTableModel extends DefaultTableModel {
6   public MyTableModel() {
7   }
8
9   /** Construct a table model with specified data and columnNames */
10  public MyTableModel(Object[][] data, Object[] columnNames) {
11    super(data, columnNames);
12  }
13
14  /** Override this method to return a class for the column */
15  public Class getColumnClass(int column) {
16    return getValueAt(0, column).getClass();
17  }
18
19  /** Override this method to return true if cell is editable */
20  public boolean isCellEditable(int row, int column) {
21    Class columnClass = getColumnClass(column);
22    return columnClass != ImageIcon.class &&
23      columnClass != Date.class;
24  }
25 }
```

column class

cell editable?

If you create a JTable using a table model created from MyTableModel, the default renderers and editors for numbers, Boolean values, dates, and icons are used to display and edit these columns. Listing 24.11 gives a test program.

LISTING 24.11   TableCellRendererEditorDemo.java

```
1 import java.awt.*;
2 import javax.swing.*;
3 import java.util.*;
4
5 public class TableCellRendererEditorDemo extends JApplet {
6   // Create table column names
7   private String[] columnNames =
8     {"Title", "Copies Needed", "Publisher", "Date Published",
9     "In-stock", "Book Photo"};
10
11  // Create image icons
12  private ImageIcon intro1eImageIcon = ImageViewer.createImageIcon(
13    "image/intro1e.gif", this);
14  private ImageIcon intro2eImageIcon = ImageViewer.createImageIcon(
15    "image/intro2e.gif", this);
16  private ImageIcon intro3eImageIcon = ImageViewer.createImageIcon(
17    "image/intro3e.jpg", this);
18
19  // Create table data
20  private Object[][] rowData = {
21    {"Introduction to Java Programming", new Integer(120),
22    "Que Education & Training",
23    new GregorianCalendar(1998, 1-1, 6).getTime(),
24    new Boolean(false), intro1eImageIcon},
25    {"Introduction to Java Programming, 2E", new Integer(220),
26    "Que Education & Training",
27    new GregorianCalendar(1999, 1-1, 6).getTime(),
28    new Boolean(false), intro2eImageIcon},
29    {"Introduction to Java Programming, 3E", new Integer(220),
30    "Prentice Hall",
```

column names

image icons

table data

table model

table

`main` method omitted

EXAMPLE 24.9 (CONTINUED)

```
31        new GregorianCalendar(2000, 12-1, 0).getTime(),
32        new Boolean(true), intro3eImageIcon},
33  };
34
35  // Create a table model
36  private MyTableModel tableModel = new MyTableModel(
37    rowData, columnNames);
38
39  // Create a table
40  private JTable jTable1 = new JTable(tableModel);
41
42  public TableCellRendererEditorDemo() {
43    jTable1.setRowHeight(60);
44    getContentPane().add(new JScrollPane(jTable1),
45      BorderLayout.CENTER);
46  }
47 }
```

Review

The example creates two classes: `MyTableModel` and `TestPredefinedTableRenderer-Editor`. `MyTableModel` is an extension of `DefaultTableModel`. The purpose of `MyTableModel` is to override the default implementation of the `getColumnClass()` method to return the class of the column, so that an appropriate predefined `JTable` can be used for the column. By default, `getColumnClass()` returns `Object.class`.

`MyTableModel` also overrides the `isCellEditable()` method. By default, `isCellEditable()` returns `true`. You can override it to prohibit editing of a cell. This example does not allow the user to edit image icons and dates. For a cell to be editable, both `isCellEditable()` in the table model and `isEditing` in the `JTable` class must be `true`.

The `TableCellRendererEditorDemo` class creates a table model using `MyTableModel`. `JTable` assigns a predefined cell renderer and a predefined editor to the cell, whose class is specified in the `getColumnClass()` method in `MyTableModel`.

24.6.7   Custom Table Renderers and Editors

Predefined renderers and editors are convenient and easy to use, but their functions are limited. The predefined image icon renderer displays the image icon in a label. The image icon cannot be scaled. If you want the whole image to fit in a cell, you need to create a custom renderer.

A custom renderer can be created by extending the `DefaultTableCellRenderer`, which is a default implementation for the `TableCellRenderer` interface. The custom renderer must override the `getTableCellRendererComponent()` to return a component for rendering the table cell. The `getTableCellRendererComponent()` is defined as follows:

```
public Component getTableCellRendererComponent
  (JTable table, Object value, boolean isSelected,
   boolean isFocused, int row, int column)
```

This method signature is very similar to the `getListCellRendererComponent()` method used to create custom list cell renderers.

This method is passed with a `JTable`, the value associated with the cell, information regarding whether the value is selected and the cell has the focus, and the row and column indices of the value. The component returned from the method is painted on the cell in the table. The following class, `MyImageCellRenderer` creates a renderer for displaying image icons in a panel:

```
1 import javax.swing.*;
2 import javax.swing.table.*;
3 import java.awt.*;
```

```
 4
 5 public class MyImageCellRenderer extends DefaultTableCellRenderer {
 6   /** Override this method in DefaultTableCellRenderer */
 7   public Component getTableCellRendererComponent
 8     (JTable table, Object value, boolean isSelected,
 9      boolean isFocused, int row, int column) {
10     Image image = ((ImageIcon)value).getImage();
11     ImageViewer imageViewer = new ImageViewer(image);
12     return imageViewer;
13   }
14 }
```

You can also create a custom editor. JTable provides the DefaultCellEditor class, which can be used to edit a cell in a text field, a check box, or a combo box. To use it, simply create a text field, a check box, or a combo box, and pass it to DefaultCellEditor's constructor to create an editor.

EXAMPLE 24.10 USING CUSTOM TABLE RENDERERS AND EDITORS

Problem

Revise Example 24.9, "Using Predefined Table Renderers and Editors," to display scaled image icons and to use a custom combo editor to edit the cells in the Publisher column, as shown in Figure 24.33.

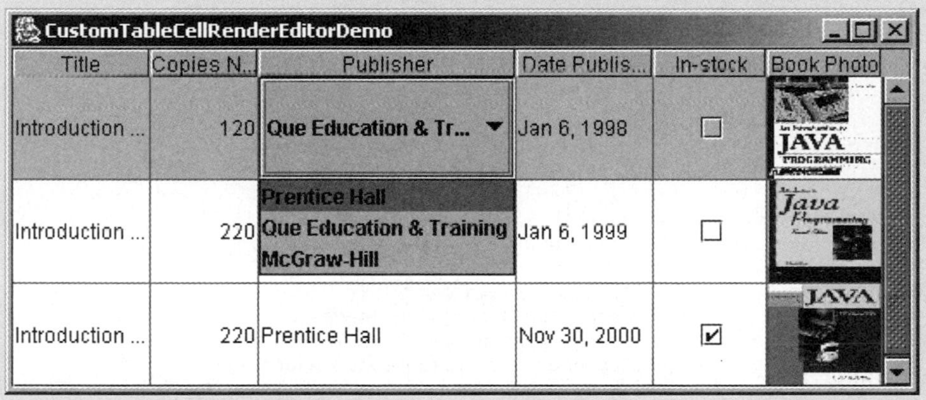

FIGURE **24.33** *A custom renderer displays a scaled image, and a custom editor edits the Publisher column using a combo box.*

Solution

A custom table cell renderer for rendering scaled images has been defined in MyImageCellRenderer. You need to create an instance of this class and set it on the Book Photo column using the setCellRenderer method in the TableColumn class.

To use a combo box to edit the Publisher cells, create a JComboBox with appropriate items and create an instance of DefaultCellEditor with the combo box. Set the instance on the Publisher column using the setCellEditor method in the TableColumn class.

The program is given in Listing 24.12.

LISTING 24.12 CustomTableCellRenderEditorDemo.java

```
1 import java.awt.*;
2 import javax.swing.*;
3 import javax.swing.table.*;
4 import java.util.*;
```

EXAMPLE **24.10** (CONTINUED)

```
5
6 public class CustomTableCellRenderEditorDemo extends JApplet {
7    // Create table column names
8    private String[] columnNames =
9      {"Title", "Copies Needed", "Publisher", "Date Published",
10     "In-stock", "Book Photo"};
11
12   // Create image icons
13   private ImageIcon intro1eImageIcon = ImageViewer.createImageIcon(
14     "image/intro1e.gif", this);
15   private ImageIcon intro2eImageIcon = ImageViewer.createImageIcon(
16     "image/intro2e.gif", this);
17   private ImageIcon intro3eImageIcon = ImageViewer.createImageIcon(
18     "image/intro3e.jpg", this);
19
20   // Create table data
21   private Object[][] rowData = {
22     {"Introduction to Java Programming", new Integer(120),
23      "Que Education & Training",
24      new GregorianCalendar(1998, 1-1, 6).getTime(),
25      new Boolean(false), intro1eImageIcon},
26     {"Introduction to Java Programming, 2E", new Integer(220),
27      "Que Education & Training",
28      new GregorianCalendar(1999, 1-1, 6).getTime(),
29      new Boolean(false), intro2eImageIcon},
30     {"Introduction to Java Programming, 3E", new Integer(220),
31      "Prentice Hall",
32      new GregorianCalendar(2000, 12-1, 0).getTime(),
33      new Boolean(true), intro3eImageIcon},
34   };
35
36   // Create a table model
37   private MyTableModel tableModel = new MyTableModel(
38     rowData, columnNames);
39
40   // Create a table
41   private JTable jTable1 = new JTable(tableModel);
42
43   public CustomTableCellRenderEditorDemo() {
44     // Set custom renderer for displaying images
45     TableColumn bookCover = jTable1.getColumn("Book Photo");
46     bookCover.setCellRenderer(new MyImageCellRenderer());
47
48     // Create a combo box for publishers
49     JComboBox jcboPublishers = new JComboBox();
50     jcboPublishers.addItem("Prentice Hall");
51     jcboPublishers.addItem("Que Education & Training");
52     jcboPublishers.addItem("McGraw-Hill");
53
54     // Set combo box as the editor for the publisher column
55     TableColumn publisherColumn = jTable1.getColumn("Publisher");
56     publisherColumn.setCellEditor(
57       new DefaultCellEditor(jcboPublishers));
58
59     jTable1.setRowHeight(60);
60     getContentPane().add(new JScrollPane(jTable1),
61       BorderLayout.CENTER);
62   }
63 }
```

Labels (left margin): column names (8), image icons (13), table data (21), table model (37), table (41), set renderer (46), combo box (49), set editor (56), main method omitted (63).

Review

This example uses the same table model (MyTableModel) that was created in the preceding example (Lines 37–38). By default, image icons are displayed using the predefined image icon renderer. To use MyImageCellRenderer to display the image, you have to explicitly specify the MyImageCellRenderer renderer for the Book Photo column (Line 46). Likewise,

Chapter 24 Advanced Swing Components 927

EXAMPLE 24.10 (CONTINUED)

you have to explicitly specify the combo box editor for the Publisher column (Lines 56–57); otherwise the default editor would be used.

When you edit a cell in the Publisher column, a combo box of three items is displayed. When you select an item from the box, it is displayed in the cell. You did not write the code for handling selections. The selections are handled by the `DefaultCellEditor` class.

When you resize the Book Photo column, the image is resized to fit into the whole cell. With the predefined image renderer, you can only see part of the image if the cell is smaller than the image.

24.6.8 Table Events

`JTable` does not fire table events. It fires events like `MouseEvent`, `KeyEvent`, and `ComponentEvent` that are inherited from its superclass `JComponent`. Table events are fired by table models, table column models, and table-selection models whenever changes are made to these models. Table models fire `TableModelEvent` when table data are changed. Table column models fire `TableColumnModelEvent` when columns are added, removed, or moved, or when the column selection changes. Table-selection models fire `ListSelectionEvent` when the selection changes.

To listen for these events, a listener must be registered with an appropriate model and implement the correct listener interface. The following example demonstrates how to use these events.

EXAMPLE 24.11 USING TABLE EVENTS

Problem

This example demonstrates handling table events. The program displays messages on a text area when a row or a column is selected, when a cell is edited, or when a column is removed. Figure 24.34 is a sample run of the program.

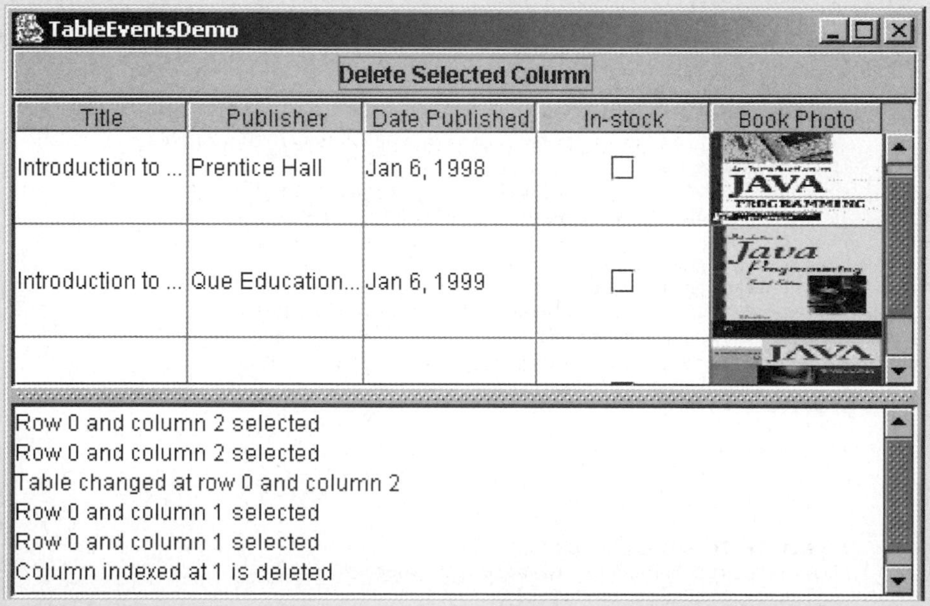

FIGURE 24.34 *Table event handlers display table events on a text area.*

EXAMPLE 24.11 (CONTINUED)

Solution

To respond to the row and column selection events, you need to implement the `valueChanged` method in `ListSelectionListener`. To respond to the cell-editing event, you need to implement the `tableChanged` method in `TableModelListener`. To respond to the column-deletion event, you need to implement the `columnRemoved` method in `TableColumnModelListener`. Let's use the same table from the preceding example, but with a button added for deleting the selected column and a text area for displaying the messages. The program is given in Listing 24.13.

LISTING 24.13   TableEventsDemo.java

```
 1 import java.awt.*;
 2 import java.awt.event.*;
 3 import javax.swing.*;
 4 import javax.swing.event.*;
 5 import javax.swing.table.*;
 6 import java.util.*;
 7
 8 public class TableEventsDemo extends JApplet {
 9   // Create table column names
10   private String[] columnNames =
11     {"Title", "Copies Needed", "Publisher", "Date Published",
12      "In-stock", "Book Photo"};
13
14   // Create image icons
15   private ImageIcon intro1eImageIcon = ImageViewer.createImageIcon(
16     "image/intro1e.gif", this);
17   private ImageIcon intro2eImageIcon = ImageViewer.createImageIcon(
18     "image/intro2e.gif", this);
19   private ImageIcon intro3eImageIcon = ImageViewer.createImageIcon(
20     "image/intro3e.jpg", this);
21
22   // Create table data
23   private Object[][] rowData = {
24     {"Introduction to Java Programming", new Integer(120),
25      "Que Education & Training",
26      new GregorianCalendar(1998, 1-1, 6).getTime(),
27      new Boolean(false), intro1eImageIcon},
28     {"Introduction to Java Programming, 2E", new Integer(220),
29      "Que Education & Training",
30      new GregorianCalendar(1999, 1-1, 6).getTime(),
31      new Boolean(false), intro2eImageIcon},
32     {"Introduction to Java Programming, 3E", new Integer(220),
33      "Prentice Hall",
34      new GregorianCalendar(2000, 12-1, 0).getTime(),
35      new Boolean(true), intro3eImageIcon},
36   };
37
38   // Create a table model
39   private MyTableModel tableModel = new MyTableModel(
40     rowData, columnNames);
41
42   // Create a table
43   private JTable jTable1 = new JTable(tableModel);
44
45   // Get table column model
46   private TableColumnModel tableColumnModel =
47     jTable1.getColumnModel();
48
49   // Get table selection model
50   private ListSelectionModel selectionModel =
51     jTable1.getSelectionModel();
52
```

column names

image icons

table data

table model

table

column model

selection model

EXAMPLE 24.11 (CONTINUED)

```
53   // Create a text area
54   private JTextArea jtaMessage = new JTextArea();
55
56   // Create a button
57   private JButton jbtDeleteColumn =
58     new JButton("Delete Selected Column");
59
60   public TableEventsDemo() {
61     // Set custom renderer for displaying images
62     TableColumn bookCover = jTable1.getColumn("Book Photo");
63     bookCover.setCellRenderer(new MyImageCellRenderer());
64
65     // Create a combo box for publishers
66     JComboBox jcboPublishers = new JComboBox();
67     jcboPublishers.addItem("Prentice Hall");
68     jcboPublishers.addItem("Que Education & Training");
69     jcboPublishers.addItem("McGraw-Hill");
70
71     // Set combo box as the editor for the publisher column
72     TableColumn publisherColumn = jTable1.getColumn("Publisher");
73     publisherColumn.setCellEditor(
74       new DefaultCellEditor(jcboPublishers));
75
76     jTable1.setRowHeight(60);
77     jTable1.setColumnSelectionAllowed(true);
78
79     JSplitPane jSplitPane1 = new JSplitPane(
80       JSplitPane.VERTICAL_SPLIT);
81     jSplitPane1.add(new JScrollPane(jTable1), JSplitPane.LEFT);
82     jSplitPane1.add(new JScrollPane(jtaMessage), JSplitPane.RIGHT);
83     getContentPane().add(jbtDeleteColumn, BorderLayout.NORTH);
84     getContentPane().add(jSplitPane1, BorderLayout.CENTER);
85
86     tableModel.addTableModelListener(new TableModelListener() {    table model listener
87       public void tableChanged(TableModelEvent e) {
88         jtaMessage.append("Table changed at row " +
89           e.getFirstRow() + " and column " + e.getColumn() + "\n");
90       }
91     });
92
93     tableColumnModel.addColumnModelListener(                        column model listener
94       new TableColumnModelListener() {
95       public void columnRemoved(TableColumnModelEvent e) {
96         jtaMessage.append("Column indexed at " + e.getFromIndex() +
97           " is deleted \n");
98       }
99       public void columnAdded(TableColumnModelEvent e) {
100       }
101       public void columnMoved(TableColumnModelEvent e) {
102       }
103       public void columnMarginChanged(ChangeEvent e) {
104       }
105       public void columnSelectionChanged(ListSelectionEvent e) {
106       }
107     });
108
109     jbtDeleteColumn.addActionListener(new ActionListener() {
110       public void actionPerformed(ActionEvent e) {
111         if (jTable1.getSelectedColumn() >= 0) {
112           TableColumnModel columnModel = jTable1.getColumnModel();
113           TableColumn tableColumn =
114               columnModel.getColumn(jTable1.getSelectedColumn());
115           columnModel.removeColumn(tableColumn);
116         }
117       }
118     });
```

EXAMPLE 24.11 (CONTINUED)

selection model listener

```
119
120    selectionModel.addListSelectionListener(
121      new ListSelectionListener() {
122      public void valueChanged(ListSelectionEvent e) {
123        jtaMessage.append("Row " + jTable1.getSelectedRow() +
124          " and column " + jTable1.getSelectedColumn() +
125          " selected\n");
126      }
127    });
128  }
129 }
```

main method omitted

Review

A table model is created using `MyTableModel` (Lines 39–40), which was given in Example 24.9, "Using Predefined Table Renderers and Editors." When a table is created (Line 43), its default column model and selection model are also created. Therefore, you can obtain the table column model and selection model from the table (Lines 46–51).

When a row or a column is selected, a `ListSelectionEvent` is fired by `selectionModel`, which invokes the handler to display the selected row and column in the text area (Lines 120–127). When the content or structure of the table is changed, a `TableModelEvent` is fired by `tableModel`, which invokes the handler to display the last row and last column of the changed data in the text area (Lines 86-91). When a column is deleted by clicking the *Delete Selected Column* button, a `ColumnModelEvent` is fired by `tableColumnModel`, which invokes the handler to display the index of the deleted column (Lines 93–107).

24.7   JTree

`JTree` is a Swing component that displays data in a treelike hierarchy, as shown in Figure 24.35.

All the nodes displayed in the tree are in the form of a hierarchical indexed list. The tree can be used to navigate structured data with hierarchical relationships. A node can have child nodes. A node is called a *leaf* if it has no children; a node with no parent is called the *root* of its tree. A tree may consist of many subtrees, each node acting as the root for its own subtree.

A nonleaf node can be expanded or collapsed by double-clicking on the node or on the node's handle in front of the node. The handle usually has a visible sign to indicate whether the node is expanded or collapsed. For example, on Windows, the $+$ symbol indicates that the node can be expanded, and the $-$ symbol indicates that it can be collapsed.

Like `JTable`, `JTree` is a very complex component with many supporting interfaces and classes. `JTree` is in the `javax.swing` package, but its supporting interfaces and classes are all included in the `javax.swing.tree` package. The supporting interfaces are `TreeModel`, `TreeSelectionModel`, `TreeNode`, and `MutableTreeNode`, and the supported classes are `DefaultTreeModel`, `Default-MutableTreeNode`, `DefaultTreeCellEditor`, `DefaultTreeCellRenderer`, and `TreePath`.

While `JTree` displays the tree, the data representation of the tree is handled by `TreeModel`, `TreeNode`, and `TreePath`. `TreeModel` represents the entire tree, `TreeNode` represents a node, and `TreePath` represents a path to a node. Unlike the `ListModel` or `TableModel`, `TreeModel` does not directly store or manage tree data. Tree data are stored and managed in `TreeNode` and `TreePath`. `DefaultTreeModel` is a concrete implementation of `TreeModel`. `MutableTreeNode` is a subinterface of `TreeNode`, which represents a tree node that can be

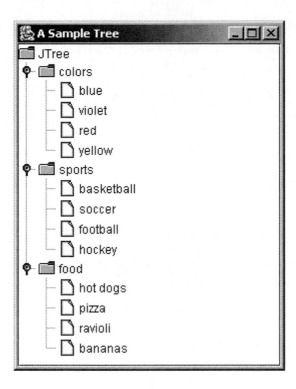

FIGURE 24.35 *JTree displays data in a treelike hierarchy.*

mutated by adding or removing child nodes, or by changing the contents of a user object stored in the node.

The `TreeSelectionModel` interface handles tree node selection. The `DefaultTreeCellRenderer` class provides a default tree node renderer that can display a label and/or an icon in a node. The `DefaultTreeCellEditor` can be used to edit the cells in a text field.

A `TreePath` is an array of `Objects` that are vended from a `TreeModel`. The elements of the array are ordered such that the root is always the first element (index 0) of the array. Figure 24.36 shows how these interfaces and classes are interrelated.

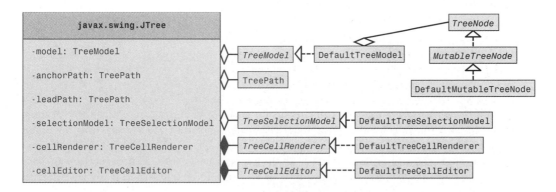

FIGURE 24.36 *JTree contains many supporting interfaces and classes.*

24.7.1 JTree Constructors, Properties, and Methods

Figure 24.37 shows the constructors, frequently used properties, and methods of JTree.

javax.swing.JTree	
#cellEditor: TreeCellEditor	Specifies a cell editor used to edit entries in the tree.
#cellRenderer: TreeCellRenderer	Specifies a cellRenderer.
#editable: boolean	Specifies whether the cells are editable (default: false).
#model: TreeModel	Maintains the tree model.
#rootVisible: boolean	Specifies whether the root is displayed (depending on the constructor).
#rowHeight: int	Specifies the height of the row for the node displayed in the tree (default: 16 pixels).
#scrollsOnExpand: boolean	If true, when a node is expanded, as many of the descendants are scrolled to be visible (default: 16 pixels).
#selectionModel: TreeSelectionModel	Models the set of selected nodes in this tree.
#showsRootHandles: boolean	Specifies whether the root handles are displayed (default: true).
#toggleClickCount: int	Number of mouse clicks before a node is expanded (default: 2).
-anchorSelectionPath: TreePath	The path identified as the anchor.
-expandsSelectedPaths: boolean	True if paths in the selection should be expanded (default: true).
-leadSelectionPaths: TreePath	The path identified as the lead.
+JTree()	Creates a JTree with a sample tree model, as shown in Figure 24.35.
+JTree(value: java.util.Hashtable)	Creates a JTree with an invisible root and the keys in the Hashtable key/value pairs as its children.
+JTree(value: Object[])	Creates a JTree with an invisible root and the elements in the array as its children.
+JTree(newModel: TreeModel)	Creates a JTree with the specified tree model.
+JTree(root: TreeNode)	Creates a JTree with the specified tree node as its root.
+JTree(root: TreeNode, asksAllowsChildren: boolean)	Creates a JTree with the specified tree node as its root and decides whether a node is a leaf node in the specified manner.
+JTree(value: Vector)	Creates a JTree with an invisible root and the elements in the vector as its children.
+addSelectionPath(path: TreePath): void	Adds the specified TreePath to the current selection.
+addSelectionPaths(paths: TreePath[]): void	Adds the specified TreePaths to the current selection.
+addSelectionRow(row: int): void	Adds the path at the specified row to the current selection.
+addSelectionRows(rows: int[]): void	Adds the path at the specified rows to the current selection.
+clearSelection(): void	Clears the selection.
+collapsePath(path: TreePath): void	Ensures that the node identified by the specified path is collapsed and viewable.
+getSelectionPath(): TreePath	Returns the path from the root to the first selected node.
+getSelectionPaths(): TreePath[]	Returns the paths from the root to all the selected nodes.
+getLastSelectedPathComponent()	Returns the last node in the first selected TreePath.
+getRowCount():int	Returns the number of rows currently being displayed.
+removeSelectionPath(path: TreePath): void	Removes the node in the specified path.
+removeSelectionPaths(paths: TreePath[]): void	Removes the node in the specified paths.

FIGURE 24.37 *The JTree class is for creating, customizing, and manipulating trees.*

The JTree class contains seven constructors for creating trees. You can create a tree using its no-arg constructor, a tree model, a tree node, a Hashtable, an array, or a vector. Using the no-arg constructor, a sample tree is created as shown in Figure 24.35. Using a Hashtable, an array, or a vector, a root is created but not displayed. All the keys in a Hashtable, all the objects in an array, and all the elements in a vector are added into the tree as children of the root. If you wish the root to be displayed, set the rootVisible property to true.

All the methods related to path selection are also defined in the TreeSelectionModel interface, which will be covered in Section 24.7.5, "TreeSelectionModel and DefaultTree-SelectionModel."

EXAMPLE 24.12 SIMPLE TREE DEMO

Problem

Write a program to create four trees: a default tree using the no-arg constructor, a tree created from an array of objects, a tree created from a vector, and a tree created from a hash table, as shown in Figure 24.38. Enable the user to dynamically set the properties for rootVisible, rowHeight, and showsRootHandles.

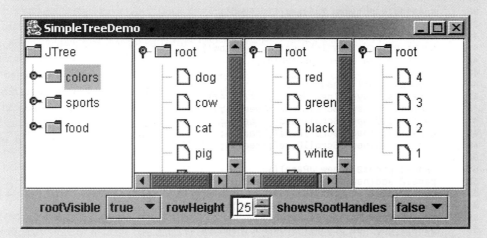

FIGURE 24.38   *You can dynamically set the properties for* rootVisible, rowHeight, *and* showRootHandles *in a tree.*

Solution

Listing 24.14 gives the solution.

LISTING 24.14   SimpleTreeDemo.java

```
 1 import java.awt.*;
 2 import java.awt.event.*;
 3 import javax.swing.*;
 4 import javax.swing.event.*;
 5 import java.util.*;
 6
 7 public class SimpleTreeDemo extends JApplet {
 8   // Create a default tree
 9   private JTree jTree1 = new JTree();                              tree
10
11   // Create a tree with an array of Objects.
12   private JTree jTree2 = new JTree(new String[]                    tree
13     {"dog", "cow", "cat", "pig", "rabbit"});
14
15   // Create a tree with a Hashtable
16   private Vector vector = new Vector(Arrays.asList(
17     new Object[]{"red", "green", "black", "white", "purple"}));
18   private JTree jTree3 = new JTree(vector);                        tree
19
20   private Hashtable hashtable = new Hashtable();                   tree
21   private JTree jTree4;
22
23   // Create a combo box for selecting rootVisible
24   private JComboBox jcboRootVisible = new JComboBox(
25     new String[]{"false", "true"});
26
27   // Create a combo box for selecting showRootHandles
28   private JComboBox jcboShowsRootHandles = new JComboBox(
29     new String[] {"false", "true"});
```

To create a tree model, you first create an instance of TreeNode to represent the root of the tree, and then create an instance of DefaultTreeModel fitted with the root.

javax.swing.tree.TreeNode	
+children(): java.util.Enumeration	Returns the children of this node.
+getAllowsChildren(): boolean	Returns true if this node can have children.
+getChildAt(childIndex: int): TreeNode	Returns the child TreeNode at index childIndex.
+getChildCount(): int	Returns the number of children under this node.
+getIndex(node: TreeNode): int	Returns the index of the specified node in the current node's children.
+getParent(): TreeNode	Returns the parent of this node.
+isLeaf(): boolean	Returns true if this node is a leaf.

javax.swing.tree.MutableTreeNode	
+insert(child: MutableTreeNode, index: int): void	Adds the specified child under this node at the specified index.
+remove(index: int): void	Removes the child at the specified index from this node's child list.
+remove(node: MutableTreeNode): void	Removes the specified node from this node's child list.
+removeFromParent(): void	Removes this node from its parent.
+setParent(newParent: MutableTreeNode): void	Sets the parent of this node to the specified newParent.
+setUserObject(object: Object): void	Resets the user object of this node to the specified object.

javax.swing.tree.DefaultMutableTreeNode	
#allowsChildren: Boolean	True if the node is able to have children.
#parent: MutableTreeNode	Stores the parent of this node.
#userObject: Object	Stores the content of this node.
+DefaultMutableTreeNode()	Creates a tree node without user object, and allows children.
+DefaultMutableTreeNode(userObject: Object)	Creates a tree node with the specified user object, and allows children.
+DefaultMutableTreeNode(userObject: Object, allowsChildren: boolean)	Creates a tree node with the specified user object and the specified mode to indicate whether children are allowed.
+add(newChild: MutableTreeNode)	Adds the specified node to the end of this node's child vector.
+getChildAfter(aChild: TreeNode): TreeNode +getChildBefore(aChild: TreeNode): TreeNode	These two methods return the next (previous) sibling of the specified child in this node's child vector.
+getFirstChild(): TreeNode +getLastChild(): TreeNode	These two methods return this node's first (last) child in the child's vector of this node.
+getFirstLeaf(): DefaultMutableTreeNode +getLastLeaf(): DefaultMutableTreeNode +getNextLeaf(): DefaultMutableTreeNode +getPreviousLeaf(): DefaultMutableTreeNode	These four methods return the first (last, next, and previous) leaf that is a descendant of this node. The first (last, next, and previous) leaf is recursively defined as the first (last, next, and previous) child's first (last, next, and previous) leaf.
+getLeafCount(): int	Returns the total number of leaves that are descendants of this node.
+getDepth(): int	Returns the depth of the tree rooted at this node.
+getLevel(): int	Returns the distance from the root to this node.
+getNextNode(): DefaultMutableTreeNode +getPreviousNode(): DefaultMutableTreeNode	These two methods return the node that follows (precedes) this node in a preorder traversal of this node.
+getSiblingCount(): int	Returns the number of siblings of this node.
+getNextSibling(): DefaultMutableTreeNode	Returns the next sibling of this node in the parent's child vector.
+getPath(): TreeNode[]	Returns the path from the root to this node.
+getRoot(): TreeNode	Returns the root of the tree that contains this node.
+isRoot(): boolean	Returns true if this node is the root of the tree.
+breadthFirstEnumeration(): Enumeration +depthFirstEnumeration(): Enumeration +postorderEnumeration(): Enumeration +preorderEnumeration(): Enumeration	These four methods create and return an enumeration that traverses the subtree rooted at this node in breadth-first order (depth-first order, postorder, preorder). These traversals were discussed in Section 17.4.3, "Tree Traversal."

FIGURE 24.40   TreeNode represents a node.

24.7.3   `TreeNode`, `MutableTreeNode`, and `DefaultMutableTreeNode`

While `TreeModel` represents the entire tree, `TreeNode` stores a single node in the tree. `MutableTreeNode` defines a subinterface of `TreeNode` with additional methods for changing the content of the node, for inserting and removing a child node, for setting a new parent, and for removing the node itself.

`DefaultMutableTreeNode` is a concrete implementation of `MutableTreeNode` that maintains a list of children in a vector and provides the operations for creating nodes, for examining and modifying a node's parent and children, and also for examining the tree to which the node belongs. Normally, you should use `DefaultMutableTreeNode` to create a tree node. Figure 24.40 shows `TreeNode`, `MutableTreeNode`, and `DefaultMutableTreeNode`.

 NOTE

In graph theory, depth-first traversal is defined the same as preorder traversal, but in the `depthFirstEnumeration()` method in `DefaultMutableTreeNode`, it is same as postorder traversal.

EXAMPLE 24.13 TREE MODEL DEMO

Problem

Write a program to create two trees that display world, continents, countries, and states. The two trees display identical contents. The program also displays the properties of the tree in a text area, as shown in Figure 24.41.

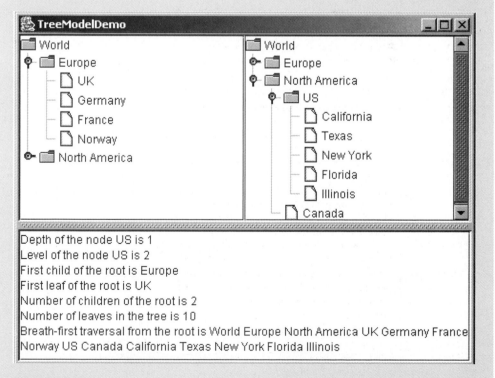

FIGURE 24.41   *The two trees have the same data because their roots are the same.*

EXAMPLE **24.13** (CONTINUED)

Solution

Listing 24.15 gives the solution.

LISTING 24.15 TreeModelDemo.java

```java
1 import java.awt.*;
2 import javax.swing.*;
3 import javax.swing.tree.*;
4 import java.util.*;
5
6 public class TreeModelDemo extends JApplet {
7   public TreeModelDemo() {
8     // Create the first tree
9     DefaultMutableTreeNode root, europe, northAmerica, us;
10
11    europe = new DefaultMutableTreeNode("Europe");
12    europe.add(new DefaultMutableTreeNode("UK"));
13    europe.add(new DefaultMutableTreeNode("Germany"));
14    europe.add(new DefaultMutableTreeNode("France"));
15    europe.add(new DefaultMutableTreeNode("Norway"));
16
17    northAmerica = new DefaultMutableTreeNode("North America");
18    us = new DefaultMutableTreeNode("US");
19    us.add(new DefaultMutableTreeNode("California"));
20    us.add(new DefaultMutableTreeNode("Texas"));
21    us.add(new DefaultMutableTreeNode("New York"));
22    us.add(new DefaultMutableTreeNode("Florida"));
23    us.add(new DefaultMutableTreeNode("Illinois"));
24    northAmerica.add(us);
25    northAmerica.add(new DefaultMutableTreeNode("Canada"));
26
27    root = new DefaultMutableTreeNode("World");
28    root.add(europe);
29    root.add(northAmerica);
30
31    JPanel panel = new JPanel();
32    panel.setLayout(new GridLayout(1, 2));
33    panel.add(new JScrollPane(new JTree(root)));
34    panel.add(new JScrollPane(new JTree(new DefaultTreeModel(root))));
35
36    JTextArea jtaMessage = new JTextArea();
37    jtaMessage.setWrapStyleWord(true);
38    jtaMessage.setLineWrap(true);
39    getContentPane().add(new JSplitPane(JSplitPane.VERTICAL_SPLIT,
40      panel, new JScrollPane(jtaMessage)), BorderLayout.CENTER);
41
42    // Get tree information
43    jtaMessage.append("Depth of the node US is " + us.getDepth());
44    jtaMessage.append("\nLevel of the node US is " + us.getLevel());
45    jtaMessage.append("\nFirst child of the root is " +
46      root.getFirstChild());
47    jtaMessage.append("\nFirst leaf of the root is " +
48      root.getFirstLeaf());
49    jtaMessage.append("\nNumber of the children of the root is " +
50      root.getChildCount());
51    jtaMessage.append("\nNumber of leaves in the tree is " +
52      root.getLeafCount());
53    String breadthFirstSearchResult = "";
54
55    // Breadth-first traversal
56    Enumeration bf = root.breadthFirstEnumeration();
57    while (bf.hasMoreElements())
58      breadthFirstSearchResult += bf.nextElement().toString() + " ";
59    jtaMessage.append("\nBreath-first traversal from the root is "
60      + breadthFirstSearchResult);
61  }
62 }
```

tree nodes

add children

add children

main method omitted

EXAMPLE 24.13 (CONTINUED)

Review

You can create a JTree using a TreeNode root (Line 33) or a TreeModel (Line 34), whichever is convenient. A TreeModel is actually created using a TreeNode root (Line 34). The two trees have the same contents because the root is the same. However, it is important to note that the two JTree objects are different, and so are their TreeModel objects, although both trees have the same root.

A tree is created by adding the nodes to the tree (Lines 9–29). Each node is created using the DefaultMutableTreeNode class. This class provides many methods to manipulate the tree (e.g., adding a child, removing a child) and obtaining information about the tree (e.g., level, depth, number of children, number of leaves, traversals). Some examples of using these methods are given in Lines 43–60.

As shown in this example, often you don't have to directly use TreeModel. Using Default-MutableTreeNode is sufficient, since the tree data are stored in individual DefaultMutable-TreeNodes, and DefaultMutableTreeNode contains all the methods for modifying the tree and obtaining tree information.

24.7.4   The TreePath Class

The TreePath class represents a path from an ancestor to a descendant in a tree. Figure 24.42 shows TreePath.

javax.swing.tree.TreePath	
+TreePath(singlePath: Object)	Constructs a TreePath containing only a single element.
+TreePath(path: Object[])	Constructs a path from an array of objects.
+getLastPathComponent(): Object	Returns the last component of this path.
+getParentPath(): TreePath	Returns a path containing all but the last path component.
+getPath(): Object[]	Returns an ordered array of objects containing the components of this TreePath.
+getPathComponent(element: int): Object	Returns the path component at the specified index.
+getPathCount(): int	Returns the number of elements in the path.
+isDescendant(aTreePath: TreePath): boolean	Returns true if aTreePath contains all the components in this TreePath.
+pathByAddingChild(child: Object): TreePath	Returns a new path containing all the elements of this TreePath plus child.

FIGURE 24.42   *TreePath represents a path from an ancestor to a descendant in a tree.*

You can construct a TreePath from a single object or an array of objects, but often instances of TreePath are returned from the methods in JTree and TreeSelectionModel. For instance, the getLeadSelectionPath() method in JTree returns the path from the root to the selected node. There are many ways to extract the nodes from a tree path. Often you use the getLast-PathComponent() method to obtain the last node in the path, and then the getParent() method to get all the nodes in the path upward through the link.

24.7.5   TreeSelectionModel and DefaultTreeSelectionModel

The selection of tree nodes is defined in the TreeSelectionModel interface, as shown in Figure 24.43. The DefaultTreeSelectionModel class is a concrete implementation of the TreeSelectionModel that maintains an array of TreePath objects representing the current selection. The last TreePath selected, called the *lead path*, can be obtained using the getLeadSelectionPath() method. To obtain all the selection paths, use the getSelectionPaths() method, which returns an array of tree paths.

```
                 javax.swing.tree.TreeSelectionModel

+addSelectionPath(path: TreePath): void              Adds the specified TreePath to the current selection.
+addSelectionPaths(paths: TreePath[]): void          Adds the specified TreePaths to the current selection.
+clearSelection(): void                              Clears the selection.
+getLeadSelectionPath(): TreePath                    Returns the last path in the selection.
+getSelectionCount(): int                            Returns the number of paths in the selection.
+getSelectionPath(): TreePath                        Returns the first path in the selection.
+getSelectionPaths(): TreePath[]                     Returns all the paths in the selection.
+getSelectionMode(): int                             Returns the current selection mode.
+removeSelectionPath(path: TreePath): void           Removes path from the selection.
+removeSelectionPaths(paths: TreePath[]): void       Removes paths from the selection.
+setSelectionMode(mode: int): void                   Sets the selection mode.
+setSelectionPath(path: TreePath): void              Sets the selection to path.
+setSelectionPaths(paths: TreePath[]): void          Sets the selection to paths.
+addTreeSelectionListener(x: TreeSelectionListener): void      Registers a TreeSelectionListener.
+removeTreeSelectionListener(x: TreeSelectionListener): void   Removes a TreeSelectionListener.
```

```
                 javax.swing.tree.DefaultTreeSelectionModel
```

FIGURE 24.43 *The* TreeSelectionModel *handles selection in a tree.*

TreeSelectionModel supports three selection modes: contiguous selection, discontiguous selection, and single selection. *Single selection* allows only one item to be selected. *Contiguous selection* allows multiple selections, but the selected items must be contiguous. *Discontiguous selection* is the most flexible; it allows any item to be selected at a given time. The default tree selection mode is discontiguous. To set a selection mode, use the setSelectionMode(int mode) method in TreeSelectionModel. The constants for the three modes are:

✦ CONTIGUOUS_TREE_SELECTION

✦ DISCONTIGUOUS_TREE_SELECTION

✦ SINGLE_TREE_SELECTION

> ❀ **NOTE**
> When you create a JTree, a DefaultTreeSelectionModel is automatically created. So you rarely need to create an instance of TreeSelectionModel explicitly. Since most of the methods in TreeSelectionModel are also in JTree, you can get selection paths and process the selection without directly dealing with TreeSelectionModel.

EXAMPLE 24.14 MODIFYING TREES

Problem

Write a program to create two trees that display the same contents: world, continents, countries, and states, as shown in Figure 24.44. For the tree on the left, enable the user to choose a selection mode, add a new child under the first selected node, and remove all the selected nodes.

When you click the *Add Node* button, if there are no nodes currently selected in the left tree, a message dialog box is displayed, as shown in Figure 24.45(a). Otherwise, an input dialog box is displayed to prompt the user to enter a value for the new node, as shown in Figure 24.45(b). The new node becomes a child of the first selected node.

EXAMPLE 24.14 (CONTINUED)

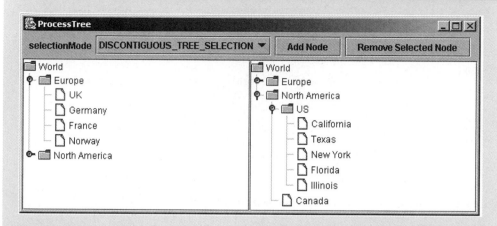

FIGURE 24.44 *The* DefaultMutableTreeNode *class is used to modify trees and obtain tree information.*

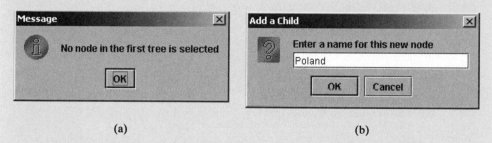

(a)   (b)

FIGURE 24.45 *You can add a new node to the tree.*

Solution

Listing 24.16 gives the solution.

LISTING 24.16 ProcessTree.java

```
 1 import java.awt.*;
 2 import java.awt.event.*;
 3 import javax.swing.*;
 4 import javax.swing.tree.*;
 5
 6 public class ProcessTree extends JApplet {
 7   // Create a combo box for choosing selection modes
 8   private JComboBox jcboSelectionMode = new JComboBox(new String[]{          combo box
 9     "CONTIGUOUS_TREE_SELECTION", "DISCONTIGUOUS_TREE_SELECTION",
10     "SINGLE_TREE_SELECTION"});
11
12   // Create two buttons
13   private JButton jbtAdd = new JButton("Add Node");                          buttons
14   private JButton jbtRemove = new JButton("Remove Selected Node");
15
16   // Declare two trees
17   private JTree jTree1, jTree2;                                              tree
18
19   public ProcessTree() {
20     // Create the first tree
21     DefaultMutableTreeNode root, europe, northAmerica, us;                   grow tree
22
```

EXAMPLE 24.14 (CONTINUED)

```
23    europe = new DefaultMutableTreeNode("Europe");
24    europe.add(new DefaultMutableTreeNode("UK"));
25    europe.add(new DefaultMutableTreeNode("Germany"));
26    europe.add(new DefaultMutableTreeNode("France"));
27    europe.add(new DefaultMutableTreeNode("Norway"));
28
29    northAmerica = new DefaultMutableTreeNode("North America");
30    us = new DefaultMutableTreeNode("US");
31    us.add(new DefaultMutableTreeNode("California"));
32    us.add(new DefaultMutableTreeNode("Texas"));
33    us.add(new DefaultMutableTreeNode("New York"));
34    us.add(new DefaultMutableTreeNode("Florida"));
35    us.add(new DefaultMutableTreeNode("Illinois"));
36    northAmerica.add(us);
37    northAmerica.add(new DefaultMutableTreeNode("Canada"));
38
39    root = new DefaultMutableTreeNode("World");
40    root.add(europe);
41    root.add(northAmerica);
42
43    jcboSelectionMode.setSelectedIndex(1);
44
45    JPanel p1 = new JPanel();
46    p1.add(new JLabel("selectionMode"));
47    p1.add(jcboSelectionMode);
48    p1.add(jbtAdd);
49    p1.add(jbtRemove);
50
51    JPanel p2 = new JPanel();
52    p2.setLayout(new GridLayout(1, 2));
53    p2.add(new JScrollPane(jTree1 = new JTree(root)));
54    p2.add(new JScrollPane(jTree2 =
55      new JTree(new DefaultTreeModel(root))));
56
57    getContentPane().add(p1, BorderLayout.NORTH);
58    getContentPane().add(p2, BorderLayout.CENTER);
59
60    // Register listeners
61    jcboSelectionMode.addActionListener(new ActionListener() {
62      public void actionPerformed(ActionEvent e) {
63        if (jcboSelectionMode.getSelectedItem().
64          equals("CONTIGUOUS_TREE_SELECTION"))
65          jTree1.getSelectionModel().setSelectionMode(
66            TreeSelectionModel.CONTIGUOUS_TREE_SELECTION);
67        else if (jcboSelectionMode.getSelectedItem().
68          equals("DISCONTIGUOUS_TREE_SELECTION"))
69          jTree1.getSelectionModel().setSelectionMode(
70            TreeSelectionModel.DISCONTIGUOUS_TREE_SELECTION);
71        else
72          jTree1.getSelectionModel().setSelectionMode(
73            TreeSelectionModel.SINGLE_TREE_SELECTION);
74      }
75    });
76
77    jbtAdd.addActionListener(new ActionListener() {
78      public void actionPerformed(ActionEvent e) {
79        DefaultMutableTreeNode parent = (DefaultMutableTreeNode)
80          jTree1.getLastSelectedPathComponent();
81
82        if (parent == null) {
83          JOptionPane.showMessageDialog(null,
84            "No node in the first tree is selected");
85          return;
86        }
87
88        // Enter a new node
89        String nodeName = JOptionPane.showInputDialog(
90          null, "Enter a name for this new node", "Add a Child",
91          JOptionPane.QUESTION_MESSAGE);
```

combo box listener

button listener

EXAMPLE 24.14 (CONTINUED)

```
92
93          // Insert the new node as a child of treeNode
94          parent.add(new DefaultMutableTreeNode(nodeName));
95
96          // Reload the model since a new tree node is added
97          ((DefaultTreeModel)(jTree1.getModel())).reload();
98          ((DefaultTreeModel)(jTree2.getModel())).reload();
99        }
100     });
101
102     jbtRemove.addActionListener(new ActionListener() {
103       public void actionPerformed(ActionEvent e) {
104         // Get all selected paths
105         TreePath[] paths = jTree1.getSelectionPaths();
106
107         if (paths == null) {
108           JOptionPane.showMessageDialog(null,
109             "No node in the left tree is selected");
110           return;
111         }
112
113         // Remove all selected nodes
114         for (int i = 0; i < paths.length; i++) {
115           DefaultMutableTreeNode node = (DefaultMutableTreeNode)
116             (paths[i].getLastPathComponent());
117
118           if (node.isRoot()) {
119             JOptionPane.showMessageDialog(null,
120               "Cannot remove the root");
121           }
122           else
123             node.removeFromParent();
124         }
125
126         // Reload the model since a new tree node is added
127         ((DefaultTreeModel) (jTree1.getModel())).reload();
128         ((DefaultTreeModel) (jTree2.getModel())).reload();
129       }
130     });
131   }
132 }
```

button listener

main method omitted

Review

Two JTree objects (jTree1 and jTree2) are created with the same root (Lines 53–55), but each has its own TreeModel and TreeSelectionModel. When you choose a selection mode in the combo box, the new selection mode is set in jTree1's selection model (Line 61–75). The selection mode for jTree2 is not affected.

When you click the *Add Node* button, the first selected node is returned as parent (Lines 79–80). Suppose you selected Europe, UK, and US in this order, parent is Europe. If parent is null, no node is selected in the left tree (Lines 82–86). Otherwise, prompt the user to enter a new node from an input dialog box (Lines 89–91) and add this node as a child of parent (Line 94). Since the tree has been modified, you need to invoke the reload() method to notify that the models for both trees have been changed (Lines 97–98). Otherwise, the new node may not be displayed in jTree1 and jTree2.

When you click the *Remove Selected Node* button, all the tree paths for each selected node are obtained in paths (Line 105). Suppose you selected Europe, UK, and US in this order, three tree paths are obtained. Each path starts from the root to a selected node. If no node is selected, paths is null. To delete a selected node is to delete the last node in each selected tree path (114–125). The last node in a path is obtained using getLastPathComponent(). If the node is the root, it cannot be removed (Lines 118–121). The removeFromParent() method removes a node (Line 123).

24.7.6 Tree Node Rendering and Editing

JTree delegates node rendering to a renderer. All renderers are instances of the TreeCellRenderer interface, which defines a single method, getTreeCellRendererComponent, as follows:

```
public Component getTreeCellRendererComponent
  (JTree tree, Object value, boolean selected, boolean expanded,
    boolean leaf, int row, boolean hasFocus);
```

You can create a custom tree cell renderer by implementing the TreeCellRenderer interface, or use the DefaultTreeCellRenderer class, which provides a default implementation for Tree-CellRenderer. When a new JTree is created, an instance of DefaultTreeCellRenderer is assigned to the tree renderer. The DefaultTreeCellRenderer class maintains three icon properties named leafIcon, openIcon, and closedIcon for leaf nodes, expanded nodes, and collapsed nodes. It also provides colors for text and background. The following code sets new leaf, open and closed icons, and new background selection color in the tree:

```
DefaultTreeCellRenderer renderer =
  (DefaultTreeCellRenderer)jTree1.getCellRenderer();
renderer.setLeafIcon(yourCustomLeafImageIcon);
renderer.setOpenIcon(yourCustomOpenImageIcon);
renderer.setClosedIcon(yourCustomClosedImageIcon);
renderer.setBackgroundSelectionColor(Color.red);
```

❀ **NOTE**

The default leaf, open icon, and closed icon are dependent on the look-and-feel. For instance, on Windows look-and-feel, the open icon is −, and the closed icon is +.

JTree comes with a default cell editor. If JTree's editable property is true, the default editor activates a text field for editing when the node is clicked three times. By default, this property is set to false. To create a custom editor, you need to extend the DefaultCellEditor class, which is the same class you used in table cell editing. You can use a text field, a check box, or a combo box, and pass it to DefaultCellEditor's constructor to create an editor. The following code uses a combo box for editing colors:

```
// Customize editor
JComboBox jcboColor = new JComboBox();
jcboColor.addItem("red");
jcboColor.addItem("green");
jcboColor.addItem("blue");
jcboColor.addItem("yellow");
jcboColor.addItem("orange");

jTree1.setCellEditor(new javax.swing.DefaultCellEditor(jcboColor));
jTree1.setEditable(true);
```

The combo box editor is shown in Figure 24.46.

There are two annoying problems with the editor created in the preceding code. First, it is activated with just one mouse click. Second, it overlaps the node's icon, as shown in Figure 24.46. These problems can be fixed by using the DefaultTreeCellEditor, as shown in the following code:

```
jTree1.setCellEditor
  (new javax.swing.tree.DefaultTreeCellEditor(jTree1,
    new javax.swing.tree.DefaultTreeCellRenderer(),
    new javax.swing.DefaultCellEditor(jcboColor)));
```

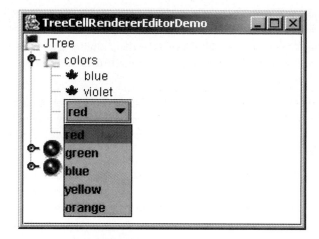

FIGURE 24.46 *You can supply a custom editor for editing tree nodes.*

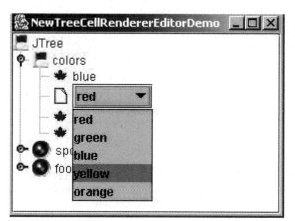 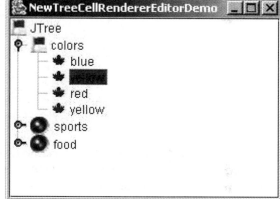

FIGURE 24.47 *The* DefaultTreeCellEditor *displays an editor that does not overlap a node's icon.*

The new editor is shown in Figure 24.47. Editing using DefaultTreeCellEditor starts on a triple mouse click. The combo box does not overlap the node's icon.

24.7.7 Tree Events

JTree can fire TreeSelectionEvent and TreeExpansionEvent, among many other events. Whenever a new node is selected, JTree fires a TreeSelectionEvent. Whenever a node is expanded or collapsed, JTree fires a TreeExpansionEvent. To handle the tree selection event, a listener must implement the TreeSelectionListener interface, which contains a single handler named valueChanged method. TreeExpansionListener contains two handlers named treeCollapsed and treeExpanded for handling node expansion or node closing.

The following code displays a selected node:

```java
public void valueChanged(TreeSelectionEvent e) {
  TreePath path = e.getNewLeadSelectionPath();
  TreeNode treeNode = (TreeNode)path.getLastPathComponent();
  System.out.println("The selected node is " + treeNode.toString());
}
```

KEY CLASSES AND METHODS

✦ **javax.swing.JSpinner** is a GUI component that contains a text field with a pair of tiny arrow buttons on its right side. A spinner is often used to let the user select numbers, dates, or values from an ordered sequence.

✦ **javax.swing.SpinnerModel** is a root interface for JSpinner data models. By default, JSpinner uses **javax.swing.SpinnerNumberModel** to display a sequence of integers. To display dates, use **javax.swing.SpinnerDateModel** and to display an enumeration list, use **javax.swing.SpinnerListModel**.

✦ **javax.swing.JList** is a GUI component that enables the user to choose a single value or multiple values from a list. JList contains methods to get and set list properties, but you cannot add or remove elements from a list without using list models. JList has two supporting models: a list model and a list-selection model. The *list model* is for storing and processing data. The *list-selection model* is for selecting items.

✦ **javax.swing.ListModel** is a root interface for JList data models. **javax.swing.Abstract-ListModel** is a convenience abstract class that partially implements ListModel. **javax.swing.DefaultListModel** is a default list model that uses java.util.Vector to implement the list.

✦ **javax.swing.ListSelectionModel** is an interface for list-selection models. By default, JList uses DefaultListSelectionModel.

✦ **javax.swing.ListCellRenderer** is an interface for displaying cells in a list. **javax.swing.DefaultListCellRenderer** is a concrete implementation of ListCellRenderer.

✦ **javax.swing.JComboBox** is a GUI component that enables the user to choose a single value from a list.

✦ **javax.swing.ComboBoxModel** is a root interface for JComboBox data models. ComboBox-Model is a subinterface of ListModel. By default, JComboBox uses **javax.swing.DefaultComboBoxModel.**

✦ **javax.swing.JTable** is a GUI component that displays data in rows and columns in a two-dimensional grid. JTable has three supporting models: a table model, a column model, and a list-selection model. The *table model* is for storing and processing data. The *column model* represents all the columns in the table. The *list-selection model* is the same as the one used by JList for selecting rows, columns, and cells in a table.

✦ **javax.swing.table.TableModel** is an interface for storing table data. **javax.swing.table.AbstractTableModel** is a convenient class that provides partial implementations for most of the methods in TableModel. **javax.swing.table.DefaultTableModel** is the default implementation for TableModel.

✦ **javax.swing.table.TableColumnModel** is an interface for storing column information. **javax.swing.table.DefaultTableColumnModel** is a concrete class that implements DefaultTableColumnModel.

✦ **javax.swing.JTree** is a GUI component that displays data in a treelike hierarchy. While JTree displays the tree, the data representation of the tree is handled by **javax.swing.tree.TreeModel**, **javax.swing.tree.TreeNode**, and **javax.swing.tree.TreePath**. TreeModel represents the entire tree, TreeNode represents a node, and TreePath represents a path to a node. Unlike the ListModel or TableModel, the tree model does not directly store or manage tree data. Tree data are stored and managed in TreeNode and TreePath. DefaultTreeModel is a concrete implementation of TreeModel. MutableTreeNode is a subinterface of `TreeNode` that represents a tree node that can be mutated by adding or removing child nodes, or by changing the contents of a user object stored in the node.

CHAPTER SUMMARY

✦ Every Swing user interface component (e.g., `JButton`, `JTextField`, `JList`, and `JComboBox`) has a property named `model` that refers to its data model. The data model is defined in an interface whose name ends with `Model` (e.g., `SpinnerModel`, `ListModel`, `ComboBoxModel`, `TableModel`, and `TreeModel`).

✦ Most simple Swing components (e.g., `JButton`, `JTextField`, `JTextArea`) contain some properties of their models, and these properties can be accessed and modified directly from the component without knowing the existence of the model.

✦ A `JSpinner` is displayed as a text field with a pair of tiny arrow buttons on its right side that enable the user to select numbers, dates, or values from an ordered sequence. A `JSpinner`'s sequence value is defined by the `SpinnerModel` interface. `AbstractSpinnerModel` is a convenient abstract class that implements `SpinnerModel` and provides the implementation for its registration/deregistration methods. `SpinnerListModel`, `SpinnerNumberModel`, and `SpinnerDateModel` are concrete implementations of `SpinnerModel`. `SpinnerNumberModel` represents a sequence of numbers with properties `maximum`, `minimum`, and `stepSize`. `SpinnerDateModel` represents a sequence of dates. `SpinnerListModel` can store a list of any object values.

✦ A `JSpinner` has a single child component, called the *editor*, which is responsible for displaying the current element or value of the model. Four editors are defined as static inner classes inside `JSpinner`: `JSpinner.DefaultEditor`, `JSpinner.NumberEditor`, `JSpinner.DateEditor`, and `JSpinner.ListEditor`.

✦ `JList` has two supporting models: a list model and a list-selection model. The *list model* is for storing and processing data. The *list-selection model* is for selecting items. By default, items are rendered as strings or icons. You can also create a custom renderer implementing the `ListCellRenderer` interface.

✦ `JComboBox` delegates the responsibilities of storing and maintaining data to its data model. All combo box models implement the `ComboBoxModel` interface, which extends the `ListModel` interface and defines the `getSelectedItem` and `setSelectedItem` methods for retrieving and setting a selected item. The methods for adding and removing items are defined in the `MutableComboBoxModel` interface, which extends `ComboBoxModel`. When an instance of `JComboBox` is created without explicitly specifying a model, an instance of `DefaultComboBoxModel` is used. The `DefaultComboBoxModel` class extends `AbstractListModel` and implements `MutableComboBoxModel`.

✦ Combo boxes render cells exactly like lists, because the combo box items are displayed in a list contained in a popup menu. Therefore, a combo box cell renderer can be created exactly like a list cell renderer by implementing the `ListCellRenderer` interface.

✦ `JTable` has three supporting models: a table model, a column model, and a list-selection model. The *table model* is for storing and processing data. The *column model* represents all the columns in the table. The *list-selection model* is the same as the one used by `JList` for selecting rows, columns, and cells in a table. JTable also has two useful supporting classes, TableColumn and JTableHeader. TableColumn contains the information on a particular column. JTableHeader contains the information on the header of a JTable. Each column has a default editor and renderer. You can also create a custom editor by implementing the TableCellEditor interface, and you can create a custom renderer by implementing the TableCellRenderer interface.

✦ Like JTable, JTree is a very complex component with many supporting interfaces and classes. JTree is in the javax.swing package, but its supporting interfaces and classes are all included in the javax.swing.tree package.

✦ While JTree displays the tree, the data representation of the tree is handled by TreeModel, TreeNode, and TreePath. TreeModel represents the entire tree, TreeNode represents a node, and TreePath represents a path to a node. Unlike the ListModel or TableModel, the tree model does not directly store or manage tree data. Tree data are stored and managed in TreeNode and TreePath. A TreePath is an array of Objects that are vended from a TreeModel. The elements of the array are ordered such that the root is always the first element (index 0) of the array. The TreeSelectionModel interface handles tree node selection. The DefaultTreeCellRenderer class provides a default tree node renderer that can display a label and/or an icon in a node. The DefaultTreeCellEditor can be used to edit the cells in a text field. The TreePath class is a support class that represents a set of nodes in a path.

REVIEW QUESTIONS

Section 24.2 Swing Model-View-Controller Architecture

24.1   Does each Swing GUI component (except containers such as JPanel) have a property named model? Is the type of model the same for all the components?

24.2   Does each model interface have a default implementation class? If so, does a Swing component use the default model class if no model is specified?

Section 24.3 JSpinner

24.3   If you create a JSpinner without specifying a data model, what is the default model?

24.4   What is the internal data structure for storing data in SpinnerListModel? How do you convert an array to a list?

Section 24.4 JList

24.5   Does JList have a method, such as addItem, for adding an item to a list? How do you add items to a list? Can JList display icons and custom GUI objects in a list? Can a list item be edited? How do you initialize data in a list? How do you specify the maximum number of visible rows in a list without scrolling? How do you specify the height of a list cell? How do you specify the horizontal margin of list cells?

24.6   How do you create a list model? How do you add items to a list model? How do you remove items from a list model?

24.7   What are the three list-selection modes? Can you set the selection modes directly in an instance of JList? How do you obtain the selected item(s)?

24.8   How do you create a custom list cell renderer?

24.9   What is the handler for handling the ListSelectionEvent?

Section 24.5 `JComboBox`

24.10 Can multiple items be selected from a combo box? Can a combo box item be edited? How do you specify the maximum number of visible rows in a combo box without scrolling? Can you specify the height of a combo box cell using a method in `JComboBox`? How do you obtain the selected item in a combo box?

24.11 How do you add or remove items from a combo box?

24.12 Why is the cell renderer for a combo box the same as the renderer for a list?

Section 24.6 `JTable`

24.13 How do you initialize a table? Can you specify the maximum number of visible rows in a table without scrolling? How do you specify the height of a table cell? How do you specify the horizontal margin of table cells?

24.14 How do you modify table contents? How do you add or remove a row? How do you add or remove a column?

24.15 What is auto-resizing of a table column? How many types of auto-resizing are available?

24.16 What are the properties that show grids, horizontal grids, and vertical grids? What are the properties that specify the table row height, vertical margin, and horizontal margin?

24.17 What are the default table renderers and editors? How do you create a custom table cell renderer and editor?

Section 24.7 `JTree`

24.18 How do you create a tree? How do you specify the row height of a tree node? How do you obtain the default tree model and tree selection model from an instance of `JTree`?

24.19 How do you initialize data in a tree using `TreeModel`? How do you add a child to an instance of `DefaultMutableTreeNode`?

24.20 How do you add or remove a node from a tree?

24.21 How do you obtain a selected tree node?

Programming Exercises

Section 24.3 `JSpinner`

24.1* (*Revising Example 24.2, "Using Spinner Models and Editors"*) The date spinner is synchronized with the day, month, and year spinners in Example 24.2. Improve Example 24.2 to synchronize the day, month, and year spinners with the date spinner. In other words, when a new value is selected in the date spinner, the values in the day, month, and year spinners are updated accordingly.

24.2* (*Developing a custom spinner model for a sequence of numbers of power 2*) Develop a custom spinner model that represents a sequence of numbers of power 2, that is, 1, 2, 4, 8, 16, 32, and so on. Your model should implement `AbstractSpinnerModel`. The registration/deregistration methods for `ChangeListener` have already been implemented in `AbstractSpinnerModel`. You need to implement `getNextValue()`, `getPreviousValue()`, `getValue()`, and `setValue(Object)` methods.

24.3* (*Reversing the numbers displayed in a spinner*) The numbers displayed in a spinner increase when the up-arrow button is clicked and decrease when the down-arrow button is clicked. You can reverse the sequence by creating a new model that extends `Spinner-NumberModel` and overrides the `getNextValue` and `getPreviousValue` methods.

Section 24.4 `JList`

24.4* (*Removing selected items in a list*) Modify Example 24.4, "List Model Demo," to meet the following requirements:

✦ Remove all the selected items from the list when the *Remove selected item* button is clicked.

✦ Enable the items to be deleted using the DELETE key.

24.5* (*Deleting a selected item in a combo box using the DELETE key*) Modify Example 24.6, "Combo Box Cell Renderer Demo," to delete the selected item from the combo box using the DELETE key.

24.6** (*Creating custom cell renderer in a list*) Create a program that shows a list of geometrical shapes along with a label in an instance of `JList`, as shown in Figure 24.48. Display the selected figure in a panel when selecting a figure from the list. The figures are represented in the `FigurePanel` class in Example 22.9, "Using `JTabbedPane`."

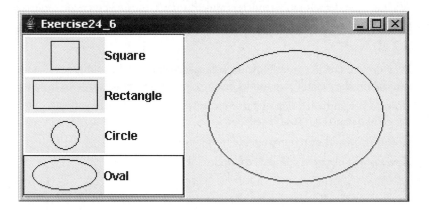

FIGURE 24.48 *The list displays geometrical shapes and their names.*

Section 24.5 `JComboBox`

24.7** (*Creating custom cell renderer in a combo box*) Create a program that shows a list of geometrical shapes along with a label in a combo box, as shown in Figure 24.49. This exercise may share the list cell renderer with the preceding exercise.

24.8** (*Creating a combo box cell renderer for standard colors*) Write a program that enables the user to choose the foreground colors for a label, as shown in Figure 24.50. The combo box contains thirteen standard colors (`BLACK`, `BLUE`, `CYAN`, `DARK_GRAY`, `GRAY`, `GREEN`, `LIGHT_GRAY`, `MAGENTA`, `ORANGE`, `PINK`, `RED`, `WHITE`, `YELLOW`). Each color name in the combo box uses its own color for its foreground.

Section 24.6 `JTable`

24.9* (*Creating a table for the loan schedule*) Exercise 20.5 displays an amortization schedule in a text area. Write a program that enables the user to enter or choose the loan amount, number of years, and interest rate from spinners and displays the schedule in a table, as shown in Figure 24.51.

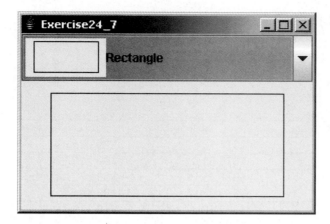

FIGURE 24.49   *The combo box contains a list of geometrical shapes and the shape names.*

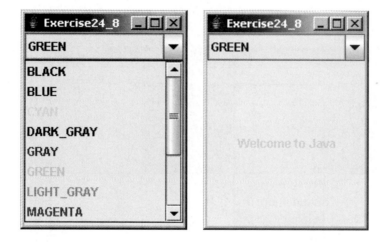

FIGURE 24.50   *The combo box contains a list of color names, each of which uses its own color for its foreground.*

24.10*   (*Modifying Example 24.8, "Modifying Rows and Columns"*) Example 24.8 deletes only the first selected row or column. Enable the program to delete all the selected rows or columns. Also enable the program to delete a row or a column by pressing the DELETE key.

24.11***   (*Creating a student table*) Create a table for student records. Each record consists of name, birthday, class status, in-state, and a photo, as shown in Figure 24.52. The name is of the String type; birthday is of the Date type; class status is one of the following five values: Freshman, Sophomore, Junior, Senior, or Graduate; in-state is a boolean value indicating whether the student is a resident of the state; and photo is an image icon. Use the default editors for name, birthday, and in-state. Supply a combo box as custom editor for class status.

24.12*   (*Displaying a table for data from a text file*) Suppose that a table named Exercise24_12Table.txt is stored in a text file. The first line in the file is the header, and

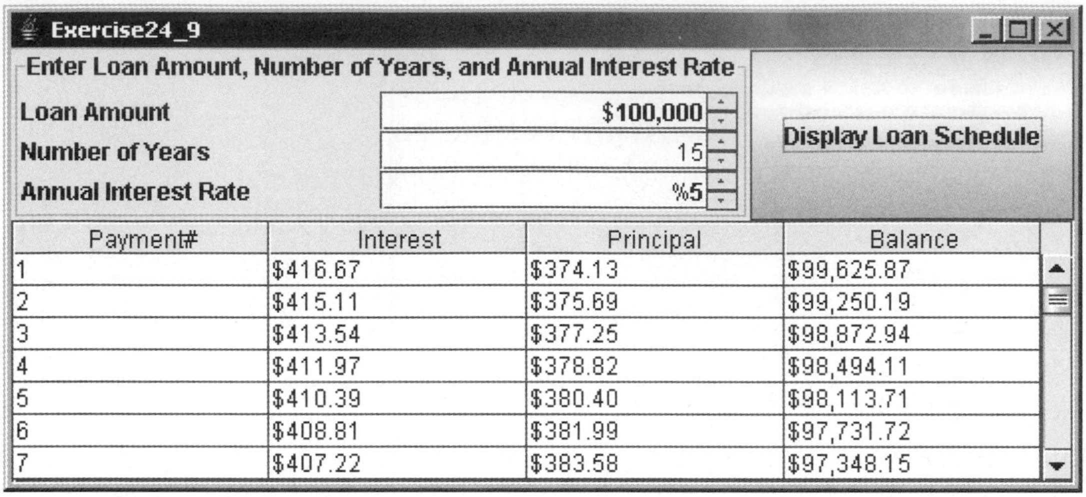

FIGURE 24.51 *The table shows the loan schedule.*

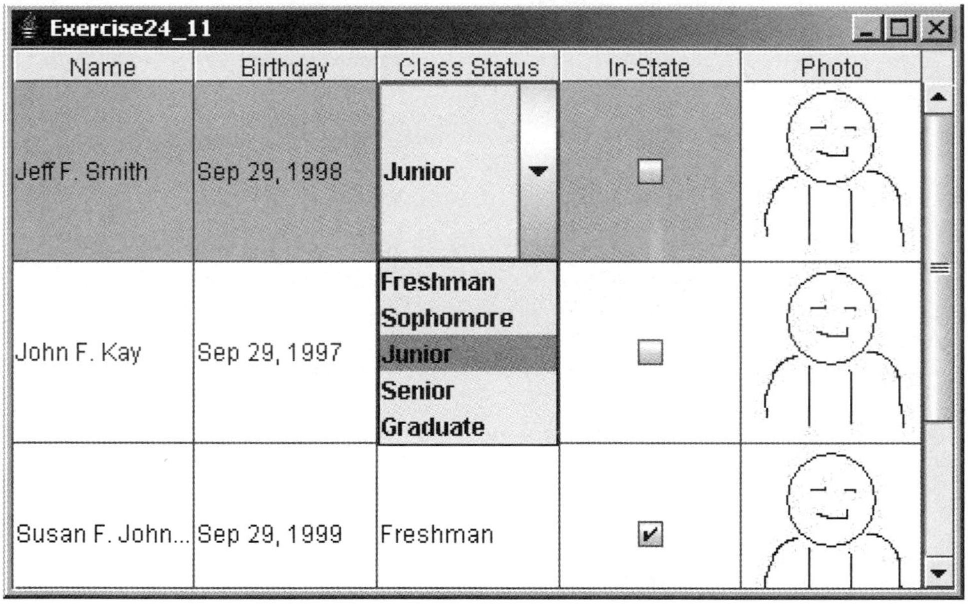

FIGURE 24.52 *The table displays student records and supports add, remove, and edit operations.*

the remaining lines correspond to rows in the table. The elements are separated by the commas. Write a program to display the table using the JTable component. For example, the following text file is displayed in a table, as shown in Figure 24.53.

```
Country, Capitol, Population, Democracy
USA, Washington DC, 280, true
Canada, Ottawa, 32, true
United Kingdom, London, 60, true
Germany, Berlin, 83, true
France, Paris, 60, true
Norway, Oslo, 4.5, true
India, New Deli, 1046, true
```

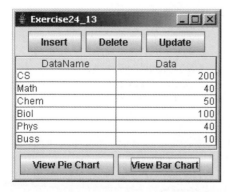

FIGURE 24.53 *The data in the file are displayed in a table.*

24.13** (*Creating a controller using* JTable) In Exercise 21.6, you created a chart model (ChartModel) and two views (PieChart and BarChart). Create a controller that enables the user to modify the data, as shown in Figure 24.54. You will see the changes take effect in the pie chart view and the bar chart view. Your exercise consists of the following classes:

✦ The controller named Exercise24_13ChartController. This class uses a table to display data. You can modify the data in the table. Click the *Insert* button to insert a new row above the selected row in the table, click the *Delete* button to delete the selected row in the table, and click the *Update* button to update the changes you made in the table.

✦ The class MyTableModel. This class extends DefaultTableModel to override the getColumnClass method so that you can use the JTable's default editor for numerical values. This class is same as in Example 24.9, "Using Predefined Table Renderers and Editors."

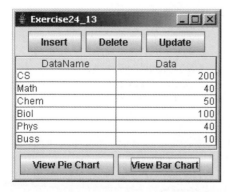
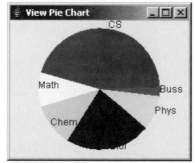
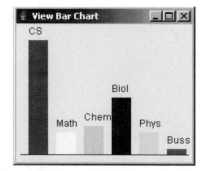

FIGURE 24.54 *You can modify the data in the controller. The views are synchronized with the controller.*

◆ The classes ChartModel, PieChart, and BarChart from Exercise 21.6.

◆ The main class Exercise24_13. This class creates a user interface with a controller and two buttons, *View Pie Chart* and *View Bar Chart*. Click the *View Pie Chart* button to pop up a frame to display a pie chart, and click the *View Bar Chart* button to pop up a frame to display a bar chart.

Section 24.7 JTree

24.14* (*Creating a tree for book chapters*) Create a tree to display the table of contents for a book. When a node is selected in the tree, display a paragraph to describe the selected node, as shown in Figure 24.55.

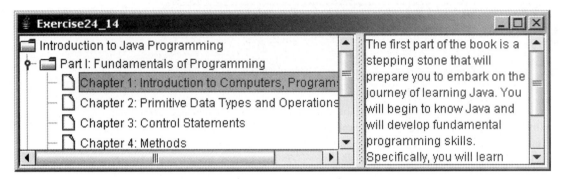

FIGURE 24.55 *The content of the node is displayed in a text area when a node is clicked.*

24.15** (*Adding and deleting tree nodes using the INSERT and DELETE keys*) Modify Example 24.14, "Modifying Trees," to add a new child node by pressing the INSERT key, and delete a node by pressing the DELETE key.

24.16* (*Traversing trees*) Create a tree using the default JTree constructor and traverse the nodes in breadth-first, depth-first, preorder, and postorder.

PART VIII

WEB PROGRAMMING

This part is devoted to the development of Web applications using Java. Chapter 25 introduces the use of Java to develop database projects, and Chapters 26 and 27 introduce how to use Java servlets and JSP to generate dynamic contents from Web servers.

Chapter 25
Java Database Programming

Chapter 26
Servlets

Chapter 27
JavaServer Pages

Prerequisites for Part VIII

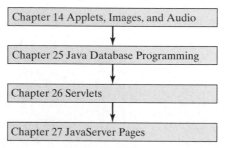

Chapter 14 Applets, Images, and Audio

Chapter 25 Java Database Programming

Chapter 26 Servlets

Chapter 27 JavaServer Pages

JAVA DATABASE PROGRAMMING

Objectives

✦ To understand the concept of database and database management systems (§25.2).

✦ To understand the relational data model: relational data structures, constraints, and languages (§25.2).

✦ To use SQL to create and drop tables, and to retrieve and modify data (§25.3).

✦ To become familiar with the JDBC API (§25.4).

✦ To learn how to load a driver, connect to a database, execute statements, and process result sets using JDBC (§25.4).

✦ To use prepared statements to execute precompiled SQL statements (§25.5).

✦ To handle transactions in the Connection interface (§25.6).

✦ To explore database metadata using the DatabaseMetaData and ResultSetMetaData interfaces (§25.7 Optional).

✦ To execute SQL statements in a batch mode (§25.8 Optional).

✦ To process updateable and scrollable result sets (§25.9 Optional).

✦ To store and retrieve images in JDBC (§25.10 Optional).

25.1   Introduction

You may have heard a lot about database systems. Database systems are everywhere. Your social security information is stored in a database by the government. If you shop online, your purchase information is stored in a database by the company. If you attend a university, your academic information is stored in a database by the university. Database systems not only store data, they also provide means of accessing, updating, manipulating, and analyzing data. Your social security information is updated periodically, and you can register in courses online. Database systems play an important role for society and for commerce.

This chapter introduces database systems, SQL, and how to develop database applications using Java. If you already know SQL, you may skip Sections 25.2 and 25.3.

25.2   Relational Database Systems

database system

A *database system* consists of a database, the software that stores and manages data in the database, and the application programs that present data and enable the user to interact with the database system, as shown in Figure 25.1.

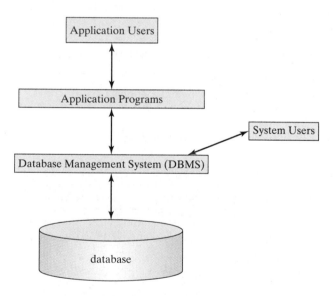

FIGURE 25.1   *A database system consists of data, database management software, and application programs.*

A database is a repository of data that form information. When you purchase a database system from a software vendor, such as MySQL, Oracle, IBM, Microsoft, or Sybase, you actually purchase the software comprising a *database management system* (DBMS) from the vendor. Database management systems are designed for use by professional programmers and are not suitable for ordinary customers. Application programs are built on top of the DBMS for customers to access and update the database. Thus application programs can be viewed as the interfaces between the database system and its users. The application programs may be standalone GUI applications or Web applications, and may access several different database systems in the network, as shown in Figure 25.2.

DBMS

Most of today's database systems are *relational database systems*, based on the relational data model. A relational data model has three key components: structure, integrity, and language. *Structure* defines the representation of the data. *Integrity* imposes constraints on the data. *Language* provides the means for accessing and manipulating data.

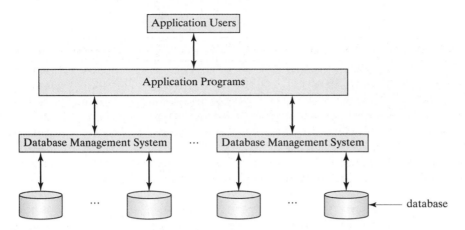

FIGURE 25.2 *An application program may access multiple database systems.*

25.2.1 Relational Structures

The *relational model* is built around a simple and natural structure. A relation is actually a table that consists of non-duplicate rows. Tables are easy to understand and easy to use. The relational model provides a simple yet powerful way to represent data.

relational model

A row of a table represents a record, and a column of a table represents the value of a single attribute of the record. In relational database theory, a row is called a *tuple* and a column is called an *attribute*. Figure 25.3 shows a sample table that stores information about the courses offered by a university. The table has eight tuples, and each tuple has five attributes.

tuple

attribute

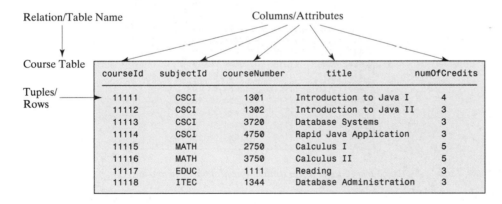

FIGURE 25.3 *A table has a table name, column names, and rows.*

Tables describe the relationship among data. Each row in a table represents a record of related data. For example, "11111", "CSCI", "1301", "Introduction to Java I", and "4" are related to form a record (the first row in Figure 25.3) in the Course table. Just as data in the same row are related, so too data in different tables may be related through common attributes. Suppose the database has two other tables named Student and Enrollment, as shown in Figures 25.4 and 25.5. The Course table and the Enrollment table are related through their common attribute courseId, and the Enrollment table and the Student table are related through ssn.

25.2.2 Integrity Constraints

An *integrity constraint* imposes a condition that all the legal values in a table must satisfy. Figure 25.6 shows an example of some integrity constraints in the Subject and Course tables.

integrity constraint

Student Table

ssn	firstName	mi	lastName	phone	birthDate	street	zipCode	deptID
444111110	Jacob	R	Smith	9129219434	1985-04-09	99 Kingston Street	31435	BIOL
444111111	John	K	Stevenson	9129219434	null	100 Main Street	31411	BIOL
444111112	George	K	Smith	9129213454	1974-10-10	1200 Abercorn St.	31419	CS
444111113	Frank	E	Jones	9125919434	1970-09-09	100 Main Street	31411	BIOL
444111114	Jean	K	Smith	9129219434	1970-02-09	100 Main Street	31411	CHEM
444111115	Josh	R	Woo	7075989434	1970-02-09	555 Franklin St.	31411	CHEM
444111116	Josh	R	Smith	9129219434	1973-02-09	100 Main Street	31411	BIOL
444111117	Joy	P	Kennedy	9129229434	1974-03-19	103 Bay Street	31412	CS
444111118	Toni	R	Peterson	9129229434	1964-04-29	103 Bay Street	31412	MATH
444111119	Patrick	R	Stoneman	9129229434	1969-04-29	101 Washington St.	31435	MATH
444111120	Rick	R	Carter	9125919434	1986-04-09	19 West Ford St.	31411	BIOL

FIGURE 25.4 *A* Student *table stores student information.*

Enrollment Table

ssn	courseId	dateRegistered	grade
444111110	11111	2004-03-19	A
444111110	11112	2004-03-19	B
444111110	11113	2004-03-19	C
444111111	11111	2004-03-19	D
444111111	11112	2004-03-19	F
444111111	11113	2004-03-19	A
444111112	11114	2004-03-19	B
444111112	11115	2004-03-19	C
444111112	11116	2004-03-19	D
444111113	11111	2004-03-19	A
444111113	11113	2004-03-19	A
444111114	11115	2004-03-19	B
444111115	11115	2004-03-19	F
444111115	11116	2004-03-19	F
444111116	11111	2004-03-19	D
444111117	11111	2004-03-19	D
444111118	11111	2004-03-19	A
444111118	11112	2004-03-19	D
444111118	11113	2004-03-19	B

FIGURE 25.5 *An* Enrollment *table stores student enrollment information.*

In general, there are three types of constraints: domain constraints, primary key constraints, and foreign key constraints. *Domain constraints* and *primary key constraints* are known as *intra-relational constraints*, meaning that a constraint involves only one relation. The *foreign key constraint* is *inter-relational*, meaning that a constraint involves more than one relation.

25.2.2.1 Domain Constraints

domain constraint

Domain constraints specify the permissible values for an attribute. Domains can be specified using standard data types, such as integers, floating-point numbers, fixed-length strings, and variant-length strings. The standard data type specifies a broad range of values. Additional constraints can be specified to narrow the ranges. For example, you can specify that the numOfCredits attribute (in the Course table) must be greater than 0 and less than 5. You can also specify whether an attribute can be null, which is a special value in database meaning unknown or not applicable. As shown in the Student table, birthDate may be null.

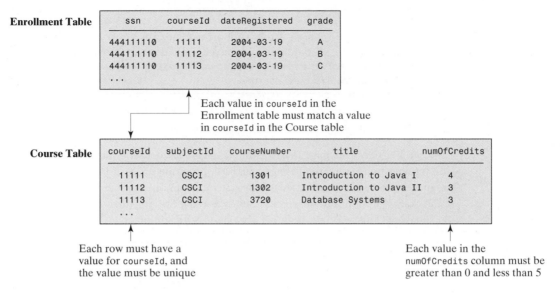

FIGURE 25.6 *The Enrollment table and the Course table have integrity constraints.*

25.2.2.2 Primary Key Constraints

To understand primary keys, it is helpful to know superkeys, keys, and candidate keys. A *superkey* is an attribute or a set of attributes that uniquely identifies the relation. That is, no two tuples have the same values on a superkey. By definition, a relation consists of a set of distinct tuples. The set of all attributes in the relation forms a superkey.

A *key* K is a minimal superkey, meaning that any proper subset of K is not a superkey. A relation can have several keys. In this case, each of the keys is called a *candidate key*. The *primary* key is one of the candidate keys designated by the database designer. The primary key is often used to identify tuples in a relation. As shown in Figure 25.6, courseId is the primary key in the Course table.

25.2.2.3 Foreign Key Constraints

In a relational database, data are related. Tuples in a relation are related, and tuples in different relations are related through their common attributes. Informally speaking, the common attributes are foreign keys. The *foreign key constraints* define the relationships among relations.

Formally, a set of attributes *FK* is a *foreign key* in a relation *R* that references relation *T* if it satisfies the following two rules:

✦ The attributes in *FK* have the same domain as the primary key in *T*.

✦ A non-null value on *FK* in *R* must match a primary key value in *T*.

As shown in Figure 25.6, courseId is the foreign key in Enrollment that references the primary key courseId in Course. Every courseId value must match a courseId value in Course.

25.2.2.4 Enforcing Integrity Constraints

The database management system enforces integrity constraints and rejects operations that would violate them. For example, if you attempt to insert a new record ('11113', '3272', 'Database Systems', 0) into the Course table, it would fail because the credit hours must be greater than or equal to 0; if you attempt to insert a record with the same primary key as an existing record in the table, the DBMS would report an error and reject the operation; if you attempt to delete a record from the Course table whose primary key value is referenced by the records in the Enrollment table, the DBMS would reject this operation.

NOTE

All relational database systems support primary key constraints and foreign key constraints. Not all database systems support domain constraints. For example, you cannot specify the constraint that `numOfCredits` is greater than 0 and less than 5 on the Microsoft Access database.

25.3 SQL

Structured Query Language (SQL) is the language for defining tables and integrity constraints and for accessing and manipulating data. SQL (pronounced "S-Q-L" or "sequel") is the universal language for accessing relational database systems. Application programs may allow users to access a database without directly using SQL, but these applications themselves must use SQL to access the database. This section introduces some basic SQL commands.

 NOTE

There are hundreds of relational database management systems. They share the common SQL language but do not all support every feature of SQL. Some systems have their own extensions to SQL. This section introduces standard SQL supported by all systems.

25.3.1 Creating and Dropping Tables

Tables are the essential objects in a database. To create a table, use the `create table` statement to specify a table name, attributes, and types, as in the following example:

```
create table Course (
  courseId char(5),
  subjectId char(4) not null,
  courseNumber integer,
  title varchar(50) not null,
  numOfCredits integer,
  primary key (courseId)
);
```

This statement creates the `Course` table with attributes `courseId`, `subjectId`, `courseNumber`, `title`, and `numOfCredits`. Each attribute has a data type that specifies the type of data stored in the attribute. `char(5)` specifies that `courseId` consists of five characters. `varchar(50)` specifies that `title` is a variant-length string with a maximum of fifty characters. `integer` specifies that `courseNumber` is an integer. The primary key is `courseId`.

The tables `Student` and `Enrollment` can be created as follows:

```
create table Student (
  ssn char(9),
  firstName varchar(25),
  mi char(1),
  lastName varchar(25),
  birthDate date,
  street varchar(25),
  phone char(11),
  zipCode char(5),
  deptId char(4),
  primary key (ssn)
);

create table Enrollment (
  ssn char(9),
  courseId char(5),
  dateRegistered date,
  grade char(1),
  primary key (ssn, courseId),
```

```
    foreign key (ssn) references Student,
    foreign key (courseId) references Course
);
```

 NOTE

SQL keywords are not case-sensitive. This book adopts the following naming
conventions: Tables are named in the same way as Java classes, and attributes are
named in the same way as Java variables. SQL keywords are named in the same
way as Java keywords.

naming convention

If a table is no longer needed, it can be dropped permanently using the `drop table` command.
For example, the following statement drops the `Course` table:

```
drop table Course;
```

If a table to be dropped is referenced by other tables, you have to drop the other tables first. For
example, if you have created the tables `Course`, `Student`, and `Enrollment` and want to drop
`Course`, you have to first drop `Enrollment`, because `Course` is referenced by `Enrollment`.

25.3.2   Using SQL on a Relational Database

SQL can be used on MySQL, Oracle, Sybase, IBM DB2, IBM Informix, Borland Interbase, MS
Access, or any other relational database system. This chapter uses MySQL to demonstrate SQL
and uses MySQL, Access, and Oracle to demonstrate JDBC programming. The Companion
Website contains the following supplements on how to install and use SQL on three popular
databases, MySQL, Oracle, and Access:

- ✦ Supplement K: Tutorial for MySQL

- ✦ Supplement L: Tutorial for Oracle

- ✦ Supplement M: Tutorial for Microsoft Access

Assume that you have installed MySQL with the default configuration; you can access
MySQL from the DOS command prompt using the command `mysql` from the c:\mysql\bin directory, as shown in Figure 25.7.

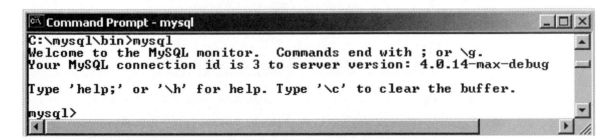

FIGURE 25.7 *You can access a MySQL database server from the command window.*

 NOTE

On Windows, your MySQL database server starts every time your computer starts.
You can stop it by typing the command `net stop mysql` and restart it by typing the
command `net start mysql`.

By default, the server contains two databases named mysql and test. You can see these two
databases displayed in Figure 25.8(a) using the command `show databases`.

FIGURE 25.8 *(a) The* show databases *command displays all available databases in the MySQL database server. (b) The* use test *command selects the test database.*

The mysql database contains the tables that store information about the server and its users. This database is intended for the server administrator to use. For example, the administrator can use it to create users and grant or revoke user privileges. Since you are the owner of the server installed on your system, you have full access to the mysql database. However, you should not create user tables in the mysql database. You can use the test database to store data or create new databases. You can also create a new database using the command create database databasename or drop an existing database using the command drop database databasename.

To select a database for use, type the use databasename command. Since the test database is created by default in every MySQL database, let us use it to demonstrate SQL commands. As shown in Figure 25.8(b), the test database is selected. Enter the statement to create the Course table, as shown in Figure 25.9.

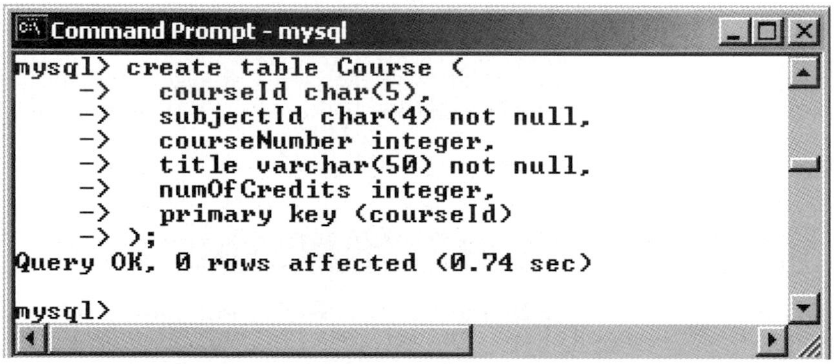

```
mysql> create table Course (
    ->     courseId char(5),
    ->     subjectId char(4) not null,
    ->     courseNumber integer,
    ->     title varchar(50) not null,
    ->     numOfCredits integer,
    ->     primary key (courseId)
    -> );
Query OK, 0 rows affected (0.74 sec)

mysql>
```

FIGURE 25.9 *The execution result of the SQL statements is displayed in the MySQL monitor.*

If you make typing errors, you have to retype the whole command. To avoid retyping the whole command, you can save the command in a file, and then run the command from the file. To do so, create a text file to contain the commands, named, for example, test.sql. You can create the text file using any text editor, such as NotePad, as shown in Figure 25.10. To comment a line, precede it with two dashes. You can now run the script file by typing source test.sql from the MySQL command prompt, as shown in Figure 25.11.

25.3.3 Simple Insert, Update, and Delete

Once a table is created, you can insert data into it. You can also update and delete records. This section introduces simple insert, update, and delete statements.

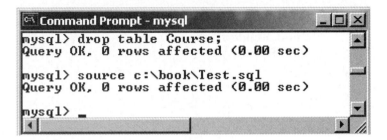

FIGURE 25.10 *You can use Notepad to create a text file for SQL commands.*

```
Command Prompt - mysql
mysql> drop table Course;
Query OK, 0 rows affected (0.00 sec)

mysql> source c:\book\Test.sql
Query OK, 0 rows affected (0.00 sec)

mysql>
```

FIGURE 25.11 *You can run the SQL commands in a script file from MySQL.*

The general syntax to insert a record into a table is:

```
insert into tableName [(column1, column2, …, column]]
values (value1, value2, …, valuen);
```

For example, the following statement inserts a record into the Course table. The new record has the courseId '11113', subjectId 'CSCI', courseNumber 3720, title 'Database Systems', and numOf-Credit 3:

```
insert into Course (courseId, subjectId, courseNumber, title, numOfCredits)
values ('11113', 'CSCI', '3720', 'Database Systems', 3);
```

The column names are optional. If the column names are omitted, all the column values for the record must be entered even though the columns have default values. String values are case-sensitive and enclosed inside single quotation marks in SQL.

The general syntax to update a table is:

```
update tableName
set column1 = newValue1 [, column2 = newValue2, ...]
[where condition];
```

For example, the following statement changes the numOfCredits for the course whose title is Database Systems to 4:

```
update Course
set numOfCredits = 4
where title = 'Database Systems';
```

The general syntax to delete records from a table is:

```
delete [from] tableName
[where condition];
```

For example, the following statement deletes the Database Systems course from the Course table:

```
delete Course
where title = 'Database System';
```

The following statement deletes all the records from the Course table:

```
delete Course;
```

25.3.4   Simple Queries

To retrieve information from tables, use a `select` statement with the following syntax:

```
select column-list
from table-list
[where condition];
```

The `select` clause lists the columns to be selected. The `from` clause refers to the tables involved in the query. The optional `where` clause specifies the conditions for the selected rows.

Query 1: Select all the students in the CS department, as shown in Figure 25.12:

```
select firstName, mi, lastName
from Student
where deptId = 'CS';
```

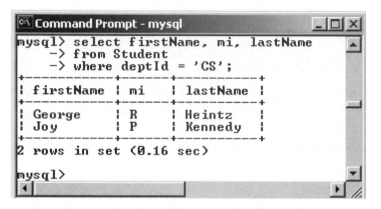

FIGURE 25.12   *The result of the select statement is displayed in a window.*

25.3.5   Comparison and Boolean Operators

SQL has six comparison operators, as shown in Table 25.1, and three Boolean operators, as shown in Table 25.2.

TABLE 25.1   Comparison Operators

Operator	Description
=	Equal to
<> or !=	Not equal to
<	Less than
<=	Less or equal to
>	Greater than
>=	Greater or equal to

TABLE 25.2   Boolean Operators

Operator	Description
not	logical negation
and	logical conjunction
or	logical disjunction

 NOTE

The comparison and Boolean operators in SQL have the same meaning as in Java. In SQL the equals to operator is =, but it is == in Java.

In SQL the not equal to operator is <> or !=, but it is != in Java. The not, and, and or operators are !, && (&), and ¦¦ (¦) in Java.

Query 2: Get the names of the students who are in the CS department and live in the zip code 31411:

```
select firstName, mi, lastName
from Student
where deptId = 'CS' and zipCode = '31411';
```

 NOTE

To select all the attributes from a table, you don't have to list all the attribute names in the select clause. Instead you can just specify an *asterisk* (*), which stands for all the attributes. For example, the following query displays all attributes of the students who are in the CS department and live in the zip code 31411:

```
select *
from Student
where deptId = 'CS' and zipCode = '31411';
```

25.3.6   The `like`, `between-and`, and `is null` Operators

SQL has a `like` operator that can be used for pattern matching. The syntax to check whether a string s has a pattern p is s `like` p or s `not like` p

You can use the wild card characters `%` (percent symbol) and `_` (underline symbol) in the pattern p. `%` matches zero or more characters, and `_` matches any single character in s. For example, `lastName like '_mi%'` matches any string whose second and third letters are m and i. `lastName not like '_mi%'` excludes any string whose second and third letters are m and i.

 NOTE

On the earlier version of MS Access, the wild card character is *, and the character ? matches any single character.

The `between-and` operator checks whether a value v is between two other values, v1 and v2, using the following syntax:

```
v between v1 and v2 or v not between v1 and v2
```

`v between v1 and v2` is equivalent to `v >= v1 and v <= v2`, and `v not between v1 and v2` is equivalent to `v < v1 and v > v2`.

The `is null` operator checks whether a value v is null using the following syntax:

```
v is null or v is not null
```

Query 3: Get the social security numbers of the students whose grades are between 'C' and 'A':

```
select ssn
from Enrollment
where grade between 'C' and 'A';
```

25.3.7   Column Alias

When a query result is displayed, SQL uses the column names as column headings. Usually the user gives abbreviated names for the columns, and the columns cannot have spaces when the table is created. Sometime it is desirable to give more descriptive names in the result heading. You can use the column aliases with the following syntax:

```
select columnName [as] alias
```

Query 4: Get the last name and zip code of the students in the CS department. Display the column headings as Last Name for lastName and Zip Code for zipCode. The query result is shown in Figure 25.13:

```
select lastName as "Last Name", zipCode as "Zip Code"
from Student
where deptId = 'CS';
```

```
Command Prompt - mysql                                    _ □ ×
mysql> select lastName as "Last Name", zipCode as "Zip Code"
    -> from Student
    -> where deptId = 'CS';
+-----------+----------+
| Last Name | Zip Code |
+-----------+----------+
| Heintz    | 31419    |
| Kennedy   | 31412    |
+-----------+----------+
2 rows in set (0.00 sec)

mysql>
```

FIGURE 25.13 *You can use a column alias in the display.*

> **Note**
>
> The as keyword is optional in MySQL and Oracle but is required in MS Access.

25.3.8   The Arithmetic Operators

You can use the arithmetic operators * (multiplication), / (division), + (addition), and - (subtraction) in SQL.

Query 5: Assume that a credit hour is fifty minutes of lectures; get the total minutes for each course with the subject CSCI. The query result is shown in Figure 25.14.

```
select title, 50 * numOfCredits as "Lecture Minutes Per Week"
from Course
where subjectId = 'CSCI';
```

```
Command Prompt - mysql                                              _ □ ×
mysql> select title, 50 * numOfCredits as "Lecture Minutes Per Week"
    -> from Course
    -> where subjectId = 'CSCI';
+-----------------------+--------------------------+
| title                 | Lecture Minutes Per Week |
+-----------------------+--------------------------+
| Intro to Java I       |                      200 |
| Intro to Java II      |                      150 |
| Database Systems      |                      150 |
| Rapid Java Application |                     150 |
+-----------------------+--------------------------+
4 rows in set (0.00 sec)

mysql>
```

FIGURE 25.14 *You can use arithmetic operators in SQL.*

25.3.9   Displaying Distinct Tuples

SQL provides the distinct keyword, which can be used to suppress duplicate tuples in the output. For example, the following statement displays all the subject IDs used by the courses:

```
select subjectId as "Subject ID"
from Course;
```

This statement displays all the subject IDs. To display distinct tuples, add the distinct keyword in the select clause, as follows:

```
select distinct subjectId as "Subject ID"
from Course;
```

When there is more than one item in the select clause, the distinct keyword applies to all the items that find distinct tuples.

25.3.10   Displaying Sorted Tuples

SQL provides the order by clause to sort the output using the following general syntax:

```
select column-list
from table-list
[where condition]
[order by columns-to-be-sorted];
```

In the syntax, columns-to-be-sorted specifies a column or a list of columns to be sorted. By default, the order is ascending. To sort in descending order, append the desc keyword. You could also append the asc keyword, but it is not necessary. When multiple columns are specified, the rows are sorted based on the first column, then the rows with the same values on the second column are sorted based on the second column, and so on.

Query 6: List the full names of the students in the CS department, ordered primarily on their last names in descending order and secondarily on their first names in ascending order. The query result is shown in Figure 25.15.

```
select lastName, firstName, deptId
from Student
where deptId = 'CS'
order by lastName desc, firstName asc;
```

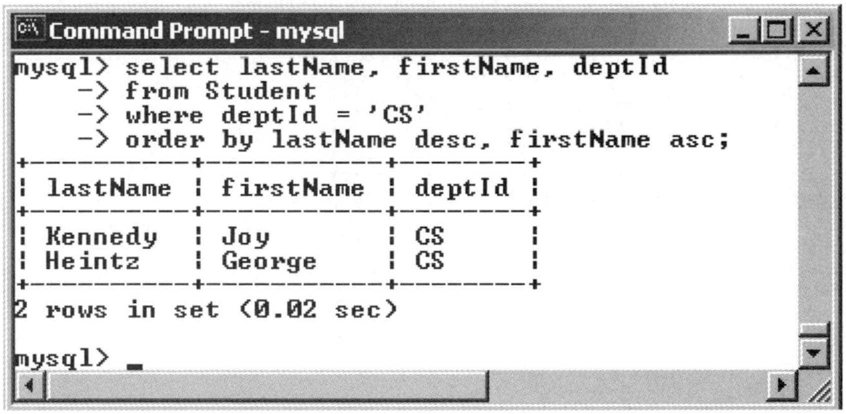

FIGURE 25.15   *You can sort results using the order by clause.*

25.3.11   Joining Tables

Often you need to get information from multiple tables, as demonstrated in the next query.

Query 7: List the courses taken by student Jacob Smith. To solve this query, you need to join tables Student and Enrollment, as shown in Figure 25.16.

You can write the query in SQL:

```
select distinct lastName, firstName, courseId
from Student, Enrollment
where Student.ssn = Enrollment.ssn and
  lastName = 'Smith' and firstName = 'Jacob';
```

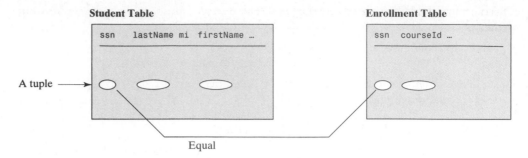

FIGURE 25.16 *Student and Enrollment are joined on ssn.*

The tables Student and Enrollment are listed in the from clause. The query examines every pair of rows, each made of one item from Student and another from Enrollment, and selects the pairs that satisfy the condition in the where clause. The rows in Student have the last name, Smith, and the first name, Jacob, and both rows from Student and Enrollment have the same ssn values. For each pair selected, lastName and firstName from Student and courseId from Enrollment are used to produce the result, as shown in Figure 25.17. Student and Enrollment have the same attribute ssn. To distinguish them in a query, use Student.ssn and Enrollment.ssn.

```
Command Prompt - mysql

mysql> select distinct lastName, firstName, courseId
    -> from Student, Enrollment
    -> where Student.ssn = Enrollment.ssn and
    ->    lastName = 'Smith' and firstName = 'Jacob';
+----------+-----------+----------+
| lastName | firstName | courseId |
+----------+-----------+----------+
| Smith    | Jacob     | 11111    |
| Smith    | Jacob     | 11112    |
| Smith    | Jacob     | 11113    |
+----------+-----------+----------+
3 rows in set (0.06 sec)

mysql>
```

FIGURE 25.17 *Query 7 demonstrates queries involving multiple tables.*

25.4 JDBC

The Java API for developing Java database applications is called *JDBC*. JDBC is the trademarked name of a Java API that supports Java programs that access relational databases. JDBC is not an acronym, but it is often thought to stand for Java Database Connectivity.

JDBC provides Java programmers with a uniform interface for accessing and manipulating a wide range of relational databases. Using the JDBC API, applications written in the Java programming language can execute SQL statements, retrieve results, present data in a user-friendly interface, and propagate changes back to the database. The JDBC API can also be used to interact with multiple data sources in a distributed, heterogeneous environment.

The relationships between Java programs, JDBC API, JDBC drivers, and relational databases are shown in Figure 25.18. The JDBC API is a set of Java interfaces and classes used to write Java

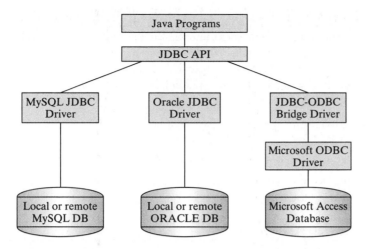

FIGURE 25.18 *Java programs access and manipulate databases through JDBC drivers.*

programs for accessing and manipulating relational databases. Since a JDBC driver serves as the interface to facilitate communications between JDBC and a proprietary database, JDBC drivers are database-specific. You need MySQL JDBC drivers to access the MySQL database, and Oracle JDBC drivers to access the Oracle database. Even with the same vendor, the drivers may be different for different versions of a database. For instance, the JDBC driver for Oracle 9 is different from the one for Oracle 8. A JDBC-ODBC bridge driver is included in JDK to support Java programs that access databases through ODBC drivers. An ODBC driver is preinstalled on Microsoft Windows 98, NT, 2000, and XP. You can use the JDBC-ODBC driver to access Microsoft Access database.

25.4.1 Developing Database Applications Using JDBC

The JDBC API is a Java application program interface to generic SQL databases that enables Java developers to develop DBMS-independent Java applications using a uniform interface.

The JDBC API consists of classes and interfaces for establishing connections with databases, sending SQL statements to databases, processing the results of the SQL statements, and obtaining database metadata. Four key interfaces are needed to develop any database application using Java: `Driver`, `Connection`, `Statement`, and `ResultSet`. These interfaces define a framework for generic SQL database access. The JDBC driver vendors provide implementation for them. The relationship of these interfaces is shown in Figure 25.19. A JDBC application loads an appropriate driver

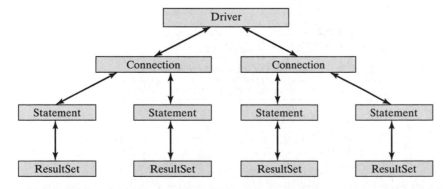

FIGURE 25.19 *JDBC classes enable Java programs to connect to the database, send SQL statements, and process results.*

using the `Driver` interface, connects to the database using the `Connection` interface, creates and executes SQL statements using the `Statement` interface, and processes the result using the `ResultSet` interface if the statements return results. Note that some statements, such as SQL data definition statements and SQL data modification statements, do not return results.

The JDBC interfaces and classes are the building blocks in the development of Java database programs. A typical Java program takes the steps outlined below to access the database.

1. **Loading drivers**. An appropriate driver must be loaded using the statement shown below before connecting to a database:

   ```
   Class.forName("JDBCDriverClass");
   ```

   A driver is a concrete class that implements the `java.sql.Driver` interface. The drivers for Access, MySQL, and Oracle are listed in Table 25.3.

   TABLE 25.3 JDBC Drivers

Database	Driver Class	Source
Access	`sun.jdbc.odbc.JdbcOdbcDriver`	Already in JDK
MySQL	`com.mysql.jdbc.Driver`	Companion Website
Oracle	`oracle.jdbc.driver.OracleDriver`	Companion Website

   The JDBC-ODBC driver for Access is bundled in JDK. The MySQL JDBC driver is contained in mysqljdbc.jar and Oracle JDBC driver is contained in classes12.jar. Both files are in the source code directory on the Companion Website. To use the MySQL and Oracle drivers, you have to add mysqljdbc.jar and classes12.jar in the classpath using the following DOS command in Windows:

   ```
   classpath=%classpath%;c:\book\mysqljdbc.jar;c:\book\classes12.jar
   ```

   If your program accesses several different databases, all their respective drivers must be loaded.

2. **Establishing connections**. To connect to a database, use the static method `getConnection(databaseURL)` in the `DriverManager` class, as follows:

   ```
   Connection connection = DriverManager.getConnection(databaseURL);
   ```

   where `databaseURL` is the unique identifier of the database on the Internet. Table 25.4 lists the URLs for the MySQL, Oracle, and Access databases.

   TABLE 25.4 JDBC URLs

Database	URL Pattern
Access	`jdbc:odbc:dataSource`
MySQL	`jdbc:mysql://hostname/dbname`
Oracle	`jdbc:oracle:thin:@hostname:port#:oracleDBSID`

   For an ODBC data source, the `databaseURL` is `jdbc:odbc:dataSource`. An ODBC data source can be created using the ODBC Data Source Administrator on Windows. See Supplement M, "Tutorial for Microsoft Access," on how to create an ODBC data source for an Access database. Suppose a data source named ExampleMDBDataSource has been created for an Access database. The following statement creates a `Connection` object:

connect Access DB

```
Connection connection = DriverManager.getConnection
  ("jdbc:odbc:ExampleMDBDataSource");
```

The databaseURL for a MySQL database specifies the host name and database name to locate a database. For example, the following statement creates a Connection object for the local MySQL database test:

```
Connection connection = DriverManager.getConnection
  ("jdbc:mysql://localhost/test");
```

connect MySQL DB

Recall that by default MySQL contains two databases named *mysql* and *test*. You can create a custom database using the MySQL SQL command create database *databasename*.

The databaseURL for an Oracle database specifies the *host name*, the *port#* where the database listens for incoming connection requests, and the *oracleDBSID* database name to locate a database. For example, the following statement creates a Connection object for the Oracle database on liang.armstrong.edu with *user name* scott and password tiger:

```
Connection connection = DriverManager.getConnection
  ("jdbc:oracle:thin:@liang.armstrong.edu:1521:ora9i",
   "scott", "tiger");
```

connect Oracle DB

3. **Creating statements**. If a Connection object can be envisioned as a cable linking your program to a database, an object of Statement or its subclass can be viewed as a cart that delivers SQL statements for execution by the database and brings the result back to the program. Once a Connection object is created, you can create statements for executing SQL statements as follows:

```
Statement statement = connection.createStatement();
```

4. **Executing statements**. An SQL DDL or update statement can be executed using executeUpdate(String sql), and an SQL query statement can be executed using executeQuery(String sql). The result of the query is returned in ResultSet. For example, the following code executes the SQL statement create table Temp (col1 char(5), col2 char(5)):

```
statement.executeUpdate
  ("create table Temp (col1 char(5), col2 char(5))");
```

The next code executes the SQL query select firstName, mi, lastName from Student where lastName = 'Smith':

```
// Select the columns from the Student table
ResultSet resultSet = statement.executeQuery
  ("select firstName, mi, lastName from Student where lastName "
   + " = 'Smith'");
```

5. **Processing ResultSet**. The ResultSet maintains a table whose current row can be retrieved. The initial row position is null. You can use the next method to move to the next row and the various get methods to retrieve values from a current row. For example, the code given below displays all the results from the preceding SQL query:

```
// Iterate through the result and print the student names
while (resultSet.next())
  System.out.println(rset.getString(1) + " " + rset.getString(2)
   + ". " + rset.getString(3));
```

The getString(1), getString(2), and getString(3) methods retrieve the column values for firstName, mi, and lastName, respectively. Alternatively, you can use getString. ("firstName"), getString("mi"), and getString("lastName") to retrieve the same three column values. The first execution of the next() method sets the current row to the first row in the result set, and subsequent invocations of the next() method set the current row to the second row, third row, and so on, to the last row.

Listing 25.1 is a complete example that demonstrates connecting to a database, executing a simple query, and processing the query result with JDBC. The program connects to a local MySQL database and displays the students whose last name is Smith.

LISTING 25.1   SimpleJDBC.java

```
 1  import java.sql.*;
 2
 3  public class SimpleJdbc {
 4    public static void main(String[] args)
 5        throws SQLException, ClassNotFoundException {
 6      // Load the JDBC driver
 7      Class.forName("com.mysql.jdbc.Driver");
 8      System.out.println("Driver loaded");
 9
10      // Establish a connection
11      Connection connection = DriverManager.getConnection
12        ("jdbc:mysql://localhost/test");
13      System.out.println("Database connected");
14
15      // Create a statement
16      Statement statement = connection.createStatement();
17
18      // Execute a statement
19      ResultSet resultSet = statement.executeQuery
20        ("select firstName, mi, lastName from Student where lastName "
21        + " = 'Smith'");
22
23      // Iterate through the result and print the student names
24      while (resultSet.next())
25        System.out.println(resultSet.getString(1) + "\t" +
26          resultSet.getString(2) + "\t" + resultSet.getString(3));
27
28      // Close the connection
29      connection.close();
30    }
31  }
```

load driver *(margin note, line 7)*

connect database *(margin note, line 11)*

create statement *(margin note, line 16)*

execute statement *(margin note, line 19)*

get result *(margin note, line 24)*

close connection *(margin note, line 29)*

The statement in Line 7 loads a JDBC driver for MySQL, and the statement in Lines 11–12 connects to a local MySQL database. You may change them to connect to an Access or Oracle database. The last statement (Line 29) closes the connection and releases resource related to the connection.

NOTE

Do not use a semicolon (;) to end the Oracle SQL command in a Java program. The semicolon does not work with the Oracle JDBC drivers. It does work, however, with the other drivers used in the book.

NOTE

The `Connection` interface handles transactions and specifies how they are processed. By default, a new connection is in auto-commit mode, and all its SQL statements are executed and committed as individual transactions. The commit occurs when the statement completes or the next execute occurs, whichever comes first. In the case of statements returning a result set, the statement completes when the last row of the result set has been retrieved or the result set has been closed. If a single statement returns multiple results, the commit occurs when all the results have been retrieved. You can use the `setAutoCommit(false)` method to disable auto-commit, so that all SQL statements are grouped into one transaction that is terminated by a call to either the `commit()` or the `rollback()` method. The `rollback()` method undoes all changes made by the transaction.

EXAMPLE 25.1   ACCESSING A DATABASE FROM A JAVA APPLET

Problem

This example demonstrates connecting to a database from a Java applet. The applet lets the user enter the SSN and the course ID to find a student's grade, as shown in Figure 25.20.

EXAMPLE 25.1 (CONTINUED)

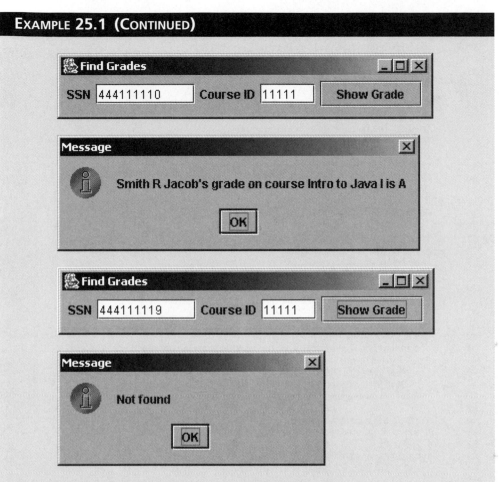

FIGURE 25.20 *A Java applet can access the database on the server.*

Solution

Using the JDBC-ODBC bridge driver, your program cannot run as an applet from a Web browser because the ODBC driver contains non-Java native code. The JDBC drivers for MySQL and Oracle are written in Java and can run from the JVM in a Web browser. The code in Listing 25.2 uses the MySQL database on the host liang.armstrong.edu:

LISTING 25.2   FindGrade.java

```
1 import javax.swing.*;
2 import java.sql.*;
3 import java.awt.*;
4 import java.awt.event.*;
5
6 public class FindGrade extends JApplet {
7   private JTextField jtfSSN = new JTextField(9);
8   private JTextField jtfCourseId = new JTextField(5);
9   private JButton jbtShowGrade = new JButton("Show Grade");
10
11  // Statement for executing queries
12  private Statement stmt;
13
14  /** Initialize the applet */
15  public void init() {
16    // Initialize database connection and create a Statement object
17    initializeDB();
18
```

EXAMPLE 25.1 (CONTINUED)

button listener
```
19      jbtShowGrade.addActionListener(
20        new java.awt.event.ActionListener() {
21        public void actionPerformed(ActionEvent e) {
22          jbtShowGrade_actionPerformed(e);
23        }
24      });
25
26      JPanel jPanel1 = new JPanel();
27      jPanel1.add(new JLabel("SSN"));
28      jPanel1.add(jtfSSN);
29      jPanel1.add(new JLabel("Course ID"));
30      jPanel1.add(jtfCourseId);
31      jPanel1.add(jbtShowGrade);
32
33      this.getContentPane().add(jPanel1, BorderLayout.NORTH);
34    }
35
36    private void initializeDB() {
37      try {
38        // Load the JDBC driver
```
load MySQL driver
Oracle driver commented
```
39        Class.forName("com.mysql.jdbc.Driver");
40 //       Class.forName("oracle.jdbc.driver.OracleDriver");
41        System.out.println("Driver loaded");
42
43        // Establish a connection
```
connect database
```
44        Connection connection = DriverManager.getConnection
45          ("jdbc:mysql://liang.armstrong.edu/test");
```
connect to Oracle
commented
```
46 //       ("jdbc:oracle:thin:@liang.armstrong.edu:1521:ora9i",
47 //        "scott", "tiger");
48        System.out.println("Database connected");
49
50        // Create a statement
```
create statement
```
51        stmt = connection.createStatement();
52      }
53      catch (Exception ex) {
54        ex.printStackTrace();
55      }
56    }
57
58    private void jbtShowGrade_actionPerformed(ActionEvent e) {
59      String ssn = jtfSSN.getText();
60      String courseId = jtfCourseId.getText();
61      try {
62        String queryString = "select firstName, mi, " +
63          "lastName, title, grade from Student, Enrollment, Course " +
64          "where Student.ssn = '" + ssn + "' and Enrollment.courseId "
65          + "= '" + courseId +
66          "' and Enrollment.courseId = Course.courseId " +
67          " and Enrollment.ssn = Student.ssn";
68
```
execute statement
```
69        ResultSet rset = stmt.executeQuery(queryString);
70
```
show result
```
71        if (rset.next()) {
72          String lastName = rset.getString(1);
73          String mi = rset.getString(2);
74          String firstName = rset.getString(3);
75          String title = rset.getString(4);
76          String grade = rset.getString(5);
77
78          // Display result in a dialog box
79          JOptionPane.showMessageDialog(null, firstName + " " + mi +
80            " " + lastName + "'s grade on course " + title + " is " +
81            grade);
82        } else {
83          // Display result in a dialog box
84          JOptionPane.showMessageDialog(null, "Not found");
85        }
86      }
```

EXAMPLE 25.1 (CONTINUED)

```
87      catch (SQLException ex) {
88         ex.printStackTrace();
89      }
90   }
91 }
```

main method omitted

Review

The `initializeDB()` method (Lines 36–56) loads the MySQL driver (Line 39), connects to the MySQL database on host liang.armstrong.edu (Lines 44–45), and creates a statement (Line 51).

You can run the applet standalone from the main method (note that the listing for the main method is omitted for all the applets in the book for brevity) or test the applet using the appletviewer utility, as shown in Figure 25.20. If this applet is deployed on the server where the database is located, any client on the Internet can run it from a Web browser. Since the client may not have a MySQL driver, you should make the driver available along with the applet in one archive file. This archive file can be created as follows:

1. Copy c:\book\mysqljdbc.jar to a new file named FindGrade.zip.

2. Add FindGrade.class into FindGrade.zip using the WinZip utility.

3. Add FindGrade$1.class into FindGrade.zip using the WinZip utility. FindGrade$1.class is for the anonymous inner event adapter class for listening to the button action.

You need to deploy FindGrade.zip and FindGrade.html on the server. FindGrade.html should use the applet tag with a reference to the Zip file, as follows:

```
<applet
   code="FindGrade"
   archive="FindGrade.zip"
   width=380
   height=80
>
</applet>
```

 NOTE
To access the database from an applet, security restrictions make it necessary for the applet to be downloaded from the server where the database is located. Therefore you have to deploy the applet on the server.

25.5 PreparedStatement

Once a connection to a particular database is established, it can be used to send SQL statements from your program to the database. The `Statement` interface is used to execute static SQL statements that contain no parameters. The `PreparedStatement` interface, extending `Statement`, is used to execute a precompiled SQL statement with or without IN parameters. Since the SQL statements are precompiled, they are efficient for repeated executions.

A `PreparedStatement` object is created using the `preparedStatement` method in the `Connection` interface. For example, the following code creates a `PreparedStatement` pstmt on a particular `Connection` connection for an SQL insert statement:

```
Statement pstmt = connection.prepareStatement
   ("insert into Student (firstName, mi, lastName) +
     values (?, ?, ?)");
```

This insert statement has three question marks as placeholders for parameters representing values for firstName, mi, and lastName in a record of the Student table.

As a subinterface of Statement, the PreparedStatement interface inherits all the methods defined in Statement. It also provides the methods for setting parameters in the object of PreparedStatement. These methods are used to set the values for the parameters before executing statements or procedures. In general, the set methods have the following name and signature:

```
setX(int parameterIndex, X value);
```

where X is the type of the parameter, and parameterIndex is the index of the parameter in the statement. The index starts from 1. For example, the method setString(int parameterIndex, String value) sets a String value to the specified parameter.

The following statements pass the parameters "Jack", "A", "Ryan" to the placeholders for first-Name, mi, and lastName in PreparedStatement pstmt:

```
pstmt.setString(1, "Jack");
pstmt.setString(2, "A");
pstmt.setString(3, "Ryan");
```

After setting the parameters, you can execute the prepared statement by invoking executeQuery() for a SELECT statement and executeUpdate() for a DDL or update statement.

The executeQuery() and executeUpdate() methods are similar to the ones defined in the Statement interface except that they have no parameters, because the SQL statements are already specified in the preparedStatement method when the object of PreparedStatement is created.

EXAMPLE 25.2 USING PreparedStatement TO EXECUTE DYNAMIC SQL STATEMENTS

Problem

This example rewrites the preceding example using PreparedStatement.

Solution

Listing 25.3 gives the solution.

LISTING 25.3 FindGradeUsingPreparedStatement.java

```java
1  import javax.swing.*;
2  import java.sql.*;
3  import java.awt.*;
4  import java.awt.event.*;
5
6  public class FindGradeUsingPreparedStatement extends JApplet {
7    boolean isStandalone = false;
8    private JTextField jtfSSN = new JTextField(9);
9    private JTextField jtfCourseId = new JTextField(5);
10   private JButton jbtShowGrade = new JButton("Show Grade");
11
12   // PreparedStatement for executing queries
13   private PreparedStatement pstmt;
14
15   /** Initialize the applet */
16   public void init() {
17     // Initialize database connection and create a Statement object
18     initializeDB();
19
20     jbtShowGrade.addActionListener(
21       new java.awt.event.ActionListener() {
22       public void actionPerformed(ActionEvent e) {
23         jbtShowGrade_actionPerformed(e);
24       }
25     });
```

EXAMPLE 25.2 (CONTINUED)

```
26
27        JPanel jPanel1 = new JPanel();
28        jPanel1.add(new JLabel("SSN"));
29        jPanel1.add(jtfSSN);
30        jPanel1.add(new JLabel("Course ID"));
31        jPanel1.add(jtfCourseId);
32        jPanel1.add(jbtShowGrade);
33
34        this.getContentPane().add(jPanel1, BorderLayout.NORTH);
35      }
36
37      private void initializeDB() {
38        try {
39          // Load the JDBC driver
40          Class.forName("com.mysql.jdbc.Driver");                      load driver
41 //         Class.forName("oracle.jdbc.driver.OracleDriver");
42          System.out.println("Driver loaded");
43
44          // Establish a connection
45          Connection connection = DriverManager.getConnection          connect database
46            ("jdbc:mysql://liang.armstrong.edu/test");
47 //         ("jdbc:oracle:thin:@liang.armstrong.edu:1521:ora9i",
48 //          "scott", "tiger");
49          System.out.println("Database connected");
50
51          String queryString = "select firstName, mi, " +
52            "lastName, title, grade from Student, Enrollment, Course " +
53            "where Student.ssn = ? and Enrollment.courseId = ? " +     placeholder
54            "and Enrollment.courseId = Course.courseId";
55
56          // Create a statement
57          pstmt = connection.prepareStatement(queryString);            prepare statement
58        }
59        catch (Exception ex) {
60          ex.printStackTrace();
61        }
62      }
63
64      private void jbtShowGrade_actionPerformed(ActionEvent e) {
65        String ssn = jtfSSN.getText();
66        String courseId = jtfCourseId.getText();
67        try {
68          pstmt.setString(1, ssn);
69          pstmt.setString(2, courseId);
70          ResultSet rset = pstmt.executeQuery();                       execute statement
71
72          if (rset.next()) {                                           show result
73            String lastName = rset.getString(1);
74            String mi = rset.getString(2);
75            String firstName = rset.getString(3);
76            String title = rset.getString(4);
77            String grade = rset.getString(5);
78
79            // Display result in a dialog box
80            JOptionPane.showMessageDialog(null, firstName + " " + mi +
81              " " + lastName + "'s grade on course " + title + " is " +
82              grade);
83          }
84          else {
85            // Display result in a dialog box
86            JOptionPane.showMessageDialog(null, "Not found");
87          }
88        }
89        catch (SQLException ex) {
90          ex.printStackTrace();
91        }
92      }
93 }                                                                     main method omitted
```

EXAMPLE **25.1** (CONTINUED)

Review

This example does exactly the same thing as Example 25.1, "Accessing a Database from a Java Applet," except that it uses the prepared statement to dynamically set the parameters. The code in this example is almost the same as in the preceding example. The new code is highlighted.

A prepared query string is defined in Lines 51–54 with ssn and course ID as parameters. An SQL prepared statement is obtained in Line 57. Before executing the query, the actual values of ssn and courseId are set to the parameters in Lines 68–69. Line 70 executes the prepared statement.

25.6   Retrieving Metadata

The Connection interface establishes a connection to a database. It is within the context of a connection that SQL statements are executed and results are returned. A connection also provides access to database metadata information that describes database tables, supported SQL grammar, stored procedures, the capabilities of the database, and so on.

JDBC provides the DatabaseMetaData interface for obtaining database-wide information and the ResultSetMetaData interface for obtaining information on the specific ResultSet. To obtain an instance of DatabaseMetaData for a database, use the getMetaData method on a connection object like this:

```
DatabaseMetaData dbMetaData = connection.getMetaData();
```

If your program connects to a local MySQL database, the following statements display the database information, as shown in Figure 25.21:

```
DatabaseMetaData dbMetaData = connection.getMetaData();
System.out.println("database URL: " + dbMetaData.getURL());
System.out.println("database username: " +
  dbMetaData.getUserName());
System.out.println("database product name: " +
  dbMetaData.getDatabaseProductName());
System.out.println("database product version: " +
  dbMetaData.getDatabaseProductVersion());
System.out.println("JDBC driver name: " +
  dbMetaData.getDriverName());
System.out.println("JDBC driver version: " +
  dbMetaData.getDriverVersion());
System.out.println("JDBC driver major version: " +
  dbMetaData.getDriverMajorVersion());
System.out.println("JDBC driver minor version: " +
  dbMetaData.getDriverMinorVersion());
System.out.println("Max number of connections: " +
  dbMetaData.getMaxConnections());
System.out.println("MaxTableNameLength: " +
  dbMetaData.getMaxTableNameLength());
System.out.println("MaxColumnsInTable: " +
  dbMetaData.getMaxColumnsInTable());
```

The ResultSetMetaData interface describes information pertaining to the result set. A ResultSetMetaData object can be used to find out about the types and properties of the columns in a ResultSet. To obtain an instance of ResultSetMetaData, use the getMetaData method on a result set like this:

```
ResultSetMetaData rsMetaData = resultSet.getMetaData();
```

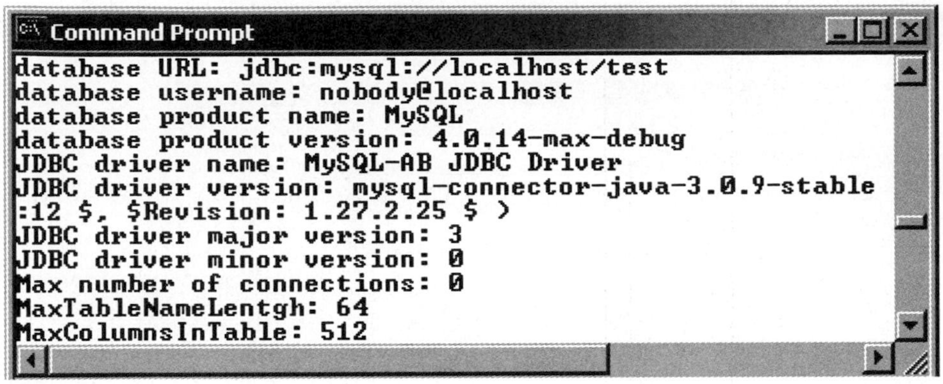

```
database URL: jdbc:mysql://localhost/test
database username: nobody@localhost
database product name: MySQL
database product version: 4.0.14-max-debug
JDBC driver name: MySQL-AB JDBC Driver
JDBC driver version: mysql-connector-java-3.0.9-stable
:12 $, $Revision: 1.27.2.25 $ )
JDBC driver major version: 3
JDBC driver minor version: 0
Max number of connections: 0
MaxTableNameLentgh: 64
MaxColumnsInTable: 512
```

FIGURE 25.21   *The* DatabaseMetaData *interface enables you to obtain database information.*

You can use the getColumnCount() method to find the number of columns in the result and the getColumnName(int) method to get the column names. For example, the following code displays all the column names and contents resulting from the SQL SELECT statement select * from Student:

```
// Execute a statement
ResultSet resultSet = statement.executeQuery
  ("select * from Student");

ResultSetMetaData rsMetaData = resultSet.getMetaData();
for (int i = 1; i <= rsMetaData.getColumnCount(); i++)
  System.out.print(rsMetaData.getColumnName(i) + "\t");
System.out.println();

// Iterate through the result and print the student names
while (resultSet.next()) {
  for (int i = 1; i <= rsMetaData.getColumnCount(); i++)
    System.out.print(resultSet.getString(i) + "\t");
  System.out.println();
}
```

25.7   A Universal SQL Client (Optional)

So far you have used various drivers to connect to the database, created statements for executing SQL statements, and processed the results from SQL queries. This section presents a universal SQL client that enables you to connect to any relational database and execute SQL commands.

EXAMPLE 25.3   CREATING AN INTERACTIVE SQL CLIENT

Problem

This example creates a Java applet for submitting and executing SQL commands interactively, as shown in Figure 25.22. The client can connect to any JDBC data source, and can submit SQL SELECT commands and non-SELECT commands for execution. The execution result is displayed for the SELECT queries, and the execution status is displayed for the non-SELECT commands.

Solution

Listing 25.4 gives the solution to the problem.

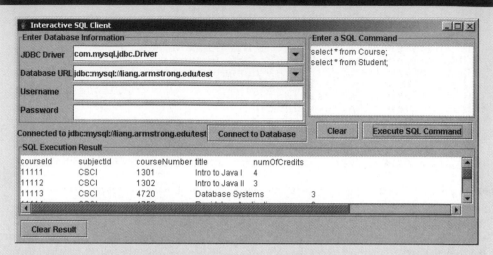

EXAMPLE 25.3 (CONTINUED)

FIGURE **25.22** *You can connect to any JDBC data source and execute SQL commands interactively.*

LISTING **25.4** SQLClient.java

```
 1 import java.awt.*;
 2 import java.awt.event.*;
 3 import javax.swing.*;
 4 import javax.swing.border.*;
 5 import java.sql.*;
 6 import java.util.*;
 7
 8 public class SQLClient extends JApplet {
 9   // Connection to the database
10   private Connection connection;
11
12   // Statement to execute SQL commands
13   private Statement statement;
14
15   // Text area to enter SQL commands
16   private JTextArea jtasqlCommand = new JTextArea();
17
18   // Text area to display results from SQL commands
19   private JTextArea jtaSQLResult = new JTextArea();
20
21   // JDBC info for a database connection
22   JTextField jtfUsername = new JTextField();
23   JPasswordField jpfPassword = new JPasswordField();
24   JComboBox jcboURL = new JComboBox(new String[] {
25     "jdbc:mysql://liang.armstrong.edu/test",
26     "jdbc:odbc:exampleMDBDataSource",
27     "jdbc:oracle:thin:@liang.armstrong.edu:1521:ora9i"});
28   JComboBox jcboDriver = new JComboBox(new String[] {
29     "com.mysql.jdbc.Driver", "sun.jdbc.odbc.JdbcOdbcDriver",
30     "oracle.jdbc.driver.OracleDriver"});
31
32   JButton jbtExecuteSQL = new JButton("Execute SQL Command");
33   JButton jbtClearSQLCommand = new JButton("Clear");
34   JButton jbtConnectDB1 = new JButton("Connect to Database");
35   JButton jbtClearSQLResult = new JButton("Clear Result");
36
37   // Create titled borders
38   Border titledBorder1 = new TitledBorder("Enter an SQL Command");
39   Border titledBorder2 = new TitledBorder("SQL Execution Result");
40   Border titledBorder3 = new TitledBorder(
41     "Enter Database Information");
```

connection

statement

URLs

drivers

EXAMPLE 25.3 (CONTINUED)

```
42
43    JLabel jlblConnectionStatus = new JLabel("No connection now");
44
45    /** Initialize the applet */
46    public void init() {
47      JScrollPane jScrollPane1 = new JScrollPane(jtasqlCommand);
48      jScrollPane1.setBorder(titledBorder1);
49      JScrollPane jScrollPane2 = new JScrollPane(jtaSQLResult);
50      jScrollPane2.setBorder(titledBorder2);
51
52      JPanel jPanel1 = new JPanel(new FlowLayout(FlowLayout.RIGHT));
53      jPanel1.add(jbtClearSQLCommand);
54      jPanel1.add(jbtExecuteSQL);
55
56      JPanel jPanel2 = new JPanel();
57      jPanel2.setLayout(new BorderLayout());
58      jPanel2.add(jScrollPane1, BorderLayout.CENTER);
59      jPanel2.add(jPanel1, BorderLayout.SOUTH);
60
61      JPanel jPanel3 = new JPanel();
62      jPanel3.setLayout(new BorderLayout());
63      jPanel3.add(jlblConnectionStatus, BorderLayout.CENTER);
64      jPanel3.add(jbtConnectDB1, BorderLayout.EAST);
65
66      JPanel jPanel4 = new JPanel();
67      jPanel4.setLayout(new GridLayout(4, 1, 10, 5));
68      jPanel4.add(jcboDriver);
69      jPanel4.add(jcboURL);
70      jPanel4.add(jtfUsername);
71      jPanel4.add(jpfPassword);
72
73      JPanel jPanel5 = new JPanel();
74      jPanel5.setLayout(new GridLayout(4, 1));
75      jPanel5.add(new JLabel("JDBC Driver"));
76      jPanel5.add(new JLabel("Database URL"));
77      jPanel5.add(new JLabel("Username"));
78      jPanel5.add(new JLabel("Password"));
79
80      JPanel jPanel6 = new JPanel();
81      jPanel6.setLayout(new BorderLayout());
82      jPanel6.setBorder(titledBorder3);
83      jPanel6.add(jPanel4, BorderLayout.CENTER);
84      jPanel6.add(jPanel5, BorderLayout.WEST);
85
86      JPanel jPanel7 = new JPanel();
87      jPanel7.setLayout(new BorderLayout());
88      jPanel7.add(jPanel3, BorderLayout.SOUTH);
89      jPanel7.add(jPanel6, BorderLayout.CENTER);
90
91      JPanel jPanel8 = new JPanel();
92      jPanel8.setLayout(new BorderLayout());
93      jPanel8.add(jPanel2, BorderLayout.CENTER);
94      jPanel8.add(jPanel7, BorderLayout.WEST);
95
96      JPanel jPanel9 = new JPanel(new FlowLayout(FlowLayout.LEFT));
97      jPanel9.add(jbtClearSQLResult);
98
99      jcboURL.setEditable(true);
100     jcboDriver.setEditable(true);
101
102     this.getContentPane().add(jPanel8, BorderLayout.NORTH);
103     this.getContentPane().add(jScrollPane2, BorderLayout.CENTER);
104     this.getContentPane().add(jPanel9, BorderLayout.SOUTH);
105
106     jbtExecuteSQL.addActionListener(new ActionListener() {
107       public void actionPerformed(ActionEvent e) {
```

create UI

EXAMPLE 25.3 (CONTINUED)

execute SQL

connect database

clear command

clear result

```
108              executeSQL();
109            }
110          });
111          jbtConnectDB1.addActionListener(new ActionListener() {
112            public void actionPerformed(ActionEvent e) {
113              connectToDB();
114            }
115          });
116          jbtClearSQLCommand.addActionListener(new ActionListener() {
117            public void actionPerformed(ActionEvent e) {
118              jtasqlCommand.setText(null);
119            }
120          });
121          jbtClearSQLResult.addActionListener(new ActionListener() {
122            public void actionPerformed(ActionEvent e) {
123              jtaSQLResult.setText(null);
124            }
125          });
126        }
127
128        /** Connect to DB */
129        private void connectToDB() {
130          // Get database information from the user input
131          String driver = (String)jcboDriver.getSelectedItem();
132          String url = (String)jcboURL.getSelectedItem();
133          String username = jtfUsername.getText().trim();
134          String password = new String(jpfPassword.getPassword());
135
136          // Connection to the database
137          try {
138            Class.forName(driver);
139            connection = DriverManager.getConnection(
140              url, username, password);
141            jlblConnectionStatus.setText("Connected to " + url);
142          }
143          catch (java.lang.Exception ex) {
144            ex.printStackTrace();
145          }
146        }
147
148        /** Execute SQL commands */
149        private void executeSQL() {
150          if (connection == null) {
151            jtaSQLResult.setText("Please connect to a database first");
152            return;
153          }
154          else {
155            String sqlCommands = jtasqlCommand.getText().trim();
156            StringTokenizer commands =
157              new StringTokenizer(sqlCommands.replace('\n', ' '), ";");
158
159            while (commands.hasMoreTokens()) {
160              String aCommand = commands.nextToken().trim();
161
162              if (aCommand.toUpperCase().startsWith("SELECT")) {
163                processSQLSelect(aCommand);
164              }
165              else {
166                processSQLNonSelect(aCommand);
167              }
168            }
169          }
170        }
171
172        /** Execute SQL SELECT commands */
173        private void processSQLSelect(String sqlCommand) {
174          try {
```

load driver
connect database

process select

process nonselect

EXAMPLE 25.3 (CONTINUED)

```
175        // Get a new statement for the current connection
176        statement = connection.createStatement();
177
178        // Execute a SELECT SQL command
179        ResultSet resultSet = statement.executeQuery(sqlCommand);
180
181        // Find the number of columns in the result set
182        int columnCount = resultSet.getMetaData().getColumnCount();
183        String row = "";
184
185        // Display column names
186        for (int i = 1; i <= columnCount; i++) {
187          row += resultSet.getMetaData().getColumnName(i) + "\t";
188        }
189
190        jtaSQLResult.append(row + '\n');
191
192        while (resultSet.next()) {
193          // Reset row to empty
194          row = "";
195
196          for (int i = 1; i <= columnCount; i++) {
197            // A non-String column is converted to a string
198            row += resultSet.getString(i) + "\t";
199          }
200
201          jtaSQLResult.append(row + '\n');
202        }
203      }
204    catch (SQLException ex) {
205        jtaSQLResult.setText(ex.toString());
206      }
207  }
208
209  /** Execute SQL DDL, and modification commands */
210  private void processSQLNonSelect(String sqlCommand) {
211    try {
212      // Get a new statement for the current connection
213      statement = connection.createStatement();
214
215      // Execute a non-SELECT SQL command
216      statement.executeUpdate(sqlCommand);
217
218      jtaSQLResult.setText("SQL command executed");
219    }
220    catch (SQLException ex) {
221      jtaSQLResult.setText(ex.toString());
222    }
223  }
224 }
```

main method omitted

Review

The user selects or enters the JDBC driver, database URL, username, and password, and clicks the *Connect to Database* button to connect to the specified database using the connectToDB() method (Lines 129–146).

When the user clicks the *Execute SQL Command* button, the executeSQL() method is invoked (Lines 149–170) to get the SQL commands from the text area (jtaSQLCommand), and extracts each command separated by a semicolon (;). It then determines whether the command is a SELECT query or a DDL or data modification statement (Lines 162–167). If the command is a SELECT query, the processSQLSelect method is invoked (Lines 173–206). This method uses the executeQuery method (Line 179) to obtain the query result. The result is displayed in the text area (jtaSQLResult). If the command is a non-SELECT

EXAMPLE 25.3 (CONTINUED)

query, the `processSQLNonSelect()` method is invoked (Lines 210–223). This method uses the `executeUpdate` method (Line 216) to execute the SQL command.

The `getMetaData` method (Lines 182, 187) in the `ResultSet` interface is used to obtain an instance of `ResultSetMetaData`. The `getColumnCount` method (Line 182) returns the number of columns in the result set, and the `getColumnName(i)` method (Line 187) returns the column name for the *i*th column.

25.8   Batch Processing (Optional)

In all the preceding examples, SQL commands are submitted to the database for execution one at a time. This is inefficient for processing a large number of updates. For example, suppose you wanted to insert a thousand rows into a table. Submitting one INSERT command at a time would take nearly a thousand times longer than submitting all the INSERT commands in a batch at once. To improve performance, JDBC 2 introduced the batch update for processing nonselect SQL commands. A batch update consists of a sequence of nonselect SQL commands. These commands are collected in a batch and submitted to the database all together.

To use the batch update, you add nonselect commands to a batch using the `addBatch` method in the `Statement` interface. After all the SQL commands are added to the batch, use the `execute-Batch` method to submit the batch to the database for execution.

For example, the following code adds a create table command, two insert statements in a batch, and executes the batch:

```
Statement statement = connection.createStatement();

// Add SQL commands to the batch
statement.addBatch("create table T (C1 integer, C2 varchar(15))");
statement.addBatch("insert into T values (100, 'Smith')");
statement.addBatch("insert into T values (200, 'Jones')");

// Execute the batch
int count[] = statement.executeBatch();
```

The `executeBatch()` method returns an array of counts, each of which counts the number of rows affected by the SQL command. The first count returns 0 because it is a DDL command. The other counts return 1 because only one row is affected.

 NOTE

To find out whether a driver supports batch updates, invoke `supportsBatchUpdates()` on a `DatabaseMetaData` instance. If the driver supports batch updates, it will return true. The JDBC drivers for MySQL, Access, and Oracle all support batch updates.

EXAMPLE 25.4 COPYING TEXT FILES TO TABLES

Problem

In this example, you will write a program that gets data from a text file and copies the data to a table, as shown in Figure 25.23. The text file consists of lines that each correspond to a row in the table. The fields in a row are separated by commas. The string values in a row are enclosed in single quotes. You can view the text file by clicking the View File button and copy the text to the table by clicking the Copy button. The table must already be defined

EXAMPLE 25.4 (CONTINUED)

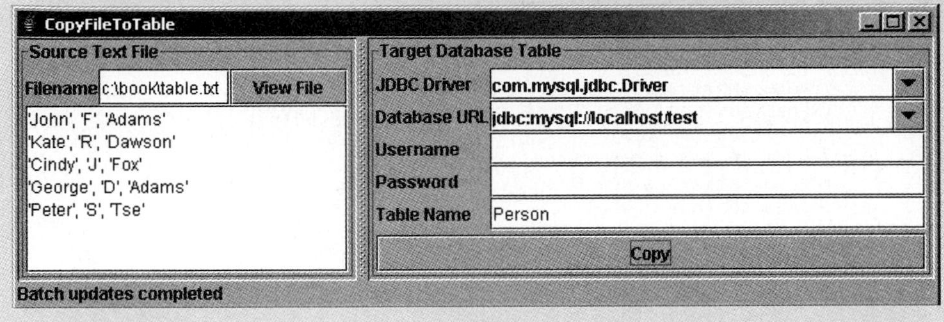

FIGURE 25.23 *The* CopyFileToTable *utility copies text files to database tables.*

in the database. Figure 25.23 shows the text file table.txt copied to table Person. Person is created using the following statement:

```
create table Person (
  firstName varchar(20),
  mi char(1),
  lastName varchar(20)
)
```

Solution

Listing 25.5 gives the solution to the problem.

LISTING 25.5 CopyFileToTable.java

```
 1 import javax.swing.*;
 2 import javax.swing.border.*;
 3 import java.awt.*;
 4 import java.awt.event.*;
 5 import java.io.*;
 6 import java.sql.*;
 7
 8 public class CopyFileToTable extends JFrame {
 9   // Text file info
10   private JTextField jtfFilename = new JTextField();
11   private JTextArea jtaFile = new JTextArea();
12
13   // JDBC and table info
14   private JComboBox jcboDriver = new JComboBox(new String[] {          drivers
15     "com.mysql.jdbc.Driver", "sun.jdbc.odbc.JdbcOdbcDriver",
16     "oracle.jdbc.driver.OracleDriver"});
17   private JComboBox jcboURL = new JComboBox(new String[] {             URLs
18     "jdbc:mysql://localhost/test", "jdbc:odbc:exampleMDBDataSource",
19     "jdbc:oracle:thin:@liang.armstrong.edu:1521:ora9i"});
20   private JTextField jtfUsername = new JTextField();
21   private JPasswordField jtfPassword = new JPasswordField();
22   private JTextField jtfTableName = new JTextField();
23
24   private JButton jbtViewFile = new JButton("View File");
25   private JButton jbtCopy = new JButton("Copy");
26   private JLabel jlblStatus = new JLabel();
27
28   public CopyFileToTable() {                                            create UI
29     JPanel jPane1 = new JPanel();
30     jPane1.setLayout(new BorderLayout());
31     jPane1.add(new JLabel("Filename"), BorderLayout.WEST);
32     jPane1.add(jbtViewFile, BorderLayout.EAST);
33     jPane1.add(jtfFilename, BorderLayout.CENTER);
```

EXAMPLE 25.4 (CONTINUED)

```
34
35       JPanel jPane2 = new JPanel();
36       jPane2.setLayout(new BorderLayout());
37       jPane2.setBorder(new TitledBorder("Source Text File"));
38       jPane2.add(jPane1, BorderLayout.NORTH);
39       jPane2.add(new JScrollPane(jtaFile), BorderLayout.CENTER);
40
41       JPanel jPane3 = new JPanel();
42       jPane3.setLayout(new GridLayout(5, 0));
43       jPane3.add(new JLabel("JDBC Driver"));
44       jPane3.add(new JLabel("Database URL"));
45       jPane3.add(new JLabel("Username"));
46       jPane3.add(new JLabel("Password"));
47       jPane3.add(new JLabel("Table Name"));
48
49       JPanel jPane4 = new JPanel();
50       jPane4.setLayout(new GridLayout(5, 0));
51       jcboDriver.setEditable(true);
52       jPane4.add(jcboDriver);
53       jcboURL.setEditable(true);
54       jPane4.add(jcboURL);
55       jPane4.add(jtfUsername);
56       jPane4.add(jtfPassword);
57       jPane4.add(jtfTableName);
58
59       JPanel jPane5 = new JPanel();
60       jPane5.setLayout(new BorderLayout());
61       jPane5.setBorder(new TitledBorder("Target Database Table"));
62       jPane5.add(jbtCopy, BorderLayout.SOUTH);
63       jPane5.add(jPane3, BorderLayout.WEST);
64       jPane5.add(jPane4, BorderLayout.CENTER);
65
66       getContentPane().add(jlblStatus, BorderLayout.SOUTH);
67       getContentPane().add(new JSplitPane(JSplitPane.HORIZONTAL_SPLIT,
68         jPane2, jPane5), BorderLayout.CENTER);
69
70       jbtViewFile.addActionListener(new ActionListener() {
71         public void actionPerformed(ActionEvent evt) {
72           showFile();
73         }
74       });
75
76       jbtCopy.addActionListener(new ActionListener() {
77         public void actionPerformed(ActionEvent evt) {
78           try {
79             copyFile();
80           }
81           catch (Exception ex) {
82             jlblStatus.setText(ex.toString());
83           }
84         }
85       });
86     }
87
88     /** Display the file in the text area */
89     private void showFile() {
90       // Use a BufferedReader to read text from the file
91       BufferedReader infile = null;
92
93       // Get file name from the text field
94       String filename = jtfFilename.getText().trim();
95
96       String inLine;
97
98       try {
99         // Create a buffered stream
100        infile = new BufferedReader(new FileReader(filename));
```

view file

to table

EXAMPLE 25.4 (CONTINUED)

```
101
102      // Read a line and append the line to the text area
103      while ((inLine = infile.readLine()) != null) {
104        jtaFile.append(inLine + '\n');
105      }
106    }
107    catch (FileNotFoundException ex) {
108      System.out.println("File not found: " + filename);
109    }
110    catch (IOException ex) {
111      System.out.println(ex.getMessage());
112    }
113    finally {
114      try {
115        if (infile != null) infile.close();
116      }
117      catch (IOException ex) {
118        System.out.println(ex.getMessage());
119      }
120    }
121  }
122
123  private void copyFile() throws Exception {
124    // Load the JDBC driver
125    System.out.println((String)jcboDriver.getSelectedItem());
126    Class.forName(((String)jcboDriver.getSelectedItem()).trim());      load driver
127    System.out.println("Driver loaded");
128
129    // Establish a connection
130    Connection conn = DriverManager.getConnection              connect database
131      (((String)jcboURL.getSelectedItem()).trim(),
132      jtfUsername.getText().trim(),
133      String.valueOf(jtfPassword.getPassword()).trim());
134    System.out.println("Database connected");
135
136    // Read each line from the text file and insert it to the table
137    insertRows(conn);                                            insert row
138  }
139
140  private void insertRows(Connection connection) {
141    // Build the INSERT statement
142    String sqlInsert = "insert into " + jtfTableName.getText()
143      + " values (";
144
145    // Use a BufferedReader to read text from the file
146    BufferedReader infile = null;
147
148    // Get file name from the text field
149    String filename = jtfFilename.getText().trim();
150
151    String inLine;
152
153    try {
154      // Create a buffered stream
155      infile = new BufferedReader(new FileReader(filename));
156
157      // Create a statement
158      Statement statement = connection.createStatement();        statement
159
160      System.out.println("Driver major version? " +
161      connection.getMetaData().getDriverMajorVersion());
162
163      // Determine if the supportsBatchUpdates method supported in
164      // DatabaseMetaData
165      boolean batchUpdatesSupported = false;
166
```

EXAMPLE 25.4 (CONTINUED)

```
167        try {
168          if (connection.getMetaData().supportsBatchUpdates()) {
169            batchUpdatesSupported = true;
170            System.out.println("batch updates supported");
171          }
172          else {
173            System.out.println("The driver is of JDBC 2 type, but " +
174            "does not support batch updates");
175          }
176        }
177        catch (UnsupportedOperationException ex) {
178          System.out.println("The driver does not support JDBC 2");
179        }
180
181        // Determine if the driver is capable of batch updates
182        if (batchUpdatesSupported) {
183          // Read a line and add the insert table command to the batch
184          while ((inLine = infile.readLine()) != null) {
185            statement.addBatch(sqlInsert + inLine + ")");
186          }
187
188          statement.executeBatch();
189
190          jlblStatus.setText("Batch updates completed");
191        }
192        else {
193          // Read a line and execute insert table command
194          while ((inLine = infile.readLine()) != null) {
195            statement.executeUpdate(sqlInsert + inLine + ")");
196          }
197
198          jlblStatus.setText("Single row update completed");
199        }
200      }
201      catch (SQLException ex) {
202        System.out.println(ex);
203      }
204      catch (FileNotFoundException ex) {
205        System.out.println("File not found: " + filename);
206      }
207      catch (IOException ex) {
208        System.out.println(ex.getMessage());
209      }
210      finally {
211        try {
212          if (infile != null) infile.close();
213        }
214        catch (IOException ex) {
215          System.out.println(ex.getMessage());
216        }
217      }
218    }
219 }
```

batch (margin note at line 185)

execute batch (margin note at line 188)

main method omitted (margin note at line 219)

Review

The `insertRows` method (Lines 140–218) uses the batch updates to submit SQL INSERT commands to the database for execution, if the driver supports batch updates. Lines 168–175 check whether the driver supports batch updates. If the driver is not JDBC 2 compatible, an `UnsupportedOperationException` exception will be thrown (Line 177) when the `supportsBatchUpdates()` method is invoked.

The tables must already be created in the database. The file format and contents must match the database table specification. Otherwise, the SQL INSERT command will fail.

In Exercise 25.4, you will write a program to insert a thousand records to a database and compare the performance with and without batch updates.

25.9 Scrollable and Updatable Result Set (Optional)

The result sets used in the preceding examples are read sequentially. A result set maintains a cursor pointing to its current row of data. Initially the cursor is positioned before the first row. The next() method moves the cursor forward to the next row. This is known as *sequential forward reading*. It is the only way of processing the rows in a result set that is supported by JDBC 1.

With JDBC 2, you can scroll the rows both forward and backward and move the cursor to a desired location using the first, last, next, previous, absolute, or relative method. Additionally, you can insert, delete, or update a row in the result set and have the changes automatically reflected in the database.

To obtain a scrollable or updateable result set, you must first create a statement with an appropriate type and concurrency mode. For a static statement, use

```
Statement statement = connection.createStatement
  (int resultSetType, int resultSetConcurrency);
```

For a prepared statement, use

```
PreparedStatement statement = connection.prepareStatement
  (String sql, int resultSetType, int resultSetConcurrency);
```

The possible values of resultSetType are the constants defined in the ResultSet:

✦ TYPE_FORWARD_ONLY: The result set is accessed forward sequentially.

✦ TYPE_SCROLL_INSENSITIVE: The result set is scrollable, but not sensitive to changes in the database.

✦ TYPE_SCROLL_SENSITIVE: The result set is scrollable and sensitive to changes made by others. Use this type if you want the result set to be scrollable and updateable.

The possible values of resultSetConcurrency are the constants defined in the ResultSet:

✦ CONCUR_READ_ONLY: The result set cannot be used to update the database.

✦ CONCUR_UPDATABLE: The result set can be used to update the database.

For example, if you want the result set to be scrollable and updateable, you can create a static statement:

```
Statement statement = connection.createStatement
  (ResultSet.TYPE_SCROLL_SENSITIVE, ResultSet.CONCUR_UPDATABLE)
```

You use the executeQuery method in a Statement object to execute an SQL query that returns a result set as follows:

```
ResultSet resultSet = statement.executeQuery(query);
```

The methods first(), next(), previous(), and last() are used to move the cursor to the first row, next row, previous row, and last row; the absolute(int row) method moves the cursor to the specified row; and the getXxx(int columnIndex) or getXxx(String columnName) method is used to retrieve the value of a specified field at the current row. The methods insertRow(), deleteRow(), and updateRow() can also be used to insert, delete, and update the current row. Before applying insertRow or updateRow, you need to use the method update(int columnIndex, Xxx value) or update(String columnName, Xxx value) to write a new value to the field at the current row. The cancelRowUpdates() method cancels the updates made to a row. The close() method closes the result set and releases its resource. The boolean wasNull() method indicates whether the last column read had a value of SQL NULL.

EXAMPLE 25.5 SCROLLING AND UPDATING TABLES

Problem

In this example, you will develop a useful utility that displays all the rows of a database table in a JTable and uses a scrollable and updateable result set to navigate the table and modify its contents.

As shown in Figure 25.24, you enter or select a JDBC driver and database, enter a username and a password, and specify a table name to connect the database and display the table contents in the JTable. You can then use the buttons First, Next, Prior, and Last to move the cursor to the first row, next row, previous row, and last row in the table, and use the buttons Insert, Delete, and Update to modify the table contents. When you click the Insert button, a dialog box is displayed to receive input, as shown in Figure 25.25.

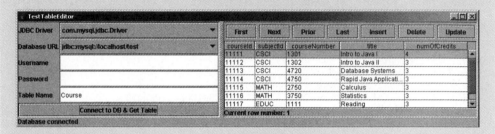

FIGURE 25.24 *The program enables you to navigate and modify the table.*

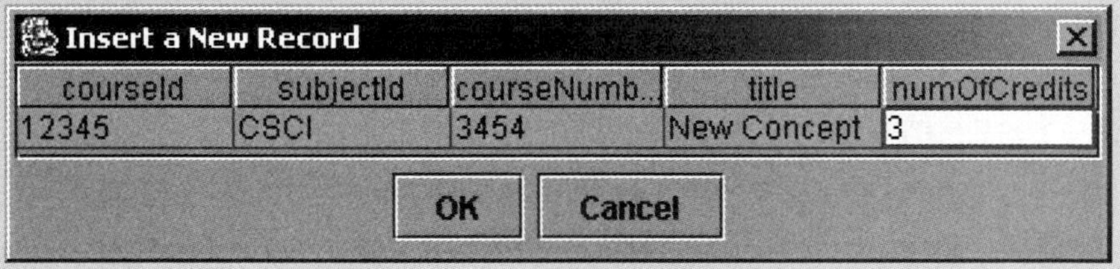

FIGURE 25.25 *The Insert a New Record dialog box lets the user enter a new record.*

The status bar at the bottom of the window shows the current row in the result set and the JTable. The cursor in the result set and the row in the JTable are synchronized. You can move the cursor by using the navigation buttons or by selecting a row in the JTable.

Solution

Create three classes: TestTableEditor (Listing 25.6), TableEditor (Listing 25.7), and NewRecordDialog (Listing 25.8). TestTableEditor is the main class that enables the user to enter the database connection information and a table name. Once the database is connected, the table contents are displayed in an instance of TableEditor. The TableEditor class can be used to browse a table and modify a table. An instance of NewRecordDialog is displayed to let you enter a new record when you click the Insert button in TableEditor.

LISTING 25.6 TestTableEditor.java

```
1 import javax.swing.*;
2 import java.awt.*;
3 import java.awt.event.*;
4 import java.sql.*;
5
```

EXAMPLE 25.5 (CONTINUED)

```
 6 public class TestTableEditor extends JApplet {                          drivers
 7   private JComboBox jcboDriver = new JComboBox(new String[] {
 8     "com.mysql.jdbc.Driver", "oracle.jdbc.driver.OracleDriver",
 9     "sun.jdbc.odbc.JdbcOdbcDriver"});
10   private JComboBox jcboURL = new JComboBox(new String[] {             URLs
11     "jdbc:mysql://localhost/test", "jdbc:odbc:exampleMDBDataSource",
12     "jdbc:oracle:thin:@liang.armstrong.edu:1521:ora9i"});
13
14   private JButton jbtConnect =
15     new JButton("Connect to DB & Get Table");
16   private JTextField jtfUserName = new JTextField();
17   private JPasswordField jpfPassword = new JPasswordField();
18   private JTextField jtfTableName = new JTextField();
19   private TableEditor tableEditor1 = new TableEditor();
20   private JLabel jlblStatus = new JLabel();
21
22   /** Creates new form TestTableEditor */
23   public TestTableEditor() {
24     JPanel jPane1 = new JPanel();                                      create UI
25     jPane1.setLayout(new GridLayout(5, 0));
26     jPane1.add(jcboDriver);
27     jPane1.add(jcboURL);
28     jPane1.add(jtfUserName);
29     jPane1.add(jpfPassword);
30     jPane1.add(jtfTableName);
31
32     JPanel jPanel2 = new JPanel();
33     jPanel2.setLayout(new GridLayout(5, 0));
34     jPanel2.add(new JLabel("JDBC Driver"));
35     jPanel2.add(new JLabel("Database URL"));
36     jPanel2.add(new JLabel("Username"));
37     jPanel2.add(new JLabel("Password"));
38     jPanel2.add(new JLabel("Table Name"));
39
40     JPanel jPane3 = new JPanel();
41     jPane3.setLayout(new BorderLayout());
42     jPane3.add(jbtConnect, BorderLayout.SOUTH);
43     jPane3.add(jPanel2, BorderLayout.WEST);
44     jPane3.add(jPane1, BorderLayout.CENTER);
45     tableEditor1.setPreferredSize(new Dimension(400, 200));
46
47     getContentPane().add(new JSplitPane(JSplitPane.HORIZONTAL_SPLIT,
48       jPane3, tableEditor1), BorderLayout.CENTER);
49     getContentPane().add(jlblStatus, BorderLayout.SOUTH);
50
51     jbtConnect.addActionListener(new ActionListener() {                connect database
52       public void actionPerformed(ActionEvent evt) {
53         try {
54           // Connect to the database
55           Connection connection = getConnection();
56           tableEditor1.setConnectionAndTable(connection,
57             jtfTableName.getText().trim());
58         }
59         catch (Exception ex) {
60           jlblStatus.setText(ex.toString());
61         }
62       }
63     });
64   }
65
66   /** Connect to a database */
67   private Connection getConnection() throws Exception {
68     // Load the JDBC driver
69     System.out.println((String)jcboDriver.getSelectedItem());
70     Class.forName(((String)jcboDriver.getSelectedItem()).trim());    load driver
71     System.out.println("Driver loaded");
72
```

EXAMPLE 25.5 (CONTINUED)

```
73       // Establish a connection
74       Connection connection = DriverManager.getConnection
75         (((String)jcboURL.getSelectedItem()).trim(),
76           jtfUserName.getText().trim(), (jpfPassword.getPassword()));
77       jlblStatus.setText("Database connected");
78
79       return connection;
80     }
81 }
```

main method omitted

LISTING 25.7 TableEditor.java

```
1 import java.util.*;
2 import java.sql.*;
3 import javax.swing.table.*;
4 import javax.swing.event.*;
5 import javax.swing.*;
6 import java.awt.*;
7 import java.awt.event.*;
8
9 public class TableEditor extends JPanel {
10   // Dialog box for inserting a new record
11   private NewRecordDialog newRecordDialog = new NewRecordDialog();
12
13   // JDBC Connection
14   private Connection connection;
15
16   // Table name
17   private String tableName;
18
19   // JDBC Statement
20   private Statement statement;
21
22   // Result set for the table
23   private ResultSet resultSet;
24
25   // Table model
26   private DefaultTableModel tableModel = new DefaultTableModel();
27
28   // Table selection model
29   private DefaultListSelectionModel listSelectionModel =
30     new DefaultListSelectionModel();
31
32   // New row vector
33   private Vector rowVectors = new Vector();
34
35   // columnHeaderVector to hold column names
36   private Vector columnHeaderVector = new Vector();
37
38   // Column count
39   private int columnCount;
40
41   private JButton jbtFirst = new JButton("First");
42   private JButton jbtNext = new JButton("Next");
43   private JButton jbtPrior = new JButton("Prior");
44   private JButton jbtLast = new JButton("Last");
45   private JButton jbtInsert = new JButton("Insert");
46   private JButton jbtDelete = new JButton("Delete");
47   private JButton jbtUpdate = new JButton("Update");
48
49   private JLabel jlblStatus = new JLabel();
50   private JTable jTable1 = new JTable();
51
52   /** Creates new form TableEditor */
53   public TableEditor() {
54     jTable1.setModel(tableModel);
55     jTable1.setSelectionModel(listSelectionModel);
56
```

connect database (line 74)

table model (line 26)

row data (line 33)

column names (line 36)

column count (line 39)

buttons (line 41)

table model / *selection model* (lines 54–55)

EXAMPLE 25.5 (CONTINUED)

```
57        JPanel jPanel1 = new JPanel();
58        setLayout(new BorderLayout());
59        jPanel1.add(jbtFirst);
60        jPanel1.add(jbtNext);
61        jPanel1.add(jbtPrior);
62        jPanel1.add(jbtLast);
63        jPanel1.add(jbtInsert);
64        jPanel1.add(jbtDelete);
65        jPanel1.add(jbtUpdate);
66
67        add(jPanel1, BorderLayout.NORTH);
68        add(new JScrollPane(jTable1), BorderLayout.CENTER);
69        add(jlblStatus, BorderLayout.SOUTH);
70
71        jbtFirst.addActionListener(new ActionListener() {              button listeners
72          public void actionPerformed(ActionEvent evt) {
73            moveCursor("first");
74          }
75        });
76        jbtNext.addActionListener(new ActionListener() {
77          public void actionPerformed(ActionEvent evt) {
78            moveCursor("next");
79          }
80        });
81        jbtPrior.addActionListener(new ActionListener() {
82          public void actionPerformed(ActionEvent evt) {
83            moveCursor("previous");
84          }
85        });
86        jbtLast.addActionListener(new ActionListener() {
87          public void actionPerformed(ActionEvent evt) {
88            moveCursor("last");
89          }
90        });
91        jbtInsert.addActionListener(new ActionListener() {
92          public void actionPerformed(ActionEvent evt) {
93            insert();
94          }
95        });
96        jbtDelete.addActionListener(new ActionListener() {
97          public void actionPerformed(ActionEvent evt) {
98            delete();
99          }
100       });
101       jbtUpdate.addActionListener(new ActionListener() {
102         public void actionPerformed(ActionEvent evt) {
103           update();
104         }
105       });
106       listSelectionModel.addListSelectionListener(
107         new ListSelectionListener() {
108           public void valueChanged(ListSelectionEvent e) {
109             listSelectionModel_valueChanged(e);
110           }
111         });
112     }
113
114   private void delete() {
115     try {
116       // Delete the record from the database
117       resultSet.deleteRow();                                          db row
118       refreshResultSet();
119
120       // Remove the row in the table
121       tableModel.removeRow(                                            JTable row
122         listSelectionModel.getLeadSelectionIndex());
123     }
124     catch (Exception ex) {
```

EXAMPLE 25.5 (CONTINUED)

```
125            jlblStatus.setText(ex.toString());
126          }
127        }
128
129        private void insert() {
130          // Display the dialog box
131          newRecordDialog.displayTable(columnHeaderVector);
132          Vector newRecord = newRecordDialog.getNewRecord();
133
134          if (newRecord == null) return;
135
136          // Insert the record to the Swing table
137          tableModel.addRow(newRecord);
138
139          // Insert the record to the database table
140          try {
141            for (int i = 1; i <= columnCount; i++) {
142              resultSet.updateObject(i, newRecord.elementAt(i - 1));
143            }
144
145            resultSet.insertRow();
146            refreshResultSet();
147          }
148          catch (Exception ex) {
149            jlblStatus.setText(ex.toString());
150          }
151        }
152
153        /** Set cursor in the table and set the row number in the status */
154        private void setTableCursor() throws Exception {
155          int row = resultSet.getRow();
156          listSelectionModel.setSelectionInterval(row - 1, row - 1);
157          jlblStatus.setText("Current row number: " + row);
158        }
159
160        private void update() {
161          try {
162            // Get the current row
163            int row = jTable1.getSelectedRow();
164
165            // Gather data from the UI and update the database fields
166            for (int i = 1;
167              i <= resultSet.getMetaData().getColumnCount(); i++) {
168              resultSet.updateObject(i, tableModel.getValueAt(row, i - 1));
169            }
170
171            // Invoke the update method in the result set
172            resultSet.updateRow();
173            refreshResultSet();
174          }
175          catch (Exception ex) {
176            jlblStatus.setText(ex.toString());
177          }
178        }
179
180        /** Move cursor to the next record */
181        private void moveCursor(String whereToMove) {
182          try {
183            if (whereToMove.equals("first"))
184              resultSet.first();
185            else if (whereToMove.equals("next"))
186              resultSet.next();
187            else if (whereToMove.equals("previous"))
188              resultSet.previous();
189            else if (whereToMove.equals("last"))
190              resultSet.last();
191            setTableCursor();
192          }
```

new row — JTable row — db row — db row / JTable row — JTable row — db row

EXAMPLE 25.5 (CONTINUED)

```
193      catch (Exception ex) {
194        jlblStatus.setText(ex.toString());
195      }
196    }
197
198    /** Refresh the result set */
199    private void refreshResultSet() {
200      try {
201        resultSet = statement.executeQuery(
202          "SELECT * FROM " + tableName);
203        // Set the cursor to the first record in the table
204        moveCursor("first");
205      }
206      catch (SQLException ex) {
207        ex.printStackTrace();
208      }
209    }
210
211    /** Set database connection and table name in the TableEditor */
212    public void setConnectionAndTable(Connection newConnection,
213        String newTableName) {
214      connection = newConnection;
215      tableName = newTableName;
216      try {
217        statement = connection.createStatement(ResultSet.
218          TYPE_SCROLL_SENSITIVE, ResultSet.CONCUR_UPDATABLE);
219        showTable();
220        moveCursor("first");
221      }
222      catch (SQLException ex) {
223        ex.printStackTrace();
224      }
225    }
226
227    /** Display database table to a Swing table */
228    private void showTable() throws SQLException {
229      // Clear vectors to store data for a new table
230      rowVectors.clear();
231      columnHeaderVector.clear();
232
233      // Obtain table contents
234      resultSet = statement.executeQuery(
235        "select * from " + tableName + ";");
236
237      // Get column count
238      columnCount = resultSet.getMetaData().getColumnCount();
239
240      // Store rows to rowVectors
241      while (resultSet.next()) {
242        Vector singleRow = new Vector();
243        for (int i = 0; i < columnCount; i++)
244          // Store cells to a row
245          singleRow.addElement(resultSet.getObject(i + 1));
246        rowVectors.addElement(singleRow);
247      }
248
249      // Get column name and add to columnHeaderVector
250      ResultSet rsColumns = connection.getMetaData().getColumns(
251        null, null, tableName, null);
252      while (rsColumns.next()) {
253        columnHeaderVector.addElement(
254          rsColumns.getString("COLUMN_NAME"));
255      }
256
257      // Set new data to the table model
258      tableModel.setDataVector(rowVectors, columnHeaderVector);
259    }
260
```

db to JTable

EXAMPLE 25.5 (CONTINUED)

```
261    /** Handle the selection in the table */
262    void listSelectionModel_valueChanged(ListSelectionEvent e) {
263      int selectedRow = jTable1.getSelectedRow();
264
265      try {
266        resultSet.absolute(selectedRow + 1);
267        setTableCursor();
268      }
269      catch (Exception ex) {
270        jlblStatus.setText(ex.toString());
271      }
272    }
273 }
```

LISTING 25.8   NewRecordDialog.java

```
 1 import java.util.*;
 2 import java.awt.*;
 3 import java.awt.event.*;
 4 import javax.swing.*;
 5 import javax.swing.table.*;
 6
 7 public class NewRecordDialog extends JDialog {
 8   private JButton jbtOK = new JButton("OK");
 9   private JButton jbtCancel = new JButton("Cancel");
10
11   private DefaultTableModel tableModel = new DefaultTableModel();
12   private JTable jTable1 = new JTable(tableModel);
13   private Vector newRecord;
14
15   /** Creates new form NewRecordDialog */
16   public NewRecordDialog(Frame parent, boolean modal) {
17     super(parent, modal);
18     setTitle("Insert a New Record");
19     setModal(true);
20
21     JPanel jPanel1 = new JPanel();
22     jPanel1.add(jbtOK);
23     jPanel1.add(jbtCancel);
24
25     jbtOK.addActionListener(new ActionListener() {
26       public void actionPerformed(ActionEvent evt) {
27         setVisible(false);
28       }
29     });
30     jbtCancel.addActionListener(new ActionListener() {
31       public void actionPerformed(ActionEvent evt) {
32         newRecord = null;
33         setVisible(false);
34       }
35     });
36
37     getContentPane().add(jPanel1, BorderLayout.SOUTH);
38     getContentPane().add(new JScrollPane(jTable1), BorderLayout.CENTER);
39   }
40
41   public NewRecordDialog() {
42     this(null, true);
43   }
44
45   public Vector getNewRecord() {
46     return newRecord;
47   }
48
49   /** Display the table */
50   void displayTable(Vector columnHeaderVector) {
51     this.setSize(new Dimension(400, 100));
```

table model
table
row

EXAMPLE 25.5 (CONTINUED)

```
52
53      tableModel.setColumnIdentifiers(columnHeaderVector);
54
55      // Must create a new vector for a new record
56      tableModel.addRow(newRecord = new Vector());                      one row
57      setVisible(true);
58   }
59 }
```

Review

The key class in this example is `TableEditor`, which can be used to navigate and modify the table contents. To use it, simply create an instance of `TableEditor` (Line 19 in TestTableEditor.java), set the database connection and the table name in the instance, and place it in a graphical user interface. The `setConnectionAndTableName` method (Lines 56–57 in TestTableEditor.java) involves creating a statement, obtaining a result set, and displaying the result set in the Swing table. The statement is created with the arguments `TYPE_SCROLL_SENSITIVE` and `CONCUR_UPDATABLE` for obtaining scrollable and updateable result sets (Lines 217–218 in TableEditor.java).

The `showTable()` method (Lines 228–256 in TableEditor.java) is responsible for transferring data from the database table to the Swing table. The column names and column count are obtained using the `ResultSetMetaData` interface. An instance of the `ResultSetMetaData` interface is obtained using the `getMetaData` method for the result set. Each record from the result set is copied to a row vector. The row vector is added to another vector that stores all the rows for the table model (`tableModel`) for the `JTable`.

The handling of the navigation buttons First, Next, Prior, and Last is simply to invoke the methods `first()`, `next()`, `previous()`, and `last()` to move the cursor in the result set and, at the same time, set the selected row in the Swing table.

The handling of the Insert button involves displaying the "Insert a New Record" dialog box (`newRecordDialog1`) for receiving the new record. Once the record is entered, clicking the OK button dismisses the dialog box. The new record is obtained by invoking the `newRecordDialog1.getNewRecord()` method. To insert the new record into the database, use the `updateObject` method (Line 142 in TableEditor.java) to update the fields, and then use the `insertRow` method to insert the record to the database table. Finally, you need to refresh the result set by re-executing the query. Theoretically, you should not have to refresh the result set (Line 146 in TableEditor.java). The driver should automatically reflect the changes in the database to the result set. However, none of the drivers I have tested supports this. So it is safe to refresh the result set.

To implement the Delete button, invoke the `deleteRow()` method (Line 117 in TableEditor.java) in the result set to remove the record from the database, and use the `removeRow` method in `TableModel` to remove a row from `JTable`.

To implement the Update button, invoke the `updateObject` method (Line 168 in TableEditor.java) in the result set, and then invoke the `updateRow` method (Line 172 in TableEditor.java) to update the result set.

To implement the handler for list-selection events on `jTable1`, set the cursor in the result set to match the row selected in `jTable1`.

 NOTE

The `TableEditor` class in this example uses only the `updateObject-(columnIndex, object)` method. This updates a string column. To update a column of `double` type, you have to use `updateDouble(columnIndex, doubleValue)`. See Exercise 25.7 to revise the program to handle all types of columns.

EXAMPLE 25.5 (CONTINUED)

 TIP
To ensure the effect of editing a field in the table, you need to press the Enter key or move the cursor to other fields.

 NOTE
Many JDBC drivers, including the MySQL and Oracle drivers, support the read-only scrollable result set but not the updateable scrollable result set. Thus you cannot modify the result set. You can use `supportsResultSetType(int type)` and `supportsResultSetConcurrency (int type, int concurrency)` in the `DatabaseMetaData` interface to find out which result type and currency modes are supported by the JDBC driver. But even if a driver supports the scrollable and updateable result set, a result set for a complex query might not be able to perform an update. For example, the result set for a query that involves several tables is likely not to support update operations.

25.10 Storing and Retrieving Images in JDBC (Optional)

A database can store not only numbers and strings, but also images. SQL3 introduced a new data type called BLOB (*B*inary *L*arge *OB*ject) for storing binary data, which can be used to store images. Another new SQL3 type is CLOB (*C*haracter *L*arge *OB*ject), for storing a large text in the character format. JDBC 2 introduced the interfaces `java.sql.Blob` and `java.sql.Clob` to support mapping for these new SQL types. JBDC 2 also added new methods in the interfaces `ResultSet` and `PreparedStatement`, such as `getBlob`, `setBinaryStream`, `getClob`, `setBlob` and `setClob`, to access SQL BLOB, and CLOB values.

To store an image into a cell in a table, the corresponding column for the cell must be of the BLOB type. For example, the following SQL statement creates a table whose type for the flag column is BLOB:

```
create table Country(name varchar(30), flag blob,
   description varchar(255));
```

In the preceding statement, the `description` column is limited to 255 characters, which is the upper limit for MySQL. For Oracle, the upper limit is 32,672 bytes. For a large character field, you can use the CLOB type for Oracle, which can store up to two GB characters. MySQL does not support CLOB. However, you can use BLOB to store a long string and convert binary data into characters.

 NOTE
Access does not support the BLOB and CLOB types.

To insert a record with images to a table, define a prepared statement like this one:

```
PreparedStatement pstmt = connection.prepareStatement(
   "insert into Country values(?, ?, ?)");
```

Images are usually stored in files. You may first get an instance of `InputStream` for an image file and then use the `setBinaryStream` method to associate the input stream with a cell in the table, as follows:

```
// Store image to the table cell
File file = new File(imageFilename);
```

```
InputStream inputImage = new FileInputStream(file);
pstmt.setBinaryStream(2, inputImage, (int)(file.length()));
```

To retrieve an image from a table, use the getBlob method, as shown below:

```
// Store image to the table cell
Blob blob = rs.getBlob(1);
ImageIcon imageIcon = new ImageIcon(
  blob.getBytes(1, (int)blob.length()));
```

EXAMPLE 25.6 STORING AND RETRIEVING IMAGES IN JDBC

Problem

In this example, you will create a table, populate it with data, including images, and retrieve and display images. The table is named Country. Each record in the table consists of three fields: name, flag, and description. Flag is an image field. The program first creates the table and stores data to it. Then the program retrieves the country names from the table and adds them to a combo box. When the user selects a name from the combo box, the country's flag and description are displayed, as shown in Figure 25.26.

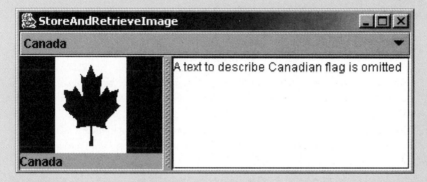

FIGURE 25.26 *The program enables you to retrieve data, including images, from a table and displays them.*

Solution

First create the Country table using the following SQL statement:

```
create table Country(name varchar(30), flag blob,
  description varchar(255));
```

Create two classes: DescriptionPanel and StoreAndRetrieveImage. DescriptionPanel is a component for displaying a country (name, flag, and description). This component was presented in Example 13.5, "Using Text Areas." StoreAndRetrieveImage (Listing 25.9) initializes the table and creates the user interface using a DescriptionPanel and a combo box.

LISTING 25.9 StoreAndRetrieveImage.java

```
1 import java.sql.*;
2 import java.io.*;
3 import javax.swing.*;
4 import java.awt.*;
5 import java.awt.event.*;
6
7 public class StoreAndRetrieveImage extends JApplet {
8   // Connection to the database
9   private Connection connection;
```

EXAMPLE 25.6 (CONTINUED)

```
10
11    // Statement for static SQL statements
12    private Statement stmt;
13
14    // Prepared statement
15    private PreparedStatement pstmt = null;
16    private DescriptionPanel descriptionPanel1 = new DescriptionPanel();
17
18    private JComboBox jcboCountry = new JComboBox();
19
20    /** Creates new form StoreAndRetrieveImage */
21    public StoreAndRetrieveImage() {
22      try {
23        connectDB(); // Connect to DB
24        storeDataToTable(); //Store data to the table (including image)
25        fillDataInComboBox(); // Fill in combo box
26        retrieveFlagInfo((String)(jcboCountry.getSelectedItem()));
27      }
28      catch (Exception ex) {
29        ex.printStackTrace();
30      }
31
32      jcboCountry.addItemListener(new ItemListener() {
33        public void itemStateChanged(ItemEvent evt) {
34          retrieveFlagInfo((String)(evt.getItem()));
35        }
36      });
37
38      getContentPane().add(jcboCountry, BorderLayout.NORTH);
39      getContentPane().add(descriptionPanel1, BorderLayout.CENTER);
40    }
41
42    private void connectDB() throws Exception {
43      // Load the driver
44      Class.forName("com.mysql.jdbc.Driver");
45      System.out.println("Driver loaded");
46
47      // Establish connection
48      connection = DriverManager.getConnection
49        ("jdbc:mysql://localhost/test");
50      System.out.println("Database connected");
51
52      // Create a statement for static SQL
53      stmt = connection.createStatement();
54
55      // Create a prepared statement to retrieve flag and description
56      pstmt = connection.prepareStatement("select flag, description " +
57        "from Country where name = ?");
58    }
59
60    private void storeDataToTable() {
61      String[] countries = {"Canada", "UK", "USA", "Germany",
62        "Indian", "China"};
63
64      String[] imageFilenames = {"image/ca.gif", "image/uk.gif",
65        "image/us.gif", "image/germany.gif", "image/india.gif",
66        "image/china.gif"};
67
68      String[] descriptions = {"A text to describe Canadian " +
69        "flag is omitted", "British flag ...", "American flag ...",
70        "German flag ...", "Indian flag ...", "Chinese flag ..."};
71
```

load driver

connect database

create statement

prepare statement

data to database

EXAMPLE 25.6 (CONTINUED)

```
72      try {
73        // Create a prepared statement to insert records
74        PreparedStatement pstmt = connection.prepareStatement(        insert
75          "insert into Country values(?, ?, ?)");
76
77        // Store all predefined records
78        for (int i = 0; i < countries.length; i++) {
79          pstmt.setString(1, countries[i]);
80
81          // Store image to the table cell
82          java.net.URL url =                                          get image URL
83            this.getClass().getResource(imageFilenames[i]);
84          InputStream inputImage = url.openStream();
85          pstmt.setBinaryStream(2, inputImage,                         binary stream
86            (int)(inputImage.available()));
87
88          pstmt.setString(3, descriptions[i]);
89          pstmt.executeUpdate();
90        }
91
92        System.out.println("Table Country populated");
93      }
94      catch (Exception ex) {
95        ex.printStackTrace();
96      }
97    }
98
99    private void fillDataInComboBox() throws Exception {
100     ResultSet rs = stmt.executeQuery("select name from Country");
101     while (rs.next()) {
102       jcboCountry.addItem(rs.getString(1));                         fill combo box
103     }
104   }
105
106   private void retrieveFlagInfo(String name) {
107     try {
108       pstmt.setString(1, name);                                     set name
109       ResultSet rs = pstmt.executeQuery();
110       if (rs.next()) {
111         Blob blob = rs.getBlob(1);
112         ImageIcon imageIcon = new ImageIcon(                        get image icon
113           blob.getBytes(1, (int)blob.length()));
114         descriptionPanel1.setImageIcon(imageIcon);
115         descriptionPanel1.setName(name);
116         String description = rs.getString(2);
117         descriptionPanel1.setDescription(description);              set description
118       }
119     }
120     catch (Exception ex) {
121       System.err.println(ex);
122     }
123   }
124 }                                                                    main method omitted
```

Review

Not all databases and their drivers support the SQL BLOB type. This example works on MySQL and Oracle, but not on Access.

The storeDataToTable method (Lines 60–97) populates the table with data. The fillDataInComboBox method (Lines 99–104) retrieves the country names and adds them to the combo box. The retrieveFlagInfo(name) method (Lines 106–123) retrieves the flag and description for the specified country name.

KEY TERMS

database system   958
domain constraint   960
foreign key constraint   961
integrity constraint   959

primary key constraint   960
relational database   958
Structured Query Language (SQL)   962

KEY CLASSES AND METHODS

◆ **java.sql.DriverManager** is a class for managing JDBC drivers and connecting data sources. Use getConnection(databaseURL) or getConnection(databaseURL, username, password) to create a Connection.

◆ **java.sql.Connection** is an interface that represents a connection to a database. Use createStatement() to create a static statement and prepareStatement(String sql) to create a prepared statement. You may obtain a scrollable or updateable statement using createStatement(int resultSetType, int resultSetConcurrency) and prepareStatement(String sql, int resultSetType, int resultSetConcurrency).

◆ **java.sql.Statement** is an interface that represents a statement. Use executeUpdate() to execute a data declaration statement, and use executeQuery(query) to execute a query. Use addBatch(sqlStatement) to add SQL statements for batch execution.

◆ **java.sql.ResultSet** is an interface that represents a query result. Use next() to move the cursor to the next row. Use getString(i) to get the ith element as a string from the current row in the result set. For a scrollable result set, you can use the method first(), last(), next(), previous(), absolute(), or relative() to move the cursor. For an updateable result set, you can use the methods insertRow(), deleteRow(), and updateRow() to insert, delete, and update rows.

◆ **java.sql.DatabaseMetadata** is an interface for retrieving database metadata. An instance of DatabaseMetadata can be obtained from a Connection instance using its getMetaData() method.

◆ **java.sql.ResultSetMetadata** is an interface for retrieving metadata of a result set. An instance of ResultSetMetadata can be obtained from a ResultSet instance using its getMetaData() method. You can use the getColumnCount() method to find the number of columns in the result and the getColumnName(int) method to get the column names.

CHAPTER SUMMARY

◆ This chapter introduced the concepts of database systems, relational databases, relational data models, data integrity, and SQL. You learned how to develop database applications using Java.

◆ The Java API for developing Java database applications is called *JDBC*. JDBC provides Java programmers with a uniform interface for accessing and manipulating a wide range of relational databases.

◆ The JDBC API consists of classes and interfaces for establishing connections with databases, sending SQL statements to databases, processing the results of SQL statements, and obtaining database metadata.

✦ Since a JDBC driver serves as the interface to facilitate communications between JDBC and a proprietary database, JDBC drivers are database-specific. A JDBC-ODBC bridge driver is included in JDK to support Java programs that access databases through ODBC drivers. If you use a driver other than the JDBC-ODBC bridge driver, make sure it is on the classpath before running the program.

✦ Four key interfaces are needed to develop any database application using Java: `Driver`, `Connection`, `Statement`, and `ResultSet`. These interfaces define a framework for generic SQL database access. The JDBC driver vendors provide implementation for them.

✦ A JDBC application loads an appropriate driver using the `Driver` interface, connects to the database using the `Connection` interface, creates and executes SQL statements using the `Statement` interface, and processes the result using the `ResultSet` interface if the statements return results.

✦ The `PreparedStatement` interface is designed to execute dynamic SQL statements with parameters. These SQL statements are precompiled for efficient use when repeatedly executed.

✦ Database *metadata* is information that describes the database itself. JDBC provides the `DatabaseMetaData` interface for obtaining database-wide information and the `ResultSetMetaData` interface for obtaining information on the specific `ResultSet`.

REVIEW QUESTIONS

Section 25.2 Relational Database Systems

25.1 What are superkeys, candidate keys, and primary keys? How do you create a table with a primary key?

25.2 What is a foreign key? How do you create a table with a foreign key?

25.3 Can a relation have more than one primary key or foreign key?

25.4 Does a foreign key need to be a primary key in the same relation?

25.5 Does a foreign key need to have the same name as its referenced primary key?

25.6 Can a foreign key value be null?

Section 25.3 SQL

25.7 Create the tables `Course`, `Student`, and `Enrollment` using the `create table` statements in Section 25.3.1, "Creating and Dropping Tables." Insert rows into `Course`, `Student`, and `Enrollment` using the data in Figures 25.3, 25.4, and 25.5.

25.8 List all CSCI courses with at least four credit hours.

25.9 List all students whose last name contains the letter *e* two times.

25.10 List all students whose birthday is null.

25.11 List all students who take Math courses.

25.12 List the number of the courses in each subject.

25.13 Assume that each credit hour is fifty minutes of lectures. Get the total minutes for the courses that each student take.

Section 25.4 JDBC

25.14 What are the advantages of developing database applications using Java?

25.15 Describe the following JDBC interfaces: `Driver`, `Connection`, `Statement`, and `ResultSet`.

25.16 How do you load a JDBC driver? What are driver classes for MySQL, Access, and Oracle?

25.17 How do you create a database connection? What are the URLs for MySQL, Access, and Oracle?

25.18 How do you create a `Statement` and execute an SQL statement?

25.19 How do you retrieve values in a `ResultSet`?

25.20 Does JDBC automatically commit a transaction? How do you set auto-commit to false?

Section 25.5 `PreparedStatement`

25.21 Describe prepared statements. How do you create instances of `PreparedStatement`? How do you execute a `PreparedStatement`? How do you set parameter values in a `PreparedStatement`?

25.22 What are the benefits of using prepared statements?

Section 25.6 Retrieving Metadata

25.23 What is `DatabaseMetaData` for? Describe the methods in `DatabaseMetaData`. How do you get an instance of `DatabaseMetaData`?

25.24 What is `ResultSetMetaData` for? Describe the methods in `ResultSetMetaData`. How do you get an instance of `ResultSetMetaData`?

25.25 How do you find the number of columns in a result set? How do you find the column names in a result set?

Section 25.8 Batch Processing

25.26 What is batch processing in JDBC? What are the benefits of using batch processing?

25.27 How do you add an SQL statement to a batch? How do you execute a batch?

25.28 Can you execute a SELECT statement in a batch?

25.29 How do you know whether a JDBC driver supports batch updates?

Section 25.9 Scrollable and Updateable Result Set

25.30 What is a scrollable result set? What is an updateable result set?

25.31 How do you create a scrollable and updateable `ResultSet`?

25.32 How do you know whether a JDBC driver supports a scrollable and updateable `ResultSet`?

Section 25.10 Storing and Retrieving Images in JDBC

25.33 How do you store images into a database?

25.34 How do you retrieve images from a database?

25.35 Does Oracle support SQL3 BLOB type and CLOB type? How about MySQL and Access?

PROGRAMMING EXERCISES

25.1* (*Accessing and updating Staff table*) Write a Java applet that views, inserts, and updates staff information stored in a database, as shown in Figure 25.27. The Staff table is created as follows:

```
create table Staff (
  id char(9) not null,
  lastName varchar(15),
  firstName varchar(15),
  mi char(1),
  address varchar(20),
  city varchar(20),
  state char(2),
  telephone char(10),
  email varchar(40),
  primary key (id)
);
```

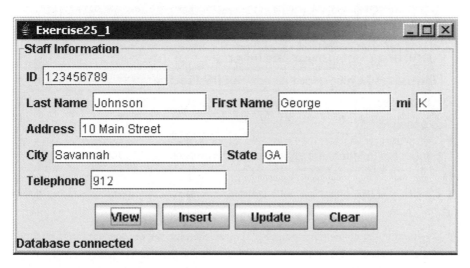

FIGURE 25.27   *The applet lets you view, insert, and update staff information.*

25.2** (*Displaying data*) Write a program that displays the number of students in each department in a pie chart and a bar chart, as shown in Figure 25.28. The number of students for each department can be obtained from the Student table (see Figure 25.4) using the following SQL statement:

```
select deptId, count(*)
from Student
group by deptId;
```

Use the `PieChart` component and the `BarChart` component created in Exercise 21.6 to display the data.

25.3* (*Connection dialog*) Develop a JavaBeans component named `DBConnectionPanel` that enables the user to select or enter a JDBC driver and a URL and to enter a username and password, as shown in Figure 25.29. When the OK button is clicked, a `Connection` object for the database

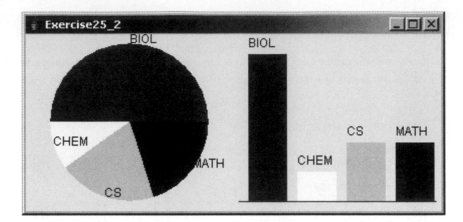

FIGURE 25.28   *The* PieChart *and* BarChart *components display the query data obtained from the data module.*

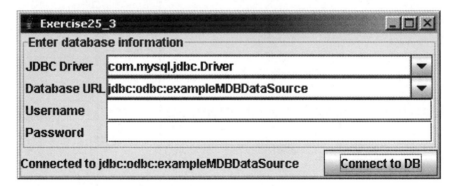

FIGURE 25.29   *The* DBConnectionPanel *component enables the user to enter database information.*

is stored in the connection property. You can then use the getConnection() method to return the connection.

25.4*   (*Batch update*) Write a program that inserts a thousand records to a database, and compare the performance with and without batch updates, as shown in Figure 25.30. Suppose the table is defined as follows:

```
create table Temp(num1 double, num2 double, num3 double)
```

Use the Math.random() method to generate random numbers for each record. Create a dialog box that contains DBConnectionPanel, discussed in the preceding exercise. Use this dialog box to connect to the database.

25.5**   (*Scrollable result set*) Write a program that uses the buttons First, Next, Prior, Last, Insert, Delete, and Update display, and modify a single record in the Address table, as shown in Figure 25.31.

25.6*   (*Storing images*) Write a program that uses JTable to display the Country table created in Example 25.6, "Storing and Retrieving Images in JDBC," as shown in Figure 25.32.

25.7**   (*Handling all types of columns*) Revise Example 25.5, "Scrolling and Updating Tables," to enable it to insert all types of columns (not just strings).

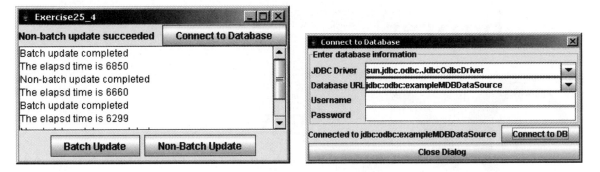

FIGURE 25.30   *The program demonstrates the performance improvements that result from using batch updates.*

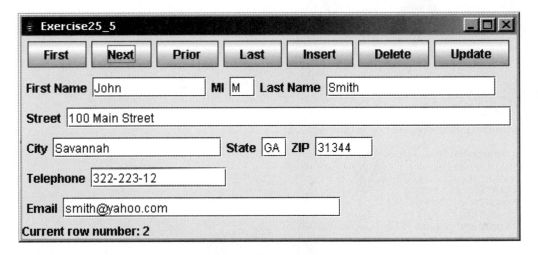

FIGURE 25.31   *You can use the buttons to display and modify a single record in the Address table.*

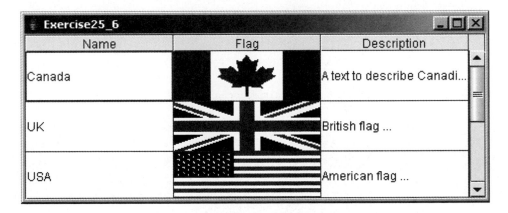

FIGURE 25.32   *The Country table is displayed in a* JTable *instance.*

chapter

26

SERVLETS

Objectives

- ✦ To understand the concept of servlets (§26.2).
- ✦ To run servlets with Tomcat (§26.3).
- ✦ To know the servlets API (§26.4).
- ✦ To create simple servlets (§26.5).
- ✦ To create and process HTML forms (§26.6).
- ✦ To develop servlets to access databases (§26.7).
- ✦ To use hidden fields, cookies, and HttpSession to track sessions (§26.8).
- ✦ To send images from servlets (§26.9).

26.1   Introduction

Servlet technology is primarily designed for use with the HTTP protocol of the Web. *Servlets* are
Java programs that run on a Web server. Java servlets can be used to process client requests or produce dynamic Web pages. For example, you can write servlets to generate dynamic Web pages
that display stock quotes or process client registration forms and store registration data in a database. This chapter introduces the concept of Java servlets. You will learn how to write Java servlets
and run them from Tomcat. Tomcat is a Web server that supports Java servlets and JSP. It can be
downloaded free.

servlet

26.2   HTML and Common Gateway Interface

Java servlets run in the Web environment. To understand Java servlets, let us review HTML and
the Common Gateway Interface (CGI).

26.2.1   Static Web Contents

You create Web pages using HTML. Your Web pages are stored as files on the Web server. The files
are usually stored in the htdocs directory on Unix, as shown in Figure 26.1. A user types a URL for
the file from a Web browser. The browser contacts the Web server and requests the file. The server
finds the file and returns it to the browser. The browser then displays the file to the user. This
works fine for static information that does not change regardless of who requests it or when it is requested. Static information is stored in HTML files. The information in the files can be updated,
but at any given time every request for the same document returns exactly the same result.

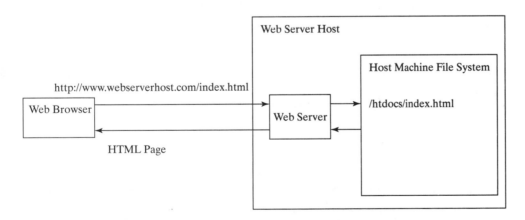

FIGURE 26.1   *A Web browser requests a static HTML page from a Web server.*

26.2.2   Dynamic Web Contents and Common Gateway Interface

Not all information, however, is static in nature. Stock quotes are updated every minute. Election
vote counts are updated constantly on Election Day. Weather reports are frequently updated. The
balance in a customer's bank account is updated whenever a transaction takes place. To view up-
to-date information on the Web, the HTML pages for displaying this information must be generated dynamically. Dynamic Web pages are generated by Web servers. The Web server needs to

run certain programs to process user requests from Web browsers in order to produce a customized response.

CGI

The *Common Gateway Interface*, or *CGI*, was proposed to generate dynamic Web content. The interface provides a standard framework for Web servers to interact with external programs, known as *CGI programs*. As shown in Figure 26.2, the Web server receives a request from a Web browser and passes it to the CGI program. The CGI program processes the request and generates a response at runtime. CGI programs can be written in any language, but the *Perl* language is the most popular choice. CGI programs are typically stored in the /cgi-bin directory. Here is a pseudocode example of a CGI program for displaying a customer's bank account balance:

1. Obtain account ID and password.

2. Verify account ID and password. If it fails, generate an HTML page to report incorrect account ID and password, and exit.

3. Retrieve account balance from the database; generate an HTML page to display the account ID and balance.

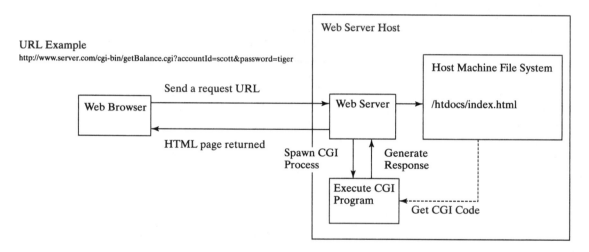

FIGURE 26.2 *A Web browser requests a dynamic HTML page from a Web server.*

26.2.3 The GET and POST Methods

The two most common HTTP requests, also known as *methods*, are GET and POST. The Web browser issues a request using a URL or an HTML form to trigger the Web server to execute a CGI program. HTML forms will be introduced in Section 26.6, "HTML Forms." When issuing a CGI request directly from a URL, the GET method is used. This URL is known as a *query string*. The URL query string consists of the location of the CGI program, parameters, and their values. For example, the following URL causes the CGI program `getBalance` to be invoked on the server side:

```
http://www.webserverhost.com/cgi-bin/
  getBalance.cgi?accountId=scott+smith&password=tiger
```

The ? symbol separates the program from the parameters. The parameter name and value are associated using the = symbol. Parameter pairs are separated using the & symbol. The + symbol denotes a space character.

When issuing a request from an HTML form, either a GET method or a POST method can be used. The form explicitly specifies which of the two is used. If the GET method is used, the data in the form are appended to the request string as if they were submitted using a URL. If the POST method is used, the data in the form are packaged as part of the request file. The server program obtains the data by reading the file.

 NOTE

The GET and POST methods both send requests to the Web server. The POST method always triggers the execution of the corresponding CGI program. The GET method may not cause the CGI program to be executed if the previous same request is cached in the Web browser. Web browsers often cache Web pages so that the same request can be quickly responded to without contacting the Web server. The browser checks the request sent through the GET method as a URL query string. If the results for the exact same URL are cached on a disk, then the previous Web pages for the URL may be displayed. To ensure that a new Web page is always displayed, use the POST method. For example, use a POST method if the request will actually update the database. If your request is not time-sensitive, such as finding the address of a student in the database, use the GET method to speed up the performance.

26.2.4   From CGI to Java Servlets

CGI provides a relatively simple approach for creating dynamic Web applications that accept a user request, process it on the server side, and return responses to the Web browser. But CGI is very slow when handling a large number of requests simultaneously, because the Web server spawns a process for executing each CGI program. Each process has its own runtime environment that contains and runs the CGI program. It is not difficult to imagine what will happen if many CGI programs are executed simultaneously. System resource would be quickly exhausted, potentially causing the server to crash.

Several new approaches have been developed to remedy the performance problem of CGI programs. Java servlets are one successful technology for this purpose. Java servlets are Java programs that function like CGI programs. They are executed upon request from a Web browser. All servlets run inside a *servlet container*, also referred to as a *servlet server* or a *servlet engine*. A servlet container is a single process that runs a Java Virtual Machine. The JVM creates a thread to handle each servlet. Java threads have much less overhead than full-blown processes. All the threads share the same memory allocated to the JVM. Since the JVM persists beyond the life cycle of a single servlet execution, servlets can share objects already created in the JVM. For example, if multiple servlets access the same database, they can share the connection object. Servlets are much more efficient than CGI.

servlet engine

Servlets have other benefits that are inherent in Java. As Java programs, they are object-oriented, portable, and platform-independent. Since you know Java, you can develop servlets immediately with the support of Java API for accessing databases and network resources.

26.3   Creating and Running Servlets

To run Java servlets, you need a servlet container. Many servlet containers are available. *Tomcat*, developed by Apache (`www.apache.org`), is a standard reference implementation for Java servlets and Java Server Pages. It can be used standalone as a Web server or be plugged into a Web server like Apache, Netscape Enterprise Server, or Microsoft Internet Information Server. You can download it from `jakarta.apache.org/tomcat`.

26.3.1   Creating a Servlet

Before introducing the servlet API, it is helpful to use a simple example to demonstrate how servlets work. A servlet resembles an applet to some extent. Every Java applet is a subclass of the `Applet` class. You need to override appropriate methods in the `Applet` class to implement the applet. Every servlet is a subclass of the `HttpServlet` class. You need to override appropriate methods in the `HttpServlet` class to implement the servlet. Listing 26.1 is a servlet that generates a response in HTML using the `doGet` method.

LISTING 26.1 FirstServlet.java

```
 1 import javax.servlet.*;
 2 import javax.servlet.http.*;
 3
 4 public class FirstServlet extends HttpServlet {
 5   /** Handle the HTTP GET method.
 6    * @param request servlet request
 7    * @param response servlet response
 8    */
 9   protected void doGet(HttpServletRequest request,
10       HttpServletResponse response)
11       throws ServletException, java.io.IOException {
12     response.setContentType("text/html");
13     java.io.PrintWriter out = response.getWriter();
14     // output your page here
15     out.println("<html>");
16     out.println("<head>");
17     out.println("<title>Servlet</title>");
18     out.println("</head>");
19     out.println("<body>");
20     out.println("Hello, Java Servlets");
21     out.println("</body>");
22     out.println("</html>");
23     out.close();
24   }
25 }
```

process GET

content type
output to browser

close stream

26.3.2 Compiling the Servlet

Suppose you have installed Tomcat 4.1.27 or higher in c:\jakarta-tomcat-4.1.27. To compile FirstServlet.java, you need to add c:\jakarta-tomcat-4.1.27\common\lib\servlet.jar to the classpath from DOS prompt, as shown below:

classpath

```
set classpath=%classpath%;c:\jakarta-tomcat-4.1.27\common\lib\servlet.jar
```

servlet.jar contains the classes and interfaces to support servlets. Use the following command to compile the servlet:

```
javac FirstServlet.java
```

Copy the resultant .class file into c:\jakarta-tomcat-4.1.27\webapps\examples\WEB-INF\classes so that it can be found at runtime.

 TIP

You can compile FirstServlet directly into the target directory by using the –d option in the javac command:

```
javac FirstServlet.java -d targetdirectory
```

26.3.3 Starting Tomcat

Before running the servlet, you need to start the Tomcat servlet engine. To start Tomcat, you have to first set the JAVA_HOME environment variable to the JDK home directory using the command given below (please note that there is no space before or after the = sign in the following line):

```
set JAVA_HOME=c:\Program Files\java\jdk1.5.0
```

The JDK home directory is where your JDK is stored. On my computer, it is c:\Program Files\java\jdk1.5.0. You may have a different directory. You can now start Tomcat using the command **startup** from c:\jakarta-tomcat-4.1.27\bin, as follows:

```
c:\jakarta-tomcat-4.1.27\bin>startup
```

 NOTE

> By default, Tomcat runs on port 8080. An error occurs if this port is currently being used. You can change the port number in c:\jakarta-tomcat-4.1.27\conf\server.xml.

 NOTE

> To terminate Tomcat, use the **shutdown** command from c:\jakarta-tomcat-4.1.27\bin.

To prove that Tomcat is running, type the URL `http://localhost:8080` from a Web browser, as shown in Figure 26.3.

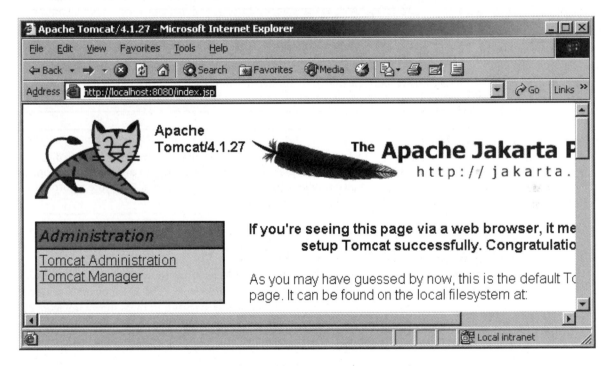

FIGURE 26.3   *The default Tomcat page is displayed.*

26.3.4   Running the Servlet

To run the servlet, start a Web browser and type `http://localhost:8080/examples/servlet/FirstServlet` in the URL, as shown in Figure 26.4.

 NOTE

> You can use the servlet from anywhere on the Internet if your Tomcat is running on a host machine on the Internet. Suppose the host name is liang.armstrong.edu; use the URL `http://liang.armstrong.edu:8080/examples/servlet/FirstServlet` to test the servlet.

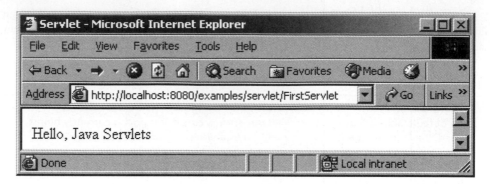

FIGURE 26.4   *You can request a servlet from a Web browser.*

 NOTE

If you have modified the servlet, you need to shut down and restart Tomcat.

 TIP

If your servlet class uses packages (e.g., package chapter26), you have to create a directory named chapter26 under c:\jakarta-tomcat-4.1.27\webapps\examples\WEB-INF\classes and copy the .class into the new directory. You have to use the URL http://localhost:8080/examples/servlet/chapter26.FirstServlet to invoke the servlet.

 NOTE

The easiest way to run a servlet is to store all the servlet class files in c:\Jakarta-tomcat-4.1.27\wepapps\examples\WEB-INF\classes. You can also configure Tomcat so that you can place servlets anywhere in your computer. For more information, see Supplement O, "Tutorial for Tomcat."

26.4   The Servlet API

You have to know the servlet API in order to understand the source code in FirstServlet.java. The servlet API provides the interfaces and classes that support servlets. These interfaces and classes are grouped into two packages, javax.servlet and javax.servlet.http, as shown in Figure 26.5. The

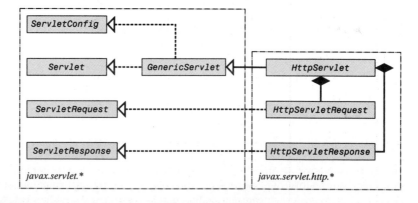

FIGURE 26.5   *The servlet API contains interfaces and classes that you use to develop and run servlets.*

javax.servlet package provides basic interfaces, and the javax.servlet.http package provides classes and interfaces derived from them, which provide specific means for servicing HTTP requests.

26.4.1   The *Servlet* Interface

The javax.servlet.Servlet interface defines the methods that all servlets must implement. The methods are listed below:

```
/** Invoked for every servlet constructed */
public void init() throws ServletException;

/** Invoked to respond to incoming requests */
public void service(ServletRequest request, ServletResponse response)
  throws ServletException, IOException;

/** Invoked to release resource by the servlet */
public void destroy();
```

The init, service, and destroy methods are known as *life-cycle methods* and are called in the following sequence (see Figure 26.6):

life-cycle

1. The init method is called when the servlet is first created, and is not called again as long as the servlet is not destroyed. This resembles an applet's init method, which is invoked after the applet is created, and is not invoked again as long as the applet is not destroyed.

2. The service method is invoked each time the server receives a request for the servlet. The server spawns a new thread and invokes service.

3. The destroy method is invoked after a timeout period has passed or the Web server is being terminated. This method releases resources for the servlet.

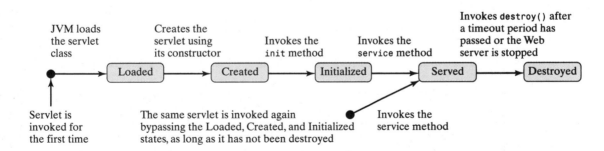

FIGURE 26.6 *The JVM uses the init, service, and destroy methods to control the servlet.*

26.4.2   The *GenericServlet* Class, *ServletConfig* Interface, and *HttpServlet* Class

The javax.servlet.GenericServlet class defines a generic, protocol-independent servlet. It implements javax.servlet.Servlet and javax.servlet.ServletConfig. ServletConfig is an interface that defines four methods (getInitParameter, getInitParameterNames, getServletContext, and getServletName) for obtaining information from a Web server during initialization. All the methods in `Servlet` and `ServletConfig` are implemented in `GenericServlet` except `service`. Therefore, `GenericServlet` is an abstract class.

The `javax.servlet.http.HttpServlet` class defines a servlet for the HTTP protocol. It extends `GenericServlet` and implements the `service` method. The `service` method is implemented as a dispatcher of HTTP requests. The HTTP requests are processed in the following methods:

◆ `doGet` is invoked to respond to a GET request.

◆ `doPost` is invoked to respond to a POST request.

◆ `doDelete` is invoked to respond to a DELETE request. Such a request is normally used to delete a file on the server.

◆ `doPut` is invoked to respond to a PUT request. Such a request is normally used to send a file to the server.

◆ `doOptions` is invoked to respond to an OPTIONS request. This returns information about the server, such as which HTTP methods it supports.

◆ `doTrace` is invoked to respond to a TRACE request. Such a request is normally used for debugging. This method returns an HTML page that contains appropriate trace information.

All these methods have the same signature:

```
protected void doXxx(HttpServletRequest req, HttpServletResponse resp)
  throws ServletException, java.io.IOException
```

The `HttpServlet` class provides default implementation for these methods. You need to override `doGet`, `doPost`, `doDelete`, and `doPut` if you want the servlet to process a GET request, POST request, DELETE request, or PUT request. By default, nothing will be done. Normally, you should not override the `doOptions` method unless the servlet implements new HTTP methods beyond those implemented by HTTP 1.1. Nor is there any need to override the `doTrace` method.

 NOTE

GET and POST requests are often used, whereas DELETE, PUT, OPTIONS, and TRACE are not. For more information about these requests, please refer to the HTTP 1.1 specification from www.cis.ohio-state.edu/htbin/rfc/rfc2068.html.

 NOTE

Although the methods in `HttpServlet` are all nonabstract, `HttpServlet` is defined as an abstract class. Thus you cannot create a servlet directly from `HttpServlet`. Instead you have to define your servlet by extending `HttpServlet`.

The relationship of these interfaces and classes is shown in Figure 26.7.

26.4.3 The *ServletRequest* Interface and *HttpServletRequest* Interface

Every `doXxx` method in the `HttpServlet` class has a parameter of the `HttpServletRequest` type, which is an object that contains HTTP request information, including parameter name and values, attributes, and an input stream. `HttpServletRequest` is a subinterface of `ServletRequest`. `ServletRequest` defines a more general interface to provide information for all kinds of clients. The frequently used methods in these two interfaces are shown in Figure 26.8.

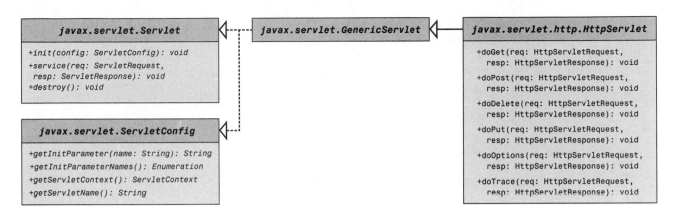

FIGURE 26.7 *HttpServlet inherits abstract class* GenericServlet, *which implements interfaces* Servlet *and* ServletConfig.

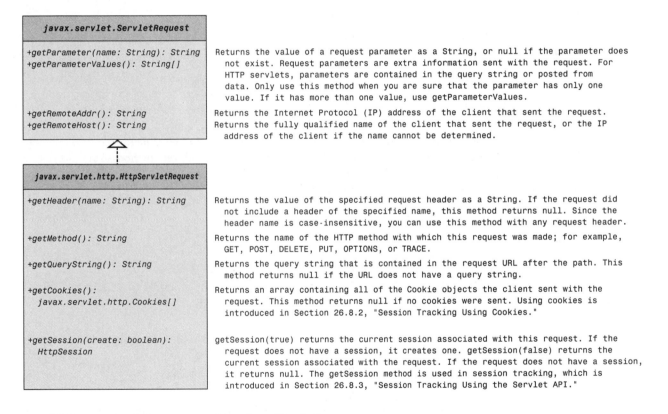

FIGURE 26.8 *HttpServletRequest is a subinterface of ServletRequest.*

26.4.4 The *ServletResponse* Interface and *HttpServletResponse* Interface

Every do*Xxx* method in the HttpServlet class has a parameter of the HttpServletResponse type, which is an object that assists a servlet in sending a response to the client. HttpServletResponse is a subinterface of ServletResponse. ServletResponse defines a more general interface for sending output to the client.

The frequently used methods in these two interfaces are shown in Figure 26.9.

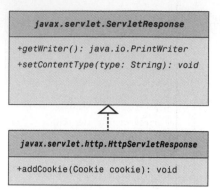

javax.servlet.ServletResponse	
+getWriter(): java.io.PrintWriter	Returns a PrintWriter object that can send character text to the client.
+setContentType(type: String): void	Sets the content type of the response being sent to the client before writing response to the client. When you are writing HTML to the client, the type should be set to "text/html." For plain text, use "text/plain." For sending a gif image to the browser, use "image/gif."

javax.servlet.http.HttpServletResponse	
+addCookie(Cookie cookie): void	Adds the specified cookie to the response. This method can be called multiple times to set more than one cookie.

FIGURE 26.9   *HttpServletResponse is a subinterface of ServletResponse.*

26.5   Creating Servlets

Servlets are the opposite of Java applets. Java applets run from a Web browser on the client side. To write Java programs, you define classes. To write a Java applet, you define a class that extends the `Applet` class. The Web browser runs and controls the execution of the applet through the methods defined in the `Applet` class. Similarly, to write a Java servlet, you define a class that extends the `HttpServlet` class. The servlet container runs and controls the execution of the servlet through the methods defined in the `HttpServlet` class. Like a Java applet, a servlet does not have a `main` method. A servlet depends on the servlet server to call the methods. Every servlet has a structure like the one shown below:

```java
import javax.servlet.*;
import javax.servlet.http.*;
import java.io.*;

public class MyServlet extends HttpServlet {
  /** Called by the servlet engine to initialize servlet */
  public void init() throws ServletException {
    ...
  }

  /** Process the HTTP Get request */
  public void doGet(HttpServletRequest request, HttpServletResponse
    response) throws ServletException, IOException {
    ...
  }

  /** Process the HTTP Post request */
  public void doPost(HttpServletRequest request, HttpServletResponse
    response) throws ServletException, IOException {
    ...
  }

  /** Called by the servlet engine to release resource */
  public void destroy() {
    ...
  }

  // Other methods if necessary
}
```

The servlet engine controls the servlets using `init`, `doGet`, `doPost`, `destroy`, and other methods. By default, the `doGet` and `doPost` methods do nothing. To handle a GET request, you need to override the `doGet` method; to handle a POST request, you need to override the `doPost` method.

EXAMPLE 26.1 OBTAINING THE CURRENT TIME FROM THE SERVER

Problem

This example gives a simple Java servlet that generates a dynamic Web page for displaying the current time, as shown in Figure 26.10.

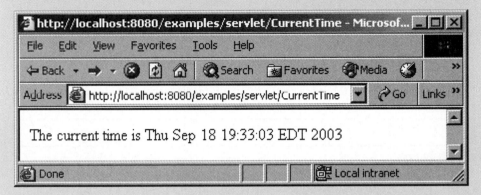

FIGURE **26.10**   *Servlet* CurrentTime *displays the current time.*

Solution

Create the servlet named CurrentTime in Listing 26.2. Compile it into c:\jakarta-tomcat-4.1.27\webapps\examples\WEB-INF\classes.

 TIP

The destination directory for CurrentTime.class is c:\jakarta-tomcat-4.1.27\webapps\examples\WEB-INF\classes. You may compile CurrentTime.java to generate CurrentTime.class and then move it into the destination directory, or use the following command to compile and save the .class directly into the destination directory:

```
javac -d destinationDirectory CurrentTime.java
```

Run the servlet using the URL

```
http://localhost:8080/examples/servlet/CurrentTime
```

LISTING 26.2   CurrentTime.java

```
 1 import javax.servlet.*;
 2 import javax.servlet.http.*;
 3 import java.io.*;
 4
 5 public class CurrentTime extends HttpServlet {
 6   /** Process the HTTP Get request */
 7   public void doGet(HttpServletRequest request, HttpServletResponse    process GET
 8       response) throws ServletException, IOException {
 9     response.setContentType("text/html");                             content type
10     PrintWriter out = response.getWriter();                           output to browser
11     out.println("<p>The current time is " + new java.util.Date());
12     out.close(); // Close stream                                      close stream
13   }
14 }
```

Review

The HttpServlet class has a doGet method. The doGet method is invoked when the browser issues a request to the servlet using the GET method. So your servlet class should override the doGet method to respond to the GET request. In this case, you write the code to display the current time.

EXAMPLE 26.1 (CONTINUED)

Servlets return responses to the browser through an `HttpServletResponse` object. Since the `setContentType("text/html")` method sets the content type to "text/html," the browser will display the response in HTML. The `getWriter` method returns a `PrintWriter` stream (out) for sending HTML back to the client.

> **NOTE**
> The URL query string uses the GET method to issue a request to the servlet. The current time may not be current if the Web page for displaying the current time is cached. To ensure that a new current time is displayed, refresh the page in the browser. In the next example, you will write a new servlet that uses the POST method to obtain the current time.

> **NOTE**
> If you experience problems after Tomcat was successfully started, you may have to shut down and restart Tomcat after new servlet class files are added to the c:\jakarta-tomcat-4.1.27\webapps\examples\WEB-INF\classes directory.

26.6   HTML Forms

HTML forms enable you to submit data to the Web server in a convenient form. As shown in Figure 26.11, the form can contain text fields, text area, check boxes, combo boxes, lists, radio buttons, and buttons.

The HTML code for creating the form in Figure 26.11 is given in Listing 26.3. (If you are unfamiliar with HTML, please see Supplement E, "HTML Tutorial.")

LISTING 26.3   Student_Registration_Form.html

```
1  <!--An HTML Demo -->
2  <html>
3  <head>
4  <title>Student Registration Form</title>
5  </head>
6  <body>
7  Student Registration Form
8
9  <form action="http://localhost:8080/examples/servlet/GetParameters"
10   method="GET">
11  Last Name <input type="text" name="lastName" size="20">
12  First Name <input type="text" name="firstName" size="20">
13  MI <input type="text" name="mi" size="1">
14  <p>Gender:
15    <input type="radio" name="gender" value="M" checked> Male
16    <input type="radio" name="gender" value="F"> Female</p>
17  <p>Major <select name="major" size="1">
18    <option value="CS">Computer Science
19    <option value="Math">Mathematics
20    <option>English
21    <option>Chinese
22    </select>
23  Minor <select name="minor" size="2" multiple>
24    <option>Computer Science
25    <option>Mathematics
26    <option>English
27    <option>Chinese
28    </select></p>
```

form tag

text fields

combo box

list

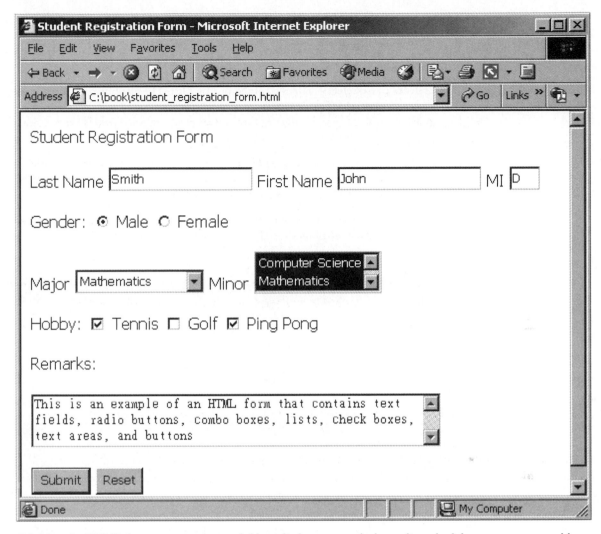

FIGURE 26.11   *An HTML form may contain text fields, radio buttons, combo boxes, lists, check boxes, text areas, and buttons.*

```
29   <p>Hobby:
30     <input type="checkbox" name="tennis"> Tennis                          check box
31     <input type="checkbox" name="golf"> Golf
32     <input type="checkbox" name="pingPong" checked> Ping Pong</p>
33   <p>Remarks:</p>
34   <p><textarea name="remarks" rows="3" cols="56"></textarea></p>         text area
35   <p><input type="submit" value="Submit">                                submit button
36     <input type="reset" value="Reset"></p>                               reset button
37   </form>
38   </body>
```

The following HTML tags are used to construct HTML forms:

✦ **<form> . . . </form>** defines a form body. The attributes for the <form> tag are **action** and **method**. The action attribute specifies the server program to be executed on the Web server when the form is submitted. The method attribute is either **GET** or **POST**.

✦ **<input>** defines an input field. The attributes for this tag are **type, name, value, checked, size,** and **maxlength**. The type attribute specifies the input type. Possible types are **text** for a one-line text field, **radio** for a radio button, and **checkbox** for a check box. The name attribute gives a formal name for the attribute. This name is used by the servlet program to retrieve its associated value. The names of radio buttons in a group must be identical. The value attribute specifies a default value for a text field and text area. The checked attribute indicates whether a radio button or a check box is initially checked. The size attribute specifies the size of a text field, and the maxlength attribute specifies the maximum length of a text field.

✦ **<select> . . . </select>** defines a combo box or a list. The attributes for this tag are **name, size,** and **multiple**. The size attribute specifies the number of rows visible in the list. The multiple attribute specifies that multiple values can be selected from a list. Set size to 1 and do not use a multiple for a combo box.

✦ **<option>** defines a selection list within a <select> . . . </select> tag. This tag may be used with the value attribute to specify a value for the selected option (e.g., **<option value="CS">Computer Science**). If no value is specified, the selected option is the value.

✦ **<textarea> . . . </textarea>** defines a text area. The attributes are **name, rows,** and **cols**. The rows and cols attributes specify the number of rows and columns in a text area.

EXAMPLE 26.2 OBTAINING PARAMETER VALUES FROM HTML FORMS

Problem

This example demonstrates how to obtain parameter values from an HTML form. Write a servlet to obtain all the parameter values from the student registration form in Figure 26.11 and display their values, as shown in Figure 26.12.

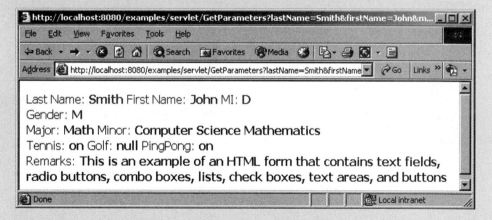

FIGURE 26.12 *The servlet displays the parameter values entered in Figure 26.11.*

Solution

Create the servlet named GetParameters in Listing 26.4 and compile it into c:\jakarta-tomcat-4.1.27\webapps\examples\WEB-INF\classes.

LISTING 26.4 GetParameters.java

```
1 import javax.servlet.*;
2 import javax.servlet.http.*;
3 import java.io.*;
4
5 public class GetParameters extends HttpServlet {
6   /** Process the HTTP POST request */
7   public void doGet(HttpServletRequest request, HttpServletResponse
8       response) throws ServletException, IOException {
```

process GET

EXAMPLE 26.2 (CONTINUED)

```
9    response.setContentType("text/html");
10   PrintWriter out = response.getWriter();
11
12   // Obtain parameters from the client
13   String lastName = request.getParameter("lastName");
14   String firstName = request.getParameter("firstName");
15   String mi = request.getParameter("mi");
16   String gender = request.getParameter("gender");
17   String major = request.getParameter("major");
18   String[] minors = request.getParameterValues("minor");
19   String tennis = request.getParameter("tennis");
20   String golf = request.getParameter("golf");
21   String pingPong = request.getParameter("pingPong");
22   String remarks = request.getParameter("remarks");
23
24   out.println("Last Name: <b>" + lastName + "</b> First Name: <b>"
25     + firstName + "</b> MI: <b>" + mi + "</b><br>");
26   out.println("Gender: <b>" + gender + "</b><br>");
27   out.println("Major: <b>" + major + "</b> Minor: <b>");
28
29   if (minors != null)
30     for (int i = 0; i < minors.length; i++)
31       out.println(minors[i] + " ");
32
33   out.println("</b><br> Tennis: <b>" + tennis + "</b> Golf: <b>" +
34     golf + "</b> PingPong: <b>" + pingPong + "</b><br>");
35   out.println("Remarks: <b>" + remarks + "</b>");
36   out.close(); // Close stream
37   }
38 }
```

content type
output to browser

get parameters

close stream

Review

The HTML form is already created in student_registration_form.html and displayed in Figure 26.11. Since the action for the form is http://localhost:8080/examples/servlet/GetParameters, clicking the *Submit* button invokes the GetParameters servlet.

Each GUI component in the form has a name attribute. The servlet uses the name attribute in the getParameter(attributeName) method to obtain the parameter value as a string. In case of a list with multiple values, use the getParameterValues(attributeName) method to return the parameter values in an array of strings (e.g., getParameterValues("minor") in Line 18).

You may optionally specify the value attribute in a text field, text area, combo box, list, check box, and radio button in an HTML form. For text field and text area, the value attribute specifies a default value to be displayed in the text field and text area. The user can type in new values to replace it. For combo box, list, check box, and radio button, the value attribute specifies the parameter value to be returned from the getParameter and getParameterValues methods. If the value attribute is not specified for a combo box or a list, it returns the selected string from the combo box or the list. If the value attribute is not specified for a radio button or a check box, it returns string "on" for a checked radio button or a checked check box, and returns null for an unchecked check box.

 NOTE

If an attribute does not exist, the getParameter(attributeName) method returns null. If an empty value of the parameter is passed to the servlet, the getParameter(attributeName) method returns a string with empty value. In this case, the length of the string is 0.

EXAMPLE 26.3 OBTAINING CURRENT TIME BASED ON LOCALE AND TIME ZONE

Problem

This example creates a servlet that processes the GET and POST requests. The GET request generates a form that contains a combo box for locale and a combo box for time zone, as shown in Figure 26.13(a). The user can choose a locale and a time zone from this form to submit a POST request to obtain the current time based on the locale and time zone, as shown in Figure 26.13(b).

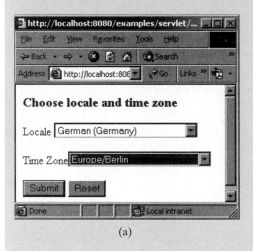
(a)

(b)

FIGURE 26.13 *The GET method in the* TimeForm *servlet displays a form in (a), and the* POST *method in the* TimeForm *servlet displays the time based on locale and time zone in (b).*

Solution

Create the servlet named TimeForm in Listing 26.5 and compile it into c:\jakarta-tomcat-4.1.27\webapps\examples\WEB-INF\classes. Run the servlet using the URL

```
http://localhost:8080/examples/servlet/TimeForm
```

LISTING 26.5   TimeForm.java

```java
1  import javax.servlet.*;
2  import javax.servlet.http.*;
3  import java.io.*;
4  import java.util.*;
5  import java.text.*;
6
7  public class TimeForm extends HttpServlet {
8    private static final String CONTENT_TYPE = "text/html";
9    private Locale[] allLocale = Locale.getAvailableLocales();
10   private String[] allTimeZone = TimeZone.getAvailableIDs();
11
12   /** Process the HTTP GET request */
13   public void doGet(HttpServletRequest request, HttpServletResponse
14     response) throws ServletException, IOException {
15     response.setContentType(CONTENT_TYPE);
16     PrintWriter out = response.getWriter();
17     out.println("<h3>Choose locale and time zone</h3>");
18     out.println("<form method=\"POST\" action=" +
19       "/examples/servlet/TimeForm>");
20     out.println("Locale <select size=\"1\" name=\"locale\">");
21
22     // Fill in all locales
23     for (int i = 0; i < allLocale.length; i++) {
```

process GET

content type
output to browser

create form

EXAMPLE 26.3 (CONTINUED)

```
24        out.println("<option value=\"" + i +"\">" +
25          allLocale[i].getDisplayName() + "</option>");
26      }
27      out.println("</select>");
28
29      // Fill in all time zones
30      out.println("<p>Time Zone<select size=\"1\" name=\"timezone\">");
31      for (int i = 0; i < allTimeZone.length; i++) {
32        out.println("<option value=\"" + allTimeZone[i] +"\">" +
33          allTimeZone[i] + "</option>");
34      }
35      out.println("</select>");
36
37      out.println("<p><input type=\"submit\" value=\"Submit\" >");
38      out.println("<input type=\"reset\" value=\"Reset\"></p>");
39      out.println("</form>");
40      out.close(); // Close stream                                        close stream
41    }
42
43    /** Process the HTTP POST request */
44    public void doPost(HttpServletRequest request, HttpServletResponse   process POST
45        response) throws ServletException, IOException {
46      response.setContentType(CONTENT_TYPE);                             content type
47      PrintWriter out = response.getWriter();                           output to browser
48      out.println("<html>");
49      int localeIndex = Integer.parseInt(                               get locale
50        request.getParameter("locale"));
51      String timeZoneID = request.getParameter("timezone");             get time zone
52      out.println("<head><title>Current Time</title></head>");
53      out.println("<body>");
54      Calendar calendar =                                               create calendar
55        new GregorianCalendar(allLocale[localeIndex]);
56      TimeZone timeZone = TimeZone.getTimeZone(timeZoneID);
57      DateFormat dateFormat = DateFormat.getDateTimeInstance(
58        DateFormat.FULL, DateFormat.FULL, allLocale[localeIndex]);
59      dateFormat.setTimeZone(timeZone);
60      out.println("Current time is " +
61        dateFormat.format(calendar.getTime()) + "</p>");
62      out.println("</body></html>");
63      out.close(); // Close stream                                       close stream
64    }
65  }
```

Review

When you use the URL `http://localhost:8080/examples/servlet/TimeForm`, the servlet `TimeForm`'s `doGet` method is invoked to generate the time form dynamically. The method of the form is POST, and the action invokes the same servlet, `TimeForm`. When the form is submitted to the server, the `doPost` method is invoked to process the request.

The variables `allLocale` and `allTimeZone` (Lines 9–10), respectively, hold all the available locales and time zone IDs. The names of the locales are displayed in the locale list. The values for the locales are the indexes of the locales in the array `allLocale`. The time zone IDs are strings. They are displayed in the time zone list. They are also the values for the list. The indexes of the locale and the time zone are passed to the servlet as parameters. The `doPost` method obtains the values of the parameters (Lines 49–51) and finds the current time based on the locale and time zone.

26.7   Database Programming in Servlets

Many dynamic Web applications use databases to store and manage data. Servlets can connect to any relational database via JDBC. In Chapter 25, "Java Database Programming," you learned how to create Java programs to access and manipulate relational databases via JDBC. Connecting a servlet to a database is no different from connecting a Java application or applet to a database. If you know Java servlets and JDBC, you can combine them to develop interesting and practical Web-based interactive projects. The following example demonstrates connecting to a database from a servlet.

EXAMPLE 26.4 REGISTERING A STUDENT IN A DATABASE

Problem

This example creates a servlet that processes a registration form. The client enters data in an HTML form and submits it to the server, as shown in Figure 26.14. The result of the submission is shown in Figure 26.15. The server collects the data from the form and stores them in a database.

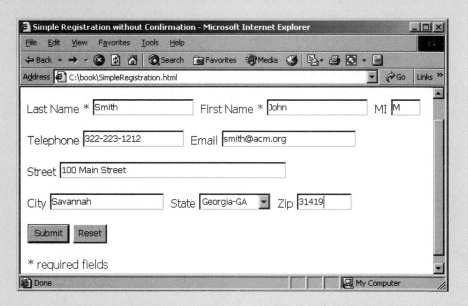

FIGURE 26.14 *The HTML form enables the user to enter student information.*

FIGURE 26.15 *The servlet processes the form and stores data in a database.*

EXAMPLE 26.4 (CONTINUED)

Solution

The registration data are stored in an `Address` table consisting of the following fields: `firstName`, `mi`, `lastName`, `street`, `city`, `state`, `zip`, `telephone`, and `email`, defined in the following statement:

```
create table Address (
  firstname varchar(25),
  mi char(1),
  lastname varchar(25),
  street varchar(40),
  city varchar(20),
  state varchar(2),
  zip varchar(5),
  telephone varchar(10),
  email varchar(30)
)
```

MySQL, Oracle, and Access were used in Chapter 25, "Java Database Programming." You can use any relational database. An ODBC data source ExampleMDBDataSource was used in Chapter 25. This example assumes that the table is stored in this data source. If the servlet uses a database driver other than the JDBC-ODBC driver (e.g., the MySQL JDBC driver and the Oracle JDBC driver), you need to place the JDBC driver (e.g., mysqljdbc.jar for MySQL and classes12.jar for Oracle) into c:\jakarta-tomcat-4.1.27\common\lib.

Create an HTML file named SimpleRegistration.html in Listing 26.6 for collecting the data and sending the data to the database using the POST method. This file is almost identical to Listing 26.3.

LISTING 26.6   SimpleRegistration.html

```
1  <!-- SimpleRegistration.html -->
2  <html>
3  <head>
4  <title>Simple Registration without Confirmation</title>
5  </head>
6  <body>
7  Please register to your instructor's student address book.</font>
8
9  <form method="POST" action=
10   "http://localhost:8080/examples/servlet/SimpleRegistration">
11 <p>Last Name <font color="#FF0000">*</font>
12     <input type="text" name="lastName"> 
13   First Name <font color="#FF0000">*</font>
14     <input type="text" name="firstName"> 
15   MI <input type="text" name="mi" size="3"></p>
16 <p>Telephone <input type="text" name="telephone" size="20"> 
17   Email <input type="text" name="email" size="28"> </p>
18 <p>Street <input type="text" name="street" size="50"></p>
19 <p>City <input type="text" name="city" size="23"> 
20   State <select size="1" name="state">
21           <option value="GA">Georgia-GA</option>
22           <option value="OK">Oklahoma-OK</option>
23           <option value="IN">Indiana-IN</option>
24         </select> 
25   Zip <input type="text" name="zip" size="9"></p>
26 <p><input type="submit" name="Submit" value="Submit">
27   <input type="reset" value="Reset"></p>
28 </form>
29 <p><font color="#FF0000">* required fields</font></p>
30 </body>
31 </html>
```

action

submit form

EXAMPLE 26.4 (CONTINUED)

Create the servlet named `SimpleRegistration` in Listing 26.7 and compile it into
c:\jakarta-tomcat-4.1.27\webapps\examples\WEB-INF\classes.

LISTING 26.7   SimpleRegistration.java

```java
 1 import javax.servlet.*;
 2 import javax.servlet.http.*;
 3 import java.io.*;
 4 import java.sql.*;
 5
 6 public class SimpleRegistration extends HttpServlet {
 7   // Use a prepared statement to store a student into the database
 8   private PreparedStatement pstmt;
 9
10   /** Initialize variables */
11   public void init() throws ServletException {
12     initializeJdbc();
13   }
14
15   /** Process the HTTP Post request */
16   public void doPost(HttpServletRequest request, HttpServletResponse
17       response) throws ServletException, IOException {
18     response.setContentType("text/html");
19     PrintWriter out = response.getWriter();
20
21     // Obtain parameters from the client
22     String lastName = request.getParameter("lastName");
23     String firstName = request.getParameter("firstName");
24     String mi = request.getParameter("mi");
25     String phone = request.getParameter("telephone");
26     String email = request.getParameter("email");
27     String address = request.getParameter("street");
28     String city = request.getParameter("city");
29     String state = request.getParameter("state");
30     String zip = request.getParameter("zip");
31
32     try {
33       if (lastName.length() == 0 || firstName.length() == 0) {
34         out.println("Last Name and First Name are required");
35         return; // End the method
36       }
37
38       storeStudent(lastName, firstName, mi, phone, email, address,
39         city, state, zip);
40
41       out.println(firstName + " " + lastName +
42         " is now registered in the database");
43     }
44     catch(Exception ex) {
45       out.println("Error: " + ex.getMessage());
46     }
47     finally {
48       out.close(); // Close stream
49     }
50   }
51
52   /** Initialize database connection */
53   private void initializeJdbc() {
54     try {
55       // Declare driver and connection string
56       String driver = "sun.jdbc.odbc.JdbcOdbcDriver";
57       String connectionString = "jdbc:odbc:exampleMDBDataSource";
58       // For Oracle
59       // String driver = "oracle.jdbc.driver.OracleDriver";
60       // String connectionString = "jdbc:oracle:" +
61       //   "thin:scott/tiger@liang.armstrong.edu:1521:ora9i";
```

Margin notes:
- initialize db (line 12)
- process POST (line 16)
- content type (line 18)
- output to browser (line 19)
- get parameters (line 22)
- store record (line 38)
- close stream (line 48)
- load driver (line 56)
- Oracle driver commented (line 59)

EXAMPLE 26.4 (CONTINUED)

```
62
63      // Load the driver
64      Class.forName(driver);                                    load driver
65
66      // Connect to the sample database
67      Connection conn = DriverManager.getConnection           connect db
68        (connectionString);
69
70      // Create a Statement
71      pstmt = conn.prepareStatement("insert into Address " +   prepare statement
72        "(lastName, firstName, mi, telephone, email, street, city, "
73        + "state, zip) values (?, ?, ?, ?, ?, ?, ?, ?, ?)");
74    }
75    catch (Exception ex) {
76      System.out.println(ex);
77    }
78  }
79
80  /** Store a student record to the database */
81  private void storeStudent(String lastName, String firstName,
82    String mi, String phone, String email, String address,
83    String city, String state, String zip) throws SQLException {
84    pstmt.setString(1, lastName);                             set values
85    pstmt.setString(2, firstName);
86    pstmt.setString(3, mi);
87    pstmt.setString(4, phone);
88    pstmt.setString(5, email);
89    pstmt.setString(6, address);
90    pstmt.setString(7, city);
91    pstmt.setString(8, state);
92    pstmt.setString(9, zip);
93    pstmt.executeUpdate();                                    execute SQL
94  }
95 }
```

Review

The init method (Line 11) is executed once when the servlet starts. After the servlet has started, the servlet can be invoked many times as long as it is alive in the servlet container. Load the driver, and connect to the database from the servlet's init method. If a prepared statement or a callable statement is used, it should also be created in the init method. In this example, a prepared statement is desirable, because the servlet always uses the same insert statement with different values.

A servlet can connect to any relational database via JDBC. The initializeJdbc method in this example loads a JDBC-ODBC bridge driver (Line 56). Use of the Oracle Thin driver is commented in the code (Line 59). Once connected, it creates a prepared statement for inserting a student record into the database. The Access database and the Oracle database are the same as were used in Chapter 25, "Java Database Programming." To use the MS Access database, the ODBC data source exampleMDBDataSource must be created. To use the Oracle database, you must have the Oracle JDBC Thin driver in the library of the project.

Last name and first name are required fields. If either of them is empty, the servlet sends an error message to the client (Lines 33–36). Otherwise, the servlet stores the data in the database using the prepared statement.

26.8 Session Tracking

Web servers use Hyper-Text Transport Protocol (HTTP). HTTP is a stateless protocol. An HTTP Web server cannot associate requests from a client, and therefore treats each request independently. This protocol works fine for simple Web browsing, where each request typically results in an HTML file or in a text file being sent back to the client. Such simple requests are isolated. However, the requests in interactive Web applications are often related. Consider the two requests in the following scenario:

Request 1: A client sends registration data to the server; the server then returns the data to the user for confirmation.

Request 2: The client confirms the data by resubmitting them.

In Request 2, the data submitted in Request 1 were sent back to the server. These two requests are related in a session. A *session* can be defined as a series of related interactions between a single client and the Web server over a period of time. Tracking data among requests in a session is known as *session tracking*.

This section introduces three techniques for session tracking: *using hidden values, using cookies,* and *using the session tracking tools from servlet API.*

26.8.1 Session Tracking Using Hidden Values

You can track a session by passing data from the servlet to the client as hidden values in a dynamically generated HTML form by including a field like this one:

```
<input type="hidden" name="lastName" value="Smith">
```

The next request will submit the data back to the servlet. The servlet retrieves this hidden value just like any other parameter value using the `getParameter` method.

EXAMPLE 26.5 USING HIDDEN VALUES IN THE REGISTRATION FORM

Problem

This example creates a servlet that processes a registration form. The client submits the form using the GET method, as shown in Figure 26.16. The server collects the data in the form, displays them to the client, and asks the client for confirmation, as shown in Figure 26.17. The client confirms the data by submitting the request with the hidden values using the POST method. Finally, the servlet writes the data to a database.

FIGURE 26.16 *The registration form collects user information.*

EXAMPLE 26.5 (CONTINUED)

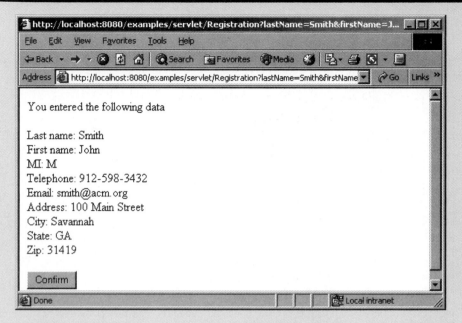

FIGURE 26.17   *The servlet asks the client for confirmation of the input.*

Solution

Create an HTML form named Registration.html in Listing 26.8 for collecting the data and sending the data to the database using the GET method for confirmation. This file is almost identical to Listing 26.6 except that it uses a different action URL.

LISTING 26.8   Registration.html

```
 1 <!-- Registration.html -->
 2 <html>
 3 <head>
 4 <title>Registration Using Hidden Data for Session Tracking</title>
 5 </head>
 6 <body>
 7 Please register to your instructor's student address book.</font>
 8
 9 <form method="GET"
10   action="http://localhost:8080/examples/servlet/Registration">
11 <p>Last Name <font color="#FF0000">*</font>
12    <input type="text" name="lastName"> 
13   First Name <font color="#FF0000">*</font>
14    <input type="text" name="firstName"> 
15   MI <input type="text" name="mi" size="3"></p>
16 <p>Telephone <input type="text" name="telephone" size="20"> 
17    Email <input type="text" name="email" size="28"> </p>
18 <p>Street <input type="text" name="street" size="50"></p>
19 <p>City <input type="text" name="city" size="23"> 
20    State <select size="1" name="state">
21          <option value="GA">Georgia-GA</option>
22          <option value="OK">Oklahoma-OK</option>
23          <option value="IN">Indiana-IN</option>
24       </select> 
25    Zip <input type="text" name="zip" size="9"></p>
26 <p><input type="submit" name="Submit" value="Submit">
27    <input type="reset" value="Reset"></p>
28 </form>
```

action

submit form

EXAMPLE 26.5 (CONTINUED)

```
29 <p><font color="#FF0000">* required fields</font></p>
30 </body>
31 </html>
```

Create the servlet named Registration in Listing 26.9 and compile it into c:\jakarta-tomcat-4.1.27\webapps\examples\WEB-INF\classes.

LISTING 26.9   Registration.java

```
 1 import javax.servlet.*;
 2 import javax.servlet.http.*;
 3 import java.io.*;
 4 import java.sql.*;
 5
 6 public class Registration extends HttpServlet {
 7   // Use a prepared statement to store a student into the database
 8   private PreparedStatement pstmt;
 9
10   /** Initialize variables */
11   public void init() throws ServletException {
12     initializeJdbc();
13   }
14
15   /** Process the HTTP GET request */
16   public void doGet(HttpServletRequest request, HttpServletResponse
17       response) throws ServletException, IOException {
18     response.setContentType("text/html");
19     PrintWriter out = response.getWriter();
20
21     // Obtain data from the form
22     String lastName = request.getParameter("lastName");
23     String firstName = request.getParameter("firstName");
24     String mi = request.getParameter("mi");
25     String telephone = request.getParameter("telephone");
26     String email = request.getParameter("email");
27     String street = request.getParameter("street");
28     String city = request.getParameter("city");
29     String state = request.getParameter("state");
30     String zip = request.getParameter("zip");
31
32     if (lastName.length() == 0 || firstName.length() == 0) {
33       out.println("Last Name and First Name are required");
34       return; // End the method
35     }
36
37     // Ask for confirmation
38     out.println("You entered the following data");
39     out.println("<p>Last name: " + lastName);
40     out.println("<br>First name: " + firstName);
41     out.println("<br>MI: " + mi);
42     out.println("<br>Telephone: " + telephone);
43     out.println("<br>Email: " + email);
44     out.println("<br>Address: " + street);
45     out.println("<br>City: " + city);
46     out.println("<br>State: " + state);
47     out.println("<br>Zip: " + zip);
48
49     // Set the action for processing the answers
50     out.println("<p><form method=\"POST\" action=" +
51       "registration>");
52     // Set hidden values
53     out.println("<p><input type=\"hidden\" " +
54       "value=" + lastName + " name=\"lastName\">");
55     out.println("<p><input type=\"hidden\" " +
56       "value=" + firstName + " name=\"firstName\">");
57     out.println("<p><input type=\"hidden\" " +
```

initialize db

process GET

content type
output to browser

get parameters

client verification

EXAMPLE 26.5 (CONTINUED)

```
58        "value=" + mi + " name=\"mi\">");
59      out.println("<p><input type=\"hidden\" " +
60        "value=" + telephone + " name=\"telephone\">");
61      out.println("<p><input type=\"hidden\" " +
62        "value=" + email + " name=\"email\">");
63      out.println("<p><input type=\"hidden\" " +
64        "value=" + street + " name=\"street\">");
65      out.println("<p><input type=\"hidden\" " +
66        "value=" + city + " name=\"city\">");
67      out.println("<p><input type=\"hidden\" " +
68        "value=" + state + " name=\"state\">");
69      out.println("<p><input type=\"hidden\" " +
70        "value=" + zip + " name=\"zip\">");
71      out.println("<p><input type=\"submit\" value=\"Confirm\" >");
72      out.println("</form>");
73
74      out.close(); // Close stream
75    }
76
77    /** Process the HTTP POST request */
78    public void doPost(HttpServletRequest request, HttpServletResponse
79        response) throws ServletException, IOException {
80      response.setContentType("text/html");
81      PrintWriter out = response.getWriter();
82
83      try {
84        String lastName = request.getParameter("lastName");
85        String firstName = request.getParameter("firstName");
86        String mi = request.getParameter("mi");
87        String telephone = request.getParameter("telephone");
88        String email = request.getParameter("email");
89        String street = request.getParameter("street");
90        String city = request.getParameter("city");
91        String state = request.getParameter("state");
92        String zip = request.getParameter("zip");
93
94        storeStudent(lastName, firstName, mi, telephone, email,
95          street, city, state, zip);
96
97        out.println(firstName + " " + lastName +
98          " is now registered in the database");
99      }
100     catch(Exception ex) {
101       out.println("Error: " + ex.getMessage());
102       return; // End the method
103     }
104   }
105
106   /** Initialize database connection */
107   private void initializeJdbc() {
108     try {
109       // Declare driver and connection string
110       String driver = "sun.jdbc.odbc.JdbcOdbcDriver";
111       String connectionString = "jdbc:odbc:exampleMDBDataSource";
112       /* For Oracle
113       String driver = "oracle.jdbc.driver.OracleDriver";
114       String connectionString = "jdbc:oracle:" +
115         "thin:scott/tiger@liang.armstrong.edu:1521:ora9i";
116       */
117       // Load the Oracle JDBC Thin driver
118       Class.forName(driver);
119
120       // Connect to the sample database
121       Connection conn = DriverManager.getConnection
122         (connectionString);
123
```

process POST

content type
output to browser

get parameters

store record

EXAMPLE 26.5 (CONTINUED)

```
124        // Create a Statement
125        pstmt = conn.prepareStatement("insert into Address " +
126          "(lastName, firstName, mi, telephone, email, street, city, "
127          + "state, zip) values (?, ?, ?, ?, ?, ?, ?, ?, ?)");
128      }
129      catch (Exception ex) {
130        System.out.println(ex);
131      }
132    }
133
134    /** Store a student record to the database */
135    private void storeStudent(String lastName, String firstName,
136        String mi, String phone, String email, String address,
137        String city, String state, String zip) throws SQLException {
138      pstmt.setString(1, lastName);
139      pstmt.setString(2, firstName);
140      pstmt.setString(3, mi);
141      pstmt.setString(4, phone);
142      pstmt.setString(5, email);
143      pstmt.setString(6, address);
144      pstmt.setString(7, city);
145      pstmt.setString(8, state);
146      pstmt.setString(9, zip);
147      pstmt.executeUpdate();
148    }
149  }
```

Review

The servlet processes the GET request by generating an HTML page that displays the client's input and asks for the client's confirmation. The input data are hidden values in the newly generated forms, so they will be sent back in the confirmation request. The confirmation request uses the POST method. The servlet retrieves the hidden values and stores them in the database.

Since the first request does not write anything to the database, it is appropriate to use the GET method. Since the second request results in an update to the database, the POST method must be used.

 NOTE

The hidden values could also be sent from the URL query string if the request uses the GET method.

26.8.2   Session Tracking Using Cookies

You can track sessions using cookies, which are small text files that store sets of name-value pairs on the disk in the client's computer. Cookies are sent from the server through the instructions in the header of the HTTP response. The instructions tell the browser to create a cookie with a given name and its associated value. If the browser already has a cookie with the key name, the value will be updated. The browser will then send the cookie with any request submitted to the same server. Cookies can have expiration dates set, after which they will not be sent to the server. The javax. servlet.http.Cookie is used to create and manipulate cookies, as shown in Figure 26.18.

To send a cookie to the browser, use the addCookie method in the HttpServletResponse class, as shown below:

```
response.addCookie(cookie);
```

where response is an instance of HttpServletResponse.

javax.servlet.http.Cookie	
+Cookie(name: String, value: String)	Creates a cookie with the specified name-value pair.
+getName(): String	Returns the name of the cookie.
+getValue(): String	Returns the value of the cookie.
+setValue(newValue: String): void	Assigns a new value to a cookie after the cookie is created.
+getMaxAge(): int	Returns the maximum age of the cookie, specified in seconds.
+setMaxAge(expiration: int): void	Specifies the maximum age of the cookie. By default, this value is –1, which implies that the cookie persists until the browser exits. If you set this value to 0, the cookie is deleted.
+getSecure(): boolean	Returns true if the browser is sending cookies only over a secure protocol.
+setSecure(flag: boolean): void	Indicates to the browser whether the cookie should only be sent using a secure protocol, such as HTTPS or SSL.
+getComment(): String	Returns the comment describing the purpose of this cookie, or null if the cookie has no comment.
+setComment(purpose: String): void	Sets the comment for this cookie.

FIGURE 26.18 *Cookie stores a name-value pair and other information about the cookie.*

To obtain cookies from a browser, use

```
request.getCookies();
```

where request is an instance of HttpServletRequest.

EXAMPLE 26.6 USING COOKIES IN THE REGISTRATION FORM

Problem

This example accomplishes the same task as Example 26.5, "Using Hidden Values in the Registration Form." Instead of using hidden values for session tracking, it uses cookies.

Solution

Create the servlet named RegistrationWithHttpCookie in Listing 26.10. Compile it into c:\jakarta-tomcat-4.1.27\webapps\examples\WEB-INF\classes.

Create an HTML file named RegistrationWithCookie.html that is identical to Registration.html except that the action is replaced by

```
http://localhost:8080/examples/servlet/RegistrationWithCookie
```

LISTING 26.10   RegistrationWithCookie.java

```
 1 import javax.servlet.*;
 2 import javax.servlet.http.*;
 3 import java.io.*;
 4 import java.sql.*;
 5
 6 public class RegistrationWithCookie extends HttpServlet {
 7   private static final String CONTENT_TYPE = "text/html";
 8   // Use a prepared statement to store a student into the database
 9   private PreparedStatement pstmt;
10
11   /** Initialize variables */
12   public void init() throws ServletException {
13     initializeJdbc();
14   }
15
16   /** Process the HTTP GET request */
17   public void doGet(HttpServletRequest request, HttpServletResponse
```

process GET

EXAMPLE 26.6 (CONTINUED)

```
18        response) throws ServletException, IOException {
19      response.setContentType("text/html");
20      PrintWriter out = response.getWriter();
21
22      // Obtain data from the form
23      String lastName = request.getParameter("lastName");
24      String firstName = request.getParameter("firstName");
25      String mi = request.getParameter("mi");
26      String telephone = request.getParameter("telephone");
27      String email = request.getParameter("email");
28      String street = request.getParameter("street");
29      String city = request.getParameter("city");
30      String state = request.getParameter("state");
31      String zip = request.getParameter("zip");
32
33      // Create cookies and send cookies to browsers
34      Cookie cookieLastName = new Cookie("lastName", lastName);
35      // cookieLastName.setMaxAge(1000);
36      response.addCookie(cookieLastName);
37      Cookie cookieFirstName = new Cookie("firstName", firstName);
38      response.addCookie(cookieFirstName);
39      // cookieFirstName.setMaxAge(0);
40      Cookie cookieMi = new Cookie("mi", mi);
41      response.addCookie(cookieMi);
42      Cookie cookieTelephone = new Cookie("telephone", telephone);
43      response.addCookie(cookieTelephone);
44      Cookie cookieEmail = new Cookie("email", email);
45      response.addCookie(cookieEmail);
46      Cookie cookieStreet = new Cookie("street", street);
47      response.addCookie(cookieStreet);
48      Cookie cookieCity = new Cookie("city", city);
49      response.addCookie(cookieCity);
50      Cookie cookieState = new Cookie("state", state);
51      response.addCookie(cookieState);
52      Cookie cookieZip = new Cookie("zip", zip);
53      response.addCookie(cookieZip);
54
55      System.out.println("MaxAge? " + cookieLastName.getMaxAge());
56      System.out.println("MaxAge fir? " + cookieFirstName.getMaxAge());
57
58      if (lastName.length() == 0 || firstName.length() == 0) {
59        out.println("Last Name and First Name are required");
60        return; // End the method
61      }
62
63      // Ask for confirmation
64      out.println("You entered the following data");
65      out.println("<p>Last name: " + lastName);
66      out.println("<br>First name: " + firstName);
67      out.println("<br>MI: " + mi);
68      out.println("<br>Telephone: " + telephone);
69      out.println("<br>Email: " + email);
70      out.println("<br>Street: " + street);
71      out.println("<br>City: " + city);
72      out.println("<br>State: " + state);
73      out.println("<br>Zip: " + zip);
74
75      // Set the action for processing the answers
76      out.println("<p><form method=\"POST\" action=" +
77        "/examples/servlet/RegistrationWithCookie>");
78      out.println("<p><input type=\"submit\" value=\"Confirm\" >");
79      out.println("</form>");
80      out.close(); // Close stream
81    }
82
83    /** Process the HTTP POST request */
84    public void doPost(HttpServletRequest request, HttpServletResponse
```

get parameters (line 23)

create cookies (line 34)

send cookies (line 36)

client verification (line 63)

process POST (line 84)

EXAMPLE 26.6 (CONTINUED)

```
85        response) throws ServletException, IOException {
86      response.setContentType(CONTENT_TYPE);
87      PrintWriter out = response.getWriter();
88
89      String lastName = "";
90      String firstName = "";
91      String mi = "";
92      String telephone = "";
93      String email = "";
94      String street = "";
95      String city = "";
96      String state = "";
97      String zip = "";
98
99      // Read the cookies
100     Cookie[] cookies = request.getCookies();
101
102     // Get cookie values
103     for (int i = 0; i < cookies.length; i++) {
104       if (cookies[i].getName().equals("lastName"))
105         lastName = cookies[i].getValue();
106       else if (cookies[i].getName().equals("firstName"))
107         firstName = cookies[i].getValue();
108       else if (cookies[i].getName().equals("mi"))
109         mi = cookies[i].getValue();
110       else if (cookies[i].getName().equals("telephone"))
111         telephone = cookies[i].getValue();
112       else if (cookies[i].getName().equals("email"))
113         email = cookies[i].getValue();
114       else if (cookies[i].getName().equals("street"))
115         street = cookies[i].getValue();
116       else if (cookies[i].getName().equals("city"))
117         city = cookies[i].getValue();
118       else if (cookies[i].getName().equals("state"))
119         state = cookies[i].getValue();
120       else if (cookies[i].getName().equals("zip"))
121         zip = cookies[i].getValue();
122     }
123
124     try {
125       storeStudent(lastName, firstName, mi, telephone, email, street,
126         city, state, zip);
127
128       out.println(firstName + " " + lastName +
129         " is now registered in the database");
130
131       out.close(); // Close stream
132     }
133     catch(Exception ex) {
134       out.println("Error: " + ex.getMessage());
135       return; // End the method
136     }
137   }
138
139   /** Initialize database connection */
140   private void initializeJdbc() {
141     try {
142       // Declare driver and connection string
143       String driver = "sun.jdbc.odbc.JdbcOdbcDriver";
144       String connectionString = "jdbc:odbc:exampleMDBDataSource";
145       // For Oracle
146       // String driver = "oracle.jdbc.driver.OracleDriver";
147       // String connectionString = "jdbc:oracle:" +
148       //   "thin:scott/tiger@liang.armstrong.edu:1521:ora9i";
149
150       // Load the Oracle JDBC Thin driver
151       Class.forName(driver);
152       System.out.println("Driver " + driver + " loaded");
```

get cookies

store record

EXAMPLE 26.6 (CONTINUED)

```
153
154        // Connect to the sample database
155        Connection conn = DriverManager.getConnection
156          (connectionString);
157        System.out.println("Database " + connectionString +
158          " connected");
159
160        // Create a Statement
161        pstmt = conn.prepareStatement("insert into Address " +
162          "(lastName, firstName, mi, telephone, email, street, city, "
163          + "state, zip) values (?, ?, ?, ?, ?, ?, ?, ?, ?)");
164      }
165      catch (Exception ex) {
166        System.out.println(ex);
167      }
168    }
169
170    /** Store a student record to the database */
171    private void storeStudent(String lastName, String firstName,
172        String mi, String telephone, String email, String street,
173        String city, String state, String zip) throws SQLException {
174      pstmt.setString(1, lastName);
175      pstmt.setString(2, firstName);
176      pstmt.setString(3, mi);
177      pstmt.setString(4, telephone);
178      pstmt.setString(5, email);
179      pstmt.setString(6, street);
180      pstmt.setString(7, city);
181      pstmt.setString(8, state);
182      pstmt.setString(9, zip);
183      pstmt.executeUpdate();
184    }
185  }
```

Review

You have to create a cookie for each value you want to track, using the Cookie class's only constructor, which defines a cookie's name and value as shown below (Line 34):

```
Cookie cookieLastName = new Cookie("lastName", lastName);
```

To send the cookie to the browser, use a statement like this one (Line 36):

```
response.addCookie(cookieLastName);
```

If a cookie with the same name already exists in the browser, its value is updated; otherwise, a new cookie is created.

Cookies are automatically sent to the Web server with each request from the client. The servlet retrieves all the cookies into an array using the getCookies method (Line 100):

```
Cookie[] cookies = request.getCookies();
```

To obtain the name of the cookie, use the getName method (Line 104):

```
String name = cookies[i].getName();
```

The cookie's value can be obtained using the getValue method (Line 105):

```
String value = cookies[i].getValue();
```

Cookies are stored as strings just like form parameters and hidden values. If a cookie represents a numeric value, you have to convert it into an integer or a double, using the parseInt method in the Integer class or the parseDouble method in the Double class.

By default, a newly created cookie persists until the browser exits. However, you can set an expiration date, using the setMaxAge method, to allow a cookie to stay in the browser for up to 2,147,483,647 seconds (approximately 24,855 days).

26.8.3   Session Tracking Using the Servlet API

You have now learned both session tracking using hidden values and session tracking using cookies. These two session-tracking methods have problems. They send data to the browser either as hidden values or as cookies. The data are not secure, and anybody with knowledge of computers can obtain them. The hidden data are in HTML form, which can be viewed from the browser. Cookies are stored in the Cache directory of the browser. Because of security concerns, some browsers do not accept cookies. The client can turn the cookies off and limit their number. Another problem is that hidden data and cookies pass data as strings. You cannot pass objects using these two methods.

To address these problems, Java servlet API provides the `javax.servlet.http.HttpSession` interface that provides a way to identify a user across more than one page request or visit to a Web site and to store information about that user. The servlet container uses this interface to create a session between an HTTP client and an HTTP server. The session persists for a specified time period, across more than one connection or page request from the user. A session usually corresponds to one user, who may visit a site many times. The session enables tracking of a large set of data. The data can be stored as objects and are secure because they are kept on the server side.

To use the Java servlet API for session tracking, first create a session object using the `getSession()` method in the `HttpServletRequest` interface:

```
HttpSession session = request.getSession();
```

This obtains the session or creates a new session if the client does not have a session on the server.

The `HttpSession` interface provides the methods for reading and storing data to the session, and for manipulating the session, as shown in Figure 26.19.

javax.servlet.http.HttpSession	
+getAttribute(name: String): Object	Returns the object bound with the specified name in this session, or null if no object is bound under the name.
+setAttribute(name: String, value: Object): void	Binds an object to this session, using the specified name. If an object of the same name is already bound to the session, the object is replaced.
+getId(): String	Returns a string containing the unique identifier assigned to this session. The identifier is assigned by the servlet container and is implementation dependent.
+getLastAccessedTime(): long	Returns the last time the client sent a request associated with this session, as the number of milliseconds since midnight January 1, 1970 GMT, and marked by the time the container received the request.
+invalidate(): void	Invalidates this session, then unbinds any objects bound to it.
+isNew(): boolean	Returns true if the session was just created in the current request.
+removeAttribute(name: String): void	Removes the object bound with the specified name from this session. If the session does not have an object bound with the specified name, this method does nothing.
+getMaxInactiveInterval(): int	Returns the time, in seconds, between client requests before the servlet container will invalidate this session. A negative time indicates that the session will never time-out. Use setMaxInactiveInterval to specify this value.
+setMaxInactiveInterval(interval: int): void	

FIGURE 26.19 *HttpSession establishes a persistent session between a client with multiple requests and the server.*

 NOTE

HTTP is stateless. So how does the server associate a session with multiple requests from the same client? This is handled behind the scenes by the servlet container and is transparent to the servlet programmer.

EXAMPLE 26.7 USING HttpSession IN THE REGISTRATION FORM

Problem

This example accomplishes the same task as Examples 26.5 and 26.6, "Using Hidden Values in the Registration Form," and "Using Cookies in the Registration Form." Instead of using hidden values or cookies for session tracking, it uses servlet HttpSession.

Solution

Create the servlet named `RegistrationWithHttpSession` in Listing 26.11. Compile it into c:\jakarta-tomcat-4.1.27\webapps\examples\WEB-INF\classes. Note that this servlet contains two class files, RegistrationWithHttpSession.class and RegistrationWithHttpSession$Student.class.

Create an HTML file named RegistrationWithHttpSession.html that is identical to Registration.html except that the action is replaced by

```
http://localhost:8080/examples/servlet/RegistrationWithHttpSession
```

LISTING 26.11   RegistrationWithHttpSession.java

```java
 1 import javax.servlet.*;
 2 import javax.servlet.http.*;
 3 import java.io.*;
 4 import java.sql.*;
 5 import java.util.*;
 6
 7 public class RegistrationWithHttpSession extends HttpServlet {
 8   // Use a prepared statement to store a student into the database
 9   private PreparedStatement pstmt;
10
11   /** Initialize variables */
12   public void init() throws ServletException {
13     initializeJdbc();
14   }
15
16   /** Process the HTTP GET request */
17   public void doGet(HttpServletRequest request, HttpServletResponse
18       response) throws ServletException, IOException {
19     // Set response type and output stream to the browser
20     response.setContentType("text/html");
21     PrintWriter out = response.getWriter();
22
23     // Obtain data from the form
24     String lastName = request.getParameter("lastName");
25     String firstName = request.getParameter("firstName");
26     String mi = request.getParameter("mi");
27     String telephone = request.getParameter("telephone");
28     String email = request.getParameter("email");
29     String street = request.getParameter("street");
30     String city = request.getParameter("city");
31     String state = request.getParameter("state");
32     String zip = request.getParameter("zip");
33
34     if (lastName.length() == 0 || firstName.length() == 0) {
35       out.println("Last Name and First Name are required");
36       return; // End the method
37     }
38
39     // Create a Student object
40     Student student = new Student(lastName, firstName,
41       mi, telephone, email, street, city, state, zip);
42
43     // Get an HttpSession or create one if it does not exist
44     HttpSession httpSession = request.getSession();
45
```

process GET

get parameters

create student

create session

Example 26.7 (Continued)

```
46      // Store student object to the session
47      httpSession.setAttribute("student", student);
48
49      // Ask for confirmation
50      out.println("You entered the following data");
51      out.println("<p>Last name: " + lastName);
52      out.println("<p>First name: " + firstName);
53      out.println("<p>MI: " + mi);
54      out.println("<p>Telephone: " + telephone);
55      out.println("<p>Email: " + email);
56      out.println("<p>Address: " + street);
57      out.println("<p>City: " + city);
58      out.println("<p>State: " + state);
59      out.println("<p>Zip: " + zip);
60
61      // Set the action for processing the answers
62      out.println("<p><form method=\"POST\" action=" +
63        "/examples/servlet/RegistrationWithHttpSession>");
64      out.println("<p><input type=\"submit\" value=\"Confirm\" >");
65      out.println("</form>");
66
67      out.close(); // Close stream
68    }
69
70    /** Process the HTTP POST request */
71    public void doPost(HttpServletRequest request, HttpServletResponse
72        response) throws ServletException, IOException {
73      // Set response type and output stream to the browser
74      response.setContentType("text/html");
75      PrintWriter out = response.getWriter();
76
77      // Obtain the HttpSession
78      HttpSession httpSession = request.getSession();
79
80      // Get the Student object in the HttpSession
81      Student student = (Student)(httpSession.getAttribute("student"));
82
83      try {
84        storeStudent(student);
85
86        out.println(student.firstName + " " + student.lastName +
87          " is now registered in the database");
88        out.close(); // Close stream
89      }
90      catch(Exception ex) {
91        out.println("Error: " + ex.getMessage());
92        return; // End the method
93      }
94    }
95
96    /** Initialize database connection */
97    private void initializeJdbc() {
98      try {
99        // Declare driver and connection string
100       String driver = "sun.jdbc.odbc.JdbcOdbcDriver";
101       String connectionString = "jdbc:odbc:exampleMDBDataSource";
102
103       // Load the Oracle JDBC Thin driver
104       Class.forName(driver);
105       System.out.println("Driver " + driver + " loaded");
106
107       // Connect to the sample database
108       Connection conn = DriverManager.getConnection
109         (connectionString);
110       System.out.println("Database " + connectionString +
111         " connected");
```

set attribute

process POST

get session

get student

store student

EXAMPLE 26.7 (CONTINUED)

```
112
113        // Create a Statement
114        pstmt = conn.prepareStatement("insert into Address " +
115          "(lastName, firstName, mi, telephone, email, street, city, "
116          + "state, zip) values (?, ?, ?, ?, ?, ?, ?, ?, ?)");
117      }
118      catch (Exception ex) {
119        System.out.println(ex);
120      }
121    }
122
123    /** Store a student record to the database */
124    private void storeStudent(Student student) throws SQLException {
125      pstmt.setString(1, student.getLastName());
126      pstmt.setString(2, student.getFirstName());
127      pstmt.setString(3, student.getMi());
128      pstmt.setString(4, student.getTelephone());
129      pstmt.setString(5, student.getEmail());
130      pstmt.setString(6, student.getAddress());
131      pstmt.setString(7, student.getCity());
132      pstmt.setString(8, student.getState());
133      pstmt.setString(9, student.getZip());
134      pstmt.executeUpdate();
135    }
136
137    class Student {
138      private String lastName = "";
139      private String firstName = "";
140      private String mi = "";
141      private String telephone = "";
142      private String email = "";
143      private String street = "";
144      private String city = "";
145      private String state = "";
146      private String zip = "";
147
148      Student(String lastName, String firstName,
149        String mi, String telephone, String email, String street,
150        String city, String state, String zip) {
151        this.lastName = lastName;
152        this.firstName = firstName;
153        this.mi = mi;
154        this.telephone = telephone;
155        this.email = email;
156        this.street = street;
157        this.city = city;
158        this.state = state;
159        this.zip = zip;
160      }
161
162      public String getLastName() {
163        return lastName;
164      }
165
166      public String getFirstName() {
167        return firstName;
168      }
169
170      public String getMi() {
171        return mi;
172      }
173
174      public String getTelephone() {
175        return telephone;
176      }
177
```

inner class

EXAMPLE 26.7 (CONTINUED)

```
178      public String getEmail() {
179        return email;
180      }
181
182      public String getAddress() {
183        return street;
184      }
185
186      public String getCity() {
187        return city;
188      }
189
190      public String getState() {
191        return state;
192      }
193
194      public String getZip() {
195        return zip;
196      }
197    }
198  }
```

Review

The statement (Line 44)

```
HttpSession httpSession = request.getSession();
```

obtains a session, or creates a new session if the session does not exist.

Since objects can be stored in HttpSession, this program defines a Student class. A Student object is created and is stored in the session using the setAttribute method, which binds the object with a name like the one shown below (Line 47):

```
httpSession.setAttribute("student", student);
```

To retrieve the object, use the following statement (Line 81):

```
Student student = (Student)(httpSession.getAttribute("student"));
```

There is only one session between a client and a servlet. You can store any number of objects in a session. By default, a session stays alive as long as the servlet is not destroyed. You can explicitly set the session active time using the setMaxInactiveInterval method.

26.9   Sending Images from Servlets

So far you have learned how to write Java servlets that generate dynamic HTML text. Java servlets are not limited to sending text to a browser. They can return images on demand. The images can be stored in files or created from programs.

26.9.1   Sending Image from Files

You can use the HTML <img> tag to send images from files. The syntax for the tag is:

```
<img src=URL alt=text align = [top ¦ middle ¦ bottom ¦ texttop]>
```

The attribute src specifies the source of the image. The attribute alt specifies an alternative text to be displayed in case the image cannot be displayed on the browser. The attribute align tells the browser where to place the image.

EXAMPLE 26.8 GETTING IMAGES FROM SERVLETS

Problem

This example creates a servlet that dynamically generates the flag of a country and a text that describes the flag, as shown in Figure 26.20. The flag is stored in an image file and the text that describes the flag is stored in a text file.

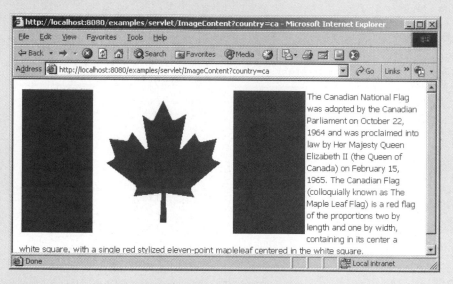

FIGURE 26.20   *The servlet returns an image along with the text.*

Solution

Create the servlet named `ImageContent` in Listing 26.12. Compile it into c:\jakarta-tomcat-4.1.27\webapps\examples\WEB-INF\classes. Run the servlet using the URL

```
http://localhost:8080/examples/servlet/ImageContent?country=ca
```

LISTING 26.12   **ImageContent.java**

```java
1 import javax.servlet.*;
2 import javax.servlet.http.*;
3 import java.io.*;
4
5 public class ImageContent extends HttpServlet {
6   /** Process the HTTP GET request */
7   public void doGet(HttpServletRequest request, HttpServletResponse
8       response) throws ServletException, IOException {
9     response.setContentType("text/html");
10    PrintWriter out = response.getWriter();
11
12    String country = request.getParameter("country");
13
14    out.println("<img src = \"/examples/images/" + country + ".gif"
15      + "\" align=left>");
16
17    // Read description from a file and send it to the browser
18    BufferedReader in = new BufferedReader(new FileReader(
19      "c:\\book\\" + country + ".txt"));
20
21    // Text line from the text file for flag description
22    String line;
23
24    // Read a line from the text file and send it to the browser
25    while ((line = in.readLine()) != null) {
26      out.println(line);
27    }
```

image tag

read file

EXAMPLE 26.8 (CONTINUED)

```
28
29    out.close();
30  }
31 }
```

Review

You should store the image files in c:\jakarta-tomcat-4.1.27\webapps\examples\images.

The country parameter determines which image file and text file are displayed. The servlet sends the HTML contents to the browser. The contents contain an <img> tag (Lines 14–15) that references to the image file.

The servlet reads the characters from the text file and sends them to the browser (Lines 18–27).

26.9.2 Sending Images from the Image Object

The preceding example displays an image stored in an image file. You can also send an image dynamically created in the program.

Before the image is sent to a browser, it must be encoded into a format acceptable to the browser. Image encoders are not part of the Java API, but several free encoders are available. One of them is the GifEncoder class (http://www.acme.com/java/software/Acme.JPM.Encoders.GifEncoder.html), which is included in \book\acme.jar. Use the following statement to encode and send the image to the browser:

```
new GifEncoder(image, out, true).encode();
```

where out is a binary output stream from the servlet to the browser, which can be obtained using the following statement:

```
OutputStream out = response.getOutputStream();
```

EXAMPLE 26.9 CREATING IMAGES BY DRAWING

Problem

This example creates a servlet that displays a clock to show the current time, as shown in Figure 26.21.

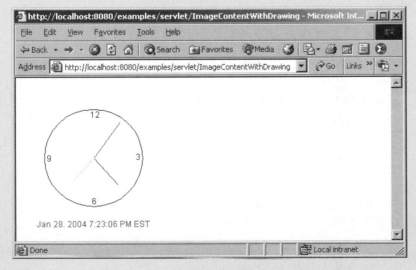

FIGURE 26.21 *The servlet returns a clock that displays the current time.*

EXAMPLE 26.9 (CONTINUED)

Solution

Create the servlet named `ImageContentWithDrawing` in Listing 26.13. Compile it into c:\jakarta-tomcat-4.1.27\webapps\examples\WEB-INF\classes. Run the servlet using the URL

```
http://localhost:8080/examples/servlet/ImageContentWithDrawing
```

LISTING 26.13   ImageContentWithDrawing.java

```java
1  import javax.servlet.*;
2  import javax.servlet.http.*;
3  import java.io.*;
4  import java.util.*;
5  import java.text.*;
6  import java.awt.*;
7  import java.awt.image.BufferedImage;
8  import Acme.JPM.Encoders.GifEncoder;
9
10 public class ImageContentWithDrawing extends HttpServlet {
11   /** Initialize variables */
12   private final static int width = 300;
13   private final static int height = 300;
14
15   /** Process the HTTP GET request */
16   public void doGet(HttpServletRequest request, HttpServletResponse
17     response) throws ServletException, IOException {
18     response.setContentType("image/gif");
19     OutputStream out = response.getOutputStream();
20
21     // Create image
22     Image image = new BufferedImage(width, height,
23       BufferedImage.TYPE_INT_ARGB);
24
25     // Get Graphics context of the image
26     Graphics g = image.getGraphics();
27
28     drawClock(g); // Draw a clock on graphics
29
30     // Encode the image and send to the output stream
31     new GifEncoder(image, out, true).encode();
32
33     out.close(); // Close stream
34   }
35
36   private void drawClock(Graphics g) {
37     // Initialize clock parameters
38     int clockRadius =
39       (int)(Math.min(width, height) * 0.7 * 0.5);
40     int xCenter = (width) / 2;
41     int yCenter = (height) / 2;
42
43     // Draw circle
44     g.setColor(Color.black);
45     g.drawOval(xCenter - clockRadius,yCenter - clockRadius,
46       2 * clockRadius, 2 * clockRadius);
47     g.drawString("12", xCenter - 5, yCenter - clockRadius + 12);
48     g.drawString("9", xCenter - clockRadius + 3, yCenter + 5);
49     g.drawString("3", xCenter + clockRadius - 10, yCenter + 3);
50     g.drawString("6", xCenter - 3, yCenter + clockRadius - 3);
51
52     // Get current time using GregorianCalendar
53     TimeZone timeZone = TimeZone.getDefault();
54     GregorianCalendar cal = new GregorianCalendar(timeZone);
55
56     // Draw second hand
57     int second = (int)cal.get(GregorianCalendar.SECOND);
58     int sLength = (int)(clockRadius * 0.9);
```

(margin notes)
import GifEncoder
process GET
gif type
image
graphics
draw graphics
close stream
draw clock

EXAMPLE 26.9 (CONTINUED)

```
59    int xSecond = (int)(xCenter + sLength * Math.sin(second *
60      (2 * Math.PI / 60)));
61    int ySecond = (int)(yCenter - sLength * Math.cos(second *
62      (2 * Math.PI / 60)));
63    g.setColor(Color.red);
64    g.drawLine(xCenter, yCenter, xSecond, ySecond);
65
66    // Draw minute hand
67    int minute = (int)cal.get(GregorianCalendar.MINUTE);
68    int mLength = (int)(clockRadius * 0.75);
69    int xMinute = (int)(xCenter + mLength * Math.sin(minute *
70      (2 * Math.PI / 60)));
71    int yMinute = (int)(yCenter - mLength * Math.cos(minute *
72      (2 * Math.PI / 60)));
73    g.setColor(Color.blue);
74    g.drawLine(xCenter, yCenter, xMinute, yMinute);
75
76    // Draw hour hand
77    int hour = (int)cal.get(GregorianCalendar.HOUR_OF_DAY);
78    int hLength = (int)(clockRadius * 0.6);
79    int xHour = (int)(xCenter + hLength * Math.sin((hour + minute
80      / 60.0) * (2 * Math.PI / 12)));
81    int yHour = (int)(yCenter - hLength * Math.cos((hour + minute
82      / 60.0) * (2 * Math.PI / 12)));
83    g.setColor(Color.green);
84    g.drawLine(xCenter, yCenter, xHour, yHour);
85
86    // Set display format in specified style, locale and timezone
87    DateFormat formatter = DateFormat.getDateTimeInstance
88      (DateFormat.MEDIUM, DateFormat.LONG);
89
90    // Display current date
91    g.setColor(Color.red);
92    String today = formatter.format(cal.getTime());
93    FontMetrics fm = g.getFontMetrics();
94    g.drawString(today, (width -
95      fm.stringWidth(today)) / 2, yCenter + clockRadius + 30);
96  }
97 }
```

Review

Before you start the Tomcat server, place acme.jar in the c:\jarkata-tomcat-4.1.27\common\lib directory to ensure that GifEncoder and its supporting classes are available at runtime for the server. You also need to add acme.jar to the classpath to be able to compile the servlet.

Since the image is sent to the browser as binary data, the content type of the response is set to image/gif (Line 18). The GifEncoder class is used to encode the image into content understood by the browser (Line 31). The content is sent to the OutputStream object out.

The program creates an image with the specified width, height, and image type, using the BufferedImage class (Lines 22–23):

```
Image image = new BufferedImage(width, height,
  BufferedImage.TYPE_INT_ARGB);
```

To draw things on the image, you need to get its graphics context using the getGraphics method (Line 26):

```
Graphics g = image.getGraphics();
```

You can use various drawing methods in the Graphics class to draw simple shapes, or you can use Java 2D to draw more sophisticated graphics. This example uses simple drawing methods to draw a clock that displays the current time.

26.9.3 Sending Images and Text Together

The servlets in the preceding example return images. Often images are mixed with other content. In this case, you have to set the content type to "image/gif" before sending images, and set the content type to "text/html" before sending the text. However, the content type cannot be changed in one request. To circumvent this restriction, you may embed a GET request for displaying the image in a `<img>` tag in the HTML content. When the HTML content is displayed, a separate GET request for retrieving the image is then sent to the server. Thus text and image are obtained through two separate GET requests.

EXAMPLE 26.10 MIXING IMAGES AND TEXTS

Problem

This example mixes the clock image created in the preceding example with some text, as shown in Figure 26.22.

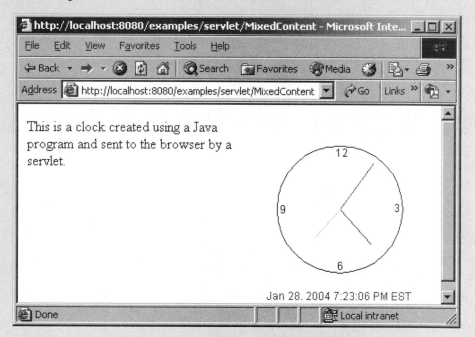

FIGURE 26.22 *The servlet returns an image along with the text.*

Solution

Create the servlet named `MixedContent` in Listing 26.14 and compile it into c:\jakarta-tomcat-4.1.27\webapps\examples\WEB-INF\classes. Run the servlet using the URL

```
http://localhost:8080/examples/servlet/MixedContent
```

LISTING 26.14 MixedContent.java

```
1 import javax.servlet.*;
2 import javax.servlet.http.*;
3 import java.io.*;
4
5 public class MixedContent extends HttpServlet {
6   /** Process the HTTP GET request */
7   public void doGet(HttpServletRequest request, HttpServletResponse
```

EXAMPLE 26.10 (CONTINUED)

```
 8        response) throws ServletException, IOException {
 9      response.setContentType("text/html");
10      PrintWriter out = response.getWriter();
11
12      String country = request.getParameter("country");
13
14      out.println("<img src = \"/examples/servlet/" +
15        "ImageContentWithDrawing\" align=right>");
16
17      out.println("This is a clock created using a Java program " +
18        "and sent to the browser by a servlet.");
19
20      out.close();
21    }
22 }
```

content type

get parameter

image tag

close stream

Review

When you test the servlet using the URL

    http://localhost:8080/examples/servlet/MixedContent?country=ca,

it generates an HTML file with the image tag

    <img src = "/examples/servlet/ImageContentWithDrawing align=right>

followed by the text from the file ca.txt.

The HTML file is rendered by the browser. When the browser sees the image tag, it sends the request to the server. The servlet ImageContentWithDrawing created in Example 26.9, "Getting Images by Drawing," is invoked to send the image to the browser.

KEY TERMS

CGI programs   1012
Common Gateway Interface   1012
Cookie   1036
GET and POST methods   1013
HTML form   1022

life-cycle methods   1017
URL query string   1012
servlet   1013
servlet container (servlet engine)   1013
Tomcat   1013

KEY CLASSES AND METHODS

✦ **javax.servlet.Servlet** is a root interface that defines the methods init, service, and destroy for controlling how a servlet is executed.

✦ **javax.servlet.http.HttpServlet** is an abstract class that implements javax.servlet. Servlet for HTTP protocol. It provides default implementation for the doGet(HttpServletRequest, HttpServletResponse) and doPut(HttpServletRequest, HttpServletResponse) methods.

✦ **javax.servlet.http.HttpServletRequest** is an interface for passing HTTP client request information to a servlet.

✦ **javax.servlet.http.HttpServletResponse** is an interface for passing an HTTP response to a Web browser client.

✦ **javax.servlet.http.Cookie** is a class for creating a cookie using the constructor Cookie(String name, String value). It contains the method getName() to get the cookie's name, getValue() to get the cookie's value, and setValue(String) to set a new cookie value. A cookie is sent to the browser using `response.addCookie(Cookie)`, where response is an instance of `HttpServletResponse`.

✦ **`javax.servlet.http.HttpSession`** is an interface for establishing a persistent session between a client with multiple requests and the server. An `HttpSession` can be obtained using `request.getSession()`, where request is an instance of `HttpServletRequest`. To set a value, use `setAttribute(String name, Object value)`. To get a value, use `getAttribute(String name)`.

CHAPTER SUMMARY

✦ A servlet is a special kind of program that runs from a Web server that supports servlets. Tomcat is a Web server that can run servlets. You start Tomcat using the **startup** command and stop Tomcat using the **shutdown** command from the Tomcat bin directory.

✦ A servlet URL is specified by the hostname, port, and request string (e.g., `http://localhost:8080/examples/servlet/ServletClass`). There are several ways to invoke a servlet: (1) by typing a servlet URL from a Web browser, (2) by placing a hyper reference link in an HTML page, and (3) by embedding a servlet URL in an HTML form. All the requests trigger the GET method except that you explicitly specify the POST method in the HTML form.

✦ You develop a servlet by defining a class that extends the `HttpServlet` class, implements the `doGet(HttpServletRequest, HttpServletResponse)` method to respond to the GET method, and implements the `doPost(HttpServletRequest, HttpServletResponse)` method to respond to the POST method.

✦ The request information passed from a client to the servlet is contained in an object of `HttpServletRequest`. You can use the methods `getParameter`, `getParameterValues`, `getRemoteAddr`, `getRemoteHost`, `getHeader`, `getQueryString`, `getCookies`, and `getSession` to obtain the information from the request.

✦ The content sent back to the client is contained in an object of `HttpServletResponse`. To send content to the client, first set the type of the content (e.g., html/plain) using the `setContentType(contentType)` method, then output the content through an IO stream on the `HttpServletResponse` object. You can obtain a character `PrintWriter` stream using the `getWriter()` method and obtain a binary `OutputStream` using the `getOutputStream()` method.

✦ A servlet may be shared by many clients. When the servlet is first created, its `init` method is called. It is not called again as long as the servlet is not destroyed. The `service` method is invoked each time the server receives a request for the servlet. The server spawns a new thread and invokes `service`. The `destroy` method is invoked after a timeout period has passed or the Web server is stopped.

✦ There are three ways to track a session. You can track a session by passing data from the servlet to the client as a hidden value in a dynamically generated HTML form by including a field such as `<input type="hidden" name="lastName" value="Smith">`. The next request will submit the data back to the servlet. The servlet retrieves this hidden value just like any other parameter value using the `getParameter` method.

✦ You can track sessions using cookies. A cookie is created using the constructor new `Cookie(String name, String value)`. Cookies are sent from the server through the object of `HttpServletResponce` using the `addCookie(aCookie)` method to tell the browser to add a cookie with a given name and its associated value. If the browser already has a cookie with the key name, the value will be updated. The browser will then send the cookie with any request submitted to the same server. Cookies can have expiration dates set, after which they will not be sent to the server.

✦ The Java servlet API provides a session-tracking tool that enables tracking of a large set of data. A session can be obtained using the `getSession()` method through an `HttpServletRequest` object. The data can be stored as objects and are secure because they are kept on the server side using the `SetAttribute(String name, Object value)` method.

✦ Java servlets are not limited to sending text to a browser. They can return images in GIF, JPEG, or PNG format.

REVIEW QUESTIONS

Sections 26.1–26.2

26.1   What is the common gateway interface?

26.2   What are the differences between the GET and POST methods in an HTML form?

26.3   Can you submit a GET request directly from a URL? Can you submit a POST request directly from a URL?

26.4   What is wrong in the following URL for submitting a GET request to the servlet Find-Score on host liang at port 8080 with parameter name?

`http://liang:8080/findScore?name="P Yates"`

26.5   What are the differences between CGI and servlets?

Section 26.3 Creating and Running Servlets

26.6   Can you display an HTML file (e.g., c:\test.html) by typing the complete file name in the Address field of Internet Explorer? Can you run a servlet by simply typing the servlet class file name?

26.7   Before you start Tomcat, what value should be set to the environment variable `JAVA_HOME`?

26.8   How do you start Tomcat? How do you stop Tomcat?

26.9   How do you test whether Tomcat is running?

26.10   To compile a servlet program, what library file has to be included in the classpath?

26.11   When you run Tomcat, which port does it use? What happens if the port is already in use?

Section 26.4 The Servlet API

26.12   Describe the life cycle of a servlet.

26.13   Suppose that you started Tomcat, ran the following servlet twice by issuing an appropriate URL from a Web browser, and finally stopped Tomcat. What was displayed on the console when the servlet was first invoked? What was displayed on the console when the servlet was invoked for the second time? What was displayed on the console when Tomcat was shut down?

```java
import javax.servlet.*;
import javax.servlet.http.*;
import java.io.*;

public class Test extends HttpServlet {
  public Test() {
    System.out.println("Constructor called");
  }

  /** Initialize variables */
  public void init() throws ServletException {
    System.out.println("init called");
  }

  /** Process the HTTP GET request */
  public void doGet(HttpServletRequest request, HttpServletResponse
    response) throws ServletException, IOException {
    System.out.println("doGet called");
  }

  /** Clean up resources */
  public void destroy() {
    System.out.println("destroy called");
  }
}
```

Sections 26.5–26.7

26.14   What would be displayed if you changed the content type to `"html/plain"` in Example 26.1, "Obtaining the Current Time from the Server"?

26.15   The statement `out.close()` is used to close the output stream to response. Why isn't this statement enclosed in a try-catch block?

26.16   What happens when invoking `request.getParameter(paramName)` if `paramName` does not exist?

26.17   How do you write a text field, combo box, check box, and text area in an HTML form?

26.18   How do you retrieve the parameter value for a text field, combo box, list, check box, radio button, and text area from an HTML form?

26.19   If the servlet uses a database driver other than the JDBC-ODBC driver, where should the driver be placed?

Section 26.8 Session Tracking

26.20   What is session tracking? What are three techniques for session tracking?

26.21   How do you create a cookie, send a cookie to a browser, get cookies from a browser, get the name of a cookie, set a new value in the cookie, and set cookie expiration time?

26.22   How do you get a session, set object value for the session, and get object value from the session?

Section 26.9 Sending Images from Servlets

26.23   What output stream should you use to send images to the browser? What content type do you have to set for the response?

26.24   How do you deal with dynamic contents with images and text?

PROGRAMMING EXERCISES

Section 26.5 Creating Servlets

26.1*   (*Factorial table*) Write a servlet to display a table that contains factorials for the numbers from 0 to 10, as shown in Figure 26.23.

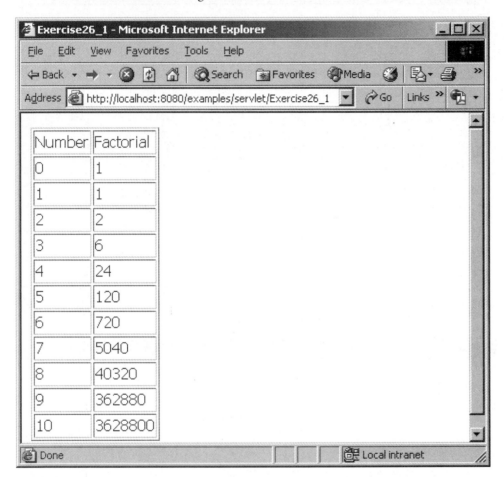

FIGURE 26.23   *The servlet displays factorials for the numbers from 0 to 10 in a table.*

26.2*   (*Multiplication table*) Write a servlet to display a multiplication table, as shown in Figure 26.24.

26.3*   (*Visit count*) Develop a servlet that displays the number of visits on the servlet. Also display the client's host name and IP address, as shown in Figure 26.25.

Implement this program in three different ways:

1. Use an instance variable to store count. When the servlet is created for the first time, count is 0. count is incremented every time the servlet's doGet method is invoked. When the Web server stops, count is lost.

2. Store the count in a file named Exercise26_3.dat, and use RandomAccessFile to read the count in the servlet's init method. The count is incremented every time the servlet's doGet method is invoked. When the Web server stops, store the count back to the file.

3. Instead of counting total visits from all clients, count the visits by each client identified by the client's IP address. Use Map to store a pair of IP addresses and visit counts. For the first visit, an entry is created in the map. For subsequent visits, the visit count is updated.

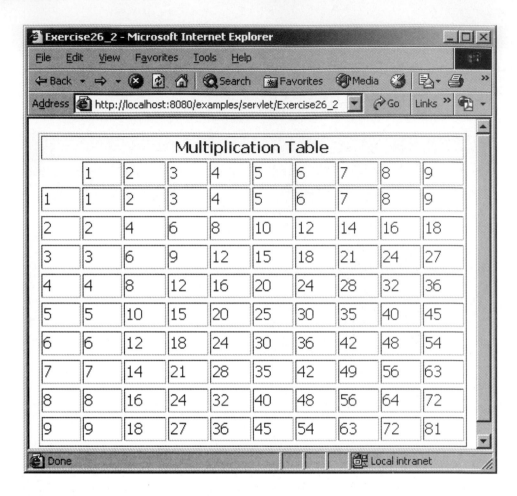

FIGURE 26.24   *The servlet displays the multiplication table.*

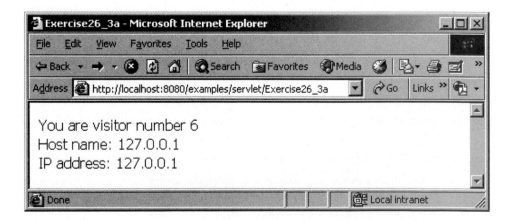

FIGURE 26.25   *The servlet displays the number of visits and the client's host name, IP address, and request URL.*

Section 26.6 HTML Forms

26.4* (*Calculating tax*) Write an HTML form to prompt the user to enter taxable income and filing status, as shown in Figure 26.26(a). Clicking the *Compute Tax* button invokes a servlet to compute and display the tax, as shown in Figure 26.26(b). Use the computeTax method in the ComputeTax class introduced in Example 5.6, "Computing Taxes Using Arrays," to compute personal income tax for the year 2002.

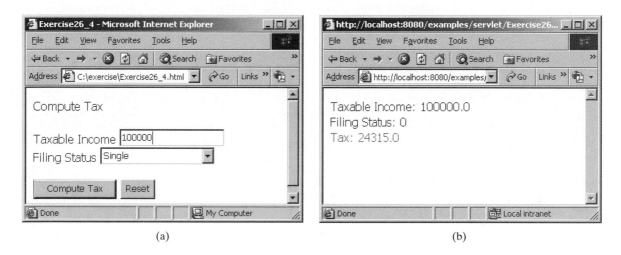

(a)   (b)

FIGURE **26.26**   *The servlet computes the tax.*

26.5* (*Calculating a loan*) Write an HTML form that prompts the user to enter loan amount, interest rate, and number of years, as shown in Figure 26.27(a). Clicking the *Compute Loan Payment* button invokes a servlet to compute and display the monthly and total loan payments, as shown in Figure 26.27(b). Use the Loan class introduced in Section 6.15, "Case Study: The Loan Class," to compute the monthly and total payments.

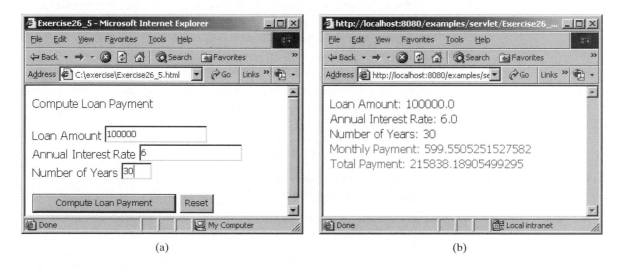

(a)   (b)

FIGURE **26.27**   *The servlet computes the loan payment.*

26.6** (*Finding scores from text files*) Write a servlet that displays the student name and the current score, given the SSN and class ID. For each class, a text file is used to store the student name, SSN, and current score. The file is named after the class ID with .txt extension. For instance, if the class ID were csci1301, the file name would be csci1301.txt. Suppose each line consists of student name, SSN, and score. These three items are separated by the # sign. Create an HTML form that enables the user to enter the SSN and class ID, as shown in Figure 26.28(a). Upon clicking the Submit button, the result is displayed, as shown in Figure 26.28(b). If the SSN or the class ID does not match, report an error.

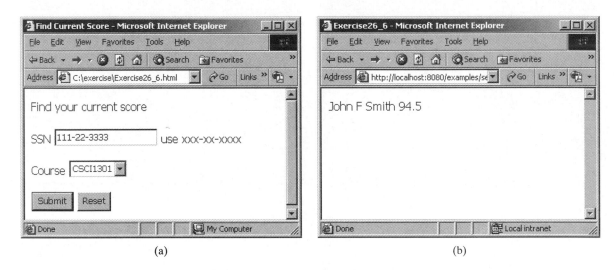

(a)   (b)

FIGURE 26.28 *The HTML form accepts the SSN and class ID from the user and sends them to the servlet to obtain the score.*

Section 26.7 Database Programming in Servlets

26.7** (*Finding scores from database tables*) Rewrite the preceding servlet. Assume that for each class, a table is used to store the student name, SSN, and score. The table name is the same as the class ID. For instance, if the class ID were csci1301, the table name would be csci1301.

26.8* (*Changing the password*) Write a servlet that enables the user to change the password from an HTML form, as shown in Figure 26.29(a). Suppose that the user information is stored in a database table named User with three columns, username, password, and name, where name is the real name of the user. The servlet performs the following tasks:

   a. Verify that the username and old password are in the table. If not, report the error and redisplay the HTML form.

   b. Verify that the new password and the confirmed password are the same. If not, report this error and redisplay the HTML form.

   c. If the user information is entered correctly, update the password and report the status of the update to the user, as shown in Figure 26.29(b).

26.9** (*Displaying database tables*) Write an HTML form that prompts the user to enter or select a JDBC driver, database URL, username, password, and table name, as shown in Figure 26.30(a). Clicking the *Submit* button displays the table content, as shown in Figure 26.30(b).

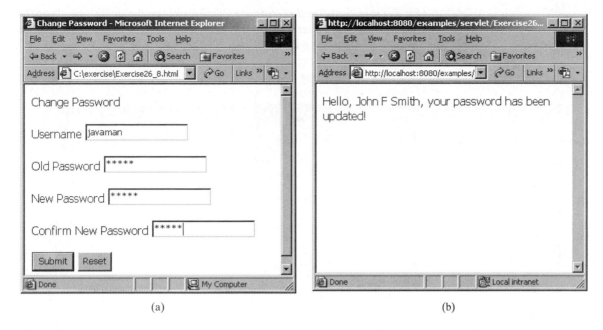

(a)   (b)

FIGURE 26.29   *The user enters the username and the old password and sets a new password. The servlet reports the status of the update to the user.*

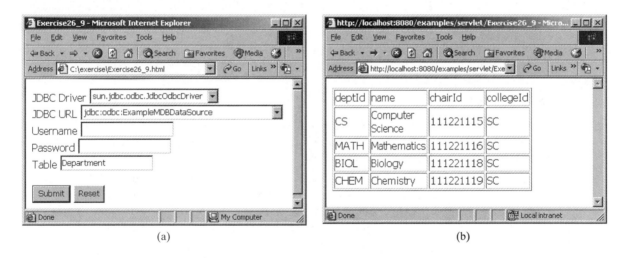

(a)   (b)

FIGURE 26.30   *The user enters database information and specifies a table to display its content.*

Section 26.8 Session Tracking

26.10* (*Storing cookies*) Write a servlet that stores the following cookies in a browser, and set their max age for two days:

Cookie 1: name is "color" and value is red.

Cookie 2: name is "radius" and value is 5.5.

Cookie 3: name is "count" and value is 2.

26.11* (*Retrieving cookies*) Write a servlet that displays all the cookies on the client. The client types the URL of the servlet from the browser to display all the cookies stored on the browser. See Figure 26.31.

FIGURE 26.31 *All the cookies on the client are displayed in the browser.*

JavaServer Pages

Objectives

- ✦ To know what a JSP page is (§27.2).

- ✦ To comprehend how a JSP page is processed (§27.3).

- ✦ To learn how to use JSP constructs (§27.4).

- ✦ To become familiar with JSP predefined variables and JSP directives (§§27.5–27.6).

- ✦ To use JavaBeans components in JSP (§§27.7–27.9).

- ✦ To develop database applications using JSP (§§27.7–27.9).

- ✦ To know how to forward requests from JSP (§27.10).

27.1   Introduction

Servlets can be used to generate dynamic Web content. One drawback, however, is that you have to embed HTML tags and text inside the Java source code. A Web page usually contains both static and dynamic content. Using servlets, you have to modify the Java source code and recompile it if changes are made to the static HTML text. If you have a lot of static HTML code mixed with some dynamic code in a servlet, the code is difficult to read and maintain, since the regular HTML code is part of the Java source code. JavaServer Pages (JSP) technology was introduced to remedy this drawback. JSP enables you to write regular static HTML code in the normal way and embed Java code to produce dynamic content.

27.2   A Simple JSP Page

JSP tag

JSP provides an easy way to create dynamic Web pages and simplify the task of building Web applications. A JavaServer page is like a regular HTML page with special tags, known as *JSP tags*, which enable the Web server to generate dynamic content. You can create a Web page with static HTML and enclose the code for generating dynamic content in the JSP tags. Here is an example of a simple JSP page:

```
<!-- CurrentTime.jsp -->
<html>
      <head>
      <title>
      CurrentTime
      </title>
      </head>
      <body>
      Current time is <%= new java.util.Date() %>
      </body>
</html>
```

JSP tag

The dynamic content is enclosed in the tag that begins with <%= and ends with %>. The current time is returned as a string by invoking the toString method of an object of the java.util.Date class.

store JSP files

To run the JSP page, you need to create a text file for the page, name the file CurrentTime.jsp, and store the file in c:\jakarta-tomcat-4.1.27\webapps\examples\jsp. Assume you have started Tomcat. You can run it from a Web browser using the URL http://localhost:8080/examples/jsp/CurrentTime.jsp, as shown in Figure 27.1.

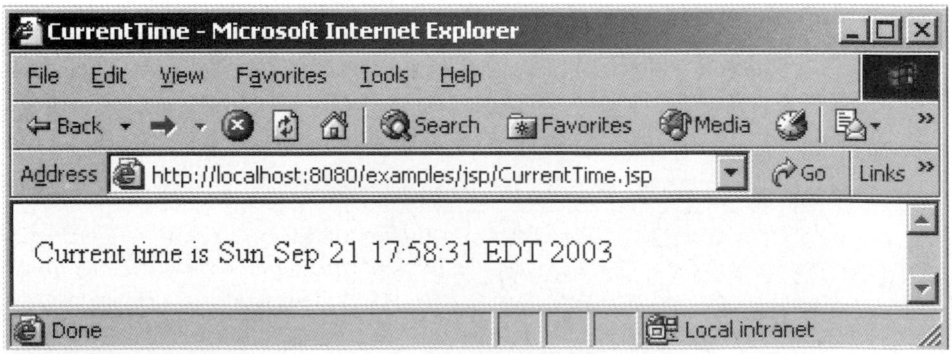

FIGURE 27.1   *A JSP page is displayed in a Web browser.*

NOTE
The easiest way to run a JSP page is to store all the JSP files in c:\jakarta-tomcat-4.1.27\webapps\examples\jsp. You can also configure Tomcat so that you can place JSP files anywhere in your computer. For more information, see Supplement O, "Tutorial on Tomcat."

27.3 How Is a JSP Page Processed?

A JSP page must first be processed by a Web server before it can be displayed in a Web browser. The Web server must support JSP, and the JSP page must be stored in a file with a .jsp extension. The Web server translates the .jsp file into a Java servlet, compiles the servlet, and executes it. The result of the execution is sent to the browser for display. Figure 27.2 shows how a JSP page is processed by a Web server. The CurrentTime.jsp in Figure 27.1 is translated into a servlet named CurrentTime_jsp.java in c:\jakarta-tomcat-4.1.27\work\standalone\localhost\examples\jsp. Viewing the file will help you to better understand that JSP is based on the servlet.

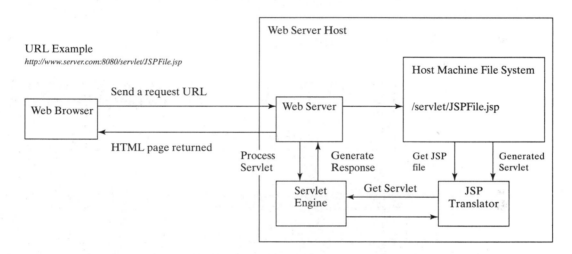

FIGURE 27.2 *A JSP page is translated into a servlet.*

 NOTE
A JSP page is translated into a servlet when the page is requested for the first time. It is not retranslated if the page is not modified. To ensure that the first-time real user does not get a delay, JSP developers may test the page after it is installed.

27.4 JSP Scripting Constructs

There are three main types of JSP constructs: scripting constructs, directives, and actions. *Scripting elements* enable you to specify Java code that will become part of the resultant servlet. *Directives* enable you to control the overall structure of the resultant servlet. *Actions* enable you to control the behavior of the JSP engine. This section introduces scripting constructs.

scripting element
directive
action

There are three types of JSP scripting constructs that can be used to insert Java code into a resultant servlet: expressions, scriptlets, and declarations.

JSP expression

A JSP *expression* is used to insert a Java expression directly into the output. It has the following form:

```
<%= Java expression %>
```

The expression is evaluated, converted into a string, and sent to the output stream of the servlet.

JSP scriptlet

A JSP *scriptlet* enables you to insert a Java statement into the servlet's jspService method, which is invoked by the service method. A JSP scriptlet has the following form:

```
<% Java statement %>
```

JSP declaration

A JSP *declaration* is for declaring methods or fields into the servlet. It has the following form:

```
<%! Java declaration %>
```

HTML comments have the following form:

```
<!-- HTML Comment -->
```

JSP comment

If you don't want the comment to appear in the resultant HTML file, use the following comment in JSP:

```
<%-- JSP Comment --%>
```

EXAMPLE 27.1 COMPUTING FACTORIALS

Problem

This example creates a JavaServer page that displays factorials for numbers from 0 to 10. Figure 27.3 shows a sample run of the JavaServer page.

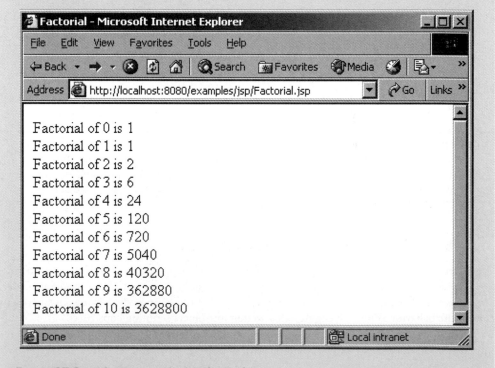

FIGURE 27.3 *The JSP page displays factorials.*

EXAMPLE 27.1 (CONTINUED)

Solution

Create a JSP named Factorial.jsp in Listing 27.1 and save it into c:\jakarta-tomcat-4.1.27\webapps\examples\jsp. Run it from the URL http://localhost:8080/examples/jsp/Factorial.jsp, as shown in Figure 27.3.

LISTING 27.1 Factorial.jsp

```
1  <html>
2  <head>
3  <title>
4  Factorial
5  </title>
6  </head>
7  <body>
8
9  <%  for (int i = 0; i <= 10; i++) { %>          JSP scriptlet
10 Factorial of <%= i %> is                        JSP expression
11 <%= computeFactorial(i) %> <br>
12 <%  } %>
13
14 <%! private long computeFactorial(int n) {       JSP declaration
15       if (n == 0)
16         return 1;
17       else
18         return n * computeFactorial(n - 1);
19     }
20 %>
21
22 </body>
23 </html>
```

Review

JSP scriptlets are enclosed between `<%` and `%>`. Thus

```
for (int i = 0; i <= 10; i++) {,      (Line 9)
```

is a scriptlet and as such is inserted directly into the servlet's jspService method.

JSP expressions are enclosed between `<%=` and `%>`. Thus

```
<%= i %>, (Line 10)
```

is an expression and is inserted into the output stream of the servlet.

JSP declarations are enclosed between `<%!` and `%>`. Thus

```
<%! private long computeFactorial(int n) {
      ...
    }
%>
```

is a declaration that defines methods or fields in the servlet.

What would be different if Line 9 is replaced by the two alternatives shown below? Both work fine, but there is an important difference. In (a), i is a local variable in the servlet, whereas in (b) i is an instance variable when translated to the servlet.

```
<% int i = 0; %>               <%! int i; %>
<% for ( ; i <= 10; i++) { %>  <% for (i = 0; i <= 10; i++) { %>
```

      (a)   (b)

EXAMPLE 27.1 (CONTINUED)

 CAUTION
For JSP, the loop body must be placed inside braces even though the body contains a single statement. It would be wrong to delete the opening brace ({) in Line 9 and the closing brace (<% } %>) in Line 12.

 CAUTION
There is no semicolon at the end of a JSP expression. For example, <%= i; %> is incorrect. But there must be a semicolon for each Java statement in a JSP scriptlet. For example, <% int i = 0 %> is incorrect.

 CAUTION
JSP and Java elements are case-sensitive, but HTML is not case-sensitive.

27.5   Predefined Variables

You can use variables in JSP. For convenience, JSP provides eight predefined variables from the servlet environment that can be used with JSP expressions and scriptlets. These variables are also known as *JSP implicit objects*.

JSP implicit object

request

response

out

session

application

config

pageContext

page

- **request** represents the client's request, which is an instance of `HttpServletRequest`. You can use it to access request parameters and HTTP headers, such as cookies and hostname.

- **response** represents the servlet's response, which is an instance of `HttpServletResponse`. You can use it to set response type and send output to the client.

- **out** represents the character output stream, which is an instance of `PrintWriter` obtained from `response.getWriter()`. You can use it to send character content to the client.

- **session** represents the `HttpSession` object associated with the request, obtained from `request.getSession()`.

- **application** represents the `ServletContext` object for storing persistent data for all clients. The difference between `session` and `application` is that session is tied to one client, but `application` is for all clients to share persistent data.

- **config** represents the `ServletConfig` object for the page.

- **pageContext** represents the `PageContext` object. `PageContext` is a new class introduced in JSP to give a central point of access to many page attributes.

- **page** is an alternative to `this`.

EXAMPLE 27.2 COMPUTING LOAN PAYMENTS

Problem

Write an HTML page that prompts the user to enter loan amount, annual interest rate, and number of years, as shown in Figure 27.4(a). Clicking the *Compute Loan Payment* button invokes a JSP to compute and display the monthly and total loan payments, as shown in Figure 27.4(b).

EXAMPLE 27.2 (CONTINUED)

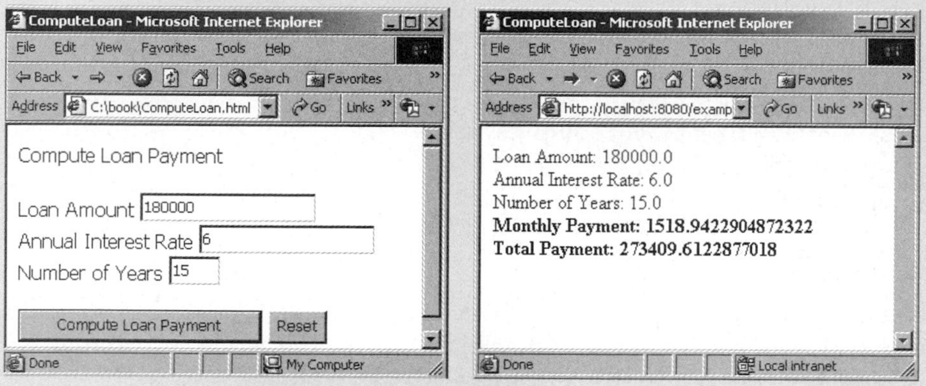

(a)   (b)

FIGURE 27.4   *The JSP computes the loan payments.*

Solution

Create an HTML file named ComputeLoan.html (Listing 27.2) in c:\book and Compute-Loan.jsp (Listing 27.3) in c:\jakarta-tomcat-4.1.27\webapps\examples\jsp.

LISTING 27.2   ComputeLoan.html

```
 1 <!-- ComputeLoan.html -->
 2 <html>
 3 <head>
 4 <title>ComputeLoan</title>
 5 </head>
 6 <body>
 7 Compute Loan Payment
 8
 9 <form method="get"
10   action="http://localhost:8080/examples/jsp/ComputeLoan.jsp">
11 <p>Loan Amount
12    <input type="text" name="loanAmount"><br>
13 Annual Interest Rate
14    <input type="text" name="annualInterestRate"><br>
15 Number of Years <input type="text" name="numberOfYears" size="3"></p>
16 <p><input type="submit" name="Submit" value="Compute Loan Payment">
17    <input type="reset" value="Reset"></p>
18 </form>
19 </body>
20 </html>
```

form
action

text field

submit

LISTING 27.3   ComputeLoan.jsp

```
 1 <!-- ComputeLoan.jsp -->
 2 <html>
 3 <head>
 4 <title>ComputeLoan</title>
 5 </head>
 6 <body>
 7 <% double loanAmount = Double.parseDouble(
 8     request.getParameter("loanAmount"));
 9    double annualInterestRate = Double.parseDouble(
10     request.getParameter("annualInterestRate"));
11    double numberOfYears = Integer.parseInt(
12     request.getParameter("numberOfYears"));
13    double monthlyInterestRate = annualInterestRate / 1200;
```

JSP scriptlet
get parameters

EXAMPLE 27.2 (CONTINUED)

```
14    double monthlyPayment = loanAmount * monthlyInterestRate /
15      (1 - 1 / Math.pow(1 + monthlyInterestRate, numberOfYears * 12));
16    double totalPayment = monthlyPayment * numberOfYears * 12; %>
17  Loan Amount: <%= loanAmount %><br>
18  Annual Interest Rate: <%= annualInterestRate %><br>
19  Number of Years: <%= numberOfYears %><br>
20  <b>Monthly Payment: <%= monthlyPayment %><br>
21  Total Payment: <%= totalPayment %><br></b>
22  </body>
23  </html>
```

JSP expression

Review

ComputeLoan.html is displayed first to prompt the user to enter the loan amount, annual interest rate, and number of years. Since this file does not contain any JSP elements, it is named with an .html extension as a regular HTML file.

http://localhost:8080/examples/jsp/ComputeLoan.jsp is invoked upon clicking the *Compute Loan Payment* button in the HTML form. The JSP page obtains the parameter values using the predefined variable request in Lines 7–12 and computes monthly payment and total payment in Lines 13–16. The formula for computing monthly payment is given in Example 2.2, "Computing Loan Payments."

What is wrong if the JSP scriptlet <% in Line 7 is replaced by the JSP declaration <%!? The predefined variables (e.g., request, response, out) correspond to local variables defined in the servlet methods doGet and doPost. They must appear in JSP scriptlets, not in JSP declarations.

 TIP

ComputeLoan.jsp can also be invoked using the following query string:
http://localhost:8080/examples/jsp/ComputeLoan.jsp?loanAmount=10000
&annualInterestRate=6&numberOfYears=15.

27.6 JSP Directives

A JSP directive is a statement that gives the JSP engine information about the JSP page. For example, if your JSP page uses a Java class from a package other than the java.lang package, you have to use a directive to import this package. The general syntax for a JSP directive is as shown below:

```
<%@ directive attribute="value" %>, or
<%@ directive attribute1="value1"
             attribute2="value2"
             ...
             attributen="valuen" %>
```

The possible directives are:

✦ **page** lets you provide information for the page, such as importing classes and setting up content type. The page directive can appear anywhere in the JSP file.

✦ **include** lets you insert a file to the servlet when the page is translated to a servlet. The include directive must be placed where you want the file to be inserted.

✦ **tablib** lets you define custom tags.

The following are useful attributes for the page directive:

✦ **import** specifies one or more packages to be imported for this page. For example, the directive <%@ page import="java.util.*, java.text.*" %> imports java.util.* and java.text.*.

✦ **contentType** specifies the content type for the resultant JSP page. By default, the content type is text/html for JSP. The default content type for servlets is text/plain.

✦ **session** specifies a boolean value to indicate whether the page is part of the session. By default, session is true.

✦ **buffer** specifies the output stream buffer size. By default, it is 8KB. For example, the directive <%@ page buffer="10KB" %> specifies that the output buffer size is 10KB. The directive <%@ page buffer="none" %> specifies that a buffer is not used.

✦ **autoFlush** specifies a boolean value to indicate whether the output buffer should be automatically flushed when it is full or whether an exception should be raised when the buffer overflows. By default, this attribute is true. In this case, the buffer attribute cannot be none.

✦ **isThreadSafe** specifies a boolean value to indicate whether the page can be accessed simultaneously without data corruption. By default, it is true. If it is set to false, the JSP page will be translated to a servlet that implements the SingleThreadModel interface.

✦ **errorPage** specifies a JSP page that is processed when an exception occurs in the current page. For example, the directive <%@ page errorPage="HandleError.jsp" %> specifies that HandleError.jsp is processed when an exception occurs.

✦ **isErrorPage** specifies a boolean value to indicate whether the page can be used as an error page. By default, this attribute is false.

EXAMPLE 27.3 COMPUTING LOAN PAYMENTS USING THE Loan CLASS

Problem

Use the Loan class created in Section 6.15, "Case Study: The Loan Class," to simplify Example 27.2, "Computing Loan Payments." You can create an object of the Loan class and use its monthlyPayment() and totalPayment() methods to compute the monthly payment and total payment.

Solution

ComputeLoan.html is the same as in Example 27.2. Replace ComputeLoan.jsp in Example 27.2 by the code in Listing 27.4.

LISTING 27.4 ComputeLoan.jsp

```
1 <!-- ComputeLoan.jsp -->
2 <html>
3 <head>
4 <title>ComputeLoan Using the Loan Class</title>
5 </head>
6 <body>
7 <%@ page import = "chapter27.Loan" %>
8 <% double loanAmount = Double.parseDouble(
9      request.getParameter("loanAmount"));
10    double annualInterestRate = Double.parseDouble(
11      request.getParameter("annualInterestRate"));
12    int numberOfYears = Integer.parseInt(
13      request.getParameter("numberOfYears"));
14    Loan loan = new Loan(annualInterestRate, numberOfYears, loanAmount);
15 %>
16 Loan Amount: <%= loanAmount %><br>
17 Annual Interest Rate: <%= annualInterestRate %><br>
18 Number of Years: <%= numberOfYears %><br>
19 <b>Monthly Payment: <%= loan.monthlyPayment() %><br>
```

JSP directive

create object

EXAMPLE 27.3 (CONTINUED)

```
20 Total Payment: <%= loan.totalPayment() %><br></b>
21 </body>
22 </html>
```

To import a class, the class must be placed in a package explicitly. Create a new `Loan` class in package chapter27 as follows:

```
package chapter27;
```

```
public class Loan {
  // Same as on Page 240, so omitted
}
```

Compile it into c:\jakarta-tomcat-4.1.27\webapps\examples\WEB-INF\classes\chapter27.

TIP

The destination directory for Loan.class is c:\jakarta-tomcat-4.1.27\web-apps\examples\WEB-INF\classes. You may create a subdirectory named chapter27 under the destination directory and then move Loan.class into it. As an alternative, you can use the following command to compile and save the .class directly into the destination directory:

```
javac -d destinationDirectory CurrentTime.java
```

This command automatically creates the subdirectory chapter27, since it is in the package statement of the `Loan` class.

Review

The directive `<%@ page import ="chapter27.Loan" %>` imports the `Loan` class in Line 7. Line 14 creates an object of `Loan` for the given loan amount, annual interest rate, and number of years. Lines 19–20 invokes the `Loan` object's `monthlyPayment()` and `totalPayment()` methods to display monthly payment and total payment.

EXAMPLE 27.4 USING ERROR PAGES

Problem

This example prompts the user to enter an integer (see Figure 27.5(a)) and displays the factorial for the integer (see Figure 27.5(b)). If a noninteger value is entered by mistake, an error page is displayed, as shown in Figure 27.5(c).

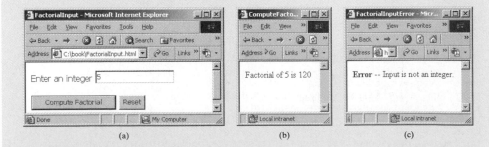

(a)   (b)   (c)

FIGURE 27.5   *You enter an integer to obtain its factorial in (a). The factorial of the integer is displayed in (b). An error page is displayed in (c) when an exception occurs.*

EXAMPLE 27.4 (CONTINUED)

Solution

Create three files named FactorialInput.html (Listing 27.5), ComputeFactorial.jsp (Listing 27.6), FactorialInputError.jsp (Listing 27.7), and save the two .jsp files into c:\jakarta-tomcat-4.1.27\webapps\examples\jsp. Display FactorialInput.html first, as shown in Figure 27.5(a).

LISTING 27.5   **FactorialInput.html**

```
 1 <!-- FactorialInput.html -->
 2 <html>
 3 <head>
 4 <title>
 5 FactorialInput
 6 </title>
 7 </head>
 8 <body>
 9 <form method="POST"
10   action="http://localhost:8080/examples/jsp/ComputeFactorial.jsp">
11   Enter an integer  <input name="number"><br><br>
12 <input type="submit" name="Submit" value="Compute Factorial">
13 <input type="reset" value="Reset">
14 </form>
15 </body>
16 </html>
```

form
action

LISTING 27.6   **ComputeFactorial.jsp**

```
 1 <!-- ComputeFactorial.jsp -->
 2 <html>
 3 <head>
 4 <title>
 5 ComputeFactorial
 6 </title>
 7 </head>
 8 <body>
 9 <%@ page import ="java.text.*" %>
10 <%@ page errorPage = "FactorialInputError.jsp" %>
11
12 <%  NumberFormat format = NumberFormat.getNumberInstance();
13     int number = Integer.parseInt(request.getParameter("number")); %>
14 Factorial of <%= number %> is
15 <%= format.format(computeFactorial(number)) %> <p>
16
17 <%! private long computeFactorial(int n) {
18       if (n == 0)
19         return 1;
20       else
21         return n * computeFactorial(n - 1);
22    }
23 %>
24 </body>
25 </html>
```

import directive
error page directive

create object

JSP declaration

LISTING 27.7   **FactorialInputError.jsp**

```
 1 <!-- FactorialInputError.jsp -->
 2 <html>
 3 <head>
 4 <title>
 5 FactorialInputError
 6 </title>
 7 </head>
 8 <body>
```

JSP directive

EXAMPLE 27.4 (CONTINUED)

```
 9 <%@ page isErrorPage = "true" %>
10
11 <b>Error</b> -- Input is not an integer.
12
13 </body>
14 </html>
```

Review

FactorialInput.html is displayed first to prompt the user to enter an integer. Upon clicking the *Compute Factorial* button, the JSP page ComputeFactorial.jsp is invoked to compute the factorial for the number. If the user enters an integer, its factorial is displayed; otherwise, the error page is displayed.

In ComputeFactorial.jsp, the directive `<%@ page import ="java.text.*" %>` (Line 9) imports the `java.text` package because the `NumberFormat` class is in this package. The directive `<%@ page errorPage = "FactorialInputError.jsp" %>` (Line 10) specifies that FactorialInputError.jsp is processed when an exception in ComputeFactorial.jsp occurs. The directive `<%@ page isErrorPage = "true" %>` (Line 9 in FactorialInputError.jsp) denotes that FactorialInputError.jsp can be used as an error page.

27.7   Using JavaBeans in JSP

You used the `computeFactorial` method to compute the factorial in Examples 27.1 and 27.3, "Computing Factorials" and "Using Error Pages." You defined the method in both examples. You could have defined the method in a class and shared it in both examples. Normally you create an instance of a class in each program and use it in that program. This method is for sharing the class, not the object. JSP allows you to share the object of a class among different pages.

To enable an object to be shared, its class must be a JavaBeans component. Recall that a class is a Java Beans component if it has the following three features:

✦ The class is public.

✦ The class has a public constructor with no arguments.

✦ The class is serializable. (This requirement is not necessary in JSP.)

To create an instance for a JavaBeans component, use the following syntax:

```
<jsp:useBean id="objectName" scope="scopeAttribute"
  class="ClassName" />
```

This syntax is equivalent to

```
<% ClassName objectName = new ClassName() %>
```

except that the scope attribute specifies the scope of the object. Listed below are four possible values for the scope attribute:

✦ **application** specifies that the object is bound to the application. The object can be shared by all sessions of the application.

✦ **session** specifies that the object is bound to the client's session. Recall that a client's session is automatically created between a Web browser and a Web server. When a client from the same browser accesses two servlets or two JSP pages on the same server, the session is the same.

◆ **page** is the default scope, which specifies that the object is bound to the page.

◆ **request** specifies that the object is bound to the client's request.

When `<jsp:useBean id="objectName" scope="scopeAttribute" class="ClassName" />` is processed, the JSP engine first searches for an object of the class with the same id and scope. If found, the pre-existing bean is used; otherwise, a new bean is created.

Here is another syntax for creating a bean:

```
<jsp:useBean id="objectName" scope="scopeAttribute"
   class="ClassName" >
statements
</jsp:useBean>
```

The statements are executed when the bean is created. If a bean with the same ID and class name already exists in the scope, the statements are not executed.

EXAMPLE 27.5 TESTING BEAN SCOPE

Problem

This example creates a JavaBeans component named Count and uses it to count the number of visits to a page, as shown in Figure 27.6.

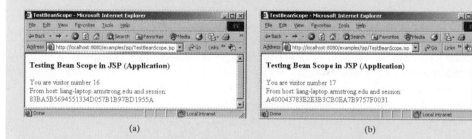

(a)   (b)

FIGURE 27.6   *The number of visits to the page is increased when the page is visited.*

Solution

Create a JavaBeans component named Count.java (Listing 27.8) and compile it into c:\jakarta-tomcat-4.1.27\webapps\examples\WEB-INF\classes\chapter27.

LISTING 27.8   Count.java

```
1  package chapter27;
2
3  public class Count {
4    private int count = 0;
5
6    /** Return count property */
7    public int getCount() {
8      return count;
9    }
10
11   /** Increase count */
12   public void increaseCount() {
13     count++;
14   }
15 }
```

package statement

Create TestBeanScope.jsp (Listing 27.9) and save it into c:\jakarta-tomcat-4.1.27\ webapps\examples\jsp. Run it from the URL `http://localhost:8080/examples/jsp/ TestBeanScope.jsp`, as shown in Figure 27.6.

EXAMPLE 27.5 (CONTINUED)

LISTING 27.9   TestBeanScope.jsp

import directive
create bean

```
1 <!-- TestBeanScope.jsp -->
2 <%@ page import = "chapter27.Count" %>
3 <jsp:useBean id="count" scope="application" class="chapter27.Count">
4 </jsp:useBean>
5 <html>
6 <head>
7 <title>TestBeanScope</title>
8 </head>
9 <body>
10 <h3>
11 Testing Bean Scope in JSP (Application)
12 </h3>
```

use bean

```
13 <% count.increaseCount(); %>
14 You are visitor number <%= count.getCount() %><br>
```

request
session

```
15 From host: <%= request.getRemoteHost() %>
16 and session: <%= session.getId() %>
17 </body>
18 </html>
```

Review

The `scope` attribute specifies the scope of the bean. `scope="application"` (Line 3) specifies that the bean is alive in the JSP engine and available for all clients to access. The bean can be shared by any client with the directive `<jsp:useBean id="count" scope="application" class="Count" >` (Lines 3–4). Every client accessing TestBeanScope.jsp causes the count to increase by 1. The first client causes `count` object to be created, and subsequent access to `TestBeanScope` uses the same object.

If `scope="application"` is changed to `scope="session"`, the scope of the bean is limited to the session from the same browser. The count will increase only if the page is requested from the same browser. If `scope="application"` is changed to `scope="page"`, the scope of the bean is limited to the page, and any other page cannot access this bean. The page will always display count 1. If `scope="application"` is changed to `scope="request"`, the scope of the bean is limited to the client's request, and any other request on the page will always display count 1.

If the page is destroyed, the count restarts from 0. You can fix the problem by storing the count in a random access file or in a database table. Assume you store the count in the Count table in a database. The `Count` class can be modified in Listing 27.10.

LISTING 27.10   Count.java (Optional)

package statement

```
1 package chapter27;
2
3 import java.sql.*;
4
5 public class Count {
6   private int count = 0;
7   private Statement statement = null;
8
9   public Count() {
10     initializeJdbc();
11   }
12
13   /** Return count property */
14   public int getCount() {
15     try {
```

execute SQL

```
16       ResultSet rset = statement.executeQuery
17         ("select countValue from Count");
18       rset.next();
19       count = rset.getInt(1);
20     }
```

EXAMPLE 27.5 (CONTINUED)

```
21      catch (Exception ex) {
22        ex.printStackTrace();
23      }
24
25      return count;
26  }
27
28  /** Increase count */
29  public void increaseCount() {
30    count++;
31    try {
32      statement.executeUpdate(
33        "update Count set countValue = " + count);
34    }
35    catch (Exception ex) {
36      ex.printStackTrace();
37    }
38  }
39
40  /** Initialize database connection */
41  public void initializeJdbc() {
42    try {
43      Class.forName("sun.jdbc.odbc.JdbcOdbcDriver");          load driver
44
45      // Connect to the sample database
46      Connection connection = DriverManager.getConnection(   connection
47        "jdbc:odbc:exampleMDBDataSource");
48
49      statement = connection.createStatement();              statement
50    }
51    catch (Exception ex) {
52      ex.printStackTrace();
53    }
54  }
55 }
```

27.8 Getting and Setting Properties

By convention, a JavaBeans component provides the get and set methods for reading and modifying its private properties. You can get the property in JSP using the syntax shown below:

```
<jsp:getProperty name="beanId" property="sample" />
```

This is equivalent to

```
<%= beanId.getSample() %>
```

You can set the property in JSP using the following syntax:

```
<jsp:setProperty name="beanId" property="sample" value="test1" />
```

This is equivalent to

```
<% beanId.setSample("test1"); %>
```

27.9 Associating Properties with Input Parameters

Often properties are associated with input parameters. Suppose you want to get the value of the input parameter named score and set it to the JavaBeans property named score. You could write the following code:

```
<% double score = Double.parseDouble(
    request.getParameter("score")); %>
<jsp:setProperty name="beanId" property="score"
  value="<%= score %>" />
```

This is cumbersome. JSP provides a convenient syntax that can be used to simplify it:

```
<jsp:setProperty name="beanId" property="score"
  param="score" />
```

Instead of using the value attribute, you use the param attribute to name an input parameter. The value of this parameter is set to the property.

 NOTE

Simple type conversion is performed automatically when a bean property is associated with an input parameter. A string input parameter is converted to an appropriate primitive data type or a wrapper class for a primitive type. For example, if the bean property is of the int type, the value of the parameter will be converted to the int type. If the bean property is of the Integer type, the value of the parameter will be converted to the Integer type.

Often the bean property and the parameter have the same name. You can use the following convenient statement to associate all the bean properties in beanId with the parameters that match the property names:

```
<jsp:setProperty name="beanId" property="*" />
```

EXAMPLE 27.6 COMPUTING LOAN PAYMENTS USING JAVABEANS

Problem

Use JavaBeans to simplify Example 27.3, "Computing Loan Payments Using the Loan Class," by associating the bean properties with the input parameters.

Solution

ComputeLoan.html is the same as in Example 27.2. Replace ComputeLoan.jsp in Example 27.2 by Listing 27.11.

LISTING 27.11 ComputeLoan.jsp (Optional)

```
 1 <!-- ComputeLoan.jsp -->
 2 <html>
 3 <head>
 4 <title>ComputeLoan Using the Loan Class</title>
 5 </head>
 6 <body>
 7 <%@ page import = "chapter27.Loan" %>
 8 <jsp:useBean id="loan" class="chapter27.Loan"></jsp:useBean>
 9 <jsp:setProperty name="loan" property="*" />
10 Loan Amount: <%= loan.getLoanAmount() %><br>
11 Annual Interest Rate: <%= loan.getAnnualInterestRate() %><br>
12 Number of Years: <%= loan.getNumOfYears() %><br>
13 <b>Monthly Payment: <%= loan.monthlyPayment() %><br>
14 Total Payment: <%= loan.totalPayment() %><br></b>
15 </body>
16 </html>
```

import
create bean

use bean

EXAMPLE 27.6 (CONTINUED)

Review

Line 8 `<jsp:useBean id="loan" class="chapter27.Loan"></jsp:useBean>` creates a bean named loan for the Loan class. Line 9 `<jsp:setProperty name="loan" property="*" />` associates the bean properties loanAmount, annualInteresteRate, and numberOfYears with the input parameter values and performs type conversion automatically.

Lines 10–12 use the accessor methods of the loan bean to get the loan amount, annual interest rate, and number of years.

This program acts the same as in Examples 27.2 and 27.3, but the coding is much simplified.

EXAMPLE 27.7 COMPUTING FACTORIALS USING JAVABEANS

Problem

This example creates a JavaBeans component named FactorialBean and uses it to compute the factorial of an input number in a JSP page named FactorialBean.jsp, as shown in Figure 27.7.

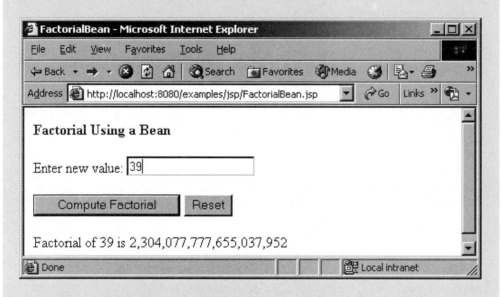

FIGURE 27.7 *The factorial of an input integer is computed using a method in FactorialBean.*

Solution

Create a JavaBeans component named FactorialBean.java (Listing 27.12) and compile it into c:\jakarta-tomcat-4.1.27\webapps\examples\WEB-INF\classes\chapter27.

LISTING 27.12 FactorialBean.java

```
1 package chapter27;
2
3 public class FactorialBean {
4   private int number;
5
```

package statement

EXAMPLE 27.7 (CONTINUED)

get

```
 6   /** Return number property */
 7   public int getNumber() {
 8     return number;
 9   }
10
```

set

```
11   /** Set number property */
12   public void setNumber(int newValue) {
13     number = newValue;
14   }
15
16   /** Obtain factorial */
17   public long getFactorial() {
18     long factorial = 1;
19     for (int i = 1; i <= number; i++)
20       factorial *= i;
21     return factorial;
22   }
23 }
```

Create FactorialBean.jsp (Listing 27.13) and save it into c:\jakarta-tomcat-4.1.27\
webapps\examples\jsp. Run it from the URL `http://localhost:8080/examples/`
`jsp/FactorialBean.jsp`, as shown in Figure 27.7.

LISTING 27.13 FactorialBean.jsp

import
create bean

form

get property

```
 1 <!-- FactorialBean.jsp -->
 2 <%@ page import = "chapter27.FactorialBean" %>
 3 <jsp:useBean id="factorialBeanId" class="chapter27.FactorialBean" >
 4 </jsp:useBean>
 5 <jsp:setProperty name="factorialBeanId" property="*" />
 6 <html>
 7 <head>
 8 <title>
 9 FactorialBean
10 </title>
11 </head>
12 <body>
13 <h3>
14 Compute Factorial Using a Bean
15 </h3>
16 <form method="POST">
17 Enter new value: <input name="number"><br><br>
18 <input type="SUBMIT" name="Submit" value="Compute Factorial">
19 <input type="RESET" value="Reset">
20 <p>Factorial of
21 <jsp:getProperty name="factorialBeanId" property="number" /> is
22 <%@ page import="java.text.*" %>
23 <% NumberFormat format = NumberFormat.getNumberInstance(); %>
24 <%= format.format(factorialBeanId.getFactorial()) %>
25 </form>
26 </body>
27 </html>
```

Review

The `jsp:useBean` tag (Lines 3–4) creates a bean `factorialBeanId` of the `FactorialBean`
class. Line 5 `<jsp:setProperty name="factorialBeanId" property="*" />` associates all
the bean properties with the input parameters that have the same name. In this case, the
bean property `number` is associated with the input parameter `number`. When you click the
Compute Factorial button, JSP automatically converts the input value for `number` from
string into `int` and sets it to `factorialBean` before other statements are executed.

The `<jsp:getProperty name="factorialBeanId" property="number" />` tag (Line 21)
is equivalent to `<%= factorialBeanId.getNumber() %>`. The method `factorialBeanId.`
`getFactorial()` (Line 24) returns the factorial for the number in `factorialBeanId`.

27.10   Forwarding Requests from JavaServer Pages

Web applications developed using JSP generally consist of many pages linked together. JSP provides a forwarding tag in the following syntax that can be used to forward a page to another page:

```
<jsp:forward page="destination" />
```

EXAMPLE 27.8   BROWSING DATABASE TABLES

Problem

This example creates a JSP database application that browses tables. When you start the application, the first page prompts the user to enter the JDBC driver, URL, username, and password for a database, as shown in Figure 27.8. After you log into the database, you can select a table to browse, as shown in Figure 27.9. Upon clicking the Browse Table Content button, the table content is displayed, as shown in Figure 27.10.

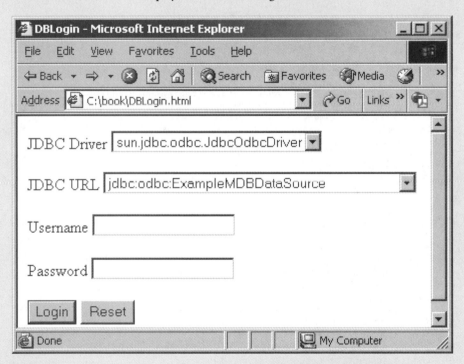

FIGURE 27.8   *To access a database, you need to provide the JDBC driver, URL, username, and password.*

Solution

Create a JavaBeans component named DBBean.java (Listing 27.14) and compile it into c:\jakarta-tomcat-4.1.27\webapps\examples\WEB-INF\classes\chapter27.

LISTING 27.14   **DBBean.jsp**

```
1 package chapter27;
2
3 import java.sql.*;
4
```

EXAMPLE 27.8 (CONTINUED)

```java
 5 public class DBBean {
 6   private Connection connection = null;
 7   private String username;
 8   private String password;
 9   private String driver;
10   private String url;
11
12   /** Initialize database connection */
13   public void initializeJdbc() {
14     try {
15       System.out.println("Driver is " + driver);
16       Class.forName(driver);
17
18       // Connect to the sample database
19       connection = DriverManager.getConnection(url, username,
20         password);
21     }
22     catch (Exception ex) {
23       ex.printStackTrace();
24     }
25   }
26
27   /** Get tables in the database */
28   public String[] getTables() {
29     String[] tables = null;
30
31     try {
32       DatabaseMetaData dbMetaData = connection.getMetaData();
33       ResultSet rsTables = dbMetaData.getTables(null, null, null,
34         new String[] {"TABLE"});
35
36       int size = 0;
37       while (rsTables.next()) size++;
38
39       rsTables = dbMetaData.getTables(null, null, null,
40         new String[] {"TABLE"});
41
42       tables = new String[size];
43       int i = 0;
44       while (rsTables.next())
45         tables[i++] = rsTables.getString("TABLE_NAME");
46     }
47     catch (Exception ex) {
48       ex.printStackTrace();
50     }
51
52     return tables;
53   }
54
55   /** Return connection property */
56   public Connection getConnection() {
57     return connection;
58   }
59
60   public void setUsername(String newUsername) {
61     username = newUsername;
62   }
63
64   public String getUsername() {
65     return username;
66   }
67
68   public void setPassword(String newPassword) {
69     password = newPassword;
70   }
71
72   public String getPassword() {
73     return password;
74   }
```

load driver

connect db

get tables

return table names

EXAMPLE 27.8 (CONTINUED)

```
75
76    public void setDriver(String newDriver) {
77      driver = newDriver;
78    }
79
80    public String getDriver() {
81      return driver;
82    }
83
84    public void setUrl(String newUrl) {
85      url = newUrl;
86    }
87
88    public String getUrl() {
89      return url;
90    }
91 }
```

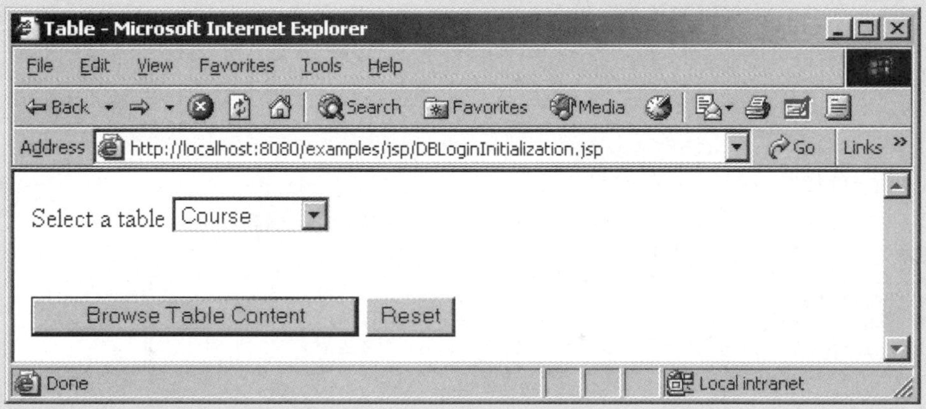

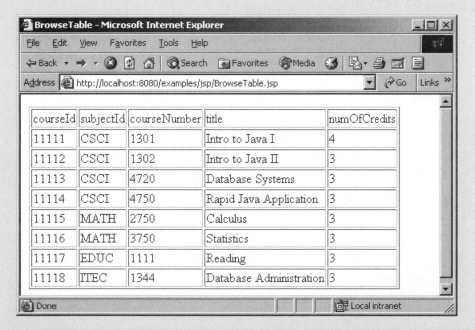

FIGURE 27.9 *You can select a table to browse from this page.*

FIGURE 27.10 *The contents of the selected table are displayed.*

EXAMPLE 27.8 (CONTINUED)

Create an HTML file named DBLogin.html (Listing 27.15) that prompts the user to enter database information and three JSP files named DBLoginInitialization.jsp (Listing 27.16), Table.jsp (Listing 27.17), and BrowseTable.jsp (Listing 27.18) to process and obtain database information. DBLogin.html is stored in c:\book, and the JSP files are stored in c:\jakarta-tomcat-4.1.27\webapps\examples\jsp.

LISTING 27.15 DBLogin.html

```
1  <!-- DBLogin.html -->
2  <html>
3  <head>
4  <title>
5  DBLogin
6  </title>
7  </head>
8  <body>
9  <form method="POST" action=
10    "http://localhost:8080/examples/jsp/DBLoginInitialization.jsp">
11 JDBC Driver
12   <select name="driver" size="1">
13     <option>sun.jdbc.odbc.JdbcOdbcDriver
14     <option>oracle.jdbc.driver.OracleDriver
15   </select><br>
16 <br>JDBC URL
17   <select name="url" size="1">
18     <option>jdbc:odbc:ExampleMDBDataSource
19     <option>jdbc:oracle:thin:@liang.armstrong.edu:1521:ora9i
20     <option>jdbc:oracle:thin:@localhost:1521:test
21   </select><br>
22 <br>Username <input name="username"><br>
23 <br>Password <input name="password"><br><br>
24 <input type="submit" name="Submit" value="Login">
25 <input type="reset" value="Reset">
26 </form>
27 </body>
28 </html>
```

form
action

combo box

combo box

submit

LISTING 27.16 DBLoginInitialization.jsp

```
1  <!-- DBLoginInitialization.jsp -->
2  <%@ page import = "chapter27.DBBean" %>
3  <jsp:useBean id="dBBeanId" scope="session" class="chapter27.DBBean">
4  </jsp:useBean>
5  <jsp:setProperty name="dBBeanId" property="*" />
6  <html>
7  <head>
8  <title>DBLoginInitialization</title>
9  </head>
10 <body>
11
12 <%-- Connect to the database --%>
13 <% dBBeanId.initializeJdbc(); %>
14
15 <% if (dBBeanId.getConnection() == null) { %>
16    Error: Login failed. Try again.
17 <% }
18   else {%>
19    <jsp:forward page="Table.jsp" />
20 <% } %>
21 </body>
22 </html>
```

import
create bean

connect db

report error

get tables

LISTING 27.17 Table.jsp

```
1  <!-- Table.jsp -->
2  <%@ page import = "chapter27.DBBean" %>
3  <jsp:useBean id="dBBeanId" scope="session" class="chapter27.DBBean">
```

import
get bean

EXAMPLE 27.8 (CONTINUED)

```
 4 </jsp:useBean>
 5 <html>
 6 <head>
 7 <title>Table</title>
 8 </head>
 9 <body>
10 <% String[] tables = dBBeanId.getTables();
11    if (tables == null) { %>
12      No tables
13 <% }
14    else { %>
15      <form method="POST" action="BrowseTable.jsp">
16      Select a table <select name="tablename" size="1">
17      <% for (int i=0; i<tables.length; i++) { %>
18        <option><%= tables[i] %>
19 <%   }
20    } %>
21            </select><br><br><br>
22 <input type="submit" name="Submit" value="Browse Table Content">
23 <input type="reset" value="Reset">
24 </form>
25 </body>
26 </html>
```

get tables

create form

LISTING 27.18 BrowseTable.jsp

```
 1 <!-- BrowseTable.jsp -->
 2 <%@ page import = "chapter27.DBBean" %>
 3 <jsp:useBean id="dBBeanId" scope="session" class="chapter27.DBBean" >
 4 </jsp:useBean>
 5 <%@ page import="java.sql.*" %>
 6 <html>
 7 <head>
 8 <title>BrowseTable</title>
 9 </head>
10 <body>
11
12 <%String tableName = request.getParameter("tablename");
13
14   ResultSet rsColumns = dBBeanId.getConnection().getMetaData().
15     getColumns(null, null, tableName, null);
16 %>
17   <table border="1">
18     <tr>
19 <%  // Add column names to the table
20     while (rsColumns.next()) { %>
21        <td> <%= rsColumns.getString("COLUMN_NAME") %> </td>
22 <%} %>
23   </tr>
24
25 <%
26   Statement statement = dBBeanId.getConnection().createStatement();
27   ResultSet rs = statement.executeQuery(
28     "select * from " + tableName);
29
30   // Get column count
31   int columnCount = rs.getMetaData().getColumnCount();
32
33   // Store rows to rowData
34   while (rs.next()) {
35     out.println("<tr>");
36     for (int i = 0; i < columnCount; i++) { %>
37       <td> <%= rs.getObject(i + 1) %> </td>
38 <%  }
39     out.println("</tr>");
40   } %>
41 </table>
42 </body>
43 </html>
```

import
get bean

get table name

table column

column names

table content

display content

EXAMPLE 27.8 (CONTINUED)

Review

You start the application from DBLogin.html. This page prompts the user to enter a JDBC driver, URL, username, and password to log in to a database. A list of accessible drivers and URLs is provided in the selection list. You must make sure that these databases are accessible from the JSP server and that their drivers are installed in c:\jakarta-tomcat-4.1.27\ common\lib.

When you click the Login button, DBLoginInitialization.jsp is invoked. When this page is processed for the first time, an instance of `DBBean` named `dBBeanId` is created. The input parameters `driver`, `url`, `username`, and `password` are passed to the bean properties. The `initializeJdbc` method loads the driver and establishes a connection to the database. If login fails, the `connection` property is `null`. In this case, an error message is displayed. If login succeeds, control is forwarded to Table.jsp.

Table.jsp shares `dBBeanId` with DBLoginInitialization.jsp in the same session, so it can access `connection` through `dBBeanId` and obtain tables in the database using the database metadata. The table names are displayed in a selection box in a form. When the user selects a table name and clicks the Browse Table Content button, BrowseTable.jsp is processed.

BrowseTable.jsp shares `dBBeanId` with Table.jsp and DBLoginInitialization.jsp in the same session. It retrieves the table contents for the selected table from Table.jsp.

JSP SCRIPTING CONSTRUCTS SYNTAX

♦ `<%= Java expression %>` The expression is evaluated and inserted into the page.

♦ `<% Java statement %>` Java statements inserted in the `jspService` method.

♦ `<%! Java declaration %>` Defines data fields and methods.

♦ `<%-- JSP comment %>` The JSP comments do not appear in the resultant HTML file.

♦ `<%@ directive attribute="value" %>` The JSP directives give the JSP engine information about the JSP page. For example, `<%@ page import="java.util.*, java.text.*" %>` imports `java.util.*` and `java.text.*`.

♦ `<jsp:useBean id="objectName" scope="scopeAttribute" class="ClassName" />` Creates a bean if new. If a bean is already created, associates the id with the bean in the same scope.

♦ `<jsp:useBean id="objectName" scope="scopeAttribute" class="ClassName" > statements </jsp:useBean>` The statements are executed when the bean is created. If a bean with the same ID and class name already exists, the statements are not executed.

♦ `<jsp:getProperty name="beanId" property="sample" />` Gets the property value from the bean, which is the same as `<%= beanId.getSample() %>`.

♦ `<jsp:setProperty name="beanId" property="sample" value="test1" />` Sets the property value for the bean, which is the same as `<% beanId.setSample("test1"); %>`.

♦ `<jsp:setProperty name="beanId" property="score" param="score" />` Sets the property with an input parameter.

✦ **`<jsp:setProperty name="beanId" property="*" />`** Associates and sets all the bean properties in `beanId` with the input parameters that match the property names.

✦ **`<jsp:forward page="destination" />`** Forwards this page to a new page.

JSP PREDEFINED VARIABLES

✦ **`application`** represents the `ServletContext` object for storing persistent data for all clients.

✦ **`config`** represents the `ServletConfig` object for the page.

✦ **`out`** represents the character output stream, which is an instance of `PrintWriter`, obtained from `response.getWriter()`.

✦ **`page`** is alternative to `this`.

✦ **`request`** represents the client's request, which is an instance of `HttpServletRequest` in the servlet's `service` method.

✦ **`response`** represents the client's response, which is an instance of `HttpServletResponse` in the servlet's `service` method.

✦ **`session`** represents the `HttpSession` object associated with the request, obtained from `request.getSession()`.

CHAPTER SUMMARY

✦ A JavaServer page is like a regular HTML page with special tags, known as *JSP tags*, which enable the Web server to generate dynamic content. You can create a Web page with static HTML and enclose the code for generating dynamic content in the JSP tags.

✦ A JSP page must be stored in a file with a .jsp extension. The Web server translates the .jsp file into a Java servlet, compiles the servlet, and executes it. The result of the execution is sent to the browser for display.

✦ A JSP page is translated into a servlet when the page is requested for the first time. It is not retranslated if the page is not modified. To ensure that the first-time real user does not get a delay, JSP developers may test the page after it is installed.

✦ In order to display a JSP page, the page must be placed in a designated directory (e.g., c:\jakarta-tomcat-4.1.27\webapps\examples\jsp) and must be accessed from a JSP-enabled Web server with an appropriate URL (e.g., `http://localhost:8080/examples/jsp/CurrentTime.jsp`).

✦ There are three main types of JSP constructs: scripting constructs, directives, and actions. *Scripting* elements enable you to specify Java code that will become part of the resultant servlet. *Directives* enable you to control the overall structure of the resultant servlet. *Actions* enable you to control the behaviors of the JSP engine.

✦ There are three types of scripting constructs that can be used to insert Java code into the resultant servlet: expressions, scriptlets, and declarations.

✦ The scope attribute (application, session, page, and request) specifies the scope of a JavaBeans object. Application specifies that the object be bound to the application. Session specifies that the object be bound to the client's session. Page is the default scope, which specifies that the object be bound to the page. Request specifies that the object be bound to the client's request.

✦ Web applications developed using JSP generally consist of many pages linked together. JSP provides a forwarding tag in the following syntax that can be used to forward a page to another page: `<jsp:forward page="destination" />`.

REVIEW QUESTIONS

Sections 27.1–27.3

27.1 What is the file name extension of a JavaServer page? How is a JSP page processed?

27.2 Where should a JSP file be placed for it to run from Tomcat?

27.3 You can display an HTML file (e.g., c:\test.html) by typing the complete file name in the Address field of Internet Explorer. Why can't you display a JSP file by simply typing the file name?

Section 27.4 JSP Scripting Constructs

27.4 What are a JSP expression, a JSP scriptlet, and a JSP declaration? How do you write these constructs in JSP?

27.5 Find three syntax errors in the following JSP code:

```
<%! int k %>
<% for (int j = 1; j <= 9; j++) %>
    <%= j; %> <br>
```

27.6 In the following JSP, which variables are instance variables and which are local variables when it is translated into in the servlet?

```
<%! int k; %>
<%! int i; %>
<% for (int j = 1; j <= 9; j++) k += 1;%>
<%= k><br> <%= i><br> <%= getTime()><br>
<% private long getTime() {
      long time = System.currentTimeMillis();
      return time; } %>
```

Section 27.5 Predefined Variables

27.7 Describe the predefined variables in JSP.

27.8 What is wrong if the JSP scriptlet `<%` in Line 7 in ComputeLoan.jsp in Example 27.2 is replaced by JSP declaration `<%!`?

27.9 Can you use predefined variables (e.g., request, response, out) in JSP declarations?

Section 27.6 JSP Directives

27.10 Describe the JSP directives and attributes for the page directive.

27.11 If a class does not have a package statement, can you import it?

27.12 If you use a custom class from a JSP, where should the class be placed?

Section 27.7 Using JavaBeans in JSP

27.13 You can create an object in a JSP scriptlet. What is the difference between an object created using the new operator and a bean created using the `<jsp:useBean ... >` tag?

27.14   What is the scope attribute for? Describe four scope attributes.

27.15   Describe how a <jsp:useBean ... > statement is processed by the JSP engine.

Sections 27.8–27.10

27.16   How do you associate bean properties with input parameters?

27.17   How do you write a statement to forward requests to another JSP page?

PROGRAMMING EXERCISES

Section 27.4 JSP Scripting Constructs

27.1   (*Factorial table in JSP*) Rewrite Exercise 26.1 using JSP.

27.2   (*Multiplication table in JSP*) Rewrite Exercise 26.2 using JSP.

Section 27.5 Predefined Variables

27.3*   (*Obtaining parameters in JSP*) Rewrite Example 26.2, "Obtaining Parameter Values from HTML Forms." Create an HTML form that is identical to student_registration_form.html in Example 26.2 except that the action is replaced by http://localhost:8080/examples/jsp/Exercise27_3.jsp for obtaining parameter values.

Section 27.6 JSP Directives

27.4   (*Calculating tax in JSP*) Rewrite Exercise 26.4 using JSP. You need to import ComputeTax in the JSP. Create a new ComputeTax.java in package chapter27 and compile it into c:\jakarta-tomcat-4.1.27\webapps\examples\WEB-INF\classes\chapter27.

27.5*   (*Displaying international time in JSP*) Use JSP to rewrite Example 26.3, "Obtaining Current Time Based on Locale and Time Zone," as shown in Figure 27.11.

FIGURE 27.11   *The JSP creates the HTML form and displays the time based on locale and time zone.*

27.6** (*Registering students in JSP*) Use JSP to rewrite Example 26.4, "Registering a Student in a Database." Create an HTML form that is identical to SimpleRegistration.html in Example 26.4 except that the action is replaced by `http://localhost:8080/examples/jsp/Exercise27_6.jsp` for processing registration.

Section 27.7 Using JavaBeans in JSP

27.7** (*Registering students using JavaBeans in JSP*) Rewrite Example 26.7, "Using `HttpSession` in the Registration Form." Create a JavaBeans component to hold all the parameter values with methods to connect to databases.

Comprehensive

27.8* (*Storing cookies in JSP*) Rewrite Exercise 26.10 using JSP. Use `response.addCookie (Cookie)` to add a cookie.

27.9 (*Retrieving cookies in JSP*) Rewrite Exercise 26.11 using JSP. Use `Cookie[] cookies = request.getCookies()` to add all cookies.

PART IX

DISTRIBUTED COMPUTING

This part introduces how to write programs that talk with each other from different hosts over the Internet. Networking is embedded in Java. Chapter 28 introduces low-level socket network programming, and Chapter 29 introduces high-level remote method invocation.

Chapter 28
Networking

Chapter 29
Remote Method Invocation

Prerequisites for Part IX

Chapter 14 Applets, Images, and Audio

Chapter 28 Networking

Chapter 29 Remote Method Invocation

NETWORKING

Objectives

✦ To comprehend socket-based communication in Java (§28.2).

✦ To understand client/server computing (§28.2).

✦ To implement Java networking programs using stream sockets (§28.2).

✦ To obtain Internet addresses using the `InetAddress` class (§28.3).

✦ To develop servers for multiple clients (§28.4).

✦ To develop applets that communicate with the server (§28.5).

✦ To send and receive objects on a network (§28.6).

✦ To create applications or applets to retrieve files from a network (§28.7).

✦ To render HTML files using the `JEditorPane` class (§28.8).

✦ To implement Java networking programs using datagram sockets (§28.10).

28.1 Introduction

socket-based

Networking is tightly integrated in Java. *Socket-based communication* is provided that enables programs to communicate through designated sockets. *Sockets* are the endpoints of logical connections between two hosts and can be used to send and receive data. Java treats socket communications much as it treats I/O operations; thus programs can read from or write to sockets as easily as they can read from or write to files.

stream socket
datagram socket

Java supports stream sockets and datagram sockets. *Stream sockets* use TCP (Transmission Control Protocol) for data transmission, whereas *datagram sockets* use UDP (User Datagram Protocol). Since TCP can detect lost transmissions and resubmit them, transmissions are lossless and reliable. UDP, in contrast, cannot guarantee lossless transmission. Because of this, stream sockets are used in most areas of Java programming, and that is why most of the discussion in this chapter is based on stream sockets. Datagram socket programming is introduced in the last section of this chapter.

28.2 Client/Server Computing

Network programming usually involves a server and one or more clients. The client sends requests to the server, and the server responds to the requests. The client begins by attempting to establish a connection to the server. The server can accept or deny the connection. Once a connection is established, the client and the server communicate through sockets.

The server must be running when a client starts. The server waits for a connection request from a client. The statements needed to create a server and a client are shown in Figure 28.1.

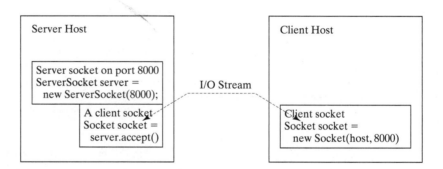

FIGURE 28.1 *The server creates a server socket and, once a connection to a client is established, connects to the client with a client socket.*

28.2.1 Server Sockets

To establish a server, you need to create a *server socket* and attach it to a port, which is where the server listens for connections. The port identifies the TCP service on the socket. Port numbers range from 0 to 65536, but port numbers 0 to 1024 are reserved for privileged services. For instance, the e-mail server runs on port 25, and the Web server usually runs on port 80. You can choose any port number that is not currently used by any other process. The following statement creates a server socket serverSocket:

server socket

```
ServerSocket serverSocket = new ServerSocket(port);
```

> ### 🌱 NOTE
> Attempting to create a server socket on a port already in use would cause the
> java.net.BindException.

BindException

28.2.2   Client Sockets

After a server socket is created, the server can use the following statement to listen for connections:

```
Socket socket = serverSocket.accept();
```
connect to client

This statement waits until a client connects to the server socket. The client issues the following statement to request a connection to a server:

```
Socket socket = new Socket(serverName, port);
```
client socket

This statement opens a socket so that the client program can communicate with the server. *serverName* is the server's Internet host name or IP address. The following statement creates a socket at port 8000 on the client machine to connect to the host drake.armstrong.edu:

```
Socket socket = new Socket("drake.armstrong.edu", 8000);
```
use host name

Alternatively, you can use the IP address to create a socket, as follows:

```
Socket socket = new Socket("130.254.204.36", 8000)
```
use IP address

An IP address, consisting of four dotted decimal numbers between 0 and 255, such as 130.254.204.36, is a computer's unique identity on the Internet. Since it is not easy to remember so many numbers, they are often mapped to meaningful names called *host names*, such as

drake.armstrong.edu.

A program can use the host name localhost or the IP address 127.0.0.1 to refer to the machine on which a client is running.

 NOTE
There are special servers on the Internet that translate host names into IP addresses. These servers are called *Domain Name Servers* (DNS). The translation is done behind the scenes. When you create a socket with a host name, the JVM asks the DNS to translate the host name into the IP address.

domain name server

28.2.3   Data Transmission through Sockets

After the server accepts the connection, communication between server and client is conducted the same as for I/O streams. The statements needed to create the streams and to exchange data between them are shown in Figure 28.2.

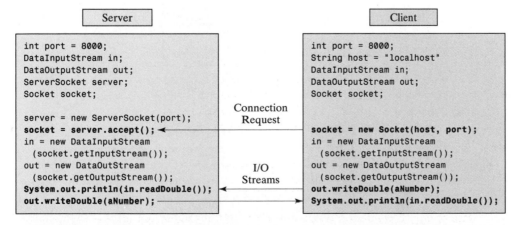

FIGURE 28.2   *The server and client exchange data through I/O streams on top of the socket.*

To get an input stream and an output stream, use the getInputStream() and getOutputStream() methods on a socket object. For example, the following statements create an InputStream stream called input and an OutputStream stream called output from a socket:

```
InputStream input = socket.getInputStream();
OutputStream output = socket.getOutputStream();
```

The InputStream and OutputStream streams are used to read or write bytes. You can use DataInput-Stream, DataOutputStream, BufferedReader, and PrintWriter to wrap on the InputStream and OutputStream to read or write data, such as int, double, or String. The following statements, for instance, create a DataInputStream stream, input, and a DataOutput stream, output, to read and write primitive data values:

```
DataInputStream input = new DataInputStream
   (socket.getInputStream());
DataOutputStream output = new DataOutputStream
   (socket.getOutputStream());
```

The server can use input.readDouble() to receive a double value from the client, and output.writeDouble(d) to send double value d to the client.

TIP

Recall that binary I/O is more efficient than text I/O because text I/O requires encoding and decoding. So, I recommend you use binary I/O for transmitting data between a server and a client to improve performance.

EXAMPLE 28.1 A CLIENT/SERVER EXAMPLE

Problem

This example presents a client program and a server program. The client sends data to a server. The server receives the data, uses them to produce a result, and then sends the result back to the client. The client displays the result on the console. In this example, the data sent from the client comprise the radius of a circle, and the result produced by the server is the area of the circle (see Figure 28.3).

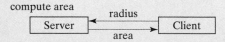

FIGURE 28.3   *The client sends the radius to the server; the server computes the area and sends it to the client.*

Solution

The client sends the radius through a DataOutputStream on the output stream socket, and the server receives the radius through the DataInputStream on the input stream socket, as shown in Figure 28.4(a). The server computes the area and sends it to the client through a DataOutputStream on the output stream socket, and the client receives the area through a DataInputStream on the input stream socket, as shown in Figure 28.4(b). The server and client programs are given in Listings 28.1 and 28.2. Figure 28.5 contains a sample run of the server and the client.

EXAMPLE 28.1 (CONTINUED)

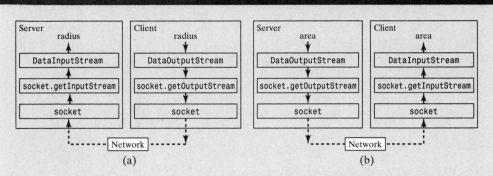

FIGURE 28.4 *(a) The client sends the radius to the server. (b) The server sends the area to the client.*

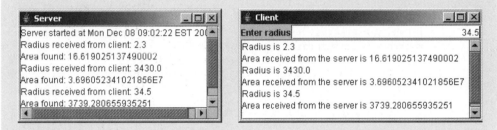

FIGURE 28.5 *The client sends the radius to the server. The server receives it, computes the area, and sends the area to the client.*

LISTING 28.1 Server.java (The Server Program)

```java
 1 import java.io.*;
 2 import java.net.*;
 3 import java.util.*;
 4 import java.awt.*;
 5 import javax.swing.*;
 6
 7 public class Server extends JFrame {
 8   // Text area for displaying contents
 9   private JTextArea jta = new JTextArea();
10
11   public static void main(String[] args) {
12     new Server();
13   }
14
15   public Server() {
16     // Place text area on the frame
17     getContentPane().setLayout(new BorderLayout());
18     getContentPane().add(new JScrollPane(jta), BorderLayout.CENTER);
19
20     setTitle("Server");
21     setSize(500, 300);
22     setDefaultCloseOperation(JFrame.EXIT_ON_CLOSE);
23     setVisible(true); // It is necessary to show the frame here!
24
25     try {
26       // Create a server socket
27       ServerSocket serverSocket = new ServerSocket(8000);
28       jta.append("Server started at " + new Date() + '\n');
29
30       // Listen for a connection request
31       Socket socket = serverSocket.accept();
32
```

launch server

server socket

connect client

EXAMPLE 28.1 (CONTINUED)

input from client

output to client

read radius

write area

```
33      // Create data input and output streams
34      DataInputStream inputFromClient = new DataInputStream(
35        socket.getInputStream());
36      DataOutputStream outputToClient = new DataOutputStream(
37        socket.getOutputStream());
38
39      while (true) {
40        // Receive radius from the client
41        double radius = inputFromClient.readDouble();
42
43        // Compute area
44        double area = radius * radius * Math.PI;
45
46        // Send area back to the client
47        outputToClient.writeDouble(area);
48
49        jta.append("Radius received from client: " + radius + '\n');
50        jta.append("Area found: " + area + '\n');
51      }
52    }
53    catch(IOException ex) {
54      System.err.println(ex);
55    }
56  }
57 }
```

LISTING 28.2 Client.java (The Client Program)

launch client

```
1 import java.io.*;
2 import java.net.*;
3 import java.awt.*;
4 import java.awt.event.*;
5 import javax.swing.*;
6
7 public class Client extends JFrame implements ActionListener {
8   // Text field for receiving radius
9   private JTextField jtf = new JTextField();
10
11  // Text area to display contents
12  private JTextArea jta = new JTextArea();
13
14  // IO streams
15  private DataOutputStream toServer;
16  private DataInputStream fromServer;
17
18  public static void main(String[] args) {
19    new Client();
20  }
21
22  public Client() {
23    // Panel p to hold the label and text field
24    JPanel p = new JPanel();
25    p.setLayout(new BorderLayout());
26    p.add(new JLabel("Enter radius"), BorderLayout.WEST);
27    p.add(jtf, BorderLayout.CENTER);
28    jtf.setHorizontalAlignment(JTextField.RIGHT);
29
30    getContentPane().setLayout(new BorderLayout());
31    getContentPane().add(p, BorderLayout.NORTH);
32    getContentPane().add(new JScrollPane(jta), BorderLayout.CENTER);
33
34    jtf.addActionListener(this); // Register listener
35
36    setTitle("Client");
37    setSize(500, 300);
38    setDefaultCloseOperation(JFrame.EXIT_ON_CLOSE);
39    setVisible(true); // It is necessary to show the frame here!
40
```

EXAMPLE 28.1 (CONTINUED)

```
41      try {
42        // Create a socket to connect to the server
43        Socket socket = new Socket("localhost", 8000);                      request connection
44        // Socket socket = new Socket("130.254.204.36", 8000);
45        // Socket socket = new Socket("drake.Armstrong.edu", 8000);
46
47        // Create an input stream to receive data from the server
48        fromServer = new DataInputStream(                                   input from server
49          socket.getInputStream());
50
51        // Create an output stream to send data to the server
52        toServer =                                                          output to server
53          new DataOutputStream(socket.getOutputStream());
54      }
55      catch (IOException ex) {
56        jta.append(ex.toString() + '\n');
57      }
58    }
59
60    public void actionPerformed(ActionEvent e) {
61      String actionCommand = e.getActionCommand();
62      if (e.getSource() instanceof JTextField) {
63        try {
64          // Get the radius from the text field
65          double radius = Double.parseDouble(jtf.getText().trim());
66
67          // Send the radius to the server
68          toServer.writeDouble(radius);                                     write radius
69          toServer.flush();
70
71          // Get area from the server
72          double area = fromServer.readDouble();                           read radius
73
74          // Display to the text area
75          jta.append("Radius is " + radius + "\n");
76          jta.append("Area received from the server is "
77            + area + '\n');
78        }
79        catch (IOException ex) {
80          System.err.println(ex);
81        }
82      }
83    }
84 }
```

Review

You start the server program first, then start the client program. In the client program, enter a radius in the text field and press Enter to send the radius to the server. The server computes the area and sends it back to the client. This process is repeated until one of the two programs terminates.

The networking classes are in the package java.net. This should be imported when writing Java network programs.

The Server class creates a ServerSocket serverSocket and attaches it to port 8000, using the following statement (Line 27 in Server.java):

```
ServerSocket serverSocket = new ServerSocket(8000);
```

The server then starts to listen for connection requests, using this statement (Line 31 in Server.java):

```
Socket socket = serverSocket.accept();
```

The server waits until a client requests a connection. After it is connected, the server reads the radius from the client through an input stream, computes the area, and sends the result to the client through an output stream.

EXAMPLE 28.1 (CONTINUED)

The `Client` class uses the following statement to create a socket that will request a connection to the server on the same machine (localhost) at port 8000 (Line 43 in Client.java):

```
Socket socket = new Socket("localhost", 8000);
```

If you run the server and the client on different machines, replace `localhost` with the server machine's host name or IP address. In this example, the server and the client are running on the same machine.

If the server is not running, the client program terminates with a `java.net.ConnectException`. After it is connected, the client gets input and output streams—wrapped by data input and output streams—in order to receive and send data to the server.

If you receive a `java.net.BindException` when you start the server, the server port is currently in use. You need to terminate the process that is using the server port and then restart the server.

What happens if the `setVisible(true)` statement in Line 23 in Server.java is moved after the `try-catch` block in Line 56 in Server.java? The frame would not be displayed because the `while` loop in the `try-catch` block will not finish until the program terminates.

28.3 The `InetAddress` Class

Occasionally, you would like to know who is connecting to the server. You can use the `InetAddress` class to find the client's host name and IP address. The `InetAddress` class models an IP address. You can use the statement shown below to create an instance of `InetAddress` for the client on a socket:

```
InetAddress inetAddress = socket.getInetAddress();
```

Next, you can display the client's host name and IP address, as follows:

```
System.out.println("Client's host name is " +
  inetAddress.getHostName());
System.out.println("Client's IP Address is " +
  inetAddress.getHostAddress());
```

You can also create an instance of `InetAddress` from a host name or IP address using the static `getByName` method. For example, the following statement creates an `InetAddress` for the host `liang.armstrong.edu`:

```
InetAddress address = InetAddress.getByName("liang.armstrong.edu");
```

28.4 Serving Multiple Clients

Multiple clients are quite often connected to a single server at the same time. Typically, a server runs constantly on a server computer, and clients from all over the Internet may want to connect to it. You can use threads to handle the server's multiple clients simultaneously. Simply create a thread for each connection. Here is how the server handles the establishment of a connection:

```
while (true) {
  Socket socket = serverSocket.accept();
  Thread thread = new ThreadClass(socket);
  thread.start();
}
```

The server socket can have many connections. Each iteration of the `while` loop creates a new connection. Whenever a connection is established, a new thread is created to handle communication between the server and the new client; and this allows multiple connections to run at the same time.

EXAMPLE 28.2 SERVING MULTIPLE CLIENTS

Problem

Write a server that serves multiple clients simultaneously. For each connection, the server starts a new thread. This thread continuously receives input (the radius of a circle) from clients and sends the results (the area of the circle) back to them (see Figure 28.6).

Solution

The client program is same as in Example 28.1. Listing 28.3 gives the new server program. A sample run of the server with two clients is shown in Figure 28.7.

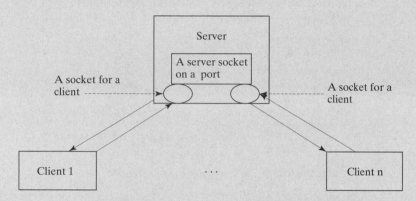

FIGURE 28.6 *Multithreading enables a server to handle multiple independent clients.*

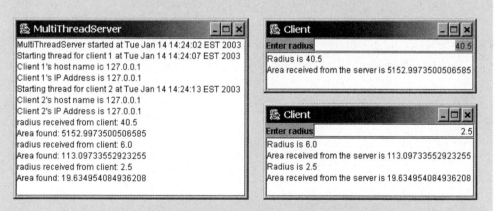

FIGURE 28.7 *The server spawns a thread in order to serve a client.*

LISTING 28.3 MultiThreadServer.java (Serving Multiple Clients)

```java
1 import java.io.*;
2 import java.net.*;
3 import java.util.*;
4 import java.awt.*;
5 import javax.swing.*;
6
7 public class MultiThreadServer extends JFrame {
8   // Text area for displaying contents
9   private JTextArea jta = new JTextArea();
10
11   public static void main(String[] args) {
12     new MultiThreadServer();
13   }
14
```

EXAMPLE 28.2 (CONTINUED)

```
15    public MultiThreadServer() {
16      // Place text area on the frame
17      getContentPane().setLayout(new BorderLayout());
18      getContentPane().add(new JScrollPane(jta), BorderLayout.CENTER);
19
20      setTitle("MultiThreadServer");
21      setSize(500, 300);
22      setDefaultCloseOperation(JFrame.EXIT_ON_CLOSE);
23      setVisible(true); // It is necessary to show the frame here!
24
25      try {
26        // Create a server socket
27        ServerSocket serverSocket = new ServerSocket(8000);
28        jta.append("MultiThreadServer started at " + new Date() + '\n');
29
30        // Number a client
31        int clientNo = 1;
32
33        while (true) {
34          // Listen for a new connection request
35          Socket socket = serverSocket.accept();
36
37          // Display the client number
38          jta.append("Starting thread for client " + clientNo +
39            " at " + new Date() + '\n');
40
41          // Find the client's host name, and IP address
42          InetAddress inetAddress = socket.getInetAddress();
43          jta.append("Client " + clientNo + "'s host name is "
44            + inetAddress.getHostName() + "\n");
45          jta.append("Client " + clientNo + "'s IP Address is "
46            + inetAddress.getHostAddress() + "\n");
47
48          // Create a new thread for the connection
49          HandleAClient thread = new HandleAClient(socket);
50
51          // Start the new thread
52          thread.start();
53
54          // Increment clientNo
55          clientNo++;
56        }
57      }
58      catch(IOException ex) {
59        System.err.println(ex);
60      }
61    }
62
63    // Inner class
64    // Define the thread class for handling new connection
65    class HandleAClient extends Thread {
66      private Socket socket; // A connected socket
67
68      /** Construct a thread */
69      public HandleAClient(Socket socket) {
70        this.socket = socket;
71      }
72
73      /** Run a thread */
74      public void run() {
75        try {
76          // Create data input and output streams
77          DataInputStream inputFromClient = new DataInputStream(
78            socket.getInputStream());
79          DataOutputStream outputToClient = new DataOutputStream(
80            socket.getOutputStream());
81
```

server socket

connect client

network information

create thread

start thread

thread class

I/O

EXAMPLE 28.2 (CONTINUED)

```
82              // Continuously serve the client
83              while (true) {
84                // Receive radius from the client
85                double radius = inputFromClient.readDouble();
86
87                // Compute area
88                double area = radius * radius * Math.PI;
89
90                // Send area back to the client
91                outputToClient.writeDouble(area);
92
93                jta.append("radius received from client: " +
94                  radius + '\n');
95                jta.append("Area found: " + area + '\n');
96              }
97            }
98            catch(IOException e) {
99              System.err.println(e);
100           }
101         }
102       }
103     }
```

Review

The server creates a server socket at port 8000 (Line 27) and waits for a connection (Line 35). When a connection with a client is established, the server creates a new thread to handle the communication (Line 49). It then waits for another connection in an infinite while loop (Lines 33–56).

The threads, which run independently of one another, communicate with designated clients. Each thread creates data input and output streams that receive and send data to a client.

This server accepts an unlimited number of clients. To limit the number of concurrent connections, you can use a thread group to monitor the number of active threads and modify the while loop (Lines 33–56), as follows:

```
ThreadGroup group = new ThreadGroup("serving clients");

while (true) {
  if (group.activeCount() >= maxThreadLimit)
    try {
      Thread.sleep(1000);
    }
    catch (InterruptedException ex) {
    }
  else {
    // Listen for a new connection request
    Socket socket = serverSocket.accept();

    // Display the client number
    jta.append("Starting thread for client " + clientNo +
      " at " + new Date() + '\n');

    // Create a new thread for the connection
    Thread thread = new Thread(group,
      new HandleAClient(socket));

    // Start the new thread
    thread.start();

    // Increment clientNo to label the next connection
    clientNo++;
  }
}
```

28.5   Applet Clients

Because of security constraints, applets can only connect to the host from which they were loaded. Therefore, the HTML file must be located on the machine on which the server is running. You can obtain the server's host name by invoking getCodeBase().getHost() on an applet. So you can write the applet without the host name fixed. Below is an example of how to use an applet to connect to a server.

EXAMPLE 28.3 CREATING APPLET CLIENTS

Problem

Write an applet that shows the number of visits made to a Web page. The count should be stored in a file on the server side. Every time the page is visited or reloaded, the applet sends a request to the server, and the server increases the count and sends it to the applet. The applet then displays the new count in a message, such as **You are visitor number 11**, as shown in Figure 28.8.

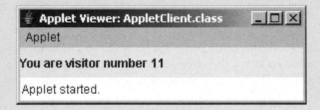

FIGURE 28.8 *The applet displays the access count on a Web page.*

Solution

The server and client programs are given in Listings 28.4 and 28.5.

LISTING 28.4   CountServer.java (Maintaining and Sending a Count)

```
 1 import java.io.*;
 2 import java.net.*;
 3
 4 public class CountServer {
 5   private RandomAccessFile raf;
 6   private int count; // Count the access to the server
 7
 8   public static void main(String[] args) {
 9     new CountServer();
10   }
11
12   public CountServer() {
13     try {
14       // Create a server socket
15       ServerSocket serverSocket = new ServerSocket(8000);
16       System.out.println("Server started ");
17
18       // Create or open the count file
19       raf = new RandomAccessFile("count.dat", "rw");
20
21       // Get the count
22       if (raf.length() == 0)
23         count = 0;
24       else
25         count = raf.readInt();
26
```

launch server

server socket

random access file

new file

get count

EXAMPLE 28.3 (CONTINUED)

```
27        while (true) {
28          // Listen for a new connection request
29          Socket socket = serverSocket.accept();        connect client
30
31          // Create a DataOutputStream for the socket
32          DataOutputStream outputToClient =              send to client
33            new DataOutputStream(socket.getOutputStream());
34
35          // Increase count and send the count to the client
36          count++;                                        update count
37          outputToClient.writeInt(count);
38
39          // Write new count back to the file
40          raf.seek(0);
41          raf.writeInt(count);
42        }
43      }
44      catch(IOException ex) {
45        ex.printStackTrace();
46      }
47    }
48 }
```

LISTING 28.5 AppletClient.java (Receiving a Count)

```
1 import java.io.*;
2 import java.net.*;
3 import java.awt.BorderLayout;
4 import java.awt.event.*;
5 import javax.swing.*;
6
7 public class AppletClient extends JApplet {
8   // Label for displaying the visit count
9   private JLabel jlblCount = new JLabel();
10
11  // Indicate if it runs as application
12  private boolean isStandAlone = false;
13
14  // Host name or ip
15  private String host = "localhost";
16
17  /** Initialize the applet */
18  public void init() {
19    getContentPane().add(jlblCount);
20
21    try {
22      // Create a socket to connect to the server
23      Socket socket;
24      if (isStandAlone)
25        socket = new Socket(host, 8000);                  for standalone
26      else
27        socket = new Socket(getCodeBase().getHost(), 8000);  for applet
28
29      // Create an input stream to receive data from the server
30      DataInputStream inputFromServer =
31        new DataInputStream(socket.getInputStream());
32
33      // Receive the count from the server and display it on label
34      int count = inputFromServer.readInt();               receive count
35      jlblCount.setText("You are visitor number " + count);
36
37      // Close the stream
38      inputFromServer.close();
39    }
40    catch (IOException ex) {
```

EXAMPLE 28.3 (CONTINUED)

```
41        ex.printStackTrace();
42      }
43    }
44 }
```

main method omitted

Review

Let us first review CountServer.java.

The server creates a `ServerSocket` in Line 15 and creates or opens a file using `RandomAccessFile` in Line 19. It reads the count from the file in Lines 22–25. The server then waits for a connection request from a client (Line 29). After a connection with a client is established, the server creates an output stream to the client (Lines 32–33), increases the count (Line 36), sends the count to the client (Line 37), and writes the new count back to the file. This process continues in an infinite `while` loop to handle all clients.

Now let us review AppletClient.java.

The client is an applet. When it runs as an applet, it uses `getCodeBase().getHost()` (Line 27) to return the IP address for the server. When it runs as an application, it passes the URL from the command line (Line 56). If the URL is not passed from the command line, by default "localhost" is used for the URL (Line 15).

The client creates a socket to connect to the server (Lines 24–27), creates an input stream from the socket (Lines 30–31), receives the count from the server (Line 34), and displays it in the text field (Line 35).

28.6   Sending and Receiving Objects

In the preceding examples, you learned how to send and receive data of primitive types. You can also send and receive objects using `ObjectOutputStream` and `ObjectInputStream` on socket streams. To enable passing, the objects must be serializable. The next example demonstrates how to send and receive objects.

EXAMPLE 28.4 PASSING OBJECTS IN NETWORK PROGRAMS

Problem

Write a program that collects student information from a client and sends it to a server, as shown in Figure 28.9.

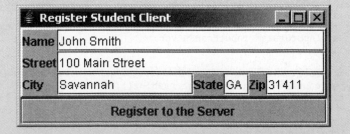

FIGURE 28.9   *The client sends the student information in an object to the server.*

EXAMPLE 28.4 (CONTINUED)

Solution

Create a serialized class named Student that contains the student information: name, street, state, and zip, in Listing 28.6.

LISTING 28.6   Student.java (Containing Student Information)

```java
1 public class Student implements java.io.Serializable {
2   private String name;
3   private String street;
4   private String city;
5   private String state;
6   private String zip;
7
8   public Student(String name, String street, String city,
9     String state, String zip) {
10    this.name = name;
11    this.street = street;
12    this.city = city;
13    this.state = state;
14    this.zip = zip;
15  }
16
17  public String getName() {
18    return name;
19  }
20
21  public String getStreet() {
22    return street;
23  }
24
25  public String getCity() {
26    return city;
27  }
28
29  public String getState() {
30    return state;
31  }
32
33  public String getZip() {
34    return zip;
35  }
36 }
```

The client sends a Student object through an ObjectOutputStream on the output stream socket, and the server receives the Student object through the ObjectInputStream on the input stream socket, as shown in Figure 28.10. The client uses the writeObject method in the ObjectOutputStream class to send a student to the server, and the server receives the student using the readObject method in the ObjectInputStream class. The server and client programs are given in Listings 28.7 and 28.8.

LISTING 28.7   StudentServer.java (Storing Student Information)

```java
1 import java.io.*;
2 import java.net.*;
3
4 public class StudentServer {
5   private ObjectOutputStream outputToFile;
6   private ObjectInputStream inputFromClient;
7
8   public static void main(String[] args) {
9     new StudentServer();
10  }
```

EXAMPLE 28.4 (CONTINUED)

```
11
12    public StudentServer() {
13      try {
14        // Create a server socket
15        ServerSocket serverSocket = new ServerSocket(8000);
16        System.out.println("Server started ");
17
18        // Create an object ouput stream
19        outputToFile = new ObjectOutputStream(
20          new FileOutputStream("student.dat", true));
21
22        while (true) {
23          // Listen for a new connection request
24          Socket socket = serverSocket.accept();
25
26          // Create an input stream from the socket
27          inputFromClient =
28            new ObjectInputStream(socket.getInputStream());
29
30          // Read from input
31          Object object = inputFromClient.readObject();
32
33          // Write to the file
34          outputToFile.writeObject(object);
35          System.out.println("A new student object is stored");
36        }
37      }
38      catch(ClassNotFoundException ex) {
39        ex.printStackTrace();
40      }
41      catch(IOException ex) {
42        ex.printStackTrace();
43      }
44      finally {
45        try {
46          inputFromClient.close();
47          outputToFile.close();
48        }
49        catch (Exception ex) {
50          ex.printStackTrace();
51        }
52      }
53    }
54 }
```

server socket

output to file

connect to client

input stream

get from client

write to file

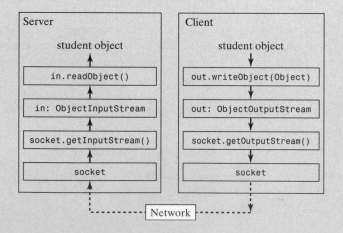

FIGURE 28.10 *The client sends a student object to the server.*

EXAMPLE 28.4 (CONTINUED)

LISTING 28.8 StudentClient.java (Obtaining Student Information)

```
1 import java.io.*;
2 import java.net.*;
3 import java.awt.*;
4 import java.awt.event.*;
5 import javax.swing.*;
6 import javax.swing.border.*;
7
8 public class StudentClient extends JApplet
9     implements ActionListener {
10   private JTextField jtfName = new JTextField(32);
11   private JTextField jtfStreet = new JTextField(32);
12   private JTextField jtfCity = new JTextField(20);
13   private JTextField jtfState = new JTextField(2);
14   private JTextField jtfZip = new JTextField(5);
15
16   // Button for sending a student to the server
17   private JButton jbtRegister = new JButton("Register to the Server");
18
19   // Indicate if it runs as application
20   private boolean isStandAlone = false;
21
22   // Host name or ip
23   String host = "localhost";
24
25   public void init() {
26     // Panel p1 for holding labels Name, Street, and City
27     JPanel p1 = new JPanel();
28     p1.setLayout(new GridLayout(3, 1));
29     p1.add(new JLabel("Name"));
30     p1.add(new JLabel("Street"));
31     p1.add(new JLabel("City"));
32
33     // Panel jpState for holding state
34     JPanel jpState = new JPanel();
35     jpState.setLayout(new BorderLayout());
36     jpState.add(new JLabel("State"), BorderLayout.WEST);
37     jpState.add(jtfState, BorderLayout.CENTER);
38
39     // Panel jpZip for holding zip
40     JPanel jpZip = new JPanel();
41     jpZip.setLayout(new BorderLayout());
42     jpZip.add(new JLabel("Zip"), BorderLayout.WEST);
43     jpZip.add(jtfZip, BorderLayout.CENTER);
44
45     // Panel p2 for holding jpState and jpZip
46     JPanel p2 = new JPanel();
47     p2.setLayout(new BorderLayout());
48     p2.add(jpState, BorderLayout.WEST);
49     p2.add(jpZip, BorderLayout.CENTER);
50
51     // Panel p3 for holding jtfCity and p2
52     JPanel p3 = new JPanel();
53     p3.setLayout(new BorderLayout());
54     p3.add(jtfCity, BorderLayout.CENTER);
55     p3.add(p2, BorderLayout.EAST);
56
57     // Panel p4 for holding jtfName, jtfStreet, and p3
58     JPanel p4 = new JPanel();
59     p4.setLayout(new GridLayout(3, 1));
60     p4.add(jtfName);
61     p4.add(jtfStreet);
62     p4.add(p3);
63
64     // Place p1 and p4 into StudentPanel
65     JPanel studentPanel = new JPanel(new BorderLayout());
```

create UI

EXAMPLE 28.4 (CONTINUED)

```
66         studentPanel.setBorder(new BevelBorder(BevelBorder.RAISED));
67         studentPanel.add(p1, BorderLayout.WEST);
68         studentPanel.add(p4, BorderLayout.CENTER);
69
70         // Add the student panel and button to the applet
71         getContentPane().add(studentPanel, BorderLayout.CENTER);
72         getContentPane().add(jbtRegister, BorderLayout.SOUTH);
73
74         // Register listener
75         jbtRegister.addActionListener(this);
76
77         // Find the IP address of the Web server
78         if (!isStandAlone)
79           host = getCodeBase().getHost();
80       }
81
82     /** Handle button action */
83     public void actionPerformed(ActionEvent e) {
84       if (e.getSource() == jbtRegister) {
85         try {
86           // Establish connection with the server
87           Socket socket = new Socket(host, 8000);
88
89           // Create an output stream to the server
90           ObjectOutputStream toServer =
91             new ObjectOutputStream(socket.getOutputStream());
92
93           // Get text field
94           String name = jtfName.getText().trim();
95           String street = jtfStreet.getText().trim();
96           String city = jtfCity.getText().trim();
97           String state = jtfState.getText().trim();
98           String zip = jtfZip.getText().trim();
99
100          // Create a Student object and send to the server
101          Student s = new Student(name, street, city, state, zip);
102          toServer.writeObject(s);
103        }
104        catch (IOException ex) {
105          System.err.println(ex);
106        }
107      }
108    }
109
110    /** Run the applet as an application */
111    public static void main(String[] args) {
112      // Create a frame
113      JFrame frame = new JFrame("Register Student Client");
114
115      // Create an instance of the applet
116      StudentClient applet = new StudentClient();
117      applet.isStandAlone = true;
118
119      // Get host
120      if (args.length == 1) applet.host = args[0];
121
122      // Add the applet instance to the frame
123      frame.getContentPane().add(applet, BorderLayout.CENTER);
124
125      // Invoke init() and start()
126      applet.init();
127      applet.start();
128
129      // Display the frame
130      frame.pack();
131      frame.setVisible(true);
132    }
133 }
```

register listener (line 75)

get server name (line 79)

server socket (line 87)

output stream (lines 90–91)

send to server (line 102)

EXAMPLE 28.4 (CONTINUED)

Review

The Student class implements the Serializable interface. Therefore, it can be sent and received using the object output and input streams.

On the client side, when the user clicks the "Register to the Server" button, the client creates a socket to connect to the host (Line 87), creates an ObjectOutputStream on the output stream of the socket (Lines 90–91), and invokes the writeObject method to send the Student object to the server through the object output stream (Line 102).

On the server side, when a client connects to the server, the server creates a thread to process the client registration (Line 24). The thread creates an ObjectInputStream on the input stream of the socket (Lines 27–28), invokes the readObject method to receive the Student object through the object input stream (Line 31), and writes the object to a file (Line 34).

This program can run either as an applet or as an application. To run it as an application, the host name is passed as a command-line argument.

28.7 Retrieving Files from Web Servers

You developed client/server applications in the preceding sections. Java allows you to develop clients that retrieve files on a remote host through a Web server. In this case, you don't have to create a custom server program. The Web server can be used to send the files, as shown in Figure 28.11.

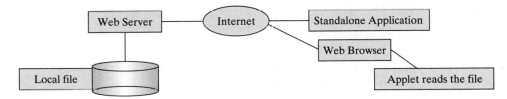

FIGURE 28.11 *The applet client or the application client retrieves files from a Web server.*

To retrieve a file, first create a URL object for the file. The java.net.URL class was introduced in Section 14.8, "The URL Class." For example, the statement given below creates a URL object for http://www.cs.armstrong.edu/liang/index.html:

```
URL url = new URL("http://www.cs.armstrong.edu/liang/index.html");
```

You can then use the openStream() method defined in the URL class to open an input stream to the file's URL:

```
InputStream inputStream = url.openStream();
```

Now you can read the data from the input stream.

EXAMPLE 28.5 RETRIEVING REMOTE FILES

Problem

This example demonstrates how to retrieve a file from a Web server. The program can run as an application or an applet. The user interface includes a text field in which to enter the URL of the filename, a text area in which to show the file, and a button that can be used to submit an action. A label is added at the bottom of the applet to indicate the status, such as File loaded successfully or Network connection problem. A sample run of the program is shown in Figure 28.12.

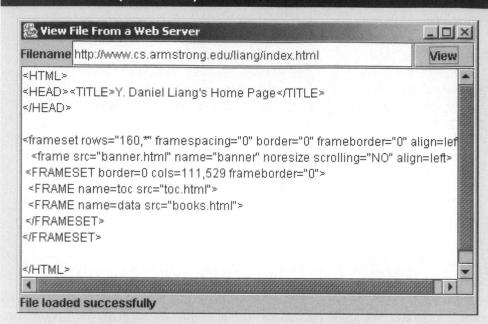

EXAMPLE 28.5 (CONTINUED)

FIGURE **28.12**   *The program displays the contents of a specified file on the Web server.*

Solution

Listing 28.9 gives the solution to the problem.

LISTING **28.9   ViewRemoteFile.java (Retrieving Remote File)**

```java
1  import java.awt.*;
2  import java.awt.event.*;
3  import java.io.*;
4  import java.net.*;
5  import javax.swing.*;
6
7  public class ViewRemoteFile extends JApplet
8      implements ActionListener {
9    // Button to view the file
10   private JButton jbtView = new JButton("View");
11
12   // Text field to receive file name
13   private JTextField jtfURL = new JTextField(12);
14
15   // Text area to store file
16   private JTextArea jtaFile = new JTextArea();
17
18   // Label to display status
19   private JLabel jlblStatus = new JLabel();
20
21   /** Initialize the applet */
22   public void init() {
23     // Create a panel to hold a label, a text field, and a button
24     JPanel p1 = new JPanel();
25     p1.setLayout(new BorderLayout());
26     p1.add(new JLabel("Filename"), BorderLayout.WEST);
27     p1.add(jtfURL, BorderLayout.CENTER);
28     p1.add(jbtView, BorderLayout.EAST);
29
30     // Place text area and panel p to the applet
31     getContentPane().setLayout(new BorderLayout());
32     getContentPane().add(new JScrollPane(jtaFile),
33       BorderLayout.CENTER);
```

create UI

EXAMPLE 28.5 (CONTINUED)

```
34      getContentPane().add(p1, BorderLayout.NORTH);
35      getContentPane().add(jlblStatus, BorderLayout.SOUTH);
36
37      // Register listener
38      jbtView.addActionListener(this);
39    }
40
41    /** Handle the "View" button */
42    public void actionPerformed(ActionEvent e) {
43      if (e.getSource() == jbtView)
44        showFile();
45    }
46
47    private void showFile() {
48      // Declare buffered stream for reading text for the URL
49      BufferedReader infile = null;
50      URL url = null;
51
52      try {
53        // Obtain URL from the text field
54        url = new URL(jtfURL.getText().trim());
55
56        // Create a buffered stream
57        InputStream is = url.openStream();
58        infile = new BufferedReader(new InputStreamReader(is));
59
60        // Get file name from the text field
61        String inLine;
62
63        // Read a line and append the line to the text area
64        while ((inLine = infile.readLine()) != null) {
65          jtaFile.append(inLine + '\n');
66        }
67
68        jlblStatus.setText("File loaded successfully");
69      }
70      catch (FileNotFoundException e) {
71        jlblStatus.setText("URL " + url + " not found.");
72      }
73      catch (IOException e) {
74        jlblStatus.setText(e.getMessage());
75      }
76      finally {
77        try {
78          if (infile != null) infile.close();
79        }
80        catch (IOException ex) {}
81      }
82    }
83  }
```

register listener

get URL

input stream

main method omitted

Review

Line 54 new URL(jtfURL.getText().trim()) creates an URL for the filename entered from the text field. Line 57 url.openStream() creates an InputStream from the URL. After the input stream is established, reading data from the remote file is just like reading data locally. A BufferedReader object is created from the input stream (Line 58). The text from the file is displayed in the text area (Line 65).

28.8 JEditorPane (Optional)

Swing provides a GUI component named javax.swing.JEditorPane that can display plain text, HTML, and RTF files automatically. Using it you don't have to write code to explicitly read data from the files. JEditorPane is a subclass of JTextComponent. Thus it inherits all the behavior and properties of JTextComponent.

To display the content of a file, use the `setPage(URL)` method, as follows:

```
public void setPage(URL url) throws IOException
```

`JEditorPane` generates `javax.swing.event.HyperlinkEvent` when a hyperlink in the editor pane is clicked. Through this event, you can get the URL of the hyperlink and display it using the `setPage(url)` method.

EXAMPLE 28.6 CREATING A WEB BROWSER

Problem

Create a simple Web browser to render HTML files. The program lets the user enter an HTML file in a text field and press the Enter key to display it in an editor pane, as shown in Figure 28.13.

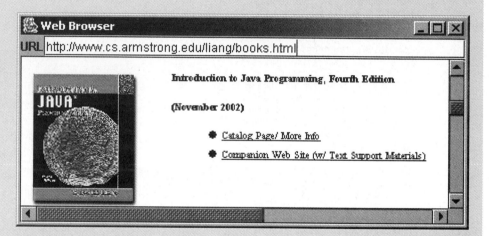

FIGURE **28.13**   *You can specify a URL in the text field and display the HTML file in an editor pane.*

Solution

Listing 28.10 gives the solution to the problem.

LISTING 28.10   **WebBrowser.java (Rendering HTML)**

```
 1  import java.awt.*;
 2  import java.awt.event.*;
 3  import java.applet.*;
 4  import javax.swing.*;
 5  import java.net.URL;
 6  import javax.swing.event.*;
 7  import java.io.*;
 8
 9  public class WebBrowser extends JApplet
10      implements ActionListener, HyperlinkListener {
11    // JEditor pane to view HTML files
12    private JEditorPane jep = new JEditorPane();
13
14    // Label for URL
15    private JLabel jlblURL = new JLabel("URL");
16
17    // Text field for entering URL
18    private JTextField jtfURL = new JTextField();
19
20    /** Initialize the applet */
21    public void init() {
22      // Create a panel jpURL to hold the label and text field
23      JPanel jpURL = new JPanel();
24      jpURL.setLayout(new BorderLayout());
```

create UI

EXAMPLE 28.6 (CONTINUED)

```
25        jpURL.add(jlblURL, BorderLayout.WEST);
26        jpURL.add(jtfURL, BorderLayout.CENTER);
27
28        // Create a scroll pane to hold JEditorPane
29        JScrollPane jspViewer = new JScrollPane();
30        jspViewer.getViewport().add(jep, null);
31
32        // Place jpURL and jspViewer in the applet
33        this.getContentPane().add(jspViewer, BorderLayout.CENTER);
34        this.getContentPane().add(jpURL, BorderLayout.NORTH);
35
36        // Set jep noneditable
37        jep.setEditable(false);
38
39        // Register listener
40        jep.addHyperlinkListener(this);                          register listeners
41        jtfURL.addActionListener(this);
42      }
43
44      public void actionPerformed(ActionEvent e) {
45        try {
46          // Get the URL from text field
47          URL url = new URL(jtfURL.getText().trim());            get URL
48
49          // Display the HTML file
50          jep.setPage(url);                                      display HTML
51        }
52        catch (IOException ex) {
53          System.out.println(ex);
54        }
55      }
56
57      public void hyperlinkUpdate(HyperlinkEvent e) {
58        try {
59          jep.setPage(e.getURL());
60        }
61        catch (IOException ex) {
62          System.out.println(ex);
63        }
64      }
65    }                                                            main method omitted
```

Review

In this example, a simple Web browser is created using the JEditorPane class (Line 12). JEditorPane is capable of displaying files in HTML format. To enable scrolling, the editor pane is placed inside a scroll pane (Lines 29–30).

The user enters the URL of the HTML file in the text field and presses the Enter key to fire an action event to display the URL in the editor pane. To display the URL in the editor pane, simply set the URL in the page property of the editor pane (Line 50).

The editor pane does not have all the functions of a commercial Web browser, but it is convenient for displaying HTML files, including embedded images.

There are two shortcomings in this program: (1) it cannot view a local HTML file, and (2) to view a remote HTML file, you have to enter a URL beginning with http://. In Exercise 28.9, you will modify the program so that it can also view an HTML file from the local host and accept URLs beginning with either http:// or www.

28.9 Case Study: Distributed TicTacToe (Optional)

In Section 14.7, "Case Study: TicTacToe," you developed an applet for the TicTacToe game that enables two players to play on the same machine. In this section, you will learn how to develop a distributed TicTacToe game using multithreads and networking with socket streams.

EXAMPLE 28.7 DISTRIBUTED TICTACTOE GAME

Problem

The TicTacToe game in Section 14.7 lets the users play the game on the same machine. Create a distributed TicTacToe game that enables users to play on different machines from anywhere on the Internet.

Solution

The example consists of a server for multiple clients. The server creates a server socket, and accepts connections from every two players to form a session. Each session is a thread that communicates with the two players and determines the status of the game. The server can establish any number of sessions, as shown in Figure 28.14.

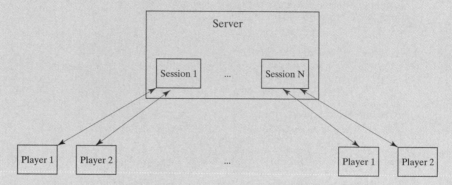

FIGURE 28.14   *The server can create many sessions, each of which facilitates a TicTacToe game for two players.*

For each session, the first client connecting to the server is identified as player 1 with token 'X', and the second client connecting to the server is identified as player 2 with token 'O'. The server notifies the players of their respective tokens. Once two clients are connected to it, the server starts a thread to facilitate the game between the two players by performing the steps repeatedly, as shown in Figure 28.15.

The server does not have to be a graphical component, but creating it as a frame in which game information can be viewed is user-friendly. You can create a scroll pane to hold a text area in the frame and display game information in the text area. The server creates a thread to handle a game session when two players are connected to the server.

The client is responsible for interacting with the players. It creates a user interface with nine cells, and displays the game title and status to the players in the labels. The client class is very similar to the TicTacToe class presented in Section 14.7. However, the client in this example does not determine the game status (win or draw), it simply passes the moves to the server and receives the game status from the server.

Based on the foregoing analysis, you can create the following classes:

✦ `TicTacToeServer` serves all the clients in Listing 28.12.

✦ `HandleASession` facilitates the game for two players in Listing 28.12. It is in the same file with TicTacToeServer.java.

✦ `TicTacToeClient` models a player in Listing 28.13.

✦ `Cell` models a cell in the game in Listing 28.13. It is an Inner class in `TicTacToeClient`.

✦ `TicTacToeConstants` is an interface that defines the constants shared by all the classes in the example in Listing 28.11.

The relationships of these classes are shown in Figure 28.16.

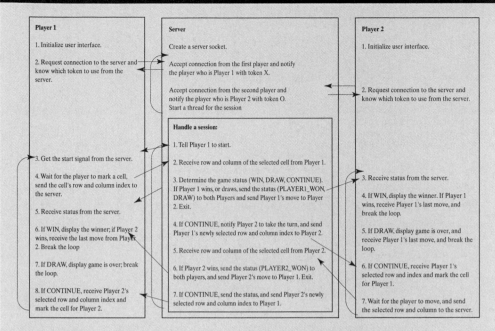

FIGURE 28.15 *The server starts a thread to facilitate communications between the two players.*

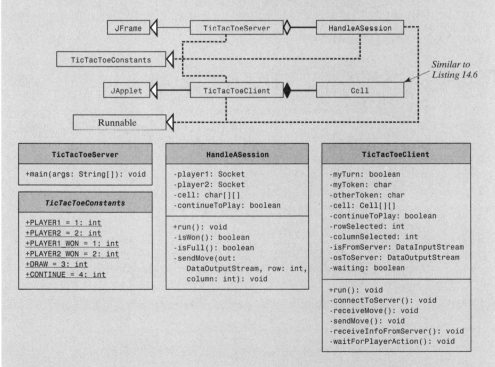

FIGURE 28.16 *TicTacToeServer creates an instance of HandleASession for each session of two players. TicTacToeClient creates nine cells in the UI.*

LISTING 28.11 TicTacToeConstants.java (Defining Constants)

```
1 public interface TicTacToeConstants {
2   public static int PLAYER1 = 1; // Indicate player 1
3   public static int PLAYER2 = 2; // Indicate player 2
4   public static int PLAYER1_WON = 1; // Indicate player 1 won
```

EXAMPLE **28.7** (CONTINUED)

```
5   public static int PLAYER2_WON = 2; // Indicate player 2 won
6   public static int DRAW = 3; // Indicate a draw
7   public static int CONTINUE = 4; // Indicate to continue
8 }
```

LISTING **28.12**   TicTacToeServer.java (Server for the Game)

```
 1 import java.io.*;
 2 import java.net.*;
 3 import javax.swing.*;
 4 import java.awt.*;
 5 import java.util.Date;
 6
 7 public class TicTacToeServer extends JFrame
 8     implements TicTacToeConstants {
 9   public static void main(String[] args) {
10     TicTacToeServer frame = new TicTacToeServer();
11   }
12
13   public TicTacToeServer() {
14     JTextArea jtaLog = new JTextArea();
15
16     // Create a scroll pane to hold text area
17     JScrollPane scrollPane = new JScrollPane(jtaLog);
18
19     // Add the scroll pane to the frame
20     getContentPane().add(scrollPane, BorderLayout.CENTER);
21
22     setDefaultCloseOperation(JFrame.EXIT_ON_CLOSE);
23     setSize(300, 300);
24     setTitle("TicTacToeServer");
25     setVisible(true);
26
27     try {
28       // Create a server socket
29       ServerSocket serverSocket = new ServerSocket(8000);
30       jtaLog.append(new Date() +
31         ": Server started at socket 8000\n");
32
33       // Number a session
34       int sessionNo = 1;
35
36       // Ready to create a session for every two players
37       while (true) {
38         jtaLog.append(new Date() +
39           ": Wait for players to join session " + sessionNo + '\n');
40
41         // Connect to player 1
42         Socket player1 = serverSocket.accept();
43
44         jtaLog.append(new Date() + ": Player 1 joined session " +
45           sessionNo + '\n');
46         jtaLog.append("Player 1's IP address" +
47           player1.getInetAddress().getHostAddress() + '\n');
48
49         // Notify that the player is Player 1
50         new DataOutputStream(
51           player1.getOutputStream()).writeInt(PLAYER1);
52
53         // Connect to player 2
54         Socket player2 = serverSocket.accept();
55
56         jtaLog.append(new Date() +
57           ": Player 2 joined session " + sessionNo + '\n');
58         jtaLog.append("Player 2's IP address" +
59           player2.getInetAddress().getHostAddress() + '\n');
60
```

run server

create UI

server socket

connect to client

to player1

EXAMPLE 28.7 (CONTINUED)

```
61              // Notify that the player is Player 2
62              new DataOutputStream(                              to player2
63                player2.getOutputStream()).writeInt(PLAYER2);
64
65              // Display this session and increment session number
66              jtaLog.append(new Date() + ": Start a thread for session " +
67                sessionNo++ + '\n');
68
69              // Create a new thread for this session of two players
70              HandleASession thread = new HandleASession(player1, player2);    a session for two players
71
72              // Start the new thread
73              thread.start();
74            }
75          }
76       catch(IOException ex) {
77         System.err.println(ex);
78       }
79     }
80 }
81
82 // Define the thread class for handling a new session for two players
83 class HandleASession extends Thread implements TicTacToeConstants {
84    private Socket player1;
85    private Socket player2;
86
87    // Create and initialize cells
88    private char[][] cell = new char[3][3];
89
90    private DataInputStream fromPlayer1;
91    private DataOutputStream toPlayer1;
92    private DataInputStream fromPlayer2;
93    private DataOutputStream toPlayer2;
94
95    // Continue to play
96    private boolean continueToPlay = true;
97
98    /** Construct a thread */
99    public HandleASession(Socket player1, Socket player2) {
100     this.player1 = player1;
101     this.player2 = player2;
102
103     // Initialize cells
104     for (int i = 0; i < 3; i++)
105       for (int j = 0; j < 3; j++)
106         cell[i][j] = ' ';
107   }
108
109   /** Implement the run() method for the thread */
110   public void run() {
111     try {
112       // Create data input and output streams
113       DataInputStream fromPlayer1 = new DataInputStream(
114         player1.getInputStream());
115       DataOutputStream toPlayer1 = new DataOutputStream(
116         player1.getOutputStream());
117       DataInputStream fromPlayer2 = new DataInputStream(
118         player2.getInputStream());
119       DataOutputStream toPlayer2 = new DataOutputStream(
120         player2.getOutputStream());
121
122       // Write anything to notify player 1 to start
123       // This is just to let player 1 know to start
124       toPlayer1.writeInt(1);
125
126       // Continuously serve the players and determine and report
127       // the game status to the players
```

EXAMPLE 28.7 (CONTINUED)

```
128          while (true) {
129            // Receive a move from player 1
130            int row = fromPlayer1.readInt();
131            int column = fromPlayer1.readInt();
132            cell[row][column] = 'X';
133
134            // Check if Player 1 wins
135            if (isWon('X')) {
136              toPlayer1.writeInt(PLAYER1_WON);
137              toPlayer2.writeInt(PLAYER1_WON);
138              sendMove(toPlayer2, row, column);
139              break; // Break the loop
140            }
141            else if (isFull()) { // Check if all cells are filled
142              toPlayer1.writeInt(DRAW);
143              toPlayer2.writeInt(DRAW);
144              sendMove(toPlayer2, row, column);
145              break;
146            }
147            else {
148              // Notify player 2 to take the turn
149              toPlayer2.writeInt(CONTINUE);
150
151              // Send player 1's selected row and column to player 2
152              sendMove(toPlayer2, row, column);
153            }
154
155            // Receive a move from Player 2
156            row = fromPlayer2.readInt();
157            column = fromPlayer2.readInt();
158            cell[row][column] = 'O';
159
160            // Check if Player 2 wins
161            if (isWon('O')) {
162              toPlayer1.writeInt(PLAYER2_WON);
163              toPlayer2.writeInt(PLAYER2_WON);
164              sendMove(toPlayer1, row, column);
165              break;
166            }
167            else {
168              // Notify player 1 to take the turn
169              toPlayer1.writeInt(CONTINUE);
170
171              // Send player 2's selected row and column to player 1
172              sendMove(toPlayer1, row, column);
173            }
174          }
175        }
176        catch(IOException ex) {
177          System.err.println(ex);
178        }
179      }
180
181      /** Send the move to other player */
182      private void sendMove(DataOutputStream out, int row, int column)
183          throws IOException {
184        out.writeInt(row); // Send row index
185        out.writeInt(column); // Send column index
186      }
187
188      /** Determine if the cells are all occupied */
189      private boolean isFull() {
190        for (int i = 0; i < 3; i++)
191          for (int j = 0; j < 3; j++)
192            if (cell[i][j] == ' ')
193              return false; // At least one cell is not filled
194
```

EXAMPLE 28.7 (CONTINUED)

```
195      // All cells are filled
196      return true;
197    }
198
199    /** Determine if the player with the specified token wins */
200    private boolean isWon(char token) {
201      // Check all rows
202      for (int i = 0; i < 3; i++)
203        if ((cell[i][0] == token)
204             && (cell[i][1] == token)
205             && (cell[i][2] == token)) {
206          return true;
207        }
208
209      /** Check all columns */
210      for (int j = 0; j < 3; j++)
211        if ((cell[0][j] == token)
212             && (cell[1][j] == token)
213             && (cell[2][j] == token)) {
214          return true;
215        }
216
217      /** Check major diagonal */
218      if ((cell[0][0] == token)
219           && (cell[1][1] == token)
220           && (cell[2][2] == token)) {
221        return true;
222      }
223
224      /** Check subdiagonal */
225      if ((cell[0][2] == token)
226           && (cell[1][1] == token)
227           && (cell[2][0] == token)) {
228        return true;
229      }
230
231      /** All checked, but no winner */
232      return false;
233    }
234 }
```

LISTING 28.13 TicTacToeClient.java (For One Player)

```
 1 import java.awt.*;
 2 import java.awt.event.*;
 3 import javax.swing.*;
 4 import javax.swing.border.LineBorder;
 5 import java.io.*;
 6 import java.net.*;
 7
 8 public class TicTacToeClient extends JApplet
 9     implements Runnable, TicTacToeConstants {
10   // Indicate whether the player has the turn
11   private boolean myTurn = false;
12
13   // Indicate the token for the player
14   private char myToken = ' ';
15
16   // Indicate the token for the other player
17   private char otherToken = ' ';
18
19   // Create and initialize cells
20   private Cell[][] cell =  new Cell[3][3];
21
22   // Create and initialize a title label
23   private JLabel jlblTitle = new JLabel();
24
25   // Create and initialize a status label
26   private JLabel jlblStatus = new JLabel();
```

EXAMPLE 28.7 (CONTINUED)

```
27
28      // Indicate selected row and column by the current move
29      private int rowSelected;
30      private int columnSelected;
31
32      // Input and output streams from/to server
33      private DataInputStream fromServer;
34      private DataOutputStream toServer;
35
36      // Continue to play?
37      private boolean continueToPlay = true;
38
39      // Wait for the player to mark a cell
40      private boolean waiting = true;
41
42      // Indicate if it runs as application
43      private boolean isStandAlone = false;
44
45      // Host name or ip
46      private String host = "localhost";
47
48      /** Initialize UI */
49      public void init() {
50        // Panel p to hold cells
51        JPanel p = new JPanel();
52        p.setLayout(new GridLayout(3, 3, 0, 0));
53        for (int i = 0; i < 3; i++)
54          for (int j = 0; j < 3; j++)
55            p.add(cell[i][j] = new Cell(i, j));
56
57        // Set properties for labels and borders for labels and panel
58        p.setBorder(new LineBorder(Color.black, 1));
59        jlblTitle.setHorizontalAlignment(JLabel.CENTER);
60        jlblTitle.setFont(new Font("SansSerif", Font.BOLD, 16));
61        jlblTitle.setBorder(new LineBorder(Color.black, 1));
62        jlblStatus.setBorder(new LineBorder(Color.black, 1));
63
64        // Place the panel and the labels to the applet
65        this.getContentPane().add(jlblTitle, BorderLayout.NORTH);
66        this.getContentPane().add(p, BorderLayout.CENTER);
67        this.getContentPane().add(jlblStatus, BorderLayout.SOUTH);
68
69        // Connect to the server
70        connectToServer();
71      }
72
73      private void connectToServer() {
74        try {
75          // Create a socket to connect to the server
76          Socket socket;
77          if (isStandAlone)
78            socket = new Socket(host, 8000);
79          else
80            socket = new Socket(getCodeBase().getHost(), 8000);
81
82          // Create an input stream to receive data from the server
83          fromServer = new DataInputStream(socket.getInputStream());
84
85          // Create an output stream to send data to the server
86          toServer = new DataOutputStream(socket.getOutputStream());
87        }
88        catch (Exception ex) {
89          System.err.println(ex);
90        }
91
92        // Control the game on a separate thread
93        Thread thread = new Thread(this);
```

create UI

connect to server

standalone

applet

input from server

output to server

EXAMPLE 28.7 (CONTINUED)

```
 94       thread.start();
 95    }
 96
 97    public void run() {
 98      try {
 99        // Get notification from the server
100        int player = fromServer.readInt();
101
102        // Am I player 1 or 2?
103        if (player == PLAYER1) {
104          myToken = 'X';
105          otherToken = 'O';
106          jlblTitle.setText("Player 1 with token 'X'");
107          jlblStatus.setText("Waiting for player 2 to join");
108
109          // Receive startup notification from the server
110          fromServer.readInt(); // Whatever read is ignored
111
112          // The other player has joined
113          jlblStatus.setText("Player 2 has joined. I start first");
114
115          // It is my turn
116          myTurn = true;
117        }
118        else if (player == PLAYER2) {
119          myToken = 'O';
120          otherToken = 'X';
121          jlblTitle.setText("Player 2 with token 'O'");
122          jlblStatus.setText("Waiting for player 1 to move");
123        }
124
125        // Continue to play
126        while (continueToPlay) {
127          if (player == PLAYER1) {
128            waitForPlayerAction(); // Wait for player 1 to move
129            sendMove(); // Send the move to the server
130            receiveInfoFromServer(); // Receive info from the server
131          }
132          else if (player == PLAYER2) {
133            receiveInfoFromServer(); // Receive info from the server
134            waitForPlayerAction(); // Wait for player 2 to move
135            sendMove(); // Send player 2's move to the server
136          }
137        }
138      }
139      catch (Exception ex) {
140      }
141    }
142
143    /** Wait for the player to mark a cell */
144    private void waitForPlayerAction() throws InterruptedException {
145      while (waiting) {
146        Thread.sleep(100);
147      }
148
149      waiting = true;
150    }
151
152    /** Send this player's move to the server */
153    private void sendMove() throws IOException {
154      toServer.writeInt(rowSelected); // Send the selected row
155      toServer.writeInt(columnSelected); // Send the selected column
156    }
157
158    /** Receive info from the server */
159    private void receiveInfoFromServer() throws IOException {
160      // Receive game status
161      int status = fromServer.readInt();
```

EXAMPLE 28.7 (CONTINUED)

```
162
163     if (status == PLAYER1_WON) {
164       // Player 1 won, stop playing
165       continueToPlay = false;
166       if (myToken == 'X') {
167         jlblStatus.setText("I won! (X)");
168       }
169       else if (myToken == 'O') {
170         jlblStatus.setText("Player 1 (X) has won!");
171         receiveMove();
172       }
173     }
174     else if (status == PLAYER2_WON) {
175       // Player 2 won, stop playing
176       continueToPlay = false;
177       if (myToken == 'O') {
178         jlblStatus.setText("I won! (O)");
179       }
180       else if (myToken == 'X') {
181         jlblStatus.setText("Player 2 (O) has won!");
182         receiveMove();
183       }
184     }
185     else if (status == DRAW) {
186       // No winner, game is over
187       continueToPlay = false;
188       jlblStatus.setText("Game is over, no winner!");
189
190       if (myToken == 'O') {
191         receiveMove();
192       }
193     }
194     else {
195       receiveMove();
196       jlblStatus.setText("My turn");
197       myTurn = true; // It is my turn
198     }
199   }
200
201   private void receiveMove() throws IOException {
202     // Get the other player's move
203     int row = fromServer.readInt();
204     int column = fromServer.readInt();
205     cell[row][column].setToken(otherToken);
206   }
207
208   // An inner class for a cell
209   private class Cell extends JPanel implements MouseListener {
210     // Indicate the row and column of this cell in the board
211     private int row;
212     private int column;
213
214     // Token used for this cell
215     private char token = ' ';
216
217     public Cell(int row, int column) {
218       this.row = row;
219       this.column = column;
220       setBorder(new LineBorder(Color.black, 1)); // Set cell's border
221       addMouseListener(this);  // Register listener
222     }
223
224     /** Return token */
225     public char getToken() {
226       return token;
227     }
228
```

model a cell

EXAMPLE 28.7 (CONTINUED)

```
229        /** Set a new token */
230        public void setToken(char c) {
231          token = c;
232          repaint();
233        }
234
235        /** Paint the cell */
236        protected void paintComponent(Graphics g) {
237          super.paintComponent(g);
238
239          if (token == 'X') {
240            g.drawLine(10, 10, getWidth() - 10, getHeight() - 10);
241            g.drawLine(getWidth() - 10, 10, 10, getHeight() - 10);
242          }
243          else if (token == 'O') {
244            g.drawOval(10, 10, getWidth() - 20, getHeight() - 20);
245          }
246        }
247
248        /** Handle mouse click on a cell */
249        public void mouseClicked(MouseEvent e) {
250          // If cell is not occupied and the player has the turn
251          if ((token == ' ') && myTurn) {
252            setToken(myToken);  // Set the player's token in the cell
253            myTurn = false;
254            rowSelected = row;
255            columnSelected = column;
256            jlblStatus.setText("Waiting for the other player to move");
257            waiting = false; // Just completed a successful move
258          }
259        }
260
261        public void mousePressed(MouseEvent e) {
262          // TODO: implement this java.awt.event.MouseListener method;
263        }
264
265        public void mouseReleased(MouseEvent e) {
266          // TODO: implement this java.awt.event.MouseListener method;
267        }
268
269        public void mouseEntered(MouseEvent e) {
270          // TODO: implement this java.awt.event.MouseListener method;
271        }
272
273        public void mouseExited(MouseEvent e) {
274          // TODO: implement this java.awt.event.MouseListener method;
275        }
276      }
277    }
```

draw X (lines 240-241)

draw O (line 244)

`main` method omitted (line 277)

Review

The server can serve any number of sessions. Each session takes care of two players. The client can be a Java applet or a Java application. To run a client as a Java applet from a Web browser, the server must run from a Web server. Figures 28.17 and 28.18 show sample runs of the server and the clients.

The `TicTacToeConstants` interface defines the constants shared by all the classes in the project. Each class that uses the constants needs to implement the interface. Centrally defining constants in an interface is a common practice in Java. For example, all the constants shared by Swing classes are defined in `java.swing.SwingConstants`.

Once a session is established, the server receives moves from the players in alternation. Upon receiving a move from a player, the server determines the status of the game. If the game is not finished, the server sends the status (`CONTINUE`) and the player's move to the

EXAMPLE 28.7 (CONTINUED)

FIGURE 28.17 *TicTacToeServer accepts connection requests and creates sessions to serve pairs of players.*

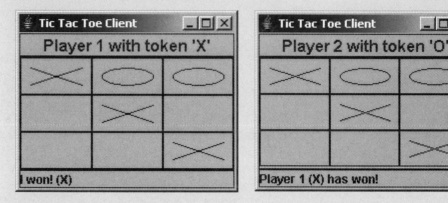

FIGURE 28.18 *TicTacToeClient can run as an applet or an application.*

other player. If the game is won or drawn, the server sends the status (PLAYER1_WON, PLAYER2_WON, or DRAW) to both players.

The implementation of Java network programs at the socket level is tightly synchronized. An operation to send data from one machine requires an operation to receive data from the other machine. As shown in this example, the server and the client are tightly synchronized to send or receive data.

28.10 Datagram Socket (Optional)

Clients and servers that communicate via a stream socket have a dedicated point-to-point channel between them. To communicate, they establish a connection, transmit the data, and then close the connection. The stream sockets use TCP (Transmission Control Protocol) for data transmission. Since TCP can detect lost transmissions and resubmit them, transmissions are lossless and reliable. All data sent via a stream socket are received in the same order in which they were sent.

In contrast, clients and servers that communicate via a datagram socket do not have a dedicated point-to-point channel. Data are transmitted using packets. Datagram sockets use UDP (User Datagram Protocol), which cannot guarantee that the packets are not lost, or not received in duplicate, or received in the order in which they were sent. A *datagram* is an independent, self-contained message sent over the network whose arrival, arrival time, and content are not guaranteed.

In an analogy, a stream socket communication between a client and a server is like a telephone connection with a dedicated link. A datagram communication is like sending a letter through the post office. Your letter is contained in an envelope (*packet*). If the letter is too large, it may be sent

datagram

packet

in several envelopes (packets). There is no guarantee that your letter will arrive or will arrive in the order it was sent. One difference is that the letter will not arrive in duplicate, whereas a datagram packet may arrive in duplicate.

Most applications require reliable transmission between clients and servers. In such cases, it is best to use stream socket network communication. Some applications that you write to communicate over the network will not require the reliable, point-to-point channel provided by TCP. In such cases, datagram communication is more efficient.

28.10.1 The `DatagramPacket` and `DatagramSocket` Classes

The `java.net` package contains two classes to help you write Java programs that use datagrams to send and receive packets over the network: `DatagramPacket` and `DatagramSocket`. An application can send and receive `DatagramPackets` through a `DatagramSocket`.

28.10.1.1 The `DatagramPacket` Class

The `DatagramPacket` class represents a datagram packet. Datagram packets are used to implement a connectionless packet delivery service. Each message is routed from one machine to another based solely on information contained within the packet. Multiple packets sent from one machine to another may be routed differently and may arrive in any order. Packet delivery is not guaranteed.

To create a `DatagramPacket` for delivery from a client, use the `DatagramPacket(byte[] buf, int length, InetAddress host, int port)` constructor. To create all other `DatagramPackets`, use the `DatagramPacket(byte[] buf, int length)` constructor, as shown in Figure 28.19. Once a datagram packet is created, you can use the `getData` and `setData` methods to obtain and set data in the packet.

java.net.DatagramPacket	
length: int	Specifies the length of the buffer with get and set methods.
address: InetAddress	Specifies the address of the machine where the packet is sent or received with get and set methods.
port: int	Specifies the port of the machine where the packet is sent or received with get and set methods.
+DatagramPacket(buf: byte[], length: int, host: InetAddress, port: int)	Constructs a datagram packet in a byte array buf of the specified length with the host and the port for which the packet is sent. This constructor is often used to construct a packet for delivery from a client.
+DatagramPacket(buf: byte[], length: int)	Constructs a datagram packet in a byte array buf of the specified length.
+getData(): byte[]	Returns the data from the packet.
+setData(buf: byte[]): void	Sets the data in the packet.

FIGURE 28.19 *The `DatagramPacket` class contains the data and information about data.*

28.10.1.2 `DatagramSocket`

The `DatagramSocket` class represents a socket for sending and receiving datagram packets. A datagram socket is the sending or receiving point for a packet delivery service. Each packet sent or received on a datagram socket is individually addressed and routed. Multiple packets sent from one machine to another may be routed differently, and may arrive in any order.

To create a server `DatagramSocket`, use the constructor `DatagramSocket(int port)`, which binds the socket with the specified port on the local host machine. *construct datagram socket*

To create a client `DatagramSocket`, use the constructor `DatagramSocket()`, which binds the socket with any available port on the local host machine.

To send data, you need to create a packet, fill in the contents, specify the Internet address and port number for the receiver, and invoke the `send(packet)` method on a `DatagramSocket`. *send packet*

To receive data, you have to create an empty packet and invoke the `receive(packet)` method on a `DatagramSocket`. *receive packet*

28.10.3 Datagram Programming

Datagram programming is different from stream socket programming in the sense that there is no concept of a `ServerSocket` for datagrams. Both client and server use `DatagramSocket` to send and receive packets, as shown in Figure 28.20.

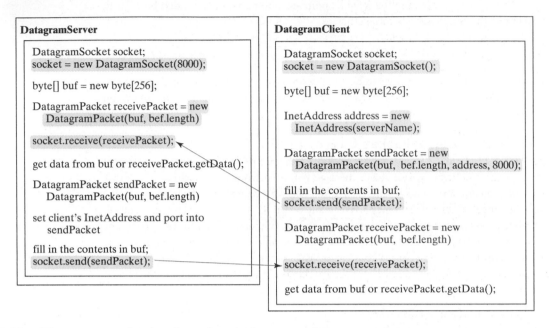

DatagramServer

```
DatagramSocket socket;
socket = new DatagramSocket(8000);

byte[] buf = new byte[256];

DatagramPacket receivePacket = new
    DatagramPacket(buf, bef.length)

socket.receive(receivePacket);

get data from buf or receivePacket.getData();

DatagramPacket sendPacket = new
    DatagramPacket(buf, bef.length)

set client's InetAddress and port into
    sendPacket

fill in the contents in buf;
socket.send(sendPacket);
```

DatagramClient

```
DatagramSocket socket;
socket = new DatagramSocket();

byte[] buf = new byte[256];

InetAddress address = new
    InetAddress(serverName);

DatagramPacket sendPacket = new
    DatagramPacket(buf, bef.length, address, 8000);

fill in the contents in buf;
socket.send(sendPacket);

DatagramPacket receivePacket = new
    DatagramPacket(buf, bef.length)

socket.receive(receivePacket);

get data from buf or receivePacket.getData();
```

FIGURE 28.20 *The programs send and receive packets via datagram sockets.*

Normally, you designate one application as the server and create a `DatagramSocket` with the specified port using the constructor `DatagramSocket(port)`. A client can create a `DatagramSocket` without specifying a port number. The port number will be dynamically chosen at runtime. When a client sends a packet to the server, the client's IP address and port number are contained in the packet. The server can retrieve it from the packet and use it to send the packet back to the client.

To demonstrate, let us rewrite Example 28.1, "A Client/Server Example," using datagrams.

EXAMPLE 28.8 CLIENT/SERVER PROGRAMMING USING DATAGRAMS

Problem

Example 28.1 presents a client program and a server program using socket streams. The client sends the radius to a server. The server receives this information, uses it to find the area, and then sends the area to the client. Rewrite the program using datagram sockets.

Solution

Listing 28.14 gives the server, and Listing 28.15 gives the client. A sample run of the program is shown in Figure 28.21.

LISTING 28.14 DatagramServer.java (Datagram Server)

```
1 import java.io.*;
2 import java.net.*;
3 import java.util.*;
4 import java.awt.*;
```

EXAMPLE 28.8 (CONTINUED)

```java
 5 import java.awt.event.*;
 6 import javax.swing.*;
 7
 8 public class DatagramServer extends JFrame {
 9   // Text area for displaying contents
10   private JTextArea jta = new JTextArea();
11
12   // The byte array for sending and receiving datagram packets
13   private byte[] buf = new byte[256];
14
15   public static void main(String[] args) {
16     new DatagramServer();
17   }
18
19   public Server() {
20     // Place text area on the frame
21     getContentPane().setLayout(new BorderLayout());
22     getContentPane().add(new JScrollPane(jta), BorderLayout.CENTER);
23
24     setTitle("DatagramServer");
25     setSize(500, 300);
26     setDefaultCloseOperation(JFrame.EXIT_ON_CLOSE);
27     setVisible(true); // It is necessary to show the frame here!
28
29     try {
30       // Create a server socket
31       DatagramSocket socket = new DatagramSocket(8000);
32       jta.append("Server started at " + new Date() + '\n');
33
34       // Create a packet for receiving data
35       DatagramPacket receivePacket =
36         new DatagramPacket(buf, buf.length);
37
38       // Create a packet for sending data
39       DatagramPacket sendPacket =
40         new DatagramPacket(buf, buf.length);
41
42       while (true) {
43         // Initialize buffer for each iteration
44         Arrays.fill(buf, (byte)0);
45
46         // Receive radius from the client in a packet
47         socket.receive(receivePacket);
48         jta.append("The client host name is " +
49           receivePacket.getAddress().getHostName() +
50           " and port number is " + receivePacket.getPort() + '\n');
51         jta.append("Radius received from client is " +
52           new String(buf).trim() +  '\n');
53
54         // Compute area
55         double radius = Double.parseDouble(new String(buf).trim());
56         double area = radius * radius * Math.PI;
57         jta.append("Area is " + area + '\n');
58
59         // Send area to the client in a packet
60         sendPacket.setAddress(receivePacket.getAddress());
61         sendPacket.setPort(receivePacket.getPort());
62         sendPacket.setData(new Double(area).toString().getBytes());
63         socket.send(sendPacket);
64       }
65     }
66     catch(IOException ex) {
67       ex.printStackTrace();
68     }
69   }
70 }
```

create UI

datagram socket

incoming packet

outgoing packet

receive packet

packet address

send packet

EXAMPLE 28.8 (CONTINUED)

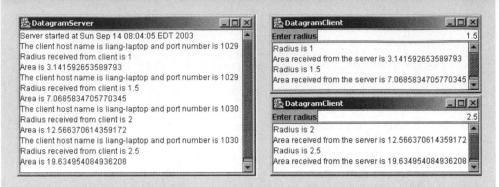

FIGURE 28.21 *The server receives a radius from a client, computes the area, and sends the area to the client. The server can serve multiple clients.*

LISTING 28.15   DatagramClient.java (Datagram Client)

```
1  import java.io.*;
2  import java.net.*;
3  import java.util.*;
4  import java.awt.*;
5  import java.awt.event.*;
6  import javax.swing.*;
7
8  public class DatagramClient extends JFrame implements ActionListener {
9    // Text field for receiving radius
10   private JTextField jtf = new JTextField();
11
12   // Text area to display contents
13   private JTextArea jta = new JTextArea();
14
15   // Datagram socket
16   private DatagramSocket socket;
17
18   // The byte array for sending and receiving datagram packets
19   private byte[] buf = new byte[256];
20
21   // Server InetAddress
22   private InetAddress address;
23
24   // The packet sent to the server
25   private DatagramPacket sendPacket;
26
27   // The packet received from the server
28   private DatagramPacket receivePacket;
29
30   public static void main(String[] args) {
31     new DatagramClient();
32   }
33
34   public Client() {
35     // Panel p to hold the label and text field
36     JPanel p = new JPanel();
37     p.setLayout(new BorderLayout());
38     p.add(new JLabel("Enter radius"), BorderLayout.WEST);
39     p.add(jtf, BorderLayout.CENTER);
40     jtf.setHorizontalAlignment(JTextField.RIGHT);
41
42     getContentPane().setLayout(new BorderLayout());
43     getContentPane().add(p, BorderLayout.NORTH);
44     getContentPane().add(new JScrollPane(jta), BorderLayout.CENTER);
45
```

create UI

EXAMPLE 28.8 (CONTINUED)

```
46       jtf.addActionListener(this); // Register listener
47
48       setTitle("DatagramClient");
49       setSize(500, 300);
50       setDefaultCloseOperation(JFrame.EXIT_ON_CLOSE);
51       setVisible(true); // It is necessary to show the frame here!
52
53       try {
54         // get a datagram socket
55         socket = new DatagramSocket();                            datagram socket
56         address = InetAddress.getByName("localhost");
57         sendPacket =
58           new DatagramPacket(buf, buf.length, address, 8000);     outgoing packet
59         receivePacket = new DatagramPacket(buf, buf.length);      incoming packet
60       }
61       catch (IOException ex) {
62         ex.printStackTrace();
63       }
64     }
65
66     public void actionPerformed(ActionEvent e) {
67       String actionCommand = e.getActionCommand();
68       if (e.getSource() instanceof JTextField) {
69         try {
70           // Initialize buffer for each iteration
71           Arrays.fill(buf, (byte)0);
72
73           // send radius to the server in a packet
74           sendPacket.setData(jtf.getText().trim().getBytes());
75           socket.send(sendPacket);                                send packet
76
77           // receive area from the server in a packet
78           socket.receive(receivePacket);                          receive packet
79
80           // Display to the text area
81           jta.append("Radius is " + jtf.getText().trim() + "\n");
82           jta.append("Area received from the server is "
83             + Double.parseDouble(new String(buf).trim()) + '\n');
84         }
85         catch (IOException ex) {
86           ex.printStackTrace();
87         }
88       }
89     }
90 }
```

Review

Since datagrams are connectionless, a DatagramPacket can be sent to multiple clients, and multiple clients can receive a packet from the same server. As shown in this example, you can launch multiple clients. Each client sends the radius to the server, and the server sends the area back to the client.

The server creates a DatagramSocket on port 8000 (Line 31 in DatagramServer.java). No DatagramSocket can be created again on the same port. The client creates a DatagramSocket on an available port (Line 55 in DatagramClient.java). The port number is dynamically assigned to the socket. You can launch multiple clients simultaneously, and each client's datagram socket will be different.

The client creates a DatagramPacket named sendPacket for delivery to the server (Lines 57–58 in DatagramClient.java). The DatagramPacket contains the server address and port number. The client creates another DatagramPacket named receivePacket (Line 59), which is used for receiving packets from the server. This packet does not need to contain any address or port number.

EXAMPLE 28.8 (CONTINUED)

A user enters a radius in the text field in the client. When the user presses the Enter key on the text field, the radius value in the text field is put into the packet and sent to the server (Lines 74–75 in DatagramClient.java). The server receives the packet (Line 47 in DatagramServer.java), extracts the data from the byte array buf, and computes the area (Lines 55–56 in DatagramServer.java). The server then builds a packet that contains the area value in the buffer, the client's address, and the port number, and sends the packet to the client (Lines 60–63). The client receives the packet (Line 78 in DatagramClient.java) and displays the result in the text area.

The data in the packet are stored in a byte array. To send a numerical value, you need to convert it into a string and then store it in the array as bytes, using the getBytes() method in the String class (Line 62 in DatagramServer.java and Line 74 in DatagramClient.java). To convert the array into a number, first convert it into a string, and then convert it into a number using the static parseDouble method in the Double class (Line 55 in DatagramServer.java and Line 83 in DatagramClient.java).

 NOTE

The port numbers for the stream socket and the datagram socket are not related. You can use the same port number for a stream socket and a datagram socket simultaneously.

KEY CLASSES AND METHODS

◆ **java.net.ServerSocket** is a class for creating a server socket. A server socket waits for a request to come in over the network using the accept() method.

◆ **java.net.Socket** is a class for creating a socket. A socket is an endpoint for communication between two machines. A client uses new Socket(serverName, port) to connect to a server socket. Use getInputStream() to obtain an InputStream and getOutputStream() to obtain an OutputStream on the socket.

◆ **java.net.InetAddress** is a class that represents an Internet Protocol (IP) address. Use getHost() to get the host name and getHostAddress() to get the host IP address.

◆ **java.net.URL** is a class that represents a URL. Use new URL(urlString) to create a URL for an Internet resource. Use openStream() to get an InputStream from the URL. Use getHost() to return the host name of the URL.

◆ **javax.swing.JEditorPane** is a subclass of JTextComponent that represents a URL. Use new URL(urlString) to create a URL for an Internet resource. Use openStream() to get an InputStream from the URL. Use getHost() to return the host name of the URL.

◆ **java.net.DatagramPacket** is a class that represents a datagram packet for sending and receiving packets. To create a DatagramPacket from a client, use new DatagramPacket (byte[] buf, int length, InetAddress host, int port). To create it from the server, use new DatagramPacket(byte[] buf, int length). Use getData() and setData- (byte[]) to obtain and set data in a packet.

◆ **java.net.DatagramSocket** is a class that represents a datagram socket. Use new DatagramSocket(int port) to create a server socket, and use new DatagramSocket() to create a client socket. Use send(DatagramPacket) to send a packet, and use receive(DatagramPacket) to receive a packet.

CHAPTER SUMMARY

✦ Java supports stream sockets and datagram sockets. *Stream sockets* use TCP (Transmission Control Protocol) for data transmission, whereas *datagram sockets* use UDP (User Datagram Protocol). Since TCP can detect lost transmissions and resubmit them, transmissions are lossless and reliable. UDP, in contrast, cannot guarantee lossless transmission.

✦ To create a server, you must first obtain a server socket, using new `ServerSocket(port)`. After a server socket is created, the server can start to listen for connections, using the `accept()` method on the server socket. The client requests a connection to a server by using new `socket(serverName, port)` to create a client socket.

✦ Stream socket communication is very much like input/output stream communication after the connection between a server and a client is established. You can obtain an input stream using the `getInputStream()` method and an output stream using the `getOutputStream()` method on the socket.

✦ A server must often work with multiple clients at the same time. You can use threads to handle the server's multiple clients simultaneously by creating a thread for each connection.

✦ Applets are good for deploying multiple clients. They can be run anywhere with a single copy of the program. However, because of security restrictions, an applet client can only connect to the server where the applet is loaded.

✦ Java programs can retrieve data from a file on a remote host through a Web server. To do so, first create a URL object using new `URL(urlString)`, then use `openStream()` to get an `InputStream` to read the data from the file.

✦ Swing provides a GUI component named `javax.swing.JEditorPane` that can be used to display text, HTML, and RTF files automatically without writing the code to read data from the file explicitly.

✦ Clients and servers that communicate via a datagram socket do not have a dedicated point-to-point channel. Data are transmitted using packets. Datagram sockets use UDP (User Datagram Protocol), which cannot guarantee that the packets are not lost, not received in duplicate, or received in the order in which they were sent. A *datagram* is an independent, self-contained message sent over the network whose arrival, arrival time, and content are not guaranteed.

REVIEW QUESTIONS

Section 28.2 Client/Server Computing

28.1 How do you create a server socket? What port numbers can be used? What happens if a requested port number is already in use? Can a port connect to multiple clients?

28.2 What are the differences between a server socket and a client socket?

28.3 How does a client program initiate a connection?

28.4 How does a server accept a connection?

28.5 How are data transferred between a client and a server?

Sections 28.3–28.4

28.6 How do you find the IP address of a client that connects to a server?

28.7 How do you make a server serve multiple clients?

Sections 28.5–28.6

28.8 Can an applet connect to a server that is different from the machine where the applet is located?

28.9 How do you find the host name of an applet?

28.10 How do you send and receive an object?

Sections 28.7–28.8

28.11 Can an application retrieve a file from a remote host? Can an application update a file on a remote host?

28.12 How do you retrieve a file from a Web server?

28.13 What types of files can be displayed in a JEditorPane? How do you display a file in a JEditorPane?

Section 28.10 Datagram Socket

28.14 What are the differences between stream sockets and datagram sockets? How do you create a datagram socket? How do you set data in the packet? How do you send and receive packets? How do you find the IP address of the sender?

PROGRAMMING EXERCISES

Sections 28.2

28.1* (*Loan server*) Write a server for a client. The client sends loan information (annual interest rate, number of years, and loan amount) to the server (see Figure 28.22(a)). The server computes monthly payment and total payment and sends them back to the client (see Figure 28.22(b)). Name the client Exercise28_1Client and the server Exercise28_1Server.

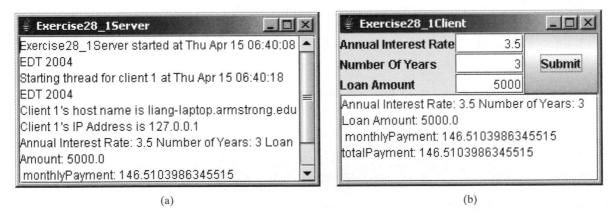

(a) (b)

FIGURE 28.22 *The client sends the annual interest rate, number of years, and loan amount to the server (a) and receives the monthly payment and total payment from the server (b).*

28.2 (*Revising Example 28.1, "A Client/Server Example"*) Rewrite Example 28.1 using a buffered reader for input and a print stream for output. Use the readLine() method to read a string from the input stream, and use the Double.parseDouble(string) to convert the string into a double value. Name the client Exercise28_2Client and the server Exercise28_2Server.

Sections 28.3–28.4

28.3* (*Loan server for multiple clients*) Revise Exercise 28.1 to write a server for multiple clients.

Sections 28.5

28.4   (*Web visit count*) Example 28.3, "Creating Applet Clients," created an applet that shows the number of visits made to a Web page. The count is stored in a file on the server side. Every time the page is visited or reloaded, the applet sends a request to the server, and the server increases the count and sends it to the applet. The count is stored using a random-access file. When the applet is loaded, the server reads the count from the file, increases it, and saves it back to the file. Rewrite the program to improve its performance. Read the count from the file when the server starts, and save the count to the file when the server stops, using the Stop button, as shown in Figure 28.23. When the server is alive, use a variable to store the count. Name the client Exercise28_4Client and the server Exercise28_4Server. The client program should be same as in Example 28.3. Rewrite the server as a GUI application with a *Stop* button that exits the server.

FIGURE 28.23   *The applet displays how many times this Web page has been accessed. The server stores the count.*

28.5   (*Creating a stock ticker in an applet*) Write an applet like the one in Exercise 14.16 (Simulating a stock ticker). Ensure that the applet gets the stock index from a file stored on the Web server. Enable the applet to run standalone.

Sections 28.6

28.6   (*Displaying and adding addresses*) Develop a client/server application to view and add addresses, as shown in Figure 28.24.

✦ Declare an Address class to hold name, street, city, state, and zip in an object.
✦ The user can use the buttons *First*, *Next*, *Previous*, and *Last* to view an address, and the *Add* button to add a new address.
✦ (Optional) Limit the concurrent connections to two clients.

Name the client Exercise28_6Client and the server Exercise28_6Server.

FIGURE 28.24   *You can view and add an address in this applet.*

Sections 28.7

28.7*   (*Retrieving remote files*) Revise Example 28.5, "Retrieving Remote Files," to use `JEditorPane` instead of `JTextArea`.

Sections 28.8

28.8*   (*Using `JEditorPane`*) Example 22.10, "Using `JSplitPane`," uses radio buttons to let the user select a `FlowLayout`, `GridLayout`, or `BoxLayout` manager dynamically for a panel. Rewrite the program to get descriptions of the layout manager from an HTML file and display it in a `JEditorPane`. The descriptions are stored in three files: FlowLayout.html, GridLayout.html, and BoxLayout.html.

28.9*   (*Web browser*) Modify Example 28.6, "Creating a Web Browser," as follows:

♦ It accepts an HTML file from a local host. Assume that a local HTML filename begins neither with http:// nor with www.

♦ It accepts a remote HTML file. A remote HTML filename begins with either http:// or www.

Sections 28.9

28.10**   (*Chat*) Write a program that enables two users to chat. Implement one user as the server (Figure 28.25(a)) and the other as the client (Figure 28.25(b)). The server has two text areas: one for entering text and the other (noneditable) for displaying text received from the client. When the user presses the Enter key, the current line is sent to the client. The client has two text areas: one for receiving text from the server, and the other for entering text. When the user presses the Enter key, the current line is sent to the server. Name the client Exercise28_10Client and the server Exercise28_10Server.

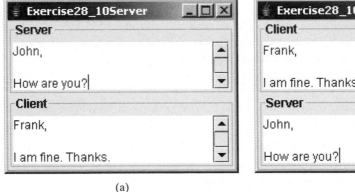
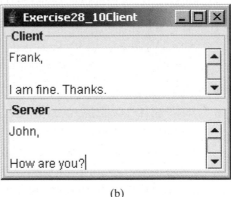

            (a)   (b)

FIGURE 28.25   *The server and client send and receive text from each other.*

Section 28.10 Datagram Socket

28.11*   (*Loan server using datagram*) Rewrite Exercise 28.1 using datagram sockets.

28.12*   (*Multiple clients using datagrams*) Rewrite Exercise 28.3 using datagram sockets.

28.13*   (*Web visit count using datagrams*) Rewrite Exercise 28.4 using datagram sockets.

28.14**   (*Displaying and adding addresses using datagrams*) Rewrite Exercise 28.6 using datagram sockets.

28.15**   (*Chat using datagrams*) Rewrite Exercise 28.10 using datagram sockets.

chapter

REMOTE METHOD INVOCATIONS

29

Objectives

- ✦ To know how RMI works (§29.2).
- ✦ To learn the process of developing RMI applications (§29.3).
- ✦ To know the differences between RMI and socket-level programming (§29.4).
- ✦ To develop three-tier applications using RMI (§29.5).
- ✦ To use callbacks to develop interactive applications (§29.6).

29.1   Introduction

Remote Method Invocation (RMI) technology provides a framework for building distributed Java systems. Using RMI, a Java object on one system can invoke a method in an object on another system on the network. A *distributed Java system* can be defined as a collection of cooperative distributed objects on the network. This chapter introduces RMI basics. You will learn how to use RMI to create useful distributed applications.

29.2   RMI Basics

RMI is the Java Distributed Object Model for facilitating communications among distributed objects. RMI is a higher-level API built on top of sockets. Socket-level programming allows you to pass data through sockets among computers. RMI enables you not only to pass data among objects on different systems, but also to invoke methods in a remote object. Remote objects can be manipulated as if they were residing on the local host. The transmission of data among different machines is handled by the JVM transparently.

In many ways, RMI is an evolution of the client/server architecture. A *client* is a component that issues requests for services, and a *server* is a component that delivers the requested services. Like the client/server architecture, RMI maintains the notion of clients and servers, but the RMI approach is more flexible than the client/server paradigm.

client
server

◆ An RMI component can act as both a client and a server, depending on the scenario in question.

◆ An RMI system can pass functionality from a server to a client, and vice versa. A client/server system typically only passes data back and forth between server and client.

29.2.1   How Does RMI Work?

All the objects you have used before this chapter are called *local objects*. *Local objects* are accessible only within the local host. Objects that are accessible from a remote host are called *remote objects*. For an object to be invoked remotely, it must be defined in a Java interface accessible to both the server and the client. Furthermore, the interface must extend the java.rmi.Remote interface. Like the java.io.Serializable interface, java.rmi.Remote is a marker interface that contains no constants or methods. It is only used to identify remote objects.

local object
remote object

The key components of the RMI architecture are listed below (see Figure 29.1):

◆ **Server object interface:** A subinterface of java.rmi.Remote that defines the methods for the server object.

◆ **Server implementation:** A class that implements the remote object interface.

◆ **Server object:** An instance of the server implementation.

◆ **RMI registry:** A utility that registers remote objects and provides naming services for locating objects.

◆ **Client program:** A program that invokes the methods in the remote server object.

◆ **Server stub:** An object that resides on the client host and serves as a surrogate for the remote server object.

◆ **Server skeleton:** An object that resides on the server host, and communicates with the stub and the actual server object.

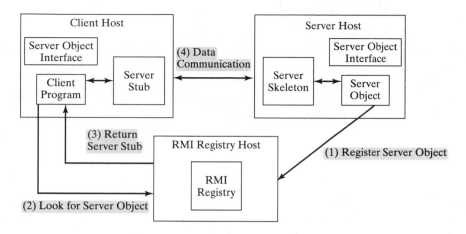

FIGURE 29.1 *Java RMI uses a registry to provide naming services for remote objects, and uses the stub and skeleton to facilitate communications between client and server.*

RMI works as follows:

1. A server object is registered with the RMI registry.

2. A client looks through the RMI registry for the remote object.

3. Once the remote object is located, its stub is returned in the client.

4. The remote object can be used in the same way as a local object. Communication between the client and the server is handled through the stub and the skeleton.

The implementation of the RMI architecture is complex, but the good news is that RMI provides a mechanism that liberates you from writing the tedious code for handling parameter passing and invoking remote methods. The basic idea is to use two helper classes known as the *stub* and the *skeleton* for handling communications between client and server.

stub
skeleton

The stub and the skeleton are automatically generated from the server implementation using an RMI utility called `rmic`. The *stub* resides on the client machine. It contains all the reference information the client needs to know about the server object. When a client invokes a method on a server object, it actually invokes a method that is encapsulated in the stub. The stub is responsible for sending parameters to the server, and for receiving the result from the server and returning it to the client.

rmic

The *skeleton* communicates with the stub on the server side. The skeleton receives parameters from the client, passes them to the server for execution, and returns the result to the stub.

29.2.2 Passing Parameters

When a client invokes a remote method with parameters, passing the parameters is handled by the stub and the skeleton. Obviously, invoking methods in a remote object on a server is very different from invoking methods in a local object on a client, since the remote object is in a different address space on a separate machine. Let us consider three types of parameters:

◆ **Primitive data types**, such as `char`, `int`, `double`, or `boolean`, are passed by value like a local call.

primitive type

◆ **Local object types**, such as `java.lang.String`, are also passed by value, but this is completely different from passing an object parameter in a local call. In a local call, an object parameter's reference is passed, which corresponds to the memory address of the object. In a remote call, there is no way to pass the object reference because the address on one machine

local object

is meaningless to a different JVM. Any object can be used as a parameter in a remote call as long as it is serializable. The stub serializes the object parameter and sends it in a stream across the network. The skeleton deserializes the stream into an object.

remote object

✦ **Remote object types** are passed differently from local objects. When a client invokes a remote method with a parameter of a remote object type, the stub of the remote object is passed. The server receives the stub and manipulates the parameter through it. Example 29.3, "Distributed TicTacToe Game Using RMI," will demonstrate passing remote objects.

29.2.3 RMI Naming Services

How does a client locate the remote object? The RMI registry provides the naming services for the server to register the object and for the client to locate the object. Each remote object has a unique name identified by a URL with the protocol `rmi`,

```
rmi://host:port/name
```

where `host` is the name or IP address of the host on which the RMI registry is running, `port` is the port number of the RMI registry, and `name` is the name bound to the remote server object.

The methods for registering and locating a server object are defined in the `java.rmi.Naming` class. All the methods in `Naming` are static, as summarized in Figure 29.2.

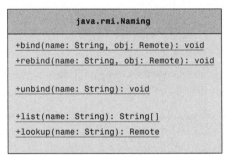

`java.rmi.Naming`	
`+bind(name: String, obj: Remote): void`	Binds the specified name with the remote object.
`+rebind(name: String, obj: Remote): void`	Binds the specified name with the remote object. Any existing binding for the name is replaced.
`+unbind(name: String): void`	Destroys the binding for the specified name that is associated with a remote object.
`+list(name: String): String[]`	Returns an array of the names bound in the registry.
`+lookup(name: String): Remote`	Returns a reference, a stub, for the remote object associated with the specified name.

FIGURE 29.2 *The* `Naming` *class provides the methods for storing and obtaining references to remote objects in a remote object registry.*

29.3 Developing RMI Applications

Now that you have a basic understanding of RMI, you are ready to write simple RMI applications. The steps in developing an RMI application are shown in Figure 29.3.

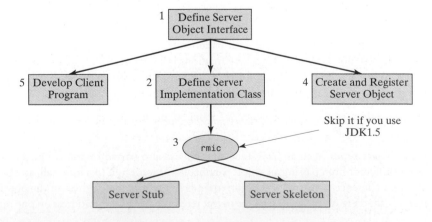

FIGURE 29.3 *The steps in developing RMI applications.*

1. Define a server object interface that serves as the contract between the server and its clients, as shown in the following outline:

```
public interface ServerInterface extends Remote {
  public void service1(...) throws RemoteException;
  // Other methods
}
```

A server object interface must extend the java.rmi.Remote interface.

2. Define a class that implements the server object interface, as shown in the following outline:

```
public class ServerInterfaceImpl extends UnicastRemoteObject
    implements ServerInterface {
  public void service1(...) throws RemoteException {
    // Implement it
  }

  // Implement other methods
}
```

The server implementation class must extend the java.rmi.server.UnicastRemoteObject class. The UnicastRemoteObject class provides support for point-to-point active object references using TCP streams.

3. (Skip this if you are using JDK 1.5.) Compile the server implementation class, and use the following command to generate the skeleton and stub for the server implementation:

```
rmic ServerInterfaceImpl
```

The generated skeleton and stub are named ServerInterfaceImpl_Skeleton and ServerInterfaceImpl_Stub, respectively. In JDK 1.5, these two files are not explicitly generated.

4. Create a server object from the server implementation class and register it with an RMI registry:

```
ServerInterfaceImpl server = new ServerInterfaceImpl(...);
Naming.rebind("rmi://host:port/name", server);
```

5. Develop a client that locates a remote object and invokes its methods, as shown in the following outline:

```
Remote remoteObj = Naming.lookup("rmi://host:port/name");
ServerInterfaceImpl server = (ServerInterfaceImpl)remoteObj;
server.service1(...);
```

The example that follows demonstrates the development of an RMI application through these steps.

EXAMPLE 29.1 RETRIEVING STUDENT SCORES FROM AN RMI SERVER

Problem

This example creates a client that retrieves student scores from an RMI server. The client, shown in Figure 29.4, displays the score for the specified name.

Solution

1. Create a server interface named StudentServerInterface in Listing 29.1. The interface tells the client how to invoke the server's findScore method to retrieve a student score.

EXAMPLE 29.1 (CONTINUED)

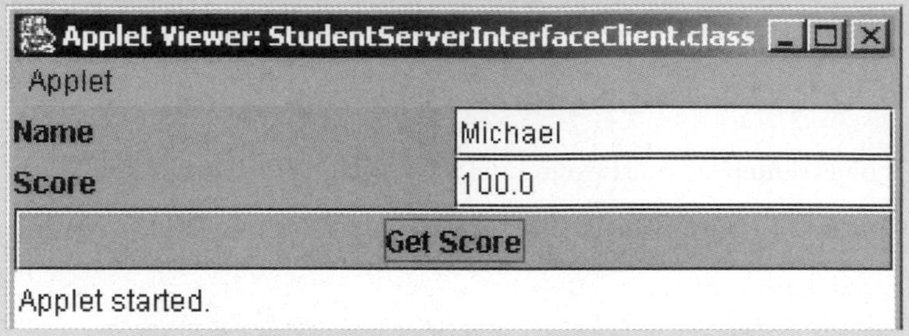

```
Applet Viewer: StudentServerInterfaceClient.class
Applet
Name          Michael
Score         100.0
              Get Score
Applet started.
```

FIGURE 29.4 *You can get the score by entering a student name and clicking the Get Score button.*

LISTING 29.1 StudentServerInterface.java

subinterface

server method

```
 1  import java.rmi.*;
 2
 3  public interface StudentServerInterface extends Remote {
 4    /**
 5     * Return the score for the specified name
 6     * @param    name    the student name
 7     * @return   a   double score or -1 if the student is not found
 8     */
 9    public double findScore(String name) throws RemoteException;
10  }
```

2. Create a server implementation named StudentServerInterfaceImpl (Listing 29.2) that implements StudentServerInterface. The findScore method returns the score for a specified student. It returns −1 if the score is not found.

LISTING 29.2 StudentServerInterfaceImpl.java

hash map

store score

get score

```
 1  import java.rmi.*;
 2  import java.rmi.server.*;
 3  import java.util.*;
 4
 5  public class StudentServerInterfaceImpl extends UnicastRemoteObject
 6      implements StudentServerInterface {
 7    // Stores scores in a map indexed by name
 8    private HashMap scores = new HashMap();
 9
10    public StudentServerInterfaceImpl() throws RemoteException {
11      initializeStudent();
12    }
13
14    /** Initialize student information */
15    protected void initializeStudent() {
16      scores.put("John", new Double(90.5));
17      scores.put("Michael", new Double(100));
18      scores.put("Michelle", new Double(98.5));
19    }
20
21    /** Implement the findScore method from the Student interface */
22    public double findScore(String name) throws RemoteException {
23      Double d = (Double)scores.get(name);
24
25      if (d == null) {
26        System.out.println("Student " + name + " is not found ");
27        return -1;
28      }
```

EXAMPLE 29.1 (CONTINUED)

```
29     else {
30       System.out.println("Student " + name + "\'s score is "
31         + d.doubleValue());
32       return d.doubleValue();
33     }
34   }
35 }
```

3. (Skip this step if you are using JDK 1.5.) Compile StudentServerInterfaceImpl.java to generate StudentServerInterfaceImpl.class. Use the JDK's rmic command to generate the skeleton from the server implementation, as follows:

```
c:\book>rmic StudentServerInterfaceImpl
```

This command generates two files named StudentServerInterfaceImpl_Skel.class and StudentServerInterfaceImpl_Stub.class.

4. Create a server object from the server implementation and register it with the RMI server (Listing 29.3).

LISTING 29.3 RegisterWithRMIServer.java (Creating a Server)

```
 1 import java.rmi.*;
 2 import java.rmi.registry.*;
 3 import java.net.MalformedURLException;
 4
 5 public class RegisterWithRMIServer {
 6   /** Main method */
 7   public static void main(String[] args) {
 8     System.setSecurityManager(new RMISecurityManager());        security manager
 9
10     try {
11       StudentServerInterfaceImpl obj =                          server object
12           new StudentServerInterfaceImpl();
13       registerToRegistry("StudentServerInterfaceImpl", obj, true);  register
14       System.out.println("Student server " + obj + " registered");
15     }
16     catch (RemoteException ex) {
17       ex.printStackTrace();
18     }
19     catch (MalformedURLException ex) {
20       ex.printStackTrace();
21     }
22   }
23
24   /** Register StudentImpl object with the RMI registry.
25    * @param name - name identifying the service in the RMI registry
26    * @param create - create local registry if necessary
27    * @throw RemoteException if cannot be exported or bound to RMI
28    *     registry
29    * @throw MalformedURLException if name cannot be used to
30    *     construct a valid URL
31    * @throw IllegalArgumentException if null passed as name
32    */
33   public static void registerToRegistry(String name, Remote obj,
34       boolean create) throws RemoteException, MalformedURLException{
35     if (name == null) throw new IllegalArgumentException(
36       "registration name can not be null");
37
38     try {
39       Naming.rebind(name, obj);
40     }
41     catch (RemoteException ex) {
42       if (create) {
43         Registry r =
```

EXAMPLE 29.1 (CONTINUED)

bind object

```
44            LocateRegistry.createRegistry(Registry.REGISTRY_PORT);
45          r.rebind(name, obj);
46        } else throw ex;
47      }
48    }
49 }
```

5. Create a client as an applet named `StudentServerInterfaceClient` in Listing 29.4. The client locates the server object from the RMI registry and uses it to find the scores.

LISTING 29.4   StudentServerInterfaceClient.java

remote object

standalone?

initialize RMI

get score

```
 1 import java.rmi.*;
 2 import javax.swing.*;
 3 import java.awt.*;
 4 import java.awt.event.*;
 5
 6 public class StudentServerInterfaceClient extends JApplet {
 7   // Declare a Student instance
 8   private StudentServerInterface student;
 9
10   private boolean isStandalone; // Is applet or application
11
12   private JButton jbtGetScore = new JButton("Get Score");
13   private JTextField jtfName = new JTextField();
14   private JTextField jtfScore = new JTextField();
15
16   public void init() {
17     // Initialize RMI
18     initializeRMI();
19
20     JPanel jPanel1 = new JPanel();
21     jPanel1.setLayout(new GridLayout(2, 2));
22     jPanel1.add(new JLabel("Name"));
23     jPanel1.add(jtfName);
24     jPanel1.add(new JLabel("Score"));
25     jPanel1.add(jtfScore);
26
27     getContentPane().add(jbtGetScore, BorderLayout.SOUTH);
28     getContentPane().add(jPanel1, BorderLayout.CENTER);
29
30     jbtGetScore.addActionListener(new ActionListener() {
31       public void actionPerformed(ActionEvent evt) {
32         getScore();
33       }
34     });
35   }
36
37   private void getScore() {
38     try {
39       // Get student score
40       double score = student.findScore(jtfName.getText().trim());
41
42       // Display the result
43       if (score < 0)
44         jtfScore.setText("Not found");
45       else
46         jtfScore.setText(new Double(score).toString());
47     }
48     catch(Exception ex) {
49       ex.printStackTrace();
50     }
51   }
52
```

EXAMPLE 29.1 (CONTINUED)

```
53   /** Initialize RMI */
54   protected void initializeRMI() {
55     String url;
56
57     if (isStandalone) {
58       url = "rmi:///";                                          standalone
59       // Use rmi://hostname/ if the server is located on hostname,
60       // i.e. rmi://liang.armstrong.edu/
61     }
62     else {
63       // Initialize RMI for an applet                          applet
64       url = getCodeBase().getHost();
65       if (url.equals("default")) url = "";
66       url = "rmi://" + url + "/";
67     }
68
69     try {
70       student = (StudentServerInterface)                       locate student
71         Naming.lookup(url + "StudentServerInterfaceImpl");
72       System.out.println("Server object " + student + " found");
73     }
74     catch(Exception ex) {
75       System.out.println(ex);
76     }
77   }
78
79   /** Main method */
80   public static void main(String[] args) {                     main method
81     StudentServerInterfaceClient applet =
82       new StudentServerInterfaceClient();
83     applet.isStandalone = true;                                standalone
84     JFrame frame = new JFrame();
85     frame.setTitle("StudentServerInterfaceClient");
86     frame.getContentPane().add(applet, BorderLayout.CENTER);
87     frame.setSize(250, 150);
88     applet.init();
89     Dimension d = Toolkit.getDefaultToolkit().getScreenSize();
90     frame.setLocation((d.width - frame.getSize().width) / 2,
91       (d.height - frame.getSize().height) / 2);
92     frame.setVisible(true);
93     frame.setDefaultCloseOperation(3);
94   }
95 }
```

6. Follow the steps below to run this example.

6.1. Start the RMI Registry by typing "**start rmiregistry**" at a DOS prompt from the book directory. By default, the port number 1099 is used by rmiregistry. To use a different port number, simply type the command "**start rmiregistry portnumber**" at a DOS prompt.

6.2. Start RegisterWithRMIServer using the following command at C:\book directory:

C:\book>java -Djava.security.policy=policy RegisterWithRMIServer

The policy file is located at c:\book with the following content to give global permission to anyone from anywhere:

```
grant {
  permission java.security.AllPermission
}
```

6.3. Run StudentServerInterfaceClient as an application. A sample run of the application is shown in Figure 29.5.

EXAMPLE 29.1 (CONTINUED)

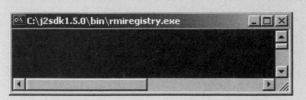

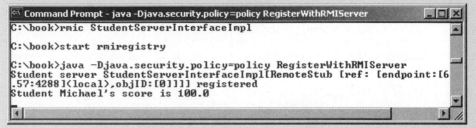

start an RMI registry

start an RMI server

start an RMI client

FIGURE 29.5 *To run an RMI program, first start the RMIRegistry, then register the server object with the registry. The client locates it from the registry.*

6.4. Run `StudentServerInterface.html` from the appletviewer. A sample run is shown in Figure 29.4.

NOTE
You must start rmiregistry from the directory where you will run the RMI server. Otherwise, you will receive an error `ClassNotFoundException` on `StudentServerInterfaceImpl_Stub`.

Review

Any object that can be used remotely must be defined in an interface that extends the `java.rmi.Remote` interface (Line 3 in StudentServerInterface.java). `StudentServerInterface`, extending `Remote`, defines the `findScore` method that can be remotely invoked by a client to find a student's score. Each method in this interface must declare that it may throw a `java.rmi.RemoteException` (Line 9). Therefore your client code that invokes this method must be prepared to catch this exception in a try-catch block.

On the server side, the `StudentServerInterfaceImpl` class implements `StudentServerInterface`. This class must also extend the `java.rmi.server.RemoteServer` class or its subclass. `RemoteServer` is an abstract class that defines the methods needed to create and export remote objects. Often its subclass `java.rmi.server.UnicastRemoteObject` is used (Line 5). This subclass implements all the abstract methods defined in `RemoteServer`.

EXAMPLE 29.1 (CONTINUED)

`StudentServerInterfaceImpl` implements the `findScore` method (Lines 22–34) defined in `StudentServerInterface`. For simplicity, three students, John, Michael, and Michelle, and their corresponding scores are stored in an instance of `java.util.HashMap` named `scores`. `HashMap` is a concrete class of the `Map` interface in the Java Collections Framework, which makes it possible to search and retrieve a value using a key. Both values and keys are of `Object` type. The `findScore` method returns the score if the name is in the hash map, and returns −1 if the name is not found.

`RegisterWithRMIServer` contains a `main` method, which is responsible for starting the server. It performs the following tasks:

1. Installing an RMI security manager to control the classes that are dynamically loaded with the following code (Line 8):

   ```
   System.setSecurityManager(new RMISecurityManager());
   ```

2. Invoking the `registerToRegistry("StudentServerInterfaceImpl", obj, true)` method (Line 13) to register the server object named `StudentServerInterfaceImpl` in the RMI registry. The code to register is (Line 39):

   ```
   Naming.rebind("StudentImpl", obj);
   ```

`java.rmi.Naming` provides the bootstrap mechanism for locating remote objects. The server registers with the service, and the client retrieves the stub of the remote object through the service. The static `bind` method binds the name to a specified remote object. You can also use the `rebind` method to rebind the name to a new object and replace any existing binding associated with the name.

`StudentServerInterfaceClient` invokes the `findScore` method on the server to find the score for a specified student. The key method in `StudentServerInterfaceClient` is the `initializeRMI` method (Lines 54–77), which is responsible for locating the server stub. The stub is specified in an RMI URL using the usual host name, port, and server name,

```
rmi://hostname:port/servername
```

where *hostname* is the host name of the RMI registry (defaults to current host), *port* is the port number of the RMI registry (defaults to the registry port number), and *servername* is the name for a remote object, such as "Student Server" in this example.

The `initializeRMI()` method treats standalone applications differently from applets. The host name should be the name where the applet is downloaded. It can be obtained using the Applet's `getCodeBase().getHost()`. For standalone applications, the host name should be specified explicitly.

The `Naming.lookup(String name)` method (Line 71) returns the remote object for the specified RMI URL. Once a remote object is found, it can be used just like a local object. The stub and the skeleton are used behind the scenes to make the remote method invocation work.

If you run the client and the server on separate machines, you need to start RMIRegistry and run `RegisterWithRMIServer` on the server machine before running `StudentServerInterfaceClient` on the client machine. To run `StudentServerInterfaceClient` standalone, you need to deploy StudentInterfaceImpl.class, and StudentServerInterfaceClient.class on the client machine, and place StudentInterfaceImpl.class, and RegisterWithRMIServer.class on the server machine. To run `StudentServerInterfaceClient` from a Web browser, you need to place StudentInterfaceImpl.class, StudentServerInterfaceClient.class, and StudentServerInterfaceClient.html on the server machine.

EXAMPLE 29.1 (CONTINUED)

 CAUTION

If you modify the remote object implementation class, you need to restart the server class to reload the object to the RMI registry. In some old versions of rmiregistry, you may have to restart rmiregistry.

29.4   RMI vs. Socket-Level Programming

RMI enables you to program at a higher level of abstraction. It hides the details of socket server, socket, connection, and sending or receiving data. It even implements a multithreading server under the hood, whereas with socket-level programming you have to explicitly implement threads for handling multiple clients.

RMI applications are scalable and easy to maintain. You can change the RMI server or move it to another machine without modifying the client program except for resetting the URL to locate the server. (To avoid resetting the URL, you can modify the client to pass the URL as a command-line parameter.) In socket-level programming, a client operation to send data requires a server operation to read it. The implementation of client and server at the socket level is tightly synchronized.

RMI clients can directly invoke the server method, whereas socket-level programming is limited to passing values. Socket-level programming is very primitive. Avoid using it to develop client/server applications. As an analogy, socket-level programming is like programming in assembly language, while RMI programming is like programming in a high-level language.

29.5   Developing Three-Tier Applications Using RMI

Three-tier applications have gained considerable attention in recent years, largely because of the demand for more scalable and load-balanced systems to replace traditional two-tier client/server database systems. A centralized database system does not just handle data access; it also processes the business rules on data. Thus, a centralized database is usually heavily loaded because it requires extensive data manipulation and processing. In some situations, data processing is handled by the client and business rules are stored on the client side. It is preferable to use a middle tier as a buffer between client and database. The middle tier can be used to apply business logic and rules, and to process data to reduce the load on the database.

A three-tier architecture does more than just reduce the processing load on the server. It also provides access to multiple network sites. This is especially useful to Java applets that need to access multiple databases on different servers, since an applet can only connect with the server from which it is downloaded.

The following example demonstrates the use of RMI to create three-tier applications.

EXAMPLE 29.2 RETRIEVING STUDENT SCORES ON A DATABASE USING RMI

Problem

This example rewrites Example 29.1, "Retrieving Student Scores from an RMI Server," to find scores stored in a database rather than a hash map. In addition, the system is capable of blocking a client from accessing a student who has not given the university permission to publish his/her score. An RMI component is developed to serve as a middle tier between client and database; it sends a search request to the database, processes the result, and returns an appropriate value to the client.

EXAMPLE 29.2 (CONTINUED)

Solution

For simplicity, this example reuses the StudentServerInterface interface and Student-ServerInterfaceClient class from Example 29.1 with no modifications. All you have to do is to provide a new implementation for the server interface and create a program to register the server with the RMI. Here are the steps to complete the program:

1. Store the scores in a database table named Score that contains three columns: name, score, and permission. The permission value is 1 or 0, which indicates whether the student has given the university permission to release his/her grade. The following is the statement to create the table and insert three records:

```
create table Scores (name varchar(20),
  score number, permission number);

insert into Scores values ('John', 90.5, 1);
insert into Scores values ('Michael', 100, 1);
insert into Scores values ('Michelle', 100, 0);
```

2. Create a new server implementation named Student3TierImpl in Listing 29.5. The server retrieves a record from the Scores table, processes the retrieved information, and sends the result back to the client.

LISTING 29.5 Student3TierImpl.java

```
1 import java.rmi.*;
2 import java.rmi.server.*;
3 import java.sql.*;
4
5 public class Student3TierImpl extends UnicastRemoteObject
6     implements StudentServerInterface {
7   // Use prepared statement for querying DB
8   private PreparedStatement pstmt;
9
10  /** Constructs Student3TierImpl object and exports it on
11   * default port.
12   */
13  public Student3TierImpl() throws RemoteException {
14    initializeDB();                                              initialize db
15  }
16
17  /** Constructs Student3TierImpl object and exports it on
18   * specified port.
19   * @param port The port for exporting
20   */
21  public Student3TierImpl(int port) throws RemoteException {
22    super(port);
23    initializeDB();
24  }
25
26  /** Load JDBC driver, establish connection and create statement */
27  protected void initializeDB() {
28    try {
29      // Load the JDBC driver
30      // Class.forName("oracle.jdbc.driver.OracleDriver");
31      Class.forName("sun.jdbc.odbc.JdbcOdbcDriver");             load driver
32      System.out.println("Driver registered");
33
34      // Establish connection
35      /*Connection conn = DriverManager.getConnection
36        ("jdbc:oracle:thin:@drake.armstrong.edu:1521:ora9i",
37        "scott", "tiger"); */
38      Connection conn = DriverManager.getConnection
39        ("jdbc:odbc:exampleMDBDataSource", "", "" );           connect db
```

EXAMPLE 29.2 (CONTINUED)

```
40            System.out.println("Database connected");
41
42            // Create a prepared statement for querying DB
43            pstmt = conn.prepareStatement(
44              "select * from Scores where name = ?");
45          }
46          catch (Exception ex) {
47            System.out.println(ex);
48          }
49        }
50
51        /** Return the score for the specified name
52         * Return -1 if score is not found.
53         */
54        public double findScore(String name) throws RemoteException {
55          double score = -1;
56          try {
57            // Set the specified name in the prepared statement
58            pstmt.setString(1, name);
59
60            // Execute the prepared statement
61            ResultSet rs = pstmt.executeQuery();
62
63            // Retrieve the score
64            if (rs.next()) {
65              if (rs.getBoolean(3))
66                score = rs.getDouble(2);
67            }
68          }
69          catch (SQLException ex) {
70            System.out.println(ex);
71          }
72
73          System.out.println(name + "\'s score is " + score);
74          return score;
75        }
76      }
```

The labels in the left margin read: `prepare statement` (line 43), `set name` (line 58), `execute SQL` (line 61), `get score` (line 66).

3. Use **javac** to compile Student3TierImpl.java to generate Student3TierImpl.class. If your JVM is not JDK 1.5, you must use rmic to generate the stub and skeleton for Student3TierImpl from Student3TierImpl.class.

4. Write a main method in the class RegisterStudent3TierServer (Listing 29.6) that registers the server object using StudentServerInterfaceImpl, the same name as in Example 29.1, so that you can use StudentServerInterfaceClient, created in Example 29.1, to test the server.

LISTING 29.6 RegisterStudent3TierServer.java

```
1 import java.rmi.*;
2 import java.rmi.registry.*;
3 import java.net.MalformedURLException;
4
5 public class RegisterStudent3TierServer {
6   public static void main(String[] args) {
7     System.setSecurityManager(new RMISecurityManager());
8
9     try {
10      Student3TierImpl obj = new Student3TierImpl();
11      // Register the server with the name StudentServerInterfaceImpl,
12      // which is the same as in Example 29.1 so it can be used
13      // by Example 29.1.
14      registerToRegistry("StudentServerInterfaceImpl", obj, true);
15      System.out.println("Server " + obj + " registered");
```

The labels in the left margin read: `security manager` (line 7), `server object` (line 10), `register` (line 14).

EXAMPLE 29.2 (CONTINUED)

```
16      } catch (RemoteException ex) {
17          ex.printStackTrace();
18      } catch (MalformedURLException ex) {
19          ex.printStackTrace();
20      }
21   }
22
23   /** Register Student3TierImpl object with the RMI registry.
24    * @param name - name identifying the service in the RMI registry
25    * @param create - create local registry if necessary
26    * @throw RemoteException if cannot be exported or bound to
27    *    RMI registry
28    * @throw MalformedURLException if name cannot be used to construct
29    *    a valid URL
30    * @throw IllegalArgumentException if null passed as name
31    */
32   public static void registerToRegistry(String name, Remote obj,
33      boolean create) throws RemoteException, MalformedURLException{
34
35      if (name == null) throw new IllegalArgumentException(
36        "registration name can not be null");
37
38      try {
39        Naming.rebind(name, obj);                              bind object
40      } catch (RemoteException ex){
41        if (create) {
42          Registry r = LocateRegistry.createRegistry(
43            Registry.REGISTRY_PORT);
44          r.rebind(name, obj);
45        } else throw ex;
46      }
47   }
48 }
```

5. Follow the steps below to run this example.

   5.1. Start RMI Registry by typing "**start rmiregistry**" at a DOS prompt from the book directory.

   5.2. Start `RegisterStudent3TierServer` using the following command at C:\book directory:

   `C:\book>java -Djava.security.policy=policy RegisterStudent3TierServer`

   5.3. Run `StudentServerInterfaceClient` as an application or applet. A sample run is shown in Figure 29.5.

Review

This example is similar to Example 29.1 except that the `Student3TierImpl` class finds the score from a JDBC data source instead from a hash map.

The table named `Scores` consists of three columns, `name`, `score`, and `permission`, where permission indicates whether the student has given permission to show his/her score. Since SQL does not support a `boolean` type, permission is defined as a number whose value of 1 indicates `true` and 0 indicates `false`.

The `initializeDB()` method (Lines 27–49) loads the appropriate JDBC driver, establishes connections with the database, and creates a prepared statement for processing the query.

The `findScore` method (Lines 54–75) sets the name in the prepared statement, executes the statement, processes the result, and returns the score for a student whose permission is true.

29.6　RMI Callbacks

In a traditional client/server system, a client sends a request to a server, and the server processes the request and returns the result to the client. The server cannot invoke the methods on a client. One of the important benefits of RMI is that it supports *callbacks*, which enable the server to invoke methods on the client. With the RMI callback feature, you can develop interactive distributed applications.

The following example demonstrates the use of the RMI callback feature to develop an interactive TicTacToe game.

EXAMPLE 29.3　DISTRIBUTED TICTACTOE GAME USING RMI

Problem

Example 28.7, "Distributed TicTacToe Game," was developed using stream socket programming. Write a new distributed TicTacToe game using RMI.

Solution

All the examples you have seen so far in this chapter have simple behaviors that are easy to model with classes. The behavior of the TicTacToe game is somewhat complex. To create the classes to model the game, you need to study and understand it and distribute the process appropriately between client and server.

Clearly, the client should be responsible for handling user interactions, and the server should coordinate with the client. Specifically, the client should register with the server, and the server can take two and only two players. Once a client makes a move, it should notify the server; the server then notifies the move to the other player. The server should determine the status of the game, that is, whether the game has been won or drawn, and should notify the players. The server should also coordinate the turns, that is, which client has the turn at a given time. The ideal approach for notifying a player is to invoke a method in the client that sets appropriate properties in the client or sends messages to a player. Figure 29.6 illustrates the relationship between clients and server.

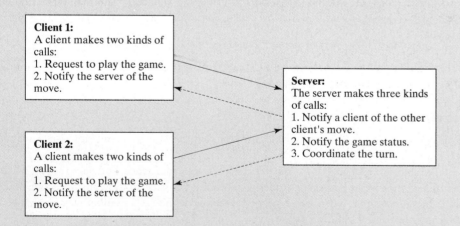

FIGURE 29.6　*The server coordinates the activities with the clients.*

All the calls a client makes can be encapsulated in one remote interface named TicTacToe (Listing 29.7), and all the calls the server invokes can be defined in another interface named CallBack (Listing 29.8). These two interfaces are defined as below:

EXAMPLE 29.3 (CONTINUED)

LISTING 29.7   TicTacToeInterface.java

```
 1 import java.rmi.*;
 2
 3 public interface TicTacToeInterface extends Remote {          subinterface
 4   /**
 5    * Connect to the TicTacToe server and return the token.
 6    * If the returned token is ' ', the client is not connected to
 7    * the server
 8    */
 9   public char connect(CallBack client) throws RemoteException;   server method
10
11   /** A client invokes this method to notify the server of its move*/
12   public void myMove(int row, int column, char token)           server method
13      throws RemoteException;
14 }
```

LISTING 29.8   CallBack.java

```
 1 import java.rmi.*;
 2
 3 public interface CallBack extends Remote {                      subinterface
 4   /** The server notifies the client for taking a turn */
 5   public void takeTurn(boolean turn) throws RemoteException;     server method
 6
 7   /** The server sends a message to be displayed by the client */
 8   public void notify(java.lang.String message)                   server method
 9      throws RemoteException;
10
11   /** The server notifies a client of the other player's move */
12   public void mark(int row, int column, char token)             server method
13      throws RemoteException;
14 }
```

What does a client need to do? The client interacts with the player. Assume that all the cells are initially empty, and that the first player takes the X token and the second player takes the O token. To mark a cell, the player points the mouse to the cell and clicks it. If the cell is empty, the token (X or O) is displayed. If the cell is already filled, the player's action is ignored.

From the preceding description, it is obvious that a cell is a GUI object that handles mouse-click events and displays tokens. The candidate for such an object could be a button or a panel. Panels are more flexible than buttons. The token (X or O) can be drawn on a panel in any size, but it only can be displayed as a label on a button.

Let `Cell` be a subclass of `JPanel`. You can declare a 3×3 grid to be an array `Cell[][] cell = new Cell[3][3]` for modeling the game. How do you know the state of a cell (marked or not)? You can use a property named `marked` of the `boolean` type in the `Cell` class. How do you know whether the player has a turn? You can use a property named `myTurn` of `boolean`. This property (initially `false`) can be set by the server through a callback.

The `Cell` class is responsible for drawing the token when an empty cell is clicked, so you need to write the code for listening to the `MouseEvent` and for painting the shape for tokens X and O. To determine which shape to draw, introduce a variable named `marker` of the `char` type. Since this variable is shared by all the cells in a client, it is preferable to declare it in the client and to declare the `Cell` class as an inner class of the client so that this variable will be accessible to all the cells.

EXAMPLE 29.3 (CONTINUED)

Now let us turn our attention to the server side. What does the server need to do? The server needs to implement `TicTacToeInterface` and notify the clients of the game status. The server has to record the moves in the cells and check the status every time a player makes a move. The status information can be kept in a 3 × 3 array of `char`. You can implement a method named `isFull()` to check whether the board is full and a method named `isWon(token)` to check whether a specific player has won.

Once a client is connected to the server, the server notifies the client which token to use; that is, X for the first client, and O for the second. Once a client notifies the server of its move, the server checks the game status and notifies the clients.

Now the most critical question is how the server notifies a client. You know that a client invokes a server method by creating a server stub on the client side. A server cannot directly invoke a client, because the client is not declared as a remote object. The `CallBack` interface was created to facilitate the server's callback to the client. In the implementation of `CallBack`, an instance of the client is passed as a parameter in the constructor of `CallBack`. The client creates an instance of `CallBack` and passes its stub to the server, using a remote method named `connect()` defined in the server. The server then invokes the client's method through a `CallBack` instance. The triangular relationship of client, `CallBack` implementation, and server is shown in Figure 29.7.

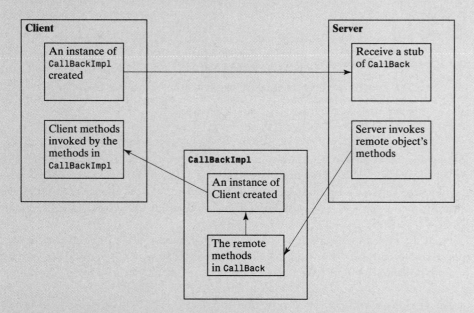

FIGURE 29.7   *The server receives a `CallBack` stub from the client and invokes the remote methods defined in the `CallBack` interface, which can invoke the methods defined in the client.*

Here are the steps to complete the example.

1. Create TicTacToeImpl.java (Listing 29.9) to implement `TicTacToeInterface`. Add a main method in the program to register the server with the RMI.

LISTING 29.9   TicTacToeImpl.java

```
1 import java.rmi.*;
2 import java.rmi.server.*;
3 import java.rmi.registry.*;
4 import java.net.MalformedURLException;
```

EXAMPLE 29.3 (CONTINUED)

```
 5
 6 public class TicTacToeImpl extends UnicastRemoteObject
 7     implements TicTacToeInterface {
 8   // Declare two players, used to call players back
 9   private CallBack player1 = null;
10   private CallBack player2 = null;
11
12   // board records players' moves
13   private char[][] board = new char[3][3];
14
15   /** Constructs TicTacToeImpl object and exports it on default port.
16    */
17   public TicTacToeImpl() throws RemoteException {
18     super();
19   }
20
21   /** Constructs TicTacToeImpl object and exports it on specified
22    * port.
23    * @param port The port for exporting
24    */
25   public TicTacToeImpl(int port) throws RemoteException {
26     super(port);
27   }
28
29   /**
30    * Connect to the TicTacToe server and return the token.
31    * If the returned token is ' ', the client is not connected to
32    * the server
33    */
34   public char connect(CallBack client) throws RemoteException {
35     if (player1 == null) {
36       // player1 (first player) registered
37       player1 = client;
38       player1.notify("Wait for a second player to join");
39       return 'X';
40     }
41     else if (player2 == null) {
42       // player2 (second player) registered
43       player2 = client;
44       player2.notify("Wait for the first player to move");
45       player2.takeTurn(false);
46       player1.notify("It is my turn (X token)");
47       player1.takeTurn(true);
48       return 'O';
49     }
50     else {
51       // Already two players
52       client.notify("Two players are already in the game");
53       return ' ';
54     }
55   }
56
57   /** A client invokes this method to notify the server of its move*/
58   public void myMove(int row, int column, char token)
59       throws RemoteException {
60     // Set token to the specified cell
61     board[row][column] = token;
62
63     // Notify the other player of the move
64     if (token == 'X')
65       player2.mark(row, column, 'X');
66     else
67       player1.mark(row, column, 'O');
68
69     // Check if the player with this token wins
70     if (isWon(token)) {
```

call back objects

implement

implement

EXAMPLE 29.3 (CONTINUED)

```
71            if (token == 'X') {
72              player1.notify("I won!");
73              player2.notify("I lost!");
74              player1.takeTurn(false);
75            }
76            else {
77              player2.notify("I won!");
78              player1.notify("I lost!");
79              player2.takeTurn(false);
80            }
81          }
82          else if (isFull()) {
83            player1.notify("Draw!");
84            player2.notify("Draw!");
85          }
86          else if (token == 'X') {
87            player1.notify("Wait for the second player to move");
88            player1.takeTurn(false);
89            player2.notify("It is my turn, (O token)");
90            player2.takeTurn(true);
91          }
92          else if (token == 'O') {
93            player2.notify("Wait for the first player to move");
94            player2.takeTurn(false);
95            player1.notify("It is my turn, (X token)");
96            player1.takeTurn(true);
97          }
98        }
99
100       /** Check if a player with the specified token wins */
101       public boolean isWon(char token) {
102         for (int i = 0; i < 3; i++)
103           if ((board[i][0] == token) && (board[i][1] == token)
104             && (board[i][2] == token))
105             return true;
106
107         for (int j = 0; j < 3; j++)
108           if ((board[0][j] == token) && (board[1][j] == token)
109             && (board[2][j] == token))
110             return true;
111
112         if ((board[0][0] == token) && (board[1][1] == token)
113           && (board[2][2] == token))
114           return true;
115
116         if ((board[0][2] == token) && (board[1][1] == token)
117           && (board[2][0] == token))
118           return true;
119
120         return false;
121       }
122
123       /** Check if the board is full */
124       public boolean isFull() {
125         for (int i = 0; i < 3; i++)
126           for (int j = 0; j < 3; j++)
127             if (board[i][j] == '\u0000')
128               return false;
129
130         return true;
131       }
132
133       public static void registerToRegistry(String name, Remote obj,
134         boolean create) throws RemoteException, MalformedURLException{
135         if (name == null) throw new IllegalArgumentException(
136           "registration name can not be null");
```

isWon

isFull

register server

EXAMPLE 29.3 (CONTINUED)

```
137
138      try {
139        Naming.rebind(name, obj);
140      } catch (RemoteException ex){
141        if (create) {
142          Registry r =
143            LocateRegistry.createRegistry(Registry.REGISTRY_PORT);
144          r.rebind(name, obj);
145        } else throw ex;
146      }
147    }
148
149    public static void main(String[] args) {
150      System.setSecurityManager(new RMISecurityManager());     security manager
151
152      try {
153        TicTacToeImpl obj = new TicTacToeImpl();
154        registerToRegistry("TicTacToeImpl", obj, true);         register object
155        System.out.println("Server " + obj + " started");
156      } catch (RemoteException ex) {
157        ex.printStackTrace();
158      } catch (MalformedURLException ex) {
159        ex.printStackTrace();
160      }
161    }
162 }
```

2. Create CallBackImpl.java (Listing 29.10) to implement the `CallBack` interface.

LISTING 29.10 CallBackImpl.java

```
1  import java.rmi.*;
2  import java.rmi.server.*;
3
4  public class CallBackImpl extends UnicastRemoteObject
5      implements CallBack {
6    // The client will be called by the server through callback
7    private TicTacToeClientRMI thisClient;
8
9    /** Constructor */
10   public CallBackImpl(Object client) throws RemoteException {
11     thisClient = (TicTacToeClientRMI)client;
12   }
13
14   /** The server notifies the client for taking a turn */
15   public void takeTurn(boolean turn) throws RemoteException {       implement
16     thisClient.setMyTurn(turn);
17   }
18
19   /** The server sends a message to be displayed by the client */
20   public void notify(String message) throws RemoteException {       implement
21     thisClient.setMessage(message);
22   }
23
24   /** The server notifies a client of the other player's move */
25   public void mark(int row, int column, char token)                 implement
26       throws RemoteException {
27     thisClient.mark(row, column, token);
28   }
29 }
```

3. Create an applet `TicTacToeClientRMI` (Listing 29.11) for interacting with a player and communicating with the server. Enable it to run standalone.

EXAMPLE 29.3 (CONTINUED)

LISTING 29.11 TicTacToeClientRMI.java

```
1 import java.rmi.*;
2 import java.awt.*;
3 import java.awt.event.*;
4 import javax.swing.*;
5 import javax.swing.border.*;
6
7 public class TicTacToeClientRMI extends JApplet {
8   // marker is used to indicate the token type
9   private char marker;
10
11   // myTurn indicates whether the player can move now
12   private boolean myTurn = false;
13
14   // Each cell can be empty or marked as 'O' or 'X'
15   private Cell[][] cell;
16
17   // ticTacToe is the game server for coordinating with the players
18   private TicTacToeInterface ticTacToe;
19
20   // Border for cells and panel
21   private Border lineBorder =
22     BorderFactory.createLineBorder(Color.yellow, 1);
23
24   private JLabel jlblStatus = new JLabel("jLabel1");
25   private JLabel jlblIdentification = new JLabel();
26
27   boolean isStandalone = false;
28
29   /** Initialize the applet */
30   public void init() {
31     JPanel jPanel1 = new JPanel();
32     jPanel1.setBorder(lineBorder);
33     jPanel1.setLayout(new GridLayout(3, 3, 1, 1));
34
35     this.getContentPane().add(jlblStatus, BorderLayout.SOUTH);
36     this.getContentPane().add(jPanel1, BorderLayout.CENTER);
37     this.getContentPane().add(jlblIdentification,
38       BorderLayout.NORTH);
39
40     // Create cells and place cells in the panel
41     cell = new Cell[3][3];
42     for (int i = 0; i < 3; i++)
43       for (int j = 0; j < 3; j++)
44         jPanel1.add(cell[i][j] = new Cell(i, j));
45
46     try {
47       initializeRMI();
48     }
49     catch (Exception ex) {
50       ex.printStackTrace();
51     }
52   }
53
54   /** Initialize RMI */
55   protected boolean initializeRMI() throws Exception {
56     String url;
57
58     if (isStandalone) {
59       // Initialize RMI for a standalone application
60       // System.setSecurityManager(new RMISecurityManager());
61       url = "rmi:///";
62       // Use rmi://hostname/ if the server is located on hostname,
63       // i.e. rmi://liangy.liangy.edu/
64     }
```

server object *(margin note at line 18)*

create UI *(margin note at line 30)*

server URL *(margin note at line 61)*

EXAMPLE **29.3** (CONTINUED)

```
65    else {
66      // Initialize RMI for an applet
67      url = getCodeBase().getHost();
68      if (url.equals("default")) url = "";
69      url = "rmi://" + url + "/";
70    }
71
72    ticTacToe = (TicTacToeInterface)Naming.lookup(url +
73      "TicTacToeImpl");
74    System.out.println("Server found");
75
76    // Create callback for use by the server to control the client
77    CallBackImpl callBackControl = new CallBackImpl(this);
78
79    if (
80      (marker = ticTacToe.connect((CallBack)callBackControl)) != ' ')
81    {
82      System.out.println("connected as " + marker + " player.");
83      jlblIdentification.setText("You are player " + marker);
84      return true;
85    }
86    else {
87      System.out.println("already two players connected as ");
88      return false;
89    }
90  }
91
92  /** Set variable myTurn to true or false */
93  void setMyTurn(boolean myTurn) {
94    this.myTurn = myTurn;
95  }
96
97  /** Set message on the status label */
98  public void setMessage(String message) {
99    jlblStatus.setText(message);
100 }
101
102 /** Mark the specified cell using the token */
103 public void mark(int row, int column, char token) {
104   cell[row][column].setToken(token);
105 }
106
107 /** Inner class Cell for modeling a cell on the TicTacToe board */
108 private class Cell extends JPanel {
109   // marked indicates whether the cell has been used
110   private boolean marked = false;
111
112   // row and column indicate where the cell appears on the board
113   int row, column;
114
115   // The token for the cell
116   private char token;
117
118   /** Construct a cell */
119   private Cell(final int row, final int column) {
120     this.row = row;
121     this.column = column;
122     addMouseListener(new MouseAdapter() {
123       public void mouseClicked(MouseEvent e) {
124         if (myTurn && !marked) {
125           // Mark the cell
126           setToken(marker);
127
128           // Notify the server of the move
129           try {
130             ticTacToe.myMove(row, column, marker);
131           }
```

server URL

server object

call back

inner class

EXAMPLE 29.3 (CONTINUED)

```
132              catch (RemoteException ex) {
133                System.out.println(ex);
134              }
135            }
136          }
137        });
138
139        setBorder(lineBorder);
140      }
141
142      /** Set token on a cell (mark a cell) */
143      public void setToken(char c) {
144        token = c;
145        marked = true;
146        repaint();
147      }
148
149      /** Paint the cell to draw a shape for the token */
150      protected void paintComponent(Graphics g) {
151        super.paintComponent(g);
152
153        // Draw the border
154        g.drawRect(0, 0, getSize().width, getSize().height);
155
156        if (token == 'X') {
157          g.drawLine(10, 10, getSize().width - 10,
158            getSize().height - 10);
159          g.drawLine(getSize().width - 10, 10, 10,
160            getSize().height - 10);
161        }
162        else if (token == 'O') {
163          g.drawOval(10, 10, getSize().width - 20,
164            getSize().height - 20);
165        }
166      }
167    }
168
169    /** Main method */
170    public static void main(String[] args) {
171      TicTacToeClientRMI applet = new TicTacToeClientRMI();
172      applet.isStandalone = true;
173      applet.init();
174      applet.start();
175      JFrame frame = new JFrame();
176      frame.setDefaultCloseOperation(JFrame.EXIT_ON_CLOSE);
177      frame.setTitle("TicTacToeClientRMI");
178      frame.getContentPane().add(applet, BorderLayout.CENTER);
179      frame.setSize(400, 320);
180      frame.setVisible(true);
181    }
182  }
```

standalone

4. Compile TicTacToeImpl.java and CallBackImpl.java to generate TicTacToeImpl.class and CallBackImpl.class. If your JVM is not JDK 1.5 or higher, you must use **rmic** to compile TicTacToeImpl.class and CallBackImpl.class to generate the stubs and skeletons for `TicTacToeImpl` and `CallBackImpl`.

5. Follow the steps below to run this example.

   5.1. Start RMI Registry by typing "**start rmiregistry**" at a DOS prompt from the book directory.

   5.2. Start `TicTacToeImpl` using the following command at C:\book directory:

   ```
   C:\book>java -Djava.security.policy=policy TicTacToeImpl
   ```

EXAMPLE 29.3 (CONTINUED)

5.3. Run `TicTacToeClientRMI` as an application or an applet. A sample run is shown in Figure 29.8.

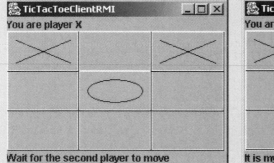 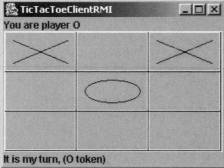

FIGURE 29.8 *Two players play each other through the RMI server.*

Review

`TicTacToeInterface` defines two remote methods, `connect(CallBack client)` and `my-Move(int row, int column, char token)`. The connect method plays two roles: one is to pass a `CallBack` stub to the server, and the other is to let the server assign a token for the player. The `myMove` method notifies the server that the player has made a specific move.

The `CallBack` interface defines three remote methods, `takeTurn(boolean turn)`, `notify (String message)`, and `mark(int row, int column, char token)`. The `takeTurn` method sets the client's `myTurn` property to `true` or `false`. The `notify` method displays a message on the client's status label. The `mark` method marks the client's cell with the token at the specified location.

`TicTacToeImpl` is a server implementation for coordinating with the clients and managing the game. The variables `player1` and `player2` are instances of `CallBack`, each of which corresponds to a client, passed from a client when the client invokes the `connect` method. The variable `board` records the moves by the two players. This information is needed to determine the game status. When a client invokes the `connect` method, the server assigns a token X for the first player and O for the second player, and only two players are accepted by the server. You can modify the program to accept additional clients as observers. See Exercise 29.7 for more details.

Once two players are in the game, the server coordinates the turns between them. When a client invokes the `myMove` method, the server records the move and notifies the other player by marking the other player's cell. It then checks to see whether the player wins or whether the board is full. If neither conditions applies and therefore the game continues, the server gives a turn to the other player.

The `CallBackImpl` implements the `CallBack` interface. It creates an instance of `TicTacToeClientRMI` through its constructor. The `CallBackImpl` relays the server request to the client by invoking the client's methods. When the server invokes the `takeTurn` method, `CallBackImpl` invokes the client's `setMyTurn()` method to set the property `myTurn` in the client. When the server invokes the `notify()` method, `CallBackImpl` invokes the client's `setMessage()` method to set the message on the client's status label. When the server invokes the `mark` method, `CallBackImpl` invokes the client's `mark` method to mark the specified cell.

EXAMPLE 29.3 (CONTINUED)

`TicTacToeClientRMI` can run as a standalone application or as an applet. The `initializeRMI` method is responsible for creating the URL for running as a standalone application or as an applet, for locating the `TicTacToeImpl` server stub, for creating the `CallBack` server object, and for connecting the client with the server.

Interestingly, obtaining the `TicTacToeImpl` stub for the client is different from obtaining the `CallBack` stub for the server. The `TicTacToeImpl` stub is obtained by invoking the `lookup()` method through the RMI registry, and the `CallBack` stub is passed to the server through the `connect` method in the `TicTacToeImpl` stub. It is a common practice to obtain the first stub with the `lookup` method, but to pass the subsequent stubs as parameters through remote method invocations.

Since the variables `myTurn` and `marker` are defined in `TicTacToeClientRMI`, the `Cell` class is defined as an inner class within `TicTacToeClientRMI` in order to enable all the cells in the client to access them. Exercise 29.7 suggests alternative approaches that implement the Cell as a non-inner class.

KEY CLASSES AND METHODS

✦ **java.rmi.Remote** is a marker interface that serves to identify interfaces whose methods may be invoked from a non-local virtual machine. A remote object must directly or indirectly implement this interface.

✦ **java.rmi.server.UnicastRemoteObject** is a class for defining a non-replicated remote object whose references are valid only while the server process is alive. The `UnicastRemoteObject` class provides support for point-to-point active object references (invocations, parameters, and results) using TCP streams.

✦ **java.rmi.RMISecurityManager** is a class that provides an example security manager for use by RMI applications that use downloaded code. RMI's class loader will not download any classes from remote locations if no security manager has been set. `RMISecurityManager` does not apply to applets, which run under the protection of their browser's security manager. To use the `RMISecurityManager` in your application, add `System.setSecurityManager(new RMISecurityManager())` to your code (it needs to be executed before RMI can download code from remote hosts, so it should appear in the main method of your application).

CHAPTER SUMMARY

✦ RMI is a high-level Java API for building distributed applications using distributed objects.

✦ The key idea of RMI is its use of stubs and skeletons to facilitate communications between objects. The stub and skeleton are automatically generated, which relieves programmers of tedious socket-level network programming.

✦ For an object to be used remotely, it must be defined in an interface that extends the `java.rmi.Remote` interface.

✦ In an RMI application, the initial remote object must be registered with the RMI registry on the server side and be obtained using the `lookup` method through the registry on the client side. Subsequent use of stubs of other remote objects may be passed as parameters through remote method invocations.

✦ RMI is especially useful for developing scalable and load-balanced multi-tier distributed applications.

REVIEW QUESTIONS

Sections 29.2–29.3

29.1 How do you define an interface for a remote object?

29.2 Describe the roles of the stub and the skeleton.

29.3 How do you generate the stub and the skeleton, if you are not using JDK 1.5 or higher?

29.4 What is an RMI registry for? How do you create an RMI registry?

29.5 What is the command to start an RMIRegistry?

29.6 How do you register a remote object with an RMI registry?

29.7 What is the command to start a custom RMI server?

29.8 How does a client locate a remote object stub through an RMI registry?

29.9 What can you do if you encounter a security violation?

Sections 29.4–29.6

29.10 What are the advantages of RMI over socket-level programming?

29.11 Describe how parameters are passed in RMI.

29.12 What is the problem if the connect method in the `TicTacToeInterface` is defined as

```
public boolean connect(CallBack client, char token)
  throws RemoteException;
```

or as

```
public boolean connect(CallBack client, Character token)
  throws RemoteException;
```

29.13 What is callback? How does callback work in RMI?

PROGRAMMING EXERCISES

Section 29.3 Developing RMI Applications

29.1* (*Limiting the number of clients*) Modify Example 29.1, "Retrieving Student Scores from an RMI Server," to limit the number of concurrent clients to ten.

29.2* (*Computing loans*) Rewrite Exercise 28.3 using RMI. You need to define a remote interface for computing monthly payment and total payment.

29.3** (*Web visit count*) Rewrite Exercise 28.4 using RMI. You need to define a remote interface for obtaining and increasing the count.

29.4** (*Displaying and adding addresses*) Rewrite Exercise 28.6 using RMI. You need to define a remote interface for adding addresses and retrieving address information.

Section 29.5 Developing Three-Tier Applications Using RMI

29.5** (*Address in a database table*) Rewrite Exercise 29.4. Assume that the address is stored in a table.

29.6** (*Three-tier application*) Use the three-tier approach to modify Exercise 25.1, as follows:

◆ Create an applet client to manipulate student information, as shown in Figure 25.27.

◆ Create a remote object interface with methods for retrieving, inserting, and updating student information, and an object implementation for the interface.

Section 29.6 RMI Callbacks

29.7** (*Improving TicTacToe*) Modify Example 29.3 as follows:

◆ Allow a client to connect to the server as an observer to watch the game.

◆ Rewrite the `Cell` class as a non-inner class.

29.8** (*Chat*) Rewrite Exercise 28.10 using RMI. You need to define a remote interface for sending and receiving a line.

APPENDIXES

Appendix

A

JAVA KEYWORDS

The following fifty keywords are reserved for use by the Java language:

abstract	double	int	super
assert	else	interface	switch
boolean	enum	long	synchronized
break	extends	native	this
byte	for	new	throw
case	final	package	throws
catch	finally	private	transient
char	float	protected	try
class	goto	public	void
const	if	return	volatile
continue	implements	short	while
default	import	static	
do	instanceof	strictfp*	

The keywords goto and const are C++ keywords reserved, but not currently used, in Java. This enables Java compilers to identify them and to produce better error messages if they appear in Java programs.

The literal values true, false, and null are not keywords, just like literal value 100. However, you cannot use them as identifiers, just as you cannot use 100 as an identifier.

assert is a keyword added in JDK 1.4 and enum is a keyword added in JDK 1.5.

---

*The strictfp keyword is a modifier for method or class to use strict floating-point calculations. Floating-point arithmetic can be executed in one of two modes: *strict* or *nonstrict*. The strict mode guarantees that the evaluation result is the same on all Java Virtual Machine implementations. The nonstrict mode allows intermediate results from calculations to be stored in an extended format different from the standard IEEE floating-point number format. The extended format is machine-dependent and enables code to be executed faster. However, when you execute the code using the nonstrict mode on different JVMs, you may not always get precisely the same results. By default, the nonstrict mode is used for floating-point calculations. To use the strict mode in a method or a class, add the strictfp keyword in the method or the class declaration. Strict floating-point may give you slightly better precision than nonstrict floating-point, but the distinction will only affect some applications. Strictness is not inherited; that is, the presence of strictfp on a class or interface declaration does not cause extended classes or interfaces to be strict.

The ASCII Character Set

Tables B.1 and B.2 show ASCII characters and their respective decimal and hexadecimal codes. The decimal or hexadecimal code of a character is a combination of its row index and column index. For example, in Table B.1, the letter A is at row 6 and column 5, so its decimal equivalent is 65; in Table B.2, letter A is at row 4 and column 1, so its hexadecimal equivalent is 41.

TABLE B.1   ASCII Character Set in the Decimal Index

	0	1	2	3	4	5	6	7	8	9
0	nul	soh	stx	etx	eot	enq	ack	bel	bs	ht
1	nl	vt	ff	cr	so	si	dle	dcl	dc2	dc3
2	dc4	nak	syn	etb	can	em	sub	esc	fs	gs
3	rs	us	sp	!	"	#	$	%	&	'
4	(	)	*	+	,	-	.	/	0	1
5	2	3	4	5	6	7	8	9	:	;
6	<	=	>	?	@	A	B	C	D	E
7	F	G	H	I	J	K	L	M	N	O
8	P	Q	R	S	T	U	V	W	X	Y
9	Z	[	\	]	^	_	`	a	b	c
10	d	e	f	g	h	i	j	k	l	m
11	n	o	p	q	r	s	t	u	v	w
12	x	y	z	{	|	}	~	del		

TABLE B.2   ASCII Character Set in the Hexadecimal Index

	0	1	2	3	4	5	6	7	8	9	A	B	C	D	E	F
0	nul	soh	stx	etx	eot	enq	ack	bel	bs	ht	nl	vt	ff	cr	so	si
1	dle	dcl	dc2	dc3	dc4	nak	syn	etb	can	em	sub	esc	fs	gs	rs	us
2	sp	!	"	#	$	%	&	'	(	)	*	+	,	-	.	/
3	0	1	2	3	4	5	6	7	8	9	:	;	<	=	>	?
4	@	A	B	C	D	E	F	G	H	I	J	K	L	M	N	O
5	P	Q	R	S	T	U	V	W	X	Y	Z	[	\	]	^	_
6	`	a	b	c	d	e	f	g	h	i	j	k	l	m	n	o
7	p	q	r	s	t	u	v	w	x	y	z	{	|	}	~	del

Appendix

OPERATOR PRECEDENCE CHART

The operators are shown in decreasing order of precedence from top to bottom. Operators in the same group have the same precedence, and their associativity is shown in the table.

Operator	Name	Associativity
( )	Parentheses	Left to right
( )	Function call	Left to right
[ ]	Array subscript	Left to right
.	Object member access	Left to right
++	Postincrement	Right to left
--	Postdecrement	Right to left
++	Preincrement	Right to left
--	Predecrement	Right to left
+	Unary plus	Right to left
-	Unary minus	Right to left
!	Unary logical negation	Right to left
(type)	Unary casting	Right to left
new	Creating object	Right to left
*	Multiplication	Left to right
/	Division	Left to right
%	Remainder	Left to right
+	Addition	Left to right
-	Subtraction	Left to right
<<	Left shift	Left to right
>>	Right shift with sign extension	Left to right
>>>	Right shift with zero extension	Left to right
<	Less than	Left to right
<=	Less than or equal to	Left to right
>	Greater than	Left to right

`>=`	Greater than or equal to	Left to right
`instanceof`	Checking object type	Left to right
`==`	Equal comparison	Left to right
`!=`	Not equal	Left to right
`&`	(Unconditional AND)	Left to right
`^`	(Exclusive OR)	Left to right
`¦`	(Unconditional OR)	Left to right
`&&`	Conditional AND	Left to right
`¦¦`	Conditional OR	Left to right
`?:`	Ternary condition	Right to left
`=`	Assignment	Right to left
`+=`	Addition assignment	Right to left
`−=`	Subtraction assignment	Right to left
`*=`	Multiplication assignment	Right to left
`/=`	Division assignment	Right to left
`%=`	Remainder assignment	Right to left

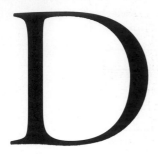

Appendix D

JAVA MODIFIERS

Modifiers are used on classes and class members (constructors, methods, data, and class-level blocks), but the final modifier can also be used on local variables in a method. A modifier that can be applied to a class is called a *class modifier*. A modifier that can be applied to a method is called a *method modifier*. A modifier that can be applied to a data field is called a *data modifier*. A modifier that can be applied to a class-level block is called a *block modifier*. The following table gives a summary of the Java modifiers.

Modifier	class	constructor	method	data	block	Explanation
(default)*	√	√	√	√	√	A class, constructor, method, or data field is visible in this package.
public	√	√	√	√		A class, constructor, method, or data field is visible to all the programs in any package.
private		√	√	√		A constructor, method or data field is only visible in this class.
protected		√	√	√		A constructor, method or data field is visible in this package and in subclasses of this class in any package.
static			√	√	√	Define a class method, or a class data field or a static initialization block.
final	√		√	√		A final class cannot be extended. A final method cannot be modified in a subclass. A final data field is a constant.
abstract	√		√			An abstract class must be extended. An abstract method must be implemented in a concrete subclass.
native			√			A native method indicates that the method is implemented using a language other than Java.
synchronized			√		√	Only one thread at a time can execute this method.
strictfp	√	√				Use strict floating-point calculations to guarantee that the evaluation result is the same on all JVMs.
transient				√		Mark a nonserializable instance data field.

*Default access has no modifier associated with it. For example: class Test {}.

Appendix

UML GRAPHICAL NOTATIONS

E

This appendix summarizes the UML notations used in this book.

Classes and Objects

A class is described using a rectangle box with three sections.

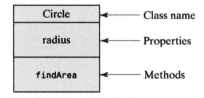

The top section gives the class name, the middle section describes the fields, and the bottom section describes the methods. The middle and bottom sections are optional, but the top section is required.

An object is described using a rectangle box with two sections.

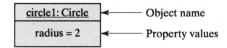

The top section is required. It gives the object's name and its defining class. The second section is optional; it indicates the object's field values.

The Modifiers `public`, `private`, `protected`, and `static`

The symbols $+$, $-$, and $\#$ are used to denote, respectively, `public`, `private`, and `protected` modifiers in the UML. The static fields and methods are underlined.

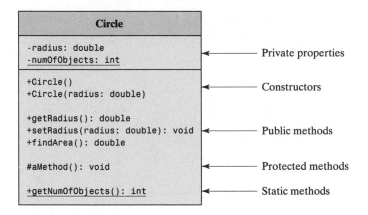

Private properties — Constructors — Public methods — Protected methods — Static methods

Class Relationships

The relationships of the classes are association, aggregation, and inheritance.

An *association* is illustrated using a solid line between the two classes with an optional label that describes their relationship.

Each class involved in an association may specify a multiplicity. A multiplicity is a number or an interval that specifies the number of objects of the class that are involved in the relationship. The character * means that the number of objects is unlimited, and an interval 1..u means that the number of objects should be between 1 and u, inclusive.

A filled diamond is attached to the composed class to denote the composition relationship, and a hollow diamond is attached to the aggregated class to denote the *aggregation* relationship, as shown below.

Inheritance models the is-a relationship between two classes, as shown below. An open triangle pointing to the superclass is used to denote the inheritance relationship between the two classes involved.

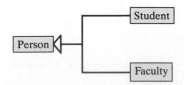

Abstract Classes and Interfaces

Abstract class names, interface names, and abstract methods are italicized. Dashed lines are used to link to the interface, as shown below:

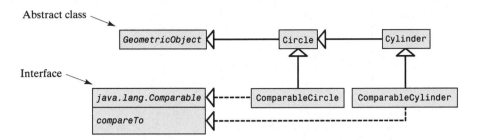

Sequence Diagrams

Sequence diagrams describe interactions among objects by depicting the time ordering of method invocations. The sequence diagram shown below consists of the following elements:

✦ Class role represents the role an object plays. The objects at the top of the diagram represent class roles.

✦ Lifeline represents the existence of an object over a period of time. A vertical dashed line extending from the object is used to denote a lifeline.

✦ Activation represents the time during which an object is performing an operation. Thin rectangles placed on lifelines are used to denote activations.

✦ Method invocation represents communications between objects. Horizontal arrows labeled with method calls are used to denote method invocations.

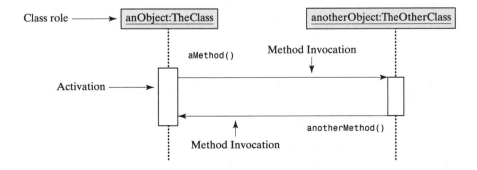

Statechart Diagrams

Statechart diagrams describe the flow of control of an object. The statechart diagram shown below contains the following elements:

◆ State represents a situation during the life of an object in which it satisfies some condition, performs some action, or waits for some event to occur. Every state has a name. Rectangles with rounded corners are used to represent states. The small filled circle is used to denote the initial state.

◆ Transition represents the relationship between two states, indicating that an object will perform some action to transfer from one state to the other. A solid arrow with appropriate method invocation is used to denote a transition.

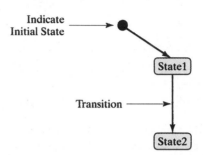

Special Floating-Point Values

Dividing an integer by zero is invalid and throws `ArithmeticException`, but dividing a floating-point value by zero does not cause an exception. Floating-point arithmetic can overflow to infinity if the result of the operation is too large for a `double` or a `float`, or underflow to zero if the result is too small for a `double` or a `float`. Java provides the special floating-point values `POSITIVE_INFINITY`, `NEGATIVE_INFINITY`, and `NaN` (Not a Number) to denote these results. These values are defined as special constants in the `Float` class and the `Double` class.

If a positive floating-point number is divided by zero, the result is `POSITIVE_INFINITY`. If a negative floating-point number is divided by zero, the result is `NEGATIVE_INFINITY`. If a floating-point zero is divided by zero, the result is `NaN`, which means that the result is undefined mathematically. The string representation of these three values are Infinity, -Infinity, and NaN. For example,

```
System.out.print(1.0 / 0); // Print Infinity
System.out.print(-1.0 / 0); // Print -Infinity
System.out.print(0.0 / 0); // Print NaN
```

These special values can also be used as operands in computations. For example, a number divided by `POSITIVE_INFINITY` yields a positive zero. Table F.1 summarizes various combinations of the /, *, %, +, and − operators.

TABLE F.1   Special Floating-Point Values

x	y	x/y	$x*y$	$x \% y$	$x + y$	$x - y$
Finite	$\pm\, 0.0$	$\pm\, \infty$	$\pm\, 0.0$	NaN	Finite	Finite
Finite	$\pm\, \infty$	$\pm\, 0.0$	$\pm\, \infty$	x	$\pm\, \infty$	∞
$\pm\, 0.0$	$\pm\, 0.0$	NaN	$\pm\, \infty$	NaN	$\pm\, 0.0$	$\pm\, 0.0$
$\pm\, \infty$	Finite	$\pm\, \infty$	$\pm\, \infty$	NaN	$\pm\, \infty$	$\pm\, \infty$
$\pm\, \infty$	$\pm\, \infty$	NaN	$\pm\, \infty$	NaN	$\pm\, \infty$	∞
$\pm\, 0.0$	$\pm\, \infty$	$\pm\, 0.0$	NaN	$\pm\, 0.0$	$\pm\, \infty$	$\pm\, 0.0$
NaN	Any	NaN	NaN	NaN	NaN	NaN
Any	NaN	NaN	NaN	NaN	NaN	NaN

 NOTE
If one of the operands is NaN, the result is NaN.

Appendix

G

BIT OPERATIONS

To write programs at the machine-level, often you need to deal with binary numbers directly and perform operations at the bit-level. Java provides the bitwise operators and shift operators defined in Table G.1.

TABLE G.1

Operator	Name	Example (using bytes in the example)	Description
&	Bitwise AND	10101110&10010010 yields 10000010	The AND of two corresponding bits yields a 1 if both bits are 1.
¦	Bitwise inclusive OR	10101110¦10010010	The OR of two corresponding bits yields a 1 if either bit is 1.
^	Bitwise exclusive OR	10101110^10010010 yields 00111100	The XOR of two corresponding bits yields a 1 only if two bits are different.
~	One's complement	~10101110 yields 01010001	The operator toggles each bit from 0 to 1 and from 1 to 0
<<	Left shift	10101110 << 2 yields 10111000	Shift bits in the first operand left by the number of bits specified in the second operand, filling with 0s on the right.
>>	Right shift with sign extension	10101110 >> 2 yields 11101011 00101110 >> 2 yields 00001011	Shift bit in the first operand right by the number of bits specified in the second operand, filling with the highest (sign) bit on the left.
>>>	Right shift with zero extension	10101110 >>> 2 yields 00101011 00101110 >>> 2 yields 00001011	Shift bit in the first operand right by the number of bits specified in the second operand, filling with 0s on the left.

The bit operators apply only to integer types (`byte`, `short`, `int`, and `long`). A character involved in a bit operation is converted to an integer. All bitwise operators can form bitwise assignment operators, such as =, ¦=, <<=, >>=, and >>>=.

INDEX